June 26–July 1, 2016
San Francisco, California, USA

Association for
Computing Machinery

Advancing Computing as a Science & Profession

PODS'16

Proceedings of the 35th ACM SIGMOD-SIGACT-SIGAI Symposium on

Principles of Database Systems

Sponsored by:

ACM SIGMOD, ACM SIGACT, & ACM SIGAI

Supported by:

Microsoft, Oracle, Tableau, Alibaba, AT&T, Facebook, Google, IBM, Infosys, Platfora, Recruit, Salesforce, SAP, Snowflake, Amazon Web Services, Cloudera, Esgyn, Hewlett Packard, Intel, Linked In, LogicBlox, MemSQL, Splice Machine, VISA Research, Hewlett-Packard Enterprise, Morgan & Claypool, Elsevier, Springer, and National Science Foundation

Association for
Computing Machinery

Advancing Computing as a Science & Profession

The Association for Computing Machinery
2 Penn Plaza, Suite 701
New York, New York 10121-0701

ISBN: 978-1-4503-4191-2 (Digital)

ISBN: 978-1-4503-4607-8 (Print)

Additional copies may be ordered prepaid from:

ACM Order Department
PO Box 30777
New York, NY 10087-0777, USA

Phone: 1-800-342-6626 (USA and Canada)
+1-212-626-0500 (Global)
Fax: +1-212-944-1318
E-mail: acmhelp@acm.org
Hours of Operation: 8:30 am – 4:30 pm ET

Printed in the USA

PODS 2016 General and Program Chairs' Welcome Message

It is our great pleasure to welcome you to the 35th ACM SIGMOD-SIGACT-SIGAI Symposium on Principles of Database Systems (PODS 2016), held in San Francisco, California, USA, on June 26 – July 1, 2016, in conjunction with the 2016 ACM SIGMOD International Conference on Management of Data. Since the first edition of the symposium in 1982, the PODS papers are distinguished by a rigorous approach to widely diverse problems in data management, often bringing to bear techniques from a variety of different areas, including computational logic, finite model theory, computational complexity, algorithm design and analysis, programming languages, and artificial intelligence. The PODS Symposia study data management challenges in a variety of application contexts, including more recently probabilistic data, parallel computation, streaming data, graph data, information retrieval, ontology and semantic web, and data-driven processes and systems. PODS has a tradition of being the premier international conference on the theoretical and foundational aspects of data management, and the interested reader is referred to the PODS web pages at http://www.sigmod.org/the-pods-pages/ for information on the history of this conference series.

This year's symposium continues this tradition and continues to explicitly invite for submission papers providing original, substantial contributions in one or more of the following categories:

a) deep theoretical exploration of topical areas central to data management;

b) new formal frameworks that aim at providing the basis for deeper theoretical investigation of important emerging issues in data management; and

c) validation of theoretical approaches from the lens of practical applicability in data management.

This volume contains the proceedings of PODS 2016, which include a paper for the keynote address by Moshe Vardi (Rice University, USA), papers based on two invited tutorials by Sara Cohen (Hebrew University of Jerusalem, Israel) and Frank Neven (Hasselt University, Belgium), and 31 contributions that were selected by the Program Committee for presentation at the symposium. In addition, it also contains an abstract and a paper from our two "Gems of PODS" speakers, Ronald Fagin (IBM Research – Almaden) and Georg Gottlob (University of Oxford). The Gems of PODS is an inaugural event where the goal is to promote understanding of past seminal PODS results to the general audience.

This year, PODS continued with two submission cycles that were introduced last year. The first cycle allowed for the possibility for papers to be revised and resubmitted. For the first cycle, 37 papers were submitted, 2 of which were directly selected for inclusion in the proceedings, and 15 were invited for a resubmission after a revision. The quality of most of the revised papers increased substantially with respect to the first submission, and 12 of 15 in the end were selected for the proceedings. For the second cycle, 57 papers were submitted, 17 of which were selected, resulting in 31 papers selected overall from a total number of 94 submissions.

With respect to the three categories mentioned above, of the 94 submissions (resp., 31 accepted papers), 71 (resp., 28) were classified by the authors in category (a), 21 (resp., 2) in category (b), and only 2 (resp., 1) in category (c). The authors were asked to select a most appropriate category for their papers when submitting their papers.

An important task for the Program Committee has been the selection of the PODS 2016 Best Paper Award. The committee selected the paper

"*FAQ: Questions Asked Frequently*" by Mahmoud Abo Khamis, Hung Ngo and Atri Rudra.

This year, the Program Committee also selected a PODS 2016 Best Student Paper Award. The following paper is selected.

> "*Shortest Paths and Distances with Differential Privacy*" by Adam Sealfon.

On behalf of the committee, we would like to extend our sincere congratulations to the authors!

Since 2008, PODS assigns the ACM PODS Alberto O. Mendelzon Test-of-Time Award to a paper or a small number of papers published in the PODS proceedings ten years prior that had the most impact over the intervening decade. This year's committee, consisting of Jan Van den Bussche (chair), Marcelo Arenas, and Peter Buneman, selected the following paper. Our warmest congratulations to their authors!

> "*Two-variable logic on data trees and XML reasoning*" by Mikołaj Bojańczyk, Claire David, Anca Muscholl, Thomas Schwentick, and Luc Segoufin.

We thank all authors who submitted papers to the symposium. We would also like to thank all members of the Program Committee and all external referees for the enormous amount of work they have done. The two submission cycles, with the revision round for the first cycle, placed an extra burden on all of them. The program committee did not meet in person, but carried out extensive discussions during the electronic program committee meeting, relying on the EasyChair System.

Our thanks go also to the members of the PODS Executive Committee for their unfailing support. They advised in the selection of the Program Committee and gave important advise on policy issues in all phases of the conference organization. We are particularly grateful to Diego Calvanese, the previous PODS PC chair, for his continuous help and advise. Special thanks go to Parachos Koutris, our Proceedings and Publicity Chair of PODS 2016, and to Wim Martens, for maintaining the PODS Web pages. We are also grateful to the SIGMOD 2016 General Chairs, Fatma Özcan and Georgia Koutrika, for their excellent coordination of the overall SIGMOD/PODS 2016 conference, and their collaboration and support in all the issues requiring coordination between SIGMOD and PODS. Finally, we thank all our sponsors, in particular the ACM Special Interest Groups on Management of Data, on Algorithms and Computation Theory, and on Artificial Intelligence, for their invaluable support.

Tova Milo
PODS 2016 General Chair

Wang-Chiew Tan
PODS 2016 Program Chair

Table of Contents

PODS 2016 Organization ix

PODS 2016 Sponsors & Supporters xi

PODS Keynote
Session Chair: Tova Milo *(Tel Aviv University)*

- **A Theory of Regular Queries** 1
  Moshe Y. Vardi *(Rice University)*

PODS Award talks + 1 regular paper
Session Chair: Jan Van den Bussche *(Hasselt University)*

- **2016 ACM PODS Alberto O. Mendelzon Test-of-Time Award** 11
  Marcelo Arenas *(PUC)*, Peter Buneman *(University of Edinburgh)*, Jan Van den Bussche *(Hasselt University)*
- **FAQ: Questions Asked Frequently** 13
  Mahmoud Abo Khamis *(LogicBlox Inc. & SUNY at Buffalo)*,
  Hung Q. Ngo *(LogicBlox Inc. & SUNY at Buffalo)*, Atri Rudra *(SUNY at Buffalo)*
- **Shortest Paths and Distances with Differential Privacy** 29
  Adam Sealfon *(Massachusetts Institute of Technology)*
- **Minimization of Tree Pattern Queries** 43
  Wojciech Czerwiński *(University of Warsaw)*, Wim Martens, Matthias Niewerth *(Universität Bayreuth)*,
  Paweł Parys *(University of Warsaw)*

Session: Gems of PODS
Session Chair: Wang-Chiew Tan *(UC Santa Cruz)*

- **Optimal Score Aggregation Algorithms** 55
  Ronald Fagin *(IBM Research – Almaden)*
- **Hypertree Decompositions: Questions and Answers** 57
  Georg Gottlob *(University of Oxford)*,
  Gianluigi Greco, Nicola Leone, Francesco Scarcello *(University of Calabria)*

Session 1: Query Rewriting, Views, and Join Algorithms
Session Chair: Dan Suciu *(University of Washington)*

- **Incremental View Maintenance For Collection Programming** 75
  Christoph Koch, Daniel Lupei *(École Polytechnique Fédérale de Lausanne)*,
  Val Tannen *(University of Pennsylvania)*
- **AJAR: Aggregations and Joins over Annotated Relations** 91
  Manas Joglekar, Rohan Puttagunta, Christopher Ré *(Stanford University)*
- **Bounded Query Rewriting Using Views** 107
  Yang Cao, Wenfei Fan *(University of Edinburgh & Beihang University)*, Floris Geerts *(University of Antwerp)*,
  Ping Lu *(Beihang University)*
- **Red Spider Meets a Rainworm: Conjunctive Query Finite Determinacy is Undecidable** 121
  Tomasz Gogacz, Jerzy Marcinkowski *(University of Wrocław)*
- **Towards a Worst-Case I/O-Optimal Algorithm for Acyclic Joins** 135
  Xiao Hu, Ke Yi *(Hong Kong University of Science and Technology)*
- **On the Complexity of Inner Product Similarity Join** 151
  Thomas D. Ahle, Rasmus Pagh *(IT University of Copenhagen)*,
  Ilya Razenshteyn *(Massachusetts Institute of Technology)*, Francesco Silvestri *(IT University of Copenhagen)*

PODS Tutorial 1

Session Chair: Marcelo Arenas *(PUC Chile)*

- **Data Management for Social Networking** 165
  Sara Cohen *(Hebrew University of Jerusalem)*

Session 2: Workflows and Incomplete Information

Session Chair: Claire David *(Université Paris-Est Marne)*

- **Verification of Hierarchical Artifact Systems** 179
  Alin Deutsch, Yuliang Li *(University of California, San Diego)*,
  Victor Vianu *(University of California, San Diego & INRIA-Saclay)*
- **Recency-Bounded Verification of Dynamic Database-Driven Systems** 195
  Parosh Aziz Abdulla, C. Aiswarya, Mohamed Faouzi Atig *(Uppsala University)*,
  Marco Montali *(Free University of Bozen/Bolzano)*, Othmane Rezine *(Uppsala University)*
- **Making SQL Queries Correct on Incomplete Databases: A Feasibility Study** 211
  Paolo Guagliardo, Leonid Libkin *(The University of Edinburgh)*
- **Designing a Query Language for RDF: Marrying Open and Closed Worlds** 225
  Marcelo Arenas *(Pontifical Catholic University of Chile)*, Martín Ugarte *(Université Libre de Bruxelles)*

Session 3: Data Streams and Indexes

Session Chair: Sudeepa Roy *(Duke University)*

- **Schema Validation via Streaming Circuits** 237
  Filip Murlak, Charles Paperman, Michał Pilipczuk *(University of Warsaw)*
- **Variability in Data Streams** 251
  David Felber, Rafail Ostrovsky *(University of California, Los Angeles)*
- **Streaming Space Complexity of Nearly All Functions of One Variable on Frequency Vectors** 261
  Vladimir Braverman *(Johns Hopkins University)*, Stephen R. Chestnut *(ETH Zurich)*, David P. Woodruff *(IBM)*,
  Lin F. Yang *(Johns Hopkins University)*
- **Efficient Top-k Indexing via General Reductions** 277
  Saladi Rahul *(University of Minnesota)*, Yufei Tao *(University of Queensland)*
- **Anti-Persistence on Persistent Storage: History-Independent Sparse Tables and Dictionaries** 289
  Michael A. Bender *(Stony Brook University)*, Jonathan W. Berry *(Sandia National Laboratories)*,
  Rob Johnson *(Stony Brook University)*, Thomas M. Kroeger *(Sandia National Laboratories)*,
  Samuel McCauley *(Stony Brook University)*, Cynthia A. Phillips *(Sandia National Laboratories)*,
  Bertrand Simon *(Ecole Normale Supérieure de Lyon)*, Shikha Singh *(Stony Brook University)*,
  David Zage *(Intel Corporation)*

PODS Tutorial 2

Session Chair: Pierre Senellart *(Télécom ParisTech, France & National University of Singapore)*

- **Logical Aspects of Massively Parallel and Distributed Systems** 303
  Frank Neven *(Hasselt University & Transnational University of Limburg)*

Session 4: Query Evaluation

Session Chair: Paris Koutris *(University of Wisconsin-Madison)*

- **Counting Answers to Existential Positive Queries: A Complexity Classification** 315
  Hubie Chen *(University of the Basque Country (UPV/EHU) & IKERBASQUE, Basque Foundation for Science)*,
  Stefan Mengel *(CNRS, CRIL UMR 8188)*
- **Computing Join Queries with Functional Dependencies** 327
  Mahmoud Abo Khamis, Hung Q. Ngo *(LogicBlox Inc. and SUNY at Buffalo)*,
  Dan Suciu *(LogicBlox Inc. & University of Washington)*

- **Semantic Acyclicity Under Constraints** ... 343
  Pablo Barceló *(University of Chile)*, Georg Gottlob *(University of Oxford)*,
  Andreas Pieris *(Vienna University of Technology)*
- **Tractable Lineages on Treelike Instances: Limits and Extensions** ... 355
  Antoine Amarilli *(LTCI, CNRS, Télécom ParisTech & Université Paris-Saclay)*,
  Pierre Bourhis *(CRIStAL, UMR 9189, CNRS, Université Lille 1)*,
  Pierre Senellart *(LTCI, CNRS, Télécom ParisTech, Université Paris-Saclay & IPAL, CNRS, NUS)*

Session 5: Data Streams and Privacy

Session Chair: Graham Comcorde *(University of Warwick)*

- **Towards Tight Bounds for the Streaming Set Cover Problem** ... 371
  Sariel Har-Peled *(University of Illinois)*,
  Piotr Indyk, Sepideh Mahabadi, Ali Vakilian *(Massachusetts Institute of Technology)*
- **An Optimal Algorithm for l1-Heavy Hitters in Insertion Streams and Related Problems** ... 385
  Arnab Bhattacharyya, Palash Dey *(Indian Institute of Science)*, David P. Woodruff *(IBM Research Almaden)*
- **Better Algorithms for Counting Triangles in Data Streams** ... 401
  Andrew McGregor, Sofya Vorotnikova, Hoa T. Vu *(University of Massachusetts, Amherst)*
- **Locating a Small Cluster Privately** ... 413
  Kobbi Nissim *(Ben-Gurion University & Harvard University)*, Uri Stemmer *(Ben-Gurion University)*,
  Salil Vadhan *(Harvard University)*

Session 6: Algorithms and Data Structures

Session Chair: Ke Yi *(Hong Kong University of Science and Technology)*

- **Parallel Algorithms for Constructing Range and Nearest-Neighbor Searching Data Structures** ... 429
  Pankaj K. Agarwal, Kyle Fox, Kamesh Munagala, Abhinandan Nath *(Duke University)*
- **Space Lower Bounds for Itemset Frequency Sketches** ... 441
  Edo Liberty *(Yahoo Research)*, Michael Mitzenmacher *(Harvard University)*, Justin Thaler *(Yahoo Research)*,
  Jonathan Ullman *(Northeastern University)*
- **Are Few Bins Enough: Testing Histogram Distributions** ... 455
  Clément L. Canonne *(Columbia University)*
- **Range-Max Queries on Uncertain Data** ... 465
  Pankaj K. Agarwal *(Duke University)*, Nirman Kumar *(University of California, Santa Barbara)*,
  Stavros Sintos *(Duke University)*, Subhash Suri *(University of California, Santa Barbara)*
- **Fast Algorithms for Parsing Sequences of Parentheses with Few Errors** ... 477
  Arturs Backurs *(Massachusetts Institute of Technology)*, Krzysztof Onak *(IBM Research)*

Author Index ... 489

PODS 2016 Organization

General Chair: Tova Milo (Tel Aviv University, Israel)

Program Chair: Wang-Chiew Tan (University of California, Santa Cruz, USA)

Proceedings & Publicity Chair: Paraschos Koutris (University of Wisconsin–Madison, USA)

Program Committee Members:
Pankaj K. Agarwal (Duke University, USA)
Marcelo Arenas (PUC Chile, Chile)
Michael Benedikt (Oxford University, UK)
Graham Cormode (University of Warwick, UK)
Claire David (Université Paris-Est Marne, France)
Daniel Deutch (Tel Aviv University, Israel)
Alin Deutsch (UC San Diego, USA)
Wenfei Fan (University of Edinburgh, UK)
Enrico Franconi (Free University of Bozen-Bolzano, Italy)
André Hernich (University of Liverpool, UK)
Kobbi Nissim (Ben-Gurion University, Israel)
Christopher Ré (Stanford University, USA)
Sudeepa Roy (Duke University, USA)
Pierre Senellart (Télécom ParisTech, France & National University of Singapore, Singapore)
Cristina Sirangelo (IRIF, Paris 7 University, France)
Sławek Staworko (University of Lille 3, France & University of Edinburgh, UK)
Dan Suciu (University of Washington, USA)
Kunal Talwar (Google, USA)
Yufei Tao (Chinese University of Hong Kong, China)
Jan Van den Bussche (Hasselt University, Belgium)
David Woodruff (IBM Almaden, USA)

Additional reviewers:
Peyman Afshani
Kook Jin Ahn
C. Aiswarya
Antoine Amarilli
Alexandr Andoni
Nikolaus Augsten
Jean-François Baget
Pablo Barceló
Raef Bassily
Benedikt Bollig
Pierre Bourhis
Gerth Stølting Brodal
Guy Van den Broeck
Amit Chakrabarti
Timothy Chan
Liang-Ting Chen
Alvin Cheung
Paolo Ciaccia
Seshadhri Comandur
Andrew Danner
Palash Dey
Gonzalo Diaz
Arnaud Durand
Alan Fekete
Sergio Flesca
Kyle Fox
Nadime Francis
Sumit Ganguly
Minos Garofalakis
Adria Gascon

Additional reviewers (continued):

Amelie Gheerbrant
Xavier Goaoc
Tomek Gogacz
Matteo Golfarelli
Benoit Groz
Paolo Guagliardo
Sudipto Guha
Anupam Gupta
Matthew Hague
Lauri Hella
Zengfeng Huang
Manas Joglekar
Hossein Jowhari
Bettina Kemme
Volha Kerhet
Roman Kontchakov
Paraschos Koutris
Nirman Kumar
Clemens Kupke
Chao Li
Leonid Libkin
Katrina Ligett
Zhenming Liu
Frederic Magniez
Dániel Marx
Andrew McGregor
Frank Mcsherry
Stefan Mengel
Morteza Monemizadeh
Kamesh Munagala
Filip Murlak
Danupon Nanongkai
Abhinandan Nath
Faisal Nawab
Jelani Nelson
Frank Neven
Hung Ngo
Nhung Ngo
Dan Olteanu
Krzysztof Onak
Jiangwei Pan
Debmalya Panigrahi
Rafael Peñaloza
Reinhard Pichler
Andreas Pieris
Dan Ports
Ilya Razenshteyn
Juan L. Reutter
Cristian Riveros
Amitabha Roy
Vladislav Ryzhikov
Barna Saha
Sylvain Schmitz
Gil Segev
Luc Segoufin
Francesco Silvestri
Stavros Sintos
Zhao Song
Daniel Stubbs
Yuthian Sun
Sergio Tessaris
Justin Thaler
Koen Verstrepen
Victor Vianu
Jan Vondrak
Domagoj Vrgoc
Zhewei Wei
Piotr Wieczorek
Virginia Vassilevska Williams
Anthony Wirth
Ryan Wisnesky
Allen Xiao
Grigory Yaroslavtsev
Ke Yi
Norbert Zeh

Alberto O. Mendelzon Test-of-Time Award Committee:

Marcelo Arenas (PUC Chile, Chile)
Peter Buneman (University of Edinburgh, UK)
Jan Van den Bussche (chair) (Hasselt University, Belgium)

Gems of PODS Committee:

Dan Suciu (University of Washington, USA)
Wang-Chiew Tan (chair) (University of California, Santa Cruz, USA)
Jan Van den Bussche (Hasselt University, Belgium)

Sponsors, Supporters, and Exhibitors

Sponsors:

Platinum Supporters:

Gold Supporters:

platfora

RECRUIT

salesforce

SAP

snowflake

Silver Supporters:

amazon web services™

cloudera

esgyn

hp

intel

LinkedIn

LogicBlox

memsql

splice MACHINE

VISA Research

Other Supporters:

Hewlett Packard Enterprise

Platinum Publisher:

Morgan & Claypool Publishers

Silver Publishers:

Elsevier

Springer

A Theory of Regular Queries

Moshe Y. Vardi
Rice University
vardi@cs.rice.edu

ABSTRACT

A major theme in relational database theory is navigating the tradeoff between expressiveness and tractability for query languages, where the query-containment problem is considered a benchmark of tractability. The query class UCQ, consisting off *unions of conjunctive queries*, is a fragment of first-order logic that has a decidable query containment problem, but its expressiveness is limited. Extending UCQ with recursion yields Datalog, an expressive query language that has been studied extensively and has recently become popular in application areas such as declarative networking. Unfortunately, Datalog has an undecidable query containment problem. Identifying a fragment of Datalog that is expressive enough for applications but has a decidable query-containment problem has been an open problem for several years.

In the area of graph databases, there has been a similar search for a query language that combines expressiveness and tractability. Because of the need to navigate along graph paths of unspecified length, transitive closure has been considered a fundamental operation. Query classes of increasing complexity – using the operations of disjunction, conjunction, projection, and transitive closure – have been studied, but the classes lacked natural closure properties. The class RQ of *regular queries* has emerged only recently as a natural query class that is closed under all of its operations and has a decidable query-containment problem.

RQ turned out to be a fragment of Datalog where recursion can be used only to express transitive closure. Furthermore, it turns out that applying this idea to Datalog, that is, restricting recursion to the expression of transitive closure, does yield the long-sought goal – an expressive fragment of Datalog with a decidable query-optimization problem.

1. INTRODUCTION

The development of declarative database-query languages is one of the great accomplishments of computer science. Following the introduction of relational databases by Codd [22], he proposed using first-order logic as a declarative database query language [23]. This led to the development of both SEQUEL [16] and QUEL [54], as practical relational query languages realizing Codd's idea, ultimately giving in 1986 rise to the SQL standard [27], which has continued to evolve over the past 30 years.

Starting in the late 1970s, Codd's definition of first-order logic as "expressively complete" came under serious criticism [4], and various proposals emerged on how to extend its expressive power [4, 6, 17], whose essence was to extend first-order logic with *recursion*, which was added to SQL in 1999 by way of *common table expressions* [29]. On the research side, the most popular relational language embodying recursion is *Datalog* [15], describe in more details below.

From the very beginning of research on relational query languages it became clear that *query optimization* is a central problem due to the declarative nature of these language [23, 32]. Fundamentally, query optimization requires us to transform a query Q to an equivalent query Q' that is easier to evaluate. Query equivalence can be reduced to query containment – Q is equivalent to Q' if Q is contained in Q' and Q' is contained in Q. Thus, query containment is a key database-theoretic problem. In fact, it has found uses in many other database contexts, including *query reuse* [47], *query reformulation* [31], *data integration* [33, 36], *cooperative query answering* [44], and more.

Unfortunately, query containment is essentially logical implication; thus, it is undecidable for first-order logic, and, consequently, for SQL [2]. A major fragment of SQL for which query containment is decidable is the class UCQ, *union of conjunctive queries*, which is the class of queries that be be defined using the relationals operator Select, Project, Join, and Union [18, 50]. In fact, UCQ is also the largest class of relational queries for which we have a robust theory and practice of query optimization [19].

Datalog is essentially the closure of UCQ under recursion. The main appeal of Datalog comes from its syntactical simplicity; a Datalog query consists of a set of rules, where each rule expresses a conjunctive query (Select-Project-Join query) [15]. Due to this syntactical simplicity, Datalog has recently found applications outside the database area, for example, in *declarative networking* [37]. Unfortunately, the presence of recursion in Datalog is sufficient to make the containment problem undecidable [52]. The only fragment of Datalog that is known to have a decidable containment problem is the class of *monadic* Datalog, in which all recursive rules return monadic relations (i.e., sets) [25]. This fragment, however, is too weak for practical applications

PODS '16, June 26–July 1, 2016, San Francisco, CA, USA.

DOI: http://dx.doi.org/10.1145/2902251.2902305

such as declarative networking, due to its inability to express network connectivity properties.

In a different development, information systems nowadays are required to deal with more complex data with respect to traditional relational data. For example, web data, social networks, or biological data are better modeled by resorting to more flexible structuring mechanisms than those provided by relational systems [10]. This development led to the emergence of the graph-database model as a data model that is less expressive but is more flexible that the classical relational model. The graph-data model conceives a database essentially as a finite directed labeled graph whose nodes represent objects, and whose edges represent relationships between objects [1], that is, an edge-labeled graph. (It is convenient to restrict attention, without loss of generality, to edge-labeled graphs.) Over the past 20 years, graph databases have been a major focus of research and practical interest [41, 49].

As in relational databases, a major research focus in graph databases is identifying a core query language that has a decidable query-containment problem. In the same way that UCQ forms the decidable core of of both SQL and Datalog, *regular-path queries* (RPQs) are considered the basic querying mechanisms for graph databases [1, 3, 10]. Query languages for graph databases must indeed be equipped with flexible mechanisms for navigating the graph representing the data. This includes the ability to follow a sequence of edges of the graph whose length is not specified a priori, something which is directly provided by RPQs via a limited form of recursion in the form of transitive closure. Thus, RPQs are simply regular expressions over the edge alphabet of the graph database.

The theory of regular languages is one of the most thoroughly studied and best understood theories in theoretical computer science [30]. Regular languages have robust definability properties. That is, different means of defining regular languages, e.g, regular expressions vs. automata, have the same expressive power. They also have robust closure properties, that is, they are closed under many set-theoretic and algebraic operations. In particular, the containment problem for regular expression can be shown to be decidable in polynomial space (in fact, PSPACE-complete) using standard automata-theoretic constructions [30]. Can this results from regular-language theory be applied to the containment problem for RPQs?

RPQs allow for navigating the edges of a graph database only in the forward direction. It is obviously of interest, however, to be able to navigate edges in both forward and backward directions, as, e.g., supported by the predecessor axis of XPath [9, 21]. RPQs extended with the ability of navigating database edges backward are called *two-way regular-path queries* (2RPQs) [12]. It turns out that while regular-expression containment techniques can be applied to RPQ containment, these techniques cannot easily be applied to 2RPQ containment, because the difference between "inverse letters" in words and "inverse edges" in graphs. That is, the theories of regular expressions over words and regular expression over graphs diverge [12]. Nevertheless, containment of 2RPQs can still be shown to be PSPACE-complete, using automata-theoretic techniques [12].

The divergence between the the theories of regular expressions over words and regular expressions over graphs expands when we consider the conjunction operation. Over words, conjunction and intersection coincide, and regular languages are closed under intersection. Thus, extending regular expressions with intersection/conjunction does not yield an increase in expressive power [30]. In contrast, over graphs, conjunction differs from intersection. Since we are seeking a graph-database analogue to the class UCQ of relational queries, it does make sense to close the class 2RPQ of 2-way regular path queries under both disjunction (which corresponds to union) and conjunction, resulting in the class UC2RPQ, which is the class of unions of conjunctions of 2RPQs. The decidability of of the containment problem for UC2RPQ cannot be shown using only automata-theoretic techniques; rather one has to combine automata-theoretic techniques with database-theoretic techniques, showing that the problem is EXPSPACE-complete [11].

Yet the class UC2RPQ cannot be considered a natural class of graph-database queries. A natural class should be defined by means of basic queries and closure under certain operations. For example, the class CQ is the class of atomic relational queries, closed under selection, conjunction, and projection, while the class UCQ is closed also under disjunction (union). In contrast, the class UC2RPQ is closed under election, isjunction, and conjunction, but it is not closed under transitive closure, which can appear only inside 2RPQs. A natural definition for the class RQ of *regular queries* is the closure of atomic queries under selection, projection, disjunction, conjunction, and transitive closure.

The query-containment problem for RQ has been open for several years. Decidability can be shown via embedding in monadic-second order logic (MSO) [34], but this yields a nonelemenary complexity upper bound, that is, a tower of exponentials of unbounded height. Only recently it was shown that the problem has elementary complexity – it is 2EXPSPACE-complete [48]. As in [11], the proof requires a combination automata-theoretic and database-theoretic techniques (cf. [20]), but these techniques are quite more sophisticated than those required for UC2RPQs.

The classes of graph-database queries we have discussed so far, namely, RPQ, 2RPQ, UC2RPQ, and RQ, can all be expressed in graph-database Datalog. Thus, they can all be viewed as fragments of Datalog with a decidable query-containment problem. The class RQ, however, is notable, as it can be viewed as Datalog where recursion can be used only to express only transitive closure.

It turns out that this restriction of recursion is the key to the decidability result for RQ. Let GRQ be the class of *generalized regular queries*, consisting of all Datalog queries where recursion is used only to express transitive closure. The query-containment problem for GRQ can be reduced to that of RQ yielding the same 2EXPSPACE bound [48]. Thus, the class GRQ provides an answer to the long-standing open question of identifying a fragment of Datalog that is expressive enough to capture connectivity properties, while still having a decidable query-containment problem.

The outline of the paper is as follows. Following the introduction, we introduce in Section 2 the relational query languages UCQ and Datalog, and review the open question of finding a fragment of Datalog that is expressive enough for applications yet has a decidable query-containment problem. In Section 3 we review the development of more and more expressive graph-database query languages with a decidable query-containment problem, culminating with the class RQ of Regular Queries. We conclude in Section 4 with the description of GRQ, the class of Generalized Regular Queries, as an expressive fragment of Datalog with an elementarily decidable query-containment problem, and discuss the practical implications of this result.

2. FROM CONJUNCTIVE QUERIES TO DATALOG

2.1 Union of Conjunctive Queries

A *conjunctive query* is a positive existential conjunctive first-order formula, i.e., the only propositional connective allowed is $\wedge$ and the only quantifier allowed is $\exists$. Without loss of generality, we can assume that conjunctive queries are given as formulas $\theta(x_1, \ldots, x_k)$ of the form $(\exists y_1, \ldots, y_m)(a_1 \wedge \ldots a_n)$ with free variables among $x_1, \ldots, x_k$, where the a_i's are atomic formulas of the form $p(z_1, \ldots, z_l)$ over the variables $x_1, \ldots, x_k, y_1, \ldots, y_m$. For example, the conjunctive query $(\exists y)(E(x,y) \wedge E(y,z))$ is satisfied by all pairs $\langle x, z\rangle$ such that there is a path of length 2 between x and z. The free variables are also called *distinguished variables.* A *union of conjunctive queries* is a disjunction

$$\bigvee_{i=1}^{k} \theta_i(x_1, \ldots, x_k)$$

of conjunctive queries. Every positive first-order formula that has only existential quantifiers can be written (with a possible blow-up in size) as a union of conjunctive queries. The class of such queries is denoted UCQ. This class is essentially the class of relational algebraic queries composed of the Select, Project, Join, and Union operators, which cover a major fraction of relational queries used in practice [2].

A union of conjunctive queries $\Theta(x_1, \ldots, x_k)$ with distinguished variables $x_1, \ldots, x_k$ can be applied to a database D. The result

$$\Theta(D) = \{(a_1, \ldots, a_k) | D \models \Theta(a_1, \ldots, a_k)\}$$

is the set of k-ary tuples representing assignments to the distinguished variables that satisfy Θ in D.

2.2 Datalog

A *Datalog* program consists of a set of Horn rules. A Horn rule consists of a single atom in the head of the rule and a conjunction of atoms in the body, where an atom is a formula of the form $p(z_1, .., z_l)$ where p is a predicate symbol and $z_1..z_l$ are variables. Note that every such rule can be viewed as a conjunctive query, under the convention that variables that appear in the body but not in the head are quantified existentially. The predicates that occur in head of rules are called *intensional* (IDB) predicates. The rest of the predicates are called *extensional* (EDB) predicates. Let Π be a Datalog program. Let $P^i_\Pi(D)$ be the collection of facts about an IDB predicate P that can be deduced from a database D by at most i applications of the rules in Π and let $P^\infty_\Pi(D)$ be the collection of facts about P that can be deduced from D by an arbitrary number of applications of the rules in Π, that is,

$$P^\infty_\Pi(D) = \bigcup_{i \geq 0} P^i_\Pi(D).$$

A Datalog query Q is a Datalog program Π with one IDB predicate P designated as the *goal predicate.* Then we have $Q(D) = P^\infty_\Pi(D)$. For detailed semantics, see [15].

It is known (cf. [46]) that the relation defined by an IDB predicate in a Datalog program Π, i.e., $Q^\infty_\Pi(D)$, can be defined by a *possibly infinite* union of conjunctive queries. That is, for each IDB predicate Q there is a possibly infinite sequence $\phi_0, \phi_1, \ldots$ of conjunctive queries such that for every database D, we have $Q^\infty_\Pi(D) = \bigcup_{i=0}^{\infty} \phi_i(D)$.

A predicate P *depends* on a predicate Q in a program Π, if Q occurs in the body of a rule r of Π and P is the predicate at the head of r. The *dependence graph* of Π is a directed graph whose nodes are the predicates of Π, and whose edges capture the dependence relation, i.e., there is an edge from Q to P if P appears in the body of a rule with Q in the head; that is Q *depends* on P. If there is a dependence-graph path from a predicate Q to itself, we say that Q is a *recursive predicate.* A program Π is *nonrecursive* if it has no recursive predicates, i.e., no predicate depends recursively on itself. It is well-known [2] that a nonrecursive program can be expressed as a *finite* union of conjunctive queries. Thus, nonrecursive Datalog is equivalent to the query class UCQ. Thus, we can view Datalog as the extension of the query class UCQ with recursion.

Datalog has been a subject of extensive research both from a theoretical, cf. [35], and applied, cf. [45], perspectives. This research led to the extension of SQL standard with recursion, *common table expressions* [29]. In recent years variants of Datalog have gained popularity in various application areas from access-control policies [28] to declarative networking [37]. These applications use recursion in an essential way, which means that nonrecursive Datalog is not expressive enough for them. For example, in declarative networking it is important to say that there is a network connection of some unknown length between nodes x and y.

2.3 Query Containment

Let Q_1 and Q_2 be two queries. We say that Q_1 is *contained* in Q_2, denoted $Q_1 \subseteq Q_2$, if $Q_1(D) \subseteq Q_2(D)$ for every database D. Clearly, if $Q_1 \subseteq Q_2$ and $Q_2 \subseteq Q_1$, then Q_1 and Q_2 are equivalent, which explains the centrality of the query-containment problem in relational database research. As discussed in Section 1, many database applications make use of query containment. A celebrated results in database theory is the decidability of query containment for CQ – the problem is NP-complete [18]. (Of course, tractability is an important issue, to be discussed in Section 4.) This was extended a few years later to UCQ, though with higher complexity [50]. As nonrecursive Datalog is equivalent to UCQ, it follows that decidability of query containment extends also to the former, but with an even higher complexity [8].

It is easy, however, to see that decidability of query containment does not extend to full Datalog. The syntactic similarity of Datalog programs and context-free grammars suggests that the containment problem for context-free grammars can be reduced to the containment problem for Datalog, implying undecidability [52]. So nonrecursive Datalog has a decidable query-containment problem but is not expressive enough for applications, yet full Datalog is expressive enough, but has an undecidable query-containment problem. Can we find a fragment of Datalog that would give us both expressiveness and decidability? That question has been open for many years.

Monadic Datalog is a fragment of Datalog. In Monadic Datalog all recursive predicates must be one-place predicates, that is, they define sets of values. Monadic Datalog is more expressive than nonrecursive Datalog, while still having a decidable query-containment problem [25]. Yet Monadic Datalog is not expressive enough for applications. In Monadic Datalog we can express reachability properties, i.e., we can capture the set Q of elements that have a path to nodes in a given set P, using the program:

$$\begin{aligned} Q(X) &\ :-E(X,Y),P(Y) \\ Q(X) &\ :-E(X,Y),Q(Y) \end{aligned}$$

Yet we cannot express in Monadic Datalog the binary relation E^+, which is the transitive closure of a binary relation, cf. E [7]. That is, we cannot express the following Datalog program:

$$\begin{aligned} E^+(X,Y) &\ :-E(X,Y) \\ E^+(X,Z) &\ :-E(X,Y),E^+(Y,Z) \end{aligned}$$

(Note that Monadic Datalog can have non-monadic goals; it is only the recursive predicates that are restricted to be monadic.) But it is exactly these kind of connectivity properties that are needed in applications such as declarative networking. Thus, Monadic Datalog does not provide a query language that is expressive enough, but with a decidable query-containment problem.

3. GRAPHH DATABASES

3.1 Regular Path Queries

Following the usual approach in modeling graph data [1], we define a *graph database* D as a finite directed graph whose edges are labeled by elements from a finite alphabet Σ. Each node represents an objects and an edge from object x to object y labeled by r, denoted $r(x,y)$, represents the fact that relation r holds between x and y. (We omit node labels, as these can be captured by edge labels.) For a given edge label r, let $r(D)$ denote the binary relation consisting of the pairs of nodes connected by an edge labeled by r.

Observe that a graph database can be seen as a (finite) relational structure over the set Σ of binary relational symbols. Thus, the edge alphabet Σ can be viewed as the relational schema of the database. But while in relational databases schema design is a "heavy duty" process and schema changes are not undertaken lightly, the edge alphabet of a graph database is simply part of the data and can be changed simply by updating the database. This flexibility is one feature of the "noSQL" movement, cf. [40].

A *regular-path query* (RPQ) Q over a graph database D is expressed as a regular expression (or, equivalently, a finite-state automaton) over the edge alphabet Σ. The *answer* $Q(D)$ to an RPQ Q over D is the set of pairs of objects connected in D by a directed path traversing a sequence of edges forming a word in the regular language $L(Q)$ defined by Q [41].

RPQs allow for navigating the edges of a semistructured databases only in the forward direction. RPQs extended with the ability of navigating database edges backward are called *two-way regular-path queries* (2RPQs) [12]. Formally, we consider an alphabet $\Sigma^{\pm} = \Sigma \cup \{r^- \mid r \in \Sigma\}$, which includes a new symbol r^- for each relation symbol r in Σ. The symbol r^- denotes the *inverse* of the binary relation r. If $p \in \Sigma^{\pm}$, then we use p^- to mean the inverse of p, i.e., if p is r, then p^- is r^-, and if p is r^-, then p^- is r. A 2RPQ over Σ is expressed as a regular expression or a finite-state automaton over $\Sigma^{\pm}$. The *answer $Q(D)$ to a 2RPQ Q over a database D* is the set of pairs of objects connected in D by a semipath that conforms to the regular language $L(Q)$. A *semipath* in D from x to y (labeled with $p_1 \cdots p_n$) is a sequence of the form $(y_0, p_1, y_1, \ldots, y_{n-1}, p_n, y_n)$, where $n \geq 0$, $y_0 = x$, $y_n = y$, and for each y_{i-1}, p_i, y_i, we have that $p_i \in \Sigma^{\pm}$, and, if $p_i = r$ then $(y_{i-1}, y_i) \in r(D)$, and if $p_i = r^-$ then $(y_i, y_{i-1}) \in r(D)$). Intuitively, a semipath $(y_0, p_1, y_1, \ldots, y_{n-1}, p_n, y_n)$ corresponds to a navigation of the database from y_0 to y_n, following edges forward or backward, according to the sequence of edge labels $p_1 \cdots p_n$. Note that the objects in a semipath are not necessarily distinct. We say that a semipath $(y_0, p_1, \ldots, p_n, y_n)$ *conforms to* a 2RPQ Q if $p_1 \cdots p_n \in L(Q)$. Summing up, a pair (x, y) of objects is in the answer $Q(D)$ if and only if, by starting from x, it is possible to reach y by navigating in D according to one of the words in $L(Q)$.

3.2 Query Containment

To solve query containment for 2RPQ, we first consider RPQs, where we do not allow inverse symbols. We characterize query containment via a fundamental lemma [14].

LEMMA 1. (Language-Theoretic Lemma 1)*: Let Q_1, Q_2 be RPQs. Then $Q_1 \sqsubseteq Q_2$ iff $L(Q_1) \subseteq L(Q_2)$.*

Since containment of regular expressions is known to be PSPACE-complete [42], it follows from Language-Theoretic Lemma 1 that containment of RPQs is PSPACE-complete. Before we try to extend this result to 2RPQs, it is instructive to recall the proof of the upper bound. The key is the observation that $L(E_1) \subseteq L(E_2)$ iff $L(E_1) - L(E_2) = \emptyset$. The algorithm for checking whether $L(E_1) \subseteq L(E_2)$ proceeds as follows, using classical automata-theoretic constructions [30]:

1. Construct nondeterministic finite-state automata (NFAs) A_1, A_2 such that $L(A_i) = L(E_i)$. This step involves a linear blow-up.

2. Construct an NFA $\overline{A_2}$ such that $L(\overline{A_2}) = \Sigma^* - L(A_2)$. This step involves an exponential blow-up, as complementation requires an application of the subset construction.

3. Construct an NFA $A = A_1 \times \overline{A_2}$ such that $L(A) = L(E_1) - L(E_2)$. This requires taking the product of A_1 and $\overline{A_2}$, involving a quadratic blow-up.

4. Check if there is a path from start state to final state in A. This requires nondeterministic logarithmic space in the size of A.

A naive application of steps (3–4) would requires exponential-space. Instead, we construct A *on the fly*, constructing states only as we search for a path from a start state to a final state in A. This can be done in polynomial space, establishing the upper bound (formally, we need to appeal to Savitch's Theorem [51] to eliminate the nondeterminism in step (4).)

Extending this result to 2RPQs encounters two difficulties. The first difficulty is that an automata-theoretic approach would most likely involve two-way automata, due to the presence of inverse letters, but extending the result of [42] to two- way automata is not straightforward. While it is known that two-way automata can be reduced to one-way automata, that reduction has an exponential cost [30], making a naive approach to containment exponentially harder. An even more fundamental difficulty is that Language-Theoretic Lemma 1 fails for 2RPQs.

Consider the 2RPQs $Q_1 = p$, and $Q_2 = pp^-p$. It is easy to see that $Q_1 \sqsubseteq Q_2$, as every semipath (x, p, y), which establishes that $(x, y) \in Q_1(\mathcal{B})$, corresponds to the semipath (x, p, y, p^-, x, p, y), establishing that $(x, y) \in Q_2(\mathcal{B})$. At the same time, we clearly do not have $L(Q_1) \subseteq L(Q_2)$, since $p \notin L(Q_2)$. Our first step in studying query containment for 2RPQs is revising the language-theoretic characterization, which requires the notion of *folding*. Let $u, v \in \Sigma^\pm$. We say that v *folds* onto u, $v \rightsquigarrow u$, if v can be "folded" on u, e.g., $abb^-bc \rightsquigarrow abc$. Formally, we say that $v = v_1 \cdots v_m$ folds onto $u = u_1 \cdots u_n$ if there is a sequence $i_0, \ldots, i_m$ of positive integers between 0 and $|u|$ such that

- $i_0 = 0$ and $i_m = n$, and
- for $0 \leq j < m$, either $i_{j+1} = i_j + 1$ and $v_{j+1} = u_{i_j+1}$, or $i_{j+1} = i_j - 1$ and $v_{j+1} = u^-_{i_{j+1}}$.

(In particular, $v_0 = u_0$ and $v_m = u_n$.) For example, the sequence demonstrating that $abb^-bc \rightsquigarrow abc$ is $0, 1, 2, 1, 2, 3$. Pictorially, $\xrightarrow{a} \cdot \xrightarrow{b} \cdot \xleftarrow{b} \cdot \xrightarrow{b} \cdot \xrightarrow{c} \rightsquigarrow \xrightarrow{a} \cdot \xrightarrow{b} \cdot \xrightarrow{c}$. Let L be a language $\Sigma^\pm$. We define $fold(L) = \{u \ : \ v \rightsquigarrow u, v \in L\}$. We can now offer a language-theoretic characterization for containment of 2RPQs [14].

LEMMA 2. (Language-Theoretic Lemma 2) *Let Q_1 and Q_2 be 2RPQs. Then $Q_1 \sqsubseteq Q_2$ iff $L(Q_1) \subseteq fold(L(Q_2))$.*

We now show that if A is an NFA, then $fold(L(A))$ can be represented by a "small" *two-way nondeterministic finite-state automaton* (2NFA). Recall that an NFA is a tuple $A = (\Sigma, S, S_0, \rho, F)$, where Σ is a finite alphabet, S is a finite state set, $S_0 \subseteq S$ is an initial-state set, $F \subseteq S$ is a final-state set, and $\rho : S \times \Sigma \to 2^S$ is a transition function, providing for each state and letter a set of possible successor states. A is a 2NFA if it has a transition function $\rho : S \times \Sigma \to 2^{S \times \{-1,0,1\}}$, providing for each state and letter a set of possible successor states and directions. An accepting run of A on a word $w = w_1 \cdots w_n$ is a sequence $(s_1, i_1), \ldots, (s_m, i_n)$, where $s_j \in S$ and $1 \leq i_j \leq n$ for $1 \leq j < m$, $s_1 \in S_0$, $i_1 = 1$, $s_m \in F$, and $i_m = n + 1$, and the following holds for $1 \leq j < m$: there is a pair $(s_{j+1}, c) \in \rho(s_j, a_{i_j})$ such that $i_{j+1} = i_j + c$.

LEMMA 3. *[14] Let A be an n-state NFA over $\Sigma^\pm$. Then there is a 2NFA for $fold(L(A))$ with $n \cdot (|\Sigma^\pm| + 1)$ states.*

According to Language-Theoretic Lemma 2, to check that $Q_1 \sqsubseteq Q_2$, we need to check $L(Q_1) \subseteq fold(L(Q_2))$. This requires the ability to complement 2NFAs. If we use the standard approach, we'd first convert the 2NFA to an NFA with an exponential blow-up and then complement the latter with another exponential blow-up [30], resulting in a doubly-exponential blow-up. Instead, we accomplish both tasks on a singly-exponential blow-up.

LEMMA 4. *[56] Let A be a 2NFA over Σ. There is an NFA A^c such that*

- $L(A^c) = \Sigma^* - L(A)$
- $||A^c|| \in 2^{O(||A||)}$

We now have the "technology" to establish complexity bounds for 2RPQ containment.

THEOREM 5. *Containment of 2RPQs is PSPACE-complete.*

PROOF. Containment of RPQs is a special case, which implies PSPACE-hardness. To establish the PSPACE upper bound, we use the following steps in order to test $Q_1 \sqsubseteq Q_2$:

1. Construct NFAs A_1, A_2 such that $L(A_i) = L(Q_i)$. This step involves a linear blow-up [30].
2. Construct a 2NFA A'_2 such that $L(A'_2) = fold(L(A_2))$. The step involves a polynomial blow-up (Lemma 3).
3. Construct an NFA A^c_2 such that $L(A^c_2) = (\Sigma^\pm)^* - L(A'_2)$. This step involves an exponential blow-up (Lemma 4).
4. Construct an NFA $A = A_1 \times A^c_2$ such that $L(A) = L(Q_1) - fold(L(Q_2))$. This requires taking the product of A_1 and A^c_2, involving a quadratic blow-up [30].
5. Check if there is a path from start state to final state in A. This requires nondeterministic logarithmic space in the size of A.

Again, we construct A on the fly, constructing states only as we search for a path from a start state to a final state in A. This can be done in polynomial space, establishing the upper bound. □

What the above treatment of query containment for 2RPQs shows is that the theory of regular expressions over the extended alphabet $\Sigma^\pm$ diverges from the theory of 2RPQs over $\Sigma^\pm$. Regular expressions over $\Sigma^\pm$ simply defines languages over $\Sigma^\pm$, while 2RPQs over $\Sigma^\pm$ definde queries by means of semipaths. Nevertheless, we were able to develop automata-theoretic technique to develop a query-containment algorithm for 2RPQs.

3.3 Adding Conjunction

The difference between regular expressions and regular path queries becomes even sharper when we consider the conjunction operator. Over word languages, conjunction corresponds to intersection. That is, the semantics of the regular expression $e_1 \wedge e_2$ is $L((e_1) \cap L(e_2)$. But regular languages are closed under intersection, which means that adding intersection to regular expressions does not make them more expressive. (Though they do make them more succint [53].) Let, however, Q_1 and Q_2 be RPQs, and consider the following two queries: $(Q_1 \cap Q_2)(x, y)$ and $Q_1(x, y) \wedge Q_2(x, y)$. The former requires x and y to be connected by a path matching both Q_1 and Q_2. In contrast, the latter requires x and y to be connected by two paths, one matching Q_1 and one matching Q_2. Thus, while conjunction does not add expressiveness to regular expressions, it does add expressiveness to regular path queries.

Thus, it makes sense to define an analogue of CQs in the context of graph databases as the class of *conjunctive* 2RPQs, or C2RPQs [11]. A C2RPQ is a conjunctive query where instead of atoms $r(x, y)$ we have atoms $\kappa(x, y)$, where κ is a 2RPQ. To evaluate a C2RPQ Q over a graph database D we first evaluate all the 2RPQs appearing in Q, instantiating each as a binary relation over the elements of D, and then evaluating Q as a conjunctive query over this collection of relations. We can then define the query class UC2RPQ as the class of unions of C2RPQ, analogously to the class UCQ over relational databases. The class UC2RPQ is not only natural as the graph-database analog of UCQ, but is also well-motivated by graph-database applications [10, 43].

EXAMPLE 1. Consider the query in C2RPQ defined by means of the following rule:

$$Q(x,y) \;:-r(x,y)\&r(x,z)\&r(y,z)$$

Here a pair (a,b) is in the answer $Q(D)$ if there is a node c, and r-edges from a to b, from a to c, and from b to c. If we now add the rule:

$$Q(x,y) \;:-r(x,y)\&r(y,z)\&r(z,x)$$

then Q is in UC2RPQ. ∎

Solving the query-containment problem requires going beyond just automata-theoretic techniques. After all, UCQs over graph databases are a special case of UC2RPQ, so a query-containment algorithm for UC2RPQ also has to solve the query-containment problem for UCQ. What is required is an algorithm that combines the automata-theoretic techniques described above for query containment for 2RPQs, with the homomorphism-based tecniques developed in [18, 50] for solving query containment for UCQs. A framework that combines automata with homomorphisms was developed in [20] for solving the containment of Datalog in UCQ. The basic idea of that framework is the observation that one needs to consider only a finite (although exponentially large) set of *homomorphism types*, which can be encoded by a finite alphabet, enabling the application of automata. This approach was pursued in [11], where the following theorem is proved:

THEOREM 6. *The query-containment problem for UC2RPQ is EXPSPACE-complete.*

3.4 Adding Transitive Closure

What are the basic operations from which queries in UC2RPQ are composed? Just like UCQ, we have selection, projection, conjunction, and unions, but we also have transitive closure that appear inside 2RPQs. But while the class UC2RPQ is sloced under all the operations of UCQs, it is not closed under transitive closure. Consider for example the "triangle query" we saw earlier:

$$Q(x,y) \;:-r(x,y)\&r(y,z)\&r(z,x)$$

(which is in C2RPQ). The syntax of UC2RPQ does not allow us to form a query expressing the transitive closure Q^+ of Q, and it us not difficult to show that Q^+ is not in UC2RPQ. Thus, unlike CQ and UCQ, which can be defined as a class of queries closed under some basic operations, this is not the case for UC2RPQ. We therefore define the class *RQ* of *regular queries* by simply closing UC2RPQ under transitive closure. That is, RQ consists of the class of queries one can form from atomic queries $r(x,y)$ using the following operations:

- If $Q(\vec{x})$ is in RQ, and y and z are variables in $\vec{x}$, then $Q \wedge y = z$ is in RQ (selection).
- If $Q(\vec{x})$ is in RQ, and y is a variable in $\vec{x}$, then $(\exists y)Q$ is in RQ (projection).
- If $Q_1(\vec{x})$ and $Q_2(\vec{y})$ are in RQ, then $Q_1 \vee Q_2$ and $Q_1 \wedge Q_2$ are in RQ (disjunction and conjunction).
- If $Q(x,y)$ is in RQ, then Q^+ is in RQ (transitive closure)

Note that the first four operations define UCQ, so RQ just add transitive closure to set of basic operations defining the query class.

It remains to consider the query-containment problem for RQ. In [34] it was argued that, one one hand, RQ can be viewed as a fragment of Datalog (see discussion below), and, on the other hand, RQ can be viewed as a fragment of monadic second-order logic (MSO). Then using MSO techniques developed by Courcelle [26], decidability of containment can be shown, cf. [20]. This approach, however, yields an upper bound of nonelementary time, that is, its time complexity cannot be bounded by a bounded-height tower of exponential, so the question of elementary decidability was left open. Finally, the following theorem was proved in [48]:

THEOREM 7. *The query-containment problem for RQ is 2EXPSPACE-complete*

The proof builds on techniques, developed in [11, 13, 20] for combining automata-theoretic techniques with database-theoretic techniques, but the techniques in [48] are quite more sophisticated than those required for UC2RPQs, pushing the upper bound (with a matching lower bound) to 2EXPSPACE. The bottom line, however, is that RQ is an expressive and natural class of graph queries, with an elementarily decidable query-containment problem.

4. BACK TO DATALOG

4.1 From RQ to Datalog

As mentioned earlier, RQ can be embedded in Datalog:

- Atoms: If $r(x,y)$ is an atom, use the rule
$$Q(x,y) \;:-r(x,y)$$
- Selection: If $Q(\vec{x})$ is IDB, and y and z are variables in $\vec{x}$, then use the rule
$$Q'(\vec{x}-y) : -Q(\vec{x}[y/x])$$
where $\vec{x}-y$ is $\vec{x}$ with y deleted, and $\vec{x}[y/x]$ is $\vec{x}$ with y replaced by x.
- Projection: If $Q(\vec{x})$ is an IDB, and y is a variable in $\vec{x}$, then use the rule
$$Q'(\vec{x} \quad y) : -Q(\vec{x})$$
,
- Union: If $Q_1(\vec{x})$ and $Q_2(\vec{x})$ are IDBs, then use the rules
$$Q(\vec{x}) : -Q_1(\vec{x})$$
$$Q(\vec{x}) : -Q_2(\vec{x})$$
- Conjunction: If $Q_1(\vec{x})$ and $Q_2(\vec{y})$ are IDBs, then use the rule
$$Q(\vec{x} \cup \vec{y}) : -Q_1(\vec{x}), Q_2(\vec{y})$$
where $\vec{x} \cup \vec{y}$ combines the variables in $\vec{x}$ and $\vec{y}$.

- Transitive Closure: If $Q(x, y)$ is IDB, then use the rules

$$Q^+(x, y) : -Q(x, y)$$

$$Q^+(x, z) : -Q^+(x, y), Q(y, z)$$

Note that there is nothing special about the first four items in the list above; they correspond to standard nonrecursive Datalog rules. The fifth items tell us that recursion can be used *only* to define transitive closure of binary relations. It is this restriction of recursion in Datalog that is the basis for the decidability of query containment for RQ.

Note that this version of Datalog is defined over graph databases. It is only the first rule that is restricted to binary atoms. If we allow arbitrary relational atoms, then we get a version of Datalog where recursion is limited to defining transitive closure of binary relations. We call this class of queries GRQ, for *Generalized Regular Queries*. The decidability results of for RQ query containments lifts fairly easily to GRQ, since it is possible to encode relation of arbitrary arity by binary relatoions [48].

THEOREM 8. *The query-containment problem for GRQ is 2EXPSPACE-complete*

So GRQ is a fragment of Datalog that can express connectivity properties, yet has an elementarily decidable query-containment problem.

4.2 Practical Aspects

The search for an expressive query languages with a decidable query-containment problem was motivated by practical applications, but it is too early to state that the main result, the decidability of query containment for GRQ, is a practical result. After all, the problem 2EXPSPACE-complete, which means that we cannot hope to have a better then a triply-exponential time upper bound. We should not confuse, however, a theoretical worst-case complexity bound with algorithmic behavior on real-world instances. Over the past 15 years we have witnessed impressive progress in the development of tools that perform well on real-world instances, in spite of pessimistic worst-case complexity bounds, cf. [24, 38]. To assess the usefulness of the algoritms underlying the decidability results here, would require careful empirical research [57, 58].

Furthermore, despite the centrality of the query-containment problem in database theory, it is far from clear that this centrality has translated to impact on database practice. The standard approach in query optimization is *cost-based optimization*, where we search for a low-cost plan in a space of alterntaive query-evaluation plans and their estimated costs [19]. (See [55] for an example of recent work in this area.) Very little empirical research has been done on *structural query optimization*, as was envisioned, say, in [5] (but see [39] for exception). Thus, the practical usefulness of query containment is still very much an open question.

5. ACKNOWLEDGMENTS:

I am grateful for my collaborators on this research project: Diego Calvanese, Giuseppe De Giacomo, Vencent Jugé, Maurizio Lenzerini, Miguel Romero, and Juan Reutter.

6. REFERENCES

[1] S. Abiteboul, P. Buneman, and D. Suciu. *Data on the Web: from Relations to Semistructured Data and XML*. Morgan Kaufmann, San Mateo, CA, 2000.

[2] S. Abiteboul, R. Hull, and V. Vianu. *Foundations of Databases*. Addison-Wesley, 1995.

[3] S. Abiteboul and V. Vianu. Regular path queries with constraints. *Journal of Computer and System Sciences*, 58(3):428–452, 1999.

[4] A. Aho and J. Ullman. Universality of data retrieval languages. In *Proc. 6th ACM Symp. on Principles of Programming Languages*, pages 110–117, 1979.

[5] A. V. Aho, Y. Sagiv, and J. D. Ullman. Efficient optimization of a class of relational expressions. *ACM Trans. Database Syst.*, 4(4):435–454, 1979.

[6] K. Apt, H. Blair, and A. Walker. Towards a theory of declarative knowledge. In J. Minker, editor, *Foundations of Deductive Databases and Logic Programming*, pages 89–148. Morgan Kaufmann, San Mateo, CA, 1988.

[7] M. Benedikt, P. Bourhis, and M. Vanden Boom. A step up in expressiveness of decidable fixpoint logics. In *Proc. 31st IEEE Symp. on Logic in Computer Science*. ACM, 2016. To Appear.

[8] M. Benedikt and G. Gottlob. The impact of virtual views on containment. *PVLDB*, 3(1):297–308, 2010.

[9] S. Boag, D. Chamberlin, M. Fernandez, D. Florescu, J. Robie, and J. Simeon. XQuery 1.0: An XML query language – w3c working draft. Technical report, World Wide Web Consortium, 2003.

[10] P. Buneman. Semistructured data. In *Proc. 16th ACM Symp. on Principles of database systems*, pages 117–121. ACM, 1997.

[11] D. Calvanese, G. De Giacomo, M. Lenzerini, and M. Vardi. Containment of conjunctive regular path queries with inverse. In *Proc. 7th Int. Conf. on the Principles of Knowledge Representation and Reasoning*, pages 176–185, 2000.

[12] D. Calvanese, G. De Giacomo, M. Lenzerini, and M. Vardi. Query processing using views for regular path queries with inverse. In *Proc. 19th ACM Symp. on Principles of Database Systems*, pages 58–66, 2000.

[13] D. Calvanese, G. De Giacomo, and M. Y. Vardi. Decidable containment of recursive queries. *Theor. Comput. Sci.*, 336(1):33–56, 2005.

[14] D. Calvanese, G. D. Giacomo, M. Lenzerini, and M. Vardi. Reasoning on regular path queries. In *SIGMOD Record*, volume 32:4, pages 83–92, 2003.

[15] S. Ceri, G. Gottlob, and L. Tanca. What you always wanted to know about datalog (and never dared to ask). *IEEE Trans. Knowledge and Data Engineering*, 1(1):146–166, 1989.

[16] D. Chamberlin and R. Boyce. SEQUEL: A structured english query language. In *Proc. ACM SIGFIDET Workshop on Data Description, Access and Control*, pages 249–264. ACM, 1974.

[17] A. Chandra and D. Harel. Horn clause queries and generalizations. *Journal of Logic Programming*, 1:1–15, 1985.

[18] A. Chandra and P. Merlin. Optimal implementation of conjunctive queries in relational databases. In *Proc.*

9th ACM Symp. on Theory of Computing, pages 77–90, 1977.

[19] S. Chaudhuri. An overview of query optimization in relational systems. In *Proc. 17th ACM Symposium on Principles of Database Systems*, pages 34–43. ACM Press, 1998.

[20] S. Chaudhuri and M. Y. Vardi. On the equivalence of recursive and nonrecursive Datalog programs. *Journal of Computer and System Sciences*, 54:61–88, 1997.

[21] J. Clark and S. DeRose. XML Path Language (XPath) version 1.0 – W3C recommendation 16 november 1999. Technical report, World Wide Web Consortium, 1999.

[22] E. Codd. A relational model for large shared data banks. *Communications of the ACM*, 13:377–387, 1970.

[23] E. Codd. Relational completeness of databases sublanguages. In R. Rustin, editor, *Data Base Systems*, pages 65–98. Prentice-Hall, Englewood Cliffs, New Jersey, 1972.

[24] B. Cook, A. Podelski, and A. Rybalchenko. Proving program termination. *Communications of the ACM*, 54(5):88–98, 2011.

[25] S. S. Cosmadakis, H. Gaifman, P. C. Kanellakis, and M. Y. Vardi. Decidable optimization problems for database logic programs. In *Proc. 20th ACM Symp. on Theory of Computing*, pages 477–490, 1988.

[26] B. Courcelle. The monadic second-order theory of graphs iii: Tree decmpositions, minors, and complexity issues. *Theoret. Inform. Applic.*, 26:257–286, 1992.

[27] C. Date and H. Darwen. *A Guide To SQL Standard*, volume 3. Addison-Wesley Reading, 1997.

[28] D. Dougherty, K. Fisler, and S. Krishnamurthi. Specifying and reasoning about dynamic access-control policies. In *Automated Reasoning*, pages 632–646. Springer, 2006.

[29] A. Eisenberg and J. Melton. Sql: 1999, formerly known as sql3. *ACM Sigmod record*, 28(1):131–138, 1999.

[30] J. Hopcroft, R. Motwani, and J. Ullman. *Introduction to Automata Theory, Languages, and Computation (2nd Edition)*. Addison-Wesley, 2000.

[31] I. I. Tatarinov and A. Halevy. Efficient query reformulation in peer data management systems. In *Proc. of the 2004 ACM Conference on Management of Data*, pages 539–550. ACM, 2004.

[32] Y. Ioannidis. Query optimization. *Computing Surveys)*, 28(1):121–123, 1996.

[33] J. D. J.D. Ullman. Information integration using logical views. In *Proc. Int'l Conf. on Database Theory*, pages 19–40. Springer, 1997.

[34] V. Jugé and M. Vardi. On the containment of Datalog in Regular Datalog. Technical report, Rice University, 2009.

[35] P. G. Kolaitis and M. Y. Vardi. On the expressive power of Datalog: tools and a case study. *Journal of Computer and System Sciences*, 51(1):110–134, 1995.

[36] M. Lanzerini. Data integration: A theoretical perspective. In *Proc. 21st ACM Symp. on Principles of Database Systems*, pages 233–246, 2002.

[37] B. Loo, T. Condie, M. Garofalakis, D. Gay, J. Hellerstein, P. Maniatis, R. Ramakrishnan, T. Roscoe, and I. Stoica. Declarative networking. *Commun. ACM*, 52(11):87–95, 2009.

[38] S. Malik and L. Zhang. Boolean satisfiability from theoretical hardness to practical success. *Commun. ACM*, 52(8):76–82, 2009.

[39] B. McMahan, G. Pan, P. Porter, and M. Vardi. Projection pushing revisited. In *Proc. 9th Int'l Conf. on Extending Database Technology*, volume 2992 of *Lecture Notes in Computer Science*, pages 441–458. Springer, 2004.

[40] E. Meijer and G. Bierman. A co-relational model of data for large shared data banks. *Communications of the ACM*, 54(4):49–58, 2011.

[41] A. Mendelzon and P. Wood. Finding regular simple paths in graph databases. *SIAM Journal on Computing*, 24(6):1235–1258, 1995.

[42] A. R. Meyer and L. J. Stockmeyer. The equivalence problem for regular expressions with squaring requires exponential time. In *Proc. of the 13th IEEE Symp. on Switching and Automata Theory*, pages 125–129, 1972.

[43] T. Milo and D. Suciu. Index structures for path expressions. In *Proc. 7th Int'l Conf. on Database Theory*, volume 1540 of *Lecture Notes in Computer Science*, pages 277–295. Springer, 1999.

[44] J. Minker. An overview of cooperative answering in databases. In *Flexible Query Answering Systems*, pages 282–285. Springer, 1998.

[45] K. Morris, J. D. Ullman, and A. Van Gelder. Design overview of the nail! system. In *Proc. 3rd Int'l Conf. on Logic Programming*, volume 225 of *Lecture Notes in Computer Science*, pages 554–568. Springer, 1986.

[46] J. Naughton. Minimizing function-free recursive inference rules. *J. ACM*, 36(1):69–91, 1989.

[47] J. Rao and K. Ross. Reusing invariants: A new strategy for correlated queries. In *ACM SIGMOD Record*, volume 27:2, pages 37–48. ACM, 1998.

[48] J. Reutter, M. Romero, and M. Vardi. Regular queries on graph databases. In *Proc. 18th Int'l Conf. on Database Theory*, volume 31 of *LIPIcs*, pages 177–194. Schloss Dagstuhl - Leibniz-Zentrum fuer Informatik, 2015.

[49] I. Robinson, J. Webber, and E. Eifrem. *Graph Databases: New Opportunities for Connected Data.* O'Reilly Media, 2015.

[50] Y. Sagiv and M. Yannakakis. Equivalences among relational expressions with the union and difference operators. *Journal of the ACM*, 27(4):633–655, 1980.

[51] W. J. Savitch. Relationship between nondeterministic and deterministic tape complexities. *Journal of Computer and System Sciences*, 4:177–192, 1970.

[52] O. Shmueli. Equivalence of Datalog queries is undecidable. *J. of Logic Programming*, 15(3):231–241, 1993.

[53] L. Stockmeyer and A. Meyer. Word problems requiring exponential time: Preliminary report. In *Proc. 5th ACM Symp. on Theory of Computing*, pages 1–9, 1973.

[54] M. Stonebraker, G. Held, E. Wong, and P. Kreps. The design and implementation of ingres. *ACM*

Transactions on Database Systems, 1(3):189–222, 1976.
[55] I. Trummer and C. Koch. An incremental anytime algorithm for multi-objective query optimization. In *Proc. ACM Int'l Conf. on Management of Data*, pages 1941–1953, 2015.
[56] M. Vardi. A note on the reduction of two-way automata to one-way automata. *Inf. Process. Lett.*, 30(5):261–264, 1989.
[57] M. Vardi. Solving the unsolvable. *Commun. ACM*, 54(7):5, 2011.
[58] M. Vardi. Boolean satisfiability: theory and engineering. *Commun. ACM*, 57(3):5, 2014.

The ACM PODS Alberto O. Mendelzon Test-of-Time Award 2016

In 2007, the PODS Executive Committee decided to establish a Test-of-Time Award, named after the late Alberto O. Mendelzon, in recognition of his scientific legacy, and his service and dedication to the database community.

Mendelzon was an international leader in database theory, whose pioneering and fundamental work has inspired and influenced both database theoreticians and practitioners, and continues to be applied in a variety of advanced settings. He served the database community in many ways; in particular, he served as the General Chair of the PODS conference, and was instrumental in bringing together the PODS and SIGMOD conferences. He also was an outstanding educator, who guided the research of numerous doctoral students and postdoctoral fellows. The Award is to be awarded each year to a paper or a small number of papers published in the PODS proceedings ten years prior, that had the most impact (in terms of research, methodology, or transfer of practice) over the intervening decade. The decision was approved by SIGMOD and ACM. The funds for the Award were contributed by IBM Toronto.

The PODS Executive Committee has appointed us to serve as the Award Committee for 2016. After careful consideration and listening to external nominations and advice, we have decided to select the following paper as the award winner for 2016:

Two-variable logic on data trees and XML reasoning
Mikołaj Bojańczyk, Claire David, Anca Muscholl, Thomas Schwentick, and Luc Segoufin

The authors introduced an influential new approach to the modeling of XML trees with data values. This means that not only purely structural queries, but also queries involving joins can be modeled. The new approach unifies earlier results, and has led to many new results, on the automated verification of XML queries under integrity constraints. The paper has been highly influential both in database and automata theory. Because database theory research on XML has greatly benefitted from an automata-theoretic approach, it is satisfying to see the circle completed in this respect.

Marcelo Arenas
PUC, Chile

Peter Buneman
University of Edinburgh, UK

Jan Van den Bussche
Hasselt University, Belgium

The Alberto O. Mendelzon Test-of-Time Award Committee for 2016

PODS 2016 Best Paper

FAQ: Questions Asked Frequently

Mahmoud Abo Khamis
LogicBlox Inc., and
SUNY at Buffalo

Hung Q. Ngo
LogicBlox Inc., and
SUNY at Buffalo

Atri Rudra
Comp. Sci. and Eng.
SUNY at Buffalo

ABSTRACT

We define and study the **F**unctional **A**ggregate **Q**uery (FAQ) problem, which encompasses many frequently asked questions in constraint satisfaction, databases, matrix operations, probabilistic graphical models and logic. This is our main conceptual contribution.

We then present a simple algorithm called InsideOut to solve this general problem. InsideOut is a variation of the traditional dynamic programming approach for constraint programming based on variable elimination. Our variation adds a couple of simple twists to basic variable elimination in order to deal with the generality of FAQ, to take full advantage of Grohe and Marx's fractional edge cover framework, and of the analysis of recent worst-case optimal relational join algorithms.

As is the case with constraint programming and graphical model inference, to make InsideOut run efficiently we need to solve an optimization problem to compute an appropriate *variable ordering*. The main technical contribution of this work is a precise characterization of when a variable ordering is 'semantically equivalent' to the variable ordering given by the input FAQ expression. Then, we design an approximation algorithm to find an equivalent variable ordering that has the best 'fractional FAQ-width'. Our results imply a host of known and a few new results in graphical model inference, matrix operations, relational joins, and logic.

We also briefly explain how recent algorithms on beyond worst-case analysis for joins and those for solving SAT and #SAT can be viewed as variable elimination to solve FAQ over compactly represented input functions.

Keywords

Join algorithm; Quantified conjunctive query; Logic; Semiring; Probabilistic graphical model; Constraint satisfaction

PODS'16, June 26-July 01, 2016, San Francisco, CA, USA
© 2016 ACM. ISBN 978-1-4503-4191-2/16/06...$15.00
DOI: http://dx.doi.org/10.1145/2902251.2902280

1. INTRODUCTION

1.1 Motivating examples

The following fundamental problems from three diverse domains share a common algebraic structure.

Example 1. (Matrix Chain Multiplication (MCM)) Given a series of matrices $\mathbf{A}_1, \dots, \mathbf{A}_n$ over some field $\mathbb{F}$, where the dimension of $\mathbf{A}_i$ is $p_i \times p_{i+1}$, $i \in [n]$, we wish to compute the product $\mathbf{A} = \mathbf{A}_1 \cdots \mathbf{A}_n$. The problem can be reformulated as follows. There are $n+1$ variables $X_1, \dots, X_{n+1}$ with domains $\mathsf{Dom}(X_i) = [p_i]$, for $i \in [n+1]$. For $i \in [n]$, matrix $\mathbf{A}_i$ can be viewed as a function of two variables

$$\psi_{i,i+1} : \mathsf{Dom}(X_i) \times \mathsf{Dom}(X_{i+1}) \to \mathbb{F},$$

where $\psi_{i,i+1}(x, y) = (\mathbf{A}_i)_{xy}$. The MCM problem is to compute the output function

$$\varphi(x_1, x_{n+1}) = \sum_{x_2 \in \mathsf{Dom}(X_2)} \cdots \sum_{x_n \in \mathsf{Dom}(X_n)} \prod_{i=1}^{n} \psi_{i,i+1}(x_i, x_{i+1}).$$

Example 2. (Maximum A Posteriori (MAP) queries in probabilistic graphical models (PGM)) Consider a discrete graphical model represented by a hypergraph $\mathcal{H} = (\mathcal{V}, \mathcal{E})$. There are n discrete random variables $\mathcal{V} = \{X_1, \dots, X_n\}$ on finite domains $\mathsf{Dom}(X_i)$, $i \in [n]$, and $m = |\mathcal{E}|$ *factors*

$$\psi_S : \prod_{i \in S} \mathsf{Dom}(X_i) \to \mathbb{R}_+, \ S \in \mathcal{E}.$$

A typical inference task is to compute the marginal MAP estimates, written in the form

$$\varphi(x_1, \dots, x_f) = \max_{x_{f+1} \in \mathsf{Dom}(X_{f+1})} \cdots \max_{x_n \in \mathsf{Dom}(X_n)} \prod_{S \in \mathcal{E}} \psi_S(\mathbf{x}_S).$$

Example 3. (# Quantified Conjunctive Query (#QCQ)) Let Φ be a first order formula of the form

$$\Phi(X_1, \dots, X_f) = Q_{f+1} X_{f+1} \cdots Q_n X_n \left(\bigwedge_{R \in \mathsf{atoms}(\Phi)} R \right),$$

where $Q_i \in \{\exists, \forall\}$, for $i > f$. The #QCQ problem is to *count* the number of tuples in relation Φ on the free variables $X_1, \dots, X_f$. To reformulate #QCQ, construct a hypergraph $\mathcal{H} = (\mathcal{V}, \mathcal{E})$ as follows: $\mathcal{V}$ is the set of all variables $X_1, \dots, X_n$, and for each $R \in \mathsf{atoms}(\Phi)$ there is a hyperedge $S = \mathsf{vars}(R)$ consisting of all variables in R. The atom R can be viewed as a function indicating whether an assignment $\mathbf{x}_S$ to its variables is satisfied by the atom; namely $\psi_S(\mathbf{x}_S) = 1$ if $\mathbf{x}_S \in R$ and 0 otherwise.

Now, for each $i \in \{f+1, \dots, n\}$ we define an aggregate operator

$$\bigoplus^{(i)} = \begin{cases} \max & \text{if } Q_i = \exists, \\ \times & \text{if } Q_i = \forall. \end{cases}$$

Then, the #QCQ problem above is to compute the *constant* function

$$\varphi = \sum_{x_1 \in \mathsf{Dom}(X_1)} \cdots \sum_{x_f \in \mathsf{Dom}(X_f)} \bigoplus_{x_{f+1}\in\{0,1\}}^{(f+1)} \cdots \bigoplus_{x_n \in \{0,1\}}^{(n)} \prod_{S\in\mathcal{E}} \psi_S(\mathbf{x}_S).$$

It turns out that these and dozens of other fundamental problems from constraint satisfaction (CSP), databases, matrix operations, PGM inference, logic, coding theory, and complexity theory can be viewed as special instances of a generic problem we call the **F**unctional **A**ggregate **Q**uery, or the FAQ problem, which we define next. The first two columns in Table 1 present eight of these problems. The full version of the paper [3] presents many more.

1.2 The FAQ problem

Throughout the paper, we use the following convention. Uppercase X_i denotes a variable, and lowercase x_i denotes a value in the domain $\mathsf{Dom}(X_i)$ of the variable. Furthermore, for any subset $S \subseteq [n]$, define

$$\mathbf{X}_S = (X_i)_{i\in S}, \qquad \mathbf{x}_S = (x_i)_{i \in S} \in \prod_{i\in S} \mathsf{Dom}(X_i).$$

In particular, $\mathbf{X}_S$ is a tuple of variables and $\mathbf{x}_S$ is a tuple of specific values with support S. The input to FAQ is a set of functions and the output is a function computed using a series of aggregates over the variables and input functions. More specifically, for each $i \in [n]$, let X_i be a variable on some discrete domain $\mathsf{Dom}(X_i)$, where $|\mathsf{Dom}(X_i)| \geq 2$. The FAQ problem is to compute the following function

$$\varphi(\mathbf{x}_{[f]}) = \bigoplus_{x_{f+1}\in \mathsf{Dom}(X_{f+1})}^{(f+1)} \cdots \bigoplus_{x_n \in \mathsf{Dom}(X_n)}^{(n)} \bigotimes_{S\in\mathcal{E}} \psi_S(\mathbf{x}_S), \quad (1)$$

where

- $\mathcal{H} = (\mathcal{V}, \mathcal{E})$ is a multi-hypergraph. $\mathcal{V} = [n]$ is the index set of the variables X_i, $i \in [n]$. Overloading notation, $\mathcal{V}$ is also referred to as the set of variables.
- The set $F = [f]$ is the set of *free variables* for some integer $0 \leq f \leq n$. Variables in $\mathcal{V} - F$ are called *bound variables*.
- $\mathbf{D}$ is a fixed domain, such as $\{0, 1\}$ or $\mathbb{R}^+$.
- For every hyperedge $S \in \mathcal{E}$, $\psi_S : \prod_{i\in S} \mathsf{Dom}(X_i) \to \mathbf{D}$ is an *input* function (also called a *factor*).
- For every bound variable $i > f$, $\oplus^{(i)}$ is a binary (aggregate) operator on the domain $\mathbf{D}$.
- And, for each bound variable $i > f$ either $\oplus^{(i)} = \otimes$ or $(\mathbf{D}, \oplus^{(i)}, \otimes)$ forms a commutative semiring [1] (with the same $\mathbf{0}$ and $\mathbf{1}$).

[1] A triple $(\mathbf{D}, \oplus, \otimes)$ is a *commutative semiring* if $\oplus$ and $\otimes$ are commutative binary operators over $\mathbf{D}$ satisfying the following: (1) $(\mathbf{D}, \oplus)$ is a commutative monoid with an additive identity, denoted by $\mathbf{0}$. (2) $(\mathbf{D}, \otimes)$ is a commutative monoid with a multiplicative identity, denoted by $\mathbf{1}$. (In the usual semiring definition, we do not need the multiplicative monoid to be commutative.) (3) $\otimes$ distributes over $\oplus$. (4) For any element $e \in \mathbf{D}$, we have $e \otimes \mathbf{0} = \mathbf{0} \otimes e = \mathbf{0}$.

If $\oplus^{(i)} = \otimes$, then $\oplus^{(i)}$ is called a *product aggregate*; otherwise, it is a *semiring aggregate*. (We assume that there is at least one semiring aggregate.)

Because for $i > f$ every variable X_i has its own aggregate $\bigoplus^{(i)}$ over all values $x_i \in \mathsf{Dom}(X_i)$, in the rest of the paper we will write $\bigoplus^{(i)}_{x_i}$ to mean $\bigoplus\limits^{(i)}_{x_i \in \mathsf{Dom}(X_i)}$.

We will often refer to φ as an FAQ-*query*. We use FAQ-SS (for FAQ on *single semiring*) to denote the special case of FAQ when there is only *one* variable aggregate, i.e. $\oplus^{(i)} = \oplus, \forall i > f$, and $(\mathbf{D}, \oplus, \otimes)$ is a semiring.

Due to space limitation, in this extended abstract we will assume that the input factors are given using the *listing representation*, i.e. each factor is a table of all tuples of the form $\langle \mathbf{x}_S, \psi_S(\mathbf{x}_S)\rangle$, such that $\psi_S(\mathbf{x}_S) \neq \mathbf{0}$. (Entries not in the table are $\mathbf{0}$-entries.) This representation is commonly used in the CSP, databases, and sparse matrix computation domains. It should be noted that our results can handle even more succinct representations such as GDNFs and decision diagrams [15] in CSP literature and algebraic decision diagrams in the PGM literature [8]. (See [3] for details.)

1.3 Paper organization

Section 2 summarizes the contributions of the paper and sketches the line of attack. Related works are discussed in Section 3. Section 4 discusses the main ideas behind InsideOut and states its runtime *given* a variable ordering. Section 5 presents most of our technical details on computing a good variable ordering for a special case of FAQ where for every $i > f$, $\oplus^{(i)}$ is a semiring aggregate. This special case illustrates many of the key ideas and concepts. Unfortunately, due to space limitation we have to leave out the analytical details of the most general case of FAQ. All the missing details can be found in [3].

2. SUMMARY OF CONTRIBUTIONS

2.1 Conceptual contribution

The formulation of FAQ has its roots in the SumProd problem formulated by Dechter [20] who solved it using variable elimination. The SumProd problem is *exactly* FAQ-SS. A later work by Aji and McEliece [5] also addressed SumProd, which they renamed marginalization over semirings.

FAQ substantially generalizes FAQ-SS, as FAQ can now capture problems in logic such as QCQ (quantified conjunctive query) or #QCQ (sharp quantified conjunctive query). We argue that FAQ is a very powerful way of thinking about these problems and related issues. FAQ can be thought of as a declarative query language over functions. For example, we show in [3] how different input representations can vastly affect the landscape of tractability of the problem, and how the output representation is related to the notion of factorized databases [43].

2.2 Algorithmic contribution

We present a single algorithm, called InsideOut, to solve FAQ. InsideOut is a variation of the variable elimination algorithm [20, 54, 53]. In PGM, variable elimination was first proposed by Zhang and Poole [53]. Then Dechter [20] observed that this strategy can be applied to problems on other semirings such as constraint satisfaction and SAT solving. In the database literature, Yannakakis' algorithm [52] can also

Problem	FAQ formulation	Previous Algo.	**Our Algo.**
#QCQ	$\sum_{(x_1,\dots,x_f)} \bigoplus^{(f+1)}_{x_{f+1}} \cdots \bigoplus^{(n)}_{x_n} \prod_{S\in\mathcal{E}} \psi_S(\mathbf{x}_S)$ where $\bigoplus^{(i)} \in \{\max, \times\}$	No non-trivial algo	$\tilde{O}(N^{\mathsf{faqw}(\varphi)} + Z)$
QCQ	$\bigoplus^{(f+1)}_{x_{f+1}} \cdots \bigoplus^{(n)}_{x_n} \prod_{S\in\mathcal{E}} \psi_S(\mathbf{x}_S)$ where $\bigoplus^{(i)} \in \{\max, \times\}$	$\tilde{O}(N^{\mathsf{PW}(\mathcal{H})} + Z)$ [14]	$\tilde{O}(N^{\mathsf{faqw}(\varphi)} + Z)$
#CQ	$\sum_{(x_1,\dots,x_f)} \max_{x_{f+1}} \cdots \max_{x_n} \prod_{S\in\mathcal{E}} \psi_S(\mathbf{x}_S)$	$\tilde{O}(N^{\mathsf{DM}(\mathcal{H})} + Z)$ [23]	$\tilde{O}(N^{\mathsf{faqw}(\varphi)} + Z)$
Joins	$\bigcup_{\mathbf{x}} \bigcap_{S\in\mathcal{E}} \psi_S(\mathbf{x}_S)$	$\tilde{O}\left(N^{\mathsf{fhtw}(\mathcal{H})} + Z\right)$ [28]	$\tilde{O}\left(N^{\mathsf{fhtw}(\mathcal{H})} + Z\right)$
Marginal Distribution	$\sum_{(x_{f+1},\dots,x_n)} \prod_{S\in\mathcal{E}} \psi_S(\mathbf{x}_S)$	$\tilde{O}(N^{\mathsf{htw}(\varphi)} + Z)$ [32]	$\tilde{O}(N^{\mathsf{faqw}(\varphi)} + Z)$
MAP query	$\max_{(x_{f+1},\dots,x_n)} \prod_{S\in\mathcal{E}} \psi_S(\mathbf{x}_S)$	$\tilde{O}(N^{\mathsf{htw}(\varphi)} + Z)$ [32]	$\tilde{O}(N^{\mathsf{faqw}(\varphi)} + Z)$
Matrix Chain Mult.	$\sum_{x_2,\dots,x_n} \prod_{i=1}^{n} \psi_{i,i+1}(x_i, x_{i+1})$	DP bound [18]	DP bound
DFT	$\sum_{(y_0,\dots,y_{m-1})\in\mathbb{Z}_p^m} b_y \cdot \prod_{0\le j+k<m} e^{i2\pi \frac{x_j \cdot y_k}{p^{m-j-k}}}$	$O(N \log_p N)$ [17]	$O(N \log_p N)$

Table 1: Runtimes of algorithms assuming optimal variable ordering is given. Problems shaded red are in CSPs and logic ($\mathbf{D} = \{0,1\}$ for CSP and $\mathbf{D} = \mathbb{N}$ for #CSP), problems shaded green fall under PGMs ($\mathbf{D} = \mathbb{R}_+$), and problems shaded blue fall under matrix operations ($\mathbf{D} = \mathbb{C}$). N denotes the size of the largest factor (assuming they are represented with the listing format). $\mathsf{htw}(\varphi)$ is the notion of integral cover width defined in [32] for PGM. $\mathsf{PW}(\mathcal{H})$ is the *optimal width of a prefix graph* of $\mathcal{H}$ from [14] and $\mathsf{DM}(\mathcal{H}) = \text{poly}(F\text{-}\mathsf{ss}(\mathcal{H}), \mathsf{fhtw}(\mathcal{H}))$, where F-$\mathsf{ss}(\mathcal{H})$ is the $[f]$-quantified star size [23]. Z is the output size in listing representation. Our width $\mathsf{faqw}(\varphi)$ is never worse than any of the three and there are classes of queries where ours is unboundedly better than all three. In DFT, $N = p^m$ is the length of the input vector. $\tilde{O}$ hides a logarithmic factor in data complexity and polynomial factor in query complexity.

be cast as variable elimination under the set semiring or Boolean semiring.[2]

InsideOut adds three minor twists to the basic variable elimination strategy. **First**, we use a backtracking-search strategy called OutsideIn to compute the intermediate results. This strategy allows us to use the *analysis* of recent worst-case optimal join algorithms [51, 40, 41] to bound the time it takes to compute the intermediate results using the fractional edge cover bound [7, 28]. **Second**, we introduce the idea of a **01**-*projection* of a function onto a support to obtain the fractional hypertree width style of runtime guarantee [29]. **Third**, in addition to making use of the distributive law to 'fold' common factors [5] when we face a semiring aggregate, we apply a swap between an aggregate and the inside product when that aggregate is also a product.

We show that InsideOut runs in time $\tilde{O}(N^{\mathsf{faqw}(\sigma)} + Z)$, where σ is a variable ordering that we choose to run the algorithm on, N is the input size, and Z is the output size (under the 'listing representation' of input and output factors), and $\mathsf{faqw}(\sigma)$ is a parameter called the (fractional) FAQ-*width* of σ. FAQ-width is the FAQ-analog of the induced fractional edge cover width of a variable ordering. (See Definition 2.)

In fact, we show (in [3]) that the variable elimination framework is still powerful in cases when the fractional hypertree width bounds are no longer applicable. These are special cases of FAQ where the input functions are compactly represented. In particular, we explain how – with a suitable modification – InsideOut can be used to recover recently known beyond worst-case results in join algorithms (Minesweeper [39], and Tetris [2]), and results on the tractability of SAT and #SAT for β-acyclic formulas [44, 11].

On the practical side, preliminary implementations of join algorithms based on fractional hypertree width for counting graph patterns have been very encouraging, as they are faster than existing commercial systems by at least an order of magnitude [1, 42] for selected queries. Far beyond graph patterns, we have implemented InsideOut within the LogicBlox database system [6] with great performance results.

2.3 Main technical contributions

The key technical problem is choosing a σ that minimizes $\mathsf{faqw}(\sigma)$. This is where the generality of FAQ requires new ideas. Traditional variable elimination for CSPs or PGM inference also requires computing a good variable ordering to minimize the *treewidth* [35] or *fractional hypertree width* [29] of the variable ordering. However, in those cases all variable orderings are valid. Hence, all we have to do in this traditional setting is to compute a tree decomposition whose maximum bag size (or maximum fractional edge cover number over the bags) is minimized, then the GYO-elimination procedure will produce a good variable ordering (see [3]). In the general setting of FAQ, just like in logic where there are alternating quantifiers, the set of semantically equivalent variable orderings depends on both the input query expression and the structure of the query hypergraph.

To see what equivalent ordering could mean, consider the following. A natural class of valid permutations to consider are those that only permute aggregates in a maximal block of identical aggregates in the query expression. However, taking the query hypergraph into account, one can do much

[2]It is well-known [5, 35] that variable elimination and message passing are equivalent in the special case of FAQ-SS.

better. Consider, for example, the FAQ-query

$$\varphi = \max_{x_1} \sum_{x_2} \max_{x_3} \cdots \sum_{x_{2k}} \psi_{\{1,3,\dots,2k-1\}} \psi_{\{2,4,\dots,2k\}}$$

where both factors have range $\mathbb{R}_+$. In this case, even though max and $\sum$ do not commute with one another, we can rewrite φ using any of the $(2k)!$ variable orderings and still obtain the same result. (The aggregates have to be permuted along with the variables to which they are attached.)

Even for the special case of FAQ-SS, where there is only one type of semiring aggregates hence all permutations are valid, computing the optimal variable ordering is already **NP**-hard in query complexity, because computing the (fractional hyper) treewidth of the query hypergraph is **NP**-hard. Hence, the extra complication of only considering 'valid' orderings for FAQ seems to make our task much harder. Somewhat surprisingly, we are able to show that the complexity of computing the optimal ordering for general FAQ is essentially the same as the complexity of computing the optimal ordering for FAQ-SS instances. As a brief summary, we have the following technical contributions:

- Given an FAQ-query φ we define the set $\mathsf{EVO}(\varphi)$ of all variable orderings *semantically equivalent* to φ. Roughly, for any $\sigma \in \mathsf{EVO}(\varphi)$, if we rewrite the expression for φ using the ordering σ (with all aggregates permuted along), then we obtain a function identical to φ, **no matter** what the input factors are. The FAQ-width of φ is $\mathsf{faqw}(\varphi) = \min_{\sigma \in \mathsf{EVO}(\varphi)} \mathsf{faqw}(\sigma)$.
- We describe how to (in poly-time, query complexity) construct an *expression tree* for the input FAQ-query. The expression tree induces a partially ordered set on the variables called the *precedence poset*. By defining a notion called *component-wise equivalence*, we completely characterize $\mathsf{EVO}(\varphi)$: $\sigma \in \mathsf{EVO}(\varphi)$ if and only if it is component-wise equivalent to some linear extension of the precedence poset.
- To prepare for the approximation algorithm for $\mathsf{faqw}(\varphi)$, we show that going through all orderings in $\mathsf{EVO}(\varphi)$ is *not* necessary. The set of linear extensions of the precedence poset is sufficient for this purpose: every linear extension of the precedence poset is semantically equivalent to φ, and every $\sigma \in \mathsf{EVO}(\varphi)$ has the same FAQ-width as some linear extension of this poset.
- Finally, using an approximation algorithm for the fractional hypertree width (fhtw) with approximation ratio $g(\mathsf{fhtw})$ as a blackbox,[3] and using the expression tree as a guide, we give an approximation algorithm computing an ordering σ such that $\mathsf{faqw}(\sigma) \leq \mathsf{faqw}(\varphi) + g(\mathsf{faqw}(\varphi))$.

2.4 Highlights of our corollaries

In light of the fact that many problems can be reduced to FAQ, Table 1 presents a selected subset of corollaries that our results imply.[4] We list the results assuming the optimal variable ordering is already given. (This holds true for both known results and our results.) When the optimal variable ordering is not given, the exponents of N in all cases have to be changed to the best known approximating factors for the corresponding width. In the FAQ case, that would be $O(\mathsf{faqw}^3(\varphi))$.

For each problem, the table lists the corresponding FAQ instance, the runtime of the previously best known algorithm, and the runtime of InsideOut. These are the problems that we would like to highlight, as they yield either new results or an alternative interpretation of known results in the FAQ framework.

The results in Table 1 roughly span three areas: (1) CSPs and Logic; (2) PGMs and (3) Matrix operations. Except for joins, problems in area (1) need the full generality of our FAQ formulation, where InsideOut either improves upon existing results or yields new results. Problems in area (2) can already be reduced to FAQ-SS. Here, InsideOut improves upon known results since it takes advantage of Grohe and Marx's more recent fractional hypertree width bounds. Finally, problems in area (3) of Table 1 are classic. InsideOut does not yield anything new here, but it is intriguing to be able to explain the textbook dynamic programming algorithm for Matrix-Chain Multiplication [18] as an algorithm to find a good variable ordering for the corresponding FAQ-instance. The DFT result is a re-writing of Aji and McEliece's observation [5].[5]

It should be noted that the prior results on #CQ [23] and QCQ [14] focused on dichotomy theorems for bounded-arity classes of input hypergraphs, not just on the best possible runtime one can get. Our faqw notion is a generalization of fractional hypertree width, which steps into the unbounded arity world. See Marx [38] for a more detailed discussion of known results on CSP in the unbounded-arity case.

3. RELATED WORK

Since FAQ encompasses so many areas, our related work discussion is necessarily incomplete. The full version [3] has pointers to many more related works.

3.1 Problems on one semiring

As was mentioned in the introduction, the FAQ-SS problem was explicitly defined by Aji and McEliece [5] who called it the MPF problem (for Marginalize the product function). They presented a message passing algorithm for FAQ-SS and essentially showed that their algorithm meets the treewidth bound. Their paper also lists a number of problems that are FAQ-SS instances, including Matrix Chain Multiplication (less specific than our result, they just argue that essentially different variable orderings give rise to different ways of parenthesizing the matrix chain multiplication) and Matrix Vector Multiplication. They showed that their general algorithm contains FFT as a special case. We re-phrase their interpretation of the FFT using InsideOut. They also showed that many basic decoding problems in coding theory can be cast as FAQ-SS instances.

Kohlas and Wilson [34] presented even more applications of the FAQ-SS problem. The paper categorized various existing message passing algorithms depending on what extra properties they need beyond $(\mathbf{D}, \oplus, \otimes)$ being a commutative semiring. Their paper also explored algorithms for approximate computations (while in this work we solely deal with

[3]The best known such algorithm due to Marx [36] has $g(\mathsf{fhtw}) = O(\mathsf{fhtw}^3)$

[4]The results listed in the table implicitly assumed the listing representation of input factors.

[5]Note that we have further results on matrix vector multiplication for structured matrices (see [3]).

exact computation). Approximate computations in PGMs have been explored under the semiring framework [48].

Most of the results in the PGM literature present algorithms that are shown to obtain the treewidth bound. To the best of our knowledge, the finest notion of hypergraph width used to bound the performance of algorithms is the integral hypertree width bound of [26], which appeared in [32, 21]. See Section 3.3 and [3] for a more detailed discussion on the various notions of widths.

In the database literature, recently Koch [33] described an algebraic query language called AGCA over 'rings of databases' which is somewhat similar in spirit to FAQ. This framework makes use of additive inverses to allow for efficient view maintenance.

3.2 Factorized databases

Bakibayev et al. [9] and Olteanu and Závodný [43] introduced the notion of *factorized databases*, and showed how one can efficiently compute join and aggregates over factorized databases. In hindsight there is much in common between their approach and InsideOut applied to the single semiring case of FAQ-SS. Both approaches have the same runtime complexity, because both are dynamic programming algorithms, InsideOut is bottom-up, and factorized database computation is top-down (memoized).

The FAQ framework is more general in that it can handle multiple aggregate types. Our contribution also involves the characterization of EVO and an approximation algorithm for faqw. On the other hand, aspects of factorized database that FAQ does not handle include the evaluation of SQL queries and output size bounds on the factorized representations.

3.3 Notions of widths

Various notions of hypergraph 'widths' have been developed over the years in PGM, CSP, and database theory. In particular, two often-used properties of the input query are *acyclicity* and *bounded width.*

When the query is acyclic, the classic algorithm of Yannakakis [52] for relational joins (and CSPs) runs in time linear in the input plus output size, modulo a log factor. Similarly, Pearl's belief propagation algorithm [45] works well for acyclic graphical models. As we briefly touch upon in [3], Yannakakis' algorithm is essentially belief propagation on the Boolean semiring or set semiring. The algorithm can also be reinterpreted using InsideOut.

Subsequent works on databases and CSPs further expand the classes of queries that can be evaluated in polynomial time. These works define progressively more general notions of width for a query, which intuitively measure how far a query is from being acyclic. Roughly, these results state that if the corresponding notion of 'width' is bounded by a constant, then the query is 'tractable,' i.e. there is a polynomial-time algorithm to evaluate it. For example, Gyssens et al. [30, 31] showed that queries with bounded *degree of acyclicity* are tractable. Then came *query width* (qw) from Chekuri and Rajaraman [12], *hypertree width* and *generalized hypertree width* (ghw) from Gottlob et al. [50, 26], and *fractional hypertree width* from Grohe and Marx [29]. More recently, Marx developed the most general width notions known to date, called *adaptive width* and *submodular width* [37, 38].

In the PGM literature, the most common notion is *treewidth* as the textbook variable elimination and message passing algorithms are often stated to run in time $O(N^{w+1})$ where w is the tree width of the model [35]. Freuder [24] and Dechter and Pearl [22] showed in late 1980s that CSP instances with bounded treewidth are tractable.

In the logic/finite model theory literature, several notions of widths were also developed [4, 23, 14]. We describe them in the relevant sections of the full version [3].

3.4 Finite model theory

In [47], Pichler and Skritek studied the #CQ problem in the special case where the query is acyclic. We refer to this special case as #ACQ. In particular, they showed that #ACQ is tractable in data complexity (i.e. when the number of variables that we are counting over is a constant) and in query complexity (i.e. when all relations have constant sizes) but not in combined complexity where the problem turns out to be #**P**-complete.

In [23], Durand and Mengel introduced a new parameter for #CQ called the *quantified star size*. It is basically a measure of how free variables are connected in the query's hypergraph. Along with bounded generalized hypertree width (or fractional hypertree width), bounded quantified star size characterizes the classes of #CQ instances that are tractable in the bounded arity (or bounded generalized hypertree width) case.

The quantified star size idea has been expanded later by applying it to the *core* of the query instead of the original query [27]. The core is a minimal subquery that is homomorphic to the original query. Because homomorphism does not preserve counts (i.e. it is not a one-to-one mapping), free variables have to be explicitly preserved by taking the core of the *color query* of the original query. Further development along with new lower bounds appeared in [16].

QCQ (second row of Table 1) has its own long line of research. An early and interesting result was the tractability of QCQ when the domain size, treewidth, and number of quantifier alternations are all constants [13]. More recently, Chen and Dalmau introduced a notion of width for QCQ based on elimination orderings [14]. In particular, they take the minimum width over some variable orderings that are equivalent to the original query. They showed the tractability of QCQ when their width is bounded.

The runtime of InsideOut for CQ, #CQ, and QCQ are unboundedly better than the above results as shown in Table 1. Our result on #QCQ is new: to the best of our knowledge no non-trivial efficient algorithms for #QCQ were known prior to our work. Essentially, InsideOut is able to unify the above results under the same umbrella.

4. THE ALGORITHM

4.1 Notation

Recall that $\mathbf{0}$ is the additive identity of the semiring(s) which also annihilates any element of $\mathbf{D}$ under multiplication. Unless specified otherwise, we also assume that there are n variables and m factors. Given any Boolean predicate P, define the *Kronecker delta* δ_P to be $\delta_P = 1$ if P holds and 0 otherwise. (Note that these are numbers 1 and 0, not the multiplicative or additive identity.)

Let $W \subseteq [n]$ be some subset of variables, and $\mathbf{y}_W \in \prod_{i \in W} \mathsf{Dom}(X_i)$ be some given value tuple. The *conditional factor* $\psi_S(\cdot \mid \mathbf{y}_W)$ is a function from $\prod_{i \in S} \mathsf{Dom}(X_i)$ to $\mathbf{D}$

defined by

$$\psi_S(\mathbf{x}_S \mid \mathbf{y}_W) = \begin{cases} \mathbf{0} & \text{if } S \cap W \neq \emptyset \text{ and } \mathbf{x}_{S\cap W} \neq \mathbf{y}_{S\cap W} \\ \psi_S(\mathbf{x}_S) & \text{otherwise.} \end{cases}$$

For each factor ψ_S, define its *size* to be the number of non-zero points under its domain:

$$|\psi_S| := \left|\{\mathbf{x}_S \mid \psi_S(\mathbf{x}_S) \neq \mathbf{0}\}\right|.$$

We often use N to denote the sum of all input factor sizes.

4.2 The algorithmic building block

Consider the FAQ-SS form of the FAQ expression (1) when there is no free variable and all aggregates are the same semiring aggregate. In this case, we write the expression as

$$\varphi = \bigoplus_{\mathbf{x}} \bigotimes_{S\in\mathcal{E}} \psi_S(\mathbf{x}_S) = \bigoplus_{x_1 \in \mathsf{Dom}(X_1)} \left(\bigoplus_{\mathbf{x}_{[n]-\{1\}}} \bigotimes_{S\in\mathcal{E}} \psi_S(\mathbf{x}_S \mid x_1) \right).$$

We can evaluate this expression by going through each value of x_1 and computing the inner expression 'conditioned' on this x_1. The naïve implementation of this strategy wastes time if there is any x_1 for which *some* conditional factor $\psi_S(\cdot \mid x_1)$ is identically $\mathbf{0}$. Thus, the obvious idea is to first compute the set I_1 of values x_1 for which $\psi_S(\cdot \mid x_1) \not\equiv \mathbf{0}$ *for all* factors ψ_S. Then, recursively compute the expression

$$\varphi = \bigoplus_{x_1 \in I_1} \left(\bigoplus_{\mathbf{x}_{[n]-\{1\}}} \bigotimes_{S\in\mathcal{E}} \psi_S(\mathbf{x}_S \mid x_1) \right).$$

This is called the OutsideIn algorithm, as it evaluates the expression from the outer-most aggregate to the inner-most. It serves as the algorithmic building block of InsideOut.

Given that the input factors are represented using the listing format (i.e. only non-$\mathbf{0}$ entries are listed), computing the above expression recursively is a join algorithm in disguise, and any of the algorithms from [40, 51, 41] works. In fact, the OutsideIn algorithm works even if there were free variables. Using the Hölder inequality analysis approach from [41], we can easily show the following. (See [3] for more details including the proofs.)

THEOREM 4.1. *Let $(\lambda_S)_{S\in\mathcal{E}}$ be any fractional edge cover of the hypergraph $\mathcal{H} = (\mathcal{V}, \mathcal{E})$ with m edges and n vertices. Algorithm* OutsideIn *applied to* FAQ-SS *runs in time*

$$\tilde{O}(mn \prod_{S\in\mathcal{E}} |\psi_S|^{\lambda_S}).$$

The expression $\prod_{S\in\mathcal{E}} |\psi_S|^{\lambda_S}$ with an optimal choice of the fractional edge cover $(\lambda_S)_{S\in\mathcal{E}}$ is called the AGM-*bound* for the query [7].

OutsideIn is backtracking search [19, 25] which was known 50 years ago in the AI and constraint programming world. In the PGM literature, the method of conditioning search is similar, but the main theoretical objective is so that the conditioning graph is acyclic [46]. The main advantage of backtracking search is that it requires very little extra space. The main disadvantage is that it might have to resolve the same subproblem multiple times. The duality between backtracking search and dynamic programming is well-known in the constraint programming literature [49]. Next section explores the other side of this duality: the dynamic programming side.

4.3 The InsideOut algorithm

4.3.1 *The* FAQ-SS *case*

To describe the intuition, we first explain InsideOut for the special instance FAQ-SS (or SumProd). The idea behind variable elimination [20, 54, 53] is to 'fold' common factors, exploiting the distributive law:

$$\bigoplus_{x_{f+1}} \cdots \bigoplus_{x_n} \bigotimes_{S\in\mathcal{E}} \psi_S(\mathbf{x}_S)$$

$$= \bigoplus_{x_{f+1}} \cdots \bigoplus_{x_{n-1}} \bigotimes_{S\in\mathcal{E}-\partial(n)} \psi_S(\mathbf{x}_S) \otimes \underbrace{\left(\bigoplus_{x_n} \bigotimes_{S\in\partial(n)} \psi_S(\mathbf{x}_S) \right)}_{\text{new factor } \psi_{U_n-\{n\}}},$$

where the equality follows from the fact that $\otimes$ distributes over $\oplus$, $\partial(n)$ denotes all edges incident to n in $\mathcal{H}$ and $U_n = \bigcup_{S\in\partial(n)} S$. Assume for the moment that we can somehow efficiently compute the intermediate factor $\psi_{U_n-\{n\}}$. Then, the resulting problem is another instance of FAQ-SS on a modified multi-hypergraph $\mathcal{H}_{n-1}$, constructed from $\mathcal{H}$ by removing vertex n along with all edges in $\partial(n)$, and *adding back* a new hyperedge $U_n - \{n\}$. Recursively, we continue this process until all variables $X_n, \ldots, X_{f+1}$ are eliminated. Textbook treewidth-based results for PGM inference are obtained this way [35]. In the database context (i.e. given an FAQ-query over the Boolean semiring), the intermediate result $\psi_{U_n-\{n\}}$ is essentially an intermediate materialized relation of a query plan.

While correct, basic variable elimination as described above is potentially not very efficient for sparse input factors, i.e. factors whose sizes are smaller than the product of the domain sizes. The main reason is that the product that was factored out might annihilate many entries of the intermediate result $\psi_{U_n-\{n\}}$, while we have spent so much time computing $\psi_{U_n-\{n\}}$. For example, for an $S \notin \partial(n)$ and tuple $\mathbf{y}_S$ such that $S \subseteq U_n$ and $\psi_S(\mathbf{y}_S) = \mathbf{0}$, we do not need to compute the entries $\psi_{U_n-\{n\}}(\mathbf{x}_{U_n-\{n\}})$ for which $\mathbf{y}_S = \mathbf{x}_S$: those entries will be killed later anyhow. The idea is then to only compute those $\psi_{U_n-\{n\}}(\mathbf{x}_{U_n-\{n\}})$ values that will 'survive' the other factors. One simple way to achieve this would be to compute the following factor instead of $\psi_{U_n-\{n\}}$:

$$\psi'_{U_n-\{n\}}(\mathbf{x}_{U_n-\{n\}})$$

$$= \bigoplus_{x_n} \left[\left(\bigotimes_{S\in\partial(n)} \psi_S(\mathbf{x}_S) \right) \otimes \left(\bigotimes_{\substack{S\notin\partial(n),\\ S\cap U_n \neq \emptyset}} \bigoplus_{\mathbf{x}_{S-U_n}} \psi_S(\mathbf{x}_S) \right) \right],$$

where $\bigoplus_{\mathbf{x}_{S-U_n}} \psi_S(\mathbf{x}_S)$ results from $\psi_S(\mathbf{x}_S)$ by marginalizing away variables in $S - U_n$. If $\mathbf{D} = \{0, 1\}$ or $\{\mathsf{true}, \mathsf{false}\}$, then the above computation of $\psi'_{U_n-\{n\}}$ is enough; indeed, this idea is precisely what is behind relational join and CSP algorithms achieving the *fractional hypertree width bound* [29]. However, for a general range $\mathbf{D}$ as in PGM inference or an aggregate query in a database, the change above can produce an incorrect result because the same $\psi_S(\mathbf{x}_S)$ can participate in the product multiple times during different elimination steps.

Our proposed fix is very simple: instead of multiplying with the actual value of $\psi_S(\mathbf{x}_S)$ for $S \notin \partial(n)$, we only multiply with an indicator factor that checks if $\psi_S(\mathbf{x}_S)$ is $\mathbf{0}$ or not. More precisely, let $\psi_{S/U_n}(\mathbf{x}_S)$ be the *projection* of ψ_S to variables in $S \cap U_n$ where all the non-zero entries become **1**. (See Definition 9 in the appendix.) Armed with this new indicator factor, InsideOut computes the following factor when marginalizing X_n away:

$$\psi_{U_n-\{n\}}(\mathbf{x}_{U_n-\{n\}}) = \bigoplus_{x_n}\left[\left(\bigotimes_{S\in\partial(n)} \psi_S(\mathbf{x}_S)\right) \otimes \left(\bigotimes_{\substack{S\notin\partial(n),\\ S\cap U_n\neq\emptyset}} \psi_{S/U_n}(\mathbf{x}_{S\cap U_n})\right)\right] \quad (2)$$

and similarly for eliminating the remaining variables.

4.3.2 *The general case*

The above strategy does not care if the variable aggregates where the same or different: As long as $(\mathbf{D}, \oplus^{(n)}, \otimes)$ is a semiring, we can fold the common factors. Thus, InsideOut works almost as is for a general FAQ instance (as opposed to FAQ-SS).

We are left to describe how InsideOut deals with the case when $\oplus^{(n)} = \otimes$. In this case, the simple idea is to swap the two (identical) operators:

$$\begin{aligned}
&\varphi(\mathbf{x}_{[f]}) \\
&= \cdots \bigoplus_{x_{n-1}}^{(n-1)} \bigoplus_{x_n}^{(n)} \bigotimes_{S\in\mathcal{E}} \psi_S(\mathbf{x}_S) \\
&= \cdots \bigoplus_{x_{n-1}}^{(n-1)} \bigotimes_{x_n\in\mathsf{Dom}(X_n)} \bigotimes_{S\in\mathcal{E}} \psi_S(\mathbf{x}_S) \\
&= \cdots \bigoplus_{x_{n-1}}^{(n-1)} \bigotimes_{S\in\mathcal{E}} \bigotimes_{x_n\in\mathsf{Dom}(X_n)} \psi_S(\mathbf{x}_S) \\
&= \cdots \bigoplus_{x_{n-1}}^{(n-1)} \bigotimes_{S\notin\partial(n)} (\psi_S(\mathbf{x}_S))^{|\mathsf{Dom}(X_n)|} \bigotimes_{S\in\partial(n)} \bigotimes_{x_n} \psi_S(\mathbf{x}_S).
\end{aligned}$$

This results in a *product marginalization* of individual factors ψ_S for $S \in \partial(n)$. In particular, for each $S \in \partial(n)$, we compute the factor with support $S - \{n\}$ defined by

$$\psi_{S-\{n\}}(\mathbf{x}_{S-\{n\}}) = \bigotimes_{x_n\in\mathsf{Dom}(X_n)} \psi_S(\mathbf{x}_S).$$

This can be computed in linear time in $|\psi_S|$. The product marginalization step is algorithmically much easier because it does not create the intermediate factor $\psi_{U_n-\{n\}}$.

As for $S \notin \partial(n)$, we replace ψ_S by the power factor

$$\psi'_S(\mathbf{x}_S) = (\psi_S(\mathbf{x}_S))^{|\mathsf{Dom}(X_n)|},$$

which can be done in linear time with a log $|\mathsf{Dom}(X_n)|$ blowup using the repeated squaring algorithm. Note the key fact that this power is with respect to the product aggregate $\otimes$. In most (if not all) applications of FAQ, there is one additional property: most of the time, $\otimes$ is an idempotent operator over the effective domain. For example, in the #QCQ problem $\otimes$ is the usual product operator and the domain that it aggregates over is $\{0, 1\}$ (before there is a sum outside). In this case, $\psi'_S(\mathbf{x}_S) = (\psi_S(\mathbf{x}_S))^{|\mathsf{Dom}(X_n)|} = \psi_S(\mathbf{x}_S)$, and we do not need to spend the linear nor log-blowup time.

The definition of what it means for an operator to act idempotently on a domain and its relationship to the position of the operator in the FAQ-formula are subtle. We leave the details to [3]. Finally, note that in this case we recurse on the hypergraph $\mathcal{H}_{n-1} = \mathcal{H} - \{n\}$.

Thus far we left open the question of how to compute $\psi_{U_n-\{n\}}$ efficiently, assuming $\oplus^{(n)}$ is a semiring aggregate. We simply apply the OutsideIn algorithm from Section 4.2. Note that computing $\psi_{U_n-\{n\}}$ is an instance of FAQ with $|U_n| - 1$ free variables.

4.3.3 *Output representation*

Let $\mathcal{E}_f$ be the set of supports of factors remaining after eliminating the non-free variables. The output to FAQ is now the expression

$$\varphi(\mathbf{x}_{[f]}) = \bigotimes_{S\in\mathcal{E}_f} \psi_S(\mathbf{x}_S), \quad (3)$$

which is an FAQ instance with all free variables. We can compute the output directly by running OutsideIn on (3). However, inspired by Olteanu and Závodný [43] we can first compute the output in the factorized representation, and then report it.

One way to think about this idea is to first compute the set of tuples $\mathbf{x}_{[f]}$ for which $\varphi(\mathbf{x}_{[f]}) \neq \mathbf{0}$, and then for each such tuple compute its value $\varphi(\mathbf{x}_{[f]})$ using (3) by multiplying the corresponding ψ_S. Computing the non-**0** output tuples *is* a join problem, which in the FAQ setting is the $(\cup, \cap)/(\vee, \wedge)$ semiring, with the runtime $\tilde{O}(N^{\mathsf{fhtw}} + Z)$ as shown in Table 1.

Implementation-wise, we can use the **01**-projection idea from Section 4.3.1 as follows. For $k = f, \ldots, 1$, we will eliminate the free variable X_k and use OutsideIn to compute the factors $\psi_{U_k}, \psi_{U_k-\{k\}}$ defined as

$$\begin{aligned}
\psi_{U_k}(\mathbf{x}_{U_k}) &:= \bigotimes_{S:S\cap U_k\neq\emptyset} \psi_{S/U_k}(\mathbf{x}_{S\cap U_k}),\\
\psi_{U_k-\{k\}}(\mathbf{x}_{U_k-\{k\}}) &:= \bigoplus_{x_k}^{(k)} \psi_{U_k}(\mathbf{x}_{U_k}),
\end{aligned}$$

where $\bigoplus_{x_k}^{(k)}$ is the **01**-OR (See Defintion 10). Finally, we run OutsideIn on the following expression instead of (3).

$$\varphi(\mathbf{x}_{[f]}) = \left(\bigotimes_{S\in\mathcal{E}_f} \psi_S(\mathbf{x}_S)\right) \otimes \left(\bigotimes_{k\in[f]} \psi_{U_k}(\mathbf{x}_{U_k})\right). \quad (4)$$

Eliminating free variables and then recovering them back by (4) are equivalent to the two phases of Yannakakis algorithm [52]. Our implementation of InsideOut in LogicBlox follows the elimination/recovery method.

4.3.4 *Runtime analysis*

The runtime of InsideOut is the sum of the runtimes of n variable elimination steps plus the time needed to report the output at the end. For $k = n, \ldots, 1$, the cost of the kth step is analyzed as follows. If $k > f$ and the aggregate $\bigoplus^{(k)}$ is a semiring aggregate, or if $k \leq f$, then the runtime is dominated by the OutsideIn algorithm's runtime to compute the intermediate factor $\psi_{U_k-\{k\}}$. From Theorem 4.1, this is bounded by the AGM-bound on the set U_k, denoted by $\mathsf{AGM}(U_k)$. On the other hand, if $k > f$ and $\bigoplus^{(k)} = \bigotimes$, then the runtime is linear in the input size modulo a log factor. The final invocation of OutsideIn on (4) reports the output (in listing representation) in linear time, just like the output phase of Yannakakis algorithm.

From there, with a bit of care we can write down a precise expression for the runtime of InsideOut. Minimizing the resulting (somewhat complicated) expression leads to the dynamic programming algorithm for the MCM problem and the FFT algorithm for the DFT. See [3] for details.

One way to simplify the runtime expression is to upper-bound each bound $\mathsf{AGM}(U_k)$ by the fractional edge cover number of the set U_k, i.e. $\mathsf{AGM}(U_k) \leq N^{\rho^*_{\mathcal{H}}(U_k)}$ [29].[6] Let

[6]For any subset $B \subseteq \mathcal{V}$ of vertices, $\rho^*_{\mathcal{H}}(B)$ is the optimal ob-

K denote the indices $f < i \leq n$ such that $\oplus^{(i)} \neq \otimes$. Then, it follows that the algorithm runs in time

$$\tilde{O}\left(N^{\max_{k \in K \cup [f]} \rho^*_{\mathcal{H}}(U_k)} + Z\right), \quad (5)$$

where Z is the output size in listing representation. In the above discussion, we eliminated the variables in order $X_n, X_{n-1}, \dots, X_1$. However, there is no reason to force InsideOut to follow this particular order. In particular, there might be a different variable ordering for which expression (5) is *a lot* smaller and the algorithm still works correctly on that ordering. (See [3] for examples.)

This is where the main technical contributions of this paper begin. We need to answer the following questions:

1. How do we know which variable orderings are equivalent to the original FAQ-query expression?
2. How do we find the best variable ordering among all equivalent variable orderings?

The next section formalizes the above two questions.

4.4 Fractional width of an FAQ-query

We first define precisely the notion of 'semantic equivalence' between two variable orderings.

Definition 1. (φ-equivalent variable ordering) Let φ be an FAQ-query written in the form (1). A *φ-equivalent variable ordering* is a vertex ordering $\sigma = (\sigma(1), \dots, \sigma(n))$ of the hypergraph $\mathcal{H}$ satisfying the following conditions:

(a) The set $\{\sigma(1), \dots, \sigma(f)\}$ is exactly $F = [f]$. In other words, in a φ-equivalent variable ordering, the free variables come first (in any order).

(b) The function φ^σ defined by

$$\varphi^\sigma(\mathbf{x}_F) := \bigoplus^{(\sigma(f+1))}_{x_{\sigma(f+1)}} \cdots \bigoplus^{(\sigma(n))}_{x_{\sigma(n)}} \bigotimes_{S \in \mathcal{E}} \psi_S(\mathbf{x}_S)$$

is identical to the function φ irrespective of the input factors.[7]

Let $\mathsf{EVO}(\varphi)$ denote the set of all φ-equivalent variable orderings.

For any φ-equivalent variable ordering σ, we could have run InsideOut on φ^σ instead of φ. In that case, the sets U_k are denoted by U^σ_k, and the recursive sequence of hypergraphs is denoted by $\mathcal{H}^\sigma_k$, $k = n, n-1, \dots$, as expected.

Definition 2. (Fractional FAQ-width of a variable ordering) Let σ be a φ-equivalent variable ordering. Define the sequence of hypergraphs $\mathcal{H}^\sigma_k$ along with the sets U^σ_k. The *fractional* FAQ *width* of a variable ordering σ is the quantity

$$\mathsf{faqw}(\sigma) := \max_{k \in K \cup [f]} \rho^*_{\mathcal{H}}(U^\sigma_k). \quad (6)$$

As analyzed in (5), InsideOut runs in time $\tilde{O}(N^{\mathsf{faqw}(\sigma)} + Z)$, where σ is the original variable ordering given in expression (1). Thus, to have the best runtime we would like to select an equivalent ordering σ with the smallest $\mathsf{faqw}(\sigma)$.

jective value of the following linear program: $\min \sum_{F \in \mathcal{E}} x_e$ subject to $\sum_{F \ni v} x_F \geq 1$ for every $v \in B$ and $x_F \geq 0$ for every $F \in \mathcal{E}$.

[7] Here, we assume that the variable domains, the range $\mathbf{D}$, and the aggregates are fixed and known in advance, but the input factors are not.

Definition 3. (FAQ-width of an FAQ-query) The FAQ-*width* of an FAQ-query φ is defined by

$$\mathsf{faqw}(\varphi) := \min\{\mathsf{faqw}(\sigma) \mid \sigma \in \mathsf{EVO}(\varphi)\}$$

It is easy to see that if φ is an instance of FAQ-SS without free variables then $\mathsf{faqw}(\varphi) = \mathsf{fhtw}(\mathcal{H})$.

The question of determining whether a given variable ordering σ belongs to $\mathsf{EVO}(\varphi)$ is a tricky question to answer formally. In particular, the answer depends on what exactly we meant by a variable aggregate, a product aggregate, the variable domain sizes, and the range $\mathbf{D}$. This difficulty is analogous to the situation in logic when one wants to decide whether two (first-order, e.g.) formulas of specific forms are logically equivalent [10][8].

We derive a complete characterization of EVO, based on a combinatorial concept of *component-wise equivalence.* However, to facilitate the approximation algorithm for the FAQ-width we show that one does not need the complete characterization.

Our approach is as follows. In the most general case, we will define a class of variable orderings for a given input FAQ-query φ. This class will be precisely the set of linear extensions $\mathsf{LinEx}(P)$ of a partially ordered set (poset) on variables called the *precedence poset* P. The precedence poset is defined on a tree called the *expression tree* of the input query φ. Every variable ordering in this class will be shown to be φ-equivalent. This is the 'soundness' of the variable ordering class.

Then, we prove that this class of variable orderings is all we need to consider to compute/approximate $\mathsf{faqw}(\varphi)$, because every φ-equivalent variable ordering σ either belongs to $\mathsf{LinEx}(P)$ or is component-wise equivalent to π (which implies that $\mathsf{faqw}(\sigma) = \mathsf{faqw}(\pi)$) for some $\pi \in \mathsf{LinEx}(P)$. This shows the 'completeness' of $\mathsf{LinEx}(P)$. The completeness result rests on the assumption that different variable aggregates do not commute. (Even this simple statement needs a technical clarification, which is done in Proposition 5.1.)

Because the final result is a bit technically involved, we shall present in the next section a special case that illustrates many of our main ideas. It should be noted, however, that in the end there is only one theorem and one approximation algorithm for all FAQ instances.

5. VARIABLE ORDERING FOR FAQ WITH ONLY SEMIRING AGGREGATES

This section presents the variable ordering results for FAQ where every variable aggregate forms a semiring with the product aggregate. (Note that there can be an arbitrary number of different types of semirings.) In particular, we consider the FAQ-query of the form

$$\varphi(\mathbf{x}_{[f]}) = \bigoplus^{(f+1)}_{x_{f+1}} \cdots \bigoplus^{(n)}_{x_n} \bigotimes_{S \in \mathcal{E}} \psi_S(\mathbf{x}_S) \quad (7)$$

where $(\mathbf{D}, \oplus^{(i)}, \otimes)$ is a semiring for every $i > f$ (i.e. the set K as defined in (5) is $\{f+1, \dots, n\}$).

The main aim in this section is to illustrate the key technical idea of the *expression tree.* The expression tree defines the *precedence poset.* One key component of our completeness results is the notion of *component-wise equivalence* between two variable orderings. Component-wise equivalence

[8] We thank Balder ten Cate for pointing out to us the essence of the difficulty and the reference.

preserves FAQ-width and φ-equivalence. We will show two important facts about the precedence poset:

- (Soundness) Every linear extension of the precedence poset is a φ-equivalent variable ordering.
- (Completeness) Every φ-equivalent variable ordering is component-wise equivalent to (hence has the same FAQ-width as) some linear extension of the precedence poset. Therefore, $\mathsf{EVO}(\varphi)$ is *completely* characterized using component-wise equivalence and the precedence poset. Moreover, to compute/approximate $\mathsf{faqw}(\varphi)$, we *only* need to consider linear extensions of the precedence poset.

We use the structure of the expression tree to compute a variable ordering to approximate $\mathsf{faqw}(\varphi)$, using an approximation algorithm for fhtw as a blackbox. Thus, the expression tree is crucial in guiding the construction of a good variable ordering.

5.1 Expression tree and and precedence poset

The expression tree is defined on a sequence of *tagged variables* along with a hypergraph. In such a sequence, every vertex i (or equivalently variable X_i) is tagged with its corresponding operator $\oplus^{(i)}$; or, if the variable is a free variable then its tag is *free*. Given a sequence σ of tagged variables, a *tag block* is a maximal subsequence of consecutive variables in σ with the same tag. The first tag block of a sequence σ of tagged variables is the longest prefix of σ consisting of variables of the same tag.

Definition 4. (Expression tree) The *expression tree* for φ is a rooted tree P. Every node of the tree is a set of variables. We construct the expression tree using two steps: the *compartmentalization step* and the *compression step.* In the compartmentalization step, we construct the expression tree based on the connected component structures of the FAQ-query relative to the hypergraph structure $\mathcal{H}$. In the compression step we collapse the tree to make it shorter whenever possible.

Compartmentalization. In this step, initially we start off with the sequence of variables with their corresponding tags exactly as written in (7). In particular, the sequence starts with f free variables (whose tags are 'free'), and then the i'th variable with tag $\oplus^{(i)}$ for $i = f+1, \dots, n$. For technical reasons, we add a dummy variable X_0 to the beginning of the sequence with a free tag too. So the sequence we start off with is the following

$$\sigma = \Big\langle (X_0, \text{'free'}), \dots, (X_f, \text{'free'}), \\ (X_{f+1}, \oplus^{(f+1)}), \dots, (X_n, \oplus^{(n)}) \Big\rangle.$$

The vertex X_0 is an isolated vertex of the hypergraph $\mathcal{H}$. Now given a tagged variable sequence σ and a hypergraph $\mathcal{H}$, we build the tree by constructing a node L containing all variables in the first tag block L of σ. This node L will be the root of the expression tree. (The effect of the dummy variable X_0 is that, even if the original query has no free variable, the first block L still has X_0 in it.) If L contains all variables already, then naturally the tree has only one node. Otherwise, for each connected component $C = (\mathcal{V}(C), \mathcal{E}(C))$ of $\mathcal{H} - L$ we construct a sequence σ_C of tagged variables by listing all variables in $\mathcal{V}(C)$ in exactly the same relative order as they appeared in σ. From the sequence σ_C and the hypergraph C, we recursively construct the expression tree P_C. Finally, we connect all the roots of (sub)expression trees P_C to the node L. This completes the compartmentalization step. After everything is done, we also remove the dummy variable X_0 from the expression tree P. If originally there was no free variable, the tree has an empty root node and the subtrees correspond to the connected components of $\mathcal{H}$. (See Example 4 and Figure 1 in Appendix A.)

Compression. Now, in the expression tree P that resulted from the compartmentalization step, as long as there is still a node L whose tag is the same as a child node L' of the tree P, we merge the child into L; namely, we set $L := L \cup L'$, remove L', and connect all subtrees under L' to become subtrees of L. Repeat this step until no further merging is possible. (See Figure 2.)

Note that the compression step can make some nodes L larger and the final tree T shorter than the tree that resulted from the compartmentalization step alone. This step is crucial for getting the correct expression tree. If φ is an instance of FAQ-SS, then P is a tree of depth ≤ 1 where the root node contains all free variables (if any) and its children (if any) contain the rest of the variables.

Definition 5. (Precedence poset) The expression tree defines a partial order on the variables. Abusing notation we will also use P to denote the partial order $([n], \preceq)$. In this poset, $u \prec v$ whenever $u \in L$, $v \in L'$, and L' is a (strict) descendant of L in the expression tree P. In particular, variables in the same node of the expression tree are not comparable in this partial order. We call this partial order the *precedence poset.* Let $\mathsf{LinEx}(P)$ denote the set of all linear extensions of the poset.

5.2 What makes two aggregates different?

Before proving soundness and completeness, we need a small technical detour. Recall that aggregates are simply binary operators under $\mathbf{D}$.

Definition 6. (Different aggregates) Two aggregates $\oplus$ and $\bar{\oplus}$ are *different* if there is a pair $a, b \in \mathbf{D}$ such that

$$a \oplus b \neq a \bar{\oplus} b.$$

Otherwise they are *identical.*

Definition 7. (Commutative aggregates) Two aggregates $\oplus$ and $\bar{\oplus}$ are said to be *commutative* if for every $a, b, c, d \in \mathbf{D}$, we have $(a \oplus b) \bar{\oplus} (c \oplus d) = (a \bar{\oplus} c) \oplus (b \bar{\oplus} d)$.

Recall that in FAQ, all semirings share the same $\mathbf{0}$ (since one '$\mathbf{0}$' must annihilate the rest). Thus, if we select $a = d = \mathbf{0}$ in the above equality, then we obtain $b \bar{\oplus} c = b \oplus c$, for every $b, c \in \mathbf{D}$. This means

Proposition 5.1. *Commutative aggregates are identical aggregates. Conversely, non-commutative aggregates are different aggregates.*

(Note that it is possible for semantically different aggregates to be identical under $\mathbf{D}$ by accident. For example, in the $\{0, 1\}$ domain min and $\times$ are identical.) In this paper, we assume that two different aggregates in the input FAQ-expression are not functionally identical. Recall that we also assumed $|\mathsf{Dom}(X_i)| \geq 2$ for every $i \in [n]$ (otherwise the aggregate on that X_i is trivial and can be ignored).

PROPOSITION 5.2. *Suppose $\oplus$ and $\bar{\oplus}$ are different binary operators (under the domain $\mathbf{D}$), then for every $i, j \in [n]$, there is a function $\phi_{ij} : \mathsf{Dom}(X_i) \times \mathsf{Dom}(X_j) \to \mathbf{D}$ for which*

$$\bigoplus_{x_i \in \mathsf{Dom}(X_i)} \bar{\bigoplus_{x_j \in \mathsf{Dom}(X_j)}} \phi_{ij}(x_i, x_j) \neq \bar{\bigoplus_{x_j \in \mathsf{Dom}(X_j)}} \bigoplus_{x_i \in \mathsf{Dom}(X_i)} \phi_{ij}(x_i, x_j). \quad (8)$$

PROOF. From the analysis above, the two operators do not commute. Hence, there are four members $a, b, c, d \in \mathbf{D}$ so that $(a \oplus b)\bar{\oplus}(c \oplus d) \neq (a\bar{\oplus}c) \oplus (b\bar{\oplus}d)$. Fix arbitrary elements $x_i^1 \neq x_i^2 \in \mathsf{Dom}(X_i)$ and $x_j^1 \neq x_j^2 \in \mathsf{Dom}(X_j)$. Define

$$\phi_{ij}(x_i, x_j) = \begin{cases} a & \text{if } (x_i, x_j) = (x_i^1, x_j^1) \\ b & \text{if } (x_i, x_j) = (x_i^2, x_j^1) \\ c & \text{if } (x_i, x_j) = (x_i^1, x_j^2) \\ d & \text{if } (x_i, x_j) = (x_i^2, x_j^2) \\ \mathbf{0} & \text{otherwise.} \end{cases} \quad (9)$$

Then, $\bigoplus_{x_i} \bar{\bigoplus}_{x_j} \phi_{ij}(x_i, x_j) = (a\bar{\oplus}c) \oplus (b\bar{\oplus}d) \neq (a \oplus b)\bar{\oplus}(c \oplus d) = \bar{\bigoplus}_{x_j} \bigoplus_{x_i} \phi_{ij}(x_i, x_j)$. □

Given $i, j \in [n]$, $x_i^1 \neq x_i^2 \in \mathsf{Dom}(X_i)$, $x_j^1 \neq x_j^2 \in \mathsf{Dom}(X_j)$, we define an 'identity' function $\phi_{ij}^{(\mathbf{I})} : \mathsf{Dom}(X_i) \times \mathsf{Dom}(X_j) \to \mathbf{D}$ as follows.

$$\phi_{ij}^{(\mathbf{I})}(x_i, x_j) = \begin{cases} \mathbf{1} & \text{if } (x_i, x_j) = (x_i^1, x_j^1) \text{ or } (x_i, x_j) = (x_i^2, x_j^2) \\ \mathbf{0} & \text{otherwise.} \end{cases} \quad (10)$$

We will use both ϕ_{ij} and $\phi_{ij}^{\mathbf{I}}$ in the proofs below.

5.3 Soundness and completeness

We are now fully equipped to show that $\mathsf{LinEx}(P)$ is sound.

THEOREM 5.3 ($\mathsf{LinEx}(P) \subseteq \mathsf{EVO}(\varphi)$). *Every linear extension of the precedence poset P is φ-equivalent.*

PROOF. Let P be the expression tree constructed using only the compartmentalization step. This expression tree already defines a poset on variables. We will first show that every linear extension of this *compartmentalization poset* is φ-equivalent. We prove this claim by induction on the number of tag blocks of the input sequence. Let σ denote the input sequence of tagged variables with input hypergraph $\mathcal{H}$.

In the base case σ has only one tag block. All variables in the sequence belong to the same node of the compartmentalization expression tree. This means every permutation of variables is a linear extension of the poset, which is what we expect because every permutation is φ-equivalent.

In the inductive step, suppose σ has at least two tag blocks with the first block being the set L of variables. Then, each sub-sequence σ_C for each connected component of $\mathcal{H} - L$ defines an FAQ-expression φ_C on the set of conditional factors $\{\psi_S(\cdot \mid \mathbf{x}_L) \mid S \in \mathcal{E} \wedge S \cap \mathcal{V}(C) \neq \emptyset\}$. When we condition on the first L variables, the expression $\varphi(\cdot \mid \mathbf{x}_L)$ completely factorizes into a product of the FAQ-expressions φ_C. (Another way to put this is that φ can be written as a series of aggregates on variables in L, with a product of φ_C inside.) By induction, every linear extension of the compartmentalization poset for σ_C is φ_C-equivalent. Those linear extensions can be put together in arbitrary interleaving way to form $\varphi(\cdot \mid \mathbf{x}_L)$. This observation completes the proof of the claim, because every linear extension of the expression poset for φ consists of variables in L, followed by arbitrary interleavings of linear extensions of the expression posets for the φ_C.

Next, we consider the expression tree after the compression step. We show that every linear extension of the final precedence poset is φ-equivalent by induction on the number of merges of a child node L' to a parent node L (which both must have the same tag). To see this, we can take a linear extension σ of the expression tree *before* the merge where all variables in L and in L' are consecutive in σ. Then, because all variables in $L \cup L'$ have the same tag, we can permute them in any way and still obtain a φ-equivalent variable ordering. □

It would have been nice if every φ-equivalent variable ordering is a linear extension of P. Unfortunately this is not true. Consider the following FAQ-query

$$\varphi = \sum_{x_1} \sum_{x_2} \max_{x_3} \max_{x_4} \sum_{x_5} \psi_{15}\psi_{25}\psi_{13}\psi_{24},$$

where all factors have range $\mathbb{R}_+$ so that all variables are semiring variables. In this case the expression tree has three nodes: one empty root, a node containing $\{1, 2, 5\}$ and two children $\{3\}$ and $\{4\}$. The linear extensions will enforce that X_1, X_2, X_5 come before X_3 and X_4. However, it is easy to see that we can rewrite φ as follows.

$$\begin{aligned} \varphi &= \sum_{x_1} \sum_{x_2} \max_{x_3} \max_{x_4} \sum_{x_5} \psi_{15}\psi_{25}\psi_{13}\psi_{24} \\ &= \sum_{x_5} \sum_{x_1} \sum_{x_2} \max_{x_3} \max_{x_4} \psi_{15}\psi_{25}\psi_{13}\psi_{24} \\ &= \sum_{x_5} \left(\sum_{x_1} \max_{x_3} \psi_{15}\psi_{13} \right) \cdot \left(\sum_{x_2} \max_{x_4} \psi_{25}\psi_{24} \right). \end{aligned}$$

This means when conditioned on X_5, the expression factorizes and we can multiply them back allowing for 4 to come before 1, or for 3 to come before 2; namely,

$$\begin{aligned} \varphi &= \sum_{x_5} \sum_{x_2} \max_{x_4} \sum_{x_1} \max_{x_3} \psi_{15}\psi_{25}\psi_{13}\psi_{24} \\ &= \sum_{x_5} \sum_{x_1} \max_{x_3} \sum_{x_2} \max_{x_4} \psi_{15}\psi_{25}\psi_{13}\psi_{24}. \end{aligned}$$

However, it can be verified that

$$\mathsf{faqw}(5, 1, 3, 2, 4) = \mathsf{faqw}(5, 2, 4, 1, 3) = \mathsf{faqw}(\sigma)$$

for any $\sigma \in \mathsf{LinEx}(P)$ where 5 comes first in σ, and where P is the expression tree of the query. Note that we can take the linear extensions of the factorized components $\{1, 3\}$ and $\{2, 4\}$ and interleave them in any way, as long as we still respect their relative order within each component. However, these interleavings do not add anything of value as far as the faqw is concerned.

Another way to think about the above example is that we could have arbitrarily selected one variable in the first tag block of φ, construct a compartmentalization expression tree with that variable as the root. (One variable at a time instead of one tag block at a time.) Then, by the same reasoning we used in the proof of Theorem 5.3, every linear extension of this 'variable-wise' poset is φ-equivalent. However, this idea alone also does not work because it will forbid the selection of X_5 as the first variable in the above example. Thus, it is crucial that we construct the compressed expression tree first, to determine which variable *can* come first in a φ-equivalent variable ordering. Ultimately, the set $\mathsf{LinEx}(P)$ gives us a canonical way of listing the variable orderings that really matter in evaluating φ.

In what follows, we implement the above informal discussion and intuition by showing that every φ-equivalent variable ordering has the same width as some ordering in $\mathsf{LinEx}(\varphi)$. The following lemma says that the expression tree indeed gives us a complete list of variables that can occur first (after the free variables) in any φ-equivalent ordering.

LEMMA 5.4. *For every variable ordering $\pi = (u_1, \dots, u_n) \in \mathsf{EVO}(\varphi)$, the variable u_{f+1} must belong to a child node of the root of the expression tree.*[9]

PROOF. Let φ^π denote the function defined by the FAQ-query with π as the variable ordering (over the same input factors as φ). Our aim is to show that if the conclusion of the lemma does not hold then there exist input factors ψ_S for which $\varphi^\pi \not\equiv \varphi$.

Suppose for the sake of contradiction that u_{f+1} belongs to a node L whose parent is L_p, and L_p is not the root of the expression tree P. Let $\overline{L}_a$ denote union of all the (strict) ancestors of L_p in the expression tree. From the construction of the expression tree, the vertices in the set $\{u_{f+1}\} \cup L_p$ belong to the same connected component of the graph $\mathcal{H} - \overline{L}_a$. Let $i_0 := u_{f+1}, i_1, \dots, i_k \in L_p$ be the shortest path in the Gaifman graph of $\mathcal{H} - \overline{L}_a$ from u_{f+1} to L_p. Then, the vertices $i_1, \dots, i_{k-1}$ do not belong to $L_p \cup \overline{L}_a$; and, there are distinct hyperedges $S_1, \dots, S_k$ of $\mathcal{H}$ such that $\{i_{j-1}, i_j\} \subseteq S_j$ for all $j \in [k]$.

For each variable $\ell \in \{i_0, \dots, i_k\}$, we fix two arbitrary values $x_\ell^1 \neq x_\ell^2 \in \mathsf{Dom}(X_\ell)$ and for each $\ell' \in [n] \setminus \{i_0, \dots, i_k\}$, we fix one arbitrary value $e_{\ell'} \in \mathsf{Dom}(X_{\ell'})$. For the sake of brevity, denote $\bigoplus = \bigoplus^{(i_0)}$ and $\bar{\bigoplus} = \bigoplus^{(i_k)}$.

Now, we construct an input set of factors ψ_S, $S \in \mathcal{E}$, for which $\varphi^\pi \not\equiv \varphi$.

- Define the factor ψ_{S_k} by

$$\psi_{S_k}(\mathbf{x}_{S_k}) := \begin{cases} \phi_{i_{k-1} i_k}(x_{i_{k-1}}, x_{i_k}) & \text{if } x_{\ell'} = e_{\ell'} \text{ for all } \ell' \\ & \in S_k \setminus \{i_0, \dots, i_k\} \\ \mathbf{0} & \text{otherwise,} \end{cases}$$

  where $\phi_{i_{k-1} i_k}$ is the function defined in (9).

- For every $j \in [k-1]$, define

$$\psi_{S_j}(\mathbf{x}_{S_j}) := \begin{cases} \phi^{(\mathbf{I})}_{i_{j-1} i_j}(x_{i_{j-1}}, x_{i_j}) & \text{if } x_{\ell'} = e_{\ell'} \text{ for all } \ell' \\ & \in S_j \setminus \{i_0, \dots, i_k\} \\ \mathbf{0} & \text{otherwise,} \end{cases}$$

  where $\phi^{(\mathbf{I})}_{i_{j-1} i_j}$ is the 'identity' function defined in (10). (Think of these factors as little 2×2 identity matrices.)

- Finally, for every $S' \in \mathcal{E} \setminus \{S_1, \dots, S_k\}$, define

$$\psi_{S'}(\mathbf{x}_{S'}) := \begin{cases} \mathbf{1} & \text{if } x_{\ell'} = e_{\ell'} \text{ for all } \ell' \in S' \setminus \{i_0, \dots, i_k\} \\ \mathbf{0} & \text{otherwise.} \end{cases}$$

[9]Recall that $\{u_1, \dots, u_f\}$ are the free variables, which are located in the root of the expression tree. And, if $f = 0$ then the root of the expression tree is empty.

Because i_0 is the first in π after the free variables, $\varphi^\pi(e_1, \dots, e_f)$ will evaluate to the left hand side of (8). (Imagine running the $\mathsf{InsideOut}$ algorithm to evaluate φ^π.) Next, to get a contradiction, we pick an ordering $\sigma \in \mathsf{LinEx}(P)$ such that i_0 precedes all variables that are at the same or lower level in the expression tree. By Theorem 5.3, we know that $\sigma \in \mathsf{EVO}(\varphi)$. In σ, i_k precedes i_0 which in turn precedes all of $\{i_1, \dots, i_{k-1}\}$. Hence, when we compute $\varphi(e_1, \dots, e_f)$ using the ordering σ (and the $\mathsf{InsideOut}$ algorithm) we get the right hand side of (8). Thus, $\varphi^\pi \not\equiv \varphi$ as desired. □

The next definition realizes the intuition that if we construct the precedence tree using the one-variable-at-a-time strategy (as opposed to the one-tag-block-at-a-time strategy), then we can interleave the linear extensions of each connected components arbitrarily and still get a variable ordering which is φ-equivalent with the same FAQ-width. Since the interleaving can happen at any level, the definition is inductive.

Definition 8. (Component-wise equivalence) Let φ be an FAQ-query where all variable aggregates are semiring aggregates. Let $\sigma = (v_1, \dots, v_n) \in \mathsf{EVO}(\varphi)$ be a variable ordering. Let $\pi = (u_1, \dots, u_n)$ be another variable ordering with $\{u_1, \dots, u_f\} = F$. Then, π is said to be *component-wise equivalent* (or CW-equivalent) to σ if and only if:

- either $n = 1$,
- or $\mathcal{H}$ has ≥ 2 connected components, and for each connected component $C = (\mathcal{V}(C), \mathcal{E}(C))$ of $\mathcal{H}$, π_C is CW-equivalent to σ_C, where σ_C (respectively, π_C) is the variable ordering ordering of $\mathcal{V}(C)$ that is consistent with σ (respectively, π),
- or $u_1 = v_1$, and for each connected component $C = (\mathcal{V}(C), \mathcal{E}(C))$ of $\mathcal{H} - \{v_1\}$, π_C is CW-equivalent to σ_C, where σ_C (respectively, π_C) is the ordering of $\mathcal{V}(C)$ that is consistent with σ (respectively, π).

Given a set of variable orderings $\Lambda \subseteq \mathsf{EVO}(\varphi)$, we use $\mathsf{CWE}(\Lambda)$ to denote the set of all variable orderings that are CW-equivalent to some variable ordering in Λ.

PROPOSITION 5.5. *Let π be a variable ordering that is CW-equivalent to $\sigma \in \mathsf{EVO}(\varphi)$. Then, we have $\pi \in \mathsf{EVO}(\varphi)$ and $\mathsf{faqw}(\sigma) = \mathsf{faqw}(\pi)$.*

The following theorem shows the completeness part. (The proof and an example are in Appendices B.2 and B.3.)

THEOREM 5.6 ($\mathsf{EVO}(\varphi) = \mathsf{CWE}(\mathsf{LinEx}(P))$). *A variable ordering σ is φ-equivalent if and only if it is CW-equivalent to some linear extension of the precedence poset P.*

Proposition 5.5 and Theorem 5.6 imply the following result, which is precisely what we need to approximate $\mathsf{faqw}(\varphi)$.

COROLLARY 5.7. $\mathsf{faqw}(\varphi) = \min\{\mathsf{faqw}(\sigma) \mid \sigma \in \mathsf{LinEx}(P)\}$.

5.4 Approximating $\mathsf{faqw}(\varphi)$

Let P be the expression tree constructed from the query φ in the form (7). We define notation that will be used through out this section. Let C be a node of the expression tree P. (This means C is a set of variables of φ, and all variables in C have the same tag.) Let L be the parent node of C (if any) in the expression tree P. We define the following sets:

$$\bar{\mathcal{E}}(C) := \{S \in \mathcal{E} \mid S \cap C' \neq \emptyset \text{ for some } C' \text{ node in the subtree of } P \text{ rooted at } C.\} \quad (11)$$

$$S_{L,C} := L \cap \left(\bigcup_{S \in \bar{\mathcal{E}}(C)} S \right) \quad (12)$$

$$U(C) := \bigcup_{L' \text{ an ancestor of } C} \left(L' \cap \bigcup_{S \in \bar{\mathcal{E}}(C)} S \right). \quad (13)$$

If C has no parent then $U(C) = \emptyset$ by default. We think of the set $S_{L,C}$ as the contribution of all the nodes in the C-branch to L, and the set $U(C)$ as the contribution of all the nodes in the C-branch to all the (strict) ancestors of C. Next, for every node L in the expression tree P, define the hypergraph $\mathcal{H}_L$ as follows.

- If L is a leaf node of P, then $\mathcal{H}_L = \mathcal{H}[L]$, the subgraph of $\mathcal{H}$ induced by L.
- If L is not a leaf node of P, then $\mathcal{H}_L = (L, \mathcal{E}_L)$, where

$$\mathcal{E}_L := \{S \cap L \mid (S \in \mathcal{E}) \wedge (S \cap L \neq \emptyset) \wedge (S \cap C = \emptyset, \forall \text{ descendant } C \text{ of } L)\} \cup \{S_{L,C} \mid C \text{ a child of } L\}.$$

  In other words, $\mathcal{E}_L$ is the set of all projections of S down to L for all hyperedges S for which S intersects L but not any descendant of L in the expression tree; and for each child C of L, $\mathcal{E}_L$ also contains the projection onto L of the union of all hyperedges S that intersect (some descendant of) C.

LEMMA 5.8. *For any node L in the expression tree,*

$$\mathsf{faqw}(\varphi) \geq \mathsf{fhtw}(\mathcal{H}_L) \quad \textit{and} \quad \mathsf{faqw}(\varphi) \geq \rho^*_{\mathcal{H}}(U(L)).$$

PROOF. To show the first inequality, by Corollary 5.7, it is sufficient to prove that $\mathsf{faqw}(\sigma) \geq \mathsf{fhtw}(\mathcal{H}_L)$ for any variable ordering $\sigma = (v_1, \dots, v_n) \in \mathsf{LinEx}(P)$ and for any node L in the expression tree.

If L is a leaf node of the expression tree, then $\mathsf{faqw}(\sigma) \geq \mathsf{fhtw}(\mathcal{H}) \geq \mathsf{fhtw}(\mathcal{H}_L)$ because $\mathcal{H}_L$ is an induced subgraph of $\mathcal{H}$. Now, suppose L is not a leaf node. For any child C of L, let k be the smallest integer such that v_k belongs to some node in the subtree rooted at C. Then, due to the fact that $\sigma \in \mathsf{LinEx}(P)$, if $v_j \in L$ then $j < k$. The set U^σ_k is *precisely* equal to $U(C) \cup \{v_k\}$. This is because each time we eliminate a vertex belonging to any node in the subtree rooted at C, we insert back a hyperedge interconnecting all its neighbors (to the next hypergraph in the hypergraph sequence). And so by the time we reach U^σ_k all of the nodes in $U(C)$ belong to the same hyperedge of $\mathcal{H}^\sigma_k$. It follows that $(U^\sigma_k - \{v_k\}) \cap L = U(C) \cap L = S_{L,C}$ (since $L \cap L' = \emptyset$ for any ancestor L' of L). From this observation we obtain:

$$\begin{aligned}
\mathsf{faqw}(\varphi) &= \min_\sigma \left(\max \{\rho^*_{\mathcal{H}}(U^\sigma_k) \mid k \in [n]\}\right) \\
&\geq \min_\sigma \left(\max \{\rho^*_{\mathcal{H}}(U^\sigma_j) \mid j \in L\}\right) \\
(\rho^* \text{ is monotone}) &\geq \min_\sigma \left(\max \{\rho^*_{\mathcal{H}}(U^\sigma_j \cap L) \mid j \in L\}\right) \\
&\geq \min_\tau \left(\max \{\rho^*_{\mathcal{H}}(U^\tau_j) \mid j \in L\}\right) \\
&= \mathsf{fhtw}(\mathcal{H}_L).
\end{aligned}$$

In the above, τ is taken only over all variable orderings of L instead of the entire set $[n]$.

We next prove the second inequality that, for any $\sigma = (v_1, \dots, v_n) \in \mathsf{LinEx}(\varphi)$, and any node C in the expression tree, we have $\mathsf{faqw}(\sigma) \geq \rho^*_{\mathcal{H}}(U(C))$. As we have observed above, let k be the smallest integer such that $v_k \in C$, then $U^\sigma_k = U(C) \cup \{v_k\}$. Hence, because ρ^* is monotone, $\mathsf{faqw}(\sigma) = \max_{j \in [n]} \rho^*_{\mathcal{H}}(U^\sigma_j) \geq \rho^*_{\mathcal{H}}(U^\sigma_k) \geq \rho^*_{\mathcal{H}}(U(C))$. □

THEOREM 5.9. *Let φ be any* FAQ *query whose hypergraph is $\mathcal{H}$ and all variable aggregates are semiring aggregates. Suppose there is an approximation algorithm that, given any hypergraph $\mathcal{H}'$, outputs a tree decomposition of $\mathcal{H}'$ with fractional hypertree width at most $g(\mathsf{fhtw}(\mathcal{H}'))$ in time $t(|\mathcal{H}'|, \mathsf{fhtw}(\mathcal{H}'))$ for some non-decreasing functions g, t. Then, we can in time $|\mathcal{H}| \cdot t(|\mathcal{H}|, \mathsf{faqw}(\varphi))$ compute a φ-equivalent vertex ordering σ such that*

$$\mathsf{faqw}(\sigma) \leq \mathsf{faqw}(\varphi) + g(\mathsf{faqw}(\varphi)).$$

PROOF. We use the blackbox approximation algorithm for fhtw to construct a tree decomposition (T_L, χ_L) for every hypergraph $\mathcal{H}_L$ where L is a node in the expression tree. Then, from each of those tree decompositions, we construct a variable ordering σ_L for variables in the set L in the standard way. Finally, we construct the variable ordering σ for $[n]$ by concatenating all the σ_L together in any way that respects the precedence partial order.

Suppose $\sigma = (v_1, \dots, v_n)$ is the resulting variable ordering. Consider an arbitrary vertex v_k. Let L be the node of the precedence tree that contains v_k. Let B be the bag in (T_L, χ_L) that v_k belonged to when it was eliminated to construct σ_L. Then, using the same argument as in the proof of Lemma 5.8, we can show that

$$U^\sigma_k \subseteq B \cup U(L). \quad (14)$$

To see this, first consider the simpler case when L is a leaf node of the expression tree. Then, when we eliminate v_k the set U_k is the union of the sets $S \in \partial(v_k)$. The part $U_k \cap L$ is covered by B because within L the elimination algorithm works on $\mathcal{H}_L$. The part $U_k \setminus L$ is covered by the maximum *residue* left over from eliminating all vertices in L. The residue is precisely the set $U(L)$, because every time we eliminate a vertex we collect all its neighbors together into a hyperedge. By the time the last vertex from L is eliminated, the entire set $U(L)$ becomes a hyperedge. Now, if L is not a leaf node, the situation is exactly the same except for the fact that we work on the graph $\mathcal{H}_L$ which is not necessarily the same as $\mathcal{H}[L]$. The graph $\mathcal{H}_L$ contains the restrictions on L of all the residues of the subtrees under L.

Next, from Lemma 5.8 and from the fact that ρ^* is subadditive, relation (14) implies

$$\begin{aligned}
\rho^*_{\mathcal{H}}(U^\sigma_k) &\leq \rho^*(B) + \rho^*(U(L)) \leq g(\mathsf{fhtw}(\mathcal{H}_L)) + \mathsf{faqw}(\varphi) \\
&\leq g(\mathsf{faqw}(\varphi)) + \mathsf{faqw}(\varphi).
\end{aligned}$$

Finally, $\mathsf{faqw}(\sigma) = \max_{k \in [n]} \rho^*_{\mathcal{H}}(U^\sigma_k) \leq g(\mathsf{faqw}(\varphi)) + \mathsf{faqw}(\varphi)$. □

Acknowledgments

This work was partly supported by NSF grants CNF-1409551, CCF-1319402, and by DARPA under agreement #FA8750-15-2-0009. The U.S. Government is authorized to reproduce and distribute reprints for Governmental purposes notwithstanding any copyright thereon.

6. REFERENCES

[1] C. R. Aberger, A. Nötzli, K. Olukotun, and C. Ré. EmptyHeaded: Boolean Algebra Based Graph Processing. *ArXiv e-prints*, Mar. 2015.

[2] M. Abo Khamis, H. Q. Ngo, C. Ré, and A. Rudra. Joins via geometric resolutions: Worst-case and beyond. In *Proceedings of the 34rd ACM SIGMOD-SIGACT-SIGART Symposium on Principles of Database Systems, PODS'15, Melbourne, VIC, AustraliaS, May 31-June 04, 2015*, 2015.

[3] M. Abo Khamis, H. Q. Ngo, and A. Rudra. FAQ: questions asked frequently. *CoRR*, abs/1504.04044, 2015.

[4] I. Adler and M. Weyer. Tree-width for first order formulae. *Logical Methods in Computer Science*, 8(1), 2012.

[5] S. M. Aji and R. J. McEliece. The generalized distributive law. *IEEE Transactions on Information Theory*, 46(2):325–343, 2000.

[6] M. Aref, B. ten Cate, T. J. Green, B. Kimelfeld, D. Olteanu, E. Pasalic, T. L. Veldhuizen, and G. Washburn. Design and implementation of the LogicBlox system. In T. Sellis, S. B. Davidson, and Z. G. Ives, editors, *Proceedings of the 2015 ACM SIGMOD International Conference on Management of Data, Melbourne, Victoria, Australia, May 31 - June 4, 2015*, pages 1371–1382. ACM, 2015.

[7] A. Atserias, M. Grohe, and D. Marx. Size bounds and query plans for relational joins. In *FOCS*, pages 739–748. IEEE Computer Society, 2008.

[8] R. I. Bahar, E. A. Frohm, C. M. Gaona, G. D. Hachtel, E. Macii, A. Pardo, and F. Somenzi. Algebraic decision diagrams and their applications. *Formal Methods in System Design*, 10(2/3):171–206, 1997.

[9] N. Bakibayev, T. Kociský, D. Olteanu, and J. Zavodny. Aggregation and ordering in factorised databases. *PVLDB*, 6(14):1990–2001, 2013.

[10] E. Börger, E. Grädel, and Y. Gurevich. *The classical decision problem.* Universitext. Springer-Verlag, Berlin, 2001. Reprint of the 1997 original.

[11] J. Brault-Baron, F. Capelli, and S. Mengel. Understanding model counting for β-acyclic cnf-formulas. *CoRR*, abs/1405.6043, 2014.

[12] C. Chekuri and A. Rajaraman. Conjunctive query containment revisited. *Theor. Comput. Sci.*, 239(2):211–229, 2000.

[13] H. Chen. Quantified constraint satisfaction and bounded treewidth. In *Proceedings of the 16th Eureopean Conference on Artificial Intelligence, ECAI'2004, including Prestigious Applicants of Intelligent Systems, PAIS 2004, Valencia, Spain, August 22-27, 2004*, pages 161–165, 2004.

[14] H. Chen and V. Dalmau. Decomposing quantified conjunctive (or disjunctive) formulas. In *Proceedings of the 27th Annual IEEE Symposium on Logic in Computer Science, LICS 2012, Dubrovnik, Croatia, June 25-28, 2012*, pages 205–214. IEEE Computer Society, 2012.

[15] H. Chen and M. Grohe. Constraint satisfaction with succinctly specified relations. *J. Comput. Syst. Sci.*, 76(8):847–860, 2010.

[16] H. Chen and S. Mengel. A trichotomy in the complexity of counting answers to conjunctive queries. *CoRR*, abs/1408.0890, 2014.

[17] J. W. Cooley and J. W. Tukey. An algorithm for the machine calculation of complex Fourier series. *Mathematics of Computation*, 19:297–301, 1965.

[18] T. H. Cormen, C. E. Leiserson, R. L. Rivest, and C. Stein. *Introduction to algorithms.* MIT Press, Cambridge, MA, second edition, 2001.

[19] M. Davis, G. Logemann, and D. W. Loveland. A machine program for theorem-proving. *Commun. ACM*, 5(7):394–397, 1962.

[20] R. Dechter. Bucket elimination: A unifying framework for reasoning. *Artif. Intell.*, 113(1-2):41–85, 1999.

[21] R. Dechter, L. Otten, and R. Marinescu. On the practical significance of hypertree vs. treewidth. In M. Ghallab, C. D. Spyropoulos, N. Fakotakis, and N. M. Avouris, editors, *ECAI 2008 - 18th European Conference on Artificial Intelligence, Patras, Greece, July 21-25, 2008, Proceedings*, volume 178 of *Frontiers in Artificial Intelligence and Applications*, pages 913–914. IOS Press, 2008.

[22] R. Dechter and J. Pearl. Tree clustering for constraint networks. *Artificial Intelligence*, 38(3):353–366, 1989.

[23] A. Durand and S. Mengel. Structural tractability of counting of solutions to conjunctive queries. In W. Tan, G. Guerrini, B. Catania, and A. Gounaris, editors, *Joint 2013 EDBT/ICDT Conferences, ICDT '13 Proceedings, Genoa, Italy, March 18-22, 2013*, pages 81–92. ACM, 2013.

[24] E. C. Freuder. Complexity of k-tree structured constraint satisfaction problems. In H. E. Shrobe, T. G. Dietterich, and W. R. Swartout, editors, *Proceedings of the 8th National Conference on Artificial Intelligence. Boston, Massachusetts, July 29 - August 3, 1990, 2 Volumes.*, pages 4–9. AAAI Press / The MIT Press, 1990.

[25] S. W. Golomb and L. D. Baumert. Backtrack programming. pages 516–524, 1965.

[26] G. Gottlob, N. Leone, and F. Scarcello. Robbers, marshals, and guards: game theoretic and logical characterizations of hypertree width. *J. Comput. Syst. Sci.*, 66(4):775–808, 2003.

[27] G. Greco and F. Scarcello. Counting solutions to conjunctive queries: structural and hybrid tractability. In R. Hull and M. Grohe, editors, *Proceedings of the 33rd ACM SIGMOD-SIGACT-SIGART Symposium on Principles of Database Systems, PODS'14, Snowbird, UT, USA, June 22-27, 2014*, pages 132–143. ACM, 2014.

[28] M. Grohe and D. Marx. Constraint solving via fractional edge covers. In *SODA*, pages 289–298. ACM Press, 2006.

[29] M. Grohe and D. Marx. Constraint solving via fractional edge covers. *ACM Transactions on Algorithms*, 11(1):4, 2014.

[30] M. Gyssens, P. Jeavons, and D. A. Cohen. Decomposing constraint satisfaction problems using database techniques. *Artif. Intell.*, 66(1):57–89, 1994.

[31] M. Gyssens and J. Paredaens. A decomposition methodology for cyclic databases. In *Advances in Data Base Theory*, pages 85–122, 1982.

[32] K. Kask, R. Dechter, J. Larrosa, and A. Dechter. Unifying tree decompositions for reasoning in graphical models. *Artif. Intell.*, 166(1-2):165–193, 2005.

[33] C. Koch. Incremental query evaluation in a ring of databases. In J. Paredaens and D. V. Gucht, editors, *Proceedings of the Twenty-Ninth ACM SIGMOD-SIGACT-SIGART Symposium on Principles of Database Systems, PODS 2010, June 6-11, 2010, Indianapolis, Indiana, USA*, pages 87–98. ACM, 2010.

[34] J. Kohlas and N. Wilson. Semiring induced valuation algebras: Exact and approximate local computation algorithms. *Artif. Intell.*, 172(11):1360–1399, 2008.

[35] D. Koller and N. Friedman. *Probabilistic graphical models*. Adaptive Computation and Machine Learning. MIT Press, Cambridge, MA, 2009. Principles and techniques.

[36] D. Marx. Approximating fractional hypertree width. *ACM Trans. Algorithms*, 6(2):29:1–29:17, Apr. 2010.

[37] D. Marx. Tractable structures for constraint satisfaction with truth tables. *Theory Comput. Syst.*, 48(3):444–464, 2011.

[38] D. Marx. Tractable hypergraph properties for constraint satisfaction and conjunctive queries. *J. ACM*, 60(6):42, 2013.

[39] H. Q. Ngo, D. T. Nguyen, C. Re, and A. Rudra. Beyond worst-case analysis for joins with minesweeper. In *Proceedings of the 33rd ACM SIGMOD-SIGACT-SIGART Symposium on Principles of Database Systems, PODS'14, Snowbird, UT, USA, June 22-27, 2014*, pages 234–245, 2014.

[40] H. Q. Ngo, E. Porat, C. Ré, and A. Rudra. Worst-case optimal join algorithms. In M. Lenzerini and M. Benedikt, editors, *PODS*, pages 37–48. ACM, 2012.

[41] H. Q. Ngo, C. Ré, and A. Rudra. Skew strikes back: New developments in the theory of join algorithms. In *SIGMOD RECORD*, pages 5–16, 2013.

[42] D. T. Nguyen, M. Aref, M. Bravenboer, G. Kollias, H. Q. Ngo, C. Ré, and A. Rudra. Join processing for graph patterns: An old dog with new tricks. In *Proceedings of the Third International Workshop on Graph Data Management Experiences and Systems, GRADES 2015, Melbourne, VIC, Australia, May 31 - June 4, 2015*, pages 2:1–2:8, 2015.

[43] D. Olteanu and J. Závodný. Size bounds for factorised representations of query results. *ACM Trans. Datab. Syst.*, 40(1), 2015.

[44] S. Ordyniak, D. Paulusma, and S. Szeider. Satisfiability of Acyclic and Almost Acyclic CNF Formulas. In *FSTTCS 2010*, volume 8, 2010.

[45] J. Pearl. Reverend bayes on inference engines: A distributed hierarchical approach. In D. L. Waltz, editor, *Proceedings of the National Conference on Artificial Intelligence. Pittsburgh, PA, August 18-20, 1982.*, pages 133–136. AAAI Press, 1982.

[46] J. Pearl. Fusion, propagation, and structuring in belief networks. *Artif. Intell.*, 29(3):241–288, Sept. 1986.

[47] R. Pichler and S. Skritek. Tractable counting of the answers to conjunctive queries. *J. Comput. Syst. Sci.*, 79(6):984–1001, Sept. 2013.

[48] E. Rollon, J. Larrosa, and R. Dechter. Semiring-based mini-bucket partitioning schemes. In F. Rossi, editor, *IJCAI 2013, Proceedings of the 23rd International Joint Conference on Artificial Intelligence, Beijing, China, August 3-9, 2013*. IJCAI/AAAI, 2013.

[49] F. Rossi, P. v. Beek, and T. Walsh. *Handbook of Constraint Programming (Foundations of Artificial Intelligence)*. Elsevier Science Inc., New York, NY, USA, 2006.

[50] F. Scarcello. Query answering exploiting structural properties. *SIGMOD Record*, 34(3):91–99, 2005.

[51] T. L. Veldhuizen. Triejoin: A simple, worst-case optimal join algorithm. In *ICDT*, pages 96–106, 2014.

[52] M. Yannakakis. Algorithms for acyclic database schemes. In *VLDB*, pages 82–94, 1981.

[53] N. Zhang and D. Poole. A simple approach to Bayesian network computations. In *Proceedings of the Tenth Canadian Conference on Artificial Intelligence*, pages 171–178, 1994.

[54] N. L. Zhang and D. Poole. Exploiting causal independence in Bayesian network inference. *J. Artificial Intelligence Res.*, 5:301–328, 1996.

APPENDIX

A. INTUITION BEHIND THE EXPRESSION TREE

Example 4. (Intuition behind expression tree) Consider the following FAQ query that has two different semiring aggregates ($\sum$ and max) and no free variables:

$$\varphi = \sum_{x_1}\sum_{x_2}\max_{x_3}\sum_{x_4}\sum_{x_5}\max_{x_6}\max_{x_7}\psi_{12}\psi_{135}\psi_{14}\psi_{246}\psi_{27}\psi_{37}.$$

(ψ_{12} above denotes a factor whose support is $\{X_1, X_2\}$, and so on.) The hypergraph of φ is depicted in Figure 1a. The compartmentalization step of the construction of the expression tree is depicted in Figures 1b through 1d. Figures 2a and 2b depict the compression step. The final expression tree appears on the right of Figure 2b.

B. OMITTED TECHNICAL DETAILS

B.1 The InsideOut Algorithm

Definition 9. (**01**-projection) For each $S \in \mathcal{E}$ and any set $U \subseteq \mathcal{V}$ such that $S \cap U \neq \emptyset$, define the **01**-*projection* of ψ_S onto U as the function

$$\psi_{S/U} : \prod_{i \in S \cap U} \mathsf{Dom}(X_i) \to \{\mathbf{0}, \mathbf{1}\},$$

where

$$\psi_{S/U}(\mathbf{x}_{S\cap U}) = \begin{cases} \mathbf{1} & \text{if } \exists \mathbf{y}_S \text{ s.t. } \psi_S(\mathbf{y}_S) \neq \mathbf{0} \text{ and } \mathbf{y}_{S\cap U} = \mathbf{x}_{S\cap U} \\ \mathbf{0} & \text{otherwise} \end{cases}$$

Definition 10. (**01**-OR) Given $a, b \in \{\mathbf{0}, \mathbf{1}\}$, the **01**-OR of a and b is $\mathbf{0}$ if $a = b = \mathbf{0}$, and $\mathbf{1}$ otherwise.

B.2 Proof of Completeness

In this section, we prove Theorem 5.6, which basically says that our characterization of $\mathsf{EVO}(\varphi)$ is complete. We start with proving Proposition 5.5, which almost immediately follows from Definition 8.

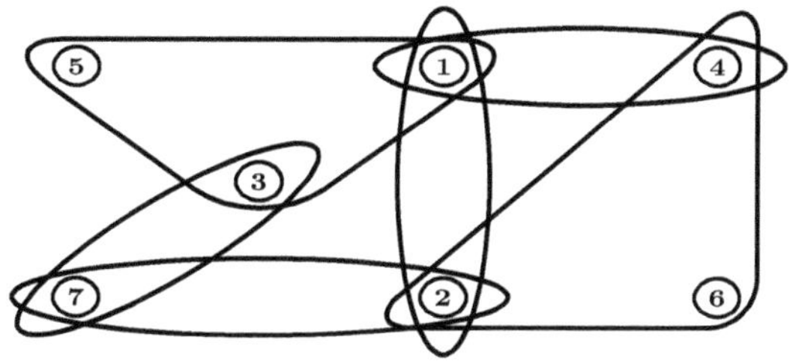

(a) $\varphi = \sum_{x_1}\sum_{x_2}\max_{x_3}\sum_{x_4}\sum_{x_5}\max_{x_6}\max_{x_7}\psi_{12}\,\psi_{135}\,\psi_{14}\,\psi_{246}\,\psi_{27}\,\psi_{37}$

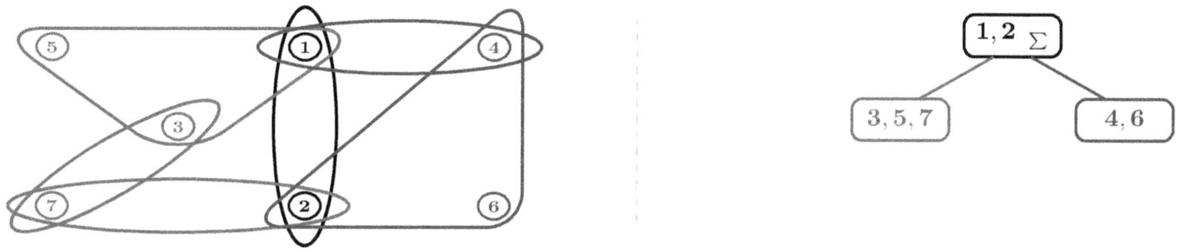

(b) $\varphi = \sum_{x_1}\sum_{x_2}\psi_{12}\left(\max_{x_3}\sum_{x_5}\max_{x_7}\psi_{135}\,\psi_{27}\,\psi_{37}\right)\left(\sum_{x_4}\max_{x_6}\psi_{14}\,\psi_{246}\right)$

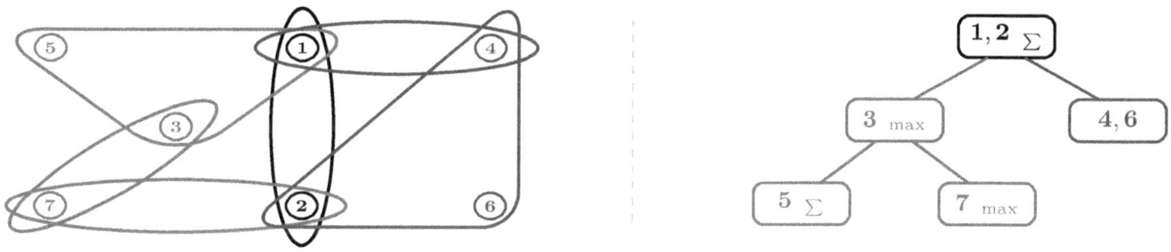

(c) $\varphi = \sum_{x_1}\sum_{x_2}\psi_{12}\left(\max_{x_3}\sum_{x_5}\psi_{135}\max_{x_7}\psi_{27}\,\psi_{37}\right)\left(\sum_{x_4}\max_{x_6}\psi_{14}\,\psi_{246}\right)$

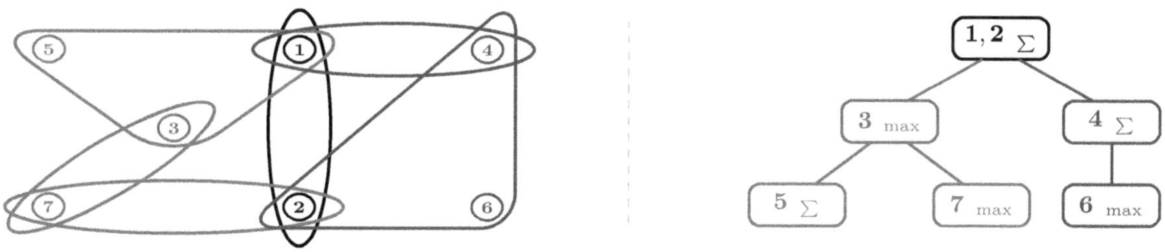

(d) $\varphi = \sum_{x_1}\sum_{x_2}\psi_{12}\left(\max_{x_3}\sum_{x_5}\psi_{135}\max_{x_7}\psi_{27}\,\psi_{37}\right)\left(\sum_{x_4}\psi_{14}\max_{x_6}\psi_{246}\right)$

Figure 1: The compartmentalization step of the expression tree from Example 4, depicted using colors. (1a) depicts the hypergraph of the FAQ query: $\varphi = \sum_{x_1}\sum_{x_2}\max_{x_3}\sum_{x_4}\sum_{x_5}\max_{x_6}\max_{x_7}\psi_{12}\psi_{135}\psi_{14}\psi_{246}\psi_{27}\psi_{37}$. For simplicity, the dummy free variable X_0 is ignored in this example. (1b) shows the first part of the compartmentalization step, where the first tag block is $L = \{1, 2\}$. After removing L, the query breaks into two connected components: the red and the blue. The expression tree at this point appears on the right. Each color is used to denote correspondence between parts of the query expression, hypergraph, and expression tree having that color. (1c) shows how to apply compartmentalization recursively on the red component, while (1d) shows the blue component compartmentalization.

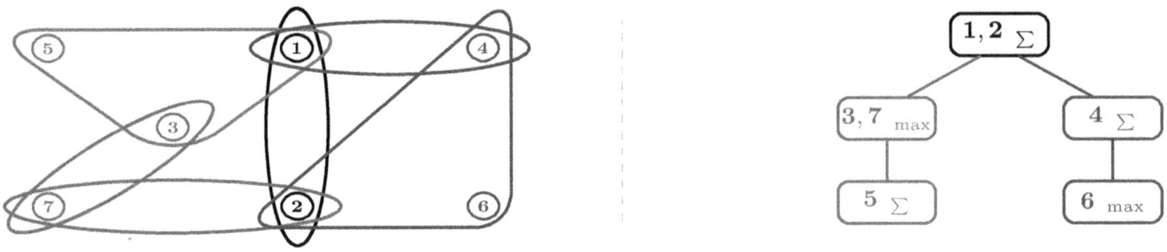

$$\text{(a)}\quad \varphi = \sum_{x_1}\sum_{x_2}\psi_{12}\left(\max_{x_3}\max_{x_7}\psi_{27}\,\psi_{37}\sum_{x_5}\psi_{135}\right)\left(\sum_{x_4}\psi_{14}\max_{x_6}\psi_{246}\right)$$

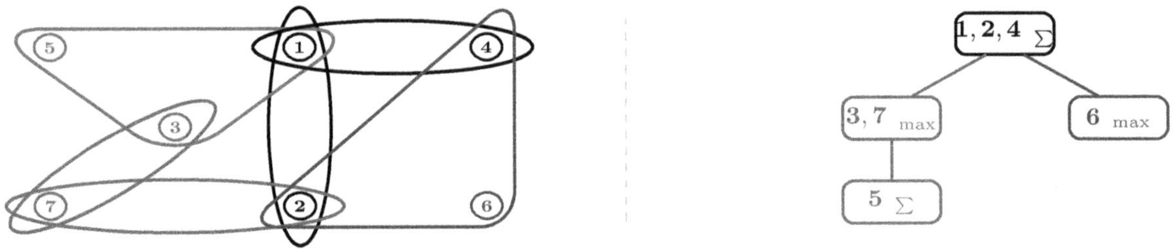

$$\text{(b)}\quad \varphi = \sum_{x_1}\sum_{x_2}\sum_{x_4}\psi_{12}\,\psi_{14}\left(\max_{x_3}\max_{x_7}\psi_{27}\,\psi_{37}\sum_{x_5}\psi_{135}\right)\left(\max_{x_6}\psi_{246}\right)$$

Figure 2: The compression step of the expression tree from Example 4. Recall that Figure (1d) (right) depicted the expression tree at the end of the compartmentalization step. (2a) shows a compression where node $\{7\}$ is merged into its parent $\{3\}$ (since they both have the same tag "max"). (2b) shows another compression where $\{4\}$ is merged into $\{1, 2\}$. Since no further compression is possible, (2b) (right) depicts the final expression tree.

Proof of Proposition 5.5. Due to the fact that the different (conditional) connected components do not interact, when we run InsideOut on σ and π for all $k \in [n]$, we have $U_k^\sigma = U_k^\pi$. This observation proves both claims. □

Proof of Theorem 5.6. We only need to show that $\mathsf{EVO}(\varphi) \subseteq \mathsf{CWE}(\mathsf{LinEx}(P))$ because the reverse containment follows from Proposition 5.5 and Theorem 5.3. Also, without loss of generality we can assume that the root of the expression tree F is empty, and it has one child node L. (If there were different connected components, they can interleave arbitrarily and we prove each of them separately.)

Fix an arbitrary $\sigma = (v_1, \dots, v_n) \in \mathsf{EVO}(\varphi)$. Then $v_1 \in L$ by Lemma 5.4. For each connected component C of $\mathcal{H} - \{v_1\}$, define a sub-query φ_C with variable ordering σ_C on the conditional factors $\{\psi_S(\cdot \mid x_{v_1}) \mid S \in \mathcal{E} \wedge S \cap \mathcal{V}(C) \neq \emptyset\}$, where σ_C is the subsequence of σ obtained by picking out vertices in $\mathcal{V}(C)$. Let P_C be the precedence poset of the expression tree for φ_C. By induction on the number of variables, we know $\sigma_C \in \mathsf{EVO}(\varphi_C) \subseteq \mathsf{CWE}(\mathsf{LinEx}(P_C))$. Hence, there exists $\pi_C \in \mathsf{LinEx}(P_C)$ that is CW-equivalent to σ_C.

The expression tree P_C for φ_C consists of an empty root (with 'free' tag). This root has only one child node L_C. The subtree rooted at L_C is called an L_C-subtree. Now, if we attach all the roots of all the L_C-subtrees together, we will create a tree whose root R is the union of the L_C. Then, we add v_1 to the root R and add an empty parent to R then we will obtain exactly the expression tree P.

From this observation, we can pick a variable ordering π that is consistent with all π_C such that π starts with v_1, followed by variables in $L - \{v_1\}$. It follows that $\pi \in \mathsf{LinEx}(P)$ and π is CW-equivalent to σ. □

B.3 Example of Completeness

Here, we give an example of component-wise equivalence (Definition 8) and the role it plays in completeness (Theorem 5.6).

Example 5. (Component-wise equivalence and completeness) Consider the following FAQ query with two different semiring aggregates ($\sum$ and max) and three variables, all are bound.

$$\varphi = \sum_{x_1}\max_{x_2}\sum_{x_3}\psi_{12}\psi_{13}.$$

(ψ_{ij} above denotes an input factor whose support is $\{X_i, X_j\}$.) For this query, $\mathsf{EVO}(\varphi) = \{(1,2,3),(1,3,2),(3,1,2)\}$. Ignoring the dummy free variable X_0, the expression tree of φ consists of a root with the tag '$\sum$' containing the variables $\{X_1, X_3\}$ and a single child node with tag 'max' containing $\{X_2\}$. Therefore, $\mathsf{LinEx}(P) = \{(1,3,2),(3,1,2)\} \subseteq \mathsf{EVO}(\varphi)$, as suggested by Theorem 5.3. Note that the original ordering $(1,2,3) \notin \mathsf{LinEx}(P)$. However, $(1,2,3)$ is component-wise equivalent to $(1,3,2)$ (See Definition 8). Therefore,

$$\mathsf{CWE}(\mathsf{LinEx}(P)) = \{(1,3,2),(1,2,3),(3,1,2)\} = \mathsf{EVO}(\varphi),$$

just as predicted by Theorem 5.6. Moreover, by Proposition 5.5, $\mathsf{faqw}((1,2,3)) = \mathsf{faqw}((1,3,2)) = 1$. Therefore, when searching for the variable ordering with the best FAQ-width, the ordering $(1,2,3)$ is redundant, hence it is sufficient to consider $\mathsf{LinEx}(P)$, just as suggested by Corollary 5.7.

PODS 2016 Best Student Paper

Shortest Paths and Distances with Differential Privacy

Adam Sealfon
MIT
asealfon@csail.mit.edu

ABSTRACT

We introduce a model for differentially private analysis of weighted graphs in which the graph topology $(\mathcal{V}, \mathcal{E})$ is assumed to be public and the private information consists only of the edge weights $w : \mathcal{E} \to \mathbb{R}^+$. This can express hiding congestion patterns in a known system of roads. Differential privacy requires that the output of an algorithm provides little advantage, measured by privacy parameters ϵ and δ, for distinguishing between neighboring inputs, which are thought of as inputs that differ on the contribution of one individual. In our model, two weight functions w, w' are considered to be neighboring if they have ℓ_1 distance at most one.

We study the problems of privately releasing a short path between a pair of vertices and of privately releasing approximate distances between all pairs of vertices. We are concerned with the *approximation error*, the difference between the length of the released path or released distance and the length of the shortest path or actual distance.

For the problem of privately releasing a short path between a pair of vertices, we prove a lower bound of $\Omega(|\mathcal{V}|)$ on the additive approximation error for fixed privacy parameters ϵ, δ. We provide a differentially private algorithm that matches this error bound up to a logarithmic factor and releases paths between all pairs of vertices, not just a single pair. The approximation error achieved by our algorithm can be bounded by the number of edges on the shortest path, so we achieve better accuracy than the worst-case bound for pairs of vertices that are connected by a low-weight path consisting of $o(|\mathcal{V}|)$ vertices.

For the problem of privately releasing all-pairs distances, we show that for trees we can release all-pairs distances with approximation error $O(\log^{2.5} |\mathcal{V}|)$ for fixed privacy parameters. For arbitrary bounded-weight graphs with edge weights in $[0, M]$ we can release all distances with approximation error $\tilde{O}(\sqrt{|\mathcal{V}|M})$.

PODS '16, June 26–July 1, 2016, San Francisco, CA, USA.

ISBN 978-1-4503-4191-2/16/06...$15.00

DOI: http://dx.doi.org/10.1145/2902251.2902291

1. INTRODUCTION

1.1 Differential privacy and our model

Privacy-preserving data analysis is concerned with releasing useful aggregate information from a database while protecting sensitive information about individuals in the database. *Differential privacy* [DMNS06] provides strong privacy guarantees while allowing many types of queries to be answered approximately. Differential privacy requires that for any pair of *neighboring* databases x and y, the output distributions of the mechanism on database x and database y are very close. In the traditional setting, databases are collections of data records and are considered to be neighboring if they are identical except for a single record, which is thought of as the information associated with a single individual. This definition guarantees that an adversary can learn very little about any individual in the database, no matter what auxiliary information the adversary may possess.

A new model We introduce a model of differential privacy for the setting in which databases are weighted graphs $(\mathcal{G}, w)$. In our setting, the graph topology $\mathcal{G} = (\mathcal{V}, \mathcal{E})$ is assumed to be public, and only the edge weights $w : \mathcal{E} \to \mathbb{R}^+$ must be kept private. Individuals are assumed to have only bounded influence on the edge weights. Consequently, two weight functions on the same unweighted graph are considered to be neighbors if they have ℓ_1 distance at most one.

The model is well suited to capture the setting of a navigation system which has access to current traffic data and uses it to direct drivers. The travel times along routes provided by the system should be as short as possible. However, the traffic data used by the system may consist of private information. For instance, navigation tools such as Google Maps and Waze estimate traffic conditions based on GPS locations of cars or based on traffic reports by users. On the other hand, the topology of the road map used by the system is non-private, since it is a static graph readily available to all users. We would like to provide information about paths and distances in the network without revealing sensitive information about the edge weights. In this paper we introduce a variant of differential privacy suitable for studying network routing, and provide both algorithms and lower bounds.

1.2 Our results

We will consider two classic problems in this model which are relevant for routing. First, we are interested in finding *short paths* between specified pairs of vertices. We cannot hope always to release the shortest path while preserving privacy, but we would like to release a path that is not much longer than the shortest path. Here the *approximation error* is the difference in length between the released path and the shortest path. Second, we would like to release *distances* between pairs of vertices. The *approximation error* here is the absolute difference between the released distance and the actual distance. As we discuss below, releasing an accurate distance estimate for a single pair of vertices in our model is a straightforward application of the Laplace mechanism of [DMNS06]. We focus on the more difficult problem of releasing *all-pairs distances* privately with low error.

Interestingly, all of our error bounds are independent of the sum of the edge weights $\|w\|_1$, which corresponds most naturally to the size of the database under the usual setting for differential privacy. Instead, they depend only on the number of vertices $|\mathcal{V}|$ and edges $|\mathcal{E}|$ in the graph and the privacy parameters ϵ and δ. Our error bounds constitute additive error. Consequently, if the edge weights are large, the error will be small in comparison.

Approximate shortest paths We consider the problem of privately releasing an approximate *shortest path.* We provide a strong reconstruction based lower bound, showing that in general it is not possible under differential privacy to release a short path between a pair of vertices with additive error better than $\Omega(|\mathcal{V}|)$. Our lower bound is obtained by reducing the problem of reconstructing many of the rows of a database to the problem of finding a path with low error.

We also show that a simple ϵ-differentially private algorithm based on the Laplace mechanism of [DMNS06] comes close to meeting this bound. If the minimum-weight path between a pair of vertices s, t consists of at most k edges, then the weight of the path released by our algorithm is greater by at most $O(k \log |\mathcal{V}|)/\epsilon$. Since $k < |\mathcal{V}|$, the weight of the released path is $O(|\mathcal{V}| \log |\mathcal{V}|)/\epsilon$ greater than optimal. Note that when the edge weights are large, the length of a path can be much larger than $(|\mathcal{V}| \log |\mathcal{V}|)/\epsilon$, in which case our algorithm provides a good approximation. Moreover, for many networks we would expect that shortest paths should be compact and consist of few vertices, in which case the accuracy obtained will be much greater. The algorithm releases not only a single path but short paths between every pair of vertices without loss of additional privacy or accuracy.

Approximate all pairs distances For the problem of privately releasing all-pairs *distances*, standard techniques yield error $O(|\mathcal{V}| \log |\mathcal{V}|)/\epsilon$ for each query under ϵ-differential privacy. We obtain improved algorithms for two special classes of graphs, trees and arbitrary graphs with edges of bounded weight.

For trees we show that a simple recursive algorithm can release all-pairs distances with error $O(\log^{2.5} |\mathcal{V}|)/\epsilon$. Implicitly, the algorithm finds a collection $\mathcal{C}$ of paths with two properties. Every edge is contained in at most $\log |\mathcal{V}|$ paths, and the unique path between any pair of vertices can be formed from at most $4 \log |\mathcal{V}|$ paths in $\mathcal{C}$ using the operations of concatenation and subtraction. The first property implies that the query consisting of the lengths of all of the paths in $\mathcal{C}$ has global ℓ_1 sensitivity $\log |\mathcal{V}|$, so we can release estimates of the lengths of all paths in $\mathcal{C}$ with error roughly $\log |\mathcal{V}|$ using the standard Laplace mechanism [DMNS06]. The second property implies that we can use these estimates to compute the distance between any pair of vertices without too much increase in error. We first reduce the approximate all-pairs distances problem to the problem of approximating all distances from a single fixed vertex. We then solve the single-source problem recursively, repeatedly decomposing the tree into subtrees of at most half the size.

In the special case of the path graph, releasing approximate all-pairs distances is equivalent to query release of threshold functions on the domain $X = \mathcal{E}$. The results of [DNPR10] yield the same error bound that we obtain for computing distances on the path graph. Consequently our algorithm for all-pairs distances on trees can be viewed as a generalization of a result for private query release of threshold functions.

For bounded-weight graphs we show that we can generate a set of vertices $\mathcal{Z} \subset \mathcal{V}$ such that distances between all pairs of vertices in $\mathcal{Z}$ suffice to estimate distances between all pairs of vertices in $\mathcal{V}$. The required property on $\mathcal{Z}$ is that every vertex $v \in \mathcal{V}$ is connected to a vertex $z_v \in \mathcal{Z}$ by a path consisting of few vertices. Since we can always find a set $\mathcal{Z}$ that is not too large, we can release distances between all pairs of vertices in $\mathcal{Z}$ with relatively small error. The distance between a pair of vertices $u, v \in \mathcal{V}$ can then be approximated by the distance between nearby vertices $z_u, z_v \in \mathcal{Z}$. In general, if edge weights are in $[0, M]$ for $\frac{1}{|\mathcal{V}|} < M\epsilon < |\mathcal{V}|$, then we can release all pairs shortest paths with an additive error of $\tilde{O}(\sqrt{|\mathcal{V}| M \epsilon^{-1} \log(1/\delta)})$ per path under (ϵ, δ)-differential privacy for any $\epsilon, \delta > 0$. Note that the distance between a pair of vertices can be as large as $|\mathcal{V}| \cdot M$, so this error bound is nontrivial. For specific graphs we can obtain better bounds by finding a smaller set $\mathcal{Z}$ satisfying the necessary requirements.

Additional problems We also consider two other problems in this model, the problem of releasing a nearly *minimal spanning tree* and the problem of releasing an almost *minimum weight perfect matching.* For these problems, the *approximation error* is the absolute difference in weight between the released spanning tree or matching and the minimum-weight spanning tree or matching.

Using a similar argument to the shortest path results of Section 5, we provide lower bounds and algorithms for these problems. Through a reduction from the problem of reconstructing many rows in a database, we show that it is not possible under differential privacy to release a spanning tree or matching with error better than $\Omega(|\mathcal{V}|)$. Using a simple algorithm based on the Laplace mechanism of [DMNS06], we can privately release a spanning tree or matching with error roughly $(|\mathcal{V}| \log |\mathcal{V}|)/\epsilon$. These results are presented in Appendix B.

Future directions In this work we describe differentially private algorithms and lower bounds for several natural graph problems related to network routing. We would like to explore how well our algorithms perform in practice on actual road networks and traffic data. We would also like to develop new algorithms for additional graph problems and to design improved all-pairs distance algorithms for additional classes of networks. In addition, lower bounds for accuracy of private all-pairs distances would be very interesting.

Scaling Our model requires that we preserve the indistinguishability of two edge weight functions which differ by at most 1 in ℓ_1 norm. The constant 1 here is arbitrary, and the error bounds in this paper scale according to it. For instance, if a single individual can only influence edge weights by $1/|\mathcal{V}|$

rather than 1 in ℓ_1 norm, then we can privately find a path between any pair of vertices whose length is only $O(\log|\mathcal{V}|)/\epsilon$ longer than optimal rather than $O(|\mathcal{V}|\log|\mathcal{V}|)/\epsilon$. The other results in this paper can be scaled similarly.

1.3 Previous work on graphs and differential privacy

Why a new model? The two main models which have been considered for applying differential privacy to network structured data are *edge* and *node* differential privacy [HLMJ09, BBDS13, KNRS13, KRSY11]. Under edge differential privacy, two graphs are considered to be neighbors if one graph can be obtained from the other by adding or removing a single edge. With node differential privacy, two graphs are neighbors if they differ only on the set of edges incident to a single vertex.

However, the notions of edge and node differential privacy are not well suited to shortest path and distance queries. Consider an algorithm that releases a short path between a specified pair of vertices. Any useful program solving this problem must usually at least output a path of edges which are in the graph. But doing so blatantly violates privacy under both the edge and node notions of differential privacy, since the released edges are private information. Indeed, an algorithm cannot release subgraphs of the input graph without violating both edge and node differential privacy because this distinguishes the input from a neighboring graph in which one of the released edges is removed.

What if we simply want to release the distance between a pair of vertices? In general it is not possible to release approximate distances with meaningful utility under edge or node differential privacy, since changing a single edge can greatly change the distances in the graph. Consider the unweighted path graph $\mathcal{P}$ and any pair of adjacent vertices x, y on the path. Removing edge (x, y) disconnects the graph, increasing the distance between x and y from 1 to ∞. Even if the graph remains connected, the removal of an edge does not preserve approximate distances. Consider any pair of adjacent vertices x, y on the cycle graph $\mathcal{C}$. Here, removing edge (x, y) increases the distance between x and y from 1, the smallest possible distance, to $|\mathcal{V}|-1$, the largest possible distance. Hence, the edge and node notions of differential privacy do not enable the release of approximate distances. This inadequacy motivates the new notion of differential privacy for graphs introduced in this work.

A histogram formulation A database consisting of elements from a data universe $\mathcal{U}$ can be described by a vector $D \in \mathbb{N}^{|\mathcal{U}|}$, where the ith component of the vector corresponds to the number of copies of the ith element of $\mathcal{U}$ in the database. More generally, we can allow the database to be a point in $\mathbb{R}^{|\mathcal{U}|}$, which corresponds to allowing a fractional number of occurrences of each element. Since an edge weight function w is an element of $\mathbb{R}^{|\mathcal{E}|}$ and the notions of sensitivity coincide, we can rephrase our model in the standard differential privacy framework.

Consequently, we can use existing tools for privately answering low sensitivity queries to yield incomparable results to those presented in this paper for the problem of releasing all-pairs distances with low error. If all edge weights are integers and the sum $\|w\|_1$ of the edge weights is known, we can release all-pairs distances with additive error

$$\tilde{O}(\sqrt{\|w\|_1 \cdot \log|\mathcal{V}|}\log^{1.5}(1/\delta)/\epsilon)$$

except with probability δ using the (ϵ, δ)-differentially private boosting mechanism of [DRV10]. The assumption that $\|w\|_1$ is known is not problematic, since we can privately release a good approximation. We can also extend the algorithm to noninteger edge weights for the queries in our setting, although we obtain a worse error bound. We do this by modifying the base synopsis generator of [DRV10] to produce a database in $(\tau\mathbb{N})^{|\mathcal{E}|}$ whose fractional counts are integer multiples of $\tau = \alpha/(2|\mathcal{V}|)$, where α will be the obtained additive approximation. The modified algorithm releases all-pairs distances with error $\tilde{O}(\sqrt[3]{\|w\|_1 \cdot |\mathcal{V}|}\log^{4/3}(1/\delta)/\epsilon^{2/3})$.

This error bound has a better dependence on $|\mathcal{V}|$ than the algorithms for all-pairs distances in general and weighted graphs described in Section 4. However, it has a substantial dependence on $\|w\|_1$, while the error bound for all algorithms in the remainder of this paper are independent of $\|w\|_1$. In addition, the running time of the algorithm of [DRV10] is exponential in the database size, while all algorithms described below run in polynomial time.

Additional related work While the private edge weight model explored in this work is new, a few previous works have considered problems on graphs in related models. Nissim, Raskhodnikova and Smith [NRS07] consider the problem of computing the cost of the minimum spanning tree of a weighted graph. They introduce the notion of smooth sensitivity, which they use to compute the approximate MST cost. In their work, edge weights are bounded, and each weight corresponds to the data of a single individual. In contrast, we allow unbounded weights but assume a bound on the effect an individual can have on the weights.

Hsu et al. [HHR$^+$14] consider the problem of privately finding high-weight matchings in bipartite graphs. In their model, which captures a private version of the allocation problem, two weightings of the complete bipartite graph are neighbors if they differ only in the weights assigned to the edges incident to a single left-vertex, which correspond to the preferences of a particular agent. They show that the problem is impossible to solve under the standard notion of differential privacy. They work instead under the relaxed notion of "joint differential privacy," in which knowledge of the edges of the matching which correspond to some of the left-vertices cannot reveal the weights of edges incident to any of the remaining left-vertices.

A series of works has explored the problem of privately computing the size of all cuts $(S, \overline{S})$ in a graph. Gupta, Roth and Ullman [GRU12] show how to answer cut queries with $O(|\mathcal{V}|^{1.5})$ error. Blocki et al. [BBDS12] improve the error for small cuts. Relatedly, Gupta et al. [GLM$^+$10] show that we can privately release a cut of close to minimal size with error $O(\log|\mathcal{V}|)/\epsilon$, and that this is optimal. Since the size of a cut is the number of edges crossing the cut, it can also be viewed as the sum of the weights of the edges crossing the cut in a $\{0, 1\}$-weighting of the complete graph. Consequently the problem can be restated naturally in our model.

As we have discussed, the problem of approximating all threshold functions on a totally ordered set is equivalent to releasing approximate distances on the path graph. In addition to the work of Dwork et al. [DNPR10] described above, additional bounds and reductions for query release and learning of threshold functions are shown in Bun et al. [BNSV15].

2. THE PRIVACY MODEL

Let $\mathcal{G} = (\mathcal{V}, \mathcal{E})$ denote an undirected graph with vertex set $\mathcal{V}$ and edge set $\mathcal{E}$, and let $w : \mathcal{E} \to \mathbb{R}^+$ be a *weight function.* (The shortest path results in Section 5 also apply to directed graphs.) Let $V = |\mathcal{V}|$ and $E = |\mathcal{E}|$ be the number of vertices and edges, respectively.

Let $\mathcal{P}_{xy}$ denote the set of paths between a pair of vertices $x, y \in \mathcal{V}$. For any path $P \in \mathcal{P}_{xy}$, the weight $w(P)$ is the sum $\sum_{e \in P} w(e)$ of the weights of the edges of P. The distance $d_w(x, y)$ from x to y denotes the weighted distance $\min_{P \in \mathcal{P}_{xy}} w(P)$. We will denote the unweighted or hop distance from x to y by $h(x, y) = \min_{P \in \mathcal{P}_{xy}} \ell(P)$, where the hop length $\ell(P)$ of path $P = (v_0, \ldots, v_\ell)$ is the number ℓ of edges on the path. Let the shortest path $\mathrm{SP}_w(x, y)$ denote a path from x to y of minimum possible weight $w(\mathrm{SP}_w(x, y)) = d_w(x, y)$.

We now formally define differential privacy in the private edge weight model.

Definition 2.1. *For any edge set $\mathcal{E}$, two weight functions $w, w' : \mathcal{E} \to \mathbb{R}^+$ are **neighboring**, denoted $w \sim w'$, if*

$$\|w - w'\|_1 = \sum_{e \in \mathcal{E}} |w(e) - w'(e)| \le 1.$$

Definition 2.2. *For any graph $\mathcal{G} = (\mathcal{V}, \mathcal{E})$, let $\mathcal{A}$ be an algorithm that takes as input a weight function $w : \mathcal{E} \to \mathbb{R}^+$. $\mathcal{A}$ is (ϵ, δ)-**differentially private** on $\mathcal{G}$ if for all pairs of neighboring weight functions w, w' and for all sets of possible outputs S, we have that*

$$\Pr[\mathcal{A}(w) \in S] \le e^\epsilon \Pr[\mathcal{A}(w') \in S] + \delta.$$

If $\delta = 0$ we say that $\mathcal{A}$ is ϵ-differentially private on $\mathcal{G}$.

For a class $\mathcal{C}$ of graphs, we say that $\mathcal{A}$ is (ϵ, δ)-differentially private on $\mathcal{C}$ if $\mathcal{A}$ is (ϵ, δ)-differentially private on $\mathcal{G}$ for all $\mathcal{G} \in \mathcal{C}$.

We now define our accuracy criteria for the approximate shortest paths and distances problems.

Definition 2.3. *For the shortest path problem, the **error** of a path $P \in \mathcal{P}_{xy}$ between vertices x, y is the difference $w(P) - d_w(x, y)$ between the length of P and the length of the shortest path between x and y.*

Definition 2.4. *For the approximate distances problem, the **error** is the absolute difference between the released distance between a pair of vertices x, y and the actual distance $d_w(x, y)$.*

3. PRELIMINARIES

We will now introduce a few basic tools which will be used throughout the remainder of this paper. A number of differential privacy techniques incorporate noise sampled according to the Laplace distribution. We define the distribution and state a concentration bound for sums of Laplace random variables.

Definition 3.1. *The **Laplace distribution** with scale b, denoted Lap(b), is the distribution with probability density function given by*

$$p(x) = \frac{1}{2b} \exp(-|x|/b).$$

If Y is distributed according to Lap(b), then for any $t > 0$ we have that $\Pr[|Y| > t \cdot b] = e^{-t}$.

Lemma 3.1. (Concentration of Laplace random variables [CSS10]) *Let $X_1, \ldots, X_t$ be independent random variables distributed according to Lap(b), and let $X = \sum_i X_i$. Then for all $\gamma \in (0, 1)$ we have that with probability at least $1 - \gamma$,*

$$|X| < 4b\sqrt{t} \ln(2/\gamma) = O(b\sqrt{t} \log(1/\gamma)).$$

One of the first and most versatile differentially private algorithms is the Laplace mechanism, which releases a noisy answer with error sampled from the Laplace distribution with scale proportional to the sensitivity of the function being computed.

Definition 3.2. *For any function $f : \mathcal{X} \to \mathbb{R}^k$, the **sensitivity***

$$\Delta f = \max_{\substack{w, w' \in \mathcal{X} \\ w \sim w'}} \|f(w) - f(w')\|_1$$

is the largest amount f can differ in ℓ_1 norm between neighboring inputs.

In our setting we have $\mathcal{X} = (\mathbb{R}^+)^{\mathcal{E}}$.

Lemma 3.2. (Laplace mechanism [DMNS06]) *Given any function $f : \mathcal{X} \to \mathbb{R}^k$, the Laplace mechanism on input $w \in \mathcal{X}$ independently samples $Y_1, \ldots, Y_k$ according to Lap($\Delta f / \epsilon$) and outputs*

$$\mathcal{M}_{f,\epsilon}(w) = f(w) + (Y_1, \ldots, Y_k).$$

The Laplace mechanism is ϵ-differentially private.

Finally, we will need the following results on the composition of differentially private algorithms.

Lemma 3.3. (Basic Composition, e.g. [DKM⁺06]) *For any ϵ, $\delta \ge 0$, the adaptive composition of k (ϵ, δ)-differentially private mechanisms is $(k\epsilon, k\delta)$-differentially private.*

Lemma 3.4. (Composition [DRV10, DR13]) *For any $\epsilon, \delta, \delta' \ge 0$, the adaptive composition of k (ϵ, δ)-differentially private mechanisms is $(\epsilon', k\delta + \delta')$-differen-tially private for*

$$\epsilon' = \sqrt{2k \ln(1/\delta')} \cdot \epsilon + k\epsilon(e^\epsilon - 1)$$

which is $O(\sqrt{k \ln(1/\delta')} \cdot \epsilon)$ provided $k \le 1/\epsilon^2$. In particular, if $\epsilon' \in (0, 1), \delta, \delta' \ge 0$, the composition of k (ϵ, δ)-differentially private mechanisms is $(\epsilon', k\delta + \delta')$-differentially private for $\epsilon = O(\epsilon' / \sqrt{k \ln(1/\delta')})$.

4. COMPUTING DISTANCES

In this section we consider the problem of releasing distance oracle queries in the private edge weights model. Since neighboring weight functions differ by at most 1 in ℓ_1 norm, the weight of any path also changes by at most 1. Consequently, a single distance oracle query is sensitivity-1, and so we can use the Laplace mechanism (Lemma 3.2) to answer it privately after adding noise proportional to $1/\epsilon$. However, what if we would like to learn all-pairs distances privately?

There are V^2 pairs (s, t) of vertices, so we can achieve ϵ-differential privacy by adding to each query Laplace noise proportional to V^2/ϵ. We can do better using approximate differential privacy ($\delta > 0$) and Lemma 3.4 (Composition). Adding Laplace noise proportional to $1/\epsilon'$ to

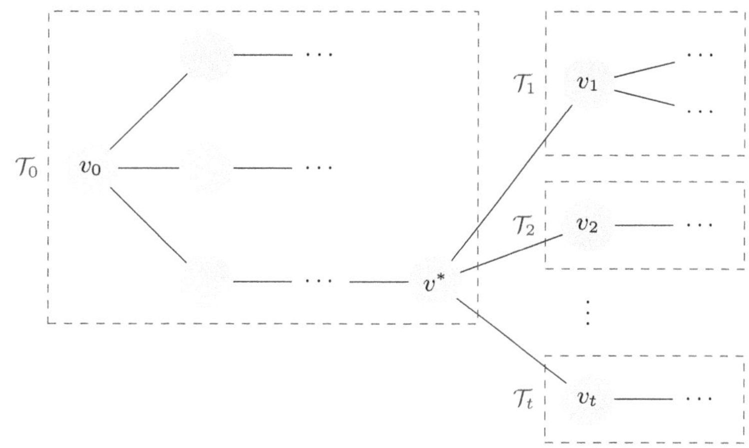

Figure 1: The partition used in Algorithm 1 to separate a tree into subtrees of size at most $V/2$.

each query results in a mechanism that is $(V\epsilon'\sqrt{2\ln(1/\delta)} + V^2\epsilon'(e^{\epsilon'}-1), \delta)$-differentially private for any $\delta > 0$. Taking $\epsilon' = \epsilon/O(V\sqrt{\ln 1/\delta})$ for $\epsilon < 1$, we obtain a mechanism that is (ϵ, δ)-differentially private by adding $O(V\sqrt{\ln 1/\delta})/\epsilon$ noise to each query.

The other natural approach is to release an ϵ-differentially private version of the graph by adding $\text{Lap}(1/\epsilon)$ noise to each edge. This will be the basis for our approach in Algorithm 3 for computing approximate shortest paths. With probability $1-\gamma$, all E Laplace random variables will have magnitude $(1/\epsilon)\log(E/\gamma)$, so the length of every path in the released synthetic graph is within $(V/\epsilon)\log(E/\gamma)$ of the length of the corresponding path in the original graph. Therefore with probability $1-\gamma$ we have that all pairs distances in the released synthetic graph will be within $(V/\epsilon)\log(E/\gamma)$ of the corresponding distances in the original graph.

Both of these approaches result in privately releasing all pairs distances with additive error roughly V/ϵ. It is natural to ask whether this linear dependance on V is the best possible. In the remainder of this section we present algorithms which substantially improve on this bound for two special classes of graphs, trees and arbitrary graphs with edges of bounded weight. For trees we can obtain all-pairs distances with error $\text{polylog}(V)/\epsilon$, and for graphs with edges in $[0, M]$ we can obtain all-pairs distances with error roughly $\sqrt{VM/\epsilon}$.

4.1 Distances in trees

For trees it turns out to be possible to release all-pairs distances with far less error. We will first show a single-source version of this result for rooted trees, which we will then use to obtain the full result. The idea is to split the tree into subtrees of at most half the size of the original tree. As long as we can release the distance from the root to each subtree with small error, we can then recurse on the subtrees.

The problem of privately releasing all-pairs distances for the path graph can be restated as the problem of privately releasing threshold functions for a totally ordered data universe of size $E = V - 1$. Dwork et al. [DNPR10] showed that we can privately maintain a running counter for T timesteps, with probability $1-\gamma$ achieving additive accuracy of $O(\log(1/\gamma)\log^{2.5} T/\epsilon)$ at each timestep. This algorithm essentially computes all threshold queries for a totally ordered universe of size T, which is equivalent to computing the distance from an endpoint to each other vertex of the path graph. We match the accuracy of the [DNPR10] algorithm and generalize the result to arbitrary trees.

In Appendix A we provide an alternate algorithm for the path graph which achieves the same asymptotic bounds. This result can be viewed as a restatement of the [DNPR10] algorithm.

THEOREM 4.1. (SINGLE-SOURCE DISTANCES ON ROOTED TREES) *Let $\mathcal{T} = (\mathcal{V}, \mathcal{E})$ be a tree with root vetex v_0, and let $\epsilon > 0$. Then there is an algorithm that is ϵ-differentially private on $\mathcal{T}$ that on input edge weights $w : \mathcal{E} \to \mathbb{R}^+$ releases approximate distances from v_0 to each other vertex, where with probability $1-\gamma$ the approximation error on each released distance is*

$$O(\log^{1.5} V \cdot \log(1/\gamma))/\epsilon$$

for any $\gamma \in (0, 1)$.

PROOF. Given the tree $\mathcal{T}$ and root v_0, we will partition $\mathcal{V}$ into subtrees of size at most $V/2$ as shown in Figure 1 and recursively obtain distances in each subtree. There exists some vertex v^* such that the subtree rooted at v^* contains more than $V/2$ vertices while the subtree rooted at each child of v^* has at most $V/2$ vertices. The topology of the graph is public, so we can release vertex v^*. Let $v_1, \ldots, v_t$ be the children of v^*, and let $\mathcal{T}_i = (\mathcal{V}_i, \mathcal{E}_i)$ be the subtree rooted at v_i for each $i \in [t]$. Let $\mathcal{T}_0 = (\mathcal{V}_0, \mathcal{E}_0)$ be the subtree rooted at v_0 consisting of the remaining vertices $\mathcal{V} \setminus (\mathcal{V}_1 \cup \cdots \cup \mathcal{V}_t)$.

We can compute and release distances between the following pairs of vertices, adding $\text{Lap}(\log V/\epsilon)$ noise to each distance:

- (v_0, v^*)
- (v^*, v_i) for each $i \in [t]$

Since v^* is the parent of $v_1, \ldots, v_t$ in the tree rooted at v_0, the path from v_0 to v^* in T contains none of the edges (v^*, v_i) for $i \in [t]$, so the function which releases these $t+1$ distances is sensitivity-1.

Algorithm 1: Rooted tree distances

Inputs: Tree $\mathcal{T} = (\mathcal{V}, \mathcal{E})$, root $v_0 \in \mathcal{V}$, edge weights $w : \mathcal{E} \to \mathbb{R}^+$, and number of vertices n of original tree.

1. Let v^* be the unique vertex such that the subtree rooted at v^* has more than $V/2$ vertices while the subtree rooted at each child of v^* has at most $V/2$ vertices.
2. Let $v_1, \ldots, v_t$ be the children of v^*.
3. Let $\mathcal{T}_i$ be the subtree rooted at v_i for $i \in [t]$, and let $\mathcal{T}_0 = \mathcal{T} \setminus \{\mathcal{T}_1, \ldots, \mathcal{T}_t\}$.
4. Sample $X_{v^*,\mathcal{T}} \leftarrow \text{Lap}(\log V/\epsilon)$ and let $d(v^*, \mathcal{T}) = d_w(v_0, v^*) + X_{v^*,\mathcal{T}}$.
5. Let $d(v_0, \mathcal{T}) = 0$.
6. For each $i \in [t]$, sample $X_{v_i,\mathcal{T}} \leftarrow \text{Lap}(\log V/\epsilon)$ and let $d(v_i, \mathcal{T}) = d(v^*, \mathcal{T}) + w((v^*, v_i)) + X_{v_i,\mathcal{T}}$.
7. Recursively compute distances in each subtree $\mathcal{T}_0, \ldots, \mathcal{T}_t$.
8. For each vertex $v \in \mathcal{V}$, if $v \in \mathcal{T}_i$, then let $d(v, \mathcal{T}) = d(v_i, \mathcal{T}) + d(v, \mathcal{T}_i)$.
9. Release $d(v, \mathcal{T})$ for all $v \in \mathcal{V}$.

We then recursively repeat the procedure on each subtree $\mathcal{T}_0, \ldots, \mathcal{T}_t$ until we reach trees containing only a single vertex, adding $\text{Lap}(\log V/\epsilon)$ noise to each released value. Each subtree has size at most $V/2$, so the depth of recursion is bounded by $\log V$. The subtrees $\mathcal{T}_0, \ldots, \mathcal{T}_t$ are also disjoint. Consequently the function which releases all of the distances at depth d in the recursion has sensitivity 1 for any d. Therefore the function which releases all distances queried in this recursive procedure has sensitivity at most $\log V$. Since we add $\text{Lap}(\log V/\epsilon)$ noise to each coordinate of this function, the algorithm outlined above is an instantiation of the Laplace mechanism (Lemma 3.2) and is ϵ-differentially private.

We now show how these queries suffice to compute the distance from root vertex v_0 to each other vertex with small error. The algorithm samples at most $2V$ Laplace random variables distributed according to $\text{Lap}(\log V/\epsilon)$, so by a union bound, with probability $1-\gamma$ all of these have magnitude $O(\log V \log(V/\gamma))/\epsilon$. Consequently to obtain an error bound of roughly $O(\log^3 V)/\epsilon$ it suffices to show that any distance in $\mathcal{T}$ can be represented as a sum of $O(\log V)$ of the noisy distances released in the algorithm. We will use Lemma 3.1 to obtain a slightly better bound on the error terms.

Let set Q consist of the pairs of vertices corresponding to distance queries made by the algorithm above. We prove the following statement by induction. For any vertex $u \in \mathcal{V}$, there is a path from v_0 to u in the graph $(\mathcal{V}, Q)$ consisting of at most $2\log V$ edges. The base case $V = 1$ is vacuous. For $V > 1$, note that since subtrees $T_0, \ldots, T_t$ partition the vertex set, u must lie in one of them. If $u \in T_i$, then by the inductive assumption on T_i, there is a path from v_i to u in (V, Q) consisting of at most $2\log(V/2) = 2\log V - 2$ edges. If $i = 0$ this already suffices. Otherwise, if $i > 0$, note that $(v_0, v^*) \in Q$ and $(v^*, v_i) \in Q$. Consequently there is a path in $(\mathcal{V}, Q)$ from v_0 to u consisting of at most $2\log V$ edges.

This means that there is a set of at most $2\log V$ distances queried such that the distance from v_0 to u consists of the sum of these distances. Consequently by adding these distances we obtain an estimate for the distance from v_0 to u whose error is the sum of at most $2\log V$ independent random variables each distributed according to $\text{Lap}(\log V/\epsilon)$. By Lemma 3.1, we have that with probability at least $1-\gamma$, we compute an estimate of $d_w(v_0, u)$ with error $O(\log^{1.5} V \cdot \log(1/\gamma))/\epsilon$ for any $\gamma \in (0,1)$. Since differentially private mechanism are preserved under post-processing, this algorithm satisfies ϵ-differential privacy and computes distances from v^* to each other vertex in T, where with probability at least $1-\gamma$ each distance has error at most $O(\log^{1.5} V \cdot \log(1/\gamma))/\epsilon$. □

We now extend this result to obtain all-pairs distances for trees.

THEOREM 4.2. (ALL-PAIRS DISTANCES ON TREES) *For any tree $\mathcal{T} = (\mathcal{V}, \mathcal{E})$ and $\epsilon > 0$ there is an algorithm that is ϵ-differentially private on $\mathcal{T}$ and on input edge weights $w : \mathcal{E} \to \mathbb{R}^+$ releases all-pairs distances such that with probability $1-\gamma$, all released distances have approximation error*

$$O(\log^{2.5} V \cdot \log(1/\gamma))/\epsilon$$

for any $\gamma \in (0,1)$. For each released distance, with probability $1-\gamma$ the approximation error is $O(\log^{1.5} V \cdot \log(1/\gamma))/\epsilon$.

PROOF. Arbitrarily choose some root vertex v_0. Use the ϵ-differentially private algorithm of Theorem 4.1 to obtain approximate distances from v_0 to each other vertex of $\mathcal{T}$. We now show that this suffices to obtain all-pairs distances.

Consider any pair of vertices x, y, and let z be their lowest common ancestor in the tree rooted at v_0. Then

$$\begin{aligned} d_w(x,y) &= d_w(z,x) + d_w(z,y) \\ &= d_w(v_0,x) + d_w(v_0,y) - 2d_w(v_0,z). \end{aligned}$$

Since with probability $1-3\gamma$ we can compute each of these three distances with error $O(\log^{1.5} V \cdot \log(1/\gamma)/\epsilon)$, it follows that we can compute the distance between x and y

Algorithm 2: Bounded-weight distances

Inputs: $\mathcal{G} = (\mathcal{V}, \mathcal{E})$, $w : \mathcal{E} \to \mathbb{R}^+$, $k, M, \gamma, \epsilon' > 0$, k-covering $\mathcal{Z}$.

1. For all $y, z \in \mathcal{Z}$, sample $X_{y,z} \leftarrow \text{Lap}(|\mathcal{Z}|/\epsilon')$ and output $a_{y,z} := d_w(y,z) + X_{y,z}$.
2. For $v \in V$, let $z(v) \in \mathcal{Z}$ denote a vertex in $\mathcal{Z}$ with $h(v, z(v)) \leq k$.
3. The approximate distance between vertices $u, v \in V$ is given by $a_{z(u),z(v)}$.

with error at most four times this, which is still $O(\log^{1.5} V \cdot \log(1/\gamma))/\epsilon$. By a union bound, for any $\gamma \in (0,1)$, with probability at least $1-\gamma$ each error among the $V(V-1)/2$ all-pairs distances released is at most $O(\log^{1.5} V \cdot \log(V/\gamma))/\epsilon = O(\log^{2.5} V \cdot \log(1/\gamma))/\epsilon$. □

4.2 Distances in bounded-weight graphs

Theorem 4.3. *For all $\mathcal{G}, \delta, \gamma, M$, and $\epsilon \in (0,1)$, if $1/V < M\epsilon < V$ then there is an algorithm $\mathcal{A}$ that is (ϵ, δ)-differentially private on $\mathcal{G}$ such that for all $w : \mathcal{E} \to [0, M]$, with probability $1-\gamma$, $\mathcal{A}(w)$ outputs approximate all-pairs distances with additive error*

$$O\left(\sqrt{VM\epsilon^{-1} \cdot \log(1/\delta)} \cdot \log(VM\epsilon/\gamma)\right)$$

per distance. For any $\epsilon > 0$, $\mathcal{G}, \gamma, M$, if $1/V < M\epsilon < V^2$ then there is an algorithm $\mathcal{B}$ that is ϵ-differentially private on $\mathcal{G}$ such that for all $w : \mathcal{E} \to [0, M]$, with probability $1-\gamma$, $\mathcal{B}(w)$ outputs approximate all-pairs distances with additive error

$$O\left((VM)^{2/3}\epsilon^{-1/3} \log(VM\epsilon/\gamma)\right)$$

per distance.

To achieve this result, we will find a small subset $\mathcal{Z}$ of $\mathcal{V}$ such that every vertex $v \in \mathcal{V}$ is near some vertex $z \in \mathcal{Z}$. We will need the following definition, introduced in [MM75].

Definition 4.1. *A subset $\mathcal{Z} \subset \mathcal{V}$ of vertices is a **k-covering** if for every $v \in \mathcal{V}$ there is some $z \in \mathcal{Z}$ such that $h(v,z) \leq k$, where h is the hop-distance.*

A k-covering is sometimes called a k-dominating set (e.g. in [CN82]). The following lemma shows that we can find a sufficiently small k-covering for any graph $\mathcal{G}$.

Lemma 4.4. *[MM75] If $V \geq k+1$, then $\mathcal{G}$ has a k-covering of size at most $\lfloor V/(k+1) \rfloor$.*

Proof. Consider any spanning tree $\mathcal{T}$ of $\mathcal{G}$ and any vertex $x \in \mathcal{V}$ that is an endpoint of one of the longest paths in $\mathcal{T}$. For $0 \leq i \leq k$, let $\mathcal{Z}_i$ be the subset of $\mathcal{V}$ consisting of vertices whose distance from x in $\mathcal{T}$ is congruent to i modulo $k+1$. It can be shown that each $\mathcal{Z}_i$ is a k-covering of $\mathcal{T}$ and therefore of $\mathcal{G}$. But the $k+1$ sets $\mathcal{Z}_i$ form a partition of $\mathcal{V}$. Therefore some $\mathcal{Z}_i$ has $|\mathcal{Z}_i| \leq \lfloor V/(k+1) \rfloor$, as desired. □

Theorem 4.5. *For any $\mathcal{G} = (\mathcal{V}, \mathcal{E}), k, \delta > 0$, and $\gamma, \epsilon \in (0,1)$, let $\mathcal{Z}$ be a k-covering of $\mathcal{G}$, and let $Z = |\mathcal{Z}|$. Then there is an algorithm $\mathcal{A}$ which is (ϵ, δ)-differentially private on $\mathcal{G}$ such that for any edge weight function $w : \mathcal{E} \to [0, M]$, with probability $1-\gamma$, $\mathcal{A}(w)$ releases all-pairs distances with approximation error*

$$O\left(kM + Z\epsilon^{-1} \log(Z/\gamma)\sqrt{\log(1/\delta)}\right)$$

per distance.

Proof. There are Z^2 pairwise distances between vertices in $\mathcal{Z}$. We can compute and release noisy versions of each of these distances, adding $\text{Lap}(Z/\epsilon')$ noise to each. For any $\gamma \in (0,1)$, with probability $1-\gamma$ we have that each of these Z^2 noise variables has magnitude at most $(Z/\epsilon') \log(Z^2/\gamma)$. By Lemma 3.4, for any $\delta > 0$ releasing this is (ϵ, δ)-differentially private for $\epsilon' = O(\epsilon/\sqrt{\ln 1/\delta})$.

But this information allows the recipient to compute approximate distances between any pair of vertices $x, y \in \mathcal{V}$, as follows. Since $\mathcal{Z}$ is a k-covering of $\mathcal{G}$, we can find $z_x, z_y \in \mathcal{Z}$ which are at most k vertices from x and y. Since the maximum weight is M, the weight of the shortest path between x and z_x is at most kM, and similarly for y and z_y. Consequently

$$|d_w(x,y) - d_w(z_x, z_y)| \leq 2kM.$$

But we have released an estimate of $d_w(z_x, z_y)$ with noise distributed according to $\text{Lap}(Z/\epsilon)$. Consequently with probability $1-\gamma$ each of these estimates differs from $d_w(z_x, z_y)$ by at most $(Z/\epsilon)\log(Z^2/\gamma)$. □

We obtain a slightly weaker result under pure differential privacy.

Theorem 4.6. *Let $\mathcal{G} = (\mathcal{V}, \mathcal{E})$. For any $k > 0$ and $\gamma \in (0,1)$, if $\mathcal{Z}$ is a k-covering of $\mathcal{G}$ of size Z, then there is an algorithm $\mathcal{A}$ that is ϵ-differentially private on $\mathcal{G}$ such that for any $w : \mathcal{E} \to [0, M]$, with probability $1-\gamma$, $\mathcal{A}(w)$ releases all-pairs distances with approximation error*

$$O(kM + Z^2\epsilon^{-1} \log(Z/\gamma))$$

per distance.

Proof. There are at most Z^2 pairwise distances between vertices in $\mathcal{Z}$, so we can release approximations of each distance, adding $\text{Lap}(Z^2/\epsilon)$ noise to each distance. With probability $1-\gamma$ each of these Z^2 noise variables has magnitude at most $(Z^2/\epsilon)\log(Z^2/\gamma)$. By Lemma 3.3, releasing these distances is ϵ-differentially private. As above, since $\mathcal{Z}$ is a k-covering of $\mathcal{G}$, we can find $z_x, z_y \in \mathcal{Z}$ which are at most k vertices from x and y. Consequently $d_w(x, z_x) \leq kM$ and $d_w(y, z_y) \leq kM$, so

$$|d_w(x,y) - d_w(z_x, z_y)| \leq 2kM.$$

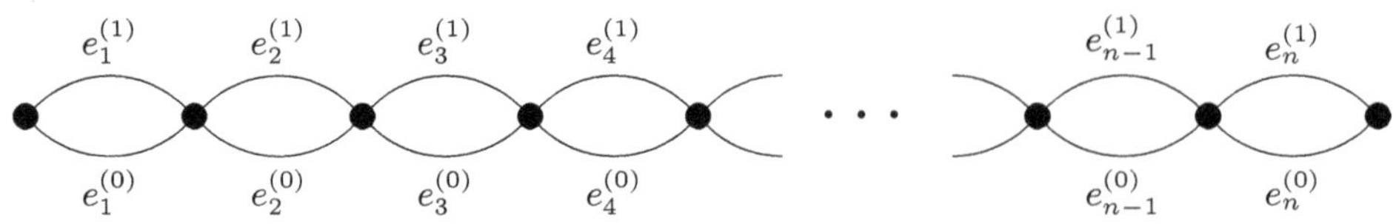

Figure 2: The graph used for the lower bound of Lemma 5.2.

But the released estimate for $d_w(z_x, z_y)$ has noise distributed according to $\mathrm{Lap}(kM)$, so with probability $1-\gamma$ each of these estimates differs from $d_w(x,y)$ by at most $O(Z^2\epsilon^{-1}\log(Z^2/\gamma))$, as desired. □

We now conclude the proof of Theorem 4.3.

PROOF OF THEOREM 4.3. Combine Lemma 4.4 with Theorem 4.5 for $k = \lfloor\sqrt{V/(M\epsilon)}\rfloor$, and combine Lemma 4.4 with Theorem 4.6 for $k = \lfloor V^{2/3}/(M\epsilon)^{1/3}\rfloor$. □

Note that if we are only interested in the $V-1$ distances from a single source, then directly releasing noisy distances and applying Lemma 3.4 yields (ϵ,δ)-differen-tial privacy with error distributed according to $\mathrm{Lap}(b)$ for $b = O(\sqrt{V\log 1/\delta})/\epsilon$, which has the same dependence on V as the bound provided by the theorem for releasing all pairs distances.

For some graphs we may be able to find a smaller k-covering than that guaranteed by Lemma 4.4. Then we can use Theorems 4.5 and 4.6 to obtain all-pairs distances with lower error. For instance, we have the following.

THEOREM 4.7. *Let $\mathcal{G}$ be the $\sqrt{V}\times\sqrt{V}$ grid. Then for any $\epsilon,\gamma\in(0,1)$ and $\delta>0$, we can release with probability $1-\gamma$ all-pairs distances with additive approximation error*

$$V^{1/3}\cdot O\left(M+\epsilon^{-1}\log(V/\gamma)\sqrt{\log 1/\delta}\right)$$

while satisfying (ϵ,δ)-differential privacy.

PROOF. Let $\mathcal{V} = [\sqrt{V}]\times[\sqrt{V}]$, and let $\mathcal{Z}\subset\mathcal{V}$ consist of vertices $(i,j)\in\mathcal{V}$ with i,j both one less than a multiple of $V^{1/3}$. Then $\mathcal{Z}$ is a $2V^{1/3}$-covering of $\mathcal{G}$, and also $|\mathcal{Z}|\le V^{1/3}$. Consequently Theorem 4.5 implies the desired conclusion. □

5. FINDING SHORTEST PATHS

5.1 Lower bound

In this section we present a lower bound on the additive error with which we can privately release a short path between a pair of vertices. The argument is based on a reduction from the problem of reconstructing a large fraction of the entries of a database. We show that an adversary can use an algorithm which outputs a short path in a graph to produce a vector with small Hamming distance to an input vector, which is impossible under differential privacy. To that end, we exhibit a "hard" graph $\mathcal{G}=(\mathcal{V},\mathcal{E})$ and a family of weight functions, and provide a correspondence between inputs $x\in\{0,1\}^n$ and weight functions $w:\mathcal{E}\to\{0,1\}$.

THEOREM 5.1. *There exists a graph $\mathcal{G}=(\mathcal{V},\mathcal{E})$ and vertices $s,t\in\mathcal{V}$ such that for any algorithm $\mathcal{A}$ that is (ϵ,δ)-differentially private on $\mathcal{G}$, there exist edge weights $w:\mathcal{E}\to\{0,1\}$ for which the expected approximation error of the path $\mathcal{A}(w)$ from s to t is at least $\alpha=(V-1)\cdot\left(\frac{1-(1+e^\epsilon)\delta}{1+e^{2\epsilon}}\right)$. In particular, for sufficiently small ϵ and δ, $\alpha\ge 0.49(V-1)$.*

Consequently, any differentially private algorithm for approximate shortest paths must on some inputs have additive error proportional to the number of vertices. Let $\mathcal{G}=(\mathcal{V},\mathcal{E})$ be the $(n+1)$-vertex graph with vertex set $\mathcal{V}=\{0,\dots,n\}$ and two parallel edges $e_i^{(0)}$ and $e_i^{(1)}$ between each pair of consecutive vertices $i-1,i$, as shown in Figure 2. (For simplicity we have defined this is a multigraph, but it can be transformed into a simple graph with the addition of n extra vertices, changing the bound obtained by a factor of 2.)

LEMMA 5.2. *Let $\mathcal{G}=(\mathcal{V},\mathcal{E})$ be the graph defined in the previous paragraph. For any α, let $\mathcal{A}$ be an algorithm that is (ϵ,δ)-differentially private on $\mathcal{G}$ that on input edge weights $w:\mathcal{E}\to\{0,1\}$ produces a path from vertex $s=0$ to vertex $t=n$ with expected approximation error at most α. Then there exists a $(2\epsilon,(1+e^\epsilon)\delta)$-differentially private algorithm $\mathcal{B}$ which on input $x\in\{0,1\}^n$ produces $y\in\{0,1\}^n$ such that the expected Hamming distance $d_H(x,y)$ is at most α.*

PROOF. Given an input $x\in\{0,1\}^n$, the corresponding edge weight function w_x is given by $w_x(e_i^{(x_i)})=0$ and $w_x(e_i^{(1-x_i)})=1$. That is, for each pair of consecutive vertices $i-1,i$, one of the edges between them will have weight 0 and the other will have weight 1 as determined by the ith bit of the input x.

The algorithm $\mathcal{B}$ is as follows. On input $x\in\{0,1\}^n$, apply $\mathcal{A}$ to $(\mathcal{G},w_x)$, and let $\mathcal{P}$ be the path produced. Define $y\in\{0,1\}^n$ as follows. Let $y_i=0$ if $e_i^{(0)}\in\mathcal{P}$ and $y_i=1$ otherwise. Output y.

We first show that this procedure is differentially private. Given neighboring inputs $x,x'\in\{0,1\}^n$ which differ only on a single coordinate $x_i\ne x_i'$, we have that the associated weight functions w_x and $w_{x'}$ have ℓ_1 distance 2, since they disagree only edges $e_i^{(0)}$ and $e_i^{(1)}$. Consequently, since $\mathcal{A}$ is (ϵ,δ)-differentially private, we have that for any set of values S in the range of $\mathcal{A}$,

$$\begin{aligned}\Pr[\mathcal{A}(w_x)\in S] &\le e^\epsilon(e^\epsilon\Pr[\mathcal{A}(w_{x'})\in S]+\delta)+\delta\\ &= e^{2\epsilon}\Pr[\mathcal{A}(w_{x'})\in S]+(1+e^\epsilon)\delta\ .\end{aligned}$$

But algorithm $\mathcal{B}$ only accesses the database x through $\mathcal{A}$. Consequently by the robustness of differential privacy to post-processing, we have that $\mathcal{B}$ is $(2\epsilon,(1+e^\epsilon)\delta)$-differentially private.

We now show that the expected number of coordinates in which y disagrees with x is at most α. The shortest path from s to t in $\mathcal{G}$ has length 0, so the expected length of the path $\mathcal{P}$ produced by $\mathcal{A}$ is at most α. Consequently in expectation $\mathcal{P}$ consists of at most α edges $e_i^{(1-x_i)}$. But

Algorithm 3: Private shortest paths

Inputs: $\mathcal{G} = (\mathcal{V}, \mathcal{E})$, $w : \mathcal{E} \to \mathbb{R}^+$, $\gamma > 0$. For each edge $e \in \mathcal{E}$, do the following:

1. Sample $X_e \leftarrow \text{Lap}(1/\epsilon)$
2. Let $w'(e) = w(e) + X_e + (1/\epsilon)\log(E/\gamma)$, where $E = |\mathcal{E}|$

Output w'.

The approximate shortest path between a pair of vertices $x, y \in \mathcal{V}$ is taken to be the shortest path $\text{SP}_{w'}(x, y)$ in the weighted graph $(\mathcal{G}, w')$.

$y_i \neq x_i$ only if $e_i^{(1-x_i)} \in \mathcal{P}$, so it follows that the expected Hamming distance $d_H(x, y) \leq \alpha$. □

We will now prove two simple and standard lemmas concerning the limits of identifying rows of the input of a differentially private algorithm. In the first lemma, we show that a differentially private algorithm cannot release a particular row of its input with probability greater than $\frac{e^\epsilon+\delta}{1+e^\epsilon}$. In essence, for $\delta = 0$ this can be interpreted as a statement about the optimality of the technique of randomized response [War65].

LEMMA 5.3. *If algorithm $\mathcal{B} : \{0,1\}^n \to \{0,1\}$ is (ϵ, δ)-differentially private, then if we uniformly sample a random input $X \leftarrow U_n$, we have that for all i,*

$$\Pr[\mathcal{B}(X) \neq X_i] \geq \frac{1-\delta}{1+e^\epsilon}$$

PROOF. We have that $\Pr[\mathcal{B}(X) = X_i]$ is given by

$$\begin{aligned}&\frac{1}{2}\Pr[\mathcal{B}(X_{-i}, 0) = 0] + \frac{1}{2}\Pr[\mathcal{B}(X_{-i}, 1) = 1]\\ &\leq \frac{e^\epsilon}{2} \cdot (\Pr[\mathcal{B}(X_{-i}, 1) = 0] + \Pr[\mathcal{B}(X_{-i}, 0) = 1]) + \delta\\ &= e^\epsilon \Pr[\mathcal{B}(X) \neq X_i] + \delta\end{aligned}$$

so since $\Pr[\mathcal{B}(X) = X_i] = 1 - \Pr[\mathcal{B}(X) \neq X_i]$,

$$\Pr[\mathcal{B}(X) \neq X_i] \geq \frac{1-\delta}{1+e^\epsilon}\ .$$

□

This immediately implies the following result.

LEMMA 5.4. *If algorithm $\mathcal{B} : \{0,1\}^n \to \{0,1\}^n$ is (ϵ, δ)-differentially private, then for some $x \in \{0,1\}^n$ we have that the expected Hamming distance $d_H(\mathcal{B}(x), x)$ is at least $\frac{n(1-\delta)}{1+e^\epsilon}$.*

PROOF. By Lemma 5.3, projecting onto any coordinate i, the probability that $\Pr[\mathcal{B}(X)_i \neq X_i]$ for uniformly random $X \leftarrow U_n$ is at least $\frac{1-\delta}{1+e^\epsilon}$. Consequently the expected number of coordinates on which $\mathcal{B}(X)$ differs from X is $\mathbf{E}(d_H(\mathcal{B}(X), X)) \geq \frac{n(1-\delta)}{1+e^\epsilon}$. Since this holds for X uniformly random, in particular we have that there exists some $x \in \{0,1\}^n$ such that

$$\mathbf{E}(d_H(\mathcal{B}(x), x)) \geq \frac{n(1-\delta)}{1+e^\epsilon}.$$

□

We now conclude the proof of Theorem 5.1.

PROOF OF THEOREM 5.1. Assume that there is some algorithm which is (ϵ, δ)-differentially private on $\mathcal{G}$ and always produces a path of error at most α between s and t. Then by Lemma 5.2 we have that there is a $(2\epsilon, (1+e^\epsilon)\delta)$-differentially private algorithm $\mathcal{B}$ which for all $x \in \{0,1\}^n$ produces $y \in \{0,1\}^n$ such that the expected Hamming distance $d_H(x, y)$ is less than α. But by Lemma 5.4, for some x the expected Hamming distance $\mathbf{E}(d_H(x, y)) \geq \frac{n(1-(1+e^\epsilon)\delta)}{1+e^{2\epsilon}} = \alpha$, yielding a contradiction. □

5.2 Upper bound

In this section we show that an extremely simple algorithm matches the lower bound of the previous section up to a logarithmic factor, for fixed ϵ, δ. Consider a direct application of the Laplace mechanism (Lemma 3.2), adding $\text{Lap}(1/\epsilon)$ noise to each edge weight and releasing the resulting values. With high probably all of these $E < V^2$ noise variables will be small, providing a bound on the difference in the weight of any path between the released graph and the original graph. Consequently we can show that if we take the shortest path in the released graph, with 99% probability the length of the same path in the original graph is $O(V \log V)/\epsilon$ longer than optimal.

This straightforward application of the Laplace mechanism almost matches the lower bound of the previous section. Surprisingly, with the same error bound it releases not just a short path between a single pair of vertices but short paths between all pairs of vertices.

One drawback of this argument is that the error depends on the size of the entire graph. In practice we may expect that the shortest path between most pairs of vertices consist of relatively few edges. We would like the error to depend on the number of hops on the shortest path rather than scaling with the number of vertices. We achieve this with a post-processing step that increases the weight of all edges, introducing a preference for few-hop paths. We show that if there is a short path with only k hops, then our algorithm reports a path whose length is at most $O(k \log V/\epsilon)$ longer.

THEOREM 5.5. *For all graphs $\mathcal{G}$ and $\gamma \in (0,1)$, Algorithm 3 is ϵ-differentially private on $\mathcal{G}$ and computes paths between all pairs of vertices such that with probability $1-\gamma$, for all pairs of vertices $s, t \in \mathcal{V}$, if there exists a k-hop path of weight W in $(\mathcal{G}, w)$, the path released has weight at most $W + (2k/\epsilon)\log(E/\gamma)$.*

In particular, if the shortest path in $\mathcal{G}$ has k hops, then Algorithm 3 releases a path only $(2k/\epsilon)\log(E/\gamma)$ longer than optimal. This error term is proportional to the number of hops on the shortest path. Noting that the shortest path between any pair of vertices consists of fewer than V hops, we obtain the following corollary.

COROLLARY 5.6. *For any $\gamma \in (0,1)$, with probability $1-\gamma$ Algorithm 3 computes paths between every pair of vertices with approximation error at most $(2V/\epsilon)\log(E/\gamma)$.*

PROOF OF THEOREM 5.5. Each random variable X_e is distributed according to $\mathrm{Lap}(1/\epsilon)$, so with probability $1-\gamma$ we have that $|X_e| \leq (1/\epsilon)\log(1/\gamma)$ for any $\gamma \in (0,1)$. By a union bound, with probability $1-\gamma$ all $E < V^2$ of these random variables have magnitude at most $(1/\epsilon)\log(E/\gamma)$. Conditioning on this event, for each edge $e \in \mathcal{E}$, the modified weight computed by the algorithm satisfies

$$w(e) \leq w'(e) \leq w(e) + (2/\epsilon)\log(E/\gamma).$$

Therefore, for any k-hop path $\mathcal{P}$ we have that

$$w(\mathcal{P}) \leq w'(\mathcal{P}) \leq w(\mathcal{P}) + (2k/\epsilon)\log(E/\gamma).$$

For any $s,t \in \mathcal{V}$, if $\mathcal{Q}$ is the path from s to t produced by the algorithm and $\mathcal{Q}'$ is any path from s to t, then we have that $\mathcal{Q}$ is a shortest path under w', so

$$w(\mathcal{Q}) \leq w'(\mathcal{Q}) \leq w'(\mathcal{Q}') \leq w(\mathcal{Q}') + (2\ell(\mathcal{Q}')/\epsilon)\log(E/\gamma).$$

□

Acknowledgments I am grateful to Salil Vadhan and Shafi Goldwasser for their guidance and encouragement throughout this project. Thanks to Jon Ullman, Tommy MacWilliam and anonymous referees for helpful suggestions. This work was supported by a DOE CSGF Fellowship, NSF Frontier CNS-1413920, DARPA W911NF-15-C-0236, and the Simons Foundation (agreement dated 6-5-12).

6. REFERENCES

[BBDS12] Jeremiah Blocki, Avrim Blum, Anupam Datta, and Or Sheffet. The johnson-lindenstrauss transform itself preserves differential privacy. In *Foundations of Computer Science (FOCS), 2012 IEEE 53rd Annual Symposium on*, pages 410–419. IEEE, 2012.

[BBDS13] Jeremiah Blocki, Avrim Blum, Anupam Datta, and Or Sheffet. Differentially private data analysis of social networks via restricted sensitivity. In *Proceedings of the 4th conference on Innovations in Theoretical Computer Science*, pages 87–96. ACM, 2013.

[BNSV15] Mark Bun, Kobbi Nissim, Uri Stemmer, and Salil Vadhan. Differentially private release and learning of threshold functions. *arXiv preprint arXiv:1504.07553*, 2015.

[CN82] GJ Chang and GL Nemhauser. The k-domination and k-stability problem on graphs. *Techn. Report*, 540, 1982.

[CSS10] TH Hubert Chan, Elaine Shi, and Dawn Song. Private and continual release of statistics. In *Automata, Languages and Programming*, pages 405–417. Springer, 2010.

[DKM+06] Cynthia Dwork, Krishnaram Kenthapadi, Frank McSherry, Ilya Mironov, and Moni Naor. Our data, ourselves: Privacy via distributed noise generation. In *Advances in Cryptology-EUROCRYPT 2006*, pages 486–503. Springer, 2006.

[DMNS06] Cynthia Dwork, Frank McSherry, Kobbi Nissim, and Adam Smith. Calibrating noise to sensitivity in private data analysis. In *Theory of cryptography*, pages 265–284. Springer, 2006.

[DNPR10] Cynthia Dwork, Moni Naor, Toniann Pitassi, and Guy N Rothblum. Differential privacy under continual observation. In *Proceedings of the forty-second ACM symposium on Theory of computing*, pages 715–724. ACM, 2010.

[DR13] Cynthia Dwork and Aaron Roth. The algorithmic foundations of differential privacy. *Theoretical Computer Science*, 9(3-4):211–407, 2013.

[DRV10] Cynthia Dwork, Guy N Rothblum, and Salil Vadhan. Boosting and differential privacy. In *Foundations of Computer Science (FOCS), 2010 51st Annual IEEE Symposium on*, pages 51–60. IEEE, 2010.

[GLM+10] Anupam Gupta, Katrina Ligett, Frank McSherry, Aaron Roth, and Kunal Talwar. Differentially private combinatorial optimization. In *Proceedings of the Twenty-First Annual ACM-SIAM Symposium on Discrete Algorithms*, pages 1106–1125. Society for Industrial and Applied Mathematics, 2010.

[GRU12] Anupam Gupta, Aaron Roth, and Jonathan Ullman. Iterative constructions and private data release. In *Theory of Cryptography*, pages 339–356. Springer, 2012.

[HHR+14] Justin Hsu, Zhiyi Huang, Aaron Roth, Tim Roughgarden, and Zhiwei Steven Wu. Private matchings and allocations. In *Proceedings of the 46th Annual ACM Symposium on Theory of Computing*, pages 21–30. ACM, 2014.

[HLMJ09] Michael Hay, Chao Li, Gerome Miklau, and David Jensen. Accurate estimation of the degree distribution of private networks. In *Data Mining, 2009. ICDM'09. Ninth IEEE International Conference on*, pages 169–178. IEEE, 2009.

[KNRS13] Shiva Prasad Kasiviswanathan, Kobbi Nissim, Sofya Raskhodnikova, and Adam Smith. Analyzing graphs with node differential privacy. In *Theory of Cryptography*, pages 457–476. Springer, 2013.

[KRSY11] Vishesh Karwa, Sofya Raskhodnikova, Adam Smith, and Grigory Yaroslavtsev. Private analysis of graph structure. *Proceedings of the VLDB Endowment*, 4(11):1146–1157, 2011.

[MM75] A Meir and JW Moon. Relations between packing and covering numbers of a tree. *Pacific J. Math*, 61(1):225–233, 1975.

[NRS07] Kobbi Nissim, Sofya Raskhodnikova, and Adam Smith. Smooth sensitivity and sampling in private data analysis. In *Proceedings of the*

thirty-ninth annual ACM symposium on Theory of computing, pages 75–84. ACM, 2007.
[War65] Stanley L Warner. Randomized response: A survey technique for eliminating evasive answer bias. *Journal of the American Statistical Association*, 60(309):63–69, 1965.

APPENDIX

A. DISTANCES IN THE PATH GRAPH

In this section we give an explicit description of the private all-pairs distance algorithm for the path graph $\mathcal{P} = (\mathcal{V}, \mathcal{E})$ with vertex set $\mathcal{V} = [V]$ and edge set $\mathcal{E} = \{(i, i+1) : i \in [V-1]\}$. This result is a restatement of a result of [DNPR10], and is generalized to trees in Section 4.1. This alternate argument for the special case of the path graph is included for illustration.

The idea behind the construction is as follows. We designate a small set of hubs and store more accurate distances between consecutive hubs. As long as we can accurately estimate the distance from any vertex to the nearest hub and the distance between any pair of hubs, we can use these distances to obtain an estimate of the distance between any pair of vertices. Given any pair of vertices $x, y \in \mathcal{V}$, in order to estimate the distance $dist(x, y)$, we first find the hubs h_x and h_y nearest to x and y. We estimate the distance $dist(x, y)$ by adding our estimates for the distances $dist(x, h_x)$, $dist(h_x, h_y)$, and $dist(h_y, y)$.

Instead of simply using a single set of hubs, we will use a hierarchical tree of hubs of different levels. There will be many hubs of low level and only a small number of hubs of high level. Each hub will store an estimate of the distance to the next hub at the same level and every lower level. Hubs higher in the hierarchy will allow us to skip directly to distant vertices instead of accruing error by adding together linearly many noisy estimates. In order to estimate the distance between a particular pair of vertices $x, y \in \mathcal{V}$, we will only consider a small number of hubs on each level of the hierarchy. Since the total number of levels is not too large, this will result in a much more accurate differentially private estimate of the distance between x and y.

THEOREM A.1. *Let $\mathcal{P} = (\mathcal{V}, \mathcal{E})$ be the path graph on V vertices. For any $\epsilon > 0$, there is algorithm $\mathcal{A}$ that is ϵ-differentially private on $\mathcal{P}$ that on input $w : \mathcal{E} \to \mathbb{R}^+$ releases approximate all-pairs distances such that for each released distance, with probability $1-\gamma$ the approximation error is $O(\log^{1.5} V \log(1/\gamma))/\epsilon$ for any $\gamma \in (0,1)$.*

PROOF. For fixed k, define nested subsets $\mathcal{V} = S_0 \supset S_1 \supset \ldots \supset S_{k-1}$ of the vertex set $\mathcal{V} = [V]$ as follows. Let

$$S_i = \{x \in [V] : V^{i/k} \mid x\}.$$

That is, S_0 consists of all the vertices, and in general S_i consists of one out of every $V^{i/k}$ vertices on the path. Then $|S_i| = V^{(k-i)/k}$. Let $s_{i,1}, s_{i,2} \ldots, s_{i,|S_i|}$ denote the elements of S_i in increasing order, for each i. Using the Laplace mechanism (Lemma 3.2), release noisy distances between each pair of consecutive vertices $s_{i,j}, s_{i,j+1}$ of each set, adding noise proportional to $\text{Lap}(k/\epsilon)$. Note that since the vertices in each S_i are in increasing order, each edge of P is only considered for a single released difference from each set. Consequently the total sensitivity to release all of these distances is k, so releasing these noisy distances is ϵ-differentially private. Using post-processing and these special distances, we will compute approximate all-pairs distances with small error.

For any pair of vertices x, y, consider the path $\mathcal{P}[x, y]$ in $\mathcal{P}$ between x and y, and let i be the largest index such that S_i contains multiple vertices of $\mathcal{P}[x, y]$. We must have that $S_i \cap \mathcal{P}[x, y] < 2V^{1/k}$, since otherwise S_{i+1} would contain at least two vertices on $\mathcal{P}[x, y]$. Let x_i, y_i denote the first and last vertices in $S_i \cap \mathcal{P}[x, y]$. For $j < i$, let x_j denote the first vertex in $S_j \cap \mathcal{P}[x, x_i]$ and let y_j denote the last vertex in $S_j \cap \mathcal{P}[y_i, y]$. There are at most $1 + V^{1/k}$ vertices of S_j in $\mathcal{P}[x_j, x_{j+1}]$, since otherwise this interval would contain another vertex of S_{j+1}. Similarly, there are at most $1 + V^{1/k}$ vertices of S_j in $\mathcal{P}[y_{j+1}, y_j]$. Therefore we can express the distance from x_j to x_{j+1} as the sum of at most $V^{1/k}$ distances which were estimated in S_j, and similarly for the distance from y_{j+1} to y_j.

Putting this all together, we can estimate the distance from $x = x_0$ to $y = y_0$ as the sum of at most $2(i+1)V^{1/k} \leq 2kV^{1/k}$ approximate distances which were released. But each of these distances is released with noise distributed according to $\text{Lap}(k/\epsilon)$. Consequently the total error on the estimated distance from x to y is the sum of at most $2kV^{1/k}$ random variables distribued according to $\text{Lap}(k/\epsilon)$. Taking $k = \log V$, the error is the sum of at most $4 \log V$ variables distributed according to $\text{Lap}(\log V/\epsilon)$. By Lemma 3.1, with probability at least $1-\gamma$ the sum of these $4 \log V$ variables is bounded by $O(\log^{1.5} V \log(1/\gamma))/\epsilon$ for any $\gamma \in (0,1)$. Consequently this is an ϵ-differentially private algorithm which releases all-pairs distances in the path graph P such that for any $\gamma \in (0,1)$, with probability at least $1-\gamma$ the error in each released distance is at most $O(\log^{1.5} V \log(1/\gamma))/\epsilon$. $\square$

B. OTHER GRAPH PROBLEMS

In this section we consider some additional queries on graphs in the private edge weights model.

B.1 Almost-minimum spanning tree

We first consider the problem of releasing a low-cost spanning tree. The work of [NRS07] showed how to privately approximate the cost of the minimum spanning tree in a somewhat related privacy setting. We seek to release an actual tree of close to minimal cost under our model. Using techniques similar to the lower bound for shortest paths from Section 5.1, we obtain a lower bound of $\Omega(V)$ for the error of releasing a low-cost spanning tree, and show that the Laplace mechanism yields a spanning tree of cost $O(V \log V)$

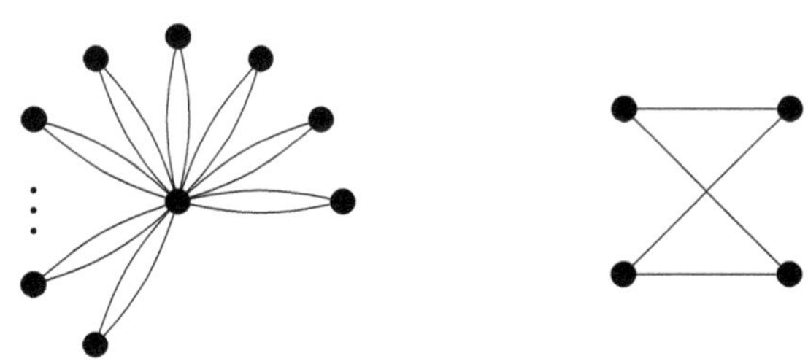

Figure 3: (Left) The graph used in the reduction of Lemma B.2. (Right) A single gadget in the graph used in the reduction of Lemma B.5.

more than optimal. Note that in this section edge weights are permitted to be negative.

THEOREM B.1. *There exists a graph $\mathcal{G} = (\mathcal{V}, \mathcal{E})$ such that for any spanning tree algorithm $\mathcal{A}$ that is (ϵ, δ)-differentially private on $\mathcal{G}$, there exist edge weights $w : \mathcal{E} \to \{0, 1\}$ such that the expected weight of the spanning tree $\mathcal{A}(w)$ is at least*

$$\alpha = (V - 1) \cdot \left(\frac{1 - (1 + e^{\epsilon})\delta}{1 + e^{2\epsilon}} \right)$$

longer than the weight of the minimum spanning tree. In particular, for sufficiently small ϵ and δ, $\alpha \geq 0.49(V - 1)$.

We first prove a lemma reducing the problem of reidentifying rows in a database to privately finding an approximate minimum spanning tree. Let $\mathcal{G} = (\mathcal{V}, \mathcal{E})$ be the $(n+1)$-vertex graph with vertex set $\mathcal{V} = \{0, \ldots, n\}$ and a pair of edges $e_i^{(0)}$ and $e_i^{(1)}$ between vertex 0 and each vertex $i > 0$, as shown in Figure 3. (As in Lemma 5.2, this is a multigraph, but we can transform it into a simple graph by adding n extra vertices, changing the bound obtained by a factor of 2.)

LEMMA B.2. *Let $\mathcal{G}$ be the graph defined in the previous paragraph, and let $\epsilon, \delta \geq 0$. For any α, let $\mathcal{A}$ be an algorithm that is (ϵ, δ)-differentially private on $\mathcal{G}$ that on input $w : \mathcal{E} \to \{0, 1\}$ produces a spanning tree whose weight in expectation is at most α greater than optimal. Then there exists a $(2\epsilon, (1 + e^{\epsilon})\delta)$-differentially private algorithm $\mathcal{B}$ which on input $x \in \{0, 1\}^n$ produces $y \in \{0, 1\}^n$ such that the expected Hamming distance $d_H(x, y)$ is at most α.*

PROOF. The outline of the proof is the same as that of Lemma 5.2. For input $x \in \{0, 1\}^n$, the corresponding edge weight function w_x is given by $w_x(e_i^{(x_i)}) = 0$ and $w_x(e_i^{(1-x_i)}) = 1$, where x_i is the ith bit of x.

We define algorithm $\mathcal{B}$ as follows. On input $x \in \{0, 1\}^n$, apply $\mathcal{A}$ to $(\mathcal{G}, w_x)$, and let $\mathcal{T}$ be the tree produced. Define $y \in \{0, 1\}^n$ by setting $y_i = 0$ if $e_i^{(0)} \in \mathcal{T}$ and $y_i = 1$ otherwise. Output y.

It is straightforward to verify that $\mathcal{B}$ is $(2\epsilon, (1 + e^{\epsilon})\delta)$-differentially private. We now bound the expected Hamming distance of x and y. The minimum spanning tree in $\mathcal{G}$ has weight 0, so the expected weight of $\mathcal{T}$ is at most α and $\mathcal{T}$ must consist of at most α edges $e_i^{(1-x_i)}$. But $y_i \neq x_i$ only if $e_i^{(1-x_i)} \in \mathcal{T}$, so in expectation $d_H(x, y) \leq w(\mathcal{T}) \leq \alpha$. □

We now complete the proof of Theorem B.1.

PROOF OF THEOREM B.1. Assume that there is some (ϵ, δ)-differentially private algorithm which on all inputs produces a spanning tree with expected weight less than α more than optimal. By Lemma B.2, there is a $(2\epsilon, (1 + e^{\epsilon})\delta)$-differentially private algorithm which for all $x \in \{0, 1\}^n$ produces $y \in \{0, 1\}^n$ with expected Hamming distance less than α. But then Lemma 5.4, for some x the expected Hamming distance $\mathbf{E}(d_H(x, y)) \geq \frac{n(1-(1+e^{\epsilon})\delta)}{1+e^{2\epsilon}} = \alpha$, yielding a contradiction. □

We now show that the Laplace mechanism (Lemma 3.2) almost matches this lower bound.

THEOREM B.3. *For any $\epsilon, \gamma > 0$ and $\mathcal{G} = (\mathcal{V}, \mathcal{E})$, there is an algorithm $\mathcal{A}$ that is ϵ-differentially private on $\mathcal{G}$ that on input $w : \mathcal{E} \to \mathbb{R}$ releases with probability $1 - \gamma$ a spanning tree of weight at most $((V - 1)/\epsilon) \log(E/\gamma)$ larger than optimal.*

PROOF. Consider the algorithm that adds noise X_e distributed according to $\text{Lap}(1/\epsilon)$ for each edge $e \in \mathcal{E}$ and releases the minimum spanning tree on the resulting graph $(\mathcal{G}, w')$. This is ϵ-differentially private, since it is post-processing of the Laplace mechanism. We now show that the resulting error is small. By a union bound, with probability $1 - \gamma$ we have that $|X_e| \leq (1/\epsilon) \log(E/\gamma)$ for every $e \in \mathcal{E}$. Consequently, conditioning on this event, if $\mathcal{T}$ is the spanning tree released by the algorithm and $\mathcal{T}^*$ is the minimum spanning tree, then we have that

$$\begin{aligned} w(\mathcal{T}) &\leq w'(\mathcal{T}) + \frac{V-1}{\epsilon} \cdot \log(E/\gamma) \\ &\leq w'(\mathcal{T}^*) + \frac{V-1}{\epsilon} \cdot \log(E/\gamma) \\ &\leq w(\mathcal{T}^*) + \frac{2(V-1)}{\epsilon} \cdot \log(E/\gamma). \end{aligned}$$

□

B.2 Low-weight matching

We now consider the problem of releasing a minimum weight matching in a graph in our model. As for the minimum spanning tree problem, a minor modification of the lower bound for shortest paths from Section 5.1 yields a similar result. For comparison, [HHR+14] use similar reconstruction techniques to obtain a lower bound for a matching problem on bipartite graphs in a somewhat different model in which all edge weights are in $[0, 1]$ and neighboring graphs can differ on the weights of the edges incident to a single left vertex. We show a lower bound of $\Omega(V)$ for the error of releasing a low-weight matching tree, and show that the matching released by the Laplace mechanism has weight $O(V \log V)$ greater than optimal.

The theorems in this section are stated for the problem of finding a minimum weight perfect matching. We can also obtain identical results for the problem of finding a minimum weight matching which is not required to be perfect, and for the corresponding maximum weight matching problems. Our results apply to both bipartite matching and general matching. Note that in this section edge weights are permitted to be negative.

THEOREM B.4. *There exists a graph $\mathcal{G} = (\mathcal{V}, \mathcal{E})$ such that for any perfect matching algorithm $\mathcal{A}$ which is (ϵ, δ)-differentially private on $\mathcal{G}$, there exist edge weights $w : \mathcal{E} \to \{0, 1\}$ such that the expected weight of the matching $\mathcal{A}(w)$ is at least*

$$\alpha = \left(\frac{V}{4} \right) \cdot \left(\frac{1 - (1 + e^{\epsilon})\delta}{1 + e^{2\epsilon}} \right)$$

larger than the weight of the min-cost perfect matching. In particular, for sufficiently small ϵ, δ, $\alpha \geq 0.12 \cdot V$.

The following lemma reduces the problem of reidentification in a database to finding a low-cost matching. Let $\mathcal{G} = (\mathcal{V}, \mathcal{E})$ be the $4n$-vertex graph with vertex set $\mathcal{V} = \{(b_1, b_2, c) : b_1, b_2 \in \{0, 1\}, c \in [n]\}$ and edges from $(0, b, c)$ to $(1, b', c)$ for every $b, b' \in \{0, 1\}$, $c \in [n]$. That is, $\mathcal{G}$ consists of n disconnected hourglass-shaped gadgets as shown in Figure 3.

LEMMA B.5. *Let $\mathcal{G} = (\mathcal{V}, \mathcal{E})$ be the graph defined in the previous paragraph. For any α, let $\mathcal{A}$ be an algorithm that is (ϵ, δ)-differentially private on $\mathcal{G}$ that on input $w : \mathcal{E} \to \{0, 1\}$ produces a perfect matching of expected weight at most α*

greater than optimal. Then there exists a $(2\epsilon, (1+e^{\epsilon})\delta)$-differentially private algorithm $\mathcal{B}$ which on input $x \in \{0,1\}^n$ produces $y \in \{0,1\}^n$ with expected Hamming distance to x at most α.

PROOF. For any input $x \in \{0,1\}^n$, the corresponding weight function w_x assigns weight 1 to the edge connecting vertex $(0,1,i)$ to $(1,1-x_i,i)$ for each $i \in [n]$, and assigns weight 0 to the other $3n$ edges. The algorithm $\mathcal{B}$ is as follows. On input $x \in \{0,1\}^n$, apply $\mathcal{A}$ to $(\mathcal{G}, w_x)$, and let $\mathcal{M}$ be the matching produced. Define $y \in \{0,1\}^n$ as follows. Let $y_i = 0$ if the edge from $(0,1,i)$ to $(1,0,i)$ is in the matching, and $y_i = 1$ otherwise. Output y.

Algorithm $\mathcal{B}$ is clearly $(2\epsilon, (1+e^{\epsilon})\delta)$-differentially private. We will have that $y_i \neq x_i$ only if the edge from $(0,1,i)$ to $(1,1-x_i,i)$ is in the matching, so the expected Hamming distance is at most the expected size of the matching produced by $\mathcal{A}$, which is at most α. □

We now conclude the proof of Theorem B.4.

PROOF OF THEOREM B.4. The result follows by combining Lemma B.5 with Lemma 5.4. □

Using the Laplace mechanism (Lemma 3.2), we obtain a nearly-matching upper bound.

THEOREM B.6. *For any $\epsilon, \gamma > 0$ and $\mathcal{G} = (\mathcal{V}, \mathcal{E})$ containing a perfect matching, there is an algorithm $\mathcal{A}$ that is ϵ-differentially private on $\mathcal{G}$ that on input $w : \mathcal{E} \to \mathbb{R}$ releases with probability $1-\gamma$ a perfect matching of weight at most $(V/\epsilon)\log(E/\gamma)$ larger than optimal.*

PROOF. Consider the algorithm that adds noise X_e distributed according to $\mathrm{Lap}(1/\epsilon)$ for each edge $e \in \mathcal{E}$ and releases the minimum-weight perfect matching on the resulting graph $(\mathcal{G}, w')$. This is ϵ-differentially private, since it is post-processing of the Laplace mechanism. We now show that the resulting error is small. With probability $1-\gamma$ we have that $|X_e| \leq (1/\epsilon)\log(E/\gamma)$ for every $e \in \mathcal{E}$. Consequently, conditioning on this event, if $\mathcal{M}$ is the matching released by the algorithm and $\mathcal{M}^*$ is the minimum-weight matching, then we have that

$$\begin{aligned} w(\mathcal{M}) &\leq w'(\mathcal{M}) + \frac{V}{2\epsilon} \cdot \log(E/\gamma) \\ &\leq w'(\mathcal{M}^*) + \frac{V}{2\epsilon} \cdot \log(E/\gamma) \\ &\leq w(\mathcal{M}^*) + \frac{V}{\epsilon} \cdot \log(E/\gamma). \end{aligned}$$

□

Minimization of Tree Pattern Queries

Wojciech Czerwiński*
University of Warsaw

Wim Martens†
Universität Bayreuth

Matthias Niewerth†
Universität Bayreuth

Paweł Parys*
University of Warsaw

ABSTRACT

We investigate minimization of tree pattern queries that use the child relation, descendant relation, node labels, and wildcards. We prove that minimization for such tree patterns is Σ_2^P-complete and thus solve a problem first attacked by Flesca, Furfaro, and Masciari in 2003. We first provide an example that shows that tree patterns cannot be minimized by deleting nodes. This example shows that the M-NR conjecture, which states that minimality of tree patterns is equivalent to their nonredundancy, is false. We then show how the example can be turned into a gadget that allows us to prove Σ_2^P-completeness.

Keywords

XPath, XML, trees, tree patterns, graph databases, optimization, complexity

1. INTRODUCTION

Tree-structured data is among us in many forms: JSON, XML, our filesystems, the secondary structure of RNA, and parse trees for linguistic data, just to name a few examples. Tree pattern queries are a fundamental tool for querying and selecting nodes in tree-structured data. They are present in most query languages for tree-structured data, most notably, XPath [33]. In fundamental research they appear in a wide range of topics. For example, they form a basis for conjunctive queries over trees [22], for models of XML with incomplete information [5], and for the closely related pattern-based XML queries [20]. They are used for specifying guards in Active XML systems [1] and for specifying schema mappings in XML data exchange [4]. Beyond trees, they are a natural language for querying graph databases [14, 27].

Optimization of tree pattern queries is therefore a very natural question. Not only do new results in this direction give us new insights on query optimization in many practical languages, they can also give us a better understanding of the foundations of the above mentioned models which are based on tree patterns. Tree pattern query optimization already attracted significant attention in the form of *query containment* [29, 31, 14], *satisfiability* [6], and *minimization* [3, 13, 18, 25, 32, 36].

In this paper we study the minimization problem for tree pattern queries that use the *child relation*, *descendant relation*, *label tests*, and *wildcards* (henceforth: tree patterns). These tree patterns are widely studied [17, 29, 37, 18, 25, 1, 8, 4, 34] but their minimization problem remained elusive. In particular, the complexity of minimization is unknown.

It is believed that a key in understanding tree pattern minimization lies in understanding the relationship between *minimality* (M) and *nonredundancy* (NR) [18, 25]. Here, a tree pattern is minimal if it has the smallest number of nodes among all equivalent tree patterns. It is nonredundant if none of its leaves or branches can be deleted while remaining equivalent. The question is if minimality and nonredundancy are the same:

> M-NR CONJECTURE (page 35 of [18], rephrased):
> A tree pattern is minimal if and only if it is nonredundant.

Clearly, every minimal tree pattern is nonredundant, so one direction of the M-NR conjecture trivially holds. The opposite direction is much less clear. If it would be true, it means that, for a given tree pattern p, a minimal tree pattern is always a substructure of p. It would also mean that tree pattern minimization can be solved by tree pattern containment. Indeed, one would be able to minimize tree patterns p by iteratively removing leaves and testing if the obtained tree pattern p' is still contained in p. If no leaf can be removed anymore, the remaining tree pattern would be nonredundant and therefore minimal. Since testing containment of tree patterns is coNP-complete [29], this would mean that one could solve minimization with a polynomial-time algorithm with a coNP oracle and that the minimization problem for tree patterns is coNP-complete.

The minimization problem for tree patterns is not entirely uncontroversial. It was claimed to be coNP-complete in 2003 [17] but the algorithm relied on the M-NR conjecture.

*Supported by Poland's National Science Centre grant no. UMO-2013/11/D/ST6/03075.

†Supported by grant number MA 4938/2–1 from the Deutsche Forschungsgemeinschaft (Emmy Noether Nachwuchsgruppe).

PODS'16, June 26-July 01, 2016, San Francisco, CA, USA

ISBN 978-1-4503-4191-2/16/06...$15.00

DOI: http://dx.doi.org/10.1145/2902251.2902295

Kimelfeld and Sagiv [25] proved that, in contrast to claims in [17], the M-NR conjecture is open and, as a consequence, the algorithms from [17] were revised in [18]. The updated work [18] proves that the M-NR conjecture holds for tree patterns in which *every wildcard node has at most one child* and presents a coNP algorithm for this case. It is needless to say that [18, 25] contain a wealth of valuable results on tree patterns and their minimization (many of which we use here), but the most central questions, that is, the status of the M-NR conjecture and the question of the complexity of tree pattern minimization, remained open.

Our main contributions are the following:

- We prove that the M-NR conjecture is false by providing a tree pattern that is nonredundant but not minimal.
- We prove that tree pattern minimization is Σ_2^P-complete. This means that, unless Σ_2^P = coNP, we have that tree pattern minimization *cannot* be solved by a polynomial-time algorithm with an oracle for tree pattern containment.
- Interestingly, our counterexample and our gadgets in the Σ_2^P-hardness proof use only two wildcard nodes with two children, which is only barely beyond the fragment for which the M-NR conjecture is known to hold.

The Bigger Picture.

This paper fits naturally in a line of research that originated in the early days of database theory. Query minimization and optimization by removing redundant parts goes back to the seminal work of Chandra and Merlin [11] and has since then been successfully adopted for many types of queries, in various data models such as relations and trees (see, e.g., [3, 10, 11, 18, 32, 36]). In this section we highlight a few parallels and differences between conjunctive queries and acyclic conjunctive queries over relational data and over tree-structured data.

Conjunctive Queries over Relations. Minimization, containment, and evaluation of conjunctive queries over relations are well known to be NP-complete [11]. For *acyclic* conjunctive queries, which have been extensively studied (see, e.g., [12, 23, 38]), the complexity of these problems is in polynomial time. **Conjunctive Queries over Trees.** Conjunctive queries over trees [22] are different from conjunctive queries over relations in two respects. First, the underlying model is based on trees instead of relations and second, conjunctive queries over trees use different built-in relations. Most notably, apart from the child relation, they can use the descendant relation and therefore have the power to reason about certain transitive closures. They therefore query a more restricted data model than their counterpart over relations but in return they have more powerful reasoning. The original definition of conjunctive queries over trees allows for many built-in relations (child, descendant, next-sibling, following-sibling, etc. [22]); we only discuss the two most basic ones, child and descendant, in the following.

Conjunctive queries over trees have an NP-complete evaluation problem [22] just like conjunctive queries over relations. Their containment problem, however, is Π_2^P-complete [7] and the complexity of their minimization problem is unknown.

Tree patterns can be seen as acyclic variants of conjunctive queries over trees. Their evaluation problem is in polynomial time [21] and their containment problem is coNP-complete [29]. By proving that minimization of tree patterns is Σ_2^P-complete, we finish a natural step in this line of research.

Tree Patterns as a Graph Query Language.

Due to their modal nature, tree patterns and XPath-like languages are also suitable languages for querying graph databases [9, 24, 27, 2, 28, 19]. In fact, the complexity of tree pattern containment does not depend on whether they are evaluated over trees or over graphs, see [29, Section 5.3] and [14, Section 7]. The same is true for the minimization problem. Therefore, the complexity results in this paper can be extended to tree patterns over graphs as well. We present all results in terms of trees because it makes proofs considerably simpler.

The problems for trees can even be extended to *data graphs* [27] and patterns that compare data values with constants (such comparisons are essentially the same as the label tests of tree patterns). However, as soon as data value *comparisons* enter the picture, such a straightforward extension to graphs does not work anymore, see e.g. [26].

Outline.

We present the counterexample to the M-NR conjecture in Section 3. We also show in Section 3 that minimal tree patterns are not unique (up to adornments). In Section 4 we prove that tree pattern minimization is Σ_2^P-complete. We discuss implications on k-ary queries and further outlooks in Section 5.

2. PRELIMINARIES

We are interested in finite, labeled, unordered trees.[1] A *labeled unordered tree* is a triple (V, E, lab), where V is a finite nonempty set of *nodes*, E is a set of *edges* $(u, v) \in V \times V$ and $\text{lab} : V \to \Sigma$ is a *labeling function* assigning to every node its label coming from an infinite set of labels Σ. If $(u, v) \in E$ then we say that u is the *parent* of v and v is a *child* of u. We demand that for every node v there is at most one $(u, v) \in E$, so in trees the parent is uniquely determined. There is a unique node without parent, which we denote $\text{root}(t)$ and call the *root* of t. The *descendant* and *ancestor* relations are transitive closures of the child and parent relations, respectively. We say that a child of a node u is a 1-*descendant* of u and a child of a k-*descendant* of u is a $(k+1)$-*descendant* of u for any $k \in \mathbb{N}$. We define k-*ancestors* similarly. A node has *depth* k if it is a k-descendant of the root. In the sequel we just use the term *trees* for referring to labeled unordered trees.

For a tree $t = (V, E, \text{lab})$ and a node $v \in V$ we denote by t^v the subtree of t rooted in node v. By $t \setminus v$ we denote the tree obtained from t by deleting the subtree rooted at v (including node v itself).

A *tree pattern* is intended to describe a set of trees. It is a special type of a tree; its set of edges is divided into two disjoint sets: *child edges* and *descendant edges* (we draw descendant edges using double lines). Its labeling function

[1]However, we don't require trees to be unordered. Our results are the same for ordered trees. Tree patterns, however, are inherently unordered.

provides every node with a label from Σ or a special label $*$ which we assume not to be in Σ and call *wildcard*. We denote $\Sigma_* = \Sigma \cup \{*\}$. The intended meaning of the wildcard is not to specify any particular label. For a tree pattern $p = (V_p, E_p, \text{lab}_p)$ and a tree $t = (V, E, \text{lab})$, a function $\pi : V_p \to V$ is a *strong embedding*[2] of p in t if it fulfills all the following conditions:

(1) if $\text{lab}_p(v) \neq *$ for $v \in V_p$ then $\text{lab}_p(v) = \text{lab}(\pi(v))$,

(2) if $(u, v) \in E_p$ is a child edge then $\pi(u)$ is a parent of $\pi(v)$ in the tree t,

(3) if $(u, v) \in E_p$ is a descendant edge then $\pi(u)$ is an ancestor of $\pi(v)$ in the tree t, and

(4) $\pi(\text{root}(p)) = \text{root}(t)$.

We say that p *strongly embeds* in t if there exists a strong embedding of p in t. We say that π is a *weak embedding* of p in t and p *weakly embeds* in t if the above conditions (1)–(3) are fulfilled, but not necessarily $\pi(\text{root}(p)) = \text{root}(t)$. Figure 1 contains examples of strong and weak embeddings. Notice that we do not require embeddings to be injective (Figure 1(c)).

Equivalence, Containment, and Minimality.

The *(strong) language of a tree pattern p*, denoted by $L_S(p)$, is the set of trees in which p strongly embeds. A tree pattern p_1 is *(strongly) contained* in a tree pattern p_2 if $L_S(p_1) \subseteq L_S(p_2)$, which we denote by $p_1 \subseteq_S p_2$. If $p_1 \subseteq_S p_2$ and $p_1 \supseteq_S p_2$ then we say that the tree patterns p_1 and p_2 are *(strongly) equivalent* and we write $p_1 \equiv_S p_2$.

We call a tree pattern p *redundant* if one of its nodes can be removed without changing its language. More formally, p is redundant if it is strongly equivalent to $p \setminus v$ for a node v of p. In this case, v is a *redundant node*. If p is not redundant we say that it is *nonredundant*. It is known that a pattern is redundant if and only if it has a redundant leaf [25, Proposition 3.3].

The *size* of a tree pattern p, denoted size(p), is the number of its nodes. A tree pattern p is said to be *minimal* if there is no tree pattern p' that is equivalent to p but has strictly smaller size.

Analogously, we define *weak language*, *weak containment*, *weak equivalence*, *weak redundancy*, and *weak nonredundancy*. The definitions are exactly the same, but use weak embeddings instead of strong embeddings. The notation for weak containment and weak equivalence is $p_1 \subseteq_W p_2$ and $p_1 \equiv_W p_2$, respectively. It is well-known that containment of tree patterns, i.e., deciding for two given tree patterns p and q if $p \subseteq_S q$, is coNP-complete.

THEOREM 2.1 ([29]). *Containment of tree patterns is* coNP*-complete.*

We now mention a weak version of the M-NR Conjecture which was proved in [18]. We require the following definition.

DEFINITION 2.2 ($*$-NARROW PATTERN). *A tree pattern is a* $*$-narrow pattern *if every wildcard node has at most one child.*

[2] A strong embedding is sometimes also called *root embedding*.

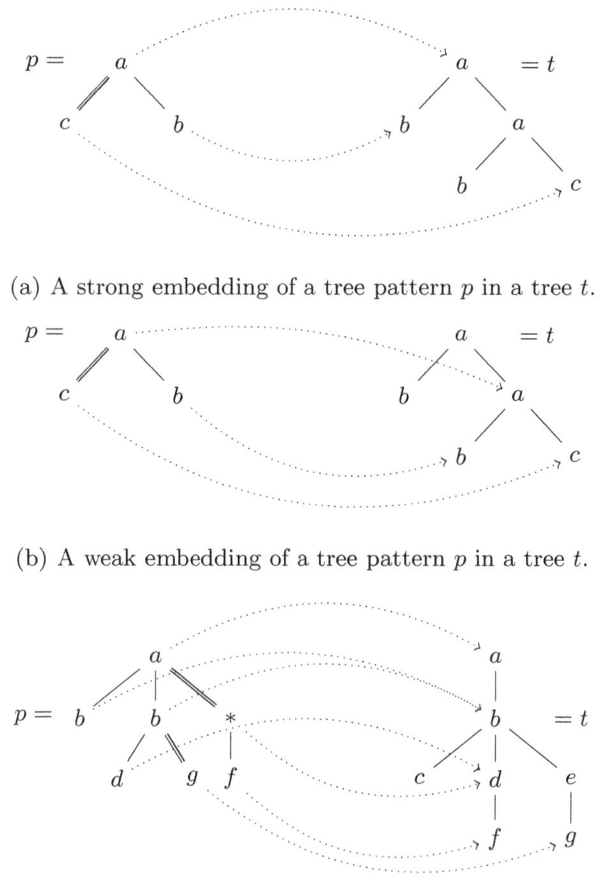

(a) A strong embedding of a tree pattern p in a tree t.

(b) A weak embedding of a tree pattern p in a tree t.

(c) A strong embedding of a tree pattern p in tree t. Embeddings are not required to be injective.

Figure 1: Examples of strong and weak embeddings.

For example, the tree patterns in Figure 1 are $*$-narrow patterns.

LEMMA 2.3 (COROLLARY 4.5 IN [18]). *If p is a $*$-narrow pattern, then p is minimal if and only if p is nonredundant.*

Canonical trees.

Canonical trees were introduced by Miklau and Suciu [29] for studying the containment problem for tree patterns. We need them in our paper to simplify proofs.

Let $z \in \Sigma$ be a special label that does not occur in any tree pattern that we consider in the paper. (We can assume that such a label exists because Σ is infinite.) A *canonical tree* of a tree pattern p is a tree obtained from p by application of the two following steps:

- for every node v such that $\text{lab}_p(v) = *$, we relabel $\text{lab}(v) = z$,
- change every descendant edge in p to a (nonempty) sequence of edges in t in such a way that all newly created nodes are labeled by z.

Notice that it is possible in the last step that no new nodes are created. This happens when each descendant edge is

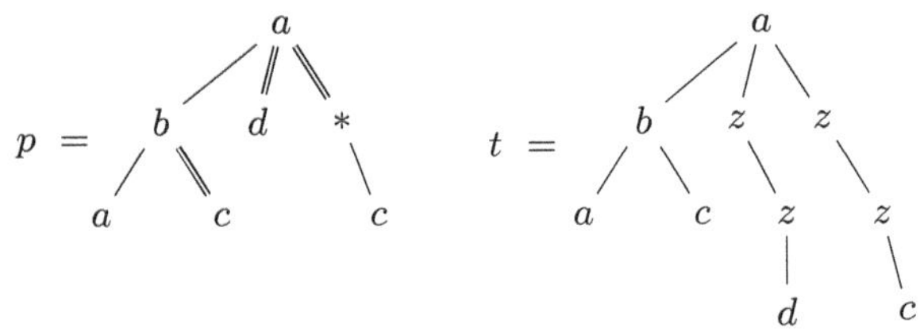

Figure 2: A tree pattern p and a canonical tree t.

replaced by a single child edge. An example of a canonical tree is given in Figure 2. We denote by Can(p) the set of all canonical trees of p.

Given a pattern p and one of its canonical trees t, there is a canonical injective embedding of the non-wildcard nodes of p into t. We sometimes use this correspondence to talk about nodes in t. That is, for a non-wildcard node u of p, we use this injective embedding to identify *the node in t corresponding to u.*

LEMMA 2.4 (PROPOSITION 3 IN [29]). *Let p_1 and p_2 be two tree patterns. Then $p_1 \subseteq_S p_2$ if and only if $Can(p_1) \subseteq L_S(p_2)$.*

A corresponding lemma for weak containment can be proved analogously as in [29].

Homomorphisms.

Let $p_1 = (V_{p_1}, E_{p_1}, \text{lab}_{p_1})$ and $p_2 = (V_{p_2}, E_{p_2}, \text{lab}_{p_2})$ be tree patterns. A *homomorphism* from p_1 to p_2 is a function $h : V_{p_1} \to V_{p_2}$ that fulfills the following conditions:

(1) $h(\text{root}(p_1)) = \text{root}(p_2)$,

(2) if $\text{lab}_{p_1}(v) \neq *$ for $v \in V_{p_1}$ then $\text{lab}_{p_1}(v) = \text{lab}_{p_2}(h(v))$,

(3) if $(u, v) \in E_{p_1}$ is a child edge then $(h(u), h(v)) \in E_{p_2}$ is a child edge, and

(4) if $(u, v) \in E_{p_1}$ is a descendant edge then $h(u)$ is an ancestor of $h(v)$ in p_2.

The existence of a homomorphism h from p_1 to p_2 is a sufficient condition for $p_2 \subseteq_S p_1$ [29]. Essentially, the reason is that, if π is a strong embedding of p_2 in a tree t, then $\pi \circ h$ is a strong embedding of p_1 in t. We make use of this fact later in the paper.

3. NONREDUNDANCY AND MINIMALITY

In this section we present a counterexample for the M-NR conjecture. We build further on this example to show that minimal tree patterns are not unique. We choose the examples in such a way that they help the reader understand the gadgets we use in Section 4.

Nonredundancy $\neq$ Minimality.

We will show that the left tree pattern p in Figure 3 is nonredundant and not minimal. One thing is easy to see: the tree pattern q on the right is smaller. Seeing that the left tree pattern p is nonredundant and equivalent to the tree pattern q on the right requires more work.

First we show that the tree pattern p is nonredundant. To this end, it suffices to show that none of its leaves can be deleted while remaining equivalent [25, Proposition 3.3].

For the purpose of this proof, we order the leaves in p from left to right, that is, the *first c_1-leaf* is the one in depth 7, the *second c_1-leaf* is the leftmost leaf on depth 8, and so on.

- If the first c_1-leaf is removed, then the resulting tree pattern matches the tree t_1 in Figure 4 by the strong embedding π which we partly illustrated in that figure. However, the tree pattern p does not match. The reason why we cannot remove the first c_2-leaf of p is analogous (replace the first c_2-leaf in t_1 by a c_1-leaf).
- If the second c_1-leaf is removed, then the resulting tree pattern matches the tree t_2 in Figure 4 using the strong embedding π which we partly illustrated in that figure. However, the tree pattern p does not match. The reason why we cannot remove the second c_2-leaf of p is analogous (replace the first c_2-leaf in t_2 by a c_1-leaf).
- Finally, if any of the other c_1- or c_2-leaves would be removed, the tree pattern would match the tree t_3 in Figure 4 in which the corresponding (circled) leaf would be removed and this is always a tree that is not matched by p.

Finally, we show that the tree pattern p is (strongly) equivalent to the tree pattern q. To this end, observe that $q \subseteq_S p$ because q is more restrictive: it has the same requirements as p but, in addition it says that the nodes onto which the second c_1- and c_2-leaves are matched have the same parent. It therefore only remains to show that $p \subseteq_S q$. By Lemma 2.4, it suffices to prove that $\text{Can}(p) \subseteq_S L_S(q)$.

Let $t \in \text{Can}(p)$. Let π_p be a strong embedding of p in t. Consider the nodes u_A and u_B in p. We make a case distinction on the number of nodes between $\pi_p(u_A)$ and $\pi_p(u_B)$ in t and show in each case how to construct a strong embedding π_q from q in t.

- If $\pi_p(u_A)$ is the parent of $\pi_p(u_B)$, then we can define $\pi_q(v_2) := \pi_p(u_4)$. For all non-descendants of v_2, we define π_q the same as π_p.
- If $\pi_p(u_A)$ is the 2-ancestor of $\pi_p(u_B)$ (see Figure 5 left), then we define $\pi_q(v_1) := \pi_p(u_2)$, and $\pi_q(v_2) := \pi_p(u_4)$, and $\pi_q(v_B) := \pi_p(u_B)$, and, since the distance between $\pi_q(v_2)$ and $\pi_q(v_A)$ is four, we map v_A to the parent of $\pi_p(u_B)$. In particular, the leftmost branch of t is not used by π_q at all.
- If $\pi_p(u_A)$ is the 3-ancestor of $\pi_p(u_B)$ (see Figure 5 right), then we define $\pi_q(v_1) := \pi_p(u_B)$ and $\pi_q(v_2) := \pi_p(u_3)$. In particular, the two leftmost branches of t are not used by π_q at all.
- If $\pi_p(u_A)$ is the k-ancestor of $\pi_b(u_B)$ for some $k \geq 4$, we proceed in the same way than in the previous case. Here, we move $\pi_q(v_A)$ downward on the path to $\pi_p(u_B)$ so that the distance between $\pi_q(v_2)$ and $\pi_q(v_A)$ is four.

This means that every canonical tree of p can be (strongly) matched by q. By Lemma 2.4 this means that p and q are strongly equivalent.

We therefore obtained that p is nonredundant but q is equivalent and smaller, which leads to the following theorem:

THEOREM 3.1. *The M-NR conjecture is false.*

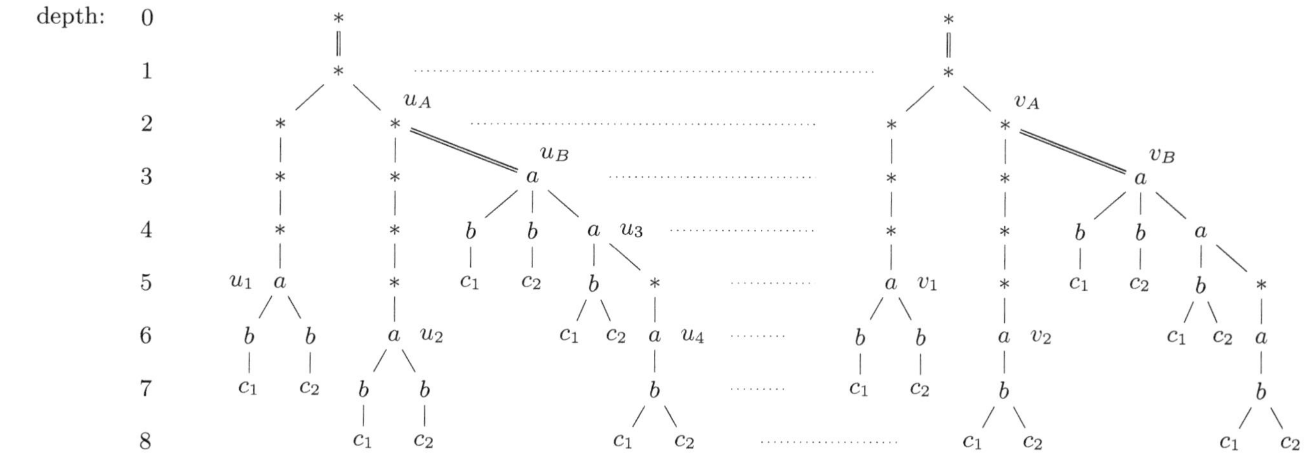

Figure 3: A non-redundant tree pattern p (left) and an equivalent tree pattern q that is smaller (right).

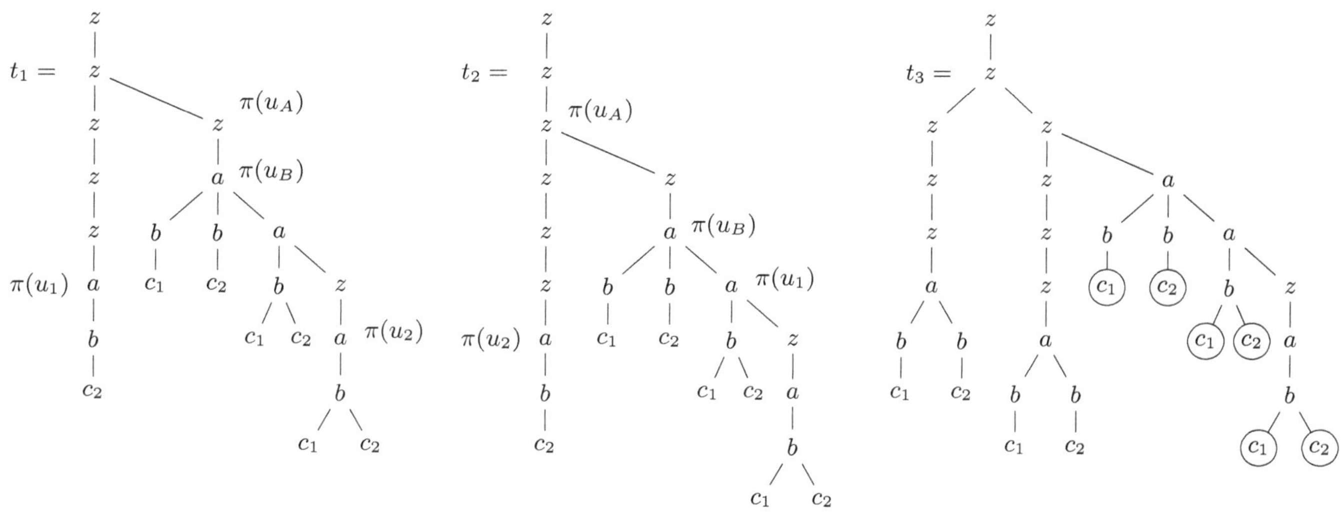

Figure 4: Trees for proving non-redundancy of p in Figure 3.

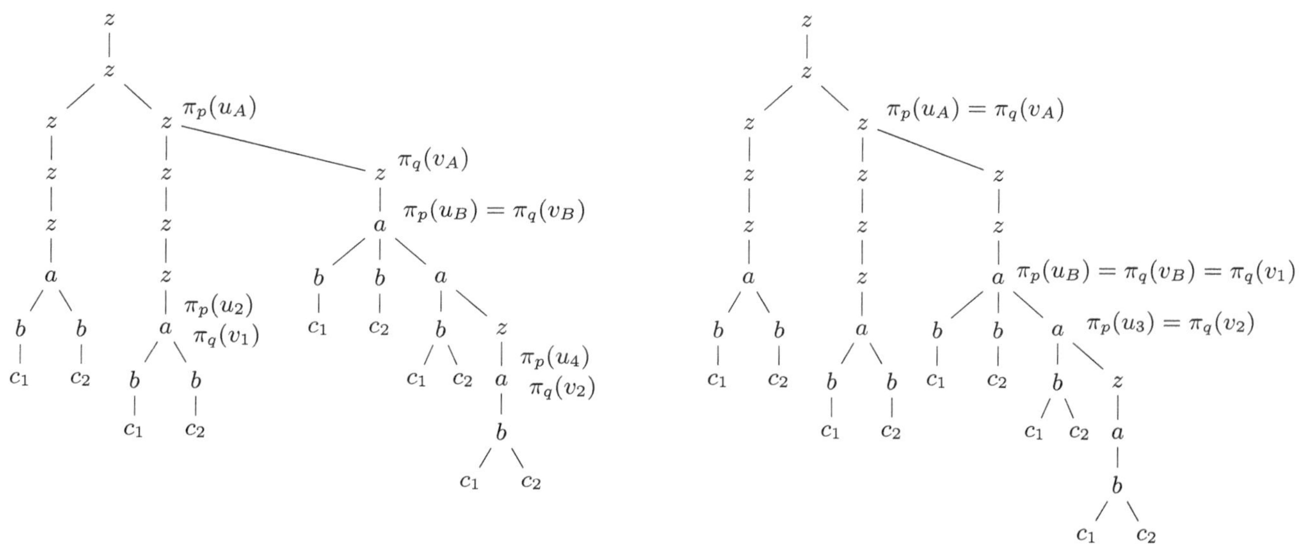

Figure 5: Canonical trees for proving that p and q in Figure 3 are equivalent.

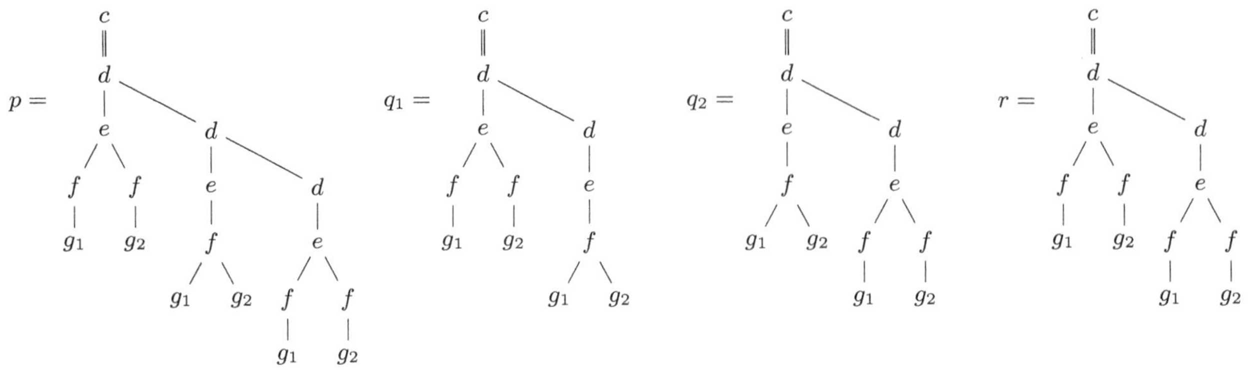

Figure 6: Tree patterns used to show that minimal tree patters can be structurally different.

Minimal Patterns are not Unique up to Adornment.

Minimal tree patterns are not unique. For example, the tree patterns in Figure 7(a) are different, minimal, and both express that there should be at least one node between an a-labeled node and a b-labeled node.

However, it can be argued that the difference between the patterns in Figure 7(a) is rather artificial. In the context of the containment problem for tree patterns, these patterns were used to illustrate that the existence of a homomorphism is not a necessary condition for containment [30, 29]. On the other hand, Milo and Suciu [30] proved that, in restricted cases, it is possible to rewrite patterns in a normal form that alleviates this problem. Miklau and Suciu [29, Section 3.2] extended this normal form to the full class of tree patterns. The patterns in normal form are called *adorned tree patterns.*

Intuitively, adorning a tree pattern corresponds to replacing some paths in the pattern by annotated descendant edges. For example, the adorned pattern equivalent to both patterns in Figure 7(a) is in Figure 7(b). The adornment "≥ 1" means that the pattern requires at least one node between the a-node and the b-node. More formally, Miklau and Suciu define adorned tree patterns as follows. For a given tree pattern, every descendant edge is initially adorned with "≥ 0". Then, adjacent edges sharing a $*$ node are combined into a descendant edge with higher adornment. Only $*$ nodes that have a unique child may be eliminated this way. (If a $*$ node has two or more children, we cannot eliminate it.) The process can also be described as a set of rewrite rules using an XPath-like syntax for tree patterns:

$$\begin{aligned} /\!\!/ &\rightarrow /\!\!/^{\geq 0} \\ /\!\!/^{\geq m} * / &\rightarrow /\!\!/^{\geq m+1} \\ / * /\!\!/^{\geq n} &\rightarrow /\!\!/^{\geq n+1} \\ /\!\!/^{\geq m} * /\!\!/^{\geq n} &\rightarrow /\!\!/^{\geq m+n+1} \end{aligned}$$

For example, these rules would rewrite $a/\!\!/*/\!\!/b/*/c/*/*/*/\!\!/d$ into $a\,/\!\!/^{\geq 1}\, b/*/c\,/\!\!/^{\geq 3}\, d$. In tree pattern syntax, they would rewrite the patterns in Figure 7(a) to the adorned pattern in Figure 7(b).

The question in this section is whether there exist equivalent minimal tree patterns that have different adorned patterns. We show that such patterns can be obtained as follows. Consider the gadget $P(X, Y, Z)$ in Figure 8. For tree patterns p, q, and r, denote by $P(p, q, r)$ the tree pattern obtained from P by instantiating the subtrees marked X, Y, and Z by p, q, and r, respectively. Consider the tree patterns p, q_1, q_2, and r from Figure 6. Then, we claim that

$$P(p, q_1, r) \text{ and } P(p, q_2, r)$$

are equivalent and minimal, but they have different adorned patterns. In fact, notice that adornment does not change anything in $P(p, q_1, r)$ or $P(p, q_2, r)$. Since $P(p, q_1, r)$ is different from $P(p, q_2, r)$, it is immediate that their adornments are also different. It remains to show that $P(p, q_1, r)$ and $P(p, q_2, r)$ are equivalent and minimal, which is non-trivial.

We first show that the tree patterns are equivalent. To this end, we first prove a lemma that already gives insight to a central property of the gadget in Figure 8.

LEMMA 3.2. *Let α, β_1, β_2, and γ be tree patterns that do not use labels in $\{a, b\}$ and such that $\alpha \subseteq_S \beta_1 \subseteq_S \gamma$ and $\alpha \subseteq_S \beta_2 \subseteq_S \gamma$. Then $P(\alpha, \beta_1, \gamma) \equiv_S P(\alpha, \beta_2, \gamma)$.*

PROOF SKETCH. The proof follows the same lines as the proof showing that the two tree patterns in Figure 3 are equivalent. Given a tree t and embedding π_1 of $P(\alpha, \beta_1, \gamma)$ in t, the corresponding embedding π_2 of $P(\alpha, \beta_2, \gamma)$ in t can be constructed using the same case distinction as for tree patterns in Figure 3 and in an analogous manner. Proving that $P(\alpha, \beta_2, \gamma) \subseteq_S P(\alpha, \beta_1, \gamma)$ is analogous. □

We are now ready to show the equivalence between the tree patterns.

PROPOSITION 3.3. *$P(p, q_1, r)$ and $P(p, q_2, r)$ are strongly equivalent.*

PROOF SKETCH. The inclusions $q_1 \subseteq_S r$ and $q_2 \subseteq_S r$ are trivial: q_1 and q_2 restrict r by additionally requiring that two nodes labeled g_1 and g_2 should have the same parent. The inclusion $p \subseteq_S q_1$ holds since q_1 is a strict subpattern of p and the inclusion $p \subseteq_S q_2$ holds since there is a homomorphism π from q_2 to p that maps the topmost d-node of q_2 to the middle d-node of p. The equivalence then follows from Lemma 3.2. □

Minimality of $P(p, q_1, r)$ and $P(p, q_2, r)$ is more technical to prove and requires material which we develop in Section 4. More precisely, minimality of $P(p, q_1, r)$ and $P(p, q_2, r)$ follows from Lemma 4.2. We briefly explain why. Since p and r are $*$-narrow, their minimality is immediate because they are nonredundant (Lemma 2.3). It remains to prove that q_1 and q_2 are smallest tree patterns such that $p \subseteq_S q_i \subseteq_S r$

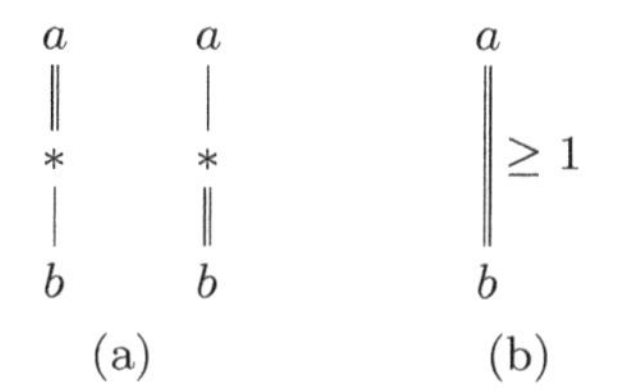

Figure 7: Two minimal but different tree patterns and their equivalent adorned pattern.

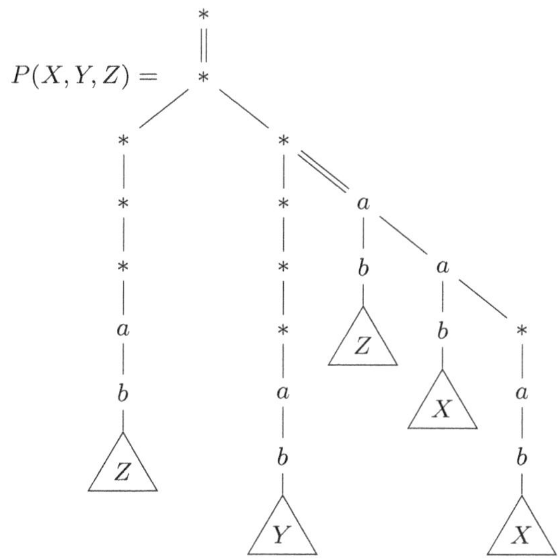

Figure 8: Gadget for constructing tree patterns (Lemma 4.3).

holds. The intuitive[3] reason is that, starting with tree pattern r, we can only get a smaller pattern q that still satisfies $q \subseteq_S r$ by merging f-nodes that are siblings. Furthermore, we can only merge one pair of f-nodes, because otherwise the pattern does not satisfy $p \subseteq_S q$ any more.

4. THE COMPLEXITY OF MINIMIZATION

In this section we study the complexity of the following problems.

	TREE PATTERN MINIMIZATION
Given:	A tree pattern p and $k \in \mathbb{N}$
Question:	Does there exist a tree pattern q such that size$(q) \leq k$ and $q \equiv_S p$?

	MINIMALITY
Given:	A tree pattern p
Question:	Is p minimal?

It was proved in [18, Theorem 5.9] that TREE PATTERN MINIMIZATION is coNP-hard. MINIMALITY is known to be NP-hard [25, Theorem 6.3]. The central theorem of this section is:

[3]A more formal proof would be analogous to the proof of Claim 4.7.

THEOREM 4.1. *TREE PATTERN MINIMIZATION is Σ_2^P-complete.*

Since testing non-redundancy of a tree pattern is NP-complete [25, Theorem 6.3], the above theorem proves that, under standard complexity theoretic assumptions, the problem TREE PATTERN MINIMIZATION is more difficult than testing non-redundancy.

We will now prove Theorem 4.1. The Σ_2^P upper bound is straightforward: given an instance of TREE PATTERN MINIMIZATION consisting of tree pattern p and $k \in \mathbb{N}$, one can guess a tree pattern q of size at most k and test if it is equivalent to p. Since we make polynomially many nondeterministic guesses and since testing equivalence is coNP-complete, this is a Σ_2^P algorithm.

To show hardness, we will introduce an intermediate problem called *relative minimization*. We will give two reductions: the first is from relative minimization to tree pattern minimization and the second one shows that relative minimization is Σ_2^P-hard.

	RELATIVE TREE PATTERN MINIMIZATION
Given:	Minimal tree patterns p and r such that $p \subseteq_S r$ and $k \in \mathbb{N}$
Question:	Is there a pattern q such that size$(q) \leq k$ and $p \subseteq_S q \subseteq_S r$?

We will use the gadget $P(X, Y, Z)$ from Figure 8. Recall that, for tree patterns p, q, and r, we denote by $P(p, q, r)$ the tree pattern obtained from P by instantiating the subtrees marked X, Y, and Z by p, q, and r, respectively.

The following lemma is the technically most difficult result in the paper. It is crucial for connecting TREE PATTERN MINIMIZATION with RELATIVE TREE PATTERN MINIMIZATION and essentially proves two things. First, if one inserts minimal patterns p, q, r in the positions X, Y and Z, then one may still be able to obtain a smaller pattern by changing q. Second, all patterns that are equivalent to $P(p, q, r)$, minimal and satisfy some side-conditions are, in a sense, similar to $P(p, q, r)$. Thus in order to show that $P(p, q, r)$ is minimal can focus only on such similar candidates for being smaller and equivalent one. It is this second part that has a very technical proof.

LEMMA 4.2. *Let p, q, and r be tree patterns that have at least one node, do not use labels in $\{a, b\}$, and such that $p \subseteq_S q \subseteq_S r$. Then $P(p, q, r)$ is minimal if and only if*

(1) p and r are minimal; and

(2) there is no tree pattern q' such that

- *$p \subseteq_S q' \subseteq_S r$ and*
- *size$(q') <$ size(q).*

Notice that condition (2) in Lemma 4.2 is subtle. If $P(p, q, r)$ is minimal, then q must also be minimal. However, minimality of q does not necessarily imply that $P(p, q, r)$ is minimal. Indeed, if there would be a pattern q' that is not equivalent to q but such that size$(q') <$ size(q) and $p \subseteq_S q' \subseteq_S r$, then $P(p, q', r)$ would be equivalent to $P(p, q, r)$ and smaller.

The proof of the lemma considers an arbitrary pattern that is minimal and equivalent to $P(p, q, r)$ and proves step by step that it must be similar to $P(p, q, r)$. In a second step, we infer that the pattern at Y must be a smallest pattern q

such that $p \subseteq_S q \subseteq_S r$. A particular challenge in the proof is the lack of methods that work for the general class of tree patterns.

LEMMA 4.3. RELATIVE TREE PATTERN MINIMIZATION *is reducible to* TREE PATTERN MINIMIZATION *in logarithmic space.*

PROOF. Consider an arbitrary instance of RELATIVE TREE PATTERN MINIMIZATION consisting of minimal tree patterns p and r such that $p \subseteq_S r$, and a number $k \in \mathbb{N}$. We can assume w.l.o.g. that p and r have at least one node. Since we can rename labels, we can also assume that p and r do not use the labels a or b. We will construct an instance p_m and $k' \in \mathbb{N}$ of TREE PATTERN MINIMIZATION so that p_m has an equivalent pattern of size at most k' if and only if there is a tree pattern q with size$(q) \le k$ and $p \subseteq_S q \subseteq_S r$.

Tree pattern p_m is $P(p, p, r)$, where the gadget P is illustrated in Figure 8. We define k' as $k + 2|p| + 2|r| + 20$.

We now prove that the reduction is correct. We need to prove two implications. For the first, assume that p, r, and k have a solution q w.r.t. RELATIVE TREE PATTERN MINIMIZATION. In this case we know from Lemma 3.2 that $p_m = P(p,p,r) \equiv_S P(p,q,r)$. Furthermore, the size of $P(p,q,r)$ is size$(q) + 2|p| + 2|r| + 20 \le k'$.

We prove the other implication. We assume that $p_m = P(p,p,r)$ has an equivalent pattern of size at most k' and we want to prove that there exists a pattern q of size at most k such that $p \subseteq_S q \subseteq_S r$. Let q be a smallest pattern such that $p \subseteq_S q \subseteq_S r$ (more precisely, there exists no pattern q' such that size$(q') <$ size(q) and $p \subseteq_S q' \subseteq_S r$).

By Lemma 3.2, we have that $P(p,q,r) \equiv_S p_m$. Tree patterns p and r are minimal and q is a smallest pattern in the set $\{q' \mid p \subseteq_S q' \subseteq_S r\}$. Therefore, by Lemma 4.2, pattern $P(p,q,r)$ is minimal. Therefore its size is at most $k' = k + 2|p| + 2|r| + 20$. This implies that $|q| \le k$ and concludes the proof. □

To prove Theorem 4.1 it therefore only remains to prove that RELATIVE TREE PATTERN MINIMIZATION is Σ_2^P-complete, which we do next. We will reduce from the following problem, which is a mild variation of the canonical satisfiability problem of quantified $\exists\forall$-formulas ($\exists\forall$-QBF).

$\exists$-VALIDITY	
Given:	A set of pairs of conjunctive clauses $\{(c_1^1, c_1^2), \ldots, (c_m^1, c_m^2)\}$ over variables $x_1, \ldots, x_n$
Question:	Is there a $(i_1, \ldots, i_m) \in \{1,2\}^m$ such that $c_1^{i_1} \vee \cdots \vee c_m^{i_m}$ is true for every valuation of $x_1, \ldots, x_n$?

Due to the similarity between $\exists$-VALIDITY and $\exists\forall$-QBF, it is not surprising that $\exists$-VALIDITY is Σ_2^P-complete.

LEMMA 4.4. $\exists$-VALIDITY *is* Σ_2^P*-complete.*

PROOF. Membership in Σ_2^P is obvious. For the other direction let

$$\Psi = \exists x_1, \ldots, x_n \forall y_1, \ldots, y_\ell \; \Phi(x_1, \ldots, x_n, y_1, \ldots, y_\ell)$$

be a QBF formula such that $\Phi = c_1 \vee \cdots \vee c_m$ is quantifier-free and in disjunctive normal form. We compute the $\exists$-VALIDITY instance

$$\{(c_i, c_i) \mid i \in [1,m]\} \cup \{(x_i, \neg x_i) \mid i \in [1,n]\} .$$

For the correctness of the reduction, we first observe, that the formula Ψ is equivalent to

$$\Psi' = \exists x_1, \ldots, x_n \forall z_1, \ldots, z_n, y_1, \ldots, y_\ell$$
$$\Phi(z_1, \ldots, z_n, y_1, \ldots, y_\ell) \vee z_1 \ne x_1 \vee \cdots \vee z_n \ne x_n .$$

Now it is easy to see the correctness, as the pairs

$$(c_1, c_1), \ldots, (c_m, c_m)$$

enforce that each original clause has to be satisfied (there is no choice) and the pairs $(x_1, \neg x_1), \ldots, (x_n, \neg x_n)$ allow an existential choice for the values of the x-variables as demonstrated in Ψ', i.e., if some x-variable x_i should be true, we choose $\neg x_i$ from the pair $(x_i, \neg x_i)$ and vice versa. □

We now use $\exists$-VALIDITY to prove that RELATIVE TREE PATTERN MINIMIZATION is Σ_2^P-complete, which is our final step in proving Theorem 4.1.

LEMMA 4.5. RELATIVE TREE PATTERN MINIMIZATION *is* Σ_2^P*-complete.*

PROOF. The upper bound follows from the straightforward algorithm: guess q and check whether $p \subseteq_S q \subseteq_S r$. Clearly, guessing q can be done by a polynomial number of guesses and the containment tests can be done in coNP by Theorem 2.1.

For the lower bound, we reduce from $\exists$-VALIDITY. We build on Miklau and Suciu's proof that containment of tree patterns is coNP-hard ([29, Proofs of Lemma 3 and Theorem 4]) and extend their idea. Let $I = \{(c_1^1, c_1^2), \ldots, (c_m^1, c_m^2)\}$ be an instance of $\exists$-VALIDITY. We compute the patterns p and r as given in Figure 9. We let $k = |r| - m$. Notice that the pattern p only depends on the *number* of clauses and variables of I (it uses m in the picture of p and n in the subpatterns C and D) and not on the clauses themselves. Furthermore, p does not contain any wildcards and only contains descendant edges in its subquery D. Pattern r does contain wildcards in the subpatterns C_i^j, but these wildcards have only one child. Therefore, p and r are $*$-narrow patterns.

The idea of p and r is that each subpattern of r that is rooted at a b-labeled node represents a pair of clauses and the subpattern C_i^j represents the clause c_i^j for each $i \in \{1, \ldots, m\}$ and $j \in \{1, 2\}$. The subpattern C_i^j has a root labeled g. For each positive literal x_i of c_i^j, the g-labeled node has an x_i-labeled child that itself has an x_i-labeled child, connected by a child edge. For each negative literal $\neg x_i$ of c_i^j, the g-labeled node has an x_i-labeled child, that has a wildcard node as child which has an x_i-labeled child connected by a descendant edge.

Since the only descendant edges of p occur in the subpattern D, the canonical trees of p only differ from p in the subtree corresponding to D.

We will show that I is a true instance of $\exists$-VALIDITY if and only if p, r, and k are a true instance of RELATIVE TREE PATTERN MINIMIZATION. To this end, we first present two claims and prove correctness of the reduction based on these claims.

The first claim states that p, r, and k are an instance of RELATIVE TREE PATTERN MINIMIZATION.

CLAIM 4.6. *The tree patterns p and r are minimal.*

We prove the claim. Since p and r both are $*$-narrow, it suffices to show that both patterns are nonredundant, according to Lemma 2.3. It is easy (but tedious) to verify that

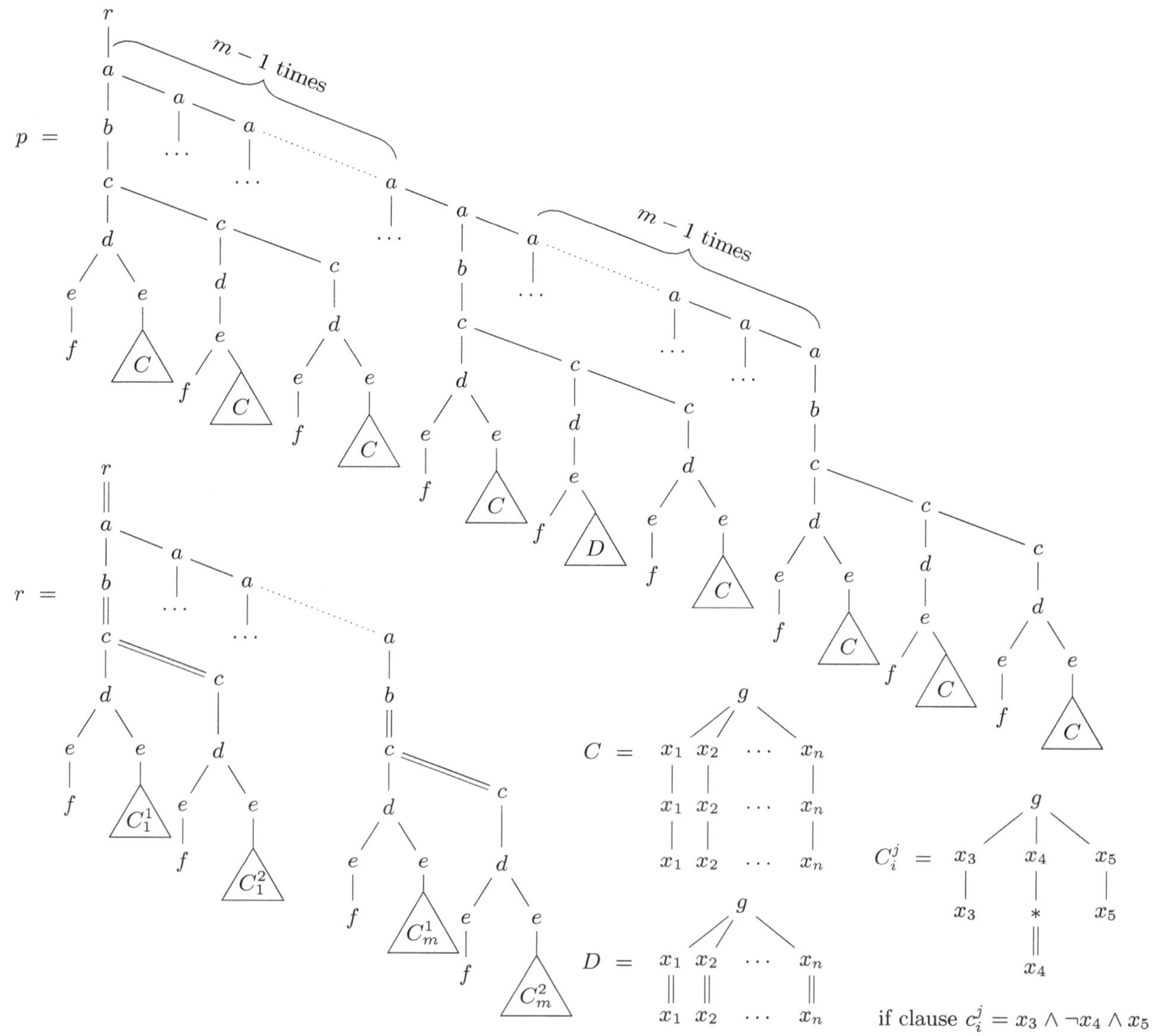

Figure 9: Patterns used in the proof of Theorem 4.1

removing any leaf from any canonical tree of p results in a tree that is not in $L(p)$. By Lemma 2.4, this means that none of the patterns obtained from p by removing a leaf is equivalent to p. This means that p is nonredundant and therefore also minimal. The proof for r is analogous. This concludes the proof of Claim 4.6.

The second claim limits the form of solutions q to the instance. We say that a tree pattern q is in *normal form* if it can be obtained from pattern r by the following algorithm: Select in each subpattern rooted at a b-labeled node at most one subpattern rooted at a d-labeled node. In each selected subpattern, merge the two nodes labeled e — the other nodes remain unchanged. Furthermore, we allow to replace descendant edges by child edges.[4]

[4]The important operation, however, is the merging of nodes, since this operation changes the size of a pattern. The only reason why we also allow replacement of descendant edges by child edges is because we cannot avoid it in Claim 4.7.

CLAIM 4.7. *Let q be a smallest pattern in the set $\{q' \mid p \subseteq_S q' \subseteq_S r\}$. Then q is in normal form.*

We sketch a proof of the claim. Consider a fixed pattern q among the smallest (possibly non-equivalent) patterns in the set

$$\{q' \mid p \subseteq_S q' \subseteq_S r\}\ .$$

Let t_q be the (unique) smallest canonical tree of q and π be an embedding of r into t_q. We note that t_q contains no information about which edges of q are descendant edges.

We first show that π is surjective. Indeed, if this is not the case, then we can construct a tree pattern q' such that $p \subseteq_S q' \subseteq_S r$ and size(q') < size(q) as follows. We remove a node of t_q not used by π, relabel every z-node as wildcard node, and change every edge $(\pi(u), \pi(v))$ of t_q for which (u, v) is a descendant edge in r into a descendant edge. We have that $p \subseteq_S q \subseteq_S q'$, as the construction only removes restrictions. Furthermore, we also have that $q' \subseteq_S r$ since there are no nodes u, v and w in r such that all of the following hold:

- v is a descendant of u;
- (u, w) is a descendant edge;
- v and w have the same label or one of the nodes is a wildcard; and
- v and w are in different subtrees, i.e., v is not a descendant of w or vice versa.

The existence of q' therefore contradicts the definition of q, which means that π is surjective.

The claim now follows from the three observations below:

(1) For each child edge (u, v) of r, the edge $(\pi(u), \pi(v))$ corresponds to a child edge of q, because otherwise we would have $p \not\subseteq_S q$. We note that it might be possible that, for some descendant edge (u, v) of r, the edge $(\pi(u), \pi(v))$ corresponds to a child edge of q.

(2) If for two nodes v and w of r we have that $\pi(v) = \pi(w)$, then both nodes have label e and are siblings. All other possibilities can be excluded by considering the relative depth of nodes in the pattern and ancestor-descendant relationships.

(3) Furthermore, in any b-subpattern, there is at most one pair of e-labeled siblings such that $\pi(v) = \pi(w)$, since otherwise we would have that $p \not\subseteq_S q$.

Indeed, from (1) and (2) we can conclude that q can be obtained from r by merging e-labeled siblings and possibly replacing some descendant edges by child edges. From (3) we can conclude that in each b-subpattern it suffices to merge one pair of e-labeled siblings, which concludes the proof of Claim 4.7.

We now proceed with the proof of Lemma 4.5. We say that a pattern q is a *solution* to I if it is has size k, satisfies $p \subseteq_S q \subseteq_S r$, and is in normal form, i.e., in every subpattern rooted at a b-labeled node, two e-labeled siblings are merged.

Let q be a tree pattern of size k in normal form. We denote by v_i^j for $i \in \{1, \dots, m\}$ and $j \in \{1, 2\}$ the d-labeled node of q that is ancestor of the C_i^j subpattern. We define a function $\mathrm{f}^q : \{1, \dots, m\} \to \{1, 2\}$ as follows:

$$\mathrm{f}^q(i) = \begin{cases} 1 & \text{if } v_i^1 \text{ has exactly one child} \\ 2 & \text{if } v_i^2 \text{ has exactly one child} \end{cases}$$

Notice that f^q is well-defined if q has size k and is in normal form.

Let t be a canonical tree of pattern p and let $d(x_i)$ denote the distance between the two x_i-labeled nodes in the subtree of t corresponding to the D-subpattern of p. With t we associate a valuation σ^t of the variables $x_1, \dots, x_n$ as follows:

$$\sigma^t(x_i) = \begin{cases} \text{true} & \text{if } d(x_i) = 1 \\ \text{false} & \text{if } d(x_i) > 1 \end{cases}$$

We can show the following points, which prove the equivalence between tree pattern minimization and ∃-VALIDITY.

(a) If q is a solution to I, then σ^t satisfies

$$c_1^{\mathrm{f}^q(1)} \vee \cdots \vee c_m^{\mathrm{f}^q(m)}$$

for every canonical tree t of r. This shows universality of the formula because there exists a canonical tree t of p such that $\sigma^t = \rho$ for each possible valuation ρ of variables.

For the other direction, let $\iota : \{0, \dots, m\} \to \{1, 2\}$ be a choice of clauses. We can show the following.

(b) If the formula $c_1^{\iota(1)} \vee \cdots \vee c_m^{\iota(m)}$ is universally true, then the normal form pattern q of size k such that

$$\mathrm{f}^q(j) = \iota(j) \text{ for all } j \in \{1, \dots, m\}$$

satisfies $r \subseteq_S q \subseteq_S p$.

Statements (a) and (b) show that the reduction to tree pattern minimization is correct. Notice that the patterns p and q and the number k can be computed using logarithmic space.

We omit the proofs of statements (a) and (b). This concludes the proof of Lemma 4.5. □

The techniques we used for proving that TREE PATTERN MINIMIZATION is Σ_2^P-complete can also be used to prove that MINIMALITY is Π_2^P-complete. The proof for minimality uses the same ideas as the proof for minimization. However it is not immediate, as MINIMALITY can be seen as a variant of TREE PATTERN MINIMIZATION for fixed $k = \text{size}(p) - 1$, and thus these two problems are a bit different. The basic observation idea is that we can compute a tree pattern q such that $p \subseteq_S q \subseteq_S r$ and

$$\text{size}(q) = k + 1 = |r| - m + 1 \,.$$

Therefore, $P(p, q, r)$ is minimal if and only if the underlying ∃-validity instance is a false instance.

THEOREM 4.8. MINIMALITY *is* Π_2^P*-complete.*

PROOF SKETCH. Membership in Π_2^P is immediate: the algorithm has to check whether each smaller pattern is non-equivalent. The non-equivalence test can be done in NP since equivalence of tree patterns is coNP-complete [29].

For Π_2^P-hardness, we use essentially the same (combined) reduction as in the proofs of Lemma 4.5 and 4.3. Let I be an instance of ∃-VALIDITY and let p and r be the patterns computed in the reduction from ∃-VALIDITY to RELATIVE TREE PATTERN MINIMIZATION in the proof of Lemma 4.5.

We compute a pattern q from p by merging the e-nodes above the subpatterns C_1^1 to C_{m-1}^1 with their siblings.

It is easy to see that $p \subseteq_S q \subseteq_S r$. The second inclusion holds again, because we restrict the trees by merging nodes. The first inclusion holds, because there exists a homomorphism from q to p which embeds the lowest b-subpattern of q on the b-subpattern containing D. The two c-labeled nodes from the q-pattern can be embedded on the upper and lower c-labeled nodes inside the b-subpattern of p.

Finally, we ask whether the pattern $P(p, q, r)$ is minimal. If the answer is yes, then I has no solution because we already know that a solution to I implies the existence of a pattern q' with $p \subseteq_S q' \subseteq_S r$ and

$$\text{size}(q') = \text{size}(r) - m < \text{size}(q) = \text{size}(r) - m + 1 \,.$$

By Lemma 3.2, we know that $P(p, q', r) \equiv_S P(p, q, r)$. Furthermore, $P(p, q', r)$ is smaller than $P(p, q, r)$.

On the other hand, if there exists a pattern $P_{\min}$ with $P_{\min} \equiv_S P(p, q, r)$ and $\text{size}(P_{\min}) < \text{size}(P(p, q, r))$, then, by Lemma 4.2, we know that there exists a pattern q' with $\text{size}(q') < \text{size}(q)$ and $p \subseteq_S q' \subseteq r$. As

$$\text{size}(q') < \text{size}(q) = \text{size}(r) - m + 1 ,$$

and therefore $\text{size}(q) \leq \text{size}(r) - m$, we know from the reduction in Lemma 4.5, that I has a solution. □

5. DISCUSSION AND OUTLOOK

Boolean versus k-ary Queries.

We proved that minimization for Boolean tree patterns is Σ_2^P-complete. This result can also be extended to k-ary tree patterns (as considered in [29, 25]). However, the technique to transfer this result is not the usual one from [25, Section 5] because, as the authors say, it is not clear if the reduction presented there preserves minimality. We can transfer the complexity directly, however. For k-ary queries, the Σ_2^P upper bound follows by applying the naive algorithm and the lower bound follows from attaching all k output nodes to the root of our gadgets.

Lessons for Minimization.

This work gives new insights on how minimal tree patterns may need to be obtained and is the first to give a tight complexity bound for doing so. Even though our main result is a hardness result, we believe that the new insights can be used to develop better tree pattern optimization algorithms. For example, we know that minimization of $*$-narrow tree patterns can always be done by (iteratively) removing leaves [18]. It was long believed that all tree patterns can be minimized in such a way (see, e.g., [17, 18]) but from this paper we now know that this is not the case. In particular, we now know that it may also be necessary to merge nodes.

This is a fact that we can use for developing better heuristics for greedy tree pattern minimization. That is, for a given tree pattern, we can approximate a minimal equivalent pattern by iteratively removing a leaf or merging two nodes and testing if the resulting tree pattern is still equivalent; until no such operation can be done anymore. Notice that this is a polynomial-time algorithm with a subroutine for equivalence tests (which can in general be coNP-complete).

It is important to note that the presented approach is still a heuristic and does not always produce a minimal pattern. For instance, if $\Pi_2^P \neq \text{coNP}$, then we know that minimal patterns cannot always be obtained from a given pattern by removing leaves and merging nodes. Indeed, assume that this would be true. Then consider a non-minimal pattern p_1 and an equivalent pattern p_2 obtained from p_1 by deleting a node or merging two nodes. By the above assumption, we should also be able to go from p_2 to a minimal pattern of p_2 (and thus also of p_1) by deleting and merging nodes. However, this would mean that the above greedy algorithm can be used to decide TREE PATTERN MINIMIZATION in coNP.

We also believe that the above argument can be strengthened so that the $\Pi_2^P \neq \text{coNP}$ condition is not needed. This proof would be based on the concrete patterns we construct in the proof of Lemma 4.5. Essentially, the argument boils down to showing that there are patterns q'' with $p \subseteq_S q'' \subseteq_S r$ from which no smallest pattern in $\{q' \mid p \subseteq_S q' \subseteq_S r\}$ can be reached by merging nodes. This means that, for the pattern $P(p, q'', r)$, it would be necessary to *split* a node in order to reach a pattern of the form $P(p, q', r)$ where q' is one of the smallest patterns in $\{q' \mid p \subseteq_S q' \subseteq_S r\}$. So, a rewriting sequence from a given pattern to an equivalent minimal one may have to perform steps that make patterns larger.

It is an interesting question which (non-trivial) set of operations would be sufficient to guarantee that a minimal pattern can always be obtained by applying a sequence of such operations to the input pattern. This line of thinking leads to questions about query rewriting and axiomatizations for tree pattern equivalence. Ten Cate and Marx [35] studied such axiomatizations for XPath 2.0 (which contains tree patterns as a sublanguage) and present a sound and complete set of axioms for query equivalence, that is, a set of axioms for rewriting patterns into equivalent ones. Fazzinga, Flesca, and Furfaro [15, 16] considered this question for tree patterns and provide a set of axioms complete up to homomorphism containment.

Acknowledgments

We are very grateful to Benny Kimelfeld for insightful discussions and for bringing the tree pattern query minimization problem to our attention.

6. REFERENCES

[1] S. Abiteboul, L. Segoufin, and V. Vianu. Static analysis of active XML systems. *ACM Trans. Database Syst.*, 34(4), 2009.

[2] N. Alechina, S. Demri, and M. de Rijke. A modal perspective on path constraints. *J. Log. Comput.*, 13(6):939–956, 2003.

[3] S. Amer-Yahia, S. Cho, L. V. S. Lakshmanan, and D. Srivastava. Tree pattern query minimization. *VLDB J.*, 11(4):315–331, 2002.

[4] M. Arenas, P. Barceló, L. Libkin, and F. Murlak. *Foundations of Data Exchange*. Cambridge University Press, 2014.

[5] P. Barceló, L. Libkin, A. Poggi, and C. Sirangelo. XML with incomplete information. *J. ACM*, 58(1):4, 2010.

[6] M. Benedikt, W. Fan, and F. Geerts. XPath satisfiability in the presence of DTDs. *J. ACM*, 55(2), 2008.

[7] H. Björklund, W. Martens, and T. Schwentick. Conjunctive query containment over trees. *J. Comput. Syst. Sci.*, 77(3):450–472, 2011.

[8] H. Björklund, W. Martens, and T. Schwentick. Validity of tree pattern queries with respect to schema information. In *International Symposium on Mathematical Foundations of Computer Science (MFCS)*, pages 171–182, 2013.

[9] S. Cassidy. Generalizing XPath for directed graphs. In *Extreme Markup Languages Conference*, 2003.

[10] E. P. F. Chan. Containment and minimization of positive conjunctive queries in OODB's. In *Symposium on Principles of Database Systems (PODS)*, pages 202–211, 1992.

[11] A. K. Chandra and P. M. Merlin. Optimal implementation of conjunctive queries in relational data bases. In *Symposium on Theory of Computing (STOC)*, pages 77–90, 1977.

[12] C. Chekuri and A. Rajaraman. Conjunctive query containment revisited. *Theor. Comput. Sci.*, 239(2):211–229, 2000.

[13] D. Chen and C. Y. Chan. Minimization of tree pattern queries with constraints. In *International Conference on Management of Data (SIGMOD)*, pages 609–622, 2008.

[14] W. Czerwiński, W. Martens, P. Parys, and M. Przybyłko. The (almost) complete guide to tree pattern containment. In *Symposium on Principles of Database Systems (PODS)*, pages 117–130, 2015.

[15] B. Fazzinga, S. Flesca, and F. Furfaro. On the expressiveness of generalization rules for xpath query relaxation. In *International Database Engineering and Applications Symposium (IDEAS)*, pages 157–168, 2010.

[16] B. Fazzinga, S. Flesca, and F. Furfaro. XPath query relaxation through rewriting rules. *IEEE Trans. Knowl. Data Eng.*, 23(10):1583–1600, 2011.

[17] S. Flesca, F. Furfaro, and E. Masciari. On the minimization of XPath queries. In *International Conference on Very Large Data Bases (VLDB)*, pages 153–164, 2003.

[18] S. Flesca, F. Furfaro, and E. Masciari. On the minimization of XPath queries. *J. ACM*, 55(1), 2008.

[19] G. H. L. Fletcher, M. Gyssens, D. Leinders, J. V. den Bussche, D. V. Gucht, S. Vansummeren, and Y. Wu. Relative expressive power of navigational querying on graphs. In *International Conference on Database Theory (ICDT)*, pages 197–207, 2011.

[20] A. Gheerbrant, L. Libkin, and C. Sirangelo. Reasoning about pattern-based XML queries. In *International Conference on Web Reasoning and Rule Systems (RR)*, pages 4–18, 2013.

[21] G. Gottlob, C. Koch, and R. Pichler. Efficient algorithms for processing XPath queries. *ACM Trans. Database Syst.*, 30(2):444–491, 2005.

[22] G. Gottlob, C. Koch, and K. U. Schulz. Conjunctive queries over trees. *J. ACM*, 53(2):238–272, 2006.

[23] G. Gottlob, N. Leone, and F. Scarcello. The complexity of acyclic conjunctive queries. *J. ACM*, 48(3):431–498, 2001.

[24] Gremlin Language. https://github.com/tinkerpop/gremlin/wiki, 2013.

[25] B. Kimelfeld and Y. Sagiv. Revisiting redundancy and minimization in an XPath fragment. In *International Conference on Extending Database Technology (EDBT)*, pages 61–72, 2008.

[26] E. V. Kostylev, J. L. Reutter, and D. Vrgoc. Containment of data graph queries. In *International Conference on Database Theory (ICDT)*, pages 131–142, 2014.

[27] L. Libkin, W. Martens, and D. Vrgoc. Querying graph databases with XPath. In *International Conference on Database Theory (ICDT)*, pages 129–140, 2013.

[28] M. Marx. XPath and modal logics of finite DAG's. In *International Conference on Automated Reasoning with Analytic Tableaux and Related Methods*, pages 150–164, 2003.

[29] G. Miklau and D. Suciu. Containment and equivalence for a fragment of XPath. *J. ACM*, 51(1):2–45, 2004.

[30] T. Milo and D. Suciu. Index structures for path expressions. In *International Conference on Database Theory (ICDT)*, pages 277–295, 1999.

[31] F. Neven and T. Schwentick. On the complexity of XPath containment in the presence of disjunction, DTDs, and variables. *Logical Methods in Computer Science*, 2(3), 2006.

[32] P. Ramanan. Efficient algorithms for minimizing tree pattern queries. In *International Conference on Management of Data (SIGMOD)*, pages 299–309, 2002.

[33] J. Robie, D. Chamberlin, M. Dyck, and J. Snelson. XML Path Language 3.0. Technical report, World Wide Web Consortium, April 2014. Recommendation, http://www.w3.org/TR/2014/REC-xpath-30-20140408/.

[34] S. Staworko and P. Wieczorek. Characterizing XML twig queries with examples. In *International Conference on Database Theory (ICDT)*, pages 144–160, 2015.

[35] B. ten Cate and M. Marx. Axiomatizing the logical core of XPath 2.0. *Theory Comput. Syst.*, 44(4):561–589, 2009.

[36] P. T. Wood. Minimising simple XPath expressions. In *WebDB*, pages 13–18, 2001.

[37] W. Xu and Z. M. Özsoyoglu. Rewriting XPath queries using materialized views. In *International Conference on Very Large Data Bases (VLDB)*, pages 121–132, 2005.

[38] M. Yannakakis. Algorithms for acyclic database schemes. In *International Conference on Very Large Data Bases (VLDB)*, pages 82–94, 1981.

Optimal Score Aggregation Algorithms

Ronald Fagin
IBM Research – Almaden
fagin@us.ibm.com

ABSTRACT

Assume that there is a set of "voters" and a set of "candidates", where each voter assigns a numerical score to each candidate. There is a scoring function (such as the mean or the median), and a consensus ranking is obtained by applying the scoring function to each candidate's scores. The problem is to find the top k candidates, while minimizing the number of database accesses. The speaker will present an algorithm that is optimal in an extremely strong sense: not just in the worst case or the average case, but in every case! Even though the algorithm is only 10 lines long (!), the paper containing the algorithm won the 2014 Gödel Prize, the top prize for a paper in theoretical computer science.

CCS Concepts

• Theory and algorithms for application domains → Database theory → Data structures and algorithms for data management

Keywords

Aggregation algorithms; score aggregation; instance optimal

Short Bio

Ronald Fagin is an IBM Fellow at IBM Research – Almaden. IBM Fellow is IBM's highest technical honor. There are currently around 90 active IBM Fellows (out of around 400,000 IBM employees worldwide), and there have been only around 250 IBM Fellows in the over 50-year history of the program. Ron received his B.A. in mathematics from Dartmouth College and his Ph.D. in mathematics from the University of California at Berkeley.

He is a Fellow of IEEE, ACM, and AAAS (American Association for the Advancement of Science).

He has co-authored four papers that won Best Paper Awards and three papers that won Test-of-time Awards, all in major conferences He was named Docteur Honoris Causa by the University of Paris. He won the IEEE Technical Achievement Award, IEEE W. Wallace McDowell Award, and ACM SIGMOD Edgar F. Codd Innovations Award (a lifetime achievement award in databases). He is a member of the US National Academy of Engineering and the American Academy of Arts and Sciences.

PODS'16, June 26–July 1, 2016, San Francisco, California, USA.
ACM 978-1-4503-4191-2/16/06.
DOI: http://dx.doi.org/10.1145/2902251.2902308

Hypertree Decompositions: Questions and Answers

Georg Gottlob
Computer Science Dep.
University of Oxford
gottlob@cs.ox.ac.uk

Gianluigi Greco
DEMACS
University of Calabria
ggreco@mat.unical.it

Nicola Leone
DEMACS
University of Calabria
leone@mat.unical.it

Francesco Scarcello
DIMES
University of Calabria
scarcello@dimes.unical.it

ABSTRACT

In the database context, the hypertree decomposition method is used for query optimization, whereby conjunctive queries having a low degree of cyclicity can be recognized and decomposed automatically, and efficiently evaluated. Hypertree decompositions were introduced at ACM PODS 1999. The present paper reviews –in form of questions and answers– the main relevant concepts and algorithms and surveys selected related work including applications and test results.

Keywords

Conjunctive queries; hypergraphs; query evaluation; tractability; acyclic queries; hypertree width; decompositions

1. INTRODUCTION

1.1 What Is This All About?

This paper is about *hypertree decompositions* [74], a hypergraph-based method for decomposing conjunctive queries (or, equivalently, their associated hypergraphs) into tree-structures called *hypertrees*, in order to process them more efficiently. Each hypertree decomposition of a query is associated with a width. The smallest width over all such decompositions is the query's *hypertree width*. Queries of bounded hypertree width can be answered efficiently [74] in combined complexity. In particular, while Boolean conjunctive queries are NP-complete to answer in general [30], in the case of bounded hypertree width, they can be processed in polynomial time. Moreover, conjunctive queries with output, in case of bounded hypertree width, can be processed in time polynomial in the size of the input plus the size of the output. Queries having bounded hypertree width are also highly parallelizable. This was already noted in [72, 68] and has gained renewed interest in the context of MapReduce [43] and more advanced models of parallel query processing [7].

PODS'16, June 26-July 01, 2016, San Francisco, CA, USA
© 2016 ACM. ISBN 978-1-4503-4191-2/16/06...$15.00
DOI: http://dx.doi.org/10.1145/2902251.2902309

The notion of bounded hypertree width generalizes the well-known concept of *query acyclicity*. The hypertree width of a query is a good measure of its degree of cyclicity. In particular, the class of all conjunctive queries (CQs) of hypertree width 1 coincides with the class of acyclic CQs. Hypertree decompositions, in a precise sense, lift the great benefits of acyclic queries to much larger and more general classes of queries which, in addition to acyclic queries, contain queries that are, so to say, *mildly cyclic*. A large number of realistic queries are of bounded hypertree width, as we shall discuss in Sections 3 and 9. Such queries can be answered efficiently, by using specific algorithms that exploit hypertree decompositions. However, the same queries would often require time exponential in their length if evaluated by classical methods. Hypertree decompositions are thus a powerful query optimization method with a huge potential for practical applications. Moreover, the problem of conjunctive query answering is equivalent to the query containment problem and, in AI, to the *constraint satisfaction problem (CSPs)* [44]. Thus, the algorithms and favorable complexity results for hypertree decompositions presented in this paper also apply to these problems.

1.2 What Is so Smart about Acyclic Queries?

Query acyclicity, which will be discussed in detail in Section 2, is one of the most fundamental and most fascinating concepts in database theory. It was introduced in [18] in the context of *acyclic database schemes* and, independently, as the *tree-query property* in [59]. In [19, 58] it was shown that these notions coincide. A query Q is acyclic if its associated hypergraph $\mathcal{H}_Q$ has a join tree. This is an appropriate arrangement of the (hyperedges associated with the) query atoms in form of a tree—see Section 2 for details. The hypergraph $\mathcal{H}_Q$ associated with a Boolean conjunctive query Q has as nodes its variables and has, for each query atom, a hyperedge consisting of the set of all variables appearing in that atom. Note that, unlike for graphs, for hypergraphs there are various different definitions of acyclicity. The join-tree based definition used in the present paper coincides with α-acyclicity as defined in [50]. This type of hypergraph acyclicity is the most general acyclicity notion and is far more sophisticated than graph acyclicity. To appreciate this, consider Figure 1, which shows two acyclic hypergraphs and their associated join trees. The hypergraph on the left side is intuitively acyclic, less so the one on the right side. In fact, the latter contains an obvious cycle over the nodes A, B, C, and D, which is not covered by any single hyperedge. Still, because this cycle is appropriately covered by two consecutive edges of the join tree, the hypergraph is acyclic. Note that, unlike for graphs, an acyclic hypergraph may contain a cyclic one as a sub-hypergraph.

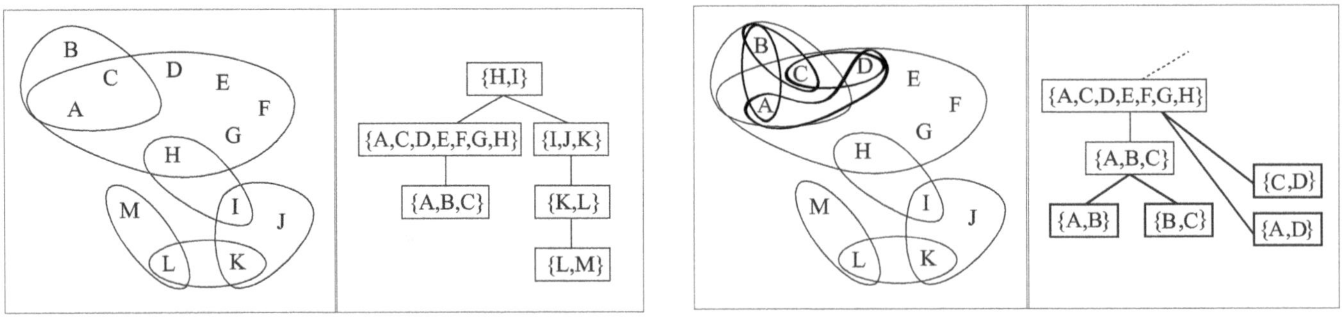

Figure 1: A hypergraph $\mathcal{H}_{Q_1}$ and a join tree for it (left), plus a hypergraph $\mathcal{H}_{Q_{0 \wedge 1}}$ and a join tree for it (right).

This is illustrated yet more drastically by the following example, which also explains how recognizing acyclicity helps processing a query in polynomial time.

EXAMPLE 1.1. Let CLIQUE$_r$ be the query expressing that a graph with edge relation E has an r-clique, i.e.,

$$\text{CLIQUE}_r \equiv \bigwedge_{1 \leq i < j \leq r} E(x_i, x_j) \wedge E(x_j, x_i).$$

Let, moreover, Q_r be the query

$$\text{CLIQUE}_r \wedge R(x_1, \ldots, x_r),$$

and define the infinite class $\mathcal{C}$ of queries by $\mathcal{C} = \{Q_r | r \geq 1\}$. Each query Q_r in C is acyclic, and can thus be answered very efficiently. In fact, to answer Q_r over some database DB, we just need to start by matching the $R(x_1, \ldots, x_r)$ atom to the polynomially many tuples of the R relation of DB one by one. Each such match binds all variables, and thus for each such match it suffices to check in linear time whether all other instantiated query atoms are in the database.

However, if we used a more naïve evaluation strategy that processes the query by performing joins from left to right, we would first solve the NP-hard CLIQUE$_r$ query and only then evaluate the $R(x_1, \ldots, x_r)$ atom. Unless P=NP, this would require an exponential effort (in combined complexity) in the worst case. $\triangleleft$

Boolean acyclic conjunctive queries (ACQs) with m atoms, where r is the size of the largest database relation relevant to the query, can be answered in time $O(m \cdot r \cdot \log r)$, while non-Boolean ACQs in time $O(m \cdot N \cdot \log N))$, where N is the size of the output plus r. This is achieved by first automatically recognizing whether a query is acyclic, which is feasible in linear time [133], and if so, by processing the query efficiently using a smart algorithm, such as Yannakakis' algorithm [137], which reduces the relevant database relations via semi-joins along the edges of the query join tree in such a way that no remaining tuple is superfluous (see Section 2).

1.3 How to Generalize Query-Acyclicity?

A significant proportion of the conjunctive queries (and the constraint satisfaction problems) arising in practice are not properly acyclic, but are in some sense nearly acyclic. Efforts have therefore been made since the 1990s to weaken the notion of acyclicity by defining appropriate concepts of near acyclicity and by finding query evaluation algorithms that are efficient for nearly acyclic queries. In this context, the degree of acyclicity of a hypergraph (or of a corresponding query) is mostly referred to as its *width*.

In defining a generalization of acyclicity, one seeks to ensure the following fundamental three conditions to hold for each fixed constant $k \geq 1$:

1. **Generalization of Acyclicity:** Queries of width k include the acyclic ones.
2. **Tractable Recognizability:** Queries of width k can be recognized in polynomial time.
3. **Tractable Query-Answering:** Queries of width k can be answered in polynomial time (in combined complexity).

In Condition 3, in case of non-Boolean queries, the polynomial-time bound is considered with respect to the combined size of the input and the output (indeed, in general, we may get exponentially many tuples in the output).

In graph theory, there is an appropriate and well-known generalization of graph acyclicity: *bounded treewidth* [124, 123]. This notion is based on tree decompositions as explained in detail in Section 3. Tree decompositions can straightforwardly be defined for hypergraphs, and thus for queries. They have been considered for conjunctive query answering (or, equivalently, CSP-solving) in [46, 31, 108]. Briefly, a tree decomposition of a hypergraph $\mathcal{H}$ consists of a tree T, whose vertices are each associated with a so called *bag*, i.e., a set of nodes of $\mathcal{H}$, such that each hyperedge is covered by some bag, and such that for each node v of $\mathcal{H}$ all vertices of the decomposition tree whose bag contains v induce a connected subtree of T. The *width* of a decomposition is $s - 1$, where s is the cardinality of the largest bag. The *treewidth* $tw(\mathcal{H})$ of $\mathcal{H}$ is the minimum treewidth among all tree decompositions of $\mathcal{H}$. The treewidth $tw(Q)$ of a query Q is defined to be the treewidth $tw(\mathcal{H}_Q)$ of its associated hypergraph $\mathcal{H}_Q$. A similar convention will be adopted for other notions of width introduced below.

Conjunctive queries of treewidth k can be answered on a database DB in time $O(m' \cdot D^{k+1} \cdot \log D)$, where m' is the number of vertices of the decomposition tree T, and D is the number of distinct values occurring in DB. So, the tree decomposition method enjoys our criterion of Tractable Query-Answering (Condition 3 above), because we can always find a tree decomposition of width k, whose number of vertices m' is at most the number of variables occurring in the query. It is also well-known that, for fixed constant k, determining whether a hypergraph has treewidth k is feasible in linear time [23], therefore tree decompositions also enjoy Tractable Recognizability (Condition 2). There is, however, a significant drawback of the tree decomposition method: it does not generalize hypergraph acyclicity, and therefore does not fulfill Condition 1. For instance, for each integer r, the acyclic query Q_r of Example 1.1 has treewidth $r - 1$. Therefore, the class C of all these queries has unbounded treewidth.

Another method introduced in an attempt to capture the degree of acyclicity of a query is the method of *biconnected components* [52]. In this method, the degree of acyclicity of a query Q is defined as the number of nodes of the largest biconnected component of $\mathcal{H}_Q$.

This method, too, satisfies conditions 2 and 3, but not Condition 1, as it does not generalize acyclicity. According to this method, for each integer r, the acyclic query Q_r of Example 1.1 has degree of acyclicity r. Further methods that do not suitably generalize acyclicity are reviewed and compared in [70].

A significantly more appropriate, but still not fully satisfactory approach to the generalization of query acyclicity is the notion of *query width* [31], which is based on the concept of *query decompositions*. Essentially, a query decomposition of width k of a query Q is a tree decomposition of $\mathcal{H}_Q$ each of whose bags coincides with the union of k or fewer hyperedges from $\mathcal{H}_Q$, and where at least one bag is the union of precisely k such hyperedges—as shown in [72], this definition is equivalent to the original definition in [31]. The *query width (qw)* of Q is the minimum width among all possible query decompositions of Q. Bounded query width generalizes query acyclicity, as each join-tree is a query decomposition of query width 1. Thus, Condition 1 is satisfied. Queries of bounded query width can be answered in polynomial time by the same algorithms that are also used for hypertree decompositions (which we will discuss in Section 4), thus also Condition 3 is satisfied. Unfortunately, however, queries of bounded query width are hard to recognize. In fact, as shown in [74], deciding for a query Q whether $qw(Q) = k$ for fixed constants $k > 3$ is NP-complete. Thus, unless P=NP, Condition 2 is not satisfied. In addition, the fact that the bags need to coincide *exactly* to a union of $\leq k$ hyperedges is restrictive and gives rise to a higher than necessary width [74].

To redress the latter issue, it is sufficient to merely require that each bag of the tree decomposition of $\mathcal{H}_Q$ be *covered* by a union of k hyperedges (rather than requiring it coincides with their union). This generalization gives rise to the concept of *generalized hypertree decomposition (GHD)* and to the associated notion of *generalized hypertree width (ghw)*. Thus, a GHD of a hypergraph (or query) is a tree decomposition together with a specified covering of its bags by hyperedges. The ghw of a particular GHD is the maximum number of hyperedges used to cover a bag, and the generalized hypertree width of the original hypergraph (or query) is the minimum generalized hypertree width over all GHDs for this hypergraph. GHDs properly generalize query decompositions (query decompositions are GHDs but not vice-versa), and thus also acyclic queries. Hence, Condition 1 is satisfied. Queries of bounded ghw can be answered in polynomial time [74], thus Condition 3 is satisfied. However, as shown in [76], for fixed constants $k \geq 3$, it is NP-hard to decide whether for a query Q, $ghw(\mathcal{H}_Q) = k$. Thus, unless P=NP, Condition 2 is still not satisfied.

To achieve tractability, an additional restriction, called the *Descendant Condition* or also the *Special Condition*, was added to the definition of GHD. This condition, which will be defined and explained in Section 3.2, while attempting to construct a width-k GHD, reduces in a rather natural way the choice of possible child-bags of an already computed bag to a polynomial number of alternatives (each of which can be represented in logarithmic space). Based on this, a width-k decomposition of a hypergraph $\mathcal{H}$ can be computed via an alternating logspace procedure and thus in deterministic polynomial time (see Section 3.3). GHDs that satisfy the Descendant Condition are called *hypertree decompositions (HDs)*, and the associated width is the *hypertree width*, denoted by $hw(\mathcal{H})$. Hypertree decompositions were originally defined in [74], where also their fundamental properties were studied. In [70] they were carefully compared to other types of decompositions. There has been since then much further research related to (G)HDs, as well as several implementations and applications. Much of this work is reviewed in the sequel of the present paper.

1.4 What Are the Main Advantages of HDs?

We give here only a very short itemized summary of the advantages of HDs here. For more details, see Sections 3-6.

- For a fixed constant k, it can be checked in polynomial time whether a conjunctive query Q is of hypertree width $\leq k$, and if so, a HD of width $hw(\mathcal{H}_Q)$ can be computed in polynomial time. The best upper bound currently known for this is $O(m^{2k}v^2)$ time, where m and v are the number of atoms and the number of variables in Q, respectively [69]. The decision and computation problems are, moreover, at a very low level of structural complexity and are highly parallelizable problems in LOGCFL, a low class within NC^2. These results are discussed in Section 3.
- A Boolean conjunctive query Q having (generalized) hypertree width k can be answered in time $O(v \cdot r^k \cdot \log r)$ where r is the size of the largest database relation mentioned by the query. For queries with output (whose results may consist of exponentially many tuples) an output-polynomial upper bound is $O(v \cdot (r^k + s) \cdot \log(r + s))$, where s is the number of output tuples. In particular, for each query of bounded hw, we can generate in polynomial time an efficient query plan for a relational machine. This and further improved bounds are discussed in Section 4.
- Generalized hypertree decompositions (and thus, in particular, HDs) can be used for generating efficient query plans not only for standard query processing engines, but also for systems using multiway joins or for systems using parallel processing at various levels of granularity (see Section 4.1). Moreover, just as for acyclic queries, evaluating queries of bounded hw is complete for the parallel class LOGCFL [72].
- Generalized hypertree decompositions (and thus also HDs) cannot just be used for plain conjunctive query answering, but, as shown in Section 5, they are also usable for *top-k* queries, and queries with aggregation operators, such as COUNT.
- Hypertree width is not very far apart from the tighter acyclicity-measure of ghw. In fact, in [6] it was proven that for each hypergraph $\mathcal{H}$, $ghw(\mathcal{H}) \leq hw(\mathcal{H}) \leq 3 \cdot ghw(\mathcal{H}) + 1$, which implies that a class of queries has bounded ghw iff it has bounded hw.

1.5 Do HDs Have Any Disadvantage?

There is a small price we have to pay for the significant improvement HDs offer over other decompositions. While HDs of bounded width k, if they exist, can be computed in polynomial time, the exponent of the polynomial in the upper bound involves k as a factor. It is deemed very unlikely that we can get rid of the factor k in the exponent, because the problem of deciding whether a query has hypertree width k was shown to be fixed-parameter intractable [66].

In the database context this is not really a problem. First, as we will see below, in all benchmarks analyzed so far, the hypertree width of queries is extremely low. For an effective practical query optimization, it actually suffices to detect queries of hw 2 or 3. Second, while conjunctive queries can become quite large in practice, they hardly reach sizes of over, say, 50 atoms. With these figures, even exact HD algorithms can be used very effectively. Finally, note that in database applications it is very often the case that the same query is repeated extremely frequently over constantly changing data. It is then worthwhile first spending a little computational effort so as to get a really good decomposition and being rewarded a myriad of times afterwards by running a highly optimized query.

The situation is more problematic in the context of large constraint satisfaction problems. Such problems may have hundreds or even thousands of constraint atoms and we may want to look for decompositions of hypertree width around 20. For such problems, the current exact HD algorithms often cause memory overflow or take very long time to complete. However, more efficient algorithms have been developed that use heuristics that do not necessarily aim at an optimal HD (see Section 3.4). Moreover, for such problems, if the constraint *relations* are relatively small, then methods of computing the answer of a query by implicitly exploiting an assumed small hw, but without computing the decomposition explicitly, may be appropriate. Such methods are discussed in Section 4.2.

1.6 Do HDs Matter in Practice?

Yes, definitely. As discussed in Section 6, and as noted by many authors, hypertree decompositions are a significant and very beneficial query optimization technique. The low hypertree width of all queries in the database benchmarks we and others have analyzed, and the fact that a substantial part of the queries are not plainly acyclic supports this. HDs have been used profitably in experimental systems [1, 7, 10, 8], and we believe the time is ripe for using them in for query optimization in commercial DBMSs too.

1.7 Which Applications Are HDs Suited For?

As already discussed, hypertree decompositions are, in the first place, useful for database query optimization, not only in the classical DBMS setting, but also in the context of more modern query processing using multiway joins, and for parallel and distributed query processing. In each of this contexts, HDs can be used for generating smart and efficient query plans.

Another large application area is constraint satisfaction (see Section 7.1). The constraint satisfaction problem (CSP) has been recognized to be equivalent to conjunctive query evaluation—see [92, 108, 25]. In particular, Kolaitis and Vardi [108] pointed out that both problems are, in turn, equivalent to the *homomorphism* problem between finite relational structures. However, as already noted, practical CSPs may differ from conjunctive query answering in that they have many more constraint atoms but often (though not always) quite small relations. Therefore, with CSPs, approximate algorithms using heuristics may work better than exact decomposition algorithms, for some applications.

Other applications, which we discuss in Section 7, relate to computing Nash equilibria of games, and to the problem of winner determination in combinatorial auctions. More in general, any application that is any easier on restrictions characterized by acyclic hypergraph structures may find useful to exploit (G)HDs.

1.8 Can the Concept of HD Be Improved?

It is shown in [76] that if, in addition to the original hyperedges of a hypergraph $\mathcal{H}$, we also use some proper subsets of these hyperedges for covering the bags of a tree decomposition of $\mathcal{H}$, then we still obtain a correct decomposition, whose associated width may be smaller than $hw(\mathcal{H})$. In particular, if *all* subsets of the hyperedges of H are allowed, then the obtained width coincides with $ghw(H)$. However, this causes an exponential blow-up, as there is an exponential number of hyperedge-subsets. If, on the other hand, we use a polynomial-time function that associates a *polynomial number* of such subsets with each hypergraph, then we may obtain an improvement of HD-decompositions yielding in some cases a smaller width, while still fulfilling Conditions 1-3. This is precisely the idea of subset-based decompositions as defined in [76]. Specific subset-based decompositions are the *component decompositions* defined in [76] and the *spread-cut* decompositions defined in [37], while an interesting way of computing a subset-based decomposition *dynamically* provides the new notion of *greedy hypertree decomposition* [82, 88]. In essence, however, subset-based decompositions are generalizations of HDs that are mainly based on the same principles.

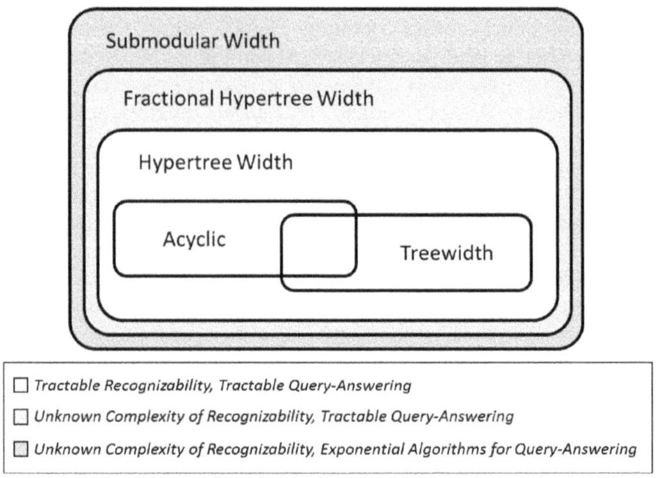

Figure 2: Relationships among hypertree decompositions and more general decomposition methods.

A more radical approach to improve HDs and even GHDs, was taken by Grohe and Marx [90], who defined *fractional hypertree decompositions (FHDs)*, giving rise to the *fractional hypertree width* $fhw(\mathcal{H})$ of a hypergraph $\mathcal{H}$ (or of a query). While hypertree decompositions exploit low cyclicity, which in a sense means a loose coherence of the variables in a query, FHDs manage to exploit, *in addition*, certain types of strong coherence between sets of variables. Moreover, even for hypergraphs $\mathcal{H}$ of low cyclicity, FHDs may yield width $fhw(\mathcal{H}) < ghw(\mathcal{H})$. The current problem with FHDs is that it is unknown whether $fhw(\mathcal{H}) \leq k$, for a fixed k, is recognizable in polynomial time. Thus, Condition 2 is not known to be satisfied. An approximate decomposition whose width is bounded by a cubic function of the fractional hypertree width can be computed in polynomial time [113]. A yet more general width-concept is *submodular width* [115]. Unfortunately, recognizing queries of bounded submodular width is not known to be tractable. Moreover, having bounded submodular width (smw) does (unfortunately) not guarantee a polynomial-time combined complexity as for GHDs, but just fixed-parameter tractability where the query hypergraph is used as a parameter. This means that we have a polynomial-time data complexity of the form $O(f_1(\mathcal{H}_Q) \cdot |\mathrm{DB}|^{f_2(\mathrm{smw})})$, where f_1 is an exponential function of the query size. Unlike the previous methods, the decompositions used to answer the query depend not only on the hypergraph $\mathcal{H}_Q$, but on the actual database DB, too. The relationships among these methods are illustrated in Figure 2—see also Section 8.

In summary, to the best of our knowledge, except for improvements such as subset-based decompositions that are essentially HD-based, there is no other improvement of hypertree decompositions that fulfills the three fundamental conditions of (1) Generalization of Acyclicity, (2) Tractable Recognizability, and (3) Tractable Query-Answering.

2. WHAT IS HYPERGRAPH ACYCLICITY?

We will adopt the standard convention of identifying a relational database instance with a logical theory consisting of ground facts [3, 134]. Accordingly, a tuple $\langle a_1, \ldots, a_k \rangle$ of constants belonging to relation r of a database DB is simply denoted by $r(a_1, \ldots, a_k) \in$ DB. The set of all constants in DB is denoted by $dom(\mathrm{DB})$.

2.1 Conjunctive Queries and Hypergraphs

A *conjunctive query* Q is a rule of the form

$$ans(\mathbf{u}) \leftarrow r_1(\mathbf{u_1}) \wedge ... \wedge r_m(\mathbf{u_m}),$$

where $r_1, ..., r_m$ are relation symbols, and $\mathbf{u}, \mathbf{u_1}, ..., \mathbf{u_m}$ are lists of terms (i.e., variables or constants). We denote by $atoms(Q)$ the set of all atoms in the right-hand side, i.e., $atoms(Q) = \{r_1(\mathbf{u_1}), ..., r_m(\mathbf{u_m})\}$. For a set A of atoms, $vars(A)$ is the set of all variables in A, and $vars(Q)$ is used for short in place of $vars(atoms(Q))$. If $\mathbf{u}$ is empty, then the query Q is said *Boolean*.

The *answer* of Q on a database DB, denoted by Q^{DB}, consists of the set of all ground facts $ans(\theta(\mathbf{u}))$ where $\theta : vars(Q) \mapsto dom(\text{DB})$ is a substitution such that:

$$\theta'(r_i(\mathbf{u_i})) \in \text{DB holds,}^1 \text{ for each } i \in \{1, ..., m\},$$

where $\theta'(t) = \theta(t)$ if $t \in vars(Q)$ and $\theta'(t) = t$ otherwise (i.e., if the term t is a constant).

There is a very natural way to associate a hypergraph $\mathcal{H}_Q = (N, H)$ with a conjunctive query Q: The set N of nodes consists of all variables in Q; for each atom in Q, the set H of hyperedges contains a hyperedge including all its variables; and no other hyperedge is in H. Note that the cardinality of H can be smaller than the cardinality of $atoms(Q)$, because two query atoms having exactly the same set of variables in their arguments give rise to only one edge in H. In the following the set of the nodes and the set of the hyperedges of any hypergraph $\mathcal{H}$ will be shortly denoted by $nodes(\mathcal{H})$ and $edges(\mathcal{H})$, respectively.

EXAMPLE 2.1. Consider the following conjunctive query Q_0 over the set $\{A, B, C, D\}$ of variables:

$$ans() \leftarrow c_1(A, B) \wedge c_2(B, C) \wedge c_3(C, D) \wedge c_4(D, A).$$

This is a Boolean query whose associated hypergraph $\mathcal{H}_{Q_0}$ is actually a graph, because each query atom is defined over precisely two variables. Indeed, $nodes(\mathcal{H}_{Q_0}) = \{A, B, C, D\}$ and $edges(\mathcal{H}_{Q_0}) = \{\{A, B\}, \{B, C\}, \{C, D\}, \{D, A\}\}$. ◁

A hypergraph $\mathcal{H}$ is *acyclic* iff it has a join tree [20]. A *join tree* $JT(\mathcal{H})$ for a hypergraph $\mathcal{H}$ is a tree whose vertices are the hyperedges of $\mathcal{H}$ such that, whenever the same node $X \in V$ occurs in two hyperedges h_1 and h_2 of $\mathcal{H}$, then X occurs in each vertex on the unique path linking h_1 and h_2 in $JT(\mathcal{H})$. This is equivalent to requiring that the decomposition vertices where X appears induce a connected subtree of T (connectedness condition). Note that this notion of hypergraph acyclicity, known as α-acyclicity, is the most general one [50]. Moreover, it is efficiently recognizable: Deciding whether a hypergraph is acyclic is feasible in linear time [133], and also in deterministic logspace. This latter property follows from the fact that hypergraph acyclicity belongs to symmetric logspace [72], and that this is equal to deterministic logspace [122].

EXAMPLE 2.2. The (hyper)graph $\mathcal{H}_{Q_0}$ associated with the query in Example 2.1 contains a cycle over A,B, C, and D. In fact, it is not possible to build a join tree for it.

Consider, then, the following conjunctive query Q_1 over the set $\{A, ..., M\}$ of variables:

$$ans() \leftarrow r_1(A, B, C) \wedge r_2(A, C, D, E, F, G, H) \wedge$$
$$r_3(H, I) \wedge r_4(I, J, K) \wedge r_5(K, L) \wedge r_6(L, M).$$

The hypergraph $\mathcal{H}_{Q_1}$ associated with the query Q_1 is the one discussed in the introduction (and reported in the left part of Figure 1). The hypergraph is acyclic as witnessed by the join tree depicted for it. More interestingly, if we consider the conjunctive query $Q_{0\wedge 1}$ such that $atoms(Q_{0\wedge 1}) = atoms(Q_0) \cup atoms(Q_1)$, i.e., the query obtained by joining all the atoms occurring in Q_0 and Q_1, then we obtain a hypergraph $\mathcal{H}_{Q_{0\wedge 1}}$ that is acyclic. Indeed, the cycle in Q_0, due to the atoms $c_1(A, B)$, $c_2(B, C)$, $c_3(C, D)$, and $c_4(D, A)$ is now "absorbed" by two hyperedges of Q_1. In fact, a join tree for $\mathcal{H}_{Q_{0\wedge 1}}$ can be easily obtained from the one shown on the left in Figure 1, by just appending the fresh vertices $\{A, B\}$, $\{B, C\}$, $\{C, D\}$, and $\{D, A\}$ as children of the vertex $\{A, C, D, E, F, G, H\}$ and $\{A, B, C\}$, as illustrated on the right of the same figure.

Instead, for the query Q_2 obtained from Q_1 by adding the atom $r_7(B, M)$ to Q_1, the associated hypergraph $\mathcal{H}_{Q_2}$ is not acyclic. This hypergraph is shown on the left of Figure 4. Note that there is no way to build a join tree for it. In particular, every attempt to add a vertex for the hyperedge $\{B, M\}$ to the join tree in Figure 1 does not satisfy the connectedness condition for B or M. ◁

2.2 Basic Properties

Acyclic queries, i.e., queries whose associated hypergraphs are acyclic, can be *efficiently answered*. More precisely, using Yannakakis' algorithm [137], Boolean acyclic queries can be evaluated by processing any of their join trees bottom-up, by performing upward semijoins between the relations associated with the query atoms, thus keeping the size of the intermediate relations small. At the end, if the relation associated with the root of the join tree is not empty, then the query evaluates to true.

For non-Boolean queries, after the bottom-up step we have described above, one can perform the opposite top-down step by filtering each child vertex from those tuples that do not match with its parent tuples. The filtered database enjoys the *global consistency* property: every tuple in every relation participates in some solution. By exploiting this property, all solutions can be computed with a backtrack-free procedure (i.e., with backtracks used to look for further solutions, and never caused by wrong choices).

Combining the fact that acyclic queries can be efficiently answered with the fact that acyclicity is efficiently recognizable, such queries identify a so-called (accessible) "island of tractability" for the query answering problem [107]—and for equivalent problems, such as conjunctive query containment, constraint satisfaction problems, and so on [72].

3. HOW TO GENERALIZE ACYCLICITY?

While acyclic queries would be very desirable due to the properties discussed in the previous section, queries arising from real applications are often precisely of this kind. As an example, consider the following query Q_3 extracted from the well-known TPC-H benchmark (*www.tpc.org/tpch*)—the original specification was given in the SQL language, and for further details we refer to [56]:

$$\begin{array}{l} ans(Name, ExtendedPrice, Discount) \leftarrow \\ \quad customer(CustKey, NationKey) \wedge orders(OrdKey, NationKey) \wedge \\ \quad lineitem(SuppKey, OrdKey, ExtendedPrice, Discount) \wedge \\ \quad supplier(SuppKey, NationKey) \wedge region(RegionKey) \wedge \\ \quad nation(Name, NationKey, RegionKey). \end{array}$$

Its associated hypergraph $\mathcal{H}_{Q_3}$, shown in Figure 3, is not acyclic. However, the hypergraph is not very intricate and its "degree of cyclicity" appears to be rather limited. Accordingly, one might naturally hope that, for queries of this kind, the nice properties of acyclic queries can be preserved. Motivated by such observations, significant efforts have been spent to investigate hypergraph properties that are best suited for identifying and efficiently processing nearly-acyclic queries. This led to the definition of a number of so-called *(purely) structural decomposition methods*.

[1]As usual, if $\mathbf{u_i}$ is the list of terms $t_1, ..., t_m$, then we denote $r_i(\theta'(t_1), ..., \theta'(t_m))$ by $\theta'(r_i(t_1, ..., t_m))$.

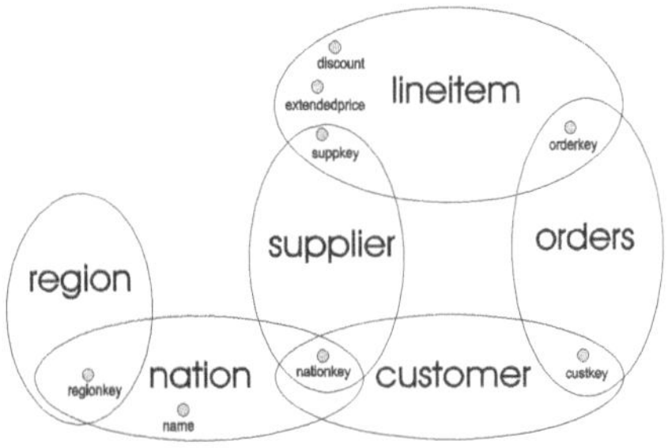

Figure 3: Hypergraph $\mathcal{H}_{Q_3}$.

3.1 Tree Decompositions

The notion of tree decomposition [123] represents a significant success story in Computer Science (see, e.g., [65]). The associated notion of *treewidth* was meant to provide a measure of the degree of cyclicity in graphs and hypergraphs.[2]

Formally, a *tree decomposition* [123] of a hypergraph $\mathcal{H}$ is a pair $\langle T, \chi \rangle$, where $T = (V, F)$ is a tree, and χ is a labeling function assigning to each vertex $p \in V$ a set of vertices $\chi(p) \subseteq nodes(\mathcal{H})$, such that the following three conditions are satisfied: (1) for each node b of $\mathcal{H}$, there exists $p \in V$ such that $b \in \chi(p)$; (2) for each hyperedge $h \in edges(\mathcal{H})$, there exists $p \in V$ such that $h \subseteq \chi(p)$; and (3) for each node b in $nodes(\mathcal{H})$, the set $\{p \in V \mid b \in \chi(p)\}$ induces a connected subtree of T. The *width* of $\langle T, \chi \rangle$ is the number $\max_{p \in V}(|\chi(p)| - 1)$. The *treewidth* of $\mathcal{H}$, denoted by $tw(\mathcal{H})$, is the minimum width over all its tree decompositions.

Recall from the introduction that the notion of treewidth does not generalize hypergraph acyclicity. For instance, consider the query Q_1 and its associated hypergraph shown in Figure 1. We have already observed that the hypergraph is acyclic (see Example 2.2), but the treewidth of this acyclic hypergraph is 6—note that there is a hyperedge defined over the variables $\{A, C, D, E, F, G, H\}$.

On the other hand, treewidth is a true generalization of graph acyclicity. Indeed, a graph is acyclic if, and only if, it has treewidth 1. In particular, note that the treewidth of a hypergraph $\mathcal{H}$ coincides with the treewidth of its *primal graph*, which is defined over the same set $nodes(\mathcal{H})$ of nodes of $\mathcal{H}$ and contains an edge for each pair of nodes included in some hyperedge of $edges(\mathcal{H})$. In fact, the notion can be applied to other graph-based representations of hypergraphs, including *dual* and *incidence* graphs representations. These approaches are contrasted with each other in [81].

Determining the treewidth of a (hyper)graph is NP-hard. However, for each fixed natural number k, checking whether its treewidth is bounded by k, and if so, computing a tree decomposition of optimal width, is achievable in linear time [23], and was shown to be achievable in logarithmic space [48]. Note that the multiplicative constant factor of Bodlaender's linear algorithm [23] is a fast growing exponential in k. However, there are algorithms that find in reasonable time tree decompositions whose width is a good upper approximation of the treewidth, in many cases of practical relevance [24].

3.2 Hypertree Decompositions

A crucial limitation for the practical use of the tree decomposition method in databases is that the method obscures, in many cases, the actual degree of cyclicity of the query hypergraph. Intuitively, many problems are easy if cycles are kept under control.

[2]Some notions strongly related to the treewidth appeared even before the 80's in the literature. It is the case of the *dimension*, defined in 1972 by Bertelé and Brioschi in the context of dynamic programming [21]. For a more detailed story, we refer to [44].

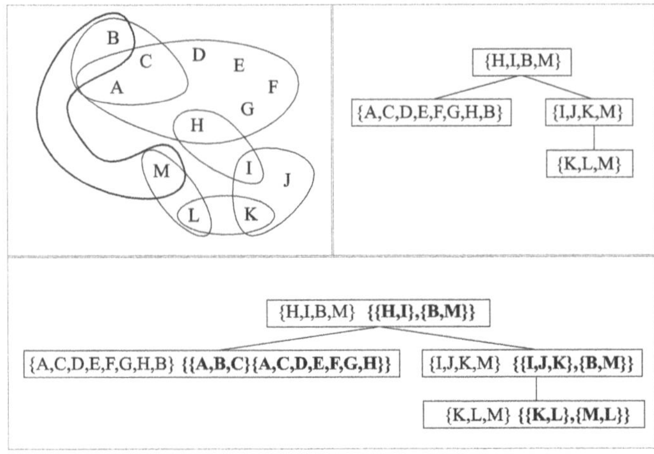

Figure 4: A hypergraph $\mathcal{H}_{Q_2}$, a tree decomposition, and a width-2 hypertree decomposition for $\mathcal{H}_{Q_2}$.

In tree decompositions, this is obtained by using suitable bags of variables in the vertices of the decomposition trees. However, in hypergraph-based problems, any hyperedge may contain a large number of variables at once, so that in order to keep cycles under control, one can exploit the power of hyperedges. Therefore, we expect that a useful measure of degree of cyclicity for hypergraphs depends on bags of hyperedges, rather than just bags of nodes. With this respect, the natural counter-part of the tree decomposition method over hypergraphs is the notion of (generalized) hypertree decomposition [74, 75].

DEFINITION 3.1 ([74]). A *generalized hypertree decomposition* of a hypergraph $\mathcal{H}$ is a triple $HD = \langle T, \chi, \lambda \rangle$, called a *hypertree* for $\mathcal{H}$, where $\langle T, \chi \rangle$ is a tree decomposition of $\mathcal{H}$, and λ is a function labeling the vertices of T by sets of hyperedges of $\mathcal{H}$ such that, for each vertex p of T, $\chi(p) \subseteq \bigcup_{h \in \lambda(v)} h$. That is, all nodes in the χ labeling are covered by hyperedges in the λ labeling.

A *hypertree decomposition* is a generalized hypertree decomposition that satisfies the following additional condition, called *Descendant Condition* or also *special condition*: for each vertex p of T and for each hyperedge $h \in \lambda(p)$, it holds that $h \cap \chi(T_p) \subseteq \chi(p)$, where T_p denotes the subtree of T rooted at p, and $\chi(T_p)$ the set of all variables occurring in the χ labeling of this subtree. Note that we are really interested in the variables occurring in the χ labels, with hyperedges in the λ labels allowing us to effectively deal with such variables. In particular, according to the Descendant Condition, if we have to deal with some variable X in the subtree T_p, then we must immediately care about it in p if it is possible (i.e., if X occurs in some hyperedge in $\lambda(p)$). This condition was introduced to simplify the computation of decompositions, as we shall see in the next section. Moreover, note that all nodes that appear in the hyperedges of $\lambda(p)$ but that are not included in $\chi(p)$ are "ineffective" for v and do not count w.r.t. the connectedness condition.

The *width* of $\langle T, \chi, \lambda \rangle$ is the number $\max_{p \in V}(|\lambda(p)|)$. The (generalized) *hypertree width* of $\mathcal{H}$, denoted by $(g)hw(\mathcal{H})$, is the minimum width over all its (generalized) hypertree decompositions. A class of hypergraphs has bounded (generalized) hypertree width if every hypergraph in the class has (generalized) hypertree width at most k, for some finite natural number $k > 0$.

The notions of hypertree width and generalized hypertree width are true generalizations of acyclicity, as the acyclic hypergraphs are precisely those hypergraphs having (generalized) hypertree width one [75]. Moreover, recall from the introduction that for each hypergraph $\mathcal{H}$, $ghw(\mathcal{H}) \leq hw(\mathcal{H}) \leq 3 \cdot ghw(\mathcal{H}) + 1$. Hence, this entails that a class of hypergraphs has bounded generalized hypertree width if, and only if, it has bounded hypertree width.

EXAMPLE 3.2. Recall the hypergraph $\mathcal{H}_{Q_2}$ shown in Figure 4. We have already observed that this hypergraph is not acyclic because it has no join tree. However, the connectedness condition can be fulfilled if one inserts additional nodes into the decomposition bags, possibly taken from multiple hyperedges. For instance, this behavior can be observed in the tree decomposition shown in the left part of Figure 4. Note that the width of this decomposition is 7, because the notion of treewidth is based on the number of nodes used in each label. However, this hypergraph is evidently quasi-acyclic. In fact, the hypertree width of $\mathcal{H}_{Q_2}$ is at most 2, because all sets of nodes used in the labels may be covered by two hyperedges at most, as witnessed by the hypertree decomposition in the bottom part of Figure 4. To complete the picture, note that the hypertree width of $\mathcal{H}_{Q_2}$ is precisely 2, because the fact that it is cyclic entails $hw(\mathcal{H}_{Q_2}) > 1$. $\lhd$

3.3 Complexity of Computing HDs

Choosing a decomposition tree and suitable labelings χ and λ in order to get a hypertree decomposition of width $\leq k$ is not that easy, and it is definitely more difficult than computing a bounded-width tree decomposition. While, as already said, deciding whether a hypergraph has generalized hypertree width at most k is NP-complete for any fixed $k \geq 3$ [76], the problem is fixed-parameter tractable if the parameter is the maximum hyperedge size (this follows from a more general result on tree projections [88]).

For those instances where the number of hyperedges and their cardinality is not small, it is convenient to look for width-k hypertree decompositions that, due to the Descendant Condition, can be computed in polynomial time [74]. Moreover, as observed above, they can differ from the best generalized hypertree decomposition of a very small constant factor. In order to get an intuition on this, it is convenient to recall here a useful characterization of hypertree decompositions in terms of the *robber and marshals game* [75].

The game is played by one robber and a number of marshals on a hypergraph. The robber moves on nodes, while marshals move on hyperedges. At each step, any marshal controls an entire hyperedge. During a move of the marshals from the set of hyperedges E to the set of hyperedges E', the robber cannot pass through the nodes in $B = (\cup E) \cap (\cup E')$, where, for a set of hyperedges F, $\cup F$ denotes the union of all hyperedges in F. Intuitively, the vertices in B are those not released by the marshals during their move from E to E'. The game is won by the marshals if they corner and capture the robber somewhere in the hypergraph, by monotonically shrinking the moving space of the robber. A hypergraph $\mathcal{H}$ has k-bounded hypertree width if, and only if, k marshals win the robber and marshals game on $\mathcal{H}$ [75]. In particular, $\mathcal{H}$ is acyclic if, and only if, one marshal wins on $\mathcal{H}$.

It can be seen that winning strategies for the marshals correspond to certain *normal form* decompositions, where the escape spaces of the robber correspond to certain components of the hypergraph and redundancies are ruled out. In such decompositions, formally defined in [74] and later strengthened in [130, 87], the number of vertices cannot exceed the number of variables of $\mathcal{H}$, and is typically much smaller. Moreover, $\mathcal{H}$ has a hypertree decomposition of width w if, and only if, it has a normal-form hypertree decomposition of the same width w. It follows that the game characterization immediately gives to us an algorithm for computing hypertree decompositions. Indeed, one can use a logspace alternating Turing machine (ATM) for deciding whether the marshals win the game in a quite natural way. It can be shown that such a machine has always polynomial space computation trees for "yes" instances, which entails that, for any fixed $k \geq 1$, deciding whether a given hypergraph has hypertree width at most k is in LOGCFL. For the sake of completeness, we recall here that the class LOGCFL consists of all decision problems that are logspace reducible to a context-free language. Note that, since LOGCFL $\subseteq$ AC^1 $\subseteq$ NC^2, deciding if a given hypergraph has hypertree width at most k is a highly parallelizable problem. Correspondingly, the problem of computing a k-bounded hypertree decomposition belongs to the functional version of LOGCFL [74].

3.4 Algorithms for Computing HDs

Based on the intuitions discussed above, a number of algorithms for computing hypertree decompositions have been proposed. The (historically) first implementation is based on dynamic programming and is a quite direct simulation of the method suggested by the game, where we evaluate a bipartite graph whose nodes encodes the possible choices of the k marshals (i.e., k-uples of hyperedges) and the possible escape spaces for the robber (i.e., components of nodes determined by the moves of the marshals) [71]. This algorithm, called `opt-`k`-decomp`, is good if we would like to compute an optimal hypertree decomposition, that is, a decomposition whose width is precisely the hypertree width of the given hypergraph. Whenever we are instead satisfied with any (possibly not optimal) width-k hypertree decomposition for some a-priori chosen width k, it may be better to tackle an opposite top-down approach, as done in the algorithm proposed in [77], which exhibits good performances by using heuristic approaches to accelerate the search for a (generalized) hypertree decomposition of width at most k (not necessarily the minimal one). The resulting algorithm `det-`k`-decomp` is based on backtracking, and can also be implemented for parallel executions.

We note however that, if the threshold width k is not very small and the hypergraph has many hyperedges, then exact algorithms may require too much time. In fact, unlike treewidth, the problem of deciding whether $hw(\mathcal{H}) \leq k$ is fixed-parameter intractable (more precisely, W[2]-hard) if the threshold k is used as parameter [66]. Therefore, unless some unlikely collapse occurs in the classes defined by the fixed-parameter complexity theory, an exponential dependency on k of the form $O(f_1(n)^{f_2(k)})$ is unavoidable. This is usually not a problem for database applications, but large hypergraphs may occur in other applications of hypertree decompositions, such as constraint satisfaction problems or those that we mention in Section 7.

For dealing with large instances, a number of algorithms based on heuristics have been proposed, in order to find efficiently (generalized) hypertree decompositions of a given hypergraph $\mathcal{H}$, without a bounded guarantee on their width. A widely used technique is to look for some tree decomposition of $\mathcal{H}$, e.g., by using the bucket elimination method by [44] or any other algorithm developed for tree decompositions [22], and then cover the bags of nodes with as few hyperedge as possible (by using set covering heuristics) in order to get a generalized hypertree decomposition. As proposed in [47, 109], this can be improved by using techniques to find good separators, that is, suitable sets of nodes that are able to partition the hypergraph to deal with the components to be decomposed—think of them as the possible escape spaces for the robber.

Other heuristic approaches aim at finding some restricted kinds of decompositions, such as the *connected* hypertree decompositions of [132]. Another technique has been discussed in [127], which shows how to use the *branch-decomposition* approach for ordinary graphs [38] for the heuristic construction of generalized hypertree decompositions (based on the fact that every branch decomposition of width k can be transformed into a tree decomposition of width at most $3k/2$). The use of tabu search for computing (generalized) hypertree decompositions was considered in [116].

A list of available implementations of algorithms for computing hypertree decompositions (and heuristics) is available at the Hypertree Decomposition HomePage [128].

4. HOW TO ANSWER A QUERY VIA HYPERTREE DECOMPOSITIONS?

There are different ways to use (generalized) hypertree decompositions for answering a query (as well as, for instance, to check query containment). We here review some of them, starting with the most natural one.

4.1 HDs and Query Plans

Let Q be a conjunctive query over a database instance DB, and let $HD = \langle T, \chi, \lambda \rangle$ be a generalized hypertree decomposition for $\mathcal{H}_Q$ whose width is k. The basic idea is to use HD as a guide for obtaining a logical query plan that allows us to answer the query in a similar way we can do for acyclic queries. A high level view of this approach is given by the following two steps.

First, for each vertex p in the decomposition tree T, we compute a fresh atom such that: its set of variables is $\chi(p)$; its relation is obtained by projecting on $\chi(p)$ the join of all relations associated with the query atoms whose sets of variables are the hyperedges in $\lambda(p)$. After that, because the χ labeling encodes a tree decomposition, it can be seen that the conjunction of these fresh atoms forms an acyclic conjunctive query, say Q', equivalent to Q. Indeed, the decomposition tree T represents a join tree of $\mathcal{H}_{Q'}$; all fresh atoms encodes subqueries of Q (hence cannot be more restrictive than the original query); and all query atoms are included in some of these subqueries (so that Q' cannot be more liberal than Q). Moreover, because the hypertree width is at most k, each subquery consists of k atoms at most and can be answered in polynomial time.

EXAMPLE 4.1. Consider the query Q_2 we have introduced in Example 2.2 and the hypertree decomposition for it depicted at the bottom of Figure 4. The root, say p_1, of the hypertree covers the hyperedges $\{H, I\}$ and $\{B, M\}$, which come from the query atoms $r_3(H, I)$ and $r_7(B, M)$. Moreover, $\chi(p_1) = \{H, I, B, M\}$, that is, all variables of these hyperedges are included in $\chi(p_1)$. Therefore, in the first phase we associate with p_1 the following query:

$$ans_1(H, I, B, M) \leftarrow r_3(H, I) \wedge r_7(B, M).$$

Similarly, for the remaining three vertices, we get:

$$\begin{aligned} ans_2(A, B, C, D, E, F, G, H) &\leftarrow r_1(A, B, C) \wedge \\ & \qquad r_2(A, C, D, E, F, G, H), \\ ans_3(I, J, K, M) &\leftarrow r_4(I, J, K) \wedge r_7(B, M), \\ ans_4(K, L, M) &\leftarrow r_5(K, L) \wedge r_6(L, M). \end{aligned}$$

Then, it can be verified immediately that the original query Q_2 is equivalent to the query Q_2' defined as follows:

$$\begin{aligned} ans() \leftarrow\ & ans_1(H, I, B, M) \wedge \\ & ans_2(A, B, C, D, E, F, G, H) \wedge \\ & ans_3(I, J, K, M) \wedge \\ & ans_4(K, L, M). \end{aligned}$$

The query Q_2' is now acyclic. Indeed, by considering the χ-labeling of the hypertree for $\mathcal{H}_{Q_2}$, we immediately get a join tree of $\mathcal{H}_{Q_2'}$. This means that, with the results for ans_1, ..., ans_4 at hand, we can answer Q_2 by using any algorithm for answering acyclic queries over Q_2'. $\lhd$

The first phase of the method is actually a polynomial-time reduction to the problem of answering an acyclic query. Indeed, from the given instance (Q, DB), we derive the acyclic instance (Q', DB') by using HD. At this point, as the second step, we can easily answer the acyclic Q' as discussed in Section 2.

Concerning the running time, let r be the size of the largest relation of the database instance DB and let m be the number of vertices of the decomposition tree, which in normal form decompositions cannot exceed the number of variables. The first phase is feasible in $O(m \cdot r^k)$, with each relation in the new database DB$'$ having at most r^k tuples. Let $r' \leq r^k$ be the actual size of the largest relation of the database DB$'$. The overall complexity immediately follows by adding the cost of evaluating the new acyclic instance, which actually dominates the overall cost: the worst-case upper bound is $O(m \cdot (r' + s) \cdot \log(r' + s))$ time and $O(m \cdot (r' + s))$ space, where s is the size of the output.

Note that the above algorithm works as well with the following *projection-free variant*: In the first phase, at each vertex p, we simply omit the projection over the $\chi(p)$ variables, and keep the full join of all the relations associated with hyperedges in $\lambda(p)$.

4.1.1 More Accurate Bounds

The above bounds are largely determined by the output size of the subqueries associated with the vertices of the decomposition tree, for which the estimate $r' = r^k$ is a very rough upper bound. In fact, a number of works recently investigated in detail how to derive more accurate bounds. For each vertex p of the decomposition tree, let Q_p be the conjunctive subquery associated with p, that is, the join of the relations associated with hyperedges in $\lambda(p)$, projected over its "local output variables" $\chi(p)$. In [67], the notion of *coloring number* $C(Q_p)$ of such a query is defined and shown to provide a tight bound, namely $r_p^{C(Q_p)}$, for the output size of Q_p, where r_p is the size of the largest relation occurring in the input database for Q_p. By using the fact that we are interested only in the output variables of the subquery Q_p, this bound improves an earlier defined bound, called *AGM bound* after the authors of [14]. This bound is based on the notion of fractional cover [90, 14] (see also Section 8). Moreover, the coloring number is able to take into account certain kinds of functional dependencies, such as keys, and can be used to provide a tight bound for the output size of the whole query Q, too.

Similar size bounds were also obtained for the factorised representations of query results [119], where relations are succinctly represented through relational algebra expressions comprising Cartesian products, relations with singleton tuples, and their unions.

The above bounds are based on structural information only, without considering (besides keys) auxiliary information about data such as relation sizes, histograms, or attributes selectivities. By using such information on the input database, yet more refined bounds can be obtained, which can also guide the search for a "good" decomposition for the given database, as we shall see later in Section 6. Besides classical estimates used in database optimization (see, e.g., [54]), we mention here the recent DBP bound, based on the notion of *degree-based packing* [97], which exploits the information on the number of tuples in which any value occurs in a relation (degree of the value).

4.1.2 Hypertree-Based Plans for Multiway Joins

Recent works have shown that traditional query optimizers are provably suboptimal on large classes of queries, and worst-case optimal algorithms have been developed [118, 136]. Such algorithms, based on a multiway join approach that may look at all atoms at once, have been implemented, e.g., in the LogicBlox system [11] and in the EmptyHeaded relational engine [1, 2]. Unfortunately, these algorithms are not able to recover the polynomial-time worst-case bounds for queries having bounded hypertree width. For instance, they may require exponential time for acyclic queries with an empty output (as long as, in principle, such queries could have an exponential number of answers). To overcome these troubles, EmptyHeaded additionally features a query compiler based on hypertrees: it searches for a GHD having the minimum possible estimated size for the intermediate results (by using fractional covers and the AGM bound), and then uses this information to determine the order of attributes to be used in the multiway joins. Such an order is also exploited for the multi-level data structures, called *tries*, used to store input and output relations, and to perform the joins efficiently. For experimental results, see Section 9. We also mention a different approach designed for the Leapfrog Trie Join algorithm [136], where (hyper)tree decompositions are used to guide a flexible caching of intermediate results [98]. The algorithm described in [103] considers also possible functional dependencies, by using the coloring number bound of [67].

Further algorithms based on multiway joins have been defined in order to guarantee the worst-case upper bound that can be obtained by using generalized hypertree decompositions of the given query (more precisely, the bound determined by its fractional hypertree width—see Section 8), without using a dynamic programming approach á la Yannakakis. This is the case in [104], where a notion of geometric resolution is defined to support different kinds of indices and even multiple indices per table. By performing such resolutions, the proposed algorithm covers the whole multidimensional (tuple) space by distinguishing the output tuples (if any) and the other infeasible (non-matching) tuples. As opposed to the standard bottom-up computation, this method can be viewed as a backtracking algorithm with memoization.

4.1.3 Parallel and Distributed Evaluation

From a computational complexity viewpoint, evaluating Boolean queries having bounded hypertree-width is LOGCFL-complete (even for binary acyclic queries) [72]. Combining the result with the techniques discussed by [73], it can be seen easily that the corresponding computation problem (output an answer) is in (functional) LOGCFL. It is known that this class contains highly parallelizable problems: Any problem in LOGCFL is solvable in logarithmic time by a concurrent-read concurrent-write *parallel random access machine* (CRCW PRAM) with a polynomial number of processors, or in $\log^2$-time by an exclusive-read exclusive-write (EREW) PRAM with a polynomial number of processors. In fact, efforts have been spent in the literature to translate these theoretical results into practical implementation of algorithms for parallel (and distributed) query evaluation.

A parallel algorithm, called DB-SHUNT, has been defined in [72] for answering Boolean acyclic queries—an extension, called ACQ, which is able to deal with acyclic queries with output variables is discussed in [68]. This algorithm is well-suited for bounded hypertree-width queries once the transformation process in Section 4.1 has been performed. The transformation itself can be done by exploiting parallelism. For instance, the data storage in the EmptyHeaded system is specifically designed to leverage SIMD parallel architectures, in particular, for the execution of the multiway joins to be performed at every vertex of the decomposition tree. Having the (equivalent) acyclic query at hand, DB-SHUNT (and ACQ) uses a special *shunt* operation based on relational algebra for contracting a join tree, akin the well-known shunt operation used for the parallel evaluation of arithmetic expressions [100]. This way, any tree can be contracted to a single node by a logarithmic number

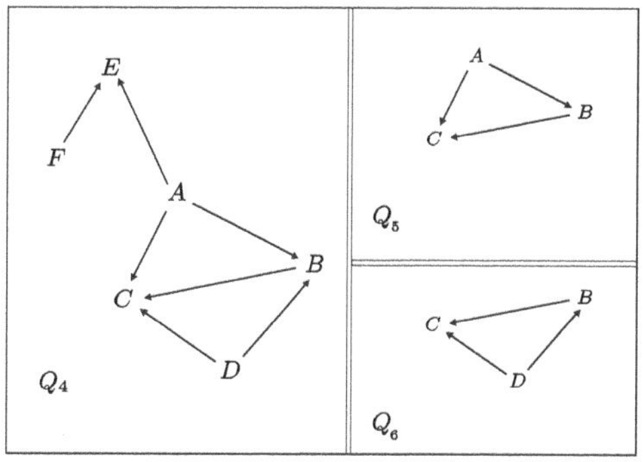

Figure 5: The (hypergraph of the) query Q_4.

of parallel steps, independently of the shape of the tree (e.g., even if the tree is a highly unbalanced chain).

More in detail, the decomposition tree T is preliminary made strictly binary, and its leaves are numbered from left to right. At each iteration, the shunt operation is applied in parallel to all odd numbered leaves of T. To avoid concurrent changes on the same relation, left and right leaves are processed in two distinct steps. Thus, after each iteration, the number of leaves is halved, and the tree-contraction ends within $2 \log m$ parallel steps by using $O(m)$ processors and $O(m)$ intermediate relations having size at most $O(r^2)$, where r is the size of the largest relation of the database instance and m is the number of vertices of T. It can be shown that, if we have a fixed number of processors $c < m/2$, then the number of parallel shunt operations becomes $2(\lceil \log c \rceil + 2\lceil m/(4c) \rceil)$. Here, transformations of query atoms and input other than relations are considered costless as long as they are polynomial. Moreover, the above cost refers to the first bottom-up processing of the decomposition tree, which is enough for the evaluation of a Boolean query. For computing the answers of a non-Boolean query, two further processing of the tree are needed, with the same cost (but for the space consumption of the final ascending phase, where we have to consider an additional cost that is linear in the output size).

An implementation of the above strategy has been recently described in [7] for the Valiant's bulk synchronous parallel (BSP) computational model [135], which can simulate the PRAM model. In this model, there are a set of connected machines that do not share any memory. The computation consists in general in a series of rounds, where machines perform some local computation in parallel and communicate messages over the network. Moreover, the same authors use generalized hypertree decompositions for parallel query answering in their GYM algorithm [7], which is a distributed and generalized version of Yannakakis' algorithm specifically designed for MapReduce [43] (as well as for other BSP-based frameworks). In fact, especially after the introduction of Google MapReduce, the problem of evaluating joins efficiently in distributed environments has been attracting much attention in the literature. In a BSP distributed environment, algorithms should mainly deal with the communication costs between the machines, and the number of global synchronizations that are needed to take place between the machines, in particular, the number of rounds of MapReduce jobs that need to be executed.

4.2 Answering Queries without Decompositions

The above approaches to answer a query need to exploit the knowledge of a suitable decomposition tree. However, approaches have been proposed in the literature that do not need this knowledge and that can answer the query by means of "local" computations only. The basic idea is, again, inspired by an interesting property of acyclic queries: local consistency entails global consistency.

4.2.1 *Answering Acyclic Queries without Join Trees*

Let DB be a database instance, let Q be a Boolean acyclic query, and let $\mathcal{V}_Q$ denote the set of relations associated with the query atoms of Q. Recall that, according to Yannakakis' algorithm [137], we can answer Q on DB by processing any join tree bottom-up, by performing upward semijoins on the relations in $\mathcal{V}_Q$.

Consider now a different approach that, at the first step, performs the semijoin between *all* pairs of relations in $\mathcal{V}_Q$, without any specific ordering. Note that the semijoin that Yannakakis' algorithm would perform as the first one is also performed at the first step of this novel approach, even though interleaved with other semijoins. The crucial observation is that these additional semijoins preserve the semantics of the query, and they can possibly help to speed up the computation: If some relation becomes empty during the process, then the answer of the query is clearly empty, too.

Let us iterate the method, by performing again semijoins between *all* pairs of relations. Of course, the semijoin that Yannakakis' algorithm would perform as the second one is also performed at this second step, even though interleaved with other semijoins that might have filtered out only tuples that will never contribute to the answer of Q.

By repeating this method for $|\mathcal{V}_Q|$ steps, since any join tree contains $|\mathcal{V}_Q|$ nodes at most, it is now clear that all semijoins that Yannakakis' algorithm would perform are also performed in the same order, just being interleaved with other semijoins—irrelevant as far as the correctness is concerned. Hence, we derive that the answer of Q is empty if, and only if, some relation becomes empty at the end of the process. Therefore, the query Q has been answered without the knowledge of any join tree, but only under the guarantee (promise) that it is actually an acyclic query. In fact, this approach involves computing $O(|\mathcal{V}_Q|^3)$ semijoins in the worst case. Hence, it is hardly useful in practice for dealing with acyclic queries, since computing a join tree is feasible in linear time [133] and since, based on it, we can answer the query with $O(|\mathcal{V}_Q|)$ semijoins only.

Actually, the approach described above is a correct query answering method not only for acyclic queries, but also for queries whose *cores* are acyclic [82, 84]. For the sake of completeness, let us recall and exemplify the concept of core. Let Q' be such that $atoms(Q') \subseteq atoms(Q)$, i.e., Q' is a subquery of Q, and assume there is a homomorphism from Q to Q'. Then, Q and Q' are *homomorphically equivalent*. Moreover, if Q' is a minimal homomorphically equivalent subquery of Q, then Q' is a *core* of Q. All cores are *isomorphic* with each other.

EXAMPLE 4.2. Consider the following query Q_4:

$$\begin{aligned} ans() \leftarrow\ & r(A,B) \wedge r(B,C) \wedge r(A,C) \wedge r(D,C) \wedge \\ & r(D,B) \wedge r(A,E) \wedge r(F,E), \end{aligned}$$

Its associated (hyper)graph is reported in Figure 5, where edge orientation just reflects the position of the variables in query atoms. Moreover, the figure reports the hypergraphs associated with the following two queries

$$\begin{aligned} Q_5 &: ans() \leftarrow r(A,B) \wedge r(B,C) \wedge r(A,C) \\ Q_6 &: ans() \leftarrow r(D,B) \wedge r(B,C) \wedge r(D,C). \end{aligned}$$

Note that Q_5 and Q_6 are two (isomorphic) cores of Q_4. ◁

Note that Yannakakis' algorithm can be still applied on queries with acyclic cores, in particular by building a join tree associated with a core. However, computing a core is a NP-hard task so that, for large queries involving many atoms or in the equivalent setting of constraint satisfaction (see Section 7), the above computation approach that does not need the knowledge of a join tree might be a more viable option. Moreover and somehow surprisingly, acyclicity of a core is a necessary condition for the approach to work. Indeed, the approach is a sound and complete query answering method for a query Q on every database instance DB if, and only if, Q has an acyclic core [82, 84].

Note that having acyclic cores characterizes the (Boolean) *semantic acyclic queries*, that is, those conjunctive queries that are equivalent to acyclic ones [17] (see also [16]). Putting it all together, we get that a Boolean conjunctive query *is a semantic acyclic query if, and only if, it can be answered by just enforcing local consistency*. However, this result stated on classes defined via "cores" is a tractability result for the *promise* version of the problem, that is, the method can be applied only if we have a guarantee on the fact that Q is a semantic acyclic query. In fact, it has been observed [129, 27] that, unless P = NP, there is no efficient way to distinguish whether a non-empty answer means that the query has a true non-empty answer, or that Q has no acyclic core.

4.2.2 *Answering Low-Width Queries without HDs*

Using algorithms for answering queries that are not acyclic, without the knowledge of a decomposition, attracted much attention in the literature (e.g., [32, 41, 13, 61]). In fact, the precise relationship between generalized hypertree decompositions and such algorithms has recently been clarified.

For any fixed natural number $k > 0$, let $\mathcal{V}_{Q,k}$ be the set of relations containing, for each k-tuple of query atoms, one relation obtained as the join of the corresponding k database relations. In this case, the idea is to repeatedly perform semijoins between all pairs of relations in $\mathcal{V}_{Q,k}$ until a fixpoint is reached. At this point, either some relation is empty or we got the so-called *k-local consistency* property. In the former case, we are sure that the answer of Q on the given database is empty. We say that a Boolean query Q can be answered by enforcing *k-local consistency* if, for any given database, its answer is non-empty if, and only if, the above procedure ends without getting empty relations (that is, we achieve k-local consistency). It has been shown that this happens if, and only if, Q has a core whose generalized hypertree width is at most k [82, 84]. Therefore, similarly to the case of acyclic queries, we can answer the query Q neither knowing the core nor knowing any generalized hypertree decomposition $\langle T, \chi, \lambda \rangle$ of $\mathcal{H}_Q$. In this extension, the semijoin operations are defined with respect to all variables occurring in the k-tuples of query atoms, that is, without considering the key role played by the variables occurring in the χ labeling in any decomposition tree. The correctness of this approach follows immediately from the correctness of the projection-free variant for answering width-k queries described in Section 4.1.

Let v be the number of variables occurring in the core of Q. Assume the core has a generalized hypertree decomposition of width k. From the results in [87] it follows that it has a decomposition of the same width which has at most v decomposition vertices. Therefore, the fixpoint for enforcing k-local consistency must end after at most $2 \cdot v$ rounds of semijoins. In particular this entails that, if a fixpoint is not reached after $2 \cdot vars(Q)$ rounds, then we are sure that the generalized hypertree width of Q (and of its core) is greater than k. Again, the notion of core plays a crucial role, so that the approach might be viewed as a viable query answering procedure in the presence of large queries for which computing a core—and a generalized hypertree decomposition (both NP-hard tasks)—may be practically infeasible. However, the tractability result holds for the promise version of the problem.

A related characterization is also known for queries that are not Boolean. In this case, k-local consistency is a sound and complete method to compute the answer of a query Q over a set W of output variables if, and only if, variables in W are covered by some vertex of a width-k generalized hypertree decomposition of some query Q' that is homomorphically equivalent to Q [82, 84]. In particular, for $k = 1$ this provides a precise characterization of the relationship between (1-)local consistency and global consistency that was missing in the classical results about acyclic queries: *local consistency entails global consistency* if, and only if, the variables occurring in each atom p of Q are covered by a join tree of some (acyclic) query homomorphically equivalent to Q. Note that we do not require the existence of a join tree covering all atoms (this would mean that Q is acyclic). Instead, we can use different equivalent queries (with their join trees/decompositions) for different atoms.

5. CAN WE GO BEYOND CONJUNCTIVE QUERIES?

Aggregation operators are very often at the basis of decision support systems examining large volumes of data, in order to obtain business intelligence. We briefly review some results based on GHDs for such queries.

5.1 Counting Query Answers

Let Q be a conjunctive query and let DB be a database instance. So far, we have focused on the problem of computing the set Q^{DB}, but in many cases we might just be interested in computing the cardinality of this set. This *counting* problem is, indeed, a natural abstraction for SQL queries specifying "COUNT" aggregates (see, e.g, [26, 28]). The challenge in counting problems is to compute the right number in polynomial time without actually computing the (possibly exponentially-many) query answers. In particular it is crucial, both in theory and in practice, to deal with queries where output variables can be specified, so that we are only interested in counting the answers projected on them. Technically, such distinguished variables are free, while all the other variables are existentially quantified. As a matter of fact, in almost all practical applications, there are many of such "auxiliary" (existentially quantified) variables whose instantiations must not be counted.

Whenever all variables are free, having bounded generalized hypertree width is a sufficient condition for the tractability of the counting problem [121]. Moreover, on fixed-arity queries, this condition is also necessary (under widely believed assumptions in parameterized complexity) [40].[3] However, in presence of projections, classical decomposition methods are not helpful. Indeed, even for acyclic queries [121], counting answers is #P-hard in this case. An algorithm counting the answers of an acyclic query Q in $O(m \cdot r^2 \cdot 4^r)$, with r being the size of the largest database relation and m the number of atoms, has been exhibited in [121]. Therefore, the evaluation is tractable over acyclic instances w.r.t. query complexity (where the database is fixed and not part of the input). The technique can be extended easily to queries having generalized hypertree width at most k, for some fixed number k (cf. [86]). Thus, to get more powerful structural results, we should distinguish the hypergraph nodes associated with free and existentially quantified variables. A sufficient condition for tractability is the existence of a homomorphically equivalent subquery Q' of Q that includes all free variables, and such that there is a width-k generalized hypertree decomposition for Q' which covers all frontiers of the free variables with the existential variables (see [86] for more information). Interestingly, it turns out that for fixed-arity queries this structural condition precisely characterizes the queries where the counting problem is tractable [33].

[3]Recall that for queries having a fixed maximum arity, bounded (generalized) hypertree width entails bounded treewidth (and vice versa), so that the two notions are interchangeable.

5.2 Further Aggregations

Answering ORDER BY queries is intimately related to the problem of computing the best solution according to the given ordering, which is incidentally another important aggregate (MAX) in SQL queries. This was first given in the context of ranking solutions to discrete optimization problems [110]. In particular, whenever the MAX problem of computing an optimal solution is feasible in polynomial time, then we can solve the problem of returning all the solutions in the ranked order with polynomial delay, as well as the more general problem of returning the best K-ranked solutions over all solutions, i.e., the top-K query evaluation problem [94].

A number of structural tractability results for MAX (so, for top-K and ORDER BY) queries are known in the literature (see, e.g., [64]). For *monotone* functions built on top of one binary aggregation operator (such as the standard $+$ and $\times$), MAX is feasible in polynomial time over queries that have bounded treewidth [45], and over queries that have bounded generalized hypertree width [106, 60]. Structural tractability results for extensions to certain (possibly) *non-monotone* functions which manipulate "small" (in fact, polynomially-bounded) values, called *smooth evaluation functions*, have also been studied [83, 64].

An implementation of some aggregation operators based on hypertree decompositions is described in [56, 57]. It can be used with any system at a logical level. For the sake of efficiency, a semijoin operator that supports the execution of these operators over decompositions is implemented in the open-source DBMS PostgreSQL. Further operators are considered in [96] for the so-called AJAR queries, that is, queries with annotated relations over which (possibly multiple) aggregations can be used. Technically, aggregations are modeled by means of semiring quantifiers that "sum over" or "marginalize out" values. It is argued that such queries can be used to extend conjunctive queries with most SQL-like aggregation operators, as well as to capture data processing problems such as probabilistic inference via message passing on graphical models [101]. The problem with these queries is finding a variable ordering that allows us to manage the aggregations by using a suitable generalized hypertree decompositions ("compatible" with the ordering), together with standard join algorithms. The proposed algorithm can efficiently be implemented in the parallel framework, by using GYM [7] and the degree-based MapReduce algorithm in [97]. Answering AJAR queries is equivalent to answering Functional Aggregate Queries [105].

6. CAN WE COMBINE STRUCTURAL AND DATA PROPERTIES?

The basic notion of hypertree decomposition ignores the quantitative aspects of data, such as attributes selectivity and degree, and cardinality of relations, as well as information on functional dependencies such as primary or external keys, and so on. Clearly enough, such knowledge, in the practice of query evaluation, may dramatically speed-up the evaluation time. In general there is an exponential number of hypertree decompositions of a given width, and every decomposition encodes a different way of aggregating groups of atoms and arranging them in a tree-like fashion. Now, as far as the theoretical tractability is concerned, we may be happy with any minimum-width decomposition, possibly measured according to the accurate bounds in Section 4. However, in practical real-world applications we have to exploit all information available about the database, and compute a decomposition that will eventually lead to the best possible evaluation performances. For instance, by using information on functional dependencies and their closure, it is possible to obtain a useful generalization of hypertree decompositions [5], while further information on the data have been used in the algorithms in [97, 2].

In order to express preferences about hypertree decompositions of a given query, a notion of *weighted* hypertree decomposition has been proposed by [130]. In a nutshell, the notion is based on fixing a weighting function that equips each (generalized) hypertree decomposition $HD = \langle T, \chi, \lambda \rangle$ of $\mathcal{H}$ with a rational number, and then on looking for a decomposition minimizing this value over all possible decompositions of some desired width.

In particular, an interesting weighting function can be obtained by estimating the cost associated with the operations required to answer Q according to the algorithm discussed in Section 4.1. Formally, if p is a vertex of T, then we define $v^*(p)$ as the cost of computing the join of all atoms associated with hyperedges in $\lambda(p)$, by eventually projecting the result over $\chi(p)$. Similarly, if p' is a child of p, then we define $e^*(p, p')$ as the cost of evaluating the semi-join between the reletion hereby computed for p and p'. These costs can be estimated via standard techniques (see, e.g., [55]), possibly combined with recent proposals [35].

Based on the functions v^* and e^*, every decomposition HD can be then associated with the weight: $\omega^*(HD) = \sum_p v^*(p) + \sum_{(p,p')} e^*(p, p')$. In [130], it has been observed that, for any fixed natural number $k > 0$, computing a normal form width-k hypertree decomposition whose ω^*-weight is the minimum possible is feasible in polynomial time. For arbitrary weighting functions, the problem has been shown to be intractable.

Further hybrid approaches, specifically designed to deal with counting problems, are discussed in [86].

7. ARE THERE APPLICATIONS OUTSIDE THE DATABASE AREA?

While originally tailored for database applications, hypertree decompositions have emerged over the years as a powerful approach to identify islands of tractability in a number of different areas of research. A few applications are discussed below. Further applications include, e.g., matrix reordering [53] and circuit design [109].

7.1 CSPs and Homomorphisms

An instance of a *constraint satisfaction problem (CSP)* (also *constraint network*) (e.g., [44]) is a triple $I = (Var, U, \mathcal{C})$, where Var is a finite set of variables, U is a finite domain of values, and $\mathcal{C} = \{C_1, C_2, \ldots, C_q\}$ is a finite set of constraints. Each constraint C_i is a pair (S_i, r_i), where S_i is a list of variables of length m_i called the *constraint scope*, and r_i is an m_i-ary relation over U, called the *constraint relation*. In fact, the tuples of r_i indicate the allowed combinations of simultaneous values for the variables S_i. A *solution* to a CSP instance is a substitution $\theta : Var \longrightarrow U$, such that for each $1 \leq i \leq q$, $S_i\theta \in r_i$. The problem of deciding whether a CSP instance has any solution is called *constraint satisfiability*. This problem is in general NP-complete.

The structure of a CSP instance I can be represented by its associated hypergraph $\mathcal{H}(I) = (V, H)$, where $V = Var$ and $H = \{S \mid (S, r) \in \mathcal{C}\}$. Constraint satisfiability is feasible in polynomial time on classes of instances having bounded hypertree width [74]. The result is the natural consequence of the fact that constraint satisfiability is essentially the same problem of answering conjunctive queries, reformulated in a different context and with a different syntax (see, e.g., [10, 93] for a recent implementation in the CSP area). Indeed, as said in Section 1.7, the two settings (CSPs and conjunctive queries) can be abstractly viewed as special instances of the *homomorphism problem*, which takes as input two finite relational structures $\mathcal{A}$ and $\mathcal{B}$, and asks whether there is a homomorphism from $\mathcal{A}$ to $\mathcal{B}$ [108]. In the CSP setting, $\mathcal{A}$ models the variables and the scopes of the constraints, while $\mathcal{B}$ models the relations associated with constraints; in the database setting, instead, $\mathcal{A}$ models the conjunctive query and $\mathcal{B}$ models the database instance.

Structural methods are used to support different techniques, too. For instance, hypertree decompositions are used for improving the performance of AND/OR search algorithms, by producing tighter bounds on the search space explored by these algorithms [120]. Some approaches also use structural methods to improve performances of algorithms based on enforcing high levels of consistencies localized to the decomposition clusters (see, e.g., [99]).

Note that the tractability results discussed in this paper refer to the so-called *uniform* CSP (homomorphism) problem, where both structures are part of the input, i.e., nothing is fixed. For completeness we recall that an interesting line of research in the CSP community looks at the so-called *non-uniform* problem, where $\mathcal{B}$ is a fixed structure (thus, any instance of such a problem just consists of some structure $\mathcal{A}$). In this case, the challenge is identifying any relational structure $\mathcal{B}$ such that all instances over this fixed structure is tractable, for any input structure $\mathcal{A}$ (see. e.g. [36]).

7.2 Strategic Games and Nash Equilibria

The theory of strategic games has important applications in economics and decision making [117]. Nash equilibria are the most prominent solution concept therein, and problems related to their computation have attracted much research in computer science [42, 34]. In general, Nash equilibria admit strategies played according to probability distributions, but in many cases it is useful to focus on *pure* strategies, which have to be played deterministically [49].

A *strategic game* [117] $\mathcal{G}$ is a tuple $\langle P, Neigh, Act, U \rangle$, where P is a non-empty set of distinct players, $Neigh : P \longrightarrow 2^P$ is a function such that for each $p \in P$, $Neigh(p) \subseteq P - \{p\}$ contains all players of interest for p, $Act : P \longrightarrow A$ is a function returning for each player p a set of possible actions $Act(p)$, and U associates a utility function $u_p : Act(p) \times_{j \in Neigh(p)} Act(j) \rightarrow \Re$ to each player p. For a player p, p_a denotes her *strategy* to play the action $a \in Act(p)$. A global strategy $\mathbf{x}$ is a set containing a strategy for each player $p \in P$ and, with a small abuse of notation, $u_p(\mathbf{x})$ denotes the output of u_p on the projection of $\mathbf{x}$ to the domain of u_p, i.e., the output of the function u_p applied to the actions played by p and her neighbors according to the strategy $\mathbf{x}$. Moreover, we denote by $\mathbf{x}_{-p}$ the set obtained by removing from $\mathbf{x}$ the strategy associated with player p. Then, we say that a global strategy $\mathbf{x}$ is a pure Nash Equilibrium for $\mathcal{G}$ if, for every player $p \in P$, there is no strategy p_a such that $u_p(\mathbf{x}) < u_p(\mathbf{x}_{-p} \cup \{p_a\})$. A game $\mathcal{G}$ is naturally associated with the *strategic dependency hypergraph* $\mathcal{H}(\mathcal{G})$, whose vertices are the players P and whose set of hyperedges is $\{\{p\} \cup Neigh(p) \mid p \in P\}$. Deciding the existence of pure Nash equilibria (and compute one, if any) is NP-hard on arbitrary strategic games. However, the problem becomes tractable on classes of games whose associated have bounded hypertree width [63]. Tractability results also hold on such structurally-restricted games, for related solution concepts [102, 80].

Decomposition methods have also been used in the related setting of *coalitional* games (see, e.g., [79, 29]), where players are not selfish and the main goal is to compute worth distributions among the agents that can be perceived as fair and stable by all of them.

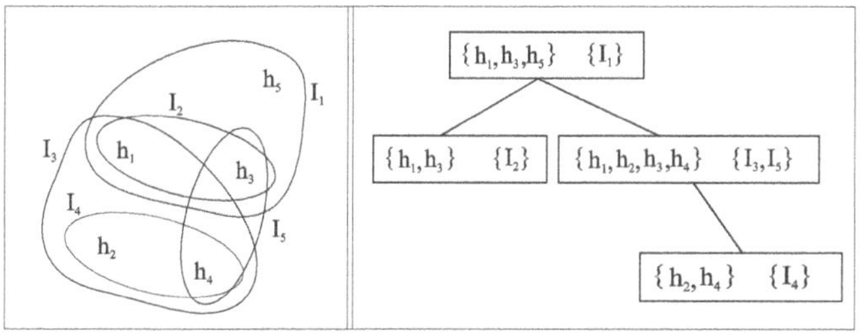

Figure 6: A dual hypergraph for a combinatorial auction, with a with-2 hypertree decomposition.

7.3 Combinatorial Auctions

Combinatorial auctions are well-known mechanisms for resource and task allocation where bidders are allowed to simultaneously bid on combinations of items. Such mechanisms apply to those situations where the bidders' valuations of bundles of items are not equal to the sum of their valuations of individual items [39].

A *combinatorial auction* is a pair $\langle \mathcal{I}, \mathcal{B} \rangle$, where $\mathcal{I} = \{I_1, ..., I_m\}$ is the set of items the auctioneer has to sell, and $\mathcal{B} = \{B_1, ..., B_n\}$ is the set of bids from the buyers interested in the items in $\mathcal{I}$. Each bid B_i has the form $\langle item(B_i), pay(B_i) \rangle$, where $pay(B_i)$ is a rational number denoting the price a buyer offers for the items in $item(B_i) \subseteq \mathcal{I}$. An outcome for $\langle \mathcal{I}, \mathcal{B} \rangle$ is a subset $\mathbf{b}$ of $\mathcal{B}$ such that $item(B_i) \cap item(B_j) = \emptyset$, for each pair B_i and B_j of bids in $\mathbf{b}$ with $i \neq j$. Bidder interaction in a combinatorial auction $\langle \mathcal{I}, \mathcal{B} \rangle$ can be represented by the so-called *dual hypergraph* $\overline{\mathcal{H}}(\langle \mathcal{I}, \mathcal{B} \rangle)$, whose nodes are the various bids in the auction and hyperedges represent items, that is, each item $\mathrm{I} \in \mathcal{I}$ is associated with a hyperedge consisting of the set of bids that contain I.

For example, the hypergraph in Figure 6, on the left, encodes an auction over items $\{\mathrm{I}_1, ..., \mathrm{I}_5\}$ and where bids are on the following bundles of items: h_1:$\{\mathrm{I}_1\}$, h_2:$\{\mathrm{I}_1, \mathrm{I}_2, \mathrm{I}_3\}$, h_3:$\{\mathrm{I}_1, \mathrm{I}_2, \mathrm{I}_5\}$, h_4:$\{\mathrm{I}_3, \mathrm{I}_4\}$, and h_5:$\{\mathrm{I}_3, \mathrm{I}_4, \mathrm{I}_5\}$. Note that this hypergraph is not acyclic and its hypertree width 2, as it is witnessed by the decomposition reported in Figure 6.

A crucial problem for combinatorial auctions is the *winner determination problem* of determining the outcome $\mathbf{b}^*$ that maximizes the sum of the accepted bid prices (i.e., $\sum_{B_i \in \mathbf{b}^*} pay(B_i)$) over all possible outcomes. The problem is in general NP-hard [125]. However, it is tractable on auctions with bounded hypertree-width dual hypergraphs [60] (see also [51]).

8. CAN WE GO BEYOND HYPERTREES?

Consider a generalized hypertree decomposition HD=$\langle T, \chi, \lambda \rangle$. The cyclicity measure used in standard generalized hypertree decompositions is based on the cardinality of the set $\lambda(p)$ in charge of covering $\chi(p)$, for each vertex p of the decomposition tree. It has been observed that a more general notion can be obtained by allowing the use of more general functions $f_{HD}(\cdot)$, to measure the weight $f_{HD}(p)$ of such a vertex, and hence to define the width of a decomposition. This is formalized in [4], where possibly infinite hypergraphs are considered, too.

In Section 1.8 a number of restrictions of GHDs, such as the *greedy hypertree decompositions* [88] and the *subset-based decompositions* [76], have been mentioned. The notion of width in such methods was however still based on the cardinality of the λ labelings. We recall some further decompositions based on more general width functions.

8.1 Fractional HDs

A *fractional hypertree decomposition* [90] of a hypergraph $\mathcal{H}$ is a pair $FHD = \langle HD, \gamma \rangle$, where $HD = \langle T, \chi, \lambda \rangle$ is a generalized hypertree decomposition of $\mathcal{H}$, and γ is a mapping associating each vertex p of T with a function $\gamma_p : \lambda(p) \mapsto \mathbb{R}$ mapping hyperedges to non-negative real numbers. For each vertex p in T, γ_p encodes a *fractional cover* of the nodes in $\chi(p)$: for each $v \in \chi(p)$, $\sum_{h \in \lambda(p), v \in h} \gamma_p(h) \geq 1$. Define $\rho(p) = \sum_{h \in \lambda(p)} \gamma_p(h)$. The *width* of FHD is the maximum of $\rho(p)$ over all vertices p in T. The *fractional hypertree width* of $\mathcal{H}$, denoted by $fhw(\mathcal{H})$, is the minimum width over all its fractional hypertree decompositions.[4]

Queries whose fhw is bounded by some constant k can be answered in polynomial time by applying the transformation of the given query Q to an acyclic query, based on the generalized hypertree decomposition HD at hand (see Section 4.1). Indeed, the maximum number of answers of the subquery Q_p associated with each vertex p is at most $|r_p|^{\rho(p)}$, where r_p is the largest database relation associated with the hyperedges in $\lambda(p)$ [90, 14]. Generalized hypertree width is obtained if in the definition of fractional hypertree decomposition we restrict the codomain of each γ_p to be integral. It is thus not surprising that there are hypergraphs where the fractional hypertree width is smaller than the (generalized) hypertree width—see Figure 2.

EXAMPLE 8.1 ([90]). For any value of $n \geq 1$, consider the hypergraph $\mathcal{H}_n$ built as follows: $\mathcal{H}_n$ has a node v_S, for each subseteq $S \subseteq \{1, ..., 2n\}$; furthermore, for every $i \in \{1, ..., 2n\}$, $\mathcal{H}_n$ has a hyperedge $h_i = \{v_S \mid i \in S\}$. It can be checked that $fhw(\mathcal{H}_n) = 2$. This is witnessed by the fractional decomposition $FHD = \langle T, \chi, \gamma \rangle$ consisting of one vertex p only and such that $\gamma_p(h_i) = 1/n$, for each hyperedge $h_i \in edges(\mathcal{H}_n)$. On the other hand, the generalized hypertree width of $\mathcal{H}_n$ is n. $\lhd$

The complexity of checking whether a hypergraph has fractional hypertree width at most w, for some fixed constant $w \geq 0$, is an open problem. However, there is a polynomial-time algorithm for deciding whether the fractional hypertree width is $f(w)$ for a function f in $O(w^3)$ [113].

8.2 Tree Projections

All the known purely-structural decomposition methods, where decompositions are only based on the (hyper)graph structure of the given query, are in fact specializations of the general and abstract framework of *tree projections* [126]. In this framework, a query Q is given together with a set $\mathcal{V}$ of atoms, called views, which are defined over the variables in Q. The question is whether (parts of) the views can be arranged as to form a tree projection (playing the role of a decomposition tree), i.e., a novel acyclic query that still "covers" Q. By representing Q and $\mathcal{V}$ via the hypergraphs $\mathcal{H}_Q$ and $\mathcal{H}_\mathcal{V}$, where hyperedges one-to-one correspond with query atoms and views, respectively, the tree projection problem reveals its graph-theoretic nature. For two hypergraphs $\mathcal{H}_1$ and $\mathcal{H}_2$, let $\mathcal{H}_1 \leq \mathcal{H}_2$ denote that each hyperedge of $\mathcal{H}_1$ is contained in some hyperedge of $\mathcal{H}_2$. Then, a tree projection of $\mathcal{H}_Q$ w.r.t. $\mathcal{H}_\mathcal{V}$ is any acyclic hypergraph $\mathcal{H}_a$ such that $\mathcal{H}_Q \leq \mathcal{H}_a \leq \mathcal{H}_\mathcal{V}$.

The existence of a tree projection is often a key to establish tractability results for decision problems [126] and for enumeration ones [85]. Moreover, it guarantees that interesting consistency properties [82] and game-theoretic characterizations [87] hold. Indeed, according to this unifying view [62], differences among the various (purely) structural decomposition methods just come in the

[4]The equivalent (original) definition in [90] does not use the λ-labeling, so that γ_p weighs all hyperedges. In practical applications, it can be convenient to consider λ, possibly for restricting the search space at each vertex. Our definition is used, e.g., in [1].

way the resource hypergraph $\mathcal{H}_2$ is defined. In particular, for a fixed natural number k, the treewidth method is obtained by considering as available hyperedges in the resource hypergraph all combinations of k nodes of $\mathcal{H}_1$; while the generalized hypertree-width method is obtained by considering, as resource hypergraph $\mathcal{H}_2$, the hypergraph $\mathcal{H}_1^k$ such that each of its hyperedge is the union of k hyperedges of $\mathcal{H}_1$. However, note that the notion of tree projection is more general then both treewidth and hypertree width, because the hyperedges of the "resource" hypergraph $\mathcal{H}_2$ may model arbitrary subproblems of the given instance whose solutions are easy to compute, or already available from previous computations (for instance, materialized views while answering database queries).

Deciding the existence of tree projections is NP-hard [76], however the problem is fixed parameter tractable, if the cardinality of the largest hyperedge of $\mathcal{H}_2$ is used as parameter [87]. A greedy technique has been proposed by [88] to identify tractable instances. This technique, when $\mathcal{H}_2 = \mathcal{H}_1^k$, provides the notion of greedy hypertree decomposition [88].

8.3 Submodular Width

While the frontier of polynomial-time tractability for conjunctive queries is still unknown, some important advances have been made with regard to a weaker notion of tractability based on parameterized complexity. Let p-CQ be the problem of answering a Boolean conjunctive query Q, parameterized by the hypergraph $\mathcal{H}_Q$. Given a set $\mathbf{H}$ of hypergraphs, let $CQ(\mathbf{H})$ denote the set of all Boolean conjunctive queries, whose associated hypergraphs belong to $\mathbf{H}$. It has been shown that, for each recursively enumerable class of hypergraphs $\mathbf{H}$, the problem p-CQ over the class of queries $CQ(\mathbf{H})$ is fixed-parameter tractable if, and only if, $\mathbf{H}$ has bounded *submodular width* (unless the Exponential Time Hypothesis [95] fails) [115]. Consider such a class $\mathbf{H}$ and assume that the submodular width of all hypergraphs in the class is at most w. Then, the result guarantees that there are two computable functions f_1 and f_2 such that each query Q in $CQ(\mathbf{H})$ can be answered over a database DB in time $O(f_1(\mathcal{H}_Q) \cdot |\text{DB}|^{f_2(w)})$. In the algorithm described in [115], f_1 has a term of the form $2^{2^{O(|V|)}}$, where V is the set of nodes in $\mathcal{H}_Q$. For the submodular width, the decompositions used to answer the query depend not only on the query hypergraph, but on the actual database DB, too. It follows that, unlike for all methods based on generalized hypertree decompositions (and tree projections), we cannot amortize the time spent in computing a good query plan beforehand through the time saved later, when Q is executed multiple times. Rather, at each query execution, we incur the same overhead exponential in the size of $\mathcal{H}_Q$.

Submodular width is more general than the fractional (and hence the generalized) hypertree width. Indeed, it has been shown that there are classes of hypergraphs having bounded submodular width, but unbounded fractional hypertree width. This follows from the results on the adaptive width in [114], and from its equivalence with the submodular width [115].

9. WHAT DO EXPERIMENTS SHOW?

Experimental evidence of the benefits gained from structural decomposition methods in query optimization (and CSP solving) has been provided in the literature by a number of different authors and in different application domains.

As already mentioned, the EmptyHeaded relational engine uses generalized hypertree decompositions in its query planner [1]. The system, supporting a rich datalog-like query language, has been tested on popular graphs datasets (Google+, Higgs, LiveJournal, Orkuts, Patent, Twitter). It emerged that graph engines supporting the same kind of high-level query language are outperformed by EmptyHeaded, which is even an order of magnitude faster than many low-level graph engines on such queries. The system has been also tested in the context of RDF processing [2], by comparing its performances with those of state-of-the-art specialized RDF engines. Experiments have been performed on the LUBM benchmark [91]. The results show that EmptyHeaded outperforms all other engines on many cyclic queries, while remaining competitive with the specialized RDF engines on the others.

In [98], similar techniques based on structural decompositions (but using a different width function) have been used to guide a flexible caching of intermediate results in the context of computing multiway joins. Experimental validation has been conducted on the SNAP collection (*https://snap.stanford.edu/data*) showing benefits over both earlier ad-hoc algorithms and standard DBMSs.

In [56, 57], a query optimizer using hypertree decompositions and taking into account the cost model discussed in Section 6 has been implemented. The optimizer can be put on top of any existing database management system supporting JDBC technology, by transparently replacing its standard optimization module. Moreover, to exploit the potential of HDs in a proper way, a special semijoin operator supporting some aggregation operators has been implemented within the PostgreSQL DBMS. The resulting prototype has been compared with standard PostgreSQL and with a well-known commercial DBMS on the TPC-H (*www.tpc.org/tpch*) benchmark, consisting of queries designed for simulating classical tasks in decision support systems. The results demonstrate a significant gain obtained by using query plans based on hypertree decompositions on queries involving more than two query atoms.

In [10], a CSP solving technique based on generalized hypertree decompositions and using compressed representations for the relations has been proposed, and its scalability has been assessed over well-known CPS benchmarks (Large bdd, VarDimacs, Modified Renault, Pret, Dubois). Another implementation focusing on large (CSP) instances is described in [112] that, in particular, focused on the so-called Modified Renault benchmark,[5] which comes from a real application concerning the configuration of a car (the Renault Megane) [9, 12]. The considered instances consist of about 150 atoms/constraints and 110 variables, with database instances where attributes have degree at most 42, and the largest constraint relation contains 48721 tuples. The generalized hypertree width is 3 for most instances (with a maximum of 4). The total number of solutions is about $2 \cdot 10^{12}$, however this information is not very meaningful, because of the many auxiliary variables occurring in the problem. Rather, by using the algorithms based on generalized hypertree decompositions, it is possible to compute the solutions of these instances (or just their number) over the actual variables of interest. None of the other available engines that we know, either in the database or in the CSP community, were able to compute such a result for those large instances. For more information, we refer to the Hypertree Decomposition Web-page [128].

10. CONCLUSION & FUTURE RESEARCH

The aim of decomposition methods is to extend the nice computational properties of acyclic queries to larger classes of queries. Hypertree decompositions serve this aim very well. They fulfill three important criteria postulated for decompositions: (1) Generalization of Acyclicity, (2) Tractable Recognizability, and (3) Tractable Query-Answering. There has been a large body of research on HDs since their introduction in 1999. However, there are still

[5] http://www.cril.univ-artois.fr/ lecoutre/benchmarks.html

many interesting questions that deserve further research, some of purely theoretical nature, some of more practical relevance.

We conclude this paper by listing those research issues which we deem most important.

- Are there substantially different decomposition methods generalizing hypertree decompositions, which still fulfill criteria 1-3?
- Are there more efficient exact algorithms for computing HDs? The best known algorithm for checking for hypertree width k runs in time exponential in $2k$. Given that the problem is fixed-parameter intractable in parameter k, we most likely cannot get rid of the constant k in the exponent, but is it maybe possible to get rid of the factor 2 in front of k?
- Further research on heuristic methods for computing HDs of "reasonably" low width would be beneficial, especially in the context of constraint satisfaction.
- In order to suitably integrate the HD method into query optimizers of existing and future DBMSs, research is needed on how this method can be effectively combined with the standard methods of logical and physical query optimization. Such combined methods could, for example, use weighted hypertree decompositions [130], see Section 6.
- It has been shown [89] (under a standard complexity assumption) that Boolean queries in a recursively enumerable class $\mathbf{Q}$ can be answered in polynomial time if, and only if, the cores of the queries in $\mathbf{Q}$ have bounded treewidth (or bounded hypertree width, as boundedness for tw and hw coincides in case of bounded arity). Is there a similar characterization for tractability for the case of unbounded arities (see also Section 8.3)? A related open question is to chart the tractability frontier for arbitrary queries, i.e., not necessarily Boolean [27, 85, 131, 15].
- Find new applications that profit from the technique of hypertree decompositions. As an example, it would be interesting to see if hypertree decompositions could be used profitably for speeding up Datalog engines (see [78, 134]), and, more specifically, widely used Datalog-based answer set programming (ASP) systems such as e.g. DLV [111]. In such systems, Datalog rules bodies essentially consist of conjunctive queries.

Acknowledgments

Georg Gottlob's work was supported by the EPSRC Programme Grant EP/M025268/"VADA: Value Added Data Systems – Principles and Architecture". The work of Gianluigi Greco and Nicola Leone was supported by the Italian Ministry of University and Research under PON project "Ba2Know (Business Analytics to Know) Service Innovation - LAB", No. PON03PE_00001_1. Gianluigi Greco's work was also supported by a Kurt Gödel Research Fellowship, awarded by the Kurt Gödel Society.

We thank Andrea Calì for comments on a draft of this paper.

11. REFERENCES

[1] C. R. Aberger, S. Tu, K. Olukotun, and C. Ré. EmptyHeaded: A Relational Engine for Graph Processing. In *Proc. of SIGMOD'16*, 2016.

[2] C. R. Aberger, S. Tu, K. Olukotun, and C. Ré. Old techniques for new join algorithms: A case study in RDF processing. *CoRR*, abs/1602.03557, 2016.

[3] S. Abiteboul, R. Hull, and V. Vianu. *Foundations of Databases: The Logical Level*. Addison-Wesley Longman Publishing Co., Inc., 1995.

[4] I. Adler. *Width functions for hypertree decompositions*. PhD thesis, Albert-Ludwigs-Universität Freiburg, 2006.

[5] I. Adler. Tree-width and functional dependencies in databases. In *Proc. of PODS'08*, pages 311–320, 2008.

[6] I. Adler, G. Gottlob, and M. Grohe. Hypertree width and related hypergraph invariants. *European Journal on Combinatorics*, 28(8):2167–2181, 2007.

[7] F. N. Afrati, M. Joglekar, C. Ré, S. Salihoglu, and J. D. Ullman. GYM: A multiround join algorithm in mapreduce. *CoRR*, abs/1410.4156, 2014.

[8] Y. Ahmad, O. Kennedy, C. Koch, and M. Nikolic. DBToaster: Higher-order delta processing for dynamic, frequently fresh views. *Proceedings of the VLDB Endowment*, 5(10):968–979, 2012.

[9] J. Amilhastre, H. Fargier, and P. Marquis. Consistency restoriation and explanations in dynamic CSPs - application to configuration. *Artificial Intelligence*, 135(1-2):199–234, 2002.

[10] K. Amroun, Z. Habbas, and W. Aggoune-Mtalaa. A compressed generalized hypertree decomposition-based solving technique for non-binary constraint satisfaction problems. *AI Communications*, 29(2):371–392, 2016.

[11] M. Aref, B. ten Cate, T. J. Green, B. Kimelfeld, D. Olteanu, E. Pasalic, T. L. Veldhuizen, and G. Washburn. Design and implementation of the logicblox system. In *Proc. of SIGMOD'15*, pages 1371–1382, 2015.

[12] J.-M. Astesana, L. Cosserat, and H. Fargier. Constraint-based vehicle configuration: A case study. In *Proc. of ICTAI'10*, pages 68–75, 2010.

[13] A. Atserias, A. Bulatov, and V. Dalmau. On the power of k-consistency. In *Proc. of ICALP'07*, pages 279–290, 2007.

[14] A. Atserias, M. Grohe, and D. Marx. Size bounds and query plans for relational joins. *SIAM Journal on Computing*, 42(4):1737–1767, 2013.

[15] G. Bagan, A. Durand, and E. Grandjean. On acyclic conjunctive queries and constant delay enumeration. In *Proc. of CSL/EACSL'07*, pages 208–222, 2007.

[16] P. Barceló, G. Gottlob, and A. Pieris. Semantic acyclicity under constraints. In *Proc. of PODS'16*, 2016.

[17] P. Barceló, M. Romero, and M. Y. Vardi. Semantic acyclicity on graph databases. In *Proc. of PODS'13*, pages 237–248, 2013.

[18] C. Beeri, R. Fagin, D. Maier, A. Mendelzon, J. Ullman, and M. Yannakakis. Properties of acyclic database schemes. In *Proc. of STOC'81*, pages 355–362, 1981.

[19] C. Beeri, R. Fagin, D. Maier, and M. Yannakakis. On the desirability of acyclic database schemes. *Journal of the ACM*, 30(3):479–513, 1983.

[20] P. A. Bernstein and N. Goodman. Power of natural semijoins. *SIAM Journal on Computing*, 10(4):751–771, 1981.

[21] U. Bertelé and F. Brioschi. *Nonserial Dynamic Programming*. Academic Press, 1972.

[22] H. Bodlaender. Treewidthlib. http://www.cs.uu.nl/research/projects/treewidthlib/.

[23] H. L. Bodlaender. A Linear Time Algorithm for Finding Tree-decompositions of Small Treewidth. In *Proc. of STOC'93*, pages 226–234, 1993.

[24] H. L. Bodlaender, F. V. Fomin, A. M. C. A. Koster, D. Kratsch, and D. M. Thilikos. On exact algorithms for

treewidth. *ACM Transactions on Algorithms*, 9(1):12:1–12:23, 2012.

[25] L. Bordeaux, Y. Hamadi, and P. Kohli, editors. *Tractability: Practical Approaches to Hard Problems*. Cambridge University Press, 2014.

[26] A. A. Bulatov. The complexity of the counting constraint satisfaction problem. *Journal of the ACM*, 60(5):34:1–34:41, 2013.

[27] A. A. Bulatov, V. Dalmau, M. Grohe, and D. Marx. Enumerating homomorphisms. *Journal of Computer and System Sciences*, 78(2):638–650, 2012.

[28] A. A. Bulatov, M. Dyer, L. A. Goldberg, M. Jerrum, and C. Mcquillan. The expressibility of functions on the boolean domain, with applications to counting CSPs. *Journal of the ACM*, 60(5):32:1–32:36, 2013.

[29] G. Chalkiadakis, G. Greco, and E. Markakis. Characteristic function games with restricted agent interactions: Core-stability and coalition structures. *Artificial Intelligence*, 232:76–113, 2016.

[30] A. K. Chandra and P. M. Merlin. Optimal implementation of conjunctive queries in relational data bases. In *Proc. of STOC'77*, pages 77–90, 1977.

[31] C. Chekuri and A. Rajaraman. Conjunctive query containment revisited. *Theoretical Computer Science*, 239(2):211–229, 2000.

[32] H. Chen and V. Dalmau. Beyond hypertree width: Decomposition methods without decompositions. In *Proc. of CP'05*, pages 167–181, 2005.

[33] H. Chen and S. Mengel. A trichotomy in the complexity of counting answers to conjunctive queries. In *Proc. of ICDT'15*, pages 110–126, 2015.

[34] X. Chen, X. Deng, and S.-H. Teng. Settling the complexity of computing two-player Nash equilibria. *Journal of the ACM*, 56(3):14:1–14:57, 2009.

[35] S. Chu, M. Balazinska, and D. Suciu. From theory to practice: Efficient join query evaluation in a parallel database system. In *Proc. of SIGMOD'15*, pages 63–78, 2015.

[36] D. A. Cohen and P. Jeavons. The complexity of constraint languages. In *Handbook of Constraint Programming*, pages 245–280. 2006.

[37] D. A. Cohen, P. Jeavons, and M. Gyssens. A unified theory of structural tractability for constraint satisfaction problems. *Journal of Computer and System Sciences*, 74(5):721–743, 2008.

[38] W. Cook and P. Seymour. Tour merging via branch-decomposition. *INFORMS Joural on Computing*, 15(3):233–248, 2003.

[39] P. Cramton, Y. Shoham, and R. Steinberg, editors. *Combinatorial Auctions*. MIT Press, 2006.

[40] V. Dalmau and P. Jonsson. The complexity of counting homomorphisms seen from the other side. *Theory of Computing Systems*, 329(1-3):315–323, 2004.

[41] V. Dalmau, P. G. Kolaitis, and M. Y. Vardi. Constraint satisfaction, bounded treewidth, and finite-variable logics. In *Proc. of CP'02*, pages 310–326, 2002.

[42] C. Daskalakis, P. W. Goldberg, and C. H. Papadimitriou. The complexity of computing a Nash equilibrium. In *Proc. of STOC'06*, pages 71–78, 2006.

[43] J. Dean and S. Ghemawat. Mapreduce: a flexible data processing tool. *Commununications of the ACM*, 53(1):72–77, 2010.

[44] R. Dechter. *Constraint Processing*. Morgan Kaufmann Publishers Inc., 2003.

[45] R. Dechter, N. Flerova, and R. Marinescu. Search Algorithms for M Best Solutions for Graphical Models. In *Proc. of AAAI'12*, pages 1895–1901, 2012.

[46] R. Dechter and J. Pearl. Tree Clustering for Constraint Networks. *Artificial Intelligence*, 38(3):353–366, 1989.

[47] A. Dermaku, T. Ganzow, G. Gottlob, B. McMahan, N. Musliu, and M. Samer. Heuristic methods for hypertree decomposition. In *Proc. of MICAI'08*, pages 1–11, 2008.

[48] M. Elberfeld, A. Jakoby, and T. Tantau. Logspace Versions of the Theorems of Bodlaender and Courcelle. In *Proc. of FOCS'10*, pages 143–152, 2010.

[49] A. Fabrikant, C. Papadimitriou, and K. Talwar. The complexity of pure Nash equilibria. In *Proc. of STOC'04*, pages 604–612, 2004.

[50] R. Fagin. Degrees of acyclicity for hypergraphs and relational database schemes. *Journal of the ACM*, 30(3):514–550, 1983.

[51] V. Fionda and G. Greco. The complexity of mixed multi-unit combinatorial auctions: Tractability under structural and qualitative restrictions. *Artificial Intelligence*, 196:1–25, 2013.

[52] E. C. Freuder. A sufficient condition for backtrack-bounded search. *Journal of the ACM*, 32(4):755–761, 1985.

[53] W. Gansterer and T. Korimort. Matrix reordering by hypertree decomposition. *AURORA TR2003-19*, 2003.

[54] H. Garcia-Molina, J. Ullman, and J. Widom. *Database Systems: The Complete Book*. Prentice-Hall, Inc., 2008.

[55] H. Garcia-Molina, J. Widom, and J. D. Ullman. *Database System Implementation*. Prentice-Hall, Inc., 1999.

[56] L. Ghionna, L. Granata, G. Greco, and F. Scarcello. Hypertree decompositions for query optimization. In *Proc. of ICDE'07*, pages 36–45, 2007.

[57] L. Ghionna, G. Greco, and F. Scarcello. H-DB: A Hybrid Quantitative-structural SQL Optimizer. In *Proc. of CIKM '11*, pages 2573–2576, 2011.

[58] N. Goodman and O. Shmueli. Characterizations of tree database schemas. *TR, Harvard University*, 1981.

[59] N. Goodman and O. Shmueli. Tree queries: A simple class of relational queries. *ACM Transactions on Database Systems*, 7(4):653–677, 1982.

[60] G. Gottlob and G. Greco. Decomposing combinatorial auctions and set packing problems. *Journal of the ACM*, 60(4):24:1–24:39, 2013.

[61] G. Gottlob, G. Greco, and B. Marnette. Hyperconsistency width for constraint satisfaction: Algorithms and complexity results. In *Graph Theory, Computational Intelligence and Thought*, pages 87–99, 2009.

[62] G. Gottlob, G. Greco, Z. Miklós, F. Scarcello, and T. Schwentick. Tree projections: Game characterization and computational aspects. In *Graph Theory, Computational Intelligence and Thought*, pages 217–226, 2009.

[63] G. Gottlob, G. Greco, and F. Scarcello. Pure Nash equilibria: hard and easy games. *Journal of Artificial Intelligence Research*, pages 357–406, 2005.

[64] G. Gottlob, G. Greco, and F. Scarcello. Tractable optimization problems through hypergraph-based structural restrictions. In *Proc. of ICALP'09*, pages 16–30, 2009.

[65] G. Gottlob, G. Greco, and F. Scarcello. Treewidth and Hypertree Width. In L. Bordeaux, Y. Hamadi, and P. Kohli, editors, *Tractability: Practical Approaches to Hard Problems*. 2012.

[66] G. Gottlob, M. Grohe, N. Musliu, M. Samer, and F. Scarcello. Hypertree decompositions: Structure, algorithms, and applications. In *Proc. of WG'05*, pages 1–15, 2005.

[67] G. Gottlob, S. T. Lee, G. Valiant, and P. Valiant. Size and Treewidth Bounds for Conjunctive Queries. *Journal of the ACM*, 59(3):1–35, 2012.

[68] G. Gottlob, N. Leone, and F. Scarcello. Advanced parallel algorithms for acyclic conjunctive queries. Technical Report DBAI-TR-98/18, Technical University of Vienna, 1998.

[69] G. Gottlob, N. Leone, and F. Scarcello. On tractable queries and constraints. In *Proc. of DEXA'99*, pages 1–15, 1999.

[70] G. Gottlob, N. Leone, and F. Scarcello. A comparison of structural CSP decomposition methods. *Artificial Intelligence*, 124(2):243–282, 2000.

[71] G. Gottlob, N. Leone, and F. Scarcello. Hypertree decompositions: A survey. In *Proc. of MFCS'01*, pages 37–57, 2001.

[72] G. Gottlob, N. Leone, and F. Scarcello. The complexity of acyclic conjunctive queries. *Journal of the ACM*, 48(3):431–498, 2001.

[73] G. Gottlob, N. Leone, and F. Scarcello. Computing LOGCFL certificates. *Theoretical Computer Science*, 270(1-2):761–777, 2002.

[74] G. Gottlob, N. Leone, and F. Scarcello. Hypertree decompositions and tractable queries. *Journal of Computer and System Sciences (conference version has appeared in PODS'99)*, 64(3):579–627, 2002.

[75] G. Gottlob, N. Leone, and F. Scarcello. Robbers, marshals, and guards: Game theoretic and logical characterizations of hypertree width. *Journal of Computer and System Sciences*, 66(4):775–808, 2003.

[76] G. Gottlob, Z. Miklós, and T. Schwentick. Generalized hypertree decompositions: NP-hardness and tractable variants. *Journal of the ACM*, 56(6):30:1–30:32, 2009.

[77] G. Gottlob and M. Samer. A backtracking-based algorithm for hypertree decomposition. *ACM Journal of Experimental Algorithmics*, 13, 2008.

[78] G. Gottlob, L. Tanca, and S. Ceri. *Logic Programming and Databases*. Springer-Verlag, 1990.

[79] G. Greco, F. Lupia, and F. Scarcello. Structural tractability of Shapley and Banzhaf values in allocation games. In *Proc. of IJCAI'15*, pages 547–553, 2015.

[80] G. Greco and F. Scarcello. On the complexity of constrained Nash equilibria in graphical games. *Theoretical Computer Science*, 410(38-40):3901–3924, 2009.

[81] G. Greco and F. Scarcello. On the power of structural decompositions of graph-based representations of constraint problems. *Artificial Intelligence*, 174(5-6):382–409, 2010.

[82] G. Greco and F. Scarcello. The power of tree projections: Local consistency, greedy algorithms, and larger islands of tractability. In *Proc. of PODS'10*, pages 327–338, 2010.

[83] G. Greco and F. Scarcello. Structural tractability of constraint optimization. In *Proc. of CP'11*, pages 340–355, 2011.

[84] G. Greco and F. Scarcello. Tree projections and structural decomposition methods: The power of local consistency. *CoRR*, abs/1205.3321, 2012.

[85] G. Greco and F. Scarcello. Structural tractability of enumerating CSP solutions. *Constraints*, 18(1):38–74, 2013.

[86] G. Greco and F. Scarcello. Counting solutions to conjunctive queries: Structural and hybrid tractability. In *Proc. of PODS'14*, pages 132–143, 2014.

[87] G. Greco and F. Scarcello. Tree projections and structural decomposition methods: Minimality and game-theoretic characterization. *Theoretical Computer Science*, 522:95–114, 2014.

[88] G. Greco and F. Scarcello. Greedy strategies and larger islands of tractability for conjunctive queries and constraint satisfaction problems. *CoRR*, abs/1603.09617, 2016.

[89] M. Grohe. The complexity of homomorphism and constraint satisfaction problems seen from the other side. *Journal of the ACM*, 54(1):1:1–1:24, 2007.

[90] M. Grohe and D. Marx. Constraint solving via fractional edge covers. *ACM Transactions on Algorithms*, 11(1):4:1–4:20, 2014.

[91] Y. Guo, Z. Pan, and J. Heflin. LUBM: A Benchmark for OWL Knowledge Base Systems. *Web Semantics*, 3(2-3):158–182, 2005.

[92] M. Gyssens, P. G. Jeavons, and D. A. Cohen. Decomposing constraint satisfaction problems using database techniques. *Artificial Intelligence*, 66(1):57–89, 1994.

[93] Z. Habbas, K. Amroun, and D. Singer. A forward-checking algorithm based on a generalised hypertree decomposition for solving non-binary constraint satisfaction problems. *Journal of Experimental and Theoretical Artificial Intelligence*, 27(5):649–671, 2015.

[94] I. F. Ilyas, G. Beskales, and M. A. Soliman. A Survey of Top-k Query Processing Techniques in Relational Database Systems. *ACM Computing Surveys*, 40(4):11:1–11:58, 2008.

[95] R. Impagliazzo, R. Paturi, and F. Zane. Which problems have strongly exponential complexity? *Journal of Computer and System Sciences*, 63(4):512–530, 2001.

[96] M. Joglekar, R. Puttagunta, and C. Ré. Aggregations over generalized hypertree decompositions. In *Proc. of PODS'16*, 2016.

[97] M. R. Joglekar and C. M. Ré. It's All a Matter of Degree: Using Degree Information to Optimize Multiway Joins. In *Proc. of ICDT'16*, volume 48, pages 11:1–11:17, 2016.

[98] O. Kalinsky, Y. Etsion, and B. Kimelfeld. Flexible caching in trie joins. *CoRR*, abs/1602.08721, 2016.

[99] S. Karakashian, R. J. Woodward, and B. Y. Choueiry. Improving the performance of consistency algorithms by localizing and bolstering propagation in a tree decomposition. In *Proc. of AAAI'13*, 2013.

[100] R. M. Karp and V. Ramachandran. Parallel algorithms for shared-memory machines. In *Handbook of Theoretical Computer Science (Vol. A)*, pages 869–941. MIT Press, 1990.

[101] K. Kask, R. Dechter, J. Larrosa, and A. Dechter. Unifying tree decompositions for reasoning in graphical models. *Artificial Intelligence*, 166(1-2):165–193, 2005.

[102] M. J. Kearns, M. L. Littman, and S. P. Singh. Graphical models for game theory. In *Proc. of UAI'01*, pages 253–260, 2001.

[103] M. A. Khamis, H. Ngo, and D. Suciu. Worst-case optimal algorithms for conjunctive queries with functional dependencies. In *Proc. of PODS'16*, 2016.

[104] M. A. Khamis, H. Q. Ngo, C. Ré, and A. Rudra. Joins via geometric resolutions: Worst-case and beyond. In *Proc. of PODS'15*, pages 213–228, 2015.

[105] M. A. Khamis, H. Q. Ngo, and A. Rudra. FAQ: questions asked frequently. In *Proc. of PODS'16*, 2016.

[106] B. Kimelfeld and Y. Sagiv. Incrementally computing ordered answers of acyclic conjunctive queries. In *Proc. of NGITS'06*, pages 141–152, 2006.

[107] P. G. Kolaitis. Constraint satisfaction, databases, and logic. In *Proc. of IJCAI'03*, pages 1587–1595, 2003.

[108] P. G. Kolaitis and M. Y. Vardi. Conjunctive-query containment and constraint satisfaction. *Journal of Computer and System Sciences*, 61(2):302–332, 2000.

[109] T. Korimort. *Heuristic Hypertree Decomposition*. PhD thesis, Technical University of Vienna, Vienna, 2003.

[110] E. L. Lawler. A procedure for computing the k best solutions to discrete optimization problems and its application to the shortest path problem. *Management Science*, 18(7):401–405, 1972.

[111] N. Leone, G. Pfeifer, W. Faber, T. Eiter, G. Gottlob, S. Perri, and F. Scarcello. The DLV system for knowledge representation and reasoning. *ACM Transactions on Computational Logics*, 7(3):499–562, 2006.

[112] F. Lupia. *Constraint Satisfaction: Algorithms, Complexity Results, and Applications*. PhD thesis, University of Calabria, 2015.

[113] D. Marx. Approximating fractional hypertree width. *ACM Transactions on Algorithms*, 6(2):29:1–29:17, 2010.

[114] D. Marx. Tractable structures for constraint satisfaction with truth tables. *Theory of Computing Systems*, 48(3):444–464, 2011.

[115] D. Marx. Tractable hypergraph properties for constraint satisfaction and conjunctive queries. *Journal of the ACM*, 60(6):42:1–42:51, 2013.

[116] N. Musliu. Generation of tree decompositions by iterated local search. In *Proc. of EvoCOP'07*, pages 130–141, 2007.

[117] J. Nash. Non-cooperative games. *Annals of Mathematics*, 54(2):286–295, 1951.

[118] H. Q. Ngo, C. Ré, and A. Rudra. Skew strikes back: new developments in the theory of join algorithms. *SIGMOD Record*, 42(4):5–16, 2013.

[119] D. Olteanu and J. Závodný. Size bounds for factorised representations of query results. *ACM Transactions on Database Systems*, 40(1):2:1–2:44, 2015.

[120] L. Otten and R. Dechter. Bounding Search Space Size via (Hyper) tree Decompositions. In *Proc. of UAI'08*, 2008.

[121] R. Pichler and S. Skritek. Tractable counting of the answers to conjunctive queries. *Journal of Computer and System Sciences*, 79(6):984–1001, 2013.

[122] O. Reingold. Undirected connectivity in log-space. *Journal of the ACM*, 55(4):17:1–17:24, 2008.

[123] N. Robertson and P. Seymour. Graph minors. II. Algorithmic aspects of tree-width. *Journal of Algorithms*, 7(3):309–322, 1986.

[124] N. Robertson and P. D. Seymour. Graph minors. III. Planar tree-width. *Journal of Combinatorial Theory, Series B*, 36(1):49–64, 1984.

[125] M. H. Rothkopf, A. Pekec, and R. M. Harstad. Computationally manageable combinatorial auctions. *Management Science*, 44:1131–1147, 1998.

[126] Y. Sagiv and O. Shmueli. Solving queries by tree projections. *ACM Transactions on Database Systems*, 18(3):487–511, 1993.

[127] M. Samer. Hypertree-decomposition via branch decomposition. In *Proc. of IJCAI'05*, pages 1535–1536, 2005.

[128] F. Scarcello. Hypertree decompositions homepage. http://www.dimes.unical.it/scarcello/Hypertrees/.

[129] F. Scarcello, G. Gottlob, and G. Greco. Uniform constraint satisfaction problems and database theory. In *Complexity of Constraints*, pages 156–195. Springer-Verlag, 2008.

[130] F. Scarcello, G. Greco, and N. Leone. Weighted hypertree decompositions and optimal query plans. *Journal of Computer and System Sciences*, 73(3):475–506, 2007.

[131] L. Segoufin. Constant delay enumeration for conjunctive queries. *SIGMOD Records*, 44(1):10–17, 2015.

[132] S. Subbarayan and H. R. Andersen. Backtracking procedures for hypertree, hyperspread and connected hypertree decomposition of CSPs. In *Proc. of IJCAI'07*, pages 180–185, 2007.

[133] R. E. Tarjan and M. Yannakakis. Simple linear-time algorithms to test chordality of graphs, test acyclicity of hypergraphs, and selectively reduce acyclic hypergraphs. *SIAM Journal on Computing*, 13(3):566–579, 1984.

[134] J. D. Ullman. *Principles of Database and Knowledge-Base Systems: Volume II: The New Technologies*. W. H. Freeman & Co., 1990.

[135] L. G. Valiant. A bridging model for parallel computation. *Commununications of the ACM*, 33(8):103–111, 1990.

[136] T. L. Veldhuizen. Triejoin: A simple, worst-case optimal join algorithm. In *Proc. of ICDT'14*, pages 96–106, 2014.

[137] M. Yannakakis. Algorithms for acyclic database schemes. In *Proc. of VLDB'81*, pages 82–94, 1981.

Incremental View Maintenance For Collection Programming*

Christoph Koch
EPFL
christoph.koch@epfl.ch

Daniel Lupei*
EPFL
daniel.lupei@epfl.ch

Val Tannen
University of Pennsylvania
val@cis.upenn.edu

ABSTRACT

In the context of incremental view maintenance (IVM), *delta* query derivation is an essential technique for speeding up the processing of large, dynamic datasets. The goal is to generate delta queries that, given a small change in the input, can update the materialized view more efficiently than via recomputation.

In this work we propose the first solution for the efficient incrementalization of positive nested relational calculus (NRC^+) on bags (with integer multiplicities). More precisely, we model the cost of NRC^+ operators and classify queries as efficiently incrementalizable if their delta has a strictly lower cost than full re-evaluation. Then, we identify IncNRC^+, a large fragment of NRC^+ that is efficiently incrementalizable and we provide a semantics-preserving translation that takes any NRC^+ query to a collection of IncNRC^+ queries. Furthermore, we prove that incremental maintenance for NRC^+ is within the complexity class NC_0 and we showcase how *recursive* IVM, a technique that has provided significant speedups over traditional IVM in the case of flat queries [25], can also be applied to IncNRC^+.

1. INTRODUCTION

Large-scale collection processing in frameworks such as Spark [41] or LINQ [33] can greatly benefit from incremental maintenance in order to minimize query latency in the face of updates. These frameworks provide collection abstractions equivalent to nested relational operators that are embarrassingly parallelizable. Also, they can be aggressively optimized using powerful algebraic laws. Language-integrated querying makes use of this algebraic framework to turn declarative collection processing queries into efficient nested calculus expressions.

Incremental view maintenance (IVM) by static query rewriting (a.k.a. delta query derivation) has proven to be a highly useful and, for instance in the context of data warehouse loading, an indispensable feature of many commercial data management systems. With delta processing, the results of a query are incrementally maintained by a delta query that, given the original input and an incremental update, computes the corresponding change of the output. Query execution can thus be staged into an offline phase for running the query over an initial database and materializing the result, followed by an online phase in which the delta query is evaluated and its result applied to the materialized view upon receiving updates. This execution model means that one can do as much as possible once and for all before any updates are first seen, rather than process the entire input every time data changes.

Delta processing is worthwhile only if delta query evaluation is much cheaper than full re-computation. In many cases deltas are actually asymptotically faster – for instance, filtering the input based on some predicate takes linear time, whereas the corresponding delta query does not need to access the database but only considers the incremental update, and thus runs in time proportional to the size of the update (in practice, usually constant time).

The benefits of incremental maintenance can be amplified if one applies it recursively [24] – the evaluation of delta queries themselves can be sped up by materializing and incrementally maintaining their results using second-order delta-queries (deltas of the delta queries). One can build a hierarchy of delta queries, where the deltas at each level are used to maintain the materialization of deltas above them, all the way up to the original query. This approach of *higher-order* delta derivation (a.k.a. recursive IVM) admits a complexity-theoretic separation between re-evaluation and incremental maintenance of positive relational queries with aggregates (RA^+_Σ) [24], and outperforms classical IVM by many orders of magnitude [25]. Unfortunately, the techniques described above target only flat relational queries and as such cannot be used to enable incremental maintenance for collection processing engines.

In this work we address the problem of delta processing for positive nested-relational calculus on bags (NRC^+). Specifically, we consider deltas for updates that are applied to the input relations via a generalized bag union $\uplus$ (which sums up multiplicities), where tuples have integer multiplicities in order to support both insertions and deletions. We formally define what it means for a nested update to be *incremental* and a NRC^+ query to be *efficiently* incrementalizable, and we propose the first solution for the efficient incremental maintenance of NRC^+ queries.

This work was supported by ERC grant 279804 and NSF grants IIS-1217798 and IIS-1302212.
*Corresponding author.

PODS'16, June 26-July 01, 2016, San Francisco, CA, USA
© 2016 ACM. ISBN 978-1-4503-4191-2/16/06...$15.00
DOI: http://dx.doi.org/10.1145/2902251.2902286

We say that a query is efficiently incrementalizable if its delta has a lower cost than recomputation. We define cost domains equipped with partial orders for every nested type in NRC$^+$ and determine cost functions for the constructs of NRC$^+$ based on their semantics and a lazy evaluation strategy. The cost domains that we use attach a cardinality estimate to each nesting level of a bag, where the cardinality of a nesting level is defined as the maximum cardinality of all the bags with the same nesting level. For example, to the nested bag $\{\{a\},\{b\},\{c,d\}\}$ we associate a cost value of $3\{2\}$, since the top bag has 3 elements and the inner bags have a maximum cardinality of 2. This choice of cost domains was motivated by the fact that data may be distributed unevenly across the nesting levels of a bag, while one can write queries that operate just on a particular nested level of the input. Even though our cost model makes several conservative approximations, it is still precise enough to separate incremental maintenance from re-evaluation for a large fragment of NRC$^+$.

We efficiently incrementalize NRC$^+$ in two steps. We first establish IncNRC$^+$, the largest fragment for which we can derive efficient deltas. Then, for queries in NRC$^+$ $\setminus$ IncNRC$^+$, we provide a semantics preserving translation into a collection of IncNRC$^+$ queries on a differently represented database.

For IncNRC$^+$ we leverage the fact that our delta transformation is *closed* (i.e. maps to the same query language) and illustrate how to further optimize delta processing using recursive IVM: if the delta of an IncNRC$^+$ query still depends on the database, it follows that it can be partially evaluated and efficiently maintained using a higher-order delta. We show that for any IncNRC$^+$ query there are only a finite number of higher-order delta derivations possible before the resulting expressions no longer depend on the database (but are purely functions of the update), and thus no longer require maintenance.

The only queries that fall outside IncNRC$^+$ are those that use the singleton bag constructor $\mathbf{sng}(e)$, where e depends on the database. This is supported by the intuition that in NRC$^+$ we do not have an efficient way to modify $\mathbf{sng}(e)$ into $\mathbf{sng}(e \uplus \Delta e)$, without first removing $\mathbf{sng}(e)$ from the view and then adding $\mathbf{sng}(e \uplus \Delta e)$, which amounts to re-computation. The challenge of efficiently applying updates to inner bags, a.k.a. *deep* updates, does not lie in designing an operator that navigates the structure of a nested object and applies the update to the right inner bag, but doing so while providing useful re-writing rules wrt. the other language constructs, which can be used to derive efficient delta queries. Previous approaches to incremental maintenance of nested views have either ignored the issue of deep updates [15], handled it by triggering recomputation of nested bags [32] or defaulted to change propagation [34, 22].

We address the problem of efficiently incrementalizing $\mathbf{sng}(e)$ with *shredding*, a semantics-preserving transformation that replaces the inner bag introduced by $\mathbf{sng}(e)$ with a label l and separately maintains the mapping between l and its defining query e. Therefore, deep updates can be applied by simply modifying the label definition corresponding to the inner bag being updated. As such, the problem of incrementalizing NRC$^+$ queries is reduced to that of incrementalizing the collection of IncNRC$^+$ queries resulting from the shredding transformation. Furthermore, based on this reduction we also show that, analogous to the flat relational case [24], incremental processing of NRC$^+$ queries is in a strictly lower complexity class than re-evaluation (NC_0 vs. TC_0).

The idea of encoding inner bags by fresh indices/labels and then keeping track of the mapping between the labels and the contents of those bags has been studied before in the literature in various contexts [9, 23, 10, 28, 38, 18]. However we are, to the best of our knowledge, the first to propose a generic and compositional shredding transformation for solving the problem of efficient IVM for NRC$^+$ queries. The compositional nature of our solution is essential for applications where nested data is exchanged between several layers of the system.

We summarize our contributions as follows:

- We define the notions of *incremental* nested update and *efficient incrementalization* of nested queries, based on cost domains and a cost interpretation over NRC$^+$'s constructs.
- We provide the first solution for the efficient incrementalization of positive nested-relational calculus (NRC$^+$).
- We show how delta processing of nested queries can be further optimized using recursive IVM [24].
- We show that incremental evaluation is in a strictly lower complexity class than re-computation (NC_0 vs. TC_0).

The rest of the paper is organized as follows. We first introduce our approach for the incrementalization of NRC$^+$ queries on a motivating example and formally define the variant of positive nested relational calculus that we use. The efficient delta processing of a large fragment of NRC$^+$ is discussed in Section 4 and in Section 5 we show how the full NRC$^+$ can be efficiently maintained. Finally, in Section 6 we review the related literature. Some of the proofs have been ommited for space reasons but can be found in the long version of this paper [26], along with additional examples/discussions.

2. MOTIVATING EXAMPLE

We follow the classical approach to incremental query evaluation, which is based on applying certain syntactic transformations called "delta rules" to the query expressions of interest (in [26] we revisit how delta processing works for the flat relational case). In the following, we give some intuition for the difficulties that arise in finding a delta rules approach to the problem of incremental computation on *nested* bag relations.

Notation. For a query Q and relation R, we denote by $Q[R]$ the fact that Q is defined in terms of input R. We will sometimes simply write Q, if R is obvious from the context.

EXAMPLE 1. *We consider the query* `related` *that computes for every movie in relation* $M(name, gen, dir)$ *a set of related movies which are either in the same genre* gen *or share the same artistic director* dir*. We define* `related` *in Spark*[1]*:*

```
case class Movie(name: String, gen: String, dir: String)
val M: RDD[Movie] = ...
val related = for(m <- M) yield (m.name, relB(m))
def relB(m: Movie) =
  for(m2 <- M if isRelated(m,m2)) yield m2.name
def isRelated(m: Movie, m2: Movie) =
  m.name != m2.name && (m.gen==m2.gen || m.dir==m2.dir)
```

[1]To improve the presentation we omitted Spark's boilerplate code.

where RDD is Spark's collection type for distributed datasets, relB(m) computes the names of all the movies related to m and isRelated tests if two different movies are related by genre or director. We evaluate related on an example instance.

M

name	*gen*	*dir*
Drive	*Drama*	*Refn*
Skyfall	*Action*	*Mendes*
Rush	*Action*	*Howard*

related[M]

name	{*name*}
Drive	{}
Skyfall	{*Rush*}
Rush	{*Skyfall*}

Now consider the outcome of updating M with ΔM via bag union $\uplus$, where ΔM is a relation with the same schema as M and contains a single tuple ⟨Jarhead, Drama, Mendes⟩.

$M \uplus \Delta M$

name	*gen*	*dir*
Drive	*Drama*	*Refn*
Skyfall	*Action*	*Mendes*
Rush	*Action*	*Howard*
Jarhead	*Drama*	*Mendes*

related[$M \uplus \Delta M$]

name	{*name*}
Drive	{*Jarhead*}
Skyfall	{*Rush, Jarhead*}
Rush	{*Skyfall* }
Jarhead	{*Drive, Skyfall*}

To incrementally update the result of **related** we design a set of delta rules that, when applied to the definition of **related**[M], give us an expression δ(**related**)[$M, \Delta M$] s.t.:

$$\texttt{related}[M \uplus \Delta M] \;=\; \texttt{related}[M] \uplus \delta(\texttt{related})[M, \Delta M].$$

For our example, in order to modify **related**[M] into **related**[$M \uplus \Delta M$], without completely replacing the existing tuples[2], one would have to add the movie Jarhead to the inner bag of related movies for Drive (same genre) and Skyfall (same director). However, our target language of Nested Relational Calculus (NRC) [6, 27, 11, 12] (with bag semantics, where tuples have integer multiplicities in order to support both insertions and deletions [29, 24]) is not equipped with the necessary constructs for expressing this kind of changes, and efficiently processing such 'deep' updates represents the main challenge in incrementally maintaining nested queries. Although update operations able to perform deep changes have been proposed in the literature [30], they lack the necessary re-write rules needed for a *closed* delta transformation, which is a prerequisite for recursive IVM.

In order to make inner bags accessible by 'deep' updates, we must first devise a naming scheme to address them. We have two options: i) we can either associate a label to each tuple in a bag and then identify an inner bag based on this label and the index of the tuple component that contains the bag, or ii) we can associate a label to each inner bag, and separately maintain a mapping between the label and the corresponding inner bag. In other words, labels can either identify the position of an inner bag within the nested value or serve as an alias for the contents of the inner bag. For example, given a value $X = \{\langle a, \{x_1, x_2\}\rangle, \langle b, \{x_3\}\rangle\}$, the first alternative decorates it with labels as follows: $\{l_1 \mapsto \langle a, \{x_1, x_2\}\rangle, l_2 \mapsto \langle b, \{x_3\}\rangle\}$, and then addresses the inner bags by $l_1.2$ and $l_2.2$. By contrast, the second approach creates the mappings $l_1 \mapsto \{x_1, x_2\}$ and $l_2 \mapsto \{x_3\}$, and then represents the original value as the flat bag $X^F = \{\langle a, l_1\rangle, \langle b, l_2\rangle\}$.

Even though both schemes faithfully represent the original nested value, we prefer the second one, a.k.a. *shredding* [9, 18], as it offers a couple of advantages. Firstly, it makes the contents of the inner bags conveniently accessible to updates via regular bag addition, without the need to introduce a custom update operation[3]. Secondly, since inner bags are represented by labels it also avoids duplicating their contents. For example, when computing the Cartesian product of X with some bag Y, one would normally create a copy of the tuples in X, along with their inner bags, for each element of Y. Moreover, any update of an inner bag from X would also have to be applied to every instance of that bag appearing in the output of $X \times Y$. By contrast, the second scheme computes the Cartesian product only between X^F and Y, while the mappings between labels and the contents of the inner bags remain untouched. Therefore, any update to an inner bag of X can be efficiently applied just by updating its corresponding mapping.

For operating over nested values represented in shredded form, we propose a semantics-preserving transformation that rewrites a query with nested output $Q[R]$ into a query Q^F returning the flat representation of the result, and a series of queries Q^Γ, computing the contents of its inner bags.

2.1 Incrementalizing related

We showcase our approach on the motivating example by first expressing it in NRC. The main constructs that we use are: i) the for-comprehension **for** x **in** Q_1 **where** $p(x)$ **union** $Q_2(x)$, which iterates over all the elements x from the output of query Q_1 that satisfy predicate $p(x)$ and unions together the results of each $Q_2(x)$, and ii) the singleton constructor **sng**(e), which creates a bag with the result of e as its only element.

$$\texttt{related} \equiv \textbf{for } m \textbf{ in } M \textbf{ union sng}(\langle m.name, \texttt{relB}(m)\rangle)$$

$$\texttt{relB}(m) \equiv \textbf{for } m_2 \textbf{ in } M \textbf{ where } \texttt{isRelated}(m, m_2)$$
$$\textbf{union sng}(m_2.name).$$

Next, we investigate the incrementalization of the constructs used by the **related** query in order to identify which one of them can lead to the problem of deep updates. The delta rule of the **for** construct is a natural generalization of the rule for Cartesian product in relational algebra[4]:

$$\begin{aligned} \delta(\textbf{for } x \textbf{ in } Q_1 \textbf{union } Q_2) = \;& \textbf{for } x \textbf{ in } \delta(Q_1) \textbf{ union } Q_2 \quad (1)\\ & \uplus \textbf{ for } x \textbf{ in } Q_1 \textbf{ union } \delta(Q_2)\\ & \uplus \textbf{ for } x \textbf{ in } \delta(Q_1) \textbf{ union } \delta(Q_2) \end{aligned}$$

assuming we can derive corresponding deltas for Q_1 and Q_2.

If the **where** clause is also present, the same rule applies because we only consider the positive fragment of nested bag languages, for which predicates are not allowed to test expressions of bag type (the reasoning behind this decision is detailed in Appendix A). Therefore the predicates in the **where** clause can only be boolean combinations of comparisons involving base type expressions and these are not affected by updates of the database.

The difficulty arises when we try to design a delta rule for singleton, specifically, how to deal with **sng**(e) when e depends on some database relation. There is plainly no way in our calculus to express the change from **sng**(M) to **sng**($M \uplus \Delta M$) in an efficient manner, i.e., one that is proportional to the size of ΔM and not the size of the output. This

[2]Maintaining the result of **related** by completely replacing the affected tuples defeats the goal of making incremental computation more efficient than full re-evaluation, as these tuples could be arbitrarily large.

[3]The authors investigated this alternative and found it particularly challenging due to the complex ways in which this custom operation would interact with the existing constructs of the language.

[4]$\delta(e_1 \times e_2) = \delta(e_1) \times e_2 \;\uplus\; e_1 \times \delta(e_2) \;\uplus\; \delta(e_1) \times \delta(e_2)$

is the same problem that we saw with the **related** example above. In Section 4 we will show that $\mathbf{sng}(e)$ is the only construct in our calculus whose efficient incrementalization relies on 'deep' updates.

2.2 Maintaining inner bags

In order to facilitate the maintenance of the bags produced by $\mathtt{relB}(m)$, we associate to each one of them a label, and we store separately a mapping between the label and its bag. Then, for implementing updates to a nested bag, we can simply modify the definition of its associated label via bag union. We note that this strategy can be applied for enacting 'deep' changes to both nested materialized views as well as nested relations in the database.

Since the bags created by $\mathtt{relB}(m)$ clearly depend on the variable m bound by the **for** construct, we also incorporate the values that m takes in the labels that replace them. The simplest way of doing so is to use labels that are pairs of indices and values, where the index uniquely identifies the inner query being replaced. In our running example, as we have just a single inner query, we only need one index ι.

The shredding of **related** yields two queries, $\mathtt{related}^F$ producing a flat version of **related** with its inner bags replaced by labels, and $\mathtt{related}^\Gamma$ that computes the value of a nested bag given a label *parameter* ℓ of the form $\langle \iota, m\rangle$

$$\mathtt{related}^F \equiv \mathbf{for}\ m\ \mathbf{in}\ M\ \mathbf{union}\ \mathbf{sng}(\langle m.name, \langle \iota, m\rangle\rangle)$$

$$\mathtt{related}^\Gamma(\ell) \equiv \mathbf{for}\ m_2\ \mathbf{in}\ M\ \mathbf{where}\ \mathtt{isRelated}(\ell.2, m_2)\ \mathbf{union}\ \mathbf{sng}(m_2.name)$$

The output of these queries on our running example is:

$\mathtt{related}^F[M]$

name	ℓ
Drive	$\langle \iota, \langle$Drive,..$\rangle\rangle$
Skyfall	$\langle \iota, \langle$Skyfall,..$\rangle\rangle$
Rush	$\langle \iota, \langle$Rush,..$\rangle\rangle$

$\mathtt{related}^\Gamma[M]$

ℓ	$\mapsto$	{*name*}
$\langle \iota, \langle$Drive,..$\rangle\rangle$	$\mapsto$	{}
$\langle \iota, \langle$Skyfall,..$\rangle\rangle$	$\mapsto$	{Rush}
$\langle \iota, \langle$Rush,..$\rangle\rangle$	$\mapsto$	{Skyfall}

Although in our example the generated queries are completely flat, this need not always be the case. In particular, in order to avoid expensive pre-/post-processing steps, one should perform shredding only down to the nesting level that is affected by the changes in the input.

Upon shredding, the strategy for incrementally maintaining **related** is to materialize and incrementally maintain $\mathtt{related}^F$ and $\mathtt{related}^\Gamma$, and then recover **related** from the results based on the following equivalence:

$$\mathtt{related} = \mathbf{for}\ r\ \mathbf{in}\ \mathtt{related}^F\ \mathbf{union}\ \mathbf{sng}(\langle r.1, \mathtt{related}^\Gamma(r.2)\rangle),$$

which holds since the values that m takes are incorporated in the labels ℓ, and $\mathtt{related}^\Gamma(\ell)$ is essentially a rewriting of the subquery $\mathtt{relB}(m)$.

We remark that, while being able to reconstruct **related** from $\mathtt{related}^F$ and $\mathtt{related}^\Gamma$ is important for proving the correctness of our transformation (see Section 5.3), it is not essential for representing the final result since the labels that appear in $\mathtt{related}^F$ can simply be seen as references to the inner bags. We also note that even though $\mathtt{related}^\Gamma$ is parameterized by ℓ, one can use standard domain maintenance techniques to materialize it since the relevant values of ℓ are ultimately those found in the tuples of $\mathtt{related}^F$. Finally, in this example the labels are in bijection with the values over which m ranges, and hence, one could use those values themselves as labels. In general however we may have several nested subqueries that depend on the same variable m.

In the process of shredding queries we replace every subquery of a singleton construct that depends on the database with a label that does not. This is the case with the subquery $\mathtt{relB}(m)$ in **related**, and we have a very simple delta rule for expressions that do not depend on the input bags: $\delta(\mathbf{sng}(\langle m.name, \langle \iota, m\rangle\rangle)) = \delta(\mathbf{sng}(m_2.name)) = \varnothing$. Therefore, applying delta rules such as (1) gives us:

$$\delta(\mathtt{related}^F) = \mathbf{for}\ m\ \mathbf{in}\ \Delta M\ \mathbf{union}\ \mathbf{sng}(\langle m.name, \langle \iota, m\rangle\rangle)$$

$$\delta(\mathtt{related}^\Gamma)(\ell) = \mathbf{for}\ m_2\ \mathbf{in}\ \Delta M\ \mathbf{where}\ \mathtt{isRelated}(\ell.2, m_2)\ \mathbf{union}\ \mathbf{sng}(m_2.name)$$

We shall prove in Section 4 that, for the class of queries to which $\mathtt{related}^F$ and $\mathtt{related}^\Gamma$ belong, the delta rules do indeed produce a proper update. We remark that since the domain of $\mathtt{related}^\Gamma$ is determined by the labels in $\mathtt{related}^F$, it may be extended by the $\delta(\mathtt{related}^F)$ update. Thus, when updating the materialization of $\mathtt{related}^\Gamma$ with the change produced by $\delta(\mathtt{related}^\Gamma)$, one must also check whether each label in its domain has an associated definition, and if not initialize it accordingly.

Cost analysis. In the following we show that maintaining **related** incrementally is more efficient than its re-evaluation (for the general case see Section 4.2). Let us assume that M and ΔM have n and d tuples, respectively, including repetitions. From the expressions above it follows that the costs of computing the original queries ($\mathtt{related}^F$ and $\mathtt{related}^\Gamma(\ell)$) is proportional to the input, while their deltas cost $O(d)$.

As previously noted, $\mathtt{related}[M \uplus \Delta M]$ can be recovered from:

$$\mathbf{for}\ r\ \mathbf{in}\ \mathtt{related}^F[M \uplus \Delta M]\ \mathbf{union}\ \mathbf{sng}(\langle r.1, \mathtt{related}^\Gamma[M \uplus \Delta M](r.2)\rangle),$$

and by the properties of delta queries and one of the general equivalence laws of the NRC [6], this becomes $V \uplus W$ where

$$V = \mathbf{for}\ r\ \mathbf{in}\ \mathtt{related}^F[M]\ \mathbf{union}\ \mathbf{sng}(\langle r.1, \mathtt{related}^\Gamma[M](r.2) \uplus \delta(\mathtt{related}^\Gamma)(r.2)\rangle) \quad (2)$$

$$W = \mathbf{for}\ r\ \mathbf{in}\ \delta(\mathtt{related}^F)\ \mathbf{union}\ \mathbf{sng}(\langle r.1, \mathtt{related}^\Gamma[M \uplus \Delta M](r.2)\rangle) \quad (3)$$

Even counting repetitions, we have $O(n)$ tuples in the materialization of $\mathtt{related}^F[M]$ while the result of computing $\delta(\mathtt{related}^F)$ has $O(d)$ tuples. From (2) the cost of computing V is $O(nd)$ and from (3) the cost of computing W is $O(d(n+d))$, where we assumed that unioning two already materialized bags takes time proportional to the smaller one, and looking up the definition of a label takes constant (amortized) time. Thus, the incremental computation of **related** costs $O(nd + d^2)$. For the costs of maintaining $\mathtt{related}^F$ and $\mathtt{related}^\Gamma$ we have $O(d)$ and $O(d(n+d))$, respectively, considering that initializing the new labels introduced by $\delta(\mathtt{related}^F)$ takes $O(dn)$ and then updating all the definitions in $\mathtt{related}^\Gamma$ takes $O((n+d)d)$ (which includes the cost of rehashing the labels in $\mathtt{related}^\Gamma$ as may be required due to its increase in size). It follows that the overall cost of IVM is $O(nd + d^2)$ and when $n \gg d$, performing IVM is clearly much better than recomputing $\mathtt{related}[M \uplus \Delta M]$ which costs $\Omega((n+d)^2)$ (in the step-counting model we have been using).

In the next sections we develop our approach in detail.

3. CALCULUS

We describe the version of the positive nested relational calculus (NRC⁺) on bags that we use. Its types are:

$$A, B, C \;:=\; 1 \mid Base \mid A \times B \mid \mathbf{Bag}(C),$$

where $Base$ is the type of the database domain and 1 denotes the "unit" type (a.k.a. the type of the 0-ary tuple $\langle\rangle$). We also use $TBase$ to denote nested tuple types with components of only $Base$ type.

In order to capture all updates, i.e., both insertions and deletions, we use a generalized notion of bag where elements have (possibly negative) integer multiplicities and bag addition $\uplus$ sums multiplicities as integers. In addition, for every bag type we have an empty bag constructor $\varnothing$, as well as construct $\ominus(e)$ that negates the multiplicities of all the elements produced by e. We remark that, semantically, bag types along with empty bag $\varnothing$, bag addition $\uplus$ and bag minus $\ominus$ exhibit the structure of a commutative group. This implies that given any two query results Q_{old} and Q_{new}, there will always exist a value ΔQ s.t. $Q_{new} = Q_{old} \uplus \Delta Q$. This rich algebraic structure that bags exhibit is also the reason why we use a calculus with bag, as opposed to set semantics.

Typed calculus expressions $\Gamma;\Pi \vdash e : \mathbf{Bag}(B)$ have two sets of type assignments to variables $\Gamma = X_1{:}\mathbf{Bag}(C_1), \cdots, X_m{:}\mathbf{Bag}(C_m)$ and $\Pi = x_1{:}A_1, \cdots, x_n{:}A_n$, in order to distinguish between variables X_i defined via **let** bindings and which reference top level bags, and variables x_i which are introduced within **for** comprehensions and bind the inner elements of a bag. We maintain this distinction since in the process of shredding we will use the latter set to generate unique labels, identifying shredded bags (section 5.1).

The typing rules and semantics of NRC⁺ are given in Figure 1, where R ranges over the relations in the database, X and x range over the variables in the contexts Γ and Π, respectively, **let** binds the result of e_1 to R and uses it in the evaluation of e_2, $\times$ performs Cartesian product of bags, **for** iteratively evaluates e_2 with x bound to every element of e_1 and then unions together all the resulting bags, **flatten** turns a bag of bags into just one bag by unioning the inner bags, **sng** places its input into a singleton bag and p stands for any predicate over tuples of primitive values. Compared to the standard formulation given in [6] we use a calculus version that is "delta-friendly" in that all expressions have bag type and more importantly most of its constructs are either linear or distributive wrt. to bag union, with the notable exception of $\mathbf{sng}(e)$. Therefore we have a bag (Cartesian) product construct instead of a pairing construct, we have a separate flattening construct, and we control carefully how singletons are constructed (note that we have four rules for singletons but they do not "overlap"). Finally, γ and ε are assignments of values to variables, and we denote their extension with a new assignment by $\gamma[X := v]$ and $\varepsilon[x := v]$, respectively. Throughout the presentation, we will omit such value assignments whenever they are not explicitly needed for resolving variable names.

Booleans are simulated by $\mathbf{Bag}(1)$, with the singleton bag $\mathbf{sng}(\langle\rangle)$ denoting *true* and the empty bag $\varnothing$ denoting *false*. Consequently, the return type of predicates $p(x)$ is also $\mathbf{Bag}(1)$. The "positivity" of the calculus is captured by the restriction put on (comparison) predicates $p(x)$ to only act on tuples of basic values since comparisons involving bags can be used to simulate negation [6](see Appendix A for a discussion about the challenges posed by negation wrt. efficient maintenance within our framework).

$$\frac{\mathrm{Sch}(R){=}B}{R : \mathbf{Bag}(B)} \qquad \frac{\Gamma;\Pi \vdash e_1{:}\, \mathbf{Bag}(C) \quad \Gamma, X{:}\mathbf{Bag}(C);\Pi \vdash e_2{:}\, \mathbf{Bag}(B)}{\Gamma;\Pi \vdash \mathbf{let}\ X := e_1\ \mathbf{in}\ e_2 : \mathbf{Bag}(B)}$$

$$\frac{}{\Gamma, X : \mathbf{Bag}(C);\Pi \vdash X : \mathbf{Bag}(C)} \qquad \frac{}{\Gamma;\Pi, x{:}TBase \vdash p(x) : \mathbf{Bag}(1)}$$

$$\frac{}{\Gamma;\Pi, x{:}A \vdash \mathbf{sng}(x) : \mathbf{Bag}(A)} \qquad \frac{}{\mathbf{sng}(\langle\rangle) : \mathbf{Bag}(1)} \qquad \frac{}{\varnothing : \mathbf{Bag}(B)}$$

$$\frac{i = 1,2}{\Gamma;\Pi, x{:}A_1{\times}A_2 \vdash \mathbf{sng}(\pi_i(x)) : \mathbf{Bag}(A_i)} \qquad \frac{e : \mathbf{Bag}(B)}{\mathbf{sng}(e) : \mathbf{Bag}(\mathbf{Bag}(B))}$$

$$\frac{\Gamma;\Pi \vdash e_1 : \mathbf{Bag}(A) \quad \Gamma;\Pi, x{:}A \vdash e_2 : \mathbf{Bag}(B)}{\Gamma;\Pi \vdash \mathbf{for}\ x\ \mathbf{in}\ e_1\ \mathbf{union}\ e_2 : \mathbf{Bag}(B)} \qquad \frac{e_{1,2} : \mathbf{Bag}(B)}{e_1 \uplus e_2 : \mathbf{Bag}(B)}$$

$$\frac{e_i : \mathbf{Bag}(B_i), i = 1,2}{e_1 \times e_2 : \mathbf{Bag}(B_1{\times}B_2)} \qquad \frac{e : \mathbf{Bag}(\mathbf{Bag}(B))}{\mathbf{flatten}(e) : \mathbf{Bag}(B)} \qquad \frac{e : \mathbf{Bag}(B)}{\ominus(e) : \mathbf{Bag}(B)}$$

$$[\![R]\!] = R \qquad [\![\mathbf{let}\ X := e_1\ \mathbf{in}\ e_2]\!]_{\gamma;\varepsilon} = [\![e_2]\!]_{\gamma[X:=[\![e_1]\!]_{\gamma;\varepsilon}];\varepsilon}$$

$$[\![X]\!]_{\gamma;\varepsilon} = \gamma(X) \qquad [\![p(x)]\!]_{\gamma;\varepsilon} = \text{ if } p(\varepsilon(x)) \text{ then } \{\langle\rangle\} \text{ else } \{\}$$

$$[\![\mathbf{sng}(x)]\!]_{\gamma;\varepsilon} = \{\varepsilon(x)\} \qquad [\![\mathbf{sng}(\pi_i(x))]\!]_{\gamma;\varepsilon} = \{\pi_i(\varepsilon(x))\}$$

$$[\![\mathbf{sng}(e)]\!] = \{[\![e]\!]\} \qquad [\![\mathbf{flatten}(e)]\!] = \biguplus\nolimits_{v\in[\![e]\!]} v$$

$$[\![\mathbf{for}\ x\ \mathbf{in}\ e_1\ \mathbf{union}\ e_2]\!]_{\gamma;\varepsilon} = \biguplus\nolimits_{v\in[\![e_1]\!]_{\gamma;\varepsilon}} [\![e_2]\!]_{\gamma;\varepsilon[x:=v]}$$

$$[\![e_1 \times e_2]\!] = \biguplus\nolimits_{v_1\in[\![e_1]\!]} \biguplus\nolimits_{v_2\in[\![e_2]\!]} \{\langle v_1, v_2\rangle\} \qquad [\![\mathbf{sng}(\langle\rangle)]\!] = \{\langle\rangle\}$$

$$[\![\varnothing]\!] = \{\} \qquad [\![e_1 \uplus e_2]\!] = [\![e_1]\!] \uplus [\![e_2]\!] \qquad [\![\ominus(e)]\!] = \ominus([\![e]\!])$$

Figure 1: Typing rules and semantics for NRC⁺.

Example 2. *Filtering an input bag R according to some predicate p can be defined in* NRC⁺ *as:*

$$\mathrm{filter}_p[R] = \mathbf{for}\ x\ \mathbf{in}\ R\ \mathbf{where}\ p(x)\ \mathbf{union}\ \mathbf{sng}(x)$$

considering that the **for** *construct with* **where** *clause (also used in Section 2) can be expressed as follows:*

$$\mathbf{for}\ x\ \mathbf{in}\ e_1\ \mathbf{where}\ p(x)\ \mathbf{union}\ e_2 =$$
$$\mathbf{for}\ x\ \mathbf{in}\ e_1\ \mathbf{union}\ \mathbf{for}\ \_\ \mathbf{in}\ p(x)\ \mathbf{union}\ e_2,$$

where we ignore the variable binding the contents of the bag returned by predicate p since its only possible value is $\langle\rangle$.

For a variable X we say that an expression e is *X-dependent* if X appears as a free variable in e, and *X-independent* otherwise. Also, among NRC⁺ expressions we distinguish between those that are *input-independent*, i.e. are *R-independent* for all relations R in the database, and those that are *input-dependent.* We define IncNRC⁺ as the fragment of NRC⁺ that uses a syntactically restricted singleton construct $\mathbf{sng}^*(e)$, where e must be *input-independent.* While this prevents IncNRC⁺ queries from adding nesting levels to their inputs[5], it does provide the useful guarantee that their deltas do not require deep updates. We take advantage of this fact in the next section, when we discuss the efficient delta-processing of IncNRC⁺. For the incrementalization of the full NRC⁺, we provide a shredding transformation taking any NRC⁺ query into a series of IncNRC⁺ queries (see Section 5).

[5]We note that the query from Section 2 does not belong to IncNRC⁺.

$$\delta_R(R) = \Delta R \qquad \delta_R(X) = \varnothing \qquad \delta_R(p(x)) = \varnothing \qquad \delta_R(\varnothing) = \varnothing$$

$$\delta_R(\textbf{let } X := e_1 \textbf{ in } e_2) = \textbf{let } X := e_1,\ \Delta X := \delta_R(e_1) \textbf{ in } \delta_R(e_2) \uplus \delta_X(e_2) \uplus \delta_R(\delta_X(e_2))$$

$$\delta_R(\textbf{sng}(x)) = \varnothing \qquad \delta_R(\textbf{sng}(\pi_i(x))) = \varnothing \qquad \delta_R(\textbf{sng}(\langle\rangle)) = \varnothing$$

$$\delta_R(\textbf{sng}^*(e)) = \varnothing \qquad \delta_R(\textbf{flatten}(e)) = \textbf{flatten}(\delta_R(e))$$

$$\delta_R(\textbf{for } x \textbf{ in } e_1 \textbf{ union } e_2) = \textbf{for } x \textbf{ in } \delta_R(e_1) \textbf{ union } e_2 \uplus \textbf{for } x \textbf{ in } e_1 \textbf{ union } \delta_R(e_2) \uplus \textbf{for } x \textbf{ in } \delta_R(e_1) \textbf{ union } \delta_R(e_2)$$

$$\delta_R(e_1 \times e_2) = \delta_R(e_1) \times e_2 \uplus e_1 \times \delta_R(e_2) \uplus \delta_R(e_1) \times \delta_R(e_2)$$

$$\delta_R(e_1 \uplus e_2) = \delta_R(e_1) \uplus \delta_R(e_2) \qquad \delta_R(\ominus(e)) = \ominus(\delta_R(e))$$

Figure 2: Delta rules for the constructs of IncNRC$^+$

4. INCREMENTALIZING IncNRC$^+$

In the following we show that any query in IncNRC$^+$ admits a delta expression with a lower cost estimate than re-evaluation. Since the derived deltas are also IncNRC$^+$ queries, their evaluation can be optimized in the same way as the original query, i.e. materialize and maintain them via delta-processing. We call the resulting expressions *higher-order* deltas. As each derivation produces 'simpler' queries, we show that the entire process has a finite number of steps and the final one is reached when the generated delta no longer depends on the database. Thus the maintenance of nested queries can be further optimized using the technique of recursive IVM, which has delivered important speedups for the flat relational case [25].

To simplify the presentation, we consider a database where a single relation R is being updated. Nonetheless, the discussion and the results carry over in a straightforward manner when updates are applied to several relations.

The delta rules for the constructs of IncNRC$^+$ wrt. the update of bag R are given in Figure 2, where ΔR is a bag containing the elements to be added/removed from R (with positive/negative multiplicity for insertions/deletions) and we use **let** $X := e_1, Y := e_2$ **in** e as a shorthand for **let** $X := e_1$ **in** (**let** $Y := e_2$ **in** e). The delta of constructs that do not depend on R is the empty bag, while the rules for the other constructs are a direct consequence of their linear or distributive behavior wrt. bag union. We show that indeed, the derived delta queries $\delta_R(h)[R, \Delta R]$ produce a correct update for the return value of h:

PROPOSITION 4.1. *Given an* IncNRC$^+$ *expression* $h[R] : \textbf{Bag}(B)$ *with input* $R : \textbf{Bag}(A)$ *and update* $\Delta R : \textbf{Bag}(A)$, *then:*

$$h[R \uplus \Delta R] \;=\; h[R] \;\uplus\; \delta_R(h)[R, \Delta R].$$

PROOF. (sketch) The proof follows via structural induction on h and from the semantics of IncNRC$^+$ constructs (extended proof in [26]). □

LEMMA 1. *The delta of an* input-independent IncNRC$^+$ *expression* h *is the empty bag,* $\delta_R(h) = \varnothing$.

The lemma above is useful for deriving in a single step the delta of *input-independent* subexpressions (as in Example 3), but it also plays an important role in showing that deltas are cheaper than the original queries (Theorem 4) and in the discussion of higher-order incrementalization (Section 4.1).

Notation. We sometimes write $\delta(h)$ instead of $\delta_R(h)$ if the updated bag R can be easily inferred from the context.

EXAMPLE 3. *Taking the delta of the* IncNRC$^+$ *query presented in Example 2 results in:*

$$\delta_R(\text{filter}_p) = \textbf{for } x \textbf{ in } \Delta R \textbf{ where } p(x) \textbf{ union } \textbf{sng}(x),$$

since $\delta_R(\textbf{for } \_ \textbf{ in } p(x) \textbf{ union } \textbf{sng}(x)) = \varnothing$ *(from Lemma 1) and* **for** x **in** e **union** $\varnothing = \varnothing$. *As expected the delta query of* filter_p *amounts to filtering the update:* $\text{filter}_p[\Delta R]$.

4.1 Higher-order delta derivation

The technique of higher-order delta derivation stems from the intuition that if the evaluation of a query can be sped up by re-using a previous result and evaluating a cheaper delta, then the same must be true for the delta query itself. This has brought about an important leap forward in the incremental maintenance of flat queries [25], and in the following we show that our approach to delta-processing enables recursive IVM for NRC$^+$ as well (since we derive 'simpler' deltas expressed in the same language as the original query).

The delta queries $\delta(h)[R, \Delta R]$ we generate may depend on both the update ΔR as well as the initial bag R. Considering that typically the updates are much smaller than the original bags and thus the cost of evaluating $\delta(h)$ is most likely dominated by the subexpressions that depend on R, it is beneficial to partially evaluate $\delta(h)[R, \Delta R]$ offline wrt. those subexpressions that depend only on R. Once ΔR becomes available, one can use the partially evaluated expression of $\delta(h)$ to quickly compute the final update for $h[R]$.

However, since the underlying bag R is continuously being updated, in order to keep using this strategy we must be able to efficiently maintain the partial evaluation of $\delta(h)$. Fortunately, $\delta(h)[R, \Delta R]$ is an IncNRC$^+$ expression just like h, and thus we can incrementally maintain its partial evaluation wrt. R based on its second-order delta $\delta^2(h)[R, \Delta R, \Delta' R]$, as in

$$\delta(h)[R \uplus \Delta' R, \Delta R] = \delta(h)[R, \Delta R] \uplus \delta^2(h)[R, \Delta R, \Delta' R],$$

where $\Delta' R$ binds the update applied to R in $\delta(h)[R, \Delta R]$.

The same strategy can be applied to $\delta^2(h)$, leading to a series $\delta^k(h)[R, \Delta R, \cdots, \Delta^{(k-1)} R]$ of partially evaluated higher-order deltas. Each is used to incrementally maintain the preceding delta $\delta^{k-1}(h)$, all the way up to the original query h.

EXAMPLE 4. *Given bag* $R : \textbf{Bag}(\textbf{Bag}(A))$ *let us consider the first and second order deltas of query* h

$$h[R] = \textbf{flatten}(R) \times \textbf{flatten}(R)$$

$$\delta(h)[R, \Delta R] = \textbf{flatten}(R) \times \textbf{flatten}(\Delta R) \uplus \textbf{flatten}(\Delta R) \times (\textbf{flatten}(R) \uplus \textbf{flatten}(\Delta R))$$

$$\delta^2(h)[\Delta R, \Delta' R] = \textbf{flatten}(\Delta' R) \times \textbf{flatten}(\Delta R) \uplus \textbf{flatten}(\Delta R) \times \textbf{flatten}(\Delta' R).$$

In the initial stage of delta-processing, besides materializing $h[R]$ *as* H_0, *we also partially evaluate* $\delta(h)$ *wrt.* R *as* $H_1[\Delta R]$. *Then, for each update* U, *we maintain* H_0 *and* $H_1[\Delta R]$ *using:*

$$H_0 = H_0 \uplus H_1[U] \qquad H_1[\Delta R] = H_1[\Delta R] \uplus \delta^2(h)[\Delta R, U].$$

We note that one can apply updates over partially evaluated expressions like $H_1[\Delta R]$ *due to the rich algebraic structure of the calculus (bags with addition and Cartesian product form a semiring) which makes it possible to factorize*

$H_1[\Delta R] \uplus \delta^2(h)[\Delta R, U]$ into subexpressions that depend on ΔR, and subexpressions that do not. Nonetheless, the process of compiling these expressions into highly optimized trigger programs is outside the scope of this work.

Finally, we remark that in the traditional IVM approach, the value of **flatten**(R) *which depends on the entire input R is recomputed for each evaluation of $\delta(h)[R, U]$, whereas with recursive IVM we evaluate it only once during the initialization phase.*

Since we can always derive an extra delta query, this process could in principle generate an infinite series of deltas and thus render the approach of recursive IVM inapplicable. By contrast, we say that a query is *recursively incrementalizable* if there exists a k such that $\delta^k(h)$ no longer depends on the input (and therefore there is no reason to continue the recursion and to derive a delta for it). In our previous example, this happened for $k = 2$. In the following we will show that any IncNRC⁺ query is *recursively incrementalizable.*

In order to determine the minimum k for which $\delta^k(h)$ is input-independent we associate to every IncNRC⁺ expression a degree $\deg_\phi(h) : \mathbb{N}$ as follows: $\deg_\phi(R) = 1$, $\deg_\phi(X) = \phi(X)$, $\deg_\phi(h) = 0$ for $h \in \{\Delta R, \varnothing, p, \mathbf{sng}(x), \mathbf{sng}(\pi_i(x)), \mathbf{sng}^*(e), \mathbf{sng}(\langle\rangle)\}$ and:

$$\deg_\phi(e_1 \uplus e_2) = \max(\deg_\phi(e_1), \deg_\phi(e_2))$$
$$\deg_\phi(\mathbf{for}\ x\ \mathbf{in}\ e_1\ \mathbf{union}\ e_2) = \deg_\phi(e_1) + \deg_\phi(e_2)$$
$$\deg_\phi(e_1 \times e_2) = \deg_\phi(e_1) + \deg_\phi(e_2)$$
$$\deg_\phi(\mathbf{flatten}(e)) = \deg_\phi(\ominus(e)) = \deg_\phi(e)$$
$$\deg_\phi(\mathbf{let}\ X := e_1\ \mathbf{in}\ e_2) = \deg_{\phi[X:=\deg_\phi(e_1)]}(e_2),$$

where ϕ associates a degree to each free variable X, corresponding to the degree of its defining expression.

We remark that the expressions h that have degree 0 are exactly those which are *input-independent.* Therefore, determining the minimum k s.t. $\delta^k(h)$ is *input-independent* means finding the minimum k s.t. $\deg(\delta^k(h)) = 0$, where $\delta^0(h) = h$. In order to show that this k is in fact the degree of h, we give the following theorem, relating the degree of an expression to the degree of its delta.

THEOREM 2. *Given an input-dependent* IncNRC⁺ *expression $h[R]$ then* $\deg(\delta(h)) = \deg(h) - 1$.

PROOF. (sketch) The proof follows by induction on the structure of h and from the definition of $\delta(\cdot)$ and $\deg(\cdot)$ (extended proof in [26]). □

Theorem 2 captures the fact that the delta of a IncNRC⁺ query is 'simpler' than the original query and we can infer from it that $\deg(\delta^k(h)) = \deg(h) - k$. It then follows that $\deg(h)$ is the minimum k s.t. $\deg(\delta^k(h))$=0, i.e. the minimum k s.t. $\delta^k(h)$ is *input-independent.*

We conclude that with recursive IVM one can avoid computing over the entire database during delta-processing by initially materializing the given query and its deltas up to $\delta^{\max(0,\deg(h)-1)}(h)$, since those are the only ones that are *input-dependent.* Then, maintaining each such materialized $H_i := \delta^i(h)$ is simply a matter of partially evaluating $\delta^{i+1}(h)$ wrt. the update and applying it to H_i. Moreover, the ability to derive higher order deltas and materialize them wrt. the database is the key result that enables the TC_0 vs. NC_0 complexity separation between nonincremental and incremental evaluation (Theorem 9).

4.2 Cost transformation

Considering that delta processing is worthwhile only if the size of the change is smaller than the original input, in this section we discuss what does it mean in the nested data model for an update to be *incremental.* Then, we provide a cost interpretation to every IncNRC⁺ expression that given the size of its input estimates the cost of generating the output. Finally, we prove that for incremental updates the derived delta query is indeed cost-effective wrt. the original query.

While for the flat relational case incrementality can be simply defined in terms of the cardinality of the input bag wrt. the cardinality of the update, this is clearly not an appropriate measure when working with nested values, since an update of small cardinality could have arbitrarily large inner bags. In order to adequately capture and compare the size of nested values we associate to every type A of our calculus a cost domain A° equipped with a partial order and minimum values. The definition of A° is designed to preserve the distribution of cost across the nested structure of A in order to accurately reflect the size of nested values and how they impact the processing of queries operating at different nesting levels. Thus, for every type in IncNRC⁺ we have:

$$Base^\circ = 1^\circ \qquad (A_1{\times}A_2)^\circ = A_1^\circ \times A_2^\circ \qquad \mathbf{Bag}(A)^\circ = \mathbb{N}^+\{A^\circ\},$$

where 1° has only the constant cost 1, we individually track the cost of each component in a tuple, and $\mathbb{N}^+\{A^\circ\}$ represents the cost of bags as the pairing between their cardinality and the least upper-bound cost of their elements[6]. Additionally, we define a family of functions $\mathrm{size}_A : A \to A^\circ$, that associate to any value $a : A$ a cost proportional to its size:

$$\mathrm{size}_{Base}(x) = 1$$
$$\mathrm{size}_{A_1\times A_2}(\langle x_1, x_2\rangle) = \langle \mathrm{size}_{A_1}(x_1), \mathrm{size}_{A_2}(x_2)\rangle$$
$$\mathrm{size}_{\mathbf{Bag}(C)}(X) = |X|\{\sup_{x_i \in X} \mathrm{size}_C(x_i)\},$$

where the supremum function is defined based on the following type-indexed partial ordering relation $\prec_A$:

$$x \prec_{Base} y \qquad = \text{false}$$
$$\langle x_1, x_2\rangle \prec_{A_1\times A_2} \langle y_1, y_2\rangle \qquad = x_1 \prec_{A_1} y_1 \text{ and } x_2 \prec_{A_2} y_2$$
$$n\{x\} \prec_{\mathbf{Bag}(C)} m\{y\} \qquad = n < m \text{ and } x \preceq_C y.$$

Finally, the $x \preceq_A y$ ordering is defined analogously to $\prec_A$ by making all the comparisons above non-strict, with the exception of *Base* values for which we have $x \preceq_{Base} y = \text{true}$. We denote by 1_A the bottom element of $(A^\circ, \prec_A)$.

We can now say that an update ΔR for a nested bag R is *incremental* if $\mathrm{size}(\Delta R) \prec \mathrm{size}(R)$.

EXAMPLE 5. *The size of bag R:*$\mathbf{Bag}(String{\times}\mathbf{Bag}(String))$, *$R = \{\langle Comedy, \{Carnage\}\rangle, \langle Animation, \{Up, Shrek, Cars\}\rangle\}$ is estimated as* $\mathrm{size}(R) : \mathbb{N}^+\{1^\circ \times \mathbb{N}^+\{1^\circ\}\} = 2\{\langle 1, 3\{1\}\rangle\}$.

Notation. Whenever the cardinality estimation of a bag is 1, we simply write $\{c\}$ as opposed to $1\{c\}$, where c is the cost estimation for its elements.

Given an IncNRC⁺ expression $e : \mathbf{Bag}(B)$, we derive its cost $\mathcal{C}[\![e]\!] : \mathbb{N}^+\{B^\circ\}$ based on the transformation in Figure 3, where γ° and ε° are cost assignments to variables. The generated costs have two components: one that computes an upper bound for the cardinality of the output bag, denoted

[6] We use $\mathbb{N}^+\{A^\circ\}$ instead of $\mathbb{N}^+ \times A^\circ$ to distinguish it from the cost domain of tuples.

$$\mathcal{C}[\![R]\!] = \text{size}(R) \qquad \mathcal{C}[\![\mathbf{sng}(x)]\!]_{\gamma^\circ;\varepsilon^\circ} = \{\varepsilon^\circ(x)\}$$
$$\mathcal{C}[\![X]\!]_{\gamma^\circ;\varepsilon^\circ} = \gamma^\circ(X) \qquad \mathcal{C}[\![\mathbf{sng}(\pi_i(x))]\!]_{\gamma^\circ;\varepsilon^\circ} = \{\pi_i(\varepsilon^\circ(x))\}$$
$$\mathcal{C}[\![p(x)]\!] = 1_{\mathbf{Bag}(1)} \qquad \mathcal{C}[\![\mathbf{sng}(\langle\rangle)]\!] = 1_{\mathbf{Bag}(1)}$$
$$\mathcal{C}[\![\varnothing]\!] = 1_{\mathbf{Bag}(B)} \qquad \mathcal{C}[\![\mathbf{sng}^*(e)]\!] = \{\mathcal{C}[\![e]\!]\}$$
$$\mathcal{C}[\![\ominus(e)]\!] = \mathcal{C}[\![e]\!] \qquad \mathcal{C}[\![e_1 \uplus e_2]\!] = \sup(\mathcal{C}[\![e_1]\!], \mathcal{C}[\![e_2]\!])$$
$$\mathcal{C}[\![\mathbf{let}\ X := e_1\ \mathbf{in}\ e_2]\!]_{\gamma^\circ;\varepsilon^\circ} = \mathcal{C}[\![e_2]\!]_{\gamma^\circ[X:=\mathcal{C}[\![e_1]\!]_{\gamma^\circ;\varepsilon^\circ}];\varepsilon^\circ}$$
$$\mathcal{C}[\![e_1 \times e_2]\!] = \mathcal{C}_o[\![e_1]\!] \cdot \mathcal{C}_o[\![e_2]\!]\{\langle \mathcal{C}_i[\![e_1]\!], \mathcal{C}_i[\![e_2]\!]\rangle\}$$
$$\mathcal{C}[\![\mathbf{flatten}(e)]\!] = \mathcal{C}_o[\![e]\!] \cdot \mathcal{C}_{oi}[\![e]\!]\{\mathcal{C}_{ii}[\![e]\!]\}$$
$$\mathcal{C}[\![\mathbf{for}\ x\ \mathbf{in}\ e_1\ \mathbf{union}\ e_2]\!] =$$
$$\mathcal{C}_o[\![e_1]\!]_{\gamma^\circ;\varepsilon^\circ} \cdot \mathcal{C}_o[\![e_2]\!]_{\gamma^\circ;\varepsilon^\circ[x:=\mathcal{C}_i[\![e_1]\!]]}\{\mathcal{C}_i[\![e_2]\!]_{\gamma^\circ;\varepsilon^\circ[x:=\mathcal{C}_i[\![e_1]\!]]}\}$$

Figure 3: The cost transformation $\mathcal{C}[\![f]\!] = \mathcal{C}_o[\![f]\!]\{\mathcal{C}_i[\![f]\!]\} : \mathbb{N}^+\{B^\circ\}$ over the constructs of IncNRC$^+$.

by $\mathcal{C}_o[\![e]\!] : \mathbb{N}^+$, and another returning the upper bound for the size of its elements $\mathcal{C}_i[\![e]\!] : B^\circ$. If B is itself a bag type $\mathbf{Bag}(C)$, we also denote the two components of $\mathcal{C}_i[\![e]\!]$ by $\mathcal{C}_{oi}[\![e]\!] : \mathbb{N}^+$ and $\mathcal{C}_{ii}[\![e]\!] : C^\circ$.

The cost transformation follows the natural semantics of the constructs in IncNRC$^+$. For example, in the case of **for** x **in** e_1 **union** e_2, the cardinality of the output is estimated as the product of the cardinalities of the bags returned by e_1 and e_2, while the elements in the output have the same cost as the elements returned by e_2. We note that in computing the cost of e_2 we assigned to x the estimated cost for the elements of e_1.

Finally, we leverage the estimated cost of an expression to obtain an upper bound on its running time:

LEMMA 3. *An* IncNRC$^+$ *expression* $h : \mathbf{Bag}(B)$ *can be evaluated in* $\Omega(\text{tcost}_{\mathbf{Bag}(B)}(\mathcal{C}[\![h]\!]))$, *where* $\text{tcost}_A : A^\circ \to \mathbb{N}$ *is defined as:*

$$\text{tcost}_{Base}(c) = 1 \qquad \text{tcost}_{\mathbf{Bag}(C)}(n\{c\}) = n \cdot \text{tcost}_C(c)$$
$$\text{tcost}_{A_1 \times A_2}(\langle c_1, c_2\rangle) = \text{tcost}_{A_1}(c_1) + \text{tcost}_{A_2}(c_2).$$

PROOF. (Sketch) In order to show that h can be computed within $\Omega(\text{tcost}_{\mathbf{Bag}(B)}(\mathcal{C}[\![h]\!])) = \Omega(\mathcal{C}_o[\![h]\!] \cdot \text{tcost}_B(\mathcal{C}_i[\![h]\!]))$ we assume that all **let**-bound variables have been replaced by their definition and we proceed in two steps. At first we compute a lazy version of the result $h^L = [\![h]\!]^L$, which instead of inner bags produces lazy bags $\beta_{e,\varepsilon}$, i.e. closures containing the expression e that would have generated the inner bag, along with ε, the value assignment for e's free variables at the time of the evaluation. The lazy evaluation strategy $[\![\cdot]\!]^L$ operates similar to the standard interpretation $[\![\cdot]\!]$, except for the singleton construct $[\![\mathbf{sng}(e)]\!]^L_\varepsilon = \beta_{e,\varepsilon}$ and for interpreting lazy values $[\![\beta_{e,\varepsilon}]\!]^L_{\varepsilon'} = [\![e]\!]^L_\varepsilon$, for which we replace the current value assignment ε' with the one stored in the closure. Considering that producing each element of h^L takes constant time (since building tuples and closures takes constant time), it follows that this step can be done in time proportional to the cardinality of the output $O(\mathcal{C}_o[\![h]\!])$.

In the second step we expand the lazy values appearing in each element of h^L in order to obtain the final value of h. To do so we use the following expansion function:

$$\text{exp}_{Base}(x) = x, \quad \text{exp}_{A_1 \times A_2}(\langle x_1, x_2\rangle) = \langle \text{exp}_{A_1}(x_1), \text{exp}_{A_2}(x_2)\rangle$$
$$\text{exp}_{\mathbf{Bag}(C)}(\beta_{e,\varepsilon}) = \mathbf{for}\ y\ \mathbf{in}\ [\![e]\!]^L_\varepsilon\ \mathbf{union}\ \mathbf{sng}(\text{exp}_C(y)).$$

We remark that, by postponing the materialization of inner bags until after the entire top level bag has been evaluated, we avoid computing the contents of nested bags that might get projected away in a later stage of the computation (as might be the case for an eager evaluation strategy).

Our result then follows from the fact that expanding each element $x : B$ from h^L takes at most $\text{tcost}_B(\mathcal{C}_i[\![h]\!])$, which can be easily shown through induction over the structure of B and considering that $\mathcal{C}_i[\![h]\!]$ represents on upper bound for the size of the elements in the output bag. □

EXAMPLE 6. *If we apply the cost transformation to the* `related`$[M]$ *query in section 2.1 we get cost estimate:*

$$\mathcal{C}[\![\texttt{related}[M]]\!] = |M|\{\langle 1, |M|\{1\}\rangle\},$$

and an upper bound for its running time as $\Omega(|M|(1+|M|))$, *which fits within the expected execution time for this query.*

We can now give the main result of this section showing that for incremental updates delta-processing is more cost-effective than recomputation.

THEOREM 4. IncNRC$^+$ *is efficiently incrementalizable, i.e. for any* input-dependent IncNRC$^+$ *query* $h[R]$ *and incremental update* ΔR, *then:*

$$\text{tcost}(\mathcal{C}[\![\delta(h)]\!]) < \text{tcost}(\mathcal{C}[\![h]\!]).$$

PROOF. (sketch) We first show by induction on the structure of h and using the cost semantics of IncNRC$^+$ constructs that $\mathcal{C}[\![\delta(h)]\!] \prec \mathcal{C}[\![h]\!]$. Then the result follows immediately from the definition of $\text{tcost}_A(\cdot)$ and $\prec_A$ (extended proof in [26]). □

It can be easily seen that $\text{filter}_p[R]$ is *efficiently incrementalizable* since its delta is $\text{filter}_p[\Delta R]$ and $\mathcal{C}[\![\text{filter}_p[R]]\!] = \mathcal{C}[\![R]\!]$, therefore $\mathcal{C}[\![\Delta R]\!] \prec \mathcal{C}[\![R]\!]$ implies $\mathcal{C}[\![\text{filter}_p[\Delta R]]\!] \prec \mathcal{C}[\![\text{filter}_p[R]]\!]$.

5. INCREMENTALIZING NRC$^+$

We now turn to the problem of efficiently incrementalizing NRC$^+$ queries that make use of the unrestricted singleton construct. As showcased in Section 2, an efficient delta rule for $\mathbf{sng}(e)$ requires deep updates which are not readily expressible in NRC$^+$. Moreover, deep updates are necessary not only for maintaining the output of a NRC$^+$ query, but also for applying local changes to the inner bags of the input. To address both problems we propose a shredding transformation that translates any NRC$^+$ query into a collection of efficiently incrementalizable expressions whose deltas can be applied via regular bag union. Furthermore, we show that our translation generates queries semantically equivalent to the original query, thus providing the first solution for the efficient delta-processing of NRC$^+$.

5.1 The shredding transformation

The essence of the shredding transformation is the replacement of inner bags by labels while separately storing their definitions in label dictionaries. Accordingly, we inductively map every type A of NRC$^+$ to a label-based/flat representation A^F along with a context component A^Γ for the corresponding label dictionaries:

$$Base^F = Base \qquad Base^\Gamma = 1$$
$$(A_1 \times A_2)^F = A_1^F \times A_2^F \qquad (A_1 \times A_2)^\Gamma = A_1^\Gamma \times A_2^\Gamma$$
$$\mathbf{Bag}(C)^F = \mathbb{L} \qquad \mathbf{Bag}(C)^\Gamma = (\mathbb{L} \mapsto \mathbf{Bag}(C^F)) \times C^\Gamma$$

For instance, the flat representation of a bag of type $\mathbf{Bag}(C)$ is a label $l : \mathbb{L}$, whereas its context includes a label dictionary $\mathbb{L}\mapsto\mathbf{Bag}(C^F)$, mapping l to the flattened contents of the bag.

The shredding transformation takes any NRC$^+$ expression $h[R] : \mathbf{Bag}(B)$ to:

$$\mathrm{sh}^F(h)[R^F, R^\Gamma] : \mathbf{Bag}(B^F) \quad \text{and} \quad \mathrm{sh}^\Gamma(h)[R^F, R^\Gamma] : B^\Gamma,$$

where $\mathrm{sh}^F(h)$ computes the flat representation of the output bag, while the set of queries in $\mathrm{sh}^\Gamma(h)$ define the context, i.e. the dictionaries corresponding to the labels introduced by $\mathrm{sh}^F(h)$. We note that the shredded expressions depend on the shredded input bag $R^F = \mathrm{sh}^F(R)$, $R^\Gamma = \mathrm{sh}^\Gamma(R)$[7], and that they make use of several new constructs for working with labels: the label constructor inL, the dictionary constructor $[l \mapsto e]$, and the label union of dictionaries $\cup$. We denote by NRC$_l^+$ and IncNRC$_l^+$, the extension with these constructs of NRC$^+$ and IncNRC$^+$, respectively, but we postpone their formal definition until the following section. Next, we discuss some of the more interesting cases of the shredding transformation, for the full definition see Appendix B.1.

Notation. We often shorthand $\mathrm{sh}^F(h)$ and $\mathrm{sh}^\Gamma(h)$ as h^F and h^Γ, respectively. We will also abuse the notation Π/ε representing the type/value assignment for the free variables of an expression introduced by **for** constructs, to also denote a tuple type/value with one component for each such free variable.

For the unrestricted singleton construct $\mathbf{sng}(e)$ we tag each of its occurrences in an expression with a unique static index ι. Given the shredding of e, $e^F : \mathbf{Bag}(B^F)$, $e^\Gamma : B^\Gamma$, we transform $\mathbf{sng}_\iota(e)$ as follows: we first replace the inner bag e^F in its output with a label $\langle\iota,\varepsilon\rangle$ using the label constructor $\mathrm{inL}_{\iota,\Pi}$, where $\varepsilon : \Pi$ represents the value assignment for all the free variables in e^F. Since e^F operates only over shredded bags, it follows that ε is a tuple of either primitive values or labels. Then we extend the context e^Γ with a dictionary $[(\iota,\Pi) \mapsto e^F]$ mapping labels $\langle\iota,\varepsilon\rangle$ to their definition e^F:

$$\mathrm{sh}^F(\mathbf{sng}_\iota(e)) : \mathbf{Bag}(\mathbb{L}) = \mathrm{inL}_{\iota,\Pi}(\varepsilon)$$
$$\mathrm{sh}^\Gamma(\mathbf{sng}_\iota(e)) : \mathbb{L} \mapsto \mathbf{Bag}(B^F) \times B^\Gamma = \langle [(\iota,\Pi) \mapsto e^F], e^\Gamma \rangle.$$

We incorporate the value assignment ε within labels as it allows us to discuss the creation of labels independently from their defining dictionary. Also, since the value assignment ε uniquely determines the definition of a label $\langle\iota,\varepsilon\rangle$, this also ensures that we do not generate redundant label definitions. Although other alternatives can be found in the literature [9], we do not explore this issue further since our results hold independently from a particular indexing scheme.

For the shredding of $\mathbf{flatten}(e), e : \mathbf{Bag}(\mathbf{Bag}(B))$, we simply expand the labels returned by $e^F : \mathbf{Bag}(\mathbb{L})$, based on the corresponding definitions stored in the first component of the context $e^\Gamma : \mathbb{L} \mapsto \mathbf{Bag}(B^F) \times B^\Gamma$:

$$\mathrm{sh}^F(\mathbf{flatten}(e)) : \mathbf{Bag}(B^F) = \mathbf{for}\ l\ \mathbf{in}\ e^F\ \mathbf{union}\ e^{\Gamma_1}(l),$$

where $e^{\Gamma_1}/e^{\Gamma_2}$ denotes the first/second component of e^Γ.

Finally, for adding two queries in shredded form via $\uplus$, we add their flat components, but we label union their contexts, i.e. their label dictionaries:

$$\mathrm{sh}^F(e_1 \uplus e_2) = e_1^F \uplus e_2^F \qquad \mathrm{sh}^\Gamma(e_1 \uplus e_2) = e_1^\Gamma \cup e_2^\Gamma.$$

[7]We consider a full shredding of the input/output down to flat relations, although the transformation can be easily fine-tuned in order to expose only those inner bags that require updates.

To complete the shredding transformation we also inductively define $\mathrm{s}_A^F : A \to \mathbf{Bag}(A^F)$ and $\mathrm{s}_A^\Gamma : A^\Gamma$, for shredding input bags $R : \mathbf{Bag}(A)$, as well as $\mathrm{u}_A[a^\Gamma] : A^F \to \mathbf{Bag}(A)$ for converting them back to nested form, as in:

$$R^F = \mathbf{for}\ r\ \mathbf{in}\ R\ \mathbf{union}\ \mathrm{s}_A^F(r) \qquad R^\Gamma = \mathrm{s}_A^\Gamma$$
$$R = \mathbf{for}\ r^F\ \mathbf{in}\ R^F\ \mathbf{union}\ \mathrm{u}_A[R^\Gamma](r^F).$$

Shredding primitive values leaves them unchanged and produces no dictionary ($Base^\Gamma = 1$), while tuples get shredded and nested back component-wise. For shredding inner bag values we rely on an association between every bag value v in the database and a label l, as given via mappings $\mathcal{D}_C, \mathcal{D}_C^{-1}$:

$$\mathcal{D}_C : \mathbf{Bag}(C) \to \mathbf{Bag}(\mathbb{L}) \qquad \mathcal{D}_C(v) = \{l\}$$
$$\mathcal{D}_C^{-1} : \mathbb{L} \mapsto \mathbf{Bag}(C) \qquad \mathcal{D}_C^{-1}(l) = v.$$

The shredding context for these labels is then obtained by mapping each label l from the dictionary $\mathcal{D}_C^{-1}$ to a shredded version of its original value v. The full details for the definition of $\mathrm{s}^F, \mathrm{s}^\Gamma$ and u can be found in Appendix B.1.

5.2 Working with labels

In the following we detail the semantics of IncNRC$_l^+$'s constructs for operating on dictionaries and we show that IncNRC$_l^+$ is indeed efficiently incrementalizable.

Given an expression $e : \mathbf{Bag}(B)$ with a value assignment for its free variables $\varepsilon : \Pi$, we define a label dictionary $[(\iota,\Pi) \mapsto e] : \mathbb{L} \mapsto \mathbf{Bag}(B)$, i.e. a mapping between labels $l = \langle\iota,\varepsilon\rangle$ and bag values $e : \mathbf{Bag}(B)$, as:

$$[(\iota,\Pi) \mapsto e](\langle\iota',\varepsilon\rangle) = \text{ if } (\iota == \iota')\ \rho_\varepsilon(e) \text{ else } \{\}$$

where $\rho_\varepsilon(e)$ replaces each free variable from e with its corresponding projection from ε. A priori, such dictionaries have infinite domain, i.e. they produce a bag for each possible value assignment ε. However, when materializing them as part of a shredding context we need only compute the definitions of the labels produced by the flat version of the query.

Example 7. *Given* $\mathtt{relB}(m) : \mathbf{Bag}(String)$, *the query from the motivating example in section 2, dictionary* $d = [(\iota, Movie) \mapsto \mathtt{relB}(m)]$ *of type* $\mathbb{L} \mapsto \mathbf{Bag}(String)$ *builds a mapping between labels* $l = \langle\iota,m\rangle$ *and the bag of related movies computed by* $\mathtt{relB}(m)$, *where* l *need only range over the labels produced by* $\mathtt{related}^F$.

Notation. We will often abuse notation and use l to refer to both the kind of a label (ι,Π), as well as an instance of a label $\langle\iota,\varepsilon\rangle$.

In order to distinguish between an empty definition, $[] = \varnothing$, and a definition that maps its label to the empty bag, $[l \mapsto \varnothing]$, we attach support sets to label definitions such that $\mathrm{supp}([]) = \varnothing$ and $\mathrm{supp}([l \mapsto e]) = \{l\}$.

For combining dictionaries of labels, i.e. $d = [l_1 \mapsto e_1, \cdots, l_n \mapsto e_n] : \mathbb{L} \mapsto \mathbf{Bag}(B)$, with $\mathrm{supp}(d) = \{l_1, \cdots, l_n\}$, we define the addition of dictionaries $(d_1 \uplus d_2)(l) = d_1(l) \uplus d_2(l)$ as well as the *label union* of dictionaries $d_1 \cup d_2$, where $d_1, d_2 : \mathbb{L} \mapsto \mathbf{Bag}(B)$, $\mathrm{supp}(d_1 \cup d_2) = \mathrm{supp}(d_1) \cup \mathrm{supp}(d_2)$ and:

$$(d_1 \cup d_2)(l) = d_1(l), \text{ if } l \in \mathrm{supp}(d_1) \setminus \mathrm{supp}(d_2)$$
$$(d_1 \cup d_2)(l) = d_2(l), \text{ if } l \in \mathrm{supp}(d_2) \setminus \mathrm{supp}(d_1)$$
$$(d_1 \cup d_2)(l) = d_1(l), \text{ if } l \in \mathrm{supp}(d_1) \cap \mathrm{supp}(d_2) \ \&\ d_1(l) = d_2(l)$$
$$(d_1 \cup d_2)(l) = \text{error}, \text{ if } l \in \mathrm{supp}(d_1) \cap \mathrm{supp}(d_2) \ \&\ d_1(l) \neq d_2(l)$$

We ensure the well definedness of the label union operation by requiring that the definitions of labels found in both input dictionaries must agree, i.e. for any $l \in \text{supp}(d_1) \cap \text{supp}(d_2)$ we must have $d_1(l) = d_2(l)$. If this condition is not met the evaluation of $\cup$ will result in an error. We remark that $\cup$ cannot modify a label definition, only $\uplus$ can (for an example contrasting their semantics see Appendix B.2). Moreover, we formalize the notion of consistent shredded values, i.e. values that do not contain undefined labels or definitions that conflict and we show that shredding produces consistent values and that given consistent inputs, shredded NRC⁺ expressions also produce consistent outputs [26].

Finally, we introduce the delta rules and the degree and cost interpretations for the new label-related constructs:

$$\delta([l \mapsto e]) = [l \mapsto \delta(e)] \quad \delta(\text{inL}_l) = \varnothing \quad \delta(e_1 \cup e_2) = \delta(e_1) \cup \delta(e_2)$$

$$\deg([l \mapsto e]) = \deg(e) \qquad \deg(\text{inL}_l) = 0$$

$$\deg(e_1 \cup e_2) = \max(\deg(e_1), \deg(e_2))$$

$$\mathcal{C}[\![[l \mapsto e](l')]\!] = \mathcal{C}[\![e]\!] \qquad \mathcal{C}[\![\text{inL}_l(a)]\!] = \{1\}$$

$$\mathcal{C}[\![(e_1 \cup e_2)(l)]\!] = \sup(\mathcal{C}[\![e_1(l)]\!], \mathcal{C}[\![e_2(l)]\!]),$$

where the cost domains for labels is 1°. Based on these definitions we prove the following result:

THEOREM 5. *IncNRC^+_l is recursively and efficiently incrementalizable, i.e. given any input-dependent IncNRC^+_l query $h[R]$, and incremental update ΔR then:*

$$h[R \uplus \Delta R] = h[R] \uplus \delta(h)[R, \Delta R], \quad \deg(\delta(h)) = \deg(h) - 1$$

$$\textit{and} \qquad \text{tcost}(\mathcal{C}[\![\delta(h)]\!]) < \text{tcost}(\mathcal{C}[\![h]\!]).$$

Theorem 5 implies that we can efficiently incrementalize any NRC⁺ query by incrementalizing the IncNRC^+_l queries resulting from its shredding. The output of these queries faithfully represents the expected nested value as we demonstrate in section 5.3.

5.3 Correctness

In order to prove the correctness of the shredding transformation, we show that for any NRC⁺ query $h[R] : \textbf{Bag}(B)$, shredding the input bag $R : \textbf{Bag}(A)$, evaluating h^F, h^Γ, and converting the output back to nested form produces the same result as $h[R]$, that is:

$$h[R] = \textbf{let } R^F := \textbf{for } r \textbf{ in } R \textbf{ union } \text{s}^F(r),\ R^\Gamma := \text{s}^\Gamma \textbf{ in}$$
$$\textbf{for } x^F \textbf{ in } h^F \textbf{ union } \text{u}[h^\Gamma](x^F), \qquad (4)$$

where $\text{s}^F(r)$ shreds each tuple in R to its flat representation, s^Γ returns the dictionaries corresponding to the labels generated by $\text{s}^F(r)$, and $\text{u}[h^\Gamma](x^F)$ places each tuple from h^F back in nested form using the dictionaries in h^Γ.

We proceed with the proof in two steps. We first show that shredding a value and then nesting the result returns back the original value (Lemma 6). Then, we show that applying the shredded version of a function over a shredded value and then nesting the result is equivalent to first nesting the input and then applying the original function (Lemma 7). The main result then follows immediately (Theorem 8). The proofs of the following lemmas rely on induction over the structure of the types or expressions involved, and are omitted for space reasons (they can be found in [26]).

LEMMA 6. *The nesting function* u *is left inverse wrt. the shredding functions* $\text{s}^F, \text{s}^\Gamma$*, i.e. for nested value* $a : A$ *we have* $\textbf{for } a^F \textbf{ in } \text{s}^F_A(a) \textbf{ union } \text{u}_A[\text{s}^\Gamma_A](a^F) = \textbf{sng}(a)$.

LEMMA 7. *For any* NRC⁺ *query* $h[R] : \textbf{Bag}(B)$ *and consistent shredded bag* R^F, R^Γ*:*

$$\textbf{let } R := (\textbf{for } r^F \textbf{ in } R^F \textbf{ union } \text{u}[R^\Gamma](r^F)) \textbf{ in } h[R]$$
$$= \textbf{for } x^F \textbf{ in } h^F \textbf{ union } \text{u}[h^\Gamma](x^F).$$

THEOREM 8. *For any* NRC⁺ *query property (4) holds.*

PROOF. The result follows from Lemma 7, if we consider the shredding of R as input, and then apply Lemma 6. □

5.4 Complexity class separation

In terms of data complexity, NRC belongs to TC_0 [39, 23], the class of languages recognizable by LOGSPACE-uniform families of circuits of polynomial size and constant depth using and-, or- and majority-gates of unbounded fan-in. The positive fragment of NRC is in the same complexity class since just the flatten operation on bag semantics requires the power to compute the sum of integers, which is in TC_0. In the following, we show that incrementalizing NRC⁺ queries in shredded form fits within the strictly lower complexity class of NC_0, which is a better model for real hardware since, in contrast to TC_0, it uses only gates with bounded fan-in. To obtain this result we require that multiplicities are represented by fixed size integers of k bits, and thus their value is computed modulo 2^k.

Assume that, for the following circuit complexity proof, shredded values are available as a bit sequence, with k bits (representing a multiplicity modulo 2^k) for each possible tuple constructible from the active domain of the shredded views and their schema, in some canonical ordering. For $k = 1$, this is the standard representation for circuit complexity proofs for relational queries with set semantics. Note that the active domain of a shredded view consists of the active domain of the nested value it is constructed from, the delimiters "⟨", "⟩", ", ", "{", "}", as well as an additional linearly-sized label set. We consider this the *natural* bit sequence representation of shredded values.

It may be worth pointing out that shredding only creates polynomial blow-up compared to a string representation of a complex value (e.g. in XML or JSON). This further justifies our representation. Generalizing the classical bit representation of relational databases (which has polynomial blow-up) to non-first normal form relations (with, for the simplest possible type $\{\langle\{Base\}\rangle\}$, one bit for every possible subset of the active domain) has exponential blow-up.

THEOREM 9. *Materialized views of* NRC⁺ *queries with multiplicities modulo* 2^k *in shredded form are incrementally maintainable in* NC_0 *wrt. constant size updates.*

PROOF. We will refer to the database and the update by d and Δd, respectively. By Theorem 8, every NRC⁺ query can be simulated by a fixed number of IncNRC⁺ queries on the shredding of the input. By Proposition 4.1, for every IncNRC⁺ query h, there is an IncNRC⁺ query $\delta_d(h)$ such that $h(d \uplus \Delta d) = h(d) \uplus \delta_d(h)(d)(\Delta d)$. We partially evaluate and materialize such delta queries as views $h' := \delta_d(h)(d)$ which then allow lookup of $h'(\Delta d)$. By Theorem 2, given an IncNRC⁺ query h, there is a a finite stack of higher-order delta queries $h_0, \cdots, h_k$ (with $h_i = \delta^{(i)}_d(h)(d)$, $0 \le i \le k$, and $\delta^{(0)}_d(h)(d) = h(d)$) such that h_k is input-independent (only depends on Δd). Thus, h_i can be refreshed as $h_i := h_i \uplus h_{i+1}(\Delta d)$ for $i < k$. We can incrementally maintain overall query h on a group of views in shredded representation using just the $\uplus$ operations and the operations of IncNRC⁺ on a constant-size input (executing queries h_i on the update). This is all the work that needs to be done, for an update, to refresh all the views.

It is easy to verify that in natural bit sequence representation of the shredded views, both $\uplus$ (on the full input representations) and IncNRC$^+$ on constantly many input bits can be modeled using NC$_0$ circuit families, one for each meaningful size of input bit sequence. For IncNRC$^+$ on constant-size inputs, this is obvious, since all Boolean functions over constantly many input bits can the captured by constant-size bounded fan-in circuits, and since there is really only one circuit, it can also be output in LOGSPACE. For $\uplus$, remember that we represent multiplicities modulo 2^k, i.e. by a fixed k bits. Since addition modulo 2^k is in NC$_0$, so is $\uplus$: The view contains aggregate multiplicities, each of which only needs to be combined with one multiplicity from the respective delta view. The overall circuit for an input size is a straightforward composition of these building blocks. □

In contrast, even when multiplicities are modeled modulo 2^k and the input is presented in flattened form, NRC$^+$ is not in NC$_0$ since multiplicities of projections (or **flatten**) depend on an unbounded number of input bits.

In Appendix B.3, we show that shredding (for the initial materialization of the views) itself is in TC$_0$; it follows immediately that shredding constant-size updates – the only shredding necessary during IVM – is in NC$_0$.

6. RELATED WORK

Delta derivation was originally proposed for datalog programs [19, 20] but it is even more natural for algebraic query languages such as the relational algebra on bags [16, 5, 8, 37, 40], simply because the algebraic structure of a group is the necessary and sufficient environment in which deltas live. In many cases the derived deltas are asymptotically faster than the original queries and the resulting speedups prompted a wide adoption of such techniques in commercial database systems. Our work is an attempt to develop similarly powerful static incrementalization tools for languages on nested collections and comes in the context of advances in the complexity class separation between recomputation and IVM [24, 42]. Compared to [24] which discusses the recursive incrementalization of a flat query language, we address the challenges raised by a nested data model, i.e. we design a *closed* delta transformation for IncNRC$^+$'s constructs and a semantics-preserving shredding transformation for implementing 'deep' updates. Furthermore, we provide cost domains and a cost interpretations for IncNRC$^+$'s constructs, according to which we define the notion of an *incremental* nested update and we show that the deltas we generate have lower upper-bound time estimates than re-evaluation.

The **nested data model** has been thoroughly studied in the literature over multiple decades and has enjoyed a wide adoption in industry in the form of data format standards like XML or JSON. However, solutions to the problem of incremental maintenance for nested queries either focus only on the fragment of the language that does not generate changes to inner collections [15], or propagate those changes based on auxiliary data structures designed to track the lineage of tuples in the view [14, 13, 22, 34]. The use of dedicated data-structures as well as custom update languages make it extremely difficult to further apply recursive IVM on top of these techniques. In contrast, our approach is fully algebraic and both the given query as well as the generated deltas belong to the same language and thus they can be further incrementalized via higher-order delta processing.

The related topic of **incremental computation** has also received considerable attention within the programming languages community, with proposals being divided between dynamic and static approaches. The dynamic solutions, such as *self-adjusting computation* [3, 1, 2], record at runtime the dependency-graph of the computation. Then, upon updates, one can easily identify the intermediate results affected and trigger their re-evaluation. As this technique makes few assumptions about its target language, it is applicable to a variety of languages ranging from Standard ML to C. Nonetheless, its generality comes at the price of significant runtime overheads for building the dependency graph. Moreover, while static solutions derive deltas that can be further optimized via global transformations, such an opportunity is mostly missed by dynamic approaches .

Delta derivation has also been proposed in the context of incremental computation, initially only for first-order languages [35], and more recently it has been extended to higher-order languages [7]. However, these approaches offer no guarantees wrt. the efficiency of the generated deltas, whereas in our work we introduce cost interpretations and discuss the requirements for cost-efficient delta processing.

The challenge of **shredding** nested queries has been previously addressed by Paredaens et al. [36], who propose a translation taking flat-to-flat nested relational algebra expressions into flat relational algebra. Van den Bussche [10] also showed that it is possible to evaluate nested queries over sets via multiple flat queries, but his solution may produce results that are quadratically larger than needed [9].

Shredding transformations have been studied more recently in the context of language integrated querying systems such as Links [31] and Ferry [17]. In order to efficiently evaluate a nested query, it is first converted to a series of flat queries which are then sent to the database engine for execution. While these transformations also replace inner collections with flat values, they are geared towards generating SQL queries and thus they make assumptions that are not applicable to our goal of efficiently incrementalizing any nested-to-nested expressions. For example, Ferry makes extensive use of On-Line Analytic Processing (OLAP) features of SQL:1999, such as `ROW_NUMBER` and `DENSE_RANK` [18], while Links relies on a normalization phase and handles only flat-to-nested expressions [9]. More importantly, none of the existing proposals translate NRC$^+$ queries to an efficiently incrementalizable language.

7. REFERENCES

[1] Umut A. Acar, Amal Ahmed, and Matthias Blume. Imperative self-adjusting computation. In *Proc. POPL*, pages 309–322, 2008.

[2] Umut A. Acar, Guy Blelloch, Ruy Ley-Wild, Kanat Tangwongsan, and Duru Turkoglu. Traceable data types for self-adjusting computation. In *Proc. PLDI*, pages 483–496, 2010.

[3] Umut A. Acar, Guy E. Blelloch, and Robert Harper. Adaptive functional programming. In *Proc. POPL*, pages 247–259, 2002.

[4] David A. M. Barrington, Neil Immerman, and H. Straubing. "On Uniformity within NC1". *Journal of Computer and System Sciences*, **41**(3):274–306, 1990.

[5] José A. Blakeley, Per-Åke Larson, and Frank Wm. Tompa. Efficiently updating materialized views. In

Proc. SIGMOD Conference, pages 61–71, 1986.

[6] Peter Buneman, Shamim A. Naqvi, Val Tannen, and Limsoon Wong. Principles of programming with complex objects and collection types. *Theor. Comput. Sci.*, 149(1):3–48, 1995.

[7] Yufei Cai, Paolo G. Giarrusso, Tillmann Rendel, and Klaus Ostermann. A theory of changes for higher-order languages: Incrementalizing λ-calculi by static differentiation. In *Proc. PLDI*, pages 145–155, 2014.

[8] Stefano Ceri and Jennifer Widom. Deriving production rules for incremental view maintenance. In *VLDB*, 1991.

[9] James Cheney, Sam Lindley, and Philip Wadler. Query shredding: Efficient relational evaluation of queries over nested multisets. In *Proc. SIGMOD*, pages 1027–1038, 2014.

[10] Jan Van den Bussche. Simulation of the nested relational algebra by the flat relational algebra, with an application to the complexity of evaluating powerset algebra expressions. *Theoretical Computer Science*, 254(1–2):363 – 377, 2001.

[11] Jan Van den Bussche, Dirk Van Gucht, and Stijn Vansummeren. Well-definedness and semantic type-checking for the nested relational calculus. *Theor. Comput. Sci.*, 371(3):183–199, 2007.

[12] Jan Van den Bussche and Stijn Vansummeren. Well-defined NRC queries can be typed - (extended abstract). In *In Search of Elegance in the Theory and Practice of Computation - Essays Dedicated to Peter Buneman*, pages 494–506, 2013.

[13] Katica Dimitrova, Maged El-Sayed, and ElkeA. Rundensteiner. Order-sensitive view maintenance of materialized xquery views. In *Conceptual Modeling - ER 2003*, volume 2813 of *Lecture Notes in Computer Science*, pages 144–157. 2003.

[14] J. Nathan Foster, Ravi Konuru, Jérôme Siméon, and Lionel Villard. An algebraic approach to view maintenance for XQuery. In *PLAN-X 2008, Programming Language Technologies for XML.*

[15] Dieter Gluche, Torsten Grust, Christof Mainberger, and MarcH. Scholl. Incremental updates for materialized oql views. In *Deductive and Object-Oriented Databases*, volume 1341 of *Lecture Notes in Computer Science*, pages 52–66. 1997.

[16] Timothy Griffin and Leonid Libkin. Incremental maintenance of views with duplicates. In *Proc. SIGMOD*, pages 328–339, 1995.

[17] Torsten Grust, Manuel Mayr, Jan Rittinger, and Tom Schreiber. Ferry: Database-supported program execution. In *Proc. Conference on Management of Data*, SIGMOD '09, pages 1063–1066, 2009.

[18] Torsten Grust, Jan Rittinger, and Tom Schreiber. Avalanche-safe linq compilation. *Proc. VLDB Endow.*, 3(1-2):162–172, 2010.

[19] Ashish Gupta, Dinesh Katiyar, and Inderpal Singh Mumick. Counting solutions to the view maintenance problem. In *Proc. Workshop on Deductive Databases, JICSLP*, 1992.

[20] Ashish Gupta, Inderpal Singh Mumick, and V. S. Subrahmanian. Maintaining views incrementally. In *SIGMOD'93*, pages 157–166.

[21] David S. Johnson. A catalog of complexity classes. In Jan van Leeuwen, editor, *Handbook of Theoretical Computer Science*, volume 1, chapter 2, pages 67–161. Elsevier Science Publishers B.V., 1990.

[22] Akira Kawaguchi, Daniel Lieuwen, Inderpal Mumick, and Kenneth Ross. Implementing incremental view maintenance in nested data models. In *In Proceedings of the Workshop on Database Programming Languages*, pages 202–221, 1997.

[23] Christoph Koch. On the complexity of nonrecursive xquery and functional query languages on complex values. In *Proc. PODS*, pages 84–97, 2005.

[24] Christoph Koch. Incremental query evaluation in a ring of databases. In *Proc. PODS*, pages 87–98, 2010.

[25] Christoph Koch, Yanif Ahmad, Oliver Kennedy, Milos Nikolic, Andres Nötzli, Daniel Lupei, and Amir Shaikhha. Dbtoaster: higher-order delta processing for dynamic, frequently fresh views. *VLDB J.*, 23(2):253–278, 2014.

[26] Christoph Koch, Daniel Lupei, and Val Tannen. Incremental view maintenance for collection programming. *CoRR*, abs/1412.4320, 2016.

[27] S. Kazem Lellahi and Val Tannen. A calculus for collections and aggregates. In *Category Theory and Computer Science, 7th International Conference, CTCS '97, Proceedings*, pages 261–280.

[28] Alon Y. Levy and Dan Suciu. Deciding containment for queries with complex objects. In *Proc. PODS*, pages 20–31, 1997.

[29] Leonid Libkin and Limsoon Wong. Query languages for bags and aggregate functions. *J. Comput. Syst. Sci.*, 55(2):241–272, 1997.

[30] Hartmut Liefke and Susan B. Davidson. Specifying updates in biomedical databases. In *Proc. SSDBM*, 1999.

[31] Sam Lindley and James Cheney. Row-based effect types for database integration. In *Proc. Workshop on Types in Language Design and Implementation*, TLDI '12, pages 91–102, 2012.

[32] Jixue Liu, Millist W. Vincent, and Mukesh K. Mohania. Incremental evaluation of nest and unnest operators in nested relations. In *Proc. of 1999 CODAS Conf*, pages 264–275, 1999.

[33] Erik Meijer, Brian Beckman, and Gavin Bierman. Linq: Reconciling object, relations and xml in the .net framework. In *Proc. SIGMOD*, pages 706–706, 2006.

[34] Hiroaki Nakamura. Incremental computation of complex object queries. OOPSLA, pages 156–165, 2001.

[35] Robert Paige and Shaye Koenig. Finite differencing of computable expressions. *ACM Trans. Program. Lang. Syst.*, 4(3):402–454, 1982.

[36] Jan Paredaens and Dirk Van Gucht. Converting nested algebra expressions into flat algebra expressions. *ACM Trans. Database Syst.*, 17(1):65–93, March 1992.

[37] Nick Roussopoulos. An incremental access method for viewcache: Concept, algorithms, and cost analysis. *ACM Transactions on Database Systems*, 16(3):535–563, 1991.

[38] Dan Suciu. Bounded fixpoints for complex objects. In *Database Programming Languages (DBPL-4), Proc. of the Fourth International Workshop on Database Programming Languages - Object Models and Languages*, pages 263–281, 1993.

[39] Dan Suciu and Val Tannen. "A Query Language for NC". In *Proc. PODS'94*, pages 167–178, 1994.

[40] Dimitra Vista. Integration of incremental view maintenance into query optimizers. In *Advances in Database Technology-EDBT'98*, volume 1377, pages 374–388, 1998.

[41] Matei Zaharia, Mosharaf Chowdhury, Michael J. Franklin, Scott Shenker, and Ion Stoica. Spark: Cluster computing with working sets. HotCloud'10, 2010.

[42] Thomas Zeume and Thomas Schwentick. Dynamic conjunctive queries. In *Proc. ICDT*, pages 38–49, 2014.

APPENDIX

A. CHALLENGES FOR EFFICIENT INCREMENTALIZATION

In the following we discuss the challenges in deriving a delta query which is cheaper than full re-evaluation for any expression in a language.

Informally, we say that the delta $\delta(e)[R, \Delta R]$ of a query $e[R]$ is more *efficient* than full recomputation (or simply *efficient*), if for any update ΔR s.t. $\text{size}(\Delta R) \ll \text{size}(R)$, evaluating $\delta(e)[R, \Delta R]$ and applying it to the output of e is less expensive than re-evaluating e from scratch, i.e.:

$$\text{cost}(\delta(e)[R, \Delta R]) \ll \text{cost}(e[R \uplus \Delta R]) \quad \text{and}$$
$$\text{size}(\delta(e)[R, \Delta R]) \ll \text{size}(e[R \uplus \Delta R]),$$

where the second equation ensures that applying the update is cheaper than re-computation considering that the cost of applying an update is proportional to its size and that the cost of evaluating an expression is lowerbounded by the size of its output ($\text{size}(e[R \uplus \Delta R]) \leq \text{cost}(e[R \uplus \Delta R])$).

One can guarantee that the delta of any expression in a language is efficient by requiring that every construct $\mathbf{p}(e)[R]$ of the language satisfies the property above, i.e. $\text{size}(\delta(e)[R, \Delta R]) \ll \text{size}(e[R])$ implies:

$$\text{cost}(\delta(\mathbf{p}(e))[R, \Delta R]) \ll \text{cost}(\mathbf{p}(e)[R \uplus \Delta R]) \quad \text{and}$$
$$\text{size}(\delta(\mathbf{p}(e))[R, \Delta R]) \ll \text{size}(\mathbf{p}(e)[R \uplus \Delta R]) \tag{5}$$

Unfortunately, this property does not hold for constructs $\mathbf{p}(e)[R]$ which take linear time in their inputs $e[R]$ (i.e. $\text{cost}(\mathbf{p}(e)[R]) = \text{size}(e[R])$) and whose delta $\delta(\mathbf{p}(e))[R, \Delta R]$ depends on the original input $e[R]$ (therefore $\text{cost}(e[R]) < \text{cost}(\delta(\mathbf{p}(e))[R, \Delta R])$), as it leads to the following contradiction:

$$\text{size}(e[R]) \leq \text{cost}(e[R]) < \text{cost}(\delta(\mathbf{p}(e))[R, \Delta R]) \ll$$
$$\ll \text{cost}(\mathbf{p}(e)[R \uplus \Delta R]) = \text{size}(e[R \uplus \Delta R]) \approx \text{size}(e[R]),$$

where the last approximation follows from the fact that:

$$e[R \uplus \Delta R] = e[R] \;\uplus\; \delta(e)[R, \Delta R] \quad \text{and}$$
$$\text{size}(\delta(e)[R, \Delta R]) \ll \text{size}(e[R]).$$

An example of such a construct is bag subtraction $(e_1 \setminus e_2)[R]$, that associates to every element v_i in $e_1[R]$ the multiplicity $\max(0, m_1 - m_2)$, where m_1, m_2 are v_i's multiplicities in $e_1[R]$ and $e_2[R]$, respectively. Indeed, the cost of evaluating bag subtraction is proportional to its input (i.e. $\text{cost}(e_1 \setminus e_2)[R] = \text{size}(e_1[R])$, assuming $e_1[R]$ and $e_2[R]$ have similar sizes) and the result of $(e_1 \setminus e_2)[R]$ can be maintained when $e_2[R]$ changes, only if the initial value of $e_1[R]$ is known at the time of the update. The singleton constructor or the emptiness test over bags also exhibit similar characteristics. By contrast, constructs that take time linear in their input, but whose delta rule depends only on the update do not present this issue (eg. **flatten**).

This problem can be addressed by materializing the result of the subquery $e[R]$, such that one does not need to pay its cost again when evaluating $\delta(\mathbf{p}(e))[R, \Delta R]$. However, this only solves half of the problem, as we also need to make sure that the outcome of $\delta(\mathbf{p}(e))[R, \Delta R]$ can be efficiently propagated through outer queries e' that may use $\mathbf{p}(e)[R \uplus \Delta R]$ as a subquery. Solving this issue requires handcrafted solutions that take into consideration the particularities of $\mathbf{p}$ and the ways it can be used. For example, in our solution for efficiently incrementalizing $\mathbf{sng}(\cdot)$ we take advantage of the fact that the only way of accessing the contents of a inner bag is via $\mathbf{flatten}(\cdot)$.

Finally, for constructs $\mathbf{p}$ with boolean as output domain (eg. testing whether a bag is empty), it no longer makes sense to distinguish between small and large values, and therefore, the condition (5) can never be satisfied. This problem extends to a class of primitives that includes bag equality, negation, and membership testing, and restricts our solution for efficient incrementalization to only the positive fragment of nested relational calculus NRC$^+$.

B. SHREDDING NRC$^+$

B.1 The shredding transformation

The full definition of the shredding transformation for the constructs of NRC$^+$ can be found in Figure 4. We remark that it produces expressions that no longer make use of the singleton combinator $\mathbf{sng}(e)$, thus their deltas do not generate any deep updates.

In addition, we note that only the shreddings of $\mathbf{sng}(e)$ and $\mathbf{flatten}(e)$ fundamentally change the contexts, whereas the shreddings of most of the other operators modify only the flat component of the output (see $\text{sh}(e_1 \times e_2)$, $\text{sh}(\ominus(e))$). In fact, if we interpret the output context B^Γ as a tree, having the same structure as the nested type B, we can see that $\text{sh}^\Gamma(\mathbf{sng}(e))$ / $\text{sh}^\Gamma(\mathbf{flatten}(e))$ are the only ones able to add / remove a level from the tree.

We define $\text{s}^F_A : A \to \mathbf{Bag}(A^F)$ and $\text{s}^\Gamma_A : A^\Gamma$, for shredding bag values $R : \mathbf{Bag}(A)$, as well as $\text{u}_A[a^\Gamma] : A^F \to \mathbf{Bag}(A)$ for converting them back to nested form:

$$R^F = \mathbf{for}\ a\ \mathbf{in}\ R\ \mathbf{union}\ \text{s}^F_A(a) \qquad R^\Gamma = \text{s}^\Gamma_A \qquad\qquad R = \mathbf{for}\ a^F\ \mathbf{in}\ R^F\ \mathbf{union}\ \text{u}_A[R^\Gamma](a^F),$$

where $\text{s}^F_A, \text{s}^\Gamma_A$ and u_A are presented in Figure 5.

$$\begin{array}{lll}
\mathrm{sh}^F(\mathbf{sng}(x)) : \mathbf{Bag}(A^F) & \mathrm{sh}^F(\mathbf{for}\ x\ \mathbf{in}\ e_1\ \mathbf{union}\ e_2) : \mathbf{Bag}(B^F) & \mathrm{sh}^F(\mathbf{sng}(\pi_i(x))) : \mathbf{Bag}(A_i^F) \\
\mathrm{sh}^F(\mathbf{sng}(x)) = \mathbf{sng}(x^F) & \mathrm{sh}^F(\mathbf{for}\ x\ \mathbf{in}\ e_1\ \mathbf{union}\ e_2) = \mathbf{let}\ x^\Gamma := e_1^\Gamma\ \mathbf{in}\ \mathbf{for}\ x^F\ \mathbf{in}\ e_1^F\ \mathbf{union}\ e_2^F & \mathrm{sh}^F(\mathbf{sng}(\pi_i(x))) = \mathbf{sng}(\pi_i(x^F)) \\
\mathrm{sh}^\Gamma(\mathbf{sng}(x)) : A^\Gamma & \mathrm{sh}^\Gamma(\mathbf{for}\ x\ \mathbf{in}\ e_1\ \mathbf{union}\ e_2) : B^\Gamma & \mathrm{sh}^\Gamma(\mathbf{sng}(\pi_i(x))) : A_i^\Gamma \\
\mathrm{sh}^\Gamma(\mathbf{sng}(x)) = x^\Gamma & \mathrm{sh}^\Gamma(\mathbf{for}\ x\ \mathbf{in}\ e_1\ \mathbf{union}\ e_2) = \mathbf{let}\ x^\Gamma := e_1^\Gamma\ \mathbf{in}\ e_2^\Gamma & \mathrm{sh}^\Gamma(\mathbf{sng}(\pi_i(x))) = x^{\Gamma_i}
\end{array}$$

$$\begin{array}{lll}
\mathrm{sh}^F(\mathbf{sng}(\langle\rangle)) : \mathbf{Bag}(1) & \mathrm{sh}^F(e_1 \times e_2) : \mathbf{Bag}(A_1^F \times A_2^F) & \mathrm{sh}^F(R) : \mathbf{Bag}(A^F) \\
\mathrm{sh}^F(\mathbf{sng}(\langle\rangle)) = \mathbf{sng}(\langle\rangle) & \mathrm{sh}^F(e_1 \times e_2) = e_1^F \times e_2^F & \mathrm{sh}^F(R) = \mathbf{for}\ r\ \mathbf{in}\ R\ \mathbf{union}\ \mathrm{s}_A^F(r) \\
\mathrm{sh}^\Gamma(\mathbf{sng}(\langle\rangle)) : 1 & \mathrm{sh}^\Gamma(e_1 \times e_2) : A_1^\Gamma \times A_2^\Gamma & \mathrm{sh}^\Gamma(R) : A^\Gamma \\
\mathrm{sh}^\Gamma(\mathbf{sng}(\langle\rangle)) = \langle\rangle & \mathrm{sh}^\Gamma(e_1 \times e_2) = \langle e_1^\Gamma, e_2^\Gamma\rangle & \mathrm{sh}^\Gamma(R) = \mathrm{s}_A^\Gamma
\end{array}$$

$$\begin{array}{lll}
\mathrm{sh}^F(e_1 \uplus e_2) : \mathbf{Bag}(B^F) & \mathrm{sh}^F(\mathbf{sng}_\iota(e)) : \mathbf{Bag}(\mathbb{L}) & \mathrm{sh}^F(\varnothing) : \mathbf{Bag}(B^F) \\
\mathrm{sh}^F(e_1 \uplus e_2) = e_1^F \uplus e_2^F & \mathrm{sh}^F(\mathbf{sng}_\iota(e)) = \mathrm{inL}_{\iota,\Pi}(\varepsilon) & \mathrm{sh}^F(\varnothing) = \varnothing \\
\mathrm{sh}^\Gamma(e_1 \uplus e_2) : B^\Gamma & \mathrm{sh}^\Gamma(\mathbf{sng}_\iota(e)) : (\mathbb{L} \to \mathbf{Bag}(B^F)) \times B^\Gamma & \mathrm{sh}^\Gamma(\varnothing) : B^\Gamma \\
\mathrm{sh}^\Gamma(e_1 \uplus e_2) = e_1^\Gamma \cup e_2^\Gamma & \mathrm{sh}^\Gamma(\mathbf{sng}_\iota(e)) = \langle[(\iota,\Pi) \mapsto e^F], e^\Gamma\rangle & \mathrm{sh}^\Gamma(\varnothing) = \varnothing_{B^\Gamma}
\end{array}$$

$$\begin{array}{lll}
\mathrm{sh}^F(\ominus(e)) : \mathbf{Bag}(B^F) & \mathrm{sh}^F(\mathbf{flatten}(e)) : \mathbf{Bag}(B^F) & \mathrm{sh}^F(p(x)) : \mathbf{Bag}(1) \\
\mathrm{sh}^F(\ominus(e)) = \ominus(e^F) & \mathrm{sh}^F(\mathbf{flatten}(e)) = \mathbf{for}\ l\ \mathbf{in}\ e^F\ \mathbf{union}\ e^{\Gamma_1}(l) & \mathrm{sh}^F(p(x)) = p(x) \\
\mathrm{sh}^\Gamma(\ominus(e)) : B^\Gamma & \mathrm{sh}^\Gamma(\mathbf{flatten}(e)) : B^\Gamma & \mathrm{sh}^\Gamma(p(x)) : 1 \\
\mathrm{sh}^\Gamma(\ominus(e)) = e^\Gamma & \mathrm{sh}^\Gamma(\mathbf{flatten}(e)) = e^{\Gamma_2} & \mathrm{sh}^\Gamma(p(x)) = \langle\rangle
\end{array}$$

$$\begin{array}{ll}
\mathrm{sh}^F(\mathbf{let}\ X := e_1\ \mathbf{in} e_2) : \mathbf{Bag}(B^F) & \mathrm{sh}^F(\mathbf{let}\ X := e_1\ \mathbf{in}\ e_2) = \mathbf{let}\ X^F := e_1^F,\ X^\Gamma := e_2^\Gamma\ \mathbf{in}\ e_2^F \\
\mathrm{sh}^\Gamma(\mathbf{let}\ X := e_1\ \mathbf{in} e_2) : B^\Gamma & \mathrm{sh}^\Gamma(\mathbf{let}\ X := e_1\ \mathbf{in}\ e_2) = \mathbf{let}\ X^F := e_1^F,\ X^\Gamma := e_2^\Gamma\ \mathbf{in}\ e_2^\Gamma
\end{array}$$

Figure 4: The shredding transformation, where s_A^F and s_A^Γ are described in Figure 5a.

$$\begin{array}{lll}
\mathrm{s}_{Base}^F : Base \to \mathbf{Bag}(Base) & \mathrm{s}_{A_1\times A_2}^F : (A_1 \times A_2) \to \mathbf{Bag}(A_1^F \times A_2^F) & \mathrm{s}_{\mathbf{Bag}(C)}^F : \mathbf{Bag}(C) \to \mathbf{Bag}(\mathbb{L}) \\
\mathrm{s}_{Base}^F(a) = \mathbf{sng}(a) & \mathrm{s}_{A_1\times A_2}^F(a) = \mathbf{for}\ \langle a_1, a_2\rangle\ \mathbf{in}\ \mathbf{sng}(a)\ \mathbf{union}\ \mathrm{s}_{A_1}^F(a_1) \times \mathrm{s}_{A_2}^F(a_2) & \mathrm{s}_{\mathbf{Bag}(C)}^F(v) = \mathcal{D}_C(v)
\end{array}$$

$$\begin{array}{llll}
\mathrm{s}_{Base}^\Gamma : 1 & \mathrm{s}_{A_1\times A_2}^\Gamma : A_1^\Gamma \times A_2^\Gamma & \mathrm{s}_{\mathbf{Bag}(C)}^\Gamma : (\mathbb{L} \mapsto \mathbf{Bag}(C^F)) \times C^\Gamma & \\
\mathrm{s}_{Base}^\Gamma = \langle\rangle & \mathrm{s}_{A_1\times A_2}^\Gamma = \langle \mathrm{s}_{A_1}^\Gamma, \mathrm{s}_{A_2}^\Gamma\rangle & \mathrm{s}_{\mathbf{Bag}(C)}^{\Gamma_1} = \mathbf{for}\ l\ \mathbf{in}\ \mathrm{supp}(\mathcal{D}_C^{-1})\ \mathbf{union}\ [l \mapsto \mathbf{for}\ c\ \mathbf{in}\ \mathcal{D}_C^{-1}(l)\ \mathbf{union}\ \mathrm{s}_C^F(c)] & \mathrm{s}_{\mathbf{Bag}(C)}^{\Gamma_2} = \mathrm{s}_C^\Gamma
\end{array}$$

(a) $\mathrm{s}_A^F : A \to \mathbf{Bag}(A^F), \mathrm{s}_A^\Gamma : A^\Gamma$

$$\begin{array}{ll}
\mathrm{u}_{Base}[\langle\rangle] : Base \to \mathbf{Bag}(Base) & \mathrm{u}_{Base}[\langle\rangle](a^F) = \mathbf{sng}(a^F) \\
\mathrm{u}_{A_1\times A_2}[a^\Gamma] : A_1^F \times A_2^F \to \mathbf{Bag}(A_1 \times A_2) & \mathrm{u}_{A_1\times A_2}[a^\Gamma](a^F) = \mathbf{for}\ \langle a_1^F, a_2^F\rangle\ \mathbf{in}\ \mathbf{sng}(a^F)\ \mathbf{union}\ \mathrm{u}_{A_1}[a^{\Gamma_1}](a_1^F) \times \mathrm{u}_{A_2}[a^{\Gamma_2}](a_2^F) \\
\mathrm{u}_{\mathbf{Bag}(C)}[a^\Gamma] : \mathbb{L} \to \mathbf{Bag}(\mathbf{Bag}(C)) & \mathrm{u}_{\mathbf{Bag}(C)}[a^\Gamma](l) = \mathbf{sng}(\mathbf{for}\ c^F\ \mathbf{in}\ a^{\Gamma_1}(l)\ \mathbf{union}\ \mathrm{u}_C[a^{\Gamma_2}](c^F))
\end{array}$$

(b) $\mathrm{u}_A[a^\Gamma] : A^F \to \mathbf{Bag}(A)$

Figure 5: Shredding and nesting bag values.

When shredding a bag value $R : \mathbf{Bag}(A)$, the flat component $R^F : \mathbf{Bag}(A^F)$ is generated by replacing every nested bag $v : \mathbf{Bag}(C)$ from R, with a label $l = \langle \iota_v, \langle\rangle\rangle$. The association between every bag $v : \mathbf{Bag}(C)$, occurring nested somewhere inside R, and the label l is given via $\mathcal{D}_C$ and $\mathcal{D}_C^{-1}$:

$$\mathcal{D}_C : \mathbf{Bag}(C) \to \mathbf{Bag}(\mathbb{L}) \qquad \mathcal{D}_C(v) = \{l\} \qquad \mathcal{D}_C^{-1} : \mathbb{L} \mapsto \mathbf{Bag}(C) \qquad \mathcal{D}_C^{-1}(l) = v.$$

For each label l introduced by $\mathcal{D}_C$, $\mathrm{s}_{\mathbf{Bag}(C)}^\Gamma$ constructs a dictionary, mapping l to the flat component of the shredded version of v. This is done by first using the dictionary $\mathcal{D}_C^{-1}$, to obtain v and applying s_C^F to shred its contents.

Converting a shredded bag $R^F : \mathbf{Bag}(A^F), R^\Gamma : A^\Gamma$, back to nested form can be done via **for** x **in** R^F **union** $\mathrm{u}_A[R^\Gamma](x)$, which replaces the labels in R^F by their definitions from the context R^Γ, as computed by $\mathrm{u}_A[a^\Gamma]$ (Figure 5b). We note that the definitions themselves also have to be recursively turned to nested form, which is done in $\mathrm{u}_{\mathbf{Bag}(C)}$.

B.2 Example: Label dictionaries

We give a couple of examples where we contrast the outcome of label unioning dictionaries with that of applying bag addition on them (we use x^n to denote n copies of x).

$$[l_1 \mapsto \{b_1\}, l_2 \mapsto \{b_2, b_3\}] \cup [l_2 \mapsto \{b_2, b_3\}, l_3 \mapsto \{b_4\}] = [l_1 \mapsto \{b_1\}, l_2 \mapsto \{b_2, b_3\}, l_3 \mapsto \{b_4\}]$$
$$[l_1 \mapsto \{b_1\}, l_2 \mapsto \{b_2, b_3\}] \uplus [l_2 \mapsto \{b_2, b_3\}, l_3 \mapsto \{b_4\}] = [l_1 \mapsto \{b_1\}, l_2 \mapsto \{b_2^2, b_3^2\}, l_3 \mapsto \{b_4\}]$$

$$[l_1 \mapsto \{b_1\}, l_2 \mapsto \{b_2, b_3\}] \cup [l_2 \mapsto \{b_5\}, l_3 \mapsto \{b_4\}] = \text{error}$$
$$[l_1 \mapsto \{b_1\}, l_2 \mapsto \{b_2, b_3\}] \uplus [l_2 \mapsto \{b_5\}, l_3 \mapsto \{b_4\}] = [l_1 \mapsto \{b_1\}, l_2 \mapsto \{b_2, b_3, b_5\}, l_3 \mapsto \{b_4\}]$$

As we can see from these examples, bag addition allows us to modify the label definitions stored inside the dictionaries, which is otherwise not possible via label unioning.

B.3 Complexity of Shredding

In this section we show that shredding nested bags can be done in TC_0. By NC_0 we refer to the class of languages recognizable by LOGSPACE-uniform families of circuits of polynomial size and constant depth using and- and or-gates of bounded fan-in. The related complexity class AC_0 differs from NC_0 by allowing gates to have unbounded fan-in, while TC_0 extends AC_0 by further permitting so-called majority-gates, that compute "true" iff more than half of their inputs are true. For details on circuit complexity and the notion of uniformity we refer to [21].

We recall that the standard way of representing flat relations when processing them via circuits is the unary representation, i.e. as a collection of bits, one for each possible tuple that can be constructed from the active domain and the schema, in some canonical ordering, where a bit being turned on or off signals whether the corresponding tuple is in the relation or not. In such a representation (denote by F^{Set} below), if the active domain has size σ, then the number of bits required for encoding a relation whose schema has n_f fields is σ^{n_f}. For example, for a relation with a single field, we need σ bits to encode which values from the active domain are present or not. We also assume a total order among the elements of the active domain, and that the bits of F^{Set} are in lexicographical order of the tuples they represent.

In the case of bags, whose elements have an associated multiplicity, we work with circuits that compute the multiplicity of tuples modulo 2^k, for some fixed k. Thus, for every possible tuple in a bag we use k bits instead of a single one, in order to encode the multiplicity of that tuple as a binary number. In the following we use F^{Bag} to refer to this representation of bags.

For nested values the F^{Set} representation discussed above is no longer feasible since it suffers from an exponential blowup with every nesting level. This becomes apparent when we consider that representing in unary an inner bag with n_t possible tuples requires 2^{n_t} bits. Consequently, for a nested value we use an alternate representation N^{Str}, as a relation $S(p, s)$ which encodes the string representation (over a non-fixed alphabet that includes the active domain, the possible atomic field values) of the value by mapping each position p in the string to its corresponding symbol s.

EXAMPLE 8. *The string representation* $\{\langle a, \{b, c\}\rangle, \langle d, \{e, f\}\rangle\}$, *of a nested value of type* **Bag**$(Base \times$**Bag**$(Base))$, *is encoded by relation* $S(p, s)$ *as follows (we show tuples as columns to save space):*

p	1	2	3	4	5	6	7	8	9	10	11	12	13	14	15	16	17	18	19	20	21
s	{	⟨	a	,	{	b	,	c	}	⟩	,	⟨	d	,	{	e	,	f	}	⟩	}

For a particular input size n, the active domain of S consists of σ_{ext} symbols including the active domain of the database, delimiting symbols "⟨", "⟩", ",", "{", "}", as well as an additional symbol for each possible position in the string (i.e. $\sigma_{ext} = \sigma + 5 + n$). We remark that the F^{Set} representation of S requires σ_{ext}^2 bits and thus remains polynomial in the size of the input.

This representation may seem to require justification, since strings over an unbounded alphabet may seem undesirable. We note that the representation is fair in the sense that it does not require a costly (exponential) blow-up from the practical string representation that could be used to store the data on a real storage device such as a disk; we use a relational representation of the string and the canonical representation of relations as bit-sequences that is standard in circuit complexity. The one way we could have been even more faithful would have been to start with exactly the bit-string representation by which an (XML, JSON, or other) nested dataset would be stored on a disk. This – breaking up the active domain values into bit sequences – is however avoided for the same reason it is avoided in the case of the study of the circuit complexity of queries on flat relations – reconstructing the active domain from the bit string dominates the cost of query evaluation.

We can now give our main results of this section.

THEOREM 10. *Shredding a nested bag from* N^{Str} *representation to a flat bag* (F^{Bag}) *representation is in* TC_0.

PROOF. To obtain our result we take advantage of the fact that first-order logic with majority-quantifiers (FOM) is in TC_0 [4], and express the shredding of a nested value as a set of FOM queries over the $S(p, s)$ relation.

We start by defining a family of queries $\text{Val}_A(i, j)$ for testing whether a closed interval (i, j) from the input contains a value of a particular type A:

$$\text{Val}_{Base}(i, j) := S_{Base}(i) \wedge i = j$$
$$\text{Val}_{A_1 \times A_2}(i, j) := S_{\langle}(i) \wedge S_{\rangle}(j) \wedge \exists k. \text{Pair}_{A_1, A_2}(i + 1, k, j - 1)$$

$$\mathrm{Pair}_{A_1,A_2}(i,k,j) := S_,(k) \wedge \mathrm{Val}_{A_1}(i,k-1) \wedge \mathrm{Val}_{A_2}(k+1,j)$$
$$\mathrm{Val}_{\mathbf{Bag}(C)}(i,j) := S_\{(i) \wedge S_\}(j) \wedge (j = i+1 \vee \mathrm{Seq}_C(i+1,j-1))$$
$$\mathrm{Seq}_C(i,j) := \exists k,l.\,\mathrm{Elem}_C(i,k,l,j) \wedge \forall k,l.\,\mathrm{Elem}_C(i,k,l,j) \to (\mathrm{EndsWith}_C(i,k) \wedge \mathrm{StartsWith}_C(l,j))$$
$$\mathrm{Elem}_C(i,k,l,j) := (i \le k \wedge l \le j \wedge \mathrm{Val}_C(k,l))$$
$$\mathrm{EndsWith}_C(i,k) := i = k \vee (S_,(k-1) \wedge \exists k'.i \le k' \wedge \mathrm{Val}_C(k',k-2))$$
$$\mathrm{StartsWith}_C(l,j) := l = j \vee (S_,(l+1) \wedge \exists l'.l' \le j \wedge \mathrm{Val}_C(l+2,l'))$$

where $S_{Base}(i)$ is true iff we have a *Base* symbol at position i in the input string (and analogously for $S_\{(i), S_\}(i), S_\langle(i), S_\rangle(i)$ and $S_,(i)$). When determining if an interval (i,j) contains a bag value of type $\mathbf{Bag}(C)$ we test if it is either empty, i.e. $j = i+1$ or if it encloses a sequence of C elements (using Seq_C), i.e. it has at least one C element and each element is preceded by another C element or is the first in the sequence, and succeeded by another C element or is the last in the sequence. We use auxiliary queries: $\mathrm{Elem}_C(i,k,l,j)$, which returns true iff the interval (i,j) contains a value of type C between indices k and l, and $\mathrm{StartsWith}_C(l,j)$ / $\mathrm{EndsWith}_C(i,k)$ which returns true iff the intervals (l,j) / (i,k) are either empty or they begin, respectively end, with a value of type C.

For shredding the value contained in an interval (i,j) of the input we define the following family of queries $\mathrm{Sh}^F_A(i,j,p,s)$:

$$\mathrm{Sh}^F_{Base}(i,j,p,s) := i \le p \wedge p \le j \wedge S(p,s)$$
$$\mathrm{Sh}^F_{A_1\times A_2}(i,j,p,s) := \exists k.\,\mathrm{Pair}_{A_1,A_2}(i+1,k,j-1) \wedge (\mathrm{Sh}^F_{A_1}(i+1,k-1,p,s) \;\vee\; \mathrm{Sh}^F_{A_2}(k+1,j-1,p,s))$$
$$\mathrm{Sh}^F_{\mathbf{Bag}(C)}(i,j,p,s) := p = i \wedge s = i,$$

where the shredding of bag values results in their replacement with a unique identifier, i.e. the index of their first symbol, that acts as a label. Additionally, the definitions of these labels, i.e. the shredded versions of the bags they replace are computed via:

$$\mathrm{Dict}_C(p,s) := \exists i,j,k,l.\,\mathrm{Val}_{\mathbf{Bag}(C)}(i,j) \wedge \mathrm{Elem}_C(i+1,k,l,j-1) \wedge ((p = k-1 \wedge s = i) \vee \mathrm{Sh}^F_C(k,l,p,s)),$$

where we prepend to each shredded element in the output the label of the bag to which it belongs (we can do that by reusing the index of the preceding "{" or "," present in the original input). We build a corresponding relation Dict_C for every bag type $\mathbf{Bag}(C)$ occurring in the input. These relations encode a flat representation of the input, as bags of type $\mathbf{Bag}(\mathbb{L}\times C^F)$, where each tuple uses a fixed number of of symbols, therefore we no longer make use of delimiting symbols.

For our example input, we only have two bag types, $\mathbf{Bag}(Base \times \mathbf{Bag}(Base))$ and $\mathbf{Bag}(Base)$, and their corresponding relations are:

$\mathrm{Dict}_{Base\times\mathbf{Bag}(Base)}(p,s) :=$

p	1	3	5	11	13	15
s	1	a	5	1	d	15

$\mathrm{Dict}_{Base}(p,s) :=$

p	5	6	7	8	15	16	17	18
s	5	b	5	c	15	e	15	f

.

The flat values that they encode are $\{\langle 1,a,5\rangle, \langle 1,d,15\rangle\} : \mathbf{Bag}(\mathbb{L}\times Base\times\mathbb{L})$ and $\{\langle 5,b\rangle,\langle 5,c\rangle,\langle 15,e\rangle,\langle 15,f\rangle\} : \mathbf{Bag}(\mathbb{L}\times Base)$.

However, the Dict_C relations cannot be immediately used to produce the sequence of tuples that they encode since the indices p associated with their symbols are non-consecutive. To address this issue we define:

$$\mathrm{ToSeq}[X](p',s) := \exists p.X(p,s) \wedge p' = \#u(\exists w.X(u,w) \wedge u \le p),$$

which maps each index p in relation $X(p,s)$ to an index p' corresponding to its position relative to the other indices in X. To do so we used predicate $p' = \#u\Phi(u)$ to count the number of positions u for which $\Phi(u)$ holds, since it is expressible in FOM [4].

Finally, we determine the shredded version of an input value $x : \mathbf{Bag}(B)$, based on its N^{Str} representation $S(p,s)$, as $S^F(p,s) := \mathrm{ToSeq}[\mathrm{Dict}_B(p,s) \wedge s \ne 1]$ where we filter out from $\mathrm{Dict}_B(p,s)$ those symbols denoting that a tuple belongs to the top level bag, identified by label 1. The shredding context is defined by a collection of relations $S^\Gamma := \mathrm{Sh}^\Gamma_B$, where:

$$\mathrm{Sh}^\Gamma_{Base} := \varnothing \qquad \mathrm{Sh}^\Gamma_{A_1\times A_2} := \langle \mathrm{Sh}^\Gamma_{A_1}, \mathrm{Sh}^\Gamma_{A_2}\rangle \qquad \mathrm{Sh}^\Gamma_{\mathbf{Bag}(C)} := \langle \mathrm{ToSeq}[\mathrm{Dict}_C], \mathrm{Sh}^\Gamma_C\rangle$$

The last step that remains is to convert the resulting flat bags from the current representation (as $X(p,s)$ relations in F^{Set} form) to the F^{Bag} representation. We recall that each such relation encodes a sequence of tuples such that each consecutive group of n_f symbols (according to their positions p) stands for a particular tuple in the bag, where n_f is the number of fields in the tuple. Additionally, since the bits in the F^{Set} representation are lexicographically ordered it follows that each consecutive group of σ_{ext} bits contains the unary representation of the symbol located at that position. Therefore, we can find out how many copies of a particular tuple t are in the bag by counting (modulo 2^k) for how many groups of $n_f \cdot \sigma_{ext}$ bits we have unary representations of symbols that match the symbols in t. By performing this counting for all possible tuples t in the output bag we obtain the F^{Bag} representation of $X(p,s)$. We note that both testing whether particular bits are set and counting modulo k are in TC_0.

Since $S^F(p,s)$ and S^Γ can be defined via FOM queries, and since their conversion from $X(p,s)$ relations in F^{Set} form to the F^{Bag} representation uses a TC_0 circuit, this concludes our proof that shredding nested values from N^{Str} to F^{Bag} representation can be done in TC_0. □

AJAR: Aggregations and Joins over Annotated Relations

Manas Joglekar
Stanford University
manasrj@stanford.edu

Rohan Puttagunta
Stanford University
rohanp@stanford.edu

Christopher Ré
Stanford University
chrismre@cs.stanford.edu

ABSTRACT

We study a class of aggregate-join queries with multiple aggregation operators evaluated over annotated relations. We show that straightforward extensions of standard multiway join algorithms and generalized hypertree decompositions (GHDs) provide best-known runtime guarantees. In contrast, prior work uses bespoke algorithms and data structures and does not match these guarantees. We extend the standard techniques by providing a complete characterization of (1) the set of orderings equivalent to a given ordering and (2) the set of GHDs valid with respect to the given ordering, i.e., GHDs that correctly answer a given aggregate-join query when provided to (simple variants of) standard join algorithms. We show by example that previous approaches are incomplete. The key technical consequence of our characterizations is a decomposition of a valid GHD into a set of (smaller) *unconstrained* GHDs, i.e., into a set of GHDs of sub-queries without aggregations. Since this decomposition is comprised of unconstrained GHDs, we are able to connect to the wide literature on GHDs for join query processing, thereby obtaining improved runtime bounds, MapReduce variants, and an efficient method to find approximately optimal GHDs.

1. INTRODUCTION

Generalized hypertree decompositions (GHDs), introduced by Gottlob et al. [9, 10] and further developed by Grohe and Marx [12], provide a means for performing early projection in join processing, which can result in dramatically faster runtimes. In this work, we extend GHDs to handle queries that include aggregations, which allows us to capture both SQL-aggregate processing and message passing problems. Motivated by our own database engine based on GHDs [1, 23, 27], we seek to more deeply understand the space of optimization for aggregate-join queries.

We build upon work by Green, Karvounarakis, and Tannen [11] on annotated relations to define our notion of aggregation. These annotations provide a general definition of aggregation, allowing us to represent a wide-ranging set of problems as aggregate-join queries. Our queries, which we call AJAR (Aggregations and Joins over Annotated Relations) queries, contain semiring quantifiers that "sum over" or "marginalize out" values. We formally define AJAR queries in Section 3, but they are easy to illustrate by example:

R

A	B	$\mathbb{Z}$
1	3	3
1	2	1
1	1	2

S

B	C	$\mathbb{Z}$
1	1	4
3	3	6

$R \bowtie S$

A	B	C	$\mathbb{Z}$
1	3	3	18
1	1	1	8

$\sum_C \sum_B R \bowtie S$

A	$\mathbb{Z}$
1	26

Figure 1: Illustrating the computation of Example 1

EXAMPLE 1. *Consider two relations with attributes $\{A, B\}$ and $\{B, C\}$ such that each tuple is annotated with some integer; we call these relations $\mathbb{Z}$-relations. Consider the query:*

$$\sum_C \sum_B R(A, B) \bowtie S(B, C)$$

Our output will then be a $\mathbb{Z}$-relation with attribute set $\{A\}$. The tuples in the relation will simply be the tuples of π_A $R(A, B) \bowtie S(B, C)$; we note that our convention of aggregation is opposite to that of projection in relational algebra. Each value a of attribute A in R is associated with a set X_a of tuples (b, c) composed of the values that appear with a in $R(A, B) \bowtie S(B, C)$; $X_a = \pi_{B,C}\sigma_{A=a}R(A, B) \bowtie S(B, C)$. Furthermore let z_R and z_S be the functions that return annotations of a given tuple for relations R and S, respectively. Then the annotation associated with a in our output will simply be

$$\sum_{(b,c)\in X_a} z_R(a, b) \times z_s(b, c).$$

AJAR queries capture both classical SQL-style project-join queries and newer data processing problems like probabilistic inference via message passing on graphical models [15]. In fact, Aji and McEliece proposed the "Marginalize a Product Function" (MPF) problem [4], which is a special case of an AJAR query, and showed how the problem and its solution capture a number of classic problems and algorithms, including fast Hadamard transforms, Viterbi's algorithm, forward-backward algorithm, FFT, and probabilistic inference in Bayesian networks. These algorithms are fundamental to

PODS'16, June 26-July 01, 2016, San Francisco, CA, USA

DOI: http://dx.doi.org/10.1145/2902251.2902293

various fields; for example the forward-backward algorithm over conditional random fields forms the basis for state of the art solutions to named entity recognition, part of speech tagging, noun phrase segmentation, and other problems in NLP [26]. We are motivated by the wide applicability of queries over annotated relations; annotated relations may provide a framework for combining classical query processing, linear algebra, and statistical inference in a single data processing system.

We consider a generalization of MPF with multiple aggregation operators. We represent an aggregate-join query as a join and an aggregation ordering, which specifies both the ordering and the aggregation of each attribute. Our class of queries directly follows from the work of Abo Khamis, Ngo, and Rudra [16], who investigated the "Functional Aggregate Query" (FAQ) problem. In addition to MPF, FAQ is a generalization of Chen and Dalmau's QCQ problem [7], in which the only aggregates are logical quantifiers (AND and OR).

The key technical challenge in these problems is characterizing the permissible aggregation orders to answer the query. A query consists of body Q and a string of attribute-operator pairs α, which we call an aggregation ordering. The challenge arises because different aggregation operators (e.g., $\sum$ and max) cannot freely commute. We show that attribute-operator pairs can commute for only two reasons: (1) their operators commute or (2) their attributes are "independent" in the query, e.g., in query $\max_B \max_A \sum_C R(A,B), S(B,C)$, the aggregations involving A and C can commute – even though max and $\sum$ do not commute as operators, the query body renders them *independent* given B. These two conditions for commuting generate equivalence classes among aggregation orderings.

Given the ordering α, we wish to identify which orderings are equivalent to α and which GHDs are compatible with an equivalent ordering. Chen and Dalmau give a complete characterization of which variable orders are equivalent for QCQ via a procedure. In the same spirit, we provide such a characterization for both equivalent orderings and compatible GHDs. We describe these characterizations in turn.

- *A Complete Characterization of Equivalent Orders:* Given an order α and two attribute-operator pairs $x, y \in \alpha$, we describe a set of constraints of the form *"in any order, x must appear after y."* Our constraints are sound and complete, i.e., a string β satisfies these constraints if and only if it is equivalent to α. In contrast, previous approaches have incomplete characterizations.

- *A Complete Characterization of GHDs Compatible with any Equivalent Order.* Given an order α and a query hypergraph Q, we call a GHD 'valid' if it is compatible with any ordering equivalent to α. We give a succinct characterization for all valid GHDs. We then describe a decomposition of the query (Q, α) into a series of *characteristic hypergraphs* (without attached aggregation orderings). GHDs for these hypergraphs can be combined into a valid GHD for the original query. We show that for any "node-monotone"[1] width function, there is a GHD with optimal width w that can be constructed with this decomposition. Treewidth, fractional hypertreewidth, and submodular width are all node-monotone.

[1]Informally, a measure is *node monotone* if adding more *nodes* to a graph does not reduce the measure, but additional edges may reduce the measure (see Definition 31).

Conceptually, the latter result is important for tying our work to existing GHD literature; the result reduces our problem to constructing standard GHDs. Pragmatically, it lets us apply existing GHD results to our characteristic hypergraphs and obtain the following results for free:

- Based on Grohe and Marx [12], we are able to describe our runtime in terms of classical metrics like fractional hypertreewidth. In turn, we can use tighter notions of width to upper bound the runtime like Marx's submodular width [18] or Joglekar's efficiently computable variant [14].

- Based on Afrati et al. [3], who bound the communication costs of join processing in terms of a "width" parameter for GHDs, we can develop efficient MapReduce algorithms for solving AJAR queries.

- Based on Marx's approximation [17] for GHDs, we can find approximately optimal GHDs for the popular fractional hypertreewidth measure in polynomial time.

We get the above results essentially for free from forging this connection to GHDs. We view this simple link as a strength of our approach.

Finally, we discuss an extension to handle "product aggregations" that allows us to aggregate away an attribute *before* we join the relations containing the attribute when the aggregation operator is the multiplication operator of the semiring. FAQ was the first to observe that this special case can improve certain types of logical queries. This opens up a new space of equivalent orderings and valid GHDs; mirroring the above results, we give a simple test and a complete characterization of the valid GHDs for queries that include this aggregation. This extension allows us to recover the results on QCQ presented by Chen and Dalmau. Moreover, we obtain similar improvements in runtime as previous work.

Outline. We discuss related work in Section 2. In Section 3, we introduce notation and algorithms that are relevant to our work before defining the AJAR problem. We also present our algorithm for answering AJAR queries. Section 4 provides a succinct characterization of all orderings that are equivalent to a given ordering. Section 5 discusses how to connect our work with recent research on GHDs, explaining how to construct valid optimal query plans and how to further improve and parallelize our results. In Section 6, we discuss how to incorporate product aggregations.

2. RELATED WORK

Join Algorithms. The Yannakakis algorithm, introduced in 1981, guarantees a runtime of $O(\text{IN} + \text{OUT})$ for α-acyclic join queries [29]. Modern multiway algorithms can process any join query and have worst-case optimal runtime. In particular, Atserias, Grohe, and Marx [5] derived a tight bound on the worst-case size of a join query given the input size and structure. Ngo et al. [20] presented the first algorithm to achieve this runtime bound, i.e., the first worst-case optimal algorithm. Soon after, Veldhuizen presented Leapfrog Triejoin, a very simple worst-case optimal algorithm that had been implemented in LogicBlox's commercial database system [28]. Ngo et al. [21] later presented the simplified and unified algorithm GenericJoin (GJ) that captured both of the previous worst-case optimal algorithms.

GHDs. First introduced by Gottlob, Leone, and Scarcello [10], hypertree decompositions and the associated hypertree width generalize the concept of tree decompositions [25]. Conceptually, the decompositions capture a hypergraph's cyclicity, allowing them to facilitate the selective use of GJ and Yannakakis in the standard hybrid join algorithm GHDJoin. There are deep connections between variable orderings and GHDs [16], which we leverage extensively. Grohe and Marx [12] introduced the idea of fractional hypertree width over GHDs, which bounds the runtime of GHDJoin by $\widetilde{O}(IN^w + OUT)$ ($\widetilde{O}$ hides poly-logarithmic factors) for w defined to be the minimum fractional hypertree width among all GHDs.

Semirings and Aggregations. Green, Karvounarakis, and Tannen developed the idea of annotations over a semiring [11]. Our notation for the annotations is superficially different from theirs, solely for notational convenience. We delve into more detail in Section 3. This also has been used as a mechanism to capture aggregation in probabilistic databases [24].

MPF. Aji and McEliece [4] defined the "Marginalize a Product Function" (MPF) problem, which is equivalent to the space of AJAR queries with only one aggregation operator. They showed that MPF generalizes a wide variety of important algorithms and problems, which also implies that AJAR queries are quite general. They also provided a message passing algorithm to solve MPF, which has since been refined [15]. We further improve runtimes over the state of the art.

Aggregate-Join Queries. There is a standard modification to Yannakakis to handle aggregations [29], but the classic analysis provides only a $O(\text{IN}\cdot\text{OUT})$ bound. Bakibayev, Kocisky, Olteanu, and Zavodny study aggregation-join queries in factorized databases [6], and later Olteanu and Zavodny connected factorized databases and GHDs/GHDJoin [22]. They develop the intuition that if output attributes are above non-output attributes, the +OUT runtime is preserved; we use the same intuition to develop and analyze AggroGHDJoin, a variant to GHDJoin for aggregate-join queries.

Abo Khamis, Ngo, and Rudra present the "Functional Aggregate Query" (FAQ) problem [16], which is equivalent to AJAR. The FAQ/AJAR problems arose out of discussions between Ngo, Rudra, and Ré at PODS12 about how to extend the worst-case result to queries using aggregation and message passing via Green et al.'s semiring formulation. We originally worked jointly on the problem, but we developed substantially different approaches, and decided to split our work. We argue that the AJAR approach is simpler and yields better runtime guarantees. We also describe new complete characterizations as described above. These completeness results let us connect more easily to existing literature. The algorithm described here has been implemented in the related database engine EmptyHeaded [1][2]. This engine has run motif finding, pagerank, and single-source shortest path queries, faster than previous high-level approaches that take datalog-like queries as input.

A primary application of multiple aggregation operators is quantified conjunctive queries (QCQ) and the counting variant, which can be expressed as AJAR queries over the semiring $(\vee, \wedge)$ with aggregations involving both operators. Here, we follow FAQ's idea to formulate this as a query with product aggregation. Chen and Dalmau [7] completely characterized the space of tractable QCQ by defining a notion of width that relies on variable orderings. Chen and Dalmau's width definition includes a complete characterization of the permissible variable orderings for a QCQ instance. Their characterization is similar in spirit to the partial ordering we define in Section 4 that characterizes the space of valid GHDs for an AJAR query. However, their results are focused on tractability rather than the optimal runtime exponents; our characterization extends theirs and has improved runtime bounds.

[2]We have been told that LogicBlox has implemented a similar algorithm recently, but their approach is not public. We shared our implementation with them several months ago.

3. DEFINING AJAR

We start by describing some background material needed to define the AJAR problem. After that, we formally define the AJAR problem and discuss our solution to it.

3.1 Background

We use the classic hypergraph representation for database schema and queries [2]. A hypergraph $\mathcal{H}$ is a pair $(\mathcal{V}_\mathcal{H}, \mathcal{E}_\mathcal{H})$, where $\mathcal{V}_\mathcal{H}$ is a non-empty set of *vertices* and $\mathcal{E}_\mathcal{H} \subseteq 2^{\mathcal{V}_\mathcal{H}}$ is a set of *hyperedges*. Each $A \in \mathcal{V}_\mathcal{H}$ is called an *attribute*. Each attribute has a corresponding *domain* $\mathcal{D}^A$.

- **Data** For each hyperedge $F \in \mathcal{E}_\mathcal{H}$, there is a corresponding relation $R_F \subseteq \prod_{A\in F} \mathcal{D}^A$; we use the notation $\mathcal{D}^F$ to denote the domain of the tuples $\prod_{A\in F} \mathcal{D}^A$.

- **Join Query** Given a set $\mathcal{E}_\mathcal{H}$ and a relation R_F for each $F \in \mathcal{E}_\mathcal{H}$, let $\mathcal{V}_\mathcal{H} = \cup_{F\in\mathcal{E}_\mathcal{H}} F$. The join query is written $\bowtie_{F\in\mathcal{E}_\mathcal{H}} R_F$ and is defined as

$$\left\{t \in \mathcal{D}^{\mathcal{V}_\mathcal{H}} \mid \forall F \in \mathcal{E} : \pi_F(t) \in R_F\right\}$$

  We use n to denote the number of attributes $|\mathcal{V}_\mathcal{H}|$ and m to denote the number of relations $|\mathcal{E}_\mathcal{H}|$. IN denotes the sum of sizes of input relations in a query, and OUT denotes the output size.

The complexity analysis in the paper is largely concerned with *data complexity*, i.e., all of our runtimes will be expressed in terms of IN and OUT. In Section 5, we develop ways to reduce query complexity as well.

A *path* from $A \in \mathcal{V}_\mathcal{H}$ to $B \in \mathcal{V}_\mathcal{H}$ in a hypergraph $\mathcal{H}$ is a sequence of attributes, starting with A and ending with B, such that each consecutive pair of attributes in the sequence occur together in a hyperedge. The number of attributes in the sequence is the *length* of the path.

We now define a GHD of a hypergraph.

DEFINITION 2. *Given a hypergraph $\mathcal{H} = (\mathcal{V}_\mathcal{H}, \mathcal{E}_\mathcal{H})$, a* generalized hypertree decomposition *is a pair $(\mathcal{T}, \chi)$ of a tree $\mathcal{T} = (\mathcal{V}_\mathcal{T}, \mathcal{E}_\mathcal{T})$ and function $\chi : \mathcal{V}_\mathcal{T} \to 2^{\mathcal{V}_\mathcal{H}}$ such that*

- *For each relation $F \in \mathcal{E}_\mathcal{H}$, there exists a tree node $t \in \mathcal{V}_\mathcal{T}$ that covers the edge, i.e., $F \subseteq \chi(t)$.*

- *For each attribute $A \in \mathcal{V}_\mathcal{H}$, the tree nodes containing A, i.e., $\{t \in \mathcal{V}_\mathcal{T} \mid A \in \chi(t)\}$, form a connected subtree.*

The latter condition is called the "running intersection property". The $\chi(t)$ sets are referred to as 'bags' of the GHD. GHDs are assumed to be 'rooted' trees, which imposes a top-down partial order on their nodes[3]. Leveraging this order, for any GHD $(\mathcal{T},\chi)$ and attribute $A \in \mathcal{V}_{\mathcal{H}}$, we define $TOP_{\mathcal{T}}(A)$ to be the top-most node $v \in \mathcal{V}_{\mathcal{T}}$ such that $A \in \chi(v)$.

When each bag of a GHD consists of the attributes of a single relation, the GHD is also called a *join tree*. Joins over a join tree can be processed using Yannakakis' algorithm [29]. The runtime of Yannakakis' algorithm is $O(\text{IN}+\text{OUT})$.

GHDs can be interpreted as query plans for joins. Given a GHD, we first join the attributes in each bag using worst case optimal algorithms [20, 28] to get one intermediate relation per bag. The intermediate relations can then be joined using Yannakakis' algorithm. We call this combined algorithm GHDJoin.

The runtime of GHDJoin can be expressed in terms of the *fractional hypertree width* of the GHD:

DEFINITION 3. *Given a hypergraph $\mathcal{H}=(\mathcal{V}_{\mathcal{H}},\mathcal{E}_{\mathcal{H}})$, a GHD $(\mathcal{T},\chi)$, and an instance I over $\mathcal{H}$, the* fractional hypertree width, *denoted $fhw(\mathcal{T},\mathcal{H},I)$, is defined to be $\max_{t\in\mathcal{T}}\rho_t^*$ in which ρ_t^* is the optimal value of the following linear program defined for each $t \in \mathcal{V}_{\mathcal{T}}$:*

$$\textit{Minimize} \sum_{F\in\mathcal{E}_{\mathcal{H}}} x_F \log_{\text{IN}}(|R_F|) \textit{ such that}$$

$$\forall A \in \chi(t): \sum_{F:A\in F} x_F \geq 1, \forall F \in \mathcal{E}_{\mathcal{H}}: x_F \geq 0$$

The fractional hypertree width is just the AGM bound [5] placed on the bags. Thus $IN^{fhw(\mathcal{T},\mathcal{H},I)}$ is an upper bound on the sizes of the intermediate relations of GHDJoin. GHDJoin runs in time $\widetilde{O}(\text{IN}^{fhw(\mathcal{T},\mathcal{H},I)}+\text{OUT})$ for join queries.

We note that GHDs are traditionally defined as a triple $(\mathcal{T},\chi,\lambda)$ where the function $\lambda:\mathcal{V}_{\mathcal{T}}\to 2^{\mathcal{E}_{\mathcal{H}}}$ assigns relations to each bag. Then the linear program in the definition of *fhw* is applied to the relations in $\lambda(t)$ for each node t. We omit this function and implicitly assign *every* relation to each bag (so $\lambda(t)=\mathcal{E}_{\mathcal{H}}$ for all $t\in\mathcal{V}_{\mathcal{T}}$). Though this makes a difference for certain notions of width, it leaves the fractional hypertree width unchanged, as adding more relations to the linear program cannot make the objective value worse. We also note that omitting function λ makes GHDs equivalent to Tree Decompositions. We use the terminology of GHDs as all related works on joins use GHDs; since there is a simple mapping between the two, it makes no difference formally.

We also note that our definition of fractional hypertree width is a little different from that originally presented by Grohe and Marx [12]; the original definition of *fhw* does not use the relation sizes in the objective value of its linear program. Inspired by AGM [5], we add the relation sizes as weights to actually form a tighter bound on runtime. And the development of worst-case join algorithms allows us to achieve this faster runtime.

Annotated Relations. To define a general notion of aggregations, we look to relations annotated with semirings [11].

[3]For ordinary join queries (without aggregation) the choice of root can be arbitrary; it does not affect the complexity or the correctness of GHDJoin. However, this top-down partial order on the nodes will play a larger role when answering AJAR queries.

DEFINITION 4. *A* commutative semiring *is a triple $(S,\oplus,\otimes)$ of a set S and operators $\oplus: S\times S\to S$, $\otimes: S\times S\to S$ where there exist $0,1\in S$ such that for all $a,b,c\in S$ the following properties hold:*

- *Identity and Annihilation: $a\oplus 0=a$, $a\otimes 1=a$, $0\otimes a=0$*
- *Associativity: $(a\oplus b)\oplus c=a\oplus(b\oplus c)$, $(a\otimes b)\otimes c=a\otimes(b\otimes c)$*
- *Commutativity: $a\oplus b=b\oplus a$, $a\otimes b=b\otimes a$*
- *Distributivity: $a\otimes(b\oplus c)=(a\otimes b)\oplus(a\otimes c)$*

Suppose we have some domain $\mathbb{K}$ and an operator set $O=\{\oplus^1,\oplus^2,\ldots\oplus^k,\otimes\}$ such that 0 is the identity for each $\oplus^i\in O$ and $(\mathbb{K},\oplus^i,\otimes)$ forms a commutative semiring for each i. We then define a relation with an annotation from $\mathbb{K}$ for each tuple.

DEFINITION 5. *An* annotated relation *with annotations from $\mathbb{K}$, or a $\mathbb{K}$-relation, over attribute set F is a set $\{(t_1,\lambda_1),(t_2,\lambda_2),\ldots,(t_N,\lambda_N)\}$ such that for all $1\leq i\leq N$, $t_i\in\mathcal{D}^F$, $\lambda_i\in\mathbb{K}$ and for all $1\leq j\leq N: i\neq j\to t_i\neq t_j$.*

Green et al. define a $\mathbb{K}$-relation to be a function $R_F:\mathcal{D}^F\to\mathbb{K}$ [11]. Our notion can be viewed as an explicit listing of this function's support. But unlike an explicit listing of the function's support, our table does allow tuples with 0 annotations. However, under our definitions of the operators below, an annotation of 0 is semantically equivalent to a tuple being absent (we discuss this further in Section 6). Note that we can have an annotated relation of the form $R_\emptyset$ of size 1 containing the empty tuple with some annotation. We now define joins and aggregations over annotated relations.

Joins over Annotated Relations. Informally, a join over annotated relations is obtained as follows. We first perform a regular join on the non-annotated part of the relations. Then, for each output tuple t of the join, we set its annotation to the product of the annotations of the input tuples used to produce t. Formally, we define a join $\bowtie_{F\in\mathcal{E}_{\mathcal{H}}} R_F$ as:

$$\{(t,\lambda)\mid t\in\mathcal{D}^{\mathcal{V}_{\mathcal{H}}},\lambda=\prod_{F\in\mathcal{E}_{\mathcal{H}}}\lambda_F:(\pi_F(t),\lambda_F)\in R_F\}$$

Aggregations over Annotated Relations. An aggregation over an annotated relation R_F is specified by a pair $(A,\oplus)$ where $A\in F$, and $\oplus\in O$. The aggregation takes groups of tuples in R_F that share values of all attributes other than A, and produces a single tuple corresponding to each group, whose annotation is the $\oplus$-aggregate of the annotations of the tuples in the group. Suppose that R has schema $R(A,B)$ in which A is a single attribute and B is a set of attributes. Then, the result of aggregation $(A,\oplus)$ has only the attributes B and

$$\sum_{(A,\oplus)} R_{A,B}=\{(t_B,\lambda)\mid t_B\in\pi_B R \text{ and } \lambda=\bigoplus_{(t,\lambda_t)\in R:\pi_B t=t_B}\lambda_t\}$$

One can define the meaning of aggregate-join queries in a straightforward way: first compute the join and then perform aggregations. Figure 2 shows some examples of operators on relations. For the remainder of our work, we assume that all relations are $\mathbb{K}$-relations.

R

A	B	$\mathbb{K}$
1	1	1
2	1	2

S

B	C	$\mathbb{K}$
1	1	3
1	2	4

$R \bowtie S$

A	B	C	$\mathbb{K}$
1	1	1	3
1	1	2	4
2	1	1	6
2	1	2	8

$\Sigma_{(C,+)} S$

A	B	$\mathbb{K}$
1	1	7
2	1	14

Figure 2: Selected examples illustrating the operators over the semiring $(\mathbf{R}_+, +, \cdot)$

3.2 The AJAR problem

DEFINITION 6. *Given some global attribute set $\mathcal{V}$ and operator set O, we define an* aggregation ordering *to be a sequence $\alpha = \alpha_1, \alpha_2, \ldots, \alpha_s$ such that for each $1 \leq i \leq s$, $\alpha_i = (a_i, \oplus_i)$ for some $a_i \in \mathcal{V}, \oplus_i \in O$.* [4] *In addition, attributes occur at most once, i.e., $a_j \neq a_k$ for each $1 \leq j < k \leq s$.*

Informally, the aggregation ordering is a sequence of attribute-operator pairs such that each attribute appears at most once. Note that the aggregation ordering specifies the order and manner in which attributes are aggregated. The ordering does not need to contain every attribute; we use the term *output attributes* to denote the attributes not in the ordering.

$V(\alpha)$ represents the set of attributes that appear in α, and $V(-\alpha)$ represents $V \setminus V(\alpha)$, i.e., the output attributes. When $F \subseteq V(\alpha)$, we use α_F to denote the restriction of α to the attributes in F, so $V(\alpha_F) = F$.

DEFINITION 7 (AJAR). *Given some hypergraph $\mathcal{H} = (\mathcal{V}, \mathcal{E})$ and an aggregation ordering α, an* AJAR *query $Q_{\mathcal{H},\alpha}$ is a function over instances of $\mathcal{H}$ such that*

$$Q_{\mathcal{H},\alpha}(\{R_F | F \in \mathcal{E}\}) = \Sigma_{\alpha_1} \cdots \Sigma_{\alpha_{|\alpha|}} \bowtie_{F \in \mathcal{E}} R_F.$$

3.3 Answering AJAR Queries

For an AJAR query, we define OUT to be the final output size, which is smaller than the output size of the join when $|\alpha| > 0$. Thus the standard GHDJoin runtime of $\text{IN}^{fhw} + \text{OUT}$ is harder to achieve. In this section, we achieve this standard runtime even with aggregations by restricting the class of acceptable GHDs.

We present a simple variant of GHDJoin, called AggroGHDJoin, that performs aggregations on annotated relations.

Algorithm 1 AggroGHDJoin($\mathcal{H} = (\mathcal{V}_{\mathcal{H}}, \mathcal{E}_{\mathcal{H}})$, α, $(\mathcal{T}(\mathcal{V}_{\mathcal{T}}, \mathcal{E}_{\mathcal{T}}), \chi)$, $\{R_F | F \in \mathcal{E}_{\mathcal{H}}\}$)

Input: Query hypergraph $\mathcal{H}$, Aggregation Ordering α, GHD $(\mathcal{T}, \chi)$, Relations R_F for each $F \in \mathcal{E}_{\mathcal{H}}$

```
S_R ← ∅
for all t ∈ V_T do
    H_t ← (χ(t), {π_χ(t) F | F ∈ E_H})
    I ← {R_F | F ⊆ χ(t), ∃a ∈ F : TOP_T(a) = t} ∪
    {π¹_χ(t) R_F | F ⊈ χ(t) or ∀a ∈ F : TOP_T(a) ≠ t}
    S_R ← S_R ∪ GJ(H_t, I)
end for
return AggroYannakakis(T, α, S_R)
```

[4]Note that, by this definition, the operators in aggregation ordering can be the product aggregation $\otimes$. However, product aggregations require different definitions, see Section 6.

The operator π^1 denotes projection that sets the annotations of all output tuples to 1. We require this operator to construct the instances I passed to GJ to ensure the annotations of a particular relation only get multiplied once in the join. AggroYannakakis is a slightly modified version of the classic project-join algorithm by Yannakakis [29], with the modifications necessary to handle the annotations correctly; we provide the details in Appendix A.

We start by reasoning about the correctness of AggroGHDJoin. We note that AJAR queries are define with aggregation orderings, but our algorithm uses GHDs instead of orderings. We now connect the two notions.

DEFINITION 8. *Given an* AJAR *query $Q_{\mathcal{H},\alpha}$, a GHD $(\mathcal{T}, \chi)$ of $\mathcal{H}$ is* compatible *with α if and only if $TOP_{\mathcal{T}}(A)$ being an ancestor of $TOP_{\mathcal{T}}(B)$ implies A either precedes B in α or is an output attribute.*

THEOREM 9. *Algorithm 1 correctly computes an* AJAR *query $Q_{\mathcal{H},\alpha}$ if it is given a GHD $(\mathcal{T}, \chi)$ of $\mathcal{H}$ that is compatible with α.*

PROOF. (Sketch) Note that Yannakakis (and AggroYannakakis) performs the projections (i.e., aggregations) in a bottom-up manner. Moreover, a GHD is compatible with a given ordering iff some top-down ordering of the attributes is equivalent to the given ordering. □

Suppose our given GHD has *fhw* w. Traditional analysis of GHDJoin and GJ tells us the portion of AggroGHDJoin before calling AggroYannakakis runs in $\widetilde{O}(\text{IN}^w)$. However, the traditional analysis of Yannakakis on project-join queries only provides a guarantee of $O(\text{IN} \cdot \text{OUT})$. The underlying cause for this blowup is that the $TOP_{\mathcal{T}}$ nodes for output attributes may occur below the $TOP_{\mathcal{T}}$ nodes of non-output attributes. We note that our definition ensures this never happens in any compatible GHD, avoiding this blowup.

THEOREM 10. *Given an* AJAR *query $Q_{\mathcal{H},\alpha}$, let w^* denote the smallest fhw for a GHD compatible with α; the runtime of our approach is $\widetilde{O}(\text{IN}^{w^*} + \text{OUT})$.*

We trace through the details of the proof in Appendix A, but it follows the spirit of the proofs of the classic Yannakakis algorithm.

4. CHARACTERIZING EQUIVALENT ORDERINGS

We discussed an algorithm to solve AJAR queries with a seemingly optimal (or near-optimal) runtime of $\widetilde{O}(\text{IN}^{w^*} + \text{OUT})$. However, note that w^* is optimal width over an extremely restrictive class of GHDs. In this section we expand the class of permissible GHDs by identifying alternative aggregation orders that produce the same output as α over any database instance; some of these new orders may allow for faster runtimes, e.g., some orders may allow early aggregation.

As suggested above, we can define a natural equivalence relation over aggregation orderings.

DEFINITION 11 (EQUIVALENT ORDERINGS). *Given a hypergraph $\mathcal{H}$, define the equivalence relation between orderings $\equiv_{\mathcal{H}}$ such that $\alpha \equiv_{\mathcal{H}} \beta$ if and only if $Q_{\mathcal{H},\alpha}(I) = Q_{\mathcal{H},\beta}(I)$ for all database instances I over the schema $\mathcal{H}$.*

To determine which orders are equivalent, we first investigate which attribute-operator pairs commute. We make two simple observations: (1) by the Eckmann-Hilton argument [8], two operators commute in general if and only if they are equal[5] and (2) aggregations can be pushed down into joins, which means two attributes commute if they are in independent parts of the join. We illustrate these forms of commuting by example and then formalize them.

EXAMPLE 12. *Suppose we have the* AJAR *query* $Q_{\mathcal{H},\alpha} = \sum_{(A,+)} \sum_{(B,+)} \sum_{(C,\max)} R(A,B) \bowtie S(A,C)$. *The first pair of aggregations can commute since they have identical operators; if* $\beta = ((B,+),(A,+),(C,\max))$, $\alpha \equiv_{\mathcal{H}} \beta$. *Similarly the second pair of aggregations can commute because the projection can be pushed down:*

$$\sum_{(B,+)} \sum_{(C,\max)} R(A,B) \bowtie S(A,C)$$
$$= \left[\sum_{(B,+)} R(A,B)\right] \bowtie \left[\sum_{(C,\max)} S(A,C)\right]$$
$$= \sum_{(C,\max)} \sum_{(B,+)} R(A,B) \bowtie S(A,C)$$

So if $\beta = ((A,+),(C,\max),(B,+))$, $\alpha \equiv_{\mathcal{H}} \beta$.

THEOREM 13. *Suppose we are given a relation* R_F *such that* $A, B \in F$ *and two operators* $\oplus', \oplus \in O$. *Then*

$$\Sigma_{(A,\oplus)}\Sigma_{(B,\oplus')}R_F = \Sigma_{(B,\oplus')}\Sigma_{(A,\oplus)}R_F$$

if one of the following conditions hold:

- $\oplus = \oplus'$
- *There exist relations* R_{F_1} *and* R_{F_2} *such that* $A \notin F_1$, $B \notin F_2$, *and* $R_{F_1} \bowtie R_{F_2} = R_F$.

The proof of this theorem is straightforward, but it provides the foundation for an algorithm to test the equivalence of two aggregation orderings. This testing algorithm combined with a modified join algorithm (discussed next) lets us recover and surpass runtimes of previous work (see our technical report [13] for details).

Note that the equivalence relation $\equiv_{\mathcal{H}}$ defines equivalence classes among the orderings that may be exponential in size. We are motivated to find a more succinct characterization that lets us enumerate all equivalent orderings with constant delay. Chen and Dalmau [7] obtained a similar order-equivalence characterization for a special case of the AJAR problem, namely for aggregations "and" and "or". The characterization was based on a procedure that generated all equivalent orderings. We provide a succinct characterization of the equivalence class of an aggregation ordering with any number of operators[6].

To that end, we develop an enumeration of the constraints that are sufficient and necessary for an ordering to be in the equivalence class of α. The constraints are of the form "A must always occur before B":

[5]Two operators $\oplus, \oplus'$ are equal over a domain $\mathbb{K}$ if $\forall x, y \in \mathbb{K}$, $x \oplus y = x \oplus' y$

[6]"and" is a product aggregation, so the generalization of Chen and Dalmau's characterization is only covered in Section 6

DEFINITION 14 (PREC). *Given an* AJAR *query* $Q_{\mathcal{H},\alpha}$, *define a constraint* $\mathsf{PREC} \subseteq \mathcal{V} \times \mathcal{V}$ *such that* $(A,B) \in \mathsf{PREC}$ *if and only if* A *precedes* B *in all orderings that are equivalent to* α.

We say $\mathsf{PREC}(A,B)$ is true if and only if $(A,B) \in \mathsf{PREC}$.

Trivially, the number of pairs in PREC is less than n^2. We note that we can use PREC to define a (strict) partial ordering on the attributes; the constraints are clearly antireflexive, antisymmetric, and transitive. We use $<_{\mathcal{H},\alpha}$ to denote this partial order. Given an AJAR query $Q_{\mathcal{H},\alpha}$, $<_{\mathcal{H},\alpha}$ is a partial order of attribute-operator pairs such that for any $(A,\oplus),(B,\oplus') \in \alpha$, $(A,\oplus) <_{\mathcal{H},\alpha} (B,\oplus')$ if $\mathsf{PREC}(A,B)$ (see Definition 23 for the exact definition). The partial order $<_{\mathcal{H},\alpha}$ is easier to use for proofs; we use the partial order to show the soundness and completeness of these constraints.

THEOREM 15 ($<_{\mathcal{H},\alpha}$ SOUNDNESS AND COMPLETENESS). *Suppose we are given a hypergraph* $\mathcal{H} = (\mathcal{V},\mathcal{E})$ *and aggregation orderings* α, β. *Then* $\alpha \equiv_{\mathcal{H}} \beta$ *if and only if* β *is a linear extension of* $<_{\mathcal{H},\alpha}$.

We first describe a procedure to compute the precedence relation PREC. After that, we reason about its completeness.

Computing PREC.

To assist in building PREC, we define a constraint of the form "A and B cannot commute":

DEFINITION 16 (DNC). *Given an* AJAR *query* $Q_{\mathcal{H},\alpha}$, *define a constraint* $\mathsf{DNC} \subseteq \mathcal{V} \times \mathcal{V}$ *such that* $(A,B) \in \mathsf{DNC}$ *if and only if* A *and* B *are in the same order in any* β *such that* $\beta \equiv_{\mathcal{H}} \alpha$.

Once again, we say $\mathsf{DNC}(A,B)$ is true if and only if $(A,B) \in \mathsf{DNC}$. We prefer to work with DNC because we have already discussed when aggregations can commute in Theorem 13; the conditions of that theorem specify when DNC is $FALSE$. However, we can immediately derive a simple relationship between PREC and DNC:

LEMMA 17. *Given an* AJAR *query* $Q_{\mathcal{H},\alpha}$, *for any* $A, B \in \mathcal{V}$, $\mathsf{PREC}(A,B)$ *iff* $\mathsf{DNC}(A,B)$ *and* A *precedes* B *in* α.

We now develop conditions when DNC is true. Recall that Theorem 13 states that two aggregations can commute if (1) they have the same operator or (2) they can be separated in the join query; the simplest structure that violates both of these conditions is an edge that contains two attributes with differing aggregating operators.

LEMMA 18. *Given an* AJAR *query* $Q_{\mathcal{H},\alpha}$, *suppose* $(A,\oplus)$, $(B,\oplus') \in \alpha$. *If* $\oplus \neq \oplus'$ *and there exists an edge* $E \in \mathcal{E}$ *such that* $A, B \in E$, *then* $\mathsf{DNC}(A,B)$.

Lemma 18 serves as a base case, but we want to extend the violation of Theorem 13's conditions beyond single edges to paths. To do so, consider the following examples of how our commuting conditions interact with paths of length two.

EXAMPLE 19. *Consider the query*

$$\sum_{(A,+)} \sum_{(B,\max)} \sum_{(C,\max)} R(A,B) \bowtie S(B,C).$$

No two attributes can be separated, which implies $\mathsf{DNC}(A,B)$ *and* $\mathsf{DNC}(A,C)$. *Lemma 18 gives us the former constraint,* *but not the latter one. This example indicates that it may be possible to extend a constraint DNC(A,B) along an edge $\{B,C\}$. On the other hand, consider the query*

$$\sum_{(B,\max)} \sum_{(A,+)} \sum_{(C,\max)} R(A,B) \bowtie S(B,C).$$

Note that A and C can be separated, which implies that only DNC(A,B) holds. Note that, as before, Lemma 18 gives us this constraint. This example suggests that we cannot extend every DNC(A,B) constraint along an additional edge.

The key difference between the two examples is the *relative order* of A and B in α, which suggests that we can only extend DNC(A,B) along an edge if A precedes B in α, i.e., if PREC(A,B).

LEMMA 20. *Given an* AJAR *query $Q_{\mathcal{H},\alpha}$, suppose $(A,\oplus)$, $(B,\oplus') \in \alpha$. If $\oplus \neq \oplus'$ and $\exists C \in \mathcal{V}, E \in \mathcal{E}$: PREC(A,C) and $B,C \in E$, then DNC(A,B).*

PREC is transitive, which implies:

LEMMA 21. *Given an* AJAR *query $Q_{\mathcal{H},\alpha}$, suppose $(A,\oplus)$, $(B,\oplus') \in \alpha$. If $\exists C$: PREC(A,C) and PREC(C,B), then DNC(A,B).*

The above transitivity condition interacts with the condition from Lemma 20 in interesting ways.

EXAMPLE 22. *Consider the query,*

$$\sum_{(A,+)} \sum_{(B,\max)} \sum_{(C,\max)} \sum_{(D,+)} R(A,B) \bowtie S(B,D) \bowtie T(C,D).$$

No attributes can be separated, which implies DNC(A,B), DNC(A,C), DNC(B,D), and DNC(C,D). Transitivity gives DNC(A,D) as well. Now let us derive these constraints using Lemmas 18, 20, and 21. Lemma 18 gives us DNC(A,C), DNC(B,D), and DNC(C,D). Note that at this point, Lemma 20 gives us no more constraints. Only after the transitivity of Lemma 21 adds the constraint DNC(A,D) can Lemma 20 add the constraint DNC(A,B), completing the set of constraints.

It turns out that these three simple lemmas provide sufficient and necessary constraints on the equivalence classes of orderings; no other conditions are necessary to complete the proofs the soundness and completeness of $<_{\mathcal{H},\alpha}$.

We note that our current specifications of PREC and DNC are mutually recursive. The PREC and DNC sets build up in rounds; Lemma 18 provides their initial values, and Lemmas 17, 20, and 21 iteratively build up the sets further. We keep applying these lemmas until the sets reach a fixed point. This takes at most $2|\alpha|^2$ iterations, as we must add at least one additional attribute pair per iteration, and there can be only $|\alpha|^2$ pairs of attributes in each set. Thus the overall runtime of computing these constraints is polynomial in the number of attributes. Please see our technical report for more details [13].

For convenience of notation, we make one modification to the definition of the partial order $<_{\mathcal{H},\alpha}$. When A is an output attribute and B is not, we define $A <_{\mathcal{H},\alpha} B$ to be true. So we can formally state the definition as:

DEFINITION 23 ($<_{\mathcal{H},\alpha}$). *Given a* AJAR *query $Q_{\mathcal{H},\alpha}$, we define $A <_{\mathcal{H},\alpha} B$ to be true if either (i) A is an output attribute and B is not or (ii) PREC(A,B) is true.*

Soundness and Completeness of $<_{\mathcal{H},\alpha}$. To prove the soundness and completeness of $<_{\mathcal{H},\alpha}$, we now state two key lemmas illustrating properties of $<_{\mathcal{H},\alpha}$. We mostly provide proof sketches, please see our technical report [13] for full proofs.

LEMMA 24. *Suppose we are given a hypergraph $\mathcal{H} = (\mathcal{V},\mathcal{E})$ and an aggregation ordering α. Suppose $(A,\oplus),(B,\oplus') \in \alpha$ for differing operators $\oplus \neq \oplus'$. Then, for any path P in $\mathcal{H}$ between A and B, there must exist some attribute in the path $C \in P$ such that $C <_{\mathcal{H},\alpha} A$ or $C <_{\mathcal{H},\alpha} B$.*

Note that the C in the statement above can be either A or B. Lemma 24 is only non-trivial if A and B are incomparable. Intuitively the lemma states that attributes incomparable under $<_{\mathcal{H},\alpha}$ with differing operators must be separated in $\mathcal{H}$ by their combined predecessors in $<_{\mathcal{H},\alpha}$.

PROOF. (Sketch) We proceed by induction on the length of the path P. We let C be the attribute between A and B that appears earliest in α and assume without loss of generality that A and C have differing operators. By the inductive hypothesis, there must exist a D on the path from A to C such that either $D <_{\mathcal{H},\alpha} A$ or $D <_{\mathcal{H},\alpha} C$. In the former case, our proof is done. In the latter case we reason that since C is defined to be the attribute that appears earliest in α between A and B, $D <_{\mathcal{H},\alpha} C$ implies $D = A$. We then prove by induction that $A <_{\mathcal{H},\alpha} X$ for all X on the path between C and B, which then implies that A and B cannot be incomparable. □

This lemma allows us to prove the soundness of $<_{\mathcal{H},\alpha}$.

LEMMA 25. *(Soundness of $<_{\mathcal{H},\alpha}$) If β is a linear extension of $<_{\mathcal{H},\alpha}$, then $\alpha \equiv \beta$.*

PROOF. We induct on the number of inversions in β with respect to the ordering α. Our base case, 0 inversion, is trivial. Now suppose β has $N > 0$ inversions, and assume the lemma is true for orderings with $< N$ inversions. There must be some β_i and β_{i+1} that are inverted with respect to α. Consider the ordering β' derived by swapping β_i and β_{i+1}. By the inductive hypothesis, $\alpha \equiv_{\mathcal{H}} \beta'$.

We now show that $\beta \equiv_{\mathcal{H}} \beta'$. Suppose $\beta_i = (A,\oplus)$ and $\beta_{i+1} = (B,\oplus')$. We have two cases to consider.

- $\oplus = \oplus'$
  By Theorem 13, we can swap β_i and β_{i+1} without affecting the output. This implies that $\beta \equiv_{\mathcal{H}} \beta'$.
- $\oplus \neq \oplus'$
  By Lemma 24, any path between A and B must go through some attribute C that appears earlier than index i in β. This implies that A and B are in separate connected components in $\pi_{V(\beta_i,\beta_{i+1},\ldots,\beta_{|\beta|})}\mathcal{H}$, which implies that we can swap β_i and β_{i+1} without affecting the output by Theorem 13. Thus $\beta \equiv_{\mathcal{H}} \beta'$.

□

Our next lemma helps us prove the completeness of $<_{\mathcal{H},\alpha}$.

LEMMA 26. *Given a hypergraph $\mathcal{H} = (\mathcal{V},\mathcal{E})$ and an aggregation ordering α, suppose $A <_{\mathcal{H},\alpha} B$ for some $A,B \in V(\alpha)$. Then there must exist a path P from A to B such that for every $C \in P, C \neq A$ we have $A <_{\mathcal{H},\alpha} C$.*

PROOF. (Sketch) We proceed by induction on the recursive definition of $<_{\mathcal{H},\alpha}$. Lemma 18 implies A and B share an edge. Lemma 20 implies the existence of a C such that either $A <_{\mathcal{H},\alpha} C, (B,C) \in \mathcal{E}$ or $B <_{\mathcal{H},\alpha} C, (A,C) \in \mathcal{E}$. Either way we inductively construct a path between C and the attribute it doesn't share an edge with. Finally, Lemma 21 implies the existence of a C such that $A <_{\mathcal{H},\alpha} C <_{\mathcal{H},\alpha} B$, which lets us inductively construct paths from A to C and C to B. □

LEMMA 27. *(Completeness of $<_{\mathcal{H},\alpha}$) If β is not a linear extension of $<_{\mathcal{H},\alpha}$, then $\alpha \not\equiv \beta$.*

PROOF. (Sketch) We first construct a particular ordering $\alpha' \equiv \alpha$ that allows us to find two attribute-ordering pairs $(A, \oplus), (B, \oplus') \in \alpha'$ such that $B <_{\mathcal{H},\alpha} A$, $\oplus \neq \oplus'$, and A precedes B in β. Since $\oplus \neq \oplus'$, there must exist $x, y \in \mathbb{K}$ such that $x \oplus y \neq x \oplus' y$. Our proof constructs an instance $\hat{I}$ such that $Q_{\mathcal{H},\alpha}(\hat{I})$ returns one tuple with annotation $x \oplus' y$ and $Q_{\mathcal{H},\beta}(\hat{I})$ returns one tuple with annotation $x \oplus y$.

Our construction relies on Lemma 26, which implies the existence of a path P from A to B such that every attribute in our path comes after B in α'. Additionally, by construction, we can guarantee that every attribute in our path comes after A in β. We then finish by constructing an instance so that only the outermost aggregation of the path P changes the relation; since the outermost aggregations of α and β have different operators, we get different annotations in the output. □

5. DECOMPOSING VALID GHDS

We express our AJAR algorithm directly in terms of GHDs, rather than in terms of aggregation orderings. As such, our goal is the characterization of GHDs that are compatible with at least one equivalent ordering, i.e., the GHDs that can be used to answer an AJAR query. We call a GHD *valid* if it is compatible with at least one equivalent ordering. We first give a simple characterization of valid GHDs. Then we demonstrate a way to reduce the problem of finding a minimum-width valid GHD to multiple subproblems on unconstrained GHDs (Section 5.1). This decomposition of the problem gets us three things:

- We can speed up our brute force search for an optimal valid GHD. We can also find approximately optimal valid GHDs in polynomial time using Marx's GHD approximation algorithm [17] (Section 5.2).
- We can apply existing MapReduce join algorithms that utilize GHDs [3], obtaining efficient parallel algorithms for solving AJAR queries (Section 5.4).
- We can apply improved join algorithms [14, 18] to further reduce our runtime exponent (Section 5.3).

5.1 Valid and Decomposable GHDs

We can easily characterize valid GHDs by combining the definition of compatible GHDs with Theorem 15.

THEOREM 28. *For an AJAR query $Q_{\mathcal{H},\alpha}$, a GHD $(\mathcal{T}, \chi)$ is* valid *if and only if for every pair of attributes A, B such that $TOP_{\mathcal{T}}(A)$ is an ancestor of $TOP_{\mathcal{T}}(B)$, $B \not<_{\mathcal{H},\alpha} A$.*

Theorem 28 gives us a criterion specifying which GHDs can act as query plans. We now consider the problem of finding a minimum width valid GHD for any AJAR query. We call a GHD *optimal* if it has the minimum width possible for valid GHDs. We show how to reduce the problem of finding an optimal valid GHD into smaller problems of finding ordinary optimal GHDs. This unlocks a trove of powerful GHD results and makes them applicable to our problem.

Given an AJAR query $Q_{\mathcal{H},\alpha}$, suppose we have a subset of the nodes $V \subseteq \mathcal{V}$. Define $\mathcal{E}_V$ to be $\{E \in \mathcal{E} | E \cap V \neq \emptyset\}$, i.e., the set of edges that intersect with V. As before, α_V denotes the aggregation ordering restricted to the nodes in V. Additionally define V^O to be $\{v \in V | \forall w \in V, w \not<_{\mathcal{H},\alpha} v\}$, i.e., the nodes in V that have no predecessors in V according to the partial ordering $<_{\mathcal{H},\alpha}$. Note that $\alpha_{V \setminus V^O}$ is then α_V with all the nodes in V^O removed (this makes the nodes in V^O output attributes). Finally, for a GHD $(\mathcal{T}, \chi)$, we will use $\chi(\mathcal{T})$ to denote $\cup_{t \in \mathcal{V}_{\mathcal{T}}} \chi(t)$.

DEFINITION 29. *Given an AJAR query $Q_{\mathcal{H},\alpha}$, we say a GHD $(\mathcal{T}, \chi)$ is* decomposable *if:*

- *There exists a rooted subtree $\mathcal{T}_0$ of $\mathcal{T}$ such that $\chi(\mathcal{T}_0) = \mathcal{V}(-\alpha)$ (i.e., output attributes).*
- *For each connected component C of $\mathcal{H} \setminus V_{-\alpha}$, there is exactly one subtree $\mathcal{T}_C \in \mathcal{T} \setminus \mathcal{T}_0$ such that $\mathcal{T}_C$ is a decomposable GHD of $Q_{(\cup_{E \in \mathcal{E}_C} E, \mathcal{E}_C), \alpha_{C \setminus C^O}}$.*

We start by connecting this idea of decomposable GHDs to valid GHDs. We only give proof sketches here; see our technical report for the full proofs.

THEOREM 30. *Every decomposable GHD is valid.*

PROOF. (Sketch) Suppose the AJAR query is $Q_{\mathcal{H},\alpha}$. We need to show for any A, B such that $TOP_{\mathcal{T}}(A)$ is an ancestor of $TOP_{\mathcal{T}}(B)$, $A \not<_{\mathcal{H},\alpha} B$. We use induction on $|\alpha|$. If $|\alpha| = 0$, all GHDs are valid and decomposable. For $|\alpha| > 0$, $\mathcal{T}_0$ ensures that the output attributes are above non-output attributes. If A and B are non-output attributes and $TOP_{\mathcal{T}}(A)$ is an ancestor of $TOP_{\mathcal{T}}(B)$, then both are in some $\mathcal{T}_C$. By the inductive hypothesis, $\mathcal{T}_C$ is valid with respect to $Q_{(\cup_{E \in \mathcal{E}_C} E, \mathcal{E}_C), \alpha_{C \setminus C^O}}$. By inspecting the partial order created by this subgraph, we conclude that $A \not<_{\mathcal{H},\alpha} B$ as desired. □

Not every valid GHD is decomposable. However, every valid GHD can be transformed into a corresponding decomposable GHD using some simple transformations. Each bag of the resulting decomposable GHD is a subset of one of the bags of the original GHD. Thus the *fhw* of the decomposable GHD is at most the *fhw* of the original valid GHD. In fact, we can make a more general claim, using a notion of node-monotone functions, defined next.

DEFINITION 31. *Given a hypergraph $\mathcal{H} = (\mathcal{V}_{\mathcal{H}}, \mathcal{E}_{\mathcal{H}})$, we define a function to be* node-monotone *if it is a function $\gamma : 2^{\mathcal{V}_{\mathcal{H}}} \to \mathbb{R}$ such that $\forall\ A \subseteq B \subseteq \mathcal{V}_{\mathcal{H}} : \gamma(A) \leq \gamma(B)$. Given any node-monotone function γ, we define the γ-width of a GHD $(\mathcal{T}, \chi)$ over $\mathcal{H}$ as $\max_{v \in \mathcal{V}_{\mathcal{T}}} \gamma(\chi(v))$.*

Many standard notions of widths can be expressed as γ-widths for a suitably chosen γ. Specifically:

PROPOSITION 1. *Suppose we are given a hypergraph $\mathcal{H} = (\mathcal{V}_{\mathcal{H}}, \mathcal{E}_{\mathcal{H}})$ and database instance I on $\mathcal{H}$. Then for each of following notions of width: (i) Treewidth (ii) Generalized Hypertree Width (iii) Fractional Hypertree Width (iv) Submodular Width, there exists a node-monotone function γ such that γ-width equals the given notion of width.*

As a simple example, tree-width can be expressed as γ-width for $\gamma(A) = |A| - 1$. We can now relate valid and decomposable GHDs with respect to their γ-widths.

THEOREM 32. *For every valid GHD $(\mathcal{T}, \chi)$, there exists a decomposable GHD $(\mathcal{T}', \chi')$ such that for all node-monotone functions γ, the γ-width of $(\mathcal{T}', \chi')$ is no larger than the γ-width of $(\mathcal{T}, \chi)$.*

PROOF. (Sketch) Suppose the AJAR query is $Q_{\mathcal{H},\alpha}$. We transform the given GHD $(\mathcal{T}, \chi)$ into $(\mathcal{T}', \chi')$ such that for each $v' \in \mathcal{V}'_{\mathcal{T}}$, there exists a $v \in \mathcal{V}_{\mathcal{T}}$ such that $\chi'(v') \subseteq \chi(v)$. The result then follows from the node-monotonicity of γ and the definition of γ-width. Any transformation of a GHD that ensures that all new bags are subsets of old bags, is called width-preserving.

We then transform the GHD $(\mathcal{T}, \chi)$ to satisfy the following properties (we describe the corresponding width-preserving transformations):

- Every $t \in \mathcal{T}$ is $TOP_{\mathcal{T}}(A)$ for exactly one attribute A.

  We can remove every node $t \in \mathcal{T}$ that is the top node for no attributes. For a node t that is the top node for multiple attributes, we create a new node t' and set it to be the parent of t such that $\chi(t') \subseteq \chi(t)$. We specify $\chi(t')$ such that t is the top node for one fewer attribute than before. We can repeat this process until our condition is met.

- For any node $t \in \mathcal{T}$ and the subtree $\mathcal{T}_t$ rooted at t, the attributes $\{v \in \mathcal{V} | TOP_{\mathcal{T}}(v) \in \mathcal{T}_t\}$ form a connected subgraph of $\mathcal{H}$.

  We transform the GHD to ensure this property in a bottom-up manner. In particular, we only consider a node $t \in \mathcal{T}$ after we know its children all satisfy the property. Then if any child's subtree is not connected to t in $\mathcal{H}$, we can safely connect the child to t's parent. This process ensures that t satisfies our property.

We can show, by induction, any valid GHD that satisfies these two properties is decomposable. Intuitively, the first transformation ensures the subtree $\mathcal{T}_0$ exists as desired. The second transformation ensures that each of the $\mathcal{T}_C$'s exists and satisfies the requisite properties. □

This theorem lets us restrict our search to the smaller space of decomposable GHDs (instead of all valid GHDs) when looking for the optimal valid GHD. Moreover, the space of decomposable GHDs is simpler; it can be factored into smaller spaces of unconstrained GHDs, as we show next. We present the definition of *characteristic hypergraphs*, which are intuitively the set of hypergraphs that specify the factors, i.e., the unconstrained GHDs.

Our goal is two-fold: (1) to be able to split a decomposable GHD into component GHDs of the characteristic hypergraphs and (2) to be able to take arbitrary GHDs of the characteristic hypergraphs and connect them to create a decomposable GHD of the original AJAR problem. The definition of decomposable GHDs decomposes a GHD into a series of sub-trees $\mathcal{T}_0, \ldots, \mathcal{T}_k$. The definition specifies that the subtrees $\mathcal{T}_1, \ldots, \mathcal{T}_k$ must be decomposable GHDs of (smaller) AJAR problems. Additionally, it is simple to show $\mathcal{T}_0$ is a GHD of the hypergraph $(V(-\alpha), \{E \in \mathcal{E} | E \subseteq V(-\alpha)\})$. If we apply this decomposition recursively to the subtrees $\mathcal{T}_1, \ldots, \mathcal{T}_k$, we can divide any decomposable GHD into a series of (unrestricted) GHDs of particular hypergraphs. This provides the basis of our definition of the characteristic hypergraphs; we define a hypergraph $\mathcal{H}_0$ that specifies the hypergraph corresponding to $\mathcal{T}_0$ and then recurse on the smaller AJAR queries specified in Definition 29.

However, if we are given arbitrary GHDs of the hypergraphs as defined thus far, we may not be able to stitch them together while preserving the running intersection property of GHDs. To ensure this stitching is possible, we need the characteristic hypergraphs to contain additional edges that we can use to guarantee the running intersection property. Intuitively the edges we add will be the intersections of the adjacent subtrees in our decomposition; for example, for any connected component C of $\mathcal{H} \setminus V(-\alpha)$, $\mathcal{T}_0$ and $\mathcal{T}_C$ are adjacent, and we will add the edge $\chi(\mathcal{T}_0) \cap \chi(\mathcal{T}_C)$ to the corresponding hypergraphs. We can use these 'intersection edges' to connect particular nodes in the adjacent subtrees.

DEFINITION 33. *Given an AJAR problem $Q_{\mathcal{H},\alpha}$, suppose $C_1, \ldots, C_k$ are the connected components of $\mathcal{H} \setminus \mathcal{V}_{-\alpha}$. Define a function $H(\mathcal{H}, \alpha)$ that maps AJAR queries to a set of hypergraphs as follows:*

- $C_i^+ = \bigcup_{E \in \mathcal{E}_{C_i}} E$ *for all* $1 \le i \le k$
- $\mathcal{H}_0 = (\mathcal{V}_{-\alpha}, \{F \in \mathcal{E} | F \subseteq \mathcal{V}_{-\alpha}\} \cup \{\mathcal{V}_{-\alpha} \cap C_i^+ | 1 \le i \le k\})$
- $\mathcal{H}_i^+ = (C_i^+, \mathcal{E}_{C_i} \cup \{\mathcal{V}_{-\alpha} \cap C_i^+\})$
- $H(\mathcal{H}, \alpha) = \{\mathcal{H}_0\} \cup \bigcup_{1 \le i \le k} H(\mathcal{H}_i^+, \alpha_{C_i \setminus C_i^O})$

The hypergraphs in the set $H(\mathcal{H}, \alpha)$ are defined to be the characteristic hypergraphs.

Note that the definition of characteristic hypergraphs depends only on $(\mathcal{H}, \alpha)$, and not on a specific GHD or the instance. Now we state a key result that lets us reduce the problem of searching for an optimal *valid* GHD over $\mathcal{H}$ to that of searching for (not necessarily valid) optimal GHDs over characteristic hypergraphs. Each decomposable GHD corresponds to a GHD over each characteristic hypergraph; conversely, a combination of GHDs for characteristic hypergraphs gives us a decomposable GHD for $\mathcal{H}$. Formally:

THEOREM 34. *For an AJAR query $Q_{\mathcal{H},\alpha}$, suppose $\mathcal{H}_0, \ldots, \mathcal{H}_k$ are the characteristic hypergraphs $H(\mathcal{H}, \alpha)$. Then GHDs $G_0, G_1, \ldots, G_k$ of $\mathcal{H}_0, \ldots, \mathcal{H}_k$ can be connected to form a decomposable GHD G for $Q_{\mathcal{H},\alpha}$. Conversely, any decomposable GHD G of $Q_{\mathcal{H},\alpha}$ can be partitioned into GHDs $G_0, G_1, \ldots, G_k$ of the characteristic hypergraphs $\mathcal{H}_0, \ldots, \mathcal{H}_k$. Moreover, in both of these cases, γ-width$(G) = \max_i \gamma$-width(G_i).*

The proof is provided in the technical report, but it is a straightforward application of definitions.

COROLLARY 35. *Given an optimal GHD for each characteristic hypergraph of an AJAR query $Q_{\mathcal{H},\alpha}$, we can construct an optimal valid GHD. The width of the optimal valid GHD equals the maximum optimal-GHD-width over its characteristic hypergraphs.*

This reduces the problem of finding the optimal valid GHD to smaller problems of finding optimal GHDs. Then we present several applications of our decomposition.

5.2 Finding optimal valid GHDs

Armed with Corollary 35, we simplify the brute force search algorithm for finding optimal valid GHDs.

THEOREM 36. *Let $Q_{\mathcal{H},\alpha}$ be an* AJAR *query. The optimal width valid GHD for this query can be found in time* $\widetilde{O}(|\mathcal{H}|2^{\widetilde{O}(\max_{\mathcal{H}' \in H(\mathcal{H},\alpha)}(|\mathcal{H}'|))})$.

This runtime for finding the optimal valid GHD can be exponentially better than the naive runtime:

EXAMPLE 37. *Consider the star query specified by* $\mathcal{H} = (\{A, B_1, \ldots, B_n\}, \{\{A, B_i\} \mid 1 \leq i \leq n\})$, $\alpha = (B_1, +), (B_2, +), \ldots, (B_n, +)$. *A is the only output attribute. Removing A breaks the hypergraph into n components, so there are $n+1$ characteristic hypergraphs, each of size ≤ 2. Finding the optimal valid GHD takes time $\widetilde{O}(n)$, whereas the standard algorithm takes time exponential in n.*

We can also approximate the GHD [17]:

THEOREM 38 (MARX'S GHD APPROXIMATION). *Let Q be a join query with hypergraph $\mathcal{H}$ and fractional hypertree width w. Then we can find a GHD for Q in time polynomial in $|\mathcal{H}|$, that has width $w' \leq w^3$.*

We can replicate Marx's result for valid GHDs.

THEOREM 39. *Let $Q_{\mathcal{H},\alpha}$ be an* AJAR *query, such that its minimum width valid GHD has width w. Then we can find a valid GHD in time polynomial in $|\mathcal{H}|$ that has width $w' \leq w^3$.*

5.3 Tighter Runtime Exponents

Marx [18] introduced the notion of submodular width (sw) that is tighter than *fhw*, and showed that a join query can be answered in time $\text{IN}^{O(sw)}$. The O in the exponent is because Marx's algorithm requires expensive preprocessing that takes $\text{IN}^{2\times sw}$ time. After the pre-processing, the join can be performed in time IN^{sw}. Despite the O in the exponent, this algorithm can be very valuable because there are families of hypergraphs that have unbounded *fhw* but bounded sw. We can apply Marx's algorithm to the characteristic hypergraphs, potentially improving our runtime. Marx also showed that joins on a family of hypergraphs are fixed parameter tractable if any only if the submodular width of the hypergraph family is bounded [18]. Moreover, adaptive width [19] (applicable only when relations are expressed as truth tables) is unbounded for a hypergraph family if and only if submodular width is unbounded. Corollary 35 gets us an analogous tractability result for AJAR queries.

THEOREM 40. *We can answer an* AJAR *query $Q_{\mathcal{H},\alpha}$ in time* $O(\text{IN}^{O(\max_{\mathcal{H}' \in H(\mathcal{H},\alpha)}(sw(\mathcal{H}')))} + \text{OUT})$.

Recent work [14] uses degree information to more tightly bound the output size of a query. The bound in the reference, called the *DBP bound*, has a tighter exponent than the AGM bound, while requiring only linear preprocessing to obtain. The authors also provide algorithms whose runtime matches the DBP bound. We can define DBP-width $dbpw(\mathcal{T}, \mathcal{H})$ such that $\text{IN}^{dbpw(\mathcal{T},\mathcal{H})}$ is the maximum value of the DBP bound over all bags of GHD T. We then use the improved algorithm in place of GJ in AggroGHDJoin. This lets us get tighter results "for free", reducing our runtime to IN^{dbpw} instead of IN^{fhw}. Formally:

THEOREM 41. *Given an* AJAR *query $Q_{\mathcal{H},\alpha}$ and a valid GHD for $\mathcal{H}$, we can answer the query in time* $O(\text{IN}^{dbpw(\mathcal{T},\mathcal{H})} + \text{OUT})$. *Equivalently, we can answer the query in time* $O(\text{IN}^{\max_{\mathcal{H}' \in H(\mathcal{H},\alpha)} dbpw(\mathcal{T},\mathcal{H})} + \text{OUT})$.

5.4 MapReduce and Parallel Processing

The GYM algorithm [3] uses GHDs to efficiently process joins in a MapReduce setting. GYM makes use of the GHD structure to parallelize different parts of the join. Given a GHD of depth d, and width w, with n attributes, GYM can perform a join in a MapReduce setting in $O(d+\log(n))$ rounds at a communication cost of $M^{-1}(\text{IN}^w + \text{OUT})^2$ where M is the memory per processor on the MapReduce cluster. Combining this with the degree-based MapReduce algorithm [14] gives us the following result:

THEOREM 42. *Given an optimal valid GHD $(\mathcal{T}^*, \chi)$ of depth d, and DBP-width dbpw, we can answer an* AJAR *query with Communication Cost equal to* $O(M^{-1}(\text{IN}^{dbpw(\mathcal{T},\mathcal{H})} + \text{OUT})^2)$ *in $d + \log(n)$ MapReduce rounds, where n is the number of attributes and M is the available memory per processor.*

A GHD can have depth up to $O(n)$, in which case the algorithm can take a very large number of MapReduce rounds ($O(n)$). To address this, the GYM paper uses the 'Log-GTA' algorithm to reduce the depth of any given GHD to $\log(n)$ while at most tripling its width. This lets it process joins in $\log(n)$ MapReduce rounds at a cost of $M^{-1}(\text{IN}^{3w} + \text{OUT})^2$.

Log-GTA involves some shuffling of the attributes in the GHD bags, so naively applying it to a valid GHD could make the GHD invalid (see technical report for an example). But our decomposition lets us apply Log-GTA to the GHD of each characteristic hypergraph, and then stitch the short GHDs together. Our decomposition is recursive in nature; let d' be the maximum recursive depth of the decomposition for a given $Q_{\mathcal{H},\alpha}$. Then the depth of the shortened GHD of each characteristic hypergraph is $O(\log(n))$, and so the depth of the valid GHD obtained by stitching them together is $O(d' \log(n))$. This gives us the result:

THEOREM 43. *If dbpw is the DBP width of an* AJAR *query, we can answer that query with Communication Cost equal to* $O(M^{-1}(\text{IN}^{3\times dbpw(\mathcal{T},\mathcal{H})} + \text{OUT})^2)$ *in $d' \log(n)$ MapReduce rounds, where n is the number of attributes and M is the available memory per processor.*

d' can vary from $O(1)$ to $O(n)$ depending on the query. The star query from example 37 has $d' = 2$, which lets us process it in $\log(n)$ MapReduce rounds. Any query that only has a single type of aggregation will have $d' = 2$ as well. On the other hand, a query with one relation having n attributes, 1 output attribute, and alternating $\sum$ and max aggregations, will have $d' = n$, and will be hard to parallelize.

6. PRODUCT AGGREGATIONS

The primary application of queries with multiple aggregations is to establish bounds for the Quantified Conjunctive Query (*QCQ*) problem [16], and its counting variant, *#QCQ*. We now introduce a new type of aggregation, called product aggregation, that lets us efficiently handle *QCQ* queries. We define the AJAR problem for product aggregations, and then extend our algorithm from Section 3 to handle this new type of AJAR query. We then define a decomposition analogous to that in Section 5. A more detailed version of this section with additional motivation, examples, and proofs can be found in our technical report [13].

6.1 AJAR queries with product aggregates

A *product aggregation* aggregates using the $\otimes$ operator. Throughout the paper, we assumed that an absent tuple effectively has an annotation of 0. Taking this into account, we formally define the product aggregation. Let $B = F \setminus A$:

DEFINITION 44. $\sum_{(A,\otimes)} R_{AB} = \{(t_B, \lambda) \mid \forall t_A \in \mathcal{D}^A, t_B \circ t_A \in R_{AB} \text{ and } \lambda = \prod_{(t,\lambda_t) \in R_{AB}: \pi_B t = t_B} \lambda_t\}$

We can adjust the definition of aggregation orderings and AJAR queries to allow this new type of aggregation. *QCQ* queries can now be expressed as AJAR queries on the $(\{0,1\}, \max, \cdot)$ semiring. We assume for this section that $\otimes$ is idempotent, i.e., $a \otimes a = a$ for all a. We describe how to work with non-idempotent products in the technical report.

6.2 Algorithms for product aggregates

For aggregation orderings that have product aggregations, the rules for determining when two orderings are equivalent are somewhat different; product aggregations can be performed *before* a join. We illustrate this with an example:

EXAMPLE 45. *In the semiring $(\{0,1\}, \max, \cdot)$, suppose we have two relations $R(A,B) = \{((0,0),x),((0,1),y)\}$ and $S(B,C) = \{((0,1),p),((1,1),q)\}$. Consider the* AJAR *query $\sum_{(B,\cdot)} R(A,B) \bowtie S(B,C)$. If we compute the join, we will get two tuples with the annotations $x \cdot p$ and $y \cdot q$, and then aggregating over B will produce a relation with the element $((0,1), x \cdot p \cdot y \cdot q)$. However, note that $x \cdot p \cdot y \cdot q = (x \cdot y) \cdot (p \cdot q)$, implying that $\sum_{(B,\cdot)} R(A,B) \bowtie S(B,C) = (\sum_{(B,\cdot)} R(A,B)) \bowtie (\sum_{(B,\cdot)} S(B,C))$.*

We now describe how to extend each of our results to handle AJAR queries with product aggregations present.

Defining AGHDs and Answering AJAR Queries.

Product aggregations change the set of GHDs compatible with a given ordering. In fact, product aggregates allow us to break the running intersection property of GHDs without causing incorrect behavior; a product aggregation attribute can appear in disconnected subtrees without causing incorrect computation. We express this using a simple variant of GHDs, called *aggregating generalized hypertree decompositions* (AGHDs). Informally, AGHDs are GHDs that can violate the running intersection property for attributes that have a product aggregation. We formally define AGHDs by creating new hypergraphs by splitting product aggregation attributes into multiple attributes; in particular, we can define new hypergraphs in which every product aggregation attribute will map to a set of attributes, and AGHDs are equivalent to GHDs over these new hypergraphs.

DEFINITION 46. *Given a hypergraph $\mathcal{H} = (\mathcal{V}, \mathcal{E})$ and aggregation ordering α, let $S = \{a \in \mathcal{V} | (a, \otimes) \in \alpha\}$ be the set of attributes with product aggregations. A* product partition *is a set $\{P_a | a \in S\}$ where P_a is a partition of $\{F \in \mathcal{E} | a \in F\}$ (the relations that contain a).*

We will duplicate each attribute a for each partition of P_a and have the partition specify which edges contain each instance of a. We will use N_a to denote the number of partitions $|P_a|$.

DEFINITION 47. *Suppose we are given a hypergraph $\mathcal{H} = (\mathcal{V}, \mathcal{E})$, aggregation ordering α, and product partition P. The* product partition hypergraph *$\mathcal{H}_P$ is the pair $(\mathcal{V}_P, \mathcal{E}_P)$ such that*

- $S = \{a \in \mathcal{V} | P_a \in P\}$
- $\mathcal{V}_P = (\bigcup_{a \in S} \{a_1, \ldots, a_{N_a}\}) \cup \mathcal{V} \setminus S$
- $p : \mathcal{V} \times \mathcal{E} \to \mathcal{V}_P$ *where $p(a,F) = a$ if $a \notin S$ and $p(a,F) = a_i$ such that F is in the ith partition of P_a otherwise*
- $\mathcal{E}_P = \{\{p(a,F) \mid a \in F\} \mid F \in \mathcal{E}\}$

DEFINITION 48. *Given a hypergraph $\mathcal{H}$ and aggregation ordering α, an* aggregating generalized hypertree decomposition *(AGHD) is a triple $(\mathcal{T}, \chi, P)$ such that $(\mathcal{T}, \chi)$ is a GHD of the product partition hypergraph $\mathcal{H}_P$.*

For any product aggregation attribute a in the AJAR query, $TOP_{\mathcal{T}}(a)$ for an AGHD $(\mathcal{T}, \chi, P)$ can be defined as the set $\{TOP_{\mathcal{T}}(a_1), TOP_{\mathcal{T}}(a_2), \ldots, TOP_{\mathcal{T}}(a_{|P_a|})\}$. Now we can define the notion of compatibility of an AGHD with an ordering.

DEFINITION 49. *A AGHD $(\mathcal{T}, \chi, P)$ for an* AJAR *query $Q_{\mathcal{H},\alpha}$ is compatible with α if for each attribute pair a, b for which there exists $v_1 \in TOP_{\mathcal{T}}(a)$, $v_2 \in TOP_{\mathcal{T}}(b)$ such that v_1 is an ancestor of v_2, a must either occur before b in the ordering α or be an output attribute.*

We now discuss how to use an AGHD to answer an AJAR query. Given a product partition P, let α^P be a modified aggregation ordering over $\mathcal{V}_P$ that replaces each occurence of $(a, \otimes)$ in α with $(a_1, \otimes), (a_2, \otimes), \ldots, (a_{N_a}, \otimes)$ for each product attribute a. Our definitions imply that if an AGHD $(\mathcal{T}, \chi, P)$ is compatible with the AJAR query $Q_{\mathcal{H},\alpha}$, $(\mathcal{T}, \chi)$ must be a compatible GHD for the AJAR query $Q_{\mathcal{H}_P,\alpha^P}$. For any instance I over $\mathcal{H}$, let I_P be the corresponding instance over $\mathcal{H}_P$ with the appropriate attributes renamed. To solve $Q_{\mathcal{H},\alpha}(I)$ with the AGHD $(\mathcal{T}, \chi, P)$, we can run AggroGHDJoin to solve $Q_{\mathcal{H}_P,\alpha^P}(I_P)$ with the GHD $(\mathcal{T}, \chi)$; we will now show that this produces the correct answer.

LEMMA 50. *For each database instance I and product partition P, $Q_{\mathcal{H},\alpha}(I) = Q_{P,\alpha^P}(I)$.*

This lemma can be proven by repeatedly applying the following lemma.

LEMMA 51. *Suppose $R'(A, C_1)$ is a copy of $R(A,C)$ with C renamed to C_1, and $S'(B, C_2)$ is a copy of $S(B,C)$ with C renamed to C_2. Then*

$$\sum_{(C_1,\otimes)} \sum_{(C_2,\otimes)} R'(A,C_1) \bowtie S'(B,C_2) = \sum_{(C,\otimes)} R(A,C) \bowtie S(B,C)$$

PROOF. Suppose the annotations for the C values in R are $n_1, n_2, \ldots, n_k$ and in S are $m_1, m_2, \ldots, m_k$ (assume all annotations are present, i.e., absent tuples have a zero-annotation). Then the RHS is $\otimes_{i=1}^k n_i m_i$. The LHS will have $\otimes_{i=1}^k n_i \otimes_{j=1}^k m_j$. The RHS is equal to the LHS because of idempotence of $\otimes$. □

We can thus solve AJAR queries that contain product aggregations with an unchanged algorithm.

Characterizing equivalent orderings. The base case and commutative Lemmas 18 and 21 still hold in our definition of PREC and DNC. However, Lemma 20 does not hold for product aggregations:

EXAMPLE 52. *Consider the* AJAR *query*

$$\sum_{(A,+)} \sum_{(B,\max)} \sum_{(C,\cdot)} R(A,C) \bowtie S(B,C).$$

By Lemma 18, we have $\mathsf{PREC}(A,C)$ *and* $\mathsf{PREC}(B,C)$, *and then Lemma 20 implies* $\mathsf{PREC}(A,B)$. *However, by pushing the aggregations past the join, our query can be rewritten*

$$\left(\sum_{(A,+)} \sum_{(C,\cdot)} R(A,C)\right) \bowtie \left(\sum_{(B,\max)} \sum_{(C,\cdot)} S(B,C)\right),$$

which implies that A *and* B *can commute.*

LEMMA 53. *Given an* AJAR *query* $Q_{\mathcal{H},\alpha}$, *suppose* $(A,\odot)$, $(B,\odot')$, $(C,\odot'') \in \alpha$. *If* $\odot \neq \odot'$, $\odot'' \neq \otimes$, *and* $\exists E \in \mathcal{E}$: $\mathsf{PREC}(A,C)$ *and* $B, C \in E$, *then* $\mathsf{DNC}(A,B)$.

We adapt Lemma 20 to handle product aggregations correctly by adding the condition that the connecting attribute C does not have a product aggregation.

The proofs to show the completeness and soundness of the resulting partial order $<_{\mathcal{H},\alpha}$ are essentially unchanged, but we do need to adjust the statement of Lemma 24 to add a special case for product aggregations.

LEMMA 54. *Suppose we are given a hypergraph* $\mathcal{H} = (\mathcal{V},\mathcal{E})$ *and an aggregation ordering* α. *Suppose* $(A,\odot),(B,\odot') \in \alpha$ *for differing operators* $\odot \neq \odot'$. *Then, for any path* P *in* $\mathcal{H}$ *between* A *and* B, *then there must exist some attribute* $C \in P$ *such that one of the following is true:*

- $C \neq A, B$ *and* $(C,\otimes) \in \alpha$
- $C <_{\mathcal{H},\alpha} A$ *or* $C <_{\mathcal{H},\alpha} B$

Decomposing AGHDs. We can apply the ideas from Section 5 to AJAR queries with product aggregates as well. We first extend the definition of compatible GHDs to valid GHDs.

DEFINITION 55. *For an* AJAR *query* $Q_{\mathcal{H},\alpha}$, *a GHD* $(\mathcal{T},\chi)$ *is* valid *if and only if for each attribute pair* a, b *for which there exists* $v_1 \in TOP_{\mathcal{T}}(a)$, $v_2 \in TOP_{\mathcal{T}}(b)$ *such that* v_1 *is an ancestor of* v_2, $b \not<_{\mathcal{H},\alpha} a$.

We can also extend the idea of decomposable GHDs as well. Conceptually the decompositions are very similar: at every stage of the decomposition, we construct a GHD of the output attributes and then we recursively construct decomposable AGHDs on the connected components of the other attributes. The only major difference is that the connected components are computed with the product attributes removed. In particular, decomposable GHDs recurse on the connected components of the hypergraph with the output attributes removed, while decomposable AGHDs recurse on the connected components of the hypergraph with the output and product aggregation attributes removed. After dividing the attributes into connected components, the product aggregation attributes can be added back to each of the connected components they share an edge with. With this definition, we can easily extend our decomposition and results to AGHDs. We provide the theorem statements here, please see our technical report for details and proofs.

THEOREM 56. *All decomposable AGHDs are valid.*

THEOREM 57. *For every valid AGHD* $(\mathcal{T},\chi,P)$, *there exists a decomposable AGHD* $(\mathcal{T}',\chi',P')$ *such that for all node-monotone functions* γ, *the* γ*-width of* $(\mathcal{T}',\chi')$ *is no larger than the* γ*-width of* $(\mathcal{T},\chi)$.

We can define characteristic hypergraphs similarly to how we did in Section 5 (again, see the technical report for a formal definition). We have the following result:

THEOREM 58. *For an* AJAR *query* $Q_{\mathcal{H},\alpha}$ *involving product aggregates, suppose* $\mathcal{H}_0,\ldots,\mathcal{H}_k$ *are the characteristic hypergraphs* $H(\mathcal{H},\alpha)$. *Then GHDs* $G_0, G_1, \ldots, G_k$ *of* $\mathcal{H}_0,\ldots,\mathcal{H}_k$ *can be connected to form a decomposable AGHD* G *for* $Q_{\mathcal{H},\alpha}$. *Conversely, any decomposable AGHD* G *of* $Q_{\mathcal{H},\alpha}$ *can be partitioned into GHDs* $G_0, G_1, \ldots, G_k$ *of the characteristic hypergraphs* $\mathcal{H}_0,\ldots,\mathcal{H}_k$. *Moreover, in both of these cases,* γ*-width*$(G) = \max_i \gamma$*-width*(G_i).

These theorems let us apply all the optimizations from Section 5.2, 5.3, and 5.4 to queries with product aggregates.

7. CONCLUSION

We investigate solutions to and the structure of AJAR queries: aggregate-join queries with multiple aggregators over annotated relations. We start by providing a simple algorithm based on a variant of GHDJoin that operates with a limited set of GHDs. We proceed to investigate the class of equivalent orderings to expand the set of GHDs that we can give our algorithm. To that end, we develop a partial ordering that fully characterizes equivalent orderings. We then develop a characterization of the corresponding valid GHDs, describing how they can be decomposed into ordinary, unrestricted GHDs. This reduction connects us to a trove of parallel work on GHDs. We finish by extending our work to handle product aggregations.

Acknowledgements. We thank Atri Rudra for invaluable insights and feedback developing our approach. CR gratefully acknowledges the support of the Defense Advanced Research Projects Agency (DARPA) XDATA Program under No. FA8750-12-2-0335, DARPAs SIMPLEX Program, DARPAs MEMEX program under No. FA8750-14-2-0240, the National Science Foundation (NSF) under CAREER Award No. IIS-1353606, Award No. CCF-1356918 and EarthCube Award under No. ACI-1343760, the Office of Naval Research (ONR) under awards No. N000141210041 and No. N000141310129, the Sloan Research Fellowship, the Moore Foundation Data Driven Investigator award, and gifts from American Family Insurance, Intel, Lightspeed Ventures, and Toshiba.

8. REFERENCES

[1] Christopher R. Aberger, Susan Tu, Kunle Olukotun, and Christopher Ré. Emptyheaded: A relational engine for graph processing. *SIGMOD (to appear)*, 2016.

[2] Serge Abiteboul, Richard Hull, and Victor Vianu, editors. *Foundations of Databases: The Logical Level.* Addison-Wesley Longman Publishing Co., Inc., Boston, MA, USA, 1st edition, 1995.

[3] Foto N. Afrati, Manas Joglekar, Christopher Ré, Semih Salihoglu, and Jeffrey D. Ullman. GYM: A multiround join algorithm in mapreduce. *CoRR*, abs/1410.4156, 2014.

[4] Srinivas M. Aji and Robert J. McEliece. The generalized distributive law. *IEEE Transactions on Information Theory*, 46(2):325–343, 2000.

[5] Albert Atserias, Martin Grohe, and Dániel Marx. Size bounds and query plans for relational joins. FOCS '08, pages 739–748, Washington, DC, USA, 2008. IEEE Computer Society.

[6] Nurzhan Bakibayev, Tomás Kociský, Dan Olteanu, and Jakub Zavodny. Aggregation and ordering in factorised databases. *PVLDB*, 6(14):1990–2001, 2013.

[7] Hubie Chen and Víctor Dalmau. Decomposing quantified conjunctive (or disjunctive) formulas. In *Proceedings of the 27th Annual IEEE Symposium on Logic in Computer Science, LICS 2012, Dubrovnik, Croatia, June 25-28, 2012*, pages 205–214, 2012.

[8] B. Eckmann and P. J. Hilton. Group-like structures in general categories i multiplications and comultiplications. *Mathematische Annalen*, 145(3):227–255.

[9] G. Gottlob, M. Grohe, M. Nysret, M. Samer, and F. Scarcello. Hypertree Decompositions: Structure, Algorithms, and Applications. In *WG*, 2005.

[10] Georg Gottlob, Nicola Leone, and Francesco Scarcello. Hypertree decompositions and tractable queries. In *PODS 1999*, pages 21–32, 1999.

[11] Todd J. Green, Grigoris Karvounarakis, and Val Tannen. Provenance semirings. PODS '07, pages 31–40, New York, NY, USA, 2007. ACM.

[12] Martin Grohe and Dániel Marx. Constraint solving via fractional edge covers. *ACM Trans. Algorithms*, 11(1):4:1–4:20, August 2014.

[13] Manas Joglekar, Rohan Puttagunta, and Christopher Ré. Ajar: Aggregations and joins over annotated relations. *CoRR*, abs/1508.07532, 2015.

[14] Manas R. Joglekar and Christopher Ré. It's all a matter of degree: Using degree information to optimize multiway joins. In *ICDT (to appear)*, 2016.

[15] Kalev Kask, Rina Dechter, Javier Larrosa, and Avi Dechter. Unifying tree decompositions for reasoning in graphical models. *Artif. Intell.*, 166:165–193, 2005.

[16] Mahmoud Abo Khamis, Hung Q. Ngo, and Atri Rudra. FAQ: questions asked frequently. *CoRR*, abs/1504.04044, 2015.

[17] Dániel Marx. Approximating fractional hypertree width. *ACM Trans. Algorithms*, 6, 2010.

[18] Dániel Marx. Tractable hypergraph properties for constraint satisfaction and conjunctive queries. In *Proceedings of the Forty-second ACM Symposium on Theory of Computing*, STOC '10, pages 735–744, New York, NY, USA, 2010. ACM.

[19] Daniel Marx. Tractable structures for constraint satisfaction with truth tables. *Theory of Computing Systems*, 48, 2011.

[20] Hung Q. Ngo, Ely Porat, Christopher Ré, and Atri Rudra. Worst-case optimal join algorithms: [extended abstract]. In *PODS 2012*, pages 37–48, 2012.

[21] Hung Q. Ngo, Christopher Ré, and Atri Rudra. Skew strikes back: new developments in the theory of join algorithms. *SIGMOD Record*, 42(4):5–16, 2013.

[22] Dan Olteanu and Jakub Závodný. Size bounds for factorised representations of query results. *ACM Trans. Database Syst.*, 40(1):2, 2015.

[23] Adam Perelman and Christopher Ré. Duncecap: Compiling worst-case optimal query plans. In *SIGMOD 2015*, pages 2075–2076, 2015.

[24] Christopher Ré and Dan Suciu. The trichotomy of HAVING queries on a probabilistic database. *VLDB J.*, 18(5):1091–1116, 2009.

[25] Neil Robertson and P.D Seymour. Graph minors. iii. planar tree-width. *Journal of Combinatorial Theory, Series B*, 36(1):49 – 64, 1984.

[26] Charles A. Sutton and Andrew McCallum. An introduction to conditional random fields. *Foundations and Trends in Machine Learning*, 4(4):267–373, 2012.

[27] Susan Tu and Christopher Ré. Duncecap: Query plans using generalized hypertree decompositions. In *SIGMOD 2015*, pages 2077–2078, 2015.

[28] Todd L. Veldhuizen. Triejoin: A simple, worst-case optimal join algorithm. In *ICDT 2014*, pages 96–106, 2014.

[29] M. Yannakakis. Algorithms for Acyclic Database Schemes. In *VLDB*, 1981.

APPENDIX

A. ALGORITHMS

We provide pseudo-code of AggroGHDJoin in Section 4. The last line of this algorithm calls AggroYannakakis, which we now outline in Algorithm 2. AggroYannakakis and the classic Yannakakis algorithm for project-join queries are essentially the same; AggroYannakakis is slightly modified to handle aggregations instead of simple projections.

In the classic analysis of Yannakakis for join queries (without projection), the runtime of the semi-join portion is bounded by $O(\text{IN})$ and the bottom-up join is bounded by $O(\text{OUT})$. Adding projection (or aggregation) leaves the semi-join portion is unchanged, but the projection reduces the size of the output, thereby making the OUT bound harder to achieve. In particular, during the bottom-up join, we may compute an intermediate relation whose attributes are not a subset of the output attributes, meaning that its size may not bounded by OUT. These potentially large intermediate relations are the underlying cause for the traditional $\text{IN} \cdot \text{OUT}$ runtime.

However, using intuition discovered in reference [6], if we require the output attributes to appear above non-output attributes, we can preserve the $\text{IN} + \text{OUT}$ runtime.

THEOREM 59. *Suppose we have a GHD such that for any output attribute A and non-output attribute B, $TOP_{\mathcal{T}}(B)$ is not an ancestor of $TOP_{\mathcal{T}}(A)$. AggroGHDJoin runs in $\widetilde{O}(\text{IN}^{fhw(\mathcal{T},\mathcal{H},I)} + \text{OUT})$ given this GHD.*

Algorithm 2 AggroYannakakis($\mathcal{T} = (\mathcal{V}, \mathcal{E})$, α, $\{R_F | F \in \mathcal{V}\}$)

Input: Join tree $\mathcal{T} = (\mathcal{V}, \mathcal{E})$, Aggregation order α, Relations R_F for each $F \in \mathcal{V}$

```
for all F ∈ V in some bottom-up order do    ▷ Semi-join reduction up
    P ← parent of F
    R_P ← R_P ⋉ R_F
end for
for all F ∈ V in some top-down order do    ▷ Semi-join reduction down
    P ← parent of F
    R_F ← R_F ⋉ R_P
end for
while F ∈ V in some bottom-up order do ▷ Aggregation
    β ← α ∩ {a ∈ V | TOP_T(a) = F}
    R_F ← Σ_β R_F
    if F is not the root then
        P ← parent of F
        R_P ← R_P ⋈ R_F                ▷ Compute the join
    end if
end while
return R_R for the root R
```

PROOF. GJ on each bag still runs in $\widetilde{O}(\text{IN}^{fhw(\mathcal{T},\mathcal{H},I)})$. We need to prove the Yannakakis portion runs in $O(\text{IN} + \text{OUT})$ after running GJ.

The semijoin portion runs in $O(IN)$ as in the original Yannakakis algorithm. In the join phase, we have two types of joins. In the first type, $F \setminus \beta \subseteq P$. This implies the join output is a subset of R_P (with different annotations). So the total runtime of this type of join is $O(\text{IN})$. For the second type, $F \setminus \beta \subsetneq P$. This means some attribute in $(F \setminus \beta) \setminus P$ must be an output attribute, and all attributes in P must be output attributes as well (as their TOP value is an ancestor of F). So the result of our join must be a subset of the output table; the total runtime of this type of join is $O(\text{OUT})$. Thus the total runtime of the algorithm is $O(\text{IN} + \text{OUT})$. □

Note that while AggroGHDJoin runs in $\widetilde{O}(\text{IN}^{fhw(\mathcal{T},\mathcal{H},I)} + \text{OUT})$ time on the GHDs above, it may not necessarily produce the right output unless the GHD satisfies additional conditions, to ensure that aggregations are done in the proper order. In particular, recall our definition a GHD $(\mathcal{T}, \chi)$ is compatible with α if for all attribute pairs A, B, $TOP_{\mathcal{T}}(A)$ being an ancestor of $TOP_{\mathcal{T}}(B)$ implies that either A is an output variable or A occurs before B in α.

THEOREM 60. *If a GHD $(\mathcal{T}, \chi)$ is compatible with α, then AggroGHDJoin given $(\mathcal{T}, \chi)$ correctly computes $Q_{\mathcal{H},\alpha}$.*

PROOF. We first show that AggroYannakakis works as expected. We note that the semi-join reduction does not change the output; it only quickens the process. We only consider the bottom-up join. For each node t in the join tree, let $R(t)$ be the relation associated with that node before this loop, i.e., after the semi-join portion. Let $R'(t)$ be the final relation associated with node t when we are processing node t, i.e., after the bottom up join with t's descendants is done and after the aggregation in t. Let $\mathcal{T}_t$ be the subtree that includes t and all of its descendants. Let $s(t)$ be the attributes aggregated at node t, i.e., $\alpha \cap \{a \in \mathcal{V} | TOP_{\mathcal{T}}(a) = t\}$, and let $s(\mathcal{T}_t) = \cup_{t \in \mathcal{T}_t} s(t)$. For each non-leaf node t, let $c(t)$ be the set of t's children.

For each node t, we claim $R'(t) = \sum_{\alpha_{s(\mathcal{T}_t)}} \Join_{t' \in \mathcal{T}_t} R(t')$. Proof by induction on the tree. For each leaf l, $R'(l) = \sum_{\alpha_{s(l)}} R(l)$ by definition.

For a non-leaf node t,

$$
\begin{aligned}
R'(t) &= \sum_{\alpha_{s(t)}} R(t) \Join (\Join_{t_c \in c(t)} R'(t_c)) \\
&= \sum_{\alpha_{s(t)}} R(t) \Join \left(\Join_{t_c \in c(t)} \sum_{\alpha_{s(\mathcal{T}_{t_c})}} \Join_{t' \in \mathcal{T}_{t_c}} R(t') \right) \\
&= \sum_{\alpha_{s(\mathcal{T}_t)}} \Join_{t' \in \mathcal{T}_t} R(t')
\end{aligned}
$$

The second step is due to the inductive hypothesis. The final step is simply "pulling out" the aggregations from the sub-orderings one at a time; we can arbitrarily interleave the aggregation orders $\alpha_{s(\mathcal{T}_{t_c})}$. We can simply interleave them to match $\alpha_{\cup_{t_c \in c(t)} s(\mathcal{T}_t)}$. Since the original GHD is compatible with α, we know the aggregations $\alpha_{s(t)}$ precede $\alpha_{s(\mathcal{T}_{t_c})}$ in α, implying that $\sum_{\alpha_{s(\mathcal{T}_t)}} \sum_{\alpha_{\cup_{t_c \in c(t)} s(\mathcal{T}_t)}} = \sum_{\alpha_{s(\mathcal{T}_t)}}$. Our output is $R'(t_r)$ where t_r is the root node, which is $\sum_{\alpha} \Join_{t \in \mathcal{T}} R(t)$ as desired.

Since AggroYannakakis works as expected, we simply need to ensure that the bags are computed appropriately. Note the GHD ensures for every relation R_F, there is a node t such that $F \subseteq \chi(t)$. This means that no tuple is lost; computing AggroYannakakis on the bags will compute the correct tuples. To ensure it computes the correct annotations, we need to ensure every annotation appears in the bags at most once; our algorithm places the annotation of a relation R_F in the top-most node that contains all of the attributes R_F. □

B. COMPARISON WITH RELATED WORK

We compare our results with prior work. We follow the structure of our paper, comparing the runtimes of AggroGHD-Join, the ordering equivalence chracterization, GHD decomposition results, and finally product aggregation results.

B.1 Section 3

In Section 3, we define a simple approach to solving AJAR queries, namely running AggroGHDJoin over a minimum width valid GHD. Our runtime is given by $O(\text{IN}^{w^*} + \text{OUT})$, where w^* is the width of the optimal GHD (Theorem 10). In contrast, the runtime of the FAQ's InsideOut algorithm (shown in Algorithm 3) is $O(\text{IN}^{faqw})$, were $faqw$ is called the FAQ-width of the query. We show that $\widetilde{O}(IN^{w^*} + \text{OUT}) \leq \widetilde{O}(IN^{faqw})$. We note that the $faqw$ exponent is actually the optimum value of $faqw(\sigma)$ over the equivalent orderings σ FAQ considers (we discuss the space of orderings it considers in the next subsection). Our approach will recognize σ as being equivalent, and will search for the best compatible GHD for σ. We will show that there exists a compatible AGHD $(\mathcal{T}, \chi, P)$ for every equivalent ordering σ such that $fhw(\mathcal{T}, \mathcal{H}, I) = faqw(\sigma)$ (as Example 62 shows, the compatible AGHD $\mathcal{T}$ we construct may not be the optimal compatible GHD).

We start by briefly summarizing FAQ's InsideOut algorithm, with the pseudo-code (written in the notation of this paper) given in Algorithm 3. Let σ be the ordering used for aggregation. Let n denote the total number of attributes

$|\mathcal{V}_\mathcal{H}|$ and f denote the number of output attributes (thus $|\sigma| = n - f$). For notational convenience, we will be using $\sigma[i]$ to denote both the attribute and the operator that make up the ith operator-attribute pair in the ordering.

Algorithm 3 InsideOut($\mathcal{H} = (\mathcal{V}_\mathcal{H}, \mathcal{E}_\mathcal{H})$, σ, $\{R_F | F \in \mathcal{E}_\mathcal{H}\}$)

Input: Hypergraph $\mathcal{H} = (\mathcal{V}_\mathcal{H}, \mathcal{E}_\mathcal{H})$, Aggregation ordering σ, Relations R_F for each $F \in \mathcal{E}_\mathcal{H}$

```
E_n ← {R_F | F ∈ E_H}
for (k = n; k > f; k − −) do
    δ(k) ← {R_F ∈ E_k | σ[k − f] ∈ F}
    if σ[k − f] is not a product aggregation then
        U_k ← ⋈_{R∈δ(k)} R
        E_{k−1} ← (E_k \ δ(k)) ∪ {Σ_{σ[k−f]} U_k}
    else
        E_{k−1} ← (E_k \ δ(k)) ∪ {Σ_{σ[k−f]} R | R ∈ δ(k)}
    end if
end for
return ⋈_{R∈E_f} R
```

FAQ relies on a worst-case optimal algorithm to compute each of the joins, implying that in the $\widetilde{O}(IN^{faqw})$ runtime guarantee, *faqw* is defined as the maximum AGM bound placed on each of the computed joins. Define $p^*_H : 2^{\mathcal{V}_\mathcal{H}} \to \mathcal{R}$ to be a function that maps a subset of the attributes to the AGM bound on the subset, i.e., the optimal value of the canonical linear program. Then $faqw = \max(\max_k p^*_H(U_k), p^*_H(V(-\sigma)))$ [16].

We will build up the compatible AGHD $(\mathcal{T}, \chi, P)$ in rounds corresponding to each of the k values of *InsideOut*. We first describe how to construct $(\mathcal{T}, \chi)$, and later describe how to obtain P. At the start of round corresponding to a particular k, we will have a forest of AGHDs, each of which will have a root mapped (by χ) to the attribute sets of E_k, and at the end of each round, the forest's roots will be mapped to the relations of E_{k-1}.

For an attribute set F, let $t(F)$ represent the node such that $\chi(t(F)) = F$. We start by creating the $|\mathcal{E}_\mathcal{H}|$ nodes $\{t(F)|F \in E_n\}$, which are simply nodes mapped to the input relations. Then for each k from n to $f+1$, let T represent the set of nodes $\{t(F)|F \in \delta(n)\}$; these are the nodes that will be processed, i.e., the nodes for whom we will create parents. If $\sigma[k-f]$ is not a product aggregation, we create a node $t(U_k)$ and set $parent(t) = t(U_k)$ for all $t \in T$. We then create a node $t(U_k \setminus \{\sigma[k-f]\})$ and set it to be $parent(t(U_k))$. Note that this process has transformed the set of the forest's roots by removing T and adding $t(U_k \setminus \{\sigma[k-f]\})$, mirroring the transformation between E_k and E_{k-1}. If $\sigma[k-f]$ is a product aggregation, then for each $F \in \delta(n)$, we create a node $t(F \setminus \{\sigma[k-f]\})$ and set it to be $parent(t(F))$; in this case as well the set of the forest's roots match E_{k-1}.

At the end of this process, we will have a forest of AGHDs whose roots map to the relations in E_f. To conclude our construction, we simply construct the node $t(V(-\sigma))$ and set it to be $parent(t(F))$ for all $F \in E_f$. If there are no product aggregations, then $(\mathcal{T}, \chi)$ forms a GHD.

$(\mathcal{T}, \chi)$ satisfies the running intersection property for all non-product attributes, but a product attribute a can be present in multiple disconnected parts of $\mathcal{T}$. We now describe a product partition P such that $(\mathcal{T}, \chi, P)$ forms an AGHD for the ordering σ. Let P_a denote the number of distinct connected components of $\mathcal{T}$ in which a is present. Then we create P_a copies of a ($a_1, a_2, \ldots, a_{|P_a|}$), and assign a copy to each component in some order. For each $F \in \mathcal{E}_\mathcal{H}$ that contains a, if the component that $t(F)$ belongs to is assigned a_i, then P assigns a_i to F. Then $(\mathcal{T}, \chi, P)$ is an AGHD for σ.

The AGHD $(\mathcal{T}, \chi, P)$ as described is trivially compatible with σ since we construct $parent(TOP_\mathcal{T}(\sigma[k-f]))$ explicitly in round k; this ensures that $TOP_\mathcal{T}(\sigma[i])$ cannot be an ancestor of $TOP_\mathcal{T}(\sigma[j])$ if $i > j$.

LEMMA 61. *Define $p^*_\mathcal{H}$ to be a function that maps a set of attributes to the AGM bound on the set (the optimal value of the canonical linear program). The AGHD $(\mathcal{T}, \chi, P)$ constructed as described satisfies*

$$fhw(\mathcal{T}, \mathcal{H}, I) = \max(p^*_\mathcal{H}(V(-\alpha)), \max_k p^*_\mathcal{H}(U_k)) = faqw(\sigma).$$

PROOF. The nodes in our tree that do not map to $V(-\alpha)$ or the U_k either map to an input relation or to a relation created by aggregating an attribute from a single child node. In the former case, $p^*_\mathcal{H}$ would evaluate to 1, so we can ignore them in our maximum. In the latter case, the attributes are a strict subset of its child's attributes, implying we can ignore them too. As such, the fractional hypertree width is simply the maximum fractional cover over $V(-\alpha)$ and the U_k. This shows the first part of the equality. The second part of the equality is the definition of *faqw* [16]. □

Our runtime comparison for regular as well as product aggregations, follows as a simple corollary. We now show an example where the runtime of InsideOut is much higher than that of AggroGHDJoin, primarily because InsideOut is not output-sensitive.

EXAMPLE 62. *Let n be an even number, and consider an* AJAR *query $Q_{\mathcal{H},\alpha}$ where $\mathcal{H} = (\{A_i \mid 1 \le i \le n\}, \{\{A_i, A_{i+1}\} \mid 1 \le i \le n-1\} \cup \{\{A_n, A_1\}\})$, and α is empty, i.e., the query is just a join. Also let each attribute take values $1, 2, 3, \ldots 2 \times \lfloor\sqrt{N}\rfloor$. Suppose each relation $\{A_i, A_{i+1}\}$ for $1 \le i \le n-1$ connects values of the same parity, while relation $\{A_n, A_1\}$ connectes values of opposite parities. Thus each relation has size N, and $\mathrm{IN} = O(N)$ (n is a constant), and the join output is empty. There is a GHD with bags $\{A_1, A_2, A_3\}, \{A_1, A_3, A_4\}, \ldots \{A_1, A_{n-1}, A_n\}$ that is compatible with the empty ordering. The fhw of this GHD is 2, so we have $w^* = 2$. Thus the runtime of our algorithm will be $\widetilde{O}(\mathrm{IN}^2)$. InsideOut will compute an intermediate output consisting of the join of $n-1$ of the relations, which has size $N^{(n-1)/2}$, so InsideOut's runtime will be at least $\widetilde{O}(\mathrm{IN}^{(n-1)/2})$.*

The FAQ paper does discuss, at a very high-level and without proofs, changes to InsideOut that will allow its runtime to be output-sensitive [16, Section 10.2]. It's most general and useful change involves building a GHD for the output variables and running a message passing algorithm between the bags, which exactly describes GHDJoin. Implementing this change would make InsideOut completely equivalent to AggroGHDJoin. We note that the FAQ paper frames these changes as decisions in how to *represent* the output, whereas we present the optimization in an algorithmic context, independent of any other storage optimizations.

B.2 Section 4

In Section 4, we define a partial order $<_{\mathcal{H},\alpha}$ that exactly characterizes the constraints an aggregation ordering must satisfy to be equivalent to a given ordering α. Our partial ordering is complete. The FAQ paper also defines its own partial ordering, which we denote $<_{FAQ}$, and it only considers orderings that are linear extensions of $<_{FAQ}$. However, $<_{FAQ}$ is not complete, as shown in the following example:

EXAMPLE 63. *Consider the* AJAR *query given by* $\sum_A \max_B \sum_C R(A,B)S(A,C)$. *By our characterization,* $A <_{\mathcal{H},\alpha} B$ *is the only constraint, giving rise to* 3 *different valid orderings. The FAQ characterization, however, has two constraints:* $A <_{FAQ} B$ *and* $C <_{FAQ} B$, *which only allows for* 2 *different valid orderings. Note that FAQ constraints preclude the original ordering* ABC.

B.3 Section 5

In Section 5, we define a decomposition that relates the width of a valid GHD to the widths of a series of ordinary GHDs. Variable orderings (as used by FAQ) are not as readily suited as GHDs are for decompositions. FAQ does have its own version of a decomposition, but the difficulties that arise when using variable orderings are exemplified in the way FAQ switches between GHDs and variable orderings in proofs [16]. In addition, the FAQ decomposition incurs some overhead costs when combining the sub-orderings to build the overall ordering, precluding a result like Corollary 35 that is required for our extensions. We briefly describe this overhead cost, and then provide an example of the runtime difference it can cause.

Output Addition. The FAQ paper uses a decomposition of the problem that is not width-preserving. It removes the set of output attributes $V(-\alpha)$ and decomposes the rest of the hypergraph into smaller hypergraphs. Then it constructs a regular Variable-Ordering/GHD for each hypergraph. Then it adds all output attributes $V(-\alpha)$ into each bag of each of the GHDs, and then stitches the GHDs together. This *output addition* to the bags of the GHDs leads to a potentially $2\times$ increase in width compared to our method which stitches the GHDs together without changing their width. As a result, FAQ's decomposition incurs higher runtime costs in each application of the decomposition, as we see in the next three subsections.

EXAMPLE 64. *Consider the query* $\sum_B \sum_C \sum_D R(A,B)\, S(B,C)\, T(C,D)\, U(D,A)$. *Suppose* $|A| = \sqrt{N}$, $|B| = 2 = |D|$, $|C| = N$, *and all of the pairwise relations are constructed as complete cross products of the attributes' values. Our decomposition will result in the chain GHD* $A - ABD - BCD$, *while the FAQ decomposition will result in the GHD* $A - ABC - ACD$. *The runtimes of both FAQ and GHDJoin using the former GHD is* $\tilde{O}(N)$, *whereas the runtimes using the latter GHD are* $\tilde{O}(N^{3/2})$. *As such, the FAQ decomposition will perform asymptotically worse than our decomposition.*

More generally, consider a query Q_n *with relations* $R_i(A_i,B)$, $S_i(B,C_i)$, $T_i(C_i,D)$, $U_i(D,A_i)$ *for* $1 \le i \le n$. *Like before, all* $|A_i|$*'s are* $\sqrt{N}$, *all* $|C_i|$*'s are* N, *and* $|B| = |D| = 2$. *And the aggregation ordering only has the* $+$ *operator, on* B, D *and all* C_i*'s. Our decomposition gives the chain* $A_1 \ldots A_n - A_1 \ldots A_n BD - C_1 \ldots C_n BD$. *This results in a runtime of* $\tilde{O}(N^n)$. *FAQ's decomposition gives* $A_1 \ldots A_n BC_1 \ldots C_n - A_1 \ldots A_n DC_1 \ldots C_n$. *This decomposition, and its corresponding ordering, give a runtime of* $\tilde{O}(N^{3n/2})$. *Thus the difference between runtime exponents caused by FAQ's decomposition and our decomposition can be arbitrarily high.*

B.4 Section 5.2

Section 5.2 shows how we can construct an approximately optimal valid GHD using Marx's approximation. FAQ [16]'s decomposition lets it apply Marx's approximation as well, but gives a weaker width guarantee of $faqw^3 + faqw$ [16, Theorem 9.49]. The extra $+faqw$ factor is due to output addition.

EXAMPLE 65. *Consider a query with output attribute* A

$$\sum_{B,+}\sum_{C,+}(R(A,B) \bowtie S(B,C)).$$

The optimal valid GHD for this query has bags $\{A,B\}$ *and* $\{B,C\}$, *and thus has fhw* 1. *The faqw is also* 1. *If we apply our decomposition, we get a GHD with bags* $\{A\}$, $\{A,B\}$, $\{B,C\}$ *which still has fhw* 1. *FAQ's decomposition on the reduced hypergraph (with output attribute* A *removed) has one bag* $\{B,C\}$. *Adding* A *to it gives a single bag* $\{A,B,C\}$ *resulting in a fhw of* 2. *More generally, consider query* Q_n *with* $\alpha = ((B_1,+),(B_2,+),\ldots(B_n,+))$ *and relations* $T(A_1,B_1)$ *and also* $R_{i,j}(A_i,A_j)$, $S_{i,j}(B_i,B_j)$ *for* $i,j \in \{1,2,\ldots,n\}$. *Our decomposition gives a GHD with bags* $\{A_1,A_2,\ldots,A_n\}$, $\{A_1,B_1\}$, $\{B_1,B_2,\ldots,B_n\}$, *which has fhw* $n/2$. *FAQ's decomposition has a single bag and fhw equal to* n.

Because of output addition, FAQ incurs an extra cost in our extensions involving DBP-width (Section 5.3) and MapReduce (Section 5.4) as well. We provide details and examples in the technical report.

B.5 Section 6

The runtime of InsideOut on a query involving idempotent product aggregations is given by $\tilde{O}(\mathrm{IN}^{faqw})$, where the $faqw$ depends on the ordering, and the presence of product aggregations. Our algorithm for handling product aggregations recovers the runtime of FAQ. Formally,

THEOREM 66. *For any* AJAR *query involving idempotent product aggregations,* $\mathrm{IN}^{w^*} + \mathrm{OUT} \le 2 \cdot \mathrm{IN}^{faqw}$.

The proof is in the technical report. By applying ideas from the FAQ paper to our setting, we can also recover the FAQ runtime on #QCQ. Our order equivalence characterization for product aggregations is both sound and complete; FAQ's characterization algorithm is sound but not complete. We also have a width-preserving decomposition for queries with product aggregates. This lets us get tighter runtime exponents in terms of submodular and DBP-widths (Theorems 40, 41) and efficient MapReduce Algorithms (Theorems 42, 43).

Bounded Query Rewriting Using Views

Yang Cao[1,3] Wenfei Fan[1,3] Floris Geerts[2] Ping Lu[3]

[1]University of Edinburgh [2]University of Antwerp [3]Beihang University

{Y.Cao-17@sms, wenfei@inf}.ed.ac.uk, floris.geerts@uantwerpen.be, luping@buaa.edu.cn

ABSTRACT

A query Q has a *bounded rewriting* using a set of views if there exists a query Q' expressed in the same language as Q, such that given a dataset D, $Q(D)$ can be computed by Q' that accesses only cached views and a small fraction D_Q of D. We consider datasets D that satisfy a set of access constraints, a combination of cardinality constraints and associated indices, such that the size $|D_Q|$ of D_Q and the time to identify D_Q are independent of $|D|$, no matter how big D is.

This paper studies the problem for deciding whether a query has a bounded rewriting given a set $\mathcal{V}$ of views and a set $\mathcal{A}$ of access constraints. We establish the complexity of the problem for various query languages, from Σ_3^p-complete for conjunctive queries (CQ), to undecidable for relational algebra (FO). We show that the intractability for CQ is rather robust even for acyclic CQ with fixed $\mathcal{V}$ and $\mathcal{A}$, and characterize when the problem is in PTIME. To make practical use of bounded rewriting, we provide an effective syntax for FO queries that have a bounded rewriting. The syntax characterizes a core subclass of such queries without sacrificing the expressive power, and can be checked in PTIME.

Keywords: Bounded rewriting; big data; complexity

1. INTRODUCTION

To make query answering feasible in big datasets, practitioners have been studying scale independence [4–6]. The idea is to compute the answers $Q(D)$ to a query Q in a dataset D by accessing a bounded amount of data in D, no matter how big the underlying D is.

This idea was formalized in [17, 18]. As suggested in [18], nontrivial queries can be scale independent under a set $\mathcal{A}$ of access constraints, a form of cardinality constraints with associated indices. A query Q is *boundedly evaluable* [17] if for all datasets D that satisfy $\mathcal{A}$, $Q(D)$ can be computed from a fraction D_Q of D, and the time for identifying and fetching D_Q, and hence the size $|D_Q|$ of D_Q are independent of $|D|$. We identify D_Q by reasoning about the cardinality constraints in $\mathcal{A}$, and fetch D_Q by using the indices of $\mathcal{A}$.

PODS'16, June 26-July 01, 2016, San Francisco, CA, USA

DOI: http://dx.doi.org/10.1145/2902251.2902294

Bounded evaluation has proven useful [10–12]. Experimenting with real-life data, we find that under a couple of hundreds of access constraints, 77% of randomly generated conjunctive queries [12], 67% of relational algebra queries [10], and 60% of graph pattern queries [11] are boundedly evaluable. Query plans for such queries outperform commercial query engines by 3 orders of magnitude, and the gap gets larger on bigger data. The results on CDR (call detail record) queries of one of our industry collaborators are even better: bounded evaluation improves 90% of their queries from 25 times to 5 orders of magnitude.

As an example of bounded evaluability, consider a Graph Search query of Facebook [15]: *find me all restaurants in NYC which I have not been to, but in which my friends have dined in May 2015.* A cardinality constraint imposed by Facebook is that a person can have at most 5000 friends [16]. Given this, we can answer the query by accessing 470000 tuples [10], as opposed to billions of user tuples and trillions of friend tuples in the Facebook dataset [22].

Still, many queries are not boundedly evaluable. Can we do better for such queries Q? An approach that has proven effective by practitioners is by making use of views [6]. The idea is to select and materialize a set $\mathcal{V}$ of small views, and answer Q in a dataset D by using views $\mathcal{V}(D)$ and an additional small fraction of D. That is, we cache $\mathcal{V}(D)$ with fast access, and compute $Q(D)$ by using $\mathcal{V}(D)$ and by restricting costly I/O operations to (possibly big) D. Many queries that are not boundedly evaluable can be efficiently answered using small views and bounded access to D [6].

Example 1: Consider a Graph Search query Q_0: *find movies that were released by Universal Studios in 2014, liked by people at NASA, and were rated 5.* The query is defined over a relational schema $\mathcal{R}_0$ consisting of four relations:

- person(pid, name, affiliation),
- movie(mid, mname, studio, release),
- rating(mid, rank) for ranks of movies, and
- like(pid, id, type), indicating that person pid likes item id of type, including but not limited to movies.

Over $\mathcal{R}_0$, Q_0 is written as a conjunctive query:

$$\begin{aligned} Q_0(\mathsf{mid}) = \exists x_p, x_p', y_m\ \big(&\mathsf{person}(x_p, x_p', \text{“NASA”}) \land \\ &\mathsf{movie}(\mathsf{mid}, y_m, \text{“Universal”}, \text{“2014”}) \land \\ &\mathsf{like}(x_p, \mathsf{mid}, \text{“movie”}) \land \mathsf{rating}(\mathsf{mid}, 5)\big). \end{aligned}$$

Consider a set $\mathcal{A}_0$ of two access constraints: (a) φ_1 = movie((studio, release) $\to$ mid, N_0), stating that each studio releases at most N_0 movies each year, where N_0 (≤ 100) is obtained by aggregating $\mathcal{R}_0$ instances; an index is built on movie such that given any (studio, release) value, it returns (at most N_0) corresponding mids; and (b) φ_2 = rating(mid $\rightarrow$ rank, 1), stating that each movie has a unique rating; an index is built on rating to fetch rank as above.

Under $\mathcal{A}_0$, query Q_0 is not boundedly evaluable: an instance D_0 of $\mathcal{R}_0$ may have billions of person and like tuples [22], and no constraints in $\mathcal{A}_0$ can help us identify a bounded fraction of these tuples to answer Q_0.

Nonetheless, suppose that we are given a view that collects movies liked by NASA folks, defined as follows:

$$V_1(\mathsf{mid}) = \exists x_p, x'_p, y'_m, z_1, z_2\ \big(\mathsf{person}(x_p, x'_p, \text{"NASA"}) \wedge \mathsf{movie}(\mathsf{mid}, y'_m, z_1, z_2) \wedge \mathsf{like}(x_p, \mathsf{mid}, \text{"movie"})\big).$$

As will be seen later, Q_0 can be rewritten into a conjunctive query Q_ξ using V_1, such that for all instances D_0 of $\mathcal{R}$ that satisfy $\mathcal{A}_0$, $Q_0(D_0)$ can be computed by Q_ξ that accesses only $V_1(D_0)$ and an additional $2N_0$ tuples from D_0, no matter how big D_0 is. Here $V_1(D_0)$ is a small set, much smaller than D_0 although its size is dependent on D_0. □

To support scale independence using views, practitioners have developed techniques for selecting views, indexing the views for fast access and for incrementally maintaining the views [6]. However, there are still fundamental issues that call for a full treatment. How should we characterize scale independence using views? What is the complexity for deciding whether a query is scale independent given a set of views and access constraints? If the complexity of the problem is high, is there any systematic way that helps us make effective use of cached views for querying big data?

Contributions. This paper tackles these questions.

(1) Bounded rewriting. We formalize scale independence using views, referred to as *bounded rewriting* (Section 2). Consider a query language $\mathcal{L}$, a set $\mathcal{V}$ of $\mathcal{L}$-definable views and a database schema $\mathcal{R}$. Informally, under a set $\mathcal{A}$ of access constraints, we say that a query $Q \in \mathcal{L}$ has a *bounded rewriting* Q' in the same $\mathcal{L}$ using $\mathcal{V}$ if for each instance D of $\mathcal{R}$ that satisfies $\mathcal{A}$, there exists a fraction D_Q of D such that

- $Q(D) = Q'(D_Q, \mathcal{V}(D))$, and
- the time for identifying D_Q and hence the size $|D_Q|$ of D_Q are independent of the size $|D|$ of D.

That is, we compute the exact answers $Q(D)$ via Q' by accessing cached $\mathcal{V}(D)$ and a *bounded* fraction D_Q of D. While $\mathcal{V}(D)$ may not be bounded, we can select small views following the methods of [6], which are cached with fast access. We formalize the notion in terms of query plans in a form of query trees commonly used in database systems [33], which have a bounded size M determined by our available resources such as processors and time constraint.

(2) Complexity. We study *the bounded rewriting problem* (Section 3), referred to as VBRP($\mathcal{L}$) for a query language $\mathcal{L}$. Given a set $\mathcal{A}$ of access constraints, a query $Q \in \mathcal{L}$ and a set $\mathcal{V}$ of $\mathcal{L}$-definable views, all defined on the same database schema $\mathcal{R}$, and a bound M, VBRP($\mathcal{L}$) is to decide whether under $\mathcal{A}$, Q has a bounded rewriting in $\mathcal{L}$ using $\mathcal{V}$ with a query plan no larger than M, referred to as *an M-bounded query plan.* The need for studying VBRP($\mathcal{L}$) is evident: if Q has a bounded rewriting, then we can find efficient query plans to answer Q on possibly big datasets D.

We investigate VBRP($\mathcal{L}$) when $\mathcal{L}$ ranges over conjunctive queries (CQ, *i.e.,* SPC), unions of conjunctive queries (UCQ, *i.e.,*SPCU), positive FO queries ($\exists$FO$^+$, select-project-join-union queries) and first-order logic queries (FO, the full relational algebra). We show that VBRP is Σ_3^p-complete for CQ, UCQ and $\exists$FO$^+$; but it becomes undecidable for FO. In addition, we explore the impact of various parameters ($\mathcal{R}$, M, $\mathcal{A}$ and $\mathcal{V}$) of VBRP on its complexity.

(3) Acyclic conjunctive queries. Worse yet, we show that the intractability of VBRP is quite robust (Section 4). It remains intractable for acyclic CQ (denoted by ACQ), when all parameters M, $\mathcal{R}$, $\mathcal{A}$ and $\mathcal{V}$ are fixed, and even when access constraints in the fixed $\mathcal{A}$ have restricted forms. In light of this, we give a characterization for VBRP(ACQ) to be in PTIME, and identify several sub-classes of ACQ and CQ for which VBRP is tractable under fixed M, $\mathcal{R}$, $\mathcal{A}$ and $\mathcal{V}$.

(4) Effective syntax. To cope with the undecidability of VBRP(FO) and the robust intractability of VBRP(CQ), we develop an effective syntax for FO queries that have a bounded rewriting (Section 5). For any $\mathcal{R}, \mathcal{V}, \mathcal{A}$ and M, we show that there exists a class of FO queries, referred to as *queries topped* by $(\mathcal{R}, \mathcal{V}, \mathcal{A}, M)$, such that under $\mathcal{A}$,

(a) every FO query that has an M-bounded rewriting using $\mathcal{V}$ is equivalent to a query topped by $(\mathcal{R}, \mathcal{V}, \mathcal{A}, M)$;

(b) every query topped by $(\mathcal{R}, \mathcal{V}, \mathcal{A}, M)$ has an M-bounded rewriting in FO using $\mathcal{V}$; and

(c) it takes PTIME in $M, |Q|, |\mathcal{V}|, |\mathcal{R}|, |\mathcal{A}|$ to check whether Q is topped by $(\mathcal{R}, \mathcal{V}, \mathcal{A}, M)$, using an oracle to check whether views in $\mathcal{V}$ have bounded output (see below).

That is, topped queries make a *core* subclass of FO queries with a bounded rewriting using $\mathcal{V}$, without sacrificing their expressive power, along the same lines as rang-safe queries for safe relational calculus (see, *e.g.,* [1]). This allows us to reduce VBRP to syntactic checking of topped queries. Given a query Q, we can check syntactically whether Q is topped by $(\mathcal{R}, \mathcal{V}, \mathcal{A}, M)$ in PTIME, by condition (c) above; if so, we can find a bounded rewriting as warranted by condition (b); moreover, if Q has a bounded rewriting, then it can be transformed to a topped query by condition (a).

To check topped queries, we need to determine whether some views of $\mathcal{V}$ have *bounded output* $\mathcal{V}(D)$ over all datasets D that satisfy $\mathcal{A}$, *i.e.,* the size $|\mathcal{V}(D)|$ is bounded by a constant. This is to ensure bounded accesses to D, since a query plan may filter and fetch data from D by using values from some views in $\mathcal{V}(D)$. This problem is, not surprisingly, undecidable for FO (Section 3). In light of this, we develop effective syntax for FO queries with bounded output. That is, given $\mathcal{A}$ and $\mathcal{R}$, we identify a class of FO queries, referred to as *size-bounded queries*, such that under $\mathcal{A}$, an FO view (query) over $\mathcal{R}$ has bounded output iff it is equivalent to a size-bounded FO, and it is in PTIME to check whether a query is size-bounded. We use this as a PTIME oracle when checking topped queries (condition (c)) above.

This work is an effort to give a formal treatment of scale independence with views, an approach that has already been put in action by practitioners. The complexity bounds reveal the inherent difficulty of the problem. The effective syntax, however, suggests a promising direction for making effective use of bounded rewriting. A variety of techniques are used in the proofs, including characterizations, algorithms and a wide range of reductions.

Related work. We classify related work as follows.

Scale independence. The idea of scale independence originated from [5], which is to execute the workload in an application by doing a bounded amount of work, regardless of the size of datasets used. The idea was incorporated into

PIQL [4], an extension of SQL by allowing users to specify bounds on the amount of data accessed. As pointed out by [6], to make complex PIQL queries scale independent, precomputed views and query rewriting using views should be employed. Techniques for view selection, indexing and incremental maintenance were also developed there.

The idea of scale independence was formalized in [18]. A query Q is defined to be *scale independent* in a dataset D *w.r.t.* a bound Θ if there exists $D_Q \subseteq D$ such that $Q(D) = Q(D_Q)$ and $|D_Q| \leq \Theta$. Access constraints, a notion of $\bar{x}$-controllability and a set of rules were also introduced in [18], to deduce dependencies on attributes needed for computing $Q(D)$; these yield a sufficient condition to determine the scale independence of FO queries when variables $\bar{x}$ are instantiated. In addition, it studied the problem to decide whether for all instances D of a relational schema, we can compute $Q(D)$ by accessing cached views and at most Θ tuples, *in the absence of* access constraints. The problem is NP-complete for CQ, and undecidable for FO. The notion of $\bar{x}$-controllability was extended to views, giving two simple sufficient conditions to decide the scale independence of query rewriting using views under access constraints.

This work differs from the prior work in the following. (a) We formalize bounded rewriting using views in terms of query plans subject to a bound M determined by available resources. This is quite different from the notion of $\bar{x}$-controllability [18]. (b) We incorporate access constraints to make the notion more practical; without such constraints, few queries have a bounded rewriting. Under the constraints, however, the analysis of bounded rewriting is more intriguing. For instance, VBRP(CQ) is Σ_3^p-complete, in contrast to NP-complete [18]. (c) We provide an effective syntax for FO queries with a bounded rewriting using views under access constraints, a sufficient and necessary condition. In contrast, the conditions of [18] via $\bar{x}$-controllability are sufficient but not necessary. Moreover, the rules of [18] do not distinguish whether views are used to just validate data or to fetch data from underlying datasets; this is critical for VBRP, and demands the bounded output analysis of views. Effective syntax and VBRP were not studied in [4–6].

Bounded evaluability. The notion of bounded evaluability was proposed in [17], based on a form of query plans that conform to access constraints. The problem for deciding whether a query is boundedly evaluable under access constraints is decidable but EXPSPACE-hard for CQ, UCQ and $\exists$FO$^+$, and is undecidable for FO [17]. A notion of effective boundedness was studied for CQ [12], based on a *restricted form* of query plans that conduct all data fetching before any relational operations start. It was shown [12] that effective boundedness is in PTIME for CQ. It was also studied for graph pattern queries via simulation and subgraph isomorphism [11], which are quite different from relational queries.

Bounded rewriting is more challenging than bounded evaluability. (a) With views comes the need for reasoning about their output size $|\mathcal{V}(D)|$. (b) We adopt query plans in a form of query trees as commonly used in database systems, and allow users to specify a bound on the size of the plans based on their available resources (see Section 2). In contrast, [17] considers query plans that are a sequence of relational and data fetching operations, of length possibly exponential in the sizes of queries and constraints. After experimenting with real-life data, we find that the plans of [17] are not very realistic, and worse yet, their CQ plans may actually encode non-recursive datalog queries without union, which yield exponential-size queries when expressed in CQ. It is because of the different notions of query plans adopted in this work and [17] that VBRP is Σ_3^p-complete for CQ, while bounded evaluability is EXPSPACE-hard [17].

Effective syntax. There has been a host of work on effective syntax (*e.g.,* [20, 35, 36]), which started decades ago to characterize safe relational queries up to equivalence. For bounded query evaluation, an effective syntax was proposed for CQ [17], and another one for FO [10].

This work develops an effective syntax for bounded rewriting of FO queries using views under access constraints. Such a syntax has not been studied before, and is quite different from their counterparts for bounded evaluability. (a) It is in PTIME to check whether an FO query is topped for rewriting, while for bounded evaluability, the syntactic condition of [17] is in PTIME to check for CQ, but Π_2^p-complete for UCQ, and is not defined for FO. (b) Effective syntax for query rewriting is more intriguing than its counterpart for bounded evaluability [10]. As remarked earlier, we have to reason about the size $|\mathcal{V}(D)|$ of cached views. It is further complicated by user-imposed bound on the size of query plans, which was not considered in [10]. (c) The class of effectively bounded queries of [12] does not make an effective syntax: not every boundedly evaluable CQ is necessarily equivalent to an effectively bounded CQ.

Query rewriting using views. Query rewriting has been extensively studied (*e.g.,* [2, 3, 13, 28, 31, 32]; see [23, 27] for surveys). In contrast to conventional query rewriting using views, bounded rewriting requires controlled access to the underlying dataset D under access constraints, in addition to cached $\mathcal{V}(D)$. This makes the analysis more challenging. For instance, it is Σ_3^p-complete to decide whether there exists a bounded rewriting for CQ with CQ views, as opposed to NP-complete in the conventional setting [28].

Access patterns. Related to the work is also query answering under access patterns, which require a relation to be only accessed by providing certain combinations of attributes [8,9,14,29,30,32] (see [7] for a survey). Proof-based methods for generating low-cost query plans under access patterns and integrity constraints are studied for CQ and FO. Query rewriting using views under access patterns has been studied for CQ [32], and for UCQ and UCQ$^\neg$ (with negated relation atoms) under fixed views and integrity constraints [14].

This work differs from the prior work in the following. (a) Unlike access patterns, access constraints impose cardinality constraints and controlled data accesses via indices. (b) Moreover, in an access constraint $R(X \to Y, N)$, $X \cup Y$ may account for a small set of the attributes of R, while an access pattern has to cover all the attributes of R. As a result, we can fetch partial tuples from the underlying dataset via an access constraint, as opposed to access patterns that are to fetch entire tuples. This complicates the proofs of bounded evaluability. (c) Bounded rewriting allows access to the underlying data with controlled I/O, which is prohibited in [14,32]. As an evidence of the difference, bounded CQ rewriting using fixed views is C_{2k+1}^p-complete under fixed access constraints (Section 3), as opposed to NP-complete for rewriting using fixed views under access patterns [14]. (d) To the best of our knowledge, no prior work has studied effective syntax for bounded FO rewriting.

2. BOUNDED QUERY REWRITING

In this section we formalize bounded query plans and bounded query rewriting using views under access constraints. We start with a review of basic notations.

Database schema. A relational (database) schema $\mathcal{R}$ consists of a collection of relation schemas $(R_1, \ldots, R_n)$, where each R_i has a fixed set of attributes. We assume a countably infinite domain $\mathbf{U}$ of data values, on which instances D of $\mathcal{R}$ are defined. We use $|D|$ to denote the size of D, measured as the total *number of tuples* in D.

Access schema. Following [17], we define an *access schema* $\mathcal{A}$ over a database schema $\mathcal{R}$ as a set of *access constraints* $\varphi = R(X \to Y, N)$, where R is a relation schema in $\mathcal{R}$, X and Y are sets of attributes of R, and N is a natural number. An instance D of R *satisfies* φ if

- for any X-value $\bar{a}$ in D, $|D_Y(X = \bar{a})| \leq N$, where $D_Y(X = \bar{a})$ is the set $\{t[Y] \mid t \in D,\ t[X] = \bar{a}\}$; and
- there exists a function (index) that given an X-value $\bar{a}$, returns $D_Y(X = \bar{a})$ from D in $O(N)$ time.

Intuitively, an access constraint is a combination of a cardinality constraint and *an index on X for Y* (*i.e.*, the function). It tells us that given any X-value, there exist at most N distinct corresponding Y-values, and these Y values can be efficiently fetched by using the index. For instance, $\mathcal{A}_0$ described in Example 1 is an access schema.

Note that functional dependencies (FDs) are a special case $R(X \to Y, 1)$ of access constraints, *i.e.*, when bound $N = 1$, provided that an index is built from X to Y. As shown in [10, 12], access constraints can be discovered from instances of $\mathcal{R}$, by extending mining tools for FDs with aggregates.

An instance D of $\mathcal{R}$ *satisfies* access schema $\mathcal{A}$, denoted by $D \models \mathcal{A}$, if D satisfies all the constraints in $\mathcal{A}$.

Query classes. We express queries and views in the same language $\mathcal{L}$, which is one of the following [1]:

- conjunctive queries (CQ), built up from relation atoms $R(\bar{x})$ for $R \in \mathcal{R}$, and equality atoms $x = y$ or $x = c$ (for constant c), by closing them under conjunction $\wedge$ and existential quantification $\exists$;
- unions of conjunctive queries (UCQ) of the form $Q = Q_1 \cup \cdots \cup Q_k$, where Q_i is a CQ for $i \in [1, k]$;
- positive existential FO queries ($\exists$FO$^+$), built from relation atoms and equality atoms by closing under $\wedge$, disjunction $\vee$ and $\exists$; and
- First-order logic queries (FO), built from atomic formulas by closing them under $\wedge$, $\vee$, negation $\neg$, $\exists$ and universal quantification $\forall$.

Query plans. Following [33], we define evaluation plans for a query Q using a set $\mathcal{V}$ of views, both defined over a database schema $\mathcal{R}$. To simplify the definition, we write Q in the relational algebra with projection π, selection σ, Cartesian product $\times$, union $\cup$, set difference $\setminus$ and renaming ρ.

A *query plan* for Q using $\mathcal{V}$, denoted by $\xi(Q, \mathcal{V}, \mathcal{R})$, is a tree T_ξ that satisfies the two conditions below.

(1) Each node u of T_ξ is labeled $S_i = \delta_i$, where S_i denotes a relation for partial results, and δ_i is as follows:

(a) $\{c\}$ for a constant in Q, if u is a leaf of T_ξ;

(b) a view V for $V \in \mathcal{V}$, if u is a leaf of T_ξ;

(c) fetch($X \in S_j, R, Y$), if u has a single child v labeled with $S_j = \delta_j$, and S_j has attributes X;

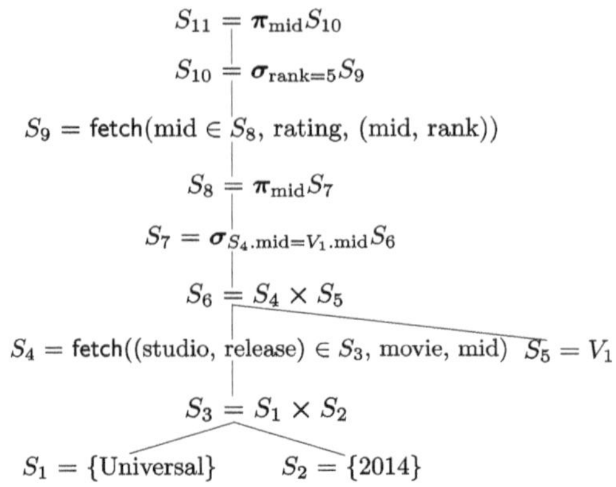

Figure 1: A query plan ξ_0 for Q_0 using view V_1

(d) $\pi_Y(S_j)$, $\sigma_C(S_j)$ or $\rho(S_j)$, if u has a single child v labeled with $S_j = \delta_j$; here Y is a set of attributes in S_j, and C is a condition defined on S_j; or

(e) $S_j \times S_l$, $S_j \cup S_l$ or $S_j \setminus S_l$, if u has two children v and v' labeled with $S_j = \delta_j$ and $S_l = \delta_l$, respectively.

Intuitively, given an instance D of $\mathcal{R}$, relations S_i's are computed by δ_i, bottom up in T_ξ as usual [33]. More specifically, δ_i may (a) extract constants from Q, (b) access cached views $V(D)$, and (c) access D via a fetch operation, which, for each $\bar{a} \in S_j$, retrieves $D_{XY}(X = \bar{a})$ from D; it may also be a relational operation ((d) and (e) above). Relation S_n associated with the root of T_ξ is the result of the computation.

(2) For each instance D of $\mathcal{R}$, the *result* $\xi(D)$ of applying $\xi(Q, \mathcal{V}, \mathcal{R})$ to D is the relation S_n at root of T_ξ computed as above. We require that $\xi(D) = Q(D)$.

The *size* of plan ξ is the number of nodes in T_ξ. We use D_Q to denote the bag of all tuples fetched for computing $\xi(D)$, *i.e.*, the multiset that collects tuples in $D_{XY}(X = \bar{a})$ for all fetch($X \in S_j, R, Y$) when applying ξ to D. Intuitively, it measures the amount of I/O operations to access D.

Example 2: A plan $\xi_0(Q_0, V_1, \mathcal{R}_0)$ for Q_0 using view V_1 given in Example 1 is depicted in Fig. 1. Given an instance D of $\mathcal{R}_0$, (a) it fetches the set S_4 of mids of all movies released by Universal Studios in 2014, using constants in Q_0; (b) filters S_4 with mids in $V_1(D)$ via join, to get a subset S_8 of S_4 of movies liked by NASA folks; (c) fetches rating tuples using the mids of S_8; and finally, (d) finds the set S_{11} of mids, which is precisely the answer $Q_0(D)$ to Q_0 in D. □

Bounded plans. To formalize bounded query rewriting, we bring into play access schema and a bound on the size of query plans. Consider an access schema $\mathcal{A}$ defined over $\mathcal{R}$.

A query plan $\xi(Q, \mathcal{V}, \mathcal{R})$ is said to *conform to* $\mathcal{A}$ if

(a) for each fetch($X \in S_j, R, Y$) operation in ξ, there exists an access constraint $R(X \to Y', N)$ in $\mathcal{A}$ such that $Y \subseteq X \cup Y'$, and

(b) there exists a constant N_Q such that for all instances D of $\mathcal{R}$ that satisfy $\mathcal{A}$, $|D_Q| \leq N_Q$.

That is, while ξ can access entire cached views, its access to the underlying D must be via fetch operations only, by making use of the indices in the access constraints of $\mathcal{A}$. Plan ξ tells us how to retrieve D_Q from D such that $Q(D)$ is computed by using the data in D_Q and $\mathcal{V}(D)$ only. Better still, D_Q is *bounded*: $|D_Q|$ is independent of possibly big $|D|$. The time for identifying and fetching D_Q is also independent of $|D|$ (assuming that given an X-value $\bar{a}$, it takes $O(N)$ time to fetch $D_{XY}(X = \bar{a})$ from D via the index for $R(X \to Y, N)$).

Given a natural number M, we say that $\xi(Q, \mathcal{V}, \mathcal{R})$ is an *M-bounded plan for Q using $\mathcal{V}$ under $\mathcal{A}$* if (a) ξ conforms to $\mathcal{A}$, and (b) the size of ξ is at most M.

Intuitively, M is a threshold picked by users and is determined by available resources. The less resources we have, the smaller M we can afford. Without the bound M, we find that rewriting plans are often of exponential length when experimenting with real-life data, which are not very practical; indeed, it would be EXPSPACE-hard to decide whether there exists a bounded rewriting even for CQ, by reduction from the problem for deciding bounded evaluability for CQ [17]. Hence we opt to let users specify M based on their resources. If $\xi(Q, \mathcal{V}, \mathcal{R})$ is M-bounded under $\mathcal{A}$, then for all datasets D that satisfy $\mathcal{A}$, we can efficiently answer Q in D by following ξ and accessing a bounded amount of data from D.

Example 3: Plan ξ_0 shown in Fig. 1 is 11-bounded for Q_0 using V_1 under $\mathcal{A}_0$. Indeed, (a) both fetch operations (S_4 and S_9) are controlled by the access constraints of $\mathcal{A}_0$, and (b) for any instance D of $\mathcal{R}_0$, ξ_0 accesses at most $2N_0$ tuples from D, where N_0 is the constant in φ_1 of $\mathcal{A}_0$, since $|S_4| \leq N_0$ by φ_1, and $|S_9| \leq N_0$ by $S_8 \subseteq S_4$ and constraint φ_2 on rating in $\mathcal{A}_0$; and (c) eleven operations are conducted in total. Note that rating tuples in D are fetched by using S_8, which is obtained by relational operations on $V_1(D)$ and S_4. While V_1 is not boundedly evaluable under $\mathcal{A}_0$, the amount of data fetched from D is independent of $|D|$. □

Bounded query rewriting. We now formalize this notion. Consider a query Q in a language $\mathcal{L}$, a set $\mathcal{V}$ of $\mathcal{L}$-definable views, and an access schema $\mathcal{A}$, all over the same database schema $\mathcal{R}$. For a bound M, we say that Q has an *M-bounded rewriting in $\mathcal{L}$ using $\mathcal{V}$ under $\mathcal{A}$*, or simply *a bounded rewriting using $\mathcal{V}$* when M and $\mathcal{A}$ are clear from the context, if it has an M-bounded query plan $\xi(Q, \mathcal{V}, \mathcal{R})$ under $\mathcal{A}$ such that ξ is *a query plan in $\mathcal{L}$, i.e.*, in each label $S_i = \delta_i$ of ξ,

- if $\mathcal{L}$ is CQ, then δ_i is a fetch, π, σ, $\times$ or ρ operation;
- if $\mathcal{L}$ is UCQ, δ_i can be fetch, π, σ, $\times$, ρ or $\cup$, and moreover, for any node labeled $\cup$, all its ancestors in the tree T_ξ of ξ are also labeled with $\cup$; that is, $\cup$ is conducted at "the top level" only;
- if $\mathcal{L}$ is $\exists\text{FO}^+$, then δ_i is fetch, π, σ, $\times$, $\cup$ or ρ; and
- if $\mathcal{L}$ is FO, δ_i can be fetch, π, σ, $\times$, $\cup$, $\setminus$ or ρ.

One can verify that if ξ is a plan in $\mathcal{L}$, then there exists a query Q_ξ in $\mathcal{L}$ such that for all instances D of $\mathcal{R}$, $\xi(D) = Q_\xi(D)$ and moreover, the size $|Q_\xi|$ of Q_ξ is linear in the size of ξ. Such query Q_ξ is unique up to equivalence. We refer to Q_ξ as the query *expressed by* ξ.

Example 4: The CQ Q_0 of Example 1 has an 11-bounded rewriting in CQ using V_1 under $\mathcal{A}_0$. Indeed, ξ_0 of Fig. 1 is such a bounded plan, which expresses

$$Q_\xi(\text{mid}) = \exists y_m \big(\text{movie}(\text{mid}, y_m, \text{"Universal"}, \text{"2014"}) \wedge V_1(\text{mid}) \wedge \text{rating}(\text{mid}, 5)\big).$$

It is a rewriting of Q_0 using V_1 in CQ. □

Notations used in this paper are summarized in Table 1.

3. DECIDING BOUNDED REWRITING

To make effective use of bounded rewriting, we need to settle *the bounded rewriting problem*, denoted by VBRP($\mathcal{L}$) for a query language $\mathcal{L}$ and stated as follows.

- INPUT: A database schema $\mathcal{R}$, a natural number M (in unary), an access schema $\mathcal{A}$, a query $Q \in \mathcal{L}$ and a set $\mathcal{V}$ of $\mathcal{L}$-definable views all defined on $\mathcal{R}$.

symbols	notations
$\mathcal{R}$, R	database schema $\mathcal{R}$ and relation schema $R \in \mathcal{R}$
$\mathcal{A}$	access schema
$D \models \mathcal{A}$	an instance D of $\mathcal{R}$ satisfies access schema $\mathcal{A}$
$Q \in \mathcal{L}$	query Q in a query language $\mathcal{L}$
$\mathcal{V}$, V	a set $\mathcal{V}$ of views and a view $V \in \mathcal{V}$
$\xi(Q, \mathcal{V}, \mathcal{R})$	a query plan ξ for Q using $\mathcal{V}$ over instances of $\mathcal{R}$
T_ξ	plan ξ represented as a query tree
$\xi(D)$	the result of applying ξ to D
VBRP($\mathcal{L}$)	the bounded rewriting problem for queries in $\mathcal{L}$
$Q \equiv_\mathcal{A} Q'$	$\mathcal{A}$-equivalence
$Q \sqsubseteq_\mathcal{A} Q'$	$\mathcal{A}$-containment
QP_Q	the set of all possible query plans of a bounded size
$\xi \sqsubseteq_\mathcal{A} Q$	$Q_\xi \sqsubseteq_\mathcal{A} Q$, query Q_ξ expressed by ξ

Table 1: Notations

- QUESTION: Under $\mathcal{A}$, does Q have an M-bounded rewriting in $\mathcal{L}$ using $\mathcal{V}$?

While VBRP($\mathcal{L}$) is important, it is nontrivial.

Theorem 1: Problem VBRP($\mathcal{L}$) is
(1) Σ_3^p-complete when $\mathcal{L}$ is CQ, UCQ or $\exists\text{FO}^+$; and
(2) undecidable when $\mathcal{L}$ is FO. □

Below we first reveal the inherent complexity of VBRP($\mathcal{L}$) by investigating problems embedded in it, and outline a proof of Theorem 1 for various $\mathcal{L}$ (Section 3.1). We then investigate the impact of parameters $\mathcal{R}$, $\mathcal{A}$, $\mathcal{V}$ and M on the complexity of VBRP($\mathcal{L}$) (Section 3.2).

3.1 The Bounded Rewriting Problem

To understand where the complexity of VBRP($\mathcal{L}$) arises, consider a problem embedded in it. Given an access schema $\mathcal{A}$, a query Q, a set $\mathcal{V}$ of views, and a query plan ξ of length M, it is to decide whether ξ is a bounded plan for Q using $\mathcal{V}$ under $\mathcal{A}$. This requires that we check the following: (a) Is the query Q_ξ expressed by ξ equivalent to Q under $\mathcal{A}$? (b) Does ξ conform to $\mathcal{A}$? None of these questions is trivial. To simplify the discussion, we focus on CQ for examples.

$\mathcal{A}$-equivalence. Consider a database schema $\mathcal{R}$. Under an access schema $\mathcal{A}$ over $\mathcal{R}$, we say that two queries Q_1 and Q_2 defined over $\mathcal{R}$ are *$\mathcal{A}$-equivalent*, denoted by $Q_1 \equiv_\mathcal{A} Q_2$, if for all instances D of $\mathcal{R}$ that satisfy $\mathcal{A}$, $Q_1(D) = Q_2(D)$. This is a notion weaker than the conventional notion of query equivalence $Q_1 \equiv Q_2$. The latter is to decide whether for all instances D of $\mathcal{R}$, $Q_1(D) = Q_2(D)$, regardless of whether $D \models \mathcal{A}$. Indeed, if $Q_1 \equiv Q_2$ then $Q_1 \equiv_\mathcal{A} Q_2$, but the converse does not hold. It is known that query equivalence for CQ is NP-complete (cf. [1]). In contrast, it has been shown that $\mathcal{A}$-equivalence is harder (unless P = NP).

Lemma 2 [17]: Given access schema $\mathcal{A}$ and two queries Q_1 and Q_2, it is Π_2^p-complete to decide whether $Q_1 \equiv_\mathcal{A} Q_2$, for Q_1 and Q_2 in CQ, UCQ or $\exists\text{FO}^+$. □

Coming back to VBRP, for a query plan ξ and a query Q, we need to check whether ξ is a query plan for Q, *i.e.*, whether $Q_\xi \equiv_\mathcal{A} Q$, where Q_ξ is the query expressed by ξ. This step is Π_2^p-hard for CQ. It is easy to show that the problem is undecidable when it comes to FO.

Bounded output. Another complication is introduced by views in $\mathcal{V}$. To decide whether a query plan ξ is bounded for a query Q using $\mathcal{V}$ under $\mathcal{A}$, we need to verify that ξ conforms to $\mathcal{A}$. This *may* require us to check whether a view $V \in \mathcal{V}$ has "bounded output".

Example 5: Consider database schema $\mathcal{R}_0$, query Q_0, and access schema $\mathcal{A}_0$ defined in Example 1.

(a) Suppose that instead of V_1, a CQ view V_2 is given:

$$V_2(\mathsf{pid}) = \exists x'_p\ \mathsf{person}(\mathsf{pid}, x'_p, \text{“NASA”}).$$

Given an instance D of $\mathcal{R}_0$, $V_2(D)$ consists of people who work at NASA. Extend $\mathcal{A}_0$ to $\mathcal{A}_1$ by including $\varphi_3 = \mathsf{like}((\mathsf{pid}, \mathsf{id}) \to (\mathsf{pid}, \mathsf{id}, \mathsf{type}), 1)$, *i.e.,* $(\mathsf{pid}, \mathsf{id})$ is a key of relation like. Then Q_0 has a rewriting Q_2 using V_2:

$$Q_2(\mathsf{mid}) = \exists x_p, y_m\ \big(V_2(x_p) \land \mathsf{like}(x_p, \mathsf{mid}, \text{“movie”}) \land \mathsf{movie}(\mathsf{mid}, y_m, \text{“Universal”}, \text{“2014”}) \land \mathsf{rating}(\mathsf{mid}, 5)\big).$$

One can verify that Q_2 is a bounded rewriting of Q_0 using V_2 under $\mathcal{A}_1$ iff there exists a constant N_1 such that for all instances D of $\mathcal{R}$, if $D \models \mathcal{A}_1$, then $|V_2(D)| \leq N_1$; that is, NASA has at most N_1 employees. For if it holds, then we can extract a set S of at most N_0 mids by leveraging constraint φ_1 of $\mathcal{A}_1$ on movie, and select pairs $(\mathsf{pid}, \mathsf{mid})$ from $V_2(D) \times S$ that are in a tuple $(\mathsf{pid}, \mathsf{mid}, \text{“movie”})$ in the like relation, by making use of constraint φ_3 given above. For each mid that passes the test, we check its rating via the index in φ_2, by accessing at most N_0 tuples in rating. Putting these together, we access at most $N_1 \cdot N_0 + N_0$ tuples from D. Conversely, if the output of $V_2(D)$ is not bounded, then Q has no bounded rewriting using V_2 under $\mathcal{A}_1$.

(b) In contrast, for rewriting some queries, we *do not* have to check whether a view has bounded output. Consider a rewriting $Q(x) = Q_3(x) \land V_3(x)$ of query Q over a database schema $\mathcal{R}$, where V_3 is a view, and Q_3 has a bounded query plan under an access schema $\mathcal{A}$ and does not use any view. Then Q has a bounded rewriting under $\mathcal{A}$ no matter whether $|V_3(D)|$ is bounded or not for instances D of $\mathcal{R}$. Indeed, all fetching operations are conducted by Q_3; for each x-value a computed by $Q_3(x)$, we only need to validate whether $a \in V(D)$. This involves only cached $V_3(D)$, without accessing D, and hence, $|V_3(D)|$ does not need to be bounded. □

To check whether views have a bounded output when it is necessary, we study *the bounded output problem*, denoted by $\mathsf{BOP}(\mathcal{L})$ and stated as follows:

- INPUT: A database schema $\mathcal{R}$, an access schema $\mathcal{A}$ and a query $V \in \mathcal{L}$, both defined over $\mathcal{R}$.
- Question: Is there a constant N such that for all instances D of $\mathcal{R}$, if $D \models \mathcal{A}$ then $|V(D)| \leq N$?

The analysis of bounded output is also nontrivial.

Theorem 3: Problem $\mathsf{BOP}(\mathcal{L})$ is

(1) coNP-complete when $\mathcal{L}$ is CQ, UCQ or $\exists\mathsf{FO}^+$; and

(2) undecidable when $\mathcal{L}$ is FO.

When database schema $\mathcal{R}$ and access schema $\mathcal{A}$ are both fixed, BOP remains coNP-hard for CQ, UCQ and $\exists\mathsf{FO}^+$, and is still undecidable for FO. □

Proof sketch: (1) We show that BOP is in coNP for $\exists\mathsf{FO}^+$and is coNP-hard for CQ. The upper bound proof is a little involved, and demands a characterization of $\exists\mathsf{FO}^+$queries with bounded output, in terms of notions of element queries and covered variables. Informally, (a) an *element query* Q_e of a query Q is a CQ obtained from Q and an access schema $\mathcal{A}$ such that its tableau representation satisfies $\mathcal{A}$. Intuitively, we do not have to worry about $\mathcal{A}$ when dealing with Q_e. We show that under $\mathcal{A}$, each query Q in $\exists\mathsf{FO}^+$is $\mathcal{A}$-equivalent to $Q_{e_1} \cup \cdots \cup Q_{e_n}$, where each Q_{e_i} is an element query. (b) A variable of Q is *covered* by $\mathcal{A}$ if its use is controlled by $\mathcal{A}$ and hence, the number of its possible valuations is bounded by the cardinality constraints of $\mathcal{A}$. Based on these, we give the characterization as follows:

Lemma 4: For an $\exists\mathsf{FO}^+$query $Q(\bar{x})$ and an access schema $\mathcal{A}$, $Q(\bar{x})$ has bounded output iff for every element query $Q_e(\bar{x}')$ of $Q(\bar{x})$, all variables in $\bar{x}'$ are in $\mathsf{cov}(Q_e, \mathcal{A})$, which is the set of variables in Q_e covered by $\mathcal{A}$. □

Capitalizing on the characterization, we can readily develop a coNP algorithm to check whether an $\exists\mathsf{FO}^+$query has bounded output under an access schema $\mathcal{A}$.

The lower bound is verified by reduction from the complement of the 3SAT problem to BOP(CQ). Given a propositional formula ψ, 3SAT is to decide whether ψ is satisfiable. It is NP-complete (cf. [19]). The reduction uses fixed database schema $\mathcal{R}$ and access schema $\mathcal{A}$, *i.e.,* they do not depend on 3SAT instance ψ. As a result, BOP(CQ) remains coNP-hard even under fixed $\mathcal{R}$ and $\mathcal{A}$.

(2) We show that BOP(FO) is undecidable by reduction from the complement of the satisfiability problem for FO. The latter is to decide, given an FO query Q defined over a database schema $\mathcal{R}$, whether there exists an instance D of $\mathcal{R}$ such that $Q(D) \neq \emptyset$. It is undecidable even when $\mathcal{R}$ is fixed (cf. [1]). The reduction uses $\mathcal{A} = \emptyset$ and a fixed relational schema $\mathcal{R}'$. Given Q, we define an FO query Q' such that Q' has bounded output over all instances of $\mathcal{R}'$ iff Q is not satisfiable. □

Using Lemma 2 and Theorem 3, we prove Theorem 1.

Proof of Theorem 1. The proof has three parts.

(1) We show that VBRP is in Σ_3^p for $\exists\mathsf{FO}^+$, by developing an algorithm for checking whether an $\exists\mathsf{FO}^+$query Q has a bounded rewriting. The algorithm works as follows: (a) guess a query plan ξ in $\exists\mathsf{FO}^+$of size at most M; (b) check whether ξ conforms to $\mathcal{A}$; if so, continue; otherwise reject the current guess; (c) check whether $Q_\xi \equiv_{\mathcal{A}} Q$ for the $\exists\mathsf{FO}^+$query Q_ξ expressed by ξ; if so, return “yes”. The algorithm is in Σ_3^p since step (b) is in Δ_2^p ($\mathsf{P}^{\mathsf{coNP}}$) as it has to check whether the polynomially many fetch operations in ξ have bounded output, and checking each fetch is in coNP by Theorem 3(1); moreover, step (c) is in Π_2^p by Lemma 2.

(2) The lower bound proof is more involved. We show that VBRP is Σ_3^p-hard for CQ, by reduction from the $\exists^*\forall^*\exists^*$3CNF problem, which is Σ_3^p-complete [34]. The latter is to decide, given a sentence $\varphi = \exists X \forall Y \exists Z\, \psi$, whether φ is true, where ψ is an instance of 3SAT defined over variables in $X \cup Y \cup Z$.

Given such a φ, the reduction employs fixed database schema $\mathcal{R}$ and access schema $\mathcal{A}$ that do not vary for different instances φ, and a fixed constant $M = 6$. We define a CQ Q and a set $\mathcal{V}$ consisting of a single view V in CQ. The encoding of V is quite intricate; it assures that whenever V is used in a bounded rewriting of Q, it must occur in the corresponding query plan ξ in the form of $\sigma_{X=\mu_X}(V)$, where μ_X denotes a truth-assignment of X. When V is used in any other form in a query plan ξ', it is shown that either ξ' does not conform to $\mathcal{A}$, or it does not help us in answering Q, and thus can be dispelled. Moreover, the access constraints in $\mathcal{A}$ and query Q are such defined that from $D \models \mathcal{A}$ and $Q(D) \neq \emptyset$, we can derive that D encodes a truth assignment μ_Y of Y. Hence, Q has a bounded rewriting using V iff ξ “corresponds” to a truth assignment μ_X for X, and when ranging over all instances D of $\mathcal{R}$ for which $D \models \mathcal{A}$ and $Q(D) \neq \emptyset$ (to simulate all truth assignments μ_Y for Y), we have that $Q(D) = \xi(D)$. By ensuring that $\xi(D) = \emptyset$ when $\exists Z\,\psi(\mu_X, \mu_Y, Z)$ is false, we show that $Q(D) = \xi(D)$ whenever $\exists Z\,\psi(\mu_X, \mu_Y, Z)$ is true. Since μ_X is fixed in ξ, and all μ_Y are considered (since $Q(D) = \xi(D)$ must hold for all $D \models \mathcal{A}$), this implies that $Q \equiv_{\mathcal{A}} \xi$ iff $\forall Y \exists Z\,\psi(\mu_X, Y, Z)$ is true, where μ_X is the chosen truth-assignment for V.

(3) We show that VBRP(FO) is undecidable also by reduction from the complement of the satisfiability problem for FO. Given an FO query Q, we define an FO query Q' such that Q' has an M-bounded rewriting iff Q is not satisfiable. We use fixed $\mathcal{A}$, $\mathcal{V}$ and M in the reduction. □

3.2 The Impact of Various Parameters

One might be tempted to think that fixing some parameters of VBRP would simplify the analysis of VBRP. As will be seen in Section 4, in practice we often have predefined database schema $\mathcal{R}$, access schema $\mathcal{A}$, bound M and views $\mathcal{V}$, while queries Q and instances D of $\mathcal{R}$ vary.

Unfortunately, fixing $\mathcal{R}$, $\mathcal{A}$, M and $\mathcal{V}$ does not simplify the analysis of VBRP for FO.

Corollary 5: There exist fixed $\mathcal{R}$, $\mathcal{A}$, M and $\mathcal{V}$ such that it is undecidable to decide, given an FO query Q, whether Q has an M-bounded rewriting in FO using $\mathcal{V}$ under $\mathcal{A}$. □

Proof sketch: It is undecidable to decide, given an FO query Q over a fixed database schema $\mathcal{R}$, whether there exists an instance D of $\mathcal{R}$ such that $Q(D) \neq \emptyset$. Indeed, a proof is by reduction from the the Post Correspondence Problem using a fixed $\mathcal{R}$ (see *e.g.,* [1]). Hence the reduction given in the proof of Theorem 3 for FO suffices to show Corollary 5, which employs $\mathcal{A} = \mathcal{V} = \emptyset$ and $M = 1$. □

We now study the impact of parameters on VBRP for CQ, UCQ and $\exists$FO$^+$. Our main conclusion is that fixing $\mathcal{R}$, $\mathcal{A}$ and M does not simplify the analysis of VBRP. When the set $\mathcal{V}$ of views is also fixed, VBRP becomes simpler for these classes of positive queries, but only to an extent.

Fixing $\mathcal{R}$, $\mathcal{A}$ and M. Fixing database schema, access schema and plan size does not help us. Indeed, the Σ_3^p lower bound for CQ is verified by using fixed $\mathcal{R}$, $\mathcal{A}$ and M (Theorem 1). From this the corollary below follows.

Corollary 6: There exist fixed $\mathcal{R}$, $\mathcal{A}$ and M such that it is Σ_3^p-complete to decide, given a query Q in $\mathcal{L}$ and a set $\mathcal{V}$ of $\mathcal{L}$-definable views over $\mathcal{R}$, whether Q has an M-bounded rewriting in $\mathcal{L}$ using $\mathcal{V}$ under $\mathcal{A}$ $\mathcal{L}$ is CQ, UCQ or $\exists$FO$^+$. □

Fixing $\mathcal{R}$, $\mathcal{A}$, M and $\mathcal{V}$. Suppose that besides $\mathcal{R}$, $\mathcal{A}$ and M, the set $\mathcal{V}$ of views is also predefined. This puts VBRP in C_{2k+1}^p for CQ, UCQ and $\exists$FO$^+$, where C_{2k+1}^p is the complexity class defined as $\mathsf{coNP} \vee \bigvee_{i=1}^{k}(\mathsf{NP} \wedge \mathsf{coNP})$ [38]. Here $\mathsf{NP} \wedge \mathsf{coNP}$ is also known as D^P, where a languages L' is in D^P iff there exist two languages $L_1' \in \mathsf{NP}$ and $L_2' \in \mathsf{coNP}$ such that $L' = L_1' \cap L_2'$. A language L' is in $\mathsf{C}_1 \vee \mathsf{C}_2$ for complexity classes C_1 and C_2 if there exist two languages $L_1' \in \mathsf{C}_1$ and $L_2' \in \mathsf{C}_2$ such that $L' = L_1' \cup L_2'$. Hence, C_{2k+1}^p consists of languages that can be written as the union of k D^P languages and a coNP language. It resides in the Boolean NP-hierarchy and is contained in $\Delta_2^p = P^{\mathsf{NP}}$. More specifically, it is known that a language L is in $\mathsf{C}_{2k+1}^\mathsf{P}$ iff there exist $2k+1$ languages $L_0, L_1, \ldots, L_{2k}$, such that each L_i is in NP, $L_0 \supseteq L_1 \supseteq L_2 \supseteq \cdots \supseteq L_{2k}$ and $L = \bar{L}_0 \cup \bigcup_{i=1}^{k}(L_{2i-1} \cap \bar{L}_{2i})$ [38].

Theorem 7: For each natural number k, there exist fixed $\mathcal{R}$, $\mathcal{A}$, M, $\mathcal{V}$ such that it is C_{2k+1}^p-complete to decide, given a query Q in $\mathcal{L}$ over $\mathcal{R}$, whether Q has an M-bounded rewriting in $\mathcal{L}$ using $\mathcal{V}$ under $\mathcal{A}$, for $\mathcal{L}$ as CQ, UCQ or $\exists$FO$^+$. □

To verify Theorem 7, we need the following notations, which will also be used in Section 4.

(a) A query Q_1 is $\mathcal{A}$-*contained* in query Q_2, denoted by $Q_1 \sqsubseteq_{\mathcal{A}} Q_2$, if for all instances D of $\mathcal{R}$ that satisfy $\mathcal{A}$, $Q_1(D) \subseteq Q_2(D)$, for Q_1 and Q_2 defined over $\mathcal{R}$.

(b) For a query Q, denote by QP_Q the set of all candidate query plans using $\mathcal{V}$ that are no larger than M.

(c) For $\xi \in \mathsf{QP}_Q$, we write $\xi \sqsubseteq_{\mathcal{A}} Q$ if $Q_\xi \sqsubseteq_{\mathcal{A}} Q$, where Q_ξ denotes the query expressed by ξ (recall Q_ξ from Section 2); similarly we write $Q \sqsubseteq_{\mathcal{A}} \xi$ if $Q \sqsubseteq_{\mathcal{A}} Q_\xi$, and $\xi \sqsubseteq_{\mathcal{A}} \xi'$ for $\xi' \in \mathsf{QP}_Q$ if $Q_\xi \sqsubseteq_{\mathcal{A}} Q_{\xi'}$. We write $\xi \equiv_{\mathcal{A}} \xi'$ if $\xi \sqsubseteq_{\mathcal{A}} \xi'$ and $\xi' \sqsubseteq_{\mathcal{A}} \xi$, and $\xi \sqsubset_{\mathcal{A}} \xi'$ if $\xi \sqsubseteq_{\mathcal{A}} \xi'$ but $\xi \not\equiv_{\mathcal{A}} \xi'$.

Proof sketch: (1) Upper bound. A query Q in $\exists$FO$^+$ has an M-bounded rewriting using $\mathcal{V}$ under $\mathcal{A}$ iff either (a) Q is not satisfiable by any instance $D \models \mathcal{A}$ of $\mathcal{R}$, *i.e.,* $Q \equiv_{\mathcal{A}} Q_\emptyset$, where $Q_\emptyset$ denotes a query that returns $\emptyset$ on all D, or (b) Q is satisfiable and $Q \equiv_{\mathcal{A}} \xi$ for a non-empty $\xi \in \mathsf{QP}_Q$. We show that condition (a) can be checked in coNP. For each non-empty $\xi \in \mathsf{QP}_Q$, condition (b) is to check whether $\xi \sqsubseteq_{\mathcal{A}} Q$ and $Q \sqsubseteq_{\mathcal{A}} \xi$, which can be decided in NP and coNP, respectively, for fixed $\mathcal{R}, \mathcal{A}, M$ and $\mathcal{V}$. Here k denotes the number of non-empty plans in QP_Q, a constant here.

In contrast, if M is fixed while $\mathcal{R}, \mathcal{A}$ or $\mathcal{V}$ is not, there are possibly exponentially many query plans in QP_Q. As an example, when $\mathcal{V}$ is not fixed, consider a view $V(\bar{x})$ with $|\bar{x}| = m$. Then, depending on how the variables in V are instantiated in a query plan ξ with constants, *i.e.,* how V is used in ξ, there are at least 2^m different plans in QP_Q. That is why VBRP(CQ) remains Σ_3^p-hard when only $M, \mathcal{R}$ and $\mathcal{A}$ are fixed but $\mathcal{V}$ is not (Corollary 6).

(2) Lower bound. For any k, take any language $L = \bar{L}_0 \cup \bigcup_{i=1}^{k}(L_{2i-1} \cap \bar{L}_{2i})$ in $\mathsf{C}_{2k+1}^\mathsf{P}$. We build fixed $\mathcal{R}$, $\mathcal{A}$, $\mathcal{V}$ and $M = 1$, *i.e.,* they depend on k only, not on L. We show that deciding whether a string $\bar{\sigma} \in L$ can be reduced to checking whether a CQ has an 1-bounded rewriting using $\mathcal{V}$ under $\mathcal{A}$.

The reduction uses the following properties. (a) Since each L_i is in NP, we have reductions f_i from L_i to 3SAT such that for each string $\bar{\sigma}$, $\bar{\sigma} \in L_i$ iff $f_i(\bar{\sigma})$ is a satisfiable 3SAT instance. Hence if $f_{i+1}(\bar{\sigma})$ is satisfiable then so is $f_i(\bar{\sigma})$, by $L_i \supseteq L_{i+1}$. We use this property to ensure that only $k+1$ possible query plans need to be considered. (b) Following [38], it can be verified that $\bar{\sigma} \in L$ iff

$$|\{i \mid f_i(\bar{\sigma}) \text{ is satisfiable, } i \in [0, 2k]\}|$$

is an even number. We show that determining the latter condition is equivalent to deciding whether a CQ Q has an 1-bounded rewriting using $\mathcal{V}$ under $\mathcal{A}$. In the reduction, we use Q to encode the $2k+1$ 3SAT instances $f_i(\bar{\sigma})$, and employ k unary fixed views and the empty view corresponding to the $k+1$ even number $0, 2, 4, \ldots, 2k$ above. □

A simple characterization. We next give a sufficient and necessary condition for query Q to have a bounded rewriting. This condition is generic: Q is not necessarily a CQ, and $\mathcal{R}, M, \mathcal{A}$ and $\mathcal{V}$ do not have to be fixed.

We use the following notations. For candidate plan $\xi \in \mathsf{QP}_Q$, we say that ξ is a *maximum plan* with $(\mathcal{A}, \mathcal{V})$ if (a)

$\xi \sqsubseteq_{\mathcal{A}} Q$, and (b) there exists no $\xi' \in \mathsf{QP}_Q$ such that $\xi' \sqsubseteq_{\mathcal{A}} Q$ and $\xi \sqsubset_{\mathcal{A}} \xi'$. We say that ξ is *unique* in QP_Q if there exists no another maximum plan $\xi' \in \mathsf{QP}_Q$ such that $\xi \not\equiv_{\mathcal{A}} \xi'$.

Lemma 8: A query Q has an M-bounded rewriting under $\mathcal{A}$ using $\mathcal{V}$ iff there exists a unique maximum plan $\xi \in \mathsf{QP}_Q$ up to $\mathcal{A}$-equivalence such that $Q \sqsubseteq_{\mathcal{A}} \xi$. □

Proof sketch: Query Q has an M-bounded rewriting under $\mathcal{A}$ using $\mathcal{V}$ iff there exists a query plan $\xi \in \mathsf{QP}_Q$ such that $Q \equiv_{\mathcal{A}} \xi$. We show that when such a plan ξ exists, it is maximum and unique up to $\mathcal{A}$-equivalence. □

4. BOUNDED REWRITING FOR ACQ

To further understand the inherent complexity of VBRP, we study VBRP under two practical conditions.

(1) *Acyclic conjunctive queries*, denoted by ACQ. A CQ Q is *acyclic* if its hypergraph has hypertree-width 1 [21]. The *hypergraph* of Q is a hypergraph (V_h, E_h) in which V_h consists of variables in Q and E_h has an edge for each set of variables that occur together in a relation atom in Q. Acyclic conjunctive queries are commonly used in practice. As an example, query Q_0 of Example 1 is an ACQ.

(2) *Fixed $\mathcal{R}, \mathcal{A}, M$ and $\mathcal{V}$.* We consider predefined database schema $\mathcal{R}$, access schema $\mathcal{A}$, bound M and views $\mathcal{V}$. After all, for an application, $\mathcal{R}$ is designed first, M is determined by our available resources (*e.g.,* processors and time constraints), access constraints are discovered from sample instances of $\mathcal{R}$, and views are selected based on the application [6]. These are determined before we start answering queries. Thus it is practical to assume fixed $\mathcal{R}$, $\mathcal{A}$, M, and $\mathcal{V}$.

In this setting, we study bounded rewriting of ACQ. Given an ACQ Q, we want to find an M-bounded query plan $\xi(Q, \mathcal{V}, \mathcal{R})$ under $\mathcal{A}$ in CQ (Section 2) such that the query Q_ξ expressed by ξ is an ACQ. Our main conclusion is that the intractability of VBRP is robust, even for ACQ under fixed $\mathcal{R}, \mathcal{A}, M$ and $\mathcal{V}$. However, we characterize when VBRP(ACQ) is tractable and identify tractable special cases.

Intractability. One might think that VBRP would become simpler for ACQ, since query evaluation and containment for ACQ are in PTIME, not to mention fixed $\mathcal{R}$, $\mathcal{A}, M$ and $\mathcal{V}$. Unfortunately, VBRP remains intractable in this setting, even under quite restrictive access constraints in a fixed $\mathcal{A}$.

Theorem 9: Given fixed $\mathcal{R}$, $\mathcal{A}$, M and $\mathcal{V}$, VBRP(ACQ) is coNP-hard when $\mathcal{A}$ has one of the following forms:

(1) when $\mathcal{A}$ consists of a single access constraint of the form $R(A \to B, N)$ and $N \geq 2$;

(2) when $\mathcal{A}$ consists of two constraints $R(A \to B, 1)$ and $R'(\emptyset \to (E, F), N)$, and $N \geq 6$; or

(3) when $\mathcal{A}$ consists of two constraints $R((A, B) \to C, 1)$ and $R'(\emptyset \to E, N)$, and $N \geq 2$. □

Proof sketch: We prove the statements by reductions from coNP-complete problems L. In the reductions we construct database schema $\mathcal{R}$, access schema $\mathcal{A}$ and query Q with care such that they do not depend on the instances ϕ of L, and ϕ is a "yes" instance of K iff $Q \equiv_{\mathcal{A}} \emptyset$, a query over $\mathcal{R}$ that returns empty for any instances $D \models \mathcal{A}$ of R. In light of these, the proofs remain intact when M is any predefined number and $\mathcal{V}$ is any predefined set of ACQ queries.

The proofs tell us that there is intricate interaction between ACQ and access constraints, and the forms of access constraints in $\mathcal{A}$ have impact on the complexity of VBRP.

(Case 1) We verify the coNP lower bound by reduction from the complement of the precoloring extension problem, which is NP-complete [26]. The latter is to decide, given an undirected graph $G = (V_G, E)$ and a 3-coloring μ of leaves of G, whether μ is extendable to a color c_i ($c_i \in \{r, g, b\}$) for all nodes v_i in V_G such that for each edge $(v_i, v_j) \in E$, $c_i \neq c_j$.

The reduction is a little complicated since we need to encode a cyclic graph with ACQ. It uses an access schema $\mathcal{A}$ consisting of a single $\phi = R(A \to B, 2)$, and a database schema $\mathcal{R}$ with a single binary relation $R(A, B)$. To ensure that query Q is acyclic, we represent the two vertices of each edge with distinct variables, and use access constraint ϕ to enforce necessary "equality" on the variables and thus, "restore" the original graph G. That is, the reduction makes use of the interaction between the access constraint and ACQ.

(Case 2) We show this case by reduction from the complement of the 3-Colorability problem, which is NP-complete (cf. [19]). The latter problem is to decide, given an undirected graph $G = (V_G, E)$, whether there exists a color c_i ($c_i \in \{r, g, b\}$) for each vertex v_i in V_G such that for every edge $(v_i, v_j) \in E$, $c_i \neq c_j$. Again the challenge is to encode cyclic G with ACQ. The reduction uses a set $\mathcal{A}$ with two access constraints $R(A \to B, 1)$ and $R'(\emptyset \to (E, F), 6)$, and a database schema $\mathcal{R}$ of two relations $R(A, B)$ and $R'(E, F)$.

(Case 3) We show this by reduction from the complement of the 3SAT problem. We use an access schema $\mathcal{A}$ having $R((A, B) \to C, 1)$ and $R'(\emptyset \to E, 2)$, and database schema $\mathcal{R}$ of a ternary relation $R(A, B, C)$ and a unary relation $R'(E)$.

The complication is introduced by encoding Boolean operations disjunction, conjunction and negated variables given the limited facility of ACQ, and restricted relations of $\mathcal{R}$ and constraints of $\mathcal{A}$. Hence the reduction is quite delicate. Given an instance $\psi(X)$ of 3SAT, we define Q to encode each clause in ψ with distinct copies of variables of X, and encode the Boolean operations in terms of distinct constants to represent their truth values. Together with the constraints, these ensure that Q correctly encodes ψ and is an ACQ.

We show that the proofs for cases (1), (2), (3) can be extended to $N > 2$, $N > 6$, $N > 2$, respectively. □

Characterization. In light of Theorem 9, we next characterize when VBRP($\mathcal{C}$) is tractable for sub-classes $\mathcal{C}$ of ACQ, and give an upper bound for VBRP(ACQ).

Theorem 10: When $\mathcal{R}$, $\mathcal{A}$, M and $\mathcal{V}$ are fixed, (1) for any sub-class $\mathcal{C}$ of ACQ, VBRP($\mathcal{C}$) is in PTIME if and only if for each query $Q \in \mathcal{C}$, it is in PTIME to check whether $Q \sqsubseteq_{\mathcal{A}} \xi$, where ξ is a query plan of size at most M, and (2) VBRP(ACQ) is in coNP. □

The result tells us that ACQ and fixed parameters, when taken together, simplify the analysis of VBRP (unless P = NP), to an extent, as opposed to the Σ_3^p-completeness of Theorem 1 and C_{2k+1}^p-completeness of Theorem 7. Putting Theorems 9 and 10 together, we can see that the cases of VBRP(ACQ) stated in Theorem 9 are coNP-complete.

The proof of Theorem 10 is based on Lemma 8 and the lemma below, which gives the complexity of basic operations that are needed for computing maximum query plans.

Lemma 11: When $\mathcal{R}$, $\mathcal{A}$, M and $\mathcal{V}$ are fixed, given a CQ Q and query plans $\xi, \xi' \in \mathsf{QP}_Q$, it is in

(a) PTIME to check whether ξ conforms to $\mathcal{A}$,

(b) PTIME to check whether $\xi \sqsubseteq_{\mathcal{A}} Q$ if Q is an ACQ,

(c) NP to check whether $Q \not\sqsubseteq_{\mathcal{A}} \xi$, and

(d) PTIME to check whether $\xi' \sqsubseteq_{\mathcal{A}} \xi$ for $\xi' \in \mathsf{QP}_Q$. □

Based on the lemmas, we prove Theorem 10.

Proof sketch of Theorem 10. We develop an algorithm that, given an ACQ Q, checks whether Q has a bounded rewriting. The algorithm first computes the unique maximum plan $\xi \in \mathsf{QP}_Q$ (up to $\mathcal{A}$-equivalence) if it exists. It then checks whether $Q \sqsubseteq_{\mathcal{A}} \xi$. Its correctness is warranted by Lemma 8. For its complexity, we show that it is in PTIME to check whether QP_Q has a unique maximum plan when $\mathcal{R}, M$, $\mathcal{A}$ and $\mathcal{V}$ are fixed, by Lemma 11 (a), (b) and (d). Hence, the algorithm is in PTIME for any sub-class $\mathcal{C}$ of ACQ as long as it is in PTIME to check whether $Q \sqsubseteq_{\mathcal{A}} \xi$ for all $Q \in \mathcal{C}$. Note that when $\mathcal{C}$ is the entire class of ACQ queries, the algorithm is in coNP since it needs to call an NP oracle to check whether $Q \sqsubseteq_{\mathcal{A}} \xi$, by Lemma 11(c). □

Theorem 10 helps us identify sub-classes of ACQ for which VBRP is tractable, such as ACQ under "FDs", *i.e.,* when all the access constraints in $\mathcal{A}$ are of the form $R(X \to Y, 1)$. As remarked earlier, FDs with associated indices are common access constraints, and can be automatically discovered by using existing tools for mining FDs. (*e.g.,* [24]).

Corollary 12: When $\mathcal{R}, \mathcal{A}, M$ and $\mathcal{V}$ are fixed, VBRP is in PTIME for ACQ if $\mathcal{A}$ consists of FDs only. □

Proof sketch: By Theorem 10, to prove Corollary 12, it suffices to show that $Q \sqsubseteq_{\mathcal{A}} \xi$ is in PTIME. Observe the following. (a) When $\mathcal{A}$ consists of FDs only, we can "chase" the tableau of Q by access constraints of $\mathcal{A}$ in PTIME [1], and get a unique query $Q_{\mathcal{A}}$ such that the tableau of $Q_{\mathcal{A}}$ satisfies $\mathcal{A}$ and $Q \equiv_{\mathcal{A}} Q_{\mathcal{A}}$. (b) Checking $Q \sqsubseteq_{\mathcal{A}} \xi$ is equivalent to checking $Q_{\mathcal{A}} \sqsubseteq \xi$. Hence we can use the conventional notion of query containment and the Homomorphism Theorem for CQ [1]. (c) The proof of Lemma 11 shows that $Q_{\mathcal{A}} \sqsubseteq Q_{\xi}$ can be checked in PTIME for fixed $\mathcal{R}, \mathcal{A}, M$ and $\mathcal{V}$. Putting these together, we have that $Q \sqsubseteq_{\mathcal{A}} \xi$ is in PTIME. □

In contrast to Corollary 12, VBRP remains intractable for CQ under FDs, although the analysis is simpler compared with Theorem 7 (unless P = NP).

Proposition 13: For fixed $\mathcal{R}, \mathcal{A}, M$ and $\mathcal{V}$, VBRP(CQ) is NP-complete if $\mathcal{A}$ consists of FDs only. It remains NP-complete when none of $\mathcal{R}, \mathcal{A}, M$ and $\mathcal{V}$ is fixed. □

Proof sketch: We show that VBRP is NP-hard by reduction from 3SAT, using fixed $\mathcal{R}, \mathcal{A}, M$ and $\mathcal{V}$, with $\mathcal{A}$ consisting of FDs. In contrast to Corollary 12, for a CQ Q, we can no longer compute its maximum query plan in QP_Q in PTIME; instead, it is an NP process.

For the upper bound, we give an algorithm to check VBRP(CQ) under FDs, which is in NP even when none of $\mathcal{R}, \mathcal{A}, M$ and $\mathcal{V}$ is fixed. It uses the following lemma.

Lemma 14: If $\mathcal{A}$ consists of FDs only, it is in PTIME to decide whether a plan $\xi \in \mathsf{QP}_Q$ conforms to $\mathcal{A}$. □

We give a PTIME algorithm to verify the lemma. □

Along the same lines as Corollary 12, one can easily verify that for fixed $\mathcal{R}, \mathcal{A}, M$ and $\mathcal{V}$, VBRP is in PTIME for the sub-class of ACQ queries such that their tableau representations satisfy the cardinality constraints in $\mathcal{A}$. A special case of this is when $\mathcal{A} = \emptyset$, *e.g.,* the setting of [6], when access constraints are not employed at all.

Theorem 10 remains intact on any class $\mathcal{C}$ of queries as long as it is in PTIME to compute a maximum plan in QP_Q for all queries in $\mathcal{C}$. Examples include (a) self-join-free CQ, *i.e.,* the class of CQ queries that contain no repeated relation names [25], and (b) CQ with a fixed number of variables, *i.e.,* for each constant k, the class of CQ queries that have at most k free variables [37]. Using Theorem 10 and Lemma 11, one can show that VBRP is also in PTIME in these two cases.

5. AN EFFECTIVE SYNTAX

We have seen that the undecidability of VBRP for FO and the intractability for CQ are rather robust. Can we still make practical use of bounded rewriting analysis when querying big data? We next show that the answer is affirmative.

We develop effective syntax for FO queries that have a bounded rewriting. For any database schema $\mathcal{R}$, views $\mathcal{V}$, access schema $\mathcal{A}$ and bound M, we identify two classes of FO queries, (a) a class of queries *topped by* $(\mathcal{R}, \mathcal{V}, \mathcal{A}, M)$, which "covers" all queries defined over $\mathcal{R}$ that have an M-bounded rewriting using $\mathcal{V}$ under $\mathcal{A}$, up to equivalence, and (b) a class of *size-bounded* queries, which "covers" all the views of $\mathcal{V}$ that have bounded output for all instances of $\mathcal{R}$ that satisfy $\mathcal{A}$. The second class helps us effectively check bounded output when deducing topped queries. It is in PTIME to decide whether a query is topped or size-bounded.

Below we first present the main results of the section in Section 5.1. We then define topped queries and size-bounded queries in Sections 5.2 and 5.3, respectively.

5.1 Practical Use of Bounded Rewriting

The main results of the section are as follows.

Theorem 15: For any $\mathcal{R}$, $\mathcal{V}$ and M, and under any $\mathcal{A}$,

(a) each FO query Q with an M-bounded rewriting using $\mathcal{V}$ is $\mathcal{A}$-equivalent to a query topped by $(\mathcal{R}, \mathcal{V}, \mathcal{A}, M)$;

(b) every FO query topped by $(\mathcal{R}, \mathcal{V}, \mathcal{A}, M)$ has an M-bounded rewriting in FO using $\mathcal{V}$ under $\mathcal{A}$; and

(c) it takes PTIME in $M, |\mathcal{R}|, |Q|, |\mathcal{V}|$ and $|\mathcal{A}|$ to check whether an FO query Q is topped by $(\mathcal{R}, \mathcal{V}, \mathcal{A}, M)$, which uses an effective syntax that checks whether FO views in $\mathcal{V}$ have bounded output in PTIME in $|Q|$.

Here $\mathcal{A}$, Q and $\mathcal{V}$ are all defined over the same $\mathcal{R}$. □

That is, topped queries are a core sub-class of FO queries with a bounded rewriting, and can be effectively checked. To check bounded output of queries, we show the following.

Theorem 16: For any $\mathcal{R}$ and under any $\mathcal{A}$,

(a) each FO query Q over $\mathcal{R}$ that has bounded output is $\mathcal{A}$-equivalent to a size-bounded query under $\mathcal{A}$;

(b) each size-bounded query has bounded output under $\mathcal{A}$;

(c) it takes PTIME in $|Q|$ to check whether an FO query Q is a size-bounded query.

Here $\mathcal{A}$ and Q are defined over the same $\mathcal{R}$. □

Before we define topped and size-bounded queries, we remark the following. (1) Theorems 15 and 16 just aim to demonstrate the existence of effective syntax for FO queries with bounded rewriting. There are other forms of effective syntax for such FO queries. (2) Theorem 15 does not contradict to Corollary 5 due to the requirement of $\mathcal{A}$-equivalence in its condition (a), which is undecidable for FO.

Practical use. Capitalizing on the effective syntax, we can develop algorithms (a) to check whether a given FO query Q is topped by $(\mathcal{R}, \mathcal{V}, \mathcal{A}, M)$ in PTIME; and if so, (b) to generate a bounded query plan ξ for Q using $\mathcal{V}$. The existence of these algorithms are warranted by Theorems 15 and 16.

We can then support bounded rewriting using views on top of commercial DBMS as follows. Given an application, a database schema $\mathcal{R}$ and a resource bound M are first determined, based on the application and available resources, respectively. Then, a set $\mathcal{V}$ of views can be selected following [6], and a set $\mathcal{A}$ of access constraints can be discovered [10]. After these are in place, given an FO query Q posed on a dataset D that satisfies $\mathcal{A}$, we check whether Q is topped by $(\mathcal{R}, \mathcal{V}, \mathcal{A}, M)$. If so, we generate a bounded query plan ξ for Q using $\mathcal{V}$, by using the algorithms described above. Then we can compute $Q(D)$ by executing ξ with the existing DBMS. Moreover, incremental methods for maintaining the views [6] and (the indices of) access constraints [10] have already been developed, in response to updates to D. Putting these together, we can expect to efficiently answer a number of FO queries Q in (possibly big) D by leveraging bounded rewriting.

5.2 Topped Queries for Bounded Rewriting

We next define topped queries and prove Theorem 15. It is nontrivial to define an effective syntax, as shown below.

Example 6: Consider a database schema $\mathcal{R}_1$ with two relations $R(A, B)$ and $T(C, E)$, an access schema $\mathcal{A}_2$ consisting of $R(A \to B, N)$ and $T(C \to E, N)$, and $\mathcal{V}_3$ with a single view $V_3(x, y) = \exists R(y, y) \wedge T(x, y)$. Consider FO query:

$$Q_3(z) = Q_4(z) \wedge \neg\exists w\, R(z, w), \text{ where}$$
$$Q_4(z) = \exists y \exists x\, (V_3(x, y) \wedge (x = 1)) \wedge R(y, z)$$

Then Q_3 has a 13-bounded rewriting as shown in Fig. 2. The plan is actually developed for an equivalent query:

$$Q_3'(z) = Q_4(z) \wedge \neg(Q_4(z) \wedge \exists w\, R(z, w)).$$

Observe the following. (1) Query Q_3' becomes bounded because it propagates z-values from Q_4 to "$\neg\exists w\, R(z, w)$". (2) Such propagated values allow us to fetch bounded data for relation atoms, *i.e.,* $R(y, z)$ and $R(z, w)$. (3) A plan for a sub-query of Q_3 may have to embed a plan for another sub-query. For instance, (i) Q_4 has a 5-bounded rewriting in Q_3; (ii) $\exists w\, R(w, z)$ has a 7-bounded rewriting, which embeds the 5-bounded plan for Q_4; and (iii) the size of the plan for Q_3 is the sum of the sizes of plans for Q_4 and $\exists w\, R(w, z)$. □

Example 6 shows that to cover queries such as Q_3, topped queries have to support value propagation among sub-queries, and keep track of the sizes of plans for sub-queries.

Topped queries. This motivates us to define two functions.

- Boolean function $\mathsf{cov}(Q_s(\bar{x}), Q(\bar{z}))$ to ensure that if $Q_s(\bar{x})$ has a bounded rewriting and $\mathsf{cov}(Q_s(\bar{x}), Q(\bar{z}))$ = true, then $Q_s(\bar{x}) \wedge Q(\bar{z})$ also has a bounded rewriting.
- Function $\mathsf{size}(Q_s(\bar{x}), Q(\bar{z}))$ to compute a natural number, which is an upper bound of the size of minimum sub-plans for sub-query $Q(\bar{z})$ in $Q_s(\bar{x}) \wedge Q(\bar{z})$.

The intuition behind these functions is as follows.

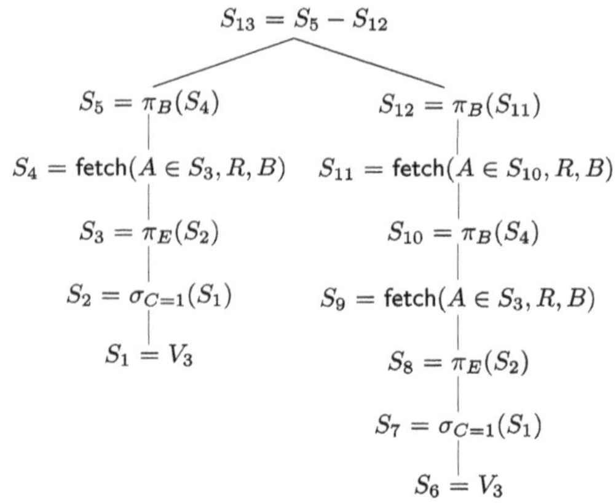

Figure 2: A bounded plan for Q_3 of Example 6

(a) Intuitively, $Q(\bar{z})$ indicates a (sub-)query we are inspecting, and $Q_s(\bar{x})$ keeps track of sub-queries from which values are propagated to $Q(\bar{z})$, to make $Q(\bar{z})$ bounded.

(b) Function $\mathsf{cov}(Q_s, Q)$ is to check whether we can propagate values from Q_s to Q, and get a bounded rewriting of Q. In particular, Q_s may include views from $\mathcal{V}$. When computing $\mathsf{cov}(Q_s, Q)$, we distinguish views that need to have bounded output from those that do not have to.

For instance, $\mathsf{cov}(Q_4, \exists w\, R(w, z))$ = true for Q_3 in Example 6, in which Q_4 is Q_s and $\exists w\, R(w, z)$ is Q. It indicates that by propagating values from bounded Q_4, we can have a bounded rewriting for sub-query $\exists w\, R(w, z)$.

(c) Function $\mathsf{size}(Q_s, Q)$ helps us ensure that our query plans do not exceed a given bound M. In Example 6, $\mathsf{size}(Q_4, \exists w\, R(w, z)) = 7$, which is the size of the plan for evaluating $\exists w\, R(w, z)$ in Q_3 by using values propagated from Q_4.

Using the functions, we now define *topped queries.* An FO query Q over $\mathcal{R}$ is in topped by $(\mathcal{R}, \mathcal{V}, \mathcal{A}, M)$ if

(1) $\mathsf{cov}(Q_\varepsilon, Q)$ = true; and

(2) $\mathsf{size}(Q_\varepsilon, Q) \leq M$.

Here Q_ε is a "tautology query" such that for any query Q, $Q_\varepsilon \wedge Q = Q$, $\mathsf{cov}(Q_\varepsilon, Q_\varepsilon)$ = true and Q_ε has a 0-bounded rewriting. That is, we compute $\mathsf{cov}(Q_s, Q)$ and $\mathsf{size}(Q_s, Q)$ starting with $Q_s = Q_\varepsilon$, and conclude that Q is topped by $(\mathcal{R}, \mathcal{V}, \mathcal{A}, M)$ if the two conditions above are satisfied.

Functions $\mathsf{cov}(Q_s(\bar{x}), Q(\bar{z}))$ and $\mathsf{size}(Q_s(\bar{x}), Q(\bar{z}))$. We next define the two functions inductively, based on the structure of FO query Q. In the process, we also give a bounded query plan. We will ensure that if $\mathsf{cov}(Q_s(\bar{x}), Q(\bar{z}))$ = true and $Q_s(\bar{x})$ has a $\mathsf{size}(Q_\varepsilon, Q_s(\bar{x}))$-bounded rewriting, then $Q_s(\bar{x}) \wedge Q(\bar{z})$ has a $\mathsf{size}(Q_\varepsilon, Q_s(\bar{x}) \wedge Q(\bar{z}))$-bounded rewriting.

To simplify the discussion, we assume *w.l.o.g.* the following [1]: (a) no variable x occurs both free and bound in Q, and there exists at most one quantifier for each x; and (b) there exists no universal quantifier in Q, *i.e.,* we replace each $\forall \bar{x}\, \psi(\bar{x})$ with $\neg\exists\bar{x}(\neg\psi(\bar{x}))$; (c) only variables occur in relation atoms, *e.g.,* $R(x, 1)$ is replaced with $\exists y\, (R(x, y) \wedge y = 1)$; and (d) no relation atoms contain repeated variables, *e.g.,* we substitute $R(x, y) \wedge x = y$ for each $R(x, x)$.

The definition is separated into 7 cases below.

(1) $Q(\bar{z})$ is $z = c$. For equality atom with a constant, $\mathsf{cov}(Q_s(\bar{x}), Q(\bar{z}))$ = true and $\mathsf{size}(Q_s(\bar{x}), Q(\bar{z})) = 1$.

(2) $Q(\bar{z})$ is $V(\bar{z})$. We can access cached views; thus, $\mathsf{cov}(Q_s(\bar{x}), Q(\bar{z}))$ = true and $\mathsf{size}(Q_s(\bar{x}), Q(\bar{z})) = 1$.

That is, constant queries and views have 1-bounded rewriting and hence, are topped queries.

(3) $Q(\bar{z})$ is $Q'(\bar{z}) \wedge C$, where C is $(x = y)$, $(x \neq y)$, $(x = c)$ or $(x \neq c)$. We define $\mathsf{cov}(Q_s(\bar{x}), Q(\bar{z})) = \mathsf{cov}(Q_s(\bar{x}), Q'(\bar{z}))$, and define $\mathsf{size}(Q_s(\bar{x}), Q(\bar{z}))$ as $\mathsf{size}(Q_s(\bar{x}), Q'(\bar{z})) + 1$ when $\mathsf{cov}(Q_s(\bar{x}), Q'(\bar{z})) = \mathsf{true}$, and as $+\infty$ otherwise.

Note that given a bounded plan ξ' for Q', a bounded plan for Q is $(T = \xi', \sigma_C(\xi'))$, increasing the size of ξ' by 1.

(4) $Q(\bar{z})$ is $Q_1(\bar{z}_1) \wedge Q_2(\bar{z}_2)$, where Q_2 is not an (in)equality. Let $\mu_i = \mathsf{cov}(Q_s(\bar{x}), Q_i(\bar{z}_i))$, $s_i = \mathsf{size}(Q_s(\bar{x}), Q_i(\bar{z}_i))$, $\mu' = \mathsf{cov}(Q_s(\bar{x}) \wedge Q_1(\bar{z}_1), Q_2(\bar{z}_2))$ and $s' = \mathsf{size}(Q_s(\bar{x}) \wedge Q_1(\bar{z}_2), Q_2(\bar{z}_2))$ $(i \in \{1, 2\})$. Then,

(a) if $\mu_1 = \mathsf{true}$ and $Q_2(\bar{z}_2)$ is of the form $\exists w\, R(\bar{z}_1, \bar{z}_2', \bar{w})$, $R(Z_1 \to Z_2', N)$ is in $\mathcal{A}$ with $Z_1 \cup Z_2' = Z_2$ and if $Q_s(\bar{x}) \wedge Q_1(\bar{z}_1)$ *has bounded output* under $\mathcal{A}$, then $\mathsf{cov}(Q_s(\bar{x}), Q(\bar{z})) = \mathsf{true}$ and $\mathsf{size}(Q_s(\bar{x}), Q(\bar{z})) = s_1 + 1$; otherwise

(b) if $\mu_1 = \mu_2 = \mathsf{true}$, $\mathsf{cov}(Q_s(\bar{x}), Q(\bar{z})) = \mathsf{true}$, $\mathsf{size}(Q_s(\bar{x}), Q(\bar{z})) = s_1 + s_2 + \lambda_{(\bar{z}_1, \bar{z}_2)}$, where $\lambda_{(\bar{z}_1, \bar{z}_2)}$ is 1 (resp. 4) if $\bar{z}_1 \cap \bar{z}_2$ is empty (resp. not empty); otherwise

(c) if $\mu_1 \wedge \mu' = \mathsf{true}$ and $|Q_2| \leq K$ for some constant K, then $\mathsf{cov}(Q_s(\bar{x}), Q(\bar{z})) = \mathsf{true}$ and $\mathsf{size}(Q_s(\bar{x}), Q(\bar{z})) = s_1 + s' + \lambda_{(\bar{z}_1, \bar{z}_2)}$ for the same $\lambda_{(\bar{z}_1, \bar{z}_2)}$ as in (b); otherwise

(d) $\mathsf{cov}(Q_s(\bar{x}), Q(\bar{z})) = \mathsf{false}$ and $\mathsf{size}(Q_s(\bar{x}), Q(\bar{z})) = +\infty$.

In this case we characterize value propagation shown in Example 6, *e.g.*, y-value from $\exists x, y\,(V(x, y) \wedge (x = 1))$ to $R(y, z)$ in sub-query Q_4 of Q_3. Note that Q_s is expanded in case (c) above to propagate $\bar{z}_1$ from $Q_1 \wedge Q_s$ to Q_2. That is, if sub-query $Q_2(\bar{z}_2)$ of Q does not have a bounded rewriting with $Q_s(\bar{x})$ (*i.e.*, $s_2 = \mathsf{false}$), we may extend $Q_s(\bar{x})$ with $Q_1(\bar{z}_1)$ to make $Q_2(\bar{z}_2)$ bounded when $\mu' = \mathsf{true}$.

When $\mathsf{cov}(Q_s(\bar{x}), Q(\bar{z})) = \mathsf{true}$, we have three cases below.

(a) If Q_1 has a bounded plan ξ_1 with Q_s, and if Q_2 is (a projection of) a relation atom covered by a constraint $R(Z_1 \to Z_2', N)$ in $\mathcal{A}$, then $Q(\bar{z})$ also has a bounded plan with $Q_s(\bar{x})$ and $Q_1(\bar{z}_1)$, as long as $Q_s(\bar{x}) \wedge Q_1(\bar{z}_1)$ has *bounded output.* Indeed, a plan for Q_2 is $(T = \xi_1, \mathsf{fetch}(X \in T, R, Z_2'))$ of size $|\xi_1| + 1$. We instantiate the Z_1 attributes of R with the output of $Q_1(\bar{z}_1)$, and ensure that the input T of fetch, *i.e.*, the output of $Q_s(\bar{x}) \wedge Q_1(\bar{z}_1)$, has bounded size.

(b) If both Q_1 and Q_2 have bounded plans with Q_s, *e.g.*, ξ_1 and ξ_2, respectively, then Q also has a bounded plan with Q_s, whose size depends on the forms of $Q_1(\bar{z}_1)$ and $Q_2(\bar{z}_2)$, as reflected by different values of $\lambda_{(\bar{z}_1, \bar{z}_2)}$. More specifically, if $\bar{z}_1$ and $\bar{z}_2$ are disjoint, then Q is a production of Q_1 and Q_2 and thus has a plan $(T_1 = \xi_1,\ T_2 = \xi_2,\ T_3 = T_1 \times T_2)$, of size $|\xi_1| + |\xi_2| + 1$. Otherwise, *i.e.*, $\bar{z}_1 \cap \bar{z}_2 \neq \emptyset$, then Q is a join of Q_1 and Q_2 and thus has a plan $(T_1 = \xi_1,\ T_2 = \xi_2,\ T_3 = \rho(T_2),\ T_4 = T_1 \times T_2,\ T_5 = \sigma_{Z_1 \cap Z_2 = \rho(Z_1 \cap Z_2)}(T_4))$, of size $|\xi_1| + |\xi_2| + 4$. Here ρ renames attributes in $Z_1 \cap Z_2$.

(c) If Q_1 has a bounded plan with Q_s while Q_2 has one with $Q_s \wedge Q_1$ instead of Q_s alone, *e.g.*, plans ξ_1 and ξ_2', respectively, then Q has a bounded query plan of size $|\xi_1| + |\xi_2'| + \lambda_{(\bar{z}_1, \bar{z}_2)}$ along the same lines as (b) above, where $|\xi_1| = \mathsf{size}(Q_s(\bar{x}), Q_1(\bar{z}_1))$ and $|\xi_2'| = \mathsf{size}(Q_s \wedge Q_1(\bar{x}), Q_2(\bar{z}_2))$.

Note that we extend $Q_s(\bar{x})$ with $Q_1(\bar{z}_1)$ only if $Q_1(\bar{z}_1)$ has a bounded plan using $\mathcal{V}$ with Q_s. One can verify that this expansion policy assures that Q_s always has a bounded plan since we start with a tautology query $Q_s = Q_\varepsilon$.

(5) $Q(\bar{z})$ is $Q_1(\bar{z}) \vee Q_2(\bar{z})$. Let $\mu_i = \mathsf{cov}(Q_s(\bar{x}), Q_i(\bar{z})$ and $s_i = \mathsf{size}(Q_s(\bar{x}), Q_i(\bar{z}))$ for $i \in \{1, 2\}$. We define $\mathsf{cov}(Q_s(\bar{z}), Q(\bar{z})) = \mu_1 \wedge \mu_2$, and $\mathsf{size}(Q_s(\bar{z}), Q(\bar{z}))$ as $s_1 + s_2 + 1$ if $\mathsf{cov}(Q_s(\bar{z}), Q(\bar{z})) = \mathsf{true}$, and as $+\infty$ otherwise.

Intuitively, if Q_1 and Q_2 have bounded plans ξ_1 and ξ_2, respectively, then $Q(\bar{z})$ has a bounded plan $(T_1 = \xi_1, T_2 = \xi_2, T_1 \cup T_2)$, of size $|\xi_1| + |\xi_2| + 1$.

(6) $Q(\bar{z})$ is $Q_1(\bar{z}) \wedge \neg Q_2(\bar{z})$. Let $\mu_i = \mathsf{cov}(Q_s(\bar{x}), Q_i(\bar{z}))$, $s_i = \mathsf{size}(Q_s(\bar{x}), Q_i(\bar{z}))$, $\mu_{12} = \mathsf{cov}(Q_s(\bar{x}), Q_1(\bar{z}) \wedge Q_2(\bar{z}))$, and $s_{12} = \mathsf{size}(Q_s(\bar{x}), Q_1(\bar{z}) \wedge Q_2(\bar{z}))$. Then

(a) if $\mu_1 \wedge \mu_2 = \mathsf{true}$, then $\mathsf{cov}(Q_s(\bar{x}), Q(\bar{z})) = \mathsf{true}$ and $\mathsf{size}(Q_s(\bar{x}), Q(\bar{z})) = s_1 + s_2 + 1$; otherwise

(b) if $\mu_1 \wedge \mu_{12} = \mathsf{true}$ and $|Q_2| \leq K$ for some constant K, $\mathsf{cov}(Q_s(\bar{x}), Q(\bar{z})) = \mathsf{true}$ and $\mathsf{size}(Q_s(\bar{x}), Q(\bar{z})) = s_1 + s_{12} + 1$; otherwise

(c) $\mathsf{cov}(Q_s(\bar{x}), Q(\bar{z}) = \mathsf{false}$ and $\mathsf{size}(Q_s(\bar{x}), Q(\bar{z})) = +\infty$.

This is the case that captures how sub-query Q_4 of Q_3 is propagated to $\exists w\, R(w, z)$ in Example 6. When $\mathsf{cov}(Q_s(\bar{x}), Q(\bar{z})) = \mathsf{true}$, we have one of the following three cases.

(a) When $\mu_1 = \mu_2 = \mathsf{true}$, it is similar to case (5) above.

(b) If $\mu_1 = \mu_{12} = \mathsf{true}$, let ξ_1 and ξ_{12} be the plans to $Q_1(\bar{z})$ and $Q_1(\bar{z}) \wedge Q_2(\bar{z})$, respectively, with $Q_s(\bar{x})$. Since $Q_1(\bar{z}) \wedge \neg Q_2(\bar{z}) = Q_1(\bar{z}) \wedge \neg(Q_1(\bar{z}) \wedge Q_2(\bar{z}))$, $Q(\bar{z})$ has bounded plan $(T_1 = \xi_1, T_2 = \xi_{12}, T_3 = T_1 - T_2)$, of size $|\xi_1| + |\xi_{12}| + 1$.

(c) Otherwise, $\mathsf{cov}(Q_s(\bar{x}), Q(\bar{z})) = \mathsf{false}$, and thus $\mathsf{size}(Q_s(\bar{x}), Q(\bar{z})) = +\infty$, *i.e.*, Q has no bounded rewriting.

(7) $Q(\bar{z})$ is $\exists \bar{w}\, Q'(\bar{w}, \bar{z})$ ($\bar{w}$ is possibly empty). Let $\mu' = \mathsf{cov}(Q_s(\bar{x}), Q'(\bar{w}, \bar{z}))$ and $s' = \mathsf{size}(Q_s(\bar{x}), Q'(\bar{w}, \bar{z}))$. Then,

(a) if Q' is $R(\bar{w}, \bar{z})$ and $R(\emptyset \to Z, N) \in \mathcal{A}$, then $\mathsf{cov}(Q_s(\bar{x}), Q(\bar{z})) = \mathsf{true}$ and $\mathsf{size}(Q_s(\bar{x}), Q(\bar{z})) = 1$;

(b) if Q' is $R(\bar{w}, \bar{z})$, $R(X \to Z', N) \in \mathcal{A}$, $X \cup Z' = Z$ and $Q_s(\bar{x})$ has *bounded output* under $\mathcal{A}$, then $\mathsf{cov}(Q_s(\bar{x}), Q(\bar{z}))$=$\mathsf{true}$, $\mathsf{size}(Q_s(\bar{x}), Q(\bar{z})) = \mathsf{size}(Q_\varepsilon, Q_s(\bar{x})) + 1$;

(c) otherwise, $\mathsf{cov}(Q_s(\bar{x}), Q(\bar{z})) = \mathsf{cov}(Q_s(\bar{x}), Q'(\bar{w}, \bar{z}))$ and $\mathsf{size}(Q_s(\bar{x}), Q(\bar{z})) = \mathsf{size}(Q_s(\bar{x}), Q'(\bar{w}, \bar{z})) + 1$ if $\mathsf{cov}(Q_s(\bar{x}), Q(\bar{z})) = \mathsf{true}$, and as $+\infty$ otherwise.

Note that $Q_s(\bar{x})$ may not have bounded output even when it has a bounded rewriting. Therefore, in case (b) above we have to ensure that $Q_s(\bar{x})$ has bounded output in order to propagate $\bar{x}$-value from $Q_s(\bar{x})$ to $R(\bar{z})$, for a fetch operation to use the $\bar{x}$-value. Moreover, observe the following.

(a) When $Q(\bar{z})$ is a projection of a relation atom, if it is covered by a constraint $R(\emptyset \to Z, N)$ in $\mathcal{A}$, then $\mathsf{fetch}(\emptyset, R, Z)$ is an 1-bounded plan for $Q(\bar{z})$. Otherwise if it is covered by $R(X \to Z', N)$ and $Q_s(\bar{x})$ has bounded output, then it has a plan $(T_1 = \xi_s, T_2 = \mathsf{fetch}(X \in T_1, R, Z'))$, where ξ_s is the plan for Q_s. Note that Q_s has a bounded plan by induction.

(b) Otherwise, $Q(\bar{z})$ has a bounded plan if $Q'(\bar{w}, \bar{z})$ has one. Let ξ' be the plan for Q' with Q_s. Then $(T_1 = \xi', T_2 = \pi_Z(T_1))$ of size $|\xi'| + 1$ is a plan for $Q(\bar{z})$ with $Q_s(\bar{x})$.

Example 7: We next show that Q_3 of Example 6 is topped by $(\mathcal{R}_1, \mathcal{A}_2, \mathcal{V}_3, 13)$. Denote the sub-queries of Q_3 as follows:

$q_1 = V_3(x, y) \wedge (x = 1)$, $q_2 = \exists x\, q_1$,

$q_3 = q_2 \wedge R(y, z)$ (thus $Q_4 = \exists y\, q_3$), $q_4 = \exists w\, R(z, w)$.

Then one can easily verify the following:

(a) $\mathsf{cov}(Q_\varepsilon, Q_3) = (\mathsf{cov}(Q_\varepsilon, Q_4) \wedge \mathsf{cov}(Q_\varepsilon, q_4)) \vee (\mathsf{cov}(Q_\varepsilon, Q_4) \wedge \mathsf{cov}(Q_\varepsilon, Q_4 \wedge q_4))$,

(b) $\mathsf{cov}(Q_\varepsilon, Q_4) = \mathsf{cov}(Q_\varepsilon, q_3) = (\mathsf{cov}(Q_\varepsilon, q_2) \wedge \mathsf{cov}(Q_\varepsilon, R(y, z)) \vee (\mathsf{cov}(Q_\varepsilon, q_2) \wedge \mathsf{cov}(q_2, R(y, z)),$

(c) $\mathsf{cov}(Q_\varepsilon, q_2) = \mathsf{cov}(Q_\varepsilon, q_1) = \mathsf{true}$,

(d) $\mathsf{cov}(q_2, R(y, z)) = \mathsf{true}$ (since q_2 has bounded output),

(e) from these it follows that $\mathsf{cov}(Q_\varepsilon, Q_4) = \mathsf{true}$,

(f) $\mathsf{cov}(Q_\varepsilon, Q_4 \wedge q_4) = (\mathsf{cov}(Q_\varepsilon, Q_3) \wedge \mathsf{cov}(Q_\varepsilon, q_4)) \vee (\mathsf{cov}(Q_\varepsilon, Q_4) \wedge \mathsf{cov}(Q_4, q_4)) = \mathsf{true}$.

Thus $\mathsf{cov}(Q_\varepsilon, Q_3) = \mathsf{true}$. One can easily verify that $\mathsf{size}(Q_\varepsilon, Q_3) = 13$. Thus Q_3 is topped by $(\mathcal{R}_1, \mathcal{A}_2, \mathcal{V}_3, 13)$. □

Having defined topped queries, we now prove Theorem 15.

Proof sketch of Theorem 15. (a) Suppose that Q is an FO query with an M-bounded rewriting, *i.e.,* Q has an M-bounded query plan $\xi(Q, \mathcal{V}, \mathcal{R})$ under $\mathcal{A}$. We show that there exists a query Q_ξ topped by $(\mathcal{R}, \mathcal{V}, \mathcal{A}, M)$ such that $\xi \equiv_\mathcal{A} Q_\xi$. This is verified by induction on M, verifying each case and step of ξ. In this direction, $Q_s = Q_\varepsilon$ suffices; in other words, we do not need to expand Q_s as described in cases (4c) and (6b) above (to be elaborated shortly).

(b) We show that every query Q topped by $(\mathcal{R}, \mathcal{V}, \mathcal{A}, M)$ has a $\mathsf{size}(Q_\varepsilon, Q)$-bounded rewriting using $\mathcal{V}$ under $\mathcal{A}$. The proof needs the following lemma: if $\mathsf{cov}(Q_s, Q) = \mathsf{true}$, and if Q_s has a $\mathsf{size}(Q_\varepsilon, Q_s)$-bounded plan, then $Q_s \wedge Q$ has a $\mathsf{size}(Q_\varepsilon, Q_s \wedge Q)$-bounded plan. This is verified by induction on the structure of Q. For instance, when $Q(\bar{z})$ is $Q_1(\bar{z}_1) \wedge Q_2(\bar{z}_2)$, $\mathsf{cov}(Q_s, Q(\bar{z}))$ is true and Q_s has a $\mathsf{size}(Q_\varepsilon, Q_s)$-bounded plan, we know that $\mathsf{cov}(Q_s, Q_1(\bar{z}_1))$ is also true. By the induction hypothesis we have that $Q_s \wedge Q_1(\bar{z}_1)$ has a $\mathsf{size}(Q_\varepsilon, Q_s \wedge Q_1(\bar{z}_1))$-bounded plan. Thus either $\mathsf{cov}(Q_s, Q_2(\bar{z}_2)) = \mathsf{true}$ or $\mathsf{cov}(Q_s \wedge Q_1(\bar{z}_1), Q_2(\bar{z}_2)) = \mathsf{true}$. In both cases, again by the induction hypothesis, $Q_s \wedge Q_1 \wedge Q_2$ has a $\mathsf{size}(Q_\varepsilon, Q_s \wedge Q_1 \wedge Q_2)$-bounded plan.

(c) It takes PTIME in $|\mathcal{R}|$, $|Q|$, $|\mathcal{V}|$, $|\mathcal{A}|$ and M to check whether an FO query is topped by $(\mathcal{R}, \mathcal{V}, \mathcal{A}, M)$. Indeed, it is easy to see that both $\mathsf{cov}(Q_\varepsilon, Q)$ and $\mathsf{size}(Q_\varepsilon, Q)$ are PTIME functions, which use a PTIME oracle to check bounded output for cases (4a) and (7b) of topped queries. □

Remark. Observe the following. (a) As mentioned above, to prove Theorem 15(1), it suffices to use $Q_s = Q_\varepsilon$ and does not need to expand Q_s (for cases (4c) and (6b)). We allow value propagation in cases (4c) and (6b) to cover queries that are commonly used and have a bounded rewriting. (b) The class of topped queries is quite different from the rules for $\bar{x}$-controllability [18] and the syntactic rules for bounded evaluability of CQ [17] and for FO [10], particularly in the use of Q_s to check bounded output of views and the function $\mathsf{size}(Q_s(\bar{x}), Q(\bar{z}))$ to ensure the bounded size of query plans.

5.3 Size Bounded Queries

We next define size-bounded queries and prove Theorem 16. We remark that there are other forms of effective syntax for FO queries with bounded output. To simplify the discussion, below we present a straightforward one.

Size-bounded queries. An FO query $Q(\bar{x})$ is *size-bounded* under an access schema $\mathcal{A}$ if it is of the following form:

$$Q(\bar{x}) = Q'(\bar{x}) \wedge \forall \bar{x}_1, \ldots, \bar{x}_{K+1} \big(Q'(\bar{x}_1) \wedge \cdots \wedge Q'(\bar{x}_{K+1}) \rightarrow \textstyle\bigvee_{i,j \in [1,K+1], i \neq j} \bar{x}_i = \bar{x}_j\big).$$

where K is a natural number, and Q' is an FO query.

Intuitively, an FO query $Q'(\bar{x})$ has bounded output under $\mathcal{A}$ if there exists a bound K such that it is $\mathcal{A}$-equivalent to $Q(\bar{x})$ of the form above, which explicitly states that $Q'(\bar{x})$ has at most K distinct answers for a constant K.

This class of size-bounded queries suffices for Theorem 16.

Proof of Theorem 16. (a) Consider an FO query $Q(\bar{x})$ having bounded output under $\mathcal{A}$. By the definition of queries with bounded-output (Section 3.1), there exists a natural number K such that for any instance D of $\mathcal{R}$, if $D \models \mathcal{A}$, then $|Q(D)| \leq K$. Construct $Q'(\bar{x})$ from $Q(\bar{x})$ as follows:

$$Q'(\bar{x}) = Q(\bar{x}) \wedge \forall \bar{x}_1, \ldots, \bar{x}_{K+1} \big(Q(\bar{x}_1) \wedge \cdots \wedge Q(\bar{x}_{K+1}) \rightarrow \textstyle\bigvee_{i,j \in [1,K+1], i \neq j} (\bar{x}_i = \bar{x}_j)\big),$$

Obviously, $Q'(\bar{x})$ is a size-bounded query. Moreover, $Q'(\bar{x}) \equiv_\mathcal{A} Q(\bar{x})$, since $Q(\bar{x})$ has output bounded by K, and hence, for any $D \models \mathcal{A}$, it is easy to see that $Q(D) = Q'(D)$.

(b) Consider a size-bounded query $Q(\bar{x})$ of the form above. Observe that for any D, if $Q'(D)$ contains more than K answer tuples, then $Q(D) = \emptyset$. Otherwise, $Q(D) = Q'(D)$ and $Q(D)$ includes at most K tuples. Putting these together, we have that $|Q(D)| \leq K$. That is, Q has bounded output.

(c) By the definition of size-bounded queries, it is immediate to syntactically check whether an FO query Q is size-bounded. It takes PTIME in the size $|Q|$ of Q. □

Queries	Complexity	Condition
FO	undecidable (Th 1)	
CQ, UCQ, $\exists$FO$^+$	Σ_3^p-complete (Th 1)	
CQ, UCQ, $\exists$FO$^+$	Σ_3^p-complete (Cor 6)	fixed $\mathcal{R}, \mathcal{A}, M$
CQ	NP-complete (Prop 13)	only FDs in $\mathcal{A}$
Fixed $\mathcal{R}, \mathcal{A}, M$ and $\mathcal{V}$ for the following		
FO	undecidable (Cor 5)	
CQ, UCQ, $\exists$FO$^+$	C_{2k+1}^p-complete (Th 7)	
CQ	NP-complete (Prop 13)	only FDs in $\mathcal{A}$
ACQ	coNP (Th 10)	
ACQ	coNP-complete (Th 9)	restricted $\mathcal{A}$
ACQ	PTIME (Cor 12)	only FDs in $\mathcal{A}$

Table 2: Complexity of VBRP($\mathcal{L}$)

6. CONCLUSION

We have formalized bounded query rewriting using views under access constraints, studied the bounded rewriting problem VBRP($\mathcal{L}$) when $\mathcal{L}$ is ACQ, CQ, UCQ, $\exists$FO$^+$or FO, and established their upper and lower bounds, all matching, when $M, \mathcal{R}, \mathcal{A}$ and $\mathcal{V}$ are fixed or not. The main complexity results are summarized in Table 2, annotated with their corresponding theorems. We have also provided an effective syntax for FO queries with a bounded rewriting, along with an effective syntax for FO queries with bounded output.

There is much more to be done. One topic for future work is to study bounded rewriting Q' in a query language more powerful than the one in which query Q and views $\mathcal{V}$ are defined, *e.g.,* when Q and $\mathcal{V}$ are CQ while Q' is a UCQ. We have only considered the setting when Q, Q' and $\mathcal{V}$ are in the same language. It is also interesting to study which language is powerful enough to express all bounded rewriting, along the same lines as [31]. Another topic concerns bounded rewriting and bounded evaluability [10, 17] when we allow the amount of data accessed from the underlying dataset D to be an α-fraction of D, for a small α in the range of $[0, 1]$, rather than to be bounded by a constant. Similarly, we may allow M to be a function of resources and workload, rather than a constant. The third topic is to study bounded view maintenance, to incrementally maintain $\mathcal{V}(D)$ by accessing a bounded amount of data in D, in response to changes to D. The fourth topic is to develop methods for selecting views $\mathcal{V}$ and discovering access constraints $\mathcal{A}$, such that under $\mathcal{A}$, the number of queries that have a bounded rewriting using $\mathcal{V}$ is maximized in a given application.

7. REFERENCES

[1] S. Abiteboul, R. Hull, and V. Vianu. *Foundations of Databases*. Addison-Wesley, 1995.

[2] F. N. Afrati. Determinacy and query rewriting for conjunctive queries and views. *TCS*, 412(11):1005–1021, 2011.

[3] F. N. Afrati, C. Li, and J. D. Ullman. Using views to generate efficient evaluation plans for queries. *JCSS*, 73(5):703–724, 2007.

[4] M. Armbrust, K. Curtis, T. Kraska, A. Fox, M. J. Franklin, and D. A. Patterson. PIQL: Success-tolerant query processing in the cloud. *PVLDB*, 5(3), 2011.

[5] M. Armbrust, A. Fox, D. A. Patterson, N. Lanham, B. Trushkowsky, J. Trutna, and H. Oh. SCADS: Scale-independent storage for social computing applications. In *CIDR*, 2009.

[6] M. Armbrust, E. Liang, T. Kraska, A. Fox, M. J. Franklin, and D. Patterson. Generalized scale independence through incremental precomputation. In *SIGMOD*, 2013.

[7] M. Benedikt, J. Leblay, B. ten Cate, and E. Tsamoura. *Generating Plans from Proofs: The Interpolation-based Approach to Query Reformulation*. Synthesis Lectures on Data Management. Morgan & Claypool Publishers, 2016.

[8] M. Benedikt, B. Ten Cate, and E. Tsamoura. Generating plans from proofs. *TODS*, 40(4), 2016.

[9] A. Calì and D. Martinenghi. Querying data under access limitations. In *ICDE*, 2008.

[10] Y. Cao and W. Fan. An effective syntax for bounded relational queries. In *SIGMOD*, 2016.

[11] Y. Cao, W. Fan, J. Huai, and R. Huang. Making pattern queries bounded in big graphs. In *ICDE*, 2015.

[12] Y. Cao, W. Fan, and W. Yu. Bounded conjunctive queries. *PVLDB*, 2014.

[13] S. Cohen, W. Nutt, and A. Serebrenik. Rewriting aggregate queries using views. In *PODS*, 1999.

[14] A. Deutsch, B. Ludäscher, and A. Nash. Rewriting queries using views with access patterns under integrity constraints. *TCS*, 371(3):200–226, 2007.

[15] Facebook. Introducing Graph Search. *https://en-gb.facebook.com/about/graphsearch*, 2013.

[16] Facebook. Constraints on the number of photos, friends and tags. *https://www.facebook.com/help*, 2014.

[17] W. Fan, F. Geerts, Y. Cao, T. Deng, and P. Lu. Querying big data by accessing small data. In *PODS*, 2015.

[18] W. Fan, F. Geerts, and L. Libkin. On scale independence for querying big data. In *PODS*, 2014.

[19] M. Garey and D. Johnson. *Computers and Intractability: A Guide to the Theory of NP-Completeness*. W. H. Freeman and Company, 1979.

[20] A. V. Gelder and R. W. Topor. Safety and translation of relational calculus queries. *TODS*, 16(2):235–278, 1991.

[21] G. Gottlob, N. Leone, and F. Scarcello. Hypertree decompositions and tractable queries. In *PODS*, 1999.

[22] I. Grujic, S. Bogdanovic-Dinic, and L. Stoimenov. Collecting and analyzing data from e-government facebook pages. In *ICT Innovations*, 2014.

[23] A. Y. Halevy. Answering queries using views: A survey. *VLDB J.*, 10(4), 2001.

[24] Y. Huhtala, J. Kärkk ainen, P. Porkka, and H. Toivonen. TANE: An efficient algorithm for discovering functional and approximate dependencies. *Comput. J.*, 42(2):100–111, 1999.

[25] P. G. Kolaitis and E. Pema. A dichotomy in the complexity of consistent query answering for queries with two atoms. *Inf. Process. Lett.*, 112(3):77–85, 2012.

[26] J. Kratochvíl. Precoloring extension with fixed color bound. *Acta Math. Univ. Comen*, 62:139–153, 1993.

[27] M. Lenzerini. Data integration: A theoretical perspective. In *PODS*, 2002.

[28] A. Y. Levy, A. O. Mendelzon, Y. Sagiv, and D. Srivastava. Answering queries using views. In *PODS*, 1995.

[29] C. Li. Computing complete answers to queries in the presence of limited access patterns. *VLDB J.*, 12(3):211–227, 2003.

[30] A. Nash and B. Ludäscher. Processing first-order queries under limited access patterns. In *PODS*, 2004.

[31] A. Nash, L. Segoufin, and V. Vianu. Views and queries: Determinacy and rewriting. *TODS*, 35(3), 2010.

[32] A. Rajaraman, Y. Sagiv, and J. D. Ullman. Answering queries using templates with binding patterns. In *PODS*, 1995.

[33] R. Ramakrishnan and J. Gehrke. *Database management systems*. McGraw Hill, 2000.

[34] L. J. Stockmeyer. The polynomial-time hierarchy. *TCS*, 3(1):1–22, 1976.

[35] A. P. Stolboushkin and M. A. Taitslin. Finite queries do not have effective syntax. In *PODS*, 1995.

[36] J. D. Ullman. *Principles of Database Systems, 2nd Edition*. Computer Science Press, 1982.

[37] M. Y. Vardi. On the complexity of bounded-variable queries. In *PODS*, 1995.

[38] K. W. Wagner. More complicated questions about maxima and minima, and some closures of NP. *TCS*, 51(1-2):53–80, 1987.

Acknowledgments. Fan, Cao and Lu are supported in part by ERC 652976, 973 Program 2014CB340302 and 2012CB316200, NSFC 61133002 and 61421003, EPSRC EP/J015377/1 and EP/M025268/1, NSF III 1302212, Shenzhen Peacock Program 1105100030834361, Guangdong Innovative Research Team Program 2011D005, Shenzhen Science and Technology Fund JCYJ20150529164656096, Guangdong Applied R&D Program 2015B010131006, Beijing Advanced Innovation Centre for Big Data and Brain Computing, and a research grant from Huawei Technologies.

Red Spider Meets a Rainworm: Conjunctive Query Finite Determinacy Is Undecidable

Tomasz Gogacz*, Jerzy Marcinkowski†
Institute of Computer Science, University Of Wrocław

ABSTRACT

We solve a well known and long-standing open problem in database theory, proving that Conjunctive Query Finite Determinacy Problem is undecidable. The technique we use builds on the top of the Red Spider method invented in our paper [11] to show undecidability of the same problem in the "unrestricted case" – when database instances are allowed to be infinite. We also show a specific instance Q_0, $\mathcal{Q} = \{Q_1, Q_2, \ldots Q_k\}$ such that the set $\mathcal{Q}$ of CQs does not determine CQ Q_0 but finitely determines it. Finally, we claim that while Q_0 is finitely determined by $\mathcal{Q}$, there is no FO-rewriting of Q_0, with respect to $\mathcal{Q}$.

1. INTRODUCTION

"Assume that a set of derived relations is available in a stored form. Given a query, can it be computed from the derived relations and, if so, how?" is the first sentence of [14]. Saying the same in today's language:

> The instance of the Conjunctive Query Finite Determinacy Problem (CQfDP) problem is a set of conjunctive queries $\mathcal{Q} = \{Q_1, \ldots Q_k\}$, and another such query Q_0. The question is whether $\mathcal{Q}$ determines Q_0, which means that for each two database instances (that is **finite** relational structures) $\mathbb{D}_1$ and $\mathbb{D}_2$ such that $Q(\mathbb{D}_1) = Q(\mathbb{D}_2)$ for each $Q \in \mathcal{Q}$, it also holds that $Q_0(\mathbb{D}_1) = Q_0(\mathbb{D}_2)$.

Answering queries using views appears in so many various contexts that it is indeed hard to imagine a more natural scenario in database theory. See for example [12], or a recent thesis [7] for a survey[1]. The contexts where such scenario appears include for example query optimization and caching [5], or – to see more recent examples – [8] where the view update problem is studied and [9] where the context are description logics. In all the examples we mentioned so far we "prefer" Q_0 to be determined by $\mathcal{Q}$. Yet another context, where it is "preferred" that Q_0 is not determined, is privacy: we would like to release some views of the database, but in a way that does not allow certain query to be computed.

Many variants of the problem were being considered, and the case we study, where both the views and the query are defined by conjunctive queries, and where the views we can see are "exact" is not the only possible (what we call "determinacy" is "losslessness under the exact view assumption" in the language of [3]). Let us just cite the most recent results: [16] shows that the problem is decidable if each query from $\mathcal{Q}$ has only one free variable; in [1] decidability is shown for $\mathcal{Q}$ and Q_0 being "path queries". This is generalized in [17] to the scenario where $\mathcal{Q}$ are path queries but Q_0 is any conjunctive query. The paper [15] is the first to present a negative result. It was shown there, that the problem is undecidable if unions of conjunctive queries are allowed rather than CQs. In [16] it was also proved that determinacy is undecidable if the elements of $\mathcal{Q}$ are CQs and Q_0 is a first order sentence (or the other way round). Another negative result is presented in [6]: determinacy is shown there to be undecidable if $\mathcal{Q}$ is a DATALOG program and Q_0 is CQ.

1.1 OUR CONTRIBUTION. FINITE VS. UNRESTRICTED CASE.

As we said, the case we study, where both the views and the query are CQs, is not the only one to be studied, but one of special importance, since CQs – as [15] puts it – are "the simplest and most common language to define views and queries". The main technical result of this paper is:

THEOREM 1. *CQfDP is undecidable.*

As usually in database theory one can consider two variants of the problem: *finite*, where all the structures in question (which in our case means $\mathbb{D}_1$ and $\mathbb{D}_2$) are assumed to be finite, and *unrestricted*, where there is no such assumption. Most of the results of [1, 15–17] that we report above hold true regardless of the finiteness assumption.

A theorem analogous to Theorem 1 but concerning the unrestricted Conjunctive Query Determinacy Problem (CQDP) is the main result of our earlier paper [11]. Since the unrestricted case is viewed by the database theory community as less natural, it is fair to say that the result from [11] was

*Supported by Polish National Science Centre grant 2013/09/N/ST6/01188
†Supported by Polish National Science Centre grant DEC-2013/09/B/ST6/01535

[1] Actually, [7] does such a good job as a survey that we will stick to an absolutely minimal introduction here, especially that we have enough of new technical material to easily overrun the page limit anyway.

PODS'16, June 26-July 01, 2016, San Francisco, CA, USA

ISBN 978-1-4503-4191-2/16/06...$15.00
DOI: http://dx.doi.org/10.1145/2902251.2902288

perceived by the community as a step forward, but not as one closing the problem (see e.g. [7]).

Since problems tend to be computationally harder in the finite case than in unrestricted, it was natural to conjecture, after [11], that Theorem 1 should hold true. But its proof is significantly more difficult than the respective proof in [11]. Let us try to explain why it is so.

As the reader is going to see in Section 4, determinacy (both finite and unrestricted) boils down to the question, whether some query (call it $red(Q_0)$) is true in **all** structures $\mathbb{M}$ (for the unrestricted case), or in all **finite** structures $\mathbb{M}$ (for the finite case) satisfying $\mathbb{M} \models \mathcal{T}_{\mathcal{Q}}$ and $\mathbb{M} \models green(Q_0)$, where $green(Q_0)$ is a structure, depending on Q_0, and $\mathcal{T}_{\mathcal{Q}}$ is a set of tuple generating dependencies, depending on $\mathcal{Q}$.

But in order to decide the above question for **all** $\mathbb{M}$ it is enough to study just **one** *universal structure*, namely $chase(\mathcal{T}_{\mathcal{Q}}, green(Q_0))$. Determinacy holds if and only if $red(Q_0)$ is true in this single structure.

This means that, when we encode some undecidable problem to show undecidability of (the unrestricted) CQDP, we only need to prove that whenever we start from a positive instance of our problem we get $\mathcal{Q}$ and Q_0 such that $chase(\mathcal{T}_{\mathcal{Q}}, green(Q_0)) \models red(Q_0)$, and whenever we start from a negative instance we get $\mathcal{Q}$ and Q_0 such that $chase(\mathcal{T}_{\mathcal{Q}}, green(Q_0)) \not\models red(Q_0)$

No such universal structure exists for the finite case. This generates problems of two sorts:

- How can we be sure (when we start from a negative instance[2]) that $\mathbb{M} \models red(Q_0)$ is true in all relevant finite structures $\mathbb{M}$? Do we have any technique that is specific for finite models?
- In order to show (when we start from a positive instance) that $\mathbb{M} \not\models red(Q_0)$, for some relevant $\mathbb{M}$, we need to built a finite model, for a set of TGDs, which omits some conjunctive query. We are dangerously close here to the issues related to finite controllability (see [2,10,18]) which are known to be difficult.

1.2 Our contribution. First Order non-rewritability

Let, as always, $\mathcal{Q} = \{Q_1 \dots Q_n\}$ be a set of CQs and let Q_0 be a CQ. Then, by (slightly restated) definition, $\mathcal{Q}$ (finitely) determines Q_0 if there is a function $h^{Q_0}_{\mathcal{Q}}$ which, for a (finite) structure $\mathbb{D}$ over Σ, takes, as its argument, the structure $\mathcal{Q}(\mathbb{D})$ and returns "yes" or "no", depending on whether $\mathbb{D} \models Q_0$ or not. Notice that $\mathcal{Q}(\mathbb{D})$ is no longer a structure over Σ. Its signature consists of one k-ary relation symbol for each query $Q_i \in \mathcal{Q}$ having k free variables.

It is known from [15] that if $\mathcal{Q}$ determines Q_0 in the unrestricted sense then function $h^{Q_0}_{\mathcal{Q}}$ can be defined by a first order formula $\Theta^{Q_0}_{\mathcal{Q}}$, called *FO-rewriting* of Q_0 with respect to $\mathcal{Q}$: $h^{Q_0}_{\mathcal{Q}}(\mathcal{Q}(\mathbb{D})) = yes$ if and only if $\mathcal{Q}(\mathbb{D}) \models \Theta^{Q_0}_{\mathcal{Q}}$. The proof is via Craig Lemma, and since this lemma does not hold for First Order Logic over finite structures, it was natural to conjecture that the result will not survive if we restrict our attention to finite database instances. And indeed, as we are going to show:

Theorem 2. *There are $\mathcal{Q}$ and Q_0 such that $\mathcal{Q}$ finitely determines Q_0 but $h^{Q_0}_{\mathcal{Q}}$ is not first order definable.*

[2]Notice that the roles of positive and negative instances have swapped. This is due to the fact that finite determinacy is co-r.e. and unrestricted determinacy is r.e.

A detailed proof of this theorem is too long for a conference paper, and will only be presented in the full version of this paper. We however outline it here, and all the important proof ideas are already present in this outline.

2. PRELIMINARIES

We need nothing beyond some standard finite model theory/database theory notions. They are only recalled here in order to fix notations.

2.1 Basic notions

When we say "structure" we mean a relational structure $\mathbb{D}$ over some signature Σ, i.e. a set of elements (vertices), denoted as $Dom(\mathbb{D})$ (or just as $\mathbb{D}$ if no confusion is possible) and a set of relational atoms, whose arguments are elements of $\mathbb{D}$ and whose predicate names are from Σ. Atoms are (of course) only positive. For an atomic formula A (or for any other formula) we use notation $\mathbb{D} \models A$ to say that A is true in $\mathbb{D}$.

Apart from predicate symbols Σ can also contain constants. If c is a constant from Σ and $\mathbb{D}$ is a structure over Σ then $c \in Dom(\mathbb{D})$.

$\mathbb{D}_1$ is a substructure of $\mathbb{D}$ (and $\mathbb{D}$ is a superstructure of $\mathbb{D}_1$) if for each atom A if $\mathbb{D}_1 \models A$ then $\mathbb{D} \models A$. This implies that $Dom(\mathbb{D}_1) \subseteq Dom(\mathbb{D})$.

For two structures $\mathbb{D}_1$ and $\mathbb{D}$ over the same signature Σ a function $h : Dom(\mathbb{D}_1) \to Dom(\mathbb{D})$ is called a homomorphism if for each $P \in \Sigma$ of arity l and each tuple $\bar{a} \in Dom(\mathbb{D}_1)^l$ if $\mathbb{D}_1 \models P(\bar{a})$ then $\mathbb{D} \models P(h(\bar{a}))$ (where $h(\bar{a})$ is a tuple of images of elements of $\bar{a}$).

A conjunctive query (over Σ), in short CQ, is a conjunction of atomic formulas (over Σ) whose arguments are either variables or the constants from Σ, preceded by existential quantifier binding some of the variables. It is important to distinguish between a CQ and its quantifier-free part.

For a conjunction of atoms Ψ (or for a CQ $Q(\bar{x}) = \exists \bar{y}\ \Psi(\bar{y}, \bar{x})$) the canonical structure of Ψ, denoted as $A[\Psi]$, is the structure whose elements are all the variables and constants appearing in Ψ and whose atoms are atoms of Ψ. It is useful to notice that for a finite structure $\mathbb{D}$ and a set $V \subseteq Dom(\mathbb{D})$ there is a unique conjunctive query Q such that $\mathbb{D} = A[Q]$ and that V is the set of free variables of Q.

For a CQ $Q(\bar{x}) = \exists \bar{y}\ \Psi(\bar{y}, \bar{x})$ with $\bar{x} = x_1, \dots x_l$, for a structure $\mathbb{D}$ and for a tuple $a_1, \dots a_l$ of elements of $\mathbb{D}$ we write $\mathbb{D} \models Q(a_1, \dots a_l)$ when there exists a homomorphism $h : A[\Psi] \to \mathbb{D}$ such that $h(x_i) = a_i$ for each i.

Sometimes we also write $\mathbb{D} \models Q$. Then we assume that all the free variables of Q are implicitly existentially quantified, so that the meaning of the notation is that there exists some homomorphism $h : A[\Psi] \to \mathbb{D}$.

The **most fundamental definition** of this paper now, needed to formulate the problem we solve: for a CQ Q and for a structure $\mathbb{D}$ by $Q(\mathbb{D})$ we denote the "view defined by Q over $\mathbb{D}$", which is the relation $\{\bar{a} : \mathbb{D} \models Q(\bar{a})\}$.

2.2 TGDs and how they act on a structure

A Tuple Generating Dependency (or TGD) is a formula of the form:

$$\forall \bar{x}, \bar{y}\ [\Phi(\bar{x}, \bar{y}) \Rightarrow \exists \bar{z}\ \Psi(\bar{z}, \bar{y})]$$

where Ψ and Φ are conjunctions of atomic formulas. The standard convention, which we usually obey, is that the universal quantifiers in front of the TGD are omitted.

From the point of view of this paper it is important to see a TGD – let it be T, equal to $\Phi(\bar{x},\bar{y}) \Rightarrow \exists \bar{z}\ \Psi(\bar{z},\bar{y})$ – as the following whose input is a structure $\mathcal{D}$ and whose output is a new structure being a superstructure of $\mathcal{D}$:

find a tuple $\bar{b}$ (with $|\bar{b}| = |\bar{y}|$) such that:
① $\mathcal{D} \models \exists \bar{x}\ \Phi(\bar{x},\bar{b})$ via homomorphism h but
② $\mathcal{D} \not\models \exists z\ \Psi(\bar{z},\bar{b})$;

create a new copy of $A[\Psi]$;

output $\mathcal{D}(T,\bar{b})$ being a union of $\mathcal{D}$ and the new copy of $A[\Psi]$, with each y from $A[\Psi]$ identified with $h(y)$ in $\mathcal{D}$.

The message, which will be **good to remember**, is that the interface between the "new" part of the structure, added by a single application of a TGD to a structure, and the "old" structure, are the free variables of the query in the right hand side of the TGD.

2.3 Chase

For a set $\mathcal{T}$ of TGDs and for a structure $\mathbb{D}$ let $chase_0(\mathcal{T},\mathbb{D}) = \mathbb{D}$. Then, $chase_{i+1}(\mathcal{T},\mathbb{D})$ is defined by the procedure:

$\mathcal{D} := chase_i(\mathcal{T},\mathbb{D})$
forall pairs $T, \bar{b}$, where T is a TGD in $\mathcal{T}$ and $\bar{b}$ is a tuple of elements of $chase_i(\mathcal{T},\mathbb{D})$ **do:**
{ **if** ① and ② hold in $\mathcal{D}$ for $\bar{b}$ and T **then** $\mathcal{D} := \mathcal{D}(T,\bar{b})$ };
$chase_{i+1}(\mathcal{T},\mathbb{D}) := \mathcal{D}$.

Then $chase(\mathcal{T},\mathbb{D})$ is defined as $\bigcup_{i\in\mathbb{N}} chase_i(\mathcal{T},\mathbb{D})$. Notice that our chase is "lazy" – we only produce new atoms and new elements when needed.

3. OUTLINE OF THE TECHNICAL PART

Most of this paper is devoted to proving Theorem 1.

Proving undecidability means encoding. Encoding means programming. Programming means the device that is being programmed, and the programming language.

In [11] we developed the device. An elementary "hardware" object there is a structure called *spider* and an elementary "instruction" able to act on a structure built out of spiders is a CQ called *spider query.*

In the Preliminaries we said that TGDs can "act on a structure". But how can a (conjunctive) query possibly do? This is explained in Section 4.

In Section 5 we try – without diving into details – to define an interface between the device from [11] and the current paper. In Section 6 we define a high level programming language to manipulate spiders. We also define what it means to compile a program in such a language and show that this compilation is correct. This is new – the problem we encoded in [11] was much simpler than what we are going to encode here, and – using our running metaphor – we could afford programming in a language which was pretty low level. Some ideas of the proof of Lemma 11 were however present already in [11].

Separating example As we already have noticed, finite determinacy is co-r.e. and unrestricted determinacy is r.e. which implies – since we know from [11] that unrestricted determinacy is undecidable – that the two notions do not coincide. But no separating example was know so far. In Section 7 we construct such an example. This is not just for curiosity. As it appears, this example is (together with Rainworm Machines) one of the two main engines of the proof of Theorem 1 which is presented in Section 8.

Finally, in Section 9 we explain the main ideas of the proof of Theorem 2. The separating example from Section 7 turns out to also be a counterexample for FO-rewritability.

4. GREEN-RED TGDS

4.1 Green-Red Signature

For a given signature Σ let Σ_G and Σ_R be two copies of Σ with new relation symbols, which have the same names and the same arities as symbols in Σ but are written in green and red respectively. Let $\bar{\Sigma}$ be the union of Σ_G and Σ_R. Notice that the constants from Σ (if there are any) are not relation symbols, so they are never colored and thus survive in $\bar{\Sigma}$ unharmed.

For any formula Ψ over Σ let $R(\Psi)$ (or $G(\Psi)$) be the result of painting all the predicates in Ψ red (green). For any formula Ψ over $\bar{\Sigma}$ let $dalt(\Psi)$ ("daltonisation of Ψ") be a formula over Σ being the result of erasing the colors from predicates of Ψ. The same convention applies to structures. For a structure $\mathcal{D}$ over $\bar{\Sigma}$, by $\mathcal{D}\restriction G$ we mean the substructure of $\mathcal{D}$ consisting of all its atoms which are over Σ_G. Analogously for $\mathcal{D}\restriction R$.

4.2 Having $\mathbb{D}$ instead of $\mathbb{D}_1$ and $\mathbb{D}_2$.

We restate CQfDP a little bit, as we prefer to be talking about one two-colored database instead of two. Clearly CQfDP can be equivalently restated as **CQfDP.2**:

> The instance of the problem is a finite set $\mathcal{Q}$ of conjunctive queries and another conjunctive query Q_0, all of them over some signature Σ. The question is whether for each finite structure $\mathbb{D}$ over $\bar{\Sigma}$ such that:
>
> ❶ $(G(Q))(\mathbb{D}) = (R(Q))(\mathbb{D})$ for each $Q \in \mathcal{Q}$
>
> it also holds that $(G(Q_0))(\mathbb{D}) = (R(Q_0))(\mathbb{D})$.

Definition 3. *For a conjunctive query Q of the form $\exists \bar{x}\ \Phi(\bar{x},\bar{y})$ where Φ is a conjunction of atoms over Σ let $Q^{G\to R}$ be the TGD* generated by Q *in the following sense:*

$$Q^{G\to R} \quad = \quad \forall \bar{x},\bar{y}\ [\ G(\Phi)(\bar{x},\bar{y}) \Rightarrow \exists \bar{z}\ R(\Phi)(\bar{z},\bar{y})\ ]$$

TGD $Q^{R\to G}$ is defined in an analogous way. For a set $\mathcal{Q}$ as above let $\mathcal{T}_\mathcal{Q}$ be the set of all TGDs of the form $Q^{G\to R}$ or $Q^{R\to G}$ with $Q \in \mathcal{Q}$. It is very easy to see that:

Lemma 4. *The above condition ❶ is satisfied by structure $\mathbb{D}$ if and only if $\mathbb{D} \models \mathcal{T}_\mathcal{Q}$.*

Now CQfDP.2 can be again restated as **CQfDP.3**:

> Given a set $\mathcal{Q}$ (as in the formulation of CQfDP.2 above), and another conjunctive query Q_0, is it true that:
>
> ❷ for each finite structure $\mathbb{D}$ and each tuple $\bar{a}$ of elements of $\mathbb{D}$, if $\mathbb{D} \models \mathcal{T}_\mathcal{Q} \wedge G(Q_0)(\bar{a})$ then also $\mathbb{D} \models R(Q_0)(\bar{a})$?

Of course the unrestricted version of CQfDP (called CQDP, see the Introduction) is equivalent to CQfDP.3 after removing, from its formulation, the word "finite".

The equivalent version of Theorem 1 which we actually prove in Sections 7 and 8 is:

THEOREM 5. **CQfDP.3** *is undecidable.*

5. BUILDING ON TOP OF [GM15]: SPIDERS AND SPIDER QUERIES.

This paper builds on top of the techniques developed in [11]. But we are of course not able to include here a presentation of the techniques from [11] which would be detailed enough to make the current paper self-contained. There are two (or three) possible ways of reading this paper:

- A good way is to first read Sections IV, V and VI.A of [11] (which is about 4 pages) and then jump to Section 6 of the current paper.
- The shortest way is to read Section 11.1 in the Appendix, where we try to outline the ideas from [11] without going into details. We believe that most of the constructions of this paper should be understandable then, with the exception of the proof of Lemma 11(1), which constitutes an interface between the techniques from [11] and the new material.
- It is of course not at all forbidden to read both Section 11.1 in the Appendix and Sections IV, V and VI.A of [11] in any chosen order.

6. CLIMBING THE ABSTRACTION LADDER

The language of spiders, whose signature is $\bar{\Sigma}$, which we briefly described in the previous section, is a very low level one – we think it is Abstraction Level Zero. But in order to show our undecidability result we need to produce pretty complicated programs in the language of spider queries from $\mathbb{F}^2$. The typical Computer Science way in such situation is to define a more abstract, higher order language, use it as the actual programming language (so that one does not need to worry about low level implementation details), and then compile the program written in this higher order language into the executable low-level form

Defining such a higher order language (or rather languages – we will first *precompile* the original program into an intermediate language and then *compile*) is precisely what we are going to do in this section. Each of the two languages we are going to define will comprise a relational signature and a set of graph rewriting rules (being TGDs, in disguise) which will act on structures over this signature.

Abstraction Level 1 language. The signature consists of one binary relation $H(\mathcal{S},\_,\_)$ for each (ideal) spider $\mathcal{S} \in \mathbb{A}$. A structure over this signature will be called a *swarm*. Now we are going to define the set $\mathbb{L}_1$ of *swarm rewriting rules.*

DEFINITION 6. *For each query $\mathbb{R}^{I_1}_{J_1} \curlyvee \mathbb{R}^{I_2}_{J_2}$ from $\mathbb{F}^2$ (and for each query $\mathbb{R}^{I_1}_{J_1} \curlywedge \mathbb{R}^{I_2}_{J_2}$ from $\mathbb{F}^2$) there will be a rule $\mathbb{R}^{I_1}_{J_1} \curlyvee \mathbb{R}^{I_2}_{J_2}$ (resp. $\mathbb{R}^{I_1}_{J_1} \curlywedge \mathbb{R}^{I_2}_{J_2}$) in $\mathbb{L}_1$, where $\mathbb{R}^{I_1}_{J_1} \curlyvee \mathbb{R}^{I_2}_{J_2}$ is a shorthand of:*

$$\bigwedge_{I'_1\subseteq I_1, J'_1\subseteq J_1, I'_2\subseteq I_2, J'_2\subseteq J_2}$$
$$[\forall x,y,y'\ \ H(☆^{I'_1}_{J'_1},x,y)\wedge H(☆^{I'_2}_{J'_2},x,y') \Rightarrow$$
$$\exists x'\ \ H(★^{I_1\setminus I'_1}_{J_1\setminus J'_1},x',y)\wedge H(★^{I_2\setminus I'_2}_{J_2\setminus J'_2},x',y')]$$
$$\wedge$$
$$[\forall x,y,y'\ \ H(★^{I'_1}_{J'_1},x,y)\wedge H(★^{I'_2}_{J'_2},x,y') \Rightarrow$$
$$\exists x'\ \ H(☆^{I_1\setminus I'_1}_{J_1\setminus J'_1},x',y)\wedge H(☆^{I_2\setminus I'_2}_{J_2\setminus J'_2},x',y')]$$

and $\mathbb{R}^{I_1}_{J_1} \curlywedge \mathbb{R}^{I_2}_{J_2}$ is a shorthand of the formula:

$$\bigwedge_{I'_1\subseteq I_1, J'_1\subseteq J_1, I'_2\subseteq I_2, J'_2\subseteq J_2}$$
$$[\forall x,x',y\ \ H(☆^{I'_1}_{J'_1},x,y)\wedge H(☆^{I'_2}_{J'_2},x',y)] \Rightarrow$$
$$\exists y'\ H(★^{I_1\setminus I'_1}_{J_1\setminus J'_1},x,y')\wedge H(★^{I_2\setminus I'_2}_{J_2\setminus J'_2},x',y')]$$
$$\wedge$$
$$[\forall x,x',y\ \ H(★^{I'_1}_{J'_1},x,y)\wedge H(★^{I'_2}_{J'_2},x',y) \Rightarrow$$
$$\exists y'\ H(☆^{I_1\setminus I'_1}_{J_1\setminus J'_1},x,y')\wedge H(☆^{I_2\setminus I'_2}_{J_2\setminus J'_2},x',y')]$$

Horrible. But this is only because we wrote the rules as FOL formulas, while they are actually easy to explain in the natural language: $\mathbb{R}^{I_1}_{J_1} \curlyvee \mathbb{R}^{I_2}_{J_2}$ means that whenever two edges can be found in the current swarm, leading from x to y and from x to y', labelled with two spiders $\mathcal{S}_1$ and $\mathcal{S}_2$, of the same color, such that, according to the rule of Spider Algebra ♣, query $\mathbb{R}^{I_1}_{J_1}$ can be applied to $\mathcal{S}_1$ and $\mathbb{R}^{I_2}_{J_2}$ can be applied to $\mathcal{S}_2$, there must be also a vertex x' in this swarm, with edges from x' to y and from x' to y', labelled with spiders $\mathbb{R}^{I_1}_{J_1}(\mathcal{S}_1)$ and $\mathbb{R}^{I_2}_{J_2}(\mathcal{S}_2)$. And analogously for $\mathbb{R}^{I_1}_{J_1} \curlywedge \mathbb{R}^{I_2}_{J_2}$.

So, at Abstraction Level One we no longer need to think about the details of spider anatomy but we are still constrained by the, hardly intuitive, rule ♣. At Abstraction Level 2 we are going to liberate ourselves also from this constraint.

Abstraction Level 2 language. Let now $\mathbb{A}_2$ be the subset of $\mathbb{A}$ consisting of all green (ideal) spiders which are of the form $☆^I$. The signature of Abstraction Level 2 language consists of one binary relation $H(\mathcal{S},\_,\_)$ for each $\mathcal{S} \in \mathbb{A}_2$. A structure over this signature will be called a *green graph.*

Notice that there is a natural bijection between $\mathbb{A}_2$ and $\bar{\mathbb{S}} = \mathbb{S} \cup \{\emptyset\}$, so we will often write[3] $H_i(x,y)$ instead of $H(☆^{\{i\}},x,y)$ and $H_\emptyset(x,y)$ instead of $H(☆,x,y)$.

Concerning the set $\mathbb{L}_2$, of *green graph rewriting rules*, for each four spiders $☆^{I_1} \neq ☆^{I_3}$, $☆^{I_2} \neq ☆^{I_4} \in \mathbb{A}_2$, there will be two rules in the set $\mathbb{L}_2$, denoted as: $I_1 \curlywedge I_2 \leftrightarrow I_3 \curlywedge I_4$ and as $I_1 \curlyvee I_2 \leftrightarrow I_3 \curlyvee I_4$ where $I_1 \curlywedge I_2 \leftrightarrow I_3 \curlywedge I_4$ is a shorthand of:

$$\forall x,x' \quad [\exists y\ \ H(☆^{I_1},x,y)\wedge H(☆^{I_2},x',y)] \Leftrightarrow$$
$$[\exists y\ \ H(☆^{I_3},x,y)\wedge H(☆^{I_4},x',y)]$$

and $I_1 \curlyvee I_2 \leftrightarrow I_3 \curlyvee I_4$ is a shorthand of:

$$\forall y,y' \quad [\exists x\ \ H(☆^{I_1},x,y)\wedge H(☆^{I_2},x,y')] \Leftrightarrow$$
$$[\exists x\ \ H(☆^{I_3},x,y)\wedge H(☆^{I_4},x,y')]$$

From now on it will be assumed that spiders $☆^3$ and $☆^4$ (that is – sets $\{3\}$ and $\{4\}$) do not occur in our sets of green graph rewriting rules.

[3] Having two alternative notations for the same object looks like asking for confusion. But see: when discussing Precompilation we need to relate Level Two language to Level One, so it is natural to use the notation where spiders are explicit. But then, in Sections 7 and 8 we do not need spiders any more, and we would hate to have the complicated tuples there as small subscripts. So $\bar{\mathbb{S}}$ fits us better than $\mathbb{A}_2$ there.

Compilation and its correctness. Swarm rewriting rules, as well as green graph rewriting rules, are first order sentences, and each of them is equivalent to a conjunction of tuple generating dependencies. So, for a set $\mathcal{T} \subseteq \mathbb{L}_1$ (or $\mathcal{T} \subseteq \mathbb{L}_2$) and a swarm (resp. green graph) $\mathbb{D}$ the statement $\mathbb{D} \models \mathcal{T}$ makes sense and also the notion of Chase applies to $\mathcal{T}$.

DEFINITION 7. *For a set* $\mathcal{T} \subseteq \mathbb{L}_1$ *let* $Compile(\mathcal{T}) =$
$= \{f \curlywedge f' : f \curlywedge f' \in \mathcal{T}\} \cup \{f \curlyvee f' : f \curlyvee f' \in \mathcal{T}\}$.

Which means "treat each rule from $\mathcal{T}$ as its analogue binary query from $\mathbb{F}^2$".

DEFINITION 8.
For a set $\mathcal{T} \subseteq \mathbb{L}_2$ *we define* $Precompile(\mathcal{T}) \subseteq \mathbb{L}_1$ *as the result of the following procedure:*

- $Precompile(\mathcal{T}) := \{\mathbb{R}_1^1 \curlywedge \mathbb{R}_2^2, \mathbb{R}_1^3 \curlywedge \mathbb{R}_2^4, \mathbb{R}^3 \curlywedge \mathbb{R}_3^4\}$
- *fix any numbering of the rules of* $\mathcal{T}$ *using natural numbers* $2, 3 \ldots k$;
- *for* $i = 2$ *to* k,

if the i'th rule in $\mathcal{T}$ *is* $I_1 \curlywedge I_2 \leftrightarrow I_3 \curlywedge I_4$ *then add to* $Precompile(\mathcal{T})$ *the rules* $\mathbb{R}_{2i+1}^{I_1} \curlywedge \mathbb{R}_{2i+2}^{I_2}$ *and* $\mathbb{R}_{2i+1}^{I_3} \curlywedge \mathbb{R}_{2i+2}^{I_4}$
and if the i'th rule in $\mathcal{T}$ *is* $I_1 \curlyvee I_2 \leftrightarrow I_3 \curlyvee I_4$ *then add to* $Precompile(\mathcal{T})$ *the rules* $\mathbb{R}_{2i+1}^{I_1} \curlyvee \mathbb{R}_{2i+2}^{I_2}$ *and* $\mathbb{R}_{2i+1}^{I_3} \curlyvee \mathbb{R}_{2i+2}^{I_4}$

REMARK 9. *The idea behind rules of the form* $\mathbb{R}_{2i+1}^{I_1} \curlywedge \mathbb{R}_{2i+2}^{I_2}$ *and* $\mathbb{R}_{2i+1}^{I_3} \curlywedge \mathbb{R}_{2i+2}^{I_4}$ *in* $Precompile(\mathcal{T})$ *is that they simulate (in a swarm), in two steps, one execution of* $I_1 \curlywedge I_2 \leftrightarrow I_3 \curlywedge I_4$ *(in a green graph). As a by-product, two red spiders are added to the swarm – labelled with* $\bigstar_{2i+1}$ *and* $\bigstar_{2i+2}$ *(the same for* $\curlyvee$ *instead of* $\curlywedge$*).*

DEFINITION 10.
- *Let* $\mathcal{Q} \subseteq \mathbb{F}^2$*. We will say that* $\mathcal{Q}$ leads to the red spider *(or* finitely leads to the red spider*) if and only if each (resp. each finite) structure* $\mathbb{D}$ *over* Σ*, such that* $\mathbb{D} \models \mathcal{T}_{\mathcal{Q}}$*, which contains a copy of the full green spider* $\star$*, also contains a copy of the full red spider* $\bigstar$.
- *Let* $\mathcal{T} \subseteq \mathbb{L}_1$*. We will say that* $\mathcal{T}$ leads to the red spider *(or* finitely leads to the red spider*) if each (resp. each finite) swarm* $\mathbb{D}$ *such that* $\mathbb{D} \models \mathcal{T}$*, which contains an atom of the relation* $H(\star, \_, \_)$*, also contains an atom of the relation* $H(\bigstar, \_, \_)$.
- *We say that a green graph contains a 1-2 pattern if contains edges* $H(\star^1, a, b)$ *and* $H(\star^2, a', b)$ *for some vertices* a, a', b.
- *Let* $\mathcal{T} \subseteq \mathbb{L}_2$*. We will say that* $\mathcal{T}$ leads to the red spider *(or* finitely leads to the red spider*) if each (resp. each finite) green graph* $\mathbb{D}$ *such that* $\mathbb{D} \models \mathcal{T}$ *which contains an atom of the relation* $H(\star, \_, \_)$ *also contains a 1-2 pattern*[4].

[4]Notice that it would make no sense to repeat, for $\mathcal{T} \subseteq \mathbb{L}_2$, the definition for $\mathcal{T} \subseteq \mathbb{L}_1$. This is because a green graph never has any atom of the relation $H(\bigstar, \_, \_)$. But (and please see it as an exercise) having a 1-2 pattern available, the set of rules $Precompile(\mathcal{T})$ will produce, in three steps, using rules $\mathbb{R}_1^1 \curlywedge \mathbb{R}_2^2$, $\mathbb{R}_1^3 \curlywedge \mathbb{R}_2^4$, $\mathbb{R}^3 \curlywedge \mathbb{R}_3^4$, an atom of $H(\bigstar, \_, \_)$.

LEMMA 11. *1. Let* $\mathcal{T} \subseteq \mathbb{L}_1$*. Then* $\mathcal{T}$ leads to the red spider *(or finitely leads to the red spider) if and only if* $Compile(\mathcal{T})$ *does.*

2. Let $\mathcal{T} \subseteq \mathbb{L}_2$*. Then* $\mathcal{T}$ leads to the red spider *(or finitely leads to the red spider) if and only if* $Precompile(\mathcal{T})$ *does.*

Proof of the Lemma can be found in the submitted version, which is available as an arXiv paper.
It is important to notice (see condition ❷ in Section 4) that:

OBSERVATION 12. *A set of queries* $\mathcal{Q} \subseteq \mathbb{F}^2$ *leads (finitely leads) to the red spider if and only if it (finitely) determines* $\exists^* dalt(\star)$ *(where* $\exists^*$ *means that all free variables are quantified, leading to a boolean query). So, by Lemma 11, since both Precompilation and Compilation are computable, in order to prove Theorem 5, it suffices to show that it is undecidable for a set* $\mathcal{T} \subseteq \mathbb{L}_2$ *whether* $\mathcal{T}$ *finitely leads to the red spider.*

From now on proof of Theorem 5 has nothing to do with spiders. It is all about green graphs and their rewriting rules.

7. A SEPARATING EXAMPLE

In this Section we are going to prove:

THEOREM 13. *There exists a set* $\mathfrak{T} \subseteq \mathbb{L}_2$ *of green graph rewriting rules which does not lead to the red spider, but finitely leads to the red spider.*

Notice that, by Lemma 11, this will imply that the set $Compile(Precompile(\mathfrak{T}))$ of conjunctive queries over Σ does not determine the query $\exists^* dalt(\star)$ but finitely determines it.

Here is how we are going to construct $\mathfrak{T}$:
Step 1. Let $\mathbb{D}_\star$ be a green graph containing just two vertices $\mathbf{a}, \mathbf{b}$ and one edge $H_\emptyset(\mathbf{a}, \mathbf{b})$ (the constants $\mathbf{a}$ and $\mathbf{b}$ from $\mathbb{D}_\star$ will be important, please befriend them). We will define a set $\mathfrak{T}_\infty$ of green graph rewriting rules such that $chase(\mathfrak{T}_\infty, \mathbb{D}_\star)$ is an infinite green graph (a sort of *infinite path*) without a 1-2 pattern.
Step 2. Another set $\mathfrak{T}_\boxplus$ of green graph rewriting rules will be constructed, and $\mathfrak{T}$ will be defined as the union of $\mathfrak{T}_\infty$ and $\mathfrak{T}_\boxplus$. The rules of $\mathfrak{T}_\boxplus$ will be quite complicated (or at least numerous) and it will follow from the construction that $\mathfrak{T}$ finitely leads to the red spider.
Step 3. We will construct (an infinite) green graph $\mathbb{M}$, containing $\mathbb{D}_\star$, without the 1-2 pattern, and such that $\mathbb{M} \models \mathfrak{T}$.

Step 1. Let $\mathfrak{T}_\infty$ consist of three green graph rewriting rules:
(I) $\emptyset \curlywedge \emptyset \leftrightarrow \alpha \curlywedge \eta_1$ (II) $\emptyset \curlyvee \eta_1 \leftrightarrow \eta_0 \curlyvee \beta_1$ (III) $\emptyset \curlywedge \eta_0 \leftrightarrow \eta_1 \curlywedge \beta_0$
where α, β_0 and η_0 are some even numbers from $\mathbb{S}$, and β_1 and η_1 are odd.

Let us try to construct $chase(\mathfrak{T}_\infty, \mathbb{D}_\star)$. We begin from a single edge $H_\emptyset(\mathbf{a}, \mathbf{b})$. The only rule that can be applied to this structure is (I). A new vertex b_1 is then created, together with two edges: $H_\alpha(\mathbf{a}, b_1)$ and $H_{\eta_1}(\mathbf{a}, b_1)$. In the next step the only way is to use rule (II), as we have $H_\emptyset(\mathbf{a}, \mathbf{b})$ and $H_{\eta_1}(\mathbf{a}, b_1)$ sharing the beginning vertex. We get a new

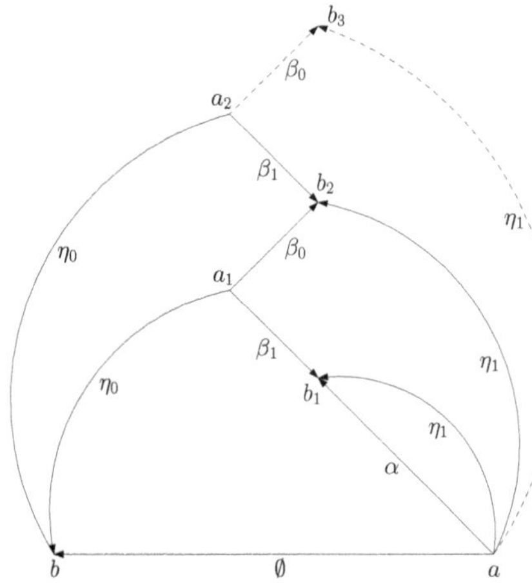

Figure 1: The structure $chase(\mathfrak{T}_\infty, \mathbb{D}_{\star})$ *in statu nascendi*. Notice (this will be important in Section 9) that $chase_{i+1}(\mathfrak{T}_\infty, \mathbb{D}_{\star})$ is always a result of exactly one application of a rule from $\mathfrak{T}_\infty$ to elements of $chase_i(\mathfrak{T}_\infty, \mathbb{D}_{\star})$.

vertex a_1 and new edges $H_{\eta_0}(a_1, \mathbf{b})$ and $H_{\beta_1}(a_1, b_1)$. In the third step we can apply rule (III) to $H_\emptyset(\mathbf{a}, \mathbf{b})$ and $H_{\eta_0}(a_1, \mathbf{b})$, creating b_2 with $H_{\eta_1}(\mathbf{a}, b_2)$ and $H_{\beta_0}(a_1, b_2)$. And so on – using rules (II) and (III) alternately we construct (see Fig. 1) infinite sequences $b_1, b_2 \dots$ of vertices with out-degree 0 and $a_1, a_2 \dots$ of vertices with in-degree 0, connected, in a regular way, with edges labelled with β_0 and β_1.

Seeing a green graph as a set of words (in parity glasses). It is standard to see paths in a directed labelled graph as words:

DEFINITION 14. *Let $\mathfrak{M}$ be a green graph with s, t among its vertices. Then paths($\mathfrak{M}, s, t$) is the set of all such words $\mathfrak{w} \in \mathbb{S}^*$ that, had $\mathfrak{M}$ been a nondeterministic finite automaton, with the initial state s and a single accepting state t, it would accept $\mathfrak{w}$, but it would not accept any nonempty proper prefix of $\mathfrak{w}$.*

It will be crucial for us to see green graphs as complicated sets of words. But unfortunately in the interesting graphs, all directed paths will have length 1. Each vertex will either have out-degree 0 or in-degree 0 (see Figure 1). This is why we need Parity Glasses (reminder: elements of $\mathbb{S}$ are natural numbers).

DEFINITION 15. *Let $\mathfrak{M}$ be a green graph containing $\mathbb{D}_{\star}$ (which means that $\mathfrak{M}$ has an edge $H_{\star}(\mathbf{a}, \mathbf{b})$). Then:*

- *$PG(\mathfrak{M})$ is the graph resulting from $\mathfrak{M}$ by:*
  1. *Removing all the edges labelled with $\emptyset$;*
  2. *reversing the direction of all edges labelled with odd numbers.*
- *$words(\mathfrak{M}) = paths(PG(\mathfrak{M}), \mathbf{a}, \mathbf{a}) \cup paths(PG(\mathfrak{M}), \mathbf{a}, \mathbf{b})$.*

Example. $words(chase(\mathfrak{T}_\infty, \mathbb{D}_{\star})) =$

$$= \{\alpha(\beta_1\beta_0)^k\eta_1 : k \in \mathbb{N}\} \cup \{\alpha(\beta_1\beta_0)^k\beta_1\eta_0 : k \in \mathbb{N}\}$$

By an $\alpha\beta$-path in a green graph $\mathbb{M}$ we mean a sequence of edges (or vertices, it will be always clear from the context),

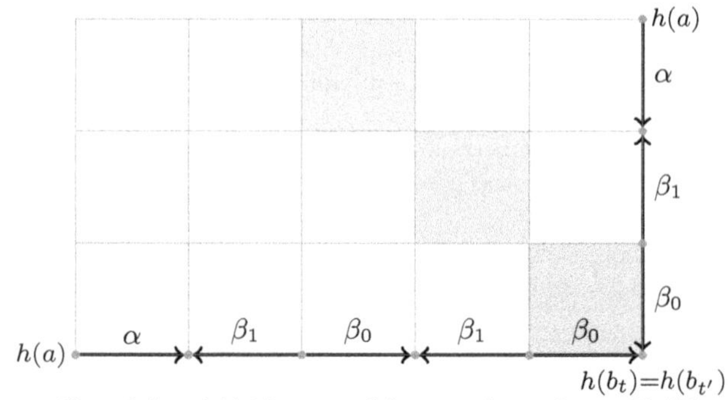

Figure 2: Long initial fragments of the two paths are also equal in $\mathbb{M}$ but we are never going to use this fact, and it is not indicated on the picture.

which seen as a word in $PG(\mathbb{M})$ is of the form $\alpha(\beta_1\beta_0)^*$. There are infinitely many $\alpha\beta$-paths in $chase(\mathfrak{T}_\infty, \mathbb{D}_{\star})$, including for example the path $\mathbf{a}, b_1, a_1, b_2$ and also the path $\mathbf{a}, b_1, a_1, b_2, a_3, b_3$ (see Figure 1).

Step 2. When a set $\mathcal{T}$ of green graph rewriting rules leads to the red spider then this fact is – at least in principle – easy to prove. One just builds $chase(\mathcal{T}, \mathbb{D}_{\star})$ until a 1-2 pattern emerges. But how could we possibly prove that $\mathfrak{T}$ (which still remains to be defined, but which is **not** going to lead to the red spider) does **finitely** lead to the red spider?

The last means that a 1-2 pattern must emerge in *every* finite model of $\mathcal{T}$ containing $\mathbb{D}_{\star}$. Is there anything that we know for sure about *every* finite model of $\mathcal{T}$ containing $\mathbb{D}_{\star}$? Yes, we know[5] that for each such model $\mathbb{M}$ there exists a homomorphism $h : chase(\mathcal{T}, \mathbb{D}_{\star}) \to \mathbb{M}$. Our $\mathfrak{T}$ is going to be a superset of $\mathfrak{T}_\infty$ so $chase(\mathfrak{T}, \mathbb{D}_{\star})$ will contain, as a substructure, the structure $chase(\mathfrak{T}_\infty, \mathbb{D}_{\star})$ that we analyzed in Step 1. This means that there for sure will be two vertices $b_t \neq b_{t'}$, such that (remember – $\mathbb{M}$ is finite) $h(b_t) = h(b_{t'})$. This means that there are two $\alpha\beta$-paths in $\mathbb{M}$: $h(a), h(b_1), h(a_1), \dots, h(b_t)$ and $h(a), h(b_1), h(a_1) \dots h(b_{t'})$), having **different** lengths, which share the endpoint (see Figure 2, do not look at the grid yet).

The set $\mathfrak{T}_{\boxplus}$ will be designed to detect such two $\alpha\beta$-paths and – after detecting them – to create a 1-2 pattern. Figure 2 explains how this will be done: the rules of $\mathfrak{T}_{\boxplus}$ will build a grid whose eastern border will be exactly the $\alpha\beta$-path $h(\mathbf{a}), h(b_1), h(a_1) \dots h(b_t)$ and whose southern border will be the path $h(\mathbf{a}), h(b_1), h(a_1) \dots h(b_{t'})$.

This will be of course done step by step – as a result of a single application of a rule from $\mathfrak{T}_{\boxplus}$ one little square of the grid will be created. For such a step a rule will need the southern and eastern edge of the little square to exist, and it will add the western and northern edge[6]. After the complete grid is built the rules of $\mathfrak{T}$ will somehow check whether the northwestern corner of the grid is on the diagonal of the grid. If it is not, then indeed the $\alpha\beta$-paths $h(\mathbf{a}), h(b_1), h(a_1) \dots h(b_t)$ and $h(\mathbf{a}), h(b_1), h(a_1) \dots h(b_{t'})$ were of different lengths.

While the idea is simple, for the real construction we need 41 green graph rewriting rules and $4 \times 2^3 = 32$ binary re-

[5]The fact that Chase is a universal structure is one of the textbook facts of database theory [13].

[6]See – adding two missing edges of a square is exactly what green graph rewriting rules are good at.

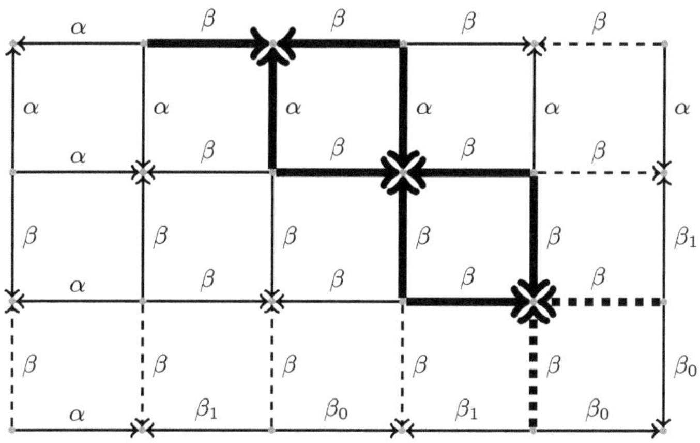

Figure 3: Grid constructed by $\mathfrak{T}_{\boxplus}$. Diagonal ("d") edges are bold and border ("b") edges are dashed. Labels of the edges in the NW-corner are $\langle n, \alpha, \bar{d}, \bar{b}\rangle$ and $\langle w, \alpha, \bar{d}, \bar{b}\rangle$ so they form a 1-2 pattern.

lations for the inner edges of the grid (by which we mean edges not belonging to one of the two $\alpha\beta$-paths, so that inner vertices, in our sense, also include western and northern border). The names of the 32 relations (or labels of the green graphs edges) will be conveniently encoded[7] as $\langle n|e|s|w, \alpha|\beta, d|\bar{d}, b|\bar{b}\rangle$ (where | is the BNF "or"). We will treat that $\langle n, \alpha, \bar{d}, \bar{b}\rangle$ is 1 and $\langle w, \alpha, \bar{d}, \bar{b}\rangle$ is 2, where 1 and 2 are the ones from 1-2-pattern.

The first parameter of a label of en edge – one of n, e, s, w – is the direction the edge heads. The second – α or β – is inherited from the "respective" element of one of the original $\alpha\beta$-paths. The parameter d (or $\bar{d}$) tells us whether one of the ends of the edge is (or is not) on the diagonal of the grid (see Figure 3). The fourth parameter (needed in Step 3) tells if an edge shares a vertex with one of the original $\alpha\beta$-paths.

Now, once we understand the sense of the parameters, it is time to see **the rules of $\mathfrak{T}_{\boxplus}$**:

$\beta_0 \curlywedge \beta_0 \leftrightarrow \langle n, \beta, d, b\rangle \curlywedge \langle w, \beta, d, b\rangle$

The above rule (call it *grid triggering rule*) creates the tile in the south-eastern corner of the grid. The next four are:

$\beta_1 \curlyvee \langle n, \beta, d, b\rangle \leftrightarrow \langle s, \beta, \bar{d}, b\rangle \curlyvee \langle e, \beta, d, \bar{b}\rangle$
$\beta_0 \curlywedge \langle s, \beta, \bar{d}, b\rangle \leftrightarrow \langle n, \beta, \bar{d}, b\rangle \curlywedge \langle w, \beta, \bar{d}, \bar{b}\rangle$
$\beta_1 \curlyvee \langle n, \beta, \bar{d}, b\rangle \leftrightarrow \langle s, \beta, \bar{d}, b\rangle \curlyvee \langle e, \beta, \bar{d}, \bar{b}\rangle$
$\alpha \curlywedge \langle s, \beta, \bar{d}, b\rangle \leftrightarrow \langle n, \beta, \bar{d}, b\rangle \curlywedge \langle w, \alpha, \bar{d}, \bar{b}\rangle$

They build the strip of tiles adjacent to the southern edge of the rectangle. Analogously, the strip of tiles adjacent to the eastern edge of the rectangle will be built by the four rules:

$\beta_1 \curlyvee \langle w, \beta, d, b\rangle \leftrightarrow \langle e, \beta, \bar{d}, b\rangle \curlyvee \langle s, \beta, d, \bar{b}\rangle$
$\beta_0 \curlywedge \langle e, \beta, \bar{d}, b\rangle \leftrightarrow \langle w, \beta, \bar{d}, b\rangle \curlywedge \langle n, \beta, \bar{d}, \bar{b}\rangle$
$\beta_1 \curlyvee \langle w, \beta, \bar{d}, b\rangle \leftrightarrow \langle e, \beta, \bar{d}, b\rangle \curlyvee \langle s, \beta, \bar{d}, \bar{b}\rangle$
$\alpha \curlywedge \langle w, \beta, \bar{d}, b\rangle \leftrightarrow \langle w, \beta, \bar{d}, b\rangle \curlywedge \langle n, \alpha, \bar{d}, \bar{b}\rangle$

Now last 32 rules of $\mathfrak{T}_{\boxplus}$ are coming, which will build the interior of the rectangle (including the strips adjacent to the northern and western borders). Due to the space limit we write them as two schemes, each representing 16 rules:

[7]Which, precisely speaking, means that we assume there is some fixed bijection between our new set of codes and some subset of $\mathbb{S}$ and that we identify a code with its image under this bijection. We of course assume that this subset is disjoint with $\{\alpha, \beta_0, \beta_1, \eta_0, \eta_1\}$.

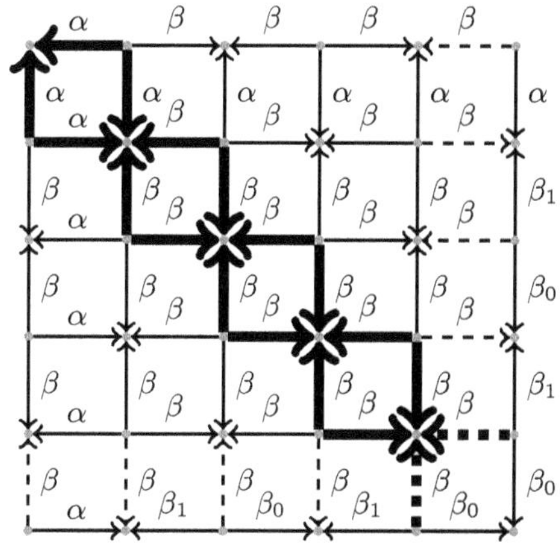

Figure 4: Grid $\mathbb{M}_3$. No 1-2 pattern.

$\langle e, \Theta, X, \bar{b}\rangle \curlywedge \langle s, \Omega, Y, \bar{b}\rangle \leftrightarrow \langle n, \Omega, X, \bar{b}\rangle \curlywedge \langle w, \Theta, Y, \bar{b}\rangle$
for each $X, Y \in \{d, \bar{d}\}$ and for each $\Theta, \Omega \in \{\alpha, \beta\}$.

$\langle w, \Theta, X, \bar{b}\rangle \curlyvee \langle n, \Omega, Y, \bar{b}\rangle \leftrightarrow \langle s, \Omega, X, \bar{b}\rangle \curlyvee \langle e, \Theta, Y, \bar{b}\rangle$
for each $X, Y \in \{d, \bar{d}\}$ and for each $\Theta, \Omega \in \{\alpha, \beta\}$.

Now it follows from the construction that:

LEMMA 16. *$\mathfrak{T} = \mathfrak{T}_{\boxplus} \cup \mathfrak{T}_{\infty}$ finitely leads to the red spider.*

Step 3. Since now we are going to build an infinite model $\mathbb{M}$ for $\mathfrak{T}$, we can afford having $chase(\mathfrak{T}_{\infty}, \mathbb{D}_{☆})$ as a substructure of $\mathbb{M}$ and we do not need to identify any of its vertices. But (unfortunately) the grid triggering rule still can be applied – this is since the edge labels in the left hand side of the first rule of $\mathfrak{T}_{\boxplus}$ are equal, which means that for each edge $H_{\beta_0}(a_t, b_{t+1})$ in $chase(\mathfrak{T}_{\infty}, \mathbb{D}_{☆})$ a new vertex, call it c_t and two new edges, both leading from a_t to c_t, will be created, namely $H_{\langle n,\beta,d,b\rangle}(a_t, c_t)$ and $H_{\langle w,\beta,d,b\rangle}(a_t, c_t)$. Then the construction from **Step 2** can be repeated, leading to a new grid $\mathbb{M}_t$ (see Figure 4), constructed in the way described in **Step 2** but without a 1-2 pattern. Notice that the picture does not fully reflect the reality here[8] – in the real green graph the respective vertices of the southern and eastern borders of $\mathbb{M}_t$ are equal.

Each of $\mathbb{M}_t$ contains some vertices and atoms of $chase(\mathfrak{T}_{\infty}, \mathbb{D}_{☆})$ so, for $t \leq t'$ the intersection of $\mathbb{M}_t$ and $\mathbb{M}_{t'}$ is exactly the $\alpha\beta$-path $\mathbf{a}, b_1, a_1 \ldots b_t$. Define the structure $\mathbb{M} = chase(\mathfrak{T}_{\infty}, \mathbb{D}_{☆}) \cup \bigcup_{t \in \mathbb{N}} \mathbb{M}_t$. Theorem 13 follows from:

LEMMA 17. 1. *$\mathbb{M}$ does not contain a 1-2 pattern.*

2. *$\mathbb{M} \models \mathfrak{T}$*

For the (easy) proof of Lemma 17 see the Appendix.

8. PROOF OF THEOREM 5

In $\mathfrak{T}_{\infty}$ we had η_0 and η_1 calling each other in an infinite loop, and creating an infinite $\alpha\beta$-path. By homomorphism argument, in presence of such a path, the rules of $\mathfrak{T}_{\boxplus}$ lead to

[8]Neither Figure 3 did, but in the context of **Step 2** we only needed to prove that some pattern **will** appear in the constructed green graph, so – as we were still able to prove it – we could pretend that we did not notice that some of the vertices were pairwise equal.

a 1-2 pattern. Now this simple mutual recursive call will be controlled by something undecidably complicated – a rainworm.

8.1 RAINWORM MACHINE. AND HOW IT CREEPS.

Rainworm machine (RM), which we will now define, is a version of (oblivious) Turing Machine, with (potentially) right-infinite tape. Alike standard Turing Machine a rainworm machine is described by the finite set of states $\mathfrak{Q}$, finite tape alphabet $\mathfrak{A}$, finite set of instructions Δ, and an initial configuration.

The "head" of a rainworm machine is always located **not** above one of the cells (like in a usual Turing Machine), but between two consecutive cells (or right to the rightmost cell). So a configuration of an RM can be in a natural way seen as a word from the language $(\mathfrak{A} + \mathfrak{Q})^*$.

The set of states $\mathfrak{Q}$ of a rainworm machine is a disjoint union of $\mathfrak{Q}_0^{\rightarrow}$, $\mathfrak{Q}_0^{\leftarrow}$, $\mathfrak{Q}_1^{\rightarrow}$, $\mathfrak{Q}_1^{\leftarrow}$, of $\mathfrak{Q}_{\gamma_0}^{\rightarrow}$, $\mathfrak{Q}_{\gamma_1}^{\rightarrow}$ and of $\{\eta_{11}, \eta_0, \eta_1\}$.

The finite tape alphabet $\mathfrak{A}$ is a disjoint union of sets $\mathfrak{A}_0$, $\mathfrak{A}_1$ and $\{\alpha, \beta_0, \beta_1, \gamma_0, \gamma_1, \omega_0\}$.

The set Δ of instructions consists of some number of instructions of any of the following forms[9]:

$\Diamond_1$: $\eta_{11} \rightsquigarrow \gamma_1\eta_0$

$\Diamond_2$: $\eta_0 \rightsquigarrow \mathfrak{b}\eta_1$ where $\mathfrak{b} \in \mathfrak{A}_0$

$\Diamond_3$: $\eta_1 \rightsquigarrow \mathfrak{q}\omega_0$ where $\mathfrak{q} \in \mathfrak{Q}_1^{\leftarrow}$

$\Diamond_4$: $\mathfrak{b}'\mathfrak{q} \rightsquigarrow \mathfrak{q}'\mathfrak{b}$ where $\mathfrak{q} \in \mathfrak{Q}_0^{\leftarrow}$, $\mathfrak{q}' \in \mathfrak{Q}_1^{\leftarrow}$, $\mathfrak{b} \in \mathfrak{A}_0$ and $\mathfrak{b}' \in \mathfrak{A}_1$
$\Diamond_{4'}$: $\mathfrak{b}\mathfrak{q}' \rightsquigarrow \mathfrak{q}\mathfrak{b}'$ where $\mathfrak{q} \in \mathfrak{Q}_0^{\leftarrow}$, $\mathfrak{q}' \in \mathfrak{Q}_1^{\leftarrow}$, $\mathfrak{b} \in \mathfrak{A}_0$ and $\mathfrak{b}' \in \mathfrak{A}_1$

$\Diamond_5$: $\gamma_1\mathfrak{q} \rightsquigarrow \beta_1\mathfrak{q}'$ where $\mathfrak{q} \in \mathfrak{Q}_0^{\leftarrow}$, $\mathfrak{q}' \in \mathfrak{Q}_{\gamma_0}^{\rightarrow}$
$\Diamond_{5'}$: $\gamma_0\mathfrak{q} \rightsquigarrow \beta_0\mathfrak{q}'$ where $\mathfrak{q} \in \mathfrak{Q}_1^{\leftarrow}$, $\mathfrak{q}' \in \mathfrak{Q}_{\gamma_1}^{\rightarrow}$

$\Diamond_6$: $\mathfrak{q}\mathfrak{b} \rightsquigarrow \gamma_1\mathfrak{q}'$ where $\mathfrak{q} \in \mathfrak{Q}_{\gamma_1}^{\rightarrow}$, $\mathfrak{q}' \in \mathfrak{Q}_0^{\rightarrow}$, $\mathfrak{b} \in \mathfrak{A}_0$
$\Diamond_{6'}$: $\mathfrak{q}\mathfrak{b} \rightsquigarrow \gamma_0\mathfrak{q}'$ where $\mathfrak{q} \in \mathfrak{Q}_{\gamma_0}^{\rightarrow}$, $\mathfrak{q}' \in \mathfrak{Q}_1^{\rightarrow}$, $\mathfrak{b} \in \mathfrak{A}_1$

$\Diamond_7$: $\mathfrak{q}'\mathfrak{b} \rightsquigarrow \mathfrak{b}'\mathfrak{q}$ where $\mathfrak{q} \in \mathfrak{Q}_0^{\rightarrow}$, $\mathfrak{q}' \in \mathfrak{Q}_1^{\rightarrow}$, $\mathfrak{b} \in \mathfrak{A}_0$ and $\mathfrak{b}' \in \mathfrak{A}_1$
$\Diamond_{7'}$: $\mathfrak{q}\mathfrak{b}' \rightsquigarrow \mathfrak{b}\mathfrak{q}'$ where $\mathfrak{q} \in \mathfrak{Q}_0^{\rightarrow}$, $\mathfrak{q}' \in \mathfrak{Q}_1^{\rightarrow}$, $\mathfrak{b} \in \mathfrak{A}_0$ and $\mathfrak{b}' \in \mathfrak{A}_1$

$\Diamond_8$: $\mathfrak{q}\omega_0 \rightsquigarrow \mathfrak{b}\eta_0$ where $\mathfrak{q} \in \mathfrak{Q}_1^{\rightarrow}$ and $\mathfrak{b} \in \mathfrak{A}_1$

We require the set Δ of instructions to be a partial function[10] – two different instructions must have different left hand sides.

The initial configuration of the machine is $\alpha\eta_{11}$.

As we said before, a configuration of an RM can be in a natural way seen as a word from the language $(\mathfrak{A} + \mathfrak{Q})^*$, so Δ is formulated in the language of Thue semisystem rules[11]. A single computation step of an RM can (should) be seen as a single application of a Thue semi-system rewriting. Following the standard Thue systems notational convention the notation $\mathfrak{w} \rightsquigarrow_\Delta \mathfrak{v}$ means that $\mathfrak{w} = \mathfrak{w}_1\mathfrak{s}\mathfrak{w}_2$ and $\mathfrak{v} = \mathfrak{w}_1\mathfrak{t}\mathfrak{w}_2$ for some rule $\mathfrak{s} \rightsquigarrow \mathfrak{t}$ in Δ. We also use $\overset{k}{\rightsquigarrow}_\Delta$ to denote the k'th power of relation $\rightsquigarrow_\Delta$, $\overset{*}{\rightsquigarrow}_\Delta$ to denote the transitive closure of $\rightsquigarrow_\Delta$ and $\overset{*}{\leftrightsquigarrow}_\Delta$ to denote the symmetric transitive closure of $\rightsquigarrow_\Delta$ (i.e. the smallest equivalence relation having $\rightsquigarrow_\Delta$ as a subset).

While a configuration of a rainworm machine can be always seen as a word, it is clear that not all words from $(\mathfrak{A} + \mathfrak{Q})^*$ make sense as configurations:

DEFINITION 18. *Call symbols in* $\{\alpha, \beta_0, \gamma_0, \eta_0\} \cup \mathfrak{Q}_0^{\rightarrow} \cup \mathfrak{Q}_0^{\leftarrow} \cup \mathfrak{Q}_{\gamma_0}^{\rightarrow} \cup \mathfrak{A}_0$ even *and symbols in* $\{\beta_1, \gamma_1, \eta_1, \eta_{11}\} \cup \mathfrak{Q}_1^{\rightarrow} \cup \mathfrak{Q}_1^{\leftarrow} \cup \mathfrak{Q}_{\gamma_1}^{\rightarrow} \cup \mathfrak{A}_1$ odd. *A word* $\mathfrak{w} \in (\mathfrak{A}+\mathfrak{Q})^*$ *is an RM configuration, if:*

1. $\mathfrak{w} \in \mathfrak{A}^+\mathfrak{Q}\mathfrak{A}^*$ *(which means there is exactly one symbol in* $\mathfrak{w}$ *which symbolizes the head of the machine);*
2. *the last symbol of* $\mathfrak{w}$ *is one of* η_{11}, η_0, η_1, ω_0;
3. *odd and even symbols occur in* $\mathfrak{w}$ *alternately (there are never two odd or two even symbols next to each other);*
4. $\mathfrak{w}$ *is of the form* $\mathfrak{w}_1\mathfrak{w}_2$ *where* $\mathfrak{w}_1$ *is of the form* $\alpha(\beta_1\beta_0)^*$ *or* $\alpha(\beta_1\beta_0)^*\beta_1$, $\mathfrak{w}_2$ *begins with* γ_0 *or* γ_1 *or an element of* $\mathfrak{Q}_{\gamma_0}^{\rightarrow}$ *or an element of* $\mathfrak{Q}_{\gamma_1}^{\rightarrow}$ *or* $\mathfrak{w}_2 = \eta_{11}$, *and none of* α, β_0, β_1 *occur in* $\mathfrak{w}_2$.

Proof of the following lemma is straightforward case inspection and induction:

LEMMA 19. *Let* $\alpha\eta_{11} \overset{*}{\rightsquigarrow}_\Delta \mathfrak{w}$. *Then* $\mathfrak{w}$ *is an RM configuration.*

Now we are going to explain – informally – how a rainworm creeps. Imagine $\mathfrak{w}$ like in Lemma 19 and let $\mathfrak{w} = \mathfrak{w}_1\mathfrak{w}_2$ be as in Definition 18(4). Suppose the last symbol of $\mathfrak{w}_2$ is η_0. Think of $\mathfrak{w}_2$ as of a rainworm (η_0 being its front and γ_0 or γ_1 being its rear end) and of $\mathfrak{w}_1$ as of the slime trail a rainworm leaves behind. Now there is at most one thing we can do (since Δ is a partial function) – we can use some rule of the form $\Diamond_2$ to rewrite η_0 into $\mathfrak{b}\eta_1$ for some $\mathfrak{b}$. Our rainworm has grown one symbol longer! In the next step we can[12] use a rule of the form $\Diamond_3$ to rewrite η_1 into $\mathfrak{q}\omega_0$ for some $\mathfrak{q} \in \mathfrak{Q}_1^{\leftarrow}$. The rainworm has grown one symbol longer again, but now the head[13] is no longer in front of the animal. The state of the head is from $\mathfrak{Q}_1^{\leftarrow} \cup \mathfrak{Q}_0^{\leftarrow}$ now. The head will now move, cell by cell, towards the rear end of the rainworm (applying rules $\Diamond_4$ and $\Diamond_4'$ alternately) rewriting the symbols from $\mathfrak{A}_0 \cup \mathfrak{A}_1$ it passes on its way. Then, after γ_1 (or γ_0) is reached, it is rewritten, by some rule of he form $\Diamond_5$ (or $\Diamond_5'$) into β_1 (or β_0). The rear end of the rainworm moves towards the front, but the slime trail gets one symbol longer!

Now – since the last rule used was one of $\Diamond_5$ (or $\Diamond_5'$) – the state is one from $\mathfrak{Q}_{\gamma_0}^{\rightarrow}$ (or $\mathfrak{Q}_{\gamma_1}^{\rightarrow}$), so the next rewriting will move the head to the right and replace the first symbol from $\mathfrak{A}_1$ it encounters with γ_0 (or, resp. the first symbol from $\mathfrak{A}_0$ with γ_1). Only rules of the form $\Diamond_7$ or $\Diamond_7'$ will be applicable then, and the head will keep moving right (and rewriting the tape symbols on its way), towards the front of the rainworm, until ω_0 is found. Then a rule of the form $\Diamond_8$ will be used, and we will be back to the original situation, with η_0 as the rightmost symbol. Notice that the rainworm is longer now (we added one symbol twice and removed one symbol once) and also the slime trail (which is an $\alpha\beta$-path in the making) is longer (we added one symbol). Given Δ, there are of course two possibilities – either the rainworm will creep forever, leaving behind an infinite $\alpha\beta$-slime trail or, at

[9]Do not give up! An informal explanation will come.

[10]In other words, this condition means that rainworm machine is a deterministic computation model.

[11]See e.g. our paper [11]. Or [4] if you prefer a more serious introduction

[12]We should repeat here, and in several other places in this paragraph, that "there is at most one thing we can do now".

[13]Head in the Turing machine sense, rainworms have neither head nor tail. They have front and rear.

some point, no rule will be applicable, and the process will terminate. It is easy to prove, using textbook techniques, that:

LEMMA 20. *The problem whether, for given Δ, the rainworm*[14] *creeps forever, is undecidable.*

8.2 CREEPING BACK AND FORTH

It is not going to surprise anyone that our next goal is to translate Δ into a set of green graph rewriting rules. But, unlike rainworm machine instructions, green graph rewriting rules are symmetric. This is how we deal with it:

LEMMA 21. *1. If $\mathfrak{w} \overset{*}{\rightsquigarrow}_\Delta \mathfrak{v}$ and $\mathfrak{v}$ is an RM-configuration then $\mathfrak{w}$ satisfies conditions (1)-(3) of Definition 18.*

2. If $\mathfrak{w}$ satisfies condition (1) of Definition 18 then there exists at most one $\mathfrak{v}$ such that $\mathfrak{w} \rightsquigarrow_\Delta \mathfrak{v}$.

3. There is a constant c_Δ, such that if $\mathfrak{v}$ satisfies condition (1) of Definition 18 then there exist at most c_Δ words $\mathfrak{w}$ such that $\mathfrak{w} \rightsquigarrow_\Delta \mathfrak{v}$.

Proof: First claim can be proved by straightforward case inspection and induction. The second and the third follow easily from the construction of Δ (remember that Δ is a partial function). □

Now suppose, till the end of this subsection, **that the computation of a rainworm machine with the set of instructions Δ terminates**, after some number k_Δ of steps, which means that there is $\mathfrak{u}_\Delta$ such that $\alpha\eta_{11} \overset{k_\Delta}{\rightsquigarrow}_\Delta \mathfrak{u}_\Delta$ and no rule from Δ can be applied to $\mathfrak{u}_\Delta$ any more. Then:

LEMMA 22. *1. $\{\mathfrak{w} : \mathfrak{w} \overset{*}{\leftrightsquigarrow}_\Delta \alpha\eta_{11}\} = \{\mathfrak{w} : \mathfrak{w} \overset{*}{\rightsquigarrow}_\Delta \mathfrak{u}_\Delta\}$.*

2. If $\mathfrak{w} \overset{*}{\rightsquigarrow}_\Delta \mathfrak{u}_\Delta$ then $\mathfrak{w}$ satisfies cond. (4) of Definition 18.

3. If $\mathfrak{w} \overset{k}{\rightsquigarrow}_\Delta \mathfrak{u}_\Delta$ then $k \leq k_\Delta$.

4. The set $\{\mathfrak{w} : \mathfrak{w} \overset{*}{\rightsquigarrow}_\Delta \mathfrak{u}_\Delta\}$ is finite.

Proof: First claim follows from Lemma 21: to reach any vertex of a tree (and, due to Lemma 21(2) the interesting part of the $\rightsquigarrow_\Delta$-graph is a tree) from a leaf, it is enough to go up to the root and then down. For the proof of the second claim notice that it of course holds for $\mathfrak{u}_\Delta$, and that if it holds for some $\mathfrak{v}_2$, and $\mathfrak{v}_1 \rightsquigarrow_\Delta \mathfrak{v}_2$ then it also holds for $\mathfrak{v}_1$.

To see why the third claim is true notice that it follows from the construction of Δ that, while of course for a configuration $\mathfrak{w}$ of Δ and for a $k \in \mathbb{N}$ there may very well be two different configurations $\mathfrak{v}$ and $\mathfrak{v}'$ such that $\mathfrak{v} \overset{k}{\rightsquigarrow}_\Delta \mathfrak{w}$ and $\mathfrak{v}' \overset{k}{\rightsquigarrow}_\Delta \mathfrak{w}$, always in such case $\mathfrak{v}$ and $\mathfrak{v}'$ will be of equal length and the machine head (that is the symbol from $\mathfrak{Q}$) will be in the same place in $\mathfrak{v}$ and $\mathfrak{v}'$.
Last claim follows from the third and from Lemma 21(3). □

[14]Given Δ, the sets $\mathfrak{Q}$ and $\mathfrak{A}$ can be reconstructed.

8.3 FROM RAINWORMS TO GREEN GRAPH RULES.

For a rainworm machine Δ we define the set $\mathfrak{T}_\Delta$ of green graph rewriting rules as follows:

- Rules $\emptyset\curlywedge\emptyset \leftrightarrow \alpha\curlywedge\eta_{11}$ and $\eta_{11}\curlyvee\emptyset \leftrightarrow \gamma_1\curlyvee\eta_0$ are in $\mathfrak{T}_\Delta$;
- $\eta_0\curlywedge\emptyset \leftrightarrow \mathfrak{b}\curlywedge\eta_1$ is in $\mathfrak{T}_\Delta$ if $\eta_0 \rightsquigarrow \mathfrak{b}\eta_1$ is in Δ;
- $\eta_1\curlyvee\emptyset \leftrightarrow \mathfrak{q}\curlyvee\omega_0$ is in $\mathfrak{T}_\Delta$ if $\eta_1 \rightsquigarrow \mathfrak{q}\omega_0$ is in Δ;
- $\mathfrak{x}\curlyvee\mathfrak{t} \leftrightarrow \mathfrak{x}'\curlyvee\mathfrak{t}'$ is in $\mathfrak{T}_\Delta$ if $\mathfrak{x}\mathfrak{t} \rightsquigarrow \mathfrak{x}'\mathfrak{t}'$ is an instruction of the form $\diamondsuit_4$, $\diamondsuit_5$, $\diamondsuit_6$, $\diamondsuit_7$ or $\diamondsuit_8$ in Δ;
- $\mathfrak{x}\curlywedge\mathfrak{t} \leftrightarrow \mathfrak{x}'\curlywedge\mathfrak{t}'$ is in $\mathfrak{T}_\Delta$ if $\mathfrak{x}\mathfrak{t} \rightsquigarrow \mathfrak{x}'\mathfrak{t}'$ is an instruction of the form $\diamondsuit'_4$, $\diamondsuit'_5$, $\diamondsuit'_6$ or $\diamondsuit'_7$ in Δ.

Now, **in view of Lemma 11 and Lemma 20, in order to prove Theorem 5 it is enough to show:**

LEMMA 23. *For given Δ, the rainworm creeps forever (i.e. rainworm machine with Δ as its set of instructions never halts) if and only if the set $\mathfrak{T}^{\boxplus}_\Delta = \mathfrak{T}_\Delta \cup \mathfrak{T}_{\boxplus}$ of green graph rewriting rules finitely leads to the red spider.*

For the proof of Lemma 23 see the Appendix.

9. FO NON-REWRITABILITY. PROOF OF THEOREM 2 (OUTLINE).

It is not hard to guess what is going to be our $\mathcal{Q}$ and Q (notations as in Section 1.2) – we only know one example of a set of CQs which finitely determines another query but does not determine it. So – let $\mathcal{Q} = \mathit{Compile}(\mathit{Precompile}(\mathfrak{T}))$ and $Q = \exists^*\mathit{dalt}(\star)$. We need to produce, for a given $l \in \mathbb{N}$, two structures, $\mathbb{D}_y$ and $\mathbb{D}_n$, over Σ (we are back to Abstraction Level 0) such that $\mathbb{D}_y$ contains a copy of $\mathit{dalt}(\star)$, $\mathbb{D}_n$ does not contain one, but the views $\mathcal{Q}(\mathbb{D}_y)$ and $\mathcal{Q}(\mathbb{D}_n)$ are not distinguishable by a FO Ehrenfeucht-Fraisse game with l rounds.

Before we go any further we need to understand well enough the sense of $\mathcal{T}_\mathcal{Q}$ – the set of green-red TGDs generated by $\mathcal{Q}$. For simplicity, instead of $\mathcal{Q}$, let us concentrate on $\mathcal{Q}_\infty = \mathit{Compile}(\mathit{Precompile}(\mathfrak{T}_\infty))$. It contains six[15] queries:

(IA) $\mathbb{R}_5 \curlywedge \mathbb{R}_6$	(IB) $\mathbb{R}_5^{\alpha} \curlywedge \mathbb{R}_6^{\eta_1}$
(IIA) $\mathbb{R}_7 \curlyvee \mathbb{R}_8^{\eta_1}$	(IIB) $\mathbb{R}_7^{\eta_0} \curlyvee \mathbb{R}_8^{\beta_1}$
(IIIA) $\mathbb{R}_9 \curlywedge \mathbb{R}_{10}^{\eta_0}$	(IIIB) $\mathbb{R}_9^{\eta_1} \curlywedge \mathbb{R}_{10}^{\beta_0}$

We imagine two viewers – Grace and Ruby – each of them is shown her own structure over Σ. Grace will see $\mathbb{D}_y$ and Ruby $\mathbb{D}_n$. The structures are uncolored, but we imagine the one seen by Grace is Green and the one seen by Ruby is Red. Our goal, as we have already said, is to have $\mathbb{D}_y$ with $\star$, $\mathbb{D}_n$ without $\bigstar$, but to make sure that each of the the two girls can see (almost) the same thing. The trick is that they do not see the real structures, but their image under the CQs in $\mathcal{Q}_\infty$.

9.1 ATTEMPT 1. $\mathbb{D}_y$ AND $\mathbb{D}_n$ AS FRAGMENTS OF $\mathit{chase}(\mathcal{T}_{\mathcal{Q}_\infty}, \star)$.

As we said, there must be a copy of the full green spider $\star$ in $\mathbb{D}_y$. Let **a** and **b** be its tail and antenna. Now, suppose some current versions of $\mathbb{D}_y$ and $\mathbb{D}_n$ are defined. One of the viewers, say Grace, can complain that "Ruby has a tuple **t** in $Q(\mathbb{D}_n)$ (for some $Q \in \mathcal{Q}_\infty$) which I do not see in $Q(\mathbb{D}_y)$". And, as we want the two girls to see the same, we must add

[15]Plus the three queries $\mathbb{R}_1^1 \curlywedge \mathbb{R}_2^2, \mathbb{R}_1^3 \curlywedge \mathbb{R}_2^4, \mathbb{R}^3 \curlywedge \mathbb{R}_3^4$, but we do not need to think about them now.

$\mathbf{t}$ to $Q(\mathbb{D}_y)$. But of course we cannot simply add a tuple to $Q(\mathbb{D}_y)$ – we add something to $\mathbb{D}_y$ in order to make sure that $\mathbf{t}$ is in $Q(\mathbb{D}_y)$. And this is exactly what $Q^{R\to G}$ is about.

So, as we see *chase* (as a procedure), with respect to $\mathcal{T}_{\mathcal{Q}_\infty}$, is all about making sure that the girls see the same. If some tuple t is in $\mathcal{Q}_\infty(dalt(chase_i(\mathcal{T}_{\mathcal{Q}_\infty}, \text{☆})\restriction G))$ then it is also in $\mathcal{Q}_\infty(dalt(chase_{i+1}(\mathcal{T}_{\mathcal{Q}_\infty}, \text{☆})\restriction R))$, and the other way round. And so, **once *chase* reaches a fixpoint, both girls really see the same**. But – and it is an important point – the structures they watch are very much different. Grace watches the daltonisation of $chase(\mathcal{T}_{\mathcal{Q}_\infty}, \text{☆})\restriction G$, and – if we abstract from the Σ-details and see the structure as a swarm – $chase(\mathcal{T}_{\mathcal{Q}_\infty}, \text{☆})\restriction G$ contains edges labelled with $\text{☆}, \text{☆}^{\alpha}, \text{☆}^{\eta_0}, \text{☆}^{\eta_1}, \text{☆}^{\beta_0}, \text{☆}^{\beta_1}$. Ruby watches the daltonisation of $chase(\mathcal{T}_{\mathcal{Q}_\infty}, \text{☆})\restriction R$, and – again seen as a swarm – structure $chase(\mathcal{T}_{\mathcal{Q}_\infty}, \text{☆})\restriction R$ contains edges labelled with $\text{☆}_4, \text{☆}_5, \text{☆}_6, \text{☆}_7, \text{☆}_8, \text{☆}_9$.

But $chase(\mathcal{T}_{\mathcal{Q}_\infty}, \text{☆})$ is infinite and we need $\mathbb{D}_y$ and $\mathbb{D}_n$ to be finite. On the other hand, we do not really require $\mathcal{Q}_\infty(\mathbb{D}_y)$ and $\mathcal{Q}_\infty(\mathbb{D}_n)$ to be equal. We just need them to be similar enough so that l-rounds Ehrenfeucht-Fraisse game cannot spot the difference. So how about having, as $\mathbb{D}_y$ and $\mathbb{D}_n$, daltonisations of $chase_i(\mathcal{T}_{\mathcal{Q}_\infty}, \text{☆})\restriction G$ and of $chase_i(\mathcal{T}_{\mathcal{Q}_\infty}, \text{☆})\restriction R$? We know from the analysis of Figure 1 and from Remark 9 that at each stage of *chase* a single execution of a rule from $\mathcal{Q}_\infty$ will be performed: *chase* begins with an application of rule (IA) (or, strictly speaking, with an application of a TGD generated by (IA), something red will be added then), then (IB), and then rules (IIA), (IIB), (IIIA), (IIIB) are used alternately, building a complicated green-red structure which, after some abstraction, looks like a long green $\alpha\beta$-path (with additional η_0 and η_1 edges leading to $\mathbf{a}$ and $\mathbf{b}$) wrapped with some red edges.

Since there is always only one match in $chase_i(\mathcal{T}_{\mathcal{Q}_\infty}, \text{☆})\restriction G$ of a TGD generated by one of the queries in $\mathcal{Q}_\infty$, the structures $\mathcal{Q}_\infty(dalt(chase_i(\mathcal{T}_{\mathcal{Q}_\infty}, \text{☆})\restriction R))$ and $\mathcal{Q}_\infty(dalt(chase_i(\mathcal{T}_{\mathcal{Q}_\infty}, \text{☆})\restriction G))$ will always differ by just one atom. Two long "paths" which differ by just one atom sounds – from the point of view of Ehrenfeucht-Fraisse games – like hope. But unfortunately, it follows from the construction of $\mathcal{Q}_\infty$, that the relation Ruby will see while watching $chase_i(\mathcal{T}_{\mathcal{Q}_\infty}, \text{☆})\restriction R$ via query (IIA) is always equal to the relation she will see watching the same structure via (IIB), and that the same holds for queries (IIIA) and (IIIB). But the two equalities never hold simultaneously for relations Grace sees in $chase_i(\mathcal{T}_{\mathcal{Q}_\infty}, \text{☆})\restriction G$. So whatever way we try to prematurely terminate this infinite chase, the single atom of difference will be enough for a FO formula to spot a difference.

9.2 ATTEMPT 2. $\mathbb{D}_y$ AND $\mathbb{D}_n$ FOR $\mathcal{Q}_\infty$.

Define $chase^L_{2i}(\mathcal{T}_{\mathcal{Q}_\infty}, \text{☆})$ (L standing for "late") as the set of atoms added to $chase_{2i}(\mathcal{T}_{\mathcal{Q}_\infty}, \text{☆})$ at some stage j, where $i \leq j \leq 2i$, together with all elements involved with these atoms (including $\mathbf{a}$ and $\mathbf{b}$). In other words, all atoms of $chase^L_{2i}(\mathcal{T}_{\mathcal{Q}_\infty}, \text{☆})$ are atoms of $chase_{2i}(\mathcal{T}_{\mathcal{Q}_\infty}, \text{☆})$ which are not in $chase_i(\mathcal{T}_{\mathcal{Q}_\infty}, \text{☆})$.

As before, structures $\mathcal{Q}_\infty(dalt(chase^L_{2i}(\mathcal{T}_{\mathcal{Q}_\infty}, \text{☆})\restriction G))$ and $\mathcal{Q}_\infty(dalt(chase^L_{2i}(\mathcal{T}_{\mathcal{Q}_\infty}, \text{☆})\restriction R))$ differ, by one atom, at the end of the path. And – unlike $\mathcal{Q}_\infty(dalt(chase_i(\mathcal{T}_{\mathcal{Q}_\infty}, \text{☆})\restriction R))$ and $\mathcal{Q}_\infty(dalt(chase_i(\mathcal{T}_{\mathcal{Q}_\infty}, \text{☆})\restriction G))$, they also differ at the "beginning": their beginnings are exactly as different as the ends of $\mathcal{Q}_\infty(dalt(chase_i(\mathcal{T}_{\mathcal{Q}_\infty}, \text{☆})\restriction R))$ and of $\mathcal{Q}_\infty(dalt(chase_i(\mathcal{T}_{\mathcal{Q}_\infty}, \text{☆})\restriction G))$ are.

Now take i Large Enough (with respect to l) and:

- define $\mathbb{D}_y$ as a disjoint union[16] of $dalt(chase_i(\mathcal{T}_{\mathcal{Q}_\infty}, \text{☆})\restriction G))$; of i copies of $dalt(chase^L_{2i}(\mathcal{T}_{\mathcal{Q}_\infty}, \text{☆})\restriction G))$ and of i copies of $dalt(chase^L_{2i}(\mathcal{T}_{\mathcal{Q}_\infty}, \text{☆})\restriction R))$;
- define $\mathbb{D}_n$ as a disjoint union of $dalt(chase_i(\mathcal{T}_{\mathcal{Q}_\infty}, \text{☆})\restriction R))$; of i copies of $dalt(chase^L_{2i}(\mathcal{T}_{\mathcal{Q}_\infty}, \text{☆})\restriction G))$ and of i copies of $dalt(chase^L_{2i}(\mathcal{T}_{\mathcal{Q}_\infty}, \text{☆})\restriction R))$;

Now an Ehrenfeucht-Fraisse games argument comes, which could not be more standard: each girl can see – via the queries of $\mathcal{Q}_\infty$ – some number of paths ($2i+1$ of them, to be precise). Among the paths Grace can see there is one whose beginning looks the same as the beginning of the Ruby's counterpart of this path (it is $dalt(chase_i(\mathcal{T}_{\mathcal{Q}_\infty}, \text{☆})\restriction G)))$, i paths whose beginnings indicate that they come from daltonisation of the green fragment of $chase^L_{2i}(\mathcal{T}_{\mathcal{Q}_\infty}, \text{☆})$ and i paths whose beginnings indicate that they come from daltonisation of the red fragment of $chase^L_{2i}(\mathcal{T}_{\mathcal{Q}_\infty}, \text{☆})$. Notice that exactly the same collection of left ends is seen by Ruby.

Now the path ends: Grace can see $i+1$ ends which indicate that they come from daltonisation of the green fragment of $chase_i(\mathcal{T}_{\mathcal{Q}_\infty}, \text{☆})$ or of $chase^L_{2i}(\mathcal{T}_{\mathcal{Q}_\infty}, \text{☆})$ (the ends of the two kinds paths are identical) and i ends which indicate that hey come from daltonisation of the red fragment of $chase_i(\mathcal{T}_{\mathcal{Q}_\infty}, \text{☆})$ or of $chase^L_{2i}(\mathcal{T}_{\mathcal{Q}_\infty}, \text{☆})$. Since i is Large, the difference between i and $i+1$ is of course not FO-noticeable[17].

Among the paths Grace can see there is one whose beginning looks the same as the beginning of the Ruby's counterpart of this path and whose end indicates being green. The end of the respective path Ruby can see indicates being red. But since the paths are Long (because i is Large) their beginnings cannot be related to their ends using a FO formula, and in consequence $\mathbb{D}_y$ and $\mathbb{D}_n$ are indeed FO-indistinguishable.

Clearly, there are details that we omitted. Most notably, for Ruby to see anything, via queries (IIA) and (IIIA), in her daltonised copies of $dalt(chase^L_i(\mathcal{T}_{\mathcal{Q}_\infty}, \text{☆})\restriction R))$, two spiders, $dalt(\bigstar_7)$ and $dalt(\bigstar_9)$, both having $\mathbf{a}$ as the tail and $\mathbf{b}$ as the antenna need to be present in $\mathbb{D}_n$. Also, while this outline is stated mainly on the Abstraction Level 1, the real construction must be at Level 0.

9.3 LAST STEP. STRUCTURES $\mathbb{D}_y$ AND $\mathbb{D}_n$ FOR $\mathcal{Q}$.

This was already complicated for $\mathcal{Q}_\infty$, and the construction we really need is for $\mathcal{Q}$. Let $\mathcal{Q}_\boxplus = Compile(Precompile(\mathfrak{T}_\boxplus))$.

Let again i be a Large Enough natural number and imagine the structure $chase(\mathcal{T}_{\mathcal{Q}_\boxplus}, chase_i(\mathcal{T}_{\mathcal{Q}_\infty}, \text{☆}))$ (or structure $chase(\mathcal{T}_{\mathcal{Q}_\boxplus}, chase^L_{2i}(\mathcal{T}_{\mathcal{Q}_\infty}, \text{☆}))$). Like in the case of structures $\mathbb{M}_t$ in Section 7, a grid will be constructed, with structures $chase_i(\mathcal{T}_{\mathcal{Q}_\infty}, \text{☆})$ playing the $\alpha\beta$-path being the southern and eastern border of this grid. But now of course the grid is two-colored: we have our old green grid, intertwining with some red edges, as explained in Remark 9. The structure of this green-red grid is unclear, but the good news is

[16]Elements $\mathbf{a}$ and $\mathbf{b}$ are seen as constants, so the word "disjoint" does not apply to them – they belong to all the copies.
[17]Saying "FO" we mean FO formula equivalent to some l-round game.

that we do not need to care: since $chase(\mathcal{T}_{\mathcal{Q}_\boxplus}, chase_i(\mathcal{T}_{\mathcal{Q}_\infty}, \star))$ reaches its fixpoint after a finite number of stages (i.e. terminates), we can be sure (as we observed in Section 9.1) that $\mathcal{Q}_\boxplus(dalt(chase(\mathcal{T}_{\mathcal{Q}_\boxplus}, chase_i(\mathcal{T}_{\mathcal{Q}_\infty}, \star))\restriction G))$ and $\mathcal{Q}_\boxplus(dalt(chase(\mathcal{T}_{\mathcal{Q}_\boxplus}, chase_i(\mathcal{T}_{\mathcal{Q}_\infty}, \star))\restriction R))$ are simply equal – using the queries in $\mathcal{Q}_\boxplus$ both girls see the same structures there. So the difference between $\mathcal{Q}(dalt(chase(\mathcal{T}_{\mathcal{Q}_\boxplus}, chase_i(\mathcal{T}_{\mathcal{Q}_\infty}, \star))\restriction G))$ and $\mathcal{Q}(dalt(chase(\mathcal{T}_{\mathcal{Q}_\boxplus}, chase_i(\mathcal{T}_{\mathcal{Q}_\infty}, \star))\restriction R))$ remains to be one atom – the same one which made $\mathcal{Q}(dalt(chase_i(\mathcal{T}_{\mathcal{Q}}, \star)\restriction R))$ and $\mathcal{Q}(dalt(chase_i(\mathcal{T}_{\mathcal{Q}}, \star)\restriction G))$ different (and the difference between $\mathcal{Q}(dalt(chase(\mathcal{T}_{\mathcal{Q}_\boxplus}, chase^L_{2i}(\mathcal{T}_{\mathcal{Q}_\infty}, \star))\restriction G))$ and $\mathcal{Q}(dalt(chase(\mathcal{T}_{\mathcal{Q}_\boxplus}, chase^L_{2i}(\mathcal{T}_{\mathcal{Q}_\infty}, \star))\restriction R))$ remains to be two atoms).

Now define $\mathbb{D}_y$ and $\mathbb{D}_n$ like in Section 9.2 but instead of each component of the form $dalt(\mathcal{D}\restriction G)$ or $dalt(\mathcal{D}\restriction R)$ of any of the two disjoint unions there (which means – instead of a part of a path) take $dalt(chase(\mathcal{T}_{\mathcal{Q}_\boxplus}, \mathcal{D})\restriction G)$ and $dalt(chase(\mathcal{T}_{\mathcal{Q}_\boxplus}, \mathcal{D})\restriction R)$ (which means – take the grid having this part of a path as two of its borders).

Now notice that the crucial argument we needed for FO-indistinguishability in Section 9.2 was that the ends of the paths in each of $\mathbb{D}_y$ and $\mathbb{D}_n$ are far enough from each other, so that they cannot be related to each other by FO. The last observation needed to see that (the new) $\mathbb{D}_y$ and $\mathbb{D}_n$ will be FO-indistinguishable is that adding the grid to the path does not decrease the distance between the ends.

10. REFERENCES

[1] Afrati, F. N. Determinacy and query rewriting for conjunctive queries and views. *Theor. Comput. Sci. 412*, 11 (2011), 1005–1021.

[2] Bárány, V., Gottlob, G., and Otto, M. Querying the guarded fragment. *Logical Methods in Computer Science 10*, 2 (2014).

[3] Calvanese, D., De Giacomo, G., Lenzerini, M., and Vardi, M. Y. Answering regular path queries using views. In *ICDE* (2000), pp. 389–398.

[4] Davis, M. Unsolvable problems. In *Handbook of Mathematical Logic*, J. Barwise, Ed. North-Holland, Amsterdam, 1977, pp. 567–594.

[5] Deutsch, A., Popa, L., and Tannen, V. Physical data independence, constraints, and optimization with universal plans. In *VLDB'99, Proceedings of 25th International Conference on Very Large Data Bases Edinburgh, Scotland, UK* (1999), pp. 459–470.

[6] Fan, W., Geerts, F., and Zheng, L. View determinacy for preserving selected information in data transformations. *Inf. Syst. 37*, 1 (2012), 1–12.

[7] Francis, N. Phd thesis.

[8] Franconi, E., and Guagliardo, P. The view update problem revisited. *CoRR abs/1211.3016* (2012).

[9] Franconi, E., Kerhet, V., and Ngo, N. Exact query reformulation over databases with first-order and description logics ontologies. *J. Artif. Intell. Res. (JAIR) 48* (2013), 885–922.

[10] Gogacz, T., and Marcinkowski, J. Converging to the chase - A tool for finite controllability. In *28th Annual ACM/IEEE Symposium on Logic in Computer Science, LICS 2013* (2013), pp. 540–549.

[11] Gogacz, T., and Marcinkowski, J. The hunt for a red spider: Conjunctive query determinacy is undecidable. In *30th Annual ACM/IEEE Symposium on Logic in Computer Science, LICS* (2015), pp. 281–292.

[12] Halevy, A. Y. Answering queries using views: A survey. *VLDB J. 10*, 4 (2001), 270–294.

[13] Johnson, D. S., and Klug, A. C. Testing containment of conjunctive queries under functional and inclusion dependencies. *J. Comput. Syst. Sci. 28*, 1 (1984), 167–189.

[14] Larson, P., and Yang, H. Z. Computing queries from derived relations. In *VLDB'85, Proceedings of 11th International Conference on Very Large Data Bases* (1985), pp. 259–269.

[15] Nash, A., Segoufin, L., and Vianu, V. Determinacy and rewriting of conjunctive queries using views: A progress report. In *Database Theory - ICDT 2007, 11th International Conference, Barcelona, Spain, January 10-12, 2007, Proceedings* (2007), pp. 59–73.

[16] Nash, A., Segoufin, L., and Vianu, V. Views and queries: Determinacy and rewriting. *ACM Trans. Database Syst. 35*, 3 (2010).

[17] Pasaila, D. Conjunctive queries determinacy and rewriting. In *Database Theory - ICDT 2011, 14th International Conference* (2011), pp. 220–231.

[18] Rosati, R. On the decidability and finite controllability of query processing in databases with incomplete information. In *Proceedings of the Twenty-Fifth ACM SIGACT-SIGMOD-SIGART Symposium on Principles of Database Systems* (2006), pp. 356–365.

11. APPENDIX

11.1 Spiders and spider queries. A crash course.

As we observed in Section 4, conjunctive query (finite) determinacy is about (finite) structures being models of $\mathcal{T}_\mathcal{Q}$, for some set $\mathcal{Q}$ of CQs. So negative results concerning determinacy (in its both versions) are about writing nontrivial logic programs in the language having $\mathcal{T}_\mathcal{Q}$ as its set of instructions. $\mathcal{T}_\mathcal{Q}$ are TGDs, and normally encoding complicated things using TGDs should not be that difficult. But the TGDs from $\mathcal{T}_\mathcal{Q}$ are of a very special form, with right-hand side being merely an opposite-color version of the left-hand side. To understand to what extent this is a restriction it is good to realize that:

Observation 24 (Very easy). *Let $\mathbb{D}$ be a structure over Σ_G and let $\mathcal{Q}$ be a set of CQs. Then there exists a homomorphism $h : dalt(chase(\mathcal{T}_\mathcal{Q}, \mathbb{D})) \to dalt(\mathbb{D})$.*

This Observation seems to imply that $\mathcal{T}_\mathcal{Q}$ cannot produce anything "non-trivial" – we never get, in $dalt(chase(\mathcal{T}_\mathcal{Q}, \mathbb{D}))$, anything we did not have in $\mathbb{D}$ anyway[18].

But, as we have discovered in [11], while daltonisation of $chase(\mathcal{T}_\mathcal{Q}, \mathbb{D})$ is indeed always an uncomplicated structure, there is a lot we can gain by playing with colors.

Let s be a natural number, large enough, and let $\mathbb{S} = \{1, 2, \ldots s\}$. We defined a structure over Σ, which we call *spider*[19] and colored versions of spider: $☆$ and $★$ (green and red spiders). Each spider has $2s$ legs, including s "upper" and s "lower" legs, and $☆^I_J$ is a green spider with his I-th upper leg and J-th lower leg being red (analogously for $★^I_J$). $I, J \subseteq \mathbb{S}$ **are always** either singletons or empty, so we can have green spiders with none, one or two red legs[20] (and *vice versa*). The set of all spiders[21] of the form $☆^I_J$ or $★^I_J$ is denoted as $\mathbb{A}$.

Then we have the set $\mathbb{F}$ of **spider queries**. Elements of $\mathbb{F}$ are denoted as $\mathbb{R}^I_J$, where I and J are as always. The crucial observation is that the left hand side of the TGD $(\mathbb{R}^I_J)^{R \to G}$ matches with $★^{I'}_{J'}$ if and only if $I' \subseteq I$ and $J' \subseteq J$, and what is produced[22] by such an application of the TGD is $☆^{I \setminus I'}_{J \setminus J'}$. The same of course holds for the colors reversed. We like this trick so much that we call it the Rule of Spider Algebra:

$$\mathbb{R}^I_J(★^{I'}_{J'}) = ☆^{I \setminus I'}_{J \setminus J'} \qquad (♣)$$

[18] When we observed this phenomenon we were pretty sure we had just discovered a key fact in a decidability proof .

[19] Spider is parametrized by $s \in \mathbb{N}$, so in [11] we call it s-pider.

[20] If $I = \emptyset$ or $J = \emptyset$ we will omit it. In particular $☆$ is short for $☆^\emptyset_\emptyset$.

[21] We should distinguish here between $2+4s+2s^2$ "ideal spiders", which are elements of $\mathbb{A}$, and "real spiders" – homomorphic copies of the elements of $\mathbb{A}$ in some bigger structure.

[22] "Matches" means in particular, that the canonical structure of the query $\mathbb{R}^I_J$ is a substructure of the respective spider. "Produced" means that $☆^{I \setminus I'}_{J \setminus J'}$ emerges somehow in the structure, after the new vertices and new edges are added, as demanded by the right-hand side of the TGD $(\mathbb{R}^I_J)^{R \to G}$. Notice that all the new edges are green, so if there are any red edges in the resulting $☆^{I \setminus I'}_{J \setminus J'}$ they are inherited from the old structure.

Binary queries. One more feature of a spider is that it has two vertices not involved in the mechanism enforcing the rule ♣. We call them *antenna* and *tail*. Also each query $\mathbb{R}^I_J$ has its antenna and its tail. Their role is to form – as we call them – *binary queries*.

The set $\mathbb{F}^2$ of binary queries contains, for each two queries $\mathbb{R}^I_J$ and $\mathbb{R}^{I'}_{J'}$ two conjunctive queries $\mathbb{R}^I_J \curlywedge \mathbb{R}^{I'}_{J'}$ and $\mathbb{R}^I_J \curlyvee \mathbb{R}^{I'}_{J'}$.

To define a conjunctive query one needs to specify its canonical structure and its set of free variables (which is a subset of the set of vertices of the canonical structure). The canonical structure of $\mathbb{R}^I_J \curlywedge \mathbb{R}^{I'}_{J'}$ is the disjoint union of canonical structures of $\mathbb{R}^I_J$ and of $\mathbb{R}^{I'}_{J'}$, with the only exception that the antennas of $\mathbb{R}^I_J$ and of $\mathbb{R}^{I'}_{J'}$ are identified. Their joint antennas are/is an existentially quantified variable in $\mathbb{R}^I_J \curlywedge \mathbb{R}^{I'}_{J'}$, and their tails are free variables in $\mathbb{R}^I_J \curlywedge \mathbb{R}^{I'}_{J'}$. All the remaining variables are free if and only if they were free in $\mathbb{R}^I_J$ or $\mathbb{R}^{I'}_{J'}$ – they do the magic of ♣ that we do not want to go into.

Now please come back to Definition 3 and notice that, when a query $Q = \mathbb{R}^I_J \curlywedge \mathbb{R}^{I'}_{J'}$ is seen as a green-red TGD $Q^{G \to R}$, the free variables in Q are what connects the new part of the structure, added by a single execution of $Q^{G \to R}$, to the old part. So, what a single execution of $Q^{G \to R}$ does is as follows: it finds, in the current structure, two green (real) spiders (call them $\mathcal{S}$ and $\mathcal{S}'$) with tails a and a', which share their antennas, and such that, according to ♣, $\mathbb{R}^I_J$ can be applied to $\mathcal{S}$ and $\mathbb{R}^{I'}_{J'}$ can be applied to $\mathcal{S}'$. Then it creates two new (real) red spiders $\mathbb{R}^I_J(\mathcal{S})$ and $\mathbb{R}^{I'}_{J'}(\mathcal{S}')$, which again share the antennas, and their shared antenna is a new vertex. They are connected to the old structure via a, which is also the tail of the new $\mathbb{R}^I_J(\mathcal{S})$, via a' which is also the tail of the new $\mathbb{R}^{I'}_{J'}(\mathcal{S}')$ and via some vertices of the old structure which correspond to other (than the two tails) free variables of $\mathbb{R}^I_J \curlywedge \mathbb{R}^{I'}_{J'}$.

The case of $\mathbb{R}^I_J \curlyvee \mathbb{R}^{I'}_{J'}$ is similar, again its canonical structure is the disjoint union of canonical structures of $\mathbb{R}^I_J$ and of $\mathbb{R}^{I'}_{J'}$. The only difference is that now the tails of $\mathbb{R}^I_J$ and of $\mathbb{R}^{I'}_{J'}$ are identified as one variable, and this variable is existentially quantified in $\mathbb{R}^I_J \curlyvee \mathbb{R}^{I'}_{J'}$. The two antennas are now free variables. The way $(\mathbb{R}^I_J \curlyvee \mathbb{R}^{I'}_{J'})^{G \to R}$ acts on a structure is analogous to the one of $(\mathbb{R}^I_J \curlywedge \mathbb{R}^{I'}_{J'})^{G \to R}$, which was explained above. Same for $(\mathbb{R}^I_J \curlywedge \mathbb{R}^{I'}_{J'})^{R \to G}$ and $(\mathbb{R}^I_J \curlyvee \mathbb{R}^{I'}_{J'})^{R \to G}$.

11.2 Proof of Lemma 17

Clearly, $\mathbb{M} \models \mathfrak{T}_\infty$, so for the proof of Lemma 17 (ii) we only need to show that $\mathbb{M} \models \mathfrak{T}_\boxplus$.

Call the edges of $\mathbb{M}$ which are labelled with ☆, $☆^\alpha$, $☆^{\beta_0}$, $☆^{\beta_1}$, $☆^{\eta_0}$, or $☆^{\eta_1}$ *skeleton*, and the edges of $\mathbb{M}$ which are labelled with any of the $☆^{\langle -,-,-,- \rangle}$ *foam*. Among the foam edges we will distinguish between $\bar{b}$-foam and b-foam (depending whether the label is of the form $☆^{\langle -,-,-,\bar{b} \rangle}$ or of the form $☆^{\langle -,-,-,b \rangle}$). We will also refer to north-edges, which are foam edges of the form $☆^{\langle n,-,-,- \rangle}$.

The next lemma follows directly from the construction of $\mathbb{M}$:

Lemma 25. *1. If e_1 and e_2 are two edges of $\mathbb{M}$ which share at least one vertex, and such that e_1 is a skeleton edge, and e_2 is a foam edge, then e_2 is b-foam.*

2. If e_1 and e_2 are two edges of $\mathbb{M}$ which share at least one vertex, and such that e_1 is a skeleton edge, and e_2 is a foam edge from some $\mathbb{M}_t$ then e_1 is also an edge of $\mathbb{M}_t$.

3. If e and e' are two foam edges of $\mathbb{M}$, e coming from $\mathbb{M}_t$ and e' coming from $\mathbb{M}_{t'}$, for some $t \neq t'$, which share at least one vertex, then they both share this vertex with some skeleton edge (and hence are – due to (1) – are both b-foam).

4. If e is a north-edge of some $\mathbb{M}_t$ and e shares its end with some edge e' in $\mathbb{M}$ then e' is also an edge of $\mathbb{M}_t$.

Now we are ready to prove claim (1) of Lemma 17. Clearly, there is no 1-2 pattern in any of the $\mathbb{M}_t$. So the only way to have it in $\mathbb{M}$ would be if (*) one of the edges of the 1-2 pattern came from $\mathbb{M}_t$ and another from $\mathbb{M}_{t'}$, for some $t \neq t'$. But the two edges of a 1-2 pattern (**) are $\bar{b}$-foam edges which share a vertex. By Lemma 25(3) conditions (*) and (**) are contradictory.

Concerning Lemma 17(2), for each $t \in \mathbb{N}$ there is $\mathbb{M}_t \models \mathfrak{T}_\boxplus$. So again, like in the proof of Lemma 17(1) the only way that $\mathbb{M} \not\models \mathfrak{T}$ could possibly happen would be if we were able to find two edges e and e' which share a vertex, do not come from the same $\mathbb{M}_t$, and such that some rule from $\mathfrak{T}_\boxplus$ applies to them. By Lemma 25(2) none of them is a skeleton edge. By Lemma 25(3) they are both b-foam edges. The only rule of $\mathfrak{T}$ which can rewrite two b-foam edges is the grid triggering rule, but this would require e and e' to share their end-vertices and one of them to be a north-edge. Which is impossible due to Lemma 25(4). □

11.3 Proof of Lemma 23

11.3.1 The "⇒" direction (the easier one).

Suppose Δ is the set of instructions of some rainworm which creeps forever. Then:

Lemma *26.*
If $\alpha\eta_{11} \overset{*}{\rightsquigarrow}_\Delta \mathfrak{w}$ then $\mathfrak{w} \in words(chase(\mathfrak{T}_\Delta, \mathbb{D}_☆))$.

*Proof:*Of course $\alpha\eta_{11} \in words(chase(\mathfrak{T}_\Delta, \mathbb{D}_☆))$, since one gets it from $\mathbb{D}_☆$ by a single application of the first rule of $\mathfrak{T}_\Delta$.
For the induction step we are going to show that if $\mathfrak{w} \rightsquigarrow_\Delta \mathfrak{v}$ and $\mathfrak{w} \in words(chase(\mathfrak{T}_\Delta, \mathbb{D}_☆))$ then also $\mathfrak{v} \in words(chase(\mathfrak{T}_\Delta, \mathbb{D}_☆))$.

So suppose $\mathfrak{w} = \mathfrak{w}_1 \mathfrak{s} \mathfrak{w}_2$ and $\mathfrak{v} = \mathfrak{w}_1 \mathfrak{t} \mathfrak{w}_2$ for a rule $\mathfrak{s} \rightsquigarrow \mathfrak{t}$ in Δ. Let (for example, as all cases are similar) $\mathfrak{s} = \mathfrak{c}_0 \mathfrak{c}_1$ and $\mathfrak{t} = \mathfrak{c}'_0 \mathfrak{c}'_1$, for some even $\mathfrak{c}_0$ and $\mathfrak{c}'_0$ and odd $\mathfrak{c}_1$ and $\mathfrak{c}'_1$. Then, by construction of $\mathfrak{T}_\Delta$, $\mathfrak{c}_0 \curlywedge \mathfrak{c}_1 \leftrightsquigarrow \mathfrak{c}'_0 \curlywedge \mathfrak{c}'_1$ is a rule of $\mathfrak{T}_\Delta$.

Let c, c' be vertices of the green graph $chase(\mathfrak{T}_\Delta, \mathbb{D}_☆)$ such

that:	$\mathfrak{w}_1 \in paths(PG(chase(\mathfrak{T}_\Delta, \mathbb{D}_☆)), \mathbf{a}, c)$,
that	$\mathfrak{s} \in paths(PG(chase(\mathfrak{T}_\Delta, \mathbb{D}_☆)), c, c')$
and that	$\mathfrak{w}_2 \in paths(PG(chase(\mathfrak{T}_\Delta, \mathbb{D}_☆)), c', \mathbf{a})$
(or	$\mathfrak{w}_2 \in paths(PG(chase(\mathfrak{T}_\Delta, \mathbb{D}_☆)), c', \mathbf{b})$).

Now, $\mathfrak{s} \in paths(PG(chase(\mathfrak{T}_\Delta, \mathbb{D}_☆)), c, c')$ means that there is a vertex d of $chase(\mathfrak{T}_\Delta, \mathbb{D}_☆)$ such that $H_{\mathfrak{c}_0}(c, d)$ and $H_{\mathfrak{c}_1}(c', d)$ are edges of $chase(\mathfrak{T}_\Delta, \mathbb{D}_☆)$. But, since $chase(\mathfrak{T}_\Delta, \mathbb{D}_☆) \models \mathfrak{T}_\Delta$, the rule $\mathfrak{c}_0 \curlywedge \mathfrak{c}_1 \leftrightsquigarrow \mathfrak{c}'_0 \curlywedge \mathfrak{c}'_1$ is also satisfied in $chase(\mathfrak{T}_\Delta, \mathbb{D}_☆)$, and thus there exists a vertex d' in $chase(\mathfrak{T}_\Delta, \mathbb{D}_☆)$ such that

$H_{\mathfrak{c}'_0}(c, d')$ and $H_{\mathfrak{c}'_1}(c', d')$ are edges of $chase(\mathfrak{T}_\Delta, \mathbb{D}_{\star})$. This means that $\mathfrak{t} \in paths(PG(chase(\mathfrak{T}_\Delta, \mathbb{D}_{\star}), c, c')$ and, in consequence, $\mathfrak{v} \in words(chase(\mathfrak{T}_\Delta, \mathbb{D}_{\star}))$. □

Since rainworm Δ creeps forever, it follows from Lemma 26 that there are $\alpha\beta$-paths of unbounded length in $chase(\mathfrak{T}_\Delta, \mathbb{D}_{\star})$, and hence in $chase(\mathfrak{T}^{\boxplus}_\Delta, \mathbb{D}_{\star})$. Now we use the machinery from Section 7 Step 2 to prove that every finite model of $\mathfrak{T}^{\boxplus}_\Delta$, containing $\mathbb{D}_{\star}$, contains a 1-2 pattern, so $\mathfrak{T}^{\boxplus}_\Delta$ finitely leads to the red spider.

11.3.2 THE "⇐" DIRECTION (THE HARDER ONE).

Now we consider a rainworm Δ whose computation terminates. Let $\mathfrak{u}_\Delta = \alpha(\beta_1\beta_0)^n\gamma_1 \ldots \omega_0$ be the final configuration[23] like in Section 8 B, and let also k_Δ be as defined there. Our goal is to construct a finite green graph $\mathfrak{M}$, without a 1-2 pattern, containing $\mathbb{D}_{\star}$ and being a model of $\mathfrak{T}^{\boxplus}_\Delta$. It would be tempting to think that $chase(\mathfrak{T}^{\boxplus}_\Delta, \mathbb{D}_{\star})$ is such a graph. But for some subtle reasons, it is not. Apparently, already $chase(\mathfrak{T}_\Delta, \mathbb{D}_{\star})$ can be infinite.

First we will apply a chase-like procedure to construct a finite structure $\mathbb{M}$ being a model of $\mathfrak{T}_\Delta$.

Let $\mathbb{M}^0$ be the structure containing nothing more than $\mathbb{D}_{\star}$ and $\mathfrak{u}_\Delta$: there is an edge $H_\emptyset(\mathbf{a}, \mathbf{b})$, then edges $H_\alpha(\mathbf{a}, b_1)$, $H_{\beta_1}(a_1, b_1)$, $H_{\beta_0}(a_1, b_2) \ldots H_{\beta_1}(a_n, b_n)$ and so on, and finally there is an edge, labelled with ω_0, from some vertex to $\mathbf{b}$. The structure $\mathbb{M}$ is defined by the following **procedure**:

- **for** m=0 **to** k_Δ **do**:

{ $\mathbb{M}^{m+1} := \mathbb{M}^m$;
for all pairs c, c' of vertices of $\mathbb{M}^m$ and **all** rules of the form $\mathfrak{c}\curlywedge\mathfrak{d} \leftrightarrow \mathfrak{c}'\curlywedge\mathfrak{d}'$ [or of the form $\mathfrak{c}\curlyvee\mathfrak{d} \leftrightarrow \mathfrak{c}'\curlyvee\mathfrak{d}'$] in $\mathfrak{T}_\Delta$ **if:**
there exists vertex d' of $\mathbb{M}^m$ such that:
(♠) $\mathbb{M}^m \models H_{\mathfrak{c}'}(c, d'), H_{\mathfrak{d}'}(c', d')$
[or $\mathbb{M}^m \models H_{\mathfrak{c}'}(d', c), H_{\mathfrak{d}'}(d', c')$]
but:
(♡) there is no such vertex d of $\mathbb{M}^m$ that:
$\mathbb{M}^m \models H_{\mathfrak{c}}(c, d), H_{\mathfrak{d}}(c', d)$ [or $\mathbb{M}^m \models H_{\mathfrak{c}}(d, c), H_{\mathfrak{d}}(d, c')$]
do:{

(i) if $\mathfrak{d} \neq \emptyset$, then add to $\mathbb{M}^{m+1}$ a new vertex d and edges $H_{\mathfrak{c}}(c, d)$ and $H_{\mathfrak{d}}(c', d)$ [resp. edges $H_{\mathfrak{c}}(d, c)$, $H_{\mathfrak{d}}(d, c')$];

(ii) if $\mathfrak{d} = \emptyset$, then add to $\mathbb{M}^{m+1}$ an edge $H_{\mathfrak{c}}(c, \mathbf{b})$ [resp. an edge $H_{\mathfrak{c}}(\mathbf{a}, c)$];
}};

- $\mathbb{M} := \mathbb{M}^{k_\Delta + 1}$.

For three reasons this procedure does not (*a priori*) build $chase(\mathfrak{T}_\Delta, \mathbb{D}_{\star})$. First, while each rule in $\mathfrak{T}_\Delta$ is an equivalence (a conjunction of two TGDs), the procedure executes only one of them, the right-to-left one. Second, in **(ii)**, instead of (as *chase* would do) creating a vertex d and two edges $H_{\mathfrak{c}}(c, d)$ and $H_\emptyset(\mathbf{a}, d)$ it reuses[24] the existing vertex $\mathbf{b}$ and edge $H_\emptyset(\mathbf{a}, \mathbf{b})$. Third reason is that it terminates after a fixed number of stages, possibly before reaching a fixpoint.

LEMMA 27. • *$\mathbb{M}$ is finite and $\mathbb{M} \models \mathfrak{T}_\Delta$.*

- *If $\mathbb{M} \models H_{\beta_0}(x, y)$, (or $\mathbb{M} \models H_{\beta_1}(x, y)$) for some vertices x, y, then x, y are already vertices of $\mathbb{M}^0$ and $\mathbb{M}^0 \models H_{\beta_0}(x, y)$, (or $\mathbb{M}^0 \models H_{\beta_1}(x, y)$).*

Proof of Lemma 27 can be found in the submitted version.

Now consider $\mathfrak{M} = chase(\mathfrak{T}^{\boxplus}, \mathbb{M})$. No two different edges labelled with β_0 share the end in $\mathbb{M}$. But, as we saw in Section 7 (Step 3) this does not stop the grid triggering rule from being applied. But again, exactly like in Section 7 (Step 3) for each $t \leq n$ (where n is the one from $\mathfrak{u}_\Delta$ above) nothing more than a harmless grid $\mathbb{M}_t$ will be constructed, not having 1-2-pattern[25]. So $\mathfrak{M} = \mathbb{M} \cup \bigcup_{t \leq n} \mathbb{M}_t$. Since the only edges in $\mathfrak{M}$ which were not in $\mathbb{M}$ are grid edges, we still have $\mathfrak{M} \models \mathfrak{T}_\Delta$, so $\mathfrak{M}$ is indeed a finite model of $\mathfrak{T}^{\boxplus}_\Delta$, without the 1-2 pattern.

[23]This is only to fix attention and simplify notations. Of course $\mathfrak{u}_\Delta$ does not need to be exactly of this form – the last symbol can also be η_0, η_1 or even η_{11}, and the symbol after last β_0 may very well be different than γ_1.

[24]It is easy to prove that in the situation of **(ii)** we have $c' = \mathbf{a}$ [or $c' = \mathbf{b}$].

[25]Notice that $\mathbb{M}_t$ has, among others, elements a_i and b_i for all $i \leq t$, and $\mathbb{M}$ also has, among others, elements a_i and b_i for all $i \leq t$. This is not a coincidence – the set union that defines $\mathfrak{M}$ would make no sense otherwise.

Towards a Worst-Case I/O-Optimal Algorithm for Acyclic Joins*

Xiao Hu Ke Yi

Hong Kong University of Science and Technology
{xhuam, yike}@cse.ust.hk

ABSTRACT

Nested-loop join is a worst-case I/O-optimal algorithm for 2 relations. Recently, a lot of efforts have been devoted to the "triangle query", for which an I/O-optimal algorithm is known. This paper extends these results to a fairly large class of acyclic joins. Acyclic joins can be computed optimally in internal memory using Yannakakis' algorithm from 1981, which simply performs a series of pairwise joins. However, no pairwise join algorithm can be I/O-optimal beyond 2 relations. To achieve I/O-optimality, the algorithm has to handle all the intermediate results carefully without writing them to disk. Unlike the optimal internal memory join algorithm which has a nice tight bound (the AGM bound), the I/O-complexity of joins turns out to be quite complex or even unknown. Yet, we are able to prove that our algorithm is I/O-optimal for certain classes of acyclic joins without deriving its bound explicitly.

Categories and Subject Descriptors

H.2.4 [**Database Management**]: Relational databases; F.2.2 [**Analysis of algorithms and problem complexity**]: Non-numerical Algorithms and Problems

Keywords

I/O-efficient algorithms, acyclic joins, worst-case optimal

1. INTRODUCTION

Evaluating join queries is one of the most central problems in relational databases, both in theory and practice. Yet surprisingly, the worst-case complexity of join evaluation has started to be unraveled just recently, largely thanks to the work of Atserials, Grohe, and Marx [2], who gave a worst-case bound on the join size. This then led to worst-case optimal[1] join algorithms [9, 13]. Ngo, Ré, and Rudra [10] presented a nice survey of these results, and also gave a simpler and unified proof for both the AGM bound and the running time of the algorithm.

These new optimal join algorithms crucially rely on retrieving tuples from a hash table, so they do not work well in external memory. On the other hand, most standard join algorithms used in existing database systems, like nested-loop join or sort-merge join, are specifically designed for limited main memory. Indeed, they achieve I/O-optimality for 2-table joins (more details to follow). Naturally, the intriguing question is if we can extend these algorithms to a broader class of joins in the external memory model.

1.1 Problem definition

Formally, a (natural) *join* is a triple $\mathcal{Q} = (\mathcal{V}, \mathcal{E}, N)$, where $\mathcal{V}$ is a set of *attributes*, $\mathcal{E} \subseteq 2^{\mathcal{V}}$ is a set of *relations*, and N is a function mapping each relation $e \in \mathcal{E}$ to a positive integer $N(e)$. Let dom(v) be the *domain* of attribute $v \in \mathcal{V}$. An *instance* of $\mathcal{Q}$ is a function R that maps each $e \in \mathcal{E}$ to a set of tuples $R(e)$ with $|R(e)| \leq N(e)$, where each tuple $t \in R(e)$ specifies a value in dom(v) for every attribute $v \in e$. The *join results* of $\mathcal{Q}$ on R, denoted by $\mathcal{Q}(R)$, consist of all combinations of tuples, one from each $R(e)$, that share common values for their common attributes. In this paper we assume that the query has constant size, namely, we consider the *data complexity* of computing the join. Indeed, the problem is intractable in terms of query size since $|\mathcal{Q}(R)|$ is exponential in $|\mathcal{E}|$ in the worst case. When the relations have subscripts as $e_1, e_2, \ldots$, we use N_i, R_i, x_i, etc., as shorthands for $N(e_i), R(e_i), x(e_i)$, etc.

We use the standard external memory model [1], which has a main memory of size M with disk block size B. For simpler presentation, we will assume that the memory size is $c \cdot M$ for a sufficiently large constant c, which will not change our results by more than a constant factor. Note that since we assume a constant query size, the sizes of the tuples do not matter asymptotically, and we may assume $O(M)$ tuples from any relation fit in memory. Here are some standard bounds in this model: scanning N tuples needs $O(\frac{N}{B})$ I/Os, and sorting N tuples can be done in $O(\frac{N}{B} \log_{\frac{M}{B}} \frac{N}{B})$ I/Os. In this paper, we will ignore this log factor, and simply say that both can be done in $\widetilde{O}(\frac{N}{B})$ I/Os, where the $\widetilde{O}$ notation suppresses possibly one $\log_{\frac{M}{B}} \frac{N}{B}$ factor. For simplicity, we

*This work is supported by HKRGC under grants GRF-621413, GRF-16211614, and GRF-16200415.

[1]Henceforth "optimal" will always mean "worst-case optimal"; it will be stated explicitly otherwise, in particular when used together with other notions of optimality like "instance optimal".

PODS'16, June 26-July 01, 2016, San Francisco, CA, USA

© 2016 ACM. ISBN 978-1-4503-4191-2/16/06...$15.00

DOI: http://dx.doi.org/10.1145/2902251.2902292

Join query	internal memory [2]	external memory	optimality	reference
Two relations	N_1N_2	$\frac{N_1N_2}{M^2}\cdot\frac{M}{B}$	yes	trivial
[1]Triangle C_3	$\sqrt{N_1N_2N_3}$	$\sqrt{\frac{N_1N_2N_3}{M^3}}\cdot\frac{M}{B}$	on equal N_i's	[7, 12]
[1]LW join LW_n	$\prod_i N_i^{\frac{1}{n-1}}$	$\prod_i(\frac{N_i}{M})^{\frac{1}{n-1}}\cdot\frac{M}{B}$	unknown	[6]
[2]General cyclic join	$\prod_i N_i^{x_i}$	open		
Line L_3	N_1N_3	$\frac{N_1N_3}{M^2}\cdot\frac{M}{B}$	yes	new
Line L_4	$\min\{N_1N_2N_4, N_1N_3N_4\}$	$\min\{\frac{N_1N_2N_4}{M^3},\frac{N_1N_3N_4}{M^3}\}\cdot\frac{M}{B}$	yes	new
Line $L_n, n\geq 5$	$\prod_i N_i^{x_i}$	complex	yes for $n\leq 8$ on balanced N_i's for all n	new
Star T_n	$\prod_{i=1}^n N_i$	complex	yes	new
General acyclic join	$\prod_i N_i^{x_i}$	complex	varies	new
[3]Acyclic join with equal $N_i = N$	N^c	$(\frac{N}{M})^c\cdot\frac{M}{B}$	yes	new

Table 1: Worst-case complexity of join algorithms in internal and external memory

[1] The bounds listed in the table are actually equivalent to the AGM bound: it can be verified that when the AGM bound is smaller than $\prod_i N_i^{\frac{1}{n-1}}$, then $\prod_i N_i^{\frac{1}{n-1}} \leq \sum N_i$, and the running time will be dominated by the omitted linear term.

[2] The x_i's are the optimal fractional edge cover.

[3] $c = \sum x_i$ is the edge cover number.

will assume $N(e) \geq M$ for every e; otherwise proper ceiling will have to be carefully added to the I/O bounds.

For each join result, the algorithm should call an *emit* function with all the participating tuples, which must reside in memory at the time of the call, but does not have to write the result to disk. This agrees with most prior work on I/O-efficient join algorithms [6, 7, 12], and also reflects how join results are usually consumed in real database systems: they are often directly fed to a process down in the pipeline; sometimes the user just wants to apply an aggregation function (standard or an UDF) on the join results in a streaming fashion. For lower bounds, we apply the same *emit* requirement, and assume that the tuples are *indivisible*, which is a standard assumption in the external memory model. The indivisibility assumption is often justified by the fact that the user may be interested in the tuples as a whole entity, e.g., the user may need the tuples' other attributes that do not participate in the join.

As with prior work on acyclic joins [14, 11], we assume that the relations are *fully reduced*, i.e., there are no "dangling" tuples. More precisely, for any relation $R(e)$ and any attribute $v \in e$, for each value $a \in \text{dom}(v)$, there is at least one tuple $t \in R(e)$ such that t has value a on attribute v. For acyclic joins, the relations can be fully reduced in linear time and linear I/Os (ignoring a log factor) in external memory, using a series of semijoins, as described in [14]. In the rest of the paper, we omit the linear term when stating the running time or I/O cost of algorithms for brevity.

1.2 Previous results

In internal memory, there is a unified optimal algorithm [9, 13], based on the AGM bound [2], for all join queries. The AGM bound is based on the optimal fractional edge cover of the query hypergraph (details given in Section 2.1). It can be simplified when considering specific join queries, as listed in Table 1.

However, the situation is much more complicated in external memory. We know that nested-loop join uses $O(\frac{N_1N_2}{MB})$ I/Os to join two relations of sizes N_1 and N_2. Since $|\mathcal{Q}(R)| = N_1N_2$ in the worst case, and the B tuples brought in by one disk I/O can join with at most $O(M)$ tuples that are currently in memory, this bound is optimal.

The *triangle query* has received particular attention [7, 12], where $\mathcal{V} = \{v_1, v_2, v_3\}, e_1 = \{v_1, v_2\}, e_2 = \{v_1, v_3\}, e_3 = \{v_2, v_3\}$. An I/O-optimal algorithm is known, but only when $N_1 = N_2 = N_3$. Hu, Qiao, and Tao [6] extended this algorithm to *Loomis-Whitney joins*, a very special class of cyclic joins, but its optimality is still unclear, even when all relations have equal size.

Most database schemas are acyclic, due to its many desirable properties [3]. Indeed, in as early as 1981, Yannakakis [14] already gave an internal memory algorithm that evaluates any acyclic join in $O(|\mathcal{Q}(R)|)$ time, which is clearly optimal (in fact, instance optimal). This algorithm easily extends to external memory, as observed in [11], yielding an algorithm with $\tilde{O}\left(\frac{|\mathcal{Q}(R)|}{B}\right)$ I/Os. This bound, however, is only optimal when the join results have to be written out to disk. In the emit model, it is even worse than a simple nested-loop join by a factor of M in the worst case for a 2-relation join, and the optimality gap gets even larger when more relations are joined, as we will see shortly.

After the relations have been fully reduced, Yannakakis' algorithm simply performs a series of pairwise joins between two relations sharing a common attribute, as in standard join processing in a database system. In internal memory, this works because these intermediate join sizes are no larger than the full join size. In external memory, however, we cannot afford to write any intermediate results in full to disk, so we will have to depart from this pairwise framework in order to achieve I/O-optimality. Note that simply pipelining the intermediate results to the next join operator will not work, as that join operator may use a nested-loop join, which requires reading one of its input relations multiple times. Thus, careful handling of the intermediate results with limited memory is a key challenge for an external memory algorithm.

1.3 Acyclicity

The acyclicity of the join $\mathcal{Q}$ is defined with respect to the hypergraph $(\mathcal{V}, \mathcal{E})$. Unlike ordinary acyclic graphs (i.e., trees or forests), there are several notions of acyclicity for hypergraphs. We adopt the most natural definition, given by Berge [4]. Consider the bipartite graph G, in which $\mathcal{V}$ corresponds to vertices on one side and $\mathcal{E}$ to vertices on the other side. There is an edge between $v \in \mathcal{V}$ and $e \in \mathcal{E}$ if $v \in e$. Then the hypergraph $(\mathcal{V}, \mathcal{E})$ is said to be acyclic if this bipartite graph is acyclic. This notion of acyclicity preserves many natural properties in ordinary acyclic graphs. For example, there is only one path between any two vertices $u, v \in \mathcal{V}$, and any subgraph of $(\mathcal{V}, \mathcal{E})$ is still acyclic. Note that this definition of acyclicity does not allow two relations to have two or more common attributes. But if these attributes always appear together in any relation, then they can be simply considered as one "combined" attribute.

We do point out that earlier work on acyclic queries, including Yannakakis' algorithm, has adopted a more relaxed notion of acyclicity, known as *α-acyclicity*. However, α-acyclicity does not preserve the two properties above. In particular, removing a hyperedge from an α-acyclic hypergraph can make it cyclic, which is quite counter-intuitive. In particular, two most commonly used types of joins, *line joins* and *star joins*, are both Berge-acyclic, to which we will pay special attention. Henceforth, "acyclic" will always mean "Berge-acyclic".

1.4 Our results

We observe from Table 1 that all existing external memory results "just" replace N_i with $\frac{N_i}{M}$ in their internal memory counterparts, plus an additional $\frac{M}{B}$ factor. Thus it is natural to make the same conjecture for other join queries. Indeed, our result on the line query L_3 confirms this, and it also trivially extends to L_4 (see Table 1). Recall that a line query L_n on n relations is a $\mathcal{Q} = (\mathcal{V}, \mathcal{E}, N)$, where $\mathcal{V} = \{v_1, v_2, ..., v_{n+1}\}$, $\mathcal{E} = \{e_1, e_2, ..., e_n\}$, and $e_i = \{v_i, v_{i+1}\}$. Interestingly, this conjecture breaks down on L_5. The AGM bound on L_5 is $N_1 N_3 N_5$, but its external memory counterpart, $\frac{N_1 N_3 N_5}{M^2 B}$, is not sufficient to characterize the query's I/O complexity. It is easy to construct an instance in which every tuple in R_1 joins with every tuple in R_4, thus applying the same argument as for the 2-relation join yields a lower bound of $\Omega(\frac{N_1 N_4}{MB})$. Note that we always have $N_1 N_4 \leq N_1 N_3 N_5$ (on fully reduced instances), but due to having different denominators, $\frac{N_1 N_4}{MB}$ is in general not comparable to $\frac{N_1 N_3 N_5}{M^2 B}$. The complication associated with the external memory model starts to manifest itself. A similar situation happens on star queries with at least 3 petals, namely, a part of the join results could impose a higher lower bound on the I/O complexity than the full join results.

We will need the following two concepts in order to state our results for those queries marked as "complex" in Table 1. For any subset of relations $S \subseteq \mathcal{E}$, we call $\Join_{e \in S} R(e)$ the *subjoin* on S. On the other hand, define the *partial join* $\mathcal{Q}(R, S)$ as the projection of $\mathcal{Q}(R)$ on the attributes of S. Note that if the relations in S are connected, $\mathcal{Q}(R, S) = \Join_{e \in S} R(e)$ for an acyclic join on fully reduced relations. If S is not connected, then $\mathcal{Q}(R, S) \subseteq \Join_{e \in S} R(e)$. Recall that the natural join of two relations without a common attribute is simply their cross product.

Figure 1 shows an instance of a line query L_3, illustrating these concepts. In the figure, attribute values are vertices, and each tuple is an edge. Thus, any path from some vertex in A to some vertex in D is a join result. Note that these relations have been fully reduced. In this example, the partial join and subjoin on R_1 and R_2 are the same, since they are connected, and includes every partial path from A to C. The subjoin on R_1 and R_3 is simply their cross product: $R_1 \Join R_3 = R_1 \times R_3$, but the partial join on R_1 and R_3 is only a subset of $R_1 \times R_3$. For example, (t_1, t_2) belongs to both the subjoin and the partial join, but (t_1, t_3) only belongs to the subjoin but not the partial join.

Because the partial join $\mathcal{Q}(R, S)$ is a projection of the full join, the algorithm has to compute $\mathcal{Q}(R, S)$ for any S implicitly or explicitly. In internal memory, $|\mathcal{Q}(R, S)| \leq |\mathcal{Q}(R)|$, so this is not an issue. However, in external memory, applying the same argument above leads to a lower bound of $\Omega\left(\frac{|\mathcal{Q}(R,S)|}{M^{|S|-1}B}\right)$. Each partial join contributes a term that is in general not comparable with others, and all of them should be taken into account to give the highest lower bound.

With this observation, we define

$$\psi(R, S) = \frac{|\mathcal{Q}(R, S)|}{M^{|S|-1}B}$$

as the minimum I/O cost for computing the partial join $\mathcal{Q}(R, S)$. Thus $\max_R \max_S \psi(R, S) = \max_S \max_R \psi(R, S)$ is a lower bound on the worst-case I/O cost for computing $\mathcal{Q}$.

Similarly, define

$$\Psi(R, S) = \frac{|\Join_{e \in S} R(e)|}{M^{|S|-1}B}$$

as the minimum I/O cost for computing the subjoin $\Join_{e \in S} R(e)$.

The main result of this paper is an algorithm for any acyclic join $\mathcal{Q} = (\mathcal{V}, \mathcal{E}, N)$, whose I/O cost on instance R is

$$\min_{\mathbf{S} \in \text{GENS}(\mathcal{Q})} \max_{S \in \mathbf{S}} \Psi(R, S),$$

where $\mathbf{S}$ is any set of subsets of $\mathcal{E}$ generatable by a nondeterministic process $\text{GENS}(\mathcal{Q})$, as described in Algorithm 3. Note that $\text{GENS}(\mathcal{Q})$ only depends on the structure of the query hypergraph.

The algorithm's worst-case I/O-cost is thus

$$\max_R \min_{\mathbf{S} \in \text{GENS}(\mathcal{Q})} \max_{S \in \mathbf{S}} \Psi(R, S), \tag{1}$$

which (for a given query hypergraph) is a function of the relation sizes, as well as M and B. Unfortunately, this function is very complex. To prove worst-case optimality, we make a connection to the partial joins directly, thus avoiding the

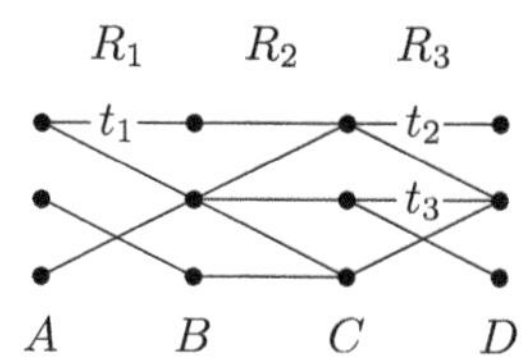

Figure 1: Illustration on subjoins and partial joins.

need to derive this function explicitly. We first rewrite (1):

$$\max_R \min_{\mathbf{S}\in\text{GENS}(\mathcal{Q})} \max_{S\in\mathbf{S}} \Psi(R,S) \le \min_{\mathbf{S}\in\text{GENS}(\mathcal{Q})} \max_R \max_{S\in\mathbf{S}} \Psi(R,S)$$
$$= \min_{\mathbf{S}\in\text{GENS}(\mathcal{Q})} \max_{S\in\mathbf{S}} \max_R \Psi(R,S).$$

Then, it suffices to show that there exists an $\mathbf{S} \in \text{GENS}(\mathcal{Q})$ such that for any $S \in \mathbf{S}$, there is an instance I on which

$$\max_R \Psi(R,S) \le \psi(I,S),$$

or

$$\max_R |\bowtie_{e\in S} R(e)| \le |\mathcal{Q}(I,S)|. \quad (2)$$

Specifically, we obtain the following results (please also refer to Table 1):

(1) Our algorithm is optimal for any star join (Section 5).

(2) For any line join in which the relation sizes satisfy a certain *balancing condition*, the algorithm is optimal (Section 6). This condition is always satisfied on any 3-relation or 4-relation line join.

(3) For line joins with 5 or more relations, the balancing condition might break. In this case, our general algorithm is not optimal, but we have designed special algorithms that are optimal for line joins with up to 8 relations.

(4) In addition to line and star joins, our algorithm is also optimal on some other types of acyclic joins (Section 7).

(5) Our algorithm is optimal on any acyclic query in which all relations have equal size (Section 7). In this case, the I/O-complexity has a closed form $(\frac{N}{M})^c \cdot \frac{M}{B}$ where c is the edge cover number of the hypergraph. Very recently, Koutris et al. [8] have given an interesting reduction from their MPC model to the I/O model, which leads to algorithms that match this edge cover bound, but only for line joins and star joins on equal-sized relations.

2. PRELIMINARIES

2.1 The AGM bound

For a query $\mathcal{Q} = (\mathcal{V}, \mathcal{E}, N)$, let x be a fractional edge cover for the hypergraph $(\mathcal{V}, \mathcal{E})$, i.e., for any $v \in \mathcal{V}$, $\sum_{e, v\in e} x(e) \ge 1$. Then the AGM bound [2] states that

$$\max_R |\mathcal{Q}(R)| = \min_x \prod_e N(e)^{x(e)}.$$

Note that the optimal fractional edge cover x can be found by solving a linear program on the $N(e)$'s, which takes $O(1)$ time for constant query size.

2.2 Properties of acyclic joins

Let $\mathcal{Q} = (\mathcal{V}, \mathcal{E}, N)$ be a join query whose corresponding hypergraph is acyclic. The following lemma can be easily proved by definition.

LEMMA 1. *In an acyclic query, there is always a relation that contains only one attribute, or an attribute that is contained in only one relation.*

This leads to the following important observation of the AGM bound on acyclic queries. Let x be the optimal fractional cover of $\mathcal{Q}$.

LEMMA 2. *For acyclic queries, $x(e) = 0$ or 1 for each e.*

PROOF. Let A be the incidence matrix of the linear program defined on x, which has a 1 at row e and column v if $v \in e$, and 0 otherwise. It is known that the optimal solution of the linear program is integral if the determinant of any square submatrix of A is ± 1 or 0. We prove this by induction on the size of the submatrix. For a 1×1 submatrix, this is trivially true. Suppose $\det(A') = \pm 1$ or 0 for any $k \times k$ submatrix A' of A. Consider any $(k+1) \times (k+1)$ submatrix A' of A, which corresponds to a subset of $k+1$ vertices $\mathcal{V}'$ and a subset of $k+1$ edges $\mathcal{E}'$ of the hypergraph. Since any sub-hypergraph of an acyclic hypergraph is acyclic, by Lemma 1 there is one relation in $\mathcal{E}'$ that contains only one attribute in $\mathcal{V}'$ or one attribute in $\mathcal{V}'$ that is contained in only one relation in $\mathcal{E}'$. In either case, A' can be rearranged as

$$A' = \begin{pmatrix} 1 & * \\ 0 & A'' \end{pmatrix},$$

where A'' is a $k \times k$ submatrix of A. Then by the induction hypothesis, $\det(A') = \pm 1 \cdot \det(A'') = \pm 1$ or 0. □

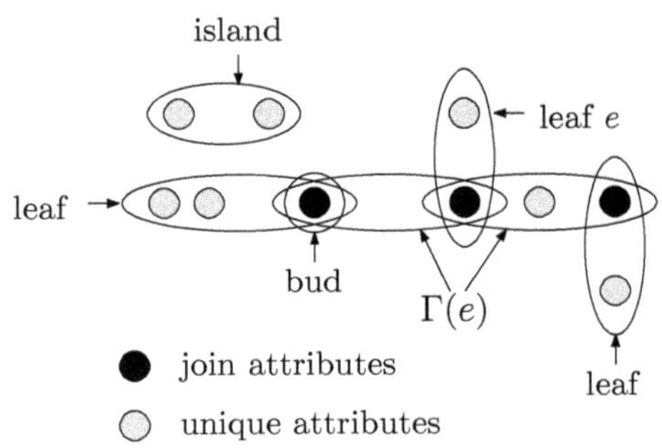

Figure 2: Attributes and edges in an acyclic hypergraph.

We classify the attributes and relations as follows. If an attribute $v \in \mathcal{V}$ appears in only one relation, it is called a *unique attribute*, otherwise a *join attribute*. Note that any two relations have at most one common join attribute due to the acyclicity requirement. A relation e is called an *island* if e has no join attribute. A *bud* is a relation with only one join attribute and no unique attribute. A relation e is called a *leaf* if it contains at least one unique attribute and exactly one join attribute. For a leaf e, let $\Gamma(e)$ be its *neighbors*, i.e., the set of other relations sharing the join attribute with e. These terms are illustrated in Figure 2.

By Lemma 1, there is always an island, a bud, or a leaf in an acyclic query. One may wonder why we consider islands and buds as they are not very meaningful in a join query. The reason, as we shall see later, is that they can appear during the recursive processing of the join in our algorithm, so we have to consider them for full generality.

2.3 Handling skew

Similar with the optimal join algorithms in internal memory [10], it is important to handle skew properly. In external memory, skew is defined with respect to the memory size M.

For a relation $R(e)$ and an attribute $v \in e$, the set of tuples in $R(e)$ with value a on attribute v is denoted as $R(e)|_{v=a}$, and let $N(e)|_{v=a} = |R(e)|_{v=a}|$.

A value a is *heavy* in $R(e)$ if $N(e)|_{v=a} \geq M$, otherwise *light*. Denote the set of heavy values in dom(v) with respect to $R(e)$ as

$$H(e, v) = \{a \in \text{dom}(v) : N(e)|_{v=a} \geq M\}.$$

Note that by sorting $R(e)$ on the v attribute, we can partition the tuples in $R(e)$ into those with heavy values on v and those with light values.

We will use the following operations in describing our algorithms. If $R(e)$ is sorted on v, we can handle the heavy and light values separately. For a heavy value a, the operation "load $R(e)|_{v=a}$ into memory as $M(e)$" means reading the next M tuples of $R(e)|_{v=a}$ into memory, and these tuples are denoted as $M(e)$. This operation is usually repeatedly invoked, and and last invocation may read less than M tuples from $R(e)|_{v=a}$. For light values, the operation "load $R(e)$ by v into memory as $M(e)$" means reading tuples from $R(e)$ by the order of v until M or more tuples are fetched, subject to the constraint that tuples with the same value on attribute v must be loaded into memory together. Note that since all values are light, no more than $2M$ tuples will be loaded to memory, with no more than M distinct values on v. This operation can also be repeatedly invoked, and the last invocation may read less than M tuples. If $R(e)$ is not sorted on any attribute, the operation "load $R(e)$ into memory as $M(e)$" means reading the next M tuples from $R(e)$ (again, the last invocation may read less than M tuples).

3. WARMING UP

Before presenting our general join algorithm, we start with a review on 2-relation join algorithms and show how we can extend them to the 3-relation line join.

For a join between 2 relations R_1 and R_2, we know that nested-loop join achieves $O(\frac{N_1 N_2}{MB})$ I/Os, which is worst-case optimal as $|\mathcal{Q}(R)|$ can be as large as $N_1 N_2$ in the worst case. In fact, by combining with sort-merge join, we can achieve instance optimality, i.e., an algorithm that runs in $\tilde{O}(\frac{|\mathcal{Q}(R)|}{MB})$ I/Os on any instance R of $\mathcal{Q}$. More precisely, we sort both relations on the join attribute v, and then "merge" them together. For each value $a \in \text{dom}(v)$, if a is heavy in both R_1 and R_2, we run a nested-loop join on $R_1|_{v=a} \bowtie R_2|_{v=a}$, costing $O(\frac{N_1|_{v=a} N_2|_{v=a}}{MB})$ I/Os; otherwise the merge can be done with a single pass of $R_1|_{v=a}$ and $R_2|_{v=a}$. Note that $|\mathcal{Q}(R)| = \sum_a N_1|_{v=a} N_2|_{v=a}$, hence the total I/O cost is as claimed. In fact, this algorithm has been described in textbooks [5], but it appears that its (I/O) instance optimality has never been formally stated.

Next we consider a 3-relation line join L_3:

$$R_1(v_1, v_2) \bowtie R_2(v_2, v_3) \bowtie R_3(v_3, v_4).$$

The naive way to extend the nested-loop join to 3 relations would result in $O(\frac{N_1 N_2 N_3}{M^2 B})$ I/Os. However, by the AGM bound, the optimal edge cover for this query is $x_1 = 1, x_2 = 0, x_3 = 1$, thus its maximum join size is only $N_1 N_3$. Below, we present an algorithm that achieves $\tilde{O}(\frac{N_1 N_3}{MB})$ I/Os (recall that we omit the linear term, so there is a hidden $\frac{N_2}{B}$ term).

We will make use of the 2-relation instance-optimal algorithm above. In fact, we will only need the observation that

---

Algorithm 1: Line join on 3 relations

1 sort R_1 by attribute v_2;
2 sort R_2 by attribute v_2, v_3 lexicographically;
3 sort R_3 by attribute v_3;
4 **foreach** $a \in H(e_1, v_2)$ **do**
5   compute $R_3' = R_2|_{v_2=a} \bowtie R_3$ by merge join, and write the results to disk;
6   compute $R_1|_{v_2=a} \bowtie R_3'$ by nested-loop join, and emit all results;
7   discard $R_1|_{v_2=a}$ and $R_2|_{v_2=a}$;
8 **while** *load* R_1 *by* v_2 *into memory as* M_1 **do**
9   compute $R_2(M_1) = R_2 \ltimes M_1$;
10   compute $R_2(M_1) \bowtie R_3$ by sort-merge join;
11   **foreach** *tuple* t *emitted* **do**
12   find any matching tuples $t' \in M_1$ and *emit*(t', t);

---

this algorithm has $\tilde{O}(\frac{N_1}{B} + \frac{N_2}{B})$ I/Os when R_1 and R_2 have no common heavy values.

Our 3-relation line join algorithm is described in Algorithm 1. It handles heavy values (line 4–7) and light values (line 8–12) on attribute v_2 in R_1 separately. For each heavy value $a \in H(e_1, v_2)$, $R_2|_{v_2=a}$ is stored continuously on disk sorted by v_3. Since R_3 is sorted by v_3, we can compute $R_3' = R_2|_{v_2=a} \bowtie R_3$ by a merge join on line 5. Note that all tuples in $R_2|_{v_2=a}$ have the same value on v_2, they must have distinct values on v_3, so no value on v_3 is heavy. Thus by the observation above, this costs $O(\frac{N_2|_{v_2=a}}{B} + \frac{N_3}{B})$ I/Os. Also, R_3' has at most N_3 tuples, so we can afford to write the results to disk. Next, computing $R_1|_{v_2=a} \bowtie R_3'$ by nested-loop join on line 6 costs $O(\frac{N_1|_{v_2=a} N_3}{MB})$ I/Os (since $N_1|_{v_2=a} \geq M$, no $\lceil \cdot \rceil$ is needed). So the total cost to handle all the heavy values in R_1 is

$$\sum_{a \in H(e_1, v_2)} \left(\frac{N_2|_{v_2=a}}{B} + \frac{N_3}{B} + \frac{N_1|_{v_2=a} N_3}{MB} \right).$$

Since there are $O(\frac{N_1}{M})$ heavy values in $H(e_1, v_2)$, this becomes $O(\frac{N_1 N_3}{MB} + \frac{N_2}{B})$.

For tuples in R_1 with light values on v_2, we load them into memory, one chunk at a time. From previous analysis, each memory chunk contains at most $2M$ tuples with at most M distinct values on v_2. Since R_1 and R_2 are both sorted by v_2, computing all the semijoins on line 9 takes just one scan through R_1 and R_2. Since M_1 has no more than M distinct values on v_2, $R_2(M_1)$ does not have any heavy value on v_3. Then by the previous observation, doing a sort-merge on $R_2(M_1) \bowtie R_3$ on line 10 has cost $\tilde{O}(\frac{|R_2(M_1)|}{B} + \frac{N_3}{B})$. Thus, the total cost to handle all the light values is

$$\tilde{O}\left(\frac{N_1}{B} + \frac{N_2}{B} + \sum_{M_1} \left(\frac{|R_2(M_1)|}{B} + \frac{N_3}{B} \right) \right).$$

Since there are $O(\frac{N_1}{M})$ memory chunks M_1, and the $R_2(M_1)$'s are disjoint, this becomes $\tilde{O}(\frac{N_1 N_3}{MB} + \frac{N_2}{B})$.

THEOREM 1. *Algorithm 1 has I/O cost $\tilde{O}(\frac{N_1 N_3}{MB})$ for any 3-relation line join.*

To see why this is optimal, simply consider the instance in Figure 3. Taking $S = \{R_1, R_3\}$, we have $\psi(R, S) = \frac{N_1 N_3}{MB}$ as a lower bound.

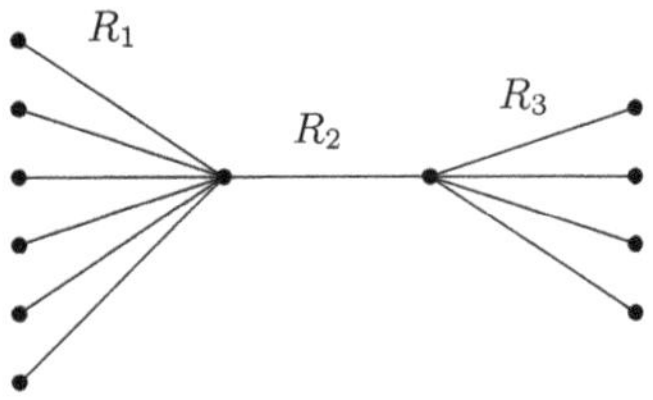

Figure 3: Worst-case instance for 3-relation line join.

4. ALGORITHM FOR ACYCLIC JOINS

4.1 The algorithm

In this section, we generalize our 3-relation line join algorithm to handle arbitrary acyclic queries. The algorithm, described in Algorithm 2, recursively "peels off" a bud, an island, or a leaf.

The base case is when only one relation remains, in which case we simply report all tuples (line 1–2). A bud can simply be ignored (line 3–4), as it has only one attribute and it appears in other relations. Since there are no dangling tuples, a bud cannot restrict other relations, either. Strictly speaking, however, ignoring a bud violates the emit model. But this can be easily fixed by attaching each tuple t in the bud to all tuples it joins with. This takes linear I/Os in total, so it is not an issue.

An island e can be peeled off by just using nested-loop join with $R(e)$ being the "outer relation" and the rest of $\mathcal{Q}$ as the "inner relation" (line 5–9). The rationale is that any tuple in $R(e)$ joins with any join result from the rest of $\mathcal{Q}$, so the I/O cost inevitably will have $\frac{N(e)}{M}$ multiplied with the cost of computing the rest of $\mathcal{Q}$.

To peel a leaf e, the idea is similar to the 3-relation line join algorithm, handling heavy (line 14–20) and light tuples (line 21–27) in $R(e)$ separately. There are two key differences, though. First, computing the join on (parts of) R_2 and R_3 will be replaced by recursion. Second, for a general acyclic join, a leaf e may share its join attribute with more than one relations, namely, there can be more than one "R_2".

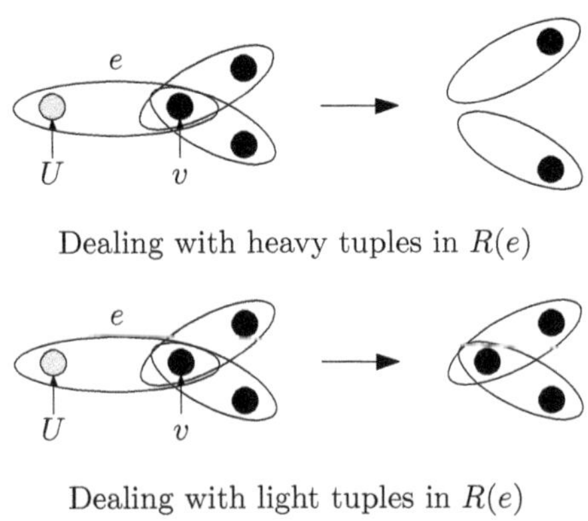

Figure 4: Different strategies for dealing with heavy and light tuples.

We provide some more explanation on the algorithm for peeling off a leaf. First, a seemingly difficult decision is which leaf to peel. Indeed, different pealing strategies may lead to different costs. For example, on L_4, we will see later that different peeling strategies would lead to two different

Algorithm 2: ACYCLICJOIN($\mathcal{V}, \mathcal{E}, R$)

```
1  if ℰ = {e} then
2  |  emit all tuples in R(e);
3  else if there is a bud e ∈ ℰ then
4  |  AcyclicJoin(𝒱, ℰ − {e}, R);
5  else if there is an island e ∈ ℰ then
6  |  while load R(e) into memory as M₁ do
7  |  |  AcyclicJoin(𝒱 − e, ℰ − {e}, R − {R(e)});
8  |  |  foreach tuple t emitted do
9  |  |  |  find any matching tuples t′ ∈ M₁ and
   |  |  |  emit(t′, t);
10 else
11 |  pick a leaf e nondeterministically;
12 |  suppose e has unique attributes U, join attribute v,
   |  and neighboring relations Γ;
13 |  sort R(e) by attribute v;
14 |  sort R(e′) by attribute v for each e′ ∈ Γ;
15 |  foreach a ∈ H(e, v) do
16 |  |  R′(a) ← R − {R(e)} − {R(e′) : e′ ∈ Γ}
   |  |  +{R(e′)|_{v=a} : e′ ∈ Γ};
17 |  |  while load R(e)|_{v=a} into memory as M₁ do
18 |  |  |  AcyclicJoin(𝒱 − U − {v}, ℰ − {e}, R′(a));
19 |  |  |  foreach tuple t emitted do
20 |  |  |  |  emit(t′, t) for each tuple t′ ∈ M₁;
21 |  |  discard R(e)|_{v=a} and R(e′)|_{v=a};
22 |  while load R(e) by v into memory as M₁ do
23 |  |  foreach e′ ∈ Γ do
24 |  |  |  compute R(e′)(M₁) = R(e′) ⋉ M₁;
25 |  |  R′(M₁) ← R − {R(e)} − {R(e′) : e′ ∈ Γ}
   |  |  +{R(e′)(M₁) : e′ ∈ Γ};
26 |  |  AcyclicJoin(𝒱 − U, ℰ − {e}, R′(M₁));
27 |  |  foreach tuple t emitted do
28 |  |  |  finding any matching tuples t′ ∈ M₁ and
   |  |  |  emit(t′, t);
```

bounds, $\tilde{O}(\frac{N_1 N_3 N_4}{M^3 B})$ and $\tilde{O}(\frac{N_1 N_2 N_4}{M^3 B})$, respectively. Thus, a "smart" algorithm should first compare N_2 and N_3, and then choose the better peeling strategy. However, as we are not trying to optimize the dependency on n, the number of relations, we chose to simply pick a leaf e nondeterministically (line 11). To convert this nondeterministic algorithm to a deterministic one, we use the standard simulation technique to explore all nondeterministic branches in a round-robin fashion, terminating the simulation as soon as any branch terminates. In effect, we attain the cost of the best peeling strategy, up to a factor that might be exponential in n, which is a constant anyway.

Next, consider a peeling a leaf e. Let U be its set of unique attributes, v its join attribute, and Γ the set of neighboring relations of e. For a heavy value a, we first find $R(e')|_{v=a}$ for each $e' \in \Gamma$, i.e., the tuples in Γ that join with a. Now we can remove both e and v from $\mathcal{Q}$, as all tuples have the same value a on v. In the case Γ has more than one relation, this will decompose $\mathcal{Q}$ into disconnected components (see Figure 4). Note that this operation may generate new islands and buds, which is exactly why we need to deal with islands and buds in each recursive call. Then, for each memory chunk of $R(e)|_{v=a}$, we do the join recursively; for each join result returned from the recursion, we combine it with all the tuples in memory since they have the same value a on the join attribute v.

For light tuples in $R(e)$, we load them into memory, one chunk M_1 at a time. Then for each $e' \in \Gamma$, we find $R(e')(M_1)$, i.e., the tuples in $R(e)$ that can join with M_1. Next, we make the recursive call. Note that in this case, we only remove e and its unique attributes, but not v, before going into the recursion, so this does not disconnect the query (see Figure 4).

4.2 Analysis

We will bound the I/O-cost of Algorithm 4 in terms of $\Psi(R, S)$, the minimum cost of computing the subjoins. The first bound, stated below, uses all subsets S of the relations.

THEOREM 2. *For an acyclic join $\mathcal{Q} = (\mathcal{V}, \mathcal{E}, N)$ and instance R, the I/O cost of Algorithm 2 is*

$$\tilde{O}\left(\max_{S \subseteq \mathcal{E}} \Psi(R, S)\right), \quad (3)$$

where S is over all subsets of $\mathcal{E}$.

The proof is by induction and naturally follows the recursion of the algorithm. The details are quite technical, though, and are given in Appendix A.1.

It is not hard to see that this bound cannot be tight. In particular, it does not depend on the peeling order, which means that this is actually a bound on the worst branch of the nondeterministic peeling process. The other source of looseness comes from a *star*. A *star* consists of a *core* e_0 that has no unique attributes, and k *petals* $e_1, \ldots, e_k, k \geq 1$, such that $e_i \cap e_0 \neq \emptyset$. Each petal contains one or more unique attributes and does not intersect with any relations except the core. The core connects with the rest of $\mathcal{Q}$ via exactly one join attribute. Please see Figure 5 for an illustration.

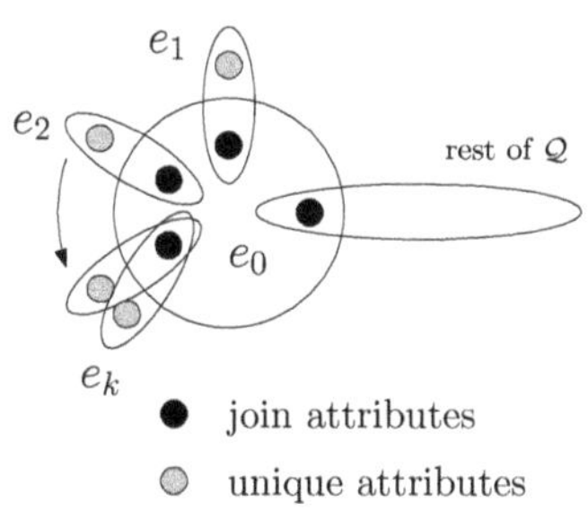

Figure 5: An illustration of a star.

When applied to a standalone star, Theorem 2 would generate all subsets of its relations. However, an observation is that we will always have

$$\Psi(R, \{e_0, e_1, \ldots, e_k\}) \leq \Psi(R, \{e_1, \ldots, e_k\}),$$

since $R_0 \bowtie R_1 \bowtie \cdots \bowtie R_k \subseteq R_1 \bowtie \cdots \bowtie R_k$ and $\Psi(R, \{e_0, e_1, \ldots, e_k\})$ has a larger denominator. This means that not all subsets S of relations have to be included in (3), and more importantly, this observation applies recursively. Specifically, whenever Algorithm 2 successively peels off the petals of a star, followed by its core, we can apply this argument: If the core is included in the recursive consideration, then not all its petals have to be included; all the petals have to be included in the same subjoin only if the core is not included.

This is more precisely defined by a nondeterministic recursive process GENS($\mathcal{Q}$) as described in Algorithm 3, which leads to the following tighter bound:

Algorithm 3: GENS($\mathcal{Q}$)

if $\mathcal{Q}$ *is empty* **then**
  return $\{\emptyset\}$;
if $\mathcal{Q}$ *contains a bud* e **then**
  return GENS($\mathcal{Q} - \{e\}$);
else if $\mathcal{Q}$ *contains a star* **then**
  pick a star $\mathcal{X}$ non-deterministically;
  let e_0 be the core of $\mathcal{X}$;
  $\mathbf{S_1} \leftarrow$ GENS($\mathcal{Q} - \mathcal{X} + \{e_0\}$);
  $\mathbf{S_1} \leftarrow \mathbf{S_1} \cup \{S \cup f \mid S \in \mathbf{S_1}, f \subsetneq \mathcal{X} - \{e_0\}\}$;
  $\mathbf{S_2} \leftarrow$ GENS($\mathcal{Q} - \mathcal{X}$);
  $\mathbf{S_2} \leftarrow \mathbf{S_2} \cup \{S \cup f \mid S \in \mathbf{S_2}, f \subseteq \mathcal{X} - \{e_0\}\}$;
  return $\mathbf{S_1} \cup \mathbf{S_2} \cup 2^{\mathcal{X}}$;
else
  pick an island e or a leaf e non-deterministically;
  $\mathbf{S} \leftarrow$ GENS($\mathcal{Q} - \{e\}$)};
  return $\mathbf{S} \cup \{S \cup \{e\} \mid S \in \mathbf{S}\}$;

THEOREM 3. *For an acyclic join $\mathcal{Q} = (\mathcal{V}, \mathcal{E}, N)$ and instance R, the I/O cost of Algorithm 2 is*

$$\tilde{O}\left(\min_{\mathbf{S} \in \text{GENS}(\mathcal{Q})} \max_{S \in \mathbf{S}} \Psi(S)\right), \quad (4)$$

where $\mathbf{S}$ is any set of subsets of $\mathcal{E}$ generatable by Algorithm 3.

The proof of Theorem 3 is given in Appendix A.2. Similar to the proof of Theorem 2, it is based on induction and the recursive structure of the algorithm. More precisely, we show that the I/O cost of any branch of the nondeterministic algorithm is captured by the corresponding branch of the nondeterministic GENS($\mathcal{Q}$) process, therefore achieving the I/O cost of the best branch by the round-robin simulation.

Here are some examples when applying Theorem 3 to some join queries.

Line query L_3: On L_3, we can either consider $\{e_1, e_2\}$ as a star (with only one petal), or $\{e_2, e_3\}$ as a star. Suppose we peel $\{e_1, e_2\}$ first. Then GENS($\mathcal{Q}$) will be recursively applied on $\{e_2, e_3\}$ and $\{e_3\}$, respectively. GENS($\{e_2, e_3\}$) will return all its subsets, and GENS($\{e_3\}$) returns $\{\{e_3\}, \emptyset\}$, each of which is unioned with $\{e_1\}$. Thus, the final $\mathbf{S}$ returned by GENS($\mathcal{Q}$) is

$$\{\{e_1, e_3\}, \{e_2, e_3\}, \{e_1, e_2\}, \{e_1\}, \{e_2\}, \{e_3\}, \emptyset\}.$$

It can be verified that if GENS($\mathcal{Q}$) peels $\{e_2, e_3\}$ first, it will generate the same $\mathbf{S}$.

On a fully reduced instance R, $\Psi(R, \{e_1, e_2\}), \Psi(R, \{e_2, e_3\})$ are dominated by $\Psi(R, \{e_1, e_3\})$, so the I/O-cost of the algorithm is $\tilde{O}(\Psi(R, \{e_1, e_3\}) + \Psi(R, \{e_2\}))$, matching the result of Theorem 1.

Line query L_4: On L_4, GENS($\mathcal{Q}$) generates different $\mathbf{S}$ on different peeling orders. If we peel the star $\{e_1, e_2\}$ first, GENS($\mathcal{Q}$) will return (subjoins that are dominated by others are omitted)

$$\{\{e_1, e_3, e_4\}, \{e_1, e_3\}, \{e_1, e_4\}, \{e_2, e_4\}\}.$$

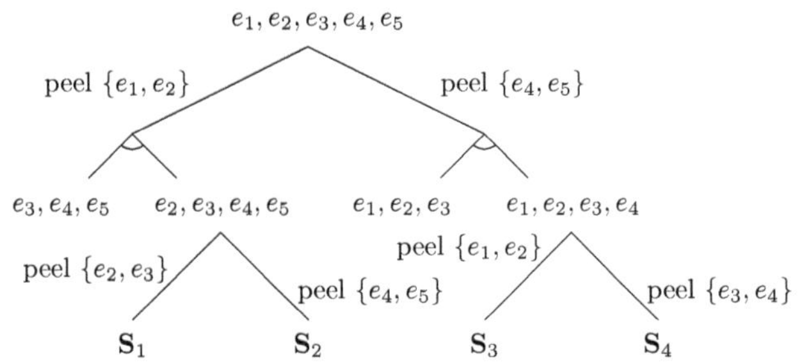

Figure 6: Applying GENS($\mathcal{Q}$) on L_5.

If we peel $\{e_3, e_4\}$ first, GENS($\mathcal{Q}$) will return

$$\{\{e_1, e_2, e_4\}, \{e_1, e_3\}, \{e_1, e_4\}, \{e_2, e_4\}\}.$$

Which one leads to a smaller bound will depend on all these subjoin sizes on the given instance. In the worst case, the former is dominated by $\Psi(R, \{e_1, e_3, e_4\}) = \frac{N_1 N_3 N_4}{M^2 B}$ and the latter dominated by $\Psi(R, \{e_1, e_2, e_4\}) = \frac{N_1 N_2 N_4}{M^2 B}$, so the I/O cost is as claimed in Table 1.

Line query L_5: On L_5, we can either peel off $\{e_1, e_2\}$ or $\{e_4, e_5\}$. In either case, GENS($\mathcal{Q}$) generates two recursive calls, one on an L_3 and one on an L_4 (see Figure 6). As seen above, GENS($\mathcal{Q}$) on an L_3 will generate a unique result, but can generate two different results on an L_4, so there are a total of 4 **S**'s generatable by GENS($\mathcal{Q}$) on L_5 (dominated subjoins are omitted):

$$\mathbf{S}_2 = \mathbf{S}_3 = \{\{e_1, e_3, e_5\}, \{e_2, e_5\}, \{e_1, e_4\}, \{e_2, e_4\}\}$$
$$\mathbf{S}_1 = \{\{e_1, e_3, e_5\}, \{e_2, e_4, e_5\}, \{e_2, e_5\}, \{e_1, e_4\}, \{e_2, e_4\}\}$$
$$\mathbf{S}_4 = \{\{e_1, e_3, e_5\}, \{e_1, e_2, e_4\}, \{e_2, e_5\}, \{e_1, e_4\}, \{e_2, e_4\}\}$$

Thus, two of the four peeling strategies are better than the others, and in terms of the worst case, they give a bound of $\tilde{O}(\frac{N_1 N_3 N_5}{M^2 B} + \frac{N_2 N_5}{MB} + \frac{N_1 N_4}{MB} + \frac{N_2 N_4}{MB})$, which will be shown to be optimal in Section 6. This is an example where the I/O-complexity is not simply replacing N_i with $\frac{N_i}{M}$ in the AGM bound.

Star query: If $\mathcal{Q}$ by itself is a standalone star, we can remove it in one shot, which would generate all subjoins. However, we could also remove all but one petal, resulting in all subjoins except the full join, which agrees with our earlier observation that the full join is dominated by the subjoin defined by all petals, thus not needed.

5. OPTIMALITY ON STAR JOINS

On a star query with n petals, our analysis above immediately yields the following result.

COROLLARY 1. *On a star join $\mathcal{Q} = (\mathcal{V}, \mathcal{E}, N)$ and an instance R, Algorithm 2 has I/O cost*

$$\tilde{O}\left(\frac{\prod_{i=1}^{n} N_i}{M^{n-1} B} + \max_{S \subsetneq \mathcal{E}, e_0 \in S} \psi(R, S)\right) \quad (5)$$

PROOF. As argued, the I/O cost has a term $\Psi(R, S)$ for each proper subset S of $\mathcal{E}$. If S does not include e_0, this is captured by the first term in (5). If $e_0 \in S$, then the subjoin becomes a partial join, thus captured by the second term of (5). □

THEOREM 4. *Algorithm 2 is worst-case optimal for any star join $\mathcal{Q}$.*

PROOF. As the second term in (5) is already optimal (actually instance-optimal). To show the first term is optimal, it suffices construct an instance I such that its partial join size on the n petals is $\prod_{i=1} N_i$. We construct I by generalizing Figure 3: The domain of each join attribute v_i has only one value, and petal R_i is a one-to-many matching from the only value in dom(v_i) to the unique attribute of R_i. The core simply consists of a single tuple connecting all the (only) values in dom(v_i), $i = 1, \ldots, n$. □

Although we have proved the optimality of our algorithm on star joins without deriving its complexity explicitly, it is still an interesting question as to what this complexity looks like, i.e., what is the second term of (5) on the worst R? The answer turns out to be a complicated function, intricately depending on N_0, the size of the core of the star, as compared to the sizes of the petals.

6. OPTIMALITY ON LINE JOINS

The optimality of Algorithm 2 on line joins is much more subtle than on star joins. Recall that a line join on n relations, L_n, is a query $\mathcal{Q} = (\mathcal{V}, \mathcal{E}, N)$, where $\mathcal{V} = \{v_1, v_2, ..., v_{n+1}\}$, $\mathcal{E} = \{e_1, e_2, ..., e_n\}$, and $e_i = \{v_i, v_{i+1}\}$, as illustrated in Figure 7.

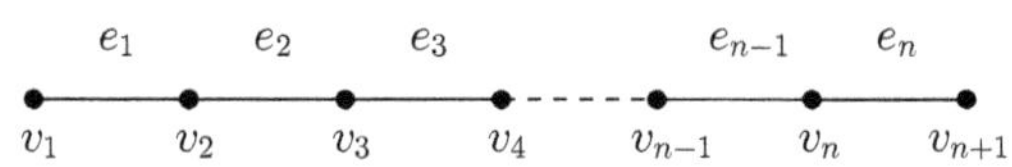

Figure 7: A line join on n relations.

6.1 Optimal edge cover

Let x be the optimal edge cover of a n-relation line join. First we give the characterization of x:

(1) $x_1 = x_n = 1$;

(2) there are no two consecutive 0's;

(3) there are no three consecutive 1's;

(4) there are no 5 consecutive x_i's being $(1, 1, 0, 1, 1)$.

The first 3 rules are obvious; the last rule follows from the observation that $(1, 0, 1, 0, 1)$ is always better than $(1, 1, 0, 1, 1)$, since the size of the middle relation is smaller than the product of its two neighbors on fully reduced relations.

Another simple observation is that x has "sub-optimality", i.e., for any $x_i = x_j = 1, i < j$, $(x_i, \ldots, x_j)$ must be an optimal edge cover for the subjoin $R_i \bowtie \cdots \bowtie R_j$. If not, we could replace $(x_i, \ldots, x_j)$ with a better one, which would improve x for the whole join.

For any $i \le j$, $(x_i, \ldots, x_j)$ is called an *alternating interval* if $(x_i, \ldots, x_j) = (1, 0, 1, 0, ..., 0, 1)$. It is easy to see that x must consist of one or more alternating intervals. A single $x_i = 1$ is also an alternating interval, but it can only appear at the two ends. For example, for $n = 4$, $x = (1, 0, 1, 1)$ or $(1, 1, 0, 1)$.

6.2 Worst-case optimality

In this subsection we give sufficient conditions under which Algorithm 2 is optimal.

When n is odd.

For an odd n, we say that an n-relation line join $\mathcal{Q}$ is *balanced* if

$$N_i N_{i+2} \cdots N_{j-2} N_j \geq N_{i+1} N_{i+3} \cdots N_{j-3} N_{j-1}$$

for any $1 \leq i < j \leq n$ such that $j-i$ is an even number. Note that any 3-relation line join is always balanced after dangling tuples are removed. A 5-relation line join is balanced if $N_1 N_3 N_5 \geq N_2 N_4$.

LEMMA 3. *On a balanced line join, the optimal edge cover x must be alternating.*

PROOF. Suppose for contradiction that x is not alternating, then by previous analysis, x must consist of 3 or more alternating intervals. Thus, the pattern $(1,1,0,1,0,\ldots,0,1,0,1,1)$ must appear somewhere, and suppose it is $(x_i,\ldots,x_j)$. By sub-optimality, this pattern has appeared only because it is better than $(1,0,1,0,\ldots,0,1,0,1)$ on the interval $(N_i,\ldots,N_j)$, which means

$$N_{i+1} N_{i+3} \cdots N_{j-3} N_{j-1} < N_{i+2} N_{i+4} \cdots N_{j-4} N_{j-2},$$

violating the balancing condition on the interval $(N_{i+1}, \ldots, N_{j-1})$. □

Applying Theorem 3 on a line join yields the following result.

COROLLARY 2. *Let $\mathcal{Q} = (\mathcal{V}, \mathcal{E}, N)$ be a line query on an odd number of relations. On instance R, Algorithm 2 has I/O cost*

$$\tilde{O}\left(\max_S \Psi(S)\right) = \tilde{O}\left(\max_S \frac{\prod_{e\in S} N(e)}{M^{|S|-1}B}\right),$$

where S is over all independent subsets of $\mathcal{E}$.

PROOF. It suffices to show that $\text{GENS}(\mathcal{Q})$ can generate an $\mathbf{S}$ such that for each $S \in \mathbf{S}$, $\Psi(S)$ is dominated by $\Psi(S')$ for some independent subset S' of $\mathcal{E}$. Let $L(i,j)$ be *a* set of subsets generatable by $\text{GENS}(\mathcal{Q})$ on $e_i \bowtie e_{i+1} \bowtie \cdots \bowtie e_j$. The proof is by induction on the length of the interval (i,j), where the interval length must be odd. The base case is trivial.

To generate $L(i,j)$, we peel off (e_i, e_{i+1}) first, which yields

$$L(i,j) = (L(i+2,j) \circ \{e_i\}) \cup L(i+1,j) \cup \{\{e_i\}\},$$

where we use the notation $\mathbf{X} \circ Y = \{X \cup Y \mid X \in \mathbf{X}\}$. By the induction hypothesis, $L(i+2,j)$ only contains subsets that are dominated by independent subsets, so $L(i+2,j) \circ \{e_i\}$ retains this property.

To deal with $L(i+1,j)$, we peel off (e_{j-1}, e_j), which gives

$$L(i+1,j) = (L(i+1,j-2) \circ \{e_j\}) \cup L(i+1,j-1) \cup \{\{e_j\}\}.$$

$L(i+1,j-1)$ is an interval of odd length and we can apply the induction hypothesis directly. For $L(i+1,j-2)$, which is an interval of even length, we peel off $\{e_{j-3}, e_{j-2}\}$:

$$L(i+1,j-2) = (L(i+1,j-4) \circ \{e_{j-2}\}) \cup L(i+1,j-3) \cup \{\{e_j - 2\}\}.$$

Again, $L(i+1,j-3)$ is an interval of odd length and we apply the induction hypothesis directly. Then we repeat the same process on $L(i+1,j-4)$, until its length reduces to 2. Thus, the only subjoin that we have not accounted for is

$$\{e_{i+1}, e_{i+2}, e_{i+4}, e_{i+6}, \ldots, e_j\}.$$

On a fully reduced instance, this subjoin is dominated by that of $\{e_i, e_{i+2}, e_{i+4}, \ldots, e_j\}$. □

THEOREM 5. *For odd n, Algorithm 2 is optimal for any balanced n-relation line join.*

PROOF. It suffices to show that for every independent subset S of $\mathcal{E}$, there exists an instance I such that the partial join size on S is the same as largest subjoin size on S, i.e., $|\mathcal{Q}(I,S)| = \prod_{e\in S} N(e)$.

It is easy to see that an instance I in which each relation is the cross product of its two domains satisfies this requirement. However, we still need to ensure that such a construction is feasible. More precisely, suppose attribute v_i has a domain size $|\text{dom}(v_i)| = z_i$. Then the following is the sufficient and necessary condition for the feasibility of such an I:

$$\begin{cases} z_i z_{i+1} = N_i, & i = 1, \ldots, n, \\ z_i \leq N_i, & i = 1, \ldots, n, \\ z_i \leq N_{i-1}, & i = 2, \ldots, n+1, \\ z_i \geq 1, & i = 1, \ldots, n+1. \end{cases}$$

Using the n equalities, we can represent all the z_i's using z_1:

$$\begin{cases} z_2 = \frac{N_1}{z_1}, \\ z_3 = \frac{z_1 N_2}{N_1}, \\ z_4 = \frac{N_1 N_3}{z_1 N_2}, \\ \ldots, \\ z_n = \frac{z_1 N_2 N_4 \cdots N_{n-1}}{N_1 N_3 \cdots N_{n-2}}, \\ z_{n+1} = \frac{N_1 N_3 \cdots N_n}{z_1 N_2 N_4 \cdots N_{n-1}}. \end{cases}$$

All the inequalities on the z_i's thus translate to those on z_1:

$$\left.\begin{matrix} 1 \\ \frac{N_1}{N_2} \\ \frac{N_1 N_3}{N_2 N_4} \\ \frac{N_1 N_3 N_5}{N_2 N_4 N_6} \\ \cdots \\ \frac{N_1 N_3 \cdots N_{n-2}}{N_2 N_4 \cdots N_{n-1}} \end{matrix}\right\} \leq z_1 \leq \left\{\begin{matrix} N_1 \\ \frac{N_1 N_3}{N_2} \\ \frac{N_1 N_3 N_5}{N_2 N_4} \\ \frac{N_1 N_3 N_5 N_7}{N_2 N_4 N_6} \\ \cdots \\ \frac{N_1 N_3 \cdots N_n}{N_2 N_4 \cdots N_{n-1}}. \end{matrix}\right.$$

By the balancing condition, any term on the right-hand side is greater than any term on the left-hand side. Thus, this construction is feasible, which concludes the proof. □

When n is even.

THEOREM 6. *For an n-relation line join $\mathcal{Q}$ where n is even, Algorithm 2 is optimal if there is an odd k such that the two subjoins $e_1 \bowtie \cdots \bowtie e_k$ and $e_{k+1} \bowtie \cdots \bowtie e_n$ are both balanced.*

PROOF. First, observe that under the above condition, the optimal edge cover consists of two alternating intervals $(x_1, \ldots, x_k)$ and $(x_{k+1}, \ldots, x_n)$.

The construction of R is the same as before, except that we set $z_{k+1} = 1$, i.e., the common attribute of R_k and R_{k+1} has only one value. Feasibility can be verified by going through the same exercise as in the proof of Theorem 5. □

The optimal bound in this case is thus $\max_S \frac{\prod_{e\in S} N(e)}{M^{|S|-1}B}$ where S is over all independent subsets of $\mathcal{E}$, except that e_k and e_{k+1} can be chosen into S together.

It may seem that the construction above can be generalized to the case where $\mathcal{Q}$ can be decomposed into any number of balanced subjoins. However, this case can never happen:

If $\mathcal{Q}$ is decomposed into 3 or more subjoins, then the pattern $(1,1,0,1,0,\ldots,0,1,0,1,1)$ must appear somewhere in the optimal edge cover, and by previous analysis, this means that one of the subjoins is not balanced.

6.3 When Algorithm 2 is not optimal

When $n = 5$.

As mentioned, L_3 is always balanced; a L_4 join can be split into an L_1 and and an L_3, both of which must be balanced. Thus, the smallest n on which Algorithm 2 might not be optimal is $n = 5$. When $N_1N_3N_5 < N_2N_4$, the construction of R above is not feasible. We have to allow R_3 to be any mapping from $\text{dom}(v_3)$ onto $\text{dom}(v_4)$, while R_2 and R_4 remain as cross products. Thus, the I/O lower bound becomes $\psi(\mathcal{Q}) = \frac{N_1N_3N_5}{MB} + \frac{N_2}{B} + \frac{N_4}{B}$, which is smaller than the bound $\frac{N_1N_3N_5}{M^2B} + \frac{N_1N_4}{MB} + \frac{N_2N_5}{MB} + \frac{N_2N_4}{MB}$ in the balanced case. For this case, we have designed a special algorithm that achieves the optimal bound, as described in Algorithm 4.

Algorithm 4: LineJoinUnbalanced5$(R_1, \ldots, R_5)$

1 call Algorithm 1 on (R_1, R_2, R_3), and write the results to disk as S;
2 call Algorithm 1 on (R_3, R_4, R_5), and write the results to disk as T;
3 sort R_3 by v_3, v_4 lexicographically;
4 sort S and T by v_3, v_4 lexicographically;
5 **foreach** $t \in R_3$ **do**
6 compute $S(t) = S \ltimes t$;
7 compute $T(t) = T \ltimes t$;
8 compute $S(t) \bowtie T(t)$ by nested-loop join, and emit all results;

The costs of the two line joins in line 1–2 are $\widetilde{O}(\frac{N_1N_3}{MB} + \frac{N_2}{B})$ and $\widetilde{O}(\frac{N_3N_5}{MB} + \frac{N_4}{B})$, but writing S and T to disk costs $\widetilde{O}(\frac{N_1N_3}{B} + \frac{N_3N_5}{B})$. The loop in line 4–7 has N_3 iterations. We can compute all the semijoins in line 5–6 with one scan of S, T and R_3 after sorting them by v_3, v_4 lexicographically. Finally, every $S(t)$ has size at most N_1 and every $T(t)$ has size at most N_5, so the nested loop join on line 8 takes $O(\frac{N_1N_5}{MB})$ I/Os. Adding up all these costs yields the desired bound.

When $n = 6$.

The only possibility where Algorithm 2 is not optimal for an L_6 is when its optimal edge cover is $(1,0,1,0,1,1)$ (or $(1,1,0,1,0,1)$), and the first 5 relations are not balanced. In this case, we can run a nested-loop join with R_6 as the outer relation and $R_1 \bowtie \cdots \bowtie R_5$ as the inner relation, computed by Algorithm 4.

When $n = 7$.

On an L_7, the optimal edge cover can be either $(1,1,0,1,0,1,1)$ or $(1,0,1,0,1,0,1)$.

The former case can be reduced to the unbalanced 5-relation case. More precisely, when the optimal edge cover is $(1,1,0,1,0,1,1)$, then the middle 5 relations must be unbalanced, i.e., $N_3N_5 > N_2N_4N_6$. Now we simply run nested-loop join on $R_1 \bowtie (R_2 \bowtie \cdots \bowtie R_6) \bowtie R_7$, while using Algorithm 4 for the 5-relation join in the middle. The I/O cost is $\widetilde{O}(\frac{N_1N_2N_4N_6N_7}{M^3B} + \frac{N_1N_3N_7}{M^2B} + \frac{N_1N_5N_7}{M^2B})$.

We can show that this bound is optimal. We construct an instance R in which R_1 and R_6 are many-to-one mappings from $\text{dom}(v_1)$ to $\text{dom}(v_2)$ and from $\text{dom}(v_6)$ to $\text{dom}(v_7)$, respectively. R_2 and R_7 are one-to-many mappings from $\text{dom}(v_2)$ to $\text{dom}(v_3)$ and $\text{dom}(v_7)$ to $\text{dom}(v_8)$, respectively. R_3 and R_5 are cross products and R_4 remains as a many-to-many mapping. It is feasible due to the condition $N_3N_5 > N_2N_4N_6$. On such an instance, we have

$$|\mathcal{Q}(R, \{e_1, e_3, e_7\})| = N_1N_3N_7,$$
$$|\mathcal{Q}(R, \{e_1, e_5, e_7\})| = N_1N_5N_7,$$
$$|\mathcal{Q}(R, \{e_1, e_3, e_5, e_7\})| = N_1N_2N_4N_6N_7.$$

When the optimal edge cover is $(1,0,1,0,1,0,1)$, 3 balancing conditions might break: $N_1N_3N_5N_6 \geq N_2N_4N_6$, $N_1N_3N_5 \geq N_2N_4$ and $N_3N_5N_7 \geq N_4N_6$. We have also designed a different algorithm, described below, which is optimal when any of these 3 balancing conditions break. Its optimality proof involves a careful case-by-case analysis, which we leave in Appendix A.3.

Algorithm 5: LineJoinUnbalanced7$(R_1, \ldots, R_7)$

call Algorithm 1 on (R_3, R_4, R_5), and write the results to disk as S;
Construct a corresponding acyclic join query $(\mathcal{V}, \mathcal{E}, R)$ with $R = \{R_1, R_2, S, R_6, R_7\}$;
AcyclicJoin$(\mathcal{V}, \mathcal{E}, R)$;

$n = 8$ and beyond.

An L_8 can be reduced to smaller joins, so can be solved optimally under all cases. However, the situation gets highly complex for $n \geq 9$. A general algorithm that can solve all the unbalanced cases optimally remains elusive.

7. GENERAL ACYCLIC JOINS

In this section, we study the optimality of Algorithm 2 on other classes of acyclic joins.

7.1 When all relations have equal sizes

Let x the optimal edge cover of $\mathcal{Q} = (\mathcal{V}, \mathcal{E}, N)$ and let $c = \sum x(e)$. When all relations have equal sizes, x is just the minimum edge cover of the hypergraph $(\mathcal{V}, \mathcal{E})$. For acyclic queries, the minimum edge cover can be found by the following simple greedy strategy:

Algorithm 6: Minimum edge cover C

$C \leftarrow \emptyset$;
while *$\mathcal{Q}$ has uncovered attributes* **do**
let e be any edge containing unique attributes;
$C \leftarrow C \cup \{e\}$;
remove e and its attributes from $\mathcal{Q}$;

We will show the Algorithm 2 is optimal in this case.

Theorem 7. *Let $\mathcal{Q} = (\mathcal{V}, \mathcal{E}, N)$ be an acyclic query where $N(e) = N$ for all $e \in \mathcal{E}$. Let c be the minimum edge cover number of $(\mathcal{V}, \mathcal{E})$. Algorithm 2 has I/O cost $\widetilde{O}\left(\left(\frac{N}{M}\right)^c \frac{M}{B}\right)$ on $\mathcal{Q}$ and this is optimal.*

PROOF. To prove the upper bound, we need to find an $\mathbf{S}$ generatable by $\text{GENS}(\mathcal{Q})$, such that for any $S \in \mathbf{S}$, $\Psi(R, S) \le \left(\frac{N}{M}\right)^c \frac{M}{B}$ on any instance R. It turns out if all relations have equal sizes, nondeterminism is not needed, and we can allow $\text{GENS}(\mathcal{Q})$ to peel any star, and peel any leaf or island if no stars exist. Buds can always be ignored as they do not appear in any $S \in \mathbf{S}$ or in the minimum edge cover.

The proof is by induction on the size of $\mathcal{Q}$. The base case when $\mathcal{Q}$ has only one relation is trivial. For the inductive step, let us first consider the case when $\text{GENS}(\mathcal{Q})$ peels off a star $\mathcal{X}$ with core e_0. Let c_1 and c_2 be the minimum edge cover number of $\mathcal{Q} - \mathcal{X} + \{e_0\}$ and $\mathcal{Q} - \mathcal{X}$, respectively. Following the greedy algorithm above for finding a minimum edge cover, we have

$$c_2 + |\mathcal{X}| - 1 = c, \quad c_1 \le c_2 + 1 \le c.$$

Let $\mathbf{S}_1$ and $\mathbf{S}_2$ respectively be the set of subsets of relations returned by $\text{GENS}(\mathcal{Q} - \mathcal{X} + \{e_0\})$ and $\text{GENS}(\mathcal{Q} - \mathcal{X})$, following any nondeterministic branch. Any S returned by $\text{GENS}(\mathcal{Q})$ must fall into one of the following cases.

1. $S \in \mathbf{S}_1$ or $S \in \mathbf{S}_2$: In this case, we have $\Psi(R, S) \le \left(\frac{N}{M}\right)^{c_1 \text{ or } c_2} \frac{M}{B} \le \left(\frac{N}{M}\right)^c \frac{M}{B}$ by invoking the induction hypothesis on $\mathcal{Q} - \mathcal{X} + \{e_0\}$ and $\mathcal{Q} - \mathcal{X}$.

2. $S \subseteq \mathcal{X}$: For such an S, we have $\Psi(R, S) \le \left(\frac{N}{M}\right)^{|S|} \frac{M}{B} \le \left(\frac{N}{M}\right)^c \cdot \frac{M}{B}$, since $|S| \le |\mathcal{X}| \le c$.

3. $S = S_1 \cup f$ where $S_1 \in \mathbf{S}_1, f \subsetneq \mathcal{X} - \{e_0\}$: We have

$$\begin{aligned}\Psi(R, S) \le& \frac{N^{|f|} \cdot |\bowtie_{e \in S_1} R(e)|}{M^{|f|+|S_1|}} \cdot \frac{M}{B} \\ =& \left(\frac{N}{M}\right)^{|f|} \cdot \Psi(R, S_1) \\ \le& \left(\frac{N}{M}\right)^{|f|+c_1} \cdot \frac{M}{B}.\end{aligned}$$

Since $|f| + c_1 \le |\mathcal{X}| - 2 + c_1 \le c$, this is bounded by $\left(\frac{N}{M}\right)^c \cdot \frac{M}{B}$.

4. $S = S_2 \cup f$ where $S_2 \in \mathbf{S}_2, f \subseteq \mathcal{X} - \{e_0\}$: Similar to above, we have

$$\Psi(R, S) \le \left(\frac{N}{M}\right)^{|f|+c_2} \cdot \frac{M}{B},$$

and the upper bound holds by the fact that $|f| + c_2 \le |\mathcal{X}| - 1 + c_2 = c$.

Next, consider the case when $\text{GENS}(\mathcal{Q})$ peels off a leaf (the case when it peels off an island is trivial). We observe that when a leaf e is peeled off by $\text{GENS}(\mathcal{Q})$, any of its neighboring edge must contain unique attributes. Otherwise, suppose e has a neighboring edge e' that does not have unique attributes, then it will become the core of a star, with e being a petal. However, when $\text{GENS}(\mathcal{Q})$ decides to peel off a leaf, it must be the case that $\mathcal{Q}$ does not have stars, which is contradictory.

Now suppose $\text{GENS}(\mathcal{Q})$ peels off a leaf e, and let c' be the minimum edge cover of $\mathcal{Q} - \{e\}$. Since every neighboring relation of e has unique attributes, all of them must be in selected in the edge cover of $\mathcal{Q} - \{e\}$. Thus we have $c' + 1 = c$. Any S returned by $\text{GENS}(\mathcal{Q})$ must take the form of $S' \cup \{e\}$ where S' is generated by $\text{GENS}(\mathcal{Q} - \{e\})$. Similar to the analysis above, we have

$$\Psi(R, S) \le \left(\frac{N}{M}\right)^{1+c'} \cdot \frac{M}{B} = \left(\frac{N}{M}\right)^c \cdot \frac{M}{B},$$

as desired.

To show that this bound is optimal, we need to construct an instance in which there are c relations whose partial join size is N^c. By LP duality, the minimum edge cover corresponds to a vertex packing such that an edge is in the cover if and only if it covers a vertex in the packing. We set the domain size of each vertex in the packing to be N, and that of each vertex not in the packing to be 1. Each relation will simply be the cross product of their domains. Note that each edge can have at most one vertex in the packing, so its relation size is at most N. On this instance, the partial join size of all relations in the edge cover is N^c. $\square$

7.2 Lollipop joins

A *lollipop join* is illustrated in Figure 8, which is a star join with one petal, say e_n, extending to another relation e_{n+1}. It is the mixture of a star join and a an L_4, so it is intuitive that Algorithm 2 should be optimal for this type of joins.

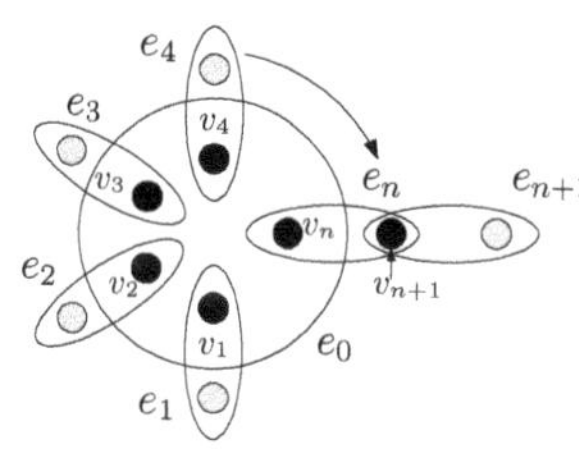

Figure 8: A lollipop join.

A lollipop join contains two stars, with e_0 and e_n as the core, respectively. Similar to the L_4 case, different peeling strategies leads to different I/O bounds, and which one is better depends on the relation sizes. When $N_0 \le N_n$, we peel off the star with e_n as the core first, otherwise we peel the star with e_0 as the core.

When $N_0 \le N_n$: In this case, we peel off the star with e_n being the core. The $\mathbf{S}$ returned by $\text{GENS}(\mathcal{Q})$ will then contain the following types of subsets: (i) $S \subseteq \{e_n, e_{n+1}\}$ (ii) $S \cup \{e_{n+1}\}$ with $S \subseteq \mathcal{E} - \{e_n, e_{n+1}\}$; (iii) $S \subseteq \mathcal{E} - \{e_{n+1}\}$. Recall that to prove optimality, for each $S \in \mathbf{S}$, we need to construct an instance I whose partial join size on S matches the maximum subjoin size, i.e.,

$$\max_R |\bowtie_{e \in S} R(e)| = |\mathcal{Q}(I, S)|.$$

Case (i) is trivial. For case (ii), the instance I is constructed as follows: Set $|\text{dom}(v_n)| = N_0$, and the domain of all the other join attributes have size 1. Each relation is simply the cross product of the domains of its attributes. Note that $|I(e_i)| = N_i$, except that $|I(e_n)| = N_0 \le N_n$. On this I, the partial join on $S \cup \{e_{n+1}\}$ has size

$$|\mathcal{Q}(I, S \cup \{e_{n+1}\})| = \prod_{e \in S \cup \{e_{n+1}\}} N(e),$$

which is clearly also the maximum subjoin size.

For (iii), if $e_0 \in S$, then the partial join size always matches the subjoin size. If $e_0 \notin S$, we construct I as follows: Set $|\text{dom}(v_n)| = N_0$, $|\text{dom}(v_{n+1})| = \frac{N_n}{N_0}$, and the domain of all the other join attributes have size 1. Each relation is the cross product of the domains of its attributes, and we have $|I(e_i)| = N_i$ for all i. Note that we will need $N_{n+1} \geq \frac{N_n}{N_0}$ for this construction to be feasible, but this is always the case on fully reduced instances.

When $N_0 \geq N_n$: In this case, we peel off the star with core e_0 first. The **S** generated by GENS($\mathcal{Q}$) contains the following types of subsets: (i) $S \subseteq \mathcal{E} - \{e_n, e_{n+1}\}$ always containing e_0; (ii) $S \cup \{e_0, e_{n+1}\}$ with $S \subsetneq \mathcal{E} - \{e_0, e_n, e_{n+1}\}$; (iii) $S \cup f$ with $S \subseteq \mathcal{E} - \{e_0, e_n, e_{n+1}\}, f \subseteq \{e_n, e_{n+1}\}$.

For any S in (i), the partial join size always matches the subjoin size. For any $S \cup \{e_0, e_{n+1}\}$ in case (ii), its subjoin size is at most

$$N_{n+1} \cdot \max_R |\mathcal{Q}(R, S \cup \{e_0\})|. \qquad (6)$$

Let $R_{\max}$ be the R that maximizes $|\mathcal{Q}(R, S \cup \{e_0\})|$. Note that in $R_{\max}$, we must have $|\text{dom}(v_n)| \leq N_n$. We construct the instance I based on $R_{\max}$: For any $e \in S \cup \{e_0\}$, $I(e) = R_{\max}(e)$; $I(e_n)$ is a many-to-one mapping from $\text{dom}(v_n)$ to $\text{dom}(v_{n+1})$; $I(e_{n+1})$ is a one-to-many mapping of size N_{n+1} from $\text{dom}(v_n)$ to $\text{dom}(v_{n+1})$. On such an I, its partial join size on $S \cup \{e_0, e_n\}$ is exactly (6).

For any $S \cup f$ in (iii), if $f = \{e_{n+1}\}$ or $f = \emptyset$, the case can be easily handled by setting $|\text{dom}(v_1)| = \cdots = |\text{dom}(v_{n+1}| = 1$. On such an I, its partial join size is simply $\prod_{e \in S \cup f} N(e)$. If $f = \{e_n\}$ or $\{e_n, e_{n+1}\}$, we just need to change $|\text{dom}(v_n)|$ to N_n. This is feasible due to condition $N_0 \geq N_n$, so that $|R(e_0)|$ does not violate its size constraint. The partial join size is then still $\prod_{e \in S \cup f} N(e)$.

We do not have a closed-form worst-case bound for lollipop joins, as it contains a star.

7.3 Dumbbell joins

A *dumbbell join* is illustrated in Figure 9, which consists of two stars connected by a common petal. One star has e_0 at its center, with n petals $e_1, \ldots, e_n$. The other star has petals $e_n, \ldots, e_{m-1}$, with e_m at its center.

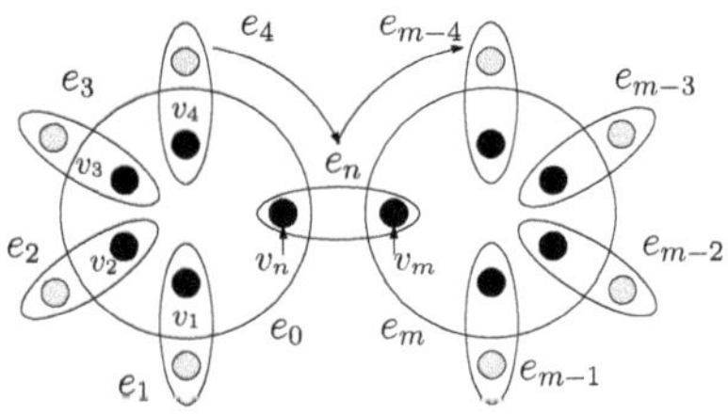

Figure 9: A dumbbell join.

Note that a dumbbell join generalizes an L_5, so Algorithm 2 is not always optimal. The optimality condition also generalizes that for L_5, becoming

$$N_i N_n N_j \geq N_0 N_m, \qquad (7)$$

for any $1 \leq i \leq n-1, n+1 \leq j \leq m-1$.

The proof of worst-case optimality on dumbbell join query is a generalization of the analysis on the lollipop join, but more involved. The details are given in Appendix A.4. Again, we do not have a closed-form bound on its optimal I/O complexity, as it contains a star.

8. CONCLUDING REMARKS

In this paper, we have designed a worst-case I/O-optimal algorithm for computing a fairly large class of acyclic joins. Interestingly, we have been able to prove its optimality without deriving its worst-case bound explicitly. This is done by relating the I/O cost of the algorithm to all the subjoins sizes, and then showing that the subjoin sizes match the corresponding partial join sizes in the worst case.

We conclude by mentioning a few interesting open problems.

1. For cases where our general algorithm is not optimal, in particular for line joins with 5 to 8 relations, we have designed special algorithms to achieve optimality. Is there a more unified way to tackle these cases?

2. Yannakakis' algorithm is instance optimal in internal memory. However, we conjecture that such an algorithm does not exist in external memory, even on 3 relations. Is there a formal proof? If it indeed does not exist, are there any conditions under which it does?

3. How about cyclic joins? So far, worst-case I/O-optimal algorithms are known only for triangle queries on relations of equal size.

9. REFERENCES

[1] A. Aggarwal, J. Vitter, et al. The input/output complexity of sorting and related problems. *Communications of the ACM*, 31(9):1116–1127, 1988.

[2] A. Atserias, M. Grohe, and D. Marx. Size bounds and query plans for relational joins. In *Proc. IEEE Symposium on Foundations of Computer Science*, pages 739–748, 2008.

[3] C. Beeri, R. Fagin, D. Maier, and M. Yannakakis. On the desirability of acyclic database schemes. *Journal of the ACM*, 30(3):479–513, 1983.

[4] C. Berge and E. Minieka. *Graphs and hypergraphs*, volume 7. North-Holland publishing company Amsterdam, 1973.

[5] H. Garcia-Molina, J. D. Ullman, and J. Widom. *Database Systems: The Complete Book.* Prentice Hall, 2008.

[6] X. Hu, M. Qiao, and Y. Tao. Join Dependency Testing, Loomis-Whitney Join, and Triangle Enumeration. In *Proc. ACM Symposium on Principles of Database Systems*, 2015.

[7] X. Hu, Y. Tao, and C.-W. Chung. Massive graph triangulation. In *Proc. ACM SIGMOD International Conference on Management of Data*, 2013.

[8] P. Koutris, P. Beame, and D. Suciu. Worst-case optimal algorithms for parallel query processing.

[9] H. Q. Ngo, E. Porat, C. Ré, and A. Rudra. Worst-case optimal join algorithms. In *Proc. ACM Symposium on Principles of Database Systems*, pages 37–48, 2012.

[10] H. Q. Ngo, C. Ré, and A. Rudra. Skew strikes back: New developments in the theory of join algorithms. *ACM SIGMOD Record*, 42(4):5–16, 2014.

[11] A. Pagh and R. Pagh. Scalable computation of acyclic joins. In *Proc. ACM Symposium on Principles of Database Systems.* ACM, 2006.

[12] R. Pagh and F. Silvestri. The input/output complexity of triangle enumeration. In *Proc. ACM Symposium on Principles of Database Systems*, 2014.

[13] T. Veldhuizen. Leapfrog triejoin: A simple, worst-case optimal join algorithm. In *Proc. International Conference on Database Theory*, 2014.

[14] M. Yannakakis. Algorithms for acyclic database schemes. In *Proc. International Conference on Very Large Data Bases*, pages 82–94, 1981.

APPENDIX

A. DETAILED PROOFS

A.1 Proof of Theorem 2

PROOF. Recall that the join between two relations with no common attribute is simply their cross product. So (3) can be written as

$$\widetilde{O}\left(\sum_{S\subseteq\mathcal{E}}\frac{\prod_{S'\in\mathcal{C}(S)}|\Join_{e'\in S'}R(e')|}{M^{|S|-1}B}\right). \quad (8)$$

where $\mathcal{C}(S)$ consists of all the connected components of S.

Let the I/O cost of Algorithm 2 be $f(\mathcal{Q})$. We will prove that $f(\mathcal{Q})$ is bounded by (8) by induction on $|\mathcal{E}|$. The base case $|\mathcal{E}|=1$ is trivial. Now suppose $f(\mathcal{Q})$ is (8) for any $\mathcal{Q}$ and R with $|\mathcal{E}|=k$ relations, and we will show that the claim holds on $k+1$ relations as well. To simplify the presentation, the analysis below hides a constant factor for each level of induction / recursion. Since we assume the query size is a constant, this does not change the asymptotic result.

First, the total costs of peeling all the buds is $\widetilde{O}(\frac{N}{B})$, which is included in (8).

Next, consider peeling off an island e. Let $\mathcal{Q}'$ be the query fed in to the recursive calls after the peeling. We have

$$f(\mathcal{V},\mathcal{E},R)=\frac{N(e)}{B}+\left\lceil\frac{N(e)}{M}\right\rceil\cdot f(\mathcal{Q}').$$

The $\frac{N(e)}{B}$ term is clearly contained in (8). If $N(e)<M$, then the algorithm just makes one recursive call, and we have $f(\mathcal{Q})=\frac{N(e)}{B}+f(\mathcal{Q}')=(8)$ by the induction hypothesis. When $N(e)>M$, we can drop the ceiling. By the induction hypothesis, $f(\mathcal{Q}')$ has a term $\frac{\prod_{S'\in\mathcal{C}(S)}|\Join_{e'\in S'}R(e')|}{M^{|S|-1}B}$ for each subset S of $\mathcal{E}-\{e\}$. Since e is disconnected from S and $S\cup\{e\}$ is a subset of $\mathcal{E}$, $\frac{N(e)}{M}\cdot\frac{\prod_{S'\in\mathcal{C}(S)}|\Join_{e'\in S'}R(e')|}{M^{|S|-1}B}$ is included in (8).

In the rest of the proof, we consider peeling off a leaf e, with join attribute v and neighboring relations Γ. The cost of the sorting in line 12–13 is $\widetilde{O}(\frac{N(e)}{B}+\sum_{e'\in\Gamma}\frac{N(e')}{B})$, which is included in (8).

Heavy tuples. Consider the heavy tuples in $R(e)$ first (line 14–20). For each a, the loop (line 16–19) has $\frac{N(e)|_{v=a}}{M}$ iterations (we must have $N(e)|_{v=a}\geq M$ because a is heavy), each recursively computing a query $\mathcal{Q}'(a)$. So the total cost of handling all the heavy tuples is

$$\sum_{a\in H(e,v)}\frac{N(e)|_{v=a}}{M}f(\mathcal{Q}'(a)).$$

Recall that for heavy values on v, we delete v before going into the recursion, which decomposes the query into $|\Gamma|$ components. And in the modified instance $R'(a)$ fed into the recursive calls, each $R(e'), e'\in\Gamma$ has been replaced with $R(e')|_{v=a}$. For any $e'\notin\Gamma$, $R(e')$ remains unchanged, i.e., $R(e')|_{v=a}=R(e')$. Thus, by the induction hypothesis, the total cost to handle all the heavy values is

$$\sum_{a\in H(e,v)}\frac{N(e)|_{v=a}}{M}\sum_{S\subseteq\mathcal{E}-\{e\}}\frac{\prod_{S'\in\mathcal{C}(S)}|\Join_{e'\in S'}R(e')|_{v=a}|}{M^{|S|-1}B}$$
$$=\sum_{S\subseteq\mathcal{E}-\{e\}}\sum_{a\in H(e,v)}\frac{N(e)|_{v=a}}{M}\frac{\prod_{S'\in\mathcal{C}(S)}|\Join_{e'\in S'}R(e')|_{v=a}|}{M^{|S|-1}B}.$$

Thus, it suffices to show that, for any $S\subseteq\mathcal{E}-\{e\}$,

$$\sum_{a\in H(e,v)}N(e)|_{v=a}\prod_{S'\in\mathcal{C}(S)}|\Join_{e'\in S'}R(e')|_{v=a}| \quad (9)$$
$$\leq\prod_{S'\in\mathcal{C}(S\cup\{e\})}|\Join_{e'\in S'}R(e')|. \quad (10)$$

Note that (9) is on the recursive calls on $\mathcal{Q}'(a)$, in which the attribute v has been removed, so the relations in Γ are not connected, while (10) considers the whole query $\mathcal{Q}$, in which all relations in Γ are connected, together with e.

First, observe that any $S'\in\mathcal{C}(S)$ that does not include any edge in Γ must be disconnected from e, thus also disconnected from any component of $\mathcal{C}(S\cup\{e\})$. Thus, it contributes the same factor

$$|\Join_{e'\in S'}R(e')|_{v=a}|=|\Join_{e'\in S'}R(e')|$$

to both (9) and (10), which cancel out. Note that if all connected components of S are like this, after all cancellation, we have

$$(9)=\sum_{a\in H(e,v)}N(e)|_{v=a}\leq N(e)=(10).$$

Thus, we can assume that each connected component of S includes a relation of Γ. Let them be $S_1,\ldots,S_r$. Note that they are disconnected in $\mathcal{Q}'(a)$, but are all connected in $\mathcal{Q}$, together with e, so $\mathcal{C}(S\cup\{e\})$ has only one component.

We then have

$$(9)=\sum_{a\in H(e,v)}N(e)|_{v=a}\prod_{i=1}^{r}|\Join_{e'\in S_i}R(e')|_{v=a}|$$
$$=\sum_{a\in H(e,v)}\left|R(e)|_{v=a}\Join\left(\Join_{e'\in S}R(e')|_{v=a}\right)\right|$$
$$=(10).$$

Light tuples. Finally, consider the light tuples (line 21–27). Different memory chunks M_1 of $R(e)$ partition each $R(e')$ into disjoint parts $R(e')(M_1)$. The total cost of computing and sorting all the $R(e')(M_1)$'s on line 22–23 is $\widetilde{O}(\frac{N}{B})$. It only remains to consider the recursive calls. By the induction hypothesis, this is

$$\sum_{M_1}f(\mathcal{Q}')=\sum_{M_1}\sum_{S\subseteq\mathcal{E}-\{e\}}\frac{\prod_{S'\in\mathcal{C}(S)}|\Join_{e'\in S'}R(e')(M_1)|}{M^{|S|-1}B}$$
$$=\sum_{S\subseteq\mathcal{E}-\{e\}}\sum_{M_1}\frac{\prod_{S'\in\mathcal{C}(S)}|\Join_{e'\in S'}R(e')(M_1)|}{M^{|S|-1}B}.$$

Here we define $R(e')(M_1)=R(e')$ if $e'\notin\Gamma$.

Thus, it suffices to show that, for any $S \subseteq \mathcal{E} - \{e\}$,

$$\sum_{M_1} \prod_{S' \in \mathcal{C}(S)} | \Join_{e' \in S'} R(e')(M_1)| \quad (11)$$

$$\leq \prod_{S' \in \mathcal{C}(S)} | \Join_{e' \in S'} R(e')|. \quad (12)$$

Note that S is also a subset of $\mathcal{E}$, so (12) is included in (8).

For any S' that does not include a relation in Γ, $R(e')(M_1) = R(e')$, it contributes the same factor to both (11) and (12), thus cancels out. Any connected component that remains after the cancellation includes some relation of Γ. Recall that for light tuples, the join attribute v is included in the recursive calls, so all relations in Γ are still connected, which means that all that is left is one connected component S. Therefore,

$$(11) = \sum_{M_1} | \Join_{e' \in S} R(e')(M_1)|$$
$$= | \Join_{e' \in S} R(e')| = (12),$$

which concludes the proof. □

A.2 Proof of Theorem 3

By the round-robin simulation of the nondeterministic algorithm, it is sufficient to prove the following:

LEMMA 4. *Let $\mathcal{Q}$ be an acyclic query, $\mathcal{A}$ be any branch of* GENS($\mathcal{Q}$)*, and* **S** *be the resulting set of subsets of relations returned by* GENS($\mathcal{Q}$) *following $\mathcal{A}$. There is a branch of Algorithm 2 whose I/O cost is $\tilde{O}(\max_{S \in \mathbf{S}} \Psi(R, S))$.*

PROOF. The proof is by induction on the size of the hypergraph of $\mathcal{Q}$. The base case when the hypergraph is empty is trivial. If $\mathcal{A}$ first peels off is a leaf, an island, or a bud, the proof is almost identical to the proof of Theorem 2, thus we will focus on the case when peeling off a star. Suppose $\mathcal{A}$ peels off a star $\mathcal{X}$ with k petals $e_1, \dots, e_k$, and the core is e_0. We assume that the petals are disjoint for now.

The set of subsets returned by GENS($\mathcal{Q}$) following $\mathcal{A}$ is

$$\text{GENS}(\mathcal{Q}) = 2^{\mathcal{X}} + 2^{\mathcal{X} - \{e_0\}} \times \text{GENS}(\mathcal{Q} - \mathcal{X}) + \left(2^{\mathcal{X} - \{e_0\}} - \{\mathcal{X} - \{e_0\}\}\right) \times \text{GENS}(\mathcal{Q} - \mathcal{X} + \{e_0\}). \quad (13)$$

Here we redefine the notation $\mathbf{X} \times \mathbf{Y} = \{X \cup Y \mid X \in \mathbf{X}, Y \in \mathbf{Y}\}$.

First consider the case where $\mathcal{X}$ has only one petal e_1. We ask Algorithm 2 to peel off e_1 and then e_0. Let v_1 be the join attribute between e_0 and e_1. Following similar analysis as in the proof of Theorem 2 and invoking the induction hypothesis on $\mathcal{Q} - \mathcal{X} = \mathcal{Q} - \{e_0, e_1\}$, the I/O-cost of handing the heavy tuples in $R(e_1)$ is

$$\sum_{a \in H(e_1, v_1)} \frac{R(e_1)|_{v_1 = a}}{M} \cdot \left(\frac{R(e_0)|_{v_1 = a}}{B} + \max_{S \in \text{GENS}(\mathcal{Q} - \mathcal{X})} \Psi(R, S) \right)$$
$$= \Psi(R, \{e_0, e_1\}) + \max_{S \in \{\{e_1\}\} \times \text{GENS}(\mathcal{Q} - \mathcal{X})} \Psi(R, S).$$

These two terms are captured by the first two terms of (13), respectively. The cost to handle the light tuples is (invoking the induction hypothesis on $\mathcal{Q} - \{e_1\}$)

$$\sum_{M_1 \in R(e_1)} \max_{S \in \text{GENS}(\mathcal{Q} - \{e_1\})} \Psi(R(M_1), S) = \sum_{S \in \text{GENS}(\mathcal{Q} - \{e_1\})} \Psi(R, S).$$

This is captured by the last term of (13), which degenerates to just GENS($\mathcal{Q} - \{e_1\}$) when $\mathcal{X}$ has only one petal.

If $\mathcal{X}$ has $k \geq 2$ petals, we ask Algorithm 2 to peel off the petals $e_k, e_{k-1}, \dots, e_1$ one by one, and finally e_0. Let v_k be the join attribute between e_0 and e_k. Recall that when dealing with heavy tuples in $R(e_k)$, we remove v_k before making the recursive call on $\mathcal{Q} - \{e_k\} - \{v_k\}$. Thus, we invoke the induction hypothesis on $\mathcal{Q} - \{e_k\} - \{v_k\}$ to bound the cost of handling the heavy tuples in $R(e_k)$:

$$\sum_{a \in H(e_k, v_k)} \frac{R(e_k)|_{v_k = a}}{M} \cdot \max_{S \in \text{GENS}(\mathcal{Q} - \{e_k\} - \{v_k\})} \Psi(R|_{v_k = a}, S)$$
$$= \Psi(R, \{e_k, e_0\}) + \max_{S \in \{\{e_k\}\} \times \text{GENS}(\mathcal{Q} - \{e_k\} - \{v_k\})} \Psi(R, S).$$

The first term is captured by the first term of (13). For the second term, observe that $e_{k-1}, \dots, e_1, e_0$ still forms a star in $\mathcal{Q} - \{e_k\} - \{v_k\}$. Consider any $S \in \{\{e_k\}\} \times$ GENS($\mathcal{Q} - \{e_k\} - \{v_k\}$). If $e_0 \notin S$, it is captured by the second term of (13); if $e_0 \in S$, then S cannot have all of $e_1, \dots, e_{k-1}$ due to the property of GENS($\mathcal{Q} - \{e_k\} - \{v_k\}$), thus captured by the third term of (13).

When dealing with the light tuples in $R(e_k)$, recall that Algorithm 2 does not remove the join attribute v_k before making the recursive call, so we invoke the induction hypothesis on $\mathcal{Q} - \{e_k\}$ to bound the cost to handle the light tuples:

$$\sum_{M_k \in R(e_k)} \max_{S \in \text{GENS}(\mathcal{Q} - \{e_k\})} \Psi(R(M_k), S)$$
$$= \Psi(R, \{e_k\}) + \max_{S \in \text{GENS}(\mathcal{Q} - \{e_k\})} \Psi(R, S).$$

The first term is captured by the first term of (13). For the second term, note that in $\mathcal{Q} - \{e_k\}$, $\mathcal{X} - \{e_k\}$ is no longer a star as e_0 contains a unique attribute v_k, and GENS will peel each of them as a leaf. So we have

$$\text{GENS}(\mathcal{Q} - \{e_k\}) = 2^{\{e_0, e_1, \dots, e_{k-1}\}} \times \text{GENS}(\mathcal{Q} - \mathcal{X}).$$

This must be a subset of GENS($\mathcal{Q}$) since it does not contain e_k.

Finally, if there are two or more petals in $\mathcal{X}$ joining with e_0 on the same join attribute, we ask Algorithm 2 to peel off the extra petals first, to transform $\mathcal{X}$ into a simple star. These extra petals will be included in every S. But since all we need to show is that not all petals can be included in S if e_0 is included, which is already guaranteed by the analysis on the simple star, this does not affect the theorem. □

A.3 Optimality of Algorithm 5

In Algorithm 2, the cost of ACYCLICJOIN in line 1 is $\tilde{O}(\frac{N_3 N_5}{MB} + \frac{N_4}{B})$, but writing S to disk costs $\tilde{O}(\frac{N_3 N_5}{B})$. The cost of ACYCLICJOIN in line 2 is $\tilde{O}(\frac{N_1 N_3 N_5 N_7}{M^2 B} + \frac{N_2 N_6}{MB} + \frac{N_1 N_6}{MB} + \frac{N_2 N_7}{MB})$. There is $\frac{N_4}{B} \leq \frac{N_3 N_5}{B} \leq \frac{N_1 N_3 N_5 N_7}{M^2 B}$ due to relation size constraints and assumptions. The upper bound is exactly $\tilde{O}(\frac{N_1 N_3 N_5 N_7}{M^2 B} + \frac{N_2 N_6}{MB} + \frac{N_1 N_6}{MB} + \frac{N_2 N_7}{MB})$.

Under this scenario, 3 balancing conditions might break: (a) $N_1 N_3 N_5 N_7 \geq N_2 N_4 N_6$, (b) $N_1 N_3 N_5 \geq N_2 N_4$, and (c) $N_3 N_5 N_7 \geq N_4 N_6$. There are eight combinations about these three conditions, but in fact only following four situations needing consideration by the dependency and symmetry among those balancing conditions.

(i) all (a)(b)(c) broken;

(ii) only (a)(b) broken, symmetric with only (a)(c) broken;

(iii) only (a) broken;

(iv) only (b) broken, symmetric with only (c) broken;

Note that if both (b)(c) are broken, (a) will definitely be broken and this case will degenerate to case (i). Next we will construct an instance for each case discussed above and show worst-case optimality of Algorithm 5.

For case (i) (ii)(iii), construct an instance I similarly as previously. Relations e_1 and e_7 are both one-to-one mapping from $\text{dom}(v_1)$ onto $\text{dom}(v_2)$ and from $\text{dom}(v_7)$ onto $\text{dom}(v_8)$ respectively. Relations e_2, e_4 and e_6 are cross products while e_3 and e_5 remain as many-to-many mappings. It is feasible by the constraints with implication $N_2 > N_1$ and $N_6 > N_7$. For such an I, only e_4 is not cross product. Thus there is $|\mathcal{Q}(I)| = N_1N_3N_5N_7$ with partial joins below.

$$\begin{aligned}|\mathcal{Q}(I, \{e_2, e_4, e_6\})| &= N_1N_3N_5N_7,\\ |\mathcal{Q}(I, \{e_2, e_7\})| &= N_2N_7,\\ |\mathcal{Q}(I, \{e_1, e_6\})| &= N_1N_6,\\ |\mathcal{Q}(I, \{e_2, e_6\})| &= N_2N_6.\end{aligned}$$

For case (iv), construct an instance I in a similar way. Relation e_1 is a one-to-one mapping from $\text{dom}(v_1)$ onto $\text{dom}(v_2)$. For attribute v_6, we set $|\text{dom}(v_6)| = 1$. Relations e_2, e_4, e_5 and e_6 are cross products while e_3 and e_7 remain as many-to-many mappings. It is feasible due to the relation size constraints and its implications $N_2 > N_1$, $N_7 > N_6$ and $N_4 > N_5$. For such an I, there is $|\mathcal{Q}(I)| = N_1N_3N_5N_7$ with partial joins below.

$$\begin{aligned}|\mathcal{Q}(I, \{e_2, e_4, e_7\})| &= N_1N_3N_5N_7,\\ |\mathcal{Q}(I, \{e_2, e_7\})| &= N_2N_7,\\ |\mathcal{Q}(I, \{e_1, e_6\})| &= N_1N_6,\\ |\mathcal{Q}(I, \{e_2, e_6\})| &= N_2N_6.\end{aligned}$$

A.4 Optimality of dumbbell joins

For a dumbbell join query $\mathcal{Q}$, we peel off the star with e_m being the core first. This generates two recursive calls, one on an lollipop join ($e_0 \bowtie \cdots \bowtie e_n \bowtie e_m$) and one on a star join ($e_n \bowtie e_{n+1} \bowtie \cdots \bowtie e_m$). For the lollipop join ($e_0 \bowtie \cdots \bowtie e_n \bowtie e_m$), we choose to peel off the star (with e_0 being the core), which generates two recursive calls on $L_3(e_0 \bowtie e_n \bowtie e_m)$ and $L_2(e_n \bowtie e_m)$. The $\mathbf{S}$ generated by GENS($\mathcal{Q}$) contains the following types of subsets. Recall that to prove optimality, for each $S \in \mathbf{S}$, we need to construct an instance I whose partial join size on S matches the maximum subjoin size, i.e.,

$$\max_R |\bowtie_{e\in S} R(e)| = |\mathcal{Q}(I, S)|$$

(i) $S = S_1 \cup S_2 \cup f$ with $S_1 \subsetneq \{e_{n+1}, e_{n+2}, \ldots, e_{m-1}\}$, $S_2 \subseteq \{e_1, \ldots, e_{n-1}\}$, $f \subseteq \{e_n, e_m\}$.

If $f = \{e_n\}$, the domain of join attribute is the solution of the following inequalities.

$$\begin{cases} N_0 = \prod_{i=1}^{n} |\text{dom}(v_i)|, \\ N_n = |\text{dom}(v_n)| \cdot |\text{dom}(v_m)|, \\ N_m = \prod_{i=n+1}^{m} |\text{dom}(v_i)|, \\ 1 \leq |\text{dom}(v_i)| \leq N_i, i = 1, 2, \cdots, m-1 \end{cases}$$

Tuples in relation $e_i, i \in [1, m-1] - \{n\}$ can be an arbitrary mapping from unique attributes onto $\text{dom}(v_i)$. This construction is always feasible by balancing condition (7). Under this instance, we obtain

$$\max_R |\bowtie_{e\in S} R(e)| = \prod_{e\in S} N(e) = |\mathcal{Q}(I, S)|.$$

If $f = \{e_m\}$, the maximum subjoin size is

$$\max_R |\bowtie_{e\in S} R(e)| \leq \prod_{e\in S_2} N(e) \cdot \max_R |\bowtie_{e\in S_1\cup f} R(e)|. \quad (14)$$

Let $R_{\max}$ be the R that maximizes $|\bowtie_{e\in S_1\cup\{e_m\}} R(e)|$ under the constraint $|\text{dom}(v_m)| \leq N_n$. We construct instance I by extending $R_{\max}$. The domain of join attribute v_i for $i \in [1, n]$ has only one value. Any relation $e_i, i \in [1, n-1]$ is a one-to-many matching from the only value in $\text{dom}(v_i)$ to the unique attribute of R_i. This construction is always feasible as $1 \cdot |\text{dom}(v_m)| \leq N_n$ in a fully reduced instance. Under this instance, we have

$$\prod_{e\in S_2} N(e) \cdot \max_R |\bowtie_{e\in S_1\cup f} R(e)| = |\mathcal{Q}(I, S)|. \quad (15)$$

If $f = \{e_n, e_m\}$, there is also (14). Let $R_{\max}$ be the R that maximizes $|\bowtie_{e\in S_1\cup f} R(e)|$ under the constraint $|\text{dom}(v_n)| \leq N_0$. We construct instance I by extending $R_{\max}$. The domain of join attribute v_i for $i \in [1, n-1]$ has only one value. Any relation $e_i, i \in [1, n-1]$ is a one-to-many matching from the only value in $\text{dom}(v_i)$ to the unique attribute of R_i. This construction is feasible as $|\text{dom}(v_n)| \leq N_0$ and (15) holds for every S.

(ii) $S = S_1 \cup S_2$ with $S_1 \subseteq \{e_{n+1}, e_{n+2}, \cdots, e_{m-1}\}$, $S_2 \subsetneq \{e_0, e_1, \cdots, e_n\}$. The instance construction I depends on two cases. If $e_0 \notin S$, the proof is the same as (i) when $f = \{e_n\}$. If $e_0 \in S$, the proof is almost the same as (i) when $f = \{e_m\}$.

(iii) $S \subseteq \{e_{n+1}, e_{n+2}, \cdots, e_{m-1}, e_m\}$. The subjoin of any S containing e_m always matches its partial join. For S not containing e_m, we construct the instance I by setting the domain of any join attribute with only one value. Each leaf can be a one-to-many matching from the only value in $\text{dom}(v_i)$ to the unique attributes in R_i. Under this instance, we achieve the same result in (i) with $f = \{e_n\}$.

(iv) $S = S_1 \cup S_2 \cup f$ with $S_1 \subsetneq \{e_{n+1}, e_{n+2}, \cdots, e_{m-1}\}$, $S_2 \subsetneq \{e_1, \cdots, e_{n-1}\}$, $f \in \{\{e_0, e_m\}, \{e_0\}, \{e_m\}, \{e_n\}\}$. If $f \in \{\{e_0\}, \{e_m\}, \{e_n\}\}$, the case degenerates to (i). If $f = \{e_0, e_m\}$, the case is different. Without loss of generality, we assume $N_i \leq N_j$ when $i \leq j$ and the balancing condition (7) becomes $N_1N_nN_{n+1} \geq N_0N_m$. For any subjoin, there is a upper bound below

$$\max_R \Psi(R, S_1 \cup \{e_m\}) \cdot \max_R \Psi(S_2 \cup \{e_0\}) \cdot \frac{B}{M}$$

under constraints $|\text{dom}(v_n)| \leq N_n$ and $|\text{dom}(v_m)| \leq N_n$. We focus on $\max_R \Psi(S_2 \cup \{e_0\})$ under $|\text{dom}(v_n)| \leq N_n$ first. When $N_0 < N_1N_n$, we know that

$$\max_{S_2} \max_R \Psi(R, S_2 \cup \{e_0\}) \leq \frac{N_0 \prod_{k=2}^{n-1} N_k}{M^{n-2}B}$$

Otherwise, $\max_{S_2} \max_R \Psi(R, S_2 \cup \{e_0\})$ is bounded by

$$\max_{S_2} \frac{\min\{N_0, \prod_{e\notin S_2} N(e)\} \cdot \prod_{e\in S_2} N(e)}{M^{|S_2|}B}$$

$$\leq \max\{\frac{\prod_{j=1}^{n} N_j}{M^{n-i}B}, \frac{N_0 \prod_{j=i+1}^{n-1} N_j}{M^{n-i-1}B}\}$$

where i is the index such that $\prod_{j=1}^{i-1} N_j \leq \frac{N_0}{N_p} < \prod_{j=1}^{i} N_j$. Note that at least one of $N_0 < N_n N_1$ and $N_m < N_n N_{n+1}$ occurs otherwise balancing condition (7) will be broken.

When $N_0 < N_n N_1$ and $N_m < N_n N_{n+1}$, the maximum subjoin is

$$\max_S \max_R \Psi(R,S) = \frac{N_0 \prod_{k=2}^{n-1} N_k}{M^{n-2}B} \cdot \frac{N_m \prod_{k=n+2}^{m-1} N_k}{M^{m-n-2}B}$$

by our analysis above. We construct instance I by setting the domain as

$$|\mathrm{dom}(v_i)| = \begin{cases} \min\{N_1, N_0\}, & i = 1 \\ \max\{\frac{N_0}{N_1}, 1\}, & i = n \\ \min\{N_{n+1}, N_m\}, & i = n+1 \\ \max\{\frac{N_m}{N_{n+1}}, 1\}, & i = m \\ 1, & otherwise \end{cases}$$

Relation R_i for $i \in [1, m-1] - \{n\}$ can be an arbitrary mapping from unique attributes onto $\mathrm{dom}(v_i)$. The construction is feasible with $|\mathrm{dom}(v_n)| \cdot |\mathrm{dom}(v_m)| \leq N_n$ implied by balancing condition (7). Under this instance, there is

$$\max_S \max_R \Psi(R,S) = \psi(I,S)$$

where $S = S_1 \cup S_2 \cup f$ with $S_1 = \{e_{n+2}, e_{n+3}, \cdots, e_{m-1}\}$, $S_2 = \{e_2, e_3, \cdots, e_{n-1}\}$, $f = \{e_0, e_m\}$.

When $N_0 < N_n N_1$ and $N_m \geq N_n N_{n+1}$, there is $\frac{N_0}{N_1} \leq \frac{N_n N_{n+1}}{N_m} \leq 1$. The maximum subjoin is

$$\max_S \max_R \Psi(R,S) = \frac{N_0 \prod_{k=2}^{n-1} N_k}{M^{n-1}} \cdot \max_R \Psi(R, S_1 \cup \{e_m\}$$

Let $R_{\max}$ be the R that maximizes $|\bowtie_{e \in S_1 \cup \{e_m\}} R(e)|$ under the constraint $|\mathrm{dom}(v_m)| \leq N_n$. We construct instance I by extending $R_{\max}$. We set $|\mathrm{dom}(v_1)| = N_0$ and the domain of join attribute v_j for $j \in [2, n]$ with only one value. This construction is always feasible as $|\mathrm{dom}(N_1)| \leq N_1$ and $|\mathrm{dom}(v_m)| \leq N_n$. We know that

$$\max_S \max_R \Psi(R,S) = \psi(I,S)$$

where $S = S_1 \cup S_2 \cup f$ with S_1 as $\arg\max_{S_1} \max_R \Psi(R, S_1 \cup \{e_m\})$, $S_2 = \{e_2, e_3, \cdots, e_{n-1}\}$, $f = \{e_0, e_m\}$.

When $N_0 \geq N_n N_1$ and $N_m < N_n N_{n+1}$, the instance construction is the same as the case $N_0 < N_n N_1$ and $N_m \geq N_n N_{n+1}$.

On the Complexity of Inner Product Similarity Join

Thomas D. Ahle
IT University of Copenhagen
thdy@itu.dk

Rasmus Pagh
IT University of Copenhagen
pagh@itu.dk

Ilya Razenshteyn
MIT CSAIL
ilyaraz@mit.edu

Francesco Silvestri
IT University of Copenhagen
fras@itu.dk

ABSTRACT

A number of tasks in classification, information retrieval, recommendation systems, and record linkage reduce to the core problem of *inner product similarity join* (IPS join): identifying pairs of vectors in a collection that have a sufficiently large inner product. IPS join is well understood when vectors are normalized and some *approximation* of inner products is allowed. However, the general case where vectors may have any length appears much more challenging. Recently, new upper bounds based on asymmetric locality-sensitive hashing (ALSH) and asymmetric embeddings have emerged, but little has been known on the lower bound side. In this paper we initiate a systematic study of inner product similarity join, showing new lower and upper bounds. Our main results are:

- Approximation hardness of IPS join in subquadratic time, assuming the strong exponential time hypothesis.
- New upper and lower bounds for (A)LSH-based algorithms. In particular, we show that asymmetry can be avoided by relaxing the LSH definition to only consider the collision probability of *distinct* elements.
- A new indexing method for IPS based on linear sketches, implying that our hardness results are not far from being tight.

Our technical contributions include new asymmetric embeddings that may be of independent interest. At the conceptual level we strive to provide greater clarity, for example by distinguishing among signed and unsigned variants of IPS join and shedding new light on the effect of asymmetry.

1. INTRODUCTION

This paper is concerned with *inner product similarity join* (*IPS join*) where, given two sets $P, Q \subseteq \mathbb{R}^d$, the task is to find for each point $q \in Q$ at least one pair[1] $(p, q) \in P \times Q$ where the inner product (or its absolute value) is larger than a given threshold s. Our results apply also to the problem where for each $q \in Q$ we seek the vector $p \in P$ that maximizes the inner product, a search problem known in literature as *maximum inner product search* (MIPS) [43, 45].

PODS'16, June 26-July 01, 2016, San Francisco, CA, USA

DOI: http://dx.doi.org/10.1145/2902251.2902285

Motivation

Similarity joins have been widely studied in the database and information retrieval communities as a mechanism for linking noisy or incomplete data. Considerable progress, in theory and practice, has been made to address metric spaces where the triangle inequality can be used to prune the search space (see e.g. [6, 61]). In particular, it is now known that in many cases it is possible to improve upon the quadratic time complexity of a naive algorithm that explicitly considers all pairs of tuples. The most prominent technique used to achieve provably subquadratic running time is locality-sensitive hashing (LSH) [25, 24]. In the database community the similarity join problem was originally motivated by applications in data cleaning [17, 10]. However, since then it has become clear that similarity join is relevant for a range of other data processing applications such as clustering, semi-supervised learning, query refinement, and collaborative filtering (see e.g. [44] for references and further examples). We refer to the recent book by Augsten and Böhlen [11] for more background on similarity join algorithms in database systems.

Inner product is an important measure of similarity between real vectors, particularly in information retrieval and machine learning contexts [31, 48], but not captured by techniques for metric similarity joins such as [26, 61]. Teflioudi et al. [50] studied the IPS join problem motivated by applications in recommender systems based on latent-factor models. In this setting, a user and the available items are represented as vectors and the preference of a user for an item is given by the inner product of the two associated vectors. Other examples of applications for IPS join are object detection [23] and multi-class prediction [22, 28]. IPS join also captures the so-called *maximum kernel search*, a general machine learning approach with applications such as image matching and finding similar protein/DNA sequences [20].

[1] Since our focus is on lower bounds, we do not consider the more general problem of finding all such pairs. Also note that from an upper bound side, it is common to limit the number of occurrences of each tuple in a join result to a given number k.

Challenges of IPS join

Large inner products do not correspond to close vectors in any metric on the vector space, so metric space techniques cannot directly be used. In fact, there are reasons to believe that inner product similarity may be inherently more difficult than other kinds of similarity search: Williams [56, 4] has shown that a truly subquadratic *exact* algorithm for IPS join would contradict the Strong Exponential Time Hypothesis, an important conjecture in computational complexity. On the upper bound side new reductions of (special cases of) *approximate* IPS join to fast matrix multiplication have appeared [51, 29], resulting in truly subquadratic algorithms even with approximation factors asymptotically close to 1. However, the approach of reducing to fast matrix multiplication does not seem to lead to practical algorithms, since fast matrix multiplication algorithms are currently not competitive on realistic input sizes. From a theoretical viewpoint it is of interest to determine how far this kind of technique might take us by extending lower bounds for exact IPS join to the approximate case.

Another approach to IPS join would be to use LSH, which has shown its utility in practice. The difficulty is that inner products do not admit locality-sensitive hashing as defined by Indyk and Motwani [45, Theorem 1]. Recently there has been progress on *asymmetric* LSH methods for inner products, resulting in subquadratic IPS join algorithms in many settings. The idea is to consider collisions between two *different* hash functions, using one hash function for query vectors and another hash function for data vectors [45, 46, 39]. However, existing ALSH methods give very weak guarantees in situations where inner products are small relative to the lengths of vectors. It is therefore highly relevant to determine the possibilities and limitations of this approach.

Problem definitions

We are interested in two variants of IPS join that slightly differ in the formulation of the objective function. For notational simplicity, we omit the term IPS and we simply refer to IPS join as join. Let $s > 0$ be a given value. The first variant is the *signed* join, where the goal is to find at least one pair $(p, q) \in P \times Q$ for each point $q \in Q$ with $p^T q \geq s$. The second variant is the *unsigned* join which finds, for each point $q \in Q$, at least one pair $(p, q) \in P \times Q$ where $|p^T q| \geq s$. We observe that the unsigned version can be solved with the signed one by computing the join between P and Q and between P and $-Q$, and then returning only pairs where the absolute inner products are larger than s. Signed join is of interest when searching for similar or preferred items with a positive correlation, like in recommender systems. On the other hand, unsigned join can be used when studying relations among phenomena where even a large negative correlation is of interest. Previous works do not make the distinction between signed and unsigned versions since they focus on settings where there are no negative dot products.

Our focus is on *approximate* algorithms for signed and unsigned joins. Indeed, approximate algorithms allow us to overcome, at least in some cases, the curse of dimensionality without significantly affecting the final results. Approximate signed joins are defined as follows.

DEFINITION 1 (APPROXIMATE SIGNED JOIN). *Given two point sets P, Q and values $0 < c < 1$ and $s > 0$, the* signed (cs, s) join *returns, for each $q \in Q$, at least one pair $(p, q) \in P \times Q$ with $p^T q \geq cs$ if there exists $p' \in P$ such that $p'^T q \geq s$. No guarantee is provided for $q \in Q$ where there is no $p' \in P$ with $p'^T q \geq s$.*

The unsigned (cs, s) join is defined analogously by taking the absolute value of dot products. Indexing versions of signed/unsigned exact/approximate joins can be defined in a similar way. For example, the signed (cs, s) search is defined as follows: given a set $P \subset \mathbb{R}^d$ of n vectors, construct a data structure that efficiently returns a vector $p \in P$ such that $p^T q > cs$ for any given query vector $q \in \mathbb{R}^d$, under the promise that there is a point $p' \in P$ such that $p^T q \geq s$ (a similar definition holds for the unsigned case).

As already mentioned, LSH is often used for solving similarity joins. In this paper, we use the following definition of asymmetric LSH based on the definition in [45].

DEFINITION 2 (ASYMMETRIC LSH). *Let $\mathcal{U}_p$ denote the data domain and $\mathcal{U}_q$ the query domain. Consider a family $\mathcal{H}$ of pairs of hash functions $h = (h_p(\cdot), h_q(\cdot))$. Then $\mathcal{H}$ is said* (s, cs, P_1, P_2)-asymmetric LSH *for a similarity function sim if for any $p \in \mathcal{U}_p$ and $q \in \mathcal{U}_q$ we have:*

1. *if $sim(p, q) \geq s$ then $\Pr_{\mathcal{H}}[h_p(p) = h_q(q)] \geq P_1$;*
2. *if $sim(p, q) < cs$ then $\Pr_{\mathcal{H}}[h_p(p) = h_q(q)] \leq P_2$.*

When $h_p(\cdot) = h_q(\cdot)$, we get the traditional (symmetric) LSH definition. The ρ value of an (asymmetric) LSH is defined as usual with $\rho = \log P_1 / \log P_2$ [6]. Two vectors $p \in \mathcal{U}_p$ and $q \in \mathcal{U}_q$ are said to collide under a hash function from $\mathcal{H}$ if $h_p(p) = h_q(q)$.

1.1 Overview of results

Hardness results

The first results of the paper are conditional lower bounds for approximate signed and unsigned IPS join that rely on a conjecture about the *Orthogonal Vectors Problem* (OVP). This problem consists in determining if two sets $A, B \subseteq \{0,1\}^d$, each one with n vectors, contain $x \in A$ and $y \in B$ such that $x^T y = 0$. It is conjectured that there cannot exist an algorithm that solves OVP in $O\left(n^{2-\epsilon}\right)$ time as soon as $d = \omega(\log n)$, for any given constant $\epsilon > 0$. Indeed, such an algorithm would imply that the Strong Exponential Time Hypothesis (SETH) is true [56].

Many recent hardness results rely on reductions from OVP, however we believe ours is the first example of using the conjecture to show the conditional hardness for an approximate problem. In particular we show the following result:

THEOREM 1. *Let $\alpha > 0$ be given and consider sets of vectors P, Q with $|Q| = n$, $|P| = n^\alpha$. Suppose there exists a constant $\epsilon > 0$ and an algorithm with running time at most $d^{O(1)} n^{1+\alpha-\epsilon}$, when d and n are sufficiently large and for all $s > 0$, for at least one of the following IPS join problems:*

1. *Signed (cs, s) join of $P, Q \subseteq \{-1,1\}^d$ where $c > 0$.*
2. *Unsigned (cs, s) join of $P, Q \subseteq \{-1,1\}^d$ where $c = e^{-o(\sqrt{\log n}/\log\log n)}$.*
3. *Unsigned (cs, s) join of $P, Q \subseteq \{0,1\}^d$ where $c = 1 - o(1)$.*

Then the OVP conjecture is false.

Discussion. For the search problem, Theorem 1 implies that, assuming the OVP conjecture, there does not exist a data structure for signed/unsigned (cs, s) inner product search with $(nd)^{O(1)}$ construction time and $n^{1-\epsilon}d^{O(1)}$ query time, for constant $\epsilon > 0$. This follows by considering a join instance with α constant small enough that we can build the data structure on P in time $o(nd)$. We can then query over all the points of Q in time $n^{1+\alpha(1-\epsilon)}d^{O(1)}$, contradicting the OVP conjecture. Our result can be seen as an explanation of why all LSH schemes for IPS have failed to provide sub-linear query times for small s. As the theorem however does not cover the case where c is very small, e.g. $n^{-\delta}$ for unsigned $\{-1,1\}^d$, we show in Section 4 that for such approximation requirements, there are indeed useful data structures.

We stress that the hardness result holds for algorithms solving signed/unsigned (cs, s) joins for *any* c in the specified range and *all* $s > 0$. It is possible to show complete relations between hard values of c, s and d, but for the sake of clearness, we have preferred to optimize the largest range of hard c's. For intuition we can say, that the exact instances of (cs, s) joins that are hard, turn out to be the ones where s/d and cs/d are very small, that is when we have to distinguish nearly orthogonal vectors from very nearly orthogonal vectors. If we inspect the proofs of Theorem 1 and Lemma 3, we see that for unsigned join in $\{-1,1\}^d$, the hard case has cs/d around $n^{1/\log\log n}$. Similarly for $\{0,1\}^d$ join, cs ends up at just barely $\omega(1)$, while the d is as high as $n^{o(1)}$. It is interesting to note for $\{0,1\}$ that if cs had been slightly lower, at $O(1)$, we could have solved the OVP problem exact in subquadratic time using an $n\binom{n^{o(1)}}{O(1)} = n^{1+o(1)}$ algorithm.

It is interesting to compare our conditional lower bound to the recent upper bounds by Karppa et al. [29], who get sub-quadratic running time for unsigned join of normalized vectors in $\{-1,1\}^d$, when $\log(s/d)/\log(cs/d)$ is a constant smaller than 1.[2] Our next Theorem 2 shows that we cannot hope to do much better than this, though it does not completely close the gap. A hardness result for $\log(s/d)/\log(cs/d) = 1 - o(1)$ is still an interesting open problem. However, while the algorithm of Karppa et al. works even for dimension $n^{1/3}$, our bound only requires the dimension to be slightly larger than polylog, so it may well be that their algorithm is optimal, while another algorithm with a higher dependency on the dimension matches our bound from above.

THEOREM 2. *Let $\alpha > 0$ be given and consider sets of vectors P, Q with $|Q| = n$, $|P| = n^\alpha$. Suppose there exists a constant $\epsilon > 0$ and an algorithm with running time at most $d^{O(1)}n^{1+\alpha-\epsilon}$, when d and n are sufficiently large and for all $s > 0$, for at least one of the following IPS join problems:*

1. *Unsigned (cs, s) over $\{-1,1\}^d$ where $\frac{\log(s/d)}{\log(cs/d)} = 1 - o(1/\sqrt{\log n})$*
2. *Unsigned (cs, s) over $\{0,1\}^d$ where $\frac{\log(s/d)}{\log(cs/d)} = 1 - o(1/\log n)$*

Then the OVP conjecture is false.

The $\{-1,1\}^d$ case seems to be harder than the $\{0,1\}^d$ case. In fact Valiant [51] reduces the general case of $P, Q \subseteq \mathbb{R}^d$ to the case $P, Q \subseteq \{-1,1\}^d$ using the Charikar hyperplane LSH [15]. Another piece of evidence is that we can achieve runtime $n^{1+\frac{\log(s/d)}{\log(cs/d)}}$ using LSH for $\{0,1\}^d$, but it is not known to be possible for $\{-1,1\}^d$. Furthermore there appears to be some hope for even better data dependent LSH, as we show in Section 4.2. The $\{0,1\}^d$ case is particularly interesting, as it is occurs often in practice, for example when the vectors represent sets. A better understanding of the upper and lower bounds for this case is a nice open problem. For an elaborate comparison of the different upper and lower bounds, see Table 1.

Techniques. From a technical point of view, the proof uses a number of different algebraic techniques to expand the gap between orthogonal and non-orthogonal vectors from the OVP problem. For the $\{-1,1\}$ we use an enhanced, deterministic version of the "Chebyshev embedding" [51], while for the interesting $\{0,1\}$ part, we initiate a study of embeddings for restricted alphabets.

Inner product LSH lower bounds

In the second part of the paper we focus on LSH functions for signed and unsigned IPS. We investigate the gap between the collision probability P_1 of vectors with inner product (or absolute inner product) larger than s and the collision probability P_2 of vectors with inner product (or absolute inner product) smaller than cs. As a special case, we get the impossibility result in [39, 45], that there cannot exist an asymmetric LSH for unbounded query vectors. Specifically we get the following theorem:

THEOREM 3. *Consider an (s, cs, P_1, P_2)-asymmetric LSH for signed IPS when data and query domains are d-dimensional balls with unit radius and radius U respectively. Then, the following upper bounds on $P_1 - P_2$ apply:*

1. *if $d \geq 1$ and $s \leq \min\{cU, U/(4\sqrt{d}\}$, we have $P_1 - P_2 = O\left(1/\log(d\log_{1/c}(U/s))\right)$ for signed and unsigned IPS;*
2. *if $d \geq 2$ and $s \leq U/(2d)$, we have $P_1 - P_2 = O\left(1/\log(dU/(s(1-c)))\right)$ for signed IPS;*
3. *if $d > \Theta\left(U^5/(c^2s^5)\right)$ and $s \leq U/8$, we have $P_1 - P_2 = O\left(\sqrt{s/U}\right)$ for signed and unsigned IPS.*

It follows that, for any given dimension d, there cannot exist an asymmetric LSH when the query domain is unbounded.

Discussion. The upper bounds for $P_1 - P_2$ translate into lower bounds for the ρ factor, as soon as P_2 is fixed. To the best of our knowledge, this is the first lower bound on ρ that holds for asymmetric LSH. Indeed, previous results [37, 40] have investigated lower bounds for symmetric LSH and it is not clear if they can be extended to the asymmetric case.

Techniques. The starting point of our proof is the same as in [39]: Use a collision matrix given by two sequences of data and query vectors that force the gap to be small. The proof in [39] then applies an asymptotic analysis of the margin complexity of this matrix [49], and it shows that for any given value of $P_1 - P_2$ there are sufficiently large data and query domains for which the gap must be smaller. Unfortunately, due to their analysis, an upper bound on the gap for a given radius U of the query domain is not possible, and so the result does not rule out very large gaps for small

[2]More precisely they need $\log(s/d)/\log(cs/d) < 2/\omega$, where ω is the matrix multiplication constant. Note that the d term is due to normalization.

Problem	Hard approx.	Permissible approx.	Hard approx.	Permissible approx.
Signed (cs, s) over $\{-1,1\}^d$	$c > 0$	-	$\frac{\log(s/d)}{\log(cs/d)} > 0$	-
Unsigned (cs, s) over $\{-1,1\}^d$	$c \geq e^{-o(\frac{\sqrt{\log n}}{\log\log n})}$	$c < n^{-\epsilon}$ [29]	$\frac{\log(s/d)}{\log(cs/d)} \geq 1 - o(\frac{1}{\log n})$ [29]	$\frac{\log(s/d)}{\log(cs/d)} = 1 - \epsilon$ [29]
		$c < n^{-\epsilon}$	$\frac{\log(s/d)}{\log(cs/d)} \geq 1 - o(\frac{1}{\sqrt{\log n}})$	$\frac{\log s/d}{\log cs/d} = 1/2 - \epsilon$
Unsigned (cs, s) over $\{0,1\}^d$	$c \geq 1 - o(1)$	$c < n^{-\epsilon}$	$\frac{\log s/d}{\log cs/d} \geq 1 - o(\frac{1}{\log n})$	$\frac{\log s/d}{\log cs/d} = 1 - \epsilon$

Table 1: The table describes the ranges of approximations that are hard, when parametrized in terms of c (second and third column) or $\log(s/d)/\log(cs/d)$ ratio (fourth and fifth column). Any algorithm for subquadratic join, which overlap with these ranges, would contradict the OVP. The permissible approximations are those ranges for which truly subquadratic algorithms are known. The upper bounds cited to [29] use fast matrix multiplication, whereas the rest don't and are usable as data structures. The bounds not cited elsewhere are new in this paper, though we are aware that other people have noted the hardness of signed $\{-1,1\}$ join and the data structure for $\{0,1\}$ join.

domains. Our method also highlights a dependency of the gap on the dimension, which is missing in [39]. In addition, our proof holds for $d = 1$ and only uses purely combinatorial arguments.

IPS upper bounds

In the third part we provide some insights on the upper bound side. We first show that it is possible to improve the asymmetric LSH in [39, 46] by just plugging the best known data structure for Approximate Near Neighbor for ℓ_2 on a sphere [9] into the reduction in [39, 12]. With data/query points in the unit ball, this LSH reaches $\rho = (1-s)/(1+(1-2c)s)$. In the $\{0,1\}$ domain, this LSH improves upon the state of the art [46] for some ranges of c and s.

Then we show how to circumvent the impossibility results in [39, 45] by showing that there exists a symmetric LSH when the data and query space coincide by allowing the bounds on collision probability to not hold when the data and query vectors are identical.

We conclude by describing a data structure based on the linear sketches for ℓ_p in [5] for unsigned (cs, s) search: for any given $0 < \kappa \leq 1/2$, the data structure yields a $c = 1/n^\kappa$ approximation with $\tilde{O}\left(dn^{2-2/\kappa}\right)$ construction time and $\tilde{O}\left(dn^{1-2/\kappa}\right)$ query time. Theorem 1 suggests that we cannot substantially improve the approximation with similar performance.

The last data structure allows us to reach truly subquadratic time for $c = 1/n^\kappa$ for the unsigned version in the $\{0,1\}$ and $\{-1,1\}$ domains for all value s. We note that the result in [29] also reaches subquadratic time for the $\{-1,1\}$ case. However, it exploits fast matrix multiplication, whereas our data structure does not.

1.2 Previous work

Similarity join

Similarity join problems have been extensively studied in the database literature (e.g. [17, 18, 19, 26, 27, 34, 36, 47, 52, 53, 58]), as well as in information retrieval (e.g. [14, 21, 59]), and knowledge discovery (e.g. [3, 13, 54, 60, 62]). Most of the literature considers algorithms for particular metrics (where the task is to join tuples that are near according to the metric), or particular application areas (e.g. near-duplicate detection). A distinction is made between methods that approximate distances in the sense that we only care about distances up to some factor $c > 1$, and methods that consider exact distances. Known exact methods do not guarantee subquadratic running time. It was recently shown how approximate LSH-based similarity join can be made I/O-efficient [41].

IPS join

The inner product similarity for the case of *normalized* vectors is known as "cosine similarity" and it is well understood [16, 33, 43]. While the general case where vectors may have any length appears theoretically challenging, *practically* efficient indexes for unsigned search were proposed in [43, 30], based on tree data structures combined with a branch-and-bound space partitioning technique similar to k-d trees, and in [12] based on principal component axes trees. For document term vectors Low and Zheng [35] showed that unsigned search can be sped up using matrix compression ideas. However, as many similarity search problems, the exact version considered in these papers suffers from the curse of dimensionality [55].

The efficiency of approximate IPS approaches based on LSH is studied in [45, 39]. These papers show that a traditional LSH does exist when the data domain is the unit ball and the query domain is the unit sphere, while it does not exist when both domains are the unit ball (the claim automatically applies to any radius by suitably normalizing vectors). On the other hand an asymmetric LSH exists in this case, but it cannot be extended to the unbounded domain $\mathbb{R}^d$. An asymmetric LSH for binary inner product is proposed in [46]. The unsigned version is equivalent to the signed one when the vectors are non-negative.

Algebraic techniques

Finally, recent breakthroughs have been made on the (unsigned) join problem in the approximate case as well as the exact. Valiant [51] showed how to reduce the problem to matrix multiplication, when $cs \approx O(\sqrt{n})$ and $s \approx O(n)$, significantly improving on the asymptotic time complexity of approaches based on LSH. Recently this technique was improved by Karppa et al. [29], who also generalized the sub-quadratic running time to the case when $\log(s)/\log(cs)$

is small. In another surprising development Alman and Williams [4] showed that for $d = O(\log n)$ dimensions, truly subquadratic algorithms for the *exact* IPS join problem on binary vectors is possible. Their algorithm is based on an algebraic technique (probabilistic polynomials) and tools from circuit complexity.

2. HARDNESS OF IPS JOIN

We first provide an overview of OVP and of the associated conjecture in next Section 2.1. Then, in Section 2.2, we prove Theorems 1 and 2 by describing some reductions from the OVP to signed/unsigned joins.

2.1 Preliminaries

The Orthogonal Vectors Problem is defined as follows:

DEFINITION 3 (OVP). *Given two sets P and Q, each one containing n vectors in $\{0,1\}^d$, detect if there exist vectors $p \in P$ and $q \in Q$ such that $p^T q = 0$.*

OVP derives its hardness from the Strong Exponential Time Hypothesis (Williams [56]), but could potentially be true even if SETH is not. We will therefore assume the following plausible conjecture:[3]

CONJECTURE 1 ([56]). *For every constant $\epsilon > 0$, there is no algorithm for OVP with $|P| = |Q| = n$ and dimension $d = \omega(\log n)$ running in $O(n^{2-\epsilon})$ time.*

The conjecture does not hold for $d = O(\log n)$: recently Aboud et al. [1] have proposed an algorithm for OVP running in time $n^{2-1/O(\gamma \log^2 \gamma)}$, when $d = \gamma \log n$. Thus, in order to disprove OVP, an algorithm must be strongly subquadratic when $d = \gamma \log n$ for *all* constant $\gamma > 0$.

The OVP conjecture, as usually stated, concerns the case where the two sets have equal size. However in order to eventually show hardness for data structures, we consider the following generalization of OVP:

LEMMA 1 (GENERALIZED OVP). *Suppose there exist constants $\epsilon > 0$ and $\alpha > 0$, and an algorithm such that for $d = \omega(\log n)$ the algorithm solves OVP for $P, Q \subseteq \{0,1\}^d$ where $|P| = n^\alpha$ and $|Q| = n$ in time $O(n^{1+\alpha-\epsilon})$. Then OVP is false.*

PROOF. Without loss of generality assume $\alpha \le 1$ (otherwise is enough to invert the role of P and Q). Suppose we have an algorithm running in time $O(n^{1+\alpha-\epsilon})$ for some $\epsilon > 0$. Take a normal OVP instance with $|P| = |Q| = n$. Split P into chunks P_i of size n^α and run the OVP algorithm on all pairs (P_i, Q). By our assumption this takes time $n^{1-\alpha} O(n^{1+\alpha-\epsilon}) = O(n^{2-\epsilon})$, contradicting OVP. □

2.2 Reductions from OVP

In this section we prove Theorems 1 and 2, about hardness of approximate joins. We will do this by showing the existence of certain efficient embeddings of the OVP problem. We need the following definition:

DEFINITION 4. *An unsigned (d_1, d_2, cs, s)-embedding into the domain $\mathcal{A}$ is a pair of functions $(f, g) : \{0,1\}^{d_1} \to \mathcal{A}^{d_2}$, where $d_1 \le d_2$, $\mathcal{A} \subseteq \mathbb{R}$, and for any $x, y \in \{0,1\}^{d_1}$:*

$$|f(x)^T g(y)| \ge s \quad \text{when} \quad x^T y = 0$$
$$|f(x)^T g(y)| \le cs \quad \text{when} \quad x^T y \ge 1$$

A signed (d_1, d_2, cs, s)-embedding is analogous, but without the absolute value symbols. We further require that the functions f and g can be evaluated in time polynomial to d_2.

Gap embeddings connect to the join problem, by the following technical lemma:

LEMMA 2. *Suppose there exist a join algorithm for (un)signed (cs, s)-join over $\mathcal{A}$ and a family of (un)signed $(d, 2^{o(d)}, cs, s)$-embeddings into $\mathcal{A}$, for all d large enough, with the following properties:*

- *The embedding can be evaluated in time $2^{o(d)}$.*
- *For given constants $\alpha \ge 0$, and $\epsilon > 0$, the join algorithm has running time $d^{O(1)} n^{1+\alpha-\epsilon}$ when $|Q| = n$ and $|P| = n^\alpha$ for all n and d large enough.*

Then OVP can be solved in $n^{1+\alpha-\epsilon}$ time, and the conjecture is false.

PROOF. First notice that for any function $d_2 = 2^{o(d)}$ we can take $d = \omega(\log n)$ growing slowly enough that $d_2 = n^{o(1)}$.

To see this, assume $d_2(d) = 2^{f(d)}$ where $f(d) = o(d)$. Then we have $f(d(n)) = o(d(n)) = o(1)d(n)$ that is $f(d(n)) = f'(n)d(n)$ for some $f'(n) = o(1)$. Now take $d(n) = \frac{\log n}{\sqrt{f'(n)}} = \omega(\log n)$ and we get $d_2(d(n)) = 2^{f'(n)d(n)} = 2^{\sqrt{f'(n)}\log n} = n^{o(1)}$ as desired.

Hence, there is a family of $(d(n), d_2(n), cs, s)$-gap embeddings for all n, where $d(n) = \omega(\log n)$ and $d_2(n) = n^{o(1)}$. By the generalized OVP lemma, for large enough n, we can thus take a hard OVP instance with $|Q| = n$, $|P| = n^\alpha$ and dimension $d(n)$. Apply the corresponding gap embedding, (f, g), to the instance, such that the maximum inner product between $f(P)$, $g(Q)$ is at least s if the OVP instance has an orthogonal pair and $\le cs$ otherwise. Now run the algorithm for (un)signed (cs, s) join on $(f(P), g(Q))$, which produces the orthogonal pair, if it exists.

It remains to show that the running time of the above procedure is $O(n^{1+\alpha-\epsilon'})$ for some $\epsilon' > 0$. But this is easy, since by assumption, performing the embedding takes time $n^{1+o(1)}$, and running the algorithm on vectors of dimension $n^{o(1)}$ takes time $n^{1+\alpha-\epsilon+o(1)}$. So letting $\epsilon' = \epsilon/2$ suffices. □

The last ingredient we need to prove Theorems 1 and 2 is a suitable family of embeddings to use with Lemma 2.

LEMMA 3. *We can construct the following embeddings:*

1. *A signed $(d, 4d-4, 0, 4)$-embedding into $\{-1, 1\}$.*
2. *An unsigned $(d, (9d)^q, (2d)^q, (2d)^q e^{q/\sqrt{d}}/2)$-embedding into $\{-1, 1\}$, for any $q \ge 1$ and $d > 1$.*
3. *An unsigned $(d, k2^{d/k}, k-1, k)$-embedding into $\{0, 1\}$, for any integer $1 \le k \le d$.*

PROOF. We will use the following notation in our constructions: Let $x \boxplus y$ be the concatenation of vectors x and

[3] We will use the name, OVP, for the problem as well as the conjecture. Sorry about that.

y;[4] Let x^n mean x concatenated with itself n times;[5] And let $x \boxtimes y$ mean the vectorial representation of the outer product xy^T. Tensoring is interesting because of the following folklore property: $(x_1 \boxtimes x_2)^T (y_1 \boxtimes y_2) = \text{trace } (x_1 x_2^T)^T (y_1 y_2^T) = \text{trace } x_2(x_1^T y_1) y_2^T = (x_1^T y_1)(x_2^T y_2)$.

(Embedding 1.) The signed embedding is a simple coordinate wise construction:

$$\hat{f}(0) := (\ 1, -1, -1) \qquad \hat{g}(0) := (\ 1,\ 1, -1)$$
$$\hat{f}(1) := (\ 1,\ 1,\ 1) \qquad \hat{g}(1) := (-1, -1, -1)$$

such that $\hat{f}(1)^T \hat{g}(1) = -3$ and $\hat{f}(0)^T \hat{g}(1) = \hat{f}(1)^T \hat{g}(0) = \hat{f}(0)^T \hat{g}(0) = 1$. This, on its own, gives a $(d, 3d, d-4, d)$ embedding, as non orthogonal vectors need to have at least one (1,1) at some position. We can then translate all the inner products by $-(d-4)$:

$$f(x) := \hat{f}(x_1) \boxplus \cdots \boxplus \hat{f}(x_n) \boxplus 1^{d-4}$$
$$g(x) := \hat{g}(x_1) \boxplus \cdots \boxplus \hat{g}(x_n) \boxplus (-1)^{d-4}$$

which gives the $(d, 4d-4, 0, 4)$ embedding we wanted. Note that the magnitudes of non orthogonal vectors may be negative $(-4d+4)$, but we do not care about those for signed embeddings.

(Embedding 2.) We recall the recursive definition of the q-th order Chebyshev polynomial of first kind, with $q \geq 0$ (see, e.g., [2] page 782):

$$T_0(x) = 1$$
$$T_1(x) = x$$
$$T_q(x) = 2xT_{q-1}(x) - T_{q-2}(x)$$

The polynomials have the following properties [51]:

$$|T_q(x)| \leq 1 \quad \text{when} \quad |x| \leq 1$$
$$|T_q(1+\epsilon)| \geq e^{q\sqrt{\epsilon}} \quad \text{when} \quad 0 < \epsilon < 1/2$$

We use the same coordinate wise transformation as in the signed embedding, but instead of translating by a negative value, we translate by adding $d+2$ ones, giving a $(d, 4d+2, 2d-2, 2d+2)$ unsigned embedding. Let the vectors created this way be called x and y.

On top of that, we would like to construct an embedding for the polynomial $T_q(u/2d)$, where T_q is the qth order Chebyshev polynomial of the first kind. However since this will not in general be integer, there is no hope for constructing it using $\{-1, 1\}$.

Luckily it turns out we can construct an embedding for $b^q T_q(u/b)$ for any integers b and q. Let (f_q, g_q) be the qth embedding of this type, defined by:

$$f_0(x),\ g_0(y) := 1,\ 1$$
$$f_1(x),\ g_1(y) := x,\ y$$
$$f_q(x) := (x \boxtimes f_{q-1}(x))^2 \boxplus f_{q-2}(x)^{(2d)^2}$$
$$g_q(y) := (y \boxtimes g_{q-1}(y))^2 \boxplus (-g_{q-2}(y))^{(2d)^2}$$

[4] $\boxplus$ for concatenation and $\boxtimes$ for tensoring stresses their dual relationship with $+$ and $\times$ on the inner products in the embedded space. We note however that in general, it is only safe to commute $\boxplus$'es and $\boxtimes$'es in an embedding (f, g), when both f and g are commuted equally.

[5] If we wanted to further stress the duality between construction and embedding, we could define $\vec{n}$ to be the all 1 vector of length n. Then $\vec{n} \boxtimes x$ would stand for repeating x n times.

We make the following observations:

- If x and y are $\{-1, 1\}$ vectors, then so are $f_q(x)$ and $g_q(y)$.
- The inner product of the embedded vectors, i.e. $f_q(x)^T g_q(x)$, is a function of the original inner product:

$$f_0(x)^T g_0(y) = 1$$
$$f_1(x)^T g_1(y) = x^T y$$
$$f_q(x)^T g_q(y) = 2x^T y\ f_{q-1}(x)^T g_{q-1}(y) - (2d)^2 f_{q-2}(x)^T g_{q-2}(y)$$

  Indeed it may be verified from the recursive definition of T_q that $f_q(x)^T g_q(y) = (2d)^n T_q(x^T y/2d)$ as wanted.
- Let d_q be the dimension of $f_q(x)$ and $g_q(y)$. Then we have:

$$d_0 = 1$$
$$d_1 = 4d - 4$$
$$d_q = 2(4d-4)d_{q-1} + (2d)^2 d_{q-2}$$

  It can be verified that $d_q \leq (9d)^q$ for any $q \geq 0$ and $d \geq 8$. Interestingly the $(2d)^2$ concatenations do not increase d_q significantly, while $d^{2+\epsilon}$ for any $\epsilon > 0$ would have killed the simple exponential dependency.
- Finally, with dynamic programming, we can compute the embeddings in linear time in the output dimension. This follows from induction over q.

By applying the transformation (f_q, g_q) to the vectors x' and y', we get a $(d, (9d)^q, (2d)^q, (2d)^q T_q(1+1/d))$-embedding for any integer $q \geq 0$. We note that the Chebyshev embedding proposed by Valiant [51] can provide similar results; however, our construction is deterministic, while Valiant's is randomized.

(Embedding 3.) The third embedding works in the $\{0, 1\}$ domain. The difficulty here is that without -1, we cannot express subtraction as in the previous argument. It turns out however, that we can construct the following polynomial:

$$(1 - x_1 y_1)(1 - x_2 y_2) \cdots (1 - x_d y_d)$$

since $\{0, 1\}$ is closed under tensoring and

$$1 - x_i y_i = (1 - x_i, 1)^T (y_i, 1 - y_i)$$

where $1 - x_i$, y_i and $1 - y_i$ are both in $\{0, 1\}$. The polynomial has the property of being 1 exactly when the two vectors are orthogonal and 0 otherwise.

However we cannot use it directly with Lemma 2, as it blows up the dimension too much, $d_2 = 2^{d_1}$. Instead we "chop up" the polynomial in k chunks and take their sum:

$$\sum_{i=0}^{k-1} \prod_{j=1}^{d/k} (1 - x_{ik/d+j} y_{ik/d+j})$$

This uses just $d_2 = k2^{d/k}$ dimensions, which is more manageable. If k does not divide d, we can let the last "chop" of the polynomial be shorter than d/k, which only has the effect of making the output dimension slightly smaller.

Finally we get the gap $s = k$ and $cs = k - 1$. The later follows because for non orthogonal vectors, at least one chunk has a $(1 - x_i y_i)$ terms which evaluates to zero. We thus have a $(d, k2^{d/k}, k-1, k)$-embedding into $\{0,1\}$. The explicit construction is thus:

$$f(x) := \boxplus_{i=0}^{k-1} \boxtimes_{j=1}^{d/k} (1 - x_{ik/d+j}, 1)$$

$$g(x) := \boxplus_{i=0}^{k-1} \boxtimes_{j=1}^{d/k} (y_{ik/d+j}, 1 - y_{ik/d+j})$$

And the running time is linear in the output dimension. □

Finally we parametrize and prove Theorem 1.

PROOF. (Theorem 1) We first prove the bounds parametrized by c. To get the strongest possible results, we want to get c as small as possible, while keeping the dimension bounded by n^δ for some $\delta > 0$.

1. The first embedding is already on the form $(d, 2^{o(d)}, 0, 4)$, showing theorem 1 for signed $(0, 4)$ join, and thus any $c > 0$.

2. In the second embedding we can take q to be any function in $o\left(\frac{d}{\log d}\right)$, giving us a family of $(d$, $2^{o(d)}$, $2^{o(d)}$, $2^{o(d)} e^{o\left(\frac{\sqrt{d}}{\log d}\right)})$. Thus by lemma 2, and for a small enough $d = \omega(\log n)$ in OVP, we get that even $c \leq e^{-o\left(\frac{\sqrt{\log n}}{\log\log n}\right)} \leq 1/\text{polylog(n)}$ is hard.

3. Finally for the third embedding, we can pick any $k = \omega(1)$ and less than d, to get a family of $(d, 2^{o(d)}, k-1, k)$ embeddings. Again picking $d = \omega(\log n)$ small enough in OVP, we have by lemma 2 that $c \leq (k-1)/k = 1 - 1/k = 1 - o(1)$ is hard. Notice that this means any c not bounded away from 1 is hard.

□

PROOF. (Theorem 2) For the bounds parametrized by $\log(s/d)/\log(cs/d)$, we need to tweak our families slightly differently. This in turn allows for hardness for shorter vectors than used in the previous results.

For embedding 1 the result follows directly as $\log(s/d)$ / $\log(cs/d) \to 0$ as $c \to 0$.

We have to remember that the results in theorem 1 are stated in terms of normalized s. For embedding 2 we calculate:

$$\begin{aligned}\frac{\log(s/d_2)}{\log(cs/d_2)} &= \frac{q\log(2/9) + q/\sqrt{d} - \log 2}{q\log(2/9)} \\ &= 1 - \frac{1}{\log(9/2)\sqrt{d}} + \frac{\log 2}{q\log(9/2)} \\ &= 1 - o\left(1/\sqrt{\log n}\right)\end{aligned}$$

Where in the last step we have taken $q = \sqrt{d}$ and $d = \omega(\log n)$ as by the OVP conjecture.

It is important to notice that we could have taken q much larger, and still satisfied lemma 2. However that wouldn't have improved the result, except by more quickly vanishing second order asymptotic terms. What we instead gain from having $d_2 = (9d)^{\sqrt{d}}$ is that, as one can verify going through the lemma, we show hardness for any join algorithm running in time $d^{o\left(\frac{\log d}{\log\log^2 d}\right)} n^{1+\alpha-\epsilon}$. That is, the hardness holds even for algorithms with a much higher dependency on the dimension than polynomial.

Similarly, we calculate for embedding 3:

$$\begin{aligned}\frac{\log(s/d_2)}{\log(cs/d_2)} &= \frac{\log\frac{k}{k2^{d/k}}}{\log\frac{k-1}{k2^{d/k}}} \\ &= 1 - \frac{k\log(1 + 1/(k-1))}{d + k\log(1 + 1/(k-1))} \\ &= 1 - 1/d + O(1/(kd)) \\ &= 1 - o(1/\log n)\end{aligned}$$

Where we have taken $k = d$ and $d = \omega(\log n)$ as by the OVP conjecture. □

3. LIMITATIONS OF LSH FOR IPS

We provide an upper bound on the gap between P_1 and P_2 for an (s, cs, P_1, P_2)-asymmetric LSH for signed/unsigned IPS. For the sake of simplicity we assume the data and query domains to be the d-dimensional balls of radius 1 and $U \geq 1$, respectively. The bound holds for a fixed set of data vectors, so it applies also to data dependent LSH [9]. A consequence of our result is that there cannot exist an asymmetric LSH for any dimension $d \geq 1$ when the set of query vectors is unbounded, getting a result similar to that of [39], which however requires even the data space to be unbounded and $d \geq 2$.

We firsts show in Lemma 4 that the gap $P_1 - P_2$ can be expressed as a function of the length h of two sequences of query and data vectors with suitable collision properties. Then we provide the proof of the aforementioned Theorem 3, where we derive some of such sequences and then apply the lemma.

LEMMA 4. *Suppose that there exists a sequence of data vectors $P = \{p_0, \ldots, p_{n-1}\}$ and a sequence of query vectors $Q = \{q_0, \ldots, q_{n-1}\}$ such that $q_i^T p_j \geq s$ if $j \geq i$ and $q_i^T p_j \leq cs$ otherwise (resp., $|q_i^T p_j| \geq s$ if $j \geq i$ and $|q_i^T p_j| \leq cs$ otherwise) . Then any (s, cs, P_1, P_2)-asymmetric LSH for signed IPS (resp., unsigned IPS) must satisfy $P_1 - P_2 \leq 1/(8\log n)$.*

PROOF. For the sake of simplicity we assume that $n = 2^\ell - 1$ for some $\ell \geq 1$; the assumption can be removed by introducing floor and ceiling operations in the proof. Let $\mathcal{H}$ denote an (s, cs, P_1, P_2)-asymmetric LSH family of hash functions, and let h be a function in $\mathcal{H}$. The following argument works for signed and unsigned IPS.

Consider the $n \times n$ grid representing the collisions between $Q \times P$, that is, a node (i, j) denotes the query-data vectors q_i and p_j. We say that a node (i, j), with $0 \leq i, j < n$, collides under h if vectors q_i and p_j collide under h. By definition of asymmetric LSH, all nodes with $j \geq i$ must collide with probability at least P_1, while the remaining nodes collide with probability at most P_2. We use *lower triangle* to refer to the part of the grid with $j \geq i$ and *P_1-nodes* to refer to the nodes within it; we refer to the remaining nodes as *P_2-nodes*.

We partition the lower triangle into squares of exponentially increasing side as shown in Figure 1. Specifically, we split the lower triangle into *squares* $G_{r,s}$ for every r and s with $0 \leq r < \log(n+1) = \ell$ and $0 \leq s < (n+1)/2^{r+1} = 2^{\ell-r-1}$, where $G_{r,s}$ includes all nodes in the square of side 2^r and top-left node $((2s+1)2^r - 1, (2s+1)2^r - 1)$. For a given square $G_{r,s}$, we define the *left squares* (resp., *top squares*)

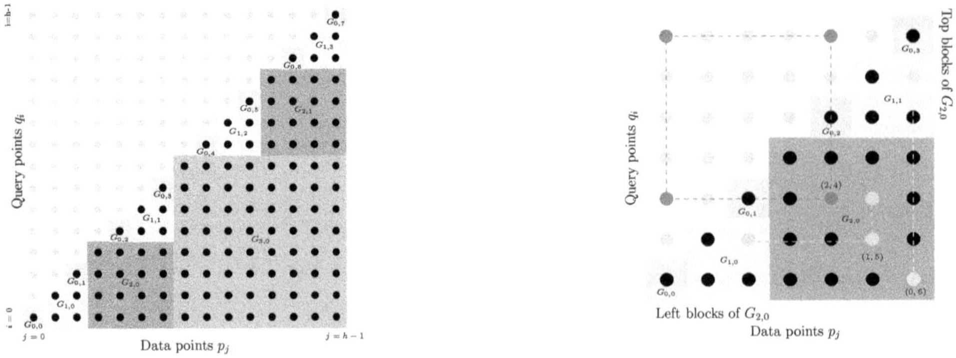

Figure 1: On the left, a 15×15 grid: black nodes are P_1-nodes, gray nodes are P_2-nodes; the colored blocks denote the partitioning of the lower triangle into squares. On the right, a zoom of the $G_{2,0}$ square and of its left and top squares: the red nodes collide under a $(2,4)$-shared function; the green nodes collide under a $(1,5)$-partially shared function; the cyan node collide under a $(0,6)$-proper function (specifically, row proper).

to be the set of squares that are on the left (resp., top) of $G_{r,s}$. We note that the left squares (resp., top squares) contain 2^{r-i-1} squares of side 2^i for any $0 \leq i < r$ and all P_1-nodes with $s2^{r+1} \leq i,j < (2s+1)2^r - 1$ (resp., $(2s+1)2^r - 1 < i,j \leq (s+1)2^{r+1} - 2)$.

We define the *mass* $m_{i,j}$ of a node (i,j) to be the collision probability, under $\mathcal{H}$, of q_i and p_j. We split the mass of a P_1-node into three contributions called shared mass, partially shared mass, and proper mass, all defined below. Consider each P_1-node (i,j) and each function $h \in \mathcal{H}$ where (i,j) collides. Let $G_{r,s}$ be the square containing (i,j) and let $K_{h,i,j}$ denote the set of P_1-nodes (i',j') on the left side of the same row or on the top of the same column of (i,j) (i.e., $i' = i$ and $i \leq j' < j$, or $j' = j$ and $i < i' \leq j$) and with the same hash value of (i,j) under h (i.e., $h(i) = h(j) = h(i') = h(j')$). Clearly all nodes in $K_{h,i,j}$ collide under h. For the given node (i,j), we classify h as follows (see Figure 1 for an example):

- *(i,j)-shared function.* $K_{h,i,j}$ contains at least a node (i,j') in a left square, and at least a node (i',j) in a top square.
- *(i,j)-partially shared function.* Function h is not in case 1 and $K_{h,i,j}$ contains at least a node node (i,j') with $j' < j$, and at least a node (i',j) with $i' > i$. That is, $K_{h,i,j}$ contains only nodes in $G_{r,s}$ and in the left blocks, or only nodes in $G_{r,s}$ and in the top blocks.
- *(i,j)-proper function.* $K_{h,i,j}$ contains no points (i,j') for any $i \leq j' < j$ or contains no points (i',j) for any $i < i' \leq j$. That is, $K_{h,i,j}$ cannot contain at the same time a point in a left square and a point in a top square. Function h is said row (resp., column) proper if there are no nodes in the same row (resp., column). We break ties arbitrary but consistently if $K_{h,i,j}$ is empty.

The *shared mass* $m^s_{i,j}$ is the sum of probabilities of all (i,j)-shared functions. The *partially shared mass* $m^{ps}_{i,j}$ is the sum of probabilities of all (i,j)-partially shared functions. The *proper mass* $m^p_{i,j}$ is the sum of probabilities of all (i,j)-proper functions (the row/column proper mass includes only row/column proper functions). We have $m_{i,j} = m^p_{i,j} + m^{ps}_{i,j} + m^s_{i,j}$. The *mass* $M_{r,s}$ of a square $G_{r,s}$ is the sum of the masses of all its nodes, while the *proper mass* $M^p_{r,s}$ is the sum of proper masses of all its nodes. The sum of row proper masses of all nodes in a row is at most one since a function h is row proper for at most one node in a row. Similarly, the sum of column proper masses of all nodes in a column is at most one. Therefore, we have that $\sum_{r,s} M^p_{r,s} \leq 2n$.

We now show that $\sum_{(i,j)\in G_{r,s}} m^s_{i,j} \leq 2^{2r} P_2$ for every $G_{r,s}$. Consider a node (i,j) in a given $G_{r,s}$. For each (i,j)-shared function h there is a P_2-node colliding under h: indeed, $K_{h,i,j}$ contains nodes (i,j') in the left blocks and (i',j) in the top blocks with $h(i) = h(j) = h(i') = h(j')$ (i.e., $s2^{r+1} \leq j' < (2s+1)2^r - 1$ and $(2s+1)2^r - 1 < i' \leq (s+1)2^{r+1} - 2$); then node (i',j') is a P_2-node since $i' > j'$ and collides under h. By considering all nodes in $G_{r,s}$, we get that all the P_2-nodes that collide in a shared function are in the square of side 2^{r-1} and bottom-right node in $((2s+1)2^r, (2s+1)2^r - 2)$. Since these P_2-nodes have total mass at most $2^{2r} P_2$, the claim follows.

We now prove that $\sum_{(i,j)\in G_{r,s}} m^{ps}_{i,j} \leq 2^{r+1} M^p_{r,s}$. A (i,j)-partially shared function is (i',j) or (i,j')-proper for some $i' < i$ and $j' > j$, otherwise there would be a node in left blocks and a node in top blocks that collide with (i,j) under h, implying that h cannot be partially shared. Since an (i,j)-proper function is partially shared for at most 2^{r+1} nodes in $G_{r,s}$, we get

$$\sum_{(i,j)\in G_{r,s}} m^{ps}_{i,j} \leq 2^{r+1} \sum_{(i,j)\in G_{r,s}} m^p_{i,j} = 2^{r+1} M^p_{r,s}.$$

By the above two bounds, we get

$$M_{r,s} \leq \sum_{(i,j)\in G_{r,s}} m^p_{i,j} + m^{ps}_{i,j} + m^s_{i,j} \leq (2^{r+1}+1) M^p_{r,s} + 2^{2r} P_2.$$

Since $M_{r,s} \geq 2^{2r} P_1$ we get $M^p_{r,s} \geq (2^{r-1} - 1)(P_1 - P_2)$. By summing among all squares, we get

$$2n \geq \sum_{r=0}^{\ell-1} \sum_{s=0}^{2^{\ell-r-1}-1} M^p_{r,s} > (P_1 - P_2) \frac{n \log n}{4}$$

from which the claim follows. □

We are now ready to prove Theorem 3.

Proof. (Theorem 3) The upper bounds to $P_1 - P_2$ in the different cases follow by applying Lemma 4 with different sequences of query and data vectors. We anticipate that in all three cases the gap $P_1 - P_2$ becomes 0 if the query ball is unbounded (i.e., $U = +\infty$), and hence there cannot exist an asymmetric LSH with $P_1 > P_2$.

First case. We now show that there exist data and query sequences of length $n = \Theta(md)$, with $m = \Theta\left(\log_{1/c}(U/s)\right)$, for signed and unsigned IPS in $d \geq 1$ dimensions if $s = O\left(U/\sqrt{d}\right)$. Note that $m \geq 1$ since we assume $s \leq cU$. As a warm-up, we start with $d = 1$. Let $Q = \{q_i, \forall\, 0 \leq i < n\}$ and $P = \{p_j, \forall\, 0 \leq j < n\}$ with

$$q_i = Uc^i, \qquad p_j = s/(Uc^j). \tag{1}$$

Let $p_j \in P$ and $q_i \in Q$. We get $p_j^T q_i = c^{i-j}s$: if $j \geq i$ then $p_j^T q_i \geq s$ and $p_j^T q_i \leq cs$ otherwise. Data and query vectors are respectively contained in the unit ball and in the ball of radius U since $i, j < \Theta\left(\log_{1/c}(U/s)\right)$. Being the sequences P and Q of length m, the claim follows.

Let now $d \geq 2$ and assume for the sake of simplicity $d = 2d'$ (the general case just requires some more tedious computations). Consider the following sequences $Q_k = \{q_{i,k}, \forall\, 0 \leq i < m\}$ and $P_k = \{p_{j,k}, \forall\, 0 \leq j < m\}$ for each $0 \leq k < d'$, where $q_{i,k}$ and $p_{j,k}$ are d-dimensional vectors defined as follows. Denote with $q_{i,k}[t]$ the t-th coordinate of $q_{i,k}$, for $0 \leq t < d$ (similarly for $p_{j,k}$). For vector $q_{i,k}$ we have: $q_{i,k}[2k] = Uc^i$; $q_{i,k}[2t+1] = 2s$ for each $k \leq t < d'$; remaining positions are set to 0. For vector $p_{i,k}$ we have: $p_{i,k}[2k] = s/(Uc^i)$; $p_{i,k}[2k-1] = 1/2$ (only when $k > 0$); remaining positions are set to 0. Intuitively, these data and query sequences follow by constructing the 1-dimensional sequences in Equation 1 on d' orthogonal dimensions and then by suitably translating each sequence. As an example, for $d = 6$ we get:

$$q_{i,0} = (Uc^i, 2s, 0, 2s, 0, 2s) \quad p_{j,0} = (s/(Uc^j), 0, 0, 0, 0, 0);$$
$$q_{i,1} = (0, 0, Uc^i, 2s, 0, 2s) \quad p_{j,1} = (0, 1/2, s/(Uc^j), 0, 0, 0);$$
$$q_{i,2} = (0, 0, 0, 0, Uc^i, 2s) \quad p_{j,2} = (0, 0, 0, 1/2, s/(Uc^j), 0).$$

The query and data sequences $Q = \{Q_0, \ldots Q_{d'-1}\}$ and $P = \{P_0, \ldots P_{d'-1}\}$ satisfy the hypothesis of Lemma 4. Indeed, it can be verified that: $p_{j,\ell}^T q_{i,\ell} = sc^{i-j}$ and thus $p_{j,\ell}^T q_{i,\ell} \geq s$ if $j \geq i$ and $p_{j,\ell}^T q_{i,\ell} \leq cs$ otherwise; $p_{j,\ell'}^T q_{i,\ell} = 0$ if $\ell' < \ell$; $p_{j,\ell'}^T q_{i,\ell} \geq s$ if $\ell' > \ell$. Further, when $s \leq U/(2\sqrt{d})$ data and query vectors are contained in balls with radius 1 and U respectively, with the exception of vectors $q_{i,k}$ for $0 \leq i < 1/(2\log(1/c))$ and $0 \leq k < d'$ which are contained in a ball of radius $2U$. However, these query vectors and the respective data vectors can be removed from the above sequences without affecting the asymptotic length. We thus get two sequences of length $n = (m - 1/(2\log(1/c)))d' = \Theta\left(d \log_{1/c}(U/s)\right)$, the claim follows. Since all inner products are non negative, the upper bound on $P_1 - P_2$ holds for signed and unsigned IPS.

Second case. Longer query and data sequences, with length $n = \Theta(md)$ for $m = \Theta\left(\sqrt{U/(s(1-c))}\right)$, can be constructed for signed IPS when $d \geq 2$. . We start considering the case $d = 2$. Let $Q = \{q_i, \forall\, 0 \leq i < m\}$ and $P = \{p_j, \forall\, 0 \leq j < m\}$ with

$$q_i = \left(\sqrt{sU}(1-(1-c)i), \sqrt{sU(1-c)}\right),$$
$$p_j = \left(\sqrt{\frac{s}{U}}, j\sqrt{\frac{s(1-c)}{U}}\right). \tag{2}$$

We observe that these sequences are similar to the one used in [39]. We have $p_j^T q_i = s(1-c)(j-i) + s$: then, $p_j^T q_i \geq s$ if $j \geq i$ and $p_j^T q_i \leq cs$ otherwise. If $s \leq U/2$, data and query vectors are within balls of radius respectively 1 and U.

Let now $d \geq 2$ and assume for the sake of simplicity $d = 2d'$ (the general case just requires some more tedious computations). Consider the following sequences $Q_k = \{q_{i,k}, \forall\, 0 \leq i < m\}$ and $P_k = \{p_{j,k}, \forall\, 0 \leq j < m\}$ for each $0 \leq k < d'$, where $q_{i,k}$ and $p_{j,k}$ are d-dimensional vectors defined as follows. For vector $q_{i,k}$ we have: $q_{i,k}[2k] = \sqrt{sU}(1-(1-c)i)$; $q_{i,k}[2k+1] = \sqrt{sU(1-c)}$; $q_{i,k}[2t] = \sqrt{Us}$ for each $k < t < d'$; remaining positions are set to 0. For vector $p_{i,k}$ we have: $p_{i,k}[2k] = \sqrt{s/U}$; $p_{i,k}[2k] = j\sqrt{s(1-c)/U}$; remaining positions are set to 0. We observe that the two sequences follow by constructing the 2-dimensional sequences in Equation 2 on d' orthogonal planes and then suitably translate. Then, it follows that data and query sequences $P = \{P_0, \ldots P_{d'-1}\}$ and $Q = \{Q_0, \ldots Q_{d'-1}\}$ satisfy the hypothesis of Lemma 4 and they are respectively contained in balls or radius one and U respectively if $s \leq U/(2d)$. Being $m = nd' = O\left(d\sqrt{U/(s(1-c))}\right)$ and the claim follows. We observe that the above sequences may generate large negative inner products and then they cannot be used for unsigned IPS.

Third case. Finally, we provide an upper bound on $P_1 - P_2$ for signed and unsigned IPS that holds for $d \geq \Theta\left(U^5/(c^2 s^5)\right)$ by providing data and query sequences of length $n = 2^{\sqrt{U/(8s)}}$. Suppose there exists a family $\mathcal{Z}$ of $2n-1$ vectors such that $|z_i^T z_j| \leq \epsilon$ and $(1-\epsilon) \leq z_i^T z_i \leq (1+\epsilon)$ for any $z_i \neq z_j$, for $\epsilon = c/(2\log^2 n)$. It can be shown with the Johnson-Lindenstrauss lemma that such a family exists when $d = \Omega\left(\epsilon^{-2}\log n\right)$ (for an analysis see e.g. [42]). For notational convenience, we denote the vectors in $\mathcal{Z}$ as follows: $z_{b_0}, z_{b_0,b_1}, \ldots, z_{b_0,b_1,\ldots,b_{\log n-1}}$ for each possible value $b_0, \ldots, b_{\log n-1} \in \{0,1\}$. Let $b_{i,\ell}$ denote the ℓ-th bit of the binary representation of i and with $\bar{b}_{i,\ell}$ its negation, where we assume $\ell = 0$ to be the most significant bit. Let $Q = \{q_i, \forall\, 0 \leq i < n\}$ and $P = \{p_j, \forall\, 0 \leq j < n\}$ with

$$q_i = \sqrt{2sU} \sum_{\ell=0}^{\log n-1} \bar{b}_{i,\ell} z_{b_{i,0},\ldots b_{i,\ell-1},\bar{b}_{i,\ell}}$$
$$p_j = \sqrt{2s/U} \sum_{\ell=0}^{\log n-1} b_{j,\ell} z_{b_{j,0},\ldots b_{j,\ell-1},b_{j,\ell}}$$

Since the inner product of two distinct vectors in $\mathcal{Z}$ is in the range $[-\epsilon, \epsilon]$, we have that $p_j^T q_i$ can be upper bounded as

$$p_j^T q_i \leq \epsilon 2s(\log^2 n - \log n) + \\ + 2s \sum_{\ell=0}^{\log n-1} b_{j,\ell}\bar{b}_{i,\ell} z_{b_{j,0},\ldots b_{j,\ell-1},b_{j,\ell}} z_{b_{i,0},\ldots b_{i,\ell-1},\bar{b}_{i,\ell}}$$

Suppose $i > j$. Then there exists a bit position ℓ' such that $b_{i,\ell'} = 1$, $b_{j,\ell'} = 0$ and $b_{i,\ell} = b_{j,\ell}$ for all $\ell < \ell'$. We get $b_{j,\ell}\bar{b}_{i,\ell} = 0$ for all $\ell \leq \ell'$ and $z_{b_{j,0},\ldots b_{j,\ell-1},b_{j,\ell}} \neq z_{b_{i,0},\ldots b_{i,\ell},\bar{b}_{i,\ell}}$ for all $\ell > \ell'$. It then follows that $p_j^T q_i < \epsilon 2s \log^2 n$ when $i > j$. On the other hand we get that $p_j^T q_i$ can be lower bounded as

$$p_j^T q_i \geq -\epsilon 2s(\log^2 n - \log n) + \\ + 2s \sum_{\ell=0}^{\log n-1} b_{j,\ell}\bar{b}_{i,\ell} z_{b_{j,0},\ldots b_{j,\ell-1},b_{j,\ell}} z_{b_{i,0},\ldots b_{i,\ell-1},\bar{b}_{i,\ell}}$$

Suppose $i \le j$. Then there exists an index ℓ' such that $b_{j,\ell'} = 1$, $b_{i,\ell'} = 0$ and $b_{j,\ell} = b_{i,\ell}$ for all $\ell < \ell'$. We get $b_{j,\ell'}\bar{b}_{i,\ell'} = 1$ and $z_{b_{j,0},\ldots b_{j,\ell'-1},b_{j,\ell'}} = z_{b_{i,0},\ldots b_{i,\ell'-1},\bar{b}_{i,\ell'}}$. It then follows that $p_j^T q_i \ge -\epsilon 2s \log^2 n + 2s$. When $d = \Omega\left((\log^5 n)/c^2\right)$, we can set $\epsilon = c/(2\log^2 n)$. From the above lower and upper bounds, it then follows that $p_j^T q_i \le cs$ if $j < i$ and $p_j^T q_i \ge s$ if $j \ge i$ and hence the sequences Q and P satisfy the hypothesis of Lemmma 4. Finally, we observe that the data and query vectors in P and Q are respectively contained in balls of radius 1 and U: each q_i (resp., p_j) is given by the sum of at most $\log n$ vectors whose norm is not larger than $\sqrt{2sU}(1+\epsilon)$ (resp., $\sqrt{2s/U}(1+\epsilon)$); being $n = 2^{\sqrt{U/(8s)}}$ the claim follows. □

4. UPPER BOUNDS

This section contains three observations with implications for IPS join and its indexing version. We first notice in Section 4.1 that by plugging the best known LSH for ℓ_2 distance on a sphere [9] into a reduction presented in [12, 39], we get a data structure based on LSH for signed IPS with search time exponent $\rho = (1-s)/(1+(1-2c)s)$.

Then, in Section 4.2, we show how to circumvent the results in [39, 45] showing that symmetric LSH is not possible when the data and query domains coincide (while an asymmetric LSH does exist). We use an slightly modified definition of LSH that disregards the collision probability of 1 for pairs of identical vectors, and assume that vectors are represented with finite precision. The LSH construction uses explicit incoherent matrices built using Reed-Solomon codes [38] to implement a symmetric version of the reduction in [12, 39].

Finally, in Section 4.3 we solve unsigned (cs, s) join using linear sketches for ℓ_p norms from [5]. Given $\kappa \ge 2$ we obtain a approximation factor $c \ge 1/n^{1/\kappa}$ using $\tilde{O}\left(dn^{2-2/\kappa}\right)$ time. Although this trade-off is not that strong, it is not far from the conditional lower bound in Theorem 1.

4.1 Asymmetric LSH for signed IPS

We assume the data and query domains to be d-dimensional balls with respective radius 1 and U. Vectors are embedded into a $(d+2)$-dimensional unit sphere using the asymmetric map as in [39]: a data vector p is mapped to $(p, \sqrt{1-||p||^2}, 0)$, while a query q is mapped to $(q/U, 0, \sqrt{1-||q||^2/U^2})$. This transformation just scales the inner product by a factor U, and hence signed inner product search can be seen as an instance of ANN in ℓ_2 with distance threshold $r = \sqrt{2(1-s/U)}$ and approximation $c' = \sqrt{(1-cs/U)/(1-s/U)}$. The latter can be solved in space $O(n^{1+\rho} + dn)$ and query time $O(n^\rho)$ using the LSH construction of [9]. We get the following ρ value (for the LSH gap as well as for the exponent of the running time):

$$\rho = \frac{1}{2c'^2 - 1} = \frac{1 - s/U}{1 + (1-2c)s/U} . \quad (3)$$

In Figure 2, we plot the ρ values of three LSH constructions: the one proposed here (with $U = 1$), the one from [39], and the one from [46]. The latter works only for binary vectors. We point out that our bound is always stronger than the one from [39] and sometimes stronger than the one from [46], despite that the latter is tailored for binary vectors. The latter conclusion is somewhat surprising, since the data structure we obtain works for non-binary vectors as well.

In practice, one may want to use a recent LSH family from [7] that—both in theory and in practice—is superior to the hyperplane LSH from [16] used in [39].

4.2 Symmetric LSH for almost all vectors

Neyshabur and Srebro [39] show that an asymmetric view on LSH for signed IPS is required. Indeed they show that a symmetric LSH for signed IPS does not exist when data and query domains are balls of the same radius, while an asymmetric LSH does exist. (On the other hand, when the data domain is a ball of given radius U and the query domain is a sphere of same radius, a symmetric LSH does exist.) In this section we show that even when data and query spaces coincide a nontrivial symmetric LSH does exist if we disregard the trivial collision probability of 1 when data and query vectors are identical.

We first show how to reduce signed IPS to the case where data and query vectors lie on a unit sphere. The reduction is deterministic and maintains inner products up to an additive error ε for all vectors x, y with $x \ne y$. We then plug in any Euclidean LSH for ANN on the sphere, for example the one from [9]. This reduction treats data and query vectors identically, unlike the one from [39], and thus we are able to obtain a symmetric LSH.

Assume that vector coordinates are encoded as k-bit numbers, and that data and query vectors are in the unit ball. The idea is the following. There are at most $N = 2^{O(dk)}$ possible data vectors and queries. Imagine a collection of N unit vectors $v_1, \ldots, v_N$ such that for every $i \ne j$ one has $|v_i^T v_j| \le \varepsilon$. Then, it is easy to check that a map of a vector p to $f(p) = (p, \sqrt{1-||p||^2} \cdot v_p)$ maps a vector from a unit ball to a unit sphere and, moreover, for $p \ne q$ one has $|f(p)^T f(q) - p^T q| \le \varepsilon$.

What remains is to construct such a collection of vectors v_i. Moreover, our collection of vectors must be explicit in a strong sense: we should be able to compute v_u given a vector u (after interpreting it as an dk-bit string). Such a constructions are well known, e.g., in [38] it is shown how to build such vectors using Reed-Solomon codes. The resulting dimension is $O\left(\varepsilon^{-2}\log N\right) = O\left(kd/\varepsilon^2\right)$ [32, 38].

After performing such a reduction we can apply any state-of-the-art LSH (or data structure for ANN) for ℓ_2 norm on a sphere, e.g. from [9, 7], with distance threshold $r^2 = 2(1-s+\epsilon)$, approximation factor $c'^2 = (1-cs-\epsilon)/r^2$. If ε is sufficiently small we get a ρ value close to the one in (3). The final result is therefore a symmetric LSH for symmetric domains that does not provide any collision bound for all pairs (q, p) with $q = p$ since the guarantees on the inner product fail for these pairs. This LSH can used for solving signed (cs, s) IPS as a traditional LSH [6], although it is required an initial step that verifies whether a query vector is in the input set and, if this is the case, returns the vector q itself if $q^T q \ge s$.

4.3 Unsigned IPS via linear sketches

In this section we propose a linear sketch for *unsigned c-MIPS*, that can be used for solving unsigned (cs, s) join. The unsigned c-MIPS is defined as follows: given a set $P \subset \mathbb{R}^d$ of n vectors, construct a data structure that efficiently returns, for a given query vector q, a vector $p \in P$ where $|p^T q| \ge c(p'^T q)$, where p' is the vector in P with maximum absolute inner product with q. The unsigned (cs, s) join between sets P and Q can be computed by constructing a data structure for

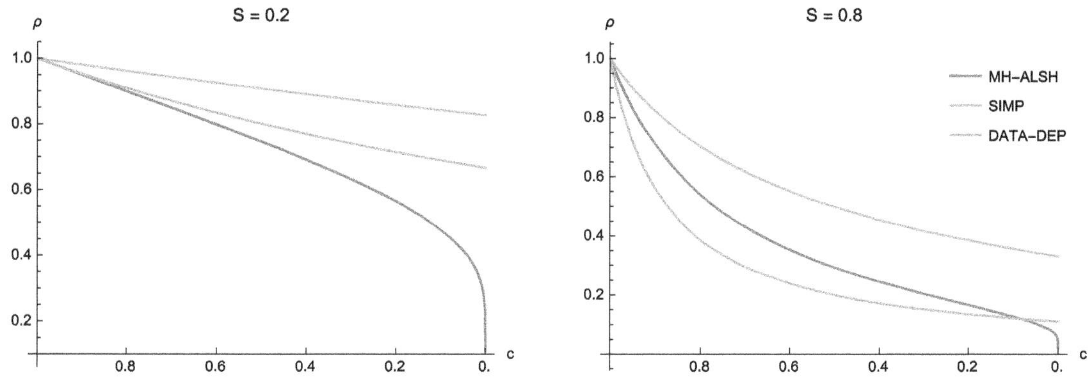

Figure 2: Our ρ value (DATA-DEP) compared to that of [39] (SIMP) and the binary data only of [46] (MH-ALSH).

unsigned c-MIPS for vectors in P and then performs a query for each vector in Q.

Of independent interest, we notice that unsigned c-MIPS can be solved by a data structure for unsigned (cs, s) search. Let $\mathcal{D}$ be a data structure for unsigned (cs, s) search on the data set P, and suppose we are given a query q and the promise that there exists $p' \in P$ such that $p'^T q > \gamma$. Then, unsigned c-MIPS can be solved by performing on $\mathcal{D}$ the queries q/c^i for any $0 \leq i \leq \lceil \log_{1/c}(s/\gamma) \rceil$. Intuitively, we are scaling up the query q until the largest inner product becomes larger than the threshold s. We notice that γ can be also considered as the smallest inner product that can be stored according to the numerical precision of the machine.

Our data structure requires $\tilde{O}\left(dn^{2-2/\kappa}\right)$ construction time and $\tilde{O}\left(dn^{1-2/\kappa}\right)$ query time and provide a $c \geq 1/n^{1/\kappa}$ approximation with high probability, for any $\kappa \geq 2$. This gives an algorithm for unsigned (cs, s) join on two sets of size n requiring time $\tilde{O}\left(dn^{2-2/\kappa}\right)$. As shown in Theorem 1, we are unlikely to significant improve further the approximation factor if the OVP conjecture is true.

First, suppose we are only interested in approximating the value of $\max_p |q^t p|$ and not to find the corresponding vector. Then, the problem is equivalent to estimating $\|Aq\|_\infty$, where A is an $n \times d$ matrix, whose rows are data vectors. This problem can be tackled using linear sketches (for an overview see [57, 8]). More specifically, we use the following result from [5]: for every $2 \leq \kappa \leq \infty$ there exists a distribution over $\tilde{O}(n^{1-2/\kappa}) \times n$ matrices Π such that for every $x \in \mathbb{R}^n$ one has:

$$\Pr_{\Pi}\left[(1-c)\|x\|_\kappa \leq \|\Pi x\|_\infty \leq (1+c)\|x\|_\kappa\right] \geq 0.99$$

for a suitable constant $0 < c < 1$. Thus, to build a data structure for computing $\|Aq\|_\infty$, we sample a matrix Π according to the aforementioned result in [5] and compute the $\tilde{O}\left(n^{1-2/\kappa}\right) \times d$ matrix $A_s = \Pi A$. Then, for every query q, we compute $\|A_s q\|_\infty$ in time $\tilde{O}\left(d \cdot n^{1-2/\kappa}\right)$, which is a $O\left(n^{1/\kappa}\right)$-approximation to $\|Aq\|_\infty$ with probability at least 0.99. Note that we can reduce the probability of error from 0.01 to $\delta > 0$ as usual, by building $O(\log(1/\delta))$ independent copies of the above data structure and reporting the median estimate.

We now consider the recovery of the vector that almost maximizes $|p^t q|$. We recover the index of the desired vector bit by bit. That is, for every bit index $0 \leq i < \log n$, we consider every binary sequence b of length i and build a data structure for the dataset containing only the vectors in $\mathcal{P}$ for which the binary representations of their indexes have prefix b. Although the number of data structures is n, the total required space is still $\tilde{O}\left(dn^{1-2/\kappa}\right)$ since each vector appears in only $\log n$ data structures. The claim stated at the beginning follows.

5. CONCLUSION

This paper has investigated different aspects of the complexity of *approximate* similarity join with inner product. In particular, we have related the hardness of this problem to the OVP conjecture. Under some assumptions on c and s, the proposed conditional lower bounds rule out algorithms for signed/unsigned (cs, s) IPS join running in $n^{2-\epsilon}$ time, for a constant $\epsilon > 0$, unless the OVP conjecture is false. Nevertheless, the data structures in section 4 show that it still possible to reach weak subquadratic time, and even truly subquadratic time for small values of the approximation factor.

The hardness of signed/unsigned IPS holds even for weak approximation factors when the vector domain is $\{-1, 1\}^d$. Indeed, the result holds if $c \geq 0$ for signed join, and if $c \geq e^{-o(\sqrt{\log n}/\log\log n)}$ for unsigned join. When $c < 1/n^{\Omega(1)}$, the data structure for unsigned IPS in section 4.3 reaches strongly subquadratic time and this gives evidence that the constraint on c of the hardness result cannot be significantly relaxed. On the other hand, when vectors are in the $\{0, 1\}^d$ domain, a stronger assumption is required on the approximation factor. In this case, the conditional lower bound holds for $c = 1 - o(1)$ and hence it does not rule out an algorithm running in $n^{2-\epsilon}$ time for a constant approximation factor. We believe that a different approach is required to show the hardness of IPS for constant approximation: indeed, the proposed reduction from OVP to IPS in the $\{0, 1\}^d$ domain strongly relies on the ability to distinguish inner products smaller than $k - 1$ and larger than k for some $k = \omega(1)$, implying $c \geq 1 - o(1)$. From an upper bound point of view, the LSH proposed in section 4.1 improves upon the state of the art [46] based on minwise hashing for different values (e.g., when $s \geq d/3$ and $c \geq 0.83$); however, it still gives weak subquadratic algorithm for signed/unsigned IPS with constant c. An interesting open question is therefore to assess if strongly subquadratic time is possible when the approximation is constant (or smaller) in the $\{0,1\}^d$ domain.

Acknowledgments

The research leading to these results has received funding from the European Research Council under the European Union's Seventh Framework Programme (FP7/2007-2013) / ERC grant agreement no. 614331.

6. REFERENCES

[1] A. Abboud, R. Williams, and H. Yu. More applications of the polynomial method to algorithm design. In *Proc. 26th ACM-SIAM Symposium on Discrete Algorithms (SODA)*, pages 218–230, 2015.

[2] M. Abramowitz and I. A. Stegun. *Handbook of mathematical functions: with formulas, graphs, and mathematical tables.* Courier Corporation, 1964.

[3] P. Achlioptas, B. Schölkopf, and K. Borgwardt. Two-locus association mapping in subquadratic time. In *Proc. 17th ACM SIGKDD International Conference on Knowledge Discovery and Data Mining (KDD)*, pages 726–734. ACM, 2011.

[4] J. Alman and R. Williams. Probabilistic polynomials and hamming nearest neighbors. In *Proc. 56th IEEE Symposium on Foundations of Computer Science (FOCS)*, 2015.

[5] A. Andoni. High frequency moments via max-stability. Unpublished manuscript, 2012.

[6] A. Andoni and P. Indyk. Near-optimal hashing algorithms for approximate nearest neighbor in high dimensions. *Commun. ACM*, 51(1):117–122, 2008.

[7] A. Andoni, P. Indyk, M. Kapralov, T. Laarhoven, I. Razenshteyn, and L. Schmidt. Practical and optimal LSH for angular distance. In *Proc. 28th Conference on Neural Information Processing Systems (NIPS)*, 2015.

[8] A. Andoni, R. Krauthgamer, and I. P. Razenshteyn. Sketching and embedding are equivalent for norms. In *Proc. 47th ACM on Symposium on Theory of Computing, (STOC)*, pages 479–488, 2015.

[9] A. Andoni and I. Razenshteyn. Optimal data-dependent hashing for approximate near neighbors. In *Proc. 47th Symposium on Theory of Computing (STOC)*, pages 793–801, 2015.

[10] A. Arasu, V. Ganti, and R. Kaushik. Efficient exact set-similarity joins. In *Proc. International Conference on Very Large Data Bases (VLDB)*, pages 918–929, 2006.

[11] N. Augsten and M. H. Böhlen. Similarity joins in relational database systems. *Synthesis Lectures on Data Management*, 5(5):1–124, 2013.

[12] Y. Bachrach, Y. Finkelstein, R. Gilad-Bachrach, L. Katzir, N. Koenigstein, N. Nice, and U. Paquet. Speeding up the xbox recommender system using a euclidean transformation for inner-product spaces. In *Proc. 8th ACM Conference on Recommender Systems*, pages 257–264, 2014.

[13] B. Bahmani, A. Goel, and R. Shinde. Efficient distributed locality sensitive hashing. In *Proc. ACM International Conference on Information and Knowledge Management (CIKM)*, pages 2174–2178, 2012.

[14] R. J. Bayardo, Y. Ma, and R. Srikant. Scaling up all pairs similarity search. In *Proc. International Conference on World Wide Web (WWW)*, pages 131–140, 2007.

[15] M. S. Charikar. Similarity estimation techniques from rounding algorithms. In *Proc. 34 ACM Symposium on Theory of computing (STOC)*, pages 380–388. ACM, 2002.

[16] M. S. Charikar. Similarity estimation techniques from rounding algorithms. In *Proc. 34th ACM Symposium on Theory of Computing (STOC)*, pages 380–388, 2002.

[17] S. Chaudhuri, V. Ganti, and R. Kaushik. A primitive operator for similarity joins in data cleaning. In *Proc.22nd International Conference on Data Engineering (ICDE)*, page 5, 2006.

[18] Y. Chen and J. M. Patel. Efficient evaluation of all-nearest-neighbor queries. In *Proc. International Conference on Data Engineering (ICDE)*, pages 1056–1065, 2007.

[19] E. Cohen, M. Datar, S. Fujiwara, A. Gionis, P. Indyk, R. Motwani, J. D. Ullman, and C. Yang. Finding interesting associations without support pruning. *IEEE Trans. Knowl. Data Eng.*, 13(1):64–78, 2001.

[20] R. R. Curtin, A. G. Gray, and P. Ram. Fast exact max-kernel search. In *Proc. 13th SIAM International Conference on Data Mining (SDM)*, pages 1–9, 2013.

[21] A. Das, M. Datar, A. Garg, and S. Rajaram. Google news personalization: scalable online collaborative filtering. In *Proc. International Conference on World Wide Web (WWW)*, pages 271–280, 2007.

[22] T. Dean, M. Ruzon, M. Segal, J. Shlens, S. Vijayanarasimhan, and J. Yagnik. Fast, accurate detection of 100,000 object classes on a single machine. In *Proc. IEEE Conference on Computer Vision and Pattern Recognition*, Washington, DC, USA, 2013.

[23] P. Felzenszwalb, R. Girshick, D. McAllester, and D. Ramanan. Object detection with discriminatively trained part-based models. *IEEE Transactions on Pattern Analysis and Machine Intelligence,*, 32(9):1627–1645, 2010.

[24] A. Gionis, P. Indyk, and R. Motwani. Similarity search in high dimensions via hashing. In *Proc. 25th International Conference on Very Large Data Bases (VLDB)*, pages 518–529, 1999.

[25] S. Har-Peled, P. Indyk, and R. Motwani. Approximate nearest neighbor: Towards removing the curse of dimensionality. *Theory of computing*, 8(1):321–350, 2012.

[26] E. H. Jacox and H. Samet. Metric space similarity joins. *ACM Transactions on Database Systems (TODS)*, 33(2):7, 2008.

[27] Y. Jiang, D. Deng, J. Wang, G. Li, and J. Feng. Efficient parallel partition-based algorithms for similarity search and join with edit distance constraints. In *Proc. Joint EDBT/ICDT Workshops*, pages 341–348. ACM, 2013.

[28] T. Joachims, T. Finley, and C.-N. J. Yu. Cutting-plane training of structural svms. *Mach. Learn.*, 77(1):27–59, 2009.

[29] M. Karppa, P. Kaski, and J. Kohonen. A faster subquadratic algorithm for finding outlier correlations. In *Proc. 27th ACM-SIAM Symposium on Discrete Algorithms (SODA16)*, 2016.

[30] N. Koenigstein, P. Ram, and Y. Shavitt. Efficient retrieval of recommendations in a matrix factorization framework. In *Proc. 21st ACM International Conference on Information and Knowledge Management (CIKM)*, pages 535–544, 2012.

[31] Y. Koren, R. Bell, and C. Volinsky. Matrix factorization techniques for recommender systems. *Computer*, 42(8):30–37, Aug. 2009.

[32] K. G. Larsen and J. Nelson. The johnson-lindenstrauss lemma is optimal for linear dimensionality reduction. *CoRR*, abs/1411.2404, 2014.

[33] D. Lee, J. Park, J. Shim, and S.-g. Lee. An efficient similarity join algorithm with cosine similarity predicate. In *Database and Expert Systems Applications*, pages 422–436. Springer, 2010.

[34] G. Li, D. Deng, J. Wang, and J. Feng. Pass-join: A partition-based method for similarity joins. *Proc. VLDB Endowment*, 5(3):253–264, 2011.

[35] Y. Low and A. X. Zheng. Fast top-k similarity queries via matrix compression. In *Proc. ACM International Conference on Information and Knowledge Management (CIKM)KM*, pages 2070–2074. ACM, 2012.

[36] J. Lu, C. Lin, W. Wang, C. Li, and H. Wang. String similarity measures and joins with synonyms. In *Proc. 2013 ACM SIGMOD International Conference on Management of Data*, pages 373–384, 2013.

[37] R. Motwani, A. Naor, and R. Panigrahi. Lower bounds on locality sensitive hashing. In *Proc. 22nd Symposium on Computational Geometry (SoCS)*, pages 154–157, 2006.

[38] J. Nelson, H. L. Nguyen, and D. P. Woodruff. On deterministic sketching and streaming for sparse recovery and norm estimation. *Linear Algebra and its Applications*, 441(0):152 – 167, 2014.

[39] B. Neyshabur and N. Srebro. On symmetric and asymmetric LSHs for inner product search. In *Proc. 32nd International Conference on Machine Learning (ICML)*, 2015.

[40] R. O'Donnell, Y. Wu, and Y. Zhou. Optimal lower bounds for locality-sensitive hashing (except when q is tiny). *ACM Trans. Comput. Theory*, 6(1):5:1–5:13, 2014.

[41] R. Pagh, N. Pham, F. Silvestri, and M. Stöckel. I/O-efficient similarity join. In *Proc. 23rd European Symposium on Algorithms (ESA)*, pages 941–952, 2015.

[42] R. Pagh, F. Silvestri, J. Sivertsen, and M. Skala. Approximate furthest neighbor in high dimensions. In *Proc. 8th International Conference on Similarity Search and Applications (SISAP)*, volume 9371 of *LNCS*, pages 3–14, 2015.

[43] P. Ram and A. G. Gray. Maximum inner-product search using cone trees. In *Proc. 18th ACM SIGKDD International Conference on Knowledge Discovery and Data Mining (KDD)*, pages 931–939, 2012.

[44] V. Satuluri and S. Parthasarathy. Bayesian locality sensitive hashing for fast similarity search. *Proc. VLDB Endowment*, 5(5):430–441, 2012.

[45] A. Shrivastava and P. Li. Asymmetric LSH (ALSH) for sublinear time maximum inner product search (MIPS). In *Proc. 27th Conference on Neural Information Processing Systems (NIPS)*, pages 2321–2329, 2014.

[46] A. Shrivastava and P. Li. Asymmetric minwise hashing for indexing binary inner products and set containment. In *Proc. 24th International Conference on World Wide Web (WWW)*, pages 981–991, 2015.

[47] Y. N. Silva, W. G. Aref, and M. H. Ali. The similarity join database operator. In *Proc. International Conference on Data Engineering (ICDE)*, pages 892–903. IEEE, 2010.

[48] N. Srebro, J. D. M. Rennie, and T. S. Jaakola. Maximum-margin matrix factorization. In *Advances in Neural Information Processing Systems 17*, pages 1329–1336. MIT Press, 2005.

[49] N. Srebro and A. Shraibman. Rank, trace-norm and max-norm. In *Proc. 18th Conference on Learning Theory COLT*, volume 3559 of *LNCS*, pages 545–560, 2005.

[50] C. Teflioudi, R. Gemulla, and O. Mykytiuk. Lemp: Fast retrieval of large entries in a matrix product. In *Proc. ACM SIGMOD International Conference on Management of Data*, pages 107–122. ACM, 2015.

[51] G. Valiant. Finding correlations in subquadratic time, with applications to learning parities and the closest pair problem. *J. ACM*, 62(2):13:1–13:45, 2015.

[52] J. Wang, G. Li, and J. Fe. Fast-join: An efficient method for fuzzy token matching based string similarity join. In *Proc. International Conference on Data Engineering (ICDE)*, pages 458–469. IEEE, 2011.

[53] J. Wang, G. Li, and J. Feng. Can we beat the prefix filtering?: an adaptive framework for similarity join and search. In *Proc. ACM SIGMOD International Conference on Management of Data*, pages 85–96. ACM, 2012.

[54] Y. Wang, A. Metwally, and S. Parthasarathy. Scalable all-pairs similarity search in metric spaces. In *Proc. ACM SIGKDD International Conference on Knowledge Discovery and Data Mining (KDD)*, pages 829–837, 2013.

[55] R. Weber, H.-J. Schek, and S. Blott. A quantitative analysis and performance study for similarity-search methods in high-dimensional spaces. In *Proc. 24rd International Conference on Very Large Data Bases (VLDB)*, pages 194–205, 1998.

[56] R. Williams. A new algorithm for optimal 2-constraint satisfaction and its implications. *Theoretical Computer Science*, 348(2):357–365, 2005.

[57] D. P. Woodruff. Sketching as a tool for numerical linear algebra. *Foundations and Trends in Theoretical Computer Science*, 10:1–157, 2014.

[58] C. Xia, H. Lu, B. C. Ooi, and J. Hu. Gorder: an efficient method for knn join processing. In *Proc. VLDB*, pages 756–767, 2004.

[59] C. Xiao, W. Wang, X. Lin, and J. X. Yu. Efficient similarity joins for near duplicate detection. In *Proc. International Conference on World Wide Web (WWW)*, pages 131–140, 2008.

[60] R. B. Zadeh and A. Goel. Dimension independent similarity computation. *The Journal of Machine Learning Research*, 14(1):1605–1626, 2013.

[61] P. Zezula, G. Amato, V. Dohnal, and M. Batko. *Similarity search: the metric space approach*, volume 32. Springer Science & Business Media, 2006.

[62] X. Zhang, F. Zou, and W. Wang. Fastanova: an efficient algorithm for genome-wide association study. In *Proc. ACM SIGKDD International Conference on Knowledge Discovery and Data Mining (KDD)*, pages 821–829. ACM, 2008.

Data Management for Social Networking

Sara Cohen*
The Rachel and Selim Benin School
of Computer Science and Engineering
Hebrew University of Jerusalem, Israel
sara@cs.huji.ac.il

ABSTRACT

Social networks are fascinating and valuable datasets, which can be leveraged to better understand society, and to make inter-personal choices. This tutorial explores the fundamental issues that arise when storing and querying social data. The discussion is divided into three main parts. First, we consider some of the key computational problems that arise over the social graph structure, such as node centrality, link prediction, community detection and information diffusion. Second, we consider algorithmic challenges that leverage both the textual content and the graph structure of a social network, e.g., social search and querying, and team formation. Finally, we consider critical aspects of implementing a social network database management system, and discuss existing systems. In this tutorial, we also point out gaps between the state-of-the-art and desired features of a data management system for social networking, and discuss open research challenges.

1. INTRODUCTION

Our lives are deeply affected by the people surrounding us, by our relationships with others, and by their activities. Thus, the ability to manage data about people, their social networks and activities, as well as the capability to query such data, are swiftly becoming one of the cornerstones of modern society. This tutorial explores the fundamental issues that arise when storing and querying social data.

The notion of a social network is commonly used narrowly, to refer to networks of friends or followers in online applications. However, social networks are in fact a broader concept, including a variety of relationships, e.g., research collaboration, email correspondence, disease transmission and organizational interactions. Both in the narrow and in the broad sense, social networks are an interesting data source, whose importance has been recognized for over a hundred years. There has been extensive research on analyzing social networks, stemming from diverse fields including psychology, anthropology, mathematics, and, more recently, computer science.

Early research in the area of social analysis already dealt with problems that are at the heart of modern social network analysis. For example, a 1922 study [8] analyzed correlations between I.Q.'s of children and their forming of social relations. This is a precursor to the well-known problem of *link prediction*, i.e., predicting which non-existing links are likely to form in a network. As another example, in 1929, [43] studied the formation of groups from social interactions. This is an early example of the *community detection problem*. Thus, key problems in social networks have been studied for almost a century, and yet take on a new twist with the explosion of online social networks.

In this tutorial, we will survey fundamental issues that arise when storing and querying social data. The discussion is divided into three main parts. First, we consider some of the key computational problems that arise over the social graph structure, such as node centrality, link prediction, community detection and information diffusion. Second, we consider algorithmic challenges that leverage both the textual content and the graph structure of a social network, e.g., social search and querying, and team formation. Finally, we consider critical aspects of implementing a social network database management system, and discuss existing systems. In this tutorial, we also point out gaps between the state-of-the-art and desired features of a data management system for social networking, and discuss open research challenges.

We note that social network database management is a research area that is huge in both breadth and depth. Thus, any finite tutorial on this topic must choose between covering more topics of interest, and discussing each selected topic in its deserved detail.[1] This tutorial has more of a breadth-wise orientation. Hence, at many places, definitions and algorithms are not presented formally, but rather are only discussed intuitively. References for further reading are provided.

2. COMPUTATIONAL PROBLEMS OVER THE SOCIAL GRAPH STRUCTURE

In this section we discuss key computational problems over

*Sara Cohen was partially supported by the Israel Science Foundation (Grant 1467/13).

[1]Indeed, several of the topics discussed here have entire books devoted to them alone.

PODS'16, June 26-July 01, 2016, San Francisco, CA, USA
© 2016 ACM. ISBN 978-1-4503-4191-2/16/06...$15.00
DOI: http://dx.doi.org/10.1145/2902251.2902306

social graphs. We adopt the traditional view that a social network is simply a graph, which may or may not be directed and weighted. Figure 1 contains a toy example of a small undirected social network.

2.1 Centrality

One important task over a social network, is finding nodes (i.e., people) who are important. The prominence of a node is also called its *centrality*, as it measures how central the node is in the network. Greater centrality values indicate higher prominence in the graph.

Centrality can be measured in a variety of ways. *Degree centrality*, is perhaps the simplest variation of centrality, and is simply the proportion of nodes in the graph that are neighbors of a given node, i.e., the degree centrality of v is

$$\frac{deg(v)}{|V(G)|},$$

where $deg(v)$ is the degree of v and $V(G)$ are the nodes of G. *Betweenness centrality* measures how critical a node is for communication between pairs of nodes in a graph. Denoting by $P_{u,w}$ the set of shortest paths from u to w, the betweenness centrality of a node v is defined as

$$\sum_{u,w \in V(G)} \frac{|\{p \in P_{u,w} \mid v \in p\}|}{|P_{u,w}|}.$$

Closeness centrality measures how close a node is to all other nodes in the graph. If $dist(u,w)$ denotes the length of the shortest path from u to w, then the closeness centrality of v is

$$\frac{1}{\sum_{u \in V(G)-\{v\}} dist(v,u)}.$$

To demonstrate these notions, in Figure 1, v_5 has the greatest degree centrality and the greatest closeness centrality, while v_4 has the greatest betweenness centrality.

Many other centrality measures have also been considered. For example, *eigenvector centrality* assigns centrality scores in such a way that edges between v and more central nodes contribute more than edges between v and less central nodes. Given an adjacency matrix A representing the relationships in a social network, the eigenvector centrality score for the nodes of a graph is the solution to the equation

$$A\vec{v} = \lambda\vec{v}$$

for the greatest eigenvalue λ. PageRank, as well as *Katz centrality,* are similar in spirit to eigenvector centrality.

Finally, *clique-overlap centrality* computes the importance of a node as a function of the number of maximal cliques in which it participates. (Only maximal cliques of size at least three are considered.) Thus, in Figure 1 node $v_2, \ldots, v_{10}$ have the clique overlap centrality of 1, while v_1, v_0 have clique overlap centrality of 0. If an edge were added between v_1 and v_2, then v_2 would have the greatest cliques overlap centrality, with a value of 3.

No single centrality measure outperforms all others on all inputs. Therefore, often machine learning techniques will be used to combine a variety of centrality scores, to find an application-dependent effective centrality measure.

2.2 Link prediction

Link prediction is the problem that asks, for a given node v, which nodes in the network that are not currently friends

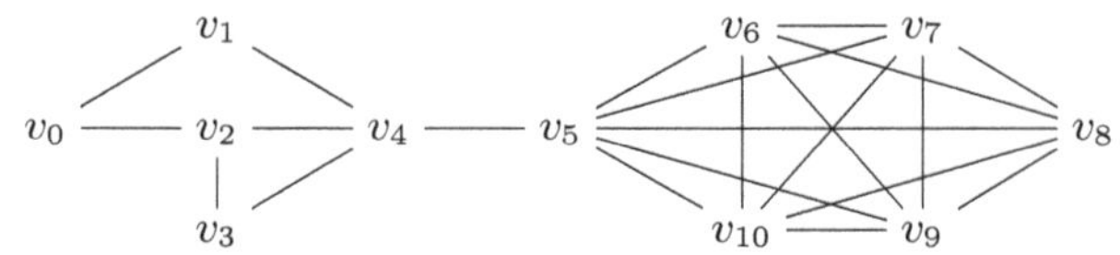

Figure 1: Toy example of a social network G.

with v are likely to become friends with v in the future. Link prediction is the basis of friend recommendation in a social network. It is an important tool that is used to predict the evolution of a network and to locate hidden or surprising links.

Multiple link prediction functions have been developed in the past. We present some of the better known functions below. These functions, as well as others, are discussed in detail in [57]. In the following, we use $N(v)$ to denote the set of neighbors of v. (To simplify the presentation, we assume that the network is undirected. Suitable adaptations for directed networks can be made.) Link prediction functions are given two unconnected nodes u, v, and produce a score indicating how likely a link is to form between them.

One of the simplest link prediction methods simply counts the number of neighbors in common to u and v, i.e., it produces the score

$$|N(u) \cap N(v)|.$$

This is based on the principle of *triadic closure*, i.e., that if a connection exists between nodes u, w and between nodes w, v, then there is likely to be a connection between nodes u, v [38]. More sophisticated adaptations of this measure exist, including the *Jaccard coefficient*

$$\frac{|N(u) \cap N(v)|}{|N(u) \cup N(v)|},$$

which takes into consideration the total number of neighbors that u and v have, as well as the *Adamic-Adar measure* [6] that weights the importance of a common neighbor w proportionately to the number of neighbors of w, i.e.,

$$\sum_{w \in N(u) \cap N(v)} \frac{1}{\log |N(w)|}.$$

Preferential attachment is based on the intuition that edges are more likely to form with popular nodes (i.e., those with many neighbors), and thus, uses the following score to predict edge formation between u and v

$$|N(u)| \times |N(v)|.$$

Much more sophisticated measures also exist, such as the *Katz measure* [49] which takes into consideration all paths between u and v, but these paths are weighted by their length, giving a score to a u, v as follows

$$\sum_{l=1}^{\infty} \beta^l \cdot |P^l_{u,v}|$$

where $P^l_{u,v}$ is the set of paths of length precisely l from u to v in G, and $0 < \beta < 1$. The parameter β is used to give lower weight to paths that are longer. Finally, *rooted PageRank* measures the stationary distribution weight of a node v under a random walk, where with probability $1-d$

(where d is the *damping factor*) one jumps back to u, while with probability d one goes to a random neighbor of the current node.

To demonstrate some of these notions, observe that the links most likely to be formed in the graph of Figure 1 are: (with equal likelihood) $\{v_1, v_2\}, \{v_0, v_4\}$ according to common neighbors; $\{v_1, v_2\}$ according to the Jaccard coefficient; $\{v_0, v_4\}$ according to the Adamic-Adar measure; and (with equal likelihood) $\{v_4, v_6\}, \ldots, \{v_4, v_{10}\}$ according to preferential attachment.

Link prediction methods vary significantly in terms of their ease of computation. (For that reason, [28] proposed using a variety of link prediction functions to measure efficiency of different types of data-stores for social networks.) As is the case for centrality measures, there is no clear winner among link prediction functions. In fact, even within a single network, different functions may be more effective for different nodes. Thus, for example, [40] states that approximately 20 different link prediction function outputs are combined within their production algorithm for link prediction. See also [32] for an axiomatic approach towards determining which link prediction function should be used in a given context, based on the underlying characteristics of the functions.

2.3 Community detection

The *community structure* of a network is a grouping of the nodes into (perhaps overlapping) sets, such that each set is densely connected, while connections between sets are sparse. Identifying the community structure of a network is called the *community detection problem* and is useful for multiple applications, e.g., for partitioning the data over server clusters, for making recommendations (based on community participation), and for finding hidden criminal activity.

Much research has focused on community detection and many different methods have been proposed. See [36] for an in-depth survey of community detection. We note that community detection comes in different flavors, depending on the form of the desired output. Some techniques partition the graph, while others allow overlap. Hierarchical methods create hierarchies of communities (nested within one another), so that the data can be examined at different degrees of granularity.

One early community detection algorithm is that of *graph partitioning*. Given a predetermined number k of communities and a predetermined size s, the goal is to divide the graph into k disjoint groups of approximately s nodes each, so that the number of inter-group edges is minimized. A distinct disadvantage of this approach is the need to known k and s, a-priori. In *hierarchical clustering*, a similarity measure is defined between pairs of nodes (e.g., by considering the similarity between their sets of neighbors). Nodes are grouped into communities based on this similarity measure, either by agglomerative merging of similar node groups (starting with groups of size 1), or by divisively splitting groups (starting with a group containing all nodes) by dividing between nodes of low similarity.

Community detection is a form of clustering, and thus, methods such as k-means clustering or spectral clustering, are popular for community detection. The *Newman-Girvan* community detection algorithm finds edges in a graph that seem to lie between communities (e.g., edges having high *betweenness*, which are on shortest paths between many pairs of nodes), and removes them, until the community structure emerges. Other community detection methods are based on *modularity maximization*.

Finally, maximal cliques have been used to detect communities, as they capture completely cohesive groups of nodes. Methods for enumerating all maximal cliques have been developed [24, 45]. While the notion of a clique captures a completely cohesive group of nodes within a graph, this definition is often overly restrictive. In practice, it is obvious that sets of nodes can represent cohesive groups even if several links are missing; for example, within a community not all pairs of people will be friends. In addition, as networks are often built from observation of empirical data, there may be real-life links that are missing within the data captured. Searching for groups of nodes that are cliques will miss highly related groups of nodes for which links have been omitted from the dataset. To overcome these limitations, relaxations to the notion of a clique have been introduced and studied [63], and enumeration algorithms for such relaxed structures have been presented [17, 44, 58].

2.4 Information Diffusion

Social networks are a powerful tool for spreading information. Understanding how information diffuses over a network (e.g., who is influential in spreading the information and what paths it will take) is critical in order to leverage social networks for campaigns of all types. Much work has studied the information diffusion problem, in order to better understand this process. See [39] for a survey.

Intuitively, information diffusion is a probabilistic process. Nodes in the network send information to their neighbors, which, in turn, may continue to spread this information further in the network. The likelihood of a neighbor spreading the information can be dependent on the strength of his tie (e.g., an edge weight or probability) with the node from whom he received the information. Threshold models assume that in addition to edge weights, the node itself has some threshold which the sum influence of the message must pass, in order for the node to continue diffusing the message.

An important task is to identify the most influential nodes for ensuring that some particular information will be effectively spread throughout the network. Different methods for identifying such nodes have been presented. In [37], influential nodes have been found by identifying nodes within the core of the network (by computing a k-core). Other works consider using PageRank [26] to measure the influence of a node. The above-mentioned approaches ignore the content of the message to be diffused. However, the likelihood of a node diffusing a message is clearly dependent on the topic of the message. This approach is taken in [77] to identify topic-relevant influential nodes. Finally, [50] considers the probabilistic process in which information diffuses in the network, in order to compute a set of k nodes that will be most effective.

2.5 Challenges

Each of the above-mentioned problems becomes extremely challenging when the underlying data is huge (and cannot fit in main memory of a single machine), and when the social network is highly dynamic. Hence, it is of great interest to develop practically efficient approximation algorithms, as

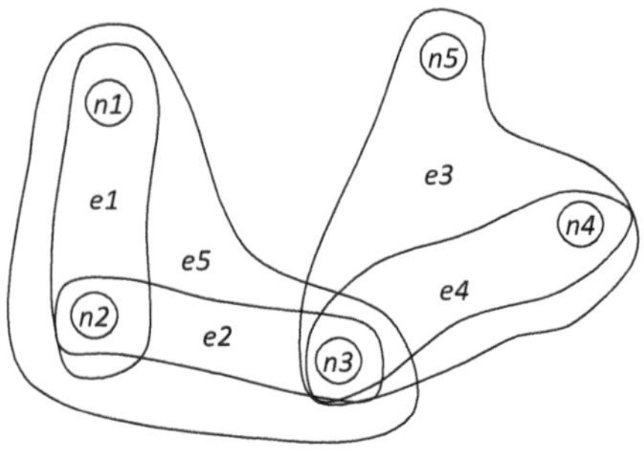

Nodes

n1	Name = Alice Age = 32
n2	Name = Bob High-school = LVHigh
n3	Name = Cindy
n4	Name = Dan Age = 35
n5	Name = Erica Hobby = Bungee jumping

Edges

e1	({n1},{n2})	Label = follows
e2	{n2,n3}	Label = friends
e3	{n3,n4,n5}	Label = co-authors Title = Bungee for Fun ISBN = 12345
e4	{n3,n4}	Label = friends
e5	({n3},{n1,n2})	Label = email Content = Check out my new book...

Figure 2: A tiny portion of a social network

well as effective and appropriate index structures. Both of these can aid in scaling up to large-scale datasets.

An interesting question that must be considered is what is the appropriate data model for a social network. So far, we have viewed a social network simply as a directed or undirected graph. However, in practice, even if labels and weights are added, this model still seems to be limiting. First, it does not explicitly model groups, a common social network element. Second, it does not model group activities (such as an email being sent to a group of users). Both of these could be accommodated by allowing the graph to contain (directed) hyper-edges. However, most work on the computational tasks considered above (centrality, link prediction, community detection and information diffusion) assumes a graph in which edges are only pairs of nodes. Hence, algorithms for these measures must be extended.

To demonstrate, Figure 2 depicts a tiny portion of a social network $\mathcal{N}$. Nodes $n_1, \ldots, n_5$ are associated with attributes and values. For example, n_1 is associated with the attribute-value pairs "Name = Alice" and "Age = 32". The network $\mathcal{N}$ also contains five edges. Observe that all edges are labeled, and some edges are associated with additional attribute-value pairs. There are several different types of edges in $\mathcal{N}$: e_1 is a directed edge, $e_2, e4$ are undirected edges, e_3 is an undirected hyper-edge and e_5 is a directed hyper-edge.[2]

An orthogonal issue is that people in social networks tend to be associated with large amounts of textual, temporal and spatial data. Query evaluation must takes these into consideration, in order to return interesting results. Explicitly incorporating such features into the data model, will drive the development of a system leveraging such features.

3. COMPUTATIONAL PROBLEMS OVER BOTH CONTENT AND STRUCTURE

In the previous section, we adopted the simplification that a social network is simply a graph. However, the textual content attached to the nodes and edges of a social network is in fact of significant importance in effectively managing a social network. This content includes attributes describing the nodes (e.g., name, age, hobbies), text produced by the nodes (e.g., tweets, posts) and labels describing relationships (e.g., friend, employee, liked). Nodes and edges can also have associated types. For example, there may be people nodes and content nodes, with edges denoting the relationships produced or read.

The information content attached to nodes and edges can be leveraged when solving the problems introduced in the previous section. For example, when detecting communities, we may give preference to grouping together nodes with similar interests. In addition, the textual content, combined with the graph structure, gives rise to new problems of interest, several of which are discussed below.

3.1 Team Formation

Given a set of necessary skills, the *team formation problem* is to find a group of people, whose expertise covers these skills, and who can "work well together." The latter is usually measured by estimating the communication cost between people, as is reflected by the graph structure. Quality solutions to this problem are useful in a variety of real-world scenarios, such as forming a program committee, and putting together teams of experts to deal with crises as they arise.

Different methods have been developed to estimate the communication cost between nodes in a social network. In [54], the goal is to form a team with a given set of skills, while minimizing the communication cost. Communication cost is measured either by considering the diameter of the subgraph induced by the team, or the cost of a minimum spanning tree connecting team nodes. Two other types of communication costs were considered in [46], i.e., measuring the sum of distances between all pairs of nodes in the team, or the sum of distances of all nodes to a designated leader node. This problem was extended to a bi-criteria minimization problem in [47], where nodes are associated with their hiring costs, and the goal is to find a team that minimizes both communication cost and team cost. The optimization problems in all of [46, 47, 54] are shown to be NP-hard, and approximation algorithms are presented.

Variations of team formation were considered in [66]. In particular, their goal was to allow realistic constraints to be specified, and then to find teams satisfying these constraints, with high subgraph density. Some of the constraints considered were inclusion of designated experts, restrictions on the

[2]Of course, all edges are simply special cases of directed or undirected hyper-edges.

size or cost of the team, and geographic and structural locality of the team.

When team formation is an oft-repeated process, it becomes important to avoid over-burdening nodes with tasks. Online team formation was considered in [9]. In the scenario considered, team formation tasks appear (in the form of required skill lists) in an online fashion. They consider how to create teams satisfying the skill requirements, and with low communication costs, while performing load balancing.

3.2 Social Search

In the most general sense, *social search* is the problem of leveraging a social network, to improve the results of searching a corpus. Thus, social search is a special type of social query, in which user requests are unstructured lists of keywords. Social relationships are leveraged to improve Web search in [69, 82]. The problem of finding people related to a set of labels is considered in [56]. This is reminiscent of the keyword search problem over arbitrary graphs.

Egocentric person search (also called *context-based person recommendation* [31]) is the problem of recommending people in a social network, when given a set of keywords k, by a member of the social network u. The goal is to return a high-quality ranked list of people who are relevant both to k and to u, and, perhaps, are of global importance. Instances of this problem include problems such as recommending an accessible expert on a medical issue, recommending a good lawyer for a legal entanglement, or recommending collaborators on a research topic.

Egocentric person search was studied in several works. In [76], queries are only names. Ranking is performed by estimating the distance of nodes with the requested name, to the initiator of the query, u. General guiding principles for this problem are considered in [31]. Machine learning techniques have also been applied to this problem, e.g., in the context of email recipient recommendation [70] and collaborator recommendation [29].

Finally, [42] considers a different twist to the social search problem. In this work, users issue free-text questions. The system, called Aardvark, aims at finding users who are likely to be able to answer a given question. Thus, much effort is made to determining user expertise, to allow effective result rankings.

3.3 Social Querying

Social querying differs from social search in the expressiveness of the user language. In particular, in social search, a user simply specifies a set of keywords, while in social querying, the user can express much richer requirements. Developing an appropriate query language is an important problem.

Query languages for graph databases have been developed and analyzed, e.g., [11, 14, 60, 79]. In the industry, the SPARQL query language is used to query RDF graphs, and Cypher is used to query the Neo4j graph database. While graph query languages are general enough to be used over arbitrary graphs, they are not necessarily a best choice for querying social networks. In particular, graph query languages focus mostly on precise queries, which can use regular path expressions (e.g., find all common co-authors of two specific authors, find people 2-hops away from a given node, find pairs of nodes whose connecting path matches a specific regular expression). These languages lack the capability to express richer imprecise queries, such as expert search, friend recommendation or recognizing communities, that are more in the spirit of social-network analysis.

Several papers have studied the problem of querying specifically social networks. Datalog [67] and RDF/SPARQL [68] have both been extended to search as query languages for social networks. In addition, specialized query languages for social networks have also been developed. These are surveyed, next.

SoQL [67], is a social-network query language that is based on SQL. In SoQL, a social network is a four-tuple

$$(N, F, T_N, T_F),$$

containing a set of nodes N, a set of undirected friend edges F, a set of node attributes T_N, and of edge attributes T_F. Nodes, sets of nodes, edges and paths of edges, are first-class citizens in the SoQL language. Thus, queries can be of two types: select-from-path queries, which return paths or aggregations over paths, and select-from-group queries, which return groups, or aggregations over groups.

We demonstrate the SoQL language with an example.

```
SELECT PATH, COUNT(PATH.nodes.*)
FROM PATH (Bob TO X)
WHERE X.company = 'Google' and
           ATMOST 0 IN PATH.nodes SATISFY
                (company='Yahoo') and
           COUNT(PATH.nodes.*) <= 4
```

This query returns paths (along with their length) starting at Bob and ending at a node X, who works at Google. In addition, the path should not pass through any person working at Yahoo, and should be of length at most 4.

SNQL [59] is inspired by GraphLog and second order tuple-generating dependencies. It includes both querying and data manipulation features. In the SNQL data model, actors, relations and attributes are all modeled as nodes. Edges are used to associate attributes with actors and relations, and to associate actors with relations. Syntactically, these are represented as triples, in a similar vein to RDF.

The SNQL query syntax allows for both graphical representations of query components, and for an SQL-like syntax, using a triple notation, e.g., the triple

```
(A1, isa, person)
```

requires variable `A1` to be bound to variable belonging to the type `person`. Advanced features, such as grouping and aggregation and computation of a transitive closure, are available. A unique feature of SNQL is the ability to construct arbitrary new portions of a social network, using a construction query. This is lacking in SoQL.

Finally, [34] combines social-network querying, data mining and clustering capabilities. This is achieved by presenting an *inductive* query language, called BiQL, for network data. A uniform representation of nodes and edges is employed, which allows the user to define different contexts on the network. As both the input and the output of a query is a network, queries can be composed.

In the data model of [34], objects have identifiers, and can have additional attribute-value pairs. Links are simply pairs of objects. The model also allows for named sets of objects (using domain names) and named sets of domain names (using context names). The query language of [34] is special in several ways, e.g., it allows the user to define a specific context over which the query should be evaluated, and allows external calls to data mining primitives. To demonstrate, consider the following query sequence:

```
CREATE CitationSimilarity AS
SELECT <X,Y>
FROM Paper P -> Cites X, Paper P -> Cites Y

CREATE G AS INSTANCE labeled_graph WITH
    Cites AS NODES,
    CitationSimilarity AS EDGES

CREATE C AS INSTANCE GraphCluster(G)
```

The first query finds pairs of nodes X, Y that are both cited by the same paper. The second query creates a graph G of citation nodes, with co-citation information as edges. Finally, the third query calls an external function to cluster G.

3.4 Challenges

As is the case with purely structural problems, computational problems over both structure and content are challenging due to the volume of social networks and to the velocity in which the data changes. In addition, a data management system, that allows for declarative access to data of interest, must be able to express key social tasks. However, the languages developed thus far cannot easily express many such information needs.

Query languages previously considered for social networks do not allow the users to utilize well-known social network notions. Hence, for example, it is not possible to express the following natural queries:

- *Matchmaking:* Find, for every female node f, the top-5 male nodes m that are not currently friends with f, and are likely to become friends with f in the near future. Note that this is simply a filtered link prediction problem.
- *Divorce Lawyer:* Find a node in the network who is a well-known expert on divorce law, and lives in the same geographic vicinity as Node 72. This query combines keyword search, a spatial distance predicate and centrality.
- *Rumor Spreading:* Find 10 people, within the community of Node 72, who can be most instrumental at spreading a "call for help" plea. Formulating this query involves ability to declaratively use elements from the community detection and information diffusion problems, while filtering by the given input data.
- *Task-force Formation:* Find 4 people, within the community of Node 72, who can form a task-force to help with a set of problems, including childcare solutions, home repairs and psychological support. This query combines community detection with team formation.

A possible approach to formulating a language that can express such queries is to develop special built-in social network functions, that can be used as building blocks for expressing interesting queries over the social network. (We note that a similar approach was taken to integrate spatial operations within relational databases.) The following built-in functions were suggested by [30].

- `imp`(v): measures the importance of a node v;
- `sim`(V): measures the similarity of a set of nodes V;
- `cls`(V): measures the closeness of a set of nodes V;
- `infl`(V): measures the influence of a set of nodes V on the rest of the network;
- `dscr`(V, t): measures the strength of the relationship between a set of nodes V and given text t.

More work is necessary to determine the best social primitives to be incorporated, as well as to analyze the expressibility of such a language.

We note that even if a choice of primitives is made, there can be many different ways to implement these primitives. For example, `imp` can be implemented using any one of many different centrality measures. Similarity (`sim`) can be measured in many different ways, e.g., by comparing sets of neighbors, or by determining community participation. In fact, it may be preferable for a system to include several different implementations of each built-in function. The choice between these implementations can be made declaratively by the user, or by leveraging machine learning techniques.

4. SYSTEMS FOR MANAGING SOCIAL NETWORKS

Previous sections considered computational problems over social networks. We now discuss systems and methodologies for managing this data. In particular, we consider benchmarks for social network data management, the problem of storing and compressing social networks, graph databases, social network analysis tools and the systems of big players in the industry.

4.1 Benchmarks

The computational problems discussed above are not, by any means, a complete listing of all interesting social network tasks. Other important challenges include effective visualization of portions of the network, using the data for collaborative filtering, and efficiently finding (shortest) paths between nodes in the network. All of the topics discussed thus far require solutions that are typically expensive. The quality of such solutions can differ greatly depending on the structure of the network, or the behavior of the users. Benchmarks for social network analysis data management include some of these tasks. However, there are additional critical, yet simpler, tasks not yet discussed, that are crucial for a benchmark.

Any database management system for a social network must efficiently support queries and updates that are generated constantly by the users. Thus, benchmarks for social networks [12, 13, 35] also focus on typical workloads including: resource updates by users (e.g., commenting or uploading a picture), reads of user profiles and associated information, listing node friends, viewing friend requests, and inviting/accepting invitations/declining invitations for friends. An effective data management system must process huge numbers of such reads and writes, with low latency and high throughput.

4.2 Storing and Compressing Social Networks

Defining methods to store a social network, while allowing efficient access for query processing, is key to achieving an efficient social database management system. One approach is to employ compression techniques that will allow the entire graph to be kept in memory on a single computer. Another approach is to partition the graph over a collection of servers, while employing some level of node duplication to achieve efficient access. Interestingly, Twitter adopted the idea of storing its entire graph in memory (with little compression) for quite a while. Currently, they seem to have mored to a partitioned approach as this allows them to store extensive auxiliary information at nodes and edges [40].

Compression of large graphs was first studied in the context of the Web graph [65]. There, two important properties were observed, when nodes were sorted lexicographically by their URLs:

- *similarity*: nodes that are close to one another, by the ordering, tend to have similar sets of neighbors.
- *locality*: neighbors of a node are often close to the node, according to the ordering.

These properties can be leveraged in order to efficiently compress a Web graph, by encoding nodes by their differences from similar, previously appearing, nodes, and by using gap encoding [20].

The nodes in a social networks do not have extrinsic information that can be leveraged for effective sorting (unlike the URLs of a Web page). Hence, much effort has been made to develop strategies that can be used to achieve effective sorting of the nodes of a social network, so that nodes close to one another are also similar (and hence, previously considered compression techniques can be applied). In particular, [27] used shingling of neighbor sets to create a node ordering (they also give reciprocal edges special treatment), [19] uses gray codes[3] to order the nodes of a social network, and [18] uses layered label propagation to label the nodes, and then sort by these labels.

As an alternative to storing the entire network, compressed, at a single location, several works have considered partitioning a graph over a set of servers. The common assumption is that queries and updates often traverse to direct neighbors of a node. Hence, it is preferable for a node, and all its neighbors, to be stored at a single machine, so as to enable efficient querying and updates. Unfortunately, due to the presence of nodes with very high degrees in a social network, satisfying this requirement would require extensive node duplication.

Another way of looking at this problem is that of partitioning the nodes of a graph, so that the number of cross-partition edges is minimized. Unfortunately, finding a balanced sized partition that minimizes cross-partition edges, is an NP-complete problem. In addition, as social networks are highly dynamic, even if such a partition could be found, it would be highly inefficient to continuously preserve optimality.

A strategy for node partitioning and duplication is given in [61]. They guarantee that a given percentage of neighbors of each node are retained locally. The choice of nodes to replicate, and how replicated nodes are kept up-to-date (using a push or pull semantics) is based on the frequency of updates at the nodes. Dynamic update of partitions, as workloads evolve, is also considered in [81]. A move from a node-centric paradigm to a graph-centric paradigm is considered in [75], allowing information about the partition to be available to the user to achieve more efficient algorithms (e.g., by avoiding partition traversal when possible). Finally, [22] considers the problem of finding a partition that is edge-balanced (as opposed to previous work that considered vertex-balanced partitions).

4.3 Graph Databases

Abstractly, social networks are often viewed simply as graphs. There has been significant work on graph databases. For example, graph database models are studied in [10, 41], and query languages for graph databases have been introduced and studied extensively [11, 14, 60, 79]. A distributed data management system for large-scale graphs is considered in [53]. Preserving privacy, while revealing statistics about a graph is considered in [48]. Several graph databases have also been developed in the industry, e.g., Neo4j[4], OrientDB[5] and Titan[6].

Some of the work on graph databases is highly relevant to managing social network data. However, much of the work is not directly applicable (or is only applicable in a limited fashion) due to the significant differences between social networks and graphs. First, using a graph as a data model may be overly simplistic. A social network may come in conjunction with a standard relational database that stores mission critical information, e.g., a university database, together with a social network of students. In addition, much interesting information in a social network is in rich textual and spatial data associated with the users. Even when restricting oneself to a graph model, most of the above works do not consider general graphs, such as hypergraphs (e.g., which can be used to model "groups" in a network) or directed hypergraphs (e.g., needed to model emails sent from a person to a set of people). Furthermore, even when taking a simplistic view of a social network as simply being a directed graph, tools for graph databases usually do not provide built-in methods to perform key social network tasks (e.g., link prediction, social search, community detection).

4.4 Social Network Analysis Tools

Many software tools are available for analysis of arbitrary social networks. In fact, Wikipedia [78] lists close to 80 social-network analysis tools. Roughly speaking, these tools usually focus on one or more of the following aspects: visualization, analysis, mining, filtering and manipulation. Some of the better known social network analysis tools include UCINET, Gephi and Pajek. The main capabilities of UCINET [21] lie in network transformations, connectivity, centrality, subgroups, positions and hypothesis testing. Gephi [15] allows for filtering, navigating, manipulating and clustering social network data. It has a 3D render engine for (dynamic) network visualization. Pajek [16] can be used to analyze and visualize large networks of thousands to millions of vertices.

While these tools are useful for social network analysis,

[3] A gray code is an ordering of binary sequences, such that consecutive sequences differ in precisely one bit.

[4] http://neo4j.com/

[5] http://orientdb.com/orientdb/

[6] http://thinkaurelius.com/

i.e., for accomplishing the tasks of Section 2, they lack the capabilities of a database system. Lacking a full-blown query language, it is difficult, in such systems, to effectively drill down on a portion of the data that is of interest. Access control capabilities are missing. Hence, data used in such systems can be leaked to unauthorized persons. Systems for social network analysis lack transaction control, and do not ensure consistency when multiple users dynamically change the data. Such systems typically have inflexible data models, which can preclude the ability to describe rich structures, such as groups of nodes, or associated tables of attributes. Finally, social network analysis systems cannot easily integrate powerful tools for geospatial analysis (such as route analysis of users) or textual analysis, which are necessary for analyzing modern social networks.

A possible solution for (some of) the above-mentioned problems is to migrate data back and forth between a database system and a system for social network analysis. Clearly such a solution has severe limitations. It does not prevent data leaks, as data is susceptible as soon as it is exported from the database management system. It makes analysis of dynamically changing data difficult, as such data must be continually exported from the DBMS. Another drawback of this approach is that it precludes optimizing of social network operations in conjunction with database operations, and cannot take advantage of index structures available within the database.

As is apparent from the above discussion, social network analysis tools are extremely useful for visualization and manipulation of social data. However, they cannot be a solution for data management of social networks.

4.5 The Big Players

There are currently several social networks of mammoth size, used by a large percentage of the world's population, and generating (tens of) terebytes of data every day. In this section, we briefly review some of the challenges and features of the data management systems of three such big players, namely LinkedIn, Facebook and Twitter. There are, of course, other huge social networks. We focus on these three because of the wealth of publications by these companies describing their data management systems, which allow non-employees to learn about the solutions deployed.

LinkedIn[7], launched in 2003, is a professional networking system. One of the goals of LinkedIn is to create an economic graph of the world, containing information about jobs, job requirements, companies and professionals worldwide. There are reportedly 400 million user accounts at LinkedIn [3]. Facebook[8], a social networking system launched in 2004, was originally geared towards college students. Since 2006, it is open to people throughout the world, and is reported to have 1.44 billion monthly active users (and 936 million daily active users) [2]. Finally, Twitter[9] is a directed information network, created in 2006. In Twitter, users can send "tweets" (i.e., short 140 character messages), and can follow one another to receive tweet updates. There are reportedly 320 million monthly users at Twitter [4].

The enormous user base of these social network systems creates significant challenges in data management. Users of the systems expect very low query latency, so as to have almost instantaneous access to the data. High throughput is critical, due to the large number of simultaneous access requests. Further complicating data management is the huge size of the data created daily. Users create data both explicitly (tweets, posts), and implicitly (page views, clickthroughs). This data must be made immediately accessible to social network users. In fact, often the most recent data is also the most interesting, and thus, must be quickly available.

In the following, we touch upon two aspects of data management within huge social networks. Obviously, it is not possible to provide all details within the scope of this tutorial, so we focus on some highlights and give references to further details for the interested reader.

Architecture

The first aspect considered is how to build a system that can meet the low latency, and high throughput requirements, on the huge and every increasing data created by social network users. Many papers have appeared in the last several years describing the various components used to manage data at these three organizations. We delineate the commonalities of their approaches.

First, all three organizations subscribe to the *"One size fits all: An idea whose time has come and gone"* [71] philosophy. Therefore, their systems are a complex combination of a variety of storage solutions, such as publish/subscribe or logging systems, key-value stores, relational databases, and OLAP systems, as discussed below:

- For a description of the LinkedIn ecosystem, see [73]. Specific LinkedIn components, such as the Kafka publish-subscribe system [51], the Voldemort key-value store [72], Espresso, a document oriented distributed database [64], and Avatara, a system for OLAP queries [80], have also been described.
- Facebook's data management solution includes Scribe, a distributed log aggregation service, which acts as a databus, moving data and actions from the website and systems into Hive tables [74]. A MySQL database is used for storage of data for which strong consistency must be preserved. Facebook has also extended HBase to meet its scalability and speed requirements [7]. Other types of data are stored in the Memcache [62] key-value store and data analytics for real-time analysis is performed with Scuba [5].
- Twitter has developed Earlybird [25], based on the open source search engine Lucene, for real-time searching of tweets and other data. As in Facebook, Twitter also builds upon Scribe for their logging infrastructure [55]. Cassovary was developed to hold the entire Twitter graph within main memory [40] (but this functionality is being redesigned based on HDFS). Other interesting components include Heron, for stream processing [52] and Summingbird, for integrating batch and online computations [23].

A second commonality that is apparent from the component description is the extensive use of a queuing (LinkedIn) or logging (Facebook and Twitter) system to serve as a databus, transferring data from component to component. This is critical, as it allows each subsystem and application to be developed independently. In fact, in all three companies, the

[7]https://www.linkedin.com
[8]https://www.facebook.com
[9]https://www.twitter.com

developers who create data (i.e., ingest data into the queuing/logging system), are typically not those who utilize this data in further applications.

In order to meet the high throughput and low latency requirements, all three aim to scale horizontally, over commodity servers, so as to deal with their mammoth data storage and processing needs. Therefore, they make extensive use of sharding and replication, to create a highly distributed system. The Hadoop framework, along with the Map-Reduce paradigm, is utilized within the systems. In fact, both offline and online Hadoop-based data-centers are maintained in order to allow effective development of new features, without degrading user experience.

Finally, in all three organizations, a large proportion of the data generated is read-only. This is true both for some user generated data (e.g., tweets), and for the large amounts of implicitly derived data, which log user and system behavior. Thus, the strong consistency capabilities of a relational database system are somewhat of an over-kill for many social network applications. In addition, for many applications, some (small) degree of staleness or incompleteness, is not detrimental. Hence, full consistency is often traded for lower latency, in a large proportion of the system. Various eventual consistency solutions are applied, such as conflict resolution at read time.

Querying

We consider the querying languages provided by Facebook, Twitter and LinkedIn. As will become apparent, the languages provided by these companies are rather limited and cannot directly express many key social network tasks. This is perhaps not surprising, as the focus here is on simple queries that can be efficiently evaluated. The more complex tasks are achieved by specially developed applications (often using Hadoop jobs).

Facebook has developed the Unicorn framework [33] for querying the graph structure of the social nework. In the Unicorn data model, nodes and edges have identifiers and types, and can be associated with key-value pairs. Queries return sets of nodes, and allow for set operations, such as intersection, union and difference. In addition, users can constrain a node or edge label to be associated with a particular value. Queries can be nested, as they are both applied to, and return, sets of nodes. For example,

```
(apply friend: (and friend:5 friend:6))
```

returns nodes that are friends of mutual friends of nodes 5 and 6.

The query language of Unicorn is quite limited. While Facebook does not provide an abstract model for their query language, it is apparently missing standard features such as node variables, and value comparisons, as well as the ability to return more complex structures than a single set. Notwithstanding, Facebook makes extensive use of query planning to achieve efficient query evaluation.

There are two additional noteworthy features of Unicorn. First, query processing does not yield all satisfying answers. Instead, only top ranking results are returned. This allows queries to be answered with lower latency. Second, Unicorn ignores privacy constraints. Instead, query results are associated with lineage, and the application requesting the query results uses a Facebook privacy service to determine which results can be displayed to the user.

Twitter allows users and developers to query the tweet stream. Thus, queries contain keywords, possibly with term operations (such as OR and NOT), and meta-data constraints. The latter can include features such as who authored the tweet, tweet language and location, as well as timing. In addition, users can constrain the tweet sentiment (to derive tweets representing positive or negative attitudes). For example, the query

```
pods since:2016-06-26 :)
```

returns tweets mentioning the keyword "pods',' sent after 26/6/2016, with a positive attitude. Currently, it does not seem to be possible to formulate richer queries, which leverage the social network graph (e.g., to return a tweet from a user who follows some other specific user).

Real-time search in Twitter is supported by the Earlybird system [25]. As in standard information retrieval systems, Earlybird is based on traditional inverted index structures. However, there are several key differences that allow Earlybird to ingest content rapidly and make it available for search immediately. In particular, Earlybird uses a single-writer, multiple reader, consistency model.

Currently, it seems that LinkedIn does not provide a query language. However, this may change soon, with project Galene [1]. The focus of Galenes is on gathering all economic data in the world, and then allowing this economic graph to be effectively queried.

4.6 Challenges

While the industry giants have their own systems for managing social network data, smaller-sized companies do not currently have a ready-to-use solution for such data. To be useful, many (or all) of the computational tasks discussed above must be implemented. A query language, that allows declarative inclusion of such tasks in a rich query, must be developed. Once such a language has been defined, new and exciting challenges immediately appear.

A primary challenge is in achieving *efficient query evaluation.* This problem is exacerbated as *(1)* evaluating social network primitives can be very expensive as they touch large portions of the network, and *(2)* precomputed values for primitives can swiftly become stale as the network changes dynamically at high speed. In addition, the huge size of a social network makes even simple network analysis operations quite expensive.

In practice, it seems that for social network queries, it is sufficient to return the most highly ranked results. Hence, the focus in query evaluation must be in quickly finding the best results, and not on complete evaluation. Techniques such as those implemented for maintenance of materialized views may be applicable here. In addition, it may be interesting to study query equivalence problems for this new query language, to allow reuse of old query results.

Another important issue is effective *privacy management.* Standard online social networks provide a very limited array of privacy controls for their users. However, a richer privacy mechanism can be of importance. For example, the user may want to allow herself to be found within specific contexts, or by specific people. As a simple example, a dentist who participates in a social network may desire to be a possible result for queries relating to dentistry (but may wish to remain anonymous for other types of queries). As another example, a database researcher may be willing to be found by any other person who is of importance in the database field, but not by others. Developing a formalism for such privacy controls is a challenge, as is determining how to evaluate built-in social network functions without inadvertently exposing private information.

Evaluating queries in a privacy-aware manner is also critical. Facebook solves this problem by evaluating queries while ignoring privacy constraints, and then using lineage of the results to determine what can be displayed to the user [33]. For a richer query language that allows for predicates expressing centrality, communities, etc., it is not clear how and if such an approach is applicable. In particular, measuring centrality often involves considering all nodes in the network. Using a lineage-based approach, such query results would be visible to a user only if all nodes in the network are visible to the user. This would seem to be very limiting.

There are many additional *advanced features* that would be invaluable within the context of a social-network database. One such feature is the ability to ask hypothetical questions (e.g., what will be the effect on the network if Bob and Alice are no longer friends). Such questions are critical in analyzing the stability of a network. Thus, such a query may be issued over the social network of some company, before determining whether an employee can be fired without a break-down of the company community structures.

Another interesting problem is that of computing and displaying provenance to the user. Consider the example queries mentioned earlier (matchmaking, divorce lawyer and rumor spreading). The answers to such a query are of significantly greater value if they also contain some explanation. This would allow the user to more effectively understand result quality.

5. ACKNOWLEDGMENTS

The author thanks Benny Kimelfeld for his helpful comments while preparing this paper.

6. REFERENCES

[1] Did you mean galene? https://engineering.linkedin.com/search/did-you-mean-galene. Accessed: 2016-02-11.

[2] Facebook reports first quarter 2015 results. http://investor.fb.com/releasedetail.cfm?ReleaseID=908022. Accessed: 2016-01-28.

[3] How linkedin's 400 million members are helping build the economic graph. http://blog.linkedin.com/2015/10/29/400-million-members/. Accessed: 2016-02-10.

[4] Twitter. https://about.twitter.com/company. Accessed: 2016-02-10.

[5] L. Abraham, J. Allen, O. Barykin, V. Borkar, B. Chopra, C. Gerea, D. Merl, J. Metzler, D. Reiss, S. Subramanian, J. L. Wiener, and O. Zed. Scuba: Diving into data at facebook. *Proc. VLDB Endow.*, 6(11):1057–1067, Aug. 2013.

[6] L. Adamic and E. Adar. Friends and neighbors on the web. *Social Networks*, 25:211–230, 2001.

[7] A. S. Aiyer, M. Bautin, G. J. Chen, P. Damania, P. Khemani, K. Muthukkaruppan, K. Ranganathan, N. Spiegelberg, L. Tang, and M. Vaidya. Storage infrastructure behind facebook messages: Using hbase at scale. *IEEE Data Eng. Bull.*, 35(2):4–13, 2012.

[8] J. Almack. The influence of intelligence on the selection of associates. *School and Society*, 16:529–530, 1922.

[9] A. Anagnostopoulos, L. Becchetti, C. Castillo, A. Gionis, and S. Leonardi. Online team formation in social networks. In *Proceedings of the 21st International Conference on World Wide Web*, WWW '12, pages 839–848, New York, NY, USA, 2012. ACM.

[10] R. Angles and C. Gutierrez. Survey of graph database models. *ACM Comput. Surv.*, 40(1):1–39, 2008.

[11] T. Antonopoulos, F. Neven, and F. Servais. Definability problems for graph query languages. In *Proceedings of the 16th International Conference on Database Theory*, ICDT '13, pages 141–152, New York, NY, USA, 2013. ACM.

[12] T. G. Armstrong, V. Ponnekanti, D. Borthakur, and M. Callaghan. Linkbench: A database benchmark based on the facebook social graph. In *Proceedings of the 2013 ACM SIGMOD International Conference on Management of Data*, SIGMOD '13, pages 1185–1196, New York, NY, USA, 2013. ACM.

[13] S. Barahmand and S. Ghandeharizadeh. BG: A benchmark to evaluate interactive social networking actions. In *CIDR 2013, Sixth Biennial Conference on Innovative Data Systems Research, Asilomar, CA, USA, January 6-9, 2013, Online Proceedings*, 2013.

[14] P. Barceló Baeza. Querying graph databases. In *Proceedings of the 32Nd Symposium on Principles of Database Systems*, PODS '13, pages 175–188, New York, NY, USA, 2013. ACM.

[15] M. Bastian, S. Heymann, and M. Jacomy. Gephi: An open source software for exploring and manipulating networks. In *Proceedings of the Third International Conference on Weblogs and Social Media, ICWSM 2009, San Jose, California, USA, May 17-20, 2009*, 2009.

[16] V. Batagelj and A. Mrvar. Pajek. In *Encyclopedia of Social Network Analysis and Mining*, pages 1245–1256. 2014.

[17] D. Berlowitz, S. Cohen, and B. Kimelfeld. Efficient enumeration of maximal k-plexes. In *Proceedings of the 2015 ACM SIGMOD International Conference on Management of Data, Melbourne, Victoria, Australia, May 31 - June 4, 2015*, pages 431–444, 2015.

[18] P. Boldi, M. Rosa, M. Santini, and S. Vigna. Layered label propagation: A multiresolution coordinate-free ordering for compressing social networks. In *Proceedings of the 20th International Conference on World Wide Web*, WWW '11, pages 587–596, New York, NY, USA, 2011. ACM.

[19] P. Boldi, M. Santini, and S. Vigna. Permuting web and social graphs. *Internet Mathematics*, 6(3):257–283, 2009.

[20] P. Boldi and S. Vigna. The webgraph framework i: Compression techniques. In *Proceedings of the 13th International Conference on World Wide Web*, WWW '04, pages 595–602, New York, NY, USA, 2004. ACM.

[21] S. P. Borgatti, M. G. Everett, and L. C. Freeman. UCINET. In *Encyclopedia of Social Network Analysis and Mining*, pages 2261–2267. 2014.

[22] F. Bourse, M. Lelarge, and M. Vojnovic. Balanced graph edge partition. In *Proceedings of the 20th ACM*

SIGKDD International Conference on Knowledge Discovery and Data Mining, KDD '14, pages 1456–1465, New York, NY, USA, 2014. ACM.

[23] O. Boykin, S. Ritchie, I. O'Connell, and J. Lin. Summingbird: A framework for integrating batch and online mapreduce computations. *Proc. VLDB Endow.*, 7(13):1441–1451, Aug. 2014.

[24] C. Bron and J. Kerbosch. Algorithm 457: Finding all cliques of an undirected graph. *Commun. ACM*, 16(9):575–577, Sept. 1973.

[25] M. Busch, K. Gade, B. Larson, P. Lok, S. Luckenbill, and J. Lin. Earlybird: Real-time search at twitter. In *Proceedings of the 2012 IEEE 28th International Conference on Data Engineering*, ICDE '12, pages 1360–1369, Washington, DC, USA, 2012. IEEE Computer Society.

[26] M. Cataldi, L. Di Caro, and C. Schifanella. Emerging topic detection on twitter based on temporal and social terms evaluation. In *Proceedings of the Tenth International Workshop on Multimedia Data Mining*, MDMKDD '10, pages 4:1–4:10, New York, NY, USA, 2010. ACM.

[27] F. Chierichetti, R. Kumar, S. Lattanzi, M. Mitzenmacher, A. Panconesi, and P. Raghavan. On compressing social networks. In *Proceedings of the 15th ACM SIGKDD International Conference on Knowledge Discovery and Data Mining*, KDD '09, pages 219–228, New York, NY, USA, 2009. ACM.

[28] S. Cohen and N. Cohen-Tzemach. Implementing link-prediction for social networks in a database system. In *Proceedings of the 3rd ACM SIGMOD Workshop on Databases and Social Networks, DBSocial 2013, New York, NY, USA, June, 23, 2013*, pages 37–42, 2013.

[29] S. Cohen and L. Ebel. Recommending collaborators using keywords. In *22nd International World Wide Web Conference, WWW '13, Rio de Janeiro, Brazil, May 13-17, 2013, Companion Volume*, pages 959–962, 2013.

[30] S. Cohen, L. Ebel, and B. Kimelfeld. A social network database that learns how to answer queries. In *CIDR 2013, Sixth Biennial Conference on Innovative Data Systems Research, Asilomar, CA, USA, January 6-9, 2013, Online Proceedings*, 2013.

[31] S. Cohen, B. Kimelfeld, G. Koutrika, and J. Vondrák. On principles of egocentric person search in social networks. In *Proceedings of the First International Workshop on Searching and Integrating New Web Data Sources - Very Large Data Search, Seattle, WA, USA, September 2, 2011*, pages 3–6, 2011.

[32] S. Cohen and A. Zohar. An axiomatic approach to link prediction. In *Proceedings of the Twenty-Ninth AAAI Conference on Artificial Intelligence, January 25-30, 2015, Austin, Texas, USA.*, pages 58–64, 2015.

[33] M. Curtiss, I. Becker, T. Bosman, S. Doroshenko, L. Grijincu, T. Jackson, S. Kunnatur, S. Lassen, P. Pronin, S. Sankar, G. Shen, G. Woss, C. Yang, and N. Zhang. Unicorn: A system for searching the social graph. *Proc. VLDB Endow.*, 6(11):1150–1161, Aug. 2013.

[34] A. Dries, S. Nijssen, and L. D. Raedt. A query language for analyzing networks. In *Proceedings of the 18th ACM Conference on Information and Knowledge Management, CIKM 2009, Hong Kong, China, November 2-6, 2009*, pages 485–494, 2009.

[35] O. Erling, A. Averbuch, J. Larriba-Pey, H. Chafi, A. Gubichev, A. Prat, M.-D. Pham, and P. Boncz. The ldbc social network benchmark: Interactive workload. In *Proceedings of the 2015 ACM SIGMOD International Conference on Management of Data*, SIGMOD '15, pages 619–630, New York, NY, USA, 2015. ACM.

[36] S. Fortunato. Community detection in graphs. *Physics Reports*, 486(3âĂŞ5):75 – 174, 2010.

[37] L. Gallos, S. Havlin, M. Kitsak, F. Liljeros, H. Makse, L. Muchnik, and H. Stanley. Identification of influential spreaders in complex networks. *Nature Physics*, 6(11):888–893, Aug 2010.

[38] M. Granovetter. The strength of weak ties. *American Journal of Sociology*, 78(6):1360–1380, May 1973s.

[39] A. Guille, H. Hacid, C. Favre, and D. A. Zighed. Information diffusion in online social networks: A survey. *SIGMOD Rec.*, 42(2):17–28, July 2013.

[40] P. Gupta, A. Goel, J. Lin, A. Sharma, D. Wang, and R. Zadeh. WTF: the who to follow service at twitter. In *Proceedings of the 22Nd International Conference on World Wide Web*, WWW '13, pages 505–514, New York, NY, USA, 2013. ACM.

[41] R. H. Güting. Graphdb: Modeling and querying graphs in databases. In J. B. Bocca, M. Jarke, and C. Zaniolo, editors, *VLDB'94, Proceedings of 20th International Conference on Very Large Data Bases, September 12-15, 1994, Santiago de Chile, Chile*, pages 297–308. Morgan Kaufmann, 1994.

[42] D. Horowitz and S. D. Kamvar. The anatomy of a large-scale social search engine. In *Proceedings of the 19th International Conference on World Wide Web*, WWW '10, pages 431–440, New York, NY, USA, 2010. ACM.

[43] R. M. Hubbard. *A method of studying spontaneous group formation*, pages 76–85. New York: Teachers College, Columbia University, Child Development Monographs, 1929.

[44] H. Ito and K. Iwama. Enumeration of isolated cliques and pseudo-cliques. *ACM Trans. Algorithms*, 5(4):40:1–40:21, Nov. 2009.

[45] D. S. Johnson, C. H. Papadimitriou, and M. Yannakakis. On generating all maximal independent sets. *Inf. Process. Lett.*, 27(3):119–123, 1988.

[46] M. Kargar and A. An. Discovering top-k teams of experts with/without a leader in social networks. In *Proceedings of the 20th ACM International Conference on Information and Knowledge Management*, CIKM '11, pages 985–994, New York, NY, USA, 2011. ACM.

[47] M. Kargar, M. Zihayat, and A. An. Finding affordable and collaborative teams from a network of experts. In *Proceedings of the SIAM International Conference on Data Mining (SDM)*, pages 587–595. SIAM, 2013.

[48] V. Karwa, S. Raskhodnikova, A. Smith, and G. Yaroslavtsev. Private analysis of graph structure. *ACM Trans. Database Syst.*, 39(3):22:1–22:33, Oct. 2014.

[49] L. Katz. A new status index derived from sociometric analysis. *Psychometrika*, 18(1):39–43, March 1953.

[50] D. Kempe, J. Kleinberg, and E. Tardos. Maximizing the spread of influence through a social network. In *Proceedings of the Ninth ACM SIGKDD International Conference on Knowledge Discovery and Data Mining*, KDD '03, pages 137–146, New York, NY, USA, 2003. ACM.

[51] J. Kreps, N. Narkhede, and J. Rao. Kafka: A distributed messaging system for log processing. In *Proceedings of the 6th International Workshop on Networking Meets Databases (NetDB)*, 2011.

[52] S. Kulkarni, N. Bhagat, M. Fu, V. Kedigehalli, C. Kellogg, S. Mittal, J. M. Patel, K. Ramasamy, and S. Taneja. Twitter heron: Stream processing at scale. In *Proceedings of the 2015 ACM SIGMOD International Conference on Management of Data*, SIGMOD '15, pages 239–250, New York, NY, USA, 2015. ACM.

[53] A. G. Labouseur, J. Birnbaum, P. W. Olsen, Jr., S. R. Spillane, J. Vijayan, J.-H. Hwang, and W.-S. Han. The g* graph database: Efficiently managing large distributed dynamic graphs. *Distrib. Parallel Databases*, 33(4):479–514, Dec. 2015.

[54] T. Lappas, K. Liu, and E. Terzi. Finding a team of experts in social networks. In *Proceedings of the 15th ACM SIGKDD international conference on Knowledge discovery and data mining*, pages 467–476. ACM, 2009.

[55] G. Lee, J. Lin, C. Liu, A. Lorek, and D. Ryaboy. The unified logging infrastructure for data analytics at twitter. *Proc. VLDB Endow.*, 5(12):1771–1780, Aug. 2012.

[56] C.-T. Li, M.-K. Shan, and S.-D. Lin. Context-based people search in labeled social networks. In *Proceedings of the 20th ACM International Conference on Information and Knowledge Management*, CIKM '11, pages 1607–1612, New York, NY, USA, 2011. ACM.

[57] D. Liben-Nowell and J. Kleinberg. The link-prediction problem for social networks. *J. Am. Soc. Inf. Sci. Technol.*, 58(7):1019–1031, May 2007.

[58] G. Liu and L. Wong. Effective pruning techniques for mining quasi-cliques. In *Proceedings of the European Conference on Machine Learning and Knowledge Discovery in Databases - Part II*, ECML PKDD '08, pages 33–49, Berlin, Heidelberg, 2008. Springer-Verlag.

[59] M. S. Martín, C. Gutierrez, and P. T. Wood. SNQL: A social networks query and transformation language. In *Proceedings of the 5th Alberto Mendelzon International Workshop on Foundations of Data Management, Santiago, Chile, May 9-12, 2011*, 2011.

[60] A. O. Mendelzon and P. T. Wood. Finding regular simple paths in graph databases. *SIAM J. Comput.*, 24(6):1235–1258, Dec. 1995.

[61] J. Mondal and A. Deshpande. Managing large dynamic graphs efficiently. In *Proceedings of the 2012 ACM SIGMOD International Conference on Management of Data*, SIGMOD '12, pages 145–156, New York, NY, USA, 2012. ACM.

[62] R. Nishtala, H. Fugal, S. Grimm, M. Kwiatkowski, H. Lee, H. C. Li, R. McElroy, M. Paleczny, D. Peek, P. Saab, D. Stafford, T. Tung, and V. Venkataramani. Scaling memcache at facebook. In *Proceedings of the 10th USENIX Conference on Networked Systems Design and Implementation*, nsdi'13, pages 385–398, Berkeley, CA, USA, 2013. USENIX Association.

[63] J. Pattillo, N. Youssef, and S. Butenko. On clique relaxation models in network analysis. *European Journal of Operational Research*, 226(1):9–18, 2013.

[64] L. Qiao, K. Surlaker, S. Das, T. Quiggle, B. Schulman, B. Ghosh, A. Curtis, O. Seeliger, Z. Zhang, A. Auradar, C. Beaver, G. Brandt, M. Gandhi, K. Gopalakrishna, W. Ip, S. Jgadish, S. Lu, A. Pachev, A. Ramesh, A. Sebastian, R. Shanbhag, S. Subramaniam, Y. Sun, S. Topiwala, C. Tran, J. Westerman, and D. Zhang. On brewing fresh espresso: Linkedin's distributed data serving platform. In *Proceedings of the 2013 ACM SIGMOD International Conference on Management of Data*, SIGMOD '13, pages 1135–1146, New York, NY, USA, 2013. ACM.

[65] K. H. Randall, R. Stata, R. G. Wickremesinghe, and J. L. Wiener. The link database: Fast access to graphs of the web. In *Data Compression Conference, 2002. Proceedings. DCC 2002*, pages 122–131. IEEE, 2002.

[66] S. S. Rangapuram, T. Bühler, and M. Hein. Towards realistic team formation in social networks based on densest subgraphs. In *Proceedings of the 22Nd International Conference on World Wide Web*, WWW '13, pages 1077–1088, New York, NY, USA, 2013. ACM.

[67] R. Ronen and O. Shmueli. Evaluating very large datalog queries on social networks. In *EDBT 2009, 12th International Conference on Extending Database Technology, Saint Petersburg, Russia, March 24-26, 2009, Proceedings*, pages 577–587, 2009.

[68] M. San Martín and C. Gutierrez. *The Semantic Web: Research and Applications: 6th European Semantic Web Conference, ESWC 2009 Heraklion, Crete, Greece, May 31–June 4, 2009 Proceedings*, chapter Representing, Querying and Transforming Social Networks with RDF/SPARQL, pages 293–307. Springer Berlin Heidelberg, Berlin, Heidelberg, 2009.

[69] R. Schenkel, T. Crecelius, M. Kacimi, S. Michel, T. Neumann, J. X. Parreira, and G. Weikum. Efficient top-k querying over social-tagging networks. In *Proceedings of the 31st Annual International ACM SIGIR Conference on Research and Development in Information Retrieval*, SIGIR '08, pages 523–530, New York, NY, USA, 2008. ACM.

[70] Z. Sofershtein and S. Cohen. Predicting email recipients. In *Proceedings of the 2015 IEEE/ACM International Conference on Advances in Social Networks Analysis and Mining, ASONAM 2015, Paris, France, August 25 - 28, 2015*, pages 761–764, 2015.

[71] M. Stonebraker and U. Cetintemel. "one size fits all": An idea whose time has come and gone. In *Proceedings of the 21st International Conference on Data Engineering*, ICDE '05, pages 2–11, Washington, DC, USA, 2005. IEEE Computer Society.

[72] R. Sumbaly, J. Kreps, L. Gao, A. Feinberg, C. Soman, and S. Shah. Serving large-scale batch computed data

with project voldemort. In *Proceedings of the 10th USENIX Conference on File and Storage Technologies*, FAST'12, pages 18–18, Berkeley, CA, USA, 2012. USENIX Association.

[73] R. Sumbaly, J. Kreps, and S. Shah. The big data ecosystem at linkedin. In *Proceedings of the 2013 ACM SIGMOD International Conference on Management of Data*, SIGMOD '13, pages 1125–1134, New York, NY, USA, 2013. ACM.

[74] A. Thusoo, Z. Shao, S. Anthony, D. Borthakur, N. Jain, J. Sen Sarma, R. Murthy, and H. Liu. Data warehousing and analytics infrastructure at facebook. In *Proceedings of the 2010 ACM SIGMOD International Conference on Management of Data*, SIGMOD '10, pages 1013–1020, New York, NY, USA, 2010. ACM.

[75] Y. Tian, A. Balmin, S. A. Corsten, S. Tatikonda, and J. McPherson. From "think like a vertex" to "think like a graph". *Proc. VLDB Endow.*, 7(3):193–204, Nov. 2013.

[76] M. V. Vieira, B. M. Fonseca, R. Damazio, P. B. Golgher, D. d. C. Reis, and B. Ribeiro-Neto. Efficient search ranking in social networks. In *Proceedings of the Sixteenth ACM Conference on Conference on Information and Knowledge Management*, CIKM '07, pages 563–572, New York, NY, USA, 2007. ACM.

[77] J. Weng, E.-P. Lim, J. Jiang, and Q. He. Twitterrank: Finding topic-sensitive influential twitterers. In *Proceedings of the Third ACM International Conference on Web Search and Data Mining*, WSDM '10, pages 261–270, New York, NY, USA, 2010. ACM.

[78] Wikipedia. Social network analysis software — Wikipedia, the free encyclopedia, 2012. [Online; Accessed Feb 2016].

[79] P. T. Wood. Query languages for graph databases. *SIGMOD Rec.*, 41(1):50–60, Apr. 2012.

[80] L. Wu, R. Sumbaly, C. Riccomini, G. Koo, H. J. Kim, J. Kreps, and S. Shah. Avatara: OLAP for web-scale analytics products. *PVLDB*, 5(12):1874–1877, 2012.

[81] S. Yang, X. Yan, B. Zong, and A. Khan. Towards effective partition management for large graphs. In *Proceedings of the 2012 ACM SIGMOD International Conference on Management of Data*, SIGMOD '12, pages 517–528, New York, NY, USA, 2012. ACM.

[82] P. Yin, W.-C. Lee, and K. C. Lee. On top-k social web search. In *Proceedings of the 19th ACM International Conference on Information and Knowledge Management*, CIKM '10, pages 1313–1316, New York, NY, USA, 2010. ACM.

Verification of Hierarchical Artifact Systems

Alin Deutsch
UC San Diego
La Jolla, California
deutsch@cs.ucsd.edu

Yuliang Li
UC San Diego
La Jolla, California
yul206@eng.ucsd.edu

Victor Vianu
UC San Diego & INRIA-Saclay
La Jolla, California
vianu@cs.ucsd.edu

ABSTRACT

Data-driven workflows, of which IBM's Business Artifacts are a prime exponent, have been successfully deployed in practice, adopted in industrial standards, and have spawned a rich body of research in academia, focused primarily on static analysis. The present work represents a significant advance on the problem of artifact verification, by considering a much richer and more realistic model than in previous work, incorporating core elements of IBM's successful Guard-Stage-Milestone model. In particular, the model features task hierarchy, concurrency, and richer artifact data. It also allows database key and foreign key dependencies, as well as arithmetic constraints. The results show decidability of verification and establish its complexity, making use of novel techniques including a hierarchy of Vector Addition Systems and a variant of quantifier elimination tailored to our context.

Keywords

data-centric workflows; business process management; temporal logic; verification

1. INTRODUCTION

The past decade has witnessed the evolution of workflow specification frameworks from the traditional process-centric approach towards data-awareness. Process-centric formalisms focus on control flow while under-specifying the underlying data and its manipulations by the process tasks, often abstracting them away completely. In contrast, data-aware formalisms treat data as first-class citizens. A notable exponent of this class is IBM's *business artifact model* pioneered in [40], successfully deployed in practice [10, 9, 17, 22, 52] and adopted in industrial standards. Business artifacts have also spawned a rich body of research in academia, dealing with issues ranging from formal semantics to static analysis (see related work).

In a nutshell, business artifacts (or simply "artifacts") model key business-relevant entities, which are updated by a set of services that implement business process tasks, specified declaratively by pre-and-post conditions. A collection of artifacts and services is called an *artifact system*. IBM has developed several variants of artifacts, of which the most recent is Guard-Stage-Milestone (GSM) [19, 34]. The GSM approach provides rich structuring mechanisms for services, including parallelism, concurrency and hierarchy, and has been incorporated in the OMG standard for Case Management Model and Notation (CMMN) [12, 37].

Artifact systems deployed in industrial settings typically specify very complex workflows that are prone to costly bugs, whence the need for verification of critical properties. Over the past few years, we have embarked upon a study of the verification problem for artifact systems. Rather than relying on general-purpose software verification tools suffering from well-known limitations, our aim is to identify practically relevant classes of artifact systems and properties for which *fully automatic* verification is possible. This is an ambitious goal, since artifacts are infinite-state systems due to the presence of unbounded data. Our approach relies critically on the declarative nature of service specifications and brings into play a novel marriage of database and computer-aided verification techniques.

In previous work [23, 18], we studied the verification problem for a bare-bones variant of artifact systems, without hierarchy or concurrency, in which each artifact consists of a flat tuple of evolving values and the services are specified by simple pre-and-post conditions on the artifact and database. More precisely, we considered the problem of statically checking whether all runs of an artifact system satisfy desirable properties expressed in LTL-FO, an extension of linear-time temporal logic where propositions are interpreted as $\exists$FO sentences on the database and current artifact tuple. In order to deal with the resulting infinite-state system, we developed in [23] a symbolic approach allowing a reduction to finite-state model checking and yielding a PSPACE verification algorithm for the simplest variant of the model (no database dependencies and uninterpreted data domain). In [18] we extended our approach to allow for database dependencies and numeric data testable by arithmetic constraints. Unfortunately, decidability was obtained subject to a rather complex semantic restriction on the artifact system and property (feedback freedom), and the verification algorithm has non-elementary complexity.

The present work represents a significant advance on the artifact verification problem on several fronts. We consider a much richer and more realistic model, called *Hierarchical Artifact System* (HAS), abstracting core elements of the GSM

PODS'16, June 26-July 01, 2016, San Francisco, CA, USA
© 2016 ACM. ISBN 978-1-4503-4191-2/16/06...$15.00
DOI: http://dx.doi.org/10.1145/2902251.2902275

model. In particular, the model features task hierarchy, concurrency, and richer artifact data (including updatable artifact relations). We consider properties expressed in a novel *hierarchical* temporal logic, HLTL-FO, that is well-suited to the model. Our main results establish the complexity of checking HLTL-FO properties for various classes of HAS, highlighting the impact of various features on verification. The results require qualitatively novel techniques, because the reduction to finite-state model checking used in previous work is no longer possible. Instead, the richer model requires the use of a hierarchy of Vector Addition Systems with States (VASS) [13]. The arithmetic constraints are handled using quantifier elimination techniques, adapted to our setting.

We next describe the model and results in more detail. A HAS consists of a database and a hierarchy (rooted tree) of *tasks*. Each task has associated to it local evolving data consisting of a tuple of artifact variables and an updatable artifact relation. It also has an associated set of *services*. Each application of a service is guarded by a pre-condition on the database and local data and causes an update of the local data, specified by a post condition (constraining the next artifact tuple) and an insertion or retrieval of a tuple from the artifact relation. In addition, a task may invoke a child task with a tuple of parameters, and receive back a result if the child task completes. A run of the artifact system consists of an infinite sequence of transitions obtained by any valid interleaving of concurrently running task services.

In order to express properties of HAS's we introduce *hierarchical* LTL-FO (HLTL-FO). Intuitively, an HLTL-FO formula uses as building blocks LTL-FO formulas acting on runs of individual tasks, called local runs, referring only to the database and local data, and can recursively state HLTL-FO properties on runs resulting from calls to children tasks. The language HLTL-FO closely fits the computational model and is also motivated on technical grounds discussed in the paper. A main justification for adopting HLTL-FO is that LTL-FO (and even LTL) properties are undecidable for HAS's.

Hierarchical artifact systems as sketched above provide powerful extensions to the variants we previously studied, each of which immediately leads to undecidability of verification if not carefully controlled. Our main contribution is to put forward a package of restrictions that ensures decidability while capturing a significant subset of the GSM model. This requires a delicate balancing act aiming to limit the dangerous features while retaining their most useful aspects. In contrast to [18], this is achieved without the need for unpleasant semantic constraints such as feedback freedom. The restrictions are discussed in detail in the paper, and shown to be necessary by undecidability results.

The complexity of verification under various restrictions is summarized in Tables 1 (without arithmetic) and 2 (with arithmetic). As seen, the complexity ranges from PSPACE to non-elementary for various packages of features. The non-elementary complexity (a tower of exponentials whose height is the depth of the hierarchy) is reached for HAS with cyclic schemas, artifact relations and arithmetic. For acyclic schemas, which include the widely used Star (or Snowflake) schemas [35, 50], the complexity ranges from PSPACE (without arithmetic or artifact relations) to double-exponential space (with both arithmetic and artifact relations). This is a significant improvement over the previous algorithm of [18], which even for acyclic schemas has non-elementary complexity in the presence of arithmetic (a tower of exponentials whose height is the square of the total number of artifact variables in the system).

The paper is organized as follows. The HAS model is presented in Section 2. We present its syntax and semantics, including a representation of runs as a tree of local task runs, that factors out interleavings of independent concurrent tasks. An example HAS modeling a simple travel booking process is provided in the appendix. The temporal logic HLTL-FO is introduced in Section 3, together with a corresponding extension of Büchi automata to trees of local runs. In Section 4 we prove the decidability of verification without arithmetic, and establish its complexity. To this end, we develop a symbolic representation of HAS runs and a reduction of model checking to state reachability problems in a set of nested VASS (mirroring the task hierarchy). In Section 5 we show how the verification results can be extended in the presence of arithmetic. Section 6 traces the boundary of decidability, showing that the main restrictions adopted in defining the HAS model cannot be relaxed. Finally, we discuss related work in Section 7 and conclude. More details and proofs are provided in the extended appendix of the full version [25] of this paper.

2. FRAMEWORK

In this section we present the syntax and semantics of Hierarchical Artifact Systems (HAS's). We begin with the underlying database schema.

DEFINITION 1. *A **database schema** $\mathcal{DB}$ is a finite set of relation symbols, where each relation R of $\mathcal{DB}$ has an associated sequence of distinct attributes containing the following:*

- *a key attribute* ID *(present in all relations),*
- *a set of foreign key attributes* $\{F_1, \ldots, F_m\}$*, and*
- *a set of non-key attributes* $\{A_1, \ldots, A_n\}$ *disjoint from* $\{\text{ID}, F_1, \ldots, F_m\}$.

To each foreign key attribute F_i of R is associated a relation R_{F_i} of $\mathcal{DB}$ and the inclusion dependency $R[F_i] \subseteq R_{F_i}[\text{ID}]$. It is said that F_i references R_{F_i}.

The domain *Dom*(A) of each attribute A depends on its type. The domain of all non-key attributes is numeric, specifically $\mathbb{R}$. The domain of each key attribute is a countable infinite domain disjoint from $\mathbb{R}$. For distinct relations R and R', $Dom(R.ID) \cap Dom(R'.ID) = \emptyset$. The domain of a foreign key attribute F referencing R is $Dom(R.ID)$. We denote by $DOM_{id} = \cup_{R \in \mathcal{DB}} Dom(R.ID)$. Intuitively, in such a database schema, each tuple is an object with a *globally* unique id. This id does not appear anywhere else in the database except as foreign keys referencing it. An *instance* of a database schema $\mathcal{DB}$ is a mapping D associating to each relation symbol R a finite relation $D(R)$ of the same arity of R, whose tuples provide, for each attribute, a value from its domain. In addition, D satisfies all key and inclusion dependencies associated with the keys and foreign keys of the schema. The active domain D, denoted $\texttt{adom}(D)$, consists of all elements of D (id's and reals). A database schema $\mathcal{DB}$ is *acyclic* if there are no cycles in the references induced by foreign keys. More precisely, consider the labeled graph FK whose nodes are the relations of the schema and in which there is an edge from R_i to R_j labeled with F if R_i has a foreign key attribute F referencing R_j. The schema $\mathcal{DB}$ is *acyclic* if the graph FK is acyclic, and it is *linearly-cyclic* if each relation R is contained in at most one simple cycle.

The assumption that the ID of each relation is a single attribute is made for simplicity, and multiple-attribute IDs can be easily handled. The fact that the domain of all non-key attributes is numeric is also harmless. Indeed, an uninterpreted domain on which only equality can be used can be easily simulated. Note that the keys and foreign keys used on our schemas are special cases of the dependencies used in [18]. The limitation to keys and foreign keys is one of the factors leading to improved complexity of verification and still captures most schemas of practical interest.

We next proceed with the definition of tasks and services, described informally in the introduction. The definition imposes various restrictions needed for decidability of verification. These are discussed and motivated in Section 6.

Similarly to the database schema, we consider two infinite, disjoint sets VAR_{id} of ID variables and $VAR_{\mathbb{R}}$ of numeric variables. We associate to each variable x its *domain* $Dom(x)$. If $x \in VAR_{id}$, then $Dom(x) = \{\texttt{null}\} \cup DOM_{id}$, where $\texttt{null} \notin DOM_{id} \cup \mathbb{R}$ (null plays a special role that will become clear shortly). If $x \in VAR_{\mathbb{R}}$, then $Dom(x) = \mathbb{R}$. An *artifact variable* is a variable in $VAR_{id} \cup VAR_{\mathbb{R}}$. If $\bar{x}$ is a sequence of artifact variables, a *valuation* of $\bar{x}$ is a mapping ν associating to each variable in $\bar{x}$ an element of its domain $Dom(x)$.

Definition 2. *A **task schema** over database schema $\mathcal{DB}$ is a triple $T = \langle \bar{x}^T, S^T, \bar{s}^T \rangle$ where $\bar{x}^T$ is a sequence of distinct artifact variables, S^T is a relation symbol not in $\mathcal{DB}$ with associated arity k, and $\bar{s}^T$ is a sequence of k distinct id variables in $\bar{x}^T$.*

We denote by $\bar{x}^T_{id} = \bar{x}^T \cap VAR_{id}$ and $\bar{x}^T_{\mathbb{R}} = \bar{x}^T \cap VAR_{\mathbb{R}}$. We refer to S^T as the *artifact relation* or *set* of T.

Definition 3. *An **artifact schema** is a tuple $\mathcal{A} = \langle \mathcal{H}, \mathcal{DB} \rangle$ where $\mathcal{DB}$ is a database schema and $\mathcal{H}$ is a rooted tree of task schemas over $\mathcal{DB}$ with pairwise disjoint sets of artifact variables and distinct artifact relation symbols.*

The rooted tree $\mathcal{H}$ defines the *task hierarchy*. Suppose the set of tasks is $\{T_1, \ldots, T_k\}$. For uniformity, we always take task T_1 to be the root of $\mathcal{H}$. We denote by $\preceq_{\mathcal{H}}$ (or simply $\preceq$ when $\mathcal{H}$ is understood) the partial order on $\{T_1, \ldots, T_k\}$ induced by $\mathcal{H}$ (with T_1 the minimum). For a node T of $\mathcal{H}$, we denote by *tree(T)* the subtree of $\mathcal{H}$ rooted at T, *child(T)* the set of children of T (also called *subtasks* of T), *desc(T)* the set of descendants of T (excluding T). Finally, $desc^*(T)$ denotes $desc(T) \cup \{T\}$. We denote by $\mathcal{S}_{\mathcal{H}}$ (or simply $\mathcal{S}$ when $\mathcal{H}$ is understood) the relational schema $\{S^{T_i} \mid 1 \le i \le k\}$. An instance of $\mathcal{S}$ is a mapping associating to each $S^{T_i} \in \mathcal{S}$ a finite relation over DOM_{id} of the same arity.

Definition 4. *An **instance** of an artifact schema $\mathcal{A} = \langle \mathcal{H}, \mathcal{DB} \rangle$ is a tuple $\bar{I} = \langle \bar{\nu}, stg, D, \bar{S} \rangle$ where D is a finite instance of $\mathcal{DB}$, $\bar{S}$ a finite instance of $\mathcal{S}$, $\bar{\nu}$ a valuation of $\bigcup_{i=1}^{k} \bar{x}^{T_i}$, and stg (standing for "stage") a mapping of $\{T_1, \ldots, T_k\}$ to $\{\texttt{init}, \texttt{active}, \texttt{closed}\}$.*

The stage $stg(T_i)$ of a task T_i has the following intuitive meaning in the context of a run of its parent: init indicates that T_i has not yet been called within the run, active says that T_i has been called and has not returned its answer, and closed indicates that T_i has returned its answer. As we will see, a task T_i can only be called once within a given run of its parent. However, it can be called again in subsequent runs.

We denote by $\mathcal{C}$ an infinite set of relation symbols, each of which has a fixed interpretation as the set of real solutions of a finite set of polynomial inequalities with integer coefficients. By slight abuse, we sometimes use the same notation for a relation symbol in $\mathcal{C}$ and its fixed interpretation. For a given artifact schema $\mathcal{A} = \langle \mathcal{H}, \mathcal{DB} \rangle$ and a sequence $\bar{x}$ of variables, a *condition* on $\bar{x}$ is a quantifier-free FO formula over $\mathcal{DB} \cup \mathcal{C} \cup \{=\}$ whose variables are included in $\bar{x}$. The special constant null can be used in equalities with ID variables. For each atom $R(x, y_1, \ldots, y_m, z_1, \ldots, z_n)$ of relation $R(ID, A_1, \ldots, A_m, F_1, \ldots, F_n) \in \mathcal{DB}$, $\{x, z_1, \ldots, z_n\} \subseteq VAR_{id}$ and $\{y_1, \ldots, y_m\} \subseteq VAR_{\mathbb{R}}$. Atoms over $\mathcal{C}$ use only numeric variables. If α is a condition on $\bar{x}$, D is an instance of $\mathcal{DB}$ and ν a valuation of $\bar{x}$, we denote by $D \cup \mathcal{C} \models \alpha(\nu)$ the fact that $D \cup \mathcal{C}$ satisfies α with valuation ν with standard semantics. For an atom $R(\bar{y})$ in α where $R \in \mathcal{DB}$ and $\bar{y} \subseteq \bar{x}$, if $\nu(y) = \texttt{null}$ for any $y \in \bar{y}$, then $R(\bar{y})$ is false.

We next define services of tasks. We start with internal services, which update the artifact variables and artifact relation of the task.

Definition 5. *Let $T = \langle \bar{x}^T, S^T, \bar{s}^T \rangle$ be a task of an artifact schema $\mathcal{A}$. An **internal service** σ of T is a tuple $\langle \pi, \psi, \delta \rangle$ where:*

- *π and ψ, called* pre-condition *and* post-condition, *respectively, are conditions over $\bar{x}^T$*
- *$\delta \subseteq \{+S^T(\bar{s}^T), -S^T(\bar{s}^T)\}$ is a set of* set updates; *$+S^T(\bar{s}^T)$ and $-S^T(\bar{s}^T)$ are called the **insertion** and **retrieval** of $\bar{s}^T$, respectively.*

Intuitively, $+S^T(\bar{s}^T)$ causes an insertion of the *current* value of $\bar{s}^T$ into S^T, while $-S^T(\bar{s}^T)$ causes the removal of some non-deterministically chosen current tuple of S^T and its assignment as the *next* value of $\bar{s}^T$. In particular, if $\delta = \{+S^T(\bar{s}^T), -S^T(\bar{s}^T)\}$, the tuple inserted by $+S^T(\bar{s}^T)$ and the one retrieved by $-S^T(\bar{s}^T)$ are generally distinct, but may be the same as a degenerate case (see definition of the semantics below).

As will become apparent, although pre-and-post conditions are quantifier-free, $\exists$FO conditions can be simulated by adding variables to $\bar{x}^T$.

An internal service of a task T specifies transitions that only modify the variables $\bar{x}^T$ of T and the contents of S^T. Interactions among tasks are specified using two kinds of special services, called the *opening-services* and *closing-services*.

Definition 6. *Let T_c be a child of a task T in $\mathcal{A}$.*
*(i) The **opening-service** $\sigma^o_{T_c}$ of T_c is a tuple $\langle \pi, f_{in} \rangle$, where π is a condition over $\bar{x}^T$, and f_{in} is a partial 1-1 mapping from $\bar{x}^{T_c}$ to $\bar{x}^T$ (called the input variable mapping). We denote dom(f_{in}) by $\bar{x}^{T_c}_{in}$, called the **input variables** of T_c, and range(f_{in}) by $\bar{x}^T_{T_c\downarrow}$ (the variables of T passed as input to T_c).*
*(ii) The **closing-service** $\sigma^c_{T_c}$ of T_c is a tuple $\langle \pi, f_{out} \rangle$, where π is a condition over $\bar{x}^{T_c}$, and f_{out} is a partial 1-1 mapping from $\bar{x}^T$ to $\bar{x}^{T_c}$ (called the output variable mapping). We denote dom(f_{out}) by $\bar{x}^T_{T_c\uparrow}$, referred to as the **returned variables** from T_c. It is required that $\bar{x}^T_{T_c\uparrow} \cap \bar{x}^T_{in} = \emptyset$. We denote by $\bar{x}^{T_c}_{ret}$ the **to-be-returned variables** (or return variables), defined as range(f_{out}).*

Intuitively, the opening-service $\langle \pi, f_{in} \rangle$ of a task T_c specifies the condition π that the parent task T has to satisfy in order to open T_c. When T_c is opened, a subset of the variables of T are sent to T_c according to the mapping f_{in}. Similarly, the closing-service $\langle \pi, f_{out}\rangle$ specifies the condition π that T_c has to satisfy in order to be closed and return to T. When T_c is closed, a subset of $\bar{x}^{T_c}$ is sent back to T, as specified by f_{out}.

For uniformity of notation, we also equip the root task T_1 with a service $\sigma^o_{T_1}$ with pre-condition *true* that initiates the computation by providing a valuation to a designated subset $\bar{x}^{T_1}_{in}$ of $\bar{x}^{T_1}$ (the input variables of T_1), and a service $\sigma^c_{T_1}$ whose pre-condition is *false* (so it never occurs in a run). For a task T we denote by Σ_T the set of its internal services, $\Sigma^{oc}_T = \Sigma_T \cup \{\sigma^o_T, \sigma^c_T\}$, $\Sigma^{obs}_T = \Sigma^{oc}_T \cup \{\sigma^o_{T_c}, \sigma^c_{T_c} \mid T_c \in child(T)\}$, and $\Sigma^{\delta}_T = \Sigma_T \cup \{\sigma^o_T\} \cup \{\sigma^c_{T_c} \mid T_c \in child(T)\}$. Intuitively, Σ^{obs}_T consists of the services observable in runs of task T and Σ^{δ}_T consists of services whose application can modify the variables $\bar{x}^T$.

DEFINITION 7. *A* Hierarchical Artifact System *(HAS) is a triple $\Gamma = \langle \mathcal{A}, \Sigma, \Pi\rangle$, where $\mathcal{A}$ is an artifact schema, Σ is a set of services over $\mathcal{A}$ including σ^o_T and σ^c_T for each task T of $\mathcal{A}$, and Π is a condition over $\bar{x}^{T_1}_{in}$ (where T_1 is the root task).*

We next define the semantics of HAS's. Intuitively, a run of a HAS on a database D consists of an infinite sequence of transitions among HAS instances (also referred to as configurations, or snapshots), starting from an initial artifact tuple satisfying pre-condition Π. At each snapshot, each active task T can open a subtask T_c if the pre-condition of the opening service of T_c holds, and the values of a subset of $\bar{x}^T$ is passed to T_c as its input variables. T_c can be closed if the pre-condition of its closing service is satisfied. When T_c is closed, the values of a subset of $\bar{x}^{T_c}$ are sent to T as T's returned variables from T_c. An internal service of T can only be applied after all active subtasks of T have returned their answer.

Because of the hierarchical structure, and the locality of task specifications, the actions of concurrently active children of a given task are independent of each other and can be arbitrarily interleaved. To capture just the essential information, factoring out the arbitrary interleavings, we first define the notion of *local run* and *tree of local runs*. Intuitively, a local run of a task consists of a sequence of services of the task, together with the transitions they cause on the task's local artifact variables and relation. The tasks's input and output are also specified. A tree of local runs captures the relationship between the local runs of tasks and those of their subtasks, including the passing of inputs and results. Then the runs of the full artifact system simply consist of all legal interleavings of transitions represented in the tree of local runs, lifted to full HAS instances (we refer to these as *global runs*). We begin by defining instances of tasks and local transitions. For a mapping M, we denote by $M[a \mapsto b]$ the mapping that sends a to b and agrees with M everywhere else.

DEFINITION 8. *Let $T = \langle \bar{x}^T, S^T, \bar{s}^T\rangle$ be a task in Γ and D a database instance over $\mathcal{DB}$. An* instance *of T is a pair (ν, S) where ν is a valuation of $\bar{x}^T$ and S an instance of S^T. For instances $I = (\nu, S)$ and $I' = (\nu', S')$ of T and a service $\sigma \in \Sigma^{obs}_T$, there is a local transition $I \xrightarrow{\sigma} I'$ if the following holds. If σ is an internal service (π, ψ), then:*

- *$D \cup \mathcal{C} \models \pi(\nu)$ and $D \cup \mathcal{C} \models \psi(\nu')$*
- *$\nu'(y) = \nu(y)$ for each y in $\bar{x}^T_{in}$*
- *if $\delta = \{+S^T(\bar{s}^T)\}$, then $S' = S \cup \{\nu(\bar{s}^T)\}$,*
- *if $\delta = \{-S^T(\bar{s}^T)\}$, then $\nu'(\bar{s}^T) \in S$ and $S' = S - \{\nu'(\bar{s}^T)\}$,*
- *if $\delta = \{+S^T(\bar{s}^T), -S^T(\bar{s}^T)\}$, then $\nu'(\bar{s}^T) \in S \cup \{\nu(\bar{s}^T)\}$ and $S' = (S \cup \{\nu(\bar{s}^T)\}) - \{\nu'(\bar{s}^T)\}$,*
- *if $\delta = \emptyset$ then $S' = S$.*

If $\sigma = \sigma^o_{T_c} = \langle \pi, f_{in}\rangle$ is the opening-service for a child T_c of T then $D \cup \mathcal{C} \models \pi(\nu)$, $\nu' = \nu$ and $S' = S$. If $\sigma = \sigma^c_{T_c}$ then $S = S'$, $\nu'|(\bar{x}^T - \bar{x}^T_{T_c\uparrow}) = \nu|(\bar{x}^T - \bar{x}^T_{T_c\uparrow})$ and $\nu'(z) = \nu(z)$ for every $z \in \bar{x}^T_{T_c\uparrow} \cap \mathrm{VAR}_{id}$ for which $\nu(z) \neq$ `null`. Finally, if $\sigma = \sigma^c_T$ then $I' = I$.

We now define local runs.

DEFINITION 9. *Let $T = \langle \bar{x}^T, S^T, \bar{s}^T\rangle$ be a non-root task in Γ and D a database instance over $\mathcal{DB}$. A* local run *of T over D is a triple $\rho_T = (\nu_{in}, \nu_{out}, \{(I_i, \sigma_i)\}_{0 \leq i < \gamma})$, where:*

- *$\gamma \in \mathbb{N} \cup \{\omega\}$*
- *for each $i \geq 0$, I_i is an instance of T and $\sigma_i \in \Sigma^{obs}_T$*
- *ν_{in} is a valuation of $\bar{x}^T_{in}$*
- *$\sigma_0 = \sigma^o_T$ and $S_0 = \emptyset$,*
- *$\nu_0|\bar{x}^T_{in} = \nu_{in}$, $\nu_0(z) =$ `null` for $z \in \mathrm{VAR}_{id} - \bar{x}^T_{in}$ and $\nu_0(z) = 0$ for $z \in \mathrm{VAR}_{\mathbb{R}} - \bar{x}^T_{in}$*
- *if for some i, $\sigma_i = \sigma^c_T$ then $\gamma \in \mathbb{N}$ and $i = \gamma - 1$ (and ρ_T is called a* returning *local run)*
- *$\nu_{out} = \nu_{\gamma-1}|\bar{x}^T_{ret}$ if ρ_T is a returning run and $\perp$ otherwise*
- *a* segment *of ρ_T is a subsequence $\{(I_i, \sigma_i)\}_{i \in J}$, where J is a maximal interval $[a, b] \subseteq \{i \mid 0 \leq i < \gamma\}$ such that no σ_j is an internal service of T for $j \in [a+1, b]$. A segment J is* terminal *if $\gamma \in \mathbb{N}$ and $b = \gamma - 1$ (and is called returning if $\sigma_{\gamma-1} = \sigma^c_T$ and blocking otherwise). Segments of ρ_T must satisfy the following properties. For each child T_c of T there is at most one $i \in J$ such that $\sigma_i = \sigma^o_{T_c}$. If J is not blocking and such i exists, there is exactly one $j \in J$ for which $\sigma_j = \sigma^c_{T_c}$, and $j > i$. If J is blocking, there is* at most *one such j.*
- *for every $0 < i < \gamma$, $I_{i-1} \xrightarrow{\sigma_i} I_i$.*

Local runs of the root task T_1 are defined as above, except that ν_{in} is a valuation of $\bar{x}^{T_1}_{in}$ such that $D \cup \mathcal{C} \models \Pi$, and $\nu_{out} = \perp$ (the root task never returns).

For a local run as above, we denote $\gamma(\rho_T) = \gamma$. Note that by definition of segment, a task can call each of its children tasks at most once between two consecutive services in Σ^{oc}_T and all of the called children tasks must complete within the segment, unless it is blocking. These restrictions are essential for decidability and are discussed in Section 6.

Observe that local runs take arbitrary inputs and allow for arbitrary return values from its children tasks. The valid interactions between the local runs of a tasks and those of its children is captured by the notion of *tree of local runs*.

DEFINITION 10. *A* tree of local runs *is a directed labeled tree **Tree** in which each node is a local run ρ_T for some task T, and every edge connects a local run of a task T with a local run of a child task T_c and is labeled with a non-negative integer i (denoted $i(\rho_{T_c})$). In addition, the following properties are satisfied. Let $\rho_T = (\nu^T_{in}, \nu^T_{out}, \{(I_i, \sigma_i)\}_{0 \leq i < \gamma})$ be a node of **Tree**, where $I_i = (\nu_i, S_i)$, $i \geq 0$. Let i be such that $\sigma_i = \sigma^o_{T_c}$ for some child T_c of T. There exists a unique edge labeled i from ρ_T to a node $\rho_{T_c} = (\nu_{in}, \nu_{out}, \{(I'_i, \sigma'_i)\}_{0 \leq i < \gamma'})$ of **Tree**, and the following hold:*

- *$\nu_{in} = f_{in} \circ \nu_i$ where[1] f_{in} is the input variable mapping of $\sigma^o_{T_c}$*

[1]Composition is left-to-right.

- ρ_{T_c} *is a returning run iff there exists* $j > i$ *such that* $\sigma_j = \sigma^c_{T_c}$; *let* k *be the minimum such* j. *Then* $\nu_k(z) = \nu_{out}(f_{out}(z))$ *for every* $z \in \bar{x}^T_{T_c\uparrow}$ *for which* $\nu_{k-1}(z) = \texttt{null}$, *where* f_{out} *is the output mapping of* $\sigma^c_{T_c}$.

Finally, for every node ρ_T *of* ***Tree***, *if* ρ_T *is blocking then there exists a child of* ρ_T *that is not returning (so infinite or blocking).*

Note that a tree of local runs may generally be rooted at a local run of any task of Γ. We say that ***Tree*** is *full* if it is rooted at a local run of T_1.

We next turn to global runs. A global run of Γ on database instance D over $\mathcal{DB}$ is an infinite sequence $\rho = \{(I_i, \sigma_i)\}_{i\geq 0}$, where each I_i is an instance (ν_i, stg_i, D, S_i) of $\mathcal{A}$ and $\sigma_i \in \Sigma$, resulting from a tree of local runs by interleaving its transitions, lifted to full HAS instances (see Appendix B.1 of [25] for the formal definition). For a tree of local runs ***Tree***, we denote by $\mathcal{L}$(***Tree***) the set of all global runs induced by the legal interleavings of ***Tree***.

3. HIERARCHICAL LTL-FO

In order to specify temporal properties of HAS's we use an extension of LTL (linear-time temporal logic). Recall that LTL is propositional logic augmented with temporal operators **X** (next), **U** (until), **G** (always) and **F** (eventually) (e.g., see [29]). An extension of LTL in which propositions are interpreted as FO sentences has previously been defined to specify properties of sequences of structures [47], and in particular of runs of artifact systems [23, 18]. The extension is denoted by LTL-FO. In order to specify properties of HAS's, we shall use a variant of LTL-FO, called *hierarchical* LTL-FO, denoted HLTL-FO. Intuitively, an HLTL-FO formula uses as building blocks LTL-FO formulas acting on local runs of individual tasks, referring only to the database and local data, and can recursively state HLTL-FO properties on runs resulting from calls to children tasks. This closely mirrors the hierarchical execution of tasks, and is a natural fit for this computation model. In addition to its naturaleness, the choice of HLTL-FO has several technical justifications. First, verification of LTL-FO (and even LTL) properties is not possible for HAS's.

THEOREM 11. *It is undecidable, given an LTL-FO formula* φ *and a HAS* $\Gamma = \langle \mathcal{A}, \Sigma, \Pi \rangle$, *whether* $\Gamma \models \varphi$. *Moreover, this holds even for LTL formulas over* Σ *(restricting the sequence of services in a global run).*

The proof, provided in Appendix B.3 of [25], is by reduction from repeated state reachability in VASS with resets and bounded lossiness, whose undecidability follows from [38].

Another technical argument in favor of HLTL-FO is that it only expresses properties that are invariant under interleavings of independent tasks. Interleaving invariance is not only a natural soundness condition, but also allows more efficient model checking by *partial-order reduction* [41]. Moreover, HLTL-FO enjoys a pleasing completeness property: it expresses, in a reasonable sense, *all* interleaving-invariant LTL-FO properties of HAS's. The proof is non-trivial, building on completeness results for propositional temporal logics on Mazurkiewicz traces [27, 28] (more details are provided in Appendix B.4 of [25]).

We next define HLTL-FO. Propositions in HLTL-FO are interpreted as conditions[2] on artifact instances in the run, or recursively as HLTL-FO formulas on runs of invoked children tasks. The different conditions may share some universally quantified global variables.

DEFINITION 12. *Let* $\Gamma = \langle \mathcal{A}, \Sigma, \Pi \rangle$ *be an artifact system where* $\mathcal{A} = \langle \mathcal{H}, \mathcal{DB} \rangle$. *Let* $\bar{y}$ *be a finite sequence of variables in* $\text{VAR}_{id} \cup \text{VAR}_{\mathbb{R}}$ *disjoint from* $\{\bar{x}^T \mid T \in \mathcal{H}\}$, *called* global variables. *We first define recursively the set* $\Psi(T, \bar{y})$ *of* basic HLTL-FO formulas *with global variables* $\bar{y}$, *for each task* $T \in \mathcal{H}$. *The set* $\Psi(T, \bar{y})$ *consists of all formulas* φ_f *obtained as follows:*

- φ *is an LTL formula with propositions* $P \cup \Sigma^{obs}_T$ *where* P *is a finite set of proposition disjoint from* Σ;
- *Let* Φ *be the set of conditions on* $\bar{x}_T \cup \bar{y}$ *extended by allowing atoms of the form* $S^T(\bar{z})$ *in which all variables in* $\bar{z}$ *are in* $\bar{y} \cap \text{VAR}_{id}$; f *is a function from* P *to*[3] $\Phi \cup \{[\psi]_{T_c} \mid \psi \in \Psi(T_c, \bar{y}), T_c \in child(T)\}$;
- φ_f *is obtained by replacing each* $p \in P$ *with* $f(p)$;

An HLTL-FO formula over $\mathcal{A}$ *is an expression* $\forall \bar{y}[\varphi_f]_{T_1}$ *where* φ_f *is in* $\Psi(T_1, \bar{y})$.

In an HLTL-FO formula of task T, each proposition is mapped to either a quantifier-free FO formula referring to the variables and set of task T, or an HLTL-FO formula of a child task of T. The intuition is the following. A proposition mapped to a quantifier-free FO formula holds in a given configuration of T if the formula is true in that configuration. A proposition mapped to an expression $[\psi]_{T_c}$ holds in a given configuration if T makes a call to T_c and the run of T_c resulting from the call satisfies ψ.

EXAMPLE 13. *Let* T_1 *be a root task with child tasks* T_2 *and* T_3. *The HLTL-FO formula (with no global variables)*

$$\varphi = [\ \mathbf{F}[\psi_2]_{T_2} \rightarrow \mathbf{G}(\sigma^o_{T_3} \rightarrow [\psi_3]_{T_3})]_{T_1}$$

states that whenever T_1 *calls child task* T_2 *and* T_2*'s local run satisfies property* ψ_2, *then if* T_3 *is also called (via the opening service* $\sigma^o_{T_3}$*), its local run must satisfy property* ψ_3.

See Appendix A.2 for a concrete HLTL-FO property of similar structure, in the context of our example for the HAS model.

Since HLTL-FO properties depend on local runs of tasks and their relationship to local runs of their descendants, their semantics is naturally defined using the full trees of local runs. We first define satisfaction by a local run of HLTL-FO formulas with no global variables. This is done recursively. Let ***Tree*** be a full tree of local runs of Γ over some database D. Let φ_f be a formula in $\Psi(T, \langle\rangle)$ (no global variables). Recall that φ is a propositional LTL formula over $P \cup \Sigma^{obs}_T$. Let $\rho_T = (\nu_{in}, \nu_{out}, \{(I_i, \sigma_i)\}_{i<\gamma})$ be a local run of T in ***Tree***. A proposition $\sigma \in \Sigma^{obs}_T$ holds in (I_j, σ_j) if $\sigma = \sigma_j$. Consider $p \in P$ and $f(p)$. If $f(p)$ is an FO formula, the standard definition applies. If $f(p) = [\psi]_{T_c}$, then (I_j, σ_j) satisfies $[\psi]_{T_c}$ iff $\sigma_j = \sigma^0_{T_c}$ and the local run of T_c connected to ρ_T in ***Tree*** by an edge labeled j satisfies ψ. The formula φ_f is satisfied if the sequence of truth values of its propositions via f satisfies φ. Note that ρ_T may be finite, in which case a finite variant of the LTL semantics is used [21].

[2]For consistency with previous notation, we denote the logic HLTL-FO although the FO interpretations are restricted to be quantifier free.

[3]$[\psi]_{T_c}$ is an expression whose meaning is explained below.

A full tree of local runs satisfies $\varphi_f \in \Psi(T_1, \langle\rangle)$ if its root (a local run of T_1) satisfies φ_f. Finally, let $\varphi_f(\bar{y})$ be a formula in $\Psi(T_1, \bar{y})$. Then $\forall\bar{y}[\varphi_f(\bar{y})]_{T_1}$ is satisfied by ***Tree***, denoted ***Tree*** $\models \forall\bar{y}[\varphi_f(\bar{y})]_{T_1}$, if for every valuation ν of $\bar{y}$, ***Tree*** satisfies φ_{f^ν} where f^ν is obtained from f by replacing each y in $f(p)$ by $\nu(y)$ for every $p \in P$. Note that $\varphi_{f^\nu} \in \Psi(T_1, \langle\rangle)$. Finally, Γ satisfies $\forall\bar{y}[\varphi_f(\bar{y})]_{T_1}$, denoted $\Gamma \models \forall\bar{y}[\varphi_f(\bar{y})]_{T_1}$, if ***Tree*** $\models \forall\bar{y}[\varphi_f(\bar{y})]_{T_1}$ for every database instance D and tree of local runs ***Tree*** of Γ on D.

The semantics of HLTL-FO on trees of local runs of a HAS also induces a semantics on the global runs of the HAS. Let $\forall\bar{y}[\varphi_f(\bar{y})]_{T_1}$ be an HLTL-FO formula and $\rho \in \mathcal{L}(\textbf{\textit{Tree}})$, where ***Tree*** is a full tree of local runs of Γ. We say that ρ satisfies $\forall\bar{y}[\varphi_f(\bar{y})]_{T_1}$ if ***Tree*** satisfies $\forall\bar{y}[\varphi_f(\bar{y})]_{T_1}$. This is well defined in view of the following easily shown fact: if $\rho \in \mathcal{L}(\textbf{\textit{Tree}}_1) \cap \mathcal{L}(\textbf{\textit{Tree}}_2)$ then $\textbf{\textit{Tree}}_1 = \textbf{\textit{Tree}}_2$.

Simplifications Before proceeding, we note that several simplifications to HLTL-FO formulas and HAS specifications can be made without impact on verification. First, although useful at the surface syntax, the global variables, as well as set atoms, can be easily eliminated from the HLTL-FO formula to be verified.It is also useful to note that one can assume, without loss of generality, two simplifications on artifact systems regarding the interaction of tasks with their subtasks: (i) for every task T, the set of variables passed to subtasks is disjoint with the set of variables returned by subtasks, and (ii) all variables returned by subtasks are non-numeric. More details and proofs of the above simplifications can be found in Appendix B.5 of [25]. In view of the above, we henceforth consider only properties with no global variables or set atoms, and artifact systems simplified as described.

Checking HLTL-FO Properties Using Automata
We next show how to check HLTL-FO properties of trees of local runs of artifact systems. Before we do so, recall the standard construction of a Büchi automaton B_φ corresponding to an LTL formula φ [49, 45]. The automaton B_φ has exponentially many states and accepts precisely the set of ω-words that satisfy φ. Recall that we are interested in evaluating LTL formulas φ on both infinite *and* finite runs. It is easily seen that for the B_φ obtained by the standard construction there is a subset Q^{fin} of its states such that B_φ viewed as a finite-state automaton with final states Q^{fin} accepts precisely the finite words that satisfy φ (details omitted).

Consider now an artifact system Γ and let $\varphi = [\xi]_{T_1}$ be an HLTL-FO formula over Γ. Consider a full tree ***Tree*** of local runs. For task T, denote by Φ_T the set of sub-formulas $[\psi]_T$ occurring in φ and by 2^{Φ_T} the set of truth assignments to these formulas. For each T and $\eta \in 2^{\Phi_T}$, let $B(T, \eta)$ be the Büchi automaton constructed from the formula

$$(\wedge_{\psi \in \Phi_T, \eta(\psi)=1}\ \psi) \wedge (\wedge_{\psi \in \Phi_T, \eta(\psi)=0}\ \neg\psi)$$

and define $\mathcal{B}_\varphi = \{B(T, \eta) \mid T \in \mathcal{H}, \eta \in 2^{\Phi_T}\}$.

We now define acceptance of ***Tree*** by $\mathcal{B}_\varphi$. An *adornment* of ***Tree*** is a mapping α associating to each edge from ρ_T to ρ_{T_c} a truth assignment in $2^{\Phi_{T_c}}$. ***Tree*** is accepted by $\mathcal{B}_\varphi$ if there exists an adornment α such that:

- for each local run ρ_T of T with no outgoing edge and incoming edge with adornment η, ρ_T is accepted by $B(T, \eta)$
- for each local run ρ_T of T with incoming edge labeled by η, $\alpha(\rho_T)$ is accepted by $B(T, \eta)$, where $\alpha(\rho_T)$ extends ρ_T by assigning to each configuration $(\rho_j, \sigma^o_{T_c})$ the truth assignment in $2^{\Phi_{T_c}}$ adorning its outgoing edge labeled j. (Recall that in configurations (I_j, σ_j) for which $\sigma_j \neq \sigma^o_{T_c}$, all formulas in Φ_{T_c} are *false* by definition.)
- $\alpha(\rho_{T_1})$ is accepted by the Büchi automaton B_ξ where $\alpha(\rho_{T_1})$ is defined as above.

The following can be shown.

LEMMA 14. *A full tree of local runs* ***Tree*** *satisfies* $\varphi = [\xi]_{T_1}$ *iff* ***Tree*** *is accepted by* $\mathcal{B}_\varphi$.

4. VERIFICATION WITHOUT ARITHMETIC

In this section we consider verification for the case when the artifact system and the HLTL-FO property have no arithmetic constraints. We show in Section 5 how our approach can be extended when arithmetic is present.

The roadmap to verification is the following. Let Γ be a HAS and $\varphi = [\xi]_{T_1}$ an HLTL-FO formula over Γ. To verify that every tree of local runs of Γ satisfies φ, we check that there is no tree of local runs satisfying $\neg\varphi = [\neg\xi]_{T_1}$, or equivalently, accepted by $\mathcal{B}_{\neg\varphi}$. Since there are infinitely many trees of local runs of Γ due so the unbounded data domain, and each tree can be infinite, an exhaustive search is impossible. We address this problem by developing a symbolic representation of trees of local runs, called *symbolic tree of runs*. The symbolic representation is subtle for several reasons. First, unlike the representations in [23, 18], it is not finite state. This is because summarizing the relevant information about artifact relations requires keeping track of the number of tuples of various isomorphism types. Second, the symbolic representation does not capture the full information about the actual runs, but just enough for verification. Specifically, we show that for every HLTL-FO formula φ, there exists a tree of local runs accepted by $\mathcal{B}_\varphi$ iff there exists a symbolic tree of runs accepted by $\mathcal{B}_\varphi$. We then develop an algorithm to check the latter. The algorithm relies on reductions to state reachability problems in Vector Addition Systems with States (VASS) [13].

One might wonder whether there is a simpler approach to verification of HAS, that reduces it to verification of a flat system (consisting of a single task). This could indeed be done in the absence of artifact relations, by essentially concatenating the artifact tuples of the tasks along the hierarchy that are active at any given time, and simulating all transitions by internal services. However, there is strong evidence that this is no longer possible when tasks are equipped with artifact relations. First, a naive simulation using a single artifact relation would require more powerful updating capabilities than available in the model. Moreover, Theorem 11 shows that LTL is undecidable for hierarchical systems, whereas the results in this section imply that it is decidable for flat ones (as it coincides with HLTL for single tasks). While this does not rule out a simulation, it shows that there can be no effective simulation natural enough to be extensible to LTL properties. A reduction to the model of [18] is even less plausible, because of the lack of artifact relations. Note that, even if a reduction were possible, the results of [18] would be of no help in obtaining our lower complexities for verification, since the algorithm provided there is non-elementary in all cases.

We next embark upon the development outlined above.

4.1 Symbolic Representation

We begin by defining the symbolic analog of a local run, called *local symbolic run*. The symbolic tree of runs is obtained by connecting the local symbolic runs similarly to the way local runs are connected in trees of local runs.

Each local symbolic run is a sequence of symbolic representations of an actual instance within a local run of a task T. The representation has the following ingredients:

1. the equality type of the artifact variables of T and the elements in the database reachable from them by navigating foreign keys up to a specified depth $h(T)$. This is called the T-*isomorphism type* of the variables.
2. the T-isomorphism type of the input and return variables (if representing a returning local run)
3. for each T-isomorphism type of the set variables of T together with the input variables, the net number of insertions of tuples of that type in S^T.

Intuitively, (1) and (2) are needed in order to ensure that the assumptions made about the database while navigating via foreign keys in tasks and their subtasks are consistent. The depth $h(T)$ is chosen to be sufficiently large to ensure the consistency. (3) is required in order to make sure that a retrieval from S^T of a tuple with a given T-isomorphism type is allowed only when sufficiently many tuples of that type have been inserted in S^T.

We now formally define the symbolic representation, starting with T-isomorphism type. Let $\bar{x}^T$ be the variables of T. We define $h(T)$ as as follows. Let FK be the foreign key graph of the schema $\mathcal{DB}$ and $F(n)$ be the maximum number of distinct paths of length at most n starting from any relation R in FK. Let $h(T) = 1 + |\bar{x}^T| \cdot F(\delta)$ where $\delta = 1$ if T is a leaf task and $\delta = \max_{T_c \in child(T)} h(T_c)$ otherwise.

We next define expressions that denote navigation via foreign keys starting from the set of id variables $\bar{x}^T_{id}$ of T. For each $x \in \bar{x}^T_{id}$ and $R \in \mathcal{DB}$, let x_R be a new symbol. An expression is a sequence $\xi_1.\xi_2.\ldots.\xi_m$, $\xi_1 = x_R$ for some $x \in \bar{x}^T_{id}$ and $R \in \mathcal{DB}$, ξ_j is a foreign key in some relation of $\mathcal{DB}$ for $2 \leq j < m$, ξ_m is a foreign key or a numeric attribute, ξ_2 is an attribute of R, and for each i, $2 < i \leq m$, if ξ_{i-1} is a foreign key referencing Q then ξ_i is an attribute of Q. We define the length of $\xi_1.\xi_2.\ldots.\xi_m$ as m. A *navigation set* $\mathcal{E}_T$ is a set of expressions such that:

- for each $x \in \bar{x}^T_{id}$ there is at most one $R \in \mathcal{DB}$ for which the expression x_R is in $\mathcal{E}_T$;
- every expression in $\mathcal{E}_T$ is of the form $x_R.w$ where $x_R \in \mathcal{E}_T$, and has length $\leq h(T)$;
- if $e \in \mathcal{E}_T$ then every expression $e.s$ of length $\leq h(T)$ extending e is also in $\mathcal{E}_T$.

Note that $\mathcal{E}_T$ is closed under prefix. We can now define T-isomorphism type. Let $\mathcal{E}^+_T = \mathcal{E}_T \cup \bar{x}^T \cup \{\texttt{null}, 0\}$. The *sort* of $e \in \mathcal{E}^+_T$ is numeric if $e \in \bar{x}^T_{\mathbb{R}} \cup \{0\}$ or $e = w.a$ where a is a numeric attribute; its sort is null if $e = \texttt{null}$ or $e = x \in \bar{x}^T_{id}$ and $x_R \notin \mathcal{E}_T$ for all $R \in \mathcal{DB}$; and its sort is ID(R) for $R \in \mathcal{DB}$ if $e = x_R$, or $e = x \in \bar{x}^T_{id}$ and $x_R \in \mathcal{E}_T$, or $e = w.f$ where f is a foreign key referencing R.

Definition 15. *A T-isomorphism type τ consists of a navigation set $\mathcal{E}_T$ together with an equivalence relation $\sim_\tau$ over $\mathcal{E}^+_T$ such that:*

- *if $e \sim_\tau f$ then e and f are of the same sort;*
- *for every $\{x, x_R\} \subseteq \mathcal{E}^+_T$, $x \sim_\tau x_R$;*
- *for every e of sort* null, *$e \sim_\tau \texttt{null}$;*
- *if $u \sim_\tau v$ and $u.f, v.f \in \mathcal{E}_T$ then $u.f \sim_\tau v.f$.*

We call an equivalence relation $\sim_\tau$ as above an *equality type* for τ. The relation $\sim_\tau$ is extended to tuples componentwise.

Note that τ provides enough information to evaluate conditions over $\bar{x}^T$. Satisfaction of a condition φ by an isomorphism type τ, denoted $\tau \models \varphi$, is defined as follows:

- $x = y$ holds in τ iff $x \sim_\tau y$,
- $R(x, y_1, \ldots, y_m, z_1, \ldots, z_n)$ holds in τ for relation $R(id, a_1, \ldots, a_m, f_1, \ldots, f_n)$ iff $\{x_R.a_1, \ldots, x_R.a_m, x_R.f_1, \ldots, x_R.f_n\} \subseteq \mathcal{E}_T$, and $(y_1, \ldots, y_m, z_1, \ldots, z_m) \sim_\tau (x_R.a_1, \ldots, x_R.a_m, x_R.f_1, \ldots, x_R.f_n)$
- Boolean combinations of conditions are standard.

Let τ be a T-isomorphism type with navigation set $\mathcal{E}_T$ and equality type $\sim_\tau$. The projection of τ onto a subset of variables $\bar{z}$ of $\bar{x}^T$ is defined as follows. Let $\mathcal{E}_T|\bar{z} = \{x_R.e \in \mathcal{E}_T | x \in \bar{z}\}$ and $\sim_\tau |\bar{z}$ be the projection of $\sim_\tau$ onto $\bar{z} \cup \mathcal{E}_T|\bar{z} \cup \{\texttt{null}, 0\}$. The projection of τ onto $\bar{z}$, denoted as $\tau|\bar{z}$, is a T-isomorphism type with navigation set $\mathcal{E}_T|\bar{z}$ and equality type $\sim_\tau |\bar{z}$. Furthermore, the projection of T-isomorphism onto $\bar{z}$ upto length k, denoted as $\tau|(\bar{z}, k)$, is defined as $\tau|\bar{z}$ with all expressions in $\mathcal{E}_T|\bar{z}$ with length more than k removed.

We apply variable renaming to isomorphism types as follows. Let f be a 1-1 partial mapping from $\bar{x}^T$ to $VAR_{id} \cup VAR_{\mathbb{R}}$ such that $f(\bar{x}^T_{id}) \subseteq VAR_{id}$, $f(\bar{x}^T_{\mathbb{R}}) \subseteq VAR_{\mathbb{R}}$ and $f(\bar{x}^T) \cap \bar{x}^T = \emptyset$. For a T-isomorphism type τ with navigation set $\mathcal{E}_T$, $f(\tau)$ is the isomorphism type obtained as follows. Its navigation set is obtained by replacing in $\mathcal{E}_T$ each variable x and x_R in $\mathcal{E}_T$ with $f(x)$ and $f(x)_R$, for $x \in dom(f)$. The relation $\sim_{f(\tau)}$ is the image of $\sim_\tau$ under the same substitution.

As seen above, a T-isomorphism type captures all information needed to evaluate a condition on $\bar{x}_T$. However, the set S^T can contain unboundedly many tuples, which cannot be represented by a finite equality type. This is handled by keeping a set of counters for projections of T-isomorphism types on the variables relevant to S^T, that is, $(\bar{x}^T_{in} \cup \bar{s}^T)$. We refer to the projection of a T-isomorphism type onto $(\bar{x}^T_{in} \cup \bar{s}^T)$ as a TS-isomorphism type, and denote by *TS*(T) the set of TS-isomorphism types of T. We will use counters to record the number of tuples in S^T of each TS-isomorphism type.

We can now define symbolic instances.

Definition 16. *A symbolic instance I of task T is a tuple $(\tau, \bar{c})$ where τ is a T-isomorphism type and $\bar{c}$ is a vector of integers where each dimension of $\bar{c}$ corresponds to a TS-isomorphism type.*

We denote by $\bar{c}(\hat{\tau})$ the value of the dimension of $\bar{c}$ corresponding to the TS-isomorphism type $\hat{\tau}$ and by $\bar{c}[\hat{\tau} \mapsto a]$ the vector obtained from $\bar{c}$ by replacing $\bar{c}(\hat{\tau})$ with a.

Definition 17. *A local symbolic run $\tilde{\rho}_T$ of task T is a tuple $(\tau_{in}, \tau_{out}, \{(I_i, \sigma_i)\}_{0 \leq i < \gamma})$, where:*

- *each I_i is a symbolic instance $(\tau_i, \bar{c}_i)$ of T*
- *each σ_i is a service in Σ^{obs}_T*
- *$\gamma \in \mathbb{N} \cup \{\omega\}$ (if $\gamma = \omega$ then $\tilde{\rho}_T$ is infinite, otherwise it is finite)*
- *τ_{in}, called the input isomorphism type, is a T-isomorphism type projected to $\bar{x}^T_{in}$. And $\tau_{in} \models \Pi$ if $T = T_1$.*
- *at the first instance I_0, $\tau_0|\bar{x}^T_{in} = \tau_{in}$, for every $x \in \bar{x}^T_{id} - \bar{x}^T_{in}$, $x \sim_{\tau_0}$ null, and for every $x \in \bar{x}^T_{\mathbb{R}} - \bar{x}^T_{in}$, $x \sim_{\tau_0} 0$. Also $\bar{c}_0 = \bar{0}$ and $\sigma_0 = \sigma^o_T$.*

- *if for some* i, $\sigma_i = \sigma^c_T$ *then* $\tilde{\rho}_T$ *is finite and* $i = \gamma - 1$ *(and* $\tilde{\rho}_T$ *is called a* returning *run)*
- τ_{out} *is* $\perp$ *if* $\tilde{\rho}_T$ *is infinite or finite but* $\sigma_{\gamma-1} \neq \sigma^c_T$*, and it is* $\tau_{\gamma-1}|(\bar{x}^T_{in} \cup \bar{x}^T_{ret})$ *otherwise*
- *a* segment *of* $\tilde{\rho}_T$ *is a subsequence* $\{(I_i, \sigma_i)\}_{i \in J}$*, where* J *is a maximal interval* $[a, b] \subseteq \{i \mid 0 \leq i < \gamma\}$ *such that no* σ_j *is an internal service of* T *for* $j \in [a+1, b]$*. A segment* J *is* terminal *if* $\gamma \in \mathbb{N}$ *and* $b = \gamma - 1$*. Segments of* $\tilde{\rho}_T$ *must satisfy the following properties. For each child* T_c *of* T *there is at most one* $i \in J$ *such that* $\sigma_i = \sigma^o_{T_c}$*. If* J *is not terminal and such* i *exists, there is exactly one* $j \in J$ *for which* $\sigma_j = \sigma^c_{T_c}$*, and* $j > i$*. If* J *is terminal, there is* at most *one such* j*.*
- *for every* $0 < i < \gamma$*,* I_i *is a* **successor** *of* I_{i-1} *under* σ_i *(see below).*

The successor relation is defined next. We begin with some preliminary definitions. A TS-isomorphism type $\hat{\tau}$ is *input-bound* if for every $s \in \bar{s}^T$, $s \not\sim_{\hat{\tau}}$ `null` implies that there exists an expression $x_R.w$ in $\hat{\tau}$ such that $x \in \bar{x}^T_{in}$ and $x_R.w \sim_{\hat{\tau}} s$. We denote by $TS_{ib}(T)$ the set of input-bound types in $TS(T)$. For $\hat{\tau}, \hat{\tau}' \in TS(T)$, update δ of the form $\{+S^T(\bar{s}^T)\}$ or $\{-S^T(\bar{s}^T)\}$ and mapping $\bar{c}_{ib}$ from $TS_{ib}(T)$ to $\{0, 1\}$, we define the mapping $\bar{a}(\delta, \hat{\tau}, \hat{\tau}', \bar{c}_{ib})$ from $TS(T)$ to $\{-1, 0, 1\}$ as follows ($\bar{a}_0$ is the mapping sending $TS(T)$ to 0):

- if $\delta = \{+S^T(\bar{s}^T)\}$, then $\bar{a}(\delta, \hat{\tau}, \hat{\tau}', \bar{c}_{ib})$ is $\bar{a}_0[\hat{\tau} \mapsto 1]$ if $\hat{\tau}$ is not input-bound, and $\bar{a}_0[\hat{\tau} \mapsto (1 - \bar{c}_{ib}(\hat{\tau}))]$ otherwise
- if $\delta = \{-S^T(\bar{s}^T)\}$, then $\bar{a}(\delta, \hat{\tau}, \hat{\tau}', \bar{c}_{ib}) = \bar{a}_0[\hat{\tau}' \mapsto -1]$
- if δ is $\{+S^T(\bar{s}^T), -S^T(\bar{s}^T)\}$ then
$$\bar{a}(\delta, \hat{\tau}, \hat{\tau}', \bar{c}_{ib}) = \bar{a}(\delta^+, \hat{\tau}, \hat{\tau}', \bar{c}_{ib}) + \bar{a}(\delta^-, \hat{\tau}, \hat{\tau}', \bar{c}_{ib})$$
where $\delta^+ = \{+S^T(\bar{s}^T)\}$ and $\delta^- = \{-S^T(\bar{s}^T)\}$.

Intuitively, the vector $\bar{a}(\delta, \hat{\tau}, \hat{\tau}', \bar{c}_{ib})$ specifies how the current counters need to be modified to reflect the update δ. The input-bound TS-isomorphism types require special handling because consecutive insertions necessarily collide so the counter's value cannot go beyond 1.

For symbolic instances $I = (\tau, \bar{c})$ and $I' = (\tau', \bar{c}')$, I' is a successor of I by applying service σ' iff:

- If σ' is an internal service $\langle \pi, \psi, \delta \rangle$, then for $\hat{\tau} = \tau|(\bar{x}^T_{in} \cup \bar{s}^T)$ and $\hat{\tau}' = \tau'|(\bar{x}^T_{in} \cup \bar{s}^T)$,
  - $\tau|\bar{x}^T_{in} = \tau'|\bar{x}^T_{in}$,
  - $\tau \models \pi$ and $\tau' \models \psi$,
  - $\bar{c}' \geq \bar{0}$ and $\bar{c}' = \bar{c} + \bar{a}(\delta, \hat{\tau}, \hat{\tau}', \bar{c}_{ib})$, where $\bar{c}_{ib}$ the restriction of $\bar{c}$ to $TS_{ib}(T)$.
- If σ' is an opening service $\langle \pi, f_{in} \rangle$ of subtask T_c, then $\tau = \tau' \models \pi$ and $\bar{c}' = \bar{c}$.
- If σ' is a closing service of subtask T_c, then for $\bar{x}^T_{const} = \bar{x}^T - \{x \in \bar{x}^T_{T_c^\uparrow} | x \sim_\tau \texttt{null}\}$, $\tau'|\bar{x}^T_{const} = \tau|\bar{x}^T_{const}$ and $\bar{c}' = \bar{c}$.
- If σ' is the closing service $\sigma^c_T = \langle \pi, f_{out} \rangle$ of T, then $\tau \models \pi$ and $(\tau, \bar{c}) = (\tau', \bar{c}')$.

Note that there is a subtle mismatch between transitions in actual local runs and in symbolic runs. In the symbolic transitions defined above, a service inserting a tuple in S^T *always* causes the correspoding counter to increase (except for the input-bound case). However, in actual runs, an inserted tuple may collide with an already existing tuple in the set, in which case the number of tuples does *not* increase. Symbolic runs do not account for such collisions (beyond the input-bound case), which raises the danger that they might overestimate the number of available tuples and allow impossible retrievals. Fortunately, the proof of Theorem 20 shows that collisions can be ignored at no peril. More specifically, it follows from the proof that for every actual local run with collisions satisfying an HLTL-FO property there exists an actual local run without collisions that satisfies the same property. The intuition is the following. First, given an actual run with collisions, one can modify it so that only new tuples are inserted in the artifact relation, thus avoiding collisions. However, this raises a challenge, since it may require augmenting the database with new tuples. If done naively, this could result in an infinite database. The more subtle observation, detailed in the proof of Theorem 20, is that only a bounded number of new tuples must be created, thus keeping the database finite.

Definition 18. *A* symbolic tree of runs *is a directed labeled tree* **Sym** *in which each node is a local symbolic run* $\tilde{\rho}_T$ *for some task* T*, and every edge connects a local symbolic run of a task* T *with a local symbolic run of a child task* T_c *and is labeled with a non-negative integer* i *(denoted* $i(\tilde{\rho}_{T_c})$*). In addition, the following properties are satisfied. Let* $\tilde{\rho}_T = (\tau_{in}, \tau_{out}, \{(I_i, \sigma_i)\}_{0 \leq i < \gamma})$ *be a node of* **Sym***. Let* i *be such that* $\sigma_i = \sigma^o_{T_c}$ *for some child* T_c *of* T*. There exists a unique edge labeled* i *from* $\tilde{\rho}_T$ *to a node* $\tilde{\rho}_{T_c} = (\tau'_{in}, \tau'_{out}, \{(I'_i, \sigma'_i)\}_{0 \leq i < \gamma'})$ *of* **Sym***, and the following hold:*

- $\tau'_{in} = f^{-1}_{in}(\tau_i)|(\bar{x}^{T_c}_{in}, h(T_c))$ *where* f_{in} *is the input variable mapping of* $\sigma^o_{T_c}$
- $\tilde{\rho}_{T_c}$ *is a returning run iff there exists* $j > i$ *such that* $\sigma_j = \sigma^c_{T_c}$*; let* k *be the minimum such* j*. Let* $\bar{x}_r = \bar{x}^T_{T_c^\downarrow}$ *and* $\bar{x}_w = \{x | x \in \bar{x}^T_{T_c^\uparrow}, x \sim_{\tau_{k-1}} \texttt{null}\}$*. Then* $\tau_k|(\bar{x}_r \cup \bar{x}_w, h(T_c)) = ((f_{in} \circ f^{-1}_{out})(\tau_{out}))|(\bar{x}_r \cup \bar{x}_w)$ *where* f_{out} *is the output variable mapping of* $\sigma^c_{T_c}$*.*

For every local symbolic run $\tilde{\rho}_T$ *where* $\gamma \neq \omega$ *and* $\tau_{out} = \perp$*, there exists a child of* $\tilde{\rho}_T$ *which is not returning.*

Now consider an HLTL-FO formula $\varphi = [\xi]_{T_1}$ over Γ. Satisfaction of φ by a symbolic tree of runs is defined analogously to satisfaction by local runs, keeping in mind that as previously noted, isomorphism types of symbolic instances of T provide enough information to evaluate conditions over $\bar{x}^T$. The definition of acceptance by the automaton $\mathcal{B}_\varphi$, and Lemma 14, are also immediately extended to symbolic trees of runs. We state the following.

Lemma 19. *A symbolic tree of runs* **Sym** *over* Γ *satisfies* φ *iff* **Sym** *is accepted by* $\mathcal{B}_\varphi$*.*

The key result enabling the use of symbolic trees of runs is the following (The proof is provided in the extended appendix of [25]).

Theorem 20. *For an artifact system* Γ *and HLTL-FO property* φ*, there exists a tree of local runs* **Tree** *accepted by* $\mathcal{B}_\varphi$*, iff there exists a symbolic tree of runs* **Sym** *accepted by* $\mathcal{B}_\varphi$*.*

The *only-if* part is relatively straightforward, but the *if* part is non-trivial. The construction of an accepted tree of local runs from an accepted symbolic tree of runs **Sym** is done in two stages. First, an accepted tree of local runs over an *infinite* database is constructed, using a global equality type that extends the local equality types by taking into account connections across instances resulting from the propagation of input variables and insertions and retrievals of tuples from S^T, and subject to satisfaction of the key constraints. In the second stage, the infinite database is turned into a finite one by carefully merging data values, while avoiding any inconsistencies.

4.2 Symbolic Verification

In view of Theorem 20, we can now focus on the problem of checking the existence of a symbolic tree of runs satisfying a given HLTL-FO property. To begin, we define a notion that captures the functionality of each task and allows a modular approach to the verification algorithm. Let φ be an HLTL-FO formula over Γ, and recall the automaton $\mathcal{B}_\varphi$ and associated notation from Section 3. We consider the relation $\mathcal{R}_T$ between input and outputs of each task, defined by its symbolic runs that satisfy a given truth assignment β to the formulas in Φ_T. More specifically, we denote by $\mathcal{H}_T$ the restriction of $\mathcal{H}$ to T and its descendants, and Γ_T the corresponding HAS, with precondition *true*. The relation $\mathcal{R}_T$ consists of the set of triples $(\tau_{in}, \tau_{out}, \beta)$ for which there exists a symbolic tree of runs $\boldsymbol{Sym}_T$ of $\mathcal{H}_T$ such that:

- β is a truth assignment to Φ_T
- $\boldsymbol{Sym}_T$ is accepted by $\mathcal{B}_\beta$
- the root of $\boldsymbol{Sym}_T$ is $\tilde{\rho}_T = (\tau_{in}, \tau_{out}, \{(I_i, \sigma_i)\}_{0 \le i < \gamma})$

Note that there exists a symbolic tree of runs $\boldsymbol{Sym}$ over Γ satisfying $\varphi = [\xi]_{T_1}$ iff $(\tau_{in}, \bot, \beta) \in \mathcal{R}_{T_1}$ for some τ_{in} satisfying the precondition of Γ, and $\beta(\xi) = 1$. Thus, if $\mathcal{R}_T$ is computable for every T, then satisfiability of $[\xi]_{T_1}$ by some symbolic tree of runs over Γ is decidable, and yields an algorithm for model-checking HLTL-FO properties of HAS's.

We next describe an algorithm that computes the relations $\mathcal{R}_T(\tau_{in}, \tau_{out}, \beta)$ recursively. The algorithm uses as a key tool Vector Addition Systems with States (VASS) [13, 32], which we review next.

A VASS $\mathcal{V}$ is a pair (Q, A) where Q is a finite set of *states* and A is a finite set of *actions* of the form $(p, \bar{a}, q)$ where $\bar{a} \in \mathbb{Z}^d$ for some fixed $d > 0$, and $p, q \in Q$. A run of $\mathcal{V} = (Q, A)$ is a finite sequence $(q_0, \bar{z}_0) \ldots (q_n, \bar{z}_n)$ where $\bar{z}_0 = \bar{0}$ and for each $i \ge 0$, $q_i \in Q$, $\bar{z}_i \in \mathbb{N}^d$, and $(q_i, \bar{a}, q_{i+1}) \in A$ for some $\bar{a}$ such that $\bar{z}_{i+1} = \bar{z}_i + \bar{a}$. We will use the following decision problems related to VASS.

- *State Reachability*: For given states $q_0, q_f \in Q$, is there a run $(q_0, \bar{z}_0) \ldots (q_n, \bar{z}_n)$ of $\mathcal{V}$ such that $q_n = q_f$?
- *State Repeated Reachability*: For given states $q_0, q_f \in Q$, is there a run $(q_0, \bar{z}_0) \ldots (q_m, \bar{z}_m) \ldots (q_n, \bar{z}_n)$ of $\mathcal{V}$ such that $q_m = q_n = q_f$ and $\bar{z}_m \le \bar{z}_n$?

Both problems are known to be EXPSPACE-complete [36, 43, 32]. In particular, [32] shows that for a n-states, d-dimensional VASS where every dimension of each action has constant size, the state repeated reachability problem can be solved in $O((\log n) 2^{c \cdot d \log d})$ non-deterministic space for some constant c. The state reachability problem has the same complexity.

VASS Construction Let T be a task, and suppose that relations $\mathcal{R}_{T_c}$ have been computed for all children T_c of T. We show how to compute $\mathcal{R}_T$ using an associated VASS. For each truth assignment β of Φ_T, we construct a VASS $\mathcal{V}(T, \beta) = (Q, A)$ as follows. The states in Q are all tuples $(\tau, \sigma, q, \bar{o}, \bar{c}_{ib})$ where τ is a T-isomorphism type, σ a service, q a state of $B(T, \beta)$, and $\bar{c}_{ib}$ a mapping from $TS_{ib}(T)$ to $\{0, 1\}$. The vector $\bar{o}$ indicates the current stage of each child T_c of T (`init`, `active` or `closed`) and also specifies the outputs of T_c (an isomorphism type or $\bot$). That is, $\bar{o}$ is a partial mapping associating to some of the children T_c of T the value $\bot$, a T_c-isomorphism type projected to $\bar{x}_{in}^{T_c} \cup \bar{x}_{ret}^{T_c}$ or the value `closed`. Intuitively, $T_c \notin dom(\bar{o})$ means that T_c is in the `init` state, and $\bar{o}(T_c) = \bot$ indicates that T_c has been called but will not return. If $\bar{o}(T_c)$ is an isomorphism type τ, this indicates that T_c has been called, has not yet returned, and will return the isomorphism type τ. When T_c returns, $\bar{o}(T_c)$ is set to `closed`, and T_c cannot be called again before an internal service of T is applied.

The set of actions A consists of all triples $(\alpha, \bar{a}, \alpha')$ where $\alpha = (\tau, \sigma, q, \bar{o}, \bar{c}_{ib})$, $\alpha' = (\tau', \sigma', q', \bar{o}', \bar{c}'_{ib})$, δ' is the update of σ', and the following hold:

- τ' is a successor of τ by applying service σ';
- $\bar{a} = \bar{a}(\delta', \hat{\tau}, \hat{\tau}', \bar{c}_{ib})$ (defined in Section 4.1), where $\hat{\tau} = \tau|(\bar{x}_{in}^T \cup \bar{s}^T)$ and $\hat{\tau}' = \tau'|(\bar{x}_{in}^T \cup \bar{s}^T)$
- $\bar{c}'_{ib} = \bar{c}_{ib} + \bar{a}$
- if σ' is an internal service, $dom(\bar{o}') = \emptyset$.
- If $\sigma' = \sigma_{T_c}^o$, then $T_c \notin dom(\bar{o})$ and for $\tau_{in}^{T_c} = f_{in}^{-1}(\tau|(\bar{x}_{T_c^\downarrow}^T, h(T_c)))$, for some output $\tau_{out}^{T_c}$ of T_c and truth assignment β^{T_c} to Φ_{T_c}, tuple $(\tau_{in}^{T_c}, \tau_{out}^{T_c}, \beta^{T_c})$ is in $\mathcal{R}_{T_c}$. Note that $\tau_{out}^{T_c}$ can be $\bot$, which indicates that this call to T_c does not return. Also, $\bar{o}' = \bar{o}[T_c \mapsto \tau_{out}^{T_c}]$.
- If $\sigma' = \sigma_{T_c}^c$, then $\bar{o}(T_c) = (f_{out} \circ f_{in}^{-1})(\tau'|(\bar{x}_{T_c^\downarrow}^T \cup \bar{x}_{T_c^\uparrow}^T, h(T_c)))$ and $\bar{o}' = \bar{o}[T_c \mapsto \texttt{closed}]$.
- q' is a successor of q in $B(T, \beta)$ by evaluating Φ_T using (τ', σ'). If $\sigma' = \sigma_{T_c}^o$, formulas in Φ_{T_c} are assigned the truth values defined by β^{T_c}.

An *initial* state of $\mathcal{V}(T, \beta)$ is a state of the form $v_0 = (\tau_0, \sigma_0, q_0, \bar{o}_0, \bar{c}_{ib}^0)$ where τ_0 is an initial T-isomorphism type (i.e., for every $x \in \bar{x}_{id}^T - \bar{x}_{in}^T$, $x \sim_{\tau_0}$ `null`, and for every $x \in \bar{x}_{\mathbb{R}}^T - \bar{x}_{in}^T$, $x \sim_{\tau_0} 0$), $\sigma_0 = \sigma_T^o$, q_0 is the successor of some initial state of $B(T, \beta)$ under (τ_0, σ_0), $dom(\bar{o}_0) = \emptyset$, and $\bar{c}_{ib}^0 = \bar{0}$.

Computing $\mathcal{R}_T(\tau_{in}, \tau_{out}, \beta)$ from $\mathcal{V}(T, \beta)$
Checking whether $(\tau_{in}, \tau_{out}, \beta)$ is in $\mathcal{R}_T$ can be done using a (repeated) reachability test on $\mathcal{V}(T, \beta)$, as stated in the following key lemma (see the extended appendix in [25] for proof).

LEMMA 21. *$(\tau_{in}, \tau_{out}, \beta) \in \mathcal{R}_T$ iff there exists an initial state $v_0 = (\tau_0, \sigma_0, q_0, \bar{o}_0, \bar{c}_{ib}^0)$ of $\mathcal{V}(T, \beta)$ for which $\tau_0|\bar{x}_{in}^T = \tau_{in}$ and the following hold:*

- *If $\tau_{out} \neq \bot$, then there exists state $v_n = (\tau_n, \sigma_n, q_n, \bar{o}_n, \bar{c}_{ib}^n)$ where $\tau_{out} = \tau_n|(\bar{x}_{in}^T \cup \bar{x}_{ret}^T)$, $\sigma_n = \sigma_T^c$, $q_n \in Q^{fin}$ where Q^{fin} is the set of accepting states of $B(T, \beta)$ for finite runs, such that v_n is reachable from v_0. A path from $(v_0, \bar{0})$ to $(v_n, \bar{z}_n)$ is called a **returning path**.*
- *If $\tau_{out} = \bot$, then one of the following holds:*
  - *there exists a state $v_n = (\tau_n, \sigma_n, q_n, \bar{o}_n, \bar{c}_{ib}^n)$ in which $q_n \in Q^{inf}$ where Q^{inf} is the set of accepting states of $B(T, \beta)$ for infinite runs, such that v_n is repeatedly reachable from v_0. A path $(v_0, \bar{0}) \ldots (v_n, \bar{z}_n) \ldots (v_n, \bar{z}'_n)$ where $\bar{z}_n \le \bar{z}'_n$ is called a **lasso path**.*
  - *There exists state $v_n = (\tau_n, \sigma_n, q_n, \bar{o}_n, \bar{c}_{ib}^n)$ in which $\bar{o}_n(T_c) = \bot$ for some child T_c of T and $q_n \in Q^{fin}$, such that v_n is reachable from v_0. The path from $(v_0, \bar{0})$ to $(v_n, \bar{z}_n)$ is called a **blocking path**.*

Complexity of Verification We now have all ingredients in place for our verification algorithm. Let Γ be a HAS and $\varphi = [\xi]_{T_1}$ an HLTL-FO formula over Γ. In view of the previous development, $\Gamma \models \varphi$ iff $[\neg\xi]_{T_1}$ is **not** satisfiable by a symbolic tree of runs of Γ. We outline a non-deterministic algorithm for checking satisfiability of $[\neg\xi]_{T_1}$, and establish

	Acyclic	Linearly-Cyclic	Cyclic
w/o. Artifact relations	$c \cdot N^{O(1)}$	$O(N^{c \cdot h})$	h- $\exp(O(N))$
w. Artifact relations	$O(\exp(N^c))$	$O(2\text{-}\exp(N^{c \cdot h}))$	$(h+2)$- $\exp(O(N))$

Table 1: Space complexity of verification without arithmetic (N: size of (Γ, φ); h: depth of hierarchy; c: constants depending on the schema)

its space complexity $O(f)$, where f is a function of the relevant parameters. The space complexity of verification (the complement) is then $O(f^2)$ by Savitch's theorem [44].

Recall that $[\neg\xi]_{T_1}$ is satisfiable by a symbolic tree of runs of Γ iff $(\tau_{in}, \bot, \beta) \in \mathcal{R}_{T_1}$ for some τ_{in} satisfying the precondition of Γ, and $\beta(\neg\xi) = 1$. By Lemma 21, membership in $\mathcal{R}_{T_1}$ can be reduced to state (repeated) reachability in the VASS $\mathcal{V}(T_1, \beta)$. For a given VASS, (repeated) reachability is decided by non-deterministically generating runs of the VASS up to a certain length, using space $O(\log n \cdot 2^{c \cdot d \log d})$ where n is the number of states, d is the vector dimension and c is a constant [32]. The same approach can be used for the VASS $\mathcal{V}(T_1, \beta)$, with the added complication that generating transitions requires membership tests in the relations $\mathcal{R}_{T_c}$'s for $T_c \in child(T_1)$. These in turn become (repeated) reachability tests in the corresponding VASS. Assuming that n and d are upper bounds for the number of states and dimensions for all $\mathcal{V}(T, \beta)$ with $T \in \mathcal{H}$, this yields a total space bound of $O(h \log n \cdot 2^{c \cdot d \log d})$ for membership testing in $\mathcal{V}(T_1, \beta)$, where h is the depth of $\mathcal{H}$.

In our construction of $\mathcal{V}(T, \beta)$, the vector dimension d is the number of TS-isomorphism types. The number of states n is at most the product of the number of T-isomorphism types, the number states in $B(T, \beta)$, the number of all possible $\bar{o}$ and the number of possible states of $\bar{c}_{ib}$. The worst-case complexity occurs for HAS with unrestricted schemas (cyclic foreign keys) and artifact relations. To understand the impact of the foreign key structure and artifact relations, we also consider the complexity for acyclic and linear-cyclic schemas, and without artifact relations. A careful analysis yields the following. For better readability, we state the complexity for HAS over a fixed schema (database and maximum arity of artifact relations). The impact of the schema is detailed in Appendix C.3 of [25].

THEOREM 22. *Let Γ be a HAS over a fixed schema and φ an HLTL-FO formula over Γ. The deterministic space complexity of checking whether $\Gamma \models \varphi$ is summarized in Table 1.* [4]

Note that the worst-case space complexity is non-elementary, as for feedback-free systems [18]. However, the height of the tower of exponentials in [18] is the square of the total number of artifact variables of the system, whereas in our case it is the depth of the hierarchy, likely to be much smaller.

5. VERIFICATION WITH ARITHMETIC

We next outline the extension of our verification algorithm to handle HAS and HLTL-FO properties whose conditions use arithmetic constraints expressed as polynomial inequalities with integer coefficients over the numeric variables (ranging over $\mathbb{R}$). We note that one could alternatively limit the arithmetic constraints to linear inequalities with integer coefficients (and variables ranging over $\mathbb{Q}$), with the same complexity results. These are sufficient for many applications.

[4] k- exp is the tower of exponential functions of height k.

The seed idea behind our approach is that, in order to determine whether the arithmetic constraints are satisfied, we do not need to keep track of actual valuations of the task variables and the numeric navigation expressions they anchor (for which the search space would be infinite). Instead, we show that these valuations can be partitioned into a finite set of equivalence classes with respect to satisfaction of the arithmetic constraints, which we then incorporate into the isomorphism types of Section 4, extending the algorithm presented there. This however raises some significant technical challenges, which we discuss next.

Intuitively, this approach uses the fact that a finite set of polynomials $\mathcal{P}$ partitions the space into a bounded number of *cells* containing points located in the same region ($= 0, < 0, > 0$) with respect to every polynomial $P \in \mathcal{P}$. Isomorphism types are extended to include a cell, which determines which arithmetic constraints are satisfied in the conditions of services and in the property. In addition to the requirements detailed in Section 4, we need to enforce cell compatibility across symbolic service calls. For instance, when a task executes an internal service, the corresponding symbolic transition from cell c to c' is possible only if the projections of c and c' on the subspace corresponding to the task's input variables have non-empty intersection (since input variables are preserved). Similarly, when the opening or closing service of a child task is called, compatibility is required between the parent's and the child's cell on the shared variables, which amounts again to non-empty intersection between cell projections. This suggests the following first-cut (and problematic) attempt at a verification algorithm: once a local transition imposes new constraints, represented by a cell c', these constraints are propagated *back* to previously guessed cells, refining them via intersection with c'. If an intersection becomes empty, the candidate symbolic run constructed so far has no corresponding actual run and the search is pruned. The problem with this attempt is that it is incompatible with the way we deal with sets in Section 4: the contents of sets are represented by associating counters to the isomorphism types of their elements. Since extended isomorphism types include cells, retroactive cell intersection invalidates the counters and the results of previous VASS reachability checks.

We develop an alternative solution that avoids retroactive cell intersection altogether. More specifically, for each task, our algorithm extends isomorphism types with cells guessed from a *pre-computed* set constructed by following the task hierarchy bottom-up and including in the parent's set those cells obtained by appropriately projecting the children's cells on shared variables and expressions. Only non-empty cells are retained. We call the resulting cell collection the Hierarchical Cell Decomposition (HCD).

The key benefit of the HCD is that it arranges the space of cells so that consistency of a symbolic run can be guaranteed by performing simple local compatibility tests on the cells involved in each transition. Specifically, (i) in the case of internal service calls, the next cell c' must *refine* the current cell c on the shared variables (that is, the projection of c' must be contained in the projection of c); (ii) in the case of

	Acyclic	Linearly-Cyclic	Cyclic
w/o. Artifact relations	$O(\exp(N^{c \cdot h}))$	$O(\exp(N^{c \cdot h^2}))$	$(h+1)\text{-}\exp(O(N))$
w. Artifact relations	$O(2\text{-}\exp(N^{c \cdot h}))$	$O(2\text{-}\exp(N^{c \cdot h^2}))$	$(h+2)\text{-}\exp(O(N)))$

Table 2: Space complexity of verification with arithmetic (N: size of (Γ, φ); h: depth of hierarchy; c: constants depending on the schema)

child task opening/closing services, the parent cell c must refine the child cell c'. This ensures that in case (i) the intersection with c' of all relevant previously guessed cells is non-empty (because we only guess non-empty cells and c' refines all prior guesses), and in case (ii) the intersection with the child's cell c' is a no-op for the parent cell. Consequently, retroactive intersection can be skipped as it can never lead to empty cells.

A natural starting point for constructing the HCD is to gather for each task all the polynomials appearing in its arithmetic constraints (or in the property sub-formulas referring to that task), and associate sign conditions to each. This turns out to be insufficient. For example, the projection from the child cell can impose on the parent variables new constraints which do not appear explicitly in the parent task. It is a priori not obvious that the constrained cells can be represented symbolically, let alone efficiently computed. The tool enabling our solution is the Tarski-Seidenberg Theorem [48], which ensures that the projection of a cell is representable by a union of cells defined by a set of polynomials (computed from the original ones) and sign conditions for them. The polynomials can be efficiently computed using quantifier elimination.

Observe that a bound on the number of newly constructed polynomials yields a bound on the number of cells in the HCD, which in turn implies a bound on the number of distinct extended isomorphism types manipulated by the verification algorithm, ultimately yielding decidability of verification. A naive analysis produces a bound on the number of cells that is hyperexponential in the height of the task hierarchy, because the number of polynomials can proliferate at this rate when constructing all possible projections, and p polynomials may produce 3^p cells. Fortunately, a classical result [3] from real algebraic geometry bounds the number of distinct *non-empty* cells to only exponential in the number of variables (the exponent is independent of the number of polynomials). This yields an upper bound of the number of cells (and also the number of extended isomorphism types) which is singly exponential in the number of numeric expressions and doubly exponential in the height of the hierarchy $\mathcal{H}$. We state below our complexity results for verification with arithmetic, relegating details (including a fine-grained analysis) to Appendix D of [25].

THEOREM 23. *Let Γ be a HAS over a fixed database schema and φ an HLTL-FO formula over Γ. If arithmetic is allowed in (Γ, φ), then the deterministic space complexity of checking whether $\Gamma \models \varphi$ is summarized in Table 2.*

6. RESTRICTIONS AND UNDECIDABILITY

We briefly review the main restrictions imposed on the HAS model and motivate them by showing that they are needed to ensure decidability of verification. Specifically, recall that the following restrictions are placed in the model:

1. in an internal transition of a given task (caused by an internal service), only the input parameters of the task are explicitly propagated from one artifact tuple to the next
2. each task may overwrite upon return only `null` variables in the parent task
3. the artifact variables of a task storing the values returned by its subtasks are disjoint from the task's input variables
4. an internal transition can take place only if all active subtasks have returned
5. each task has just one artifact relation
6. the artifact relation of a task is reset to empty every time the task closes
7. the tuple of artifact variables whose value is inserted or retrieved from a task's artifact relation is fixed
8. each subtask may be called at most once between internal transitions of its parent

These restrictions are placed in order to control the data flow and recursive computation in the system. Lifting any of them leads to undecidability of verification, as stated informally next.

THEOREM 24. *For each $i, 1 \leq i \leq 8$, let $HAS^{(i)}$ be defined identically to HAS but without restriction (i) above. It is undecidable, given a $HAS^{(i)}$ Γ and an HLTL-FO formula φ over Γ, whether $\Gamma \models \varphi$.*

The proofs of undecidability for (1)-(7) are by reduction from the Post Correspondence Problem (PCP) [42, 44]. They make no use of arithmetic, so undecidability holds even without arithmetic constraints. The only undecidability result relying on arithmetic is (8). Indeed, restriction (8) can be lifted in the absence of numeric variables, with no impact on decidability or complexity of verification. This is because restriction (2) ensures that even if a subtask is called repeatedly, only a bounded number of calls have a non-vacuous effect.

The proofs using a reduction from the PCP rely on the same main idea: removal of the restriction allows to extract from the database a path of unbounded length in a labeled graph, and check that its labels spell a solution to the PCP. For illustration, we sketch the proof of undecidability for (2) using this technique in Appendix E of [25].

We claim that the above restrictions remain sufficiently permissive to capture a wide class of applications of practical interest. This is confirmed by numerous examples of practical business processes modeled as artifact systems, that we encountered in our collaboration with IBM (see [18]). The restrictions limit the recursion and data flow among tasks and services. In practical workflows, the required recursion is rarely powerful enough to allow unbounded propagation of data among services. Instead, as also discussed in [18], recursion is often due to two scenarios:

- allowing a certain task to undo and retry an unbounded number of times, with each retrial independent of previous ones, and depending only on a context that remains unchanged throughout the retrial phase (its input parameters). A typical example is repeatedly providing credit card information until the payment goes through, while the order details remain unchanged.

- allowing a task to batch-process an unbounded collection of records, each processed independently, with unchanged input parameters (e.g. sending invitations to an event to all attendants on the list, for the same event details).

Such recursive computation can be expressed with the above restrictions, which are satisfied by our example provided in Appendix A.1.

7. RELATED WORK

We have already discussed our own prior related work in the introduction. We summarize next other related work on verification of artifact systems.

Initial work on formal analysis of artifact-based business processes in restricted contexts has investigated reachability [30, 31], general temporal constraints [31], and the existence of complete execution or dead end [11]. For each considered problem, verification is generally undecidable; decidability results were obtained only under rather severe restrictions, e.g., restricting all pre-conditions to be "true" [30], restricting to bounded domains [31, 11], or restricting the pre- and post-conditions to be propositional, and thus not referring to data values [31]. [16] adopts an artifact model variation with arithmetic operations but no database.

Decidability relies on restricting runs to bounded length. [51] addresses the problem of the existence of a run that satisfies a temporal property, for a restricted case with no database and only propositional LTL properties. All of these works model no underlying database, sets (artifact relations), task hierarchy, or arithmetic.

A recent line of work has tackled verification of artifact-centric processes with an underlying relational database. [5, 4, 6, 7, 20] evolve the business process model and property language, culminating in [33], which addresses verification of first-order μ-calculus (hence branching time) properties over business processes expressed in a framework that is equivalent to artifact systems whose input is provided by external services. [8, 15] extend the results of [33] to artifact-centric multi-agent systems where the property language is a version of first-order branching-time temporal-epistemic logic expressing the knowledge of the agents. This line of work uses variations of a business process model called DCDS (data-centric dynamic systems), which is sufficienty expressive to capture the GSM model, as shown in [46]. In their unrestricted form, DCDS and HAS have similar expressive power. However, the difference lies in the tackled verification problem and in the restrictions imposed to achieve decidability. We check satisfaction of linear-time properties for every possible choice of initial database instance, whereas the related line checks branching-time properties and assumes that the initial database is given. None of the related works address arithmetic. In the absence of arithmetic, the restrictions introduced for decidability are incomparable (neither subsumes the other).

Beyond artifact systems, there is a plethora of literature on data-centric processes, dealing with various static analysis problems and also with runtime monitoring and synthesis. We discuss the most related works here and refer the reader to the surveys [14, 24] for more. Static analysis for semantic web services is considered in [39], but in a context restricted to finite domains. The works [26, 47, 2] are ancestors of [23] from the context of verification of electronic commerce applications. Their models could conceptually (if not naturally) be encoded in HAS but correspond only to particular cases supporting no arithmetic, sets, or hierarchies. Also, they limit external inputs to essentially come from the active domain of the database, thus ruling out fresh values introduced during the run.

8. CONCLUSION

We showed decidability of verification for a rich artifact model capturing core elements of IBM's successful GSM system: task hierarchy, concurrency, database keys and foreign keys, arithmetic constraints, and richer artifact data. The extended framework requires the use of novel techniques including nested Vector Addition Systems and a variant of quantifier elimination tailored to our context. We improve significantly on previous work on verification of artifact systems with arithmetic [18], which only exhibits non-elementary upper bounds regardless of the schema shape, even absent artifact relations. In contrast, for acyclic and linearly-cyclic schemas, even in the presence of arithmetic and artifact relations, our new upper bounds are elementary (doubly-exponential in the input size and triply-exponential in the depth of the hierarchy). This brings the verification algorithm closer to practical relevance, particularly since its complexity gracefully reduces to PSPACE (for acyclic schema) and EXPSPACE in the hierarchy depth (for linearly-cyclic schema) when arithmetic and artifact relations are not present. The sole remaining case of nonelementary complexity occurs for arbitrary cyclic schemas. Altogether, our results provide substantial new insight and techniques for the automatic verification of realistic artifact systems.

Acknowledgement This work was supported in part by the National Science Foundation under award IIS-1422375.

9. REFERENCES

[1] Expedia. www.expedia.com. Accessed: 2014-12-10.

[2] S. Abiteboul, V. Vianu, B. Fordham, and Y. Yesha. Relational transducers for electronic commerce. *JCSS*, 61(2):236–269, 2000. Extended abstract in PODS 98.

[3] S. Basu, R. Pollak, and M.-F. Roy. On the number of cells defined by a family of polynomials on a variety. *Mathematika*, 43(1):120–126, 1996.

[4] F. Belardinelli, A. Lomuscio, and F. Patrizi. A computationally-grounded semantics for artifact-centric systems and abstraction results. In *IJCAI 2011, Proceedings of the 22nd International Joint Conference on Artificial Intelligence, Barcelona, Catalonia, Spain, July 16-22, 2011*, pages 738–743, 2011.

[5] F. Belardinelli, A. Lomuscio, and F. Patrizi. Verification of deployed artifact systems via data abstraction. In *Service-Oriented Computing - 9th International Conference, ICSOC 2011, Paphos, Cyprus, December 5-8, 2011 Proceedings*, pages 142–156, 2011.

[6] F. Belardinelli, A. Lomuscio, and F. Patrizi. An abstraction technique for the verification of artifact-centric systems. In *Principles of Knowledge Representation and Reasoning: Proceedings of the Thirteenth International Conference, KR 2012, Rome, Italy, June 10-14, 2012*, 2012.

[7] F. Belardinelli, A. Lomuscio, and F. Patrizi. Verification of GSM-based artifact-centric systems

through finite abstraction. In *Service-Oriented Computing - 10th International Conference, ICSOC 2012, Shanghai, China, November 12-15, 2012. Proceedings*, pages 17–31, 2012.

[8] F. Belardinelli, A. Lomuscio, and F. Patrizi. Verification of agent-based artifact systems. *J. Artif. Intell. Res. (JAIR)*, 51:333–376, 2014.

[9] K. Bhattacharya, N. S. Caswell, S. Kumaran, A. Nigam, and F. Y. Wu. Artifact-centered operational modeling: Lessons from customer engagements. *IBM Systems Journal*, 46(4):703–721, 2007.

[10] K. Bhattacharya et al. A model-driven approach to industrializing discovery processes in pharmaceutical research. *IBM Systems Journal*, 44(1):145–162, 2005.

[11] K. Bhattacharya, C. E. Gerede, R. Hull, R. Liu, and J. Su. Towards formal analysis of artifact-centric business process models. In *Proc. Int. Conf. on Business Process Management (BPM)*, pages 288–304, 2007.

[12] BizAgi and Cordys and IBM and Oracle and SAP AG and Singularity (OMG Submitters) and Agile Enterprise Design and Stiftelsen SINTEF and TIBCO and Trisotech (Co-Authors). Case Management Model and Notation (CMMN), FTF Beta 1, Jan. 2013. OMG Document Number dtc/2013-01-01, Object Management Group.

[13] M. Blockelet and S. Schmitz. Model checking coverability graphs of vector addition systems. In *Mathematical Foundations of Computer Science 2011*, pages 108–119. Springer, 2011.

[14] D. Calvanese, G. De Giacomo, and M. Montali. Foundations of data-aware process analysis: a database theory perspective. In *PODS*, pages 1–12, 2013.

[15] D. Calvanese, G. Delzanno, and M. Montali. Verification of relational multiagent systems with data types. In *Proceedings of the Twenty-Ninth AAAI Conference on Artificial Intelligence, January 25-30, 2015, Austin, Texas, USA.*, pages 2031–2037, 2015.

[16] D. Calvanese, G. D. Giacomo, R. Hull, and J. Su. Artifact-centric workflow dominance. In *ICSOC/ServiceWave*, pages 130–143, 2009.

[17] T. Chao et al. Artifact-based transformation of IBM Global Financing: A case study. In *BPM*, 2009.

[18] E. Damaggio, A. Deutsch, and V. Vianu. Artifact systems with data dependencies and arithmetic. *ACM Trans. Database Syst.*, 37(3):22, 2012. Also in ICDT 2011.

[19] E. Damaggio, R. Hull, and R. Vaculín. On the equivalence of incremental and fixpoint semantics for business artifacts with guard-stage-milestone lifecycles. *Information Systems*, 38:561–584, 2013.

[20] G. De Giacomo, R. D. Masellis, and R. Rosati. Verification of conjunctive artifact-centric services. *Int. J. Cooperative Inf. Syst.*, 21(2):111–140, 2012.

[21] G. De Giacomo and M. Y. Vardi. Linear temporal logic and linear dynamic logic on finite traces. In *Proceedings of the Twenty-Third international joint conference on Artificial Intelligence*, pages 854–860. AAAI Press, 2013.

[22] H. de Man. Case management: Cordys approach. BP Trends (`www.bptrends.com`), 2009.

[23] A. Deutsch, R. Hull, F. Patrizi, and V. Vianu. Automatic verification of data-centric business processes. In *ICDT*, pages 252–267, 2009.

[24] A. Deutsch, R. Hull, and V. Vianu. Automatic verification of database-centric systems. *SIGMOD Record*, 43(3):5–17, 2014.

[25] A. Deutsch, Y. Li, and V. Vianu. Verification of hierarchical artifact systems. *arXiv preprint*, arXiv:1604.00967v1, 2016.

[26] A. Deutsch, L. Sui, and V. Vianu. Specification and verification of data-driven web applications. *JCSS*, 73(3):442–474, 2007.

[27] V. Diekert and P. Gastin. Pure future local temporal logics are expressively complete for Mazurkiewicz traces. In *LATIN 2004: Theoretical Informatics, 6th Latin American Symposium, Buenos Aires, Argentina, April 5-8, 2004, Proceedings*, pages 232–241, 2004.

[28] V. Diekert and P. Gastin. Pure future local temporal logics are expressively complete for Mazurkiewicz traces. *Inf. Comput.*, 204(11):1597–1619, 2006.

[29] E. A. Emerson. Temporal and modal logic. In J. V. Leeuwen, editor, *Handbook of Theoretical Computer Science, Volume B: Formal Models and Sematics*, pages 995–1072. North-Holland Pub. Co./MIT Press, 1990.

[30] C. E. Gerede, K. Bhattacharya, and J. Su. Static analysis of business artifact-centric operational models. In *IEEE International Conference on Service-Oriented Computing and Applications*, 2007.

[31] C. E. Gerede and J. Su. Specification and verification of artifact behaviors in business process models. In *Proceedings of 5th International Conference on Service-Oriented Computing (ICSOC)*, Vienna, Austria, September 2007.

[32] P. Habermehl. On the complexity of the linear-time μ-calculus for petri nets. In *Application and Theory of Petri Nets 1997*, pages 102–116. Springer, 1997.

[33] B. B. Hariri, D. Calvanese, G. De Giacomo, A. Deutsch, and M. Montali. Verification of relational data-centric dynamic systems with external services. In *Proceedings of the 32nd ACM SIGMOD-SIGACT-SIGART Symposium on Principles of Database Systems, PODS 2013, New York, NY, USA - June 22 - 27, 2013*, pages 163–174, 2013.

[34] R. Hull, E. Damaggio, R. D. Masellis, F. Fournier, M. Gupta, F. H. III, S. Hobson, M. Linehan, S. Maradugu, A. Nigam, P. Sukaviriya, and R. Vaculín. Business artifacts with guard-stage-milestone lifecycles: Managing artifact interactions with conditions and events. In *ACM DEBS*, 2011.

[35] R. Kimball and M. Ross. *The data warehouse toolkit: the complete guide to dimensional modeling.* John Wiley & Sons, 2011.

[36] R. Lipton. The reachability problem requires exponential space. *Research Report 62, Department of Computer Science, Yale University, New Haven, Connecticut*, 1976.

[37] M. Marin, R. Hull, and R. Vaculín. Data centric bpm and the emerging case management standard: A short survey. In *BPM Workshops*, 2012.

[38] R. Mayr. Undecidable problems in unreliable computations. *Theoretical Computer Science*, 297(1):337–354, 2003.
[39] S. Narayanan and S. McIlraith. Simulation, verification and automated composition of web services. In *Intl. World Wide Web Conf. (WWW2002)*, 2002.
[40] A. Nigam and N. S. Caswell. Business artifacts: An approach to operational specification. *IBM Systems Journal*, 42(3):428–445, 2003.
[41] D. Peled. Combining partial order reductions with on-the-fly model-checking. In *Computer aided verification*, pages 377–390. Springer, 1994.
[42] E. L. Post. Recursive unsolvability of a problem of Thue. *J. of Symbolic Logic*, 12:1–11, 1947.
[43] C. Rackoff. The covering and boundedness problems for vector addition systems. *Theoretical Computer Science*, 6(2):223–231, 1978.
[44] M. Sipser. *Introduction to the theory of computation.* PWS Publishing Company, 1997.
[45] A. P. Sistla, M. Y. Vardi, and P. Wolper. The complementation problem for Büchi automata with applications to temporal logic. *Theoretical Computer Science*, 49:217–237, 1987.
[46] D. Solomakhin, M. Montali, S. Tessaris, and R. D. Masellis. Verification of artifact-centric systems: Decidability and modeling issues. In *Service-Oriented Computing - 11th International Conference, ICSOC 2013, Berlin, Germany, December 2-5, 2013, Proceedings*, pages 252–266, 2013.
[47] M. Spielmann. Verification of relational transducers for electronic commerce. *JCSS.*, 66(1):40–65, 2003. Extended abstract in PODS 2000.
[48] A. Tarski. A decision method for elementary algebra and geometry. *1948*, 1951.
[49] M. Y. Vardi and P. Wolper. An automata-theoretic approach to automatic program verification. In *LICS*, 1986.
[50] P. Vassiliadis and T. Sellis. A survey of logical models for olap databases. *ACM Sigmod Record*, 28(4):64–69, 1999.
[51] X. Zhao, J. Su, H. Yang, and Z. Qiu. Enforcing constraints on life cycles of business artifacts. In *TASE*, pages 111–118, 2009.
[52] W.-D. Zhu et al. Advanced Case Management with IBM Case Manager. Available at `http://www.redbooks.ibm.com/abstracts/sg247929.html?Open`.

APPENDIX

A. EXAMPLES

In this section we provide an example of HAS modeling a simple travel booking business process similar to Expedia [1]. We also show an example property that the process should satisfy, using HLTL-FO.

A.1 Example Hierarchical Artifact System

The artifact system captures a process where a customer books flights and/or makes hotel reservations. The customer starts with constructing a trip by adding a flight and/or hotel reservation to it. During this time, the customer has the choice to store the trip as a candidate or retrieve a previously stored trip. Once the customer has made a decision, she can proceed to book the trip. If a hotel reservation is made together with certain flights, a discount price may be applied to the hotel reservation. In addition, the hotel reservation can be made by itself, together with the flight, or even after the flight is purchased. After submitting a valid payment, the customer is able to cancel the flight and/or the hotel reservation and receive a refund. If the customer cancels the purchase of a flight, she cannot receive the discount on the hotel reservation.

The Hierarchical artifact system has the following database schema:

- `FLIGHTS(`<u>`id`</u>`, price, comp_hotel_id)`
  `HOTELS(`<u>`id`</u>`, unit_price, discount_price)`

In the schema, the `id`'s are key attributes, `price`, `unit_price`, `discount_price` are non-key attributes, and `comp_hotel_id` is a foreign key attribute satisfying the dependency `FLIGHTS`[*comp_hotel_id*] ⊆ `HOTELS`[*id*].

Intuitively, each flight stored in the `FLIGHTS` table has a hotel compatible for discount. If a flight is purchased together with a compatible hotel reservation, a discount is applied on the hotel reservation. Otherwise, the full price needs to be paid.

The artifact system has 6 tasks: "T1: **ManageTrips**", "T2: **AddHotel**", "T3: **AddFlight**", "T4: **BookInitialTrip**", "T5: **Cancel**" and "T6: **AlsoBookHotel**", which form the hierarchy represented in Figure 1.

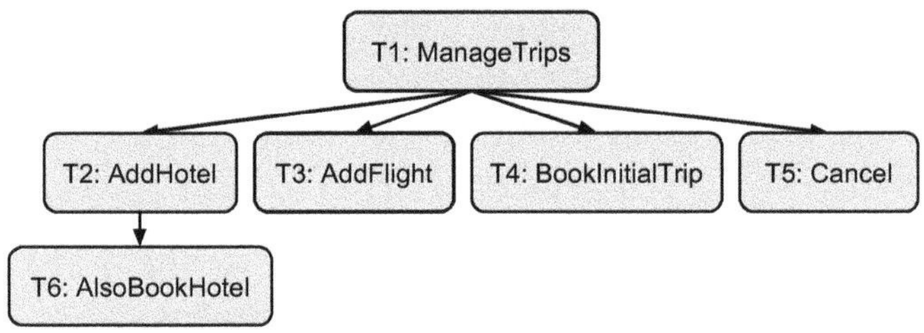

Figure 1: Tasks Hierarchy

The process can be described informally as follows. The customer starts with task **ManageTrips**, where the customer can add a flight and/or hotel to the trip by calling the **AddHotel** or the **AddFlight** tasks. The customer is also allowed to store candidate trips in an artifact relation `TRIPS` and retrieve previously stored trips. (Note that for simplicity, our example considers only outbound flights in the trip. Return flights can be added by a simple extension to the specification.) After the customer has made a decision, the **BookInitialTrip** task is called to book the trip and the payment is processed. The process also mimics a key feature of Expedia as follows. After payment is made successfully, if the customer booked the flight with no hotel reservation, then she has the opportunity to add a hotel reservation by calling the **AddHotel** task. When she does so, the task **AlsoBookHotel** needs to be called to handle the payment of the added hotel reservation. Note that the **AlsoBookHotel** task can only be called after the flight is booked for but a hotel reservation is missing in the trip. Once the payment is made, the customer can cancel the order by calling the **Cancel** task. Using **Cancel**, the customer is able to cancel the flight and/or the hotel with a full refund. It is important to note that if the customer cancels the purchase of the flight, then she cannot receive the discount on the hotel reservation.

The tasks are specified below. For convenience, we use existential quantifications in conditions, which can be simulated by adding extra variables. String values are used as syntactic sugar for numeric variables. We assume that the set of strings we used ("Unpaid", "Paid", "FlightCanceled", etc.) correspond to distinct numeric constants. In particular, the string "Unpaid" corresponds to the constant 0. Also for convenience, we use artifact variables with the same names in parent and child tasks. By default, each input/return variable is mapped to the variable in the parent/child task having the same name.

ManageTrips: This is the root task, modeling the process whereby the customer creates, stores, and retrieves candidate trips. A trip consists of a flight and/or hotel reservation. Eventually, one of the candidate trips may be chosen for booking. As the root task, its opening condition is `true` and closing condition is `false`. The task has the following artifact variables:

- ID variables: `flight_id`, `hotel_id`,
- numeric variables: `status` and `amount_paid`

It also has an artifact relation `TRIPS` storing candidate trips (`flight_id`, `hotel_id`). The customer can use the subtasks **AddFlight** and **AddHotel** (specified below) to fill in variables `flight_id` and `hotel_id`. In addition, the task has two internal services: *StoreTrip* and *RetrieveTrip*. Intuitively, when *StoreTrip* is called, the current candidate trip (`flight_id`, `hotel_id`) is inserted into `TRIPS`. When *RetrieveTrip* is called, one tuple is non-deterministically chosen and removed from `TRIPS`, and (`flight_id`, `hotel_id`) is set to be the chosen tuple. The two tasks are specified as follows:

StoreTrip:
Pre-condition: `status` = "Unpaid" ∧ (`flight_id` ≠ `null` ∨ `hotel_id` ≠ `null`)
Post-condition: `flight_id` = `null` ∧ `hotel_id` = `null` ∧ `status` = "Unpaid" ∧ `amount_paid` = 0
Set update: {+`TRIPS`(`flight_id`, `hotel_id`)}

RetrieveTrip:
Pre-condition: `status` = "Unpaid"
Post-condition: `status` = "Unpaid" ∧ `amount_paid` = 0
Set update: {−`TRIPS`(`flight_id`, `hotel_id`)}

AddFlight: This task adds a flight to the trip. It can be opened if `flight_id` = `null` and `status` = "Unpaid" in the parent task. It has no input variable and the return variable is `flight_id`. The task has a single internal service *ChooseFlight* that chooses a flight from the `FLIGHTS` database and stores it in `flight_id`, which is returned to **ManageTrips**.

AddHotel: This task adds a hotel reservation to the trip. It can be opened when `hotel_id` = `null` and `status` is either "Paid" or "Unpaid".

This task has the following artifact variables:

- ID variables: `flight_id`[5], `hotel_id`[6]
- numeric variables: `status`, `amount_paid`, `new_amount_paid` (overwriting `amount_paid` in the parent task when the task returns), `discount_price`, `unit_price` and `hotel_price`

The task has a single internal service *ChooseHotel* which picks a hotel from `HOTELS` and determines the price by checking whether the hotel is compatible with the chosen flight. If they are compatible, then `hotel_price` is set to the discount price, otherwise it is set to the full price.

A hotel can be added to the trip in two scenarios. First, if `status` is "Unpaid", which means that the trip has not been booked, then this task chooses a hotel and the id of the hotel is returned to **ManageTrips**. Second, if `status` is "Paid", which means that a flight has already been purchased without a hotel reservation, then this task chooses a hotel and then the child task **AlsoBookHotel** needs to be called to handle the payment of the newly added hotel. In **AlsoBookHotel**, a payment is received and the new total amount of payment received is written into variable `new_amount_paid` when **AlsoBookHotel** returns.

The closing service of **AddHotel** has condition `status` = "Unpaid" ∨ (`status` = "Paid" ∧ `hotel_price` = `new_amount_paid` − `amount_paid`), which means that either there is no need to call **AlsoBookHotel** or a correct payment has been received in **AlsoBookHotel**. The *ChooseHotel* service is specified as follows:

ChooseHotel:
Pre-condition: `True`
Post-condition:

$\exists cid \exists p_f$ ($\texttt{flight\_id} = \texttt{null} \rightarrow cid = \texttt{null}$)∧
($\texttt{flight\_id} \neq \texttt{null} \rightarrow \texttt{FLIGHTS}(\texttt{flight\_id}, p_f, cid)$)∧
$\texttt{HOTELS}(\texttt{hotel\_id}, \texttt{unit\_price}, \texttt{discount\_price})$∧
($cid = \texttt{hotel\_id} \rightarrow \texttt{hotel\_price} = \texttt{discount\_price}$)∧
($cid \neq \texttt{hotel\_id} \rightarrow \texttt{hotel\_price} = \texttt{unit\_price}$)∧
($\texttt{new\_amount\_paid} = 0$)

AlsoBookHotel: This task handles payment of hotel reservation made after the flight is purchased. It can be opened if `hotel_id` ≠ `null` and `status` = "Paid" in **AddHotel**. It receives input variables `hotel_price` and `amount_paid` from the parent and has local numeric variables `new_amount_paid` and `hotel_amount_paid`. It has a single service *Pay* which processes the payment. This service simply receives a hotel payment in variable `hotel_amount_paid` and the new total amount of payment received is calculated (`new_amount_paid` = `amount_paid` + `hotel_amount_paid`). The service can fail and the user can retry for unlimited number of times. This task can return only when the payment is successful, which means that the closing condition is `hotel_amount_paid` = `hotel_price`. When **AlsoBookHotel** returns, the numeric variable `new_amount_paid` is returned to **ManageTrips**.

BookInitialTrip: This task allows the customer to reserve and pay for the chosen trip. Its opening condition is `status` = "Unpaid". This task has the following variables:

- ID variables: `flight_id`, `hotel_id`
- numeric variables: `status`, `amount_paid`, `ticket_price`, `hotel_price`

The task contains a single service *Pay* to process the payment, which can fail and be retried for an unlimited number of times. Note that if the trip contains both the flight and hotel, when *Pay* is called, the payments for both of them are received.

If the payment is successful (i.e. `amount_paid` equals to the flight price plus the hotel price), `status` is set to "Paid".

[5]the underlined variables are input variables
[6]the wavy underlined variables are return variables

Otherwise it is set to "Failed". The closing condition of this task is $\texttt{status} = \text{"Paid"}$ or $\texttt{status} = \text{"Failed"}$. When **BookInitialTrip** returns, `status` and `amount_paid` in the parent task are updated by the new `status` and `amount_paid` returned by **BookInitialTrip**. The *Pay* service is specified as follows:

Pay:
Pre-condition: $\texttt{hotel\_id} \neq \texttt{null} \vee \texttt{flight\_id} \neq \texttt{null}$
Post-condition:

$$\exists cid \exists p_1 \exists p_2$$
$$(\texttt{flight\_id} = \texttt{null} \rightarrow \texttt{ticket\_price} = 0 \wedge cid = \texttt{null}) \wedge$$
$$(\texttt{flight\_id} \neq \texttt{null} \rightarrow \texttt{FLIGHTS}(\texttt{flight\_id}, \texttt{ticket\_price},$$
$$cid)) \wedge (\texttt{hotel\_id} = \texttt{null} \rightarrow \texttt{hotel\_price} = 0) \wedge$$
$$(\texttt{hotel\_id} \neq \texttt{null} \rightarrow (\texttt{HOTELS}(\texttt{hotel\_id}, p_1, p_2) \wedge$$
$$(\texttt{hotel\_id} = cid \rightarrow \texttt{hotel\_price} = p_2) \wedge$$
$$(\texttt{hotel\_id} \neq cid \rightarrow \texttt{hotel\_price} = p_1)) \wedge$$
$$(\texttt{amount\_paid} = \texttt{ticket\_price} + \texttt{hotel\_price} \rightarrow$$
$$\texttt{status} = \text{"Paid"}) \wedge (\texttt{amount\_paid} \neq \texttt{ticket\_price}+$$
$$\texttt{hotel\_price} \rightarrow \texttt{status} = \text{"Failed"})$$

Cancel: In this task, the customer can cancel the flight and/or hotel after the trip has been paid for. Its opening condition is $\texttt{status} = \text{"Paid"}$. This task has the following variables:

- ID variables: `hotel_id` and `flight_id`
- numeric variables: `amount_paid`, `ticket_price`, `discount_price`, `unit_price`, `hotel_price`, `amount_refunded` and `status`

The task has 3 services, *CancelFlight*, *CancelHotel* and *CancelBoth* which cancel the flight, the hotel reservation, or both of them, respectively. When any of these services is called, `amount_refunded` is calculated to be the correct amount needs to be refunded to the customer and `status` is set to "FlightCanceled", "HotelCanceled" and "AllCanceled" respectively. In particular, if the customer would like to cancel the flight while keeping the hotel reservation, and if a discount has been applied on the hotel reservation, then the correct `amount_refunded` equals to `ticket_price` minus the difference between the normal cost and the discounted cost of the hotel since she is no longer eligible for the discount.

The closing condition of this task is True. We show the specification of *CancelFlight* as an example. Let `Discounted` be the subformula

$$(\texttt{hotel\_id} \neq \texttt{null}) \wedge (\texttt{hotel\_price} = \texttt{discount\_price})$$

And let `Penalized` be the subformula

$$\texttt{amount\_refunded} = \texttt{ticket\_price} - (\texttt{unit\_price} - \texttt{discount\_price})$$

CancelFlight:
Pre-condition:

$$\texttt{flight\_id} \neq \texttt{null} \wedge \texttt{status} \neq \text{"FlightCanceled"} \wedge$$
$$\texttt{status} \neq \text{"HotelCanceled"} \wedge \texttt{status} \neq \text{"AllCanceled"}$$

Post-condition:

$$\exists cid\ \texttt{FLIGHTS}(\texttt{flight\_id}, \texttt{ticket\_price}, cid) \wedge$$
$$(\texttt{hotel\_price} = \texttt{amount\_paid} - \texttt{ticket\_price}) \wedge$$
$$(\texttt{hotel\_id} \neq \texttt{null} \rightarrow$$
$$(\texttt{HOTELS}(\texttt{hotel\_id}, \texttt{unit\_price}, \texttt{discount\_price}) \wedge$$
$$(\neg\texttt{Discounted} \rightarrow \texttt{amount\_refunded} = \texttt{ticket\_price}) \wedge$$
$$(\texttt{Discounted} \rightarrow \texttt{Penalized}) \wedge \texttt{status} = \text{"FlightCanceled"}$$

A.2 Example HLTL-FO Property

Suppose we wish to enforce the following policy: *if a discount is applied to the hotel reservation, then a compatible flight must be purchased without cancellation.* One typical way to defeat the policy would be for a user to first pay for the flight, then reserve the hotel with the discount price, but next cancel the flight without penalty. Detecting such bugs can be subtle, especially in a system allowing concurrency. The following HLTL-FO property of task **ManageTrips** says "If *AddHotel* is called and a hotel reservation is added with a discounted price, then at the task *Cancel*, if the customer would like to cancel the flight, a penalty must be paid".

The property is specified as $[\varphi]_{\texttt{T1}}$ where φ is the formula:

$$\varphi = \mathbf{F}[\mathbf{F}\ (\texttt{Discounted} \wedge \mathbf{X}\ \sigma^o_{\texttt{T6:AlsoBookHotel}})]_{\texttt{T2:AddHotel}} \rightarrow \mathbf{G}(\sigma^o_{\texttt{T5:Cancel}} \rightarrow [\mathbf{G}(\mathit{CancelFlight} \rightarrow \texttt{Penalized})]_{\texttt{T5:Cancel}})$$

with the subformulas `Discounted` and `Penalized` defined above.

Notice that in the specification there is no guard preventing *AddHotel* and *Cancel* to run concurrently after a successful payment is made, which can lead to a violation of this property. The problem can be fixed by adding a new variable in **ManageTrips** to indicate whether **AddHotel** or **Cancel** are currently running and modifying their opening conditions to make sure that these two tasks are mutual exclusive.

Recency-Bounded Verification of Dynamic Database-Driven Systems

Parosh Aziz Abdulla
Uppsala University
parosh@it.uu.se

C. Aiswarya
Uppsala University
aiswarya@cmi.ac.in

Mohamed Faouzi Atig
Uppsala University
mohamed_faouzi.atig@it.uu.se

Marco Montali
Free Univ. of Bozen/Bolzano
montali@inf.unibz.it

Othmane Rezine
Uppsala University
othmane.rezine@it.uu.se

ABSTRACT

We propose a formalism to model database-driven systems, called database manipulating systems (DMS). The actions of a DMS modify the current instance of a relational database by adding new elements into the database, deleting tuples from the relations and adding tuples to the relations. The elements which are modified by an action are chosen by (full) first-order queries. DMS is a highly expressive model and can be thought of as a succinct representation of an infinite state relational transition system, in line with similar models proposed in the literature. We propose monadic second order logic (`MSO-FO`) to reason about sequences of database instances appearing along a run. Unsurprisingly, the linear-time model checking problem of DMS against `MSO-FO` is undecidable. Towards decidability, we propose under-approximate model checking of DMS, where the under-approximation parameter is the "bound on recency". In a k-recency-bounded run, only the most recent k elements in the current active domain may be modified by an action. More runs can be verified by increasing the bound on recency. Our main result shows that recency-bounded model checking of DMS against `MSO-FO` is decidable, by a reduction to the satisfiability problem of MSO over nested words.

CCS Concepts

•Theory of computation → Verification by model checking; Logic and databases;

Keywords: database driven dynamic systems, data aware business processes, relational transition systems, model checking, under-approximation.

1. INTRODUCTION

In the last 15 years, research in business process management (BPM) and workflow technology has progressively shifted its emphasis from a purely control-flow, activity-centric perspective to a more holistic approach that considers also how data are manipulated and evolved by the process [25]. In particular, two lines of research emerged at the intersection of database theory, BPM and formal methods: one focused on modeling languages and technologies for specifying and enacting data-aware business processes [22], and the other tailored to their analysis and verification [10].

The first line of research gave birth to a plethora of new languages and execution platforms, culminating in the so-called *object-centric* [19] and *artifact-centric* paradigms [24], respectively exemplified by frameworks like PHILharmonicFlows [18] and IBM GSM (Guard-Stage-Milestone) [14]. Notably, GSM became the core of the recently published CMMN OMG standard on (adaptive) case management[1]. In this paper, we will use *dynamic database-driven systems* as an umbrella term for all such platforms.

The second line of research focused on understanding the boundaries of decidability and complexity for the verification of dynamic database-driven systems. Two main trends can be identified along this line. The first trend was initiated in the late 1990s with the introduction of relational transducers [2], and continued with new results over progressively richer variants of the initial model, such as systems equipped with arithmetic [15, 13], systems decomposed into interacting web services [16], and systems operating over XML databases [9]. The modelling formalisms introduced in this direction operate over a read-only, input database that is fixed during the system evolution, and use quantifier-free FO formulae to query such a database. The obtained answers can be stored into a read-write state database, whose size is fixed a-priori. Verification problems include control-state reachability [9], or model checking [15, 13] against formulae expressed in FO variants of temporal logics with a limited form of FO quantification across state. Furthermore, verification is *input-parametric*, that is, studied independently from the configuration of data in the initial input database.

In contrast, the second trend studies dynamic systems where the initial state is known. Hence their execution semantics can be captured by means of a single *relational transition system* (RTS), that is, a (possibly) infinite-state transition system whose states are labeled with database instances [27]. Further, the actions allow for bulk read-write operations over the database, possibly injecting fresh values taken from an infinite domain. The injection of such values accounts for the input of new information from the external

[1] http://www.omg.org/spec/CMMN/

PODS'16, June 26-July 01, 2016, San Francisco, CA, USA

DOI: http://dx.doi.org/10.1145/2902251.2902300

environment (e.g., through user interaction or communication with external systems/services), or the insertion of globally unique identifiers (GUIDS).

Verification of dynamic database-driven systems is challenging due to the infinite state-space generated. Several works [8, 6, 26, 11, 7, 5] succeeded in obtaining decidability by imposing restrictions that yielded finite-state abstractions of the entire system. In [21], decidability is obtained for unbounded-state dynamic database-driven systems in the restrictive case where the database schema contains a single unary relation.

In this paper we propose an under-approximation based on recency of the elements, which allows unbounded state-space. With this restriction we show decidability for the model checking problem against monadic second-order logic over sequences of database instances.

More specifically, we introduce *database-manipulating systems* (DMSs) to model dynamic database-driven systems. Salient features of DMS include guarding every action using (unrestricted) first-order queries on the current database, addition and deletion of tuples in the database, and addition of new elements in the database (which results in a growing active domain).

On top of this model, we study linear-time model checking, using *monadic second-order logic over runs* (MSO-FO) to reason about sequences of database instances appearing along the DMS runs. MSO-FO employs FO queries as its atomic formulae, and supports FO data-quantifications across distinct time points. This powerful logic can express popular verification problems such as reachability, repeated reachability, fairness, liveness, safety, FO-LTL, etc. For example, the property that "every enrolled student eventually graduates" can be formalized in MSO-FO as:

$$\forall x \forall u. \mathit{Enrolled}(u)@x \Rightarrow \exists y. y > x \wedge \mathit{Graduated}(u)@y$$

where x and y are *position* variables, used to predicate about the different time points encountered along a run, while u is a data variable, which matches with values stored in the databases present at these time points. This property corresponds to the FO-LTL formula $\forall u.\mathbf{G}\mathit{Enrolled}(u) \Rightarrow \mathbf{F}\mathit{Graduated}(u)$. More sophisticated properties can be encoded by leveraging the expressive power of MSO-FO, such as that between the enrolment of a student to a course and the moment in which the student passes that course, there is an even number of times in which the student fails that course.

As a first result we show that, unsurprisingly, already propositional reachability turns out to be undecidable to check, even for extremely limited DMSs. Instead of attacking this negative result by limiting the expressive power of the DMS specification formalism, we consider *under-approximate verification*, restricting our attention only to those runs that satisfy a given criterion. In particular, we consider as the under-approximation parameter the *bound on recency*. In a **b**-recency-bounded run, only the most recent **b** elements in the current active domain may be modified (i.e., updated or deleted) by an action, but the behavior of the action may be influenced by the entire content of the database. More runs are verified by increasing the bound on recency. In particular, model checking of safety properties converges to exact model checking in the limit.

Our main result shows that *recency-bounded model checking of DMS against MSO-FO is decidable.* Towards a proof, we encode runs of a recency-bounded DMS as an (infinite) nested word [3]. We then show that the correctness of the encoding can be expressed in MSO over nested words, consequently isolating those runs that correspond to the actual possible behaviors induced by the DMS. At the same time, we describe how to translate the MSO-FO property of interest into a corresponding MSO formula over nested words. In this way, we are able to reduce recency-bounded model checking of DMS against MSO-FO to the satisfiability problem of MSO over nested words, which is known to be decidable [3].

2. PRELIMINARIES

We start by introducing the preliminaries necessary for the development of our framework and results.

Databases. We fix a (data) domain Δ, which is a countably infinite set of data values, acting as standard names. A relational schema $\mathcal{R}$ is a finite set $\{R_1/a_1, \ldots, R_n/a_n\}$ of relation names R_i, each coming with its own arity a_i. A database instance I over schema $\mathcal{R}$ and domain Δ is the union set $\bigcup_{i:1\leq i\leq n} R_i^I$, where $R_i^I \subseteq \{R_i\} \times \Delta^{a_i}$ represents the content of relation R_i in the database instance I. If I contains a tuple (or a *fact*) $\langle R_i, e_1, \ldots, e_{a_i}\rangle$, we write $R_i(e_1, \ldots, e_{a_i}) \in I$. A nullary relation $p/0$ (also known as proposition) can be either instantiated as the singleton set $\{p()\}$ or the empty set $\emptyset$. In the former case, we say the proposition is *true*, and write $p \in I$. In the latter case $p \notin I$ and we say p is *false*.

We denote the set of all database instances over $\mathcal{R}$ and Δ by $\mathsf{DB\text{-}Inst\text{-}Set}(\mathcal{R}, \Delta)$. The *active domain* of I, denoted $\textsc{adom}(I)$, is the subset of Δ such that $e \in \textsc{adom}(I)$ if and only if e occurs in some fact in I (i.e. there exist $\langle R_i, e_1, \ldots, e_{a_i}\rangle \in I$ such that $e = e_j$ for some $j : 1 \leq j \leq a_i$). Given two database instances $I_1, I_2 \in \mathsf{DB\text{-}Inst\text{-}Set}(\mathcal{R}, \Delta)$, we define $I_1 + I_2$ to be the database instance $I \in \mathsf{DB\text{-}Inst\text{-}Set}(\mathcal{R}, \Delta)$ obtained by taking the relation-wise union. Similarly we define $I_1 - I_2$ where we take the relation-wise set difference. Simply put, $I_1 + I_2 = I_1 \cup I_2$ and $I_1 - I_2 = I_1 \setminus I_2$.

Queries. We use queries to access databases and extract data values of interest. Queries are expressed in *FOL with equality* over the schema $\mathcal{R}$ ($\mathtt{FOL}(\mathcal{R})$ for short). Let $\mathsf{Vars}_{\mathsf{data}} = \{u, v, u_1, \ldots\}$ be the set of FO data-variables ranging over the data values in Δ. A $\mathtt{FOL}(\mathcal{R})$ *query* is given by the following syntax:

$$Q ::= \mathsf{true} \mid R(u_1, \ldots, u_a) \mid \neg Q \mid Q_1 \wedge Q_2 \mid \exists u.Q \mid u_1 = u_2$$

where $R/a \in \mathcal{R}$, and u, u_i are variables from $\mathsf{Vars}_{\mathsf{data}}$. We use standard abbreviations like $Q_1 \vee Q_2 = \neg(\neg Q_1 \wedge \neg Q_2)$, $\forall u.Q = \neg\exists u.\neg Q$, etc. We also denote with $\mathsf{Free\text{-}Vars}(Q)$ the set of free variables appearing in a query Q.

For a set $V \subseteq \mathsf{Vars}_{\mathsf{data}}$, a *substitution* σ of V is a function that maps every variable in V to a value in Δ (i.e., $\sigma : V \to \Delta$). Given a substitution $\sigma : V \to \Delta$ and set $V' \subseteq V$, we define the restriction of σ on V' as the substitution $\sigma' : V' \to \Delta$ such that $\sigma'(u) = \sigma(u)$ for every $u \in V'$. We denote the restriction of σ to V' by $\sigma|_{V'}$.

Given a database instance I over $\mathcal{R}$ and Δ, a $\mathtt{FOL}(\mathcal{R})$ query Q over $\mathcal{R}$, and a substitution $\sigma : \mathsf{Free\text{-}Vars}(Q) \to \Delta$, we write $I, \sigma \models Q$ if the query Q under the substitution σ *holds* in database I. The semantics are as expected, and can be found for completeness in Appendix A. The set of *answers* of Q over I, denoted $\mathit{ans}(Q, I)$, is the set of all substitutions $\sigma : \mathsf{Free\text{-}Vars}(Q) \to \Delta$ such that $I, \sigma \models Q$. When $\mathsf{Free\text{-}Vars}(Q) = \emptyset$ (i.e., Q is a boolean query), we set $\mathit{ans}(Q, I)$ to be the empty substitution $\{\epsilon\}$ whenever

$I, \{\epsilon\} \models Q$ (or $I \models Q$ for short), and we assign $ans(Q, I)$ to the empty set $\emptyset$ whenever $I, \{\epsilon\} \not\models Q$ (or $I \not\models Q$ for short).

EXAMPLE 2.1. We describe a query $\mathsf{Active}(u)$ with a single free variable u, to check whether u is present in some tuple of some relation, no matter what the other elements of the tuple are:

$$\mathsf{Active}(u) \equiv \bigvee_{R/a \in \mathcal{R}} \exists u_1, \ldots, u_a \bigvee_{1 \leq j \leq a} R(u_1, \ldots, u_{j-1}, u, u_{j+1}, \ldots, u_a)$$

$\mathsf{Active}(u)$ characterises $\text{ADOM}(I)$. In fact, $ans(\mathsf{Active}(u), I)$ is $\{\langle u \mapsto e \rangle \mid e \in \text{ADOM}(I)\}$. ■

Substitutions in database instances. Let $V \subseteq \mathsf{Vars}_{\mathsf{data}}$ be a set of variables. Consider a substitution $\sigma : V \to \Delta$ that assigns each variable to an element from Δ. Let $I \in \mathsf{DB\text{-}Inst\text{-}Set}(\mathcal{R}, V)$ be a database instance over schema $\mathcal{R}$ and the variables V. We define $\mathsf{Substitute}(I, \sigma) \in \mathsf{DB\text{-}Inst\text{-}Set}(\mathcal{R}, \Delta)$ to be the database instance obtained from I by substituting every occurrence of variable u by $\sigma(u)$, for each variable $u \in V$.

3. FRAMEWORK

We introduce our model for dynamic database-driven systems. A *Database-Manipulating System (DMS)* over domain Δ and schema $\mathcal{R}$ is a pair $\mathcal{S} = \langle I_0, \text{ACTS} \rangle$, where:

- $I_0 \in \mathsf{DB\text{-}Inst\text{-}Set}(\mathcal{R}, \Delta)$ is the *initial database instance* over $\mathcal{R}$ and Δ, with $\text{ADOM}(I_0) = \emptyset$. I_0 gives truth-values to the nullary relations (also known as propositions), and has empty non-nullary relations
- ACTS is a set of *(guarded) actions*. An action α is a tuple $\alpha = \langle \vec{u}, \vec{v}, Q, Del, Add \rangle$, where
  - $\vec{u}$ and $\vec{v}$ are disjoint finite subsets of $\mathsf{Vars}_{\mathsf{data}}$, respectively denoting *action parameters* and *fresh-input variables.*
  - Q is a $\mathtt{FOL}(\mathcal{R})$ query, called the *guard* of α.
  - $\vec{u} = \mathsf{Free\text{-}Vars}(Q)$.
  - $Del \in \mathsf{DB\text{-}Inst\text{-}Set}(\mathcal{R}, \vec{u})$ is a database instance over the variables $\vec{u}$ and the schema $\mathcal{R}$.
  - $Add \in \mathsf{DB\text{-}Inst\text{-}Set}(\mathcal{R}, \vec{u} \uplus \vec{v})$ is a database instance over the variables $\vec{u} \uplus \vec{v}$ and $\mathcal{R}$, with $\vec{v} \subseteq \text{ADOM}(Add)$. The set $\vec{v}$ contains the so-called *fresh-input variables* of α.

Given an action $\alpha = \langle \vec{u}, \vec{v}, Q, Del, Add \rangle$, we refer to: $\vec{u}$ by $\alpha{\cdot}\mathsf{free}$, $\vec{v}$ by $\alpha{\cdot}\mathsf{new}$, Q by $\alpha{\cdot}\mathsf{guard}$, Del by $\alpha{\cdot}Del$, and Add by $\alpha{\cdot}Add$.

Intuitively, a DMS operates as follows. At any instant, it maintains a database instance from $\mathsf{DB\text{-}Inst\text{-}Set}(\mathcal{R}, \Delta)$ and a history-set $H \subseteq \Delta$ of elements encountered along its execution. It starts with the initial database instance I_0, and the empty history-set ($H = \emptyset$). At an instant, the DMS can update the current database instance and the history-set by applying an action. An action is applied in three steps. In the first step the current database is queried using Q to retrieve some elements of interest from its active domain. In the second step, some tuples involving the retrieved elements are removed from the current database, as dictated by the variable-database instance Del . Finally, new tuples may be added to the relations of the current database instance, as dictated by Add . The newly inserted tuples may contain fresh values that were not present in the history-set, and that are injected through the fresh-input variables. We give the formal execution semantics below.

Execution semantics. The execution semantics of a DMS $\mathcal{S} = \langle I_0, \text{ACTS} \rangle$ over $\mathcal{R}$ and Δ is defined in terms of a (possibly infinite) *configuration graph* $\mathcal{C}_{\mathcal{S}}$, which has the form of a relational transition system [27, 6] equipped with additional information about the data values encountered so far. Each configuration is a pair $\langle I, H \rangle$, where $I \in \mathsf{DB\text{-}Inst\text{-}Set}(\mathcal{R}, \Delta)$ is a database instance over $\mathcal{R}$ and Δ, and $H \subseteq \Delta$ is a *history-set*, i.e., the set of values encountered in the history of the current execution of the system.

Let $\langle I, H \rangle$ be a configuration and $\alpha = \langle \vec{u}, \vec{v}, Q, Del, Add \rangle$ be an action. Consider a substitution σ from $\vec{u} \uplus \vec{v}$ to Δ. We say that σ is an *instantiating substitution* for α at $\langle I, H \rangle$ if it satisfies the following:

- for every variable $u_i \in \vec{u}$, $\sigma(u_i) \in \text{ADOM}(I)$ (action parameters are substituted with values from the current active domain);
- for every variable $v_i \in \vec{v}$, $\sigma(v_i) \notin H$ (fresh-input variables are substituted with history-fresh values);
- $\sigma|_{\vec{v}}$ is injective (fresh-input variables are assigned to pairwise distinct values);
- $I, \sigma|_{\vec{u}} \models Q$ (the action guard is satisfied).

For a pair of configurations $\langle I, H \rangle$ and $\langle I', H' \rangle$, an action $\alpha = \langle \vec{u}, \vec{v}, Q, Del, Add \rangle \in \text{ACTS}$, and a substitution σ from $\vec{u} \uplus \vec{v}$ to Δ, we have an edge $\langle I, H \rangle \xrightarrow{\alpha:\sigma} \langle I', H' \rangle$ in $\mathcal{C}_{\mathcal{S}}$, if the following conditions hold:

- σ is an instantiating substitution for α at $\langle I, H \rangle$;
- $I' = (I - \mathsf{Substitute}(Del, \sigma)) + \mathsf{Substitute}(Add, \sigma)$;
- $H' = H \cup \{\sigma(v_i) \mid v_i \in \vec{v}\}$.

An *extended run* $\hat{\rho}$ of $\mathcal{S}$ is an infinite sequence

$$\langle I_0, H_0 \rangle \xrightarrow{\alpha_0:\sigma_0} \langle I_1, H_1 \rangle \xrightarrow{\alpha_1:\sigma_1} \langle I_2, H_2 \rangle \xrightarrow{\alpha_2:\sigma_2} \langle I_3, H_3 \rangle \ldots$$

where I_0 is the initial database instance of $\mathcal{S}$, and $H_0 = \emptyset$. Note that, by definition, $H_i = \cup_{0 \leq k \leq i} \text{ADOM}(I_k)$. The *run* ρ generated by the extended run $\hat{\rho}$ is the sequence $I_0, I_1, I_2 \ldots$ of database instances appearing along $\hat{\rho}$. The *set of all runs* of a DMS $\mathcal{S}$ is denoted by $\mathsf{Runs}(\mathcal{S})$.

EXAMPLE 3.1. Consider a schema $\mathcal{R} = \{p/0, R/1, Q/1\}$, and a domain $\Delta = \{e_1, e_2, \ldots\}$. Consider a DMS over $\mathcal{R}$ and Δ, $\mathcal{S} = \langle I_0 = \{p\}, \text{ACTS} = \{\alpha, \beta, \gamma, \delta\} \rangle$ where

$$\begin{aligned}
\alpha &= \langle \emptyset, \{v_1, v_2, v_3\}, \mathsf{true}, \emptyset, \{R(v_1), R(v_2), Q(v_3), p\} \rangle \\
\beta &= \langle \{u\}, \{v_1, v_2\}, p \wedge R(u), \{p, R(u)\}, \{Q(v_1), Q(v_2)\} \rangle \\
\gamma &= \langle \{u\}, \emptyset, p \wedge \neg Q(u), \{p, R(u)\}, \emptyset \rangle \\
\delta &= \langle \{u_1, u_2\}, \emptyset, \neg p \wedge Q(u_1) \wedge (R(u_2) \vee Q(u_2)), \\
&\quad \{Q(u_1), R(u_2)\}, \emptyset \rangle
\end{aligned}$$

A run of the above system is depicted in Figure 1. Notice that once an element is deleted from the current database instance, it is never re-introduced, due to the history-fresh policy. ■

DMSs are very expressive. The following example, following the artifact-centric paradigm [24, 12, 17], gives a glimpse about their modeling power.

$$\{p\} \xrightarrow{\alpha:\epsilon} \left\{ \begin{array}{c} p \\ R: e_1, e_2 \\ Q: e_3 \end{array} \right\} \xrightarrow{\beta:\{u \mapsto e_2\}} \left\{ \begin{array}{c} R: e_1 \\ Q: e_3, e_4, e_5 \end{array} \right\} \xrightarrow{\alpha:\epsilon} \left\{ \begin{array}{c} p \\ R: e_1, e_6, e_7 \\ Q: e_3, e_4, e_5, e_8 \end{array} \right\} \xrightarrow{\gamma:\{u \mapsto e_7\}} \left\{ \begin{array}{c} R: e_1, e_6 \\ Q: e_3, e_4, e_5, e_8 \end{array} \right\}$$

$$\xrightarrow{\delta:\left\{ \begin{array}{c} u_1 \mapsto e_8 \\ u_2 \mapsto e_6 \end{array} \right\}} \left\{ \begin{array}{c} R: e_1 \\ Q: e_3, e_4, e_5 \end{array} \right\} \xrightarrow{\delta:\left\{ \begin{array}{c} u_1 \mapsto e_4 \\ u_2 \mapsto e_5 \end{array} \right\}} \left\{ \begin{array}{c} R: e_1 \\ Q: e_3, e_5 \end{array} \right\} \xrightarrow{\delta:\left\{ \begin{array}{c} u_1 \mapsto e_3 \\ u_2 \mapsto e_3\} \end{array} \right\}} \left\{ \begin{array}{c} R: e_1 \\ Q: e_5 \end{array} \right\} \xrightarrow{\alpha:\epsilon} \left\{ \begin{array}{c} p \\ R: e_1, e_9, e_{10} \\ Q: e_5, e_{11} \end{array} \right\} \dots$$

Figure 1: A run of Example 3.1. Recall that the schema is $\{p/0, R/1, Q/1\}$. For ease of readability, we omit the tuple notation $\langle e \rangle$ and simply write e.

EXAMPLE 3.2. Example in the full version of the paper [4] provides the full formalization of a DMS dealing with an agency that advertises restaurant offers and manages the corresponding bookings. Specifically, the process supports B2C interactions where agents select and publish restaurant offers, while customers issue booking requests. The process is centred around the two key business artifacts of *offer* and *booking*. Intuitively, each agent can publish a dinner offer related to some restaurant; if another, more interesting offer is received by the agent, she puts the previous one on hold, so that it will be picked up again later on by the same or another agent (when it will be among the most interesting ones). Each offer can result in a corresponding booking by a customer, or removed by the agent if nobody is interested in it. Offers are customizable, hence each booking goes through a preliminary phase in which the customer indicates who she wants to bring with her to the dinner, then the agent proposes a customized prize for the offer, and finally the customer decides whether to accept it or not. This example is unbounded in many dimensions. On the one hand, unboundedly many offers can be advertised over time. On the other hand, unboundedly many bookings for the same offer can be created (and then canceled), and each such booking could lead to introduce unboundedly many hosts during the drafting stage of the booking. ■

We show in the following that several restrictions of the DMS model can be relaxed without affecting its expressive power, nor compromising our technical results. Such relaxations are essential towards capturing related models in the literature [5, 8, 6], as well as concrete specification languages like IBM GSM [26].

Adding constants to a DMS. We can extend DMS and MSO-FO to take into account a finite subset of distinguished *constant values* $\Delta_0 \subseteq \Delta$ that can be used to specify the content of the initial database instance I_0, and that may be explicitly mentioned in the definition of actions. Given a DMS equipped with constant values Δ_0, we show in [4] how to construct a constant-free DMS over the data domain $\Delta' = \Delta \setminus \Delta_0$, so that the configuration graphs of the two DMSs are isomorphic. The size of the constant-free DMS schema is exponential in the maximum arity of the relations.

Allowing Arbitrary Input Values. The semantics of a DMS requires the input values introduced via fresh variables to not have occurred in the history of the run of the DMS. We prove in Appendix D.2 that this restriction can be lifted, allowing for the input variables to be mapped to any possible value from the data domain.

Non-distinct input values. The semantics of the DMS requires that the fresh variables are injectively mapped to distinct values. We show in Appendix D.1 that this constraint is not restrictive.

Retrieving all answers of a query for bulk action in one step. We have used a *retrieve-one-answer-per-step* semantics rather than a *retrieve-all-answers-per-step* semantics, which would support the modeling of bulk operations over the database, in the style of [6].

Intuitively, in a DMS a bulk operation consists in an action that is applied *for all* the answers of its guard. Such a bulk operation can be simulated by the iterative, non-interruptible application of different standard actions, using special accessory relation to control their execution. In summary, this is done in three phases. In the first phase, the external parameters of the bulk operation are inserted into a dedicated *input relation*, so as to maintain them fixed throughout the other two phases. At the same time, a lock proposition is set, guaranteeing that no other action will interrupt the execution of the next two phases. In the second phase, an "answer accumulation" action is repeatedly executed, incrementally filling an accessory *answer relation* with the answers obtained from the guard of the bulk operation. This is needed because such answers must be computed *before* applying the bulk update. The second phase terminates when all such answers have been transferred into the accessory relation. In the third phase, the actual bulk update is applied in two passes, by iteratively considering each tuple in the answer relation, first applying all deletions, and then all additions. When the third phase terminates, the lock is unset, enabling the possibility of applying other actions. Full details of this construction are given in Appendix D.3.

4. MSO LOGIC FOR DMS: MSO-FO

We propose a powerful logical formalism to reason about the linear runs of a DMS. The formalism, called MSO-FO, combines full monadic second-order logic to reason about the linear-time properties of runs, with atomic formulae consisting of $\mathsf{FOL}(\mathcal{R})$ queries, which are used to reason about the content of the encountered database instances.

We use $\mathsf{Vars}_{\mathsf{FO}} = \{x, y, x_1, \dots\}$ to denote first-order position variables, $\mathsf{Vars}_{\mathsf{SO}} = \{X, X_1, \dots\}$ to denote second-order position variables and $\mathsf{Vars}_{\mathsf{data}} = \{u, v, u_1, \dots\}$ to denote first-order data variables. We let $\mathsf{Vars} = \mathsf{Vars}_{\mathsf{FO}} \uplus \mathsf{Vars}_{\mathsf{SO}} \uplus \mathsf{Vars}_{\mathsf{data}}$.

Syntax. Formulae ϕ of MSO-FO over schema $\mathcal{R}$ are given by the following syntax:

$$\phi ::= Q@x \mid x<y \mid x \in X \mid \neg\phi \mid \phi \wedge \phi \mid \exists x.\phi \mid \exists X.\phi \mid \exists^g u.\phi$$

where x, y are first-order position variables, X is a second-order position variable, u is a first-order data variable, and Q is a $\mathsf{FOL}(\mathcal{R})$ query. We write $\forall^g u.\phi$ to denote $\neg\exists^g u.\neg\phi$. Further we make use of standard abbreviations: $\forall x.\phi \equiv \neg\exists x.\neg\phi$, $\forall X.\phi \equiv \neg\exists X.\neg\phi$, etc.

The set of free variables of a formula ϕ is denoted $\mathsf{Free\text{-}Vars}(\phi)$. For a set $V \subseteq \mathsf{Vars}$, a substitution σ of V

is a mapping that maps every first-order position variable to a natural number (i.e., $\sigma|_{\mathsf{Vars_{FO}}} : \mathsf{Vars_{FO}} \cap V \to \mathbb{N}$), every second-order position variable to a subset of natural numbers (i.e., $\sigma|_{\mathsf{Vars_{SO}}} : \mathsf{Vars_{SO}} \cap V \to 2^{\mathbb{N}}$) and every data variable to an element from the domain Δ (i.e., $\sigma|_{\mathsf{Vars_{data}}} : \mathsf{Vars_{data}} \cap V \to \Delta$).

Semantics. A run ρ is an infinite sequence of database instances over $\mathcal{R}$ and Δ: $\rho = I_0, I_1, I_2, I_3 \ldots$

The *global active domain* of the run ρ, denoted $\textsc{Gadom}(\rho)$ is the union of all active domains along the run. $\textsc{Gadom}(\rho) = \bigcup_{i \geq 0} \textsc{adom}(I_i)$. An MSO-FO formula ϕ is evaluated over an infinite run $\rho = I_0, I_1, I_2, I_3 \ldots$ under a substitution σ of $\mathsf{Free\text{-}Vars}(\phi)$. If the formula holds in the run ρ under the substitution σ, we write $\rho, \sigma \models \phi$. The semantics is as expected for the standard cases (see Appendix B). For the particular cases, we have:

$\rho, \sigma \models Q@x$ if $I_i, \sigma' \models Q$, $i = \sigma(x)$ and $\sigma' = \sigma|_{\mathsf{Free\text{-}Vars}(Q)}$

$\rho, \sigma \models \exists^g u.\phi$ if there exists $e \in \textsc{Gadom}(\rho)$, such that $\rho, \sigma' \models \phi$, where $\textsc{Gadom}(\rho) = \bigcup_{i \geq 0} \textsc{adom}(I_i)$ and $\sigma'(u) = e$, and $\sigma'(\xi) = \sigma(\xi)$ if $\xi \neq u$.

When the formula ϕ is a sentence (i.e, $\mathsf{Free\text{-}Vars}(\phi) = \emptyset$), it can be interpreted on a run ρ under the empty substitution, denoted $\rho \models \phi$.

Example 4.1. Consider the set $\mathsf{Runs}(\mathcal{S})$ of all runs of a DMS $\mathcal{S} = \langle I_0, \textsc{acts} \rangle$. This set is MSO-FO definable by a formula $\varphi_{\mathcal{S}}^{\mathsf{Runs}}$. The formula uses set variable X_α to denote the set of positions where an α action was taken. It can be easily expressed in MSO-FO that the sets $(X_\alpha)_{\alpha \in \textsc{acts}}$ form a partition of $\mathbb{N}$. Further, we need to express the local consistency. For this, we need to say the following: $\forall x \bigwedge_{\alpha \in \textsc{acts}} (x \in X_\alpha \Rightarrow \varphi_\alpha(x))$ where $\varphi_\alpha(x)$ expresses the local consistency by action α. If $\alpha = \langle \vec{u}, \vec{v}, Q, Del, Add \rangle$, then $\varphi_\alpha(x)$ can be expressed as follows, where variables $\xi_i \in \vec{u} \uplus \vec{v}$,

$$\exists^g \vec{u}, \vec{v}. \bigwedge_{u \in \vec{u}} \mathsf{Active}(u)@x \wedge \bigwedge_{v \in \vec{v}} (\forall y.\, y \leq x \Rightarrow \neg \mathsf{Active}(v)@y) \wedge Q@x$$

$$\wedge \exists y.\mathsf{succ}(x, y) \wedge \bigwedge_{R/a \in \mathcal{R}} \begin{pmatrix} \wedge_{\langle \xi_1 \ldots \xi_a \rangle \in R^{Add}} R(\xi_1 \ldots \xi_a)@(y) \wedge \\ \wedge_{\langle \xi_1 \ldots \xi_a \rangle \in R^{Del} \setminus R^{Add}} \neg R(\xi_1 \ldots \xi_a)@(y) \end{pmatrix}$$

In the above, $\mathsf{succ}(x, y)$ states that y is the successor position of x, which can be easily expressed in MSO. ∎

Example 4.2. Many standard verification problems on DMS can be expressed in MSO-FO since we can characterise the runs of a DMS (cf. Example 4.1). Of particular interest is the simplest verification problem: propositional reachability. Given a DMS s over $\mathcal{R}$ and Δ and a proposition $p/0 \in \mathcal{R}$, is it possible that an execution of s ever reaches a database instance I with $p^I = \{p\}$? This can be reduced to the satisfiability checking of $\exists \rho. \rho \models (\varphi_{\mathcal{S}}^{\mathsf{Runs}} \wedge \exists x.p@x)$. ∎

Model checking. We now present the model checking problem of a DMS against MSO(DMS):

Problem:	MSO/DMS-MC
Input:	A DMS $\mathcal{S}$, a MSO-FO formula ϕ.
Question:	Does $\rho \models \phi$, for every $\rho \in \mathsf{Runs}(\mathcal{S})$?

The next example shows how MSO/DMS-MC can be phrased in such a way that database constraints are incorporated in the analysis of the DMS of interest.

Example 4.3. The presence of database constraints in the dynamic system under study is a key feature, which has been extensively studied in the literature [16, 15, 13, 9, 6]. In our setting, arbitrary FO constraints can be seamlessly added, adopting the semantics, as in [6], that the application of an action is blocked whenever the resulting database instance violates one of the constraints. Given a DMS $\mathcal{S}$, an MSO-FO formula ϕ and a constraint specification on the database instances as a FOL($\mathcal{R}$) sentence ϕ_c, we can reduce the model checking problem of the constrained DMS against ϕ to an unconstrained model checking problem over $\mathcal{S}$, using as formula: $(\forall x.\phi_c@x) \Rightarrow \phi$. ∎

The above model checking problem is undecidable, even by considering just simple propositional reachability properties. This is the case with related models of dynamic database-driven systems [5, 8, 6]. A proof of undecidability via a reduction from reachability over 2-counter machines can be found in [4] . Notably, undecidability for propositional reachability holds as soon as the DMS has either: *(i)* a binary predicate in $\mathcal{R}$, with all guards expressed as union of conjunctive queries (UCQ), *(ii)* two unary predicates in $\mathcal{R}$, and FOL guards.

Theorem 4.1. *MSO/DMS-MC is undecidable.*

Towards obtaining decidability of model checking for variants of FO temporal logics, the approaches in the literature either restrict the capabilities of the model, the database schema, the verification logic, or a combination thereof [10]. Here we take a different approach — that of under-approximation.

5. RECENCY-BOUNDEDNESS

As mentioned in the previous section, even propositional reachability is undecidable unless the relational schema of the database is severely restricted. This motivates the study of under-approximate analysis of the DMS. We propose an under-approximation that is parametrised (by an integer **b**) and is exhaustive. That is, more behaviours are captured (in other words, more runs can be analysed) with higher values of **b**, and in the limit it captures all finite behaviours of the DMS. The under-approximate analysis works over arbitrary (unrestricted) schema. Our under approximation is called recency boundedness.

b-restricted actions. In a recency bounded DMS the actions are restricted to act only on the **b** most recent elements in the database. The guards can query the entire database, but the data values that can be retrieved as the result of a query will be only from the **b** recent elements of the database instance. Thus the deletions cannot involve less recent elements. The newly added data values cannot participate in a relation with less recent elements either. This restriction still allows the transitions to reason about all elements in the current database instance. For example, the properties that all elements must satisfy (regardless of their recency), may be stated as a clause in the guard of an action. However, all elements cannot be *acted* on i.e. they cannot be deleted, nor new facts involving them can be added.

The most recent **b** elements are taken relatively to the current database instance. Thus it is possible that an old element which is not in the **b**-recency window eventually enters the **b**-recency window. This happens if more recent elements were deleted from the current database instance, exposing the concerned element.

Sequence numbers. In order to reason about recency, we assume that every element e gets a sequence number $\mathtt{seq\_no}(e)$ when it is added to the database. An element which is added later/more recently gets a higher sequence number. If there are multiple fresh elements that are added in one action, these elements are given different and unique sequence numbers in the order in which they appear. Thus, these fresh elements are ordered amongst themselves, and their sequence number is higher than any other sequence number present in the current active domain. Since we have a countably infinite supply of sequence numbers, we do not reuse sequence numbers. That means, even if an element is deleted from the database, its sequence number will not be used by a later element. The sequence numbers may be also thought of as a way of (abstractly) time-stamping elements as they enter the active domain.

$\mathsf{Recent}_\mathbf{b}$. Given a database instance I and a sequence-numbering $\texttt{seq\_no} : \text{ADOM}(I) \to \mathbb{N}$, we define the **b**-*recent active domain* of I wrt. $\texttt{seq\_no}$, denoted $\mathsf{Recent}_\mathbf{b}(I, \texttt{seq\_no})$, to be the *maximal* set $D \subseteq \text{ADOM}(I)$ with $|D| \leq \mathbf{b}$, such that for every (recent) element $e' \in D$ and every (non-recent) element $e \in \text{ADOM}(I) \setminus D$, we have $\texttt{seq\_no}(e) < \texttt{seq\_no}(e')$. That is, the set $\mathsf{Recent}_\mathbf{b}(I, \texttt{seq\_no})$ contains the **b** most-recent elements from $\text{ADOM}(I)$ according to the sequence numbering $\texttt{seq\_no}$. Notice that, thanks to maximality, $|\mathsf{Recent}_\mathbf{b}(I, \texttt{seq\_no})| < \mathbf{b}$ if, only if $|\text{ADOM}(I)| < \mathbf{b}$.

We are now ready to formally define the **b**-bounded execution semantics for DMSs.

The b-bounded configuration graph $\mathcal{C}_\mathcal{S}^\mathbf{b}$ of a DMS $\mathcal{S}$ is given as follows. A configuration is a tuple $\langle I, H, \texttt{seq\_no}\rangle$ where $\texttt{seq\_no} : H \to \mathbb{N}$ is an injective function assigning sequence numbers to the data values in the history-set. For an action $\alpha = \langle \vec{u}, \vec{v}, Q, Del, Add\rangle \in \text{ACTS}$ and a substitution σ from $\vec{u} \uplus \vec{v}$ to Δ, we write $\langle I, H, \texttt{seq\_no}\rangle \xrightarrow{\alpha:\sigma}_\mathbf{b} \langle I', H', \texttt{seq\_no}'\rangle$ if

1. $\langle I, H\rangle \xrightarrow{\alpha:\sigma} \langle I', H'\rangle$ in $\mathcal{C}_\mathcal{S}$.
2. $\sigma(u) \in \mathsf{Recent}_\mathbf{b}(I, \texttt{seq\_no})$ for each $u \in \vec{u}$ (That is, the values retrieved by the query must be among the b-most recent elements of the current database instance I).
3. $\texttt{seq\_no}'$ is an injective map from H' to $\mathbb{N}$. It agrees with $\texttt{seq\_no}$ on all data values in H (note that $H \subseteq H'$). For each fresh-input variable $v \in \vec{v}$, $\texttt{seq\_no}'(\sigma(v)) > \texttt{seq\_no}(e)$ for all $e \in H$ (i.e., the fresh elements that are added to the database get higher sequence numbers than the elements in H since they are more recent).
4. If $\vec{v} = \langle v_1, \ldots, v_\eta\rangle$ then for every $1 \leq i < j \leq \eta$, we have $\texttt{seq\_no}'(v_i) < \texttt{seq\_no}'(v_j)$. (The sequence number of the fresh elements are ordered according to their appearance in $\vec{v}$.)

Notice that Item 2 is a condition on the substitutions, rather than on transitions. Thus $\mathcal{C}_\mathcal{S}^\mathbf{b}$ has fewer edges than $\mathcal{C}_\mathcal{S}$. In Item 4 what is important is that each fresh element gets a pairwise different sequence number which is higher than that of the entire history. But then, in our decidability proof, we need to guess the order between fresh elements at every step. Fixing an order beforehand simplifies the encoding later on.

A **b**-*bounded extended run* $\hat{\rho}$ of $\mathcal{S}$ is an infinite sequence $\langle I_0, H_0, \texttt{seq\_no}_0\rangle \xrightarrow{\alpha_0:\sigma_0}_\mathbf{b} \langle I_1, H_1, \texttt{seq\_no}_1\rangle \xrightarrow{\alpha_1:\sigma_1}_\mathbf{b} \langle I_2, H_2, \texttt{seq\_no}_2\rangle \xrightarrow{\alpha_2:\sigma_2}_\mathbf{b} \langle I_3, H_3, \texttt{seq\_no}_3\rangle \ldots$ where I_0 is the initial database instance of $\mathcal{S}$, $H_0 = \emptyset$ and $\texttt{seq\_no}_0$ is the empty (trivial) sequence-numbering. The **b**-*bounded run* ρ generated by the **b**-bounded extended run $\hat{\rho}$ is the sequence $I_0, I_1, I_2 \ldots$ of database instances appearing along $\hat{\rho}$. The *set of all* **b**-*bounded runs* of a DMS $\mathcal{S}$ is denoted $\mathsf{Runs}_\mathbf{b}(\mathcal{S})$.

EXAMPLE 5.1. The run depicted in Figure 1 is a 2-recency-bounded run. ■

EXAMPLE 5.2. Consider the restaurant booking agency example sketched in Section 3 and detailed in [4] . Since the agency has a fixed number of agents/customers, this number indirectly witnesses also how many booking offers can be simultaneously managed by the company. Suppose now that the company works with the following strategy: an agent temporarily freezes the management of an offer because a more interesting (in terms of potential revenue and/or expiration time) offer is received. Furthermore, let us assume that once a booking is closed, it is stored in the database for historical/audit reasons, but never modified in the future courses of execution.

The DMS capturing this example can consequently query the entire (unbounded) logged history of bookings so as, e.g., to check whether a customer finalized at least a given number of bookings in the past. This query can be used to characterize when a customer is gold and, in turn, to tune the actual DMS behavior depending on this. Furthermore, the DMS can manipulate unboundedly many offers over time, following the "last-in first-out" strategy that an offer is picked up or resumed only if the management of all higher-priority offers has been completed, and no higher-priority offer is received.

If we now put a bound on the maximum number of hosts that can be added by a customer to a booking, we can derive a number k_{mb} that indicates how many values need to be simultaneously manipulated in the worst case so as to handle the current, highest-priority offers. This, in turn, tells us that recency-bounded model checking of this unbounded DMS coincides with exact model checking when the bound is $\geq k_{mb}$. ■

Recency-bounded model checking. The problem is parametrised by a bound on recency.

PROBLEM:	RECENCY-BOUNDED-MSO/DMS-MC
INPUT:	A DMS $\mathcal{S}$, a MSO-FO formula ϕ, a natural number **b**,
QUESTION:	Does $\rho \models \phi$, for every $\rho \in \mathsf{Runs}_\mathbf{b}(\mathcal{S})$?

THEOREM 5.1. RECENCY-BOUNDED-MSO/DMS-MC *is decidable.*

The proof of Theorem 5.1 is given in the next section.

6. DECIDABILITY OF RECENCY-BOUNDED MODEL CHECKING

We prove the decidability of recency bounded model checking problem by means of a symbolic encoding of runs. The symbolic encoding takes the form of finitely labelled nested words [3]. We show that the set of all valid encodings of recency bounded runs is expressible in monadic second-order logic over nested words. We also show that the MSO-FO specification over runs can be translated syntactically to monadic second-order logic over nested words. Thus we reduce the **b**-recency-bounded model checking problem to satisfiability problem of monadic second-order logic over nested words, which is decidable [3].

The encoding of **b**-bounded runs using nested words and expressing their validity in MSO over nested words is given in Section 6.3 and Section 6.4 respectively. The translation of MSO-FO specifications into MSO over nested word encodings is given in Section 6.5. First we will explain the symbolic abstraction used for the encoding in Section 6.1 and recall nested words in Section 6.2.

6.1 Symbolic abstraction

Consider a **b**-bounded run: $\rho = I_0, I_1, I_2, I_3, \ldots$. Each database instance I_i that appears on this run is potentially unbounded. For the sake of decidability we want our symbolic representation to be a word over finite alphabet.

Towards this we will first consider a **b**-bounded extended run $\hat{\rho} = \langle I_0, H_0, \texttt{seq\_no}_0 \rangle \xrightarrow{\alpha_0:\sigma_0}_{\mathbf{b}} \langle I_1, H_1, \texttt{seq\_no}_1 \rangle \xrightarrow{\alpha_1:\sigma_1}_{\mathbf{b}} \langle I_2, H_2, \texttt{seq\_no}_2 \rangle \ldots$ generating ρ, and the sequence of $\langle$action : substitution$\rangle$ pairs appearing along $\hat{\rho}$.

A sequence $\mathsf{Gen} = \langle \alpha_0 : \sigma_0 \rangle \langle \alpha_1 : \sigma_1 \rangle \langle \alpha_2 : \sigma_2 \rangle \ldots$ of $\langle$action : substitution$\rangle$ pairs generates a unique $\hat{\rho}$ (if it exists) by following the semantics. However Gen is also not finitely labelled. The substitutions σ_i maps variables to domain Δ, leaving the set of all such substitutions an infinite set.

Hence we go for the recency-indexing abstraction of a substitution. The recency-indexing abstraction, instead of mapping a variable to an element e, maps it to its relative recency in the current database. The recency-indexing abstraction s of a substitution σ is determined by the current sequence-numbering. We explain this below.

Consider a **b**-bounded extended run $\hat{\rho} =$

$$\left(\langle I_j, H_j, \texttt{seq\_no}_j \rangle \xrightarrow{\alpha_j:\sigma_j}_{\mathbf{b}} \langle I_{j+1}, H_{j+1}, \texttt{seq\_no}_{j+1} \rangle \right)_{j \geq 0}$$

For each substitution $\sigma_j : \vec{u}_j \uplus \vec{v}_j \to \Delta$ appearing in $\hat{\rho}$, where $\vec{u}_j = \alpha_j{\cdot}\mathsf{free}$ and $\vec{v}_j = \alpha_j{\cdot}\mathsf{new}$, we have $\sigma_j(u) \in \mathsf{Recent}_{\mathbf{b}}(I_j, \texttt{seq\_no}_j)$ for all $u \in \vec{u_j}$ thanks to the **b**-boundedness.

The recency-indexing abstraction of σ_j at I_j wrt. the sequence numbering $\texttt{seq\_no}_j$ is a mapping $s_j : \vec{u}_j \uplus \vec{v}_j \to \{-n, -n+1, \ldots, 0, 1, \ldots \mathbf{b}-1\}$ where $n = |\vec{v_j}|$ such that

r1. if $\vec{v}_j = \langle v_1, \ldots, v_n \rangle$ then $s_j(v_i) = -i$

r2. for $u \in \vec{u}_j$, $s_j(u) \in \{0, 1, \ldots, \mathbf{b}-1\}$

r3. for $u \in \vec{u}_j$, $s_j(u)$ represents the recency of $\sigma_j(u)$ at I wrt. the sequence-numbering $\texttt{seq\_no}_j$. More precisely, $s_j(u) = i$ if $i = |\{e \in \textsc{adom}(I_j) \mid \texttt{seq\_no}_j(e) > \texttt{seq\_no}_j(\sigma_j(u))\}|$. For example, if $\sigma_j(u)$ is the most-recent element, then $s_j(u) = 0$.

Notice that given a recency bound **b** and a DMS $\mathcal{S} = \langle I_0, \textsc{acts} \rangle$, the set of all symbolic substitutions s is finite. Let us denote this set by $\mathsf{SymSubs}(\mathcal{S}, \mathbf{b})$. Let $\mathsf{SymSubs}(\alpha, \mathbf{b}) = \{s : \vec{u} \uplus \vec{v} \to \{-n, -n+1, \ldots, 0, 1, \ldots, \mathbf{b}-1\} \mid \vec{u} = \alpha{\cdot}\mathsf{free}, \vec{v} = \alpha{\cdot}\mathsf{new}, n = |\vec{v}|$ and s satisfies conditions r1 and r2 above$\}$. We have $\mathsf{SymSubs}(\mathcal{S}, \mathbf{b}) = \uplus_{\alpha \in \textsc{acts}} \mathsf{SymSubs}(\alpha, \mathbf{b})$. Let the symbolic alphabet $\mathsf{symAlph}_{\mathcal{S},\mathbf{b}}$ be the finite set $\{\langle \alpha, s \rangle \mid \alpha \in \textsc{acts}$ and $s \in \mathsf{SymSubs}(\alpha, \mathbf{b})\}$.

To every **b**-bounded extended run $\hat{\rho}$, we can identify a corresponding word $w_{\hat{\rho}} \in (\mathsf{symAlph}_{\mathcal{S},\mathbf{b}})^{\omega}$ by taking the recency-indexing abstraction of the substitutions. Let's denote this correspondence by a mapping Abstr from **b**-bounded extended runs to $(\mathsf{symAlph}_{\mathcal{S},\mathbf{b}})^{\omega}$. That is $\mathsf{Abstr}(\hat{\rho}) = w_{\hat{\rho}}$. We extend in the natural way the definition of the abstraction function to finite prefixes of **b**-bounded extended runs.

The mapping Abstr is not injective. However, if two **b**-bounded extended runs $\hat{\rho}$ and $\hat{\rho}'$ have the same abstract generating sequence $w = \mathsf{Abstr}(\hat{\rho}) = \mathsf{Abstr}(\hat{\rho}')$, then $\hat{\rho}$ and $\hat{\rho}'$ are equivalent modulo permutations of the data domain Δ (i.e. there exists a bijection $\lambda : \textsc{Gadom}(\hat{\rho}) \to \textsc{Gadom}(\hat{\rho}')$ such that λ is an isomorphism from I_i onto I'_i for every $i \geq 0$, see Appendix C for the detailed proof). This notion of invariance under renaming is very well known in computer science and is discussed in [23]. If we assume a total ordering on the domain Δ, then we can define a canonical $\hat{\rho}$ as the representative of all such equivalent ones. Let the data domain be $\{e_1, e_2, \ldots\}$ with the ordering $e_i < e_j$ if $i < j$.

A **b**-bounded extended run $\hat{\rho}$ is canonical if it satisfies the following invariants along the run:

- For every i, for every j, if $e_j \in H_i$ then $\texttt{seq\_no}_i(e_j) = j$.
- For every i, if $v_k \in \alpha_i{\cdot}\mathsf{new}$ is the kth fresh input variable, then $\sigma(v_k) = e_{n+k}$ where $n = |H_i|$.

The second invariant implies the following:

- For every i, H_i is of the form $\{e_1, \ldots, e_n\}$ for some $n \in \mathbb{N}$. That is, there are no gaps in the history.

The mapping Abstr is not surjective either. We will define a partial concretizing function Concr from infinite words $w \in (\mathsf{symAlph}_{\mathcal{S},\mathbf{b}})^{\omega}$ to **b**-bounded extended runs such that if w is a valid abstraction then $\mathsf{Concr}(w)$ is the canonical extended run $\hat{\rho}$ with $\mathsf{Abstr}(\hat{\rho}) = w$. In order to do so, let us first denote the k-long prefix of w (respectively $\hat{\rho}$) by w_k (respectively $\hat{\rho}_k$). Similarly to the abstraction function, we also extend the concretisation function to finite prefixes of infinite words from $(\mathsf{symAlph}_{\mathcal{S},\mathbf{b}})^{\omega}$. It is easy to see that w is a valid abstract run if and only if, for every $k \geq 0$, w_k is the prefix of a valid abstract run. In that case, $\hat{\rho} = \mathsf{Concr}(w)$ amounts to the limit of $\mathsf{Concr}(w_k) = \hat{\rho}_k$ when $k \to +\infty$. Also, for $k \geq 0$, if w_k is the prefix of a valid run, then $\hat{\rho}_k = \mathsf{Concr}(w_k)$ is of the form $\left(\langle I_j, H_j, \texttt{seq\_no}_j \rangle \xrightarrow{\alpha_j:\sigma_j}_{\mathbf{b}} \langle I_{j+1}, H_{j+1}, \texttt{seq\_no}_{j+1} \rangle \right)_{0 \leq j < k}$. We define in what follows $\mathsf{Concr}(w_k)$ by induction on its length k.

For the empty word $w_0 = \epsilon \in (\mathsf{symAlph}_{\mathcal{S},\mathbf{b}})^{*}$ we define $\mathsf{Concr}(w_0) = \langle I_0, H_0, \texttt{seq\_no}_0 \rangle$ where $H_0 = \emptyset$ and $\texttt{seq\_no}_0 = \epsilon$, the empty mapping. Suppose $w_{k+1} = w_k \langle \alpha_k, s \rangle$ where $\alpha_k = \langle \vec{u}, \vec{v}, Q, Del, Add \rangle$. $\mathsf{Concr}(w_{k+1})$ is not defined if $\mathsf{Concr}(w_k)$ is not defined. Suppose $\mathsf{Concr}(w_k)$ is defined and is of the form $\left(\langle I_j, H_j, \texttt{seq\_no}_j \rangle \xrightarrow{\alpha_j:\sigma_j}_{\mathbf{b}} \langle I_{j+1}, H_{j+1}, \texttt{seq\_no}_{j+1} \rangle \right)_{0 \leq j < k}$. $\mathsf{Concr}(w_{k+1})$ is defined if, and only if, the following condition holds:

Condition Cnd : There exists a substitution $\sigma : \vec{u} \to \textsc{adom}(I_k)$ such that

- $I_k, \sigma \models Q$ and
- s restricted to $\vec{u}$ is the recency-indexing abstraction of σ at I_k wrt. $\texttt{seq\_no}_k$.

Assuming condition Cnd holds, w_{k+1} is also the prefix of a valid abstract run and $\mathsf{Concr}(w_{k+1})$ is defined as follows. Let n be the size of H_k, i.e. $n = |H_k|$. We define the substitution $\sigma_k : \vec{u} \uplus \vec{v} \to \Delta$ as follows: $\sigma_k|_{\vec{u}} = \sigma$ and $\sigma_k(v_i) = e_{n+i}$ for every $i : 1 \leq i \leq |\vec{v}|$. Notice that 1) $\sigma_k(u) = \sigma(u) \in \textsc{adom}(I_k)$ for every $u \in \vec{u}$, 2) $\sigma_k(v) \notin H_k$ for every $v \in \vec{v}$, 3) $\sigma_k|_{\vec{v}}$ is injective, and 4) since $I_k, \sigma \models Q$, and $\sigma_k|_{\vec{u}} = \sigma$, we have that $I_k, \sigma_k|_{\vec{u}} \models Q$. Thus, σ_k is an instantiating substitution for α_k at $\langle I_k, H_k \rangle$. Moreover, if we define the set $H_{k+1} = H_k \cup \{e_{n+1}, \ldots, e_{n+|\vec{v}|}\}$ and the database instance $I_{k+1} = (I_k - \mathsf{Substitute}(Del, \sigma_k)) + \mathsf{Substitute}(Add, \sigma_k)$, then we have that $\langle I_k, H_k \rangle \xrightarrow{\alpha_k, \sigma_k} \langle I_{k+1}, H_{k+1} \rangle$.

Furthermore, since the restriction of s to $\vec{u}$ is the recency-indexing abstraction of σ at I_k wrt. $\texttt{seq\_no}_k$, we deduce that $\sigma_k(u) = \sigma(u) \in \mathsf{Recent}_{\mathbf{b}}(I_k, \texttt{seq\_no}_k)$. Thus, the transition $\langle I_k, H_k \rangle \xrightarrow{\alpha_k, \sigma_k} \langle I_{k+1}, H_{k+1} \rangle$ is also allowed by the **b**-recency semantics and, assuming that we define $\texttt{seq\_no}_{k+1}$ by $\texttt{seq\_no}_{k+1}|_{H_k} = \texttt{seq\_no}_k$ and by $\texttt{seq\_no}_{k+1}(e_{n+i}) = n+i$ for every $i : 1 \leq i \leq |\vec{v}|$, we have that $\langle I_k, H_k, \texttt{seq\_no}_k\rangle \xrightarrow{\alpha_k,\sigma_k}_{\mathbf{b}} \langle I_{k+1}, H_{k+1}, \texttt{seq\_no}_{k+1}\rangle$ and $\mathsf{Concr}(w_{k+1}) = \left(\langle I_j, H_j, \texttt{seq\_no}_j\rangle \xrightarrow{\alpha_j:\sigma_j}_{\mathbf{b}} \langle I_{j+1}, H_{j+1}, \texttt{seq\_no}_{j+1}\rangle\right)_{0\leq j<k+1}$.

Now, for an infinite word $w \in (\mathsf{symAlph}_{\mathcal{S},\mathbf{b}})^\omega$, $\mathsf{Concr}(w)$ is defined to be the limit of $\hat{\rho}_k = \mathsf{Concr}(w_k)$ for $k \geq 0$. If defined, $\mathsf{Concr}(w)$ is a canonical run. Further, $\mathsf{Abstr}(\mathsf{Concr}(w)) = w$. Furthermore, for every w such that $w = \mathsf{Abstr}(\hat{\rho})$ for $\mathbf{b}$-bounded run $\hat{\rho}$, $\mathsf{Concr}(w)$ is defined, and $\mathsf{Concr}(w)$ and $\hat{\rho}$ are equivalent modulo permutations of the data domain. In particular, if $\hat{\rho}$ is a $\mathbf{b}$-bounded canonical run, then $\hat{\rho} = \mathsf{Concr}(\mathsf{Abstr}(\hat{\rho}))$.

EXAMPLE 6.1. The abstract generation sequence corresponding to the run in Figure 1 is:
$\langle \alpha : \{v_1 \mapsto -1, v_2 \mapsto -2, v_3 \mapsto -3\}\rangle$ $\langle \beta : \{u \mapsto 1, v_1 \mapsto -1, v_2 \mapsto -2\}\rangle\langle \alpha : \{v_1 \mapsto -1, v_2 \mapsto -2, v_3 \mapsto -3\}\rangle$ $\langle \gamma : \{u \mapsto 1\}\rangle$ $\langle \delta : \{u_1 \mapsto 0, u_2 \mapsto 1\}\rangle$ $\langle \delta : \{u_1 \mapsto 1, u_2 \mapsto 0\}\rangle$ $\langle \delta : \{u_1 \mapsto 1, u_2 \mapsto 1\}\rangle$ $\langle \alpha : \{v_1 \mapsto -1, v_2 \mapsto -2, v_3 \mapsto -3\}\rangle \ldots$ ■

In order to check the consistency of an abstract generating sequence, we need to check that condition Cnd holds at every step of the sequence. To achieve this within a formalism having "decidable theories", we add more structure to the abstract generating sequence by embedding it into a nested word, which we recall in the next section.

6.2 Nested words

A *visible alphabet* Σ is a finite alphabet partitioned into push letters $\Sigma_\downarrow$, pop letters $\Sigma_\uparrow$ and internal letters Σ_{int}. That is, $\Sigma = \Sigma_\downarrow \uplus \Sigma_\uparrow \uplus \Sigma_{\text{int}}$. Given a word $w = a_1 a_2 \ldots$ over the visible alphabet Σ, we say i is a $\Sigma_\downarrow$ *position* if $a_i \in \Sigma_\downarrow$. Similarly we define $\Sigma_\uparrow$ positions and Σ_{int} positions.

A nested word is a pair $(w, \rhd)$ where w is a word over a Σ and $\rhd \subset \{1, \ldots, |w|\}^2$ is the *maximal* binary nesting relation relating $\Sigma_\downarrow$ positions to $\Sigma_\uparrow$ positions such that:

- if $i \rhd j$ then $i < j$. The nesting relation preserves the linear order.
- if $i \rhd j$ and $i' \rhd j'$ are two distinct pairs (either $i \neq i'$ or $j \neq j'$) then $|\{i, i', j, j'\}| = 4$. Two different nesting edges are vertex-disjoint.
- for every $i \rhd j$ and $i' \rhd j'$ we do not have $i < i' < j < j'$. The nesting edges must not cross.
- if $i \rhd j$ and $i < i' < j$ for some $\Sigma_\downarrow$ position i', then there exists j' such that $i' \rhd j'$. Similarly if $i \rhd j$ and $i < j' < j$ for some $\Sigma_\uparrow$ position j', then there exists i' such that $i' \rhd j'$.

EXAMPLE 6.2. A nested word over the visible alphabet given by $\Sigma_\downarrow = \{\downarrow_a, \downarrow_b\}$, $\Sigma_\uparrow = \{\uparrow_a, \uparrow_b\}$ and $\Sigma_{\text{int}} = \{\bullet\}$ is given below:

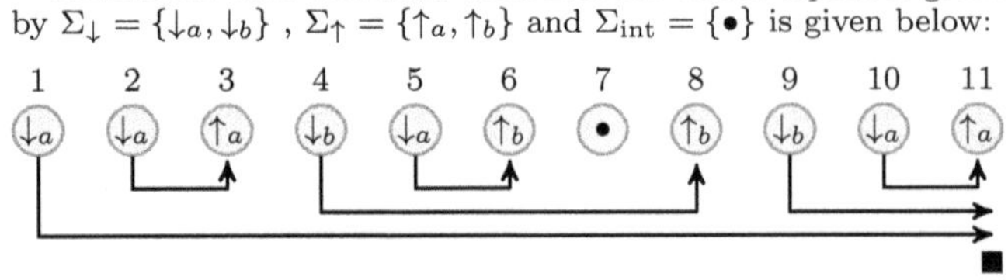

■

Note that, given a word w over a visible alphabet Σ, the nesting relation $\rhd$ is uniquely defined.

Monadic Second-Order Logic ($\texttt{MSO}_{\texttt{NW}}$) over nested words extends MSO over words with an additional binary predicate $\rhd$ that links a matching push-pop pair. This is in fact the same logic of [20] where the guessed second-order matching variable is built-in in the structure. We assume an unbounded supply of position variables $\{x, y, \ldots\}$ and set variables $\{X, Y, \ldots\}$. The syntax of $\texttt{MSO}_{\texttt{NW}}$ is given by:

$$\varphi := a(x) \mid x < y \mid x \rhd y \mid \neg\varphi \mid \varphi \vee \varphi \mid \exists x.\varphi \mid \exists X.\varphi$$

Here a ranges over the visible alphabet Σ. The position variables x, y range over positions of the nested word. The set variable X ranges over sets of positions of the nested word. The semantics is as expected.

EXAMPLE 6.3. Let x and y be two free first-order variables. Suppose we want to state that the first $\downarrow_a$ labelled position after x and the first $\uparrow_b$ labelled position after y are related by a nesting edge. This property can be stated by a formula with two free variables:

$$\begin{aligned}\varphi_{a,b}(x,y) \equiv\ & \exists x_1 \exists y_1 \downarrow_a(x_1) \wedge \uparrow_b(y_1) \wedge x < x_1 \wedge y < y_1 \wedge x_1 \rhd y_1 \\ & \wedge \forall z\, (x < z < x_1 \Rightarrow \neg\downarrow_a(z)) \wedge (y < z < y_1 \Rightarrow \neg\uparrow_b(z))\end{aligned}$$

On Example 6.2, all pairs of positions (i, j) with $2 \leq i \leq 4$ and $1 \leq j \leq 5$ satisfy the above formula. ■

FACT 1 ([3]). *Satisfiability of $\texttt{MSO}_{\texttt{NW}}$ is decidable.*

6.3 Encoding a run as a nested word

Let us fix a DMS $\mathcal{S} = \langle I_0, \text{ACTS}\rangle$, over a set of values Δ and a schema $\mathcal{R}$, and a recency bound $\mathbf{b}$ for the rest of this section. We will first provide the visible alphabet, and then describe the encoding.

Visible alphabet of the encoding. The visible alphabet $\Sigma = \Sigma_{\text{int}} \uplus \Sigma_\uparrow \uplus \Sigma_\downarrow$ where

- $\Sigma_{\text{int}} = \{\textcircled{\alpha : s} \mid \langle\alpha, s\rangle \in \mathsf{symAlph}_{\mathcal{S},\mathbf{b}}\} \cup \{\textcircled{I_0}\}$
- $\Sigma_\uparrow = \{\uparrow_0, \ldots, \uparrow_{\mathbf{b}-1}\}$
- $\Sigma_\downarrow = \{\downarrow_{-\eta}, \ldots, \downarrow_0, \ldots, \downarrow_{\mathbf{b}-1}\}$ where $\eta = \max_{\alpha\in\text{ACTS}} |\alpha{\cdot}\mathsf{new}|$

The internal letters represent the symbolic abstraction described in Section 6.1. Further, we provide a letter $\textcircled{I_0}$ to represent the initial database I_0.

The pop letters and push letters as well as the nesting relation will be used to trace the elements (or datavalues) in an encoding. We explain this more in detail when describing the encoding.

Encoding. As alluded to in Section 6.1, we need to enrich the abstract generating sequences. We go for a richer encoding where each step is followed by an encoding of the effect of the action on the database. The effect of an action involves a) adding some relational tuples to the current database instance; b) deleting some relational tuples from the current database instance. The above two items can induce 1) adding new elements to the current active domain. 2) deleting some elements from the current active domain;

The effects a) and b) are explicitly mentioned in the action α. The number of newly added fresh elements is also explicit in α. Hence the induced effect 1) as well as effects a) and b) can be deduced from the action encoding $\textcircled{\alpha : s}$.

However, the induced effect 2 is not predictable from $\textcircled{\alpha : s}$. The reason is that, even when an element is involved only in deletions, it is not clear whether this element can be removed

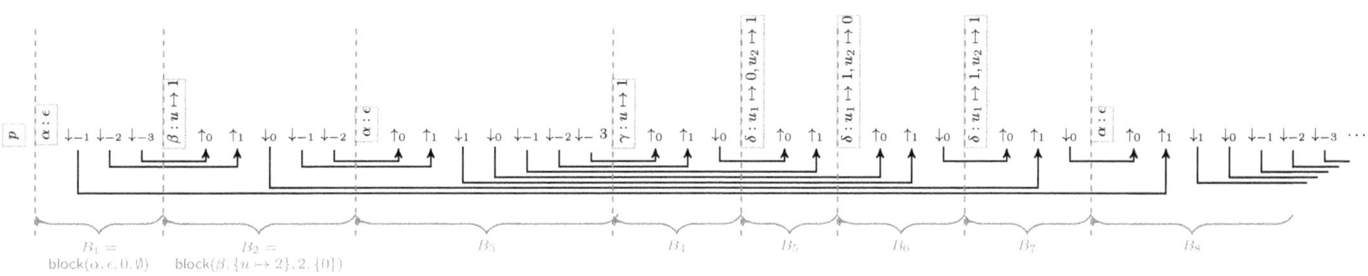

Figure 2: Nested word encoding of the run in Figure 1

from the current active domain since it may be participating in some other relations which were not tested by the action α. Thanks to recency boundedness, we know that if some element is deleted then it must be from the **b** most recent elements.

Another subtle problem is that at every configuration, the active domain need not contain **b** elements. Let m be $\min\{\mathbf{b}, |\text{ADOM}(I)|\}$, which gives the cardinality of the set $\mathsf{Recent_b}(I, \mathtt{seq\_no})$. The value of m at a configuration is not defined from an action encoding $(\alpha : s)$. Hence our encoding will also guess the value of m. Later, we will use $\mathtt{MSO_{NW}}$ to ensure that our guesses were indeed right.

We will provide an encoding which will "guess" the following: 1) the size of $\mathsf{Recent_b}(I, \mathtt{seq\_no},)$ at any configuration and 2) those recent elements which are deleted from the active domain, (or equivalently, it will "guess" those recent elements which are surviving in the active domain).

Suppose that $|\mathsf{Recent_b}(I, \mathtt{seq\_no})| = m$ in the current configuration $\langle I, H, \mathtt{seq\_no}\rangle$. Consider an action α under an abstract substitution $s : \alpha\text{-}\mathsf{free} \to \{0, 1, \dots m-1\}$. Further suppose that the elements with the recency index $J = \{i_1, i_2, \dots i_\ell\}$ with $J \subseteq \{0, 1, \dots m-1\}$ are surviving after the action. That means, the elements with recency index in $\{0, 1, \dots m-1\} \setminus J$ are deleted from the current database. The action along with its effect is encoded by the following visible word, where $n = |\alpha\text{-}\mathsf{new}|$:

$$(\alpha : s) \uparrow_0 \uparrow_1 \cdots \uparrow_{m-1} \downarrow_{i_1} \cdots \downarrow_{i_\ell} \downarrow_{-1} \cdots \downarrow_{-n}$$

with $m - 1 \geq i_1 > \cdots > i_\ell \geq 0$. The above word is parametrised by α, s, m and J. We denote it by $\mathsf{block}(\alpha, s, m, J)$.

Intuitively, we delete all the elements from $\mathsf{Recent_b}(I)$ temporarily, and insert back all the surviving ones (as dictated by J). Notice that the order of the indices of the elements from J make sure that in the later blocks a more-recent element is popped before a less-recent one. Finally, the fresh elements are pushed in.

Our encoding of a **b**-bounded run is a sequence of such blocks prefixed by (I_0):

$$(I_0)\, \mathsf{block}(\alpha_1, s_1, m_1, J_1)\, \mathsf{block}(\alpha_2, s_2, m_2, J_2) \cdots$$

The nesting edges are induced on the word due to the visibility of the alphabet. Our encoding has an interesting feature: the number of unmatched pushes in the prefix upto $(\alpha_j : s_j)$ is $|\text{ADOM}(I_j)|$ where I_j is the database instance at which α_j is executed. The set $\mathsf{Recent_b}(I_j)$ corresponds to the innermost (rightmost) $|\mathsf{Recent_b}(I_j)|$ unmatched pushes in the prefix. Note that, here an unmatched push in the prefix means it is not matched within the prefix; it may be matched after the prefix.

EXAMPLE 6.4. The nested-word encoding of the run from Figure 1 is depicted in Figure 2. It is 2-recency bounded. The indices 0 and 1 refer to the most recent and second most recent elements. Negative indices refer to freshly added elements.

Notice that in this example B_1 is the only block where $|\mathsf{Recent_b}(I)| < \mathbf{b} = 2$. On all successive blocks $|\mathsf{Recent_b}(I)| = 2$. In block B_1, indices 0 and 1 are not used.

In block B_2, the substitution uses only the second-most recent element, denoted by $u \mapsto 1$. However, the entire $\mathsf{Recent_b}(I)$ is popped. Since the second-most recent element is deleted in B_2, it is not pushed back, but the most recent element is pushed back (denoted by $\downarrow_0$). Hence for B_2, we have $J_2 = \{0\}$.

Action α of block B_3 does not use/modify any element from $\mathsf{Recent_b}(I)$. However, since $\mathsf{Recent_b}(I)$ is non-empty, it is popped entirely and pushed back. Notice the inversion in the order of the sequence of pops and that of pushes. This inversion maintains that less-recent elements are pushed before the more-recent elements.

Notice also that the number of pushes on the left of a block which are not matched on the left correspond to the number of elements in the active domain before the execution of the block. For example, the database instance I_4 just before the execution of block B_5 has 6 elements, and the $\text{ADOM}(I_7)$ has just two elements.

Notice that the abstract substitution need not be injective (cf. block B_7), and need not assign recent values to variables in the order of their recency (cf. blocks B_5 and B_6).

Notice also that the set J is not determined by the action name nor the abstract substitution s. ■

6.3.1 Conditions for valid encodings

Consider any nested word W over the visible alphabet $\Sigma = \Sigma_{\text{int}} \uplus \Sigma_\uparrow \uplus \Sigma_\downarrow$ of the form $(I_0)\, \mathsf{block}(\alpha_1, s_1, m_1, J_1)\, \mathsf{block}(\alpha_2, s_2, m_2, J_2) \ldots$. Let $w \in (\mathsf{symAlph}_{\mathcal{S},\mathbf{b}})^\omega$ be obtained by the Σ_{int} projection of W. Let W_i denote the prefix of W upto block_i, and w_i be the corresponding projection.

For $i \geq 0$, we say that a prefix W_{i+1} is *good* if $\mathsf{Concr}(w_i)$ is defined. Let $C_i = \langle I_i, H_i, \mathtt{seq\_no}_i\rangle$ be the last configuration of $\mathsf{Concr}(w_i)$ in this case. Further we require the following:

1. $m_{i+1} = |\mathsf{Recent_b}(I_i, \mathtt{seq\_no}_i)|$;
2. $j \in J_i$ iff, letting e be the element of recency-index j in C_i, there are a relation $R \in \mathcal{R}$ and a tuple t of R involving e such that t is present in I_i but not in instantiated $\alpha_{i+1}\cdot Del$, or t is present in instantiated $\alpha_{i+1}\cdot Add$; and
3. letting σ_{i+1} be the instantiation of s_{i+1} at C_i, we have $I_i, \sigma_{i+1} \models \alpha_{i+1}\cdot\mathsf{guard}$.

We say W is a *valid encoding* of a **b**-recency bounded run of $\mathcal{S}$ if W_i is good for every $i \geq 0$.

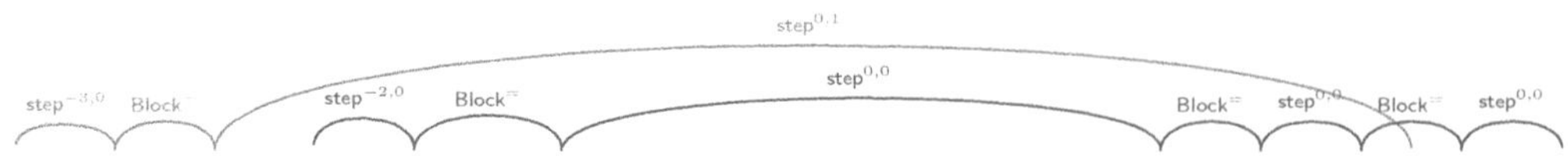

Figure 3: The relation $\mathsf{Eq}^{i,j}$ tracks the occurrences of the same element in the nested word encoding of a run. In a way it is a transitive closure of the $\mathsf{step}^{i,j}$ relations and the $\mathsf{Block}^{=}$ relations. Note that if such a transitive closure path enters a block via the relation $\mathsf{step}^{i,j}$ and exits the block via $\mathsf{step}^{i',j'}$ then $j = i'$.

$$\mathsf{Eq}^{i,j}(x,y) \equiv \forall X_{-\eta} \forall X_{-\eta+1} \dots \forall X_{\mathbf{b}-1} \left(\left(x \in X_i \wedge \forall x_1 \forall x_2. \left(\begin{array}{l} \bigwedge_{\eta \le \ell, m \le \mathbf{b}-1} (\mathsf{step}^{\ell,m}(x_1,x_2) \wedge x_1 \in X_\ell) \Rightarrow x_2 \in X_m \\ \wedge \bigwedge_{-\eta \le \ell \le \mathbf{b}-1} (\mathsf{Block}^{=}(x_1,x_2) \wedge x_1 \in X_\ell) \Rightarrow x_2 \in X_\ell \end{array} \right) \right) \Rightarrow y \in X_j \right)$$

Figure 4: Formula $\mathsf{Eq}^{i,j}$ which states that the element indexed by i in the block of the first argument is same as the element indexed by j in the block of the second argument. This is pictorially depicted in Figure 3.

Observe that, if W_i is good then $\mathsf{Concr}(w_i)$ is defined. Hence, if a nested word is not a valid encoding, it can be detected at the first index i such that W_i is not good by observing that conditions (1), (2) or (3) is violated. In this case $\mathsf{Concr}(w_{i-1})$ is defined since W_{i-1} is good. We will exploit this observation to express valid encodings in $\mathtt{MSO_{NW}}$.

In the remainder of this section we will use the above-set indexing convention for the intuitive explanations. That is, $C_i = \langle I_i, H_i, \mathtt{seq\_no}_i \rangle$ is the last configuration of $\mathsf{Concr}(w_i)$. This means that the previous configuration of block_i (or the configuration where it is being executed) is C_{i-1}.

Remark 6.1. *If W is a valid encoding then, the number of unmatched pushes in the prefix upto block_{j+1} (excluding) is $|\mathrm{ADOM}(I_j)|$. The set $\mathsf{Recent}_{\mathbf{b}}(I_j, \mathtt{seq\_no}_j)$ corresponds to the innermost (rightmost) $|\mathsf{Recent}_{\mathbf{b}}(I_j, \mathtt{seq\_no}_j)|$ unmatched pushes in the prefix. Note that, here an unmatched push in the prefix means it is not matched within the prefix; it may be matched after the prefix.*

We will now provide $\mathtt{MSO_{NW}}$ formulae stating that these three conditions are satisfied by a nested word over Σ at all of its blocks. The conjunction of the these formulae will characterise $\mathsf{Runs}_{\mathbf{b}}(\mathcal{S})$ (which we denote by $\varphi^{\mathsf{valid}}_{\mathbf{b},\mathcal{S}}$).

6.4 Expressing valid encodings in $\mathtt{MSO_{NW}}$

We first describe a few $\mathtt{MSO_{NW}}$ predicates that turn out handy when stating the validity of an encoding in MSO. Such predicates are macros/abbreviation helping towards the readability of the formula describing validity.

6.4.1 *Preliminary formulae*

We write $\Sigma_{\mathrm{int}}(x)$ as a shorthand for $\bigvee_{a \in \Sigma_{\mathrm{int}}} a(x)$. Similarly we define $\Sigma_{\downarrow}(x) \equiv \bigvee_{a \in \Sigma_{\downarrow}} a(x)$ and $\Sigma_{\uparrow}(x) \equiv \bigvee_{a \in \Sigma_{\uparrow}} a(x)$.

We write $\mathsf{Block}^{=}(x,y)$ to indicate that positions x and y belong to the same block. This is a shorthand for

$$\forall z. ((\neg \Sigma_{\mathrm{int}}(z)) \vee (z \le x \wedge z \le y) \vee (x < z \wedge y < z))$$

Notice that a block has exactly one internal letter, which indicates the action and the abstract substitution. The position labelled by such an internal letter is called *head*, and every block has a unique head. The formula $\mathsf{Block}^{=}(x,y)$ says that x and y must not be separated by an internal letter (or a head).

We now define a unary predicate with a free variable x for each relation name $R/a \in \mathcal{R}$ and choice of a recency indices $i_1, \dots i_a \in \{0, \dots, \mathbf{b}-1\}$. The predicate holds at a position if it is the head of a block and its block deletes a tuple $\langle e_1, \dots e_a \rangle$ from the relation R where e_j is indexed by i_j in its block, for all $j : 1 \le j \le a$. This predicate is denoted $\mathit{Del}(R(i_1, \dots i_a))@x$.

$$\mathit{Del}(R(i_1, \dots i_a))@x \equiv \bigvee_{\textcircled{\alpha, s} \in \Gamma} \textcircled{\alpha, s}(x)$$

where $\Gamma = \{ \textcircled{\alpha, s} \mid \alpha{\cdot}\mathit{Del}$ contains a tuple $R(u_1 \dots u_a)$ and $s(u_j) = i_j$ for all $1 \le j \le a\}$.

Similarly we define a unary predicate for adding a tuple to a relation as well. However in this case, the indices may refer to the fresh data values as well. Hence we have unary predicate $\mathit{Add}(R(i_1, \dots i_a))@x$ for each relation name $R/a \in \mathcal{R}$ and choice of a indices $i_1, \dots i_a \in \{-n, \dots, 0, \dots, \mathbf{b}-1\}$, where $n := \max_{\alpha \in \mathrm{ACTS}} |\alpha{\cdot}\mathsf{new}|$.

$$\mathit{Add}(R(i_1, \dots i_a))@x \equiv \bigvee_{\textcircled{\alpha, s} \in \Gamma} \textcircled{\alpha, s}(x)$$

where $\Gamma = \{ \textcircled{\alpha, s} \mid \alpha{\cdot}\mathit{Add}$ contains a tuple $R(\xi_1 \dots \xi_a)$ and for all $1 \le j \le a$ if $\xi_j \in \alpha{\cdot}\mathsf{free}$ then $s(\xi_j) = i_j$ and if ξ_j is the kth fresh input variable v_k then $i_j = -k\}$.

Equality between indexed elements of different blocks. Consider the encoding of the run in Figure 2. Notice that the index -2 in the block B_1 and index 1 in the block B_2 refer to the same element (e_2 in the concrete run of Figure 1). Notice also that the element referred to by index -2 in Block B_2 is the same as the element referred to by index 0 in block B_7 (e_5 in the concrete run of Figure 1).

Given two positions x and y and indices i and j, consider following question: Is *the element referred to by index i in the block of x the same as the element referred to by index j in the block of y?* In fact, this property can be expressed in $\mathtt{MSO_{NW}}$. We define below a binary predicate $\mathsf{Eq}^{i,j}(x,y)$ for the same. Indeed we will define such a predicate for every pair i, j with $-\eta \le i, j \le \mathbf{b}-1$.

Towards this, first notice that the predicate must hold

if there is a $\downarrow_i$-labelled position in the block of x that is $\rhd$-related to $\uparrow_j$-labelled position in the block of y. This forms the basic step relation towards defining $\mathsf{Eq}^{i,j}(x,y)$.

$$\mathsf{step}^{i,j}(x,y) \equiv \exists z_1 \exists z_2 . \mathsf{Block}^{=}(z_1,x) \wedge \mathsf{Block}^{=}(z_2,y) \wedge z_1 \rhd z_2 \wedge \downarrow_i(z_1) \wedge \uparrow_j(z_2)$$

Recall that $\downarrow_i(x)$ means that the position x is labelled by the letter $\downarrow_i$. Notice that our definition of $\mathsf{step}^{i,j}(x,y)$ is directional, in the sense that x must necessarily be before y for $\mathsf{step}^{i,j}(x,y)$ to hold. The transitive closure of the above step relation gives us the required predicate $\mathsf{Eq}^{i,j}(x,y)$. Suppose the element indexed i in the block of x is e. The element e may appear with different indices at the intermediate steps. Hence we need to take a zig-zag transitive closure. Our formula uses $\mathbf{b}+\eta$ second-order position variables. Intuitively the set X_k contains the set of positions such that the element e is indexed by k in its block. Using the universal quantifier, we require that the minimal of such sets which are closed under the zig-zag transitive closure must contain y in the set X_j. The formula $\mathsf{Eq}^{i,j}(x,y)$ is depicted in Figure 4.

Notice that since step is directional, so is $\mathsf{Eq}^{i,j}(x,y)$. I.e, if $\mathsf{Eq}^{i,j}(x,y)$ then necessarily $x \leq y$ or $\mathsf{Block}^{=}(x,y)$.

Recent elements participating in a relation. Consider a relation R of arity a. We define a predicate $\mathsf{Rel\text{-}R}(x_1,i_1,x_2,i_2,\dots x_a,i_a)@y^{\ominus}$ which holds iff the database instance *before* the execution of the block of y has the tuple $\langle e_1,e_2,\dots e_a\rangle$ in relation R where, the element e_j is indexed by i_j in the block of x_j for all $j : 1 \leq j \leq a$. This predicate can be expressed in MSO, as given below.

$$\exists x\, x < y \wedge \neg\mathsf{Block}^{=}(x,y) \wedge \bigvee_{-\eta\leq \ell_1,\dots \ell_a \leq \mathbf{b}-1} Add(R(\ell_1,\dots \ell_a)@x) \wedge \bigwedge_{1\leq j\leq a} \mathsf{Eq}^{\ell_j,i_j}(x,x_j)$$
$$\wedge \forall z \neg(x \leq z \wedge z < y \wedge \neg\mathsf{Block}^{=}(z,y) \wedge \bigvee_{0\leq m_1,\dots m_a\leq \mathbf{b}-1} (Del(R(m_1,\dots m_a))@z \wedge \bigwedge_{1\leq j\leq a} \mathsf{Eq}^{\ell_j,m_j}(x,z)))$$

The formula essentially says that the relation tuple has been added to the database instance at some point in the past of y, and since then it has not been deleted.

Similarly we define $\mathsf{Rel\text{-}R}(x_1,i_1,x_2,i_2,\dots x_n,i_n)@y^{\oplus}$ which holds iff the database instance *after* the execution of the block of y has a tuple in relation R as before. It can be expressed as given follows:

$$\exists x\, x \leq y \wedge \bigvee_{-\eta\leq \ell_1,\dots \ell_a\leq \mathbf{b}-1} Add(R(\ell_1,\dots \ell_a))@x \wedge \bigwedge_{1\leq j\leq a} \mathsf{Eq}^{\ell_j,i_j}(x,x_j) \wedge \forall z \neg(x \leq z \wedge z \leq y \wedge$$
$$\bigvee_{0\leq m_1,\dots,m_a\leq \mathbf{b}-1} (Del(R(m_1,\dots m_a))@z \wedge \bigwedge_{1\leq j\leq a} \mathsf{Eq}^{\ell_j,m_j}(x,z)))$$

6.4.2 *Expressing valid encodings in* $\mathtt{MSO_{NW}}$

We now show that the conditions given in Section 6.3.1 can be expressed in $\mathtt{MSO_{NW}}$.

0. Well-formedness We need to check the local consistency of each block appearing in the word, which means s_i must not assign a variable to a recency index higher than or equal to m_i, and that $J_i \subseteq \{0,\dots,m_i\}$. Further it must of the form described in Section 6.3.1. This is a syntactic check inside a block and can be easily stated in $\mathtt{MSO_{NW}}$.

1. Consistency of m. We write a formula $\varphi_m^{\text{Recent}}(x)$ to state that, just before executing the block of x, the current database I has at least $m+1$ elements in $\textsc{adom}(I)$. Thanks to Remark 6.1, this can be expressed in $\mathtt{MSO_{NW}}$ by saying that there are $m+1$ distinct pushes before the block of x which are not popped until x.

$$\varphi_m^{\text{Recent}}(x) \equiv \exists y\, \mathsf{Block}^{=}(x,y) \wedge \Sigma_{\text{int}}(y) \wedge \exists x_1,\dots x_m \bigwedge_{i\neq j} x_i \neq x_j \wedge \bigwedge_i (\Sigma_{\downarrow}(x_i) \wedge x_i < y \wedge \forall z(x_i \rhd z \Rightarrow y < z))$$

Now, consistency of m can be stated as:

$$\forall x \bigwedge_{0\leq i\leq \mathbf{b}-1} \neg\varphi_i^{\text{Recent}}(x) \vee \exists y\, (\uparrow_i(y) \wedge \mathsf{Block}^{=}(x,y))$$

2. Consistency of J. Towards this we first need to write a formula $\mathsf{live}(x,i)$ which holds only if the element with recency index i in the block of x is in $\textsc{adom}(I)$ after the execution of the block of x. This is expressed similarly to the formula $\mathsf{Active}(u)$ of Example 2.1. $\mathsf{live}(x,i) \equiv \bigvee_{R/a\in\mathcal{R}} \exists x_1,\dots,x_a \bigwedge_{1\leq j\leq a} x_i \leq x \wedge \bigvee_{-\eta\leq i_1,i_2,\dots,i_a\leq \mathbf{b}-1} \bigvee_{1\leq j\leq a} \mathsf{Rel\text{-}R}(\dots,x_{j-1},i_{j-1},x,i,x_{j+1},i_{j+1},\dots)@x^{\oplus}$ where $\eta = \max_{\alpha\in act} |\alpha\cdot\mathsf{new}|$.

Now the consistency of J can be stated by saying that a recency index is pushed in a block iff it is live:

$$\forall x \bigwedge_{0\leq i\leq \mathbf{b}-1} \mathsf{live}(x,i) \Leftrightarrow (\exists y \downarrow_i(y) \wedge \mathsf{Block}^{=}(x,y))$$

3. Consistency of action guards. We first present a syntactic translation of an $\mathtt{FOL}(\mathcal{R})$ formula into an $\mathtt{MSO_{NW}}$ formula. The translation also depends on the current block (a block is represented by the head position of the block which we denote by a free position variable x) as well as the action α and the abstract substitution s used in the block. The translation of an $\mathtt{FOL}(\mathcal{R})$ formula Q at x wrt. s and α is a $\mathtt{MSO_{NW}}$ formula denoted $\lfloor Q\rfloor_{\alpha,s,x}$.

In our translation, a first-order data variable u is represented by the position x^u and an index i^u, which is an number between $-\eta$ and $\mathbf{b}-1$ where $\eta = \max_{\alpha\in\textsc{acts}} |\alpha\cdot\mathsf{new}|$. Intuitively, instead of reasoning about an element in the domain, we reason about it symbolically by means of a (past) position where it is live and its recency index at that position. Given α, s and x, we distinguish between variables belonging to $\alpha\cdot\mathsf{free}$ and the other variables. For a variable $u \in \alpha\cdot\mathsf{free}$ we set $x^u = x$ and $i^u = s(u)$.

The translation is defined inductively as follows: (In the following $x^u = x$ and $i^u = s(u)$ if $u \in \alpha\cdot\mathsf{free}$, and $\eta = \max_{\alpha\in\textsc{acts}} |\alpha\cdot\mathsf{new}|$)

- $\lfloor R(u_1,\dots u_n)\rfloor_{\alpha,s,x} \equiv \mathsf{Rel\text{-}R}(x^{u_1},i^{u_1},\dots,x^{u_n},i^{u_n})@x^{\ominus}$
- $\lfloor u_1 = u_2\rfloor_{\alpha,s,x} \equiv \mathsf{Eq}^{i^{u_1},i^{u_2}}(x^{u_1},x^{u_2})$
- $\lfloor \exists u.\, Q\rfloor_{\alpha,s,x} \equiv \exists x^u.\, x^u < x \wedge \bigvee_{-\eta\leq i^u\leq \mathbf{b}-1} \lfloor Q\rfloor_{\alpha,s,x}$
- $\lfloor Q_1 \wedge Q_2\rfloor_{\alpha,s,x} \equiv \lfloor Q_1\rfloor_{\alpha,s,x} \wedge \lfloor Q_2\rfloor_{\alpha,s,x}$
- $\lfloor \neg Q\rfloor_{\alpha,s,x} \equiv \neg\lfloor Q\rfloor_{\alpha,s,x}$

Now we are ready to express the consistency of action guards with the run. It can be expressed by the following formula: $\forall x \bigwedge_{(\alpha : s)\in\Sigma_{\text{int}}} (\alpha, s)(x) \Rightarrow \lfloor \alpha\cdot\mathsf{guard}\rfloor_{\alpha,s,x}$.

Let $\varphi_{\mathbf{b},\mathcal{S}}^{\mathsf{valid}}$ be the conjunction of the four conditions listed above. It characterises valid encodings of $\mathbf{b}$-bounded runs of a DMS $\mathcal{S}$.

6.5 Translating MSO-FO specifications into $\mathtt{MSO}_{\mathtt{NW}}$ specifications

Here we provide a translation of the specifications in MSO-FO to an equivalent one in $\mathtt{MSO}_{\mathtt{NW}}$ over valid encodings of runs. This is similar in spirit to the translation described for action guards. As done there, we represent a first-order data variable u by the pair x^u, i^u. We extend this representation to incorporate the globally quantified data variables as well. We distinguish neither between free or bound variables, nor between globally quantified and locally quantifies variables: A data variable u is represented by the pair x^u, i^u.

A first-order position variable of MSO-FO will correspond to a block in the nested word encoding. A block is represented by its head. Thus in our translation, a first-order position variable of MSO-FO corresponds to a first-order position variable of $\mathtt{MSO}_{\mathtt{NW}}$ which varies over heads of blocks. A set variable of MSO-FO corresponds to a set variable in $\mathtt{MSO}_{\mathtt{NW}}$ relativized to head positions. The translation of a MSO-FO formula φ is denoted $\lfloor\varphi\rfloor$, and is defined inductively as follows:

- $\lfloor Q@x \rfloor \equiv \Sigma_{\text{int}}(x) \wedge \bigvee_{\textcircled{\alpha : s} \in \Sigma_{\text{int}}} \textcircled{\alpha : s}(x) \Rightarrow \lfloor Q \rfloor_{\alpha,s,x}$
- $\lfloor \exists x.\, \varphi \rfloor \equiv \exists x.\, \Sigma_{\text{int}}(x) \wedge \lfloor\varphi\rfloor$
- $\lfloor \exists X.\, \varphi \rfloor \equiv \exists X.\, (\forall x. x \in X \Rightarrow \Sigma_{\text{int}}(x)) \wedge \lfloor\varphi\rfloor$
- $\lfloor \exists^g u.\varphi \rfloor \equiv \exists x^u.\, \Sigma_{\text{int}}(x^u) \wedge \bigvee_{-\eta \le i^u \le \mathbf{b}-1} \lfloor\varphi\rfloor$ where $\eta = \max_{\alpha \in \text{ACTS}} |\alpha{\cdot}\mathsf{new}|$
- $\lfloor x < y \rfloor \equiv x < y$
- $\lfloor x \in X \rfloor \equiv x \in X$
- $\lfloor \varphi_1 \wedge \varphi_2 \rfloor \equiv \lfloor\varphi_1\rfloor \wedge \lfloor\varphi_2\rfloor$
- $\lfloor \neg\varphi \rfloor \equiv \neg\lfloor\varphi\rfloor$

6.6 Concluding the reduction

We reduce the recency bounded model checking problem to the satisfiability checking of $\mathtt{MSO}_{\mathtt{NW}}$. Given a DMS $\mathcal{S}$, recency bound $\mathbf{b}$ and an MSO-FO specification ψ, we construct $\varphi^{\mathsf{valid}}_{\mathbf{b},\mathcal{S}}$ and $\lfloor\psi\rfloor$ as described in the previous subsections. The $\mathbf{b}$ bounded model checking problem reduces to the non-satisfiability checking of $\varphi^{\mathsf{valid}}_{\mathbf{b},\mathcal{S}} \wedge \neg\lfloor\psi\rfloor$. The satisfiability checking of $\mathtt{MSO}_{\mathtt{NW}}$is decidable [3], and hence by our reduction RECENCY-BOUNDED-MSO/DMS-MC is decidable.

The construction of the $\mathtt{MSO}_{\mathtt{NW}}$ formula $\varphi^{\mathsf{valid}}_{\mathbf{b},\mathcal{S}} \wedge \neg\lfloor\psi\rfloor$ takes time $\mathcal{O}((\mathbf{b} + |\mathcal{R}| + |\text{ACTS}|)^{\mathcal{O}(\mathfrak{a}+\mathfrak{n})})$ where $|\mathcal{R}|$ denotes the number of relations in $\mathcal{R}$, $|\text{ACTS}|$ denotes the number of actions of $\mathcal{S}$, $\mathfrak{a}$ is the maximum arity of the relations in the schema (i.e., $\mathfrak{a} = \max_{R/a \in \mathcal{R}} a$) and $\mathfrak{n}$ is the number of data-variables appearing in the action guards and ψ.

7. RELATED WORK

As pointed out in the introduction, DMSs belong to the series of works on the verification of dabase-driven dynamic systems whose initial state is known [11, 7, 5, 8, 6, 26]. In [8], *artifact-centric multi-agent systems* are proposed to simultaneously account for business artifacts and for the specification of agents operating over them. Building on [11, 7], decidability of verification of FO-CTLK properties with active domain FO quantification is obtained, under the assumption that the size of the databases maintained by agents and artifacts never exceeds a pre-defined bound. This notion of *state-boundedness* is thoroughly studied in [6] on top of the framework of *data-centric dynamic systems* (DCDSs). There, decidability of verification is obtained for a sophisticated variant of FO μ-calculus with active domain FO quantification, in which the possibility of quantifying over individual objects across time is limited to those objects that persist in the active domain of the system. Our logic MSO-FO differs to those used in [8, 6] since it captures linear properties over runs, as opposed to branching properties over RTSs. Furthermore, it leverages the full power of MSO to express sophisticated temporal properties, and is equipped with unrestricted FO quantification across positions of the run, as well as the possibility of quantifying over the objects present in the whole run, as opposed to only those present in the active domain of the current state.

Both in [8] and [6], decidability is obtained by constructing a faithful, finite-state abstraction that preserves the properties to be verified. This shows that state-bounded dynamic systems are an interesting class of *essentially finite-state systems* [1]. On the other hand, state-boundedness is a too restrictive requirement when dealing with systems such as that of Example 3.2. In fact, allowing for unboundedly many tuples to be stored in the database is required to deal with *history-dependent dynamic systems*, whose behavior is influenced by the presence of certain patterns in the (unbounded) history of the system (cf. the definition of *gold customer* in Example 3.2). It is also essential to capture *last-in first-out dynamic systems*, where the currently executed task may be interrupted by a task with a higher-priority, and so on, resuming the execution of the original task only when the (unbounded) chain of higher-priority tasks is completed. See, e.g., the pre-emptive offer handling adopted in Example 5.2. Notably, as argued in Example 5.2, such classes of unbounded systems can all be subject to *exact* MSO-FO model checking, by choosing a sufficiently large bound for recency.

8. CONCLUSION

We have proposed an under-approximation of dynamic database-driven systems that allows unbounded state-space, under which we have shown decidability of model checking against MSO-FO. The decidability is obtained by a reduction to the satisfiability checking of MSO over nested words. The complexity of our model checking procedure is non-elementary in the size of the specification and the DMS. A fine-grained analysis of complexity with respect to various input parameters such as arity of the relations, size of schema, number of variables in the queries etc. is left for future work. It is interesting to study whether one can obtain model checking algorithms with elementary complexity by using other specification formalisms, like temporal logics. Expressing valid runs in temporal logic would be important in this case, and it is interesting problem on its own. Another direction for future work would be to identify other meaningful under-approximation parameters. For example, does bounding the most recently *accessed* elements as opposed to most recently added elements yield decidability? We also aim at applying under-approximation techniques in the case where the initial database is not known, and model checking is studied for every possible initial database, in the style of [15, 13, 9].

Acknowledgments

We acknowledge the support of the *Uppsala Programming for Multicore Architectures Research Center* (UPMARC), the *Programming Platform for Future Wireless Sensor Networks Project* (PROFUN), and the EU project *Optique - Scalable End-user Access to Big Data* (FP7-IP-318338).

9. REFERENCES

[1] P. A. Abdulla. Well (and better) quasi-ordered transition systems. *Bulletin of Symbolic Logic*, 16(4):457–515, 2010.

[2] S. Abiteboul, V. Vianu, B. Fordham, and Y. Yesha. Relational transducers for electronic commerce. *JCSS*, 61(2):236–269, 2000.

[3] R. Alur and P. Madhusudan. Adding nesting structure to words. *J. ACM*, 56(3), 2009.

[4] P. Aziz Abdulla, C. Aiswarya, M. Faouzi Atig, M. Montali, and O. Rezine. Recency-Bounded Verification of Dynamic Database-Driven Systems (Extended Version). http://arxiv.org/abs/1604.03413, Apr. 2016.

[5] B. Bagheri Hariri, D. Calvanese, G. De Giacomo, R. De Masellis, and P. Felli. Foundations of relational artifacts verification. In *BPM*, 2011.

[6] B. Bagheri Hariri, D. Calvanese, G. De Giacomo, A. Deutsch, and M. Montali. Verification of relational data-centric dynamic systems with external services. In *PODS*, 2013.

[7] F. Belardinelli, A. Lomuscio, and F. Patrizi. Verification of deployed artifact systems via data abstraction. In *ICSOC*, 2011.

[8] F. Belardinelli, A. Lomuscio, and F. Patrizi. An abstraction technique for the verification of artifact-centric systems. In *KR*, 2012.

[9] M. Bojanczyk, L. Segoufin, and S. Torunczyk. Verification of database-driven systems via amalgamation. In *PODS*, 2013.

[10] D. Calvanese, G. De Giacomo, and M. Montali. Foundations of data-aware process analysis: A database theory perspective. In *PODS*. ACM Press, 2013.

[11] P. Cangialosi, G. De Giacomo, R. De Masellis, and R. Rosati. Conjunctive artifact-centric services. In *ICSOC*, 2010.

[12] D. Cohn and R. Hull. Business artifacts: A data-centric approach to modeling business operations and processes. *IEEE Data Engineering Bullettin*, 32(3), 2009.

[13] E. Damaggio, A. Deutsch, and V. Vianu. Artifact systems with data dependencies and arithmetic. In *ICDT*, 2011.

[14] E. Damaggio, R. Hull, and R. Vaculín. On the equivalence of incremental and fixpoint semantics for business artifacts with guard-stage-milestone lifecycles. In *BPM*, 2011.

[15] A. Deutsch, R. Hull, F. Patrizi, and V. Vianu. Automatic verification of data-centric business processes. In *ICDT*, pages 252–267, 2009.

[16] A. Deutsch, L. Sui, and V. Vianu. Specification and verification of data-driven web applications. *JCSS*, 73(3):442–474, 2007.

[17] R. Hull. Artifact-centric business process models: Brief survey of research results and challenges. In *OTM Confederated Int. Conf.*, 2008.

[18] V. Künzle and M. Reichert. Philharmonicflows: towards a framework for object-aware process management. *Journal of Software Maintenance*, 23(4):205–244, 2011.

[19] V. Künzle, B. Weber, and M. Reichert. Object-aware business processes: Fundamental requirements and their support in existing approaches. *Int. J. of Information System Modeling and Design*, 2(2):19–46, 2011.

[20] C. Lautemann, T. Schwentick, and D. Thérien. Logics for context-free languages. In *CSL*, volume 933 of *LNCS*, pages 205–216. Springer, 1995.

[21] A. Lomuscio and J. Michaliszyn. Model checking unbounded artifact-centric systems. In *KR*. AAAIP, 2014.

[22] A. Meyer, S. Smirnov, and M. Weske. Data in business processes. Technical Report 50, Hasso-Plattner-Institut for IT Systems Engineering, Universität Potsdam, 2011.

[23] M. Montali and D. Calvanese. Soundness of data-aware, case-centric processes. *International Journal on Software Tools for Technology Transfer*, pages 1–24, 2016.

[24] A. Nigam and N. S. Caswell. Business artifacts: An approach to operational specification. *IBM Systems Journal*, 42(3), 2003.

[25] M. Reichert. Process and data: Two sides of the same coin? In *OTM*, volume 7565 of *LNCS*, pages 2–19. Springer, 2012.

[26] D. Solomakhin, M. Montali, S. Tessaris, and R. De Masellis. Verification of artifact-centric systems: Decidability and modeling issues. In *ICSOC*, 2013.

[27] M. Y. Vardi. Model checking for database theoreticians. In *ICDT*, volume 3363 of *LNCS*, pages 1–16. Springer, 2005.

APPENDIX

A. SEMANTICS OF $\mathtt{FOL}(\mathcal{R})$ QUERIES

Given a database instance I over $\mathcal{R}$ and Δ, a $\mathtt{FOL}(\mathcal{R})$ query Q over $\mathcal{R}$, and a substitution $\sigma : \mathsf{Free\text{-}Vars}(Q) \to \Delta$, we write $I, \sigma \models Q$ if the query Q under the substitution σ holds in database I. This is defined inductively:

- $I, \sigma \models \mathsf{true}$
- $I, \sigma \models R(u_1, \ldots, u_a)$ if $(e_1, \ldots, e_a) \in R^I$ where $e_i = \sigma(u_i)$ for all $i : 1 \leq i \leq a$.
- $I, \sigma \models u_i = u_j$ if $\sigma(u_i) = \sigma(u_j)$.
- $I, \sigma \models \neg Q$ if $I, \sigma \not\models Q$.
- $I, \sigma \models Q_1 \wedge Q_2$ if $I, \sigma \models Q_1$, and $I, \sigma \models Q_2$.
- $I, \sigma \models \exists u.Q$ if there exists $e \in \mathrm{ADOM}(I)$ such that $I, \sigma' \models Q$ where σ' is obataind from σ as follows: σ' is defined on u and $\sigma'(u) = e$ and $\sigma'(u') = \sigma(u')$ if $u' \neq u$.

B. SEMANTICS OF MSO-FO

A run ρ is an infinite sequence of database instances over $\mathcal{R}$ and Δ:

$$\rho = I_0, I_1, I_2, I_3 \ldots$$

An MSO formula ϕ is interpreted over a run ρ under a substitution σ of the free variables $\mathsf{Free\text{-}Vars}(\phi)$. If the formula holds in the run ρ under the substitution σ, we write $\rho, \sigma \models \phi$. The semantics is defined inductively:

- $\rho, \sigma \models Q@x$ if $I_i, \sigma' \models Q$ where $i = \sigma(x)$ and $\sigma' = \sigma|_{\mathsf{Free\text{-}Vars}(Q)}$
- $\rho, \sigma \models x < y$ if $\sigma(x) < \sigma(y)$

- $\rho, \sigma \models x \in X$ if $\sigma(x) \in \sigma(X)$
- $\rho, \sigma \models \neg\phi$ if $\rho, \sigma \not\models \phi$
- $\rho, \sigma \models \phi_1 \wedge \phi_2$ if $\rho, \sigma \models \phi_1$, and $\rho, \sigma \models \phi_2$
- $\rho, \sigma \models \exists x.\phi$ if there exists $i \in \mathbb{N}$, such that $\rho, \sigma[x \mapsto i] \models \phi$ where $\sigma[x \mapsto i](x) = i$, and $\sigma[x \mapsto i](\xi) = \sigma(\xi)$ if $\xi \neq x$
- $\rho, \sigma \models \exists X.\phi$ if there exists $J \subseteq \mathbb{N}$, such that $\rho, \sigma[X \mapsto J] \models \phi$ where $\sigma[X \mapsto J](X) = J$, and $\sigma[X \mapsto J](\xi) = \sigma(\xi)$ if $\xi \neq X$
- $\rho, \sigma \models \exists^g u.\phi$ if there exists $e \in \text{GADOM}(\rho)$, such that $\rho, \sigma[u \mapsto e] \models \phi$ where $\sigma[u \mapsto e](u) = e$, and $\sigma[u \mapsto e](\xi) = \sigma(\xi)$ if $\xi \neq u$

The semantics of database query ($I, \sigma \models Q$) is as expected (see Appendix A). The substitution of free variables is always restricted to the active domain of I in this case. That is, $\mathsf{Image}(\sigma) \subseteq \text{ADOM}(I)$ is necessary; just having $\mathsf{Image}(\sigma) \subseteq \text{GADOM}(\rho)$ is not sufficient.

Intuitively, $Q@x$ evaluates the $\mathtt{FOL}(\mathcal{R})$ query Q over the database instance present at position x in the run. Formula $x < y$ asserts that position x comes before y along the run. Formula $x \in X$ states that position x belongs to the set X of positions. Formula $\exists x.\phi$ states that there exists a position x in the run where ϕ holds, whereas formula $\exists X.\phi$ models that there exists a set X of positions in the run where ϕ holds. Finally, $\exists^g u.\phi$ states that there exists a data value u that is active in some database instance of the run and that makes ϕ true. In this light, the quantifier $\exists^g$ ranges over the *global active domain* of the run, obtained by composing all active domains of the database instances encountered therein.

C. RUNS WHICH ARE EQUIVALENT MODULO PERMUTATIONS

LEMMA C.1. *Two runs match on their abstraction, if and only if they are equivalent modulo permutations of the data domain.*

Let $\hat{\rho} = \left(\langle I_j, H_j, \mathtt{seq\_no}_j\rangle \xrightarrow{\alpha_j:\sigma_j}_{\mathsf{b}} \langle I_{j+1}, H_{j+1}, \mathtt{seq\_no}_{j+1}\rangle\right)_{j\geq 0}$

and $\hat{\rho}' = \left(\langle I'_j, H'_j, \mathtt{seq\_no}'_j\rangle \xrightarrow{\alpha'_j:\sigma'_j}_{\mathsf{b}} \langle I'_{j+1}, H'_{j+1}, \mathtt{seq\_no}'_{j+1}\rangle\right)_{j\geq 0}$

be two extended runs such that $\mathsf{Abstr}(\hat{\rho}) = \mathsf{Abstr}(\hat{\rho}') = (\langle \alpha_j : s_j\rangle)_{j\geq 0}$. That implies that $\alpha_j = \alpha'_j$ for every $j \geq 0$.

We prove in what follows the existence of a bijection $\lambda : \text{GADOM}(\hat{\rho}) \to \text{GADOM}(\hat{\rho}')$ such that, for every $i \geq 0$, λ is an isomorphism from I_i onto I'_i.

Notice that the global active domain of a given run $\hat{\rho}$ amounts to the set that contains all fresh input elements introduced in the database all along the run. That is $\text{GADOM}(\hat{\rho}) = \cup_{i\geq 0} I_i = \cup_{i\geq 0} \{\sigma_i(v) | \ v \in \alpha_i{\cdot}\mathsf{new}\}$ and $\text{GADOM}(\hat{\rho}) = \cup_{i\geq 0} I'_i = \cup_{i\geq 0} \{\sigma'_i(v) | \ v \in \alpha'_i{\cdot}\mathsf{new}\} = \cup_{i\geq 0} \{\sigma'_i(v) | \ v \in \alpha_i{\cdot}\mathsf{new}\}$ (since $\alpha'_i = \alpha_i$).

Definition of λ. Let $e \in \Delta$. We have that $e \in \text{GADOM}(\hat{\rho})$ if and only if $\exists i \geq 0$ and $\exists v \in \alpha_i{\cdot}\mathsf{new}$ such that $\sigma_i(v) = e$. Since $\alpha'_i = \alpha_i$, $\sigma'_i(v) \in \text{GADOM}(\hat{\rho}')$ is also well defined. We set $\lambda(e) = \sigma'_i(v)$. **Injectivity.** Let $e_1, e_2 \in \text{GADOM}(\hat{\rho})$ such that $e_1 \neq e_2$. That means that there are $i_1, i_2 \geq 0$, $v_1 \in \alpha_{i_1}{\cdot}\mathsf{new}$ and $v_2 \in \alpha_{i_2}{\cdot}\mathsf{new}$ such that $\sigma_{i_1}(v_1) = e_1$ and $\sigma_{i_2}(v_2) = e_2$. We have that $\lambda(e_1) = \sigma'_{i_1}(v_1)$ and $\lambda(e_1) = \sigma'_{i_2}(v_2)$. Notice that, since $e_1 \neq e_2$, we can not have $i_1 = i_2$ and $v_1 = v_2$ at the same time. That, the fact that substitutions have to be injective when applied to the fresh variables and together with the freshness condition for the newly input values, imply that $\lambda(e_1) \neq \lambda(e_2)$. Thus, λ is injective. **Surjectivity.** Let $e' \in \text{GADOM}(\hat{\rho}')$. That implies the existence of $i \geq 0$ and $v \in \alpha'_i{\cdot}\mathsf{new}$ such that $\sigma'_i(v) = e'$. Since $\alpha_i = \alpha'_i$, $\sigma_i(v)$ is also well defined and we set $e = \sigma_i(v)$. We have that $\lambda(e) = e'$. Thus, λ is surjective.

Thus, λ is a bijection. In a similar fashion, we can define yet another bijection from $\{\mathtt{seq\_no}_i(e) | \ e \in \text{GADOM}(\hat{\rho})\}$ onto $\{\mathtt{seq\_no}'_i(e) | \ e \in \text{GADOM}(\hat{\rho}')\}$ that we denote by β and such that $\beta(\mathtt{seq\_no}_i(e)) = \mathtt{seq\_no}'_i(\lambda(e))$. Moreover, we can show that β is monotonic.

Now that we have defined λ (and β), we shall prove by induction on $i \in \mathbb{N}$ that λ is an isomorphism from I_i onto I'_i.

For the base case ($i = 0$), we trivially have that $I_0 = I'_0$ and $I_0 \cap \text{GADOM}(\hat{\rho}) = \emptyset = I_0 \cap \text{GADOM}(\hat{\rho}')$. Assume now that for some $i \in \mathbb{N}$ we have that λ is an isomorphism from I_i onto I'_i. Let's prove that λ is also an isomorphism from I_{i+1} onto I'_{i+1}. Let $R(\sigma_i(u_1), \ldots, \sigma_i(u_n))$ (with $R \in \mathcal{R}$ and $u_1, \ldots, u_n \in \alpha_i{\cdot}\mathsf{free} \uplus \alpha_i{\cdot}\mathsf{new}$) be one of the facts that will be added to I_i in order to obtain I_{i+1}. Since $\alpha_i = \alpha'_i$, the fact $R(\sigma'_i(u_1), \ldots, \sigma'_i(u_n))$ is also added to I'_i in order to obtain I'_{i+1}. If $u_j \in \alpha_i{\cdot}\mathsf{new}$ then we have that $\sigma'_i(u_j) = \lambda(\sigma_i(u_j))$. In the case where $u_j \in \alpha_i{\cdot}\mathsf{free}$, since we have that i) the symbolic substitutions s_i and s'_i are equal, which free variables parts are respectively defined by the sequence numbering functions $\mathtt{seq\_no}_i$ and $\mathtt{seq\_no}'_i$, and that ii) $\beta(\mathtt{seq\_no}_i(e)) = \mathtt{seq\_no}'_i(\lambda(e))$ for every $e \in \text{ADOM}(I_i)$, we deduce that $\sigma'_i(u_j) = \lambda(\sigma_i(u_j))$. Thus, the added fact amounts to $R(\lambda(\sigma_i(u_1)), \ldots, \lambda(\sigma_i(u_n)))$. The case of deleted facts is simpler, and the inverse reasoning (from I'_i to I_i) is identical. Thus λ is also an isomorphism from I_{i+1} onto I'_{i+1}.

D. GENERALITY OF THE MODEL

We discuss the generality of the model. In particular, we consider variants of DMSs that supports:

- constant values;
- (SQL-like) *standard variable substitution* for guards and input variables, consequently tackling the repetition of matching values;
- Weakening the freshness requirement for input values, to support the possibility of matching input variables with already existing values.

In summary, we show that all such variants can be reduced back to the standard model presented in Section 3, while preserving the original system behavior.

D.1 DMSs with Possibly Overlapping Inputs

According to the DMS execution semantics, the application of an action is done by substituting the guard answer variables and by *injectively* substituting the fresh input variables with corresponding values. We show here that this is not a limitation of the approach, which can in fact seamlessly account for standard variable substitution, possibly mapping multiple fresh variables with the same value.

The algorithm in Figure 5 shows precisely how to build a set of injective actions, i.e. actions where fresh variables are mapped to different values, from a set of non-injective

procedure STANDARD-SUBSTITUTION(ACTS)
input: Set ACTS of actions, **output:** Set ACTS_{std} of actions
  $\text{ACTS}_{std} := \emptyset$
  for all $\langle Q(\vec{u}), Del(\vec{u}), Add(\vec{u}, \vec{v})\rangle \in \text{ACTS}$ **do**
    for all $\vec{p} = \langle \vec{s}_1, \ldots, \vec{s}_{|p|}\rangle$ partition of $\vec{v}$ **do**
      $Add'(\vec{u}, \langle v_i' | 1 \leq i \leq |p|\rangle) :=$
        $Add(\vec{u}, \vec{v})[v/v_i'$ **if** $v \in \vec{s}_i | 1 \leq i \leq |p|]$
      $\text{ACTS}_{std} := \text{ACTS}_{std}$
        $\cup \{\langle Q(\vec{u}), Del(\vec{u}), Add'(\vec{u}, \langle v_i' | 1 \leq i \leq |p|\rangle)\rangle\}$

Figure 5: Procedure for turning a set of actions into another set of actions that simulates standard variable substitutions. Notation $E(\vec{u})[\vec{u}/\vec{z}]$, where E is a formula or a set of facts, indicates E where variables $\vec{u}$ are consistently replaced with corresponding variables/constants $\vec{z}$. For every partition set element $\vec{s}_i$, all variables belonging to a $\vec{s}_i$ are replaced with the new fresh variable v_i'.

actions, i.e. actions where fresh variables can be mapped to the same value. A demonstration of the algorithm is given in Example D.1.

EXAMPLE D.1. Given action

$$\alpha = \langle \{u_1, u_2\}, \{v_1, v_2, v_3\}, R(u_1, u_2), \{Q(u_2)\}, \{R(u_2, v_1), R(u_2, v_2), R(u_1, v_3)\}\rangle, \text{ we get:}$$

$$\left\{\begin{array}{l} \alpha_1 = \langle \{u_1, u_2\}, \{v_1', v_2', v_3'\}, R(u_1, u_2), \{Q(u_2)\}, \\ \quad \{R(u_2, v_1'), R(u_2, v_2'), R(u_1, v_3')\}\rangle, \\ \alpha_2 = \langle \{u_1, u_2\}, \{v_1', v_2'\}, R(u_1, u_2), \{Q(u_2)\}, \\ \quad \{R(u_2, v_1'), R(u_2, v_2'), R(u_1, v_2')\}\rangle, \\ \alpha_3 = \langle \{u_1, u_2\}, \{v_1', v_2'\}, R(u_1, u_2), \{Q(u_2)\}, \\ \quad \{R(u_2, v_2'), R(u_2, v_2'), R(u_1, v_1')\}\rangle, \\ \alpha_4 = \langle \{u_1, u_2\}, \{v_1', v_2'\}, R(u_1, u_2), \{Q(u_2)\}, \\ \quad \{R(u_2, v_2'), R(u_2, v_1'), R(u_1, v_2')\}\rangle, \\ \alpha_5 = \langle \{u_1, u_2\}, \{v_1'\}, R(u_1, u_2), \{Q(u_2)\}, \\ \quad \{R(u_2, v_1'), R(u_2, v_1'), R(u_1, v_1')\}\rangle \end{array}\right\}$$

to interpret the original action using standard variable substitutions for fresh input variables v_1, v_2, v_3. In action α_2 for instance, v_1' replaces the subset $\langle v_1\rangle$, while v_2' replaces the subset $\langle v_2, v_3\rangle$. This replacement corresponds to the partition $\vec{p} = \langle \vec{s}_1 = \langle v_1\rangle, \vec{s}_2 = \langle v_2, v_3\rangle\rangle$. ■

D.2 Weakening Freshness

One may argue that inputs provided to a DMS may not necessarily be fresh. In fact, there may be cases in which a DMS action is meant to establish new relations among already existing values, but still interacting with the external world to decide which. We call *arbitrary-input DMS* a DMS that does not necessarily require the input variables to be assigned to fresh values. We provide in what follows a proof and an example illustrating this remark.

PROOF. Let $\mathcal{S} = \langle I_0, \text{ACTS}\rangle$ be an arbitrary-input DMS defined over the data domain Δ and the schema $\mathcal{R}$. We produce a corresponding standard DMS $\mathcal{S}_{fresh} = \langle I_0, \text{ACTS}'\rangle$, defined over the same data domain and over an extended schema $\mathcal{R}'$, such that:

- the schema of the $\mathcal{R}' = \mathcal{R} \cup \{Hist/1\}$ is the extension of the schema of $\mathcal{S}$ by adding the unary relation *Hist*, which role is to store all the values seen in during the run of the DMS,
- the set of actions ACTS' of the standard DMS $\mathcal{S}'$ is defined as the smallest set satisfying the following property: for every arbitrary-input action $\left\langle \vec{u}, \vec{i}, Q(\vec{u}), Del(\vec{u}), Add\left(\vec{u}, \vec{i}\right)\right\rangle \in \text{ACTS}$ with abitrary-input variables $\vec{i}$, and for every possible binary partition $\vec{h} \uplus \vec{f}$ of the set of input variables $\vec{i}$, ACTS' contains the standard DMS action $\langle \vec{u} \uplus \vec{h}, \vec{f}, Q'(\vec{u}, \vec{h}), Del(\vec{u}), Add'(\vec{u}, \vec{h}, \vec{f})\rangle$, where
  - $Q'(\vec{u}, \vec{h}) = Q(\vec{u}) \wedge \bigwedge_{h \in \vec{h}} Hist(h)$ and
  - $Add'(\vec{u}, \vec{h}, \vec{v}) = Add(\vec{u}, \vec{h} \uplus \vec{f}) \cup \left\{Hist(f) | \, f \in \vec{f}\right\}$

Thus, every action with arbitrary-input variables $\vec{i}$ is translated into $2^{|\vec{i}|}$ actions, each one handling the case in which a subset of the uniform input variables are mapped to fresh values, while the remaining ones are bound to values present in the history of the run. It is easy to see that the configuration graph obtained from $\mathcal{S}$ by removing the requirement that input variables must match with fresh values, and the standard configuration graph of $\mathcal{S}'$, indeed coincide. □

EXAMPLE D.2. Given schema $\mathcal{R} = \{R/2, Q/1\}$, we replace the arbitrary input action

$$\langle \{u_1, u_2\}, \{i_1, i_2\}, R(u_1, u_2), \{Q(u_2)\}, \{R(u_2, i_1), R(u_2, i_2)\}\rangle$$

with the standard (fresh) input set of actions

$$\left\{\begin{array}{l} \alpha_1 = \langle \{u_1, u_2\}, \{f_1, f_2\}, R(u_1, u_2), \\ \quad \{Q(u_2)\}, \{R(u_2, f_1), R(u_2, f_2), Hist(f_1), Hist(v_2)\}\rangle \\ \alpha_2 = \langle \{u_1, u_2, h_1\}, \{f\}, R(u_1, u_2) \wedge Hist(h), \\ \quad \{Q(u_2)\}, \{R(u_2, h), R(u_2, f), Hist(f)\}\rangle \\ \alpha_3 = \langle \{u_1, u_2, h_1, h_2\}, \emptyset, R(u_1, u_2) \wedge Hist(h_1) \wedge Hist(h_1), \\ \quad \{Q(u_2)\}, \{R(u_2, h_1), R(u_2, h_2)\}\rangle \end{array}\right\}$$

■

D.3 Simulating Bulk Operations

We show how *bulk actions* can be simulated by standard DMSs. Recall that DMSs adopt a *retrieve-one-answer-per-step* semantics, i.e., a DMS action $\langle \vec{u}, \vec{v}, Q, Del, Add\rangle$ is applied by nondeterministically grounding its action parameters $\vec{u}$ with *one* answer to Q. Bulk actions, instead, require the adoption of a *retrieve-all-answers-per-step* semantics, where the update specified by *Del* and *Add* would be enforced by simultaneously considering *all* answers to Q. Let $\beta = \langle \vec{u}, \vec{v}, Q, Del, Add\rangle$ be a bulk action, i.e., an action where the action parameters $\vec{u}$ are implicitly universally quantified. We show how the bulk update induced by β can be simulated in a standard DMS though a complex sequence of actions and the introduction of accessory relations.

The following accessory relations are used: *(i)* A proposition $Lock_\beta$, used to "lock" the sequence of actions simulating β, guaranteeing that it is not interrupted by other actions. *(ii)* A relation $FreshInput_\beta$ with arity $|\vec{v}|$, used to store (in a single tuple) the selected substitution for the fresh-input variables of β, enabling the consistent usage of such a substitution when reconstrucing the bulk update of β. *(iii)* A relation $ParMatch_\beta$ with arity $|\vec{u}| + 1$, used to incrementally store all answers to β·guard, then exhaustively considering them when reconstructing the bulk update induced by β. The last argument of $ParMatch_\beta$ is used to "flag" tuples that have been already considered for the corresponding deletion of tuples within the bulk update (more details are given below). *(iv)* Two propositions $DelPhase_\beta$ and $AddPhase_\beta$, identifying those portions of the sequence of actions respectively dealing with the bulk deletion/addition of β.

Whenever β is eligible for execution, those accessory relations are all empty. At the completion of the sequence of actions simulating β, such accessory relations will be empty again. To ensure the non-interruptibility of the sequence of actions used to simulate bulk actions, all actions of the DMS of interest must be modified so as to incorporate the negation of all lock propositions (like $Lock_\beta$ above), denoted in the following Φ_{NoLock}.

The simulation of β is done by structuring the sequence in three phases. The first consists of the application of a single initialization action Init_β, executable when $\beta{\cdot}\mathsf{guard}$ admits at least one answer. Init_β sets the lock, and stores the selected substitution for the fresh-input variables. Specifically, Init_β has fresh-input variables $\vec{v}$, and is defined as:

- $\mathsf{Init}_\beta{\cdot}\mathsf{guard} = (\exists \vec{u}.\beta{\cdot}\mathsf{guard}(\vec{u})) \wedge \Phi_{NoLock}$;
- $\mathsf{Init}_\beta{\cdot}Del = \emptyset$;
- $\mathsf{Init}_\beta{\cdot}Add = \{Lock_\beta, FreshInput_\beta(\vec{v})\}$.

The second phase deals with the computation of all answers to $\beta{\cdot}\mathsf{guard}$, storing them into the corresponding accessory relation. Such a phase is identified by the presence of the lock for β, and by the absence of the flags marking the bulk deletion and addition of tuples. The computation of the answers to $\beta{\cdot}\mathsf{guard}$ is handled by iteratively executing action $\mathsf{CompAns}_\beta$. This action is executable when there is at least one answer to $\beta{\cdot}\mathsf{guard}$ that has not yet been transferred. If this is the case, it nondeterministically picks one such answers, and transfers it into the accessory relation. Specifically, $\mathsf{CompAns}_\beta$ has exactly $\vec{u}$ as action parameters, no fresh-input variable, and is defined as follows:

- $\mathsf{CompAns}_\beta{\cdot}\mathsf{guard} = Lock_\beta \wedge \neg DelPhase_\beta \wedge \neg AddPhase_\beta \wedge \beta{\cdot}\mathsf{guard}(\vec{u}) \wedge \neg ParMatch_\beta(\vec{u})$;
- $\mathsf{CompAns}_\beta{\cdot}Del = \emptyset$;
- $\mathsf{CompAns}_\beta{\cdot}Add = \{ParMatch_\beta(\vec{u}, \mathsf{0})\}$.

When inserting an answer tuple into the accessory relation, the last, additional argument of $ParMatch_\beta$ is set to 0. This witnesses that such an answer tuple has still to be considered when reconstructing the deletions induced by β.

Action $\mathsf{CompAns}_\beta$ becomes non-executable when the FO sentence $\Phi_\beta^{AllSub} = \forall \vec{u}.\beta{\cdot}\mathsf{guard}(\vec{u}) \rightarrow ParMatch_\beta(\vec{u})$ holds in the current database. We consequently insert a dedicated action $\mathsf{EnableU}_\beta$, marking the end of reiterated application of $\mathsf{CompAns}_\beta$. This action is executable when all answer tuples have been transferred to the accessory relation, and has the effect of indicating that it is now time to apply the bulk update induced by β. The execution semantics of DMSs dictates that additions have priority over deletions. For this reason, the bulk update first requires to consider all deletions, and then all additions. Hence, $\mathsf{EnableU}_\beta$ raises flag $DelPhase_\beta$. Specifically, $\mathsf{EnableU}_\beta$ has no action parameters nor fresh-input variables, and is defined as follows:

- $\mathsf{EnableU}_\beta{\cdot}\mathsf{guard} =$ $Lock_\beta \wedge \neg DelPhase_\beta \wedge \neg AddPhase_\beta \wedge \Phi_\beta^{AllSub}$;
- $\mathsf{EnableU}_\beta{\cdot}Del = \emptyset$;
- $\mathsf{EnableU}_\beta{\cdot}Add = \{DelPhase_\beta\}$.

The introduction of flag $DelPhase_\beta$ marks the beginning of the third phase, which deals with the actual bulk update. As mentioned before, this phase is split into two sub-phases: a first sub-phase dealing with deletions, a second sub-phase dealing with additions. Both sub-phases consists of the iterative application of one dedicated action, which deals with the tuples to be deleted/added due to a specific answer tuple to $\beta{\cdot}\mathsf{guard}$. As for deletion, the iteratively executed action is $\mathsf{ApplyDel}_\beta$. This action nondeterministically picks an answer tuple for $\beta{\cdot}\mathsf{guard}$ that still has to be considered for deletion. This is done by extracting a tuple from $ParMatch_\beta$, checking that the last argument of such a tuple corresponds to 0. In addition, since the deletion may depend on the fresh-input of β as well, $\mathsf{ApplyDel}_\beta$ also needs to extract the single tuple present in the input accessory relation $FreshInput_\beta$. Specifically, $\mathsf{ApplyDel}_\beta$ has $\vec{u}$ as action parameters, no fresh-input variables, and is defined as follows:

- $\mathsf{ApplyDel}_\beta{\cdot}\mathsf{guard} = DelPhase_\beta \wedge ParMatch_\beta(\vec{u}, \mathsf{0})$;
- $\mathsf{ApplyDel}_\beta{\cdot}Del = \beta{\cdot}Del \cup \{ParMatch_\beta(\vec{u}, \mathsf{0})\}$;
- $\mathsf{ApplyDel}_\beta{\cdot}Add = \{ParMatch_\beta(\vec{u}, \mathsf{1})\}$.

Notice that the update over $ParMatch_\beta$ changing the last argument of the tuple $\vec{u}$ is used to track that the selected tuple has been already processed for deletion. $\mathsf{ApplyDel}_\beta$ cannot be applied anymore when all tuples in $ParMatch_\beta$ are marked with 1. This situation indicates that no more deletions have to be considered, and that bulk addition must now be handled. Such a transition is captured by the dedicated action $\mathsf{DelToAdd}_\beta$, which does not have action parameters nor fresh-input variables, and is defined as follows:

- $\mathsf{DelToAdd}_\beta{\cdot}\mathsf{guard} =$ $DelPhase_\beta \wedge \forall \vec{u}, m.ParMatch_\beta(\vec{v}, m) \rightarrow m = \mathsf{1}$;
- $\mathsf{DelToAdd}_\beta{\cdot}Del = \{DelPhase_\beta\}$;
- $\mathsf{DelToAdd}_\beta{\cdot}Add = \{AddPhase_\beta\}$.

The second sub-phase simulating the bulk update is captured by the iterative application of action $\mathsf{ApplyAdd}_\beta$, which closely resembles $\mathsf{ApplyDel}_\beta$, with three differences: *(i)* it requires to consider not only the answers to $\beta{\cdot}\mathsf{guard}$ (stored in $ParMatch_\beta$), but also the selected matching for the input variables (stored in $FreshInput_\beta$); *(ii)* it handles the insertion of tuples, hence refers to $\beta{\cdot}Add$; *(iii)* it removes a tuple from $ParMatch_\beta$ to mark that it has been considered for addition. Specifically, $\mathsf{ApplyAdd}_\beta$ has $\vec{u}$ and $\vec{v}$ as action parameters, no fresh-input variables, and is defined as:

- $\mathsf{ApplyAdd}_\beta{\cdot}\mathsf{guard} =$ $AddPhase_\beta \wedge ParMatch_\beta(\vec{u}, \mathsf{1}) \wedge FreshInput_\beta(\vec{v})$;
- $\mathsf{ApplyDel}_\beta{\cdot}Del = \{ParMatch_\beta(\vec{u}, \mathsf{1})\}$;
- $\mathsf{ApplyDel}_\beta{\cdot}Add = \beta{\cdot}Add$.

It is easy to see that this last sub-phase ends where there is no more tuple in $ParMatch_\beta$. This marks the end of the addition loop, and triggers the execution of the last action of the sequence, namely $\mathsf{Finalize}_\beta$. This last action mirrors Init_β, and has in fact a twofold effect: releasing the lock(s), and emptying the content of $FreshInput_\beta$ by removing its single tuple (recall, in fact, that $ParMatch_\beta$ is already empty). Specifically, $\mathsf{Finalize}_\beta$ has $\vec{v}$ as action parameters (since it needs to match those against the $FreshInput_\beta$ relation), has no fresh-input variable, and is defined as:

- $\mathsf{Finalize}_\beta{\cdot}\mathsf{guard} =$ $FreshInput_\beta(\vec{v}) \wedge \neg\exists \vec{u}, m.ParMatch_\beta(\vec{u}, m)$;
- $\mathsf{Finalize}_\beta{\cdot}Del = \{FreshInput_\beta(\vec{v})\}$;
- $\mathsf{Finalize}_\beta{\cdot}Add = \emptyset$.

Making SQL Queries Correct on Incomplete Databases: A Feasibility Study

Paolo Guagliardo
School of Informatics
The University of Edinburgh
pguaglia@inf.ed.ac.uk

Leonid Libkin
School of Informatics
The University of Edinburgh
libkin@inf.ed.ac.uk

ABSTRACT

Multiple issues with SQL's handling of nulls have been well documented. Having efficiency as its key goal, evaluation of SQL queries disregards the standard notion of correctness on incomplete databases – certain answers – due to its high complexity. As a result, it may produce answers that are just plain wrong. It was recently shown that SQL evaluation can be modified, at least for first-order queries, to return only correct answers. But while these modifications came with good theoretical complexity bounds, they have not been tested in practice.

The goals of this proof-of-concept paper are to understand whether wrong answers can be produced by SQL queries in real-world scenarios, and whether proposed techniques for avoiding them can be made practically feasible.

We use the TPC-H benchmark, and show that for some typical queries involving negation, wrong answers are very common. On the other hand, existing solutions for fixing the problem do not work in practice at all. By analyzing the reasons for this, we come up with a new modified way of rewriting SQL queries that restores correctness. We conduct experiments which show the feasibility of our solution: the small price tag it imposes can be often tolerated to ensure correct results, and we do not miss correct answers that the usual SQL evaluation produces. The overall conclusion is that correct evaluation can be realistically achieved in the presence of nulls, at least for the SQL fragment that corresponds to first-order queries.

1. INTRODUCTION

The way incomplete information is handled in commercial DBMSs, specifically by SQL, has been heavily criticized for producing counter-intuitive and just plain incorrect answers [7, 9]. The reason behind this behavior is that SQL designers had first and foremost efficient evaluation in mind, but correctness and efficiency do not always get along. The standard theoretical approach to answering queries on incomplete databases, which is widely accepted as providing the right notion of answers, is to compute *certain answers*. These are query answers that do not depend on how the unknown data is interpreted. However, computing them is not easy, in fact coNP-hard for most reasonable semantics, if we deal with relational calculus/algebra queries [2]. SQL's evaluation is very efficient; it is in AC^0 (a small parallel complexity class) for the same class of queries, and thus it provably cannot capture certain answers.

The gap in complexity is not yet a reason for undesirable behavior; one can easily imagine that SQL evaluation produces an approximation of certain answers. There are two ways in which certain answers and SQL's evaluation could differ:

- SQL can miss some of the tuples that belong to certain answers, thus producing *false negatives*; or
- it can return some tuples that do not belong to certain answers, that is, *false positives*.

False negatives can be accepted as the price to be paid for lowering complexity; after all, they just indicate that the correct answer is approximated. False positives, on the other hand, are outright wrong answers and therefore should not be tolerated. The problem with SQL is that it produces both kinds of errors.

To see how false positives can be generated, consider a simple query computing the difference of two relations R and S, each with a single attribute A:

```
SELECT R.A FROM R WHERE NOT EXISTS
    ( SELECT * FROM S WHERE R.A = S.A )
```

When $R = \{1\}$ and $S = \{\texttt{NULL}\}$, the output is $\{1\}$, but it is *not* a certain answer. Indeed, if the missing value represented by **NULL** is interpreted as 1, the difference $R - S$ is empty, and thus so is the set of certain answers.

The reasons behind SQL's incorrect behavior have their roots in the flawed three-valued logic approach it uses for handling nulls. Multiple attempts to fix it have been made in the past (see, e.g., [11, 15, 31]) although none of them came with formal correctness guarantees. Recently, [22] proposed a new approach to fixing SQL's evaluation scheme that provided provable correctness guarantees. It showed how to translate a query Q into a query Q' such that:

- false positives never occur: Q' returns a subset of certain answers to Q;
- data complexity of Q' is still AC^0; and
- on databases without nulls, Q and Q' produce the same results.

Given the attractive theoretical properties of the approach, we want to understand *whether these theoretical*

PODS'16, June 26-July 01, 2016, San Francisco, CA, USA

ISBN 978-1-4503-4191-2/16/06...$15.00

DOI: http://dx.doi.org/10.1145/2902251.2902297

guarantees can work in practice. To this end, we need to answer two main questions:

Question 1. Are false positives a real problem? Do they occur in real-life queries over databases with nulls?

Question 2. Can algorithms that correctly evaluate queries on databases with nulls be efficiently implemented? What is the price to pay, in terms of query evaluation performance, for correctness guarantees?

Since algorithms in [22] introduced extra steps to restore correctness, we do not expect, in general, to outperform native SQL evaluation, which was designed exclusively to optimize execution time. We can hope, however, that the overhead is sufficiently small. If this is so, one can envision two modes of evaluation: the standard one, where efficiency is the only concern, and an alternative, perhaps slightly more expensive one, that provides correctness guarantees. The difference is then the *price of correctness*, and we need to understand what it is.

This work is the first feasibility study in this direction, and it produces promising results that warrant further investment into designing algorithms with correctness guarantees for larger classes of queries. Here we consider relational calculus/algebra queries and provide the following results.

False positives. They are a real problem for queries that involve negation. We look at queries inspired by the TPC-H benchmark [28] and show that false positives are always present. Sometimes they constitute almost 100% of answers; for other queries, they quickly grow with the null rate (the probability that a null occurs in a given position), accounting for between 1.5% and 20% of answers when the null rate is 2% and rising to at least 15% even for the best behaved queries when the null rate is 10%.

Algorithms with correctness guarantees. Those presented in [22] have a very good theoretical complexity but they cannot be implemented *as-is* due to the extensive use of Cartesian product in translated queries. To overcome this, we design an alternative way of transforming queries that still guarantees correctness while producing queries that are much more implementation-friendly. For positive queries (i.e., not involving negation in any form) and on databases without nulls, it coincides with the usual SQL evaluation.

We then test our new algorithm on databases with nulls, for our sample TCP-H queries with negation, and observe two kinds of behavior. Sometimes, the performance of translated queries with correctness guarantees is very good, with the price of correctness – the overhead of executing the translated query – not exceeding 4% (and sometimes in fact making queries up to 10,000 times faster).

For other queries, the translation may "confuse" the optimizer. That is, the optimizer generates plans with astronomical costs (although in some cases these are not reflected by the actual running time). The reason is that some conditions of the form `R.A = S.B` get translated into `R.A = S.B OR R.A IS NULL` to enforce correctness, but this causes the optimizer to badly overestimate the execution time, up to the point of resorting to nested-loop implementation of joins. However, we show that simple syntactic manipulations of queries can restore sanity to the optimizer, and result in reasonable performance, with translated queries running at roughly half the speed of the original ones.

Precision and recall. We need to address them to say how good our evaluation techniques are. Precision refers to how many answers are certain, and recall to the proportion of certain answers returned. The formal correctness guarantees we prove imply that precision of our algorithms is 100% (while for some of the queries we experiment with, SQL's precision is close to zero).

It is easy to achieve high precision with low recall: just return nothing, and there are no false positives. Since SQL returns many more answers than necessary (false positives), it should not be surprising that sometimes it also returns a certain answer our procedure misses. However, in all our experiments, recall stands at 100%: our procedure returns precisely certain answers that are also returned by SQL evaluation.

The key conclusion of this study is that *achieving correctness in SQL query evaluation on databases with nulls is feasible.* As we said, this is a proof-of-concept paper, whose goal is to demonstrate that the idea of rewriting queries to achieve correctness is implementable. We have done this for first-order queries and missing-information interpretation of nulls. Of course much more is needed before one can introduce a second, fully correct, evaluation mode for SQL queries (e.g., by saying `SELECT CERTAIN`); we shall discuss particular tasks (such as handling bag semantics, aggregates, non-applicable nulls, etc.) at the end of the paper.

Organization. Basic notions and definitions are given in Section 2. Section 3 discusses the setup for our experiments. Section 4 presents experimental results on false positives in SQL query evaluation. Section 5 describes the translation of [22] and explains why it cannot be efficiently implemented. Section 6 presents our improved implementation-friendly translation. Section 7 contains the experimental results for the improved translation and describes the price of correctness for SQL query evaluation. Section 8 discusses extensions to cover other language aspects of SQL. The query translations used in our experiments are in the appendix.

2. PRELIMINARIES

We consider incomplete databases with nulls interpreted as missing information. Much of the following is standard in the literature on databases with incomplete information, see, e.g., [1, 12, 14, 22, 30]. The usual way of modeling SQL's nulls under this interpretation is to use *Codd nulls* which are a special case of the more general *marked*, or labeled, nulls. Databases are populated by two types of elements: *constants* and *nulls*, coming from countably infinite sets denoted by Const and Null, respectively. Nulls are denoted by $\bot$, sometimes with sub- or superscripts. For the purpose of the general model we follow the textbook approach assuming one domain Const for all non-null elements appearing in databases. In real life (and our experiments), such elements can be of many different types, and those appearing in the same column must be of the same type. Adjusting results and translations of queries for this setting is completely straightforward.

A relational schema, or vocabulary, is a set of relation names with associated arities. With each k-ary relation symbol S from the vocabulary, an incomplete relational instance D associates a k-ary relation S^D over $\mathsf{Const} \cup \mathsf{Null}$, that is, a finite subset of $(\mathsf{Const} \cup \mathsf{Null})^k$. When the instance is clear from the context, we write S instead of S^D for the relation itself. We denote the arity of S by $\mathsf{ar}(S)$, and use the same notation for queries.

In instances with Codd nulls, it is assumed that nulls do not repeat, i.e., each element of Null appears at most once in a database. When repetition of nulls is allowed, we speak of *labeled* or *marked* nulls; these often appear in applications such as data integration and exchange [4, 19]. Our translations work correctly on databases with Codd nulls as well as on databases with the more general marked nulls.

The sets of constants and nulls that occur in a database D are denoted by $\mathsf{Const}(D)$ and $\mathsf{Null}(D)$, respectively. The *active domain* of D is the set $\mathsf{adom}(D)$ of all elements occurring in it, i.e., $\mathsf{Const}(D) \cup \mathsf{Null}(D)$. If D has no nulls, we say that it is *complete*. A *valuation* v on a database D is a map $v : \mathsf{Null}(D) \to \mathsf{Const}$. We denote by $v(D)$ the result of replacing each null $\bot$ with $v(\bot)$ in D. The *semantics* of an incomplete database D is the set of all complete databases it can possibly represent. Under the missing value interpretation of nulls, it is defined as $\{v(D) \mid v \text{ is a valuation}\}$, and is referred to as the closed-world semantics of incompleteness [26].

Query languages. As our query language, we consider the basic fragment of SQL, corresponding to relational calculus/algebra (i.e., first-order queries). That is, we have the usual **SELECT-FROM-WHERE** queries, with (correlated) subqueries preceded by **IN** and **EXISTS**, as well as their negations.

For translations that give us correctness guarantees, we use relational algebra, with the standard operations of selection σ, projection π, Cartesian product $\times$ (or join $\bowtie$), union $\cup$, difference $-$ and intersection $\cap$. We assume that selection conditions are positive Boolean combinations of equalities of the form $A = B$ and $A = c$, where A and B are attributes and c is a constant value, and disequalities $A \neq B$ and $A \neq c$. Note that these conditions are closed under negation, which can simply be propagated to atoms: e.g., $\neg\big((A = B) \vee (B \neq 1)\big)$ is equivalent to $(A \neq B) \wedge (B = 1)$.

In the translations of queries, we also use conditions $\mathsf{const}(A)$ and $\mathsf{null}(A)$ in selections, indicating whether the value of an attribute is a constant or a null. These correspond to SQL's `A IS NOT NULL` and `A IS NULL`.

Correctness guarantees. The standard notion of correct query answering on incomplete databases is *certain answers*, that is, tuples that are present in the answer to a query regardless of the interpretation of nulls. For a query Q and a database D, these are typically defined as $\bigcap\{Q\big(v(D)\big) \mid v \text{ is a valuation}\}$; see [1, 14].

This definition has a serious drawback, though, as tuples with nulls cannot be returned, while standard query evaluation may well produce such tuples. For instance, if we have a relation $R = \{(1, \bot), (2, 3)\}$, and a query returning R, then the certain answer contains only $(2, 3)$, while intuitively it should give us the entire relation. In light of this, for correctness guarantees we use a closely-related but more general notion from [23], called certain answers with nulls in [22].

Formally, for a query Q and a database D, the *certain answer with nulls*, denoted by $\mathsf{cert}(Q, D)$, is the set of all tuples $\bar{a}$ over $\mathsf{adom}(D)$ such that $v(\bar{a}) \in Q\big(v(D)\big)$ for every valuation v on D. In the above example, certain answer with nulls contains both tuples $(1, \bot)$ and $(2, 3)$. The standard certain answers are exactly the null-free tuples in $\mathsf{cert}(Q, D)$ [22].

Definition 1. A query evaluation algorithm has *correctness guarantees* for query Q if for every database D it returns a subset of $\mathsf{cert}(Q, D)$.

In other words, with correctness guarantees, false positives are not allowed: all returned tuples must be certain answers.

Often our evaluation algorithms will be of the following form: translate Q into another query Q', and then run it on D. If $Q'(D) \subseteq \mathsf{cert}(Q, D)$, we say that Q' has correctness guarantees for Q.

Some results concerning correctness guarantees are known. By *naïve evaluation* for a fragment of relational algebra we mean the algorithm that treats elements of Null as if they were the usual database entries, i.e., each evaluation $\bot = c$ for $c \in \mathsf{Const}$ is false and $\bot = \bot'$ is true iff $\bot$ and $\bot'$ are the same element in Null.

FACT 1 ([12, 14, 22]). *Naïve evaluation has correctness guarantees for positive relational algebra, i.e., relational algebra without the difference operator and without disequalities in selection conditions. In fact it computes exactly certain answers with nulls. This remains true even if we extend the language with the division operator as long as its second argument is a relation in the database.*

Recall that division is a derived relational algebra operation; it computes tuples in a projection of a relation appearing in all possible combinations with tuples from another relation (e.g., 'find students taking all courses').

SQL evaluation. For SQL, the evaluation procedure is different, as it is based on a 3-valued logic (3VL); see [9]. In particular, comparisons such as $\bot = c$, as well as comparisons between two nulls, evaluate to *unknown*, which is then propagated through conditions using the rules of 3VL.

More precisely, selection conditions can evaluate to true ($\mathbf{t}$), false ($\mathbf{f}$), or unknown ($\mathbf{u}$). If at least one attribute in a comparison is null, the result of the comparison is $\mathbf{u}$. The interaction of $\mathbf{u}$ with Boolean connectives is as follows: $\neg\mathbf{u} = \mathbf{u}$, $\mathbf{u} \wedge \mathbf{t} = \mathbf{u} \wedge \mathbf{u} = \mathbf{u}$, $\mathbf{u} \wedge \mathbf{f} = \mathbf{f}$, and dually by De Morgan's law for $\vee$. Then, σ_θ selects tuples on which θ evaluates to $\mathbf{t}$ (that is, $\mathbf{f}$ and $\mathbf{u}$ tuples are not selected). We refer to the result of evaluating a query Q in this way as $\mathsf{Eval}_{\mathsf{SQL}}(Q, D)$.

FACT 2 ([22]). $\mathsf{Eval}_{\mathsf{SQL}}$ *has correctness guarantees for the positive fragment of relational algebra.*

The positive fragment of relational algebra corresponds to the fragment of SQL in which negation does not appear in any form, i.e., **EXCEPT** is not allowed, there are no negations in **WHERE** conditions and the use of **NOT IN** and **NOT EXISTS** for subqueries is prohibited.

3. SETUP: QUERIES AND INSTANCES

We have seen that what breaks correctness guarantees is queries with negation; the example used in the introduction was based on a **NOT EXISTS** subquery. To choose concrete queries for our experiments, we use the well established and common TPC-H benchmark that models a business application scenario and typical decision support queries [28]. Its schema contains information about customers who place orders consisting of several items, and suppliers who supply parts for those orders. There are also small relations describing geographical information (nations and regions). In terms of size, `lineitem` is by far the largest table, which records the items constituting an order and associated parts and suppliers, followed by `order` itself.

Given the decision support nature of TPC-H queries, many of them involve aggregation. However, aggregation is not important for our purposes: if a tuple without an aggregate value is a false positive, it remains false positive when an extra attribute value is added. Since we only need to measure the ratio of false positives, and the *relative* change of speed in query evaluation, we can safely drop aggregates from the output of those queries.

Most of the TPC-H queries do not have negation; they are essentially aggregate queries on top of multi-way joins. Two of them, queries 21 and 22, do use **NOT EXISTS** so we choose them for our experiments. We further supplement them with two very typical database textbook [10] queries (slightly modified to fit the TPC-H schema) that are designed to teach subqueries. We provide all these queries below, to give the reader an idea of the features involved.

Query Q_1. It is a TPC-H query meant to identify suppliers who were not able to ship required parts in a timely manner. It returns suppliers from a given nation, and multi-supplier *finalized* orders (i.e., with status 'F') where the supplier was the only one who failed to meet the committed delivery date. The query is:

```
SELECT s_suppkey, o_orderkey
FROM   supplier, lineitem l1, orders, nation
WHERE  s_suppkey = l1.l_suppkey
  AND  o_orderkey = l1.l_orderkey
  AND  o_orderstatus = 'F'
  AND  l1.l_receiptdate > l1.l_commitdate
  AND  EXISTS (
       SELECT *
       FROM   lineitem l2
       WHERE  l2.l_orderkey = l1.l_orderkey
         AND  l2.l_suppkey <> l1.l_suppkey )
  AND  NOT EXISTS (
       SELECT *
       FROM   lineitem l3
       WHERE  l3.l_orderkey = l1.l_orderkey
         AND  l3.l_suppkey <> l1.l_suppkey
         AND  l3.l_receiptdate > l3.l_commitdate )
  AND  s_nationkey = n_nationkey
  AND  n_name = $nation
```

where `$nation` is a randomly chosen value among the keys of table `nation`.

Query Q_2. It is another TPC-H query, which aims at identifying countries where there are customers who may be likely to make a purchase. It returns customers within a specific range of countries who have not recently placed orders but have a greater than average positive account balance. The query is:

```
SELECT c_custkey, c_nationkey
FROM   customer
WHERE  c_nationkey IN ($countries)
  AND  c_acctbal > (
       SELECT avg(c_acctbal)
       FROM   customer
       WHERE  c_acctbal > 0.00
         AND  c_nationkey IN ($countries) )
  AND  NOT EXISTS (
       SELECT *
       FROM   orders
       WHERE  o_custkey = c_custkey )
```

where `$countries` is a list of 7 distinct values randomly chosen among the keys of table `nation`.

Query Q_3. It is a classical textbook query that finds all orders supplied entirely by a specific supplier:

```
SELECT o_orderkey
FROM   orders
WHERE  NOT EXISTS (
       SELECT *
       FROM   lineitem
       WHERE  l_orderkey = o_orderkey
         AND  l_suppkey <> $supp_key )
```

where `$supp_key` is a randomly chosen value among the keys of table `supplier`.

Query Q_4. It is another standard textbook query illustrating a correlated subquery with **NOT EXISTS**. The subquery uses multiple relations and a complex join condition. It asks for orders not supplied with any part of a specific color by any supplier from a specific country.

```
SELECT o_orderkey
FROM   orders
WHERE  NOT EXISTS (
       SELECT *
       FROM   lineitem, part, supplier, nation
       WHERE  l_orderkey = o_orderkey
         AND  l_partkey = p_partkey
         AND  l_suppkey = s_suppkey
         AND  p_name LIKE '%'||$color||'%'
         AND  s_nationkey = n_nationkey
         AND  n_name = $nation )
```

Here `$nation` is a randomly chosen value among the keys of table `nation` and `$color` is a randomly chosen string from a list of 92 possibilities provided by TPC-H.

Generating test instances. The TPC-H benchmark comes with its own standard tool, DBGen, for generating instances. However, DBGen generates only *complete* instances (i.e., without nulls) so we need to go over them and insert nulls to make them fit for our purpose.

For that, we separate attribute into nullable and non-nullable ones; the latter are those where nulls cannot occur (due to primary key constraints, or **NOT NULL** declarations). For nullable attributes, we choose a probability, referred to as the *null rate* of the resulting instance, and simply flip a coin for each tuple to decide whether the corresponding value is to be replaced by a null. As a result, for each nullable attribute, the instance will contain a percentage of nulls roughly equal to the null rate with which nulls are generated. We consider null rates in the range 0.5%–10%.

The smallest instance DBGen generates (in line with the prescriptions of the TPC-H standard) is about 1GB in size, containing just under $9 \cdot 10^6$ tuples. We shall measure the relative performance of our translated queries w.r.t. the original ones on instances of 1GB, 3GB, 6GB, and 10GB size.

To estimate the amount of false positives in query answers, we shall generate a high number of incomplete instances, on which our sample queries are executed multiple times. False positives are detected by algorithms that are quite expensive. To speed up the process, and since in any case we are interested only in the *percentage* of false positives, for this experiment we use smaller instances. These are generated by means of a configurable data generator, DataFiller [8], and are compliant with the TPC-H specification in everything but size, which we scale down by a factor of 10^3.

All our experiments were run using a local installation of PostgreSQL 9.5.1 on a dedicated machine with an Intel Core i5-3470 quad-core CPU @ 3.20GHz and 8GB of RAM. Note that since we measure the *percentage* of false positive answers and the *relative* performance of our scheme for obtaining correct answers, the exact hardware configuration and choice of a DBMS are of less importance.

4. HOW MANY FALSE POSITIVES?

A false positive answer is a tuple that is returned by SQL evaluation and yet is not certain; that is, the set of false positives produced by a query Q on a database D is $Q(D) - \mathsf{cert}(Q, D)$. They only occur on databases with nulls (on complete databases, $Q(D) = \mathsf{cert}(Q, D)$); a simple example was given in the introduction. Our goal now is to see whether real-life queries indeed produce false positives. For this, we shall run our test queries on generated instances with nulls and compare their output with certain answers.

However, certain answers are expensive to compute: the problem is coNP-hard for queries with negation, thus a naïve computation will require exponential time. As a way around it, we design specialized algorithms to detect (some of the) false positives for queries Q_1–Q_4, and compare their results with SQL outputs. This will tell us that at least some percentage of SQL answers are false positives.

Algorithms for detecting false positives. Such algorithms take as input the bindings for the parameters of the query, a database D and an answer tuple $\bar{a}$, and return *true* if $\bar{a}$ is a false positive, thereby giving us a lower bound on the number of false positives. The underlying idea is the same for all queries: we look for the presence of null values in relevant comparisons involving nullable attributes, because in such a case the comparison can be made true or false at need in order to falsify the answer tuple. For instance, to falsify an order id k in the answer to query Q_3, we look for a tuple in table `lineitem` where the value of attribute `l_orderkey` is k and the value of `l_suppkey` is null. Intuitively, if there is a lineitem for order k where the supplier is unknown, then that supplier may well be different from the one specified by the value of parameter `$supp_key`.

Detecting false positives in query Q_2 is also simple: it suffices to check whether there is a tuple in table `orders` for which the attribute `o_custkey` is null; in that case, all answers produced by the query are false positives. Intuitively, if there is an order for which the customer is unknown, then that customer could be anybody, including the one in the answer tuple.

For the remaining two sample queries, the pseudocode to detect false positives is given in Algorithms 1 and 2.

Algorithm 1 Detect false positives in Q_1

```
for t̄ ∈ lineitem where t̄[l_orderkey] = ā[o_orderkey]:
    x ← t̄[l_suppkey]
    if x is not null and x = ā[s_suppkey]:
        continue
    d1 ← t̄[l_commitdate] ; d2 ← t̄[l_receiptdate]
    if d1 is null or d2 is null or d2 > d1:
        return true
return false
```

Algorithm 2 Detect false positives in Q_4

```
for t̄ ∈ lineitem where t̄[l_orderkey] = ā[o_orderkey]:
    P, S ← false
    for p̄ ∈ part where t̄[l_partkey] is null or
                        or equal to p̄[p_partkey]:
        if p̄[p_name] is null or has substring σ[color]:
            P ← true ; break
    if P is not true: continue
    for s̄ ∈ supplier where t̄[l_suppkey] is null or
                            equal to s̄[s_suppkey]:
        x ← s̄[s_nationkey]
        if x is null: S ← true ; break
        for n̄ ∈ nation where n̄[n_nationkey] = x:
            if n̄[n_name] equals σ[nation]:
                S ← true ; break
    if P is true and S is true: return true
return false
```

False positives: experimental results. Recall that null values in instances are randomly generated: each nullable attribute can become null with the same fixed probability, referred to as the null rate. We let null rates range from 0.5% to 6% in steps of 0.5% and from 6% to 10% in steps of 1%.

To get good estimates, we generate 100 instances for each null rate, and run each query 5 times, with randomly generated values for its parameters. At each execution, a lower bound on the percentage of false positives is calculated by means of the algorithms described above. The results of the experiment are shown in Figure 1, reporting the average over all executions.

The outcome of the experiment shows that the problem of incorrect query answers in SQL is not just theoretical but it may well occur in practical settings: all of the queries we tested produce false positives on incomplete databases with as low as 0.5% of null values.

In fact for some queries the percentage of false positives is very high: for Q_2, almost all answers are such, even when few nulls are present. For Q_3, at least a quarter of all answers are wrong when the null rate is just 3%, rising to at least half incorrect answers for the null rate of 8%. Other queries, such as Q_1 and Q_4, appear to be more robust (as we only find a lower bound on the number of false positives), but false positives are always present, even at the lowest null rate tested, and in fact they constitute at least 10% of all answers at null rates of 7% and above.

The overall conclusion is clear: false positives do occur in answers to very common queries with negation, and account for a significant portion of the answers.

5. CORRECTNESS: A SIMPLE TRANSLATION

Since false positives are a real problem, we want to devise evaluation strategies that avoid it, if correctness of query re-

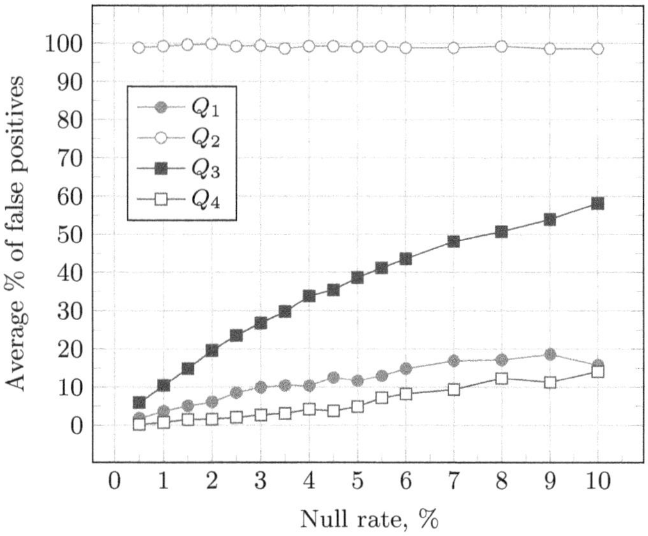

Figure 1: Average percentage of false positives produced by each query for increasing null rates.

sults is a concern. One such evaluation scheme was proposed recently [22]. We now review it, and explain why in its original form it cannot be implemented efficiently, despite good theoretical bounds.

We present it at the level of relational algebra. The key idea is to translate a query Q into a pair $(Q^{\mathsf{t}}, Q^{\mathsf{f}})$ of queries that have correctness guarantees for Q and its complement $\overline{Q}$, respectively. That is, for every database D, the tuples in $Q^{\mathsf{t}}(D)$ are certainly true, and those in $Q^{\mathsf{f}}(D)$ are certainly false:

$$Q^{\mathsf{t}}(D) \subseteq \mathsf{cert}(Q, D) \quad (1)$$

$$Q^{\mathsf{f}}(D) \subseteq \mathsf{cert}(\overline{Q}, D) \quad (2)$$

To describe the translation, we need the following.

Definition 2. Two tuples $\bar{r}$ and $\bar{s}$ of the same length over $\mathsf{Const} \cup \mathsf{Null}$ are *unifiable*, written as $\bar{r} \Uparrow \bar{s}$, if there exists a valuation v of nulls such that $v(\bar{r}) = v(\bar{s})$.

The translations of [22] are shown in Figure 2. Here adom refers to the query computing the active domain (the union of all projections on each attribute of all relations), and θ^* refers to the translation of selection conditions, which is defined inductively as follows:

$$\begin{aligned}
(A = B)^* &= (A = B) \\
(A = c)^* &= (A = c) \quad \text{if } c \text{ is a constant} \\
(A \neq B)^* &= (A \neq B) \wedge \mathsf{const}(A) \wedge \mathsf{const}(B) \\
(A \neq c)^* &= (A \neq c) \wedge \mathsf{const}(A) \\
(\theta_1 \vee \theta_2)^* &= \theta_1^* \vee \theta_2^* \\
(\theta_1 \wedge \theta_2)^* &= \theta_1^* \wedge \theta_2^*
\end{aligned}$$

While (1) and (2) ensure correctness guarantees for all relational algebra queries, and queries Q^{t} and Q^{f} have good theoretical complexity (AC^0), they suffer from a number of problems that severely hinder their practical implementation. Crucially, they require the computation of active domains and, even worse, their Cartesian products. While expressible in relational algebra, the Q^{f} translations for selections, products, projections, and even base relations become prohibitively expensive. Several optimizations have been suggested in [22] (at the price of missing some certain answers), but the cases of projection and base relations do not appear to have any reasonable alternatives. Yet another problem is the complicated structure of the queries Q^{f}. When translations are applied recursively, this leads to very complex queries Q^{t} if Q used difference.

In fact we tried a simple experiment with the translations in Figure 2, and found that they are already infeasible for much smaller databases than the smallest TPC-H compliant instance: some of the queries start running out of memory already on instances with fewer than 10^3 tuples.

All this tells us that we need an implementable alternative, which we present next.

6. AN IMPLEMENTATION-FRIENDLY TRANSLATION

To overcome the practical difficulties posed by the translation in Figure 2, we propose an alternative translation that is implementation-friendly and comes with sufficient correctness guarantees. In this translation, we do not produce a second query Q^{f} that underapproximates certain answers to the negation of the query, which was the main source of complexity. To see what we can replace it with, note that in the Q^{t} translation, Q^{f} was only used in the rule for difference: tuples that are certain answers to $Q_1 - Q_2$ are those that are certainly answers to Q_1, and certainly not answers to Q_2. That necessitated working with the complex Q^{f} translation.

But we can use a slightly different rule: if a tuple is a certain answer to Q_1, and it does not match any tuple that could possibly be an answer to Q_2, then it is a certain answer to $Q_1 - Q_2$. The advantage of this is that the query that approximates possible answers can be built in a much simpler way than Q^{f}. For instance, for a base relation R, it will be just R itself, as opposed to the complex expression involving adom we used before.

We need to formally say what "(not) matching possible answers" means. To this end, we define approximations of possible answers and two matching-based semijoin operators. There already exists a notion of *maybe-answers* [2, 30] – answers that appear in $Q\big(v(D)\big)$ for at least one valuation v – but those can be infinite, and include arbitrary elements outside of $\mathsf{adom}(D)$. What we need instead is a compact representation.

Definition 3. Given a k-ary query Q and an incomplete database D, we say that a set $A \subseteq \mathsf{adom}(D)^k$ *represents potential answers* to Q on D if $Q\big(v(D)\big) \subseteq v(A)$ for every valuation v. A query Q' *represents potential answers* to Q if $Q'(D)$ represents potential answers to Q on D, for every D.

Obviously, there are trivial ways of representing potential answers: take, e.g., $\mathsf{adom}(D)^k$. But we shall be looking for good approximations, just as we are looking for good approximations of $\mathsf{cert}(Q, D)$, for which bad ones can also be found easily (e.g., the empty set).

To express conditions involving matching, we shall need two semijoin operations based on unifiable tuples (see Definition 2).

Definition 4. For relations R, S over $\mathsf{Const} \cup \mathsf{Null}$, with the same set of attributes, the *left unification semijoin* is

$$R \ltimes_{\Uparrow} S = \big\{ \bar{r} \in R \mid \exists \bar{s} \in S \colon \bar{r} \Uparrow \bar{s} \big\}$$

$$
\begin{aligned}
R^{\mathbf{t}} &= R & R^{\mathbf{f}} &= \{ \bar{s} \in \mathsf{adom}^{\mathsf{ar}(R)} \mid \nexists \bar{r} \in R \colon \bar{r} \Uparrow \bar{s} \} \\
(Q_1 \cup Q_2)^{\mathbf{t}} &= Q_1^{\mathbf{t}} \cup Q_2^{\mathbf{t}} & (Q_1 \cup Q_2)^{\mathbf{f}} &= Q_1^{\mathbf{f}} \cap Q_2^{\mathbf{f}} \\
(Q_1 \cap Q_2)^{\mathbf{t}} &= Q_1^{\mathbf{t}} \cap Q_2^{\mathbf{t}} & (Q_1 \cap Q_2)^{\mathbf{f}} &= Q_1^{\mathbf{f}} \cup Q_2^{\mathbf{f}} \\
(Q_1 - Q_2)^{\mathbf{t}} &= Q_1^{\mathbf{t}} \cap Q_2^{\mathbf{f}} & (Q_1 - Q_2)^{\mathbf{f}} &= Q_1^{\mathbf{f}} \cup Q_2^{\mathbf{t}} \\
(\sigma_\theta(Q))^{\mathbf{t}} &= \sigma_{\theta^*}(Q^{\mathbf{t}}) & (\sigma_\theta(Q))^{\mathbf{f}} &= Q^{\mathbf{f}} \cup \sigma_{(\neg\theta)^*}(\mathsf{adom}^{\mathsf{ar}(Q)}) \\
(Q_1 \times Q_2)^{\mathbf{t}} &= Q_1^{\mathbf{t}} \times Q_2^{\mathbf{t}} & (Q_1 \times Q_2)^{\mathbf{f}} &= Q_1^{\mathbf{f}} \times \mathsf{adom}^{\mathsf{ar}(Q_2)} \cup \mathsf{adom}^{\mathsf{ar}(Q_1)} \times Q_2^{\mathbf{f}} \\
(\pi_\alpha(Q))^{\mathbf{t}} &= \pi_\alpha(Q^{\mathbf{t}}) & (\pi_\alpha(Q))^{\mathbf{f}} &= \pi_\alpha(Q^{\mathbf{f}}) - \pi_\alpha(\mathsf{adom}^{\mathsf{ar}(Q)} - Q^{\mathbf{f}})
\end{aligned}
$$

Figure 2: Relational algebra translations of [22].

$$
\begin{aligned}
R^{+} &= R && (3.1) & R^{?} &= R && (4.1)\\
(Q_1 \cup Q_2)^{+} &= Q_1^{+} \cup Q_2^{+} && (3.2) & (Q_1 \cup Q_2)^{?} &= Q_1^{?} \cup Q_2^{?} && (4.2)\\
(Q_1 \cap Q_2)^{+} &= Q_1^{+} \cap Q_2^{+} && (3.3) & (Q_1 \cap Q_2)^{?} &= Q_1^{?} \ltimes_{\Uparrow} Q_2^{?} && (4.3)\\
(Q_1 - Q_2)^{+} &= Q_1^{+} \,\overline{\ltimes}_{\Uparrow}\, Q_2^{?} && (3.4) & (Q_1 - Q_2)^{?} &= Q_1^{?} - Q_2^{+} && (4.4)\\
(\sigma_\theta(Q))^{+} &= \sigma_{\theta^*}(Q^{+}) && (3.5) & (\sigma_\theta(Q))^{?} &= \sigma_{\theta^{**}}(Q^{?}) && (4.5)\\
(Q_1 \times Q_2)^{+} &= Q_1^{+} \times Q_2^{+} && (3.6) & (Q_1 \times Q_2)^{?} &= Q_1^{?} \times Q_2^{?} && (4.6)\\
(\pi_\alpha(Q))^{+} &= \pi_\alpha(Q^{+}) && (3.7) & (\pi_\alpha(Q))^{?} &= \pi_\alpha(Q^{?}) && (4.7)
\end{aligned}
$$

Figure 3: The improved translation with correctness guarantees.

and the *left unification anti-semijoin* is

$$R \,\overline{\ltimes}_{\Uparrow}\, S = R - (R \ltimes_{\Uparrow} S) = \{ \bar{r} \in R \mid \nexists \bar{s} \in S \colon \bar{r} \Uparrow \bar{s} \}$$

These are similar to the standard definition of (anti) semijoin; we simply use unifiability of tuples as the join condition. They are definable operations: we have that $R \ltimes_{\Uparrow} S = \pi_R(\sigma_{\theta_{\Uparrow}}(R \times S))$, where the projection is on all attributes of R and condition $\theta_{\Uparrow}$ is true for a tuple $\bar{r}\bar{s} \in R \times S$ iff $\bar{r} \Uparrow \bar{s}$. The unification condition $\theta_{\Uparrow}$ is expressible as a selection condition using predicates const and null [22]. Note that, in this notation, $R^{\mathbf{f}} = \mathsf{adom}^{\mathsf{ar}(R)} \,\overline{\ltimes}_{\Uparrow}\, R$.

Now, we can see why queries that represent potential answers are useful.

LEMMA 1. *Consider the translations $Q \mapsto Q^{+}$ given in Figure 3 by (3.1)–(3.7), where the only assumption on $Q_2^{?}$ in (3.4) is that it represents potential answers to Q_2. Then Q^{+} has correctness guarantees for Q.*

PROOF SKETCH. The proof is by induction on the structure of the query; here, we show the important case of set difference. Let $Q = Q_1 - Q_2$, let D be a database, let $\bar{r}$ be in $Q^{+}(D) = Q_1^{+}(D) \,\overline{\ltimes}_{\Uparrow}\, Q_2^{?}(D)$, and let v be a valuation on D. We need to show that $v(\bar{r}) \in Q(v(D))$. As $\bar{r}$ is in $Q_1^{+}(D)$, we get that $v(\bar{r}) \in Q_1(v(D))$ by the induction hypothesis. Now, suppose that $v(\bar{r}) \in Q_2(v(D))$. Since $Q_2^{?}$ represents potential answers to Q_2 by assumption, we have $v(\bar{r}) \in v(Q_2^{?}(D))$. Hence, there exists a tuple $\bar{s} \in Q_2^{?}(D)$ that unifies with $\bar{r}$ and, as $\bar{r} \in Q_1^{+}(D)$, this implies that $\bar{r} \in Q_1^{+}(D) \ltimes_{\Uparrow} Q_2^{?}(D)$, which contradicts our assumption that $\bar{r} \in Q_1^{+}(D) \overline{\ltimes}_{\Uparrow} Q_2^{?}(D)$. This shows that $v(\bar{r}) \notin Q_2(v(D))$ and, in turn, $v(\bar{r}) \in Q(v(D))$. □

Given this lemma, our next goal is to produce a translation of queries that represent potential answers. As for queries Q^{+}, this can be done almost by mimicking the structure of queries and using a query with correctness guarantees when it comes to translating the difference operation. We also need to modify selection conditions: the new translation $\theta \mapsto \theta^{**}$ is given by $\theta^{**} = \neg(\neg\theta)^*$. Recall that negating selection conditions means propagating negations through them, and interchanging $=$ and $\neq$, and const and null. For completeness, we give it here:

$$
\begin{aligned}
(A \neq B)^{**} &= (A \neq B) \\
(A \neq c)^{**} &= (A \neq c) \quad \text{if } c \text{ is a constant} \\
(A = B)^{**} &= (A = B) \lor \mathsf{null}(A) \lor \mathsf{null}(B) \\
(A = c)^{**} &= (A = c) \lor \mathsf{null}(A) \\
(\theta_1 \lor \theta_2)^{**} &= \theta_1^{**} \lor \theta_2^{**} \\
(\theta_1 \land \theta_2)^{**} &= \theta_1^{**} \land \theta_2^{**}
\end{aligned}
$$

LEMMA 2. *Consider the translations $Q \mapsto Q^{?}$ given in Figure 3 by (4.1)–(4.7), where the only assumption on Q_2^{+} in (4.4) is that it has correctness guarantees for Q. Then $Q^{?}$ represents potential answers to Q.*

PROOF SKETCH. The proof is by induction on the structure of the query; here, we present two cases for illustration.

When $Q = Q_1 \cap Q_2$, we have that $Q^{?} = Q_1^{?} \ltimes_{\Uparrow} Q_2^{?}$. Let $\bar{r} \in Q(v(D))$; then, by the induction hypothesis, $\bar{r}$ is in $v(Q_i^{?}(D))$ for $i = 1, 2$. So, there are tuples $\bar{r}_i \in Q_i^{?}(D)$ such that $v(\bar{r}_1) = v(\bar{r}_2) = \bar{r}$. Hence, $\bar{r}_1 \Uparrow \bar{r}_2$ and thus $\bar{r} = v(\bar{r}_1) \in v(Q_1^{?}(D)) \ltimes_{\Uparrow} v(Q_2^{?}(D)) = v(Q^{?}(D))$.

Next, consider $Q = Q_1 - Q_2$ and $Q^{?} = Q_1^{?} - Q_2^{+}$. Let $\bar{r} \in Q(v(D))$. Then, $\bar{r} \in Q_1(v(D))$ and $\bar{r} \notin Q_2(v(D))$. By the induction hypothesis, $\bar{r} \in v(Q_1^{?}(D))$ and so there is $\bar{s} \in Q_1^{?}(D)$ such that $\bar{r} = v(\bar{s})$. Assume $\bar{s} \in Q_2^{+}(D)$. Since Q_2^{+} has correctness guarantees for Q by assumption, we have $\bar{r} = v(\bar{s}) \in Q_2(v(D))$, which is a contradiction. Hence, $\bar{s} \notin Q_2^{+}(D)$ and so $\bar{s} \in Q^{?}(D)$. Therefore, $\bar{r} \in v(Q^{?}(D))$ as required. □

Lemmas 1 and 2 tell us that we can now combine the two translations in Figure 3 to obtain correctness guarantees. Using the lemmas, mutual induction on the expressions in Figure 3 shows the following.

THEOREM 1. *For the translation $Q \mapsto (Q^+, Q^?)$ in Figure 3, the query Q^+ has correctness guarantees for Q, and $Q^?$ represents potential answers to Q. In particular, $Q^+(D) \subseteq \mathsf{cert}(Q, D)$ for every database D.*

The theoretical complexity bounds for queries Q^+ and $Q^{\mathbf{t}}$ are the same: both have the low AC^0 data complexity. However, the real world performance of Q^+ will be significantly better, as it completely avoids large Cartesian products. As an example, consider the query

$$Q = R - \big(\pi_\alpha(T) - \sigma_\theta(S)\big)$$

and suppose it has arity k. Its corresponding translation $Q^{\mathbf{t}}$ that follows the rules in Figure 2 is

$$R \cap \big((\pi_\alpha(\mathsf{adom}^k \,\overline{\ltimes}_{\Uparrow}\, T) - \pi_\alpha(\mathsf{adom}^k \ltimes_{\Uparrow} T)) \cup \sigma_{\theta^*}(S)\big)$$

while the translation Q^+ we propose is much simpler:

$$R \,\overline{\ltimes}_{\Uparrow}\, \big(\pi_\alpha(T) - \sigma_{\theta^*}(S)\big)$$

and avoids Cartesian products of very large sets, computed multiple times, as in $Q^{\mathbf{t}}$.

We conclude this section with a few remarks. First, the translation of Figure 3 is really a family of translations. The proof of Theorem 1 applies to show the following.

COROLLARY 1. *If in the translation in Figure 3 one replaces the right sides of rules by queries*
- *contained in those listed in (3.1)–(3.7), and*
- *containing those listed in(4.1)–(4.7),*

then the resulting translation continues to satisfy the claim of Theorem 1.

This opens up the possibility of optimizing translations (at the expense of potentially returning fewer tuples). For instance, if we modify the translations of selection conditions so that θ^* is a stronger condition than the original and θ^{**} is a weaker one, we retain overall correctness guarantees. In particular, the unification condition $\theta_{\Uparrow}$ is expressed by a case analysis that may become onerous for tuples with many attributes; the above observation can be used to simplify the case analysis while retaining correctness.

Second, the reason why queries $Q^?$ produce approximations of sets that represent potential answers is the same as for queries Q^+ to approximate certain answers, namely complexity. It can be easily seen that checking whether a set A represents potential answers to a given query Q on D is in coNP, and for some queries the problem is coNP-hard as well.

PROPOSITION 1. *There is a fixed query Q such that the following problem is coNP-complete: given a database D and a set A of tuples over $\mathsf{adom}(D)$, does A represent potential answers to Q on D?*

Next, we turn to the comparison of Q^+ with the result of SQL evaluation, i.e., $\mathsf{Eval}_{\mathsf{SQL}}(Q, D)$. Given that the latter can produce both types of errors – false positives and false negatives – it is not surprising that the two are in general incomparable. To see this, consider first a database D_1 where $R = \{(1,2), (2,\bot)\}$, $S = \{(1,2), (\bot,2)\}$ and $T = \{(1,2)\}$, and a query $Q_1 = R - (S \cap T)$. The tuple $(2,\bot)$ belongs to $\mathsf{Eval}_{\mathsf{SQL}}(Q_1, D)$ and it is a certain answer, while $Q_1^+(D) = \varnothing$. On the other hand, for D_2 with $R = \{(\bot,\bot)\}$ over attributes A, B, and $Q_2 = \sigma_{A=B}(R)$, the tuple $(\bot,\bot)$ belongs to $Q_2^+(D_2)$, but $\mathsf{Eval}_{\mathsf{SQL}}(Q_2, D_2) = \varnothing$. Nonetheless, in all our experiments Q^+ will always produce *all* of the certain answers returned by SQL.

As a final remark, note that (4.3) in Figure 3 is not the only possibility, since intersection is a commutative operation, but left unification semijoin is not. Correctness guarantees hold if we replace the left unification semijoin with the right one that keeps unifiable tuples from the second argument.

7. THE PRICE OF CORRECTNESS

Now that we have established the correctness of the translation $Q \mapsto Q^+$, our goal is to test it. For this, we take queries Q_1—Q_4 from Section 3, generate incomplete TPC-H instances, and then run Q_1—Q_4 as well as their translations to compare their performance.

Translations of SQL queries

The translation $Q \mapsto Q^+$ was given at the level of relational algebra. While there are multiple relational algebra simulators freely available, we want to carry out our experiments using a real DBMS on instances of realistic size (which rules out relational algebra simulators). Thus, we shall take SQL queries Q_1—Q_4, apply the translation $Q \mapsto Q^+$ to their relational algebra equivalents, and then run the results of the translation as SQL queries.

Expressing Q_1—Q_4 in relational algebra is standard. We remark though that traditional database texts tend to provide only simplified translations from SQL to algebra; for a full one, including nested subqueries that can themselves contain subqueries, a good source is [29] and we follow it here. As an example, consider query Q_3. Its relational algebra translation is

$$\pi_{\texttt{o\_orderkey}}\big(\texttt{orders} - \pi[\sigma_\theta(\texttt{lineitem} \times \texttt{orders})]\big)$$

where the inner projection is on the attributes of relation `orders` and the condition θ is `l_orderkey` = `o_orderkey` ∧ `l_suppkey` ≠ `$supp_key`.

Before computing Q_3^+, we need to address one more technical issue. Often, at least in the theoretical literature, SQL nulls are identified with Codd nulls (non-repeating marked nulls). While in many cases this way of modeling SQL nulls is proper, it does not always work. The main issue is that comparing a null with itself results in *true* for Codd nulls, but *unknown* for SQL nulls. For instance, computing the self-join of $R = \{\textbf{NULL}\}$ by

```
SELECT R1.A FROM R R1, R R2 WHERE R1.A = R2.A
```

results in the empty set, while for the Codd database $R = \{\bot\}$, the evaluation of $R \bowtie R$ is $\{\bot\}$. This tells us that in full generality we cannot guarantee correctness with the SQL implementation of nulls, as it is too coarse to see when null refers to the same value. However, the situation that causes this problem – when a nullable attribute is compared with itself in a self-join – is not very common, and does not affect us here as long as we make a minor adjustment of the translations Q^+ and $Q^?$ to work correctly when evaluated as SQL queries.

As expected, the adjustment occurs in selection conditions. For the Q^+ translation, we need to ensure that attributes compared for equality are not nulls (the existing translation θ^* already ensures that for disequality comparisons). For the θ^{**} translation in $Q^?$, the situation is symmetric: we need to include the possibility of attributes being nulls for disequality comparisons (the existing translation θ^{**} already does it for equalities). That is, we change the translations as follows:

$$\begin{aligned}(A = B)^* &= (A = B) \wedge \mathsf{const}(A) \wedge \mathsf{const}(B)\\ (A \neq B)^{**} &= (A \neq B) \vee \mathsf{null}(A) \vee \mathsf{null}(B)\end{aligned}$$

and likewise for $(A = c)^*$ and $(A \neq c)^{**}$. For all the queries considered here, these ensure that Q^+ continues to under-approximate certain answers and $Q^?$ continues to represent possible answers even when SQL evaluation rules are used for conditions with nulls.

Applying then the translations to Q_3 gives us Q_3^+ as

$$\pi_{\texttt{o\_orderkey}}(\texttt{orders} - \pi[\sigma_{\theta'}(\texttt{lineitem} \times \texttt{orders})])$$

where the inner projection is on the attributes of `orders` and θ' is $\texttt{l\_orderkey} = \texttt{o\_orderkey} \wedge (\texttt{l\_suppkey} \neq \texttt{\$supp\_key} \vee \mathsf{null}(\texttt{l\_suppkey}))$. The left unification anti-semijoin produced by the translation is simplified to difference in Q_3^+ due to the following observation: if R is a relation that has a key, and $S \subseteq R$, then $R \,\overline{\ltimes}_{\Uparrow}\, S = R - S$. In the above query, this applies since the inner projection is contained in `orders`. Summing up, Q_3^+ is expressed in SQL as

```
SELECT o_orderkey
FROM   orders
WHERE  NOT EXISTS (
       SELECT *
       FROM   lineitem
       WHERE  l_orderkey = o_orderkey
       AND    ( l_suppkey <> {s_key}
                OR l_suppkey IS NULL ) )
```

In fact, a key feature of all the translations is that they change some conditions of the form `A=B` to `A=B OR B IS NULL`. In general – and this has nothing to do with our translation – when several such disjunctions occur in a subquery, they may not be handled well by the optimizer. One can in fact observe that for a query of the form

```
SELECT * FROM R WHERE NOT EXISTS
   ( SELECT * FROM   S, ..., T
     WHERE   ( A=B OR B IS NULL ) AND ··· AND
             ( X=Y OR Y IS NULL ) )
```

the estimated cost of the query plan can be thousands of times higher than for the same query from which the `IS NULL` conditions are removed.

One way to overcome this is quite simple and takes advantage of the fact that such disjunctions will occur inside `NOT EXISTS` subqueries. One can then we can propagate disjunctions in the subquery, which results in a `NOT EXISTS` condition of the form $\neg\exists\bar{x} \bigvee \phi_i(\bar{x})$, where each ϕ_i now is a conjunction of atoms. This in turn can be split into conjunctions of $\neg\exists\phi_i(\bar{x})$, ending up with a query of the form

```
SELECT * FROM R WHERE NOT EXISTS
   ( SELECT * FROM S_i, i ∈ I_1 WHERE ⋀_j ψ_j^1 )
AND ··· AND NOT EXISTS
   ( SELECT * FROM S_i, i ∈ I_k WHERE ⋀_j ψ_j^k )
```

where formulae ψ_j^l are comparisons of attributes and statements that an attribute is or is not null, and relations S_i for $i \in I_l$ are those that contain attributes mentioned in the ψ_j^ls.

Translating additional features. Queries Q_1—Q_4 on which we test the approach go slightly beyond relational algebra as used in the previous section: they use $>$ and **LIKE** comparisons, and Q_2 refers to an aggregate subquery. As for the first two, looking at the SQL-adjusted translations of selection conditions, we can see that there is nothing special about (dis)equality. The same translations can be applied to other comparisons, and this is what we do. For the aggregate subquery, we just treat it as a black box, that is, we view the result of that subquery as a value c and apply the translation to condition `c_acctbal` $> c$.

Experimental results

Note that we measure *relative performance* of correct translations Q_i^+s, that is, the ratio of running times of Q_i^+s and the original queries Q_is. Intuitively, this ratio should not significantly depend on the size of generated instances. With this hypothesis in mind, we first report detailed results for the smallest allowed size of TPC-H instances (roughly 1GB). After that, we test our hypothesis using instances of 3GB, 6GB, and 10GB size, and show that indeed relative performances remain about the same for all instance sizes for queries Q_1, Q_2, and Q_3, although they can decrease slightly for Q_4 (we shall discuss this later).

For the experiments described below, we use the DBGen tool of TPC-H to generate databases of about 1GB each, and then we populate them with nulls, depending on the prescribed null rate. For each null rate in the range 1%–5%, in steps of 1%, we generate 10 incomplete databases. On each such database, we instantiate our test queries 5 times with randomly generated values for their parameters, and we run each query instance 3 times. The results that we report are averages of those runs.

Since we are interested in the *cost* of correctness, we report *relative values* of the parameters: one for the original query, and the other for the translation. Thus, if t is the time it takes a query Q to run, and t^+ is the running time of Q^+, we report the ratio t^+/t. In particular, staying close to 1 means that the price of correctness is low as correctness guarantees do not affect running time; if it drops below 1, we actually win by running a correct version of the query.

Based on the experiments we conduct, we observe three types of behavior, reported in Figure 4.

1. For queries Q_1 and Q_3, the price of correctness is *negligible* for most applications: under 4% for both.
2. For query Q_2, the translation with correctness guaranteed is *significantly faster* than the original query; in fact it is more than 3 orders of magnitude faster on average. Note that the relative performance scale in the graph for Q_2^+ ranges from $2 \cdot 10^{-4}$ to $8 \cdot 10^{-4}$.
3. For query Q_4, the behavior is the worst among those we observed, as the running time of Q_4^+ almost doubles the running time of Q_4. This is still tolerable though if correctness of results is very important.

Larger database instances. The previous results were obtained for the smallest allowed TPC-H instances. As we

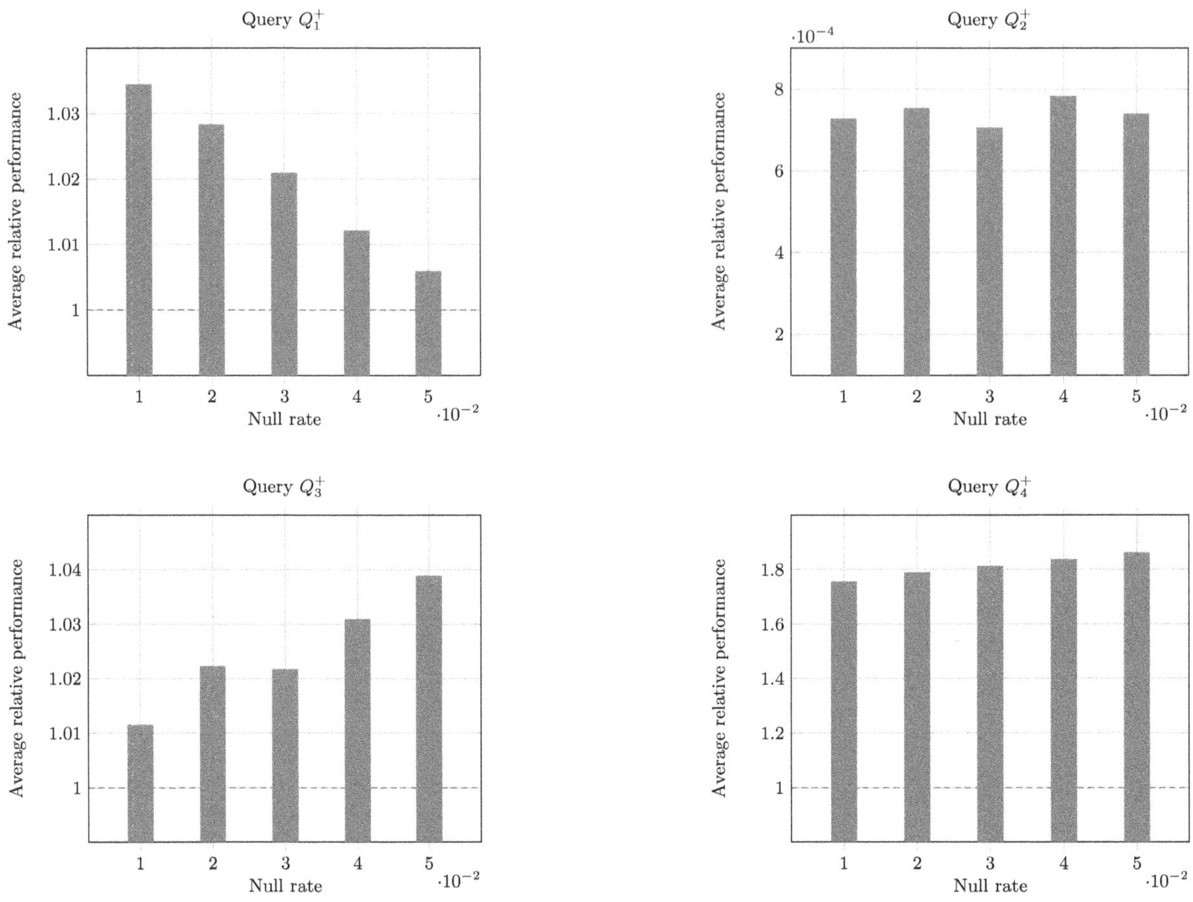

Figure 4: Average relative performance of queries with correctness guarantees.

Query	1GB	3GB	6GB	10GB
Q_1	1.0058 – 1.0344	0.9925 – 1.0148	0.9791 – 1.0113	1.0034 – 1.0201
Q_2	0.0007 – 0.0008	0.0002 – 0.0003	0.0001 – 0.0001	0.0001 – 0.0001
Q_3	1.0114 – 1.0387	1.0105 – 1.0367	0.9873 – 1.0226	1.0007 – 1.0628
Q_4	1.7530 – 1.8587	1.7986 – 1.9296	2.0532 – 2.2536	3.5354 – 3.8900

Table 1: Ranges of average relative performance – Q_i^+ vs Q_i – for instances up to 10GB.

explained, since we measure relative performance, we conjectured that the exact size of the instance should not have much impact: running times for both Q_is and Q_i^+s will increase, but proportionally so. To confirm this experimentally, we generated instances of sizes 3GB, 6GB, and 10GB, and ran similar tests (with fewer test runs for larger instances, as running times increased significantly). Our results, summarized in Table 1, validate our conjecture completely for queries Q_1, Q_2, and Q_3, as relative performances indeed change very little. For Q_4, we observe a decrease in performance from roughly half the speed of the original query for 1GB databases to one quarter of the speed for 10GB databases; we shall comment on this below.

Before analyzing these results, we address the standard measures for evaluating the quality of approximation algorithms, namely precision and recall. The first refers to the percentage of correct answers given. With the correctness guarantees proven in the previous section, we can thus state that precision of our algorithms is 100%. Recall refers to the fraction of relevant answers returned. In our case, we can look at certain answers returned by the standard SQL evaluation of a query Q, and see how many of them are returned by Q^+. The ratio of those is what we mean by recall in this scenario.

We saw that, in some artificial examples, Q^+ may miss several, or even all, certain answers returned by Q. Thus, we cannot state a theoretical bound on the recall, but we can see what it is in the scenarios represented by our test queries. For this, one needs either highly intractable algorithms for computing certain answers, or at least algorithms for identifying false positives. The latter we gave in Section 4 for the SQL evaluation of Q_1—Q_4, and tested them on smaller TPC-H instances generated by DataFiller. Thus, we ran queries Q_i^+s (modified versions for Q_2 and Q_4) on those smaller instances and observed that they returned precisely the answers to the Q_is except false positive tuples. That is, for those instances, the recall rate was 100%, and we did not miss any certain answers.

Discussion

We now discuss the factors that cause the behavior reported in Figure 4. We start with queries Q_1 and Q_3, whose behavior is quite similar. Note that the key change that our translation introduces is the change of comparisons `A op B` to `(A op B) OR B IS NULL` inside correlated **NOT EXISTS** subqueries. The number of such disjunctions is small, and they are well handled by the optimizer, resulting in small overheads. For Q_1^+, these overheads get lower as the null rate gets higher. This is most likely due to the fact that with a higher null rate it is easier to satisfy the **IS NULL** conditions in the **WHERE** clause of the **NOT EXISTS** subquery. As a result, a counterexample to the **NOT EXISTS** subquery can be found earlier, resulting in an overall faster evaluation.

For query Q_2, the translation is similar, but there is one big difference: after we split the disjunction in the correlated **NOT EXISTS** subqueries, as explained earlier, one of the resulting **NOT EXISTS** subqueries becomes *decorrelated.* It simply tests for the existence of nulls in the attribute `o_custkey` of `orders`, and once it finds it the evaluation of the entire query ends, as we know that the result will be empty. The original query, on the other hand, spends most of its time looking for incorrect answers: this is the query with a rate of false positive answers close to 100%. Hence, in this case, the translation Q_2^+ not only ensures correctness, but also speeds up the execution time by a factor of over 10^3, as it is able to detect early that the correct answer is empty. In fact, as instances grow larger, one wins even more by using the correct query Q_2^+, as the original Q_2 is forced to spend more time looking for incorrect answers.

Query Q_4 is the hardest one to deal with. Without splitting the **OR** conditions, PostgreSQL produces astronomical costs of query plans, as it resorts to nested-loop joins, even for large tables (this is due to the fact that it under-estimates the size of joins, which is a known issue for major DBMSs [18]). Hence the direct translation of this query requires some tuning. This is achieved in two steps. First, we split the disjunctions into several **NOT EXISTS** conditions, as explained earlier. Even then, **NOT EXISTS** subqueries have nested **EXISTS** subqueries, each of them appearing twice. We define those queries as views (using **WITH**) and then replace subqueries with references to those views. These modifications are sufficient to make the optimizer produce better estimates and a reasonable query plan, which runs at roughly half the speed of the original query (for 1GB databases).

What makes the performance of Q_4 the worst of the four queries is that it is the only one that has a multi-way join in the **NOT EXISTS** subquery; all others have no joins in such subqueries at all. This means that absolute running times are significantly higher for Q_4 than for other queries. The translation has four correlated subqueries, three of which use joins that involve the largest `lineitem` relation, which accounts for the decrease in relative performance (as the original query has only one multi-way join subquery). Of course the need to have these multiple subqueries has arisen from the inability of the optimizer to handle disjunctions with **IS NULL** conditions. We believe that this problem may be overcome with a proper implementation of marked nulls (see additional comments in Section 8).

Conclusions

Our main conclusion is that it is practically feasible to modify SQL query evaluation over databases with nulls to guarantee correctness of its results. This applies to the setting where nulls mean that a value is missing, and the fragment of SQL corresponds to first-order queries. This could not be achieved with the theoretical solutions presented earlier [22] and required new ways of modifying SQL queries. Depending on the exact translation involved, we saw queries running at roughly half the speed in the worst case, or almost 10^4 times faster in the best case. For several queries, the overhead was small and completely tolerable, under 4%. With these translations, we also did not miss any of the correct answers that SQL evaluation returned.

8. FUTURE WORK

Given our conclusions that wrong answers to SQL queries in the presence of nulls are not just a theoretical myth – there are real world scenarios where this happens – and correctness can be restored with syntactic changes to queries at a price that is often tolerable, it is natural to look into the next steps that will lift our solution from the first-order fragment of SQL to cover more queries and more possible interpretations of incompleteness. We shall now discuss those.

Bag semantics. SQL queries use multiset, or bag semantics, and handling duplicates is an important aspect of the language. However, at this point we do not even have a proper theory of certain answers for bag semantics, neither established notions that one can measure against, nor complexity results. We need to understand what the analog of $\mathsf{cert}(Q, D)$ is for queries under bag semantics, and how to define Q^+ in that case.

Aggregate functions. An important feature of real-life queries is aggregation; in fact it is present in most of the TPC-H queries. However, here our understanding of correctness of answers is quite poor; SQL's rules for aggregation and nulls are rather ad-hoc and have been persistently criticized [7, 9]. Thus, much theoretical work is needed in this direction before practical algorithms emerge. There is a better understanding of aggregate queries in neighboring areas such as probabilistic databases [25, 27] or inconsistent databases [5], and this could serve as a starting point.

Marked nulls. The translations $Q \mapsto Q^+, Q^?$ work at the level of marked and Codd nulls, but SQL nulls fall a bit short of Codd nulls, not being able to compare a null with itself. While sample queries used here were not affected, some queries may be. Ideally, one would use marked nulls to overcome this problem. Marked nulls should also be used to overcome issues with **OR IS NULL** conditions, as the optimizer will see them as usual disjunctions involving value comparisons. Marked nulls have been implemented in connection with data exchange systems [13, 24], and one has access to multiple querying scenarios involving marked nulls using schema mapping benchmarks [3, 6]; hence we intend to create new base types that use marked nulls and experiment with translations in that setting. If marked nulls are not available, we need to find the precise characterization of queries for which the translations proposed here restore correctness with SQL nulls.

Incorporating constraints. In the definition of certain answers, we disregarded constraints, although every real-life database will satisfy some, typically keys and foreign keys. While constraints ψ can be incorporated into a query ϕ by finding certain answers to $\psi \rightarrow \phi$, for common classes of constraints we would like to see how to make direct adjustments to rewritings. We have seen one example of this: the presence of a key constraint let us replace $R \,\overline{\ltimes}_{\Uparrow}\, S$ by $R - S$. We would like to automate such query transformations based on common classes of constraints.

Other types of incomplete information. So far we dealt with missing-information nulls, but there are other interpretations. For instance, non-applicable nulls [20, 32] arise commonly as the result of outer joins. We need to extend the notion of correct query answering and translations of queries to them. One possibility is to adapt the approach of [21] that shows how to define certainty based on the semantics of inputs and outputs of queries. At the level of missing information, we would like to see whether our translations could help with deriving partial answers to SQL queries, when parts of a database are missing, as in [16].

Direct SQL rewriting. We have rewritten SQL queries by a detour via relational algebra. We should look into both running such queries directly on a DBMS (and perhaps take advantage of good properties of semijoins [17] that feature prominently in our translations), and into direct rewriting from SQL to SQL, without an intermediate language.

Acknowledgments

We are grateful to Marco Console for many helpful discussions during the early stages of this work, and to Chris Ré and the anonymous referees for their comments. Work partially supported by EPSRC grants J015377 and M025268.

9. REFERENCES

[1] S. Abiteboul, R. Hull, and V. Vianu. *Foundations of Databases.* Addison-Wesley, 1995.

[2] S. Abiteboul, P. C. Kanellakis, and G. Grahne. On the representation and querying of sets of possible worlds. *Theoretical Computer Science*, 78(1):158–187, 1991.

[3] B. Alexe, W. C. Tan, and Y. Velegrakis. STBenchmark: Towards a benchmark for mapping systems. *PVLDB*, 1(1):230–244, 2008.

[4] M. Arenas, P. Barceló, L. Libkin, and F. Murlak. *Foundations of Data Exchange.* Cambridge University Press, 2014.

[5] M. Arenas, L. E. Bertossi, J. Chomicki, X. He, V. Raghavan, and J. P. Spinrad. Scalar aggregation in inconsistent databases. *TCS*, 296(3):405–434, 2003.

[6] P. C. Arocena, B. Glavic, R. Ciucanu, and R. J. Miller. The iBench integration metadata generator. *PVLDB*, 9(3):108–119, 2015.

[7] J. Celko. *SQL for Smarties: Advanced SQL Programming.* Morgan Kaufmann, 1995.

[8] F. Coelho. DataFiller – generate random data from database schema. https://www.cri.ensmp.fr/people/coelho/datafiller.html.

[9] C. Date and H. Darwen. *A Guide to the SQL Standard.* Addison-Wesley, 1996.

[10] C. J. Date. *An Introduction to Database Systems.* Pearson, 2003.

[11] G. H. Gessert. Four valued logic for relational database systems. *SIGMOD Record*, 19(1):29–35, 1990.

[12] A. Gheerbrant, L. Libkin, and C. Sirangelo. Naïve evaluation of queries over incomplete databases. *ACM Trans. Database Syst.*, 39(4):31:1–31:42, 2014.

[13] L. M. Haas, M. A. Hernández, H. Ho, L. Popa, and M. Roth. Clio grows up: From research prototype to industrial tool. In *SIGMOD*, pages 805–810, 2005.

[14] T. Imielinski and W. Lipski. Incomplete information in relational databases. *J. ACM*, 31(4):761–791, 1984.

[15] H. Klein. How to modify SQL queries in order to guarantee sure answers. *SIGMOD Record*, 23(3):14–20, 1994.

[16] W. Lang, R. V. Nehme, E. Robinson, and J. F. Naughton. Partial results in database systems. In *SIGMOD*, pages 1275–1286, 2014.

[17] D. Leinders, J. Tyszkiewicz, and J. Van den Bussche. On the expressive power of semijoin queries. *Inf. Process. Lett.*, 91(2):93–98, 2004.

[18] V. Leis, A. Gubichev, A. Mirchev, P. A. Boncz, A. Kemper, and T. Neumann. How good are query optimizers, really? *PVLDB*, 9(3):204–215, 2015.

[19] M. Lenzerini. Data integration: A theoretical perspective. In *PODS*, pages 233–246, 2002.

[20] N. Lerat and W. Lipski. Nonapplicable nulls. *Theor. Comput. Sci.*, 46(3):67–82, 1986.

[21] L. Libkin. Certain answers as objects and knowledge. *Artificial Intelligence*, 232:1–19, 2016.

[22] L. Libkin. SQL's three-valued logic and certain answers. *ACM TODS*, 41(1):1:1–1:28, 2016.

[23] W. Lipski. On relational algebra with marked nulls. In *PODS*, pages 201–203, 1984.

[24] B. Marnette, G. Mecca, P. Papotti, S. Raunich, and D. Santoro. ++Spicy: An opensource tool for second-generation schema mapping and data exchange. *PVLDB*, 4(12):1438–1441, 2011.

[25] C. Ré and D. Suciu. Efficient evaluation of HAVING queries on a probabilistic database. In *DBLP*, pages 186–200, 2007.

[26] R. Reiter. On closed world data bases. In *Logic and Data Bases*, pages 55–76, 1977.

[27] R. Ross, V. S. Subrahmanian, and J. Grant. Aggregate operators in probabilistic databases. *J. ACM*, 52(1):54–101, 2005.

[28] Transaction Processing Performance Council. *TPC Benchmark™ H Standard Specification*, Nov. 2014. Revision 2.17.1.

[29] J. Van den Bussche and S. Vansummeren. Translating SQL into the relational algebra. Course notes, Hasselt University and Université Libre de Bruxelles, 2009.

[30] R. van der Meyden. Logical approaches to incomplete information: A survey. In *Logics for Databases and Information Systems*, pages 307–356, 1998.

[31] K. Yue. A more general model for handling missing information in relational databases using a 3-valued logic. *SIGMOD Record*, 20(3):43–49, 1991.

[32] C. Zaniolo. Database relations with null values. *J. Comput. Syst. Sci.*, 28(1):142–166, 1984.

APPENDIX

We present the exact translations of the queries used in our experiments. Query Q_3^+ was already shown in Section 7. Queries Q_1^+, Q_2^+, and Q_4^+ are given below.

Query Q_1^+

```
SELECT s_suppkey, o_orderkey
FROM   supplier, lineitem l1, orders, nation
WHERE  s_suppkey = l1.l_suppkey
  AND  o_orderkey = l1.l_orderkey
  AND  o_orderstatus = 'F'
  AND  l1.l_receiptdate > l1.l_commitdate
  AND  s_nationkey = n_nationkey
  AND  n_name = $nation
  AND  EXISTS (
       SELECT *
       FROM   lineitem l2
       WHERE  l2.l_orderkey = l1.l_orderkey
         AND  l2.l_suppkey <> l1.l_suppkey )
  AND  NOT EXISTS (
       SELECT *
       FROM   lineitem l3
       WHERE  l3.l_orderkey = l1.l_orderkey
         AND  ( l3.l_suppkey <> l1.l_suppkey
                OR l3.l_suppkey IS NULL )
         AND  ( l3.l_receiptdate > l3.l_commitdate
                OR l3.l_receiptdate IS NULL
                OR l3.l_commitdate  IS NULL ) )
```

Query Q_2^+

```
SELECT c_custkey, c_nationkey
FROM   customer
WHERE  c_nationkey IN ($countries)
  AND  c_acctbal > (
       SELECT AVG(c_acctbal)
       FROM   customer
       WHERE  c_acctbal > 0.00
         AND  c_nationkey IN ($countries) )
  AND  NOT EXISTS (
       SELECT *
       FROM   orders
       WHERE  o_custkey = c_custkey )
  AND  NOT EXISTS (
       SELECT *
       FROM   orders
       WHERE  o_custkey IS NULL )
```

Query Q_4^+

```
WITH
part_view  AS (
    SELECT p_partkey
    FROM   part
    WHERE  p_name IS NULL
    UNION
    SELECT p_partkey
    FROM   part
    WHERE  p_name LIKE '%'||$color||'%' ),
supp_view  AS (
    SELECT s_suppkey
    FROM   supplier
    WHERE  s_nationkey IS NULL
    UNION
    SELECT s_suppkey
    FROM   supplier, nation
    WHERE  s_nationkey = n_nationkey
      AND  n_name = '$nation' )
SELECT o_orderkey
FROM   orders
WHERE  NOT EXISTS (
       SELECT *
       FROM   lineitem, part_view, supp_view
       WHERE  l_orderkey = o_orderkey
         AND  l_partkey = p_partkey
         AND  l_suppkey = s_suppkey )
  AND  NOT EXISTS (
       SELECT *
       FROM   lineitem, supp_view
       WHERE  l_orderkey = o_orderkey
         AND  l_partkey IS NULL
         AND  l_suppkey = s_suppkey
         AND  EXISTS ( SELECT * FROM part_view ) )
  AND  NOT EXISTS (
       SELECT *
       FROM   lineitem, part_view
       WHERE  l_orderkey = o_orderkey
         AND  l_partkey = p_partkey
         AND  l_suppkey IS NULL
         AND  EXISTS ( SELECT * FROM supp_view ) )
  AND  NOT EXISTS (
       SELECT *
       FROM   lineitem
       WHERE  l_orderkey = o_orderkey
         AND  l_partkey IS NULL
         AND  l_suppkey IS NULL
         AND  EXISTS ( SELECT * FROM part_view )
         AND  EXISTS ( SELECT * FROM supp_view ) )
```

Designing a Query Language for RDF: Marrying Open and Closed Worlds

Marcelo Arenas
Pontificia Universidad Católica de Chile
& Center for Semantic Web Research
marenas@ing.puc.cl

Martín Ugarte
Université Libre de Bruxelles
martin.ugarte@ulb.ac.be

Abstract

When querying an RDF graph, a prominent feature is the possibility of extending the answer to a query with optional information. However, the definition of this feature in SPARQL –the standard RDF query language– has raised some important issues. Most notably, the use of this feature increases the complexity of the evaluation problem, and its closed-world semantics is in conflict with the underlying open-world semantics of RDF. Many approaches for fixing such problems have been proposed, being the most prominent the introduction of the semantic notion of weakly-monotone SPARQL query. Weakly-monotone SPARQL queries have shaped the class of queries that conform to the open-world semantics of RDF. Unfortunately, finding an effective way of restricting SPARQL to the fragment of weakly-monotone queries has proven to be an elusive problem. In practice, the most widely adopted fragment for writing SPARQL queries is based on the syntactic notion of well designedness. This notion has proven to be a good approach for writing SPARQL queries, but its expressive power has yet to be fully understood.

The starting point of this paper is to understand the relation between well-designed queries and the semantic notion of weak monotonicity. It is known that every well-designed SPARQL query is weakly monotone; as our first contribution we prove that the converse does not hold, even if an extension of this notion based on the use of disjunction is considered. Given this negative result, we embark on the task of defining syntactic fragments that are weakly-monotone, and have higher expressive power than the fragment of well-designed queries. To this end, we move to a more general scenario where infinite RDF graphs are also allowed, so that interpolation techniques studied for first-order logic can be applied. With the use of these techniques, we are able to define a new operator for SPARQL that gives rise to a query language with the desired properties (over finite and infinite RDF graphs). It should be noticed that every query in this fragment is weakly monotone if we restrict to the case of finite RDF graphs. Moreover, we use this result to provide a simple characterization of the class of monotone CONSTRUCT queries, that is, the class of SPARQL queries that produce RDF graphs as output. Finally, we pinpoint the complexity of the evaluation problem for the query languages identified in the paper.

PODS '16, June 26–July 1, 2016, San Francisco, CA, USA.

ISBN 978-1-4503-4191-2/16/06... $15.00

DOI: http://dx.doi.org/10.1145/2902251.2902298

1. INTRODUCTION

In the last fifteen years the Semantic Web initiative has received a lot of attention. From its initial steps, the goal of this initiative has been to build a World Wide Web with *machine-understandable* information [9]. To this end, a first step was to standardize a data model for the information in the Web. This gave rise to RDF, a graph-based data model for specifying relationships between resources in the Web [25]. By 2013 more than four million Web domains offered data stored as RDF graphs, creating what is known as Linked Open Data [33]. Jointly with the release of RDF as a recommendation of the World Wide Web Consortium (W3C), the natural problem of querying this data was raised. Several designs and proposals were presented to solve this issue [15], being the query language SPARQL the one that finally got more attention. SPARQL is an SQL-flavored query language for RDF that became a W3C recommendation in 2008 [32]. The current version of this language, SPARQL 1.1, was issued in 2013 [40].

The query language SPARQL was originally designed by looking at each desired feature in isolation, but it turned out to be a rather complicated language when all of these features were put together. In [27], the authors formalized the syntax and semantics of SPARQL, presenting the first step towards understanding the fundamental properties of this language. This work was followed by studies about the complexity of query evaluation [34, 23, 5, 29], query optimisation [22, 30, 12, 13], query federation [10], expressive power analysis [3, 31, 20], and provenance tracking [17, 18]. The theoretical study of SPARQL has impacted the Semantic Web in several ways, influencing the standard definition of SPARQL by the W3C and also the form in which users query RDF.

In spite of the advance in our understanding of SPARQL, there is still a fundamental issue in the definition of this language. The semantics of SPARQL is defined under a closed-world assumption, in fact there are SPARQL queries that cannot be answered without making the assumption that the unavailable data is false. However, the information in the Web is inherently incomplete and, therefore, making such assumption about unavailable data contradicts the underlying open-world semantics of RDF. To address this problem, the authors of [28] identify a condition that is satisfied by the SPARQL queries that are appropriate for the open-world semantics of RDF, namely *weak monotonicity*.

Weak monotonicity is an important notion for the study of the query language SPARQL. However, weak monotonicity is a semantic notion that does not provide much insight on how to write well-behaved queries. In fact, this notion is not well-suited for practical applications, as the problem of verifying if a query is weakly-monotone is undecidable. Hence, finding a fragment of the class of weakly-monotone SPARQL queries with a simple syntactic definition is a fundamental task. This problem has been addressed by defining fragments of SPARQL based on some syntactic restrictions. Arguably, the most adopted of these restrictions is that of *well designedness* [28, 29, 22, 30, 1, 7, 20]. It is known that every well-designed query is weakly monotone [6], but whether the opposite direction holds is an open problem. As our first contribution, we provide a negative answer to this question proving that there are (disjunction-free) weakly-monotone queries in SPARQL that are not equivalent to any well-designed query. Moreover, we show that this is the case even if we extend well-designed queries with disjunction at the top-most level.

Given these negative results, we embark on the design of an RDF query language with a simple syntactic definition and the same expressive power as the fragment of SPARQL consisting of weakly-monotone queries. To this end, we move to a more general scenario where infinite RDF graphs are also allowed, so that interpolation techniques studied for first-order logic can be applied. Interpolation techniques have proved to be useful in establishing connections between semantic and syntactic notions for first-order logic, so they are a natural choice in this investigation. The application of these techniques to SPARQL is the most challenging contribution of this paper, and its consequences provide a significant improvement in our understanding of the notion of weak monotonicity. In particular, we make use of Lyndon's [24] and Otto's [26] interpolation theorems to obtain a result that establish a form of equivalence between the fragment of weakly-monotone SPARQL queries and the fragment of SPARQL that does not use the operator OPTIONAL (used in this query language to obtain optional information if available). This result leads to the definition of a new and simple operator for SPARQL, the not-subsumed operator (NS), that is used to remove redundant information from the answer to a query.

With the use of the operator NS, we proceed to introduce two novel fragments of weakly-monotone queries. We prove that these fragments are more expressive than the fragments based on the notion of well designedness, and we provide precise characterizations of their expressive power. In fact, we show that they capture classes of weakly-monotone queries that are widely used in practice. This, together with the fact that the syntactic definitions of these fragments are rather simple, shows that these new query languages fulfill our original goal. In fact, we think these fragments provide an interesting new approach for querying RDF graphs.

The input of a SPARQL query is an RDF graph, while its output is a set mappings. Thus, SPARQL queries cannot be composed in the sense that the result of a query cannot be used as the input of another query. To overcome this limitation, the standard definition of SPARQL by the W3C includes an operator CONSTRUCT [32, 40, 20] that can be used to produce an RDF graph as output (instead of a set of mappings). This operator is widely used in practice, so it is a relevant question whether its use in SPARQL is appropriate for the open-world semantics of RDF.

As opposed to the previous case, in the context of the CONSTRUCT operator monotonicity is the condition satisfied by the queries that are appropriate for the open-world semantics of RDF. Hence, we focus on this notion, and use the results obtained from interpolation to identify a fragment of the class of CONSTRUCT queries that captures monotonicity. This fragment has a simple syntactic definition, and, somewhat surprisingly, it uses neither the operator NS nor the operator OPTIONAL. All these properties make this fragment a promising query language that deserves further investigation.

Finally, we present a thorough study of the complexity of the evaluation problem for the query languages introduced in this paper.

Organization of the paper. We give in Section 2 the basic terminology used in the paper. Then we introduce in Section 3 the notions of well designedness and weak monotonicity, and prove that there are weakly-monotone queries in SPARQL that are not equivalent to any well-designed query. We use interpolation techniques in Section 4 to show a form of equivalence between the fragment of weakly-monotone SPARQL queries and the fragment of SPARQL that does not use the operator OPTIONAL. Inspired by this result, we define in Section 5 the operator NS. In this section, we also introduce and study two novel fragments of weakly-monotone queries. Then we consider the CONSTRUCT operator in Section 6, where we identify a query language with a simple syntactic definition that captures the class of monotone CONSTRUCT queries. Finally, we provide some concluding remarks and directions for future research in Section 8. Due to the lack of space, we only provide sketches for some of the proofs of the results in the paper. The complete proofs can be found in the extended version of the paper in https://www.dropbox.com/s/1opouuou3c4xp09/main.pdf.

2. PRELIMINARIES

In this section, we provide the basic terminology that will be used in the paper.

The Resource Description Framework (RDF) [25] is based upon *identifiers* representing Web resources. Assume that $\mathbf{I}$ is an infinite set of International Resource Identifiers (IRIs). Then a triple $(s, p, o) \in \mathbf{I} \times \mathbf{I} \times \mathbf{I}$ is called an RDF triple, where s, p and o are called the subject, predicate and object of the triple, respectively. Moreover, an RDF graph is defined to be a finite set of RDF triples. It should be noticed that constant values (like numbers and strings) and existential values (resources with unknown identifiers) are also allowed in RDF, but we disallow them here as the results of the paper are not affected by their presence. For the sake of readability, we also assume that every string can be used as an IRI, which violates the specification of these identifiers [14].

Example 2.1. Assume that we want to store in RDF information about the founders and supporters of different organizations. Then we need to state every relationship as an RDF triple; for instance, if a person s founded an organization o, then we store the triple $(s, \text{founder}, o)$. The following table stores such an RDF graph:

Subject	Predicate	Object
Gottfrid_Svartholm	founder	The_Pirate_Bay
Fredrik_Neij	founder	The_Pirate_Bay
Peter_Sunde	founder	The_Pirate_Bay
founder	sub_property	supporter
The_Pirate Bay	stands_for	sharing_rights
Carl_Lundström	supporter	The_Pirate_Bay

Notice that a resource mentioned in one triple as a property can also be mentioned in another triple as the subject or predicate. As RDF triples are relations between entities, it is also natural to represent RDF graphs as directed edge-labeled graphs, as shown in Figure 1. □

2.1 The RDF query language SPARQL

SPARQL is essentially a pattern-matching query language for RDF graphs. To define the syntax of SPARQL, assume there is an infinite set $\mathbf{V}$ of variables disjoint from $\mathbf{I}$. Elements of $\mathbf{V}$ are distinguished by using ? as a prefix (e.g. $?X$ and $?Y$ are variables).

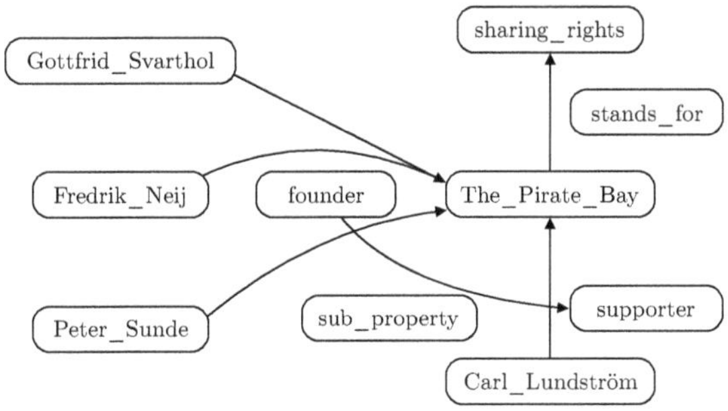

Figure 1: An RDF graph with information about founders and supporters of different organizations.

Then the set of SPARQL graph patterns is recursively defined as follows:

- A triple in $(\mathbf{I} \cup \mathbf{V}) \times (\mathbf{I} \cup \mathbf{V}) \times (\mathbf{I} \cup \mathbf{V})$ is a graph pattern (called a triple pattern).
- If P_1, P_2 are graph patterns, then $(P_1 \text{ UNION } P_2)$, $(P_1 \text{ AND } P_2)$, $(P_1 \text{ OPT } P_2)$ are graph patterns.
- If P is a graph pattern and V is a finite subset of $\mathbf{V}$, then $(\text{SELECT } V \text{ WHERE } P)$ is a graph pattern.
- If P is a graph pattern and R is a SPARQL built-in condition, then $(P \text{ FILTER } R)$ is a graph pattern.

In the previous definition, we have used the notion of SPARQL built-in condition, which is a propositional formula where atoms are equalities or inequalities over the set $(\mathbf{I} \cup \mathbf{V})$ together with some other features [32]. We restrict to the fragment of built-in conditions presented in [28], which is formally defined as follows:

- If $?X, ?Y \in \mathbf{V}$ and $c \in \mathbf{I}$, then bound$(?X)$, $?X = c$, $?X = ?Y$ are built in-conditions.
- If R_1 and R_2 are built-in conditions, then $(\neg R_1)$, $(R_1 \vee R_2)$ and $(R_1 \wedge R_2)$ are built-in conditions.

For an operator O in the set {UNION, AND, OPT, FILTER, SELECT}, we say that a graph pattern P is O-free if O does not occur in P. To refer to a fragment of SPARQL in which only some operators are allowed, we use the first letter of the these operators. For example SPARQL[AFS] represents the fragment of SPARQL where only the operators AND, FILTER and SELECT are allowed.

To define the semantics of SPARQL we need to recall some further notation. If P is a graph pattern, then var(P) and $\mathbf{I}(P)$ denote the sets of all variables and IRIs mentioned in P, respectively. If R is a built-in condition, then var(R) denotes the set of all variables mentioned in R. A mapping μ is a partial function $\mu : \mathbf{V} \to \mathbf{I}$. The domain of μ is the subset of $\mathbf{V}$ where μ is defined, and is denoted by dom(μ). Given a mapping μ and a triple pattern t such that var$(t) \subseteq$ dom(μ), we have that $\mu(t)$ is the result of replacing every variable $?X \in$ var(t) by $\mu(?X)$. A mapping μ_1 is said to be compatible with a mapping μ_2, denoted by $\mu_1 \sim \mu_2$, if for every $?X \in \text{dom}(\mu_1) \cap \text{dom}(\mu_2)$ it is the case that $\mu_1(?X) = \mu_2(?X)$. In this case, $\mu_1 \cup \mu_2$ denotes the extension of μ_1 to the variables in $\text{dom}(\mu_2) \setminus \text{dom}(\mu_1)$ defined according to μ_2. If two mappings μ_1 and μ_2 are not compatible, we write $\mu_1 \nsim \mu_2$.

Let Ω_1 and Ω_2 be two sets of mappings. Then the join of, union of, difference between, and left-outer join of Ω_1 and Ω_2 are defined, respectively, as follows [28]:

$$
\begin{aligned}
\Omega_1 \bowtie \Omega_2 &= \{\mu_1 \cup \mu_2 \mid \mu_1 \in \Omega_1, \mu_2 \in \Omega_2 \text{ and } \mu_1 \sim \mu_2\} \\
\Omega_1 \cup \Omega_2 &= \{\mu \mid \mu \in \Omega_1 \text{ or } \mu \in \Omega_2\} \\
\Omega_1 \setminus \Omega_2 &= \{\mu \in \Omega_1 \mid \text{ for all } \mu' \in \Omega_2 : \mu \nsim \mu'\} \\
\Omega_1 ⟕ \Omega_2 &= (\Omega_1 \bowtie \Omega_2) \cup (\Omega_1 \setminus \Omega_2).
\end{aligned}
$$

Finally, given a mapping μ and a set $V \subseteq \mathbf{V}$, the expression $\mu_{|V}$ represents the mapping that results from restricting μ to $\text{dom}(\mu) \cap V$.

We have now the necessary terminology to define the semantics of SPARQL. Given a mapping μ and a built-in condition R, we say that μ satisfies R, denoted by $\mu \models R$, if one of the following conditions hold (omitting the usual rules for Boolean connectives):

- R is bound$(?X)$ and $?X \in$ dom(μ);
- R is $?X = c$, $?X \in$ dom(μ) and $\mu(?X) = c$;
- R is $?X = ?Y$, $?X \in$ dom(μ), $?Y \in$ dom(μ) and $\mu(?X) = \mu(?Y)$.

Moreover, given an RDF graph G and a SPARQL graph pattern P, the evaluation of P over G, denoted by $[\![P]\!]_G$, is recursively defined as follows:

- if P is a triple pattern, then $[\![P]\!]_G = \{\mu \mid \text{dom}(\mu) = \text{var}(t) \text{ and } \mu(t) \in G\}$;
- if P is $(P_1 \text{ AND } P_2)$, then $[\![P]\!]_G = [\![P_1]\!]_G \bowtie [\![P_2]\!]_G$;
- if P is $(P_1 \text{ OPT } P_2)$, then $[\![P]\!]_G = [\![P_1]\!]_G ⟕ [\![P_2]\!]_G$;
- if P is $(P_1 \text{ UNION } P_2)$, then $[\![P]\!]_G = [\![P_1]\!]_G \cup [\![P_2]\!]_G$;
- if P is $(\text{SELECT } V \text{ WHERE } P')$, then $[\![P]\!]_G = \{\mu_{|V} \mid \mu \in [\![P']\!]_G\}$;
- if P is $(P' \text{ FILTER } R)$, then $[\![P]\!]_G = \{\mu \mid \mu \in [\![P']\!]_G \text{ and } \mu \models R\}$

The following example illustrates the syntax and semantics of SPARQL.

Example 2.2. Let G be the RDF graph shown in Figure 1. Assume we want to retrieve the founders and supporters of organizations that stand for sharing rights. This is achieved by a graph pattern $P = (\text{SELECT } \{?p\} \text{ WHERE } P_1)$, where P_1 is the the following graph pattern:

$$
\begin{aligned}
&(?o, \text{stands\_for}, \text{sharing\_rights}) \text{ AND} \\
&\qquad ((?p, \text{founder}, ?o) \text{ UNION } (?p, \text{supporter}, ?o))
\end{aligned}
$$

The evaluation of P over G is performed in a bottom-up fashion. We first evaluate the triple patterns, obtaining the following sets of mappings:

$[\![(?o, \text{stands\_for}, \text{sharing\_rights})]\!]_G =$

?o
The_Pirate_Bay

$[\![(?p, \text{founder}, ?o)]\!]_G =$

?p	?o
Gottfrid_Svartholm	The_Pirate_Bay
Fredrik_Neij	The_Pirate_Bay
Peter_Sunde	The_Pirate_Bay

$[\![(?p, \text{supporter}, ?o)]\!]_G =$

?p	?o
Carl_Lundström	The_Pirate_Bay

Then from the definition of the UNION operator, we obtain that $[\![(?p, \text{founder}, ?o) \text{ UNION } (?p, \text{supporter}, ?o)]\!]_G$ is equal to:

?p	?o
Gottfrid_Svartholm	The_Pirate_Bay
Fredrik_Neij	The_Pirate_Bay
Peter_Sunde	The_Pirate_Bay
Carl_Lundström	The_Pirate_Bay

The mappings in this table are combined with the only mapping in $[\![(?o, \text{stands\_for}, \text{sharing\_rights})]\!]_G$ through the operator AND, obtaining that $[\![P_1]\!]_G$ contains exactly the same set of mappings as in this table. Finally, the operator SELECT is used to keep only the values in the variable $?p$, thus generating the desired list of people:

?p
Gottfrid_Svartholm
Fredrik_Neij
Peter_Sunde
Carl_Lundström

□

In the previous example, we use a tabular notation for the result of a SPARQL query. In particular, a mapping μ with $\text{dom}(\mu) = \{?X_1, \ldots, ?X_n\}$ is represented as a row in a table with columns $?X_1, \ldots, ?X_n$. In what follows, we also refer to such mapping μ by using the notation $[?X_1 \to \mu(?X_1), \ldots, ?X_n \to \mu(?X_n)]$.

Finally, two graph patterns P_1 and P_2 are said to be equivalent, denoted by $P_1 \equiv P_2$, if for every RDF graph G, it holds that $[\![P_1]\!]_G = [\![P_2]\!]_G$. We use this notion of equivalence to compare fragments of SPARQL. In particular, we say that two such fragments $\mathcal{F}_1$ and $\mathcal{F}_2$ have the same expressive power if: (1) for every graph pattern $P_1 \in \mathcal{F}_1$, there exists a graph pattern $P_2 \in \mathcal{F}_2$ such that $P_1 \equiv P_2$; and (2) for every graph pattern $P_2 \in \mathcal{F}_2$, there exists a graph pattern $P_1 \in \mathcal{F}_1$ such that $P_2 \equiv P_1$. Moreover, we say $\mathcal{F}_1$ is strictly less expressive than $\mathcal{F}_2$ if: (1) for every graph pattern $P_1 \in \mathcal{F}_1$, there exists a graph pattern $P_2 \in \mathcal{F}_2$ such that $P_1 \equiv P_2$; and (2) there exists a graph pattern $P_2 \in \mathcal{F}_2$, for which there is no graph pattern $P_1 \in \mathcal{F}_1$ such that $P_2 \equiv P_1$.

3. WEAK MONOTONICITY VERSUS WELL DESIGNEDNESS

In this section, we formally introduce the notions of weak monotonicity and well designedness, and discuss their role in identifying fragments of SPARQL that are appropriate for the open-world semantics of RDF. Moreover, we show that there exist weakly monotone graph patterns that are not expressible as well-designed graph patterns, thus giving a negative answer to the question of whether these two notions are equivalent.

3.1 The notion of weak monotonicity

Intuitively, a query language is said to conform to the open-world assumption if its semantics is defined in a way such that, no assumption is made about the information that is not present when evaluating a query. This is particularly important when considering Web data, as in general we cannot make any assumption about the information that is not available. In fact, the semantics of RDF is based on an open-world assumption [25]. A notion that captures this idea for relational query languages is that of monotonicity. A query is said to be monotone if whenever it outputs an answer over a database, it outputs that same answer over all extensions of that database.

The notion of monotonicity is defined as follows for the case of SPARQL: a graph pattern P is said to be monotone if for every two RDF graphs G_1 and G_2 such that $G_1 \subseteq G_2$, it holds that $[\![P]\!]_{G_1} \subseteq [\![P]\!]_{G_2}$. On the contrary to the relational scenario, monotonicity is not the right property when trying to capture the idea

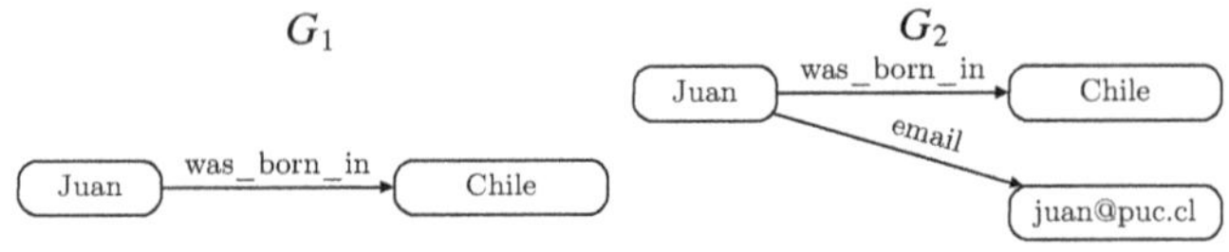

Figure 2: Two RDF graphs G_1 and G_2 such that $G_1 \subseteq G_2$.

of a query that is appropriate for the the open-world semantics of RDF. This occurs because SPARQL graph patterns allow for optional information, and hence one answer (mapping) to a query can contain *more information* than another answer to the same query. This does not occur in relational databases, where different answers to the same query have incomparable information.

Example 3.1. Consider the graph pattern

$$P \;=\; (?X, \text{was\_born\_in}, \text{Chile}) \text{ OPT } (?X, \text{email}, ?Y),$$

and let G_1 and G_2 be the RDF graphs shown in Figure 2. On the one hand, the answer to P over G_1 contains only the mapping $\mu_1 = [?X \to \text{juan}]$, as $(?X, \text{email}, ?Y)$ does not match any triple in G_1. On the other hand, the evaluation of P over G_2 contains only the mapping $\mu_2 = [?X \to \text{juan}, ?Y \to \text{juan@puc.cl}]$. Thus, we have that $[\![P]\!]_{G_1} \not\subseteq [\![P]\!]_{G_2}$ as μ_1 is not present in the answer to P over G_2, from which we conclude that P is not monotone as $G_1 \subseteq G_2$. However, in this case we can safely say that no information is lost when evaluating P over G_2, as every piece of information in μ_1 can be retrieved from the information in μ_2. □

In [6], the authors address the issue mentioned in the previous example by introducing a weaker notion of monotonicity that is appropriate for the semantics of SPARQL and, in particular, for the semantics of the OPT operator. To define this concept we need to introduce some terminology. Given two mappings μ_1 and μ_2, the mapping μ_1 is said to be subsumed by μ_2, denoted by $\mu_1 \preceq \mu_2$, if $\text{dom}(\mu_1) \subseteq \text{dom}(\mu_2)$ and $\mu_1(?X) = \mu_2(?X)$ for every $?X \in \text{dom}(\mu_1)$. Moreover, μ_1 is said to be properly subsumed by μ_2, denoted by $\mu_1 \prec \mu_2$, if $\mu_1 \preceq \mu_2$ and $\mu_1 \neq \mu_2$. Finally, given two sets of mappings Ω_1 and Ω_2, we have that Ω_1 is subsumed by Ω_2, denoted by $\Omega_1 \sqsubseteq \Omega_2$, if for every mapping $\mu_1 \in \Omega_1$, there is a mapping $\mu_2 \in \Omega_2$ such that $\mu_1 \preceq \mu_2$. With this notation we have the following:

Definition 3.2 ([6]). *A graph pattern P is said to be weakly monotone if for every two RDF graphs G_1 and G_2 such that $G_1 \subseteq G_2$, it is the case that $[\![P]\!]_{G_1} \sqsubseteq [\![P]\!]_{G_2}$.*

Weak-monotonicity overcomes the issues with monotonicity when capturing the idea of making no assumptions about unknown information when evaluating a SPARQL query. In fact, if a graph pattern P is weakly monotone and the evaluation of P over an RDF graph G produces a mapping μ, then the evaluation of P over any extension of G produces a mapping that contains at least as much information as μ. As an example of this, notice that the graph pattern in Example 3.1 is not monotone but weakly monotone.

3.2 The notion of well designedness

The operators in SPARQL are all positive in nature; in fact, neither a difference operator nor a general form of negation were included in the first version of this language [32]. However, as opposed to the intuition behind the OPT operator, there exist SPARQL graph patterns which are not weakly monotone.

Example 3.3. Let P be the graph pattern defined by:

$$P \;=\; (?X, \text{was\_born\_in}, \text{Chile}) \text{ AND } ((?Y, \text{was\_born\_in}, \text{Chile}) \text{ OPT } (?Y, \text{email}, ?X)),$$

and assume that G_1 and G_2 are the RDF graphs depicted in Figure 2. In the evaluation of P over G_1, we can see that (?X, was_born_in, Chile) and (?Y, was_born_in, Chile) match the RDF triple (Juan, was_born_in, Chile). Thus, given that the triple pattern (?Y, email, ?X) does not match any triple in G_1, we obtain that $[\![P]\!]_{G_1} = \{[?X \rightarrow \text{Juan}, ?Y \rightarrow \text{Juan}]\}$. On the other hand, if we evaluate P over G_2, we obtain the same results for the triple patterns (?X, was_born_in, Chile) and (?Y, was_born_in, Chile). Nevertheless, in this case the triple (?Y, email, ?X) matches (Juan, email, juan@puc.cl), from which we conclude that:

$$[\![(?Y, \text{was\_born\_in}, \text{Chile}) \text{ OPT } (?Y, \text{email}, ?X)]\!]_{G_2} = \{[?Y \rightarrow \text{Juan}, ?X \rightarrow \text{juan@puc.cl}]\}.$$

Hence, given that $[\![(?X, \text{was\_born\_in}, \text{Chile})]\!]_{G_2} = \{[?X \rightarrow \text{Juan}]\}$, the mappings coming from the two sides of the AND operator are not compatible. We conclude that $[\![P]\!]_{G_2} = \emptyset$ and, therefore, P is not weakly-monotone as $G_1 \subseteq G_2$ and $[\![P]\!]_{G_1} \not\sqsubseteq [\![P]\!]_{G_2}$. □

Arguably, the graph pattern P in the previous example is unnatural. In fact, the triple pattern (?Y, email, ?X) offers optional information to (?Y, was_born_in, Chile), but at the same time is intended to match the results of the triple pattern (?X, was_born_in, Chile). To avoid such patterns the notion of well designedness was introduced in [28], with the specific goal in mind of disallowing the odd use of variables shown in the previous example.

Definition 3.4 ([28]). *Let P be a graph pattern in* SPARQL[AOF]. *Then P is said to be well designed if it satisfies the following conditions:*

- *for every sub-pattern of P of the form (P_1 FILTER R), it is the case that $var(R) \subseteq var(P_1)$; and*
- *for every sub-pattern of P of the form (P_1 OPT P_2) and every variable $?X \in var(P_2)$, if $?X$ occurs in P outside (P_1 OPT P_2), then $?X \in var(P_1)$.*

For instance, the graph pattern P given in Example 3.3 is not well designed. To see why this is the case, consider the sub-pattern (P_1 OPT P_2) of P with P_1 = (?Y, was_born_in, Chile) and P_2 = (?Y, email, ?X). We have that $?X \in \text{var}(P_2)$, and also that ?X occurs in P outside (P_1 OPT P_2) in the triple pattern (?X, was_born_in, Chile). However, $?X \notin \text{var}(P_1)$, thus violating the second condition in the definition of well designedness. On the other hand, the graph pattern shown in Example 3.1 is well designed.

3.3 On the relationship between weak monotonicity and well designedness

It is well known that well designed patterns are weakly monotone, and thus they are appropriate for the open-world semantics of RDF [28, 6]. However, the rather syntactic definition of well designedness does not shed light on how close is this notion to weak monotonicity. In fact, the question of whether every weakly-monotone graph pattern in SPARQL[AOF] is equivalent to a well-designed graph pattern is still open. The first contribution of this paper is to give a negative answer to this question.

Theorem 3.5. *There exists a weakly-monotone graph pattern in* SPARQL[AOF] *that is not equivalent to any well-designed graph pattern in* SPARQL[AOF].

The notion of well designedness was defined in [28] without considering the UNION operator. Thus, it is natural to ask whether the lack of disjunction is the reason behind Theorem 3.5. To show that this is not the case, consider the following extension of the notion of well designedness. A graph pattern in SPARQL[AUOF] is said to be well designed if it is of the form

$$P_1 \text{ UNION } P_2 \text{ UNION } \cdots \text{ UNION } P_n,$$

where every disjunct P_i $(1 \leq i \leq n)$ is a well-designed graph pattern in SPARQL[AOF]. It is important to notice that every graph pattern in this class is weakly monotone, and also that this class has been widely adopted as a good practice for writing SPARQL queries (see, e.g, [30]). However, the following result shows that this fragment of SPARQL is not expressive enough to capture weak monotonicity.

Theorem 3.6. *There exists a weakly-monotone graph pattern in* SPARQL[AUOF] *that is not equivalent to any well-designed graph pattern in* SPARQL[AUOF].

The previous theorems help to improve the understanding of the expressive power of well-designed graph patterns, and also motivate the search for more expressive weakly-monotone fragments of SPARQL with simple syntactic definitions.

4. CAPTURING WEAK MONOTONICITY UNDER SUBSUMPTION EQUIVALENCE

Interpolation techniques have proved to be useful in establishing connections between semantic and syntactic notions for first-order logic (FO); an example of this is the use of Lyndon's interpolation theorem [24] to show that the semantic notion of monotonicity for FO is characterized by the syntactic notion of being positive. Interpolation techniques have also proved to be useful in the database area, for instance to generate plans for answering queries over physical repositories [37] or with restricted access to some data sources [8]. Thus, they are an obvious choice to address the issue of defining an RDF query language that captures the fragment of weakly-monotone SPARQL queries, which is the motivation of this section.

It is important to notice that interpolations techniques are known to fail when restricted to finite models [2], so infinite database instances are considered in the investigations that use these techniques for relational databases [37, 8]. By following the same idea, we consider in this paper both finite and infinite RFD graphs, and we define an *unrestricted* RDF graph as a (possible infinite) subset of $\mathbf{I} \times \mathbf{I} \times \mathbf{I}$. It is also important to notice that in this new setting, the semantics of SPARQL is defined in the same way as for the finite case. Moreover, the notions of weak monotonicity and equivalence of graph patterns are also defined as for the finite case; but to avoid confusion we say that a graph pattern P is unrestricted weakly monotone if for every pair G_1, G_2 of unrestricted RDF graphs such that $G_1 \subseteq G_2$, it holds that $[\![P]\!]_{G_1} \sqsubseteq [\![P]\!]_{G_2}$, and we use notation $P_1 \equiv^{\text{inf}} P_2$ if for every unrestricted RDF graph G, it holds that $[\![P_1]\!]_G = [\![P_2]\!]_G$. Finally, it should also be observed that if a graph pattern is unrestricted weakly monotone then it is also weakly monotone. Therefore, any query language obtained by using the results of this section is appropriate for the open-world semantics of RDF, as every graph pattern in it would be weakly monotone (in the sense defined in the previous section).

Before stating the main result of this section, we need to dig deeper into the notion of equivalence for SPARQL graph patterns. So far we have considered the usual definition of equivalence for graph patterns P_1 and P_2, which imposes the condition that the set of mappings $[\![P_1]\!]_G$ and $[\![P_2]\!]_G$ contain exactly the same elements for every (unrestricted) RDF graph G. But we have argued in Section 3 that if a mapping μ_1 is subsumed by a mapping μ_2, then μ_2 contains at least as much information as μ_1, so if $[\![P_1]\!]_G \sqsubseteq [\![P_2]\!]_G$ and $[\![P_2]\!]_G \sqsubseteq [\![P_1]\!]_G$ then we can claim that the set of mappings $[\![P_1]\!]_G$ and $[\![P_2]\!]_G$ are equally informative. Hence, it is also natural to consider a notion of equivalence of SPARQL graph patterns based on subsumption. More precisely, two graph patterns P_1 and P_2 are said to be subsumption-equivalent [1, 7], denoted by $P_1 \equiv_s P_2$ (resp., $P_1 \equiv_s^{\text{inf}} P_2$), if for every RDF graph G (resp., unrestricted RDF graph G), it holds that $[\![P_1]\!]_G \sqsubseteq [\![P_2]\!]_G$ and $[\![P_2]\!]_G \sqsubseteq [\![P_1]\!]_G$.

We are finally ready to present the main result of this paper. Notice that this result is stated in terms of the notion of subsumption-equivalence, which is a concept that has received a lot of attention in the last few years [22, 30, 1, 7].

THEOREM 4.1. *For every unrestricted weakly-monotone graph pattern P, there exists a graph pattern Q in* SPARQL[AUFS] *such that $P \equiv_s^{\text{inf}} Q$.*

As a corollary of this theorem and the fact that every graph pattern in SPARQL[AUFS] is unrestricted weakly monotone (in fact, monotone), we obtain the following result that shows that the query language SPARQL[AUFS] captures the fragment of unrestricted weakly-monotone SPARQL queries under subsumption equivalence.

COROLLARY 4.2. *A* SPARQL *graph pattern P is unrestricted weakly-monotone if and only if there exists a graph pattern Q in* SPARQL[AUFS] *such that $P \equiv_s^{\text{inf}} Q$.*

PROOF SKETCH OF THEOREM 4.1. This theorem is obtained by applying Lyndon's [24] and Otto's [26] interpolation theorems. Here we provide a sketch of the proof of this result.

Let P be a graph pattern. We first need to provide a translation from RDF and SPARQL to a setting in FO. This transformation is inspired by the translations given in [4, 31, 20], but with some modifications needed to apply interpolation techniques. Define $\mathcal{L}^P_{\text{RDF}}$ as the vocabulary that contains a ternary relation symbol T, a unary relation symbol Dom, a constant symbol c_i for each $i \in \mathbf{I}(P)$, and a constant symbol n. We say that an $\mathcal{L}^P_{\text{RDF}}$-structure $\mathfrak{A} = \langle D, T^{\mathfrak{A}}, Dom^{\mathfrak{A}}, \{c_i^{\mathfrak{A}}\}_{i\in I}, n^{\mathfrak{A}}\rangle$ corresponds to an unrestricted RDF graph G if

- D is a set of IRIs plus an additional element N;
- $G = T^{\mathfrak{A}} \cap (Dom^{\mathfrak{A}} \times Dom^{\mathfrak{A}} \times Dom^{\mathfrak{A}})$;
- for every $i \in \mathbf{I}(G)$, it is the case that $c_i^{\mathfrak{A}} = i$; and
- $n^{\mathfrak{A}} = N$ and N occurs neither in $Dom^{\mathfrak{A}}$ nor in $T^{\mathfrak{A}}$.

For every graph pattern P and unrestricted RDF graph G, there is an infinite set of $\mathcal{L}^P_{\text{RDF}}$-structures that correspond to G. We denote this set by $\mathcal{A}^P_G$. At this stage, the constant n and the unary relation Dom might seem unnecessary; their importance will become clear later.

Now we need to define a relation between mappings and tuples. To this end, assume an arbitrary order $\leq$ over the set of variables $\mathbf{V}$. Let $\{?X_1, \ldots, ?X_\ell\}$ be the set of variables in P ordered under $\leq$. Given a mapping $\mu : \text{var}(P) \to \mathbf{I}$, we define the extension of μ to var(P) as the function $\mu^P : \text{var}(P) \to \mathbf{I}$ such that $\mu^P(?X) = \mu(?X)$ for every $?X \in \text{dom}(\mu)$, and $\mu^P(?X) = N$ for $?X \in \text{var}(P) \setminus \text{dom}(\mu)$. Using this function we define the tuple corresponding to μ as $t^P_\mu = (\mu^P(?X_1), \ldots, \mu^P(?X_\ell))$. We extend the notion of subsumption to tuples: given two tuples $\bar{a} = (a_1, \ldots, a_\ell)$ and $\bar{b} = (b_1, \ldots, b_\ell)$, we define $\bar{a} \preceq \bar{b}$ as

$$\bar{a} \preceq \bar{b} \quad = \quad \bigwedge_{i\in[1..\ell]} a_i = b_i \vee a_i = N.$$

With the previous FO setting, we embark on the task of defining an FO formula $\varphi_P(\bar{x})$ that is equivalent to P in the following sense: for every mapping μ, unrestricted RDF graph G and $\mathcal{L}^P_{\text{RDF}}$-structure $\mathfrak{A} \in \mathcal{A}_G$, it is the case that $\mu \in [\![P]\!]_G$ if and only if $\mathfrak{A} \models \varphi_P(t^P_\mu)$. For the application of Otto's interpolation theorem, the formula φ_P should be quantified relative to Dom, meaning that every quantifier in φ_P is either of the form $\forall x(Dom(x) \to \psi)$ or $\exists x(Dom(x) \wedge \psi)$. This condition makes the construction of φ_P a particularly technical procedure which is performed by induction over the structure of P; we skip the details here. A corollary of this construction is that for every weakly monotone graph pattern there is an equivalent FO formula with Dom-relativized quantification.

Now we have a formula φ_P that is related to P under a precise notion of equivalence and is quantified relative to Dom. The next step is to define a formula asserting that φ_P corresponds to an unrestricted weakly-monotone graph pattern, for which we need to move to a new vocabulary. Let $\mathcal{L}^{P2}_{\text{RDF}}$ be defined as $\mathcal{L}^P_{\text{RDF}} \cup \{T', Dom'\}$, where T' is a ternary relation symbol and Dom' is a unary relation symbol. This vocabulary is intended to define structures *corresponding* to a pair of unrestricted RDF graphs. We say that an $\mathcal{L}^{P2}_{\text{RDF}}$-structure $\mathfrak{A}$ corresponds to an unrestricted RDF graph G if the restriction of $\mathfrak{A}$ to $\mathcal{L}^P_{\text{RDF}}$ corresponds to G.

Now consider the following $\mathcal{L}^{P2}_{\text{RDF}}$-formula:

$$[\varphi_P(T, Dom, \bar{x}) \wedge T \subseteq T' \wedge Dom \subseteq Dom'] \to \exists\bar{y}\,(\bar{x} \preceq \bar{y} \wedge \varphi_P(T', Dom', \bar{y})). \quad (1)$$

Here $\varphi_P(T', Dom', \bar{y})$ represents the formula $\varphi_P(\bar{y})$ but replacing every occurrence of T by T', and every occurrence of Dom by Dom'. Besides, the sentence $T \subseteq T'$ indicates that T is contained in T', which is expressed in FO as $\forall u \forall v \forall w\,(T(u, v, w) \to T'(u, v, w))$, and likewise for the formula $Dom \subseteq Dom'$. It is not hard to prove that (1) is satisfied by every $\mathcal{L}^{P2}_{\text{RDF}}$-structure corresponding to an RDF graph if and only if P is unrestricted weakly-monotone. However, we will see that to apply interpolation we need a tautology, and we cannot assert that (1) is a tautology since not every $\mathcal{L}^{P2}_{\text{RDF}}$-structure corresponds to an unrestricted RDF graph. To overcome this problem, we define a formula Φ_{RDF} that is satisfied precisely by those $\mathcal{L}^{P2}_{\text{RDF}}$-structures that correspond to an unrestricted RDF graph. Now we add Φ_{RDF} to the left-hand side of the implication:

$$[\Phi_{\text{RDF}} \wedge \varphi_P(T, Dom, \bar{x}) \wedge T \subseteq T' \wedge Dom \subseteq Dom'] \to \exists\bar{y}(\bar{x} \preceq \bar{y} \wedge \varphi_P(T', Dom', \bar{y})). \quad (2)$$

It is not hard to prove that if P is unrestricted weakly-monotone, then this formula is a tautology.

Now we proceed to apply interpolation. Lyndon's interpolation theorem [24] asserts that if an implication $\alpha \to \beta$ is a tautology, then there is a formula θ such that $\alpha \to \theta$ and $\theta \to \beta$ are both tautologies, and every relational symbol occurring on θ must occur in both α and β. Moreover, if a relation R only occurs positively in α or β, then R can only occur positively in θ. Otto extended this result by proving that if α and β are quantified relative to a set U, then θ is also quantified relative to U [26]. From these theorems and formula (2), we can deduce the existence of a new formula

$\theta(T', Dom', \bar{x})$ such that the following formulas are tautologies:

$$[\Phi_{\mathrm{RDF}} \wedge \varphi_P(T, Dom, \bar{x}) \wedge T \subseteq T' \wedge$$
$$Dom \subseteq Dom'] \rightarrow \theta(T', Dom', \bar{x}) \quad (3)$$
$$\theta(T', Dom', \bar{x}) \rightarrow \exists \bar{y}\, (\bar{x} \preceq \bar{y} \wedge \varphi_P(T', Dom', \bar{y})) \quad (4)$$

Let G be an unrestricted RDF graph. By considering an $\mathcal{L}^{P2}_{\mathrm{RDF}}$-structure $\mathfrak{A}$ that corresponds to G such that $T^{\mathfrak{A}} = T'^{\mathfrak{A}}$ and $Dom^{\mathfrak{A}} = Dom'^{\mathfrak{A}}$, and by carefully inspecting (3), we can deduce that for every $\mathcal{L}^{P}_{\mathrm{RDF}}$-structure $\mathfrak{A} \in \mathcal{A}_G$, if $\mathfrak{A} \models \varphi_P(T, Dom, \bar{x})$, then $\mathfrak{A} \models \theta(T, Dom, \bar{x})$. Furthermore, from the same structure and (4) we can deduce that for every $\mathcal{L}^{P}_{\mathrm{RDF}}$-structure $\mathfrak{A} \in \mathcal{A}_G$, if $\mathfrak{A} \models \varphi_P(T, Dom, \bar{x})$, then there is a tuple $\bar{y}$ such that $\bar{x} \preceq \bar{y}$ and $\mathfrak{A} \models \varphi_P(T, Dom, \bar{y})$. We conclude that for every tuple $\bar{a}$ and every structure $\mathfrak{A}$ corresponding to an unrestricted RDF graph, it holds that $\bar{a}$ is a maximal tuple such that $\mathfrak{A} \models \varphi_P(\bar{a})$ if and only if $\bar{a}$ is a maximal tuple such that $\mathfrak{A} \models \theta(\bar{a})$ (under the order $\preceq$).

Now we proceed to inspect the syntax of formula $\theta(T', Dom', \bar{x})$. From the construction of (2), we can see that in the left-hand side of the implication the relations T' and Dom' occur only positively. Therefore, these two relations must occur positively in $\theta(T', Dom', \bar{x})$. Moreover, every quantifier in (2) is relativized w.r.t. either Dom or Dom', and hence $\theta(T', Dom', \bar{x})$ is quantified relative to Dom'. From these two facts we are able to prove that θ is equivalent to a UCQ with inequalities θ'. This proof requires several technical details that we have to skip due to the lack of space.

The final step is to define a translation from FO to SPARQL. The goal of this translation is to transform θ' (a UCQ with inequalities) into a SPARQL[AUFS] graph pattern Q. Although this translation might sound simple, it is not straightforward to define a graph pattern equivalent to θ' under the same notion of equivalence used for P and φ_P. Therefore, we use a weaker notion of equivalence: for every RDF graph G and every structure $\mathfrak{A} \in \mathcal{A}_G$ such that $T^{\mathfrak{A}} = G$, a mapping μ belongs to $[\![Q]\!]_G$ if and only if $\mathfrak{A} \models \theta'(t^Q_\mu)$. Due to the lack of space, we omit the details of the construction of the graph pattern Q satisfying the previous condition.

Summarizing the previous procedure, given a graph pattern P we constructed an FO-formula φ_P that is equivalent to P. By using interpolation techniques, we showed the existence of a new formula θ that is equivalent in terms of the obtained maximal tuples to φ_P, over structures corresponding to unrestricted RDF graphs. We defined a UCQ with inequalities θ' equivalent to θ, from which we obtained a SPARQL[AUFS] graph pattern Q that is equivalent to θ' under a weaker notion of equivalence. By inspecting every performed step, it can be shown that for every unrestricted RDF graph G, it is the case that $[\![P]\!]_G \subseteq [\![Q]\!]_G$ and $[\![Q]\!]_G \sqsubseteq [\![P]\!]_G$. This implies that $P \equiv^{\inf}_s Q$, which was to be shown. □

Recall that we introduce in Section 3 the notion of well designed graph pattern, which is a stronger condition than weak monotonicity. It is interesting to notice that Theorem 4.1 can be proved for well-designed graph patterns using techniques similar to those presented in [20]. However, it is not clear how to prove it over unrestricted weakly-monotone graph patterns without using a translation to FO and interpolation techniques.

In the rest of the paper, we will see that Theorem 4.1 turns out to be a powerful tool for characterizing and capturing semantic properties over different fragments of SPARQL. It is important to mention that Theorem 4.1 provides, for every unrestricted weakly-monotone pattern P, a subsumption-equivalent graph pattern Q that is monotone (as Q is in SPARQL[AUFS]). Hence, we will need some further operators to obtain unrestricted weakly-monotone graph patterns, which is the motivation for the next section.

5. CAPTURING WEAKLY MONOTONE FRAGMENTS OF SPARQL

The goal of this section is to introduce RDF query languages that capture important (and widely used) weakly-monotone fragments of SPARQL. Inspired by the results in the previous section, we start by defining in Section 5.1 a new operator for SPARQL. Then we use this operator in Section 5.2 to define a query language with a simple syntax and capturing the fragment of unrestricted weakly-monotone SPARQL queries where subsumed answers are not allowed. Finally, we extend this result in Section 5.3 to consider the UNION operator.

5.1 A new operator for SPARQL

The result presented in Theorem 4.1 can be reformulated in terms of the notion of *maximal* answer for a graph pattern. More precisely, given a graph pattern P and an unrestricted RDF graph G, the set of maximal answers of P over G, denoted by $[\![P]\!]^{\max}_G$, is defined as the set of mappings $\mu \in [\![P]\!]_G$ for which there is no mapping $\mu' \in [\![P]\!]_G$ such that $\mu \prec \mu'$. Then Theorem 4.1 tell us that given an unrestricted weakly-monotone graph pattern P, there exists a graph pattern Q in SPARQL[AUFS] that preserves the maximal answer to P, that is, $[\![P]\!]^{\max}_G = [\![Q]\!]^{\max}_G$ for every unrestricted RDF graph G.

The idea of preserving only the maximal answers, or removing the properly subsumed answers, naturally gives rise to a "not subsumed" (NS) operator for SPARQL. More precisely, let NS–SPARQL be the extension of SPARQL with the following recursive rule for graph patterns:

- If P is a graph pattern, then NS(P) is a graph pattern. Moreover, given an unrestricted RDF graph G:

$$[\![\mathrm{NS}(P)]\!]_G \;=\; [\![P]\!]^{\max}_G.$$

A graph pattern of the form (P_1 OPT P_2) is equivalent to NS(P_1 UNION (P_1 AND P_2)). Thus, the operator NS can be simply considered as an alternative way of obtaining optional information in the context of incomplete data. In fact, a similar operator for obtaining maximal answers called *minimal union relation* was already studied in the context of relational databases with incomplete information [16].

A first question about NS–SPARQL is whether it has the same expressive power as SPARQL, in the sense that for every graph pattern P in NS–SPARQL, there exists a graph pattern Q in SPARQL such that $P \equiv Q$ (the opposite direction trivially holds as NS–SPARQL is an extension of SPARQL). We have already shown that the operator OPT can be easily simulated by using the operator NS. But unlike that case, the simulation of the operator NS in SPARQL is not trivial. In fact, this is proven by providing an algorithm that takes as input a graph pattern P in NS–SPARQL, and outputs a graph pattern Q in SPARQL such that $P \equiv Q$ and the size of Q is double-exponential in the size of P.

THEOREM 5.1. *The languages* SPARQL *and* NS–SPARQL *have the same expressive power.*

Given that NS–SPARQL is an extension of SPARQL, we have that not every graph pattern in NS–SPARQL is weakly monotone. However, in the following sections we use the operator NS to identify query languages with simple syntactic definitions, with good expressive power and whose graph patterns are all weakly monotone.

5.2 Capturing weak monotonicity for subsumption-free graph patterns

As mentioned before, the fact that the answer to a SPARQL query can contain subsumed mappings has given rise to two different notions of equivalence for graph patterns. We start our search for a fragment of NS–SPARQL capturing weak monotonicity by putting us in an scenario where subsumption is no longer an issue. More precisely, a graph pattern P in SPARQL is said to be subsumption-free if for every unrestricted RDF graph G, it holds that $[\![P]\!]_G = [\![P]\!]_G^{\max}$. Notice that for every pair P_1, P_2 of subsumption-free graph patterns, it holds that $P_1 \equiv^{\text{inf}} P_2$ if and only if $P_1 \equiv_s^{\text{inf}} P_2$. Moreover, also notice that subsumption-free graph patterns are the rule, not the exception, in practice.

As a corollary of Theorem 4.1, we obtain the following:

Corollary 5.2. *Let P be a subsumption-free graph pattern. If P is unrestricted weakly monotone, then there exists a graph pattern Q in* SPARQL[AUFS] *such that* $P \equiv^{\text{inf}} \text{NS}(Q)$.

This corollary motivates the introduction of the notion of simple graph pattern.

Definition 5.3. *A graph pattern is simple if it is of the form* NS(P)*, where P is in* SPARQL[AUFS].

Let SP–SPARQL be an RDF query language consisting of all simple graph patterns, that is, every query in SP–SPARQL is of the form NS(P) with P in SPARQL[AUFS]. From Corollary 5.2 and the fact that every simple graph pattern is subsumption-free, we obtain the following corollary showing that SP–SPARQL is a query language appropriate for the open-world semantics of RDF, with a simple syntactic definition and with good expressive power:

Theorem 5.4. *Over unrestricted RDF graphs,* SP–SPARQL *has the same expressive power as the fragment of unrestricted weakly-monotone and subsumption-free* SPARQL *graph patterns.*

Notice that in this theorem we compare the expressive power of two query languages over unrestricted RDF graphs; thus, we use $\equiv^{\text{inf}}$ instead of $\equiv$ when indicating that the query languages have the same expressive power.

We conclude this section by considering the important fragments SPARQL[AOF] and SPARQL[AFS] of SPARQL. The latter includes the class of conjunctive queries with inequalities, and it is widely used in practice. The former was extensively studied in [28], where the notion of well designedness introduced in Section 3 was originally defined.

It is easy to see that every graph pattern in SPARQL[AFS] is subsumption free. Moreover, from the results proved in [28], it is possible to conclude that every graph pattern in SPARQL[AOF] is also subsumption free. Thus, we obtain from Theorem 5.4 the following result:

Corollary 5.5. *Let P be a graph pattern in* SPARQL[AOF] *or* SPARQL[AFS]. *If P is unrestricted weakly-monotone, then there exists a graph pattern in* SP–SPARQL *such that* $P \equiv^{\text{inf}} Q$.

Moreover, for the case of (finite) RDF graphs, it is posible to establish the following connection between well designedness and simple graph patterns:

Proposition 5.6. *The fragment of well-designed graph patterns in* SPARQL[AOF] *is strictly less expressive than* SP–SPARQL.

The existence of a graph pattern in SP–SPARQL which is not equivalent to any well-designed graph pattern in SPARQL[AOF] is not surprising, as the operator UNION is allowed in SP–SPARQL. What is interesting from the previous result is that, a well-designed graph pattern containing arbitrarily nested OPT operators can always be translated into an equivalent graph pattern with a single operator NS on the top-most level.

5.3 Including the UNION operator

In Sections 4 and 5.2, we have argued that SPARQL[AUOF] and SP–SPARQL are good query languages for the open-world semantics of RDF, in particular because of their expressive power. But these languages are incomparable, as in the former every graph pattern is monotone but not necessarily subsumption-free, while in the latter every graph pattern is subsumption-free and weakly monotone but not necessarily monotone. Thus, it is natural to ask whether there exists a query language that contains both, and where every graph pattern is still weakly monotone. This is the motivating question for this section.

We start our search by allowing the use of disjunction in simple patterns.

Definition 5.7. *A graph pattern P is an* ns-pattern *if it is of the form* $(P_1 \text{ UNION } \cdots \text{ UNION } P_n)$*, where each* P_i $(1 \leq i \leq n)$ *is a simple pattern.*

Let USP–SPARQL be an RDF query language consisting of all ns-patterns. As our first result, we prove that USP–SPARQL is indeed more expressive than both SPARQL[AUFS] and SP–SPARQL.

Proposition 5.8. USP–SPARQL *is strictly more expressive that both* SPARQL[AUFS] *and* SP–SPARQL.

From the fact that every simple pattern is unrestricted weakly monotone, it is easy to conclude that every ns-pattern is unrestricted weakly monotone. Thus, we conclude from the previous result that USP–SPARQL is an answer to our motivating question. Moreover, we obtain the following corollary from Theorem 4.1:

Corollary 5.9. *Let P be a graph pattern in* SPARQL. *Then P is unrestricted weakly-monotone if and only if there exists a graph pattern Q in* USP–SPARQL *such that* $P \equiv_s^{\text{inf}} Q$.

Finally, we obtain the following characterization of the expressive power of USP–SPARQL by using Theorem 5.4:

Corollary 5.10. *Over unrestricted RDF graphs,* USP–SPARQL *has the same expressive power as the fragment of unions of unrestricted weakly-monotone and subsumption-free* SPARQL *graph patterns.*

From the results of this section, we can conclude that USP–SPARQL is also an appropriate query language for the open-world semantics of RDF, in particular because of their expressive power and the fact that every graph pattern in USP–SPARQL is weakly monotone.

6. CAPTURING CONSTRUCT QUERIES

The input of a SPARQL graph pattern is an RDF graph, while its output is a set mappings. Thus, SPARQL graph patterns cannot be composed in the sense that the result of a query cannot be used as the input of another query. Besides, SPARQL queries cannot be used to define views that will later used by other queries, a common functionality in relational database systems. To overcome this limitation, the standard definition of SPARQL by the World Wide Web Consortium includes an operator CONSTRUCT [32] that can be used to produce as output an RDF graph instead of set of mapping.

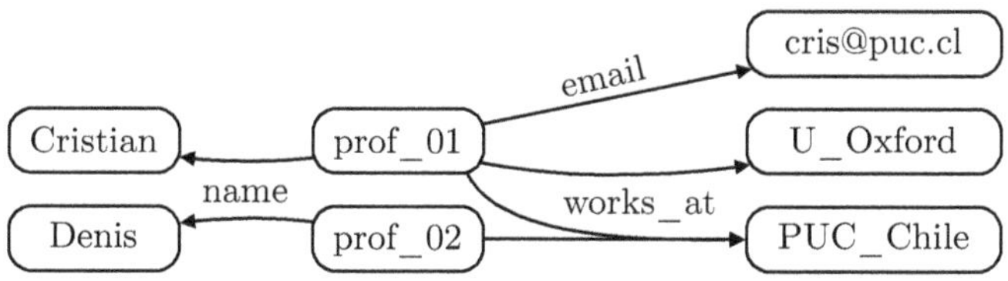

Figure 3: An RDF graph containing information about professors and universities.

This operator is widely used in practice, so it is a relevant question whether its use in SPARQL is appropriate for the open-world semantics of RDF.

The goal of this section is to answer this question. More precisely, we provide a formal definition of the CONSTRUCT operator in Section 6.1, and then we identify in Section 6.2 a query language with a simple syntactic definition and the same expressive power at the class of monotone queries using the CONSTRUCT operator. It should be noticed that Theorem 4.1 plays a crucial role in the proof of this latter result.

6.1 The CONSTRUCT operator

We follow the terminology introduced in [20] to define the CONSTRUCT operator. Let P be a SPARQL graph pattern and H a finite set of triple patterns. Then

$$Q \;=\; (\text{CONSTRUCT } H \text{ WHERE } P)$$

is a CONSTRUCT query, where P and H are called the graph pattern and the template of Q, respectively. Moreover, given an RDF graph G, the evaluation of Q over G is defined as follows:

$$\text{ans}(Q, G) = \{\mu(t) \mid \mu \in [\![P]\!]_G, t \in H \text{ and } \text{var}(t) \subseteq \text{dom}(\mu)\}.$$

Example 6.1. Let G be the RDF graph shown in Figure 3, which stores information about professors and universities. In this scenario, we want to construct an RDF graph that contains for each professor his/her name, the universities he/she is affiliated to, and his/her email if this information is available. We achieve this with a CONSTRUCT query Q of the form (CONSTRUCT H WHERE P), where $H = \{(?n, \text{affiliated\_to}, ?u), (?n, \text{email}, ?e)\}$ and P is the following graph pattern:

$$((?p, \text{name}, ?n) \text{ AND } (?p, \text{works\_at}, ?u)) \quad \text{OPT } (?p, \text{email}, ?e)$$

Notice that in this case the template H contains IRIs that are not mentioned in G. The evaluation of the graph pattern of P over G results in the following set of mappings:

	?p	?n	?u	?e
μ_1	prof_02	Denis	PUC_Chile	
μ_2	prof_01	Cristian	U_Oxford	cris@puc.cl
μ_3	prof_01	Cristian	PUC_Chile	cris@puc.cl

In the left-hand side of this table we have included names for the mappings. Then to evaluate Q, we consider the mapping in this table separately. For the mapping μ_1, we have that each variable in the triple pattern $(?n, \text{affiliated\_to}, ?u) \in H$ is contained in the domain of μ_1, so the triple $(\mu_1(?n), \text{affiliated\_to}, \mu_1(?u)) =$ (Denis, affiliated_to, PUC_Chile) is included in the output ans(Q, G). On the other hand, the variable $?e$ is not in the domain of μ_1, so no triple is produced by this mapping and the triple pattern $(?n, \text{email}, ?e) \in H$. The result of the evaluation process

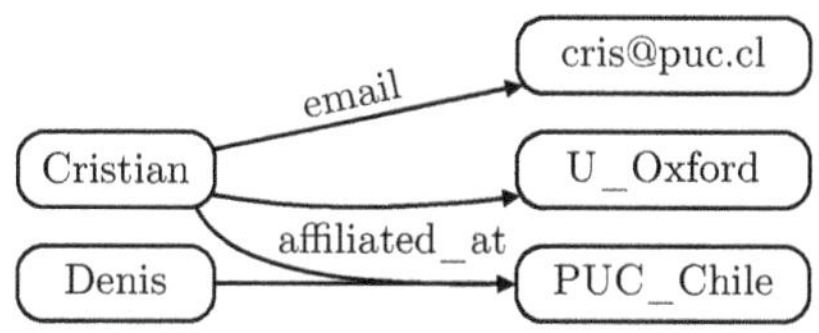

Figure 4: The RDF graph obtained by evaluating the CONSTRUCT query Q in Example 6.1 over the RDF graph in Figure 3.

is the RDF graph depicted in Figure 4. Notice that the triple (Cristian, email, cris@puc.cl) is generated when considering the mapping μ_2 and μ_3 and the triple pattern $(?n, \text{email}, ?e) \in H$. However, as the semantics of the CONSTRUCT operator is defined as a set of triples, (Cristian, email, cris@puc.cl) can occur only once in the output ans(Q, G). □

6.2 Capturing monotone CONSTRUCT queries

In Section 3, we concluded that the notion of monotonicity is too restrictive when trying to identify fragments of SPARQL that are appropriate for the open-world semantics of RDF. In that section, we also argue that the notion of weak monotonicity is appropriate for this goal, as to compare the answers of two graph patterns one has to consider the fact that a mapping can be more informative than another one. However, the situation is different for CONSTRUCT queries, as the answer for such a query is a set of RDF triples (an RDF graph), and an RDF triple is an atomic piece of information. In fact, one RDF triple cannot be more informative than another one. Thus, in the context of CONSTRUCT queries we consider the notion of monotonicity when trying to identify which fragment of these queries is appropriate for the open-world semantics of RDF. The notion of monotonicity is defined as follows in this context:

Definition 6.2. *A CONSTRUCT query Q is monotone if for every pair G_1, G_2 of RDF graphs such that $G_1 \subseteq G_2$, it holds that* ans$(Q, G_1) \subseteq$ ans(Q, G_2).

Exactly as in the case of weak monotonicity for graph patterns, this definition provides no insight about how to find a syntactic characterization of monotone CONSTRUCT queries, which is aggravated by the fact the problem of verifying whether a CONSTRUCT query is monotone is undecidable.[1] Nevertheless, CONSTRUCT queries enjoy some properties that allow us to address this issue. The key observation here is that when evaluating the graph pattern of a CONSTRUCT query, it suffices to look only at the non-subsumed graph patterns. This observation can be formalized by using the operator NS introduced in Section 5:

Lemma 6.3. *For every graph pattern P and template H, the query* (CONSTRUCT H WHERE P) *is equivalent to the query* (CONSTRUCT H WHERE NS(P)).

Next we show that this lemma plays a key role in the characterization of the monotone fragment of the class of CONSTRUCT

[1]This is a corollary of the fact that SPARQL and first-order logic have the same expressive power [4, 35] and the fact that the problem of verifying whether a first-order logic formula is monotone is undecidable. In turn, the latter result about monotonicity for first-order logic is a corollary of the undecidability of the finite satisfiability problem for this logic [38].

queries. As it is done in Sections 4 and 5, from now on we consider unrestricted RDF graphs, for which the semantics of the CONSTRUCT operator is defined in the same way as for the case of (finite) RDF graphs.

Lemma 6.3 has the following consequence. Assume that we have a CONSTRUCT query Q = (CONSTRUCT H WHERE P) in which P is unrestricted weakly monotone. From Theorem 4.1, we have that there exists a graph pattern $P^\star$ in SPARQL[AUFS] such that $P^\star \equiv_s^{\text{inf}} P$. Thus, given that the condition $P^\star \equiv_s^{\text{inf}} P$ holds if and only if the condition NS($P^\star$) $\equiv^{\text{inf}}$ NS(P) holds, we obtain the following by applying Lemma 6.3:

$$\begin{array}{rcl} Q & = & (\text{CONSTRUCT } H \text{ WHERE } P) \\ & \equiv & (\text{CONSTRUCT } H \text{ WHERE NS}(P)) \\ & \equiv^{\text{inf}} & (\text{CONSTRUCT } H \text{ WHERE NS}(P^\star)) \\ & \equiv & (\text{CONSTRUCT } H \text{ WHERE } P^\star) \end{array}$$

Hence, we obtain the following corollary.

Corollary 6.4. *Let* Q = (CONSTRUCT H WHERE P) *be a CONSTRUCT query in which P is unrestricted weakly monotone. Then there exists a graph pattern* $P^\star$ *in* SPARQL[AUFS] *such that* $Q \equiv^{\text{inf}}$ (CONSTRUCT H WHERE $P^\star$).

It is easy to prove that if the graph pattern of a CONSTRUCT query is weakly monotone, then the CONSTRUCT query is monotone. However, the opposite direction is not true, as there exist CONSTRUCT queries that are monotone but whose graph patterns are not weakly monotone. This prevents the previous corollary from establishing a general characterization of monotone CONSTRUCT queries. However, we overcome this limitation with the following lemma.

Lemma 6.5. *For every monotone CONSTRUCT query Q, there is a template H and an unrestricted weakly monotone* SPARQL *graph pattern P such that* $Q \equiv^{\text{inf}}$ (CONSTRUCT H WHERE P).

From this lemma and Corollary 6.4, we can finally obtain a syntactic characterization of monotonicity for CONSTRUCT queries. To simplify notation, given a set of SPARQL operators O, we denote by CONSTRUCT[O] the set of CONSTRUCT queries of the form (CONSTRUCT H WHERE P) such that P is a graph pattern in SPARQL[O].

Theorem 6.6. *Over unrestricted RDF graphs, the class of monotone CONSTRUCT queries has the same expressive power as* CONSTRUCT[AUFS].

Next we strengthen this result by proving that the SELECT operator can be removed from the fragment CONSTRUCT[AUFS].

Proposition 6.7. CONSTRUCT[AUF] *has the same expressive power as* CONSTRUCT[AUFS].

Thus, we obtain a simpler characterization of the class of monotone CONSTRUCT queries.

Corollary 6.8. *Over unrestricted RDF graphs, the class of monotone CONSTRUCT queries has the same expressive power as* CONSTRUCT[AUF].

This result culminates our study of CONSTRUCT queries. We have presented a clean and simple syntactic characterization of the class of monotone CONSTRUCT queries. It is interesting to notice that the only allowed operators in this characterization are FILTER, AND and UNION. We think this provides evidence to place CONSTRUCT[AUF] as an interesting query language for RDF that should be further investigated.

7. THE COMPLEXITY OF THE EVALUATION PROBLEM

So far, we have introduced a new operator and several syntactic fragments with good properties in terms of expressive power. At this point, it is natural to ask what is the complexity of the evaluation problem for these fragments, and whether this complexity is lower than for some well-known fragments of SPARQL. To answer this question, we study the combined complexity [39] of the evaluation problem. More precisely, we pinpoint the exact complexity of this problem for simple patterns and ns-patterns in Section 7.2, and for queries in CONSTRUCT[AUF] in Section 7.3.

7.1 A bit of background on computational complexity

We use complexity classes that might not be familiar to the reader, and hence we briefly recall their definition. In particular, we present the Boolean Hierarchy and the complexity class $\text{P}_{\parallel}^{\text{NP}}$.

The Boolean Hierarchy is an infinite family of complexity classes based on boolean combinations of languages in NP [41]. The most popular class in this hierarchy is DP, which consists of all languages that can be expressed as $L_1 \cap L_2$ with $L_1 \in$ NP and $L_2 \in$ coNP. The levels of the boolean hierarchy are denoted by $\{\text{BH}_i\}_{i \in \mathbb{N}}$, and are recursively defined as follows:

- BH_1 is the complexity class NP.
- BH_{2k} consists of all languages that can be expressed as $L_1 \cap L_2$, where $L_1 \in \text{BH}_{2k-1}$ and $L_2 \in$ coNP.
- BH_{2k+1} consists of all languages that can be expressed as $L_1 \cup L_2$, where $L_1 \in \text{BH}_{2k}$ and $L_2 \in$ NP.

Notice that DP = BH_2. The complexity class $\text{P}_{\parallel}^{\text{NP}}$ [19] contains all problems that can be solved in polynomial time by a Turing machine that can query a polynomial amount of times (in terms of the input's length) an NP oracle, with the restriction that all of these queries need to be issued in parallel. The parallel access to the NP oracle prevents the queries to depend on previous oracle answers. The class $\text{P}_{\parallel}^{\text{NP}}$ is equivalent to $\Delta_2^P[\log n]$, the complexity class of all problems that can be solved in polynomial time by a Turing machine that can make $O(\log n)$ queries to an NP oracle, not necessarily in parallel [11].

7.2 The evaluation problem for simple patterns and ns-patterns

Consider a fragment $\mathcal{F}$ of NS–SPARQL. Then the evaluation problem for $\mathcal{F}$ is defined as follows:

Problem	:	Eval($\mathcal{F}$)
Input	:	An RDF graph G, a graph pattern $P \in \mathcal{F}$ and a mapping μ
Question	:	Is $\mu \in [\![P]\!]_G$?

As usual, we only consider inputs of finite length and, therefore, we do not consider in this section unrestricted RDF graphs. Our complexity results are built upon several studies of the complexity of evaluating SPARQL graph patterns [30, 28, 34, 6, 21]. In particular, the key ideas rely on the fact that the evaluation problem is NP-complete for SPARQL[AUFS] [34] and is coNP-complete for well-designed graph patterns in SPARQL[AOF] [27].

We start by considering the evaluation problem for simple graph patterns.

Theorem 7.1. Eval(SP–SPARQL) *is* DP-*complete.*

It is interesting to notice that the complexity of evaluating simple patterns is already higher than that of evaluating well-designed graph patterns in SPARQL[AOF], which is coNP-complete. This is to be expected as the former fragment is more expressive than the latter (see Proposition 5.6).

We continue our study by considering the evaluation problem for ns-patterns. As an ns-pattern is of the form (P_1 UNION $\cdots$ UNION P_k) with each P_i being a simple pattern, an important parameter for the evaluation problem in this context is the maximum number of disjunct P_i in these patterns. Let USP–SPARQL$_k$ be the fragment of USP–SPARQL consisting of all ns-patterns having at most k disjuncts each. Then we have that:

THEOREM 7.2. *For every $k > 0$, it holds that* EVAL(USP–SPARQL$_k$) *is* BH_{2k}*-complete.*

Finally, we obtain the following combined complexity when considering ns-patterns with an unbounded number of disjuncts.

THEOREM 7.3. EVAL(USP–SPARQL) *is* $\mathrm{P}_{\|}^{\mathrm{NP}}$*-complete.*

It is important to mention that, although the evaluation problem for well-designed graph patterns in SPARQL[AOF] is coNP-complete, these patterns do not allow for projection. If projection is allowed only on the top-most level, then the evaluation problem for well-designed graph patterns already increases to Σ_2^p-complete [22], which is higher than the complexity of the evaluation problem for USP–SPARQL (unless the polynomial-time hierarchy [36] collapses to its second level as $\mathrm{P}_{\|}^{\mathrm{NP}} \subseteq \Delta_2^P \subseteq \Sigma_2^P$).

7.3 The evaluation problem for CONSTRUCT queries

Consider a class $\mathcal{G}$ of CONSTRUCT queries. Then the evaluation problem for $\mathcal{G}$ is defined as follows:

Problem	:	EVAL($\mathcal{G}$)
Input	:	An RDF graph G, a CONSTRUCT query $Q \in \mathcal{G}$ and a tripe t
Question	:	Is $t \in \mathrm{ans}(Q, G)$?

As mentioned before, the fragment CONSTRUCT[AUF] is one of the most important fragments defined in this paper, as it captures the class of CONSTRUCT queries that are monotone. It should be noticed that establishing the combined complexity of CONSTRUCT[AUF] is straightforward, as we rely on the fact that the evaluation problem for SPARQL[AUF] is NP-complete.

THEOREM 7.4. EVAL(CONSTRUCT[AUF]) *is* NP*-complete.*

This concludes our study of the complexity of the evaluation problem for the query languages introduced in this paper. As a final remark, it is important to mention that the results of this section provide more evidence in favor of CONSTRUCT[AUF] as an appropriate query language for RDF, as this language not only captures the notion of monotonicity for CONSTRUCT queries (over unrestricted RDF graphs), but also has an evaluation problem with a lower complexity than for well-designed graph patterns with projection on top (Σ_2^p-complete), and general CONSTRUCT queries (PSPACE-complete).

8. CONCLUDING REMARKS AND FUTURE WORK

We have presented a thorough study of the relationship between different fragments of SPARQL and the notion of weak monotonicity. We showed that one of the most adopted fragments of SPARQL, namely the class of unions of well-designed graph patterns, has lower expressive power than the fragment of weakly-monotone graph patterns. We further strengthen this result by proving that it also holds if disjunction is disallowed in both fragments. Given this negative result, we moved to a new setting in which RDF graphs can also be infinite. In this setting, we developed a framework for applying interpolation techniques for first-order logic to SPARQL, which resulted in a powerful theorem relating the fragment of weakly-monotone graph patterns with SPARQL[AUFS]. This theorem suggested the definition of the operator NS, which is a natural replacement for the operator OPTIONAL. Using the operator NS, we defined the weakly-monotone fragments of simple patterns and ns-patterns, and proved that they have higher expressive power than the fragments defined in terms of well designedness. Then we focused on the fragment of CONSTRUCT queries. We applied the results obtained from the use of interpolation techniques, from which we proved that the fragment of CONSTRUCT queries restricted to CONSTRUCT, AND, FILTER and UNION precisely characterizes the notion of monotonicity. Finally, we provided a thorough study of the combined complexity of the evaluation problem for the query languages introduced in the paper.

Our results open new research possibilities, starting by the search for useful extensions of the identified query languages. For example, allowing for projection on top of simple and ns-patterns preserves weak monotonicity, and hence this extension could lead to the definition of new weakly-monotone fragments with higher expressivity.

Finally, the focus of this paper has been mostly theoretical. Therefore, the development of more practical studies of the proposed query languages is a promising direction for future research. For instance, it is important to understand what are the practical consequences of replacing the operator OPTIONAL by the operator NS, and whether the aforementioned fragment of CONSTRUCT queries covers the needs of real-world applications. Moreover, these new lines of research are open to the development of implementations and optimizations, potentially leading to real-world applications of the techniques developed in this paper.

Acknowledgements

The authors would like to thank the anonymous referees for many helpful comments. M. Arenas was funded by the Millennium Nucleus Center for Semantic Web Research under Grant NC120004, and M. Ugarte was partially funded by the scholarship CONICYT-PCHA - 21120368, by the Millennium Nucleus Center for Semantic Web Research under Grant NC120004, and by the SPICES research project funded by Innoviris, the Brussels Institute for Research and Innovation under the Bridge strategic platform program.

9. REFERENCES

[1] S. Ahmetaj, W. Fischl, R. Pichler, M. Simkus, and S. Skritek. Towards reconciling SPARQL and certain answers. In *Proceedings of the 24th International Conference on World Wide Web, WWW 2015*, pages 23–33, 2015.

[2] M. Ajtai and Y. Gurevich. Monotone versus positive. *J. ACM*, 34(4):1004–1015, Oct. 1987.

[3] R. Angles and C. Gutierrez. The expressive power of SPARQL. In *ISWC*, pages 114–129, 2008.

[4] R. Angles and C. Gutierrez. *The expressive power of SPARQL*. Springer, 2008.

[5] M. Arenas, S. Conca, and J. Pérez. Counting beyond a yottabyte, or how SPARQL 1.1 property paths will prevent adoption of the standard. In *Proceedings of the 21st international conference on World Wide Web*, pages 629–638. ACM, 2012.

[6] M. Arenas and J. Pérez. Querying semantic web data with sparql. In *Proceedings of the thirtieth ACM SIGMOD-SIGACT-SIGART symposium on Principles of database systems*, pages 305–316. ACM, 2011.

[7] P. Barceló, R. Pichler, and S. Skritek. Efficient evaluation and approximation of well-designed pattern trees. In *Proceedings of the 34th ACM Symposium on Principles of Database Systems, PODS 2015*, pages 131–144, 2015.

[8] M. Benedikt, B. ten Cate, and E. Tsamoura. Generating low-cost plans from proofs. In *Proceedings of the 33rd ACM SIGMOD-SIGACT-SIGART Symposium on Principles of Database Systems, PODS'14*, pages 200–211, 2014.

[9] T. Berners-Lee, J. Hendler, O. Lassila, et al. The semantic web. *Scientific american*, 284(5):28–37, 2001.

[10] C. Buil-Aranda, M. Arenas, Ó. Corcho, and A. Polleres. Federating queries in SPARQL 1.1: Syntax, semantics and evaluation. *J. Web Sem.*, 18(1):1–17, 2013.

[11] S. R. Buss and L. Hay. On truth-table reducibility to sat. *Information and Computation*, 91(1):86 – 102, 1991.

[12] M. W. Chekol, J. Euzenat, P. Genevès, and N. Layaïda. SPARQL query containment under $\mathcal{SHI}$ axioms. In *AAAI*, 2012.

[13] M. W. Chekol, J. Euzenat, P. Genevès, and N. Layaïda. SPARQL query containment under RDFS entailment regime. In *IJCAR*, pages 134–148, 2012.

[14] M. Durst and M. Suignard. Rfc 3987, internationalized resource identifiers (iris), 2005.

[15] T. Furche, B. Linse, F. Bry, D. Plexousakis, and G. Gottlob. RDF querying: Language constructs and evaluation methods compared. In *Reasoning Web*, pages 1–52. Springer, 2006.

[16] C. A. Galindo-Legaria. Outerjoins as disjunctions. *SIGMOD Rec.*, 23(2):348–358, May 1994.

[17] F. Geerts, G. Karvounarakis, V. Christophides, and I. Fundulaki. Algebraic structures for capturing the provenance of SPARQL queries. In *ICDT*, 2013.

[18] H. Halpin and J. Cheney. Dynamic provenance for SPARQL updates. In *ISWC*, 2014.

[19] L. A. Hemachandra. The strong exponential hierarchy collapses. *Journal of Computer and System Sciences*, 39(3):299 – 322, 1989.

[20] E. V. Kostylev, J. L. Reutter, and M. Ugarte. CONSTRUCT queries in SPARQL. In *18th International Conference on Database Theory, ICDT 2015, March 23-27, 2015, Brussels, Belgium*, pages 212–229, 2015.

[21] A. Letelier, J. Pérez, R. Pichler, and S. Skritek. Static analysis and optimization of semantic web queries. In *Proceedings of the 31st Symposium on Principles of Database Systems*, PODS '12, pages 89–100. ACM, 2012.

[22] A. Letelier, J. Pérez, R. Pichler, and S. Skritek. Static analysis and optimization of semantic web queries. *ACM TODS*, 38(4):25, 2013.

[23] K. Losemann and W. Martens. The complexity of evaluating path expressions in SPARQL. In *Proceedings of the 31st symposium on Principles of Database Systems*, pages 101–112. ACM, 2012.

[24] R. C. Lyndon. An interpolation theorem in the predicate calculus. *Pacific J. of Mathematics*, 9(1):129–142, 1959.

[25] F. Manola and E. Miller. RDF Primer. W3C Recommendation, 10 February 2004. Available at http://www.w3.org/TR/2004/REC-rdf-primer-20040210/.

[26] M. Otto. An interpolation theorem. *Bulletin of Symbolic Logic*, 6(4):447–462, 2000.

[27] J. Pérez, M. Arenas, and C. Gutierrez. Semantics and complexity of sparql. In *ISWC*, pages 30–43, 2006.

[28] J. Pérez, M. Arenas, and C. Gutierrez. Semantics and complexity of SPARQL. *ACM TODS*, 34(3), 2009.

[29] F. Picalausa and S. Vansummeren. What are real SPARQL queries like? In *SWIM*, 2011.

[30] R. Pichler and S. Skritek. Containment and equivalence of well-designed SPARQL. In *Proceedings of the 33rd ACM SIGMOD-SIGACT-SIGART symposium on Principles of database systems*, pages 39–50. ACM, 2014.

[31] A. Polleres and J. P. Wallner. On the relation between SPARQL1.1 and answer set programming. *Journal of Applied Non-Classical Logics*, 23(1-2):159–212, 2013.

[32] E. Prud'hommeaux and A. Seaborne. SPARQL query language for RDF. W3C Recommendation, 2008. Available at http://www.w3.org/TR/rdf-sparql-query/.

[33] V. G. Ramanathan. Light at the end of the tunnel. 2013.

[34] M. Schmidt, M. Meier, and G. Lausen. Foundations of sparql query optimization. In *Proceedings of the 13th International Conference on Database Theory*, ICDT '10, pages 4–33. ACM, 2010.

[35] J. Sequeda, M. Arenas, and D. P. Miranker. On directly mapping relational databases to RDF and OWL. In *Proceedings of the 21st World Wide Web Conference 2012, WWW 2012*, pages 649–658, 2012.

[36] L. J. Stockmeyer. The polynomial-time hierarchy. *Theor. Comput. Sci.*, 3(1):1–22, 1976.

[37] D. Toman and G. E. Weddell. *Fundamentals of Physical Design and Query Compilation*. Synthesis Lectures on Data Management. Morgan & Claypool Publishers, 2011.

[38] B. Trakhtenbrot. The impossibility of an algorithm for the decidability problem on finite classes. *Proceedings of the USSR Academy of Sciences (in Russian)*, 70(4):569–572, 1950.

[39] M. Y. Vardi. The complexity of relational query languages. In *Proceedings of the fourteenth annual ACM symposium on Theory of computing*, pages 137–146. ACM, 1982.

[40] W3C SPARQL Working Group. SPARQL 1.1 Query language. W3C Recommendation, 21 March 2013. Available at http://www.w3.org/TR/sparql11-query/.

[41] G. Wechsung. On the boolean closure of NP. In *Fundamentals of Computation Theory*, pages 485–493. Springer, 1985.

Schema Validation via Streaming Circuits*

Filip Murlak
University of Warsaw
fmurlak@mimuw.edu.pl

Charles Paperman
University of Warsaw
paperman@mimuw.edu.pl

Michał Pilipczuk
University of Warsaw
michal.pilipczuk@mimuw.edu.pl

ABSTRACT

XML schema validation can be performed in constant memory in the streaming model if and only if the schema admits only trees of bounded depth—an acceptable assumption from the practical view-point. In this paper we refine this analysis by taking into account that data can be streamed block-by-block, rather then letter-by-letter, which provides opportunities to speed up the computation by parallelizing the processing of each block. For this purpose we introduce the model of streaming circuits, which process words of arbitrary length in blocks of fixed size, passing constant amount of information between blocks. This model allows us to transfer fundamental results about the circuit complexity of regular languages to the setting of streaming schema validation, which leads to effective constructions of streaming circuits of depth logarithmic in the block size, or even constant under certain assumptions on the input schema. For nested-relational DTDs, a practically motivated class of bounded-depth XML schemas, we provide an efficient construction yielding constant-depth streaming circuits with particularly good parameters.

Categories and Subject Descriptors

H.2.1 [**Database Management**]: Logical Design; F.4.3 [**Mathematical Logic and Formal Languages**]: Formal Languages

Keywords

semi-structured data; XML; streaming; schema validation; Boolean circuits; nested-relational DTDs

*These results were obtained when Charles Paperman and Michał Pilipczuk held post-doc positions at the Warsaw Centre of Mathematics and Computer Science. Michał Pilipczuk was supported by the Foundation for Polish Science (FNP) via the START stipend program. Filip Murlak was supported by Poland's National Science Centre grant no. 2013/11/D/ST6/03075.

PODS'16, June 26-July 01, 2016, San Francisco, CA, USA
 ISBN 978-1-4503-4191-2/16/06...$15.00
DOI: http://dx.doi.org/10.1145/2902251.2902299

1. INTRODUCTION

Over tree-structured data, like XML documents or JSON files, schemas impose restrictions on the structure of trees modeling the data. Popular schema formalisms, like DTDs and especially XML Schema, are able to express very complex properties, bringing their expressive power close to tree automata, which are often used as theoretical abstractions of schemas. With such expressive power, the task of schema validation—that is, verifying that a given data instance conforms to the schema—is not entirely trivial even if we have direct access to the whole data instance. When the data are streamed, schema validation becomes a major challenge.

In their seminal paper [31], Segoufin and Vianu consider streaming validation in constant memory. An algorithm over streamed data that works in constant memory can be seen as a finite automaton. Whether such an algorithm exists for a given schema depends on whether the set of word representations of the instances of the schema is a regular language. Segoufin and Vianu show that the word representation of a regular tree language (covering all popular schema formalisms) is regular if and only if there exists a uniform bound on the depth of the trees in the language. In this paper we refine this result by looking more closely at the way data are streamed. Due to the result of Segoufin and Vianu, we focus mostly on tree languages of bounded depth.

Our starting point is the observation that data need not be fed to the algorithm letter-by-letter. For instance, if the data stream serves as an abstraction of sequential access to a mass storage device, the algorithm is fed entire blocks of data that are fetched to a moderately-sized cache. This requires evaluating the finite automaton over a word read in block-sized portions. We could process each block sequentially in time linear in its size, but we would like to do better, assuming certain ability to parallelize computation over each block. As a model of parallelism we choose Boolean circuits. The most important reason is that their relation with regular languages is well understood and documented [3, 19, 20, 32], but Boolean circuits have several other advantages. On one hand, they are very close to hardware implementation: from a Boolean circuit of small depth one can directly obtain a hardware description that could be compiled into, say, an FPGA. On the other hand, Boolean circuits are also a commonly accepted theoretical model for higher-level parallelism, providing abstraction for various concrete practical models. For example, on a multi-core machine different cores could be assigned to evaluating different parts of the circuit. We remark that combining the challenges of streaming data access and parallelization has been considered from the practical perspective [5, 6, 12, 17], in particular in the context of the standard MapReduce approach (see e.g. [24]); however, to the best of our knowledge, hardly any theoretical models have been proposed so far.

In order to reconcile the random-access parallelism of Boolean circuits with the streaming setting, we introduce a model of computation called streaming circuits. Intuitively, a streaming circuit takes a block of the input word together with additional feedback information of constant size (the state of the underlying finite automaton) and outputs updated feedback. This model allows us to talk about the complexity of streaming algorithms in a way that does not abstract away the size of the block, and to transfer the huge body of results on the circuit complexity of regular languages to the streaming setting. It also avoids the inherent flaw of the classical Boolean circuit setting: the nonuniformity. While having a separate circuit for each size of the input data is entirely impractical, in our setting this is not an issue any more, as the circuit is nonuniform in the block size, which can be chosen and fixed in advance. With the right choice of the block size, the time needed to process a block can (potentially) be made close to the time needed to fetch it, thus avoiding bottlenecks.

Any finite automaton can be transformed into a streaming circuit of chosen block size. The challenge is to get the circuit as simple as possible. In the context of schema validation we are interested in how the complexity of tree language is reflected in the streaming circuits recognizing their word encodings. As we shall see, one can always build an NC^1-streaming circuit for any bounded-depth regular tree language. That is, in the block-by-block access model, one can efficiently do streaming validation in parallel—by a circuit that has polynomial size, constant fan-in, and logarithmic depth. Can we do better than that? For any class $\mathcal{C}$ of circuits one can ask about $\mathcal{C}$ streaming circuits for regular tree languages. A full positive answer to this question should include:

- an algorithm to decide if a given tree language has a $\mathcal{C}$ streaming circuit;
- an algorithm to construct a recognizing $\mathcal{C}$ streaming circuit, if it exists; and
- a syntactic fragment (a restricted schema language) that corresponds to languages that can be recognized with a $\mathcal{C}$ streaming circuit.

From the practical point of view, the crucial part of the answer is a restricted schema language guaranteeing feasibility and an efficient algorithm to build the circuit from the schema definition in this restricted language. Ideally, the schema language should cover all feasible schemas, but this should not be achieved at the expense of its simplicity and usability.

We consider two restricted classes of circuits: AC^0 and $WLAC^0$. Recall that AC^0 comprises circuit families with polynomial size and constant depth bounds, and an AC^0 circuit family is in $WLAC^0$ (for *wire-linear* AC^0) if the number of wires is bounded linearly. Unlike for NC^1, not all bounded-depth regular tree languages admit AC^0 streaming circuits, but we can decide effectively if a given bounded-depth regular language admits one. We also show that if one additionally assumes that the tree language is definable in first order logic, then the answer is always affirmative. For a practically relevant class of languages defined by nested-relational DTDs [1, 2], we provide an efficient construction of AC^0 streaming circuits with particularly good properties. For $WLAC^0$ we observe that one cannot even check the correctness of the usual XML encodings of bounded-depth trees. We propose a new encoding, enriched with the information about ancestors of nodes. Under the new encoding we can validate nested-relational schemas with $WLAC^0$ streaming circuits. We also show that this encoding can be computed from the usual encoding by an AC^0 streaming circuit that does not depend on the schema, only on the depth and the alphabet.

2. STREAMING CIRCUITS

In this article we use several well-known classes of circuits. We recall the basics very briefly and refer to the book by Straubing [32] for a more detailed presentation.

Basics of circuit complexity. We work with Boolean circuits with AND, OR, and NOT gates, taking as input words over alphabet $\Sigma = \{a_1, a_2, \ldots, a_k\}$. The letters of the input word are encoded *in unary*; that is, each input gate is modeled with k binary gates, and letter a_i is encoded as the binary sequence $0^{i-1}10^{k-i}$. A family

$$(C_n)_{n\in\mathbb{N}}$$

of circuits recognizes a language $L \subseteq \Sigma^*$ if C_n has n input gates and a single binary output gate, and returns 1 if and only if the input word is in L. We shall refer to this model of recognition as the random-access model. Whenever we consider the size of the circuit, we mean the number of gates.

Since we consider mainly regular languages (of words and of trees), we restrict ourselves to languages recognizable with NC^1 circuit families: Boolean circuit families of polynomial size, logarithmic depth and bounded fan-in. Two other classes of interest are AC^0 circuit families, which have polynomial size, constant depth and unbounded fan-in, and $WLAC^0$ circuit families, which are AC^0 circuit families with a linear number of wires (hence, also gates). The interaction of these classes with the class of regular languages is well understood, and we will use this knowledge to design adequate devices in the context of streaming schema validation.

We shall say that a language is in class $\mathcal{C}$ if it is recognized by a $\mathcal{C}$ circuit family. Some important examples separating the three classes described above:

- the parity language $(c + ac^*a)^*$ is in NC^1 (with linear-size circuits) but not in AC^0 [14];
- $(c + ac^*b)^*$ is in AC^0 (with quadratic-size circuits) but not in $WLAC^0$ [19].

Streaming circuits. In the streaming circuit setting, a single circuit is used to recognize words of all lengths, by processing them sequentially in blocks of fixed size with the help of a feedback mechanism.

A *streaming circuit* over alphabet Σ with block size n and feedback size m is a circuit C with n input gates, m feedback gates and m output gates, together with an acceptor circuit A with m input gates and 1 output gate. The computation of such a circuit on an input word w is carried out in stages. In each stage the circuit C is given the output from the previous stage (initially, the bit sequence 10^{m-1}) and the next size n block of the input word (in unary encoding, as explained above). The output of the last stage is fed to the acceptor circuit A and the word w is *accepted* if and only if the acceptor circuit A returns 1. If the last block of the input word is shorter than n symbols, a designated padding symbol \$ (encoded as a sequence of zeros) is used to fill it up. More formally, let $u_0 = 10^{m-1}$ and for $i < \lceil \frac{|w|}{n} \rceil$ let

$$u_{i+1} = C(u_i, w_{ni+1} w_{ni+2} \dots w_{ni+n})$$

where $w_j = \$$ for $j > |w|$; the word w is accepted if

$$A(u_{\lceil \frac{|w|}{n} \rceil}) = 1\,.$$

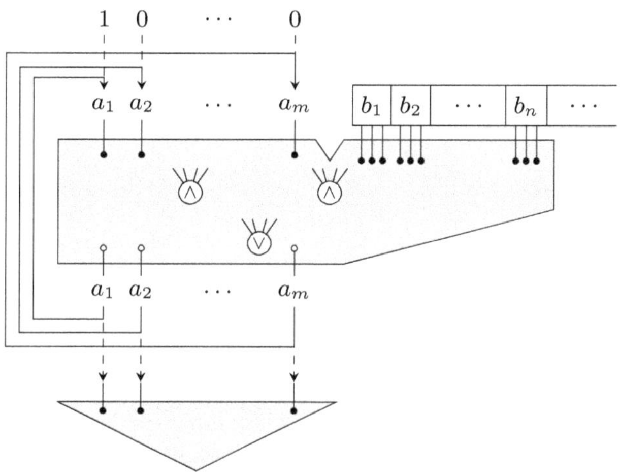

Such a streaming circuit can be interpreted as a deterministic automaton over the alphabet $\Gamma = \Sigma^n$: the state space is $\{0,1\}^m$ with the initial state 10^{m-1}, and the transition function and the set of accepting states are given by circuits C and A. Consequently, languages recognized by streaming circuits are regular.

In fact, streaming circuits give precise description of the implementation of finite automata over words read by fixed-size blocks. Indeed, if one takes an automaton and makes it read blocks of n letters instead of one letter, one obtains an automaton with the same state space over the alphabet Σ^n, but with the set of transitions growing exponentially with n (if $|\Sigma| \geq 2$). Circuits allow us to represent (and carry out) transitions more efficiently.

We can therefore talk about streaming-circuit complexity of regular languages: a regular language L has *streaming-circuit complexity* $\mathcal{C}$ if for some m there exists a $\mathcal{C}$ circuit family $(C_n)_{n\in\mathbb{N}}$ with m feedback gates and m output gates and an acceptor circuit A with m input gates, such that for each n, the streaming circuit (C_n, A) recognizes L. We say that $(C_n)_{n\in\mathbb{N}}$ is a $\mathcal{C}$ *streaming circuit family* for L (with feedback m and acceptor A). In general, $(C_n)_{n\in\mathbb{N}}$ need not have a finite description, but all families constructed in this paper will have one.

Streaming vs random access. Over regular languages of words, random-access recognizability and streaming recognizability coincide for reasonable classes of circuits. The following theorem provides efficient translation from circuits to streaming circuits, and *vice versa*. A class $\mathcal{C}$ of circuits families is *closed under shifts* if for each circuit family $(C_n)_{n\in\mathbb{N}}$ from $\mathcal{C}$, each family obtained from $(C_{n+1})_{n\in\mathbb{N}}$ by hard-wiring a chosen input gate is in $\mathcal{C}$. By *parallel composition* we mean running two circuits on the same input and concatenating the outputs, and by *sequential composition* we mean wiring the output gates of one circuit to the input gates of another circuit.

THEOREM 1. *Let $\mathcal{C}$ be a class of circuit families closed under shifts, parallel compositions, and sequential compositions with constant-size circuits. Then a regular language $L \subseteq \Sigma^*$ has streaming-circuit complexity $\mathcal{C}$ if and only if it is in $\mathcal{C}$.*

More precisely, if the recognizing family of circuits has depth and size bounded by non-decreasing functions $d(n)$ and $s(n)$, the resulting streaming circuit for block size n has feedback k, depth $d(n+k+k^2)+\mathcal{O}(1)$, and size $k^3 \cdot s(n+k+k^2)+\mathcal{O}(k^3)$, where k is the number of states of the minimal deterministic automaton for L.

PROOF. The left-to-right implication is almost immediate. Let $(C_n)_{n\in\mathbb{N}}$ be a $\mathcal{C}$ streaming circuit family for L with feedback m and acceptor A. The family of circuits recognizing L is

$$\big(A(C_n(10^{m-1},\cdot))\big)_{n\in\mathbb{N}}\,;$$

that is, we hardwire the initial values in the feedback gates of C_n, and feed the output of C_n to A. Since circuit A is fixed, by the closure properties of $\mathcal{C}$, the resulting circuit family is indeed in $\mathcal{C}$, and so is L.

The right to left implication is more complicated. Let $\mathcal{A}$ be the minimal deterministic automaton for L and $(C_n)_{n\in\mathbb{N}}$ a $\mathcal{C}$ family of circuits recognizing L. Let p,q be states of $\mathcal{A}$. We shall construct a $\mathcal{C}$ family of circuits recognizing the language

$$L_{p,q} = \{w \in \Sigma^* \mid \delta_w(p) = q\}\,,$$

where $\delta_w(p)$ is the state to which the automaton moves from state p after reading word w. Let u be the shortest word that reaches p from the initial state; by pumping, $|u| \leq k$, where k is the number of states of $\mathcal{A}$. By minimality, for all distinct states q,q' there is a word v of size at most k^2 such that $\delta_v(q) \in F$ if and only if $\delta_v(q') \notin F$. Consequently, $L_{p,q}$ is a Boolean combination of $k-1$ *residual* languages of the form

$$u^{-1} L v^{-1} = \{w \mid uwv \in L\}\,,$$

where $|u| \leq k$ and $|v| \leq k^2$. Each of these languages can be recognized with a $\mathcal{C}$ family of circuits $(C'_n)_{n\in\mathbb{N}}$ where C'_n is obtained from $C_{n+|u|+|v|}$ by hardwiring the first $|u|$ input gates to u and the last $|v|$ input gates to v. An appropriate Boolean combination of these circuits gives circuits for $L_{p,q}$. Assuming that i-th state is coded as $0^{i-1}10^{k-i}$ on the feedback gates and the first state is initial, it is easy to obtain a $\mathcal{C}$ family of streaming circuits for L from the circuits for languages $L_{p,q}$. We simply add on top of these circuits an additional circuit of depth $\mathcal{O}(1)$ and size $\mathcal{O}(k^2)$ that computes the state after processing the current block from the previous state passed in the feedback. To verify the required size bound, observe that in total we construct k^2 circuits for languages $L_{p,q}$. Every such circuit consists of $k-1$ circuits for residual languages, each of size at most $s(n+k+k^2)$. Since k is considered a constant, by the closure properties of $\mathcal{C}$ we have that the obtained circuit family belongs to $\mathcal{C}$. □

One could easily make the feedback logarithmic in k by encoding the state in binary. However, this would not improve the parameters of the circuit, as they depend on the number of states, not the size of their representation.

The fact that the circuit has access, thanks to its non-uniformity, to additional numerical information, sometimes allows to simplify drastically the ongoing computation. For instance, the language $(a_1 a_2 \cdots a_n)^*$ requires an automaton with $n+1$ states, but assuming block size n it can be recognized by a streaming circuit with feedback 1, which corresponds to 2 states:

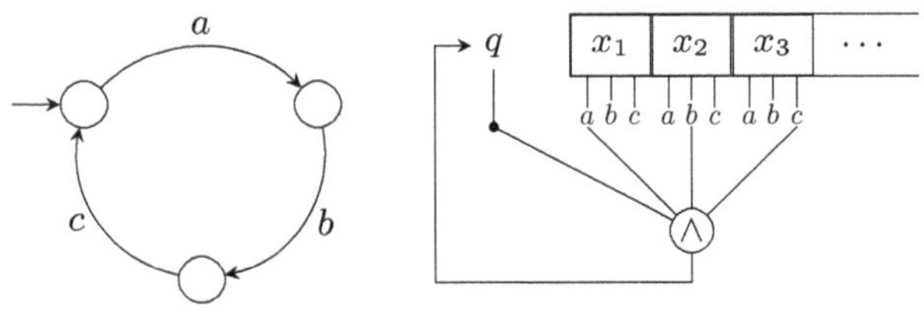

This kind of behavior is difficult to analyze, but always beneficial in the construction of streaming circuits.

3. VALIDATION: A GENERAL BOUND

Following Segoufin and Vianu [31], we work with ordered unranked trees, node-labelled with letters from a finite alphabet Σ. We denote by Trees(Σ) the set of all such trees.

For technical convenience, we model schemas as "previous sibling, last child" tree automata. A *nondeterministic tree automaton*

$$\mathcal{A} = (\Sigma, Q, q_0, F, \delta)$$

consists of a finite input alphabet Σ, a finite set of states Q with an initial state q_0, a set of accepting states $F \subseteq Q$, and a transition relation

$$\delta \subseteq Q \times Q \times \Sigma \times Q\,.$$

Being in a node v of the input tree $t \in \text{Trees}(\Sigma)$, the automaton has processed t_v, the subtree of t rooted at v. The state q for node v depends on the label σ of v and the states q_1, q_2 from the previous sibling and the last child of v, respectively, in the way specified by the transition relation:

$$(q_1, q_2, \sigma, q) \in \delta$$

(in leftmost siblings and leaves we use the initial state q_0 instead of q_1 and q_2, respectively). The tree t is *accepted* by $\mathcal{A}$ if states can be chosen for nodes in such a way that the root gets a state from F. We write $L(\mathcal{A})$ for the set of accepted trees. If $L = L(\mathcal{A})$, we say that L is *regular*, and that it is recognized by $\mathcal{A}$.

A schema language that is simpler, but often sufficient in practice, is offered by *document type definitions*, or DTDs for short. A DTD

$$\mathcal{D} = (\Sigma, r, P)$$

consists of a finite alphabet Σ with a distinguished root label $r \in \Sigma$, and a function P that assigns to each label $a \in \Sigma$ a regular expression $P(a)$ over Σ, called the production for a, and written as

$$a \to P(a)\,.$$

A tree $t \in \text{Trees}(\Sigma)$ conforms to $\mathcal{D}$ if its root is labelled with r and for each label $a \in \Sigma$ and each node v in t with label a, the sequence of labels of v's children forms a word generated by the regular expression $P(a)$.

A practically relevant class of *nested-relational* DTDs, covering a large proportion of real life schemas [4], is obtained by assuming non-recursiveness (that is, no a-labelled node has an a-labelled descendant) and allowing only productions of the form

$$a \to \widehat{a}_1 \widehat{a}_2 \ldots \widehat{a}_\ell\,,$$

where $a_1, a_2, \ldots a_\ell$ are distinct elements of Σ, and $\widehat{a}_i$ is equal to a_i, $a_i? = (\varepsilon + a_i)$, a_i^*, or $a_i^+ = a_i a_i^*$.

In the context of streaming processing we need a string representation of trees. Under the *XML encoding* trees are represented as words over $\Sigma \cup \overline{\Sigma}$, the elements of Σ and $\overline{\Sigma}$ being, respectively, the *opening* and *closing tags*,

$$\text{flat}\Big(\overset{a}{t_1 \;\cdots\; t_k} \Big) = a \cdot \text{flat}(t_1) \cdots \text{flat}(t_k) \cdot \overline{a}\,.$$

We call flat(t) the *flattening of* t, and

$$\text{flat}(L) = \big\{ \text{flat}(t) \;\big|\; t \in L \big\}$$

the *flattening of* L. Another natural possibility is the *term encoding*, which is similar to the XML encoding except that we only have one closing tag symbol $\#$,

$$\text{flat}_{\#}\Big(\overset{a}{t_1 \;\cdots\; t_k} \Big) = a \cdot \text{flat}_{\#}(t_1) \cdots \text{flat}_{\#}(t_k) \cdot \#\,.$$

Intuitively, the XML encoding corresponds to recognition by a *visibly push-down automaton* [22] (or input driven automaton [13]). The term encoding requires only one stack symbol, which corresponds to visibly counter automata [8]. In the sequel we work with the XML encoding for concreteness, but for most of our results, the choice of the encoding does not matter.

As observed by Segoufin and Vianu [31], the flattening of a regular tree language is a regular word language if and only if the tree language has bounded depth (there exists a uniform bound on the depth of all trees in L).

PROPOSITION 1 (SEGOUFIN, VIANU [31]). *For each regular tree language L the following conditions are equivalent:*

- *L has bounded depth;*
- flat(L) *is a regular word language.*

Thus, to have any chance for streaming-circuit validation, we restrict our attention to bounded-depth trees. For practical purposes this is an acceptable assumption, as real-life schemas tend to be bounded-depth [4].

Translation from bounded-depth tree automata to *deterministic* word automata over encodings involves only single-exponential blow-up.

PROPOSITION 2. *Let $\mathcal{A}$ be a tree automaton with k states recognizing a bounded-depth language $L \subseteq$ Trees(Σ). One can construct a deterministic automaton with $\mathcal{O}(|\Sigma|^k \cdot 2^{k^2})$ states recognizing* flat(L).

PROOF. As $L(\mathcal{A})$ has bounded depth, each accepting run of $\mathcal{A}$ uses each state at most once on each branch of the input tree. Indeed, if this was not the case, one could construct an arbitrarily deep tree accepted by $\mathcal{A}$ by repeating the part of the tree corresponding to the segment of the branch between two occurrences of the same state. Consequently, $L(\mathcal{A})$ has depth at most k.

Let $\mathcal{B} = (\Sigma, Q, q_0, \delta, F)$ be a deterministic automaton recognizing L obtained from $\mathcal{A}$ by the standard power-set construction; we have $|Q| = 2^k$. The automaton for $\text{flat}(L)$ simulates stack of depth at most k in its states. Its state-space is

$$(\Sigma \times Q)^{\leq k} \cup \{\bot, \top\},$$

where the empty sequence ε is the initial state and $\top$ is the only final state. The transitions are given as follows: upon reading symbol $\sigma \in \Sigma$ in state $\alpha \notin \{\bot, \top\}$,

- if $|\alpha| < k$, move to $\alpha\,(\sigma, q_0)$,
- if $|\alpha| = k$, move to $\bot$;

upon reading symbol $\overline{\sigma} \in \overline{\Sigma}$ in state $\alpha \notin \{\bot, \top\}$,

- if $\alpha = \varepsilon$, move to $\bot$,
- if $\alpha = (\sigma, q_1)$ and $\delta(q_0, q_1, \sigma) \in F$, move to $\top$,
- if $\alpha = (\sigma, q_1)$ and $\delta(q_0, q_1, \sigma) \notin F$, move to $\bot$,
- if $\alpha = \beta\,(\sigma', q')(\sigma, q)$, move to $\beta\,(\sigma', \delta(q', q, \sigma))$,
- if $\alpha = \beta\,(\tau, q)$ with $\tau \neq \sigma$, move to $\bot$;

upon reading any symbol in state $\bot$ or $\top$, move to $\bot$. $\square$

We finish this section with a general NC^1-upper bound for streaming circuit complexity of bounded-depth regular tree languages. Assuming the usual interpretation of NC^1 as the class of problems that can be solved efficiently in parallel, this shows that streaming validation parallelizes. The bound combines Theorem 1, Proposition 2 and a folklore fact that all regular languages are in NC^1 (i.e., random-access validation parallelizes).

PROPOSITION 3. *Each regular language L can be recognized by an NC^1 streaming circuit family. More precisely, for a given block size n one can construct a recognizing circuit with feedback k, depth $\mathcal{O}(\log n)$, and size $\mathcal{O}(k^3 n)$, where k is the number of states of the minimal deterministic automaton for L.*

PROOF. The first part of the claim follows by Theorem 1 from the fact that all regular languages are in NC^1. To achieve the claimed bounds, we adapt the standard construction to obtain directly a streaming circuit.

Let $\mathcal{A} = (\Sigma, Q, q_0, \delta, F)$ be the minimal automaton for L, and let $|Q| = k$. Any function $f\colon Q \to Q$ can be represented as a $k \times k$ binary matrix, which in turn can be seen as a k^2-bit word. From a single input letter σ one can compute function δ_σ, represented as a k^2-bit word, using a circuit that has depth 1 and size $\mathcal{O}(k^2)$; note that this circuit hardwires the transition function of $\mathcal{A}$. Given two $k \times k$ matrices (as k^2-bit words), one can compute their product (over the Boolean algebra) with a circuit of depth 2 and size $\mathcal{O}(k^3)$. Finally, for an input word w of length $n = 2^k$ one can compute the function δ_w by first computing functions δ_{w_i}, and then composing them in pairs to obtain functions for pairs of consecutive letters, quadruples, octuples, etc. The resulting circuit C_n has depth $\mathcal{O}(\log n)$ and size $\mathcal{O}(k^3 n)$. If $|w|$ is not a power of two, take $C_{2^{\lceil \log n \rceil}}$ and hardwire identity function in place of the functions for last $2^{\lceil \log n \rceil} - |w|$ input letters; this preserves the bounds. From the family $(C_n)_{n \in \mathbb{N}}$ one easily constructs a streaming circuit family for L: one simply computes the value of the function computed by C_n on the state represented (in unary) by the values in the feedback gates. This can be done easily with a circuit of depth 2 and size $\mathcal{O}(k^2)$. $\square$

Propositions 2 and 3 immediately yield the following.

THEOREM 2. *For each regular bounded-depth language $L \subseteq \text{Trees}(\Sigma)$, $\text{flat}(L)$ can be recognized by an NC^1 streaming circuit family. More precisely, for block size n, one can construct a recognizing streaming circuit with feedback $\mathcal{O}(|\Sigma|^k \cdot 2^{k^2})$, depth $\mathcal{O}(\log n)$, and size $\mathcal{O}(|\Sigma|^{3k} \cdot 2^{3k^2} \cdot n)$, where k is the number of states of the given nondeterministic automaton recognizing L.* $\square$

As remarked in [31], if the input tree language is given as a DTD with productions defined by *unambiguous* regular expressions (as required by the DTD specification), one can construct a finite automaton recognizing the flattening, whose number of states is bounded by a polynomial of degree at most $|\Sigma|$. This immediately improves the bounds in the theorem above.

As we have seen in Theorem 1, for regular word languages streaming and random-access recognition with circuits is the same for any reasonable class of circuits. For flattenings of regular tree languages, this is not the case. In the streaming model, the flattening must be regular to be recognized by any circuit family; in the random-access model, the flattening of each regular tree language can be recognized by an NC^1 circuit family [13].

4. VALIDATION IN CONSTANT DEPTH

In the last section we saw a generic construction translating a description of a bounded-depth tree language (an automaton or a DTD) into a streaming circuit with relatively good parameters: logarithmic depth, constant fan-in, and polynomial size. However, this construction is largely suboptimal as shown by the following example.

EXAMPLE 1. *Let L be given by the following DTD*

$$r \to a^* \,;$$

that is, L consists of trees of the form

Then, $\text{flat}(L) = r(a\overline{a})^*\overline{r}$ can be easily recognized by an AC^0 streaming circuit family (of linear size).

On the other hand, any regular language not in AC^0 gives a depth-2 regular tree language whose flattening is not recognizable by an AC^0 streaming circuit family.

EXAMPLE 2. *From the parity lower bound [14] we immediately get that for the tree language L given by*

$$r \to (ab^*a + b)^* \,,$$

$\text{flat}(L)$ cannot be recognized by an AC^0 family of streaming circuits.

Yet again, a simple modification can turn a hard tree language into an easy one, by adding more structure.

Example 3. *For the language L given by the DTD*

$$r \to (c+b)^*\,, \quad c \to ab^*a\,,$$

the flattening $\mathrm{flat}(L)$, *given by*

$$r\big(c(a\bar{a}(b\bar{b})^*a\bar{a})\bar{c} + b\bar{b}\big)^*\bar{r}\,,$$

is recognized by an AC^0 *streaming circuit family.* (♣) [1]

As regular languages in AC^0 have an exact logical characterization, and membership in AC^0 is decidable, one could decide whether the flattening of a given regular bounded-depth tree language can be recognized by an AC^0 family of circuits. To explain it in more detail, we need to recall some classical results in descriptive complexity. Then, we shall look at practical fragments of the DTD formalism that guarantee the existence of AC^0 streaming circuit families.

First order logic and constant-depth circuits. We consider first order logic over words, encoded as relational structures over universe $\{0,\dots,n-1\}$ where n is the length of the word. Formulas are generated by the first order logic grammar with two kinds of atomic predicates: the *letter predicates* of the form $\mathbf{a}(x)$ that are true if and only if the position x in the word is labelled by a, and *numerical predicates* which are predicates speaking about the word stripped of labels. For conciseness, we also allow numerical constants min and max for the first and last positions in the word.

Example 4. *The language*

$$\{a^n b^n \mid n \in \mathbb{N}\}$$

is defined by the formula

$$\max \equiv 1 \bmod 2 \ \wedge\ \forall y\ y < \frac{\max}{2} \leftrightarrow \mathbf{a}(y)\,.$$

It is well known that word languages definable in FO with arbitrary numerical predicates are exactly languages in AC^0 (see [16] for instance). The simplest way to translate an FO sentence φ into a constant-depth circuit is to introduce a gate for each subformula $\psi(x_1,\dots,x_k)$ and each choice of positions $i_1,\dots,i_k$ in the word. The most external logical symbol in ψ determines the type of the gate: $\vee$, $\wedge$, $\neg$ correspond to OR, AND or NOT gates, and quantifiers are interpreted as disjunctions and conjunctions over all positions of the word. The gate is connected to the gates corresponding to appropriate subformulas of $\psi(x_1,\dots,x_k)$ with variables valuated accordingly. The gates for the letter predicates are simply the binary input gates encoding the input symbols. If P is a numeric predicate, the gate for $P(i_1,\dots,i_k)$ is either constantly 0 or constantly 1, depending on P and $i_1,\dots,i_k$ (this is where we use non-uniformity). The depth of this circuit is bounded by the depth of the formula, seen as a term. The number of gates is bounded by $\|\varphi\|\cdot n^k$, where $\|\varphi\|$ is the number of different subformulas in φ and k is the maximal number of free variables in a subformula.

This construction can be optimized for FO^k, that is, for formulas using (and reusing) only k variables (see [21, 26]). Such a formula can be written in a normal form in which quantification is always of the form

$$\exists x_1\ \delta(x_1,\dots,x_k) \wedge \psi_2 \wedge \dots \wedge \psi_k$$

such that $\delta(x_1,\dots,x_k)$ is a quantifier-free formula using only numerical predicates, and the set of free variables of ψ_j does not contain x_j. Then, it essentially suffices to have gates for subformulas with at most $k-1$ free variables: for each valuation of variables $x_2,\dots,x_k$, we have an OR gate connected to the ANDs of the gates for ψ_j with the variable x_1 valuated in all ways that make $\delta(x_1,\dots,x_k)$ hold. The size of the resulting circuit is bounded by $\|\varphi\|\cdot n^{k-1}$.

Regular languages and logic. The connection between logic and regular languages is a field of research on its own that takes its root into the celebrated results of McNaughton and Papert [25] and Schützenberger [29], who characterized regular languages of FO[<], that is languages definable in first order logic with the linear order over positions. By extending this result to a slightly more complicated fragment, and by using the parity lower bounds for AC^0, Barrington et al. [3] proved that regular languages in AC^0 are exactly those definable in FO[<, MOD]; that is, in first order logic with (strict) order and the unary modulo predicates of the form $x \equiv r \mod q$ for arbitrary $r, q \in \mathbb{N}$. Furthermore, this class of regular languages has decidable membership thanks to its algebraic characterization.

Thus, we get the following corollary from Theorem 1.

Corollary 1. *Given a bounded-depth regular tree language L, one can decide if* $\mathrm{flat}(L)$ *can be recognized with an* AC^0 *streaming circuit family; a recognizing streaming circuit for a given block size can be constructed effectively.*

Checking whether a regular word language is definable in FO[<, MOD] is PSPACE-complete [10]. The algorithm to construct a circuit from an automaton runs in time linear in the size of the *syntactic monoid* of the recognized language, and is therefore efficient as long as the syntactic monoid is not too large. In general, the syntactic monoid has size at most exponential in the size of the minimal automaton recognizing the language.

A more practical approach to providing AC^0 streaming circuits is to define a subclass of DTDs that are directly transformable into AC^0 streaming circuit families. In order to identify such a subclass, we first show that for bounded-depth tree languages, definability in FO is equivalent to FO[<]-definability of the flattening.

FO-definable tree languages. First order logic over trees uses the letter predicates $\mathbf{a}(x)$ and the navigational predicates child(x,y), descendant(x,y), nextSibling(x,y), and followingSibling(x,y), which hold if and only if y is respectively a child, descendant, the next sibling or a following sibling of x.

Example 5. *The language of trees over a single-letter alphabet with only one branch is defined by the formula*

$$\forall x,y\ \mathit{descendant}(x,y) \vee \mathit{descendant}(y,x)\,.$$

Note that the flattening of this language is exactly the one given in Example 4 (with $b=\bar{a}$).

We begin with a lemma which shows that, assuming bounded depth, the tree structure can be recovered from the

[1] Claims marked with (♣) can be verified using, e.g., an on-line tool available at: `paperman.cadilhac.name/sage`.

flattening with FO[<] formulas. In the flattening, we think of the positions with the opening tags as the ones representing the nodes of the tree.

Lemma 1. *For all $d > 0$ there exist* FO[<] *formulas*

$$tree_d(x,y)\,, \quad forest_d(x,y)$$

expressing that the segment from x to y is, respectively, the flattening of a tree of depth at most d, and a concatenation of such flattenings.

Consequently, for all $d > 0$ there exist FO[<] *formulas*

$$child_d(x,y)\,, \quad desc_d(x,y)\,, \quad next_d(x,y)\,, \quad foll_d(x,y)$$

expressing (over flattenings of trees of depth at most d) that the node represented by position x and the node represented by position y are, respectively, in relation child, descendant, next sibling, and following sibling.

Proof. The formulas tree_d and forest_d are defined by mutual recursion. Let

$$\mathrm{tree}_0(x,y) = \mathrm{forest}_0(x,y) = \mathrm{false}\,.$$

For $d > 0$, the formula $\mathrm{forest}_d(x,y)$ expresses that each position between x and y has a matching position between x and y such that the corresponding segment is the flattening of a tree of depth at most d,

$$\begin{aligned}\mathrm{forest}_d(x,y) :=\ & x < y\ \wedge \\ & \wedge\ \forall u \in (x,y)\, \exists v \in (x,y)\ \big(\mathrm{tree}_d(u,v) \vee \mathrm{tree}_d(v,u)\big)\,,\end{aligned}$$

and $\mathrm{tree}_d(x,y)$ checks that x and y are labelled by matching tags and the segment between them is a concatenation of the flattenings of trees of depth at most $d-1$,

$$\mathrm{tree}_d(x,y) := \Big(\bigvee_{a\in\Sigma} \mathbf{a}(x) \wedge \bar{\mathbf{a}}(y)\Big) \wedge \mathrm{forest}_{d-1}(x,y)\,.$$

It is not difficult to verify that tree_d and forest_d indeed define, respectively, flattenings of trees of depth at most d and concatenations of such flattenings.

The remaining formulas,

$$\begin{aligned}&\mathrm{desc}_d(x,y) := \exists x'\ \mathrm{tree}_d(x,x') \wedge y \in (x,x') \wedge \Big(\bigvee_{a\in\Sigma} \mathbf{a}(y)\Big)\,,\\ &\mathrm{child}_d(x,y) := \mathrm{desc}_d(x,y)\ \wedge \\ &\qquad\qquad \wedge\ \neg\exists z \in (x,y)\ \mathrm{desc}_d(x,z) \wedge \mathrm{desc}_d(z,y)\,,\\ &\mathrm{foll}_d(x,y) := x < y \wedge \exists z\ \mathrm{child}_d(z,x) \wedge \mathrm{child}_d(z,y)\,,\\ &\mathrm{next}_d(x,y) := \mathrm{foll}_d(x,y) \wedge \neg\exists z \in (x,y)\ \mathrm{foll}_d(x,z)\,,\end{aligned}$$

are straightforward. □

Lemma 1 and Theorem 1 give the following result.

Theorem 3. *For each bounded-depth tree language L, L is* FO*-definable if and only if* $\mathrm{flat}(L)$ *is* FO[<]*-definable. In consequence, flattenings of* FO*-definable tree languages are recognized by* AC^0 *streaming circuit families; the recognizing streaming circuit for a given block size can be constructed effectively.*

Proof. The formula defining the flattening of L is obtained by taking the conjunction of $\mathrm{tree}_d(\min,\max)$ and the formula defining L with each occurrence of child, descendant, next-sibling, and following-sibling replaced with the appropriate formula given by Lemma 1.

For the converse implication, we begin by rewriting each FO[<]-formula over the flattenings so that quantification is in one of the following forms:

$$\exists x^o\ \Big(\bigvee_{a\in\Sigma} \mathbf{a}(x^o)\Big) \wedge \varphi\,, \qquad \exists x^c\ \Big(\bigvee_{a\in\Sigma} \bar{\mathbf{a}}(x^c)\Big) \wedge \varphi\,;$$

the resulting formula is at most exponentially larger. Then, each variable has its type, opening or closing. We now rewrite each atomic predicate for all possible types of variables. For an opening variable x^o, $\mathbf{a}(x^o)$ remains unchanged and $\bar{\mathbf{a}}(x^o)$ is rewritten as *false*; for a closing variable x^c, $\mathbf{a}(x^c)$ is rewritten as *false*, and $\bar{\mathbf{a}}(x^c)$ as $\mathbf{a}(x^c)$. For a closing variable x^c and an opening variable y^o, the atomic formula $x^c < y^o$ is rewritten as $\mathrm{right}(x^c, y^o)$, where $\mathrm{right}(x,y)$ is the formula

$$\begin{aligned}\exists z \exists z'\ &(\mathrm{descendant}(z,x) \vee z = x)\ \wedge\\ &\wedge\ \mathrm{followingSibling}(z,z')\ \wedge\\ &\wedge\ (\mathrm{descendant}(z',y) \vee z' = y)\,.\end{aligned}$$

Similarly, the formulas

$$\begin{aligned}&\mathrm{descendant}(x^o,y^o) \vee \mathrm{right}(x^o,y^o)\,,\\ &\mathrm{descendant}(x^o,y^c) \vee \mathrm{right}(x^o,y^c)\ \vee\\ &\qquad\qquad \vee\ \mathrm{descendant}(y^c,x^o) \vee x^o = y^c\,,\\ &\mathrm{right}(x^c,y^c) \vee \mathrm{descendant}(y^c,x^c)\end{aligned}$$

are used for the remaining three cases. We obtain a formula of FO on trees, easily seen to be equivalent to the original formula of FO[<] on flattenings. □

Theorem 3 gives an effective sufficient condition for the existence of an AC^0 streaming circuit family for the flattening: as FO[<] definability is decidable for regular languages, so is FO-definability for bounded-depth regular tree languages. We remark that for regular tree languages of unbounded depth, it is a major open problem whether FO-definability is decidable [7].

The condition given by Theorem 3 is not necessary. As shown in the next example, capturing the entire class of bounded-depth regular tree languages admitting AC^0 streaming circuit families for the flattenings would require intricate artificial syntactic restrictions over the basic formalism, with an unclear gain in expressivity.

Example 6. *Consider the following two DTDs:*

$$r \to (aa)^*\,,\ a \to (bb)^*\,; \qquad r \to (aa)^*\,,\ a \to (bbb)^*\,.$$

The flattening of the language given by the left DTD is in AC^0*, whereas for the right DTD it is not.* (♣)

The argument in Theorem 3 does not give good complexity bounds: the FO formula for the flattening has size linear in the original formula (and exponential in the depth), but the automaton constructed from the formula, needed to invoke Theorem 1, may have non-elementary size. And even if there was a more efficient way to do it, FO is not a natural schema definition language. A desirable language should be a natural fragment of a known schema definition language. We discuss such a fragment in the following subsection.

We finish this subsection with a remark that without the bounded-depth assumption one can recognize flattenings of FO-definable tree languages in TC^0 in the random-access model. Recall that TC^0 is defined like AC^0, except that Majority gates can also be used.

PROPOSITION 4. *Let L be an FO-definable language of trees. Then* $\mathrm{flat}(L)$ *is in* TC^0.

PROOF SKETCH. We repeat the proof of Lemma 1 and Theorem 3, but this time using circuits rather than formulas. In the course of the structural induction, we need to deal with formulas with free variables. We work with words over the alphabet

$$\{0,1\}^n \times (\Sigma \cup \overline{\Sigma}),$$

for sufficiently large n. Over such words we evaluate a formula $\varphi(x_1, x_2, \ldots, x_n)$ by assuming that x_i is assigned the *unique* position that has 1 in the i-th coordinate of its label.

It is sufficient to prove that the formula $\mathrm{tree}(x_i, x_j)$, saying that the infix from position x_i to position x_j is the flattening of a tree, is definable in TC^0: to conclude we simply note that TC^0 is closed under FO quantification (and Boolean connectives), so all predicates from Lemma 1, and all FO formulas using them, can be defined in TC^0 as well.

To express $\mathrm{tree}(x_i, x_j)$ with a TC^0 circuit, we proceed as follows. For every position $y \in [x_i, x_j]$ which is labelled by an opening tag, we find a position $z \in [y+1, x_j]$ such that z is labelled by the matching closing tag and the number of open tags between y and z is exactly the number of closing tags. This last test can be implemented as the AND of two Majority gates, checking that the number of opening tags is at most the number closing tags, and *vice versa*. □

Even the flattening of the set of all trees is TC^0-hard, but not all flattenings of regular languages of unbounded depth are: for instance the language of trees with only one branch over unary alphabet is FO-definable and its flattening is in AC^0 (see Example 4).

A practical formalism for validation in constant-depth.

A natural formalism allowing validation with constant-depth streaming circuits can be obtained by restricting the productions in DTDs to FO[<]-definable languages. Over words, being FO[<]-definable is equivalent to being definable with a *star-free* regular expression [25]; that is, an expression built from symbols from the alphabet and the empty set by means of concatenation and all Boolean operations, including complement.

COROLLARY 2. *Each language $L \subseteq \mathrm{Trees}(\Sigma)$ defined by a non-recursive DTD with star-free productions can be defined in* FO *on trees, and so can be recognized by an* AC^0 *streaming circuit family.*

PROOF. For each $a \in \Sigma$ there is an FO[<] sentence φ_a defining the word language generated by the production for a. As the DTD is non-recursive, all generated trees have depth at most $|\Sigma|$. We define L with the formula

$$\exists x\, \mathbf{r}(x) \wedge \forall y\, \neg \mathrm{descendant}(y, x) \wedge \forall z \bigwedge_{a \in \Sigma} \mathbf{a}(z) \rightarrow \widehat{\varphi}_a(z),$$

where r is the root label of the DTD, and the formula $\widehat{\varphi}_a(z)$ is obtained from the sentence φ_a by replacing each occurrence of the predicate $<$ with the predicate followingSibling and restricting all quantifiers to the children of z; that is, subformulas $\exists y\, \psi$ and $\forall y\, \psi$ are replaced, respectively, with

$$\exists y\, \mathrm{child}(z, y) \wedge \psi \qquad \text{and} \qquad \forall y\, \mathrm{child}(z, y) \rightarrow \psi$$

(assuming that variable z is not used in φ_a). □

The popular class of nested-relational DTDs is a special case, which admits constant-depth streaming circuits with particularly good parameters.

THEOREM 4. *The flattening of each language $L \subseteq \mathrm{Trees}(\Sigma)$ defined by a nested-relational DTD can be recognized by an AC^0 streaming circuit family with feedback $\mathcal{O}(d \cdot |\Sigma|)$, depth $\mathcal{O}(d)$ and size $\mathcal{O}(d^3 \cdot |\Sigma|^2 \cdot n^2)$ for block size n, where $d \leq |\Sigma|$ is the maximal depth of trees in L.*

PROOF. We shall directly construct a streaming circuit, using FO formulas over separate blocks of the input word as an intermediate formalism. Since the language is defined by a nested-relational DTD, its depth is bounded by some $d \leq |\Sigma|$. Before we look at the DTD any further, we construct a circuit that for each position x in the block computes $\mathit{open}(x) \in \Sigma^{\leq d}$, the sequence of unmatched opening tags in the prefix of the entire input word up to (and including) position x. Note that $\mathit{open}(x)$ is equal to the sequence of labels on the path from the root to the node corresponding to x in the encoded tree, including this node if the tag of x is opening, and not including it otherwise. As the feedback we shall use $\mathit{open}(\min - 1)$, where $\min - 1$ is the last position of the previous block. We use the padding symbol \$ (encoded as a sequence of zeros) to fill up $\mathit{open}(\min - 1)$ to d symbols.

First, we compute the values of the formula $\mathrm{forest}_d(x, y)$ from Lemma 1 for all positions within the block. Note that $\mathrm{forest}_d(x, y)$ has quantifier rank $\mathcal{O}(d)$ and uses only 3 variables. Its size is exponential if the recursive definition is unravelled, but it has only $\mathcal{O}(d + |\Sigma|)$ different subformulas. Thus, the standard translation for formulas with 3 variables gives a streaming circuit of depth $\mathcal{O}(d)$ and size $\mathcal{O}((d + |\Sigma|) \cdot n^2)$; the circuit has n^2 output gates, one for each pair of values of x and y. From now on, we shall treat $\mathrm{forest}_d(x, y)$ as an atomic formula.

Similarly, we can assume the existence of atomic formulas $\overline{f}_p(x)$ for $p = 1, 2, \ldots, d$ expressing that position x has the closing tag corresponding to the p-th letter stored in the feedback. Their values for all x can be computed with a circuit of depth $\mathcal{O}(1)$ and size $\mathcal{O}(d \cdot |\Sigma| \cdot n)$.

How does $v = \mathit{open}(x)$ depend on $u = \mathit{open}(\min - 1)$? The situation can be illustrated as follows:

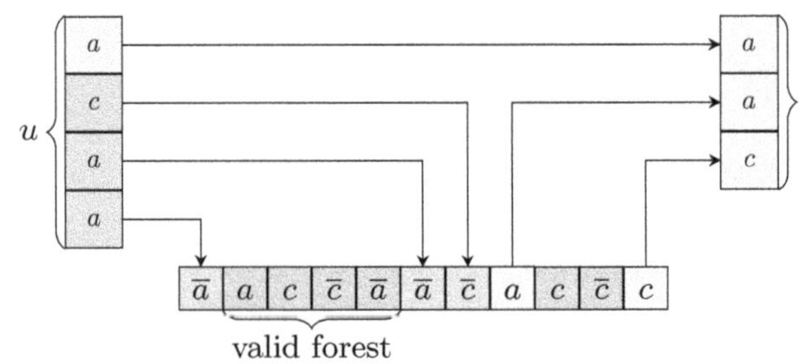

We express this with formulas

$$\varphi_{i,a}(x)$$

for $i = 1, 2, \ldots, d$, and $a \in \Sigma$, saying that the i-th symbol of $\mathit{open}(x)$ is a, assuming that the feedback stores $\mathit{open}(\min - 1)$. The formula is a disjunction over $0 \leq j \leq k, \ell \leq d$ with $\ell \geq i$ of conditions saying that

- the first \$ in the feedback is at position $k + 1$,
- there exist positions $x \geq y_\ell > y_{\ell-1} > \cdots > y_{j+1}$ with opening tags,

- there exist positions $y_{j+1} > z_{j+1} > z_{j+2} > \cdots > z_k$ with closing tags $\overline{f}_{j+1}, \overline{f}_{j+2}, \ldots, \overline{f}_k$, such that
- all segments between these positions (including $\min -1$ and x) are flattenings of forests, and
- $a = f_i$ if $i \leq j$, and $a(y_i)$ if $i > j$,

where f_p is the symbol in the p-th feedback gate.

This resulting formula uses $\mathcal{O}(d)$ quantifiers and can be written with 2 variables only. It has $\mathcal{O}(d^3)$ different subformulas (with $\text{forest}_d(x, y)$ and $\overline{f}_p(x)$ treated as atomic formulas). Thus, the standard translation gives a streaming circuit of depth $\mathcal{O}(d)$ and size $\mathcal{O}(d^3 \cdot n^2)$ for block size n; the circuit has n output gates, one for each value of x. Note that we cannot use the optimized construction giving linear-size circuit, because the formula forest_d does not define a numerical predicate; that is, it depends on the labels of positions.

The $d \cdot |\Sigma|$ circuits for formulas $\varphi_{i,a}(x)$ compute $open(x)$ for all x. If for some x and i we have 0 for all a's, it means that $open(x)$ has less than i symbols. Note that the total size of the constructed circuits is $\mathcal{O}(d^4 \cdot |\Sigma| \cdot n^2)$.

Local correctness of the encoding can be checked by verifying that $open(x)$ is nonempty throughout the computation; as soon as it becomes empty, the remaining positions in the block should store the padding symbol \$, and it should be the last block. All this can be tested with a circuit of depth $\mathcal{O}(1)$ and size $\mathcal{O}(n^2)$.

Once we have built the circuit computing $open(x)$ for each position x, we have access to the label of the parent of each node whose closing tag is within the block: it is the last letter of $open(x)$. The labelling restrictions enforced by the DTD can be expressed with the formula

$$\forall x \in [\min -1, \max) \bigwedge_{a \in \Sigma} \left(\mathbf{a}(x) \to \bigvee_{c \in N(a)} \mathbf{c}(x+1)\right) \wedge \wedge \bigwedge_{a,b \in \Sigma} \left(open(x) \in \Sigma^* a \$^* \wedge \overline{\mathbf{b}}(x) \to \bigvee_{c \in N(a,b)} \mathbf{c}(x+1)\right).$$

where $N(a)$ is the set of labels that can succeed the opening tag a, and $N(a, b)$ is the set of labels that can succeed the closing tag $\overline{b}$ in the scope of tag a. Both sets are determined by the production for a. Assume the production is

$$a \to \widehat{a}_1 \widehat{a}_2 \ldots \widehat{a}_k .$$

There are two cases, depending on whether there is i such that $\widehat{a}_i$ is either a_i^+ or a_i. If there is such i, let us take the minimal one. Then, $N(a) = \{a_1, a_2, \ldots, a_i\}$. If there is no such i, $N(a) = \{a_1, a_2, \ldots, a_k\} \cup \{\overline{a}\}$. The set $N(a, a_j)$ is characterized analogously: if there is $i > j$ such that $\widehat{a}_i$ is either a_i^+ or a_i, then for the minimal such i we have

$$N(a, a_j) = \begin{cases} \{a_j, a_{j+1}, \ldots, a_i\} & \text{for } \widehat{a}_j \in \{a_j^*, a_j^+\}, \\ \{a_{j+1}, \ldots, a_i\} & \text{for } \widehat{a}_j \in \{a_j, a_j?\}. \end{cases}$$

If no such i exists,

$$N(a, a_j) = \begin{cases} \{a_j, a_{j+1}, \ldots, a_k\} \cup \{\overline{a}\} & \text{for } \widehat{a}_j \in \{a_j^*, a_j^+\}, \\ \{a_{j+1}, \ldots, a_k\} \cup \{\overline{a}\} & \text{for } \widehat{a}_j \in \{a_j, a_j?\}. \end{cases}$$

Note that to evaluate the formula we need access to $open(\min -1)$ and the tag at position $\min -1$. We have already pointed out that $open(\min -1)$ is included in the feedback; now we see that also the label at position $\min -1$ should be a part of the feedback. Assuming unary encoding of letters, the size of the feedback is $\mathcal{O}(|\Sigma|^2)$. The standard translation of the formula gives a circuit of depth $\mathcal{O}(1)$ and size $\mathcal{O}\big((|\Sigma|^2 + d \cdot |\Sigma|) \cdot n\big)$. The output of the circuit is used to propagate the information about the lack of error so far, which is done by means of a designated error feedback gate.

Combining the two stages we obtain a circuit of depth $\mathcal{O}(d) = \mathcal{O}(|\Sigma|)$ and size $\mathcal{O}(d^3 \cdot |\Sigma|^2 \cdot n^2)$. □

Let us remark that the construction can be extended to productions with thresholds $a^{\ell..k}$, $a^{\geq k}$, at the cost of including more information in the feedback: for each label in $open(y)$ we would need the number of its repetitions among its siblings so far (up to threshold k).

5. WIRE-LINEAR CIRCUITS

While having an AC^0 streaming circuit family guarantees depth independent of the block size, it is still possible that the number of gates and the number of wires makes implementation for larger block sizes unreasonable. We now turn to *wire-linear circuit families*, $WLAC^0$; that is, bounded-depth circuit families in which the number of wires (and thus the number of gates) grows linearly with the size of the input (or block in case of streaming circuits). As for AC^0, $WLAC^0$ has been studied and regular languages in $WLAC^0$ are characterized.

Regular languages in $WLAC^0$. The logical characterization of regular languages in $WLAC^0$ is given by the following result, extending a similar characterization of regular languages with a *neutral letter* in $WLAC^0$ [19].

THEOREM 5 ([26]). *A regular language is in* $WLAC^0$ *if and only if it is definable in* $FO^2[+1, <, MOD]$.

Note that the signature includes the successor relation $+1$, which cannot be defined from $<$ with just 2 variables.

Unlike for AC^0, both directions are involved. The lower bound relies on an effective algebraic characterization of languages definable in $FO^2[+1, <, MOD]$ from [11] (which also makes definability decidable) and the fact that the language $(c + ac^*b)^*$ is not in $WLAC^0$ [19]. The upper bound, which we care mostly about, uses a clever circuit construction for *prefix functions* [9]. For completeness, we sketch this construction and explain how to use it to construct a $WLAC^0$ circuit family from a formula of $FO^2[+1, <, MOD]$. To get a $WLAC^0$ streaming circuit family we use Theorem 1.

Consider the language

$$\Sigma^* a \Sigma^* a \Sigma^*$$

of words with at least two letters a. It can be defined by the formula

$$\exists x\ \mathbf{a}(x) \wedge \exists y\ y < x \wedge \mathbf{a}(y)$$

The standard translation from FO, which introduces a gate for each subformula with free variables valuated in all possible ways, gives a circuit of quadratic size. The optimized construction for FO^2 formulas gives a circuit with linearly many gates, but quadratically many wires: for each value of x we have an OR gate connected to the circuits for $\mathbf{a}(y)$ for all $y < x$.

To obtain a wire-linear circuit, we use *prefix functions.* The prefix-OR is a function $f\colon \{0,1\}^n \to \{0,1\}^n$ such that

$$f(u)_i = \bigvee_{j \le i} u_j \,;$$

suffix-OR, prefix-AND, and suffix-AND are defined similarly. A WLAC^0 circuit for prefix-OR is constructed by evaluating prefix-OR naïvely (with quadratically many wires) over the ORs of size-$\sqrt{n}$ blocks, and then over each block separately with the additional knowledge of the bit computed by the first stage for the previous block. If we use a separate circuit for each block, we get a circuit with $\mathcal{O}(n\sqrt{n})$ wires. To avoid this we note that we need to compute the prefix-OR only for the single block where 0's switch to 1's in the prefix-OR for block ORs. The remaining prefix and suffix functions can be computed similarly. For more details we refer to the original article [9].

Coming back to our example, a WLAC^0 circuit for the language $\Sigma^* a \Sigma^* a \Sigma^*$ can be obtained by computing the prefix-OR of *being letter a* and checking if there exists an input gate which contains a such that the prefix-OR for the previous position evaluates to 1:

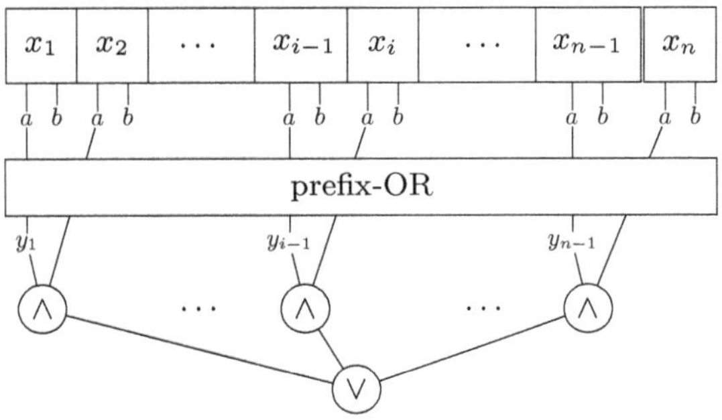

This construction can be nested: for the language of words having at least k occurrences of a, one uses k prefix-OR circuits with n inputs interleaved with k layers of AND gates of fan-in 2, with the last layer of AND gates connected to a single OR gate. The size of the resulting circuit is therefore $\mathcal{O}(kn)$ and is independent from the size of the input alphabet.

To build a circuit for an arbitrary FO^2 formula we proceed by structural induction over formulas in the classical normal form. The basic cases are unary predicates $\mathbf{a}(x)$ and $x \equiv r \bmod q$, for which the naïve construction gives wire-linear circuits. As WLAC^0 is closed under Boolean connectives, the only difficulty in the inductive step is the quantification. In the normal form, the quantification is always of the form $\exists y\ \delta(x,y) \wedge \varphi(y)$ where $\delta(x,y)$ only uses predicates $x < y$ and $x = y + k$ for $k \in \mathbb{Z}$. We deal with it like in the example above, by computing prefix functions for $\varphi(1), \dots, \varphi(n)$ and then for each x adding an OR gate wired appropriately to the outputs of $\varphi(1), \dots, \varphi(n)$ and the prefix functions; details can be adapted from [19] or found in [26].

Tree languages and WLAC^0 *validation.* Using the described results on regular languages in WLAC^0, and Theorem 1, we obtain the following corollary.

COROLLARY 3. *Given a regular bounded-depth tree language L, one can decide if* $\mathrm{flat}(L)$ *can be recognized with a* WLAC^0 *streaming circuit family; a recognizing streaming circuit for a given block size can be constructed effectively.* □

XML flattenings of the sets of trees of depth 1 and 2 (over a singleton alphabet), that is, languages $(ab)^*$ and $(a(ab)^*b)^*$, are in WLAC^0, but for depth 3 the flattening is the language $(a(a(ab)^*b)^*b)^*$, which is not in WLAC^0. (♣) Hence, unlike for full FO, the two-variable fragment of FO over trees is not captured by WLAC^0 (and thus by FO^2 over words). In fact, it is not easy to imagine a nontrivial schema formalism that guarantees recognizability with a WLAC^0 streaming circuit family. We shall eventually propose such a formalism, but for now we shift the perspective and ask: what if we change the way trees are encoded as words?

We propose an encoding giving even more information than the XML encoding: the path-from-the-root encoding. Trees of depth at most d over alphabet Σ are encoded as words over alphabet

$$\Sigma \cup \overline{\Sigma} \cup \{\$\}\,,$$

where \$ is a padding symbol, used to simplify the circuits. For $0 < i \le d$, a word $u \in \Sigma^{i-1}$, a tree t with root $a \in \Sigma$, and children that are trees $t_1, \dots, t_k$ we set

$$\Delta^d_u(t) = ua\$^{d-i} \cdot \Delta^d_{ua}(t_1) \cdots \Delta^d_{ua}(t_k) \cdot u\overline{a}\$^{d-i}$$

and let the *path-from-the-root* encoding of tree t be

$$\Delta^d(t) = \Delta^d_\varepsilon(t)\,.$$

For instance, for a tree t consisting of an r-root with one a-child and one c-child, $\Delta^2(t) = r\$\,ra\,r\overline{a}\,rc\,r\overline{c}\,\overline{r}\$$.

For this new encoding, we still have that the flattening

$$\Delta^d(L) = \{\Delta^d(t) \mid t \in L\}$$

of a regular bounded-depth tree language L is a regular language of words. Moreover, the correctness of the encoding can be checked by a WLAC^0 streaming circuit family. We shall write $\Delta(L)$ for the encoding of L, assuming that the parameter d is clear from the context.

LEMMA 2. *Let* $\mathrm{Trees}_d(\Sigma)$ *be the set of trees over Σ of depth at most d. The language* $\Delta(\mathrm{Trees}_d(\Sigma))$ *is recognized by a* WLAC^0 *streaming circuit family with feedback* $\mathcal{O}(d \cdot |\Sigma|)$*, depth* $\mathcal{O}(1)$*, and* $\mathcal{O}(|\Sigma| \cdot (n+d))$ *wires.*

PROOF. To encode consecutive tags in the flattening, the path-from-the-root encoding uses blocks of d consecutive symbols: at most d symbols on the path to the root, padded to length d with symbol \$. These blocks will be called *d-slabs.* For simplicity, in the following we assume that n is divisible by d, so that d-slabs fit exactly into blocks processed by the circuit. If this is not the case, we can adapt the construction by passing the previous incomplete block in the feedback, together with the length $r < d$ of the passed fragment, encoded in unary. This increases the number of feedback gates by $\mathcal{O}(d)$. All the congruences used in the following constructions can be easily adjusted to take in the account the fact that the d-slabs in the block are shifted by r.

The feedback consists of the last d-slab of the previously processed block, and a special error gate that passes the information whether an error has been encountered so far. In the first block, we assume that the initial feedback encodes a d-slab consisting only of symbols \$. As such d-slabs will never appear again throughout the computation, from this feedback we can recognize that the first block is being processed. Henceforth we assume that the circuit has the access to symbols at positions between $\min - d$ and $\min - 1$, or to the information that these positions do not exist.

Let us introduce an auxiliary formula $\text{last}(x)$ expressing that x is the last position with a non-padding symbol within its d-slab:

$$\text{last}(x) := \neg\$(x) \wedge \big(\$(x+1) \vee x \equiv d-1 \bmod d\big)\,.$$

We can compute this formula for all positions x using $\mathcal{O}(n)$ gates and depth $\mathcal{O}(1)$.

Let us now see how to verify that the block's description is correct. For this, we check that certain conditions hold for every position $x \in [\min -d, \max -d)$ (respectively, $x \in [0, \max -d)$ for the first block) using a formula whose encoding as a circuit will be straightforward. We first express that the padding symbols behave as expected:

$$\begin{aligned} x \equiv 0 \bmod d &\to \neg\$(x)\,, \\ \$(x) \wedge \neg\$(x+1) &\to x \equiv d-1 \bmod d\,, \\ \$(x) \wedge \neg\$(x+d) &\to \text{last}(x-1)\,. \end{aligned}$$

The first implication asserts that no d-slab contains the \$ symbol at its front. The second one asserts that after any \$ symbol, we necessarily have \$ symbols up to the end of the d-slab. The third one asserts that the only \$ symbol that can be replaced by a letter in the next d-slab is the first one. Finally, we introduce the following implications for all $a \in \Sigma$:

$$\begin{aligned} \mathbf{a}(x) &\to \bar{\mathbf{a}}(x+d) \vee \big(\mathbf{a}(x+d) \wedge \neg\text{last}(x+d)\big)\,, \\ \bar{\mathbf{a}}(x+d) &\to \text{last}(x+d) \wedge \mathbf{a}(x)\,. \end{aligned}$$

The first implication asserts that an opening tag either changes to the matching closing tag or remains the same and another symbol is added after it. In particular, an opening tag is never replaced by \$. The second implication asserts that a closing tag has to be produced from the last position of the previous d-slab. In particular, in the next d-slab it can be replaced by an opening tag or a \$ symbol, but not by a closing tag. The described formula can be turned directly into a wire-linear streaming circuit with a single gate of unbounded fan-in, connected to $|\Sigma| \cdot n$ subcircuits of size $\mathcal{O}(1)$ and constant fan-in.

The circuit described above verifies that the description of the block is correct. The error gate passed as the feedback to the next iteration is its conjunction with the error gate received in the feedback from the previous iteration. The acceptor circuit just checks that no error has occurred. □

Even if some structural properties of the input trees are accessible under the new encoding, WLAC^0 circuits still fail to capture FO^2 definable tree languages, as shown in the next example.

EXAMPLE 7. *Let L be the language given by the DTD*

$$a \to b^*\,, \quad b \to (c+d)^*$$

restricted to trees in which one of the root's children has only c-children. It is clearly definable in FO^2. The flattening $\Delta(L)$ is (up to relabelling) the language

$$(a(b(c\bar{c}+d\bar{d})^*\bar{b})^*\bar{a} \cap \Sigma^* b(c\bar{c})^*\bar{b}\Sigma^*\,,$$

which is not in WLAC^0. (♣)

This latter example works mainly because the language is not defined by a DTD. Of course, it is hopeless to believe that we can have a good streaming circuit for any bounded-depth DTD, but what if we restrict the productions to $\text{FO}^2[<]$-definable languages? As it turns out we can still get a tree language whose path-from-the-root encoding is not recognizable with a WLAC^0 streaming circuit family.

EXAMPLE 8. *For the language L given by the DTD*

$$r \to (a)^*\,, \quad a \to b^*c^*b^*\,,$$

the flattening $\Delta(L)$ is (up to relabelling) the language

$$r(a(b\bar{b})^*(c\bar{c})^*(b\bar{b})^*\bar{a})^*\bar{r}\,,$$

which is not in WLAC^0. (♣)

What we can tackle are nested-relational DTDs.

PROPOSITION 5. *Let L be a tree language defined by a nested-relational DTD. Then $\Delta(L)$ is definable in $\text{FO}^2[<, +1, \text{MOD}]$ and is recognized by a WLAC^0 streaming circuit family with feedback $\mathcal{O}(|\Sigma|^2)$, depth $\mathcal{O}(1)$, and $\mathcal{O}(|\Sigma|^2 \cdot n)$ wires for block size n.* □

PROOF. It suffices to combine the construction from Lemma 2, which guarantees correctness of the encoding, with the second stage of the construction in Theorem 4. □

Unlike for Theorem 4, we cannot directly extend the construction to DTDs with more general thresholds.

EXAMPLE 9. *For the language L defined by the DTD*

$$r \to a^*\,, \quad a \to bb\,, \quad b \to c^*$$

the flattening $\Delta(L)$ is (up to relabelling) the language

$$r(ab(c\bar{c})^*\bar{b}b(c\bar{c})^*\bar{b}\bar{a})^*\bar{r}\,,$$

which is not in WLAC^0. (♣)

A new encoding may seem an easy way out, since we add exactly the information needed to validate nested-relational DTDs with circuits having good parameters. However, it is possible to benefit from this solution even without using the path-from-the-root encoding: if we have control over the design of the schema, by adjusting the tags we can assume that each label uniquely determines the label of the father. This ensures WLAC^0 validation at the cost of a mild restriction of the practical scope of nested-relational DTDs. For instance, when a relational database is exported to XML (a major usage of nested-relational DTDs), the XML schema is obtained from a *covering forest* of the ER diagram [23]. As long as each entity in the ER diagram is covered by one branch, our condition is satisfied. If some entity is covered by more branches, we can use different element names for each branch and re-unify them into a single entity later. We could also use a *spanning forest* instead and represent the remaining relationships with foreign keys, but verifying such constraints is beyond the scope of our setting.

If we cannot or would not modify the schema nor change the encoding into path-from-the-root, we can enrich the given encoding before feeding it to the validating streaming circuit. The enriching can be done by a fixed transducer (dependent only on the alphabet, not the schema itself), implemented with an AC^0 streaming circuit family with additional outputs. This should be viewed as a (rather complicated) fixed device that could be optimized and implemented in hardware once for all. Meanwhile, the proper validation stage can be realized with a reprogrammable hardware device of adapted size, that can be readjusted as the schema changes.

A *streaming circuit with output* with input alphabet Σ, output alphabet Γ, block size n, and feedback size m is like a streaming circuit, except that it has two kinds of output gates: immediate and pass-on. The output word over a given input word is obtained by concatenating the values on the immediate output gates for subsequent blocks of the input word; the values on the pass-on output gates are sent to the feedback gates when the next block is processed. The immediate output gates encode letters from Γ in unary, just as the input letters are encoded: i-th letter is encoded as $0^{i-1}10^{|\Gamma|-i}$. The output value is returned only if the acceptor circuit returns 1; if it returns 0, the output is undefined.

PROPOSITION 6. *Let Σ be a finite alphabet and let $d \in \mathbb{N}$. For trees over Σ of depth at most d, one can compute the path-from-the-root flattening from the XML flattening with a streaming circuit with output that has feedback $\mathcal{O}(d \cdot |\Sigma|)$, depth $\mathcal{O}(d)$, and size $\mathcal{O}(d^4 \cdot |\Sigma| \cdot n^2)$ for block size n.*

PROOF. The first stage of the construction in the proof of Theorem 4 gives almost the circuit we need: it remains to append $\bar{a}$ to $open(x)$ for positions x labelled with $\bar{a}$; this does not influence the bounds. □

6. CONCLUSIONS

We have introduced streaming circuits, which model parallel processing of streamed data in a way compatible with the schema validation task. We have shown that general results on the circuit complexity of regular languages can be used directly to reason about the existence of good streaming circuits for bounded-depth regular tree languages, giving effective but inefficient criteria. For a restricted, but practically crucial, class of languages defined by nested-relational DTDs we have provided a direct construction of circuits with excellent parameters: compositions of a quadratic-size AC^0 circuits dependent only on the depth of trees and the alphabet, and wire-linear AC^0 circuits dependent on the DTD. This construction can be extended easily to schemas with more general thresholds. Extending it further would be very relevant practically.

We have seen how to get a constant-depth polynomial-size streaming circuit from a bounded-depth tree language definable in first order logic. This relies on the fact that FO-definability of word languages is decidable and effective. There is a certain trade-off between the depth of the circuits and the degree of the polynomial bounding their size. We have seen that all FO-definable languages have quadratic circuits, but achieving this requires increasing the depth. It is even possible to achieve near-linear upper bound for these languages by increasing the depth sufficiently (see [20]). However, one may want to optimize the depth at the cost of increasing the degree of the polynomial. This question is related to the famous dot-depth conjecture, which is equivalent to deciding levels of the alternation hierarchy of first-order logic. Indeed, if a language belongs to the k-th level of this hierarchy then it is a finite Boolean combination of regular languages recognized by depth-k circuits. Straubing conjectures that the languages in k-th level of the hierarchy (enriched with the modulo predicates) are exactly the Boolean combinations of regular languages recognized by depth-k circuits [32].

Another related problem is the question of the circuit complexity of word encodings of regular tree languages (of unbounded depth). While there are TC^0-complete and NC^1-complete examples, no good characterizations are known. We conjecture that each regular tree language is either NC^1-complete or in TC^0. It would be very interesting to have an effective characterization of NC^1-complete regular tree languages such that languages that do not satisfy it are in TC^0. Such a characterization exists in the classical setting of word languages and relies on an algebraic decomposition of finite automata [32]. Since such a decomposition for tree automata is unknown and related to the open question of deciding FO-definability of regular tree languages [7], we believe this question might be very hard.

Checking correctness of the encoding has a huge impact on validation. A way to isolate it is to consider *weak validation*, where the input is assumed to be a correct encoding of a tree (a *well-formed* document, under XML encoding). While no tree language of unbounded depth can be validated in constant memory, some can be weakly validated [30, 31]. For instance, for the set of trees whose each a node's leftmost child has label b, we only need to check that each opening a tag is followed by an opening b tag. However, it remains an open question to decide whether a given language can be weakly validated in constant memory. When restricted to bounded-depth tree languages, this question can be seen as a special case of the *separation* problem for regular word languages, which has rich bibliography of its own. The problem of *separation of languages from class $\mathcal{K}$ by languages from class $\mathcal{S}$* is to decide for given languages $K, M \in \mathcal{K}$ if there exists a language $S \in \mathcal{S}$ such that $K \subseteq S$ and $M \cap S = \emptyset$. Weak validation for a tree language L amounts to separating the flattening of L from the flattening of the complement of L. Separation of regular word languages by FO[<]-definable languages is known to be decidable [15, 27], and similarly for $FO^2[+1,<]$ [28]. One can use these results as a black box to find, respectively, AC^0 and $WLAC^0$ streaming circuits for the weak validation. Unfortunately, the separation abstraction is too powerful for tree languages of *unbounded* depth: as showed recently by Kopczyński, separation of flattenings of regular tree languages with regular word languages is undecidable under both XML and term encoding [18]. In contrast, the weak validation problem under term encoding is decidable [8], and still open under XML encoding.

Acknowledgments

We thank the anonymous reviewers of PODS 2016 for their useful and inspiring comments.

7. REFERENCES

[1] Serge Abiteboul, Luc Segoufin, and Victor Vianu. Representing and querying XML with incomplete information. *ACM Trans. Database Syst.*, 31(1):208–254, 2006.
[2] Marcelo Arenas and Leonid Libkin. XML data exchange: Consistency and query answering. *J. ACM*, 55(2), 2008.
[3] David A. Mix Barrington, Kevin Compton, Howard Straubing, and Denis Thérien. Regular languages in NC^1. *J. Computer and System Sciences*, 44(3):478–499, 1992.
[4] G. J. Bex, F. Neven, and J. Van den Bussche. DTDs versus XML Schema: a practical study. In *WEBDB 2004*, pages 79–84, 2004.

[5] David Black-Schaffer. *Block-Parallel Programming for Real-Time Applications on Multi-Core Processors.* PhD thesis, Humboldt-Universität zu Berlin, 2008. Available at http://cva.stanford.edu/people/davidbbs/black-schaffer_thesis_final.pdf.

[6] David Black-Schaffer and William J. Dally. Block-parallel programming for real-time embedded applications. In *ICPP 2010*, pages 297–306. IEEE Computer Society, 2010.

[7] Mikołaj Bojańczyk, Howard Straubing, and Igor Walukiewicz. Wreath products of forest algebras, with applications to tree logics. *Logical Methods in Computer Science*, 8(3), 2012.

[8] Vince Bárány, Christof Löding, and Olivier Serre. Regularity problems for visibly pushdown languages. In Bruno Durand and Wolfgang Thomas, editors, *STACS 2006*, volume 3884 of *Lecture Notes in Computer Science*, pages 420–431. Springer Berlin Heidelberg, 2006.

[9] Ashok K. Chandra, Steven Fortune, and Richard J. Lipton. Lower bounds for constant depth circuits for prefix problems. In Josep Díaz, editor, *ICALP 1983*, volume 154 of *Lecture Notes in Computer Science*, pages 109–117. Springer, 1983.

[10] Sang Cho and Dung T. Huynh. Finite-automaton aperiodicity is PSPACE-complete. *Theoretical Computer Science*, 88(1):99 – 116, 1991.

[11] Luc Dartois and Charles Paperman. Alternation hierarchies of first order logic with regular predicates. In Adrian Kosowski and Igor Walukiewicz, editors, *FCT 2015*, volume 9210 of *Lecture Notes in Computer Science*, pages 160–172. Springer, 2015.

[12] Tathagata Das, Yuan Zhong, Ion Stoica, and Scott Shenker. Adaptive stream processing using dynamic batch sizing. In Ed Lazowska, Doug Terry, Remzi H. Arpaci-Dusseau, and Johannes Gehrke, editors, *SoCC 2014*, pages 16:1–16:13. ACM, 2014.

[13] Patrick Dymond. Input-driven languages are in log n depth. *Inf. Process. Lett.*, 26(5):247–250, January 1988.

[14] Merrick Furst, James B. Saxe, and Michael Sipser. Parity, circuits, and the polynomial-time hierarchy. *Theory of Computing Systems*, 17:13–27, 1984.

[15] Karsten Henckell. Pointlike sets: the finest aperiodic cover of a finite semigroup. *Journal of Pure and Applied Algebra*, 55(1):85 – 126, 1988.

[16] Neil Immerman. Languages that capture complexity classes. *SIAM J. Computing*, 16(4):760–778, 1987.

[17] Rashid Khogali, Olivia Das, and Kaamran Raahemifar. Mobile parallel computing algorithms for single-buffered, speed-scalable processors. In *TrustCom 2013 / ISPA-13 / IUCC-2013*, pages 1832–1839. IEEE Computer Society, 2013.

[18] Eryk Kopczyński. Invisible pushdown languages. In *LICS 2016 (to appear)*, 2016. Available at http://arxiv.org/abs/1511.00289.

[19] Michal Koucký, Pavel Pudlák, and Denis Thérien. Bounded-depth circuits: separating wires from gates. In Harold N. Gabow and Ronald Fagin, editors, *STOC 2005*, pages 257–265. ACM, 2005.

[20] Michal Koucký. Circuit complexity of regular languages. *Theory of Computing Systems*, 45(4):865–879, 2009.

[21] Michal Koucký, Clemens Lautemann, Sebastian Poloczek, and Denis Thérien. Circuit lower bounds via Ehrenfeucht-Fraissé games. In *CCC 2006*, pages 190–201, 2006.

[22] Viraj Kumar, P. Madhusudan, and Mahesh Viswanathan. Visibly pushdown automata for streaming XML. In *WWW 2007*, pages 1053–1062. ACM, 2007.

[23] Dongwon Lee, Murali Mani, Frank Chiu, and Wesley W. Chu. Net & cot: translating relational schemas to XML schemas using semantic constraints. In *Proceedings of the 2002 ACM CIKM International Conference on Information and Knowledge Management, McLean, VA, USA, November 4-9, 2002*, pages 282–291. ACM, 2002.

[24] Kyong-Ha Lee, Yoon-Joon Lee, Hyunsik Choi, Yon Dohn Chung, and Bongki Moon. Parallel data processing with MapReduce: a survey. *SIGMOD Record*, 40(4):11–20, 2011.

[25] Robert McNaughton and Seymour Papert. *Counter-Free Automata.* The MIT Press, Cambridge, Mass., 1971.

[26] Charles Paperman. *Circuits booléens, prédicats modulaires et langages réguliers.* PhD dissertation, Université Paris Diderot, 2014. In French.

[27] Thomas Place and Marc Zeitoun. Separating regular languages with first-order logic. In Thomas A. Henzinger and Dale Miller, editors, *CSL-LICS 2014*, pages 75:1–75:10. ACM, 2014.

[28] Thomas Place and Marc Zeitoun. Separation and the successor relation. In Ernst W. Mayr and Nicolas Ollinger, editors, *STACS 2015*, volume 30 of *Leibniz International Proceedings in Informatics (LIPIcs)*, pages 662–675, Dagstuhl, Germany, 2015. Schloss Dagstuhl–Leibniz-Zentrum fuer Informatik.

[29] Marcel-Paul Schützenberger. On finite monoids having only trivial subgroups. *Information and Control*, 8(2):190–194, 1965.

[30] Luc Segoufin and Cristina Sirangelo. Constant-memory validation of streaming XML documents against DTDs. In Thomas Schwentick and Dan Suciu, editors, *ICDT 2007*, volume 4353 of *Lecture Notes in Computer Science*, pages 299–313. Springer, 2007.

[31] Luc Segoufin and Victor Vianu. Validating streaming XML documents. In Lucian Popa, Serge Abiteboul, and Phokion G. Kolaitis, editors, *PODS 2002*, pages 53–64. ACM, 2002.

[32] Howard Straubing. *Finite Automata, Formal Logic, and Circuit Complexity.* Birkhäuser, Boston, 1994.

Variability in Data Streams

David Felber
UCLA
dvfelber@ucla.edu

Rafail Ostrovsky
UCLA
rafail@cs.ucla.edu

ABSTRACT

We consider the problem of tracking with small relative error an integer function $f(n)$ defined by a distributed update stream $f'(n)$ in the distributed monitoring model. In this model, there are k sites over which the updates $f'(n)$ are distributed, and they must communicate with a central coordinator to maintain an estimate of $f(n)$.

Existing streaming algorithms with worst-case guarantees for this problem assume $f(n)$ to be monotone; there are very large lower bounds on the space requirements for summarizing a distributed non-monotonic stream, often linear in the size n of the stream. However, the input streams obtaining these lower bounds are highly variable, making relatively large jumps from one timestep to the next; in practice, the impact on $f(n)$ of any single update $f'(n)$ is usually small. What has heretofore been lacking is a framework for non-monotonic streams that admits algorithms whose worst-case performance is as good as existing algorithms for monotone streams and degrades gracefully for non-monotonic streams as those streams vary more quickly.

In this paper we propose such a framework. We introduce a stream parameter, the "variability" v, deriving its definition in a way that shows it to be a natural parameter to consider for non-monotonic streams. It is also a useful parameter. From a theoretical perspective, we can adapt existing algorithms for monotone streams to work for non-monotonic streams, with only minor modifications, in such a way that they reduce to the monotone case when the stream happens to be monotone, and in such a way that we can refine the worst-case communication bounds from $\Theta(n)$ to $\tilde{O}(v)$. From a practical perspective, we demonstrate that v can be small in practice by proving that v is $O(\log f(n))$ for monotone streams and $o(n)$ for streams that are "nearly" monotone or that are generated by random walks. We expect v to be $o(n)$ for many other interesting input classes as well.

PODS '16, June 26–July 1, 2016, San Francisco, CA, USA.

DOI: http://dx.doi.org/10.1145/2902251.2902277

CCS Concepts

•**Theory of computation** → **Data structures and algorithms for data management;** *Sketching and sampling; Lower bounds and information complexity;* Streaming models; •**Information systems** → *Data streams;*

Keywords

data stream; non-monotonic stream; distributed monitoring model; tracking; counting; variability

1. INTRODUCTION

In the distributed monitoring model, there is a single central monitor and several (k) observers. The observers receive data and communicate with the monitor, and the goal is to maintain at the monitor a summary of the data received at the observers while minimizing the communication between them.

This model was introduced by Cormode, Muthukrishnan, and Yi [4, 5] with the motivating application of minimizing radio energy usage in sensor networks, but can be applied to other distributed applications like determining network traffic patterns. Since the monitor can retain all messages received, algorithms in the model can be used to answer historical queries too, making the model useful for auditing changes to and verifying the integrity of time-varying datasets.

The distributed monitoring model has also yielded several theoretical results. These include algorithms and lower bounds for tracking total count [4, 5, 10, 11], frequency moments [4, 5, 8, 14, 15], item frequencies [8, 14, 15, 16, 17], quantiles [8, 14, 15, 16, 17], and entropy [1, 14, 15] to small relative error.

However, nearly all of the upper bounds assumed that data is only inserted and never deleted. This assumption is unfortunate because in the standard turnstile streaming model, all of these problems have similar algorithms that permit both insertions and deletions. In general, this unfortunate assumption is unavoidable; existing lower bounds for the distributed model [1] demonstrate that it is not possible to track even the total item count in small space when data is permitted to be deleted.

That said, when restrictions are placed on the types of allowable input, the lower bounds evaporate, and very nice upper bounds exist. Tao, Yi, Sheng, Pei, and Li [13] developed algorithms for the problem of summarizing the order statistics history of a dataset D over an insertion/deletion stream of size n, which has an $\Omega(n)$-bit lower bound in general; however, they performed an interesting analysis that yielded online and offline upper bounds proportional to $\sum_{t=1}^{n} 1/|D(t)|$, with a nearly matching lower bound. A year or two later, Liu, Radunović, and Vojnović [10, 11] considered the problem of tracking $|D|$ under random inputs; for general inputs, there is an $\Omega(n)$-bit lower bound, but Liu et. al. obtained (among other results) expected communication costs proportional to $\sqrt{n}\log n$ when the insertion/deletion pattern is the result of fair coin flips.

In fact, the pessimistic lower bounds for the general case can occur only when the input stream is such that the quantity being tracked is forced to vary quickly. In the problems considered by Tao et. al. and Liu et. al., this occurs when $|D|$ is usually small. These two groups avoid this problem in two different ways: Tao et. al. provide an analysis that yields a worst-case upper bound that is small when $|D|$ is usually large, and Liu et. al. consider input classes for which $|D|$ is usually large in expectation.

Our contributions.

In this paper we propose a framework that extends the analysis of Tao et. al. to the distributed monitoring model and that permits worst-case analysis that can be specialized for random input classes considered by Liu et. al. In so doing, we explain the intuition behind the factor of $\sum_{t=1}^{n} 1/|D(t)|$ in the bounds of Tao et. al. and how we can separate the different sources of randomness that appear in the algorithms of Liu et. al. to obtain worst-case bounds for the random input classes we also consider.

In the next section we derive a stream parameter, the variability v, that is a function of the distributed update stream $f'(n)$. We prove that v is $O(\log f(n))$ for monotone streams and $o(n)$ for streams that are "nearly" monotone or that are generated by random walks, and find that the bounds of Tao et. al. and Liu et. al. are stated nicely in terms of v. In section 3 we combine ideas from the upper bounds of Tao et. al. [13] with the existing distributed counting algorithms of Cormode et. al. [4, 5] and Huang, Yi, and Zhang [8] to obtain upper bounds for distributed counting that are proportional to v. In section 4 we show that our dependence on v is essentially necessary by developing deterministic and randomized space+communication lower bounds that hold even when v is small. We round out the piece in section 5 with a discussion of the suitability of variability as a general framework, in which we extend the ideas of section 3 to the problems of distributed tracking of item frequencies and of tracking general aggregates when $k = 1$.

But before we jump into the derivation of variability, we define our problem formally and abstract away unessential details.

Problem definition.

The problem is that of tracking at the coordinator an integer function $f(n)$ defined by an update stream $f'(n)$ that arrives online at the sites. Time occurs in discrete steps; to be definite, the first timestep is 1, and we define $f(0) = 0$ unless stated otherwise. At each new current time n the value $f'(n) = f(n) - f(n-1)$ appears at a single site $i(n)$.

There is an error parameter ε that is specified at the start. The requirement is that, after each timestep n, the coordinator must have an estimate $\hat{f}(n)$ for $f(n)$ that is usually good. In particular, for deterministic algorithms we require that $\forall n,\ |f(n) - \hat{f}(n)| \le \varepsilon f(n)$, and for randomized algorithms we require that $\forall n,\ P(|f(n)-\hat{f}(n)| \le \varepsilon f(n)) \ge 2/3$.

2. VARIABILITY

In the original distributed monitoring paper [4], Cormode et. al. define a general thresholded problem $(k, f, \tau, \varepsilon)$. A dataset D arrives as a distributed stream across k sites. At any given point in time, the coordinator should be able to determine whether $f(D) \ge \tau$ or $f(D) \le (1-\varepsilon)\tau$.

In continuous tracking problems, there is no single threshold, and so $f(n)$ is tracked to within an additive $\varepsilon\tau(n)$, where $\tau(n)$ also changes with the dataset $D(n)$. Since τ is now a function, it needs to be defined; the usual choice is f itself, except for tracking item frequencies and order statistics, for which (following the standard streaming model) τ is chosen to be $|D|$. That is, the continuous monitoring problem (k, f, ε) is, at all times n maintain at the coordinator an estimate $\hat{f}(n)$ of $f(n)$ so that $|f(n)-\hat{f}(n)| \le \varepsilon f(n)$.

To define variability we use ideas implicit in the bounds of Tao et. al. to generalize the $\sum_{t=1}^{n} 1/|D(t)|$ term in those bounds to apply to arbitrary functions $f(n)$ of the dataset $D(n)$. The intuition behind our definition is as follows. We expect that we would need to communicate each time that f changes by $\pm\varepsilon f$. Further, at each timestep t we know that f changes by $f'(t)$. Therefore, at each timestep we should have $|\frac{f'(t)}{\varepsilon f(t)}|$ communication. In sum, we would expect the total number of messages to look like $\sum_{t=1}^{n} |\frac{f'(t)}{\varepsilon f(t)}|$. In sections 3 and 4 we find that, modulo the number k of sites and constant factors, this is indeed the case.

Being a parameter of the problem rather than the stream, we can move the $1/\varepsilon$ factor out of our definition of variability and bring it back in along with the appropriate functions of k when we state upper and lower bounds for our problem. This permits us to treat the stream parameter v independently of the problem. We also need to handle the case $f = 0$ specially, which we can do by communicating at each timestep that case occurs.

With all this in mind, we define the f-*variability* of a stream to be $v(n) = \sum_{t=1}^{n} \min\{1, |\frac{f'(t)}{f(t)}|\}$. We also write $v'(t) = \min\{1, |\frac{f'(t)}{f(t)}|\}$ to be the increase in variability at time t. We say "variability" for f-variability in the remainder of this paper.

From a practical perspective, we believe low variability streams to be common. In many database applications the database is interesting primarily because it tends to grow more than it shrinks, so it is common for the size of the dataset to have low variability; as more items are inserted, the rate of change of $|D|$ shrinks relative to itself, and about as many deletions as insertions would be required to keep the ratio constant. In the following subsection, we prove that monotone and nearly monotone functions have low variability and that random walks have low variability in expectation, lending evidence to our belief.

From a theoretical perspective, variability is a way to analyze algorithms for ε relative error in the face of non-monotonicity and generate provable worst-case bounds that degrade gracefully as our assumptions about the input become increasingly pessimistic. For our counting problem, it allows us to adapt the existing distributed counting algorithms of Cormode et. al. [4, 5] and Huang et. al. [8] with only minor modifications, and the resulting analyses show that the dependence on k and ε remains unchanged.

2.1 Interesting cases with small variability

We start with functions that are nearly monotone in the sense that they are eventually mostly nondecreasing. We make this precise in the theorem statement. Of course, since the $(-f)$-variability of a stream is equal to its f-variability, the result holds for functions that are eventually mostly nonincreasing as well.

THEOREM 2.1. *Let $f^-(n) = \sum_{t:f'(t)<0}^{n} |f'(t)|$ be the total of negative updates and $f^+(n) = \sum_{t:f'(t)>0}^{n} f'(t)$ be the total of positive updates, so that $f(n) = f^+(n) - f^-(n)$.*

If there is a monotone nondecreasing function $\beta(t) \geq 1$ and a constant t_0 such that for all $n \geq t_0$ we have that $f^-(n) \leq \beta(n)f(n)$, then the variability $\sum_{t=1}^{n} |f'(t)/f(t)|$ of the function is $O(\beta(n)\log(\beta(n)f(n)))$.

The proof, which we defer to appendix A, partitions time into intervals over which $f^+(t)$ doubles and shows the variability in each interval to be $O(\beta(n))$. When $f(n)$ is strictly monotone, $\beta(n) = 1$ suffices, and the theorem reduces to the result claimed in the abstract. As we will see in section 3, our upper bounds will simplify in the monotone case to those of Cormode et. al. [4, 5] and Huang et. al. [8].

Next, we compute the variability for two random input classes considered by Liu et. al. [10, 11]. This will permit us to decouple the randomness of their algorithms from the randomness of their inputs. This means, for example, that even our deterministic algorithm of section 3 has $o(n)$ cost in expectation for these input classes. The first random input class we consider is the symmetric random walk.

THEOREM 2.2. *If $f'(t)$ is a stream of i.i.d. ± 1 coin flips then the expected variability $E(v(n)) = O(\sqrt{n}\log n)$.*

PROOF. The update sequence defines a random walk for $f(t)$, and the expected variability is

$$\sum_{t=1}^{n} P(f(t)=0) + \sum_{t=1}^{n}\sum_{s=1}^{t} 2P(f(t)=s)/s$$

We use the following fact, mentioned and justified in Liu et. al. [10]:

FACT 2.3. *For any $t \geq 1$ and $s \in [-t, t]$ we have that $P(f(t)=s) \leq c_1/\sqrt{t}$, where c_1 is some constant.*

Together, these show the expected cost to be at most

$$c_1 \sum_{t=1}^{n} (1 + 2H_t)/\sqrt{t} \;\leq\; c_2 \log(n) \sum_{t=1}^{n} 1/\sqrt{t} \;\leq\; c_3 \log(n)\sqrt{n}$$

since $(1+2H_n) \leq \frac{c_2}{c_1}\log(n)$ and $\sum_{t=1}^{n} \frac{1}{\sqrt{t}} \leq \frac{c_3}{2c_2}\int_1^n \frac{1}{\sqrt{t}}\,dt$. □

The second random input class we consider is i.i.d. increments with a common drift rate of $\mu > 0$. The case $\mu < 0$ is symmetric. We assume that μ is constant with respect to n. The proof is a simple application of Chernoff bounds and is deferred to appendix B.

THEOREM 2.4. *If $f'(t)$ is a sequence of i.i.d. ± 1 random variables with $P(f'(t) = 1) = (1 + \mu)/2$ then the expected variability $E(v(n)) = O(\frac{\log n}{\mu})$.*

Remarks.

We can restate the results of Liu et. al. [10, 11] and Tao et. al. [13] in terms of variability. For unbiased coin flips, Liu et. al. obtain an algorithm that uses $O(\frac{\sqrt{k}}{\varepsilon}\sqrt{n}\log n)$ messages (of size $O(\log n)$ bits each) in expectation, and for biased coin flips with constant μ, an algorithm that uses $O(\frac{\sqrt{k}}{\varepsilon}\frac{1}{|\mu|}(\log n)^{1+c})$ messages in expectation. If we rewrite these bounds in terms of expected variability, they become $O(\frac{\sqrt{k}}{\varepsilon}E(v(n)))$ and $O(\frac{\sqrt{k}}{\varepsilon}(\log n)^c E(v(n)))$, respectively. In the next section, we obtain (when $k = O(1/\varepsilon^2)$) a randomized bound of $O(\frac{\sqrt{k}}{\varepsilon}v(n))$. In marked contrast to the bounds of Liu et. al., our bound is a worst-case lower bound that is a function of $v(n)$; if the input happens to be generated by fair coin flips, then our expected cost happens to be $O(\frac{\sqrt{k}}{\varepsilon}\sqrt{n}\log n)$.

The results of Tao et. al. are for a different setting, but having used them as a starting point for our definition of variability we can restate their bounds terms of the $|D|$-variability $v(n)$: for the problem of tracking the historical record of order statistics, they obtain a lower bound of $\Omega(\frac{1}{\varepsilon}v(n))$, an offline upper bound of $O((\frac{1}{\varepsilon}\log^2\frac{1}{\varepsilon})v(n))$, and an online upper bound of $O(\frac{1}{\varepsilon^2}v(n))$. We adapt ideas from both their upper and lower bounds in sections 3 and 4.

3. UPPER BOUNDS

In this section we develop deterministic and randomized algorithms for maintaining at the coordinator an estimate $\hat{f}(n)$ for $f(n)$ that is usually good. In particular, for deterministic algorithms we require the deterministic guarantee that $\forall n$, $|f(n) - \hat{f}(n)| \leq \varepsilon f(n)$, and for randomized algorithms we require the probabilistic guarantee that $\forall n$, $P(|f(n)-\hat{f}(n)| \leq \varepsilon f(n)) \geq 2/3$. We obtain deterministic and randomized upper bounds of $O(\frac{k}{\varepsilon}v(n))$ and $O((k+\frac{\sqrt{k}}{\varepsilon})v(n))$ messages, respectively. For comparison, the analogous algorithms of Cormode et. al. [4, 5] and Huang et. al. [8] for the monotone case use $O(\frac{k}{\varepsilon}\log n)$ and $O((k+\frac{\sqrt{k}}{\varepsilon})\log n)$ messages, respectively.

For our upper bounds we assume that $f'(n)$ is always ± 1. If $|f'(n)| > 1$ we could simulate it with $|f'(n)|$ arrivals of ± 1 updates with $O(\log \max f'(n))$ overhead, as shown in appendix C.

3.1 Partitioning time

We use an idea from Tao et. al. [13] to first divide time into manageable blocks. At the end of each block we know the values n and $f(n)$ exactly. Within each block, we know these values only approximately. The division into blocks is deterministic and the same for both our deterministic and randomized algorithms. Our division ensures that the change in $v(n)$ over each block is at least $1/5$, which simplifies our analysis. Specifically, we prove

THEOREM 3.1. *There is an algorithm to divide time into blocks $B_0, B_1, \ldots$, where $B_j = [n_j+1, n_{j+1}]$, such that $n_0=0$, the change $v_j = v(n_{j+1})-v(n_j)$ in variability over each block B_j is at least $1/5$, the value $f(n)$ within block B_j differs from its start value $f(n_j)$ by no more than $\max\{\frac{5}{2}|f(n_j)|, k\}$, and the partitioning algorithm uses at most $25kv + 3k$ messages of size $O(\log n)$ bits each.*

The algorithm is as follows. A precise pseudocode description appears in appendix D.

- The coordinator requests the sites' values c_i and f_i at times $n_0=0, n_1, n_2, \ldots$ and then broadcasts a value r. These values will be defined momentarily.
- Each site i maintains a variable c_i that counts the number of stream updates $f'(n)$ it received since the last time it sent c_i to the coordinator. It also maintains f_i that counts the change in f it received since the last broadcast n_j. Whenever $c_i = \lceil 2^{r-1} \rceil$, site i sends c_i to the coordinator. This is in addition to replying to requests from the coordinator.
- The coordinator maintains a variable $\hat{t}$. After broadcasting r, $\hat{t}$ is reset to zero. Whenever site i sends c_i, the coordinator updates $\hat{t} = \hat{t} + c_i$ and $n_j = n_j + c_i$.
- The coordinator also maintains variables $\hat{f}$, j, and t_j. At the first time $n_j > n_{j-1}$ at which $\hat{t} \geq t_j$, the coordinator requests the c_i and f_i values, updates $\hat{f}$ and r, sets $t_{j+1} = \lceil 2^{r-1} \rceil k$, broadcasts r, and increments j.
- When r is updated at the end of time n_j, it is set to r if $2^r 2k \leq |f(n_j)| < 2^r 4k$ and zero if $|f(n_j)| < 4k$.

PROOF. Algebra tells us some facts:

- $\lceil 2^{r-1} \rceil k \leq n_{j+1} - n_j \leq 2^r k$.
- $|f(n) - f(n_j)| \leq 2^r 5k$ for all n in B_j.
- If $r \geq 1$ then $|f(n) - f(n_j)| \geq 2^r k$ for all n in B_j.

The total number of messages sent in block B_j is at most $5k$: we have at most $2k$ updates from sites, k requests from the coordinator, k replies from each site, and k broadcast at n_{j+1}.

The change in variability v_j over block B_j is

$$v_j = \sum_{t=n_j+1}^{n_{j+1}} \frac{1}{\min\{1, |f(t)|\}} \geq 2^r k / 2^r 5k \geq 1/5$$

And therefore the total number of messages is bounded by $25kv + 3k$. □

3.2 Estimation inside blocks

What remains is to estimate $f(n)$ within a given block, which we do by adapting the existing monotone algorithms of Cormode et. al. [4, 5] and Huang et. al. [8] to positive and negative updates within a block. Both our deterministic and randomized algorithms use the following template, changing only CONDITION, MESSAGE, and UPDATE:

- Site i maintains a variable d_i that tracks the drift at site i, defined as the sum of $f'(n)$ updates received at site i during the block. That is, $f(n) - f(n_j) = \sum_i d_i$.
- Site i also maintains a variable δ_i that tracks the change in d_i since the last time site i sent a MESSAGE. δ_i is initially zero.
- The coordinator maintains an estimate $\hat{d}_i$ for each value d_i. These are initially zero. It also defines two estimates based on these $\hat{d}_i$:
  - For the global drift: $\hat{d} = \sum_i \hat{d}_i$.
  - For $f(n)$: $\hat{f}(n) = f(n_j) + \hat{d}(n)$.
- When site i receives stream update $f'(n)$, it updates d_i. It then checks its CONDITION. If true, it sends a MESSAGE to the coordinator and resets $\delta_i = 0$.
- When the coordinator receives a MESSAGE from a site i it UPDATEs its estimates.

3.3 The deterministic algorithm

Our method guarantees that $|f(n) - \hat{f}(n)| \leq \varepsilon |f(n)|$ holds at all times n. It uses $O(kv/\varepsilon)$ messages in total. In the following, r is the value of r for the current block.

- CONDITION: true if $|\delta_i| = 1$ and $r = 0$, or if $|\delta_i| \geq \varepsilon 2^r$. Otherwise, false.
- MESSAGE: the new value of d_i.
- UPDATE: set $\hat{d}_i = d_i$.

PROOF. Let $\delta = \sum_i \delta_i$ be the error with which $\hat{d}$ estimates $d = \sum_i d_i$. The error in $\hat{f}$ is

$$\begin{aligned} |f(n) - \hat{f}(n)| &= |(f(n_j) + d(n)) - (\hat{f}(n_j) + d(n) + \delta(n))| \\ &= |\delta(n)| \end{aligned}$$

When $r \geq 1$ we have $|B_j| \leq 2^r k$, and we always have that $\delta \leq |B_j|$. Since we constrain $\delta_i < \varepsilon 2^r$ at the end of each timestep, we have $|f(n) - \hat{f}(n)| < \varepsilon 2^r k \leq \varepsilon |f(n)|$.

We also use at most $2k/\varepsilon$ messages for the block. If $r = 0$ then the number of messages is at most k. If $r \geq 1$, then since a site must receive $\varepsilon 2^r$ new stream updates to send a new message, and since there are at most $2^r k$ stream updates in the block, there are at most k/ε messages.

In each block the change in v is at least $1/5$, so the total number of messages is at most $5kv/\varepsilon$. □

3.4 The randomized algorithm

Our method uses $O(\sqrt{k}v/\varepsilon)$ messages (plus the time partitioning) and guarantees $P(|f(n) - \hat{f}(n)| > \varepsilon |f(n)|) < 1/3$ holds for all times n.

The idea is to estimate the sums d_i^+ and d_i^- of $+1$ and -1 updates separately. The estimators for those values are independent and monotone, so we can use the method of Huang et. al. [8] to estimate the two and then combine them.

Specifically, the coordinator and each site run two independent copies A^+ and A^- of the algorithm. Whenever $f'(n) = +1$ arrives at site i, a $+1$ is fed into algorithm A^+ at site i. Whenever $f'(n) = -1$ arrives at site i, a $+1$ is fed into algorithm A^- at site i. So the drifts d_i^+ and d_i^- at every site will always be nonnegative. At the coordinator, the estimates $\hat{d}_i^\pm$ and $\hat{d}^\pm$ are tracked independently also. However, the coordinator also defines $\hat{d} = \hat{d}^+ - \hat{d}^-$ and $\hat{f}(n) = f(n_j) + \hat{d}(n)$. The definitions for algorithm $A^\pm$ are

- CONDITION: true with probability $p = \min\{1, \frac{3}{\varepsilon 2^r k^{1/2}}\}$.
- MESSAGE: the new value of $d_i^\pm$.
- UPDATE: set $\hat{d}_i^\pm = d_i^\pm - 1 + 1/p$.

PROOF. The following fact 3.2 is lemma 2.1 of Huang et. al. [8]. For each block B_j our algorithm effectively divides the stream $f'(B_j)$ into two streams $|f'(B_j^\pm)|$. Since these streams consist of $+1$ increments only we run the algorithm of Huang et. al. separately on each of them. At any time n, stream $|f'(B_j^\pm)|$ has seen $d_i^\pm(n)$ increments at site i, and lemma 2.1 of Huang et. al. guarantees that the estimates $\hat{d}_i^\pm(n)$ for the counts $d_i^\pm(n)$ are good.

FACT 3.2. *$E(\hat{d}_i^\pm) = d_i^\pm$ and $Var(\hat{d}_i^\pm) \leq 1/p^2$.*

This means that $E(\hat{d}^\pm) = \sum_i E(\hat{d}_i^\pm) = \sum_i d_i^\pm$, and therefore that $E(\hat{d}) = \sum_i E(d_i^+ - d_i^-) = \sum_i d_i$. Since the estimators

$\hat{d}_i^{\pm}$ are independent, the variance of the global drift is at most $2k/p^2$. By Chebyshev's inequality,

$$P(|\delta(n)| > \varepsilon 2^r k) \leq \frac{2k/p^2}{(\varepsilon 2^r k)^2} < 1/3$$

Further, the expected cost of block B_j is bounded above by $p|B_j| \leq (3/\varepsilon 2^r k^{1/2})(2^r 2k) \leq 30k^{1/2} v_j/\varepsilon$. □

4. LOWER BOUNDS

In this section we show that the dependence on v is essentially necessary by developing deterministic and randomized lower bounds on space+communication that hold even when v is small. Admittedly, this is not as pleasing as a pure communication lower bound would be. On the other hand, a distributed monitoring algorithm with high space complexity would be impractical for monitoring sensor data, network traffic patterns, and other applications of the model. Note that in terms of space+communication, our deterministic lower bound is tight up to factors of k, and our randomized lower bound is within a factor of $\log(n)$ of that.

For these lower bounds we use a slightly different problem. We call this problem the tracing problem. The streaming model for the tracing problem is the standard turnstile streaming model with updates $f'(n)$ arriving online. The problem is to maintain in small space a summary of the sequence f so that, at any current time n, if we are given an earlier time t as a query, we can return an estimate $\hat{f}(t)$ so that $P(|f(t)-\hat{f}(t)| \leq \varepsilon f(t))$ is large (one in the deterministic case, 2/3 in the randomized case). We call this the tracing problem because our summary traces f through time, so that we can look up earlier values.

In appendix E we show that a space lower bound for the tracing problem implies a space+communication lower bound for the distributed tracking problem. Here, we develop deterministic and randomized space lower bounds for the tracing problem.

4.1 The deterministic bound

The deterministic lower bound that follows is similar in spirit to the lower bound of Tao et. al. [13]. It uses a simple information-theoretic argument.

THEOREM 4.1. *Let $\varepsilon = 1/m$ for some integer $m \geq 2$, let $n \geq 2m$, let $c < 1$ constant, and let $r \leq n^c$ and even. If a deterministic summary $S(f)$ guarantees for all $t \leq n$ that $|f(t) - \hat{f}(t)| \leq \varepsilon f(t)$, even only for sequences for which $v(n) = \frac{6m+9}{2m+6}\varepsilon r$, then that summary must use $\Omega(\frac{\log n}{\varepsilon} v(n))$ bits of space.*

The full proof appears in appendix F. At a high level, the sequences in the family take only values m or $m+3$, and each sequence is defined by r of the n timesteps. If the new timestep t is one of the r chosen for our sequence, then we flip from m to $m+3$ or vice-versa. All of these sequences are unique and there are $2^{\Omega(r \log n)}$ of them.

4.2 The randomized bound

We use a construction similar to the one in our deterministic lower bound to produce a randomized lower bound. In order to make the analysis simple we forego a single variability value for all sequences in our constructed family, but still maintain that they all have low variability. C is a universal constant to be defined later.

THEOREM 4.2. *Choose $\varepsilon \leq 1/2$, $v \geq 32400\varepsilon \ln C$, and $n > 3v/\varepsilon$. If a summary $S(f)$ guarantees for all $t \leq n$ that $P(|f(t) - \hat{f}(t)| \leq \varepsilon f(t)) \geq 99/100$, even only for sequences for which $v(n) \leq v$, then that summary must use $\Omega(v/\varepsilon)$ bits of space.*

We prove this theorem in two lemmas. In the first lemma, we reduce the claim to a claim about the existence of a hard family of sequences. In the second lemma we show the existence of such a family.

First a couple of definitions. For any two sequences f and g define the *number of overlaps between f and g* to be the number of positions $1 \leq t \leq n$ for which

$$|f(t) - g(t)| \leq \varepsilon \max\{f(t), g(t)\}$$

Say that f and g *match* if they have at least $\frac{6}{10}n$ overlaps.

LEMMA 4.3. *Let $\mathcal{F}$ be a family of sequences of length n and variabilities $\leq v$ such that no two sequences in $\mathcal{F}$ match. If a summary $S(f)$ guarantees for all f in $\mathcal{F}$ and all $t \leq n$ that $P(|f(t) - \hat{f}(t)| \leq \varepsilon f(t)) \geq 99/100$, then that summary must use $\Omega(\log |\mathcal{F}|)$ bits of space.*

The full proof appears in appendix G. At a high level, if $S(f)$ is the summary for a sequence f, we can use it to generate an approximation $\hat{f}$ that at least 90% of the time overlaps with f in at least $\frac{9}{10}n$ positions. Since no two sequences in $\mathcal{F}$ overlap in more than $\frac{6}{10}n$ positions, at least 90% of the time we can determine f given $\hat{f}$. We then solve the one-way Index_N problem by deterministically generating $\mathcal{F}$ and sending a summary $S(f(x))$, where x is Alice's input of size $N = \log_2 |\mathcal{F}|$, and $f(x)$ is the xth sequence in $\mathcal{F}$.

LEMMA 4.4. *For all $\varepsilon \leq 1/2$, all $v \geq 32400\varepsilon \ln C$, and all $n > 3v/\varepsilon$, there is a family $\mathcal{F}$ of size $e^{\Omega(v/\varepsilon)}$ of sequences of size n such that no two sequences match and every sequence has variability at most v.*

The full proof appears in appendix H. At a high level, sequences again switch between $m = 1/\varepsilon$ and $m+3$, except that these switches are chosen independently. We model the overlap with a Markov chain; the overlap between any two sequences is the sum over times t of a function y applied to the states of a chain modeling their interaction. We then apply a result of Chung, Lam, Liu, and Mitzenmacher [2] to show that the probability that any two sequences match is low. Lastly, we show that not too many sequences have variability more than v, by proving that they usually don't switch between m and $m+3$ many times.

5. VARIABILITY AS A FRAMEWORK

In section 2 we proposed f-variability as a way to analyze algorithms for the continuous monitoring problem (k, f, ε) over general update streams. However, our discussion so far has focused on distributed counting. In this final section we revisit the suitability of our definition by mentioning extensions to tracking other functions of a dataset defined by a distributed update stream. We include fuller discussions of these extensions in the appendices.

5.1 Tracking item frequencies

We can extend our deterministic algorithm of section 3 to the problem of tracking item frequencies, in a manner similar to that in which Yi and Zhang [16, 17] extend the ideas of Cormode et. al. [4] to this problem. The definition of this problem, the required changes to our algorithm of section 3 needed to solve it, and a discussion of the difficulties in finding a randomized algorithm, are discussed in appendix I.

5.2 Aggregate functions with one site

In this subsection we consider general single-integer-valued functions f of a dataset, including highly non-linear functions such as high-order frequency moments. When there is a single site, the site always knows the exact value of $f(n)$, and the only issue is updating the coordinator to have an approximation $\hat{f}(n)$ so that $|f(n) - \hat{f}(n)| \leq \varepsilon f(n)$ for all n. We can show that this problem of tracking f to ε relative error when $k = 1$ has an $O(\frac{1}{\varepsilon}v(n))$-word upper bound, where here $v(n)$ is the f-variability. The algorithm is: whenever $|f - \hat{f}| > \varepsilon f$, send f to the coordinator. The proof is a simple potential argument and is deferred to appendix J. Along with our lower bounds of section 4, this upper bound lends evidence to our claim that variability captures some or all of the difficulty of communicating changes in general functions f that are due to the non-monotonicity of the input stream.

Acknowledgments

We thank the anonymous reviewers for their many useful comments and suggestions.

Research supported in part by NSF grants CCF-0916574; IIS-1065276; CCF-1016540; CNS-1118126; CNS-1136174; US-Israel BSF grant 2008411, OKAWA Foundation Research Award, IBM Faculty Research Award, Xerox Faculty Research Award, B. John Garrick Foundation Award, Teradata Research Award, and Lockheed-Martin Corporation Research Award. This material is also based upon work supported by the Defense Advanced Research Projects Agency through the U.S. Office of Naval Research under Contract N00014-11-1-0392. The views expressed are those of the author and do not reflect the official policy or position of the Department of Defense or the U.S. Government.

6. REFERENCES

[1] C. Arackaparambil, J. Brody, and A. Chakrabarti. Functional monitoring without monotonicity. In *Automata, Languages and Programming*, pages 95–106. Springer, 2009.

[2] K.-M. Chung, H. Lam, Z. Liu, and M. Mitzenmacher. Chernoff-hoeffding bounds for markov chains: Generalized and simplified. *arXiv preprint arXiv:1201.0559*, 2012.

[3] G. Cormode and S. Muthukrishnan. An improved data stream summary: the count-min sketch and its applications. *Journal of Algorithms*, 55(1):58 – 75, 2005.

[4] G. Cormode, S. Muthukrishnan, and K. Yi. Algorithms for distributed functional monitoring. In *Proceedings of the Nineteenth Annual ACM-SIAM Symposium on Discrete Algorithms*, SODA '08, pages 1076–1085, Philadelphia, PA, USA, 2008. Society for Industrial and Applied Mathematics.

[5] G. Cormode, S. Muthukrishnan, and K. Yi. Algorithms for distributed functional monitoring. *ACM Transactions on Algorithms (TALG)*, 7(2):21, 2011.

[6] S. Ganguly and A. Majumder. Cr-precis: A deterministic summary structure for update data streams. *CoRR*, abs/cs/0609032, 2006.

[7] S. Ganguly and A. Majumder. Cr-precis: A deterministic summary structure for update data streams. In B. Chen, M. Paterson, and G. Zhang, editors, *Combinatorics, Algorithms, Probabilistic and Experimental Methodologies*, volume 4614 of *Lecture Notes in Computer Science*, pages 48–59. Springer Berlin Heidelberg, 2007.

[8] Z. Huang, K. Yi, and Q. Zhang. Randomized algorithms for tracking distributed count, frequencies, and ranks. In *Proceedings of the 31st symposium on Principles of Database Systems*, pages 295–306. ACM, 2012.

[9] E. Kushilevitz and N. Nisan. *Communication Complexity*. Cambridge University Press, New York, NY, USA, 1997.

[10] Z. Liu, B. Radunović, and M. Vojnović. Continuous distributed counting for non-monotonic streams. In *Technical Report MSR-TR-2011-128*, 2011.

[11] Z. Liu, B. Radunović, and M. Vojnović. Continuous distributed counting for non-monotonic streams. In *Proceedings of the 31st symposium on Principles of Database Systems*, pages 307–318. ACM, 2012.

[12] S. Muthukrishnan. *Data streams: Algorithms and applications*. Now Publishers Inc, 2005.

[13] Y. Tao, K. Yi, C. Sheng, J. Pei, and F. Li. Logging every footstep: quantile summaries for the entire history. In *Proceedings of the 2010 ACM SIGMOD International Conference on Management of data*, SIGMOD '10, pages 639–650, New York, NY, USA, 2010. ACM.

[14] D. P. Woodruff and Q. Zhang. Tight bounds for distributed functional monitoring. *CoRR*, abs/1112.5153, 2011.

[15] D. P. Woodruff and Q. Zhang. Tight bounds for distributed functional monitoring. In *Proceedings of the 44th symposium on Theory of Computing*, pages 941–960. ACM, 2012.

[16] K. Yi and Q. Zhang. Optimal tracking of distributed heavy hitters and quantiles. In *Proceedings of the Twenty-eighth ACM SIGMOD-SIGACT-SIGART Symposium on Principles of Database Systems*, PODS '09, pages 167–174, New York, NY, USA, 2009. ACM.

[17] K. Yi and Q. Zhang. Optimal tracking of distributed heavy hitters and quantiles. *Algorithmica*, 65(1):206–223, 2013.

APPENDIX

A. VARIABILITY OF NEARLY MONOTONE FUNCTIONS, THEOREM 2.1

THEOREM A.1. *Let $f^-(n) = \sum_{t:f'(t)<0}^{n} |f'(t)|$ be the total of negative updates and $f^+(n) = \sum_{t:f'(t)>0}^{n} f'(t)$ be the total of positive updates, so that $f(n) = f^+(n) - f^-(n)$.*

If there is a monotone nondecreasing function $\beta(t) \geq 1$ and a constant t_0 such that for all $n \geq t_0$ we have that $f^-(n) \leq \beta(n) f(n)$, then the variability $\sum_{t=1}^{n} |f'(t)/f(t)|$ of the function is $O(\beta(n)\log(\beta(n)f(n)))$.

PROOF. Note that $f^-(n) \leq \beta(n)f(n)$ and $\beta(n) \geq 1$ imply that $f(n) \geq 0$. For $i = 1, \ldots, k$, define t_i to be the earliest time t such that $f^+(t_i) > 2f^+(t_{i-1})$, where k is the smallest index such that $t_k > n$. (If k is undefined, define $k = n+1$.)

The cost $\sum_{t=1}^{t_0-1} |f'(t)/f(t)|$ is constant. We bound the cost $\sum_{t=t_0}^{n} |f'(t)|/f(t)$ as follows. We partition the interval $[t_0, t_k)$ into subintervals $[t_0, t_1), \ldots, [t_{k-1}, t_k)$ and sum over the times t in each one. There are at most $1 + \log f^+(n)$ of these subintervals.

$$\begin{aligned}
\sum_{t=t_0}^{n} \frac{|f'(t)|}{f(t)} &\leq \sum_{i=1}^{k} \sum_{t=t_{i-1}}^{t_i-1} \frac{|f'(t)|}{f(t)} \\
&\leq \sum_{i=1}^{k} \frac{1+\beta(n)}{f^+(t_{i-1})} \sum_{t=t_{i-1}}^{t_i-1} |f'(t)| \\
&\leq \sum_{i=1}^{k} (1+\beta(n)) \frac{f^+(t_i-1) + f^-(t_i-1)}{f^+(t_{i-1})} \\
&\leq 4(1+\beta(n))(1+\log f^+(t_i-1)) \\
&\leq 4(1+\beta(n))(1+\log(2(1+\beta(n))f(n)))
\end{aligned}$$

where the second inequality follows from

$$f^+(t) = f(t) + f^-(t) \leq (1+\beta(n))f(t)$$

and the fourth holds because

$$f^+(t_i - 1) + f^-(t_i - 1) \leq 2f^+(t_i - 1)$$

(because $f(t) \geq 0$ implies $f^+(t) \geq f^-(t)$). □

B. VARIABILITY OF BIASED COIN FLIPS, THEOREM 2.4

THEOREM B.1. *If $f'(t)$ is a sequence of i.i.d. ± 1 random variables with $P(f'(t) = 1) = (1+\mu)/2$ then the expected variability $E(v(n)) = O(\frac{\log n}{\mu})$.*

PROOF. We show that, with high probability, $f(t) \geq \mu t/2$ for times $t \geq t_0 = t_0(n)$ when n is large enough with respect to μ.

We write $f(t) = -t + 2Y_t$, where $Y_t = \sum_{s=1}^{t} y_s$, and y_s is a Bernoulli variable with mean $\frac{1+\mu}{2}$. We have that $P(f(t) \leq \mu t/2) = P(Y_t \leq \frac{2+\mu}{4}t)$ and that $E(Y_t) = \frac{1+\mu}{2}t$. Further, $P(Y_t \leq \frac{2+\mu}{4}t) \leq \exp(-\mu t/16)$ using a Chernoff bound. Let A be the event $\exists t \geq t_0\, (f(t) \leq \mu t/2)$. Then $P(A) \leq \sum_{t=t_0}^{n} e^{-\mu t/16}$ by the union bound. We can upper bound this sum by

$$\sum_{t=t_0}^{n} e^{-\mu t/16} \leq e^{-\mu t_0/16} + \int_{t_0}^{n} e^{-\mu t/16}\, dt \leq 17e^{-\mu t_0/16}/\mu$$

Taking $t_0 = (16/\mu)\ln(17n/\mu)$ gives us $P(A) \leq 1/n$. Thus

$$E\left(\sum_{t=1}^{n} \min\left\{1, \left|\frac{f'(t)}{f(t)}\right|\right\}\right)$$

$$\leq t_0 + \left(\frac{1}{n}\right)n + \left(1 - \frac{1}{n}\right)\sum_{t=t_0}^{n} \frac{2}{\mu t}$$

$= O\left(\frac{\log n}{\mu}\right)$, yielding the theorem. □

C. SIMULATING LARGE UPDATES, SECTION 3

We noted in section 3 that we can simulate $|f'(n)| > 1$ with $|f'(n)|$ arrivals of ± 1 updates with $O(\log \max f'(n))$ overhead. To simplify notation we define $1/f(n) = 1$ when $f(n) = 0$ and assume that $f(n) \geq 0$ always.

THEOREM C.1. *$\sum_{t=1}^{f'(n)} \frac{1}{f(n-1)+t} \leq \frac{f'(n)}{f(n)} H(f'(n))$ when $f'(n) > 1$ and $\sum_{t=0}^{-1-f'(n)} \frac{1}{f(n)+t} \leq \frac{|f'(n)|}{f(n)}$ when $f'(n) < -1$, where $H(x)$ is the xth harmonic number.*

PROOF. If $f'(n) > 1$, then

$$\begin{aligned}
\sum_{t=1}^{f'(n)} \frac{1}{f(n-1)+t} &= \frac{1}{f(n)} \sum_{t=1}^{f'(n)} \frac{f(n-1)+f'(n)}{f(n-1)+t} \\
&\leq \frac{1}{f(n)} \sum_{t=1}^{f'(n)} \frac{f'(n)}{t}
\end{aligned}$$

If $f'(n) < -1$ and $f(n) \geq 1$, then

$$\sum_{t=0}^{-1-f'(n)} \frac{1}{f(n)+t} \leq \sum_{t=0}^{-1-f'(n)} \frac{1}{f(n)} = \frac{|f'(n)|}{f(n)}$$

and if $f(n) = 0$ we have $\frac{|f'(n)|}{f(n)} = |f'(n)| \cdot (1/f(n))$. □

D. BLOCK ALGORITHM, THEOREM 3.1

The algorithm of theorem 3.1 that divides time into blocks has two unique processes, one that runs at the coordinator and one that runs at each of the k sites. Implicit assumptions of the model are that all of the initialization occurs prior to receiving any stream items, and that no stream items arrive while communication occurs.

The following algorithm, figure 1, is a precise pseudocode description of the coordinator process.

Initialize $j = 0$, $n_j = 0$, $t_{j+1} = k$, $\hat{t} = 0$, $\hat{f} = 0$, and $r = 0$.
Request sites' values c_i and f_i, and broadcast r.
on *receiving c_i from site i* **do**
  Update $\hat{t} = \hat{t} + c_i$ and $n_j = n_j + c_i$.
  if $\hat{t} \geq t_{j+1}$ **then**
    Increment j.
    Request sites' values c_i and f_i.
    Update $\hat{f} = \hat{f} + \sum_{i=1}^{k} f_i$. *(Now, $\hat{f} = f$.)*
    Update $n_j = n_j + \sum_{i=1}^{k} c_i$. *(Now, $n_j = n$.)*
    if $|f(n_j)| < 4k$ **then**
      Update $r = 0$.
    else
      Update $r = \lfloor \log_2(|f(n_j)|/2k) \rfloor$.
        (Now, $2^r 2k \leq |f(n_j)| < 2^r 4k$.)
    Set $t_{j+1} = \lceil 2^{r-1} \rceil k$.
    Broadcast r.

Figure 1: Coordinator process for algorithm of theorem 3.1.

The following algorithm, figure 2, is a precise pseudocode description of the process running at site i.

Initialize $c_i = 0$, $f_i = 0$, and $r = 0$.
on *receiving an update* $f'(n)$ **do**
  Update $c_i = c_i + 1$ and $f_i = f_i + f'(n)$.
  if $c_i = \lceil 2^{r-1} \rceil$ **then**
    Send c_i to the coordinator and reset $c_i = 0$.
on *receiving a request from the coordinator* **do**
  Send the coordinator c_i and f_i.
on *receiving a broadcast r from the coordinator* **do**
  Update r to the broadcasted value.
  Reset $c_i = 0$ and $f_i = 0$.

Figure 2: Site i process for algorithm of theorem 3.1.

E. REDUCING DISTRIBUTED TRACKING TO TRACING, SECTION 4

LEMMA E.1. *Fix some ε. Suppose that the tracing problem has an $\Omega(L_\varepsilon(n))$-bit space deterministic lower bound. Also suppose that there is a deterministic algorithm A for the distributed tracking problem that uses $C_\varepsilon(n)$ bits of communication and $S_\varepsilon(n)$ bits of space at the site and coordinator combined. Then we must have $C + S = \Omega(L)$.*

Further, if we replace "deterministic" with "randomized" in the preceding paragraph, the claim still holds.

PROOF. Toward a contradiction, suppose that for all constants $c < 1$ and all n_0 there is an $n > n_0$ such that $C(n) + S(n) < cL(n)$. Then we can write an algorithm B for the tracing problem that uses $L'(n) < cL(n)$ bits of space: simulate A, recording all communication, and on a query t, play back the communication that occurred through time t.

At no point did we use the fact that A guarantees that $P(|f(t) - \hat{f}(t)| \leq \varepsilon f(t)) = 1$, so the claim still holds if we change the correctness requirement to $P \geq 2/3$. □

F. DETERMINISTIC LOWER BOUND, THEOREM 4.1

THEOREM F.1. *Let $\varepsilon = 1/m$ for some integer $m \geq 2$, let $n \geq 2m$, let $c < 1$ constant, and let $r \leq n^c$ and even. If a deterministic summary $S(f)$ guarantees for all $t \leq n$ that $|f(t) - \hat{f}(t)| \leq \varepsilon f(t)$, even only for sequences for which $v(n) = \frac{6m+9}{2m+6}\varepsilon r$, then that summary must use $\Omega(\frac{\log n}{\varepsilon} v(n))$ bits of space.*

PROOF. We construct a family of input sequences of length n and variability $\frac{6m+9}{2m+6}\varepsilon r$. Choose sets of r different indices $1 \ldots n$ so that there are choose(n, r) such sets.

For each set S we define an input sequence f_S. We define $f_S(0) = m$ and the rest of f_S recursively: $f_S(t) = f_S(t-1)$ if t is not in S, and $f_S(t) = (2m + 3) - f_S(t-1)$ if t is in S. (That is, switch between m and $m + 3$.)

If A and B are two different sets, then $f_A \neq f_B$: let i be the smallest index that is in one and not the other; say i is in A. Then $f_A(1 \ldots (i-1)) = f_B(1 \ldots (i-1))$, but $f_A(i) \neq f_A(i-1) = f_B(i-1) = f_B(i)$.

The variability of any f_S is $\frac{6m+9}{2m+6}\varepsilon r$: There are $r/2$ changes from m to $m+3$ and another $r/2$ from $m+3$ to m. When we switch from m to $m+3$, we get $|f'(t)/f(t)| = 3/(m+3)$, and when we switch from $m+3$ to m, we get $|f'(t)/f(t)| = 3/m$. Thus $\sum_t |\frac{f'(t)}{f(t)}| = \frac{r}{2}\frac{6m+9}{m(m+3)} = \frac{6m+9}{2m+6}\varepsilon r$.

There are choose$(n, r) \geq (n/r)^r$ input sequences in our family, so to distinguish between any two input sequences we need at least $r \log(n/r) = \Omega(r \log n)$ bits. Any summary that can determine for each t the value $f(t)$ to within $\pm\varepsilon f(t)$, must also distinguish between $f(t) = m$ and $f(t) = m + 3$, since there is no value within εm of m that is also within $\varepsilon(m + 3)$ of $m + 3$. Since this summary must distinguish between $f(t) = m$ and $f(t) = m + 3$ for all t, it must distinguish between any two input sequences in the family, and therefore needs $\Omega(r \log n)$ bits. □

G. RANDOMIZED LOWER BOUND, LEMMA 4.3

LEMMA G.1. *Let $\mathcal{F}$ be a family of sequences of length n and variabilities $\leq v$ such that no two sequences in $\mathcal{F}$ match. If a summary $S(f)$ guarantees for all f in $\mathcal{F}$ and all $t \leq n$ that $P(|f(t) - \hat{f}(t)| \leq \varepsilon f(t)) \geq 99/100$, then that summary must use $\Omega(\log |\mathcal{F}|)$ bits of space.*

PROOF. Let $S(f)$ be the summary for a sequence f, and sample $\hat{f}(1) \ldots \hat{f}(n)$ once each using $S(f)$ to get $\hat{f}$. Let A be the event that $|\{t : |f(t) - \hat{f}(t)| \leq \varepsilon f(t)\}| \geq \frac{90}{100}n$. By Markov's inequality and the guarantee in the premise, we must have $P(A) \geq 9/10$.

Let ω define the random bits used in constructing $S(f)$ and in sampling $\hat{f}$. For any choice ω in A we have that $\hat{f}$ overlaps with f in at least $\frac{9}{10}n$ positions, which means that $\hat{f}$ overlaps with any other $g \in \mathcal{F}$ in at most $\frac{7}{10}n$ positions: at most the $\frac{6}{10}n$ in which f and g could overlap, plus the $\frac{1}{10}n$ in which $\hat{f}$ and f might not overlap.

Define $F \subseteq \mathcal{F}$ to be the sequences g that overlap with $\hat{f}$ in at least $\frac{9}{10}n$ positions. This means that when $\omega \in A$ we have $|F| = 1$, and therefore with probability at least $9/10$ we can identify which sequence f had been used to construct $S(f)$.

We now prove our claim by reducing the Index$_N$ problem to the problem of tracing the history of a sequence f. The following statement of Index$_N$ is roughly as in Kushilevitz and Nisan [9]. There are two parties, Alice and Bob. Alice has an input string x of length $N = \log_2 |\mathcal{F}|$ and Bob has an input string i of length $\log_2 N$ that is interpreted as an index into x. Alice sends a message to Bob, and then Bob must output x_i correctly with probability at least $9/10$.

Consider the following algorithm for solving Index$_N$. Alice deterministically generates a family $\mathcal{F}$ of sequences of length n and variabilities $\leq v$ such that no two match, by iterating over all possible sequences and choosing each next one that doesn't match any already chosen. Her $\log_2 |\mathcal{F}|$ bits of input x index a sequence f in $\mathcal{F}$. Alice computes a summary $S(f)$ and sends it to Bob. After receiving $S(f)$, Bob computes $\hat{f}(t)$ for every $t = 1 \ldots n$, to get a sequence $\hat{f}$. He then generates $\mathcal{F}$ himself and creates a set F of all sequences in $\mathcal{F}$ that overlap with $\hat{f}$ in at least $\frac{9}{10}n$ positions. If $F = \{f\}$, which it is with probability at least $9/10$, then Bob can infer every bit of x.

Since the Index$_N$ problem is known to have a one-way communication complexity of $\Omega(N)$, it must be the case that $|S(f)| = \Omega(\log |\mathcal{F}|)$. □

H. RANDOMIZED LOWER BOUND, LEMMA 4.4

LEMMA H.1. *For all $\varepsilon \le 1/2$, all $v \ge 32400\varepsilon \ln C$, and all $n > 3v/\varepsilon$, there is a family $\mathcal{F}$ of size $e^{\Omega(v/\varepsilon)}$ of sequences of size n such that (1) no two sequences match and (2) every sequence has variability at most v.*

PROOF. We construct $\mathcal{F}$ so that each of the two conditions holds (separately) with probability at least 4/5. Let $m = 1/\varepsilon$. To construct one sequence in $\mathcal{F}$, first define $f(0) = m$ with probability 1/2, else $f(0) = m+3$. Then, for $t = 1 \ldots n$: define $f(t) = (2m+3) - f(t-1)$ with probability $p = v/6\varepsilon n$, else $f(t) = f(t-1)$. That is, switch from m to $m+3$ (or vice-versa) with probability $p = v/6\varepsilon n$.

We first prove that the probability is at most 1/5 that any two sequences f and g match. We have that

$$P(f(0) = g(0)) \;=\; 1/2$$

If at any point in time we have $f(t) = g(t)$, then

$$\begin{aligned} P(f(t+1)=g(t+1)) \;&=\; 1 - 2p(1-p) \;=:\; \alpha \\ \text{and } P(f(t+1)\neq g(t+1)) \;&=\; 2p(1-p) \;=\; 1-\alpha \end{aligned}$$

Similarly, if $f(t) \neq g(t)$, then

$$\begin{aligned} P(f(t+1)=g(t+1)) \;&=\; 1-\alpha \\ \text{and } P(f(t+1)\neq g(t+1)) \;&=\; \alpha \end{aligned}$$

The overlap between f and g is the number of times t that $f(t) = g(t)$. We model this situation with a Markov chain M with two states, c for "same" (that is, $f = g$) and d for "different" ($f \neq g$). Let s_t be the state after t steps, and let $p_t = (p_t(c), p_t(d))$ be the probabilities that M is in state c and d after step t. The stationary distribution $\pi = (1/2, 1/2)$, which also happens to be our initial distribution. We can model the overlap between f and g by defining a function $y(s_t) = 1$ if $s_t = c$ and $y(s_t) = 0$ otherwise; then $Y = \sum_{t=1}^{n} y(s_t)$ is the overlap between f and g.

The expected value $E(y(\pi))$ of y evaluated on π is 1/2. The (1/8)-mixing time T is defined as the smallest time T such that $\frac{1}{2}||M^t r_0 - \pi||_1 \le 1/8$ over all initial distributions r_0. Let r_0 be any initial distribution and $r_t = M^t r_0$. If we define $\Delta_t = r_t(c) - \pi(c)$, then $\Delta_t = (2\alpha-1)^t \Delta_0$. We can similarly bound $|r_t(d) - \pi(d)|$, so we can bound

$$\begin{aligned} T \;&\le\; \frac{\ln(8)}{\ln(1/(2\alpha-1))} \;\le\; \frac{3}{(1-(2\alpha-1))} \;\le\; \frac{3}{2p(1-p)} \;\le\; \frac{3}{2p} \\ &=\; \frac{9\varepsilon n}{v} \end{aligned}$$

since $1 - p \ge 1/2$ and since $1/\ln(1/x) \le 1/(1-x)$ for x in $(0, 1)$. With this information we can now apply a sledgehammer of a result by Chung, Lam, Liu, and Mitzenmacher [2]. Our fact H.2 is their theorem 3.1, specialized a bit to our situation:

FACT H.2. *Let M be an ergodic Markov chain with state space S. Let T be its (1/8)-mixing time. Let $(s_1, \ldots, s_n)$ denote an n-step random walk on M starting from its stationary distribution π. Let y be a weight function such that $E(y(\pi)) = \mu$. Define the weight of $\{s_t\}$ by $Y = \sum_{t=1}^{n} y(s_t)$. Then there exists some universal constant C such that for all $0 < \delta < 1$ we have $P(Y \ge (1+\delta)\mu n) \;\le\; C \exp(-\delta^2 \mu n / 72T)$.*

Specifically, this means that

$$P(Y \ge \tfrac{6}{10}n) \;\le\; C\exp(-v/(25 \cdot 72 \cdot 9 \cdot \varepsilon))$$

Since $v \ge 32400\varepsilon \ln C$, we can also write

$$P(Y \ge \tfrac{6}{10}n) \;\le\; \exp(-v/32400\varepsilon)$$

If $|\mathcal{F}| = \frac{1}{5}\exp(v/(2 \cdot 32400\varepsilon))$, then by the union bound, with probability at least 4/5, no pair of sequences f, g matches.

We also must prove that there are enough sequences with variability at most v. The change in variability due to a single switch from m to $m+3$ (or vice-versa) is at most $3/m = 3\varepsilon$. For any sequence f, let $U_t = 1$ if f switched at time t, else $U_t = 0$. The expected number of switches is $v/6\varepsilon$; using a standard Chernoff bound,

$$P(\textstyle\sum_t U_t \ge 2v/6\varepsilon) \;\le\; \exp(-v/18\varepsilon) \;\le\; 1/10$$

Suppose we sample N sequences and B of them have more than $2v/6\varepsilon$ switches. In expectation $E(B) \le \frac{1}{10}N$ of them have too many switches. By Markov's inequality we have that $P(B \ge N/2) \;\le\; 1/5$, so we can toss out the fewer than $N/2$ bad sequences. This gives us a final size of $\mathcal{F}$ of $\frac{1}{10}\exp(v/(2 \cdot 32400\varepsilon))$. □

I. TRACKING ITEM FREQUENCIES, SECTION 5.1

Problem definition.
The problem of tracking item frequencies is only slightly different than the counting problem we've considered so far. In this problem there is a universe U of items and we maintain a dataset $D(t)$ that changes over time. At each new timestep n, either some item ℓ from U is added to D, or some item ℓ from D is removed. This update is told to a single site i; that is, site $i(n)$ receives an update $f'_\ell(n) = \pm 1$.

The frequency $f_\ell(t)$ of item ℓ at time t is the number of copies of ℓ that appear in $D(t)$. The first frequency moment $F_1(t)$ at time t is the total number of items $|D(t)|$. The problem is to maintain estimates $\hat{f}_\ell(n)$ at the coordinator so that $P(|f_\ell(n) - \hat{f}_\ell(n)| \le \varepsilon F_1(n))$ is close to 1, for all times n and all items ℓ.

Since in this problem we are tracking each item frequency to $\varepsilon F_1(n)$, we use F_1-variability instead, defining the change $v'(t) = \min\{1, 1/F_1(t)\}$.

I.1 Item frequencies with low communication

We first partition time into blocks as in section 3.1, using $f = F_1$. That is, at the end of each block we know the values n and $F_1(n)$ deterministically, and also that either $r = 0$ holds or that $F_1(n_j)$ is within a factor of two of $F_1(n_{j-1})$.

For tracking during blocks we modify the deterministic algorithm so that each site i holds counters $d_{i\ell}$ and $\delta_{i\ell}$ for every item ℓ. It also holds counters $f_{i\ell}$ of the total number of copies of ℓ seen at site i across all blocks.

At the end of each block, each site i reports all $f_{i\ell} \ge \varepsilon 2^r/3$ (using the new value of r). If site i reports counter $f_{i\ell}$ then it starts the next block with $d_{i\ell} = \delta_{i\ell} = 0$; otherwise, $d_{i\ell}$ is updated to $d_{i\ell} + \delta_{i\ell}$ and then $\delta_{i\ell}$ is reset to zero. Within a block $r \ge 1$, the CONDITION is true when $\delta_{i\ell} \ge \varepsilon 2^r/3$.

The coordinator maintains estimates $\hat{f}_{i\ell}$ of $f_{i\ell}$ for each site i and item ℓ. Upon receiving an update $\delta_{i\ell}$ during a block the coordinator updates its estimate $\hat{f}_{i\ell} = \hat{f}_{i\ell} + \delta_{i\ell}$.

Estimation error.
The total error in the estimate $\hat{f}_{i\ell}(n)$ at any time n is the error due to $d_{i\ell}$ plus the error due to $\delta_{i\ell}$. In both cases these quantities are bounded by $\varepsilon 2^r/3 \le \varepsilon F_1(n)/3$.

Communication.
The total communication for a block is the total communicated within and at the end of the block. Within a block, all $\delta_{i\ell}$ start at zero, and there are at most $2^r k$ updates, so the total number of messages sent is $3k/\varepsilon$. At the end of a block, $f_{i\ell} \ge \varepsilon 2^r/3$ is true for at most $12k/\varepsilon$ counters $f_{i\ell}$. Therefore the total number of messages $O(\frac{k}{\varepsilon}v(n))$.

I.2 Item frequencies in small space + communication

The algorithm so far uses $|U|$ counters per site, which is prohibitive in terms of space. In [3] Cormode and Muthukrishnan show that in order to track over a non-distributed update stream each $f_\ell(n)$ so that for all ℓ and all times n we have $P(|f_\ell(n) - \hat{f}_\ell(n)| \le \varepsilon F_1(n)/3) \ge 8/9$, it suffices to randomly partition each item in U into one of $27/\varepsilon$ classes using a pairwise-independent hash function h, and to estimate $f_\ell(n)$ as $f_{h(\ell)}(n)$. The $27/\varepsilon$ counters and the hash function h together form their Count-Min Sketch [3].

Similarly, in [6, 7] Ganguly and Majumder adapt a data structure of Gasieniec and Muthukrishnan [12], which they call the CR-precis, to deterministically track each $f_\ell(n)$ to $\varepsilon F_1(n)/3$ error. This data structure uses $\frac{3}{\varepsilon}$ rows of $\frac{6 \log |U|}{\varepsilon \log 1/\varepsilon}$ counters, and estimates $f_\ell(n)$ as the average over rows r of $f_{h(r,\ell)}(n)$. (Ganguly and Majumder actually take the minimum over the rows r, but the average works too and yields a linear sketch.)

In either case, we can first reduce our set of items ℓ to a small number of counters c, and instead of tracking $f_{i\ell}$ we track f_{ic} for each counter c. The coordinator can then linearly combine its estimates $\hat{f}_{ic}$ to obtain estimates $\hat{f}_{i\ell}$ for each item ℓ. This introduces another $\varepsilon F_1(n)/3$ error, yielding algorithms that guarantee

- $P(|f_{i\ell}(n) - \hat{f}_{i\ell}(n)| \le \varepsilon F_1(n)) = 1$ in
$$O\left(\frac{k \log |U|}{\varepsilon^2 \log 1/\varepsilon} v(n) \log n\right)$$
bits of space + communication, and
- $P(|f_{i\ell}(n) - \hat{f}_{i\ell}(n)| \le \varepsilon F_1(n)) \ge 8/9$ in
$$O(k \log |U| + \tfrac{k}{\varepsilon} v(n) \log n)$$
bits of space + communication.

I.3 Remarks

We obtain a randomized communication bound of $O(\frac{k}{\varepsilon}v(n))$ messages, but it might be possible to do better. In [8] Huang et. al. both develop a randomized counting algorithm ($O(\frac{\sqrt{k}}{\varepsilon}\log n)$ messages) and also extend it to the problem of tracking item frequencies to get the same communication bound. Unfortunately, their algorithm appears to require the total variance in their estimate at any time $t < n$ to be bounded by a constant factor of the variance at time n. This is only guaranteed to be true when item deletions are not permitted (and F_1 grows monotonically). We avoid this problem in section 3.4 for tracking $f = F_1$ by deterministically updating F_1 at the end of each block. For this problem, though, deterministically updating all of the large $\hat{f}_{i\ell}$ at the end of each block could incur $O(k/\varepsilon)$ messages. Whether it is also possible to probabilistically track item frequencies over general update streams in $O(\frac{\sqrt{k}}{\varepsilon}v(n))$ messages remains open.

J. AGGREGATE FUNCTIONS WITH ONE SITE, SECTION 5.2

The single-site algorithm of section 5.2 is: whenever we have $|f - \hat{f}| > \varepsilon f$ we send f to the coordinator.

Proof. If $f(n) = 0$ then $v'(n) = 1$. Also, if $f(n)$ changes sign from $f(n-1)$, then $v'(n) = 1$. So consider intervals over which $f(n)$ is nonzero and doesn't change sign. Over such an interval, let $\Phi(n) = |\frac{f(n) - \hat{f}(n)}{f(n)}|$. If at time n we update $\hat{f}$ then $\Phi(n) = 0$. Otherwise,

$$\begin{aligned}
\Phi(n) &= \frac{|f(n-1) - \hat{f}(n-1) + f'(n)|}{|f(n)|} \\
&\le \frac{|f(n-1) - \hat{f}(n-1)|}{|f(n)|} + \frac{|f'(n)|}{|f(n)|} \\
&= \frac{|f(n-1)|}{|f(n)|}\Phi(n-1) + \frac{|f'(n)|}{|f(n)|} \\
&\le \frac{|f(n)| + |f'(n)|}{|f(n)|}\Phi(n-1) + \frac{|f'(n)|}{|f(n)|} \\
&\le \Phi(n-1) + \frac{(1+\Phi(n-1))|f'(n)|}{|f(n)|}
\end{aligned}$$

Since $\Phi(n) \le \varepsilon$ we have $|\Phi'(n)| \le (1+\varepsilon)|\frac{f'(n)}{f(n)}|$. We only send a message each time that Φ would be more than ε, so the total number of messages sent is at most the total increase in Φ, which is at most $\frac{1+\varepsilon}{\varepsilon}\sum_{t=1}^{n} \min\{1, |\frac{f'(t)}{f(t)}|\}$. □

Streaming Space Complexity of Nearly All Functions of One Variable on Frequency Vectors

Vladimir Braverman*
Johns Hopkins University
vova@cs.jhu.edu

Stephen R. Chestnut†
ETH Zurich
stephenc@ethz.ch

David P. Woodruff
IBM, Almaden Research Center
dpwoodru@us.ibm.com

Lin F. Yang†
Johns Hopkins University
lyang@pha.jhu.edu

ABSTRACT

A central problem in the theory of algorithms for data streams is to determine which functions on a stream can be approximated in sublinear, and especially sub-polynomial or polylogarithmic, space. Given a function g, we study the space complexity of approximating $\sum_{i=1}^{n} g(|f_i|)$, where $f \in \mathbb{Z}^n$ is the frequency vector of a turnstile stream. This is a generalization of the well-known frequency moments problem, and previous results apply only when g is monotonic or has a special functional form. Our contribution is to give a condition such that, except for a narrow class of functions g, there is a space-efficient approximation algorithm for the sum if and only if g satisfies the condition. The functions g that we are able to characterize include all convex, concave, monotonic, polynomial, and trigonometric functions, among many others, and is the first such characterization for non-monotonic functions. Thus, for nearly all functions of one variable, we answer the open question from the celebrated paper of Alon, Matias and Szegedy (1996).

Keywords

data streams, sketching, frequency moments

1. INTRODUCTION

One of the main open problems in the theory of data stream computation is to characterize functions of a frequency vector that can be computed, or approximated, efficiently. Here we characterize nearly all functions of the form $\sum_{i=1}^{n} g(|v_i|)$, where $v = (v_1, \ldots, v_n) \in \mathbb{Z}^n$ is the frequency vector of the stream. This is a generalization of the famous frequency moments problem, where $g(x) = x^k$ for some $k \geq 0$, described by Alon, Matias, and Szegedy [1], who also asked:
"It would be interesting to determine or estimate the space complexity of the approximation of $\sum_{i=1}^{n} v_i^k$ for non-integral values of k for $k < 2$, or the space complexity of estimating other functions of the numbers v_i." The first question was answered by Indyk and Woodruff [15] and Indyk [14] who were the first to determine, up to polylogarithmic factors, the space complexity of the frequency moments for all $k > 0$. We address the second question.

Braverman and Ostrovsky [6] and Braverman and Chestnut [5], answer the second question for sums of the form given above when g is monotone. We extend their characterizations to nearly all nonmonotone functions of one variable. Specifically, we characterize the set of functions g for which there exists a sub-polynomial $(1 \pm \epsilon)$-approximation algorithm for the sum above. Our results can be adapted to characterize the set of functions approximible in polylogarithmic, rather than sub-polynomial, space. Among the main techniques we use is the layering method developed by Indyk and Woodruff [15] for approximating the frequency moments, and one may view our results as an exploration of the power of this technique.

Our results also partially answer an open question of Guha and Indyk at the IIT Kanpur workshop in 2006 [12] about characterizing sketchable distances - our results characterize nearly all distances that can be expressed in the form $d(u, v) = \sum_i g(|u_i - v_i|)$. Besides the aforementioned work on the frequency moments and monotone functions, other past work on this question was done by Guha, Indyk, and McGregor [13] as well as Andoni, Krauthgamer, and Razenshteyn [2]. Both of those papers address the same problem, but in domains different from ours. In the realm of general streaming algorithms, a result of Li, Nguyen, and Woodruff [20] shows that for any function g with a $(1 \pm \epsilon)$-approximation algorithm implementable in sub-polynomial space, there exists a linear sketch that demonstrates its tractability. However, a drawback of that work is that the space complexity of maintaining the sketching matrix, together with computing the output, may be polynomially large. Our paper deals with a smaller class of functions than [20], but we provide a zero-one law and explicit algorithms.

While several of our lower bounds can be shown via re-

*This material is based upon work supported in part by the National Science Foundation under Grant No. 1447639, by the Google Faculty Award and by DARPA grant N660001-1-2-4014. Its contents are solely the responsibility of the authors and do not represent the official view of DARPA or the Department of Defense.

†This material is based upon work supported in part by the National Science Foundation under Grant No. 1447639.

PODS'16, June 26-July 01, 2016, San Francisco, CA, USA

DOI: http://dx.doi.org/10.1145/2902251.2902282

duction from the standard index and set-disjointness communication problems, to prove lower bounds for the widest class of functions we develop a new class of communication problems and prove lower bounds for them, which may be of independent interest. The problem, which we call ShortLinearCombination, is: given a finite set $\{0, a_1, \ldots, a_r, b\}$ of possible frequencies, is there a frequency in the stream of value b? Perhaps surprisingly, the communication complexity of ShortLinearCombination depends on the magnitudes of the coefficients in any linear combination expressing b in terms of $a_1, \ldots, a_r$. We develop optimal communication bounds for this problem. This hints at the subtleties in proving lower bounds for a wide class of functions g, since by defining $g(b) \geq n \cdot \max_i g(a_i)$, the communication problem just described is a special case of characterizing the streaming complexity of all functions g. Our lower bounds provide a significant generalization of the set-disjointness problem, which has found many applications to data streams.

1.1 Applications

We now describe potential applications of this work.

1.1.1 Log-likelihood Approximation

One use for the approximation of non-monotonic functions is the computation of log-likelihoods. Here, the coordinates of the streamed vector v are taken to be i.i.d. samples from a discrete probability distribution. The likelihood of the vector v, under a distribution with probability mass function $p(x)$, $x \in \mathbb{Z}$, is $L(v) = \prod_{i=1}^n p(v_i)$, and its log-likelihood is $\ell(v) = -\sum_{i=1}^n \log p(v_i)$. Notice that $\ell(v)$ is of the form $\sum_{i=1}^n g(v_i)$, for $g(x) = -\log p(x)$. When $p(\cdot;\theta)$ is the distribution of a non-negative random variable or if $p(x;\theta)$ is symmetric about $x = 0$, our results can be applied to determine whether there is a streaming algorithm that efficiently approximates ℓ. In general, $-\log p(x)$ is not a monotonic function of x. For example, $p(x) = \lambda \frac{x^\alpha}{x!} e^{-\alpha} + (1-\lambda)\frac{x^\beta}{x!} e^{-\beta}$ is a mixture of two Poissons, which is generally not monotonic. For any constants $\lambda, \alpha, \beta > 0$, the Poisson mixture log-likelihood $-\log p(x)$ satisfies our three criteria (to be described later), hence the log-likelihood of the stream can be approximated in poly-logarithmic space. Continuous distributions can be handled similarly by discretization.

Suppose that the distribution p comes from a family of probability distributions $p(\cdot;\theta)$ parameterized by $\theta \in \Theta$. When an efficient approximation algorithm exists, we describe a linear sketch from which a $(1 \pm \epsilon)$-approximation $\hat{\ell}$ to $\ell(v)$ can be extracted with probability at least 2/3. The form of the sketch is independent of the function g, so if $-\log p(x;\theta)$ satisfies our conditions for approximability for all $\theta \in \Theta$, we derive an approximation to each of the log-likelihoods $\ell(v;\theta)$ that are separately correct with probability 2/3 each. If Θ is a discrete set then this allows us to find an approximate maximum likelihood estimator for θ with only an $O(\log|\Theta|)$ factor increase in storage. Recall, the maximum likelihood estimator is $\hat{\theta} = \text{argmin}_{\theta\in\Theta}\, \ell(\theta, v)$. Indeed, as usual we can drive the error probability down to any $\delta > 0$ with $O(\log 1/\delta)$ repetitions of the algorithm, so an additional factor of $O(\log|\Theta|)$ in the space complexity is enough. If $\hat{\ell}(\theta; v)$ denote our approximations, then $\hat{t} = \text{argmin}_{\theta\in\Theta}\, \hat{\ell}(\theta; v)$ is the approximate maximum likelihood estimate, which has the guarantee that $\ell(\hat{t}; v) \leq (1 + \epsilon)\ell(\hat{\theta}; v)$. When Θ is not finite one may still be able to apply our results by discretizing Θ with poly(n) points and proceeding as above; whether this works depends on the behavior of $p(x;\theta)$ as a function of θ.

1.1.2 Utility Aggregates

Consider an online advertising service that charges its customers based on the number of clicks on the ad by web users. More clicks should result in a higher fee, but an exceptionally high number of clicks from one user make it likely that he is a bot or spammer. Customers may demand that the service discount the cost of these spam clicks, which means that the fee is a non-monotonic function of the number of clicks from each user.

The ads application is an example of a non-monotonic utility function. Many utility functions are naturally non-monotonic, and they can appear in streaming settings. For example, extremely low or high trading volume in a stock indicates abnormal market conditions. A low volume of network traffic might be a sign of damaged or malfunctioning equipment whereas a high volume of network traffic is one indicator of a denial-of-service attack.

1.1.3 Database Query Optimization

A prominent application for streaming algorithms, indeed one of the initial motivations [1], is to database query optimization. A query optimizer is a piece of software that uses heuristics and estimates query costs in order to intelligently organize the processing of a database query with the goal of reducing resource loads (time, space, network traffic, etc.). Scalable query optimizers are needed for scalable database processing [22, 16], and poor query efficiency has been cited as one of the main drawbacks of existing implementations of the MapReduce framework [19]. Streaming algorithms and sketches are a natural choice for such heuristics because of their low computational overhead and amenability to distributed processing. By expanding the character of statistics that can be computed efficiently over data streams, our results could allow database query optimizers more expressive power when creating heuristics and estimating query costs.

1.1.4 Encoding Higher Order Functions

An obvious generalization of the problem we consider is to replace the frequency vector f_i, $i \in [n]$, with a frequency matrix f_{ij}, $i \in [n]$ and $j \in [k]$, and ask whether there is a space efficient streaming algorithm that approximates $\sum_{i=1}^n g(f_{i,1}, \ldots, f_{i,k})$. These could, for example, allow one to express more complicated database queries which first filter records based on one attribute and then sum up the function values applied to another attribute on the remaining records.

Let us demonstrate that when the coordinates of f are bounded and k is not too large, we can replace this sum with a function of a single variable. Suppose that $0 \leq f_{ij} \leq b-1 \in \mathbb{N}$, for all i, j. Upon receiving an update to coordinate (i, j) we replace it with b^j copies of i. The new frequencies are polynomially bounded if $b^k = \text{poly}(n)$.

Call the new frequency vector $f' \in \mathbb{Z}^n$. The sequence of values $f_{i1}, \ldots, f_{ik}$ is immediately available as the base-b expansion of the number f'_i, so we are able to write $g'(f'_i) = g(f_{i1}, \ldots, f_{ik})$, where g' first recovers the base-b expansion and then applies g. Our desire is to approximate $\sum_i g'(f'_i)$. Given even a well behaved function g, it is very unlikely that g' will be monotone, hence the need for an approximation algorithm for non-monotonic functions if this approach is taken. It is also very likely that, because of the construction, g' has high local variability. This is a significant problem for algorithms that use only one pass over the stream (as we show by way of a lower bound), but we also present a two pass algorithm that is not sensitive to local variability.

1.2 Problem Definition

A stream of length m with domain $[n]$ is a list $D = \langle(i_1, \delta_1), (i_2, \delta_2), \ldots (i_m, \delta_m)\rangle$, where $i_j \in [n]$ and $\delta_j \in \mathbb{Z}$ for every $j \in [m]$. The *frequency vector* of a stream D is the vector $V(D) \in \mathbb{Z}^n$ with i^{th} coordinate $v_i = \sum_{j:i_j=i} \delta_j$. A processor can read the stream some number $p \geq 1$ times, in the order in which it is given, and is asked to compute a function of the stream. We allow the processor to use randomness and we only require that its output is correct with probability at least 2/3.

Our algorithms are designed for the *turnstile* streaming model. In particular, there exists $M \in \mathbb{N}$ and it is promised that $V(D) \in \{-M, -M+1, \ldots, M\}^n$ and the same holds for any prefix of the list D. Our lower bounds, on the other hand, hold in the more restrictive *insertion-only* model which has $\delta_j = 1$, for all j. We use $\mathcal{D}(n, m)$ to denote the set of all turnstile streams with domain $[n]$ and length at most m.

Given a function $g : \mathbb{R} \to \mathbb{R}$ and vector $V = (v_1, v_2, \ldots, v_n)$, let

$$g(V) := \sum_{i=1}^{n} g(|v_i|).$$

DEFINITION 1. *Given $g : \mathbb{Z}_{\geq 0} \to \mathbb{R}$, $\epsilon > 0$, and $D \in \mathcal{D}(n, m)$ the problem of (g, ϵ)-SUM on stream D is to output an estimate $\hat{G}$ of $g(V(D))$ such that*

$$P\Big((1-\epsilon)g(V(D)) \leq \hat{G} \leq (1+\epsilon)g(V(D))\Big) \geq 2/3.$$

We often omit ϵ and refer simply to g-SUM when the value of ϵ is clear from the context.

The choice of 2/3 here is arbitrary, since given a g-SUM algorithm the success probability can be improved to $1 - 1/\text{poly}(n)$ by repeating it $O(\log n)$ times in parallel and taking the median outcome.

Our goal is to classify the space complexity of g-SUM. We ask: for which functions g can (g, ϵ)-SUM be solved in space that is sub-polynomial in n? We call such functions *tractable*. An $\Omega(\epsilon^{-1})$ lower bound applies for nearly every function g, thus we only require that the algorithm solve (g, ϵ)-SUM whenever ϵ decreases sub-polynomially. Our main results separately answer this question in the case in which the processor is allowed one pass over the stream and in the case in which $O(1)$ passes are allowed. We are able to classify the space complexity of almost all functions, though a small set of functions remains poorly understood.

1.3 Organization

Section 2 gives a high-level description of our results and states our main theorems. We put off some of the more technical definitions until Section 3, which gives the definitions needed to precisely state our main results as well as background on the main techniques for our proofs. Next, Section 4 includes the intuition and proofs for our main theorems. It describes one and two-pass algorithms and lower bounds. Section 5 discusses the functions that we are unable to characterize in more depth.

2. OUR RESULTS

To begin with, we separate the class of functions $g : \mathbb{Z}_{\geq 0} \to \mathbb{R}$ into two complementary classes: "normal functions" and "nearly periodic functions". In fact, we do this differently for 1-pass g-SUM than for multi-pass g-SUM. We define $\mathbb{S}$-normal functions, for studying one pass streaming space complexity, and $\mathbb{P}$-normal functions for multiple passes. The complements of these two sets are the $\mathbb{S}$-nearly periodic functions and $\mathbb{P}$-nearly periodic functions, respectively. The distinction between $\mathbb{S}$ and $\mathbb{P}$ is not important to understand our results at a high level, so we omit them for the rest of this section. See Section 5 for more about this class of functions. We postpone the technical definitions until Section 3, and give an informal overview here.

We are able to characterize the normal functions based on three properties which we call *slow-jumping*, *slow-dropping*, and *predictable*. Slow-jumping depends on the rate of increase. Roughly, a function is slow-jumping if it doesn't grow much faster than $y = x^2$ at every scale. Slow-dropping governs the rate of decrease of a function. A function is slow dropping if decreases no faster than sub-polynomially at every point. Finally, if a function is predictable then it satisfies a particular tradeoff between its growth rate and local variability. Interestingly, not just the properties themselves are important for our proofs, but so is the interplay between them. Precise definitions for these properties are given in Section 3.

Our proofs are by finding heavy hitters, for the upper bound, and by reductions from communication complexity for the lower bound. See Section 4.1 for more thorough discussion of how the three properties relate to heavy-hitters and the other techniques we use.

Zero-One Laws for Normal Functions

A nonnegative function f is called a sub-polynomial function if, for all $\alpha > 0$, $\lim_{x\to\infty} x^{\alpha} f(x) = \infty$ and $\lim_{x\to\infty} x^{-\alpha} f(x) = 0$. Formally, we study the class of functions g such that g-SUM can be solved with sub-polynomial accuracy $\epsilon = \epsilon(n)$ using only an amount of space which is sub-polynomial. We call such functions p-pass tractable if the algorithm uses p passes. In this paper we prove the following theorems.

THEOREM 2 (1-PASS ZERO-ONE LAW). *A function $g \in \mathcal{G}$ is 1-pass tractable and normal if and only if it is slow-jumping, slow-dropping, and predictable.*

THEOREM 3 (2-PASS ZERO-ONE LAW). *A function $g \in \mathcal{G}$ is 2-pass tractable and normal if and only if it is slow-dropping and slow-jumping.*

The main difference between the two theorems is that predictability is not needed in two passes. The message is that large local variability can rule out 1-pass approximation algorithms but not 2-pass approximation algorithms. Theorem 3 extends to any subpolynomial number of passes.

Most functions one encounters are normal, which include convex, concave, monotonic, polynomial, or trigonometric functions, as well as functions of regular variation and unbounded Lipschitz-continuous functions.

3. PRELIMINARIES

In describing the requirements and space efficiency of our algorithms for g-SUM, we use the set of sub-polynomial functions.

Definition 4. *A function $f : \mathbb{R}_{\geq 0} \to \mathbb{R}_{\geq 0}$ is* sub-polynomial *if for any $\alpha > 0$, the following two conditions are satisfied: a) $\lim_{x\to\infty} x^{\alpha} f(x) = \infty$ and b) $\lim_{x\to\infty} x^{-\alpha} f(x) = 0$.*

We use subpoly(x) to represent the set of sub-polynomial functions in the variable x. Examples of sub-polynomial functions include polylogarithmic functions and some with faster growth, like $2^{\sqrt{\log n}}$. The set of poly-logarithmic functions is a subset of the sub-polynomial functions. Formally, we study the class of functions g such that (g, ϵ)-SUM can be solved with any accuracy $\epsilon \in$ subpoly(n), using only sub-polynomial space. Our algorithms assume an oracle for computing g and that the storage required for the value $g(x)$ is sub-polynomial in x. Regardless, our sketches are sub-polynomial in size, but without these assumptions it could take more than sub-polynomial space to compute the approximation from the sketch. We restrict ourselves to the case $M \in$ poly(n). This restriction is reasonable because if it grows, say, exponentially in n, then an algorithm can store the entire frequency vector and compute $g(V(D))$ exactly in polylog(nM) space.

Definition 5. *A function $g : \mathbb{Z}_{\geq 0} \to \mathbb{R}$ is* p-pass tractable *if given any sub-polynomial function $h(x)$ and any $\epsilon \geq 1/h(nM)$ there exists a sub-polynomial function $h^*(x)$ and a p-pass algorithm $\mathcal{A}$ that solves (g, ϵ)-SUM for all streams in $\mathcal{D}(n, m)$ and $n, M \geq 1$ using no more than $h^*(nM)$ space in the worst case.*

Replacing the storage requirement, which is $h^*(nM)$, with $h^*(n) \log M$ would also be natural, but since we consider $M \in$ poly(n) the two definitions are equivalent. It simplifies our notation a little bit to write $h^*(nM)$. Unless otherwise noted, for the rest of this paper we require that $g(0) = 0$ and $g(x) > 0$, for all $x > 0$. The choice $g(0) = 0$ is equivalent to requiring that $g(V(D))$ does not depend on the particular choice of n in the model; specifically it avoids the following behavior: if $g(0) \neq 0$ then given a single stream D the value of $g(V(D))$ differs depending on the choice of the dimension, even though the stream remains the same. Functions with $g(0) \neq 0$ may be of interest for some applications. The laws for these functions are very similar to the case when $g(0) = 0$ and we provide them in Appendix A.

As shown in [10], functions with $g(x) = 0$, for some integer $x > 0$, are not n^{α}-pass tractable for any $\alpha < 1$, unless g is nonnegative and periodic with period $\min\{x > 0 \mid g(x) = 0\}$, which must exist if g is periodic and $g(0) = 0$. It is also shown in [10] that if a non-linear function g takes both positive and negative values, then g is not n^{α}-pass tractable, for any $\alpha < 1$. Without loss of generality, we can assume $g(1) = 1$ because a multiplicative approximation algorithm for the function $g'(x) := g(x)/g(1)$ is also a multiplicative approximation algorithm for g. Finally, for simplicity of notation we will often extend the domain of g symmetrically to $\mathbb{Z}$, i.e., setting $g(x) = g(-x)$, for all $x \in \mathbb{Z}_{\geq 0}$, which allows us the simpler notation $g(|v_i|) = g(v_i)$. In summary, we study the functions in the class

$$\mathcal{G} \equiv \{g : \mathbb{Z}_{\geq 0} \to \mathbb{R}, g(0) = 0, g(1) = 1, \forall x > 0, g(x) > 0\}$$

Our results are based on three characterizations of the variation of the functions. We now state the technical definitions mentioned in Section 2.

Definition 6. *A function $g \in \mathcal{G}$ is* slow-jumping *if for any $\alpha > 0$, there exists $N > 0$, such that for any $x < y$ if $y \geq N$, then $g(y) \leq \lfloor \frac{y}{x} \rfloor^{2+\alpha} x^{\alpha} g(x)$.*

Slow-jumping is a characterization of the rate of growth of a function. Examples of slow-jumping functions are x^p, for $p \leq 2$, $x^2 2^{\sqrt{\log x}}$, and $(2 + \sin x)\, x^2$, while functions like 2^x and x^p, for any $p > 2$, are not slow jumping because they grow too quickly.

Definition 7. *A function $g \in \mathcal{G}$ is* slow-dropping *if for any $\alpha > 0$ there exists $N > 0$, such that for any $x < y$, if $y \geq N$, then $g(y) \geq g(x)/y^{\alpha}$.*

Whether a function is slow-dropping is determined by its rate of decrease. The functions[1] $(\log_2 1 + x)^{-1}\mathbf{1}(x > 0)$ and $(2 + \sin x)\, x^2$ are slow-dropping, but any function with polynomial decay, i.e. x^{-p}, for $p > 0$, is not slow-dropping.

Given a function g, $x \in \mathbb{N}$, and $\epsilon > 0$ define the set: $\delta_{\epsilon}(g, x) := \{y \in \mathbb{N} \mid |g(y) - g(x)| \leq \epsilon g(x)\}$.

Definition 8. *A function g is* predictable *if for every $0 < \gamma < 1$ and sub-polynomial ϵ, there exists N such that for all $x \geq N$ and $y \in [1, x^{1-\gamma})$ with $x + y \notin \delta_{\epsilon(x)}(g, x)$ we have $g(y) \geq x^{-\gamma} g(x)$.*

Predictability is governed by the local variability of a function and its rate of growth. For example, the function $g(x) = x^2$ is predictable because $g(x+y)/g(x) = (1+\frac{y}{x})^2 \approx 1$ when $y \ll x$, or more precisely $\pi_{\epsilon}(x) \supseteq \{y \mid |x - y| \leq \epsilon x/3\}$. That function has low local variability. On the other hand, the function $(2 + \sin x)\mathbf{1}(x > 0)$ is locally highly variable but still predictable. Notice that even $x + 1 \notin \pi_{\epsilon}(x)$, for say $\epsilon = 0.01$, but $g(1)/g(x) \geq 1/3$ so the inequality in the definition of predictability is satisfied. A negative example is the function $(2 + \sin x)x^2$, which is not predictable because it varies quickly (by a multiplicative factor of 3) and grows with x.

As we will show, the three conditions above can be used to characterize nearly every function in $\mathcal{G}$ in both the single-pass and $O(1)$-pass settings. We remark here that the characterization has already been completed for monotonic functions. The tractability condition for nondecreasing g proved by [6] is equivalent to g being slow-jumping and predictable. For nonincreasing functions, it is a consequence of [5] that polynomially decreasing functions are not tractable while sub-polynomially decreasing functions are tractable. The "nearly periodic" functions are formally defined next.

Let $\mathbb{S}$ be the set of non-increasing sub-polynomial functions on domain $\mathbb{Z}_{\geq 0}$ and $\mathbb{P}$ be the set of strictly increasing polynomial functions on $\mathbb{Z}_{\geq 0}$. We now define the sets of $\mathbb{S}$-nearly periodic functions and $\mathbb{P}$-nearly periodic functions. The motivation for these definitions jumps ahead to our lower bounds, but we will explain it here. The reductions used in some of our lower bounds boil down to finding three integers $x < y$ and $x + y$ such that $g(x) \gg g(y)$ and $g(x) \not\approx g(x + y)$. The reductions fail when $g(x) \approx g(x + y)$, where the meaning of "$\approx$" depends on whether we are bounding 1-pass or multi-pass algorithms. For the 1-pass reduction

[1] $\mathbf{1}(\cdot)$ denotes the indicator function.

to fail it is necessary that $\frac{1}{g(x)}|g(x)-g(x+y)|$ decreases as x increases, hence the $\mathbb{S}$-nearly periodic functions. The 2-pass reduction fails as long as $\max(\frac{g(x)}{g(x+y)}, \frac{g(x+y)}{g(x)})$ is not polynomially large in y, hence the $\mathbb{P}$-nearly periodic functions.

DEFINITION 9. *Given a set of functions $\mathcal{S}$, call $g(x)$ $\mathcal{S}$-*nearly periodic, *if the following two conditions are satisfied.*

1. *There exists $\alpha > 0$ such that for any constant $N > 0$ there exists $x, y \in \mathbb{N}$, $x < y$ and $y \geq N$ such that $g(y) \leq g(x)/y^\alpha$. Call such a y an* α-period *of g;*
2. *For any $\alpha > 0$ and any error function $h \in \mathcal{S}$ there exists $N_1 > 0$ such that for all α-periods $y \geq N_1$ and all $x < y$ such that $g(y)y^\alpha \leq g(x)$, we have $|g(x+y) - g(x)| \leq \min\{g(x), g(x+y)\}h(y)$.*

*A function g is $\mathcal{S}$-*normal *if it is not $\mathcal{S}$-nearly periodic.*

The first condition states that the function is not slow-dropping. For example, if g is bounded then there is an increasing subsequence along which g converges to 0 polynomially fast. To understand the second condition, take h to be a decreasing function or a small constant. In loose terms, it states that if $x < y$ and $g(x) \gg g(y)$, then $g(x) \approx g(x+y)$. The choice of the set of functions $\mathcal{S}$ determines the relative accuracy implied by "$\approx$". We will apply the definition with $\mathcal{S}$ set to either $\mathbb{S}$ or $\mathbb{P}$, that is, with either subpolynomially or polynomially small relative accuracy.

An $\mathbb{S}$-nearly periodic function (it is also $\mathbb{P}$-nearly periodic) can be constructed as follows. For each $x \in \mathbb{N}$, let $i_x = \max\{j : 2^j | x\}$ and let $g_{np}(0) = 0$ and $g_{np}(x) = 2^{-i_x}$. For example, $g_{np}(1) = 1$, $g_{np}(2) = 1/2$, $g_{np}(3) = 1$, $g_{np}(4) = 1/4$, etc. The proof that g is nearly periodic appears in Section 5, but for now notice that it satisfies the first part of the definition because $g_{np}(2^k) = 2^{-k}$ and, as an example of the second part, we have $g_{np}(2^k+1) = g_{np}(1) = 1$. One may guess that a streaming algorithm for such an erratic function requires a lot of storage. In fact, g_{np} can be approximated in polylogarithmic space! Section 5 has the proof.

The following containment follows directly from the definition of the nearly periodic functions.

PROPOSITION 10. *Every $\mathbb{S}$-nearly periodic function is also $\mathbb{P}$-nearly periodic. Every $\mathbb{P}$-normal function is $\mathbb{S}$-normal.*

3.1 Heavy Hitters, Communication Complexity, and CountSketch

Our sub-polynomial space algorithm is based on the Recursive Sketch of Braverman and Ostrovsky [7], which reduces the problem to that of finding heavy hitters.

DEFINITION 11. *Given a stream $D \in \mathcal{D}(n,m)$ and a function g, call $j \in [n]$ a (g,λ)-*heavy hitter *of $V(D)$ if $g(|v_j|) \geq \lambda \sum_{i \neq j} g(|v_i|)$. We will use the terminology λ-heavy hitter when g is clear from the context.*

Given a heaviness parameter λ and approximation accuracy ϵ, a heavy hitters algorithm returns a set $\{i_1, i_2, \ldots\}$ containing every (g,λ)-heavy hitter and also returns a $(1\pm\epsilon)$-approximations to $g(v_{i_j})$ for each i_j in the set. Such a collection of pairs is called a (g,λ,ϵ)-cover.

DEFINITION 12. *Given a stream $D \in \mathcal{D}(n,m)$, a (g,λ,ϵ)-cover of $V(D)$ is a set of pairs $\{(i_1,w_1),(i_2,w_2),\ldots,(i_t,w_t)\}$, where $t \leq n$ and the following are true:*

1. *$\forall k \in [t]$, $|w_k - g(|v_{i_k}|)| \leq \epsilon g(|v_{i_k}|)$, and*
2. *if j is a (g,λ)-heavy hitter of $V(D)$, then there exists $k \in [t]$ such that $i_k = j$.*

Formally, a p-pass $(g,\lambda,\epsilon,\delta)$-heavy hitter algorithm is a p-pass streaming algorithm that outputs a (g,λ,ϵ)-cover of $V(D)$ with probability at least $(1-\delta)$.

THEOREM 13 ([7]). *Let $\lambda = \frac{\epsilon^2}{\log^3 n}$ and $\delta = \frac{1}{\log n}$. If there exists a $(g,\lambda,\epsilon,\delta)$-heavy hitter algorithm using s bits of space, then there exists a (g,ϵ)-SUM algorithm using $O(s \log n)$ bits of space.*

A similar approach has been used in other streaming algorithms; it was pioneered by Indyk and Woodruff [15] for the problem of approximating the frequency moments. Their algorithm uses the streaming algorithm CountSketch of Charikar, Chen, and Farach-Colton [9], and ours will as well. Given λ, ϵ, and δ, a CountSketch using space $O(\frac{1}{\lambda\epsilon^2}\log\frac{n}{\delta}\log M)$ gives an approximation $\hat{v}_i$ to the frequency of every item $i \in [n]$ with the following guarantee: with probability at least $(1-\delta)$, $|v_i - \hat{v}_i| \leq \epsilon\sqrt{\lambda F_2}$ for all $i \in [n]$. By adjusting the parameters slightly we can treat the output of CountSketch$(\lambda,\epsilon,\delta)$ as a set of $k = O(1/\lambda)$ pairs $(i_j, \hat{v}_{i_j})$ such that $\{i_j\}_{j=1}^k$ contains all of the λ-heavy hitters for F_2 and $|v_{i_j} - \hat{v}_{i_j}| \leq \epsilon\left(\sum_{j>k}\bar{v}_j^2\right)^{1/2} \leq \epsilon\sqrt{\lambda F_2}$, for all $j = 1,2,\ldots,k$, where $(\bar{v}_1,\ldots,\bar{v}_n)$ is a reordering of the frequency vector from largest to smallest absolute magnitude.

We establish our lower bounds using communication and information complexity. Several of our lower bounds can be shown by reduction from standard INDEX and DISJ problems, as well as a combination of them (related combined problems were used in [10, 21]). In the INDEX(n) problem, there are two players Alice, given a set $A \subseteq [n]$, and Bob, given $b \in [n]$. Alice sends a message to Bob, and with probability at least 2/3, Bob must determine whether $b \in A$. Any randomized one-way protocol for INDEX(n) requires Alice to send $\Omega(n)$ bits [18]. In an instance of $\mathsf{DISJ}(n,t)$ there are t players each receiving a subset of $[n]$ with the promise that either the sets are pairwise disjoint, or there is a single item that every set contains and other than this single item, the sets are pairwise disjoint. The players must determine which case they are in. The randomized, unrestricted communication complexity of $\mathsf{DISJ}(n,t)$ is $\Omega(n/t)$ [4, 8, 11, 17]. In the $\mathsf{DISJ{+}IND}(n,t)$ problem, $t+1$ players are given sets $A_1, A_2, \ldots, A_{t+1} \subseteq [n]$, such that $|A_{t+1}| = 1$, with the promise that either the sets are disjoint or there is a single element contained in every set and they are otherwise disjoint. A standard argument shows the one-way communication complexity of $\mathsf{DISJ{+}IND}(n,t)$ is $\Omega(n/t(\log n))$ (see Theorem 47).

To obtain stronger lower bounds for the nearly periodic function sums, we use the information complexity framework.

DEFINITION 14 (ShortLinearCombination PROBLEM). *Let $u = (u_1, u_2, \ldots u_r)$ be a vector in $\mathbb{Z}^r$ for some integer r. Let $d > 0$ be an integer not in $\{|u_1|, |u_2|, \ldots, |u_r|\}$. A stream S with frequency vector v is given to the player, v is promised to be from $V_0 = \{u_1, u_2, \ldots, u_r, 0\}^n$ or $V_1 = \{EMB(v,i,e) \mid v \in V_0, i \in [n], e \in \{-d, d\}\}$, where $EMB(v,i,e)$ is to embed e onto the i-th coordinate. The (u,d)-DIST problem is to distinguish whether $v \in V_0$ or $v \in V_1$.*

This problem is a generalization of the DISJ(n, t) problem. We show a $\Omega(n/q^2)$ bits lower bound for it where $q = \sum_{i=1}^{r} |q_i|$ and q_i are the integers such that $\min_q\{q_1, q_2, \ldots, q_r \mid \sum_{i=1}^{r} q_i u_i = d\}$. For more details, we refer the reader to Appendix C.

4. ZERO-ONE LAWS FOR NORMAL FUNCTIONS

First, we develop some intuition about why the three conditions, slow-dropping, slow-jumping, and predictable, characterize tractable normal functions. Next comes the two pass and one pass algorithms followed by the lower bounds. Finally, we prove Theorem 2 and 3 in Section 4.6.

4.1 Our Techniques

The upper and lower bounds are both established using heavy hitters. Using a $\frac{\epsilon^2}{\log^3 n}$-heavy hitters subroutine that identifies each heavy hitter H and also approximates $g(f_H)$, the algorithm of Braverman and Ostrovsky [7] (Theorem 13) solves g-SUM with $O(\log n)$ storage overhead. We will show that if g is tractable then a subpolynomially sized CountSketch suffices to find heavy hitters for g. On the lower bounds side, typical streaming lower bounds, going back to the work of Alon, Matias, and Szegedy, are derived from reductions to communication complexity that only require the streaming algorithm to detect the presence of a heavy hitter. Thus the problem of characterizing tractable functions can be reduced to characterizing the set of functions admitting subpolynomial heavy hitters algorithms.

Now let us explain how each of the three properties relates to heavy hitters. For this discussion let $\alpha = \epsilon^2/\log^3 n$ be the heaviness parameter needed by Braverman's and Ostrovsky's algorithm and let $H \in [n]$ be the identity of some α-heavy hitter.

Slow-jumping and Slow-dropping.

A function that satisfies these two conditions cannot increase much faster than a quadratic function nor can it decreasy rapidly. This means that if H is a heavy hitter for g then it is also a heavy hitter for F_2. Concretely, suppose that there exists an increasing subpolynomial function h such that $g(y)/g(x) \leq (y/x)^2 h(y)$ and $g(x) \geq g(y)/h(y)$, for all $x \leq y$, so that g is slow-jumping and slow-dropping (Propositions 15 and 16 show that such an h always exists if g is slow-jumping and slow-dropping). A bit of algebra shows that $g(f_H) \geq \alpha \sum_i g(f_i)$ implies $f_H^2 \geq \frac{\alpha}{h(M)^2} \sum_j f_j^2$, so H is a $\alpha' := \frac{\alpha}{h(M)^2}$-heavy hitter for F_2. CountSketch suffices to identify all α'-heavy hitters for F_2 with $O(\alpha' \log^2 n)$ bits, so this gives an α-heavy hitters algorithm for g that still uses subpolynomial space.

If a function is not slow-jumping then a heavy hitter may be too small to detect and we prove a lower bound by reduction from DISJ+IND in a very similar fashion to the original lower bound for approximating the frequency moments by Alon, Matias, and Szegedy.

If a function is not slow-dropping then f_H may be hidden below many small frequencies. In this case, a reduction from the communication complexity of INDEX usually works to establish a one-pass lower bound (two player DISJ can be used for a multipass lower bound). Here is a preview of the reduction that will also explain the genesis of the nearly periodic functions. Suppose $g(1) = 1$ and there is an increasing sequence $n_k \in \mathbb{N}$ such that $g(n_k) \leq 1/n_k$. Alice and Bob can solve an instance $(A \subseteq [n_k], b \in [n_k])$ of INDEX as follows. Alice creates a stream where every item in A has frequency n_k and the items in $[n_k] \setminus A$ do not appear. To Alice's stream Bob adds one copy of his item and they jointly run a streaming algorithm to approximate $g(f)$. The result is an approximation to either $|A|g(n_k) + 1$ or $(|A| - 1)g(n_k) + g(n_k + 1)$. If $g(n_k + 1)$ differs significantly from $g(n_k) + 1 \approx 1$ then Bob can determine whether $b \in A$ by checking the approximation to $g(f)$. The reduction fails if $g(n_k + 1) \approx 1$ and such a fuction may be tractable! A prime example is g_{np} from Section 3, which we demonstrate in Section 5.

At this point, one might have in mind our two pass heavy hitters algorithm. The algorithm is to use a CountSketch on the first pass to identify a subpolynomial size set of items containing all α-heavy hitters and then use the second pass just to tabulate the frequency of each of those items exactly. The details and proof of correctness for that algorithm are in Section 4.2. Local variability of the function is irrelevant for two passes because we can compute the frequencies exactly during the second pass, and that is why a function need not satisfy predictability to be two pass tractable. A one pass algorithm will have to get by with approximate frequencies.

Predictable.

Predictability is a condition on the local variability of the function. It roughly says that if $y \ll x$ then either $g(x + y) \approx g(x)$ or $g(y)$ is on the same scale[2] as $g(x)$. The first conclusion has an obvious interpretation; it means that substituting an approximation to x yields an approximation to $g(x)$. CountSketch returns an approximation to the frequency of every heavy hitter, so, in the first case, we can just as well use the approximation and there is no need to determine the frequency exactly.

The second conclusion allows local variability, but it must be accompanied by some "global" property of g, namely, g does not change a whole lot over the interval $[y, x]$. For an illustration of how predictability works, suppose that H is a heavy hitter and there is some $y \ll f_H$ such that $g(y) \geq 2g(f_H)$. Our algorithm cannot substitute $f_H + y$ for f_H because this could lead to too much error. But, approximating f_H to better accuracy than $\pm y$ using a CountSketch, one would generally need more than $(f_H/y)^2$ counters, which could be very large. Notice that y, if it occurs as a frequency in the stream and suppose it does, is a heavy hitter, and if g is slow-jumping and slow-dropping then y is also a heavy hitter for F_2 by our previous argument. It follows that the error in the frequency estimate derived from the CountSketch is less than y, in particular an estimate of f_H derived from the CountSketch will be more accurate than $\pm y$. The result is that we get an error estimate for the CountSketch that is improved over a naïve analysis. The approximate frequency $\hat{f}_H$ satisfies $g(\hat{f}_H) \approx g(f_H)$ and is accurate enough for Braverman and Ostrovsky's algorithm. When g is locally variable but not predictable, we get a one pass lower bound by a reduction from INDEX.

[2]More precisely, $g(y)$ is not much smaller than $g(x)$, if g is slow-dropping then $g(y)$ cannot be much larger than $g(x)$, either.

4.2 Two Pass Algorithm

We we will now show that any λ-heavy hitter for a slow-dropping, slow-jumping, $\mathbb{S}$-normal function is also F_2 λ'-heavy for λ' modestly smaller than λ. This means that we can use the CountSketch to identify heavy hitters in one pass for the Recursive Sketch. For a heavy hitters algorithm we also need a $(1\pm\epsilon)$-approximation to each item's contribution to g-SUM, we can easily accomplish this in the second pass by exactly tabulating the frequency of each heavy hitter identified in the first pass. This algorithm works as long as we identify every heavy hitter in the first pass, which CountSketch guarantees, and the space required remains small provided that we do not misclassify too many non-heavy hitters (so that we do not tabulate too many values in the second pass). The procedure is formally defined in Algorithm 1. Note that by Proposition 10 $\mathbb{P}$-normal functions are also $\mathbb{S}$-normal, hence, the algorithm works for slow-dropping and slow-jumping $\mathbb{P}$-normal functions.

The next two propositions describe equivalent definitions of slow-dropping and slow-jumping that are useful in describing the algorithm.

PROPOSITION 15. *$g \in \mathcal{G}$ is slow-dropping if and only if there exists a sub-polynomial function h such that for all $y \in \mathbb{N}$ and $x < y$ we have $g(x) \leq g(y)h(y)$.*

PROOF. The "if" direction follows immediately from the definition of the class of sub-polynomial functions.

For the "only if", suppose that $g(x)$ is slow-dropping. Specifically, for any $\alpha > 0$ there exists $N > 0$ such that for all $y \geq N$ and $x < y$ we have $y^\alpha g(y) \geq g(x)$. Let N_i be the least integer such that $y^{1/i} g(y) \geq g(x)$, for all $y > N_i$ and $x < y$. The sequence N_i is nondecreasing. Consider the increasing function $i(y) = \max\{i : N_i \leq y\}$ and set $h(y) = y^{1/i(y)}$. For all $x < y$ we have $h(y)g(y) \geq g(x)$ by construction.

To see that h is sub-polynomial, let $\beta > 0$. First, $h \geq 1$ hence $h(y)y^\beta \to \infty$. Second, let $i^* \geq 2/\beta$ then for all $y \geq N_{i^*}$ we have

$$h(y) \leq y^{1/i^*} \leq y^{\beta/2}.$$

Thus $h(y)y^{-\beta} \to 0$, which completes the proof. □

PROPOSITION 16. *$g \in \mathcal{G}$ is slow-jumping if and only if there exists a sub-polynomial function $h(x)$ such that for any $x < y$ we have $g(y) \leq \lfloor y/x \rfloor^2 h(\lfloor y/x \rfloor x) g(x)$.*

PROOF. Again, the "if" direction follows immediately from the definition of the class of sub-polynomial function. The reverse direction follows from the same argument as Proposition 15. □

Given g and a sub-polynomial accuracy ϵ, Propositions 15 and 16 each imply the existence of a non-decreasing sub-polynomial function. By taking the point-wise maximum, we can assume that these are the same sub-polynomial function $H : \mathbb{N} \to \mathbb{R}$. In particular H satisfies:

- $g(y) \geq g(x)/H(y)$, for all $x < y$, and
- $g(y) \leq (y/x)^2 y^\alpha H(y) g(x)$, for all $x < y$.

The space used by our algorithm depends on the sub-polynomial functions governing the slow-dropping and slow-jumping of g. If these are polylogarithmic then the algorithm is limited to polylogarithmic space.

LEMMA 17. *Let g be a function that is slow-jumping and slow-dropping. There exists a sub-polynomial function h such that for any $D \in \mathcal{D}(n, m)$ with frequencies $v_1, v_2, \ldots, v_n$, if $g(v_i) \geq \lambda \sum_j g(v_j)$ then*

$$v_i^2 \geq \frac{\lambda}{h(|v_i|)} \sum_{|v_j|<|v_i|} v_j^2.$$

PROOF. By Proposition 16, there exists a nondecreasing sub-polynomial function h such that for all $y \in \mathbb{N}$ and $x < y$ we have $g(y) \leq (y/x)^2 h(y) g(x)$.

For any j that satisfies $|v_j| < |v_i|$, we have $g(v_i) \leq g(v_j)(\frac{v_i}{v_j})^2 h(|v_i|)$. Therefore,

$$g(v_i) \geq \lambda \sum_j g(v_j) \geq \lambda \sum_{|v_j|<|v_i|} \frac{g(v_i)}{h(|v_i|)} \left(\frac{v_j}{v_i}\right)^2.$$

By rearranging, we find

$$v_i^2 \geq \frac{\lambda}{h(|v_i|)} \sum_{|v_j|<|v_i|} v_j^2 \geq \frac{\lambda}{h(|v_i|)} \sum_{|v_j|<|v_i|} v_j^2.$$

□

Algorithm 1 A 2-pass $(g, \lambda, 0, \delta)$-heavy hitters algorithm.

procedure 2-PASS HEAVY HITTERS(g, λ, ϵ, δ)
  First Pass:
    $S \leftarrow$CountSketch($\frac{\lambda}{2H(M)}, \frac{1}{3}, \delta$) discarding the frequency estimates
  Second Pass:
    Compute v_j for all $i \in S$
  return (j, v_j), for all $j \in S$

Algorithm 1 computes CountSketch[3] with $r = O(\log n)$ and $b = O(\frac{H(M)}{\lambda\epsilon^2})$ over the stream and extracts the $2H(M)/\lambda$ items with the highest estimated frequencies. Denote this list as $(i_j, \hat{v}_{i_j})_{j=1}^{2H(M)/\lambda}$. The 2-pass algorithm then discards the estimated frequencies $\hat{v}_{i_j}$ and tabulates the true frequency of each item i_j on the second pass.

LEMMA 18. *If g is a function that is slow-dropping and slow-jumping then the CountSketch used by Algorithm 1 finds all of the (g, λ)-heavy hitters.*

PROOF. From the slow-dropping condition and Lemma 17, for every $x < y \in \mathbb{N}$ we have

1. $g(y)H(y) \geq g(x)$ and
2. $g(v_i) \geq \lambda \sum_j g(v_j)$ implies

$$v_i^2 \geq \frac{\lambda}{H(M)} \sum_{|v_j|<|v_i|} v_j^2.$$

Let $D \in \mathcal{D}(n, m)$, suppose i satisfies $g(v_i) \geq \lambda \sum_j^n g(v_j)$. Since

$$g(v_i) \geq \lambda \sum_{|v_j|\geq|v_i|} g(v_j) \geq \frac{\lambda}{H(M)} \sum_{|v_j|\geq|v_i|} g(v_i),$$

there are at most $H(M)\lambda^{-1}$ items with frequencies as large or larger than v_i in magnitude.

[3] A CountSketch is a matrix with r and b rows. See [9] for details about these parameters.

Thus, a CountSketch for $\lambda/2H(M)$-heavy hitters, as is used by Algorithm 1, serves to identify the λ-heavy heavy hitters for g in one pass. □

THEOREM 19. *A function $g \in \mathcal{G}$ is 2-pass tractable and $\mathbb{S}$-normal if it is slow-dropping and slow-jumping.*

PROOF. If a function is slow-dropping then it is $\mathbb{S}$-normal. By Theorem 13, it is sufficient to show that Algorithm 1 is a sub-polynomial memory $(g, \lambda, \epsilon, \delta)$-heavy hitters algorithm for $\lambda = \frac{\epsilon^2}{\log^3 n}$, $\epsilon = \frac{1}{H(Mn)}$, and $\delta \leq \frac{1}{\log n}$.

This is a 2-pass $(g, \lambda, 0, \delta)$-heavy hitters algorithm, and it requires $O(\frac{h(M)}{\epsilon^2} \log^4 n \log nM \log\log n)$ space. The algorithm is correct with probability at least $(1-\delta)$ because this is true for the CountSketch. Therefore, g is a 2-pass tractable function. □

4.3 One Pass Algorithm

The only impediment to reducing the two pass algorithm to a single pass is local variability of the function. The algorithm must simultaneously identify heavy hitters and estimate their frequencies, but local variability could require tighter estimates than seem to be available from a sub-polynomial space CountSketch data structure. If an $\mathbb{S}$-normal function is predictable then we almost immediately overcome this barrier. In particular, the definition means that given any point x and a small error $y = o(x)$ either $|g(x+y) - g(x)| \leq \epsilon g(x)$ or $g(y)$ is reasonably large, and while it is clear how the first case helps us with the approximation algorithm, the second is less clear. The slow-dropping and slow-jumping conditions play a role, as we now explain.

PROPOSITION 20. *A function g is predictable if and only if for every sub-polynomial $\epsilon > 0$ there exists a sub-polynomial function h such that for all $x \in \mathbb{N}$ and $y \in [1, x/h(x))$ satisfying $x + y \notin \delta_{\epsilon(x)}(g, x)$ it holds that $g(y) \geq g(x)/h(x)$.*

PROOF. The "if" direction follows directly from the definition of sub-polynomial functions.

To prove the "only if" direction, let $\gamma_i = 1/i$. Since g is predictable, there exists N_i such that either $x + y \in \delta_{\epsilon(x)}(g, x)$ or $g(y) \geq x^{-\gamma} g(x)$ for $x \geq N_i$ and $y \in [1, x^{1-\gamma})$. Let $i(z) = \max\{i \in \mathbb{N} \mid N_i \leq z\}$, for $z \geq N_1$, and define $h(z) = z^{1/i(z)}$, for $z \geq N_1$, and $h(z) = \max_{1 \leq x', y' < N_1} g(x')/g(y')$, for $z < N_1$. Then h is a sub-polynomial function. The claim is that h satisfies the conclusion of the lemma. Let $x \in \mathbb{N}$ and $y \in [1, x/h(x))$. If $x < N_1$ then $y \leq x < N_1$ because $h \geq 1$. Furthermore,

$$g(y)h(x) = g(y) \max_{1 \leq x', y' < N_1} \frac{g(x')}{g(y')} \geq g(y)\frac{g(x)}{g(y)} = g(x).$$

If $x \geq N_1$, let $i = i(x) \geq 1$, so that $x \geq N_i$ and $h(x) = x^{1/i}$. Since g is predictable, if $y \in [1, x/h(x))$ and $y + x \notin \delta_{\epsilon(x)}(g, x)$ then $g(y) \geq x^{-1/i} g(x) = g(x)/h(x)$. □

Let $r_\epsilon(x) := \max\{y \mid x + y' \in \delta_\epsilon(x), \text{ for all } |y'| \leq y\}$.

LEMMA 21 (PREDICTABILITY BOOSTER). *If g is slow-dropping, slow-jumping, and predictable, then there is a sub-polynomial function h such that for all $y \in [r_\epsilon(x)+1, x/h(x))$ we have $g(y) \geq g(x)/h(x)$.*

PROOF. According to Proposition 20, there exists a sub-polynomial function h' such that for all $y \in [1, x/h'(x))$ if $x + y \notin \delta_{\epsilon/2}(x)$ then $g(y) \geq g(x)/h'(x)$. Without loss of generality h' governs the slow-jumping of g as well, hence $g(x) \leq (x/x')^2 h'(x) g(x')$ for all $x' \leq x$.

We consider two cases:

1. $|g(x) - g(x + r_\epsilon(x) + 1)| > \epsilon g(x)$ and
2. $|g(x) - g(x - r_\epsilon(x) - 1)| > \epsilon g(x)$.

In the first case, by the definition of r_ϵ and predictability we have $g(r_\epsilon(x) + 1) \geq g(x)/h'(x)$. In the second case, let $x' = x - r_\epsilon - 1$. If $g(x') \geq 2g(x)$ then $|g(x') - g(x)| > \epsilon g(x')$, as long as $\epsilon < 1/2$. Otherwise, $|g(x') - g(x)| \geq \epsilon g(x) \geq \frac{\epsilon}{2} g(x')$. Now, from predictability at x' and the definition of h', we find that

$$g(r_\epsilon(x) + 1) = g(x - x') \geq \frac{g(x')}{h'(x')} \geq \frac{g(x)}{4h'(x)^2},$$

where the last inequality follows because g is slow-jumping and $x' \geq x/2$ (w.l.o.g., choose $h'(x) > 2$).

Now, since g satisfies the slow dropping condition there exists a nondecreasing sub-polynomial function h'' such that $g(y') \geq g(r')/h''(y')$ for all $y' \in \mathbb{N}$ and $r' \leq y'$. Thus, if $y \in [r_\epsilon(x) + 1, x/h(x))$

$$g(y) \geq \frac{g(r_\epsilon(x) + 1)}{h''(y)} \geq \frac{g(x)}{4h'(x)^2 h''(x)},$$

so we take h to be the product of $4(h')^2$ and h''. □

Recall the sub-polynomial function H from the last section and let it also satisfy Lemma 21 with ϵ replaced by $\epsilon/2$. In particular H now satisfies three conditions:

- $g(y) \geq g(x)/H(y)$, for all $x < y$, and
- $g(y) \leq (y/x)^2 H(y) g(x)$, for all $x < y$.
- for all $y \in [r_{\epsilon/2}(x)+1, x/h(x))$ we have $g(y) \geq g(x)/H(x)$.

Let y be the (additive) error in our estimate of frequency x of a (g, λ)-heavy hitter. If $r_\epsilon(x) > |y|$ then we are fine. If not, consider the point $x + r_\epsilon(x) + 1$ (or $x - r_\epsilon(x) - 1$), which has $|g(x + r_\epsilon(x) + 1) - g(x)| > \epsilon g(x)$ and therefore $g(r_\epsilon(x) + 1) > g(x)/H(M)$. Now, since x is the frequency of a (g, λ)-heavy hitter it happens that $r_\epsilon(x) + 1$, were it a frequency in the stream, would be $(g, \lambda/H(M))$-heavy and thus $\lambda/H(M)^2$-heavy for F_2. Presuming that there are not too many items in the stream with frequency larger than $r_\epsilon(x)$, this implies that CountSketch produces an estimate for x with error smaller than $r_\epsilon(x)$. Now, since g satisfies the slow dropping condition there cannot be too many frequencies larger than $r_\epsilon(x)$ in the stream because

$$g(z) \geq \frac{g(r_\epsilon(x) + 1)}{H(M)} \geq \frac{g(x)}{H(M)^2}, \text{ for all } z > r_\epsilon,$$

which implies that there are at most $\frac{1}{\lambda} H(M)^2$ frequencies in this range.

4.4 One Pass Lower Bounds

The proof of the following theorem is broken up into Lemmas 23, 24 and 25.

THEOREM 22. *If $g \in \mathcal{G}$ is a 1-pass tractable $\mathbb{S}$-normal function, then g is slow-jumping, slow-dropping, and predictable.*

PROOF. Immediate from Lemmas 23 , 24, and 25. □

Algorithm 2 A 1-pass $(g, \lambda, \epsilon, \delta)$-heavy hitters algorithm.

procedure 1-PASS HEAVY HITTERS(g, λ, ϵ, δ)
  $\hat{S}, \hat{V} \leftarrow$CountSketch$(\frac{\lambda}{3H(M)}, \frac{\epsilon}{2H(M)}, \delta/2)$
  $\hat{F}_2 \leftarrow$AMS$(\epsilon, \delta/2)$
  $S \leftarrow \{i \in \hat{S} : |g(\hat{v}_i) - g(\hat{v}_i + y)| \leq \epsilon g(\hat{v}_i + y),$
    for all $-\frac{\epsilon}{2H(M)}\sqrt{\hat{F}_2} \leq y \leq \frac{\epsilon}{2H(M)}\sqrt{\hat{F}_2}\}$
  return $(j, \hat{v}_j)$, for all $j \in S$

LEMMA 23. *If an $\mathbb{S}$-normal function $g \in \mathcal{G}$ is not slow-dropping, then g is not 1-pass tractable.*

PROOF. Suppose g is not slow-dropping. Then there exist $0 < \alpha \leq 1$ and integer sequences $y_1, y_2, \ldots \in \mathbb{N}$ and $x_1, x_2, \ldots \in \mathbb{N}$, with y_k increasing, such that $x_k < y_k$ and $g(x_k) \geq y_k^\alpha g(y_k)$, for all $k \geq 1$. Furthermore, since g is $\mathbb{S}$-normal we may choose the sequences so that there exists a sub-polynomial function h satisfying

$$|g(x_k + y_k) - g(x_k)| > \frac{1}{h(y_k)} \min\{g(x_k), g(x_k + y_k)\}, \quad (1)$$

for all k. We claim that one can take $|g(x_k + y_k) - g(x_k)| > g(x_k)/h(y_k)$. If $g(x_k+y_k) < \frac{1}{2}g(x_k)$ then this is true because the constant function 2 is sub-polynomial. On the other hand, if $g(x_k + y_k) \geq \frac{1}{2}g(x_k)$ then replacing h by $2h$ in (1) does the job. Also, note that $1/h(x)$ is still a sub-polynomial function.

Let $\mathcal{A}$ be a 1-pass (g, ϵ)-SUM algorithm with $\epsilon = (3h(n))^{-1}$. We will show that $\mathcal{A}$ uses $\Omega(n^\alpha)$ bits on a sequence of g-SUM problems with $n = y_1, y_2, \ldots$, hence g is not tractable. Let $n = y_k$ and $x = x_k$ and consider the following protocol for INDEX(n^α) using $\mathcal{A}$. Alice receives a set $A \subseteq [n^\alpha]$ and Bob receives an index $b \in [n^\alpha]$. Alice and Bob jointly create a notional stream D and run $\mathcal{A}$ on it. Alice contributes n copies of i for each $i \in A$ to the stream and Bob contributes x copies of his index b. If $b \notin A$ there are $|A|$ items in the stream with frequency n and one with frequency x; whereas if $b \in A$ then $|A| - 1$ frequencies are equal to n and one is $n + x$. Alice runs $\mathcal{A}$ on her portion of the stream and sends the memory to Bob along with the value $|A|$. Bob completes the computation with his portion of the stream. Let $\hat{G}$ be the value returned to Bob by $\mathcal{A}$. Bob decides that there is an intersection if $\frac{\hat{G}}{|A|g(n)+g(x)} \notin [1 - \epsilon, 1 + \epsilon]$.

With probability at least 2/3, $\hat{G}$ is a $(1 \pm \epsilon)$-approximation to $g(V(D))$; suppose that this is so. If $b \in A$ then $g(V(D)) = (|A|-1)g(n)+g(x+n)$ and otherwise the result is $g(V(D)) = |A|g(n)+g(x)$. Without loss of generality $g(n) < \epsilon g(x)$, thus the difference between these values is

$$\begin{aligned}|g(n) + g(x) - g(x + n)| &> |g(x) - g(x + n)| - \epsilon g(x)\\ &\geq 2\epsilon g(x)\\ &\geq \epsilon(g(x) + n^\alpha g(n))\\ &\geq \epsilon(g(x) + |A|g(n)).\end{aligned}$$

Thus Bob's decision is correct and g-SUM inherits the $\Omega(n^\alpha)$ lower bound from INDEX(n^α). □

LEMMA 24. *If an $\mathbb{S}$-normal function $g \in \mathcal{G}$ is not slow-jumping, then g is not 1-pass tractable.*

PROOF. Since g is not slow-jumping, there exist $\alpha > 0$, a strictly increasing sequence $y_1, y_2, \ldots \in \mathbb{N}$, and a sequence $x_1, x_2, \ldots \in \mathbb{N}$ such that $x_k \leq y_k$ and $g(y_k) > s_k^{2+\alpha} x_k^\alpha g(x_k)$, where $s_k = \lfloor y_k/x_k \rfloor$. Without loss of generality y_k is strictly increasing. According to Lemma 23, we can assume that g is slow-dropping, since otherwise it is not 1-pass tractable. Hence, there exists $N \in \mathbb{N}$ such that for all $x \geq N$ and $r \leq x$ we have $\frac{1}{2}x^\alpha g(x) \geq g(r)$. If $x_k \leq N$ for all but finitely many k, we may assume this holds for all k. Otherwise, by taking a subsequence, we can assume $x_k > N$ holds for all k.

Let $r_k = y_k - s_k x_k$ be the sequence remainders. Before proceeding with the reduction we will establish the bound $2g(r_k) \leq g(y_k)$. If $x_k \leq N$, for all k, then s_k is unbounded while $x_k g(x_k)$ is bounded away from zero. This means that $g(y_k)$ is unbounded while $g(r_k)$ is bounded and we can assume y_1 is large enough that $g(y_k) \geq 2g(r_k)$ holds for all k. Otherwise $x_k > N$, for every k, hence $2g(r_k) \leq x_k^\alpha g(x_k) \leq g(y_k)$, for each k, from the definition of N.

Let $\mathcal{A}$ be a (g, ϵ)-SUM algorithm with accuracy $\epsilon = 1/12$. Consider the DISJ+IND(n, t) problem, where $t = s_k$ and $n = s_k^{2+\alpha} x_k^\alpha$. Denote $x := x_k$, $y := y_k$, $s := s_k$ and $r := r_k$. The $t + 1$ players receive sets $A_1, A_2, \ldots, A_t \subseteq [n]$ and an index $b \in [n]$. As before, the players jointly run $\mathcal{A}$ on a notional stream and share $|A_i|$. Each player i places x copies of each $j \in A_i$ into the stream except for the final player who places r copies of his index b. Let $n' = \sum_i |A_i|$ be the total size of the t players' sets. On an intersecting instance the result of g-SUM is $a_1 := (n' - t)g(x) + g(y)$, and on a disjoint instance the result is $a_2 := n'g(x) + g(r)$.

The difference is

$$\begin{aligned}a_1 - a_2 &\geq g(y) - g(r) - tg(x) > \frac{1}{2}g(y) - tg(x)\\ &\geq \frac{1}{6}(g(y) + (2s^{2+\alpha}x^\alpha)g(x)) - sg(x)\\ &= \frac{1}{6}(g(y) + (s^{2+\alpha}x^\alpha + s^{2+\alpha}x^\alpha - 6s)g(x))\\ &\geq 2\epsilon(g(y) + s^{2+\alpha}x^\alpha g(x))\\ &= 2\epsilon(n'g(x) + g(y)), \quad (2)\end{aligned}$$

where the last inequality holds for all sufficiently large n. Thus, the index player can correctly distinguish which case has occurred, and the algorithm requires $\Omega(n/t^2) = \Omega(y^\alpha)$ bits. □

LEMMA 25. *If an $\mathbb{S}$-normal function $g \in \mathcal{G}$ is not predictable, then g is not 1-pass tractable.*

PROOF. Since g is not predictable, there exists a sub-polynomial function ϵ and constant $\gamma > 0$ such that some infinite sequence x_k, y_k satisfies the following:

- $x_k \to \infty$ and $y_k \in [1, x_k^{1-\gamma})$,
- $x_k + y_k \notin \delta_{\epsilon(x_k)}(g, x_k)$, and
- $x_k^\gamma g(y_k) < g(x_k)$.

The proof is by a reduction from INDEX(n) with $n = \epsilon(x_k)x_k^\gamma/4$. Suppose $\mathcal{A}$ is an algorithm for $(g, \epsilon/4)$-SUM. Alice receives a set $A \subseteq [n]$ and Bob receives an index $b \in [n]$. Alice adds y_k copies of i to the stream, for each $i \in A$, runs $\mathcal{A}$ on her portion of the stream, and sends the contents of the memory to Bob. Bob adds x_k copies of b to the stream and completes the computation.

The stream has $|A|$ frequencies equal to y_k and one equal to x_k, if there is no intersection, or $|A| - 1$ equal to y_k and one equal to $x_k + y_k$, if there is an intersection. Recall that $x_k + y_k \notin \delta_\epsilon(g, x_k)$, hence $|g(x_k) - g(x_k + y_k)| > \epsilon g(x_k)$, and by construction

$$|A|g(y_k) \leq \frac{\epsilon(x_k)}{4} x_k^\gamma g(y_k) \leq \frac{\epsilon(x_k)}{4} g(x_k).$$

Therefore, Bob can correctly distinguish whether $b \in A$ when $\mathcal{A}$ yields a $(1 \pm \epsilon/4)$-approximation. Thus $(g, \epsilon/4)$-SUM requires $\Omega(n)$ bits. □

4.5 Two Pass Lower Bounds

THEOREM 26. *If a $\mathbb{P}$-normal function $g \in \mathcal{G}$ is tractable then g is slow-dropping and slow-jumping.*

PROOF. Immediate from Lemmas 27 and 28. □

LEMMA 27. *If a $\mathbb{P}$-normal function $g \in \mathcal{G}$ is not slow-dropping, then g is not $O(1)$-pass tractable.*

PROOF. Suppose $\mathcal{A}$ is a $p = O(1)$ pass algorithm that solves (g, ϵ)-SUM and g does not satisfy slow-dropping condition. Then there exists $\alpha > 0$ such that for any $N > 0$, there exists $y > N$ and $x < y$ satisfying $g(y) < g(x)/y^\alpha$. Separately, since g is $\mathbb{P}$-normal, there exists $\beta > 0$ such that for any $N > 0$ if g has an α-period $y > N$ then there is an α-period $y > N$ and $x < y$ such that $g(y) \leq g(x)/y^\alpha$ and $|g(x + y) - g(x)| > y^\beta \min(g(x), g(x + y))$.

Let $\gamma = \min(\alpha, \beta)$. Consider the following protocol for DISJ$(n, 2)$, where $n = y^{\gamma/2}$.

First, consider $g(x + y) \leq g(x)$. Since $|g(x + y) - g(x)| > y^\gamma g(x+y)$ and $y^\gamma g(x+y) \geq g(x+y)$, then $g(x) \geq y^\gamma g(x+y)$. The players jointly create a stream where Player 1 inserts x copies of each element of her set S_1 into the stream, and Player 2 inserts y copies of every element a not in her set S_2. First Player 1 creates her portion of the stream, runs the first pass of $\mathcal{A}$ on it, and sends the memory to Player 2. She completes the first pass with her portion of the stream, and returns the memory to Player 1. The players continue in this way for a total of p passes over the stream.

Let V denote the frequency vector of the resulting stream. If there is an intersection, let $S_1 \cap S_2 = \{a\}$. Then $S_1 \cap \bar{S}_2 = S_1 \backslash \{a\}$, and $g(V)$ is $r_1 = (|S_1| - 1)g(x + y) + (n - |S_2| - |S_1|)g(y) + g(x) + g(y)$. If there is no intersection, the value of $g(V)$ is $r_2 = (|S_1| - 1)g(x+y) + (n - |S_2| - |S_1|)g(y) + g(x+y)$. Notice that

$$\frac{|r_2 - r_1|}{r_1} \geq \frac{|g(x + y) - g(x)|}{g(x)} \geq \frac{1}{2},$$

for sufficiently large n. For any $\epsilon < 1/2$, $\mathcal{A}$ is able to distinguish the 2 cases, which gives a lower bound on the memory bits used by $\mathcal{A}$ is $\Omega(n/p)$.

The case $g(x + y) > g(x)$ is the same except Player 2 inserts y copies of each element that *is* in her set S_2. Thus, $\mathcal{A}$ uses $\Omega(n/p)$ bits of memory, hence g is not $O(1)$-pass tractable. □

LEMMA 28. *If a $\mathbb{P}$-normal function $g \in \mathcal{G}$ is not slow-jumping, then g is not $O(1)$-pass tractable.*

PROOF. Suppose $\mathcal{A}$ is a $p = O(1)$ pass algorithm for (g, ϵ)-SUM. If g is not slow-jumping, then there exists $\alpha > 0$ such that for any $N > 0$, there exists $x < y \in \mathbb{N}$ and $y \geq N$ but $g(y) > \lfloor y/x \rfloor^{2+\alpha} x^\alpha g(x)$. Notice that for $y > x$ we have $\lfloor y/x \rfloor \geq y/2x$, so by adjusting α we can assume $g(y) > (y/x)^2 y^\alpha g(x)$.

We can further assume g is slow dropping, since otherwise g is not $O(1)$-pass tractable by Lemma 27. Thus, there exists a nondecreasing sub-polynomial function $h(x) > 1$ such that $g(x) \leq h(y)g(y)$.

Consider an instance $A_1, A_2, \ldots, A_t \subseteq [n]$ of $\mathsf{DISJ}(n, t)$, where $t = \lceil y/x \rceil$ and $n = (\frac{y}{x})^2 \frac{y^\alpha}{2h(y)}$. Each of the first $t - 1$ players, inserts x copies of her elements into the stream and the tth player inserts $y - (t - 1)x < x$ copies of her elements into the stream. The players pass the memory and repeat to run the p passes of $\mathcal{A}$ as before. Notice that $g(y - (t - 1)x) \leq h(x)g(x)$ by the slow dropping condition.

Let $n' = \sum_i |A_i|$, and let V be the frequency vector of the stream created. If there is no intersection, the value of $g(V)$ is

$$\begin{aligned}(n' - |A_t|)g(x) + |A_t|g(y - (t - 1)x) &\leq n'h(x)g(x)\\ &\leq nh(x)g(x) \leq \frac{1}{2}g(y).\end{aligned}$$

On the other hand, if there is an intersection then y is the frequency of some item in the stream, and therefore $g(V) \geq g(y)$. Thus $\mathcal{A}$ distinguishes between the cases. The algorithm uses $\Omega(n/pt^2) = \Omega(y^{\alpha/2}/p)$ bits of memory, which proves that g is not p-pass tractable. □

4.6 Zero-One Law Proofs

THEOREM 2 (1-PASS ZERO-ONE LAW). *A function $g \in \mathcal{G}$ is 1-pass tractable and $\mathbb{S}$-normal if and only if it is slow-jumping, slow-dropping, and predictable.*

PROOF. The lower bound is proved as Theorem 26, hence the algorithm remains. With the Recursive Sketch of Theorem 13, it is enough to show that Algorithm 2 is a $(g, \lambda, \epsilon, \delta)$-heavy hitters algorithm for $\lambda = \epsilon^2/\log^3 n$ and $\delta = 1/\log n$.

By Lemma 18, the Count Sketch used by Algorithm 2 returns a list of pairs $(i_j, \hat{v}_{i_j})$ containing all of the $\lambda/3H(M)$-heavy elements for F_2. By definition, any item i_j that survives the pruning stage has $|g(\hat{v}_{i_j}) - g(v_j)| \leq \epsilon g(v_j)$. Hence, it only remains to show that every (g, λ)-heavy hitter survives the pruning stage.

Suppose i' is the index of the (g, λ)-heavy hitter that minimizes $r_{\epsilon/2}(v_{i'})$. Now suppose that we insert a new item i'' in the stream with frequency $v_{i''} = r_{\epsilon/2}(v_{i'}) + 1$. Then

$$\frac{g(v_{i'})}{H(M)} \leq g(v_{i''}) \leq H(M)g(v_{i'}),$$

where the first inequality follows from Lemma 21 and the second because g is slow-dropping. Thus, this item is a $(g, \frac{\lambda}{3H(M)})$-heavy hitter and the constant term on the parameter b for the Count Sketch can be chosen to guarantee additive error no more than $v_{i''}/3 \leq r_{\epsilon/2}(v_{i'})/3$. The same guarantee holds for the stream without i'', thus for every (g, λ)-heavy hitter i_j we have

$$|\hat{v}_{i_j} - v_{i_j}| \leq \frac{1}{3} r_{\epsilon/2}(v_{i'}) \leq \frac{1}{3} r_{\epsilon/2}(v_{i_j}),$$

where the last inequality holds by the choice of i'. Furthermore, for every $-r_{\epsilon/2}(v_{i'})/3 \leq y \leq r_{\epsilon/2}(v_{i'})/3$ we have $|(\hat{v}_{i_j} + y) - v_{i_j}| \leq r_{\epsilon/2}(v_{i_j})$ and thus

$$\begin{aligned}|g(\hat{v}_{i_j}) - g(\hat{v}_{i_j} + y)| \leq& |g(\hat{v}_{i_j}) - g(v_{i_j})|\\ &+ |g(v_{i_j}) - g(\hat{v}_{i_j} + y)|\\ \leq& \epsilon g(\hat{v}_{i_j} + y).\end{aligned}$$

With probability at least $1-2\delta/2 = 1-\delta$ both the Count Sketch and the AMS approximation of F_2 meet their obligations, in this case the output is correct. By the guarantee of CountSketch, we can safely assume that $r_{\epsilon/2}(v_i') \geq \epsilon/2H(M)\sqrt{\hat{F}_2}$, heavy hitters will survive the pruning stage. □

THEOREM 3 (2-PASS ZERO-ONE LAW). *A function $g \in \mathcal{G}$ is 2-pass tractable and $\mathbb{P}$-normal if and only if it is slow-dropping and slow-jumping. Furthermore, every slow-dropping and slow-jumping $\mathbb{S}$-normal function is also 2-pass tractable.*

PROOF. The lower bound is proved as Theorem 26. The upper bound is governed by Proposition 10 and Theorem 19. □

Here are a few examples. The functions $x^2 \lg(1+x)$, $(2+\sin\log(1+x))\, x^2$, and $e^{\log^{1/2}(1+x)}$ are all 1-pass tractable because they are all slow-dropping, slow-jumping, and predictable. On the other hand, $1/x$ is not slow-dropping, x^3 is not slow-jumping, and $(2+\sin\sqrt{x})\, x^2$ is not predictable, so none of these functions is 1-pass tractable. The last of the three is, however, slow-jumping and slow-dropping, and hence it is 2-pass tractable.

5. NEARLY PERIODIC FUNCTIONS

Nearly periodic functions are highly constrained to *almost* repeat themselves like a periodic function. These functions admit large changes in value that would imply a large lower bound on their space complexities, if they did not satisfy the many constraints.

5.1 Example Nearly Periodic Function

Constructing a tractable nearly periodic function turns out to be a non-trivial exercise. This section provides such a construction.

DEFINITION 29. *Let $x = \sum_{j=0}^{\infty} a_j 2^j \in \mathbb{N}$, for $a_j \in \{0,1\}$, be the binary expansion of the integer x. Define $i_x := \min\{j : a_j = 1\}$, the location of the first non-zero bit of x. The function is $g_{np}(x) = 2^{-i_x}$, for $x > 0$, and $g_{np}(0) = 0$.*

PROPOSITION 30. *g_{np} is $\mathbb{S}$-nearly periodic.*

PROOF. Since there is an infinite sequence $\{1, 2, 4, \ldots, 2^n \ldots\}$ such that $g_{np}(x) = 1/x$, the first condition of near-periodicity is satisfied. It is remains to show that the second condition is also satisfied.

Let $\gamma > 0$ be a constant. Consider any integer $x > 0$. By construction $g_{np}(x) = 2^{-i_x}$. Let $y > x$ be another integer. Similarly, we have $g_{np}(y) = 2^{-i_y}$. If $g_{np}(x)/g_{np}(y) = 2^{i_y - i_x} \geq y^{\gamma}$, then $i_y - i_x \geq \gamma \lg y$. Choose $N = \lceil 2^{1/\gamma} \rceil$. For any $y > N$, we have $i_y - i_x > 1$ and therefore $i_{x+y} = i_x$. Thus, $g_{np}(x+y) = g_{np}(x)$. □

PROPOSITION 31. *g_{np} is 1-pass tractable.*

PROOF. We demonstrate that one can find (g_{np}, λ)- heavy hitters in $\mathrm{poly}(\lambda^{-1} \log n \log M)$ space. It is sufficient to demonstrate an algorithm that will find a single (g_{np}, λ)-heavy hitter, since we can reduce the heavy hitters problem to this case by hashing the stream $O(\lambda^{-2})$ ways and running this algorithm on each substream.

Suppose that j^* is the single (g_{np}, λ)-heavy hitter with frequency x. Let $v_1, v_2, \ldots, v_n \geq 0$ be the frequencies in the stream, and let $U = \{j : i_{v_j} \leq i_x\}$. By definition $g_{np}(v_j) \geq g_{np}(x)$ for $j \in U$, hence $|U| \leq 1 + \lambda^{-1} \leq 2\lambda^{-1}$.

Let $C = O(\lambda^{-2})$. Apply a uniform hash function $h : [n] \to [C]$ to separate the stream into C substreams $S_1, S_2, \ldots, S_C$. With constant probability, no two elements of U are in the same substream, so suppose that this happens.

On each substream S_k with frequencies $v_1^{(k)}, \ldots, v_n^{(k)}$ we run the following algorithm $D = O(\log n)$ times independently in parallel: (i) Sample pairwise independent Bernoulli(1/2) random variables $X_1, \ldots, X_n$. (ii) Compute $m = \sum_j X_j v_j^{(k)}$ and i_m. (iii) Output 2^{-i_m}.

Consider the set of D values output by this algorithm. If there is a single item j^* with minimum $i^* := i_{v_{j^*}^{(k)}}$, then a Chernoff bound implies that very nearly $D/2$ values are equal to 2^{-i^*}, and this is the maximum value among all of the pairs. In this case, the label j^* can be found in post-processing by binary search. Let $X_{j,\ell}$ denote the value of the jth Bernoulli variable on the ℓth trial. Specifically, one finds the set $M \subseteq [D]$ of trials for which 2^{-i_m} is equal to the maximum among the D values, and with high probability, only j^* will satisfy $X_{j,\ell} = 1$ for all $\ell \in M$ and $X_{j,\ell} = 0$ for all $\ell \in [D] \setminus M$. We can detect the case where there is more than one item with minimum $i_{v_j^{(k)}}$ because either the number of maximizing values will be too large or the binary search will fail to yield a unique element.

The single-heavy-hitter algorithm now outputs the pair $(j^*, 2^{-i^*})$ if the number of maximizing values is correct and the binary search yields a unique element or nothing if either of those conditions fails. With the extra hashing step mentioned at the beginning this yields a 1-pass $O(\lambda^{-4} \log n \log M)$-space (g_{np}, λ)-heavy hitters algorithm, thus g_{np} is 1-pass tractable. □

5.2 More Lower Bounds

The set of nearly-periodic function defeat the standard reduction from the DISJ and INDEX problems. Theorem 35 shows how one can use the SHORTLINEARCOMBINATION problem, of Definition 14, to provide space lower bounds on g-SUM algorithms for some nearly periodic functions g.

DEFINITION 32. *For any $N > 0$ and non-increasing sub-polynomial function $h(x)$, define the (N, h)-dropping set of f to be $\mathcal{D}_{N,h}(f) = \{x \mid 1 \leq x \leq N, f(x) \leq h(N)/N\}$.*

PROPOSITION 33. *Let f be a nearly-periodic function, then for all $n_0 > 0$, there exists $N > n_0$ and a sub-polynomial function h such that $|D_{N,h}| > 0$.*

PROOF. Choose $N = n_0 + 1, h(x) = f(1)N$, i.e. $h(x)$ is a constant function. Then 1 in $D_{N,h}$ because $1 \leq N$ and $f(1) = h(N)/N$. □

DEFINITION 34. *An α-indistinguishable frequency set of $[n]$ is a tuple (s, d), where $s \subseteq [n]$ is a subset and $d \in [n], d \notin s$ is a integer such that (s, d)-DIST problem requires $\Omega(n^{\alpha})$ space.*

THEOREM 35. *Let function $f : \mathbb{R} \to \mathbb{R}^+$, symmetric, nearly-periodic and $f(0) = 0$. If there exists a non-increasing sub-polynomial function $h(x)$ and constants $\alpha > 0, 0 < \delta < 1$, such that for any $n_0 > 0$, there exists $N > n_0$ and a integer set $|S| > 0$ satisfying the follows,*

1. *$0 < |\mathcal{D}_{N,h}(f)| \leq N^{1-\delta}$;*
2. *$S \subseteq |\mathcal{D}_{N,h}(f)|$ and $d \in [N]$ such that (S, d) is a α-indistinguishable frequency set of N;*

3. $f(d) \geq h(d)$,

then for any $n_0 > 0$*, there exists a stream of domain* $N > n_0$*, any one-pass randomized streaming algorithm* $\mathcal{A}$ *that outputs a* $1 \pm \epsilon(N)$ *approximation of f-SUM with probability at least* $2/3$*, requires space* $\Omega(n_0^\alpha)$ *bits, where* $\epsilon(x) < 1$ *is a sub-polynomial function.*

PROOF. Suppose we have an algorithm $\mathcal{A}$ that gives a $1 \pm \epsilon(N)$ approximation to f-SUM with probability at least 2/3. We can now use $\mathcal{A}$ to construct a protocol that solves (S, d)-DIST problem on domain N. The algorithm is straightforward: run $\mathcal{A}$ on the input stream. If the result $\mathcal{A}$ outputs is $\leq h(d)/N^\delta$, then there is no frequency of absolute value d in the stream. This is so since the g-SUM is at most $\sum_{a \in S} f(a) \leq N^{1-\delta}/N$. Otherwise, if the output is at least $h(d)(1 - \epsilon(N))$. By the guarantee of $\mathcal{A}$, it can distinguish the 2 cases. The space needed of $\mathcal{A}$ inherits the lower bound of (S, d)-DIST problem, thus $\Omega(N^\alpha)$ bits. □

6. REFERENCES

[1] Noga Alon, Yossi Matias, and Mario Szegedy. The space complexity of approximating the frequency moments. In *Proceedings of the 28th annual ACM Symposium on Theory of Computing*, pages 20–29. ACM, 1996.

[2] Alexandr Andoni, Robert Krauthgamer, and Ilya Razenshteyn. Sketching and embedding are equivalent for norms. In *Proceedings of the 47th annual ACM Symposium on Theory of Computing.* ACM, 2015.

[3] Ziv Bar-Yossef. *The complexity of massive data set computations.* PhD thesis, University of California at Berkeley, 2002.

[4] Ziv Bar-Yossef, TS Jayram, Ravi Kumar, and D Sivakumar. An information statistics approach to data stream and communication complexity. In *Proceedings of the 43rd annual IEEE Symposium on Foundations of Computer Science*, pages 209–218. IEEE, 2002.

[5] Vladimir Braverman and Stephen R Chestnut. Universal sketches for the frequency negative moments and other decreasing streaming sums. *Approximation, Randomization, and Combinatorial Optimization. Algorithms and Techniques*, page 591, 2015.

[6] Vladimir Braverman and Rafail Ostrovsky. Zero-one frequency laws. In *Proceedings of the 42nd annual ACM Symposium on Theory of Computing*, pages 281–290. ACM, 2010.

[7] Vladimir Braverman and Rafail Ostrovsky. Generalizing the layering method of Indyk and Woodruff: Recursive sketches for frequency-based vectors on streams. In *Approximation, Randomization, and Combinatorial Optimization. Algorithms and Techniques*, pages 58–70. Springer, 2013.

[8] Amit Chakrabarti, Subhash Khot, and Xiaodong Sun. Near-optimal lower bounds on the multi-party communication complexity of set disjointness. In *Proceedings of the 18th annual Conference on Computational Complexity*, pages 107–117. IEEE, 2003.

[9] Moses Charikar, Kevin Chen, and Martin Farach-Colton. Finding frequent items in data streams. In *Automata, Languages and Programming*, pages 693–703. Springer, 2002.

[10] Stephen R Chestnut. *Stream sketches, sampling, and sabotage.* PhD thesis, Johns Hopkins University, 2015. https: //jscholarship.library.jhu.edu/handle/1774.2/37935.

[11] André Gronemeier. Asymptotically optimal lower bounds on the NIH-multi-party information complexity of the AND-function and disjointness. In *STACS 2009: 26th International Symposium on Theoretical Aspects of Computer Science*, volume 3 of *LIPIcs. Leibniz Int. Proc. Inform.*, pages 505–516. Schloss Dagstuhl. Leibniz-Zent. Inform., Wadern, 2009.

[12] Sudipto Guha and Piotr Indyk. Problem 5: Characterizing Sketchable Distances. http://sublinear.info/5, 2006.

[13] Sudipto Guha, Piotr Indyk, and Andrew McGregor. Sketching information divergences. In *Learning Theory*, pages 424–438. Springer, 2007.

[14] Piotr Indyk. Stable distributions, pseudorandom generators, embeddings and data stream computation. In *Proceedings of the 41st annual IEEE Symposium on Foundations of Computer Science*, pages 189–197. IEEE, 2000.

[15] Piotr Indyk and David Woodruff. Optimal approximations of the frequency moments of data streams. In *Proceedings of the 37th annual ACM Symposium on Theory of Computing*, pages 202–208. ACM, 2005.

[16] Eaman Jahani, Michael J Cafarella, and Christopher Ré. Automatic optimization for mapreduce programs. *Proceedings of the VLDB Endowment*, 4(6):385–396, 2011.

[17] T. S. Jayram. Hellinger strikes back: A note on the multi-party information complexity of AND. In *Approximation, Randomization, and Combinatorial Optimization. Algorithms and Techniques*, pages 562–573, 2009.

[18] Ilan Kremer, Noam Nisan, and Dana Ron. On randomized one-round communication complexity. *Computational Complexity*, 8(1):21–49, 1999.

[19] Kyong-Ha Lee, Yoon-Joon Lee, Hyunsik Choi, Yon Dohn Chung, and Bongki Moon. Parallel data processing with mapreduce: a survey. *ACM SIGMOD Record*, 40(4):11–20, 2012.

[20] Yi Li, Huy L Nguyen, and David P Woodruff. Turnstile streaming algorithms might as well be linear sketches. In *Proceedings of the 46th annual ACM Symposium on Theory of Computing*, pages 174–183. ACM, 2014.

[21] Yi Li and David P Woodruff. A tight lower bound for high frequency moment estimation with small error. In *Approximation, Randomization, and Combinatorial Optimization. Algorithms and Techniques*, pages 623–638. Springer, 2013.

[22] Sai Wu, Feng Li, Sharad Mehrotra, and Beng Chin Ooi. Query optimization for massively parallel data processing. In *Proceedings of the 2nd ACM Symposium on Cloud Computing*, page 12. ACM, 2011.

APPENDIX

A. THE CASE OF $G(0) \neq 0$

When $g(0) = 0$, we have to re-address the lower bound of using INDEX since the elements not contributing to the frequency vector still contribute to the g-SUM. Therefore, we re-define the nearly periodic functions in the next section. We further show that functions crossing the axis are not 1-pass tractable and functions with zero points are not tractable unless they are periodic in Section A.2. We prove the same 1-pass zero one law in the remaining 2 sections. The proof turns out to be very similar to the $g(0) = 0$ cases with small number of additional tweaks. Note that we only provide the turnstile model lower bounds.

A.1 Redefinition of Nearly Periodic

For the $g(0) \neq 0$ case, we have the following definition of nearly-periodic.

DEFINITION 36. *Given a set of functions $\mathcal{S}$, call $g(x)$ $\mathcal{S}$-nearly periodic, if the following two conditions are satisfied.*

1. *There exists $\alpha > 0$ such that for any constant $N > 0$ there exists $x, y \in \mathbb{N}$, $x < y$ and $y \geq N$ such that $g(y) \leq g(x)/y^{\alpha}$. Call such a y α-period of g;*
2. *For any $\alpha > 0$ and any error function $h \in \mathcal{S}$ there exists $N_1 > 0$ such that for all α-periods $y \geq N_1$ all $x < y$ such that $g(y)y^{\alpha} \leq g(x)$ we have $|g(x) - g(x-2y)| \leq \min\{g(x), g(x-2y)\}h(y)$.*

A function g is $\mathcal{S}$-normal if it is not $\mathcal{S}$-nearly periodic.

Let all functions be $\mathcal{G}_0^* = \{g : \mathbb{N} \to \mathbb{R}^+, g(x) = g(-x), \text{and } g(0) = 1\}$.

A.2 Crossing the Axis

If $g \in \mathcal{G}_0^*$ and there exist $x, y \in \mathbb{N}$ such that $g(x) > 0 > g(y)$, we have the following lemma.

LEMMA 37. *Let $g \in \mathcal{G}_0^*$, if $g(1) < 0$, then any algorithm solves g-SUM requires $\Omega(n)$ space.*

PROOF. Consider the following INDEX(n) reduction. Alice and Bob jointly create a stream as following. Let A be Alice's set. $n_1 = |A|$. Let $n_2 = \lfloor \frac{n-n_1}{-g(1)} \rfloor$. Let $C = (n_1 + n_2)g(1) + (n - n_1)$. We have $0 \leq C < g(1)$. Alice choose a domain $[n+n_2]$ for the algorithm and output 1 copy of each of her element. Bob receives the memory content of the algorithm from Alice as well as n, n_1, n_2. Bob outputs -1 copy of his index and also adds to the stream one copy of each of the following elements: $n+1, n+2, \ldots, n+n_2$.
If there is an intersection, the result of g-SUM is

$$(n - n_1) + (n_1 + n_2 - 1)g(1) + g(0) = C + g(0) - g(1);$$

If there is no intersection, the result is

$$(n - n_1 - 1) + (n_1 + n_2)g(1) + g(1) = C + g(1) - g(0).$$

Then a constant approximation algorithm can distinguish the two cases. The algorithm inherits an $\Omega(n)$ bound from INDEX. □

LEMMA 38. *Let $g \in \mathcal{G}_0^*$ and $g(1) > 0$, if there exists $y \in \mathbb{N}$ such that $g(y) < 0 < g(1)$, then there exits $z \in \mathbb{N}$ such that $g(1+z) \neq g(1-z)$.*

PROOF. If for every z, $g(1+z) = g(1-z)$, we have $g(2) = g(0) = 1$ and for any w, $g(w+2) = g(w)$. Therefore 2 is a period of the function. Now, consider the following cases, 1) if y even, then $g(y) = g(2\lfloor y/2 \rfloor)) = g(0)$ (2 is a period), which is a contradiction that $g(y) < 0$; 2) if y odd, then $g(y) = g(2\lfloor y/2 \rfloor + 1) = g(1) > 0$, contradicting $g(y) < 0$. □

PROPOSITION 39. *Let $g \in \mathcal{G}_0^*$ and $g(1) > 0$, if there exists $y \in \mathbb{N}$ such that $g(y) < 0$, then any algorithm solves g-SUM requires $\Omega(n)$ space.*

PROOF. Consider the following reduction from INDEX(n). Let $n' = \lfloor -(n-1)g(1)/g(y) \rfloor$ and $z \in N$ be the integer given by Lemma 38. Let $C = (n-1)g(1) + n'g(y)$. We have $0 < C < -g(y)$. Alice and Bob jointly create a data stream in domain $n + n'$: Alice outputs 1 copy of every element in her set, and -1 copy of every element not in her set. Bob outputs y copy of each of the elements $i+1, i+2, \ldots, i+n'$ and z copy of his index. If there is no intersection, the result of g-SUM is

$$(n-1)g(x) + n'g(y) + g(z-1) = C + g(z-1).$$

If there is an intersection, the result of g-SUM is

$$(n-1)g(x) + n'g(y) + g(z+1) = C + g(z+1)$$

Therefore any constant approximation algorithm can distinguish the two cases, implying an $\Omega(n)$ bound for the memory of the algorithm. □

PROPOSITION 40. *Let $g \in \mathcal{G}_0^*$ if $g(x) = 0$ and $g(2x) \neq g(0)$ then g is not 1-pass tractable.*

PROOF. Consider the INDEX(n) reduction. Alice and Bob jointly create a stream as following, Alice output x for every element in her set, $-x$ for every element not in her set. Bob output x for his index. If there is an intersection, the g-SUM result is $g(2x)$. If there is no intersection, the result is $g(0)$. □

PROPOSITION 41. *If function $g \in \mathcal{G}_0^*$ with $g(x) = 0$ for some $x \in \mathbb{N}$ is tractable, then g is periodic.*

PROOF. By reduction from INDEX(n), Alice output x for each of her elements and $-x$ for each of her non-elements. Bob output $k+x$ for his index. If there is an intersection, the g-SUM result is $g(k+2x)$. If there is no intersection, g-SUM is $g(k)$. If $g(k+2x) \neq g(k)$ for any k, a constant approximation algorithm can distinguish the 2 cases. Therefore, $2x$ is a period of the function. □

Therefore, we only consider the following set of functions,

$$\mathcal{G}_0 = \{g : \mathbb{N} \to \mathbb{R}^+, g(x) = g(-x) > 0, \text{and } g(0) = 1\}$$

A.3 Lower Bounds

THEOREM 42. *If an $\mathbb{S}$-normal function $g \in \mathcal{G}_0$ does not satisfy slow dropping, then g is not 1-pass tractable.*

PROOF. The reduction to INDEX(n^{α}) is similar to the case of $g(0) = 0$. Now Alice outputs n copies of the elements in A and also outputs $-n$ copies of i if $i \notin A$. Bob output $x - n$ copies of his index. If there is an intersection the g-SUM result is $g(V(D)) = (n^{\alpha} - 1)g(n) + g(x)$ and otherwise is $g(V(D)) = (n^{\alpha} - 1)g(n) + g(x - 2n)$. Since g is not nearly periodic, the algorithm is able to distinguish the two cases. □

THEOREM 43. *If an $\mathbb{S}$-normal function $g \in \mathcal{G}_0$ is not slow-jumping, then g is not 1-pass tractable.*

PROOF. The reduction to DISJ+IND is the same to the case of $g(0) = 0$.

Now by slow dropping, there exists a sub-polynomial function $h(x)$ such that $g(0) \leq g(x)h(x)$. The g-SUM result differs from $g(0) = 0$ case by $(n - n')g(0)$ (or $(n - n' + t)g(0)$), which is comparable to $(n - n')g(x)$. Therefore, we can apply the same analysis. □

THEOREM 44. *If an $\mathbb{S}$-normal function $g \in \mathcal{G}_0$ is not predictable, then g is not 1-pass tractable.*

PROOF. Still use the same reduction to INDEX with the $g(0) = 0$ case. Now the g-SUM results differs by $(n - |A|)g(0)$. By slow dropping, there exists a sub-polynomial function $h(x)$ such that $g(0) \leq h(y)g(y)$. Therefore, all the analyses remain the same. □

A.4 Upper Bound

The algorithm should still work by the following 2 lemmas.

LEMMA 45. *Let $g \in \mathcal{G}_0$ be an $\mathbb{S}$-normal function that is slow-jumping and slow-dropping. There exists a sub-polynomial function h such that for any $D \in \mathcal{D}(n,m)$ with frequencies $v_1, v_2, \ldots, v_n$, if $g(v_i) \geq \lambda \sum_j g(v_j)$ then $v_i^2 \geq \frac{\lambda}{h(|v_i|)} \sum_{|v_j|<|v_i|} v_j^2$.*

PROOF. The proof is the same as in the $g(0) = 0$ case with additional care of $g(0) = 1$. □

LEMMA 46. *If $g \in \mathcal{G}_0$ is slow-dropping, slow-jumping, and predictable, then there is a sub-polynomial function h such that for all $y \in [r_\epsilon(x) + 1, x/h(x))$ we have $g(y) \geq g(x)/h(x)$.*

PROOF. The proof is the same as in the $g(0) = 0$ case with additional care of $g(0) = 1$. □

B. LOWER BOUND FOR DISJ+IND

THEOREM 47. *The randomized one-way communication complexity of DISJ+IND(n, t) is $\Omega(n/t \log n)$.*

PROOF. We give a reduction from DISJ$(n, t + 1)$. Let $\mathcal{P}$ be any randomized protocol for DISJ+IND(n, t). Run in parallel $\ell = \lceil 96 \log n \rceil$ independent copies of $\mathcal{P}$ through the first t players. This produces ℓ transcripts. Player $t + 1$ now takes the each of the transcripts and computes the final value of each once for every element he holds, as if it was the only element he held. No communication is need for this part because $\mathcal{P}$ is a one-way protocol and $t + 1$ is the final player.

Player $t + 1$ then takes the majority vote among the independent copies of $\mathcal{P}$ for each element. If any vote signals an intersection then he reports intersection; otherwise he reports disjoint.

If every one of the $|A_{t+1}| \leq n$ majorities is correct then the final player's report is correct. Let X_i, for $i \in A_{t+1}$, be the number among the ℓ copies of $\mathcal{P}$ with the correct outcome when the final player completes protocol using $i \in A_{t+1}$. Then X_i is Binomially distributed from ℓ trials with success probability at least 2/3. Using a Chernoff Bound we find

$$P(X_i \leq \ell/2) = P\left(X_i \leq (1 - \frac{1}{4})\frac{2}{3}\ell\right) \leq \exp\left\{\frac{-1}{32}\mu\right\}$$
$$\leq \exp\left\{\frac{-1}{32} \cdot \frac{2}{3}\ell\right\} \leq \frac{1}{n^2}.$$

Thus, with probability at least $1 - \frac{1}{n}$ every majority vote is correct, hence our DISJ(n, t) protocol is correct for $n \geq 3$.

Let $T_1, T_2, \ldots, T_\ell$ be the transcripts. The total cost of this DISJ protocol is $\sum_{i=1}^{\ell} |T_i|$. Since DISJ$(n, t+1)$ requires $\Omega(n/t)$ bits of communication, at least one of the protocols has length $\Omega(n/t\ell) = \Omega(n/t \log n)$, hence $|\mathcal{P}| = \Omega(n/t \log n)$ bits of communication. □

C. LOWER BOUND FOR SHORTLINEARCOMBINATION

C.1 The 3-frequency Distinguishing Problem

We first define the ShortLinearCombination problem for three frequencies, which we call (a, b, c)-DIST for short.

DEFINITION 48. *A stream S with frequency vector v is given to a one-pass streaming algorithm. v is promised to be from $V_0 = \{-a, a, -b, b, 0\}^n$ or $V_1 = \{EMB(v, i, e) \mid v \in V_0, i \in [n], e \in \{-c, c\}\}$, where $a, b, c > 0$ and*

$$EMB(v, i, e)_j = \begin{cases} v_i & i \neq j \\ e & i = j \end{cases}$$

(in other words, V_1 is given by replacing a coordinate of a vector v from V_0 with $-c$ or c). The (a, b, c)-DIST problem is for the algorithm to distinguish whether $v \in V_0$ or $v \in V_1$.

To study this problem, we first consider the special case where $c = \gcd(a, b) = 1$.

PROPOSITION 49. *If $\gcd(a, b) = 1$, then any randomized algorithm solving $(a, b, 1)$-DIST with probability at least 2/3 requires $\Omega(n/\max(a, b)^2)$ bits of memory.*

PROOF. We use the same notation as in [4], and in particular refer to that work for background on information complexity. Without loss of generality, we assume $a > b$. Consider a communication problem in which Alice is given a vector v_1 and Bob is given a vector v_2, for which $v = v_1 - v_2 \in V_0 \cup V_1$. The players are asked to solve the $(a, b, 1)$-DIST on v. This problem is OR-decomposable with primitive DIST(x, y), where DIST$(x, y) = 1$ if and only if $|x - y| = 1$. Consider a randomized protocol Π which succeeds with probability at least 2/3 in solving this problem, and suppose Π has the minimum communication cost of all such protocols. We now call $(a, b, 1)$-DIST f for short. The following is well known (see, e.g., [4]),

$$R_{2/3}(f) \geq IC_{\mu,2/3}(f),$$

where $R_{2/3}(f)$ is the communication complexity of the best randomized protocol (with error probability at most 2/3) on the worst case input, μ is any distribution over the input space, and IC_μ is the information complexity of the best protocol over the input distribution μ. We now construct an input distribution μ as follows. Let D be chosen uniformly at random over {Alice, Bob}, E is chosen uniformly from $\{a, a+1, a+2, \ldots, m-a\}$, where $m \gg a$ is a sufficiently large integer for which the coordinates of the vector jointly created by Alice and Bob will never exceed m. Denote by ξ the joint distribution of (D, E). Based on the value of D and E, the input distribution γ of Alice and Bob is decided as follows: if D chooses Alice, then the input X of Alice is chosen uniformly at random from the multiset $\{E - a, E - b, E, E, E, E, E + a, E + b\}$, and Bob is given E; if D chooses

Bob, γ just swaps the role of Alice and Bob. Clearly, γ is a product distribution conditioned on (D, E). We have that $\zeta = (\gamma, \xi)$ is a mixture of product distributions. Let $\eta = \zeta^n$, and let μ be the distribution obtained by marginalizing $(\mathbf{D}, \mathbf{E})$ from η. Since every joint vector created above is from V_0, μ is a *collapsing distribution* for f (see [4]). Then by Lemma 5.1 and Lemma 5.5 of [4], we have the following direct sum result:

$$I(\mathbf{X}, \mathbf{Y}; \Pi(\mathbf{X}, \mathbf{Y}) \mid \mathbf{D}, \mathbf{E}) \geq n \cdot \mathrm{CIC}_{\zeta,2/3}(\mathrm{DIST}).$$

We now expand the terms of $\mathrm{CIC}_{\zeta,2/3}(\mathrm{DIST})$. Let $[a, m-a] = \{a, a+1, a+2, \ldots, m-a\}$, U_e be the random number from the uniform distribution on multiset $K \equiv \{e-a, e+a, e, e, e, e, e-b, e+b\}$, and Ψ be the transcript of a communication-optimal randomized protocol for the primitive function DIST. Let $\beta_{e,y}$ be the distribution of $\Psi(e, y)$ and $\beta_e = \frac{1}{8}\sum_{y \in K} \beta_{e,y}$ be the average distribution. The following inequalities follow from Lemma 2.45 and Lemma 2.52 in Bar-Yossef's PhD thesis [3], the Cauchy-Schwarz inequality, and the triangle inequality.

$$\begin{aligned}
&\mathrm{CIC}_{\zeta,2/3}(\mathrm{DIST}) \\
&= \frac{1}{2|m-2a|} \sum_{e \in [a, m-a]} [I(U_e; \Psi(U_e, e)) \\
&\quad + I(U_e; \Psi(e, U_e))] \\
&= \sum_{\substack{e \in [a, m-a] \\ e_j \in K}} \frac{Pr[U_e = e_j]}{2(m-2a)} [KL(\beta_{e,e_j} || \beta_e) \\
&\quad + KL(\beta_{e_j,e} || \beta_e)] \\
&\quad \text{(Bar-Yossef's Thesis Proposition 2.45)} \\
&\geq \frac{1}{8 \ln 2(m-2a)} \sum_{\substack{e \in [a, m-a] \\ j \in \{-a, -b, 0, ..0, a, b\}}} [h^2(\beta_{e+j,e}, \beta_e) \\
&\quad + h^2(\beta_{e,e+j}, \beta_e)] \\
&\quad \text{(Cauchy-Schwarz)} \\
&\geq \frac{1}{16 \ln 2(m-2a)} \sum_{e \in [a, m-a]} [(h(\beta_{e,e}, \beta_e) + h(\beta_{e,e+a}, \beta_e))^2 \\
&\quad + (h(\beta_{e-a,e}, \beta_e) + h(\beta_{e,e}, \beta_e))^2 \\
&\quad + (h(\beta_{e,e}, \beta_e) + h(\beta_{e,e+b}, \beta_e))^2 \\
&\quad + (h(\beta_{e-b,e}, \beta_e) + h(\beta_{e,e}, \beta_e))^2] \\
&\quad \text{(Triangle inequality and Cauchy-Schwarz)} \\
&\geq \frac{C}{m} \sum_{e \in [2a, m-2a]} h^2(\beta_{e,e}, \beta_{e+a,e+a}) + h^2(\beta_{e,e}, \beta_{e+b,e+b}),
\end{aligned} \tag{3}$$

where C is a constant. Now we are able to group the terms. By the Euclidean algorithm, there exist integers p and q such that $pa + qb = 1$. Let q be such an integer with smallest absolute value. We then have $a/b \leq |q| \leq a$ and $|p| \leq |q|$. Therefore, for any $i \in [4, m/4a - 4]$, we can select up to $|p| + |q|$ terms from the range $[4ai - 2a, 4ai + 2a]$ to group in the above equation. Without loss of generality, assume $y > 0$. First, using the Cauchy-Schwarz inequality, we have

$$\begin{aligned}
\mathrm{CIC}_{\zeta,2/3}(\mathrm{DIST}) \geq \frac{C}{4ma} \sum_i \Bigg(\sum_{e \in [4ai-2a, 4ai+2a]} & h(\beta_{e,e}, \beta_{e+a,e+a}) + h(\beta_{e,e}, \beta_{e-a,e-a}) \\
& + h(\beta_{e,e}, \beta_{e+b,e+b}) + h(\beta_{e,e}, \beta_{e-b,e-b}) \Bigg)^2.
\end{aligned}$$

Next, group the terms using the triangle inequality such that whenever combining an a-term $h(\beta_{e,e}, \beta_{e'+a,e'+a})$, follow this by combining $\lfloor q/p \rfloor$ b-terms $h(\beta_{e,e}, \beta_{e''-b,e''-b})$. Therefore, the combined term e' is always guaranteed to be in $[4ai - 2a, 4ai + 2a]$. There might be a concern that a term is combined twice, namely, that there exist $|q_1| \leq |q_2| \leq |q|$, $|p_1| \leq |p_2| \leq |p|$ and $(q_1, p_1) \neq (q_2, p_2)$ such that $p_1 a + q_1 b = p_2 a + q_2 b$. But this is impossible since $\gcd(a, b) = 1$ and $(p - (p_2 - p_1))a + (q - (q_2 - q_1))b = 1$ contradicts that q has the smallest absolute value. Therefore, we are left with,

$$\mathrm{CIC}_{\zeta,2/3}(\mathrm{DIST}) \geq \frac{C'}{ma} \sum_{\substack{i \in [4, m/4a-4] \\ e = 4ai}} h^2(\beta_{e,e}, \beta_{e+1,e+1}). \tag{4}$$

Now invoke the Pythagorean lemma of [4], stating that $h^2(\beta_{e,e}, \beta_{e+1,e+1}) \geq 1/2(h^2(\beta_{e,e}, \beta_{e+1,e}) + h^2(\beta_{e+1,e}, \beta_{e+1,e+1}))$, as well as the correctness of the protocol, stating that the $h^2(\beta_{e,e}, \beta_{e,e+1})$ terms can each be lower bounded by a positive constant. Thus,

$$\mathrm{CIC}_{\zeta,2/3}(\mathrm{DIST}) \geq \frac{C''}{a^2}. \tag{5}$$

□

The above proof also makes use of the following lemma.

Lemma 50. *Let a, b be two integers such that $\gcd(a, b) = 1$ and $b < a$. Then there exist integers x, y such that $ax + by = 1$. Let y be such an integer with smallest absolute value. Then $b/a \leq |y| \leq a$ and $|x| \leq |y|$.*

Proof. To see that $|y| \leq a$, w.l.o.g., we assume $y > a$. Then $y = qa + r$, where $r < a < y$ and $q < y$. Thus $ax + b(qa + r) = 1$, and $(qb + x)a + rb = 1$ contradicts that y has the smallest absolute value. It is clear that $|y| \geq a/b$. It remains to show that $|x| \leq |y|$. This holds since $x = (1 - by)/a$ and $b < a$. □

Now we look at a more general case.

Theorem 51. *Let a, b, c be positive integers such that $c \neq a$ and $c \neq b$. Suppose there exist integers p, q such that $ap + bq = c$. Let q be such an integer with smallest absolute value. Then any randomized algorithm solving (a, b, c)-DIST with probability at least $2/3$ requires $\Omega(n/q^2)$ bits of memory.*

Proof. The proof of this theorem is a modification of the proof of the previous proposition. With a similar distribution (replacing 1 with c), we have that Equation (3) holds. The remaining task is to show a partition scheme of the terms such that $\Theta(m/(|p|+|q|)^2)$ terms survive. Choose an arbitrary $e \in [4a^2, m - 4a^2]$. W.l.o.g. assume $p > 0$. We can combine the following $|p| + |q|$ terms,

$$
\begin{aligned}
& h^2(\beta_{e,e}, \beta_{e+a,e+a}) + h^2(\beta_{e+a,e+a}, \beta_{e+2a,e+2a}) \\
& \quad + \ldots + \\
& \quad + h^2(\beta_{e+pa-a,e+pa-a}, \beta_{e+pa,e+pa}) \\
& \quad + h^2(\beta_{e+pa,e+pa}, \beta_{e+pa-b,e+pa-b}) \\
& \quad + h^2(\beta_{e+pa-b,e+pa-b}, \beta_{e+pa-2b,e+pa-2b}) \\
& \quad + \ldots + \\
& \quad + h^2(\beta_{e+pa+qb+b,e+pa+qb+b}, \beta_{e+pa+qb,e+pa+qb}) \\
& \quad \geq \frac{1}{|p|+|q|}[\sum_{i=1}^{p} h(\beta_{e+(i-1)a,e+(i-1)a}, \beta_{e+ia,e+ia}) \\
& \quad + \sum_{j=1}^{|q|} h(\beta_{e+pa-(j-1)b,e+pa-(j-1)b}, \beta_{e+pa-jb,e+pa-jb})]^2 \\
& \qquad \text{(Cauchy-Schwarz)} \\
& \quad \geq \frac{h^2(\beta_{e,e}, \beta_{e+1,e+1})}{|p|+|q|} \qquad \text{(Triangle inequality)}.
\end{aligned}
$$

Choose an e. This forbids the choice of another e from the above terms. In fact, e uniquely determines two arithmetic progressions: $e, e+a, e+2a, \ldots, e+pa$ and $e+pa-b, e+pa-2b\ldots, e+pa+qb$. Now, in order to choose a new e', the value e' cannot be a number from the above two progressions, and the progressions determined by e' cannot share a term with one of e. Therefore, because we chose e, $2(|p|+|q|)$ terms are not available for a new choice of e'. By choosing e from $[4a^2, m-4a^2]$ one at a time, we can find $(m-8a^2)/a$ different e for the purpose of combining terms. Denote the set of these e by S. In summary, we have,

$$
\mathrm{CIC}_{\varsigma,2/3}(\mathrm{DIST}) \geq \frac{C}{m(|p|+|q|)} \sum_{e \in S} h^2(\beta_{e,e}, \beta_{e+1,e+1}). \quad (6)
$$

Since $h^2(\beta_{e,e}, \beta_{e+1,e+1})$ is bounded below by a constant as indicated in the previous proposition, and since $|S| = m - 8a^2 = \Omega(m)$, we have $\mathrm{CIC}_{\varsigma,2/3}(\mathrm{DIST}) = \Omega(1/q^2)$. □

The above lower bound is tight in the sense that there is a protocol that uses $O(n/q^2)$ memory bits and solves (a, b, c)-DIST.

PROPOSITION 52. *Let a, b, c, p, q be integers satisfying the same conditions as in the previous theorem. Then there is a randomized algorithm solving (a, b, c)-DIST with probability at least $2/3$ using $O(n/q^2) \cdot poly(\log n)$ bits of memory.*

PROOF. Before the beginning of the stream, we partition $[n]$ into t contiguous pieces each of size n/t, where $t = \tilde{O}(n/q^2)$, and the $\tilde{O}$ notation hides logarithmic factors in n. For the i-th piece of the universe, let the corresponding substream restricted to elements in the i-th piece be denoted by S_i. For each S_i, we maintain a counter C_i for which

$$
C_i = \sum_{l:h[l]=i} v_l \xi_l = \sum_{x \in \{a,b,1\}} z_{i,x} x
$$

where $\xi_l \sim \{-1,+1\}$ are uniform 4-wise independent random bits and $z_{i,x} = \sum_{l:h[l]=i,|v_l|=x} \xi_l$. Let $y_{i,x}$ denote the number of occurrence of $|x|$ in the i-th stream. We have $y_{i,x} \leq n/t$. By standard concentration arguments, we have that with arbitrarily large constant probability, $|z_{i,x}| = \tilde{O}(\sqrt{y_{i,x}}) = \tilde{O}(\sqrt{n/t})$. We can select an appropriate $t = \tilde{O}(n/q^2)$ for which this implies $|z_{i,x}|$ is at most $|q|/4$. Now the claim is that by reading the value $C_i \mod a$, this is enough to distinguish whether there is a frequency of absolute value "c" in the stream or not. This follows since the sets of values of $C_i \mod a$ in the two cases are disjoint. To see why, note that if $z'_b b = z_b b + c \mod a$, then we have $(z'_b - z_b) - ra = c$. However, since $|z'_b - z_b| < |q|$, by the minimality of $|q|$, this is a contradiction. □

C.2 ShortLinearCombination Problem for Multiple of Frequencies

DEFINITION 53. *Let $u = (u_1, u_2, \ldots u_r)$ be a vector in $\mathbb{Z}^r$ for an integer r. Let $d > 0$ be an integer not in the vector u. A stream S with frequency vector v is given to an algorithm, where v is promised to be from $V_0 = \{u_1, u_2, \ldots, u_r, 0\}^n$ or $V_1 = \{EMB(v, i, e) \mid v \in V_0, i \in [n], e \in \{-d, d\}\}$. The (u, d)-DIST problem is to distinguish whether $v \in V_0$ or $v \in V_1$.*

THEOREM 54. *Let $u = (a_1, a_2, \ldots, a_r)$ be a set of integers and $d > 0$ be a positive integer such that $d = q_1 a_1 + q_2 a_2 + \ldots q_r a_r$ where $q_1, q_2, \ldots q_r$ are integers. These integers are choosen such that $q = \sum_i |q_i|$ is minimal. Then any randomized algorithm solving (u, d)-DIST with probability at least $2/3$ requires $\Omega(n/q^2)$ bits of memory.*

PROOF. The proof of the lower bound is a straightforward extension of the previous argument for three frequencies. Let $a = \max(a_1, a_2, \ldots, a_r)$. The number of combined terms is $m/(|q_1|+|q_2|+\ldots|q_r|)$. Therefore, the lower bound is $\Omega(n/q^2)$. The upper bound is a also a straightforward extension of the three frequency case. □

Efficient Top-k Indexing via General Reductions

Saladi Rahul
University of Minnesota
USA
sala0198@umn.edu

Yufei Tao
University of Queensland
Australia
taoyf@itee.uq.edu.au

ABSTRACT

Let D be a set of n elements each associated with a real-valued weight, and $\mathbb{Q}$ be the set of all possible predicates allowed on those elements. Given a predicate in $\mathbb{Q}$ and integer k, a *top-k query* returns the k elements with the largest weights among the elements of D satisfying q. The corresponding data structure problem aims to store D in small space to allow every query to be answered efficiently. It is already known that, before settling the problem, one *must* be able to solve two degenerated accompanying problems: (i) *prioritized reporting*: given a predicate $q \in \mathbb{Q}$ and a real value τ, return all the elements of D satisfying q and having weights at least τ; (ii) *max reporting*: top-k queries with k fixed to 1.

In this paper we prove general reductions in external memory that explore the opposite direction. Our first reduction shows that, (under mild conditions) any prioritized reporting structure yields a static top-k structure with only a slowdown in query time by a factor of $O(\log_B n)$, where B is the block size. Our second reduction shows that if one additionally has a max reporting structure, then combining the two structures yields a top-k structure with no performance slow down (in space, query, and update) in expectation. These reductions significantly simplify the design of top-k structures, as we showcase on numerous problems including halfspace reporting, circular reporting, interval stabbing, point enclosure, and 3d dominance. All the techniques proposed work directly in the RAM model as well.

Keywords

Top-k; Reductions; Data Structures; Algorithms; External Memory; RAM

1. INTRODUCTION

Reporting queries—which constitute a main type of operations in database systems—can be abstracted at a high level as follows. The input is a set D of n elements drawn from a certain domain $\mathbb{D}$. Let $\mathbb{Q}$ be the set of all possible *predicates* that are allowed on the elements of $\mathbb{D}$. A *query* chooses a predicate $q \in \mathbb{Q}$, and reports all the elements $e \in D$ such that e satisfies q—we denote the set of such elements as $q(D)$.

The result size $|q(D)|$ of a reporting query is often exceedingly large, especially in today's big-data era. In many applications, on the other hand, a user is interested only in those elements of $q(D)$ with high "priorities". This motivates the augmentation of each element e in D with a *weight* $w(e) \in \mathbb{R}$ (where $\mathbb{R}$ represents the real domain). Accordingly, every reporting query spawns two variants:

- **Prioritized Reporting:** Given a predicate $q \in \mathbb{Q}$ and a real value τ, a query reports all the elements $e \in q(D)$ such that $w(e) \geq \tau$.
- **Top-k Reporting:** Given a predicate $q \in \mathbb{Q}$ and an integer $k \geq 1$, a query reports the k elements in $q(D)$ with the highest weights; specially, if $|q(D)| < k$, then the entire $q(D)$ is reported.

For each query type, the corresponding indexing problem aims to store D in a data structure of small space to guarantee attractive query efficiency. Note that a structure for prioritized reporting must support queries with any q and τ, while a structure for top-k reporting must support queries with any q and k.

1.1 Computation Models and Math Conventions

We will carry out most of our analysis in the standard external memory (EM) model [8]. A machine is equipped with M words of memory, and a disk that has been formatted into *blocks* of B words each (this paper assumes $B \geq 64$). The values of M and B satisfy $M \geq 2B$. An I/O either reads a disk block into memory, or writes B words of memory into a disk block. The *time* of an algorithm is measured in the number of I/Os performed, while the *space* of a structure is measured in the number of disk blocks occupied.

By setting M and B to appropriate constants, all our EM results also hold in the classic RAM model, whose definition can be found in almost every textbook on algorithms, e.g., [16].

We consider that each element is stored in $O(1)$ words, and that the elements of D have distinct weights, as is a standard assumption in the top-k literature (whose purpose is to avoid ambiguity in the top-k result caused by tie-breaking in weights).

All complexities by default hold in the worst case. We

PODS'16, June 26-July 01, 2016, San Francisco, CA, USA
© 2016 ACM. ISBN 978-1-4503-4191-2/16/06...$15.00
DOI: http://dx.doi.org/10.1145/2902251.2902290

(i) define $\log^*(n)$ as the number of times that we need to perform $\log_2(.)$ on n to get a value no more than 2, and (ii) use notation $\tilde{O}(.)$ to hide a factor polylogarithmic to n when such a factor is insignificant. All the logarithm bases are equal to 2 if omitted.

Finally, we say that a function $f(n)$ is *geometrically converging* if it satisfies two conditions:

- For any $n \geq B$:

$$\sum_{i=0}^{h} f\left(\frac{n}{c^i}\right) = O(f(n))$$

  for any value $c \geq 2$, where h is the largest integer i satisfying $n/c^i \geq B$.

- For any $n < B$, $f(n) = O(1)$.

1.2 Motivation

Recent years have witnessed considerable research aiming to design top-k data structures for a large variety of problems (see Section 2 for a survey), which differ in their concrete specifications of $\mathbb{D}$ and $\mathbb{Q}$. Most solutions, interestingly, share a common two-step process:

- First, design a structure for prioritized reporting.
- Second, reduce top-k reporting to prioritized reporting.

Typically, the prioritized-reporting structure is easy to obtain (if not readily available), such that the challenge lies in the second step.

The community has come to realize that this process is *necessary*. Specifically, it has been shown [26, 28, 29] that *prioritized reporting can be reduced to top-k reporting.* Suppose that there is a structure that consumes $\mathcal{S}_{top}(n)$ space on n elements, and answers a top-k query in $\mathcal{Q}_{top}(n) + O(k/B)$ I/Os. Then, there is a prioritized-reporting structure of $\mathcal{S}_{pri}(n)$ space that answers a query in $\mathcal{Q}_{pri}(n) + O(t/B)$ I/Os—where t is the number of reported elements—such that

$$\mathcal{S}_{pri}(n) = O(\mathcal{S}_{top}(n))$$
$$\mathcal{Q}_{pri}(n) = O(\mathcal{Q}_{top}(n)).$$

The reduction does not rely on the underlying problems, i.e., prioritized reporting is no harder than top-k reporting, regardless of $\mathbb{D}$ and $\mathbb{Q}$. Therefore, if one does not even have a structure for the former, there is no hope for the latter.

What is much more intriguing is the opposite: *how much harder is top-k reporting than prioritized reporting*? To phrase this differently, let us assume that we already have a structure of $\mathcal{S}_{pri}(n)$ space that answers a prioritized query in $\mathcal{Q}_{pri} + O(t/B)$ time. We want to use the structure as a *black box* to design a top-k structure of space $\mathcal{S}_{top}(n)$ and query cost $\mathcal{Q}_{top} + O(k/B)$. The question is how good the functions $\mathcal{S}_{top}(n)$ and $\mathcal{Q}_{top}(n)$ can be.

Resolving the question has an important technical implication. Since prioritized reporting structures are already known for numerous problems, such a black-box reduction will give us top-k structures *immediately* for all those problems! Unfortunately, not much progress has been made towards this direction. The best understanding is the rather primitive relationships below[1] [28]:

$$\mathcal{S}_{top}(n) = O(\mathcal{S}_{pri}(n)) \quad (1)$$
$$\mathcal{Q}_{top}(n) = O(\mathcal{Q}_{pri}(n)\log_2 n) + O\left(\frac{k}{B}\log_2 n\right) \quad (2)$$

The multiplicative term $\log_2 n$ on k/B essentially prevents the reduction from producing any structure with linear output-sensitive cost $O(k/B)$.

Ideally, we would like to have $\mathcal{S}_{top}(n) = O(\mathcal{S}_{pri}(n))$ and $\mathcal{Q}_{top}(n) = O(\mathcal{Q}_{pri}(n))$—in order words, no performance deterioration—which would prove the asymptotic equivalence of prioritized and top-k reporting. If such a strong reduction still remains elusive, the next obvious question is what other "assisting problem" needs to be settled to make a no-deterioration reduction possible.

1.3 Our Results 1: Reductions

Our first contribution is to show that, under mild conditions, there only needs to be an $O(\log_B n)$ gap in the query cost between top-k and prioritized reporting:

THEOREM 1. Suppose that there is a prioritized structure of $\mathcal{S}_{pri}(n)$ space and query cost $\mathcal{Q}_{pri}(n) + O(t/B)$ such that $\mathcal{S}_{pri}(n)$ is geometrically converging, and

$$\mathcal{Q}_{pri}(n) \geq \log_B n.$$

Furthermore, suppose that the problem is *polynomially bounded*, namely, for any input D of n elements, there are only $n^{O(1)}$ distinct outcomes for $q(D)$ over all the possible predicates $q \in \mathbb{Q}$.

Then, there is a top-k structure of space $\mathcal{S}_{top}(n)$ and query time $\mathcal{Q}_{top}(n) + O(k/B)$ with

$$\mathcal{S}_{top}(n) = O(\mathcal{S}_{pri}(n)) \quad (3)$$

$$\mathcal{Q}_{top}(n) = O\left(\mathcal{Q}_{pri}(n) \cdot \frac{\log n}{\log B + \log \frac{\mathcal{Q}_{pri}(n)}{\log_B n}}\right) \quad (4)$$

It is worth mentioning that most of the known reporting problems are polynomially bounded. Consider, for example, D to be a set of n points in $\mathbb{R}^2$. In *halfspace reporting*, given a halfspace q (the region on one side of a line), we want to report the set $q(D)$ of points in $D \cap q$. It is easy to see that $O(n^2)$ different subsets $q(D)$ exist, ranging over all possible q, because there are only $\binom{n}{2}$ different lines passing two points in D.

Two remarks are in order:

- Since the denominator in (4) is at least $\log B$, it holds that $\mathcal{Q}_{top}(n) = O(\mathcal{Q}_{pri}(n) \cdot \log_B n)$.
- If $\mathcal{Q}_{pri}(n) \geq (n/B)^\epsilon$ for an arbitrarily small constant $\epsilon > 0$, (4) becomes $\mathcal{Q}_{top}(n) = O(\mathcal{Q}_{pri}(n))$. In other words, top-$k$ reporting is asymptotically as difficult as prioritized reporting for "hard" queries.

Our techniques for establishing Theorem 1 are drastically different from those behind (1) and (2), which are obtained by binary search on the weight threshold τ [28]. We prove

[1] Assuming that $\mathcal{S}_{pri}(n)$ is geometrically converging.

Theorem 1 mainly with two new ideas. The first one is to show the existence of a core-set that allows us to process queries with large k through prioritized reporting. The second one is a recursive mechanism that "fine-tunes" the results of queries with small k using nested core-sets.

An important special case of top-k reporting is *max reporting* where all queries have $k = 1$. Before solving queries of all k, one must at least be able to design an efficient structure for max reporting. In other words, just like prioritized reporting, max reporting is also a *necessary* step towards settling top-k reporting. Our second contribution is to show that the two necessary structures are *sufficient* as well:

THEOREM 2. Suppose that there is

- A prioritized-reporting structure of $\mathcal{S}_{pri}(n)$ space that answers a query in $\mathcal{Q}_{pri}(n) + O(t/B)$ I/Os;
- A max-reporting structure of $\mathcal{S}_{max}(n)$ space that answers a query (i.e., $k = 1$) in $\mathcal{Q}_{max}(n)$ I/Os. It is required that
  - $\mathcal{S}_{max}(n) = O(n^2/B)$ for any $n \geq B$.
  - $\mathcal{S}_{max}(n)$ is geometrically converging.

Then, there is a top-k structure of expected space $\mathcal{S}_{top}(n)$ and expected query time $\mathcal{Q}_{top}(n) + O(k/B)$ with

$$\mathcal{S}_{top}(n) = O\left(\mathcal{S}_{pri}(n) + \mathcal{S}_{max}\left(\frac{6n}{B \cdot \mathcal{Q}_{pri}(n)}\right)\right) \quad (5)$$

$$\mathcal{Q}_{top}(n) = O\left(\mathcal{Q}_{pri}(n) + \mathcal{Q}_{max}(n)\right). \quad (6)$$

Furthermore, if the prioritized and max structures support an update in $\mathcal{U}_{pri}(n)$ and $\mathcal{U}_{max}(n)$ I/Os respectively, then the top-k structure supports an update in $O(\mathcal{U}_{pri}(n) + \mathcal{U}_{max}(n))$ expected I/Os. If any of $\mathcal{U}_{pri}(n)$ and $\mathcal{U}_{max}(n)$ is amortized, the update cost of the top-k structure is amortized expected. In the above, every expectation is taken over the random choices made by our algorithms.

Three remarks are in order:

- The above reduction is optimal in the sense that there is no performance degradation (in expectation): the space, query, and update costs of the top-k structure are all determined by the worse between the prioritized and max structures.
- Somewhat surprisingly, $\mathcal{S}_{top}(n)$ may even be smaller than $O(\mathcal{S}_{max}(n))$. For instance, consider $\mathcal{S}_{pri}(n) = O(n/B)$, $\mathcal{S}_{max}(n) = O((n/B)\log_B n)$, while $\mathcal{Q}_{pri}(n) \geq \log_B n$—which will give $\mathcal{S}_{top}(n) = O(n/B)$. This implies, interestingly, that one does not need to try very hard to minimize the space of the max structure: our reduction comes with "bootstrapping power" that automatically reduces the expected space of the final top-k structure.
- The condition $\mathcal{S}_{max}(n) = O(n^2/B)$ essentially captures all the max structures useful in practice. The power 2 is not compulsory at all; it can be replaced by any larger constant by adjusting the other constants in our analysis appropriately.

We establish Theorem 2 by sampling from the input set D so that the element with the highest weight in the sample set is approximately the k-th in D. This, at the conceptual level, may be reminiscent of a method by Aronov and Har-Peled [9] that reduces approximate counting to *emptiness queries*. However, our approach differs substantially in both algorithmic and technical details, a quick proof of which is the following fact: the counting structure of [9] suffers from performance degradation by a logarithmic factor compared to the emptiness structure, while as pointed out earlier Theorem 2 incurs no performance degradation.

Both theorems are applicable in RAM by setting B to appropriate constants.

1.4 Our Results 2: New Top-k Structures

The reduction results in the preceding subsection lead to top-k structures for a large number of problems. We discuss several representatives that (i) are of immediate interest to database systems, (ii) are either new or improve previous work, and (iii) nicely demonstrate the applications of Theorems 1 and 2.

Halfspace and Circular Range Reporting. In *halfspace reporting*, $\mathbb{D}$ is the set of points in $\mathbb{R}^d$, where d is a fixed integer. Each predicate in $\mathbb{Q}$ specifies a halfspace, i.e., all the $\boldsymbol{x}$ satisfying $\boldsymbol{x} \cdot \boldsymbol{q} \geq c$, where $\boldsymbol{q}$ and c are the query parameters ($\boldsymbol{x}$ and $\boldsymbol{q}$ are d-dimensional vectors, and c a real value). An element $e \in \mathbb{D}$ satisfies the predicate if e falls in the halfspace. The importance of halfspace reporting—in general, searching with linear constraints—has long been recognized in the database community; e.g., see [6]. We obtain:

THEOREM 3. For top-k halfspace reporting:

- When $d = 2$, there is a RAM structure of $O(n \log n)$ space and $O(\log n + k)$ query time, both in expectation.
- When $d \geq 4$, there is a RAM structure of $O(n \log n)$ space and $\tilde{O}(n^{1-1/\lfloor d/2 \rfloor}) + O(k)$ query time, both in the worst case.
- When $d \geq 4$, there is an EM structure of $O(n/B)$ space and $O((n/B)^{1-1/\lfloor d/2 \rfloor + \epsilon} + k/B)$ query time, both in the worst case, where $\epsilon > 0$ is an arbitrarily small constant.

The first bullet compares favorably to a structure obtained by combining [5], [15], and [28] that uses $O(n \log n)$ space, and answers a query in $O(\log^2 n + k)$ time. For $d \geq 4$, [28] gave a RAM structure that, when matching our query time, requires $O(n^{1+\epsilon})$ space for some constant $\epsilon > 0$; no EM structures were known previously.

Circular range reporting is a closely related problem. Again, $\mathbb{D}$ is the set of points in $\mathbb{R}^d$, but each predicate in $\mathbb{Q}$ specifies a ball in $\mathbb{R}^d$, i.e., all the $\boldsymbol{x}$ satisfying $dist(\boldsymbol{x}, \boldsymbol{q}) \leq r$, where $dist$ is the Euclidean distance between vectors $\boldsymbol{x}$ and $\boldsymbol{q}$, and r is a positive real value (query parameters are $\boldsymbol{q}$ and r). Circular reporting is fundamental in spatial databases and similarity retrieval; e.g., see [36]. By the standard "lifting trick" [17], we obtain directly from Theorem 3:

COROLLARY 1. For top-k circular reporting with $d \geq 3$, there is:

- A RAM structure of $O(n \log n)$ space and $\tilde{O}(n^{1-1/\lfloor (d+1)/2 \rfloor}) + O(k)$ query time, both in the worst case.
- An EM structure of $O(n/B)$ space and $O((n/B)^{1-1/\lfloor (d+1)/2 \rfloor + \epsilon} + k/B)$ query time, both in the worst case, where $\epsilon > 0$ is an arbitrarily small constant.

The RAM structure improves a structure of [28], which again requires $O(n^{1+\epsilon})$ space to match our query time. No EM structures were known for this problem.

Interval Stabbing. This problem is among the most classic problems in the database area; e.g., see [21]. Here, $\mathbb{D}$ is the set of all intervals in $\mathbb{R}$, namely, $\mathbb{D} = \{[x, y] \mid x, y \in \mathbb{R}\}$. Each predicate in $\mathbb{Q}$ specifies a point q, such that an element $e = [x, y]$ in $\mathbb{D}$ satisfies the predicate if $q \in [x, y]$. We obtain:

THEOREM 4. *For top-k interval stabbing, there is an EM structure of*

- *$O(n/B)$ space and $O(\log_B n + k/B)$ query time, both in expectation. The structure can be updated in $O(\log_B n)$ I/Os amortized expected per insertion and deletion.*
- *$O(n/B)$ space and $O(\log_B^2 n + k/B)$ query time, both in the worst case.*

The second bullet improves a structure of [28] that uses $O((n/B) \log n)$ space to ensure query time $O(\log n \cdot \log_B n + k/B)$.

2D Point Enclosure. In this problem, $\mathbb{D}$ is the set of all rectangles in $\mathbb{R}^2$, namely, $\mathbb{D} = \{[x_1, x_2] \times [y_1, y_2] \mid x_1, x_2, y_1, y_2 \in \mathbb{R}\}$. Each predicate in $\mathbb{Q}$ specifies a point $q \in \mathbb{R}^2$, such that an element $e \in \mathbb{D}$ satisfies the predicate if $q \in e$.

To emphasize on the relevance of a top-k query of this type to databases, let us consider a dating website, where a person registers requirements on her/his ideal significant other: age in $[x_1, x_2]$, and height in $[y_1, y_2]$. A reasonable top-k point enclosure query from, say, a lady is:

> "Find the 10 gentlemen with the highest salaries such that my age and height fall into their preferred ranges."

We obtain:

THEOREM 5. *For top-k point enclosure, there is a RAM structure of*

- *$O(n \log^*(n))$ space and $O(\log n \log \log n + k)$ query time, both in expectation.*
- *$O(n \log^*(n))$ space and $O(\log^2 n \frac{\log \log n}{\log \log \log n} + k)$ query time, both in the worst case.*

Both structures compare favorably to a structure obtained by combining [28] and [13] that uses $O(n \log n)$ space, and answers a query in $O(\log^2 n + k)$ time.

3D Dominance. In this problem, $\mathbb{D}$ is the set of points in $\mathbb{R}^3$. Each predicate in $\mathbb{Q}$ specifies a point $q = (x, y, z)$, such that an element $e = (e_x, e_y, e_z)$ in $\mathbb{D}$ satisfies the predicate if $e_x \leq x$, $e_y \leq y$, and $e_z \leq z$. A practical top-k query of this type is

> "Find the 10 best-rated hotels whose (i) prices are at most x dollars per night, (ii) distances from the town center are at most y km, and (iii) security rating is at least z."

We obtain:

THEOREM 6. *For top-k 3D dominance, there is a RAM structure of $O(n \log n / \log \log n)$ space and $O(\log^{1.5} n + k)$ query time, both in expectation.*

This compares favorably to a structure obtained by combining [28] and [5] that uses $O(n \log n)$ space and $O(\log^2 n + k)$ query time.

2. PREVIOUS WORK

The existing research on top-k can be classified into two categories: (i) general reductions (to which this paper belongs) and (ii) exploration of individual problems.

The first category, to our knowledge, contains only the work by Rahul and Janardan [28]. Besides the reduction giving (1) and (2), they also showed that top-k reporting can be converted to approximate counting[2] and conventional reporting queries. Specifically, consider a reporting problem defined by $\mathbb{D}$ and $\mathbb{Q}$ as formulated in Section 1. Given a predicate $q \in \mathbb{Q}$, an *approximate counting* query returns a value that is guaranteed to be between $|q(D)|$ and $c|q(D)|$ where $c > 1$ is a constant integer fixed for all queries. Suppose that we have:

- A structure that uses space $\mathcal{S}_{rep}(n)$ and answers a query in the original (unweighted) problem in $\mathcal{Q}_{rep}(n) + O(t/B)$ time, where t is the number of elements reported;
- A structure that uses $\mathcal{S}_{cnt}(n)$ space and answers an approximate counting query in $\mathcal{Q}_{cnt}(n)$ time.

Then, there is a top-k structure with space $\mathcal{S}_{top}(n)$ and query time $\mathcal{Q}_{top}(n) + O(k/B)$ such that

$$\mathcal{S}_{top}(n) = O((\mathcal{S}_{rep}(n) + \mathcal{S}_{cnt}(n)) \log_2 n)$$
$$\mathcal{Q}_{top}(n) = O((\mathcal{Q}_{rep}(n) + \mathcal{Q}_{cnt}(n)) \log_2 n).$$

The reduction also works in RAM by setting B to an appropriate constant. The competing results in Section 1.4 are obtained from the above reduction by plugging in suitable reporting and counting structures.

[2][28] requires *exact* counting; our discussion here in fact improves that of [28].

Regarding the second category, [20] is an excellent survey on top-k research that focuses on system implementation that does not necessarily have attractive performance guarantees. In the theory line, the work of [10] appears to be the first attempt to incorporate top-k features into conventional reporting queries. Since then, the topic has grown into a sizable literature. The most extensively studied (and hence, the best understood) problem is *top-k range reporting*, whose 1D version was studied in [3, 11, 12, 33, 35], and 2D (orthogonal) version in [28, 29]. See also [25] for a colored version of the problem in 1D. The work [30] investigated more sophisticated colored top-k versions of several computational geometry problems. Finally, top-k queries on text retrieval problems have been considered in [19, 24, 25, 32]; see also a recent survey [22].

3. REDUCTION WITH WORST-CASE EFFICIENCY

This section serves as a proof of Theorem 1. We will need the Chernoff bounds given in the appendix.

3.1 Top-k Core-Set

Rank Sampling. Let S be a set of elements. By independently sampling each element of S with probability p, we obtain a *p-sample set* R. Furthermore, let us further assume that the elements of S are distinct, and drawn from an ordered domain. We say that an element $e \in S$ has *rank* i, if e is the i-th greatest in S. Intuitively, given an integer k that is reasonably large, the element with rank kp in R ought to have rank roughly k in S. The next lemma formalizes this intuition.

LEMMA 1. *Let S be a set of n elements, and R be a p-sample set of S. Suppose that integer $k \geq 1$ and real value $\delta \in (0,1)$ satisfy $kp \geq 3\ln(3/\delta)$ and $n \geq 4k$. Then, the following hold simultaneously with probability at least $1-\delta$:*

- $|R| > 2kp$
- *The element with rank $\lceil 2kp \rceil$ in R has rank between k and $4k$ in S.*

PROOF. The first bullet fails with probability

$$\begin{aligned}
\mathbf{Pr}[|R| \leq 2kp] &= \mathbf{Pr}[|R| \leq (2k/n)\cdot np] \\
&\leq \mathbf{Pr}[|R| \leq (1/2)np] \\
\text{(Chernoff bound (16))} &\leq \exp(-np/12) \\
&\leq \exp(-kp/3) \\
&\leq \delta/3.
\end{aligned}$$

Let e be the element with rank $\lceil 2kp \rceil$ in R, and $\hat{k}$ be the rank of e in S. Next, we bound the probability of the event $\hat{k} > 4k$. For $i \in [1, 4k]$, define x_i to be 1 if the i-th greatest element in S is sampled, or 0 otherwise. Let $X = \sum_{i=1}^{4k} x_i$, and thus, $\mathbf{E}[X] = 4kp \geq 12\ln(3/\delta)$. Event $\hat{k} > 4k$ implies $X \leq \lceil 2kp \rceil - 1$. We have:

$$\begin{aligned}
\mathbf{Pr}[\hat{k} > 4k] &\leq \mathbf{Pr}[X \leq \lceil 2kp \rceil - 1] \\
&= \mathbf{Pr}[X < 2kp] \\
&= \mathbf{Pr}[X < (1/2)\cdot \mathbf{E}[X]] \\
\text{(Chernoff bound (16))} &\leq \exp(-\mathbf{E}[X]/12). \\
&\leq \delta/3.
\end{aligned}$$

Finally, we bound the probability of the event $\hat{k} < k$. Define $Y = \sum_{i=1}^{k} x_i$, and thus, $\mathbf{E}[Y] = kp \geq 3\ln(3/\delta)$. Event $\hat{k} < k$ implies that $Y \geq \lceil 2kp \rceil$. We have:

$$\begin{aligned}
\mathbf{Pr}[\hat{k} < k] &\leq \mathbf{Pr}[Y \geq 2kp] \\
&= \mathbf{Pr}[Y \geq 2\mathbf{E}[Y]] \\
\text{(Chernoff bound (17))} &\leq \exp(-\mathbf{E}[Y]/3) \\
&\leq \delta/3.
\end{aligned}$$

By the union bound, the two bullets in the lemma hold simultaneously with probability at least $1-\delta$. □

Core-Set. As stated in Theorem 1, suppose that the underlying problem is polynomially bounded. More specifically, we say that the problem is *λ-polynomially bounded* if for any input D of n elements, there are at most n^λ distinct outcomes for $q(D)$ over all $q \in \mathbb{Q}$, where λ is a constant.

Given a subset R of D, we say that an element $e \in R$ has *weight rank i* in R if it has the i-th greatest weight in R. The next lemma proves the existence of a small-size core-set that approximately captures a specific rank for all the "large" queries whose predicates are satisfied by many elements.

LEMMA 2 (TOP-K CORE-SET LEMMA). *For any integer $K \geq 4\lambda \ln n$, there is a subset R of D such that*

- $|R| \leq 12\lambda \cdot (n/K)\ln n$.
- *For any $q \in \mathbb{Q}$ satisfying $|q(D)| \geq 4K$, it holds that*
  - $|q(R)| > 8\lambda \ln n$
  - *The element with weight rank $\lceil 8\lambda \ln n \rceil$ in $q(R)$ has weight rank between K and $4K$ in $q(D)$.*

PROOF. Set $p = 4(\lambda/K)\ln n$, and $\delta = 1/(2n^\lambda)$. These values ensure:

$$Kp = 4\lambda \ln n \geq 3\ln(3/\delta). \tag{7}$$

Let R be a p-sample set of D. We will prove that R satisfies all the conditions in the lemma with a non-zero probability.

Fix a $q \in \mathbb{Q}$ satisfying $|q(D)| \geq 4K$. Clearly, $q(R)$ is a p-sample set of $q(D)$. Applying Lemma 1 on $S = q(D)$ (the application is enabled by (7)), we know that with probability at least $1-\delta$, the following hold simultaneously:

- $|q(R)| > 2Kp = 8\lambda \ln n$.
- The element with rank $\lceil 2Kp \rceil$ has rank between K and $4K$ in $q(D)$.

By λ-polynomially boundedness and the union bound, the above holds for all queries with probability at least $1 - \delta n^\lambda = 1/2$.

Finally, as $|R|$ equals np in expectation, by Markov's inequality, $|R| \leq 3np = 12\lambda(n/K)\ln n$ with probability at least $2/3$. It thus follows that all the conditions of the lemma hold with probability at least $1-(1/2+1/3) > 0$. □

3.2 Structure

We proceed to explain how to use a prioritized reporting structure to design a top-k reporting structure on a problem that is λ-polynomially bounded for a constant λ. Recall that the former structure consumes space $\mathcal{S}_{pri}(n)$ space on n

elements, and answers a prioritized query in $\mathcal{Q}_{pri}(n)+O(t/B)$ I/Os.

Define:

$$g = \frac{\mathcal{Q}_{pri}(n)}{\log_B n} \quad (8)$$
$$f = 12\lambda B \cdot \mathcal{Q}_{pri}(n). \quad (9)$$

Note that $g \geq 1$ (as required by Theorem 1), and for $B \geq 64$, both the following are fulfilled:

$$\frac{12\lambda}{f} \cdot \ln n \leq \frac{1}{g\sqrt{B}} \quad (10)$$
$$f \geq \lceil 8\lambda \ln n \rceil. \quad (11)$$

To prove Theorem 1, next we first describe our solution to top-k queries with $k \leq f$, and then, queries with larger k.

Queries with $k \leq f$. It suffices, in fact, to consider $k = f$. Given a query q with $k < f$, we first treat it as a top-f query, i.e., retrieving the set of f elements with the greatest weights in $q(D)$. Then, the final result of q can be easily obtained by performing *k-selection* [8] on these elements in $O(f/B) = O(\mathcal{Q}_{pri}(n))$ I/Os. Apart from this, the cost depends only on the top-f query.

Given a top-f query q, we answer it directly using a prioritized structure on D, if $|q(D)| \leq 4f$. We do *not* need any counting structure for estimating $q(D)$. Instead, we can achieve the purpose by issuing a *prioritized query* with predicate q and threshold $\tau = -\infty$ in a *cost monitoring* manner:

- Either the query terminates by itself
- Or we terminate it manually as soon as $4f+1$ elements have been reported.

In both cases, the number of I/Os performed by the query is at most $\mathcal{Q}_{pri}(n)+O(f/B) = O(\mathcal{Q}_{pri}(n))$. In the former case, we obtain the final result of the top-f query by performing k-selection on the elements fetched by the prioritized query. In the latter case, it must hold that $|q(D)| > 4f$; we answer such queries with a structure constructed as follows.

Take a core-set R_1 of D using Lemma 2 with $K = f$, and build a prioritized structure on R_1. This process is then carried out recursively: for every $i \geq 2$, we take a core-set R_{i+1} of R_i with the same $K = f$, and build a prioritized structure on R_{i+1}. The recursion ends at some $i = h$ where $|R_h| \leq 4f$.

For convenience, let us treat D as R_0. For each R_i ($0 \leq i \leq h-1$), it holds that $f \geq 4\lambda \ln n \geq 4\lambda \ln |R_i|$; hence, by Lemma 2:

$$|R_{i+1}| \leq \frac{12\lambda \cdot |R_i|}{f} \ln |R_i| \leq \frac{12\lambda \cdot |R_i|}{f} \ln n$$
$$\text{(by (10))} \leq \frac{|R_i|}{g\sqrt{B}}. \quad (12)$$

The total space of all the prioritized structures is therefore $O(\mathcal{S}_{pri}(n))$ by the fact that $\mathcal{S}_{pri}(n)$ is geometrically converging. Furthermore, (12) indicates that

$$h = O(\log_{g\sqrt{B}} n).$$

We now explain inductively how to answer a top-f query on any R_i for $i \in [0, h]$ in no more than

$$c \cdot (h - i + 1) \cdot \mathcal{Q}_{pri}(n) \quad (13)$$

I/Os, for some constant $c \geq 1$. At the bottom level $i = h$, the purpose can be easily achieved by scanning the entire R_h in $O(f/B)$ I/Os, which is at most $c_1 \cdot \mathcal{Q}_{pri}(n)$ for some constant $c_1 \geq 1$. Assuming that this can be done for all $i \geq j+1$, consider $i = j$, at which level we distinguish two scenarios:

- $|q(R_j)| \leq 4f$: Answer the query in the cost monitoring manner as explained earlier using the prioritized structure on R_j. The cost is $\mathcal{Q}_{pri}(|R_j|) + O(f/B) \leq c_2 \cdot \mathcal{Q}_{pri}(n)$ for some constant $c_2 \geq 1$.
- $|q(R_j)| > 4f$: According to Lemma 2, $q(R_{j+1})$ must have size at least $\lceil 8\lambda \ln |q(R_j)| \rceil$. By (11), it must hold:

  $$f \geq \lceil 8\lambda \ln |q(R_j)| \rceil.$$

  Therefore, we can retrieve the element e with weight rank $\lceil 8\lambda \ln |q(R_j)| \rceil$ in $q(R_{j+1})$ by issuing a top-f query on R_{j+1} in at most

  $$c \cdot (h - i) \cdot \mathcal{Q}_{pri}(n)$$

  I/Os. Lemma 2 indicates that the weight rank of e in $q(R_j)$ is between f and $4f$. We deploy the prioritized structure on R_j to fetch all the elements of $q(R_j)$ with weights at least $w(e)$ in $\mathcal{Q}_{pri}(|R_j|) + O(f/B) \leq c_2 \cdot \mathcal{Q}_{pri}(n)$ I/Os. The result of the top-f query can be obtained from these objects with "k-selection" in no more than $c_3 \cdot \mathcal{Q}_{pri}(n)$ I/Os for some constant $c_3 \geq 1$.

We choose c to be $\max\{c_1, c_2 + c_3\}$, which ensures:

$$c \cdot (h-i) \cdot \mathcal{Q}_{pri}(n) + (c_2 + c_3) \cdot \mathcal{Q}_{pri}(n)$$
$$\leq c \cdot (h - i + 1) \cdot \mathcal{Q}_{pri}(n)$$

and hence, completing our claim in (13). It thus becomes clear that the cost of answering a query on D is

$$O(h \cdot \mathcal{Q}_{pri}(n)) = O(\mathcal{Q}_{pri}(n) \cdot \log_{g\sqrt{B}} n).$$

Plugging in the definition equation (8) of g gives the claimed complexity in Theorem 1.

Queries with $k > f$. We apply Lemma 2 to take a core-set $R[i]$ of D with $K = 2^{i-1}f$, for $i = 1, 2, ..., h$, where h is the largest integer i satisfying $2^{i-1}f \leq n$. It is easy to verify from (9) that

$$h = O(\log(n/B)). \quad (14)$$

Our structure has two components:

- A prioritized structure on D.
- On each $R[i]$ where $1 \leq i \leq h$, build a *top-f structure*, namely, the structure we just explained for answering queries with $k \leq f$. Since $|R[i]| \leq 12\lambda(n/(2^{i-1}f)) \ln n$, all these top-$f$ structures use in total

  $$O\left(\sum_{i=1}^{h} \mathcal{S}_{pri}\left(\frac{12\lambda \cdot n \ln n}{2^{i-1}f}\right)\right)$$
  $$= O(\mathcal{S}_{pri}(n) + h) = O(\mathcal{S}_{pri}(n))$$

  space, where the derivation used the facts that (i) $\mathcal{S}_{pri}(n)$ is geometrically converging, (ii) $\mathcal{S}_{pri}(n)$ obviously needs to be $\Omega(n/B)$, and hence, by (14), $h = O(\mathcal{S}_{pri}(n))$.

The total space of our structure is therefore $O(\mathcal{S}_{pri}(n))$.

Now consider a top-k query q with $f < k \leq n$. First, if $k \geq n/2$, we answer it by simply scanning the entire D in $O(n/B) = O(k/B)$ I/Os. Next, we consider $k < n/2$.

Identify the smallest $i \in [1, h]$ such that $2^{i-1} f \geq k$. Fix the value of K to $2^{i-1} f$ in the rest of the section. Note that $k \leq K < 2k$. We then proceed as follows:

- If $|q(D)| \leq 4K$, we answer the query with cost monitoring through the prioritized structure on D in $\mathcal{Q}_{pri}(n) + O(K/B)$ I/Os.
- If $|q(D)| > 4K$, Lemma 2 indicates that $q(R[i])$ has size at least $\lceil 8\lambda \ln n \rceil$, and that the element e with weight rank $\lceil 8\lambda \ln n \rceil$ in $q(R[i])$ has weight rank between K and $4K$ in $q(D)$.

  Retrieve e by issuing a top-f query on $R[i]$. By searching the top-f structure on $R[i]$, the query finishes in $O(\mathcal{Q}_{pri}(n) \log_{g\sqrt{B}} n)$ I/Os, as proved earlier. Extract from the prioritized structure on D the elements in $q(D)$ whose weights are at least $w(e)$; this entails $\mathcal{Q}_{pri}(n) + O(K/B)$ I/Os. Finally, the query result can be produced with k-selection in $O(K/B)$ I/Os.

Overall, the query performs $O(\mathcal{Q}_{pri}(n) \log_{g\sqrt{B}} n + K/B)$ I/Os. This completes the whole proof of Theorem 1.

4. REDUCTION WITH EXPECTED EFFICIENCY

In this section, we provide a reduction to establish the correctness of Theorem 2. Our discussion focuses on $n \geq B \cdot \mathcal{Q}_{max}(n)$; otherwise, a top-$k$ query can be trivially answered by performing k-selection on the whole D in $O(n/B) = O(\mathcal{Q}_{max}(n))$ I/Os.

Rank Sampling, Again. Our current rank sampling lemma, i.e., Lemma 1, falls short for the subsequent discussion. That lemma governs the behavior of the sample with rank $\lceil 2kp \rceil$ which—given the working condition $kp \geq 3\ln(3/\delta)$—is strictly greater than 1. Intuitively, this is problematic because, to apply max (i.e., top-1) queries, we need to understand the behavior of rank 1 in the sample set, i.e., the largest sample.

Fortunately, we are able to get around the obstacle by proving an alternative result, which is less general than Lemma 1, but serves exactly the purpose that Lemma 1 does not.

LEMMA 3. *Let S be a set of n elements, and $K \geq 2$ a real value satisfying $n \geq 4K$. For a $(1/K)$-sample set R of S, the following hold simultaneously with probability at least 0.09:*

- $|R| \geq 1$
- *The largest element in R has rank in S greater than K but at most $4K$.*

PROOF. The first bullet fails only if none of the elements in D were sampled, which occurs with a probability

$$(1 - 1/K)^n \leq (1 - 1/K)^{4K} \leq 1/e^4$$

where the last inequality used the fact that $(1 - x)^{1/x} < 1/e$ for all $x \geq 0$.

Let e be the largest element in R (note: this should be distinguished from the base of natural logarithm; the semantics of each occurrence of "e" should be clear from the context throughout the paper). Denote by $\hat{K}$ the rank of e in D. Next, we bound the probability of the event $\hat{K} > 4K$, which occurs only if none of the $4K$ largest elements in D were sampled. Hence:

$$\mathbf{Pr}[\hat{K} > 4K] = (1 - 1/K)^{4K} \leq 1/e^4.$$

Finally, we bound the probability of the event $\hat{K} \leq K$, which occurs only if at least one of the K largest elements in D was sampled. Hence:

$$\mathbf{Pr}[\hat{K} \leq K] = 1 - (1 - 1/K)^K.$$

Applying the fact that $(1 - 1/x)^x \geq 1/e^2$ for all $x \geq 2$, we know:

$$\mathbf{Pr}[\hat{K} \leq K] \leq 1 - 1/e^2.$$

The union bound now shows that the probability of violating at least one bullet of Lemma 3 is at most

$$2/e^4 + (1 - 1/e^2) < 0.91.$$

We thus complete the proof. □

Structure. We now describe how to design a top-k structure from (i) a prioritized structure, which uses $\mathcal{S}_{pri}(n)$ space on n elements and answers a prioritized query in $\mathcal{Q}_{pri}(n) + O(t/B)$ I/Os, and (ii) a max structure, which uses $\mathcal{S}_{max}(n)$ space and answers a max query in $\mathcal{Q}_{max}(n)$ I/Os.

Fix a constant $\sigma = 1/20$. For each integer $i \geq 1$, define:

$$K_i \quad = \quad B \cdot \mathcal{Q}_{max}(n) \cdot (1 + \sigma)^{i-1}.$$

Let h be the largest i such that $K_i \leq n/4$; clearly, $h = O(\log(n/B))$. We create a prioritized structure on D. Also, for each $i \in [1, h]$, we take a $(1/K_i)$-sample set R_i of D, and create a max structure on R_i.

Query. Let us first eliminate queries with $k < B \cdot \mathcal{Q}_{max}(n)$. Given such a query q, we first treat it as a top-$(B \cdot \mathcal{Q}_{max}(n))$ query, i.e., extracting the $B \cdot \mathcal{Q}_{max}(n)$ elements with the greatest weights in $q(D)$. Then, the final result of the original query can be obtained by performing k-selection on those elements. The total cost is $O(\mathcal{Q}_{max}(n))$ plus the time of the top-$(B \cdot \mathcal{Q}_{max}(n))$ query.

Let us now focus on a top-k query q with $k \geq B \cdot \mathcal{Q}_{max}(n)$. If $k > K_h$, the query is answered naively by reading the whole D in $O(n/B)$ I/Os, which is $O(k/B)$ because $k > K_h \geq n/(4(1 + \sigma)) = \Omega(n)$.

If $k \leq K_h$, identify the smallest i such that $K_i \geq k$; note that $K_i = \Theta(k)$. Setting $j = i$, we carry out a *round* with the steps below:

1. If $|q(D)| \leq 4K_j$, solve the query with the prioritized structure on D in the cost-monitoring manner (see Section 3.2), which costs $\mathcal{Q}_{pri}(n) + O(K_j/B)$ I/Os. The algorithm declares the round *succeeded* and terminates.
2. Otherwise, identify the element e in $q(R_j)$ with the maximum weight from the max structure on R_j in $\mathcal{Q}_{max}(n)$ I/Os. In the special case where $q(R_j)$ is empty, treat e as a dummy element with $w(e) = -\infty$.

3. Perform a prioritized query on D with q and threshold $\tau = w(e)$ in a cost-monitoring manner:
   (a) Either the query terminates by itself—let S be the set of elements retrieved,
   (b) Or we terminate it as soon as $4K_j + 1$ elements have been reported.

   In both cases, the cost is $\mathcal{Q}_{pri}(n) + O(K_j/B)$.
4. Declare this round *failed* if either of the following is true:
   - Case 3(a) occurred, but $|S| \le K_j$.
   - Case 3(b) occurred.

   Otherwise, declare this round *succeeded.*
5. If succeeded, perform k-selection on S to produce the k elements in $q(D)$ with the largest weights, and terminate the algorithm by returning them as the final answer.
6. Otherwise (i.e., failed), increase j by 1.
   (a) If $j \le h$, start the next round from Step 1.
   (b) Else (i.e., $j = h + 1$), answer the top-k query naively by reading the whole D in $O(n/B) = O(K_h/B)$ I/Os; the algorithm then terminates. This is the only scenario where termination can happen in a failed round.

To analyze the cost of the algorithm, notice that a round fails only if (i) $|q(|D|)| > 4K_j$ (otherwise, Line 1 terminates the algorithm), and (ii) one of the two bullets in Step 4 is true. Thus, Lemma 3 tells us that failure happens with probability at most 0.91, noticing that $q(R_i)$ is a $(1/K_j)$-sample set of $q(D)$. This implies that round j—for a specific $j \ge i$—is executed only with probability 0.91^{j-i}, namely, only when all the preceding rounds have failed. Also observe that round j, regardless of whether it fails, performs at most

$$\mathcal{Q}_{pri}(n) + \mathcal{Q}_{max}(n) + O(K_j/B)$$

I/Os. Thus, the expected cost of the algorithm is bounded by

$$\sum_{j=i}^{h} O\Big(\Big(\mathcal{Q}_{pri}(n) + \mathcal{Q}_{max}(n) + \frac{K_j}{B}\Big) \cdot 0.91^{j-i}\Big)$$
$$= O\Big(\mathcal{Q}_{pri}(n) + \mathcal{Q}_{max}(n) + \sum_{j=i}^{h} \frac{K_j}{B} 0.91^{j-i}\Big) \quad (15)$$

Notice that $K_j = K_i \cdot (1+\sigma)^{j-i} = O(k) \cdot (1+\sigma)^{j-i}$. Plugging these into (15) shows that the expected cost is

$$O\left(\mathcal{Q}_{pri}(n) + \mathcal{Q}_{max}(n) + \frac{k}{B} \sum_{j=i}^{h} ((1+\sigma) \cdot 0.91)^{j-i}\right)$$

which is $O(\mathcal{Q}_{pri}(n) + \mathcal{Q}_{max}(n) + k/B)$ because $(1+\sigma) \cdot 0.91 < 1$.

Space. The prioritized structure on D obviously takes up $\mathcal{S}_{pri}(n)$ space. We claim that all the max structures occupy $o(n/B) + O(\mathcal{S}_{max}(\frac{6n}{B \cdot \mathcal{Q}_{max}(n)}))$ expected space in total, which implies the space result in Theorem 2 (because $\mathcal{S}_{pri}(n) = \Omega(n/B)$).

The claim is fairly intuitive because $\mathbf{E}[|R_i|] = n/K_i$ geometrically decreases as i increases, which, together with the fact that $\mathcal{S}_{max}(n)$ is geometrically converging, seems to yield the claim immediately. The complication, however, is that $\mathcal{S}_{max}(n)$ may be a convex function, such that $\mathbf{E}[\mathcal{S}_{max}(|R_i|)]$ is *not* necessarily $O(\mathcal{S}_{max}(\mathbf{E}[|R_i|]))$. Next, we show how to circumvent this obstacle.

We will prove that all the max structures occupy $o(n/B) + O(\mathcal{S}_{max}(\frac{6n}{B \cdot \mathcal{Q}_{max}(n)}))$ space in total with probability at least $1 - 1/n^2$. Combining this with the fact that all those structures obvious demand no more than $O(\mathcal{S}_{max}(n) \cdot h) = O((n^2/B) \cdot \log(n/B))$ gives the target claim.

Let i^* be the largest i such that $K_i \le n/(3 \ln n)$. Consider an $i \in [1, i^*]$. Since $|R_i|$ is the sum of n independent Bernoulli variables each of which equals 1 with probability $1/K_i$, by Chernoff bound (17), we have:

$$\begin{aligned} \mathbf{Pr}[|R_i| \ge 6 \cdot \mathbf{E}[|R_i|]] &\le \exp(-\mathbf{E}[|R_i|]) \\ &= \exp(-n/K_i) \le 1/n^3. \end{aligned}$$

Therefore, with probability at least $1 - h/n^3$, the max structures on $R_1, R_2, ..., R_{i^*}$ use at most

$$\begin{aligned} &\sum_{i=1}^{i^*} O\left(\mathcal{S}_{max}\left(\frac{6n}{B \cdot \mathcal{Q}_{max}(n) \cdot (1+\sigma)^{i-1}}\right)\right) \\ =\ &O\left(h + \mathcal{S}_{max}\left(\frac{6n}{B \cdot \mathcal{Q}_{max}(n)}\right)\right) \end{aligned}$$

space overall.

Let us now concentrate on $i \in [i^* + 1, h]$. Notice that there are only $O(\log\log n)$ such values of i. Also, by definition of i^*, we know that $\mathbf{E}[|R_i|] = n/K_i$ is in the range from 4 to $O(\log n)$. Again, by Chernoff bound (17), we have :

$$\begin{aligned} \mathbf{Pr}[|R_i| \ge (\ln n^4) \cdot \mathbf{E}[|R_i|]] &\le \exp(-(\ln n^4) \cdot \mathbf{E}[|R_i|]/6) \\ &\le \exp(-(\ln n^{4 \cdot 2/3}) \\ &= 1/n^{8/3}. \end{aligned}$$

Hence, with probability at least $1 - O(\log\log n)/n^{8/3}$, it holds that for all $i \in [i^* + 1, h]$:

$$|R_i| \le 4 \ln n \cdot \mathbf{E}[|R_i|] = O(\log^2 n).$$

By the fact that $\mathcal{S}_{max}(n) = O(1 + n^2/B)$, the max structures on R_{i^*}, R_{i^*+1}, ..., R_h together consume no more than $O(h + (\log\log n \cdot \log^4 n)/B) = o(n/B)$ space. We thus conclude that, with probability at least $1 - h/n^3 - O(\log\log n)/n^{8/3} > 1 - 1/n^2$, all the max structures use $o(n/B) + O(\mathcal{S}_{max}(\frac{6n}{B \cdot \mathcal{Q}_{max}(n)}))$ space.

Update. It remains to discuss how to support insertions and deletions on the input set D. This is in fact fairly easy, if one observes that each element $e \in D$ has in expectation only $O(1)$ copies in the entire structure—recall that the sampling rate of R_i equals $1/K_i$, which geometrically decreases as i increases. Hence, the insertion of e triggers one insertion into the prioritized structure, and one insertion into $O(1)$ max structures in expectation. The total cost is thus $O(\mathcal{U}_{pri} + \mathcal{U}_{max})$ expected. Also, we can record in $O(1)$ expected words which max structures include e. By hashing, this "bookkeeping" itself can be maintained in $O(1)$ expected I/Os as e is inserted/deleted, without increasing the overall space complexity. In this way, a deletion of e can also be supported in $O(\mathcal{U}_{pri} + \mathcal{U}_{max})$ expected I/Os.

The above argument still works even if one or both of $\mathcal{U}_{pri}$ and $\mathcal{U}_{max}$ are amortized. This completes the whole proof of Theorem 2.

5. NEW STRUCTURES FROM REDUCTIONS

Next, we utilize our reductions to derive the new top-k structures claimed in Section 1.4, specifically, in Theorems 3-6. While those theorems were presented essentially in descending order of their importance to databases, next we will prove them in a different order: from the least sophisticated to the most.

5.1 Top-*k* Interval Stabbing (Theorem 4)

The theorem now becomes almost a pleasure to prove:

- The prioritized-reporting version of the problem has been studied by Tao [34] (where the version is called *ray stabbing*), who gave an $O(n/B)$-size structure that answers a query in $O(\log_B n + t/B)$ I/Os, and supports an update in $O(\log_B n)$ amortized I/Os.
- The max-reporting version has been studied by Agarwal et al. [7], who gave an $O(n/B)$-size structure that answers a query in $O(\log_B n)$ I/Os, and supports an update in $O(\log_B n)$ amortized I/Os.

Therefore, the first and second bullets of Theorem 4 follow from Theorems 2 and Theorem 1, respectively.

5.2 Top-*k* Point Enclosure (Theorem 5)

The prioritized-reporting version of the problem has been studied by Rahul [27], who gave a structure of $O(n \log^* n)$ size and $O(\log n \log\log n + t)$ query time.

Next, we explain how to solve the max-reporting version with a structure that uses $O(n \log n)$ space and answers a query in $O(\log n)$ time. Based on the above, the first and second bullets of Theorem 5 follow from Theorems 2 and Theorem 1, respectively. Note that the application of Theorem 2 demonstrates the "bootstrapping power" as remarked in Section 1.4.

1D Stabbing Max. Section 5.1 already mentioned a dynamic structure for solving the max-reporting version of interval stabbing. In fact, if the goal is to design a *static* structure, that problem can be settled with a very simple structure of $O(n)$ space and $O(\log n)$ time. Although this should be folklore, we give the details nonetheless because it will be helpful later.

Let D be a set of n weighted intervals in $\mathbb{R}$. The $2n$ endpoints of the intervals divide $\mathbb{R}$ into at most $2n+1$ disjoint subintervals. With each subinterval I, we associate the maximum weight of all the intervals in D that span I. Given a value $q \in \mathbb{R}$, a query returns the maximum weight of the intervals of D containing q. This is precisely the weight associated with the subinterval containing q. Finding the subinterval is essentially predecessor search, which can be carried out in $O(\log n)$ time by performing binary search on the endpoints.

2D Stabbing Max (Point Enclosure Max). Now we return to the max-reporting version of point enclosure. The input is a set D of n weighted axis-parallel rectangles. Create a segment tree T on the x-projections of those rectangles. For each node u of T, define D_u to be the set of segments assigned to u. Build a 1D stabbing max structure on D_u. The overall space is clearly $O(n \log n)$.

Given a point $q = (x, y)$, a query returns the maximum weight of the rectangles of D containing q. To process the query, we descend a root-to-leaf path Π of T according to x, and then, on each node $u \in \Pi$, issue a 1D stabbing max query on D_u with y. The final answer is the maximum of the results of these 1D queries. The algorithm takes $O(\log^2 n)$ time, which can be improved to $O(\log n)$ with fractional cascading [14] because, as mentioned earlier, each 1D query performs nothing but predecessor search on a sorted list.

5.3 Top-*k* 3D Dominance (Theorem 6)

The prioritized-reporting version of the problem has been studied by Afshani et al. [2] (where the version is called *4D dominance reporting*), who gave a structure with size $O(n \log n / \log\log n)$ and query time $O(\log^{1.5} n + t)$.

Next, we explain how to solve the max-reporting version with a structure that uses $O(n)$ space and answers a query in $O(\log^{1.5} n)$ time. Plugging in these bounds into Theorem 2 proves Theorem 6.

In this setting, D is a set of n weighted points in $\mathbb{R}^3$. Let $e_1, e_2, ..., e_n$ be the sequence of points in descending order of weight. With each point e_i, we associate a region ρ_i in $\mathbb{R}^3$ satisfying the following constraint: any point $q = (x, y, z)$ belongs to ρ_i if and only if e_i is the point with the maximum weight in $(-\infty, x] \times (-\infty, y] \times (-\infty, z]$. The region assignment below ensures the constraint for all points $e_i = (e_{ix}, e_{iy}, e_{iz})$:

- $\rho_1 = [e_{1x}, \infty) \times [e_{1y}, \infty) \times [e_{1z}, \infty)$.
- For $i \in [2, n]$:

$$\rho_i = [e_{ix}, \infty) \times [e_{iy}, \infty) \times [e_{iz}, \infty) \setminus \bigcup_{j=1}^{i-1} \rho_j.$$

Each non-empty region ρ_i is decomposed into axis-parallel disjoint cuboids by performing a *vertical decomposition.* If ρ_i has n_i vertices, then the number of cuboids in the decomposition of ρ_i will be $O(n_i)$. It can be verified [1] that $\sum_{i=1}^{n} n_i = O(n)$.

Therefore, the max reporting problem can be transformed to a point location problem: Given a query point q, find the cuboid (if any) containing q from a set of $O(n)$ disjoint axis-parallel cuboids. Rahul [27] presented a structure of size $O(n)$ to answer such a query in $O(\log^{1.5} n)$ time.

5.4 Top-*k* Halfspace Reporting: $d = 2$ (Theorem 3: 1st Bullet)

We will show:

- The prioritized-reporting version of the problem can be settled by an $O(n \log n)$-size structure that answers a query in $O(\log n + t)$ time.
- The max-reporting version can be settled by an $O(n)$-size structure that answers a query in $O(\log n)$ time.

Plugging in these results into Theorem 2 proves the first bullet of Theorem 3.

Prioritized Reporting. Chazelle et al. [15] settled the *original* 2D halfspace reporting problem. Specifically, they showed that n points in $\mathbb{R}^2$ can be stored in an $O(n)$-size structure such that, given a halfspace q, all the t input points falling in q can be reported in $O(\log n + t)$ time. Their query algorithm, in fact, starts with finding the predecessor of some query value (that depends on q) in a pre-computed list of real values. This accounts for the $O(\log n)$ term. Once the predecessor is found, the rest of the algorithm finishes in $O(1 + t)$ time.

Next, we leverage the above structure to attack the prioritized-reporting version. In this setting, the input is a set D of n weighted points in $\mathbb{R}^2$. Create a balanced binary search tree T on their weights, with each weight stored in a leaf, which is associated with the corresponding point in D. For each node u of T, denote by D_u the set of points stored in the subtree of u. Create a halfspace reporting structure of [15] on D_u. The total space is $O(n \log n)$.

Given a halfspace q and a threshold τ, a query returns all the points $e \in D$ such that $e \in q$ and weight $w(e) \geq \tau$. We answer it as follows. First, collect the *canonical* set $U(\tau)$ of nodes $u_1, u_2, ..., u_m$ with the smallest m such that D_{u_1}, D_{u_2}, ..., D_{u_m} are disjoint, and their union equals $\{e \in D \mid w(e) \geq \tau\}$. It is rudimentary to find these $m = O(\log n)$ nodes in $O(\log n)$ time. Then, perform a halfspace reporting query using q on D_{u_i}, for each $i \in [1, m]$. The final answer is the union of the outputs of all these m queries.

As explained earlier, each halfspace reporting query spends $O(\log n)$ time on a predecessor search, which makes the total query time $O(\log^2 n + t)$. A standard application of fractional cascading reduces the time to $O(\log n + t)$.

Max Reporting. The input is again a set D of n weighted points. Given a halfspace q, a query returns the maximum weight of the points of D covered by q. By standard duality, we consider instead the following equivalent *stabbing max* problem. The input is a set D' of n weighted halfspaces in $\mathbb{R}^2$. The goal is to store D' in a data structure such that, given a point q' in $\mathbb{R}^2$, we can efficiently report the maximum weight of the halfspaces of D' containing q'. Below we describe an $O(n)$-size structure with $O(\log n)$ query time.

Using the idea in Section 5.3, we can transform the problem into a point location problem on a planar subdivision of complexity $O(n)$. Let $e'_1, e'_2, ..., e'_n$ be the halfspaces of D', in descending order of weight. For each e'_i, define a region ρ_i in $\mathbb{R}^2$ satisfying the following constraint: any point q belongs to ρ_i if and only if e'_i is the halfspace with the maximum weight among all the halfspaces containing q. The region assignment below ensures the constraint:

- $\rho_1 = e'_1$.
- For $i \in [2, n]$, $\rho_i = e'_i \setminus \bigcup_{j=1}^{i-1} \rho_j$.

ρ_1, ρ_2, ..., ρ_n are disjoint polygons such that the planar subdivision they induce has at most n vertices. To see this, imagine generating ρ_i in ascending order of i as follows. If e'_i falls entirely in $\bigcup_{j=1}^{i-1} \rho_j$, then e'_i introduces no vertex on the subdivision. Otherwise, at least one point p on the boundary line of e'_i must be outside $\bigcup_{j=1}^{i-1} \rho_j$. Walk from p along the boundary line towards one direction, and stop as soon as hitting the boundary line of any of the halfspaces already considered. The stopping point is a new vertex on the subdivision. Similarly, walking from p towards the other direction will determine another new vertex.

Given a query point q', it suffices to find the polygon of the subdivision containing q'. This can be done in $O(\log n)$ time with an $O(n)$-size structure [31].

5.5 Top-k Halfspace Reporting: $d \geq 4$ (Theorem 3: 2nd and 3rd Bullets)

The subsequent discussion demonstrates the power of Theorem 1 in showing the asymptotic equivalence between top-k reporting and prioritized reporting, when the query time is large.

RAM. We will show that the prioritized-reporting version of the problem can be settled by an $O(n \log n)$-size structure that answers a query in $\tilde{O}(n^{1-1/\lfloor d/2 \rfloor}) + O(t)$ time. Plugging this into Theorem 1 yields the second bullet of Theorem 3.

In the *original* halfspace reporting problem, we want to store n points in $\mathbb{R}^d$ in a structure such that, given any halfspace q in $\mathbb{R}^d$, all the input points falling in q can be reported efficiently. Afshani and Chan [4] gave a structure of $O(n)$ space and query time $\tilde{O}(n^{1-1/\lfloor d/2 \rfloor}) + O(t)$.

Recall that Section 5.4 presented a prioritized reporting structure in 2D space, where there is a 2D halfspace reporting structure on each D_u. To obtain a prioritized reporting structure for $\mathbb{R}^d$, we simply replace that 2D structure with the d-dimensional halfspace reporting structure of [4]. A prioritized query is answered in the way as described in Section 5.4, excluding the part about fractional cascading. The claimed space and query bounds follow from the same analysis as in Section 5.4.

EM. We will show that the prioritized-reporting version of the problem can be settled by an $O(n/B)$-size structure that answers a query in $O((n/B)^{1-1/\lfloor d/2 \rfloor + \epsilon} + t/B)$ time. Plugging this into Theorem 1 yields the third bullet of Theorem 3.

For the *original* halfspace reporting problem, Agarwal et al. [6] gave a structure of $O(n/B)$ space and query time $O((n/B)^{1-1/\lfloor d/2 \rfloor + \epsilon'} + t/B)$ for any arbitrarily small constant $\epsilon' > 0$, which we utilize below to design the required structure for prioritized reporting.

The input is a set D of n weighted points in $\mathbb{R}^d$, which we denote as $e_1, e_2, ..., e_n$ in descending order of weight. Set $f = (n/B)^{\epsilon/2}$. Build a B-tree T on the weights of the n points with leaf capacity B and internal fanout f. Store each point together with its weight in the corresponding leaf. For each node u of T, denote by D_u the set of points stored in the subtree of u; we create a structure of [6] on D_u by setting $\epsilon' = \epsilon/2$. The overall space consumption is $O(n/B)$—noticing that T has $O(1)$ levels.

To answer a query with halfspace q and threshold τ, we collect the canonical set $U(\tau)$ of nodes $u_1, u_2, ..., u_m$ with the smallest m such that $D_{u_1}, ..., D_{u_m}$ are disjoint, and their union equals $\{e \in D \mid w(e) \geq \tau\}$. It is rudimentary to find these $m = O(f)$ nodes in $O(1 + f/B)$ I/Os. We then perform a halfspace reporting query using q on D_{u_i}, for all $i \in [1, m]$. The final answer is the union of the outputs of all these m

queries. The query cost is

$$\begin{aligned} & O\left(m \cdot (n/B)^{1-1/\lfloor d/2 \rfloor+\epsilon'} + t/B\right) \\ = \; & O\left((n/B)^{1-1/\lfloor d/2 \rfloor+\epsilon} + t/B\right) \end{aligned}$$

I/Os.

6. REFERENCES

[1] Peyman Afshani. On dominance reporting in 3D. In *Proceedings of European Symposium on Algorithms (ESA)*, pages 41–51, 2008.

[2] Peyman Afshani, Lars Arge, and Kasper Green Larsen. Higher-dimensional orthogonal range reporting and rectangle stabbing in the pointer machine model. In *Proceedings of Symposium on Computational Geometry (SoCG)*, pages 323–332, 2012.

[3] Peyman Afshani, Gerth Stolting Brodal, and Norbert Zeh. Ordered and unordered top-k range reporting in large data sets. In *Proceedings of the Annual ACM-SIAM Symposium on Discrete Algorithms (SODA)*, pages 390–400, 2011.

[4] Peyman Afshani and Timothy M. Chan. Optimal halfspace range reporting in three dimensions. In *Proceedings of the Annual ACM-SIAM Symposium on Discrete Algorithms (SODA)*, pages 180–186, 2009.

[5] Peyman Afshani, Chris H. Hamilton, and Norbert Zeh. A general approach for cache-oblivious range reporting and approximate range counting. *Computational Geometry*, 43(8):700–712, 2010.

[6] Pankaj K. Agarwal, Lars Arge, Jeff Erickson, Paolo Giulio Franciosa, and Jeffrey Scott Vitter. Efficient searching with linear constraints. *Journal of Computer and System Sciences (JCSS)*, 61(2):194–216, 2000.

[7] Pankaj K. Agarwal, Lars Arge, Haim Kaplan, Eyal Molad, Robert Endre Tarjan, and Ke Yi. An optimal dynamic data structure for stabbing-semigroup queries. *SIAM Journal of Computing*, 41(1):104–127, 2012.

[8] Alok Aggarwal and Jeffrey Scott Vitter. The input/output complexity of sorting and related problems. *Communications of the ACM (CACM)*, 31(9):1116–1127, 1988.

[9] Boris Aronov and Sariel Har-Peled. On approximating the depth and related problems. *SIAM Journal of Computing*, 38(3):899–921, 2008.

[10] Iwona Bialynicka-Birula and Roberto Grossi. Rank-sensitive data structures. In *String Processing and Information Retrieval (SPIRE)*, pages 79–90, 2005.

[11] Gerth Stolting Brodal. External memory three-sided range reporting and top-k queries with sublogarithmic updates. In *Proceedings of Symposium on Theoretical Aspects of Computer Science (STACS)*, volume 47, pages 23:1–23:14. 2016.

[12] Gerth Stolting Brodal, Rolf Fagerberg, Mark Greve, and Alejandro Lopez-Ortiz. Online sorted range reporting. In *International Symposium on Algorithms and Computation (ISAAC)*, pages 173–182, 2009.

[13] Bernard Chazelle. A functional approach to data structures and its use in multidimensional searching. *SIAM Journal of Computing*, 17(3):427–462, 1988.

[14] Bernard Chazelle and Leonidas J. Guibas. Fractional cascading: I. A data structuring technique. *Algorithmica*, 1(2):133–162, 1986.

[15] Bernard Chazelle, Leonidas J. Guibas, and D. T. Lee. The power of geometric duality. *BIT Numerical Mathematics*, 25(1):76–90, 1985.

[16] Thomas H. Cormen, Charles E. Leiserson, Ronald L. Rivest, and Clifford Stein. *Introduction to Algorithms, Second Edition*. The MIT Press, 2001.

[17] Mark de Berg, Otfried Cheong, Marc van Kreveld, and Mark Overmars. *Computational Geometry: Algorithms and Applications*. Springer-Verlag, 3rd edition, 2008.

[18] Torben Hagerup and Christine Rub. A guided tour of chernoff bounds. *Information Processing Letters (IPL)*, 33(6):305–308, 1990.

[19] Wing-Kai Hon, Rahul Shah, Sharma V. Thankachan, and Jeffrey Scott Vitter. Space-efficient frameworks for top-k string retrieval. *Journal of the ACM (JACM)*, 61(2):9:1–9:36, 2014.

[20] Ihab F. Ilyas, George Beskales, and Mohamed A. Soliman. A survey of top-k query processing techniques in relational database systems. *ACM Computing Surveys*, 40(4), 2008.

[21] Hans-Peter Kriegel, Marco Potke, and Thomas Seidl. Managing intervals efficiently in object-relational databases. In *Proceedings of Very Large Data Bases (VLDB)*, pages 407–418, 2000.

[22] Moshe Lewenstein. Orthogonal range searching for text indexing. In *Space-Efficient Data Structures, Streams, and Algorithms*, pages 267–302, 2013.

[23] Rajeev Motwani and Prabhakar Raghavan. *Randomized Algorithms*. Cambridge University Press, 1995.

[24] S. Muthukrishnan. Efficient algorithms for document retrieval problems. In *Proceedings of the Annual ACM-SIAM Symposium on Discrete Algorithms (SODA)*, pages 657–666, 2002.

[25] Gonzalo Navarro and Yakov Nekrich. Top-k document retrieval in optimal time and linear space. In *Proceedings of the Annual ACM-SIAM Symposium on Discrete Algorithms (SODA)*, pages 1066–1077, 2012.

[26] Manish Patil, Sharma V. Thankachan, Rahul Shah, Yakov Nekrich, and Jeffrey Scott Vitter. Categorical range maxima queries. In *Proceedings of ACM Symposium on Principles of Database Systems (PODS)*, pages 266–277, 2014.

[27] Saladi Rahul. Improved bounds for orthogonal point enclosure query and point location in orthogonal subdivisions in $\mathbb{R}^3$. In *Proceedings of the Annual ACM-SIAM Symposium on Discrete Algorithms (SODA)*, pages 200–211, 2015.

[28] Saladi Rahul and Ravi Janardan. A general technique for top-k geometric intersection query problems. *IEEE Transactions on Knowledge and Data Engineering (TKDE)*, 26(12):2859–2871, 2014.

[29] Saladi Rahul and Yufei Tao. On top-k range reporting in 2d space. In *Proceedings of ACM Symposium on Principles of Database Systems (PODS)*, pages 265–275, 2015.

[30] Biswajit Sanyal, Prosenjit Gupta, and Subhashis Majumder. Colored top-k range-aggregate queries.

Information Processing Letters (IPL), 113(19-21):777–784, 2013.

[31] Neil Sarnak and Robert Endre Tarjan. Planar point location using persistent search trees. *Communications of the ACM (CACM)*, 29(7):669–679, 1986.

[32] Rahul Shah, Cheng Sheng, Sharma V. Thankachan, and Jeffrey Scott Vitter. Top-k document retrieval in external memory. In *Proceedings of European Symposium on Algorithms (ESA)*, pages 803–814, 2013.

[33] Cheng Sheng and Yufei Tao. Dynamic top-k range reporting in external memory. In *Proceedings of ACM Symposium on Principles of Database Systems (PODS)*, 2012.

[34] Yufei Tao. Stabbing horizontal segments with rays. In *Proceedings of Symposium on Computational Geometry (SoCG)*, 2012.

[35] Yufei Tao. A dynamic I/O-efficient structure for one-dimensional top-k range reporting. In *Proceedings of ACM Symposium on Principles of Database Systems (PODS)*, pages 256–265, 2014.

[36] David A. White and Ramesh Jain. Similarity indexing with the SS-tree. In *Proceedings of International Conference on Data Engineering (ICDE)*, pages 516–523, 1996.

Appendix: Chernoff Bounds

Let $X_1, ..., X_n$ be independent Bernoulli variables such that $\mathbf{Pr}[X_i = 1] = p_i$. Let $X = \sum_{i=1}^{n} X_i$ and $\mu = \mathbf{E}[X] = \sum_{i=1}^{n} p_i$. It holds for any $\alpha \in (0,1)$ that

$$\mathbf{Pr}[X \le (1-\alpha)\mu] \quad \le \quad e^{-\alpha^2\mu/3}. \qquad (16)$$

For any $\alpha \ge 2$, it holds that

$$\mathbf{Pr}[X \ge \alpha\mu] \quad \le \quad e^{-\alpha\mu/6}. \qquad (17)$$

The above inequalities can be found in many papers and textbooks, e.g., [18, 23]

Anti-Persistence on Persistent Storage: History-Independent Sparse Tables and Dictionaries

Michael A. Bender* Stony Brook University

Jonathan W. Berry† Sandia National Laboratories

Rob Johnson* Stony Brook University

Thomas M. Kroeger‡ Sandia National Laboratories

Samuel McCauley* Stony Brook University

Cynthia A. Phillips† Sandia National Laboratories

Bertrand Simon§ Ecole Normale Supérieure de Lyon

Shikha Singh* Stony Brook University

David Zage¶ Intel Corporation

ABSTRACT

We present history-independent alternatives to a B-tree, the primary indexing data structure used in databases. A data structure is history independent (HI) if it is impossible to deduce any information by examining the bit representation of the data structure that is not already available through the API.

We show how to build a history-independent cache-oblivious B-tree and a history-independent external-memory skip list. One of the main contributions is a data structure we build on the way—a history-independent packed-memory array (PMA). The PMA supports efficient range queries, one of the most important operations for answering database queries.

Our HI PMA matches the asymptotic bounds of prior non-HI packed-memory arrays and sparse tables. Specifically, a PMA maintains a dynamic set of elements in sorted order in a linear-sized array. Inserts and deletes take an amortized $O(\log^2 N)$ element moves with high probability. Simple experiments with our implementation of HI PMAs corroborate our theoretical analysis. Comparisons to regular PMAs give preliminary indications that the practical cost of adding history-independence is not too large.

Our HI cache-oblivious B-tree bounds match those of prior non-HI cache-oblivious B-trees. Searches take $O(\log_B N)$ I/Os; inserts and deletes take $O(\frac{\log^2 N}{B} + \log_B N)$ amortized I/Os with high probability; and range queries returning k elements take $O(\log_B N + k/B)$ I/Os.

Our HI external-memory skip list achieves optimal bounds with high probability, analogous to in-memory skip lists: $O(\log_B N)$ I/Os for point queries and amortized $O(\log_B N)$ I/Os for inserts/deletes. Range queries returning k elements run in $O(\log_B N + k/B)$ I/Os. In contrast, the best possible high-probability bounds for inserting into the folklore B-skip list, which promotes elements with probability $1/B$, is just $\Theta(\log N)$ I/Os. This is no better than the bounds one gets from running an in-memory skip list in external memory.

*Department of Computer Science, Stony Brook University, Stony Brook, NY 11794-2424 USA. Email: {bender, rob, smccauley, shiksingh}@cs.stonybrook.edu.

†MS 1326, PO Box 5800, Albuquerque, NM 87185 USA. Email: {jberry, caphill}@sandia.gov.

‡PO Box 969, MS 9011, Livermore, CA 94551 USA. Email: tmkroeg@sandia.gov.

§LIP, ENS de Lyon, 46 allee d'Italie, 69364 Lyon, France. Email: bertrand.simon@ens-lyon.fr.

¶Intel Corporation, 2200 Mission College Blvd, Santa Clara, CA 95054 USA. Email: zage@cerias.net.

PODS'16, June 26-July 01, 2016, San Francisco, CA, USA

© 2016 ACM. ISBN 978-1-4503-4191-2/16/06...$15.00

DOI: http://dx.doi.org/10.1145/2902251.2902276

1. INTRODUCTION

A data structure is ***history independent*** (HI) if its internal representation reveals nothing about the sequence of operations that led to its current state [43, 47]. In this paper, we study history independence for persistent, disk-resident dictionary data structures.

We give two efficient history-independent alternatives to the B-tree, the primary indexing data structure used in databases. Specifically, we give an HI external-memory skip list and an HI cache-oblivious[1] B-tree.

One of the main contributions of the paper is a data structure we build on the way: a history-independent packed-memory array (PMA). As we explain, the PMA [14, 18] is an unlikely candidate data structure to be made history independent, since traditional PMAs rely on history so fundamentally. The HI PMA is one of the primary building blocks in the HI cache-oblivious B-tree. However, it can also be bolted onto any dictionary data structure, using the PMA to hold the actual elements and deliver fast range queries.

Notions of History Independence

Informally, history independence partially protects a disk-resident data structure when the disk is stolen by—or given to—a third party (the "observer"). This observer can access the data structure through the normal API but can also see

[1]A ***cache-oblivious*** [29, 30, 51] algorithm or data structure is memory-hierarchy universal, in that it has no memory-hierarchy-specific parameterization (see Section 1.1).

its bit and pointer representation on disk. An HI data structure's bit representation never leaks any information to the observer that he could not learn through the API.

There are two notions of history independence, ***weak history independence*** (WHI) and ***strong history independence*** (SHI) [47]. The notions are distinguished by how many times the observer can look at the data structure—that is by how many times an interloper can steal (or otherwise gain access to) the disk on which the data structure resides. A weakly history-independent data structure is history independent against an observer who can see the memory representation once. A strongly history-independent data structure is history independent against an observer who can see the memory representation multiple times.

In this paper, we focus on weak history independence. From a performance perspective, weak HI is a stronger notion because it allows provably stronger performance guarantees (see Section 2). Protecting against multiple observations reduces achievable performance.

Weak history independence is the appropriate notion of history independence in situations where only one observation is possible. For example, when the data is on a device that can be separated from the owner (say a portable or embedded device), the owner no longer interacts with the device. WHI provides the same level of protection in this case with significantly better performance compared to SHI.

History Independence and Data

History independence in a database can have major advantages, depending on the kind of data that is being stored and the security requirements.

HI data structures naturally support information-theoretically-secure delete. In contrast, with more standard secure delete (where the file system overwrites deleted data with zeros), information about deleted data can leak from the memory representation. For example, it reveals how much data was deleted and where in the keyspace it might have been. In fact, a long history of failed redactions is one of the original motivations for history independence [36]. History independence guarantees that the memory representation will leak no information about these previous (now secure) deletes. Encryption is not a panacea to protect history unconditionally, since determined attackers can recover the key used to encrypt on-disk data [35].

In a database, the source of the data can be more sensitive than the data itself. As a toy example, consider a database of known organized crime members maintained by the police. The police might want to share such a database with select individuals without revealing the order and times in which the data was added to the database. Revealing this order might leak information about how and when the data was collected, which could reveal sources that the police want to stay hidden. Journalists may desire the same property to ensure their sources' anonymity.

In such cases, we need to be particularly careful about avoiding information leaks by side channels. Since leakage can be subtle and hard to quantify, it is beneficial to have a guarantee that nothing extraneous is revealed, which is exactly what history independence guarantees. HI data structures naturally hide the order in which data was inserted.

History Independence in Persistent Storage

This paper focuses on history independence for external-memory dictionaries. This area of history independence was initiated by Golovin [32, 33]; see Section 1.4 for details.

The ubiquitous (non-history-independent) external-memory dictionary is the B-tree.

Our objective is to build history-independent, I/O efficient external-memory dictionaries.We support standard dictionary operations: insertions, deletions, searches, and range queries. Our two external-storage computational models (the external-memory model [3] and the cache-oblivious model [29, 30, 51]) apply to both rotating disks and SSDs.

We give weakly history-independent data structures for persistent storage; these are easy to implement and retain strong performance guarantees. We show that even range-query data structures that seem to be inherently history *dependent*—in particular, packed-memory array or sparse tables [14, 16–18, 38, 41, 66]—can be made weakly history independent. Overall, our results demonstrate that it is possible to build efficient external-memory (and even cache-oblivious) history-independent data structures for indexing.

History Independence in Persistent Storage vs. RAM

History independence has been vigorously explored in the context of data structures that reside in RAM [20, 21, 23, 36, 43, 46, 47, 61] (see Section 1.4), but significantly less so in external memory. Although there is some theoretical work on history-independent on-disk data structures [31–33] and experimental work on history-independent file systems [10–12, 56], the area is substantially less explored.

This lacuna may seem surprising, since many of the classical arguments in support of history independence especially apply to disks. Hard drives are more vulnerable than RAM because they are persistent and easier to steal, making it easier for an attacker to observe on-disk data.

1.1 I/O and Cache-Oblivious Models

We prove our results using the classic models for analyzing on-disk algorithms and data structures: the disk-access machine (DAM) model of Aggarwal and Vitter [3] and the cache-oblivious model of Frigo et al. [29, 30, 51]. The DAM has an internal memory (RAM) of size M and an arbitrarily large external memory (disk). Data is transferred between RAM and disk in blocks of size $B < M$. The performance measure is transfers (I/Os). Computation is free.

The cache-oblivious model extends the DAM model. Now parameters B and M are unknown to the algorithm designer or coder. They can only be used as parameters in analyses.

Thus, an optimal cache-oblivious data structure is not parameterized by any block, cache or RAM size, or memory- or disk-access times. Remarkably, many problems have optimal (and practical) cache-oblivious solutions, including B-trees [14, 15, 22]. Informally, a cache-oblivious B-tree has approximately optimal memory or I/O performance at every level of an unknown multilevel memory hierarchy.

1.2 Packed-Memory Arrays and External-Memory Dictionaries

In this paper, we give a history-independent PMA and two external-memory dictionaries: a history-independent external skip list and a history-independent cache-oblivious B-tree. This subsection puts our results in context.

We first define a PMA. Then we describe the technical issues involved in making a history-independent PMA. We (this paper's authors) were surprised when we first suspected that a history-independent PMA could indeed exist. Here, we try to articulate why the PMA might seem to be an unlikely candidate data structure to make history independent, but why it is nonetheless possible.

We next explain why a history independent PMA leads, almost directly, to an HI cache-oblivious B-tree, the first nontrivial history-independent cache-oblivious data structure.

Finally, we discuss the history-independent external-memory skip list. This HI data structure still offers high-probability guarantees, analogous to in-memory skip lists. See Section 2 for the definition of with high probability, which we also write as "whp".

Although the idea of a B-skip list, which promotes elements with probability $1/B$ rather than probability $1/2$ is folklore and has appeared in the literature repeatedly [1, 25, 26, 33], we prove that its high-probability I/O guarantees are asymptotically no better than those of an in-memory skip list run in external memory.

Packed-Memory Arrays

One of the classic data-structural problems is called ***sequential file maintenance***: maintain a dynamic set of elements in sorted order in a linear-sized array. If there are N elements, then the array has $\Theta(N)$ empty array positions or *gaps* interspersed among the elements to accommodate future insertions. The gaps allow some elements to shift left or right to open slots for new elements—like shifting books on a bookshelf to make room for new books.

Remarkably, there are data structures for these problems that are efficient even for *adversarial* inserts and deletes. Indeed, the number of element moves per update is only $O(\log^2 N)$ both amortized [38, 63] and in the worst case [64–66], which is optimal [24].

In external memory, this data structure is called a ***packed-memory array*** [14, 18]. It supports inserts, deletes, and range queries. Given the location where we want to insert or delete (which can be found using a separate indexing structure, e.g., [15, 22]), it takes only $O(1 + (\log^2 N)/B)$ amortized I/Os to shift the elements. Given the starting point, a range query returning k elements costs $\Theta(1 + k/B)$ I/Os.[2]

Prior PMAs operate as follows. To insert a new element after an existing element or to delete an element, find an enclosing subarray or ***range***, and ***rebalance***. This spreads out the elements (and gaps) within that range. The rebalance range is chosen based upon the density within the range, where ranges have minimum and maximum allowed densities. These thresholds depend upon the size of the range: small ranges have high thresholds for the maximum density and low thresholds for the minimum density. The larger a range is, the less variability is allowed in its density. The algorithmic subtlety has to do with choosing the right rebalance ranges and the right minimum and maximum density thresholds for each range size.

However, range densities are very history *dependent*. For example, if you repeatedly insert towards the front of an array or if you repeatedly delete from the back of the array, then the front of the array will be denser than the back. How could we possibly make a version of this data structure, that is history independent—that is, where newly inserted (or deleted) elements do not seem to increase (or decrease) some local density? We answer this question in this paper.

To use a more evocative image, picture a long trough where you are pouring sand in one location (corresponding to inserts) and letting out sand in another location (corresponding to deletes). As the sand piles up, the pile gradually flattens (corresponding to local rebalances). Although rebalances may flatten out the pile, we may still expect a bump for newly arrived sand, and a depression for recently departed sand. Perhaps surprisingly, we can avoid bumps and depressions with mostly local rebalances.

[2]This scanning bound is a further requirement on how the elements are distributed. Beyond the $O(N)$ overall space limitation, only $O(1)$ gaps can separate two consecutive elements.

Cache-Oblivious B-Trees

A B-tree is a dictionary supporting search, insert, delete, and range query operations. There are cache-oblivious versions [13, 15, 22, 40, 55].

A history-independent PMA can immediately yield a history-independent cache-oblivious B-tree. The idea is to take a PMA and "glue" it to a static cache-oblivious B-tree [51]. For details, see [15, 22]. We use a similar method to construct our history-independent cache-oblivious B-tree in Section 3.

External-Memory Skip Lists

The skip list is an elegant search-tree alternative introduced by Pugh [53]. Skip lists are randomized data structures having a weakly history independent pointer structure [31, 53].

Skip lists with N elements support searches, inserts, and deletes in $O(\log N)$ operations whp and range queries returning k elements in $O(\log N + k)$ operations whp [27, 42, 50]. They are heavily used in internal-memory algorithms [5, 8, 9, 28, 34, 37, 39, 49, 57].

This paper gives a simple and provably good external-memory history-independent skip list, which has high probability guarantees. Specifically, our skip list supports insert, deletes, and searches with $O(\log_B N)$ I/Os whp, and range queries returning k elements with $O(\log_B N + k/B)$ whp—which is just the search plus scan cost. Thus, our history independent, external memory skip list has high-probability bounds matching those of a B-tree.

Our challenge is to tweak the folklore B-skip list [1, 25, 26, 33] as little as possible (and in a history-independent way) so that we can achieve high-probability bounds for searches and inserts while maintaining optimal range queries.

1.3 Results

We begin by giving an efficient, history-independent packed memory array.

THEOREM 1. *There exists a weakly history-independent packed-memory array on N elements which can perform inserts and deletes in $O(\log^2 N)$ amortized element moves with high probability. This PMA requires $O(N)$ space, can perform inserts and deletes in amortized $O\big(\frac{\log^2 N}{B} + \log_B N\big)$ I/Os with high probability, and can perform a range query for k elements in $O(1 + k/B)$ I/Os.*

When $B = \Omega(\log N \log\log N)$ (reasonable on today's systems), then $\frac{\log^2 N}{B} = O(\log_B N)$, so inserts and deletes in our PMA have the same I/O complexity as in a B-tree.

Theorem 1 directly yields a history-independent cache-oblivious B-tree with these performance bounds:

THEOREM 2. *There exists a weakly history-independent, cache-oblivious B-tree on N elements which can perform inserts and deletes in $O\big(\frac{\log^2 N}{B} + \log_B N\big)$ amortized I/Os with high probability. This cache-oblivious B-tree requires $O(N)$ space and can answer a range query for k elements in $O(\log_B N + k/B)$ I/Os, i.e., the search plus the scan cost.*

We give a simple and provably good external-memory history-independent skip list, which has high probability guarantees analogous to in-memory skip lists.

THEOREM 3. *There exists a weakly history-independent, external-memory skip list on N elements which can perform look-ups in $O(\log_B N)$ I/Os with high probability. For a parameter $\varepsilon > 0$, the skip-list requires $O(\log_B N)$ amortized I/Os for inserts and deletes, with a worst case of $O(B^\varepsilon \log N)$ I/Os, all with high probability. This skip-list requires $O(N)$ space and can answer a range query for k elements in $O(\frac{1}{\varepsilon}\log_B N + k/B)$ I/Os with high probability.*

The parameter ε indicates a small trade-off between the worst-case rebuild cost after an update and the cost of medium-size range queries (see Section 6).

We contrast our data structure with the B-skip list, which promotes elements from one level to the next with probability $1/B$. We prove that with high probability, there exist at least $\Omega(\sqrt{NB})$ elements where the cost to search for any one of them is $O(\log \frac{N}{B})$. Thus, the high-probability I/O bounds for searching in a B-skip list are not asymptotically better than for searching in a regular (internal-memory) skip list that is implemented in external memory.

1.4 Related Work

History of History Independence

The history of history independence spans nearly four decades. The central notions of history independence predate its formalism.

One of the key ideas of history independence is unique representation, which was studied as far back as 1977 by Snyder [59]. Many uniquely represented data structures were published before the conception of history independence [4, 6, 7, 52–54, 59, 60]. Similar to unique representation, the idea of randomized structures that are *uniformly represented*, that is, have representations drawn from a distribution irrespective of the past history, emerged with Pugh's skip list [52, 53] and Aragon and Seidel's treap [7].

Nearly a decade later, Micciancio [43] defined ***oblivious data structures*** as those whose topology does not reveal the sequence of operations that led to the current state. In 2001, Naor and Teague [47] strengthened obliviousness to ***history independence*** ("anti-persistence"), generalizing it to include the entire *bit representation* of the structure, including memory addresses.

Hartline et al. [36] proved that a reversible data structure (i.e. one whose state graph is strongly connected) is SHI if and only if it fixes a ***canonical representation*** for each state depending only on initial (possibly random) choices made before any operations are performed.

Buchbinder and Petrank [23] further explored strong versus weak history independence, proving a separation between the two notions for heaps and queues in a comparison-based model.

History-independent data structures are well-studied when the objective is to minimize RAM computations. Examples include SHI hashing [20, 46, 47], dictionaries and order-maintenance [20], and history-independent data structures for computational geometry [21, 61].

Golovin [32, 33] began an algorithmic study of history-independent data structures in external-memory. First, Golovin proposed the B-treap [32], a strongly history-independent external-memory B-tree variant based on treaps [7].

Golovin notes that while the B-treap is a unique-representation data structure supporting B-tree operations with low overhead, from a practical point of view, it is complicated and difficult to implement [33]. Golovin thus proposes a strongly history-independent B-skip list [33] as a simpler alternative to the B-treap. This data structure achieves $O(\log_B N)$ I/Os in expectation for searches and updates and $O(k/B + \log_B N)$ I/Os in expectation for range queries returning k elements.

Golovin's B-skip list builds upon the folklore extension of skip lists (see e.g., [1, 25, 26, 33]): promote an element from one level to the next with probability $1/B$, rather than $1/2$. The folklore B-skip list's I/O bounds are only in expectation, and do not extend to good high probability bounds (see Lemma 15).

Other Applications of History Independence

The theoretical work on history independence in external memory complements the security and experimental work on history-independent data structures for persistent storage, such as file systems, cloud storage, voting systems and databases [10–12, 19, 44, 45, 56].

History independence has many applications in security and privacy. For example, history-independent data structures help to guarantee privacy in incremental signature schemes [43] and vote-storage mechanisms [19, 44, 45].

History-independent data structures often have nice properties. For example, skip lists [53] have weakly history-independent topologies, and are weight balanced [48] in a randomized sense. Canonical representations [36] find applications in other areas besides security, e.g. concurrent data structures [58], equality testing [60] and dynamic and incremental algorithms [2, 52].

2. PRELIMINARIES

An event E_n on a problem of size n occurs ***with high probability (whp)*** if $\Pr[E_n] \geq 1 - 1/n^c$ for some constant c. Often the event E_n is parametrized by some constant d, in particular, because the event is defined using Big Oh notation. (See, e.g., Theorem 11.) In this case, we can say more strongly that for every c, there is a d so that $\Pr[E_n] \geq 1 - 1/n^c$. We use high probability guarantees to bound a data structure's performance more tightly than can be done using expectation alone. Even if a data structure performs well in expectation, it may have a large number of poorly-performing operations (see, for example, Lemma 15).

Two instances I_1 and I_2 of a data structure are in the same ***state*** if they cannot be distinguished via any sequence of operations on the data structure. The ***memory representation*** of an instance I of a data structure is the bit representation of I, including data, pointers, unused buffer space, and all auxiliary parts of the structure, along with the physical addresses at which they are stored.

DEFINITION 4 (WEAK HISTORY INDEPENDENCE). *A data structure is weakly history independent (WHI) if, for any two sequences of operations X and Y that take the data structure from initialization to the same state, the distribution over memory representations after X is performed is identical to the distribution after Y.*

2.1 Building Blocks for History Independence

We use history-independent allocation [47] as a black box. We also use the weak history-independent dynamic arrays [36], rather than strongly independent dynamic arrays [36,47].[3]

Weakly history-independent dynamic arrays take constant amortized time per update with high probability. The idea is to maintain the following invariants. For array A storing n elements: (1) the size $|A|$ is uniformly and randomly chosen from $\{n, \ldots, 2n-1\}$, and, (2) after each insert or delete resize with probability $\Theta(1/|A|)$.

2.2 Performance Advantages of WHI over SHI

We focus on weak history independence because of its performance benefits. In particular, weak history independence allows us to have high-probability guarantees in our data structures.

Strong history independence for reversible data structures requires a canonical representation [36].[4] While canonical representations are useful to have, maintaining them imposes strict limitations on the design and efficiency of the data structure, as argued by several authors [23,36]. Moreover, amortization, strong history independence, and high-probability guarantees are largely incompatible.

In particular, SHI dynamic arrays cannot achieve the same with high probability guarantees as WHI dynamic arrays.

OBSERVATION 1. *No strongly-history-independent dynamic array can achieve $o(N)$ amortized resize cost per insert or delete with high probability.*

PROOF. Consider a strongly-history-independent dynamic array that needs to be strictly greater than 50% full. (The proof generalizes to arbitrary capacity constraints.) For integer k, the adversary chooses a random $\ell \in \{k, k+1, \ldots, 2k\}$. Then the adversary inserts up to ℓ elements into the array, and then alternates between adding and removing an element from the array, so that the array alternates between having ℓ and $\ell+1$ elements.

Given the capacity constraints on the array, there must be at least two different canonical representations for the arrays of sizes $k, k+1, \ldots, 2k$. Thus, there is a probability of at least $1/k$ that the adversary forces an array resize (with cost $\Omega(N)$) on every insert and delete in the alternation phase.

Observe that k can be arbitrarily large. No matter how long the data structure runs, it cannot avoid an $\Omega(N)$ resize with probability greater than $1-1/k$. □

Most importantly, this observation applies to PMAs as well. A PMA with N elements at a given time is required to have size $\Theta(N)$, so it generalizes the dynamic array. That is, Observation 1 lets us conclude the following:

REMARK 1. *A strongly history-independent PMA cannot give any $o(N)$ amortized with high probability operation bounds. In contrast, our weakly history-independent PMA has a $O(\log^2 N)$ bound (Theorem 1).*

[3]Here it is assumed the contents of the dynamic array are stored (internally) in a history independent manner—thus the size of the array should not depend on the history of inserts and deletes.

[4]A data structure is reversible if the state-transition graph is strongly connected [36], which is true of all structures in this paper and most structures that support deletes.

Observation 1 similarly generalizes to other amortized data structures with large worst-case costs. Thus, while strong history independence provides stronger security guarantees, it can come at a high performance cost.

2.3 Oblivious Adversary and Oblivious Observer

Our performance analyses assume an ***oblivious adversary***, which determines the sequence of operations presented to the data structure. The oblivious adversary cannot see the outcomes of the data structure's coin flips nor the current state of memory. Said differently, the adversary is required to choose the entire sequence of operations before the data structure even starts running. The oblivious adversary is used for analyzing randomized structures such as skip lists [53] or treaps [7].

Our (weak) history-independence analyses assume an ***oblivious observer***. The observer cannot control the input sequence and does not see the data structure's coin flips. The observer gets to observe the data structure's memory representation once. We prove history independence by showing that for every state of the data structure, the distribution of memory representations is the same, regardless of how the data structure got to that state.

3. HISTORY-INDEPENDENT PACKED MEMORY ARRAY

This section gives a history-independent packed memory array (PMA). A PMA is an $\Theta(N)$-sized array that stores a sequence of elements in a user-specified order. There are up to $O(1)$ gaps between consecutive elements to support efficient insertions and deletions.

A PMA with N elements supports the following:

- `Query`(i, j)—return the ith through jth elements of the PMA, inclusive, where $0 \le i \le j < N$.
- `Insert`(i, x)—insert x as the ith element of the PMA, where $0 \le i \le N$. Elements with rank i through $N-1$ before the insert become the elements with $i+1$ though N after the insert.
- `Delete`(i)—delete the ith element of the PMA, where $0 \le i < N$.

The PMA's performance is given in Theorem 1.

3.1 High-Level Structure of HI PMA

Packed-memory arrays and sparse tables in the literature [14, 16–18, 38, 41, 66] are not history independent; the size of the array, densities of the subarrays, and rebalances depend strongly on the history.

We guarantee history independence for our PMA as follows. First, we ensure the size of the PMA is history independent. We resize using the HI dynamic array allocation strategy [36], as summarized in Section 2.1.

Next, we ensure that the N elements in the array of size $N_S = \Theta(N)$ are spread throughout the array according to a distribution (given below) that is independent of past operations.

We maintain this history-independent layout recursively. At the topmost level of recursion, we (implicitly) maintain a set of size $\Theta(N_S/\log N_S)$, which we call the ***candidate set***. The candidate set consists of elements that have rank $N/2 \pm \Theta(N_S/\log N_S)$. We pick a random element from the candidate set, which we call the ***balance element***. If the balance element has rank r, then we recursively store the first $r-1$ elements in the first half of the array and the remaining $N-r-1$ elements in the second half of the array.

In general, when we are spreading elements out within a subarray A of the PMA, the candidate set has size $\Theta(|A|/\log N_S)$, and as before, the balance element is randomly chosen from this set. The base case is when $|A| = \Theta(\log N_S)$, at which point the elements are spread evenly throughout A.

Thus, how the elements are spread throughout the PMA depends only on the size N_S (which is randomly chosen as described in Section 2.1), the number of elements in the PMA N, and the random choices of all the balance elements.

We maintain the balance elements in each candidate set using a simple generalization of reservoir sampling [62] in which there are deletes, described below. In this particular instance of reservoir sampling, the size of a candidate set at any given level of recursion stays the same, unless the size of the entire PMA changes.

See Figure 1 for an illustration of our PMA. The top part represents how each level of recursion partions the elements into ranges. We show repeated elements across levels to aid visualization; they are only stored once in the data structure (at the bottom level). The division of elements into ranges at each level helps in maintaining the balance elements, which are stored in a separate structure.

3.2 Reservoir Sampling with Deletes

We first review a small tweak on standard reservoir sampling [62], ***reservoir sampling with deletes***, which we use to help build the PMA.

Game: We have a dynamic set of elements. The objective is to maintain a uniformly and randomly chosen ***leader*** of the set, where each element in the set has equal probability of being selected as leader. In other words, we are interested in reservoir sampling with a reservoir of size 1.

Since the set is dynamic, at each step t, an element may be added to or deleted from the set. The adversary is oblivious, which means that the input sequence cannot depend on the particular element chosen as leader.

We can maintain the leader using the following technique. Let n_t denote the number of elements in the set at time t (including any newly-arrived element). Initially, if the set is nonempty, we choose the leader uniformly at random. When a new element y arrives, y becomes the leader with probability $1/n_t$; otherwise the old leader remains. When an element is deleted, there are two cases. If that element was the leader, then we choose a new leader uniformly at random from the remaining elements in the set. If the deleted element was not the leader, the old leader remains.

LEMMA 5 ([62]). *At any time step t, if there are n_t elements in the pool, then each element has a probability $1/n_t$ to be the leader.*

3.3 Detailed Structure of the HI PMA

The size N_S of our history-independent PMA is a random variable that depends on the number of elements N stored in the PMA (similar to dynamic arrays in Section 2.1). We select parameter $\hat{N}$ randomly from $\{N, \ldots, 2N-1\}$, and N_S is a function of $\hat{N}$ (as described below).

We view the PMA as a complete binary tree of ranges, where a ***range*** is a contiguous sequence of array slots. This tree has height $h = \lceil \log \hat{N} - \log\log \hat{N} \rceil$. The root is the entire PMA and has depth 0. The leaves in the binary tree are ranges comprising $\lceil C_L \log \hat{N} \rceil$ slots, and C_L is a constant to be determined later. Thus, the PMA has a total of $N_S = 2^h \lceil C_L \log \hat{N} \rceil \leq (2C_L+1)\hat{N} = \Theta(N)$ slots.

Consider a range R in the binary tree with left child R_1 and right child R_2. Recall from Section 3.1 that the ***balance element*** b_R of R is the first element of R_2; all the elements in R of smaller rank than b_R are stored in R_1. The values of b_R for each range/node are stored in a separate tree.

For each non-leaf range R at depth d, define the ***candidate set*** M_R to be the $\lceil c_1 \hat{N} 2^{-d} / \log \hat{N} \rceil$ middle elements of R. More precisely, if R holds ℓ elements, then we fix the size of M_R and set the first element of M_R to be the $1 + \lceil \ell/2 \rceil - \lceil |M_R|/2 \rceil$th element of R.

Our PMA is parameterized by a constant $0 < c_1 < 1 - 6/\log \hat{N}$.[5] A larger c_1 reduces the amortized update time and increases the space. We require $C_L \geq 1 + c_1 + 6/\log \hat{N}$. The value of C_L and c_1 need not change as $\hat{N}$ changes—values such as $c_1 = 1/2$ and $C_L = 2$ will work for sufficiently large $\hat{N}$ (over 4096 in this case).

3.4 Dynamically Maintaining Balance Elements

As elements are inserted into or deleted from the PMA, the candidate set M_R for some range R could change. This change might be caused by a newly inserted or deleted element that belongs to M_R or just because insertions at one end of R cause the median element of R to change.

As the candidate set M_R changes, we maintain the invariant that the balance element b_R is selected uniformly and randomly from M_R. (In particular, this means that b_R is selected history-independently.) We use reservoir sampling with deletes as the basis for maintaining this invariant.

INVARIANT 6. *After each operation, for each range R, balance element b_R is uniformly distributed over the candidate set M_R.*

Whenever one element leaves their candidate set, another one joins, since the candidate set size of each range is fixed between rebuilds of the entire PMA. Thus, we describe how to maintain the candidate set when exactly one element is added, and one leaves.

If the balance element is the element leaving the candidate set, we select the new balance element uniformly at random. Otherwise, when a new element enters the candidate set, it has a $1/|M_R|$ chance of becoming the new balance element (as in reservoir sampling).

When the balance element of a range changes, we rebuild the entire range and all of its subranges. Rebuilding a range of $|R|$ slots can be done in $\Theta(|R|)$ time; see Lemma 10.

3.5 Detecting Changes to the Candidate Set

In order to determine how inserts and deletes affect the candidate set of a range R, we need to know the rank of the element being inserted or deleted, the current candidate set of R, and the rank of the current balance element of R.

The rank of the element being inserted and deleted is specified as part of the insert or delete operation.

To compute the other information, our PMA maintains an auxiliary data structure containing the number of elements

[5]When $\hat{N} \leq 64$, no such c_1 exists. For such small $\hat{N}$, we use a dynamic array instead.

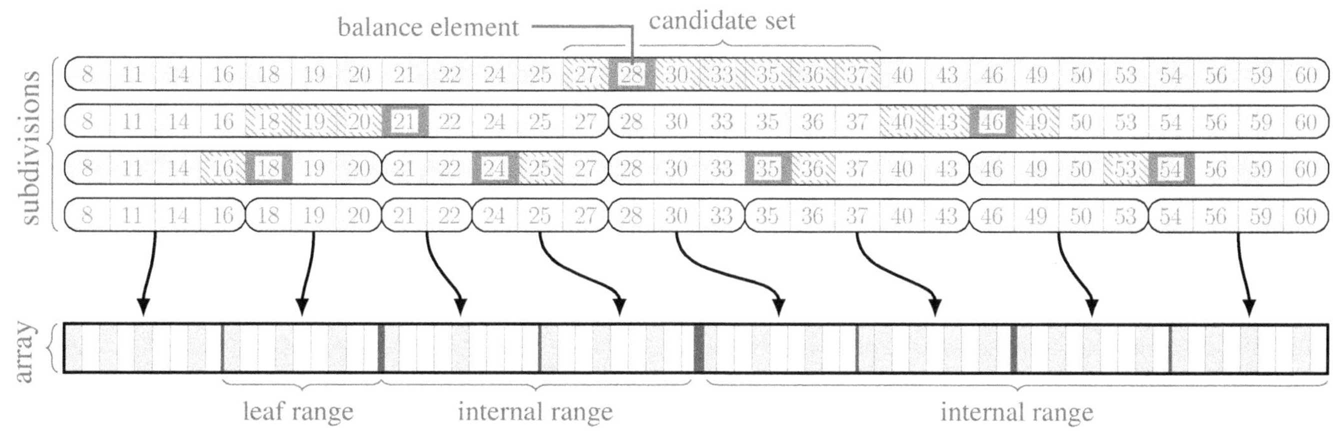

Figure 1: Illustration of our PMA showing the subdivisions of elements into ranges. In each range, the balance element is framed and the candidate set is hatched. The actual array is represented in the bottom, where occupied slots are shaded. The candidate-set size at any given level does not depend on the range. The rank of each balance element is stored in a separate tree.

ℓ_R in each range R. During an insert or delete, as we descend the tree of ranges, we keep track of the ranks of the first and last element in each range as follows. Suppose we are at range R whose first element has rank x. If we descend to R_1, then we know the rank of the first element of R_1 is also x. If we descend to R_2, then the rank of its first element is $x + \ell_{R_1}$. Given the rank of the first element of a range and the number of elements in that range, it is easy to compute its candidate set. Note also that the rank of the balance element of a range R whose first element has rank x is $x + \ell_{R_1}$.

We need to store ℓ_R for each range so that it can be accessed efficiently, both in terms of operations and I/Os. Since the ranges form a complete binary tree, we store the numbers ℓ_R in a binary tree organized in a Van Emde Boas layout (see [14,51]). We call this auxiliary data structure the ***rank tree***.

The Van Emde Boas layout is a deterministic, static, cache-oblivious—and hence history-independent—layout of a complete binary tree. It supports traversing a root-to-leaf path in $O(\log N)$ operations and $O(\log_B N)$ I/Os. Thus, the rank tree is history independent.

Whenever the size of a range changes due to an insert or delete, we update the corresponding entry in the rank tree. Whenever we rebuild a range R in the PMA, we update all entries of the rank tree corresponding to descendants of R. Whenever we rebuild the entire PMA, we rebuild the entire rank tree.

4. CORRECTNESS AND PERFORMANCE

4.1 Balance-Element Structural Lemmas

First, we show correctness—the data structure always finds a slot for any element it needs to store.

LEMMA 7. *At all times, the size of a range is larger than the number of elements it contains.*

PROOF. Consider a range at depth d. This range has $N_S/2^d = 2^{h-d}\lceil C_L \log \hat{N}\rceil \geq C_L\hat{N}/2^d$ slots. We will show that the maximum number of elements it can contain is smaller than this number of slots.

The number of elements in the range is at most half of the elements in its parents range, plus half of the size of the parent's candidate set (rounding up). In other words, if $S(d)$ is the maximum number of elements in a range at depth d, $S(0) \leq \hat{N}$ and

$$\begin{aligned} S(d) &\leq \lceil S(d-1)/2\rceil + \lceil M_R/2\rceil \\ &\leq \lceil S(d-1)/2\rceil + \frac{1}{2}\left\lceil \frac{c_1\hat{N}}{2^{d-1}\log \hat{N}}\right\rceil + \frac{1}{2} \\ &\leq \frac{S(d-1)}{2} + \frac{c_1\hat{N}}{2^d \log \hat{N}} + \frac{3}{2}. \end{aligned}$$

By induction,

$$S(d) \leq \frac{\hat{N}}{2^d} + \frac{c_1 d\hat{N}}{2^d \log \hat{N}} + 3.$$

Since $d \leq \log \hat{N}$, and $\hat{N}/2^d \geq \hat{N}/2^h \geq (\log \hat{N})/2$,

$$S(d) \leq \frac{\hat{N}}{2^d}(1 + c_1) + 3 \leq \frac{\hat{N}}{2^d}\left(1 + c_1 + \frac{6}{\log \hat{N}}\right).$$

Since we choose $C_L \geq 1 + c_1 + 6/\log \hat{N}$, we have $S(d) \leq C_L\hat{N}/2^d$. □

As Lemma 7 establishes, each leaf range in the PMA (which has $\Theta(\log N)$ slots) never fills up completely. Using a similar argument, it can be shown that each leaf also contains $\Omega(\log N)$ elements if $c_1 < 1 - 6/\log \hat{N}$. Because the elements are spread out evenly in the leaves, this implies there are $O(1)$ gaps between two consecutive elements.

LEMMA 8. *If $c_1 < 1 - 6/\log \hat{N}$, the leaves are always constant-factor full. There is $O(1)$ space between two consecutive elements in the array.*

Next, we prove weak history independence. As mentioned in Section 3.1, when we are spreading elements out within a subarray A of the PMA, the balance element is randomly chosen from the candidate set. The elements of A are recursively split between its children according to this balance element. The base case is when $|A| = \Theta(\log \hat{N})$, at which point the elements are spread evenly throughout A.

Thus, how the elements are spread throughout the PMA depends only on $\hat{N}$ (and the related N_S), the number of elements in the PMA N, and the random choices of all the balance elements. This immediately gives weak history-independence, as formalized in the following lemma.

LEMMA 9. *This PMA is weakly history independent.*

PROOF. We show that the memory representation of the PMA is based only on N and some randomness (in particular, the random choices made during balance element selection and the random choice of $\hat{N}$).

Let the PMA contain a set of elements S of size N, with a set of balance elements P. Then P partitions the elements of S into leaf ranges.

Since the elements are evenly spaced in each leaf range, the position of each element within the leaf is determined by the number of elements in that leaf. Since S is partitioned into leaf ranges by P, P determines the position of each element in the PMA. Thus P, $\hat{N}$, and N determine the memory representation of the data structure. By Invariant 6, P is selected from a distribution based only on N and $\hat{N}$.

Thus, any two sequences of operations X and Y that insert S into the PMA result in the same distribution on P, and the same distribution on memory representations. □

4.2 Proving the Performance Bounds

We begin by bounding the cost of a rebalance. Then we bound the total number of rebalances.

LEMMA 10. *Rebuilding a range R containing $|R|$ slots takes $O(|R|)$ RAM operations and $O(|R|/B+1)$ I/Os.*

PROOF. The algorithm first recursively chooses the balance elements for all ranges contained in this range R and updates them in the rank tree; this takes $O(|R|)$ time and $O(|R|/B + \log_B |R| + 1) = O(|R|/B + 1)$ I/Os. Then, all elements in R are gathered, and inserted into the appropriate leaf range using a sequence of linear scans. □

Our goal is to bound the cost of our PMA operations. Specifically, we want to show Theorem 11.

THEOREM 11. *Consider k (not necessarily consecutive) operations on a PMA during which its maximum size is N_M, its minimum size is $\Omega(N_M)$, and $k = \Omega(N_M)$. The amortized cost of these operations is $O(\log^2 N_M)$ with high probability with respect to k: in other words, these k operations require $O(k \log^2 N_M)$ total RAM operations with high probability.*

Before proving this theorem, we need some supporting lemmas and definitions.

DEFINITION 12. *A rebuild that is not charged to a range R is called a* **free rebuild**. *Free rebuilds come from two sources: (1) they are rebuilds of an ancestor range (whose cost is charged to the ancestor), or (2) they are triggered by the interstitial operations between the nonconsecutive operations of Theorem 11.*

We further categorize non-free rebuilds by their causes. An **out-of-bounds rebuild** *is a rebuild caused by the pivot leaving the candidate set. A* **lottery rebuild** *is a rebuild caused by deleting the pivot or by inserting into the candidate set an element that becomes a new pivot.*

Gearing up to Lemma 13, we concentrate on the cost of all rebalances at a single depth d. Let M_d be the size of the candidate set at depth d.

We give a lower bound on the probability that two out-of-bounds rebuilds happen in quick succession. This lemma holds regardless of the number of free and lottery rebuilds that happen in between.

LEMMA 13. *After any rebuild of a range R at depth d, consider a sequence of t operations on R, for any $t \in \{1, \ldots, \lfloor M_d/2 \rfloor\}$, with arbitrary free and lottery rebuilds occurring during these operations. The probability $p(t)$ that no out-of-bounds rebuild happens during these t operations is at least $1 - 2t/M_d$.*

PROOF. Let $p_i(t)$ be the probability that no out-of-bounds rebuild happens in the first t time steps, given that exactly i free and lottery rebuilds happen during the first t time steps. We prove the lemma by induction on i.

Define the ***guard number*** as the number of elements between the pivot and the closest endpoint of the candidate set.

First, the base case: for any t, $p_0(t)$ is at least the probability that the guard number after a rebuild is larger than t. Indeed, the balance element cannot be moved closer to an endpoint of the candidate set by more than one element per operation. As the pivot is sampled uniformly after any type of rebuild, we have

$$p_0(t) \geq \Pr\left[\text{guard number} > t\right] \geq 1 - 2t/M_d.$$

Now, assume by induction that $p_i(t) \geq 1 - 2t/M_d$ and we want to show $p_{i+1}(t) \geq 1 - t/M_d$. Let t' be the last time step before the $(i+1)$st non-out-of-bounds rebuild.

The following conditions ensure that there are no out-of-bounds rebuilds in the first t operations:

1. there is no out-of-bounds rebuild in the first t' operations, and
2. there is no out-of-bounds rebuild in the subsequent $t - t'$ operations.

These two events are independent since there is a fixed (free or lottery) rebuild between them. The first occurs with probability $p_i(t')$ and the second with probability $p_0(t-t')$. Thus, we have

$$\begin{aligned} p_{i+1}(t) &\geq p_i(t')\, p_0(t-t') \\ &\geq (1 - 2t'/M_d)\,(1 - 2(t-t')/M_d) \geq 1 - 2t/M_d, \end{aligned}$$

and the induction is complete. □

DEFINITION 14. *Consider an out-of-bounds rebuild of a range R at depth d.*

We call this rebuild a **good out-of-bounds rebuild** *if R has only free and lottery rebuilds for the next $M_d/4$ operations.*

By Lemma 13, an out-of-bounds rebuild is good with probability at least $1/2$.

We are now ready to prove Theorem 11.

PROOF OF THEOREM 11. Consider the sequence of rebuilds of ranges at a given depth d. We analyze lottery rebuilds and out-of-bounds rebuilds separately. Since variations in $\hat{N}$ slightly change the candidate set size, let M denote the smallest candidate-set size at depth d over the k operations. However, since $N = \Theta(N_M)$ at all times, $M = \Theta(|M_d|)$.

We give a (weak) bound on k/M which helps show that the high-probability bounds hold with respect to k.

In particular,

$$k/M \geq \frac{k \log N_M}{N_M} \geq \frac{k \log k \log N_M}{N_M \log k} = \Omega(\log k),$$

since $k/\log k = \Omega(N_M/\log N_M)$ if $k = \Omega(N_M)$.

Each operation has probability at most $1/M$ of causing a lottery rebuild. Thus, there are k/M lottery rebuilds in expectation. Then using Chernoff bounds, the probability that we have more than $(1+\delta)k/M$ rebuilds is less than $e^{-\delta k/3M}$. Recall that $k/M = \Omega(\log k)$. Substituting, there are $O(k/M)$ lottery rebuilds with high probability.

Now, we bound the out-of-bounds rebuilds. By the pigeonhole principle, there cannot be more than $k/(M/4) + 2^d = O(k/M)$ good out-of-bounds rebuilds (the second term comes from the number of ranges at depth d).

We bound how many bad out-of-bounds rebuilds can happen before reaching this limit on good out-of-bounds rebuilds. Any out-of-bounds rebuild is good with probability at least $1/2$. Then after $k/M = \Omega(\log k)$ out-of-bounds rebuilds, we obtain $\Theta(k/M)$ good out-of-bounds rebuilds with high probability, again by Chernoff bounds. As we can only get $O(k/M)$ good rebuilds, we have $O(k/M)$ out-of-bounds rebuilds in total.

Therefore, every k operations, there are $O(k/M)$ out-of-bounds and lottery rebuilds of ranges at depth d with high probability. Each rebuild costs $O(M \log N_M)$ RAM operations by Lemma 10 (because that is the number of slots in a range at depth d). Thus, the total rebuild cost for depth d is $O(k \log N_M)$.

Having determined the cost of rebalancing at each depth, we account for the total cost. The amortized rebalance cost, summing over all $h = O(\log N_M)$ levels, is $O(\log^2 N_M)$.

Each resize costs $O(N_M)$ and occurs with probability $O(1/N_M)$ after every insertion. Using Chernoff bounds, there are $O((k \log N_M)/N_M) = \Omega(\log k)$ resizes after k operations with high probability, leading to an additional amortized cost of $O(\log N_M)$.

Finally, each insert or delete requires extra bookkeeping: we must find the appropriate leaf range to insert the element by traversing the rank tree. This traversal takes $O(\log N_M)$ RAM operations, and rebuilding the leaf so that the elements are still evenly spaced takes $O(\log N_M)$ RAM operations.

This gives a total of $O(k \log^2 N_M)$ total RAM operations with high probability.

Using similar analysis, we can also bound the I/O performance. Recall that rebalancing a range of size R takes $O(R/B + 1)$ I/Os, and traversing a tree in the Van Emde Boas layout requires $O(\log_B N_M)$ I/Os. Carrying these terms through the above proof gives the desired bounds. □

To complete the proof of Theorem 1, we need to extend this analysis to handle the PMA changing size significantly.

PROOF OF THEOREM 1. We partition the $k = \Omega(N)$ operations on the PMA into types based on the size of the PMA. In particular, let $\hat{N}_t$ be the value of $\hat{N}$ during the tth operation. Then operation t is of type 0 if $N \geq \hat{N}_t > N/2$, type 1 if $N/2 \geq \hat{N}_t > N/4$, and type i if $N/2^i \geq \hat{N}_t > N/2^{i+1}$ for $0 \leq i \leq \lceil \log N \rceil$.

We analyze each type of operations as a whole, and bound its total cost, summing to $O(k \log^2 N)$ RAM operations in total. Each type is analyzed using two cases.

First, consider a type i which has at least $\sqrt{N}$ total operations. Then by Theorem 11, these operations take amortized $O(\log^2 N)$ RAM operations with high probability.

Second, consider a type i which has less than $\sqrt{N}$ operations. We call the operations of these types ***small-type operations***. We show that the total cost of all small-type operations is a lower-order term.

Since the PMA begins as empty, and each operation can only insert one element, there are at least $N/2^{i+1}$ operations of type i. Thus, each small-type operation t has $\hat{N}_t \leq \sqrt{N}$.

Then overall, a type which has less than $\sqrt{N}$ operations must operate on a PMA of size $\leq \sqrt{N}$. Thus, each type has total cost $O(N)$. Summing over the $O(\log N)$ such types, we get a worst-case total cost of $O(N \log N)$ for small-type operations; amortizing gives a cost of $O(\log N)$ RAM operations.

Thus the total amortized cost is $O(\log^2 N)$ with high probability with respect to N. The I/O cost to rebuild range R is $|R|/B$ by Lemma 10; carrying this term through the above analysis, we obtain the desired I/O bounds. □

4.3 Experimental Results

We implemented a normal PMA and our history-independent PMA. We found that while there was approximately a factor of 7 overhead in the run time, the asymptotic performance matched our analysis.

We also examined the number of element moves required during an insert. Figure 2 shows the number of moves required divided by $N \log^2 N$ vs. the number of elements inserted. The linear nature of this data supports our theoretical analysis.

These tests were run on a Dell server with an Intel Xeon processor (E5-2450 @ 2.10GHz). In these tests, inserting 100 million random numbers took approximately 23 minutes. Additionally the space overhead ranged from 1.8 to 5 times the number of elements.

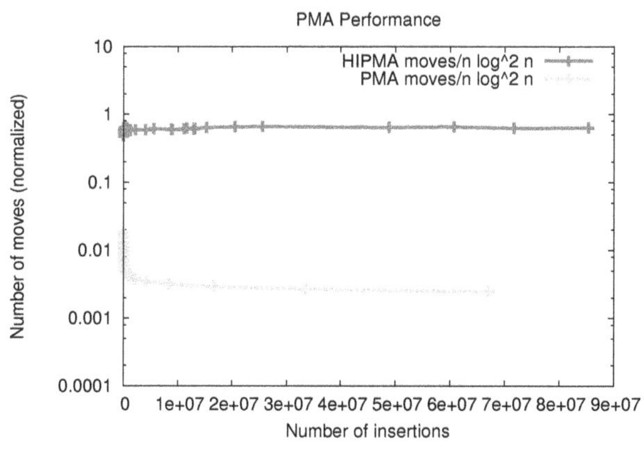

Figure 2: Experimental results of runtime for random inserts on normal and history-independent PMAs.

The history-independence of our PMA depends on the balance elements being uniformly distributed across the candidate set; see Lemma 5. To test this, we inserted values of 1-100,000 sequentially into a history-independent PMA and recorded the position of the balance for each range within this PMA where the candidate set size was eight or greater. We did this test 10,000 times and used the χ^2 goodness-of-fit test to compare these balance elements with a uniform distribution. To ensure enough samples we only looked at ranges where the expected count for each bucket was ten or greater. This resulted in 148 p-values. If our null hypothesis, that these balances are uniformly distributed, holds, these p-values themselves should be uniformly distributed. Running the χ^2 goodness-of-fit test across these p-values showed a result consistent with data coming from a uniform distribution (p=0.47, n=148). As a result we can say there is no statistically significant evidence of that our balance elements have a deviation from a uniform distribution.

5. HISTORY-INDEPENDENT CACHE-OBLIVIOUS B-TREE

In this section we prove Theorem 2, which establishes the performance of our history-independent cache-oblivious B-tree. This N-element data structure, must, without knowledge of the block size B,

- insert or delete items with $O((\log^2 N)/B + \log_B N)$ amortized I/Os with high probability,
- use $O(N)$ space, and
- answer range queries containing k elements in $O(\log_B N + k/B)$ I/Os.

When $B = \Omega(\log N \log\log N)$, which is reasonable on today's systems, $\frac{\log^2 N}{B} + \log_B N = O(\log_B N)$, so that our history-independent cache-oblivious B-tree matches the I/O complexity of a standard B-tree.

The requirements above are similar to those achieved by our PMA. The key difference is that PMA items are searched by rank (before being inserted, deleted, or completing a range search) rather than value.

By slightly augmenting our PMA, we obtain a cache-oblivious B-tree achieving the above bounds. We call our data structure the ***augmented PMA***.

The augmented PMA has an additional, static-topology tree associated with it. Recall that our PMA has the sizes of each range stored in a complete binary tree, in a Van Emde Boas layout. We store an additional tree storing the *values* of each balance element. The two trees are identically structured, and identically maintained. Thus, this leads to only a constant factor increase in both space and running time. To search (by value) in the augmented PMA, we traverse a path in the new tree of balance-element values. This costs $O(\log_B N)$ I/Os and $O(\log N)$ operations. Once we have found the element, we can determine its rank by traversing the rank tree, summing the sizes of any left children each time we go to a right child.

Once the rank of the element is known, we insert, delete, or perform range queries as in the normal PMA, establishing the desired bounds.

6. HISTORY-INDEPENDENT EXTERNAL-MEMORY SKIP LIST

In this section we prove Theorem 3. We give a history-independent external-memory skip list.

In-memory skip lists support updates and queries in $O(\log N)$ time whp. The natural extension to external memory [1, 25, 26, 33] promotes elements with probability $1/B$ rather than probability $1/2$. We prove that for this extension, the high-probability I/O bounds are asymptotically no better than those of an in-memory skip list run in external memory (Lemma 15).

We build an external-memory skip list with good (i.e., B-tree-like) high-probability bounds for searches, updates, and range queries, while retaining the structure of the folklore B-skip list as much as possible.

6.1 High-Level Structure of the HI External-Memory Skip List

First, we describe why the folklore B-skip list fails to achieve high-probability I/O bounds. Then, we present the approach used in our skip list.

Golovin and others [1, 25, 26, 33] promote elements with probability $1/B$ (rather than $1/2$, as in the in-memory skip list). Consider an ***array***, a sequence of contiguous elements at any level that have not been promoted to the next level (i.e., lie between two ***promoted elements***). These arrays can have size $O(B \log N)$ whp, which is $O(\log N)$ times larger than the expected length. When this list is embedded in an array (analogous to the nodes in a B-tree), then a scan to search for these elements costs $O(\log N)$ I/Os whp.

We change the promotion probability to $1/B^\gamma$, where $1/2 < \gamma < 1 - \log\log B/\log B$. Now, all arrays have size $O(B^\gamma \log N)$ whp, so searches and updates take $O(B^\gamma \log N/B) = O(\log_B N)$ I/Os whp.

While a promotion probability of $1/B^\gamma$ results in fast searches and updates, it slows down range queries. If we pack arrays at the leaf level (the ***leaf arrays***) of the skip list into disk blocks [33], then most disk blocks will be underutilized, containing only B^γ elements on average. Thus, a range query returning k elements may require $O(\log_B N + k/B^\gamma)$ I/Os, which is worse than the target of $O(\log_B N + k/B)$ I/Os.

For efficient range queries, we pack multiple arrays into disk blocks at the leaf level as follows. Contiguous arrays, delimited by elements promoted twice, are packed together into a ***leaf node***. A leaf node is stored consecutively on disk; see Figure 3.

The packing strategy described above permits some leaf nodes to get too large, achieving size $\Theta(B^{2\gamma} \log N)$. If we pack elements as densely as possible, then every new insert would require rewriting the entire node at a cost of $O(B^{2\gamma-1} \log N)$ I/Os, which is worse than $\Theta(\log_B N)$ I/Os.

Similar to PMAs and HI dynamic arrays [36], we leave empty spaces between the elements in the leaves to support efficient inserts. We do so in a way that maintains history independence; see Invariant 16.

6.2 Detailed Structure of the HI External-Memory Skip List

A skip list S is a series of linked lists $\{S_0, S_1, \ldots, S_h\}$, where $S_0 \supseteq S_1 \supseteq \ldots \supseteq S_h$. Let $H = \{0, 1, \ldots, h\}$ be the ***levels*** of the skip list, and h the ***height*** of the skip list. The base list S_0 contains all the elements in the skip list; we call level 0 the ***leaf level***.

Each S_i, for $0 < i \leq h$, stores a sorted subset of the elements from S_{i-1}, along with the special element `front` to mark the beginning of the list; see Figure 3. The function *level* : $S_0 \to H$ determines the highest list that contains an element x, that is, if *level* $(x) = i$ then $x \in S_j$ for all $j \leq i$ and $x \notin S_k$ for $i < k \leq h$.

The height of each element is determined randomly, according to ***promotion probability*** p. Specifically, for $i \in H - \{0\}$, if an element is in S_{i-1}, it is also in S_i with probability p. Thus, *level* (x) of an element x is the number of coin flips before we see a tail, when using a biased coin with probability p of flipping a head.

Next, we show that the folklore B-skip list, which has a

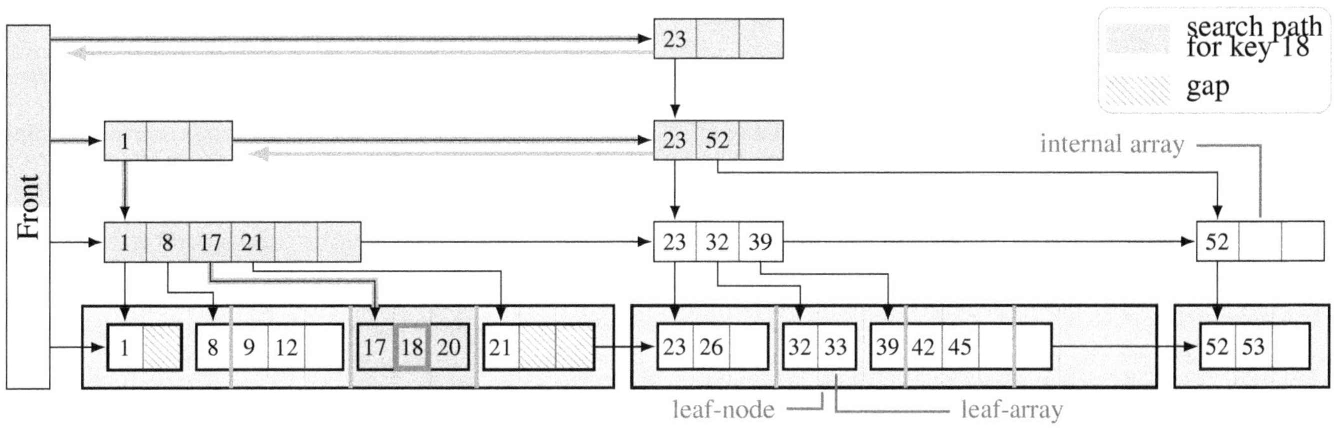

Figure 3: Illustration of a search path for element key 18 in the external skip list ($B = 3$ and $p = 1/2$).

promotion probability of $1/B$, performs poorly for some elements with high probability.

LEMMA 15. *In a B-skip list with promotion probability $p = 1/B$, there exist $\Omega(\sqrt{NB})$ elements with search cost $\Omega(\log(N/B))$ with high probability with respect to N/B.*

For our history-independent external-memory skip list, we choose promotion probability $p = 1/B^{\gamma}$, where $1/2 < \gamma \leq 1 - \log\log B/\log B$ is a constant. Let $1/p = B^{\gamma}$ be integral to simplify analysis. We parameterize our running times by $\varepsilon > 0$, with $\gamma = (\varepsilon + 1)/2$.

The parameter γ can be tuned—there is a trade-off between the cost of a range query and the worst-case cost of insertion. Specifically, a range query returning k elements has a cost of $O(\frac{1}{\varepsilon}\log_B N + k/B)$, while the worst-case insert cost is $O(B^{\varepsilon}\log N)$ I/Os. The expected insert cost remains $O(\log_B N)$ I/Os for all allowed values of γ.

We now describe how to partition the elements into arrays at nonleaf levels. We also describe how to pack the leaf arrays into leaf nodes.

Partitioning Non-Leaf Levels. We partition the list S_i at each level i for $1 \leq i \leq h$ into ***arrays***. The array at level i starts with a ***promoted element***, i.e., element x with *level* $(x) \geq i + 1$. It contains all elements up to (and not including) the next promoted element. The ***size*** of an array is the number of elements stored in it plus any empty slots. We maintain these sorted arrays history independently [36].

Partitioning the Leaf Level. We store the leaf level compactly to support I/O-efficient range queries. The ***leaf arrays*** at the leaf level are packed into a ***leaf node***. Formally, a leaf node $\mathcal{B}$ is a set of contiguous leaf arrays starting at some element x that has been promoted twice, that is, *level* $(x) \geq 2$.

We store the leaf arrays history independently (see Section 2.1), with the following modification: even when a leaf array has n elements with $n \leq B^{\gamma}$ elements, we maintain its size $n_s \geq B^{\gamma}$. We call the extra $n_s - n$ array slots ***gaps***. This modification retains history independence.

INVARIANT 16. *Let n be the number of elements in a leaf array of total size n_s then:*
- *If $n \leq B^{\gamma}$, then n_s is uniform in $[B^{\gamma}, 2B^{\gamma} - 1]$.*
- *If $n \geq B^{\gamma}$, then n_s is uniform in $[n, 2n - 1]$.*

Searches, Insertions, and Deletions. Search is implemented exactly as in a standard skip list: for an element y, start at the top list S_h, and scan right till a value $x > y$ is reached, in which case, descend a level down and continue till y is found or shown not to exist.

To insert or delete an element y, search for the leaf array where y belongs and insert or delete it. This involves shifting elements in the leaf array and causes an array resize with probability $O(1/B^{\gamma})$ by Invariant 16. If a resize occurs, rebuild the entire leaf node containing the array.

When inserting y, determine *level* $(y) = \ell$ by tossing a biased coin with probability of heads p. At levels $1 \leq i < \ell$, y starts an array, splitting the existing array into two. If $\ell \geq 2$, y starts a leaf node, splitting the existing leaf node into two.

When deleting y, at levels $1 \leq i < \ell$, merge the leaf array that y started with its predecessor. If $\ell \geq 2$ then merge the leaf node that y started with its predecessor.

6.3 History Independence of External-Memory Skip List

The history independence of our external-memory skip list follows immediately from the following facts:
- *level* (x) for each element x is generated randomly,
- the elements within an array appear in sorted order,
- the size of each array is chosen history-independently (by Invariant 16 for leaf arrays and [36] for non-leaf arrays),
- within a leaf node, the leaf arrays are packed contiguously in sorted order, and,
- each array is allocated in blocks of size $\Theta(B)$ history-independently [47].

6.4 Performance Analysis

We bound the height of the external-memory skip list. The proof is similar to standard skip lists.

LEMMA 17. *An external-memory skip list with promotion probability p has height $h = O(\log_{1/p} N)$ whp.*

PROOF. For any element x, the probability that its level is more than $O(\log_{1/p} N)$ is given by: $\Pr[\textit{level}(x) \geq c\log_{1/p} N] \leq p^{c\log_{1/p} N} = 1/N^c$.

Applying the union bound we get, $\Pr[\forall x, \textit{level}(x) \geq c\log_{1/p} N] \leq N(1/N^c) = 1/N^{c-1}$. □

Thus, the height of our external-memory skip list with $p = 1/B^{\gamma}$ is $O(\log_B N)$.

Search. To analyze searches, we bound the size of the arrays and leaf nodes.

An array contains elements between two consecutive promoted elements. Thus, the size of an array is bounded by the length of the longest sequence of tails, when flipping a biased coin with $\Pr[head] = 1/B^\gamma$, which is $O(B^\gamma \log N)$.

LEMMA 18. *The number of I/Os required to perform a search is $O(\log_B N)$ with high probability.*

PROOF. Similar to the *backward analysis* in standard skip lists [53], examine the search path from bottom up starting at the leaf level. Each element visited by the path was either promoted and the search path came from the top, or was not promoted and the search path came from the left. The number of down moves is bounded by the height $h = c \log_B N$ (Lemma 17). At each level, the search path traverses at most two arrays.

The total length of the arrays touched by the search path is bounded by the number of coin flips required to obtain $c \log_B N$ heads, where $\Pr[head] = 1/B^\gamma$. We need $O(B^\gamma \log N)$ coin flips whp. Thus, the number of I/Os during the search at nonleaf levels is $O(\log N/B^{1-\gamma} + \log_B N) = O(\log_B N)$ whp, since $\gamma \leq 1 - \log\log B/\log B$. At the leaf level, the search scans one leaf array, which costs $O(B^\gamma \log N/B) = O(\log_B N)$. □

Insert. To bound the insert cost, we bound the cost of rebuilding a leaf node. The size of a leaf node is the number of elements stored in it plus the number of gaps.

The number of elements in a leaf node is bounded by the length of the longest sequence of tails in N coin flips with $\Pr[head] = p^2 = 1/B^{2\gamma}$, which is $O(B^{2\gamma} \log N)$ whp.

The number of gaps between any k consecutive leaf elements can be shown by a Chernoff bound argument to be $O(k + B^\gamma \log N)$. Thus, the size of a leaf node is $O(B^{2\gamma} \log N)$ whp. Rebuilding it costs $O(B^{2\gamma} \log N/B) = O(B^\varepsilon \log N)$ I/Os.

LEMMA 19. *The cost of performing an insert or delete operation is amortized $O(\log_B N)$ I/Os whp, with a worst case cost of $O(B^\varepsilon \log N)$ I/Os whp.*

PROOF. When an element y is inserted or deleted, the splits and merges at levels $1 \leq i < level(y)$ are dominated by the search cost of $O(\log_B N)$.

The cost of inserting in a leaf array is dominated by the cost of rebuilding the leaf node: $O(B^\varepsilon \log N)$ I/Os whp. The rebuild occurs with probability $O(1/B^\gamma)$. The amortized I/O cost is then $O(B^{2\gamma-1} \log N/B^\gamma) = O(\log N/B^{1-\gamma}) = O(\log_B N)$ in expectation and whp with respect to the number of operations, since $\gamma \leq 1 - \log\log B/\log B$. □

Range Query. To analyze a range query on a range of size k, we bound the number of leaf nodes across which the k elements are spread. That is, we bound the number of heads obtained on k biased coin flips with $\Pr[head] = 1/B^{2\gamma}$.

LEMMA 20. *The number of leaf nodes across which k consecutive leaf elements are stored is $O(\frac{1}{\varepsilon}\log_B N + k/B)$ with high probability.*

LEMMA 21. *A range query returning k elements costs $O(\frac{1}{\varepsilon}\log_B N + k/B)$ I/Os with high probability.*

PROOF. We break the analysis into several cases depending on the source of the cost.

- If the k consecutive elements fit in a single leaf node and there are no gaps, then the size of each such leaf array is $O(B^\gamma \log N)$ whp. Thus, $O(B^\gamma \log N/B + k/B) = O(\log_B N + k/B)$ I/Os suffice.
- If the k consecutive elements span across arrays with gaps. The sum of sizes of the gaps between these elements is $O(k + B^\gamma \log N)$. Thus, a range query takes $O(k/B + B^\gamma \log N/B) = O(\log_B N + k/B)$ I/Os.
- If the k consecutive elements span several leaf nodes, by Lemma 20 they span $O(k/B + \frac{1}{\varepsilon}\log_B N)$ leaf nodes. Every time the range query scan crosses a leaf node boundary, we incur an I/O to bring in the next leaf node, which requires $O(k/B + \frac{1}{\varepsilon}\log_B N)$ I/Os.

Thus, overall a range query scanning k consecutive elements takes $O(\frac{1}{\varepsilon}\log_B N + k/B)$. □

Space. Finally, we bound the space used.

LEMMA 22. *The external skip list on N elements requires $\Theta(N)$ space with high probability.*

PROOF. The non leaf levels of the external skip list store $\Theta(N)$ elements with only constant factor space. At the leaf level, the number of gaps between N elements is $O(N + B^\gamma \log N) = \Theta(N)$ whp. □

Lemmas 18, 19, 21, and 22 prove Theorem 3.

7. CONCLUSION

We show that adding history independence to some external-memory data structures can come at low cost. We focus on history-independent indexing structures, alternatives to the traditional B-tree, the primary indexing structure used in databases. We give HI PMAs and cache-oblivious B-trees with the same asymptotic time and space bounds as their non-HI counterparts. We give a HI skip list that performs even better than the non-HI B-skip list because the bounds are given with high probability rather than in expectation.

Acknowledgments

This research was supported in part by NSF grants CCF 1114809, CCF 1217708, IIS 1247726, IIS 1251137, CNS 1408695, and CCF 1439084, and by the Laboratory Directed Research and Development program at Sandia National Laboratories, a multi-program laboratory managed and operated by Sandia Corporation, a wholly owned subsidiary of Lockheed Martin Corporation, for the U.S. Department of Energy's National Nuclear Security Administration under contract DE-AC04-94AL85000.

8. REFERENCES

[1] I. Abraham, J. Aspnes, and J. Yuan. Skip B-trees. In *Proc. of the 9th Annual International Conference on Principles of Distributed Systems (OPODIS)*, page 366, 2006.

[2] U. A. Acar, G. E. Blelloch, R. Harper, J. L. Vittes, and S. L. M. Woo. Dynamizing static algorithms, with applications to dynamic trees and history independence. In *Proc. of the 15th Annual ACM-SIAM Symposium on Discrete Algorithms (SODA)*, pages 531–540, 2004.

[3] A. Aggarwal and J. S. Vitter. The input/output complexity of sorting and related problems. *Communications of the ACM*, 31(9):1116–1127, Sept. 1988.

[4] O. Amble and D. E. Knuth. Ordered hash tables. *The Computer Journal*, 17(2):135–142, 1974.
[5] A. Anagnostopoulos, M. Goodrich, and R. Tamassia. Persistent authenticated dictionaries and their applications. *Information Security*, pages 379–393, 2001.
[6] A. Andersson and T. Ottmann. Faster uniquely represented dictionaries. In *Proc. of the 32nd Annual IEEE Symposium on Foundations of Computer Science (FOCS)*, pages 642–649, 1991.
[7] C. R. Aragon and R. G. Seidel. Randomized search trees. In *Proc. of the 30th Annual IEEE Symposium on Foundations of Computer Science (FOCS)*, pages 540–545, 1989.
[8] L. Arge, D. Eppstein, and M. T. Goodrich. Skip-webs: efficient distributed data structures for multi-dimensional data sets. In *Proc. of the 24th Annual ACM Symposium on Principles of Distributed Computing (PODS)*, pages 69–76, 2005.
[9] J. Aspnes and G. Shah. Skip graphs. *ACM Transactions on Algorithms*, 3(4):37, 2007.
[10] S. Bajaj, A. Chakraborti, and R. Sion. The foundations of history independence. *arXiv preprint arXiv:1501.06508*, 2015.
[11] S. Bajaj and R. Sion. Ficklebase: Looking into the future to erase the past. In *Proc. of the 29th IEEE International Conference on Data Engineering (ICDE)*, pages 86–97, 2013.
[12] S. Bajaj and R. Sion. HIFS: History independence for file systems. In *Proc. of the ACM SIGSAC Conference on Computer & Communications Security (CCS)*, pages 1285–1296, 2013.
[13] M. A. Bender, R. Cole, and R. Raman. Exponential structures for efficient cache-oblivious algorithms. In *Proc. of the 29th Annual International Colloquium on Automata, Languages, and Programming (ICALP)*, pages 195–207, 2002.
[14] M. A. Bender, E. D. Demaine, and M. Farach-Colton. Cache-oblivious B-trees. *SIAM Journal on Computing*, 35(2):341–358, 2005.
[15] M. A. Bender, Z. Duan, J. Iacono, and J. Wu. A locality-preserving cache-oblivious dynamic dictionary. *Journal of Algorithms*, 3(2):115–136, 2004.
[16] M. A. Bender, M. Farach-Colton, and B. C. Kuszmaul. Cache-oblivious string B-trees. In *Proc. of the 25th Annual ACM Symposium on Principles of Database Systems (PODS)*, pages 233–242, 2006.
[17] M. A. Bender, J. T. Fineman, S. Gilbert, and B. C. Kuszmaul. Concurrent cache-oblivious B-trees. In *Proc. of the 17th Annual ACM Symposium on Parallelism in Algorithms and Architectures (SPAA)*, pages 228–237, 2005.
[18] M. A. Bender and H. Hu. An adaptive packed-memory array. *ACM Transactions on Database Systems*, 32(4):26, 2007.
[19] J. Bethencourt, D. Boneh, and B. Waters. Cryptographic methods for storing ballots on a voting machine. In *Proc. of the 14th Network and Distributed System Security Symposium (NDSS)*, 2007.
[20] G. E. Blelloch and D. Golovin. Strongly history-independent hashing with applications. In *Proc. of the 48th Annual IEEE Symposium on Foundations of Computer Science (FOCS)*, pages 272–282, 2007.
[21] G. E. Blelloch, D. Golovin, and V. Vassilevska. Uniquely represented data structures for computational geometry. In *Proc. of the 11th Scandinavian Workshop on Algorithm Theory (SWAT)*, pages 17–28, 2008.
[22] G. S. Brodal, R. Fagerberg, and R. Jacob. Cache oblivious search trees via binary trees of small height. In *Proc. of the 13th Annual ACM-SIAM Symposium on Discrete Algorithms (SODA)*, pages 39–48, 2002.
[23] N. Buchbinder and E. Petrank. Lower and upper bounds on obtaining history independence. In *Advances in Cryptology*, pages 445–462, 2003.
[24] J. Bulánek, M. Koucký, and M. Saks. Tight lower bounds for the online labeling problem. In *Proc. of the 44th Annual ACM Symposium on Theory of Computing (STOC)*, pages 1185–1198, 2012.
[25] P. Callahan, M. T. Goodrich, and K. Ramaiyer. Topology B-trees and their applications. In *Proc. of the 4th International Workshop on Algorithms and Data Structures (WADS)*, pages 381–392, 1995.
[26] V. Ciriani, P. Ferragina, F. Luccio, and S. Muthukrishnan. Static optimality theorem for external memory string access. In *Proc. of the 43rd Annual IEEE Symposium on Foundations of Computer Science (FOCS)*, pages 219–227, 2002.
[27] L. Devroye. A limit theory for random skip lists. *The Annals of Applied Probability*, pages 597–609, 1992.
[28] M. Fomitchev and E. Ruppert. Lock-free linked lists and skip lists. In *Proc. of the 23rd Annual ACM Symposium on Principles of Distributed Computing (PODS)*, pages 50–59, 2004.
[29] M. Frigo, C. E. Leiserson, H. Prokop, and S. Ramachandran. Cache-oblivious algorithms. In *Proc. of the 40th Annual IEEE Symposium on the Foundations of Computer Science (FOCS)*, pages 285–298, 1999.
[30] M. Frigo, C. E. Leiserson, H. Prokop, and S. Ramachandran. Cache-oblivious algorithms. *ACM Transactions on Algorithms*, 8(1):4, 2012.
[31] D. Golovin. *Uniquely Represented Data Structures with Applications to Privacy*. PhD thesis, Carnegie Mellon University, Pittsburgh, PA, 2008, 2008.
[32] D. Golovin. B-treaps: A uniquely represented alternative to B-trees. In *Proc. of the 36th Annual International Colloquium on Automata, Languages, and Programming (ICALP)*, pages 487–499. 2009.
[33] D. Golovin. The B-skip-list: A simpler uniquely represented alternative to B-trees. *arXiv preprint arXiv:1005.0662*, 2010.
[34] M. T. Goodrich and R. Tamassia. Efficient authenticated dictionaries with skip lists and commutative hashing. *US Patent App*, 10(416,015), 2000.
[35] J. A. Halderman, S. D. Schoen, N. Heninger, W. Clarkson, W. Paul, J. A. Calandrino, A. J. Feldman, J. Appelbaum, and E. W. Felten. Lest we remember: Cold-boot attacks on encryption keys. *Communications of the ACM*, 52(5):91–98, 2009.
[36] J. D. Hartline, E. S. Hong, A. E. Mohr, W. R. Pentney, and E. C. Rocke. Characterizing history independent data structures. *Algorithmica*, 42(1):57–74, 2005.

[37] M. Herlihy, Y. Lev, V. Luchangco, and N. Shavit. A simple optimistic skiplist algorithm. *Proc. of the 14th Annual Colloquium on Structural Information and Communication Complexity (SIROCCO)*, page 124, 2007.

[38] A. Itai, A. Konheim, and M. Rodeh. A sparse table implementation of priority queues. *Proc. of the 8th Annual International Colloquium on Automata, Languages, and Programming (ICALP)*, pages 417–431, 1981.

[39] R. Jacob, A. Richa, C. Scheideler, S. Schmid, and H. Täubig. A distributed polylogarithmic time algorithm for self-stabilizing skip graphs. In *Proc. of the 28th ACM Symposium on Principles of Distributed Computing (PODS)*, pages 131–140, 2009.

[40] Z. Kasheff. Cache-oblivious dynamic search trees. M.eng., Department of Electrical Engineering and Computer Science, Massachusetts Institute of Technology, June 2004.

[41] I. Katriel. Implicit data structures based on local reorganizations. Master's thesis, Technion – Israel Inst. of Tech., Haifa, May 2002.

[42] P. Kirschenhofer and H. Prodinger. The path length of random skip lists. *Acta Informatica*, 31(8):775–792, 1994.

[43] D. Micciancio. Oblivious data structures: applications to cryptography. In *Proc. of the 29th Annual ACM Symposium on Theory of Computing (STOC)*, pages 456–464, 1997.

[44] D. Molnar, T. Kohno, N. Sastry, and D. Wagner. Tamper-evident, history-independent, subliminal-free data structures on prom storage-or-how to store ballots on a voting machine. In *Proc. of the 27th Annual IEEE Symposium on Security and Privacy (S&P)*, 2006.

[45] T. Moran, M. Naor, and G. Segev. Deterministic history-independent strategies for storing information on write-once memories. In *Proc. of the 34th International Colloquium on Automata, Languages and Programming (ICALP)*, 2007.

[46] M. Naor, G. Segev, and U. Wieder. History-independent cuckoo hashing. In *Proc. of the 35th International Colloquium on Automata, Languages and Programming (ICALP)*, pages 631–642. Springer, 2008.

[47] M. Naor and V. Teague. Anti-persistence: history independent data structures. In *Proc. of the 33rd Annual ACM Symposium on Theory of Computing (STOC)*, pages 492–501, 2001.

[48] J. Nievergelt and E. M. Reingold. Binary search trees of bounded balance. *SIAM Journal on Computing*, 2(1):33–43, 1973.

[49] R. Oshman and N. Shavit. The SkipTrie: low-depth concurrent search without rebalancing. In *Proc. of the 32nd Annual ACM Symposium on Principles of Distributed Computing (PODS)*, pages 23–32, 2013.

[50] T. Papadakis, J. I. Munro, and P. V. Poblete. Analysis of the expected search cost in skip lists. In *Proc. of the 2nd Scandinavian Workshop on Algorithm Theory (SWAT)*, pages 160–172, 1990.

[51] H. Prokop. Cache oblivious algorithms. Master's thesis, Department of Electrical Engineering and Computer Science, Massachusetts Institute of Technology, June 1999.

[52] W. Pugh. *Incremental computation and the incremental evaluation of functional programs*. PhD thesis, Cornell University, 1988.

[53] W. Pugh. Skip lists: a probabilistic alternative to balanced trees. *Communications of the ACM*, 33(6):668–676, 1990.

[54] W. Pugh and T. Teitelbaum. Incremental computation via function caching. In *Proc. of the 16th ACM SIGPLAN-SIGACT Symposium on Principles of Programming Languages (POPL)*, pages 315–328, 1989.

[55] N. Rahman, R. Cole, and R. Raman. Optimised predecessor data structures for internal memory. In *Proc. of the 5th International Workshop on Algorithm Engineering (WAE)*, pages 67–78, 2001.

[56] D. S. Roche, A. J. Aviv, and S. G. Choi. Oblivious secure deletion with bounded history independence. *arXiv preprint arXiv:1505.07391*, 2015.

[57] N. Shavit and I. Lotan. Skiplist-based concurrent priority queues. In *Proc. of the 14th International Parallel and Distributed Processing Symposium (IPDPS)*, pages 263–268, 2000.

[58] J. Shun and G. E. Blelloch. Phase-concurrent hash tables for determinism. In *Proc. of the 26th Annual ACM Symposium on Parallelism in Algorithms and Architectures (SPAA)*, pages 96–107, 2014.

[59] L. Snyder. On uniquely represented data straucturess. In *Proc. of the 18th Annual IEEE Symposium on Foundations of Computer Science (FOCS)*, pages 142–146, 1977.

[60] R. Sundar and R. E. Tarjan. Unique binary search tree representations and equality-testing of sets and sequences. In *Proc. of the 22nd Annual ACM Symposium on Theory of Computing (STOC)*, pages 18–25, 1990.

[61] T. Tzouramanis. History-independence: a fresh look at the case of R-trees. In *Proc. of the 27th Annual ACM Symposium on Applied Computing (SAC)*, pages 7–12, 2012.

[62] J. S. Vitter. Random sampling with a reservoir. *ACM Transactions on Mathematical Software*, 11(1):37–57, 1985.

[63] D. E. Willard. Inserting and deleting records in blocked sequential files. Technical Report TM81-45193-5, Bell Labs Tech Reports, 1981. (Cited in [66]).

[64] D. E. Willard. Maintaining dense sequential files in a dynamic environment. In *Proc. of the 14th Annual ACM Symposium on Theory of Computing (STOC)*, pages 114–121, 1982.

[65] D. E. Willard. Good worst-case algorithms for inserting and deleting records in dense sequential files. In *ACM SIGMOD Record*, volume 15:2, pages 251–260, 1986.

[66] D. E. Willard. A density control algorithm for doing insertions and deletions in a sequentially ordered file in a good worst-case time. *Information and Computation*, 97(2):150–204, 1992.

Logical Aspects of Massively Parallel and Distributed Systems

Frank Neven
Hasselt University and transnational University of Limburg
frank.neven@uhasselt.be

ABSTRACT

Database research has witnessed a renewed interest for data processing in distributed and parallel settings. While distributed and parallel data management systems have been around for quite some time, it is the rise of cloud computing and the advent of Big Data that presents the community with new challenges. This paper highlights recent research concerning the logical foundations of massively parallel and distributed systems. The first part of the paper concerns massively parallel systems where computation proceeds in a number of synchronized rounds. Here, the focus is on evaluation algorithms for conjunctive queries as well as on reasoning about correctness and optimization of such algorithms. The second part of the paper addresses a distributed asynchronous setting where eventual consistency comes into play. Here, the focus is on coordination-free computation and its relationship to logical monotonicity and Datalog programs.

1. INTRODUCTION

The rise of cloud computing and the popularity of Big data lead to a renewed interest for data processing in parallel and distributed settings. The purpose of this paper is to highlight research directions addressing questions related to the logical foundations of these areas. We focus on two particular settings.

The first setting is motivated by query evaluation for very large data sets where data is simply too large to be handled on a single machine. Programs for querying such data typically consist of a number of rounds (or steps) where in each round the data is reshuffled (or repartitioned) over a number of servers followed by a computation at each server. In this model there is a synchronization step after each round. We follow the MPC model as introduced by Koutris and Suciu [40] and focus on single-round MPC programs of which Shares [9] and the HyperCube algorithm [20] are typical examples. We discuss a framework for reasoning about the correctness and optimization of such programs for evaluating conjunctive queries.

PODS'16, June 26-July 01, 2016, San Francisco, CA, USA

ISBN 978-1-4503-4191-2/16/06...$15.00

DOI: http://dx.doi.org/10.1145/2902251.2902307

The second setting is motivated by declarative distributed computing (see, e.g., [13]) where the specific data partitioning is given and data can not be reshuffled. Communication is asynchronous and queries adopt an eventually consistent semantics. The focus is on relating coordination-free computations with logical monotonicity and Datalog programs.

Outline. In Section 2, we introduce some notation. We consider the massively parallel communication (MPC) model as our prime example of the setting for synchronous computation in Section 3. We discuss parallel-correctness for single-round algorithms within MPC in Section 4. We consider the asynchronous setting in Section 5 where we focus on coordination-free computations. We conclude in Section 6.

2. PRELIMINARIES

Even though the setup of the paper is rather informal, it still makes sense to fix some of the notation and to at least formally define the most important class of queries that we consider: the class of conjunctive queries.

Throughout the rest of the paper, we assume an infinite domain **dom** and a database scheme consisting of relation names with associated arities. A *(database) instance* I is simply a finite set of facts. For a fact f, we denote by $adom(f)$ the set of **dom**-values occurring in f. Furthermore, $adom(I) = \bigcup_{f \in I} adom(f)$. A *conjunctive query (CQ)* Q is an expression of the form

$$H(\mathbf{x}) \leftarrow R_1(\mathbf{y_1}), \ldots, R_m(\mathbf{y_m})$$

where every R_i is a relation name and every $\mathbf{y_i}$ matches the arity of R_i. We require that every variable in $\mathbf{x}$ occurs in some $\mathbf{y}_i$. We refer to the *head atom* $H(\mathbf{x})$ by $head_Q$ and to the set $\{R_1(\mathbf{y_1}), \ldots, R_m(\mathbf{y_m})\}$ by $body_Q$.

We denote by $vars(Q)$ the set of all variables occurring in Q. A *valuation* for a CQ Q is a total function $V : vars(Q) \to$ **dom**. We refer to $V(body_Q)$ as the facts *required* by V. A valuation V *satisfies* Q on instance I if all facts required by V are in I. In that case, V *derives* the fact $V(head_Q)$. The *result* of Q on instance I, denoted $Q(I)$, is defined as the set of facts that can be derived by satisfying valuations for Q on I.

3. MASSIVELY PARALLEL COMMUNICATION MODEL

The Massively Parallel Communication (MPC) model was introduced by Koutris and Suciu [40] to study the parallel complexity of conjunctive queries. The presentation of this model here is adapted from [22]. The setting is motivated by query processing on big data that is typically performed on a shared-nothing parallel architecture where data is stored on a large number of servers interconnected by a fast network. In the MPC model, computation is performed by p servers connected by a complete network of private channels. Examples of such systems include Pig [49], Hive [53], Dremel [43], and Spark [57]. The computation proceeds in steps or rounds where each round consists of two distinct phases:

- *Communication Phase:* The servers exchange data by communicating with all other servers (sending and receiving of data).
- *Computation Phase:* Each server performs only local computation (on the data currently stored at that server).

The number of rounds then corresponds to the number of synchronization barriers that an algorithm requires. The input data is initially partitioned among the p servers and every server receives $1/p$-th of the data. There are no assumptions on the particular partitioning scheme. At the end of the execution, the output must be present in the union of the p servers. As the model focuses primarily on quantifying the amount of communication there is no a priori bound on the computational power of a server.

A relevant measure is the *load* at each server which is the amount of data received by a server during a particular round. Let m be the number of tuples in the database.[1] Then, during any point in the execution of the parallel algorithm, the load should always be a number in the interval $[m/p, m]$. Here, m/p is optimal in that the data is optimally distributed whereas a load of m means that a server has access to all of the data and can (theoretically) compute any query locally. The load is usually represented as $m/p^{1-\varepsilon}$ where $\varepsilon \in [0, 1[$. Examples of optimization goals are minimizing total load (e.g., [8]) and minimizing maximum load (e.g., [40]).

At various places below, we talk about skew. The notion refers to the presence of skewed values in the database, so-called heavy hitters, whose frequency is much higher than some predefined threshold.

To get a feeling for the model, we next present simple examples of single- and multi-round algorithms in the MPC model for evaluating specific conjunctive queries.

Example 3.1. (1) Consider the query Q_1

$$H(x, y, z) \leftarrow R(x, y), S(y, z)$$

joining two binary relations R and S over a common attribute. We consider two different strategies for computing Q_1:

(1a) Let h be a hash function mapping every domain value to one of the p servers. The following single-round algorithm then computes Q_1. In the communication phase, executed by every server on its local data, every tuple $R(a, b)$ is sent to server $h(b)$ while every tuple $S(c, d)$ is sent to server $h(c)$. In the subsequent computation phase, every server evaluates Q_1 on the received data. The output of the algorithm then is the union of the results computed at the computation phase. This strategy is called a repartition join in [23]. This approach is not resilient to skew as it is quite possible that a large part of the database is sent to one server. However, in the absence of skew, for instance, when every domain element occurs at most once in every relation, the maximum load is $O(m/p)$.

(1b) Next, we present a strategy that is resilient to skew. It is based on Ullman's drug interaction example [55] and is used explicitly in the algorithm DYM-n of [6]. For simplicity, we assume that R and S consist of m tuples. The algorithm divides R and S into $p^{1/2}$ disjoint groups of size $m/p^{1/2}$. Every combination of an R-group and an S-group can now be sent to a different server (as there are p such combinations) in the communication phase. The computation phase then consists of evaluating Q_1 on the local data. The load per server is $O(m/p^{1/2})$ independent of any skew in the database.

(2) Let Q_2 be the triangle query:

$$H(x, y, z) \leftarrow R(x, y), S(y, z), T(z, x).$$

One way to evaluate Q_2 is through a cascade of binary joins leading to a two-round algorithm. That is, first joining R and S followed by a join of T. Either the approach in (1a) or (1b) can be followed. Assuming two hash functions h and h', we only exemplify the hashing strategy of (1a). In the first round, all tuples $R(a, b)$ and $S(c, d)$ are sent to server $h(b)$ and $h(c)$, respectively. The computation phase then computes the join of R and S at each server in a relation K. In the second round, each resulting triple $K(e, f, g)$ is sent to $h'(e, g)$, while each tuple $T(i, j)$ is sent to $h'(j, i)$. Again, the computation phase then joins K and T at each server. □

We note that every MapReduce [28] program can be seen as an algorithm within the MPC model since the map phase and reducer phase readily translate to the communication and computation phase of MPC. Conceptually, a MapReduce job is a pair (μ, ρ) of functions, where μ is called the map and ρ the reduce function. The execution of a job on an input dataset then proceeds in two stages. In the first stage, called the *map stage*, each fact f from the input data set is processed by μ, generating a collection $\mu(f)$ of key-value pairs of the form $\langle k : v \rangle$. The total collection $\bigcup_f \mu(f)$ of key-value pairs generated during the map phase is then grouped on the key value resulting in a number of groups, say $\langle k_1 : V_1 \rangle, \ldots, \langle k_n : V_n \rangle$ where each V_i is set of values. Each group $\langle k_i : V_i \rangle$ is then processed by the reduce function ρ resulting again in a collection of key-value pairs per group. The total collection $\bigcup_i \rho(\langle k_i : V_i \rangle)$ is the output of the MapReduce job. Finally, a MapReduce program then is a sequence of MapReduce jobs. As MapReduce provides a higher level of abstraction, it is a relevant formalism to specify MPC algorithms.

3.1 Single-round MPC

We focus next on the one-round evaluation of multi-way joins and start off with an example.

Example 3.2. Consider again the triangle query Q_2 of Example 3.1:

$$H(x, y, z) \leftarrow R(x, y), S(y, z), T(z, x).$$

[1] In, e.g., [22], a distinction is made between the number of tuples m in the database and the number of bits M needed to represent the data. We are a bit sloppy here and stick to m.

Let α_x, α_y, and α_z be positive natural numbers such that $\alpha_x\alpha_y\alpha_z = p$. Every server can then uniquely be identified by a triple in $[1,\alpha_x] \times [1,\alpha_y] \times [1,\alpha_z]$. For $c \in \{x,y,z\}$, let h_c be a hash function mapping each domain value to a number in $[1,\alpha_c]$. The algorithm then operates as follows. In the communication phase, every fact

- $R(a,b)$ is sent to every server with coordinate $(h_x(a), h_y(b), \alpha)$ for every $\alpha \in [1,\alpha_z]$ (replicating every R-tuple α_z times);
- $S(b,c)$ is sent to every server with coordinate $(\alpha, h_y(b), h_z(c))$ for every $\alpha \in [1,\alpha_x]$ (replicating every S-tuple α_x times); and,
- $T(c,a)$ is sent to every server with coordinate $(h_x(a), \alpha, h_z(c))$ for every $\alpha \in [1,\alpha_y]$ (replicating every T-tuple α_y times).

The computation phase then consists of evaluating Q_2 on the local data at each server. The algorithm is correct as for every valuation V for Q_2, mapping variables to domain values, there is a server that contains the facts

$$\{V(R(x,y)), V(S(y,z)), V(T(z,x))\}$$

if and only if the (hypothetical) centralized database contains those facts. In this sense, the algorithm distributes the space of all valuations of Q_2 over the computing servers in an instance independent way through hashing of domain values. In the special case that $\alpha_x = \alpha_y = \alpha_z = p^{1/3}$, each tuple is replicated $p^{1/3}$ times. Assuming each relation consists of m tuples and there is no skew, each server will receive $m/p^{2/3}$ tuples for each of the relations R, S, and T. So, the maximum load per server is $O(m/p^{2/3})$. □

The technique in Example 3.2 can be generalized to arbitrary conjunctive queries and was first introduced in the context of MapReduce by Afrati and Ullman [9] under the name of Shares. The values α_x, α_y, and α_z are called shares (hence, the name of the algorithm) and the algorithm focuses on computing optimal values for the shares minimizing the total load. The latter measure is termed the communication cost in [9] and defined as the amount of data transferred from the mappers to the reducers. Afrati et al. [7] provide a generalization of the Shares algorithm incorporating skew by distinguishing tuples that are heavy hitters. In [27] it is shown that there is a trade-off between the replication rate and the reducer size for several classes of problems.

Beame, Koutris, and Suciu [20] obtained that the strategy underlying Shares is optimal when the goal is to minimize the expected maximum load per server. More specifically, let Q be a full conjunctive query. Assuming that the sizes of all relations are equal to m and under the assumption that there is no skew, the maximum load per server is bounded by $O(m/p^{1/\tau^*})$ with high probability. Here, τ^* depends on the structure of Q and corresponds to the optimal fractional edge packing (which for Q_2 is $\tau^* = 3/2$). The algorithm is referred to as HyperCube in [20]. Additionally, the authors show that the just provided bound is tight for all one-round MPC algorithms (in the absence of skew). In the case when the relations are skewed and the heavy hitters and their frequencies are known, upper and lower bounds are provided in terms of packings of residual queries obtained by specializing the query to a heavy hitter [21]. In [39], the same authors consider a different share allocation of HyperCube to obtain a worst-case optimal algorithm for multiway join processing.

Chu, Balazinska, and Suciu [26], provide an empirical study of HyperCube (in combination with a worst-case optimal algorithm for sequential evaluation) for complex join queries, and establish, among other things, that HyperCube performs well for join queries with large intermediate results. On the other hand, HyperCube can perform badly on queries with small output.

3.2 Multi-Round MPC

Multi-round MPC has been studied in less depth. We highlight some of the results on multi-round algorithms for evaluating classes of queries.

Yannakakis algorithm [58] for acyclic conjunctive queries consists of a semi-join phase aimed at eliminating dangling tuples followed by a join phase such that the sizes of the intermediate results are never larger than the final output. Afrati et al. [6] present a generalization of this idea to the distributed setting in the algorithm GYM (Generalized Yannakakis in MapReduce). The latter algorithm takes a tree decomposition of a possibly cyclic query as input, evaluates joins of relations grouped at the same node through the Shares algorithm and executes Yannakis' algorithm on the resulting tree taking advantage of the structure of the tree to perform some joins and semi-joins in parallel. The shapes of possible tree compositions (in particular, their depth) delineate trade-offs between the number of rounds and the total amount of communication. Interestingly, the approach is resilient to skew.

Neven et al. [47] provide a formalization of MapReduce where reducers are modelled as extensions of register automata [36, 48] and obtain fragments that can express the semi-join algebra and the complete relational algebra. Employing the latter model, Tan considered multi-round algorithms for evaluating relational algebra queries that are input- as well as output-balanced [52]. Afrati and Ullman investigated ways to evaluate transitive closure and Datalog in MapReduce (see, e.g., [5, 10]).

When restricted to a single round, skewed data is provably harder to process. For instance, the maximum load for a join increases from m/p to $m/p^{1/2}$ while the load for the triangle query increases from $m/p^{2/3}$ to $m/p^{1/2}$. Beame, Koutris and Suciu [39] show that for some queries, the maximum load for skewed data can be brought down to the load of skew-free data by using multiple rounds. For example, the triangle query can be computed with load $m/p^{2/3}$ in two rounds, even if the data is skewed, while it is provably at least $m/p^{1/2}$ for one round. In contrast, the join of skewed data requires a load of $m/p^{1/2}$, no matter how many rounds one is willing to spend. Finally, Beame, Koutris, and Suciu [20] present nearly matching lower and upper bounds for multiple round algorithms computing tree-like conjunctive queries on skew-free databases of a specific form called matching databases.

4. PARALLEL-CORRECTNESS

Shares and HyperCube are a particular kind of one-round MPC algorithm where the communication phase can be seen as an initial distribution or repartitioning of the data followed by the evaluation of a single query at every server. Ameloot et al. [14] present a framework for reasoning about the correctness of such one-round MPC algorithms for the evaluation of queries but under *arbitrary* distribution policies. To target the widest possible range of repartitioning strategies, the initial distribution phase is modeled by a distribution policy that can be *any* mapping from facts to subsets of servers.

In this setting, they study two fundamental problems:

Parallel-Correctness: Given a distribution policy and a query, can we be sure that the corresponding one-round algorithm will always compute the query result correctly — no matter the actual data?

Parallel-Correctness Transfer: Given two queries Q and Q', can we infer from the fact that Q is computed correctly under the current distribution policy, that Q' is computed correctly as well?

The presentation in this section is based on [16]. The latter is a more elaborate introduction to the material contained in [14].

4.1 Parallel-Correctness

Before we can start, we need to introduce a bit of notation. A *network* $\mathcal{N}$ is a nonempty finite set of node names. A *distribution policy* $\boldsymbol{P} = (U, \mathit{rfacts}_{\boldsymbol{P}})$ for a network $\mathcal{N}$ consists of a universe U and a total function $\mathit{rfacts}_{\boldsymbol{P}}$ that maps each node of $\mathcal{N}$ to a subset of facts from $\mathit{facts}(U)$.[2] Here, $\mathit{facts}(U)$ denotes the set of all possible facts over U. A node κ is *responsible for a fact* $\boldsymbol{f}$ (under policy $\boldsymbol{P}$) if $\boldsymbol{f} \in \mathit{rfacts}_{\boldsymbol{P}}(\kappa)$. For an instance I and a $\kappa \in \mathcal{N}$, let $\mathit{loc\text{-}inst}_{\boldsymbol{P},I}(\kappa)$ denote $I \cap \mathit{rfacts}_{\boldsymbol{P}}(\kappa)$, that is, the set of facts in I for which node κ is responsible. We refer to a given instance I as the *global instance* and to $\mathit{loc\text{-}inst}_{\boldsymbol{P},I}(\kappa)$ as the *local instance on node* κ.

Notice that every primary horizontal fragmentation (see, e.g., [50]) can be modeled as a distribution policy. Consider, for instance, a range partitioning on a relation Customer that assigns tuples to network nodes determined by a threshold on the area code.

The result $[Q, \boldsymbol{P}](I)$ of the distributed evaluation in one round of a query Q on an instance I under a distribution policy $\boldsymbol{P}$ is defined as the union of the results of Q evaluated over every local instance. Formally,

$$[Q, \boldsymbol{P}](I) \stackrel{\text{def}}{=} \bigcup_{\kappa \in \mathcal{N}} Q(\mathit{loc\text{-}inst}_{\boldsymbol{P},I}(\kappa)).$$

Example 4.1. Let I_e be the example database instance

$$\{R(a,b), R(b,a), R(b,c), S(a,a), S(c,a)\},$$

and Q_e be the example CQ

$$H(x_1, x_3) \leftarrow R(x_1, x_2), R(x_2, x_3), S(x_3, x_1).$$

Consider a network $\mathcal{N}_e$ consisting of two nodes $\{\kappa_1, \kappa_2\}$. Let $\boldsymbol{P}_1 = (\{a,b,c\}, \mathit{rfacts}_{\boldsymbol{P}})$ be the distribution policy that assigns all R-facts to both nodes κ_1 and κ_2, and every fact $S(d_1, d_2)$ to node κ_1 when $d_1 = d_2$ and to node κ_2 otherwise. Then,

$$\mathit{loc\text{-}inst}_{\boldsymbol{P}_1, I_e}(\kappa_1) = \{R(a,b), R(b,a), R(b,c), S(a,a)\},$$

and

$$\mathit{loc\text{-}inst}_{\boldsymbol{P}_1, I_e}(\kappa_2) = \{R(a,b), R(b,a), R(b,c), S(c,a)\}.$$

Furthermore,

$$[Q_e, \boldsymbol{P}_1](I_e) = Q_e(\mathit{loc\text{-}inst}_{\boldsymbol{P}_1, I_e}(\kappa_1)) \cup Q_e(\mathit{loc\text{-}inst}_{\boldsymbol{P}_1, I_e}(\kappa_2)),$$

which is just $\{H(a,b)\} \cup \{H(a,c)\}$.

Next, consider the alternative distribution policy $\boldsymbol{P}_2$ that assigns all R-facts to node κ_1 and all S-facts to node κ_2, then $[Q_e, \boldsymbol{P}_2](I_e) = \emptyset$. □

Definition 4.2. A query Q is *parallel-correct on instance I under distribution policy $\boldsymbol{P}$* if $Q(I) = [Q, \boldsymbol{P}](I)$. Furthermore, Q is *parallel-correct under $\boldsymbol{P}$*, if Q is parallel-correct on all instances $I \subseteq \mathit{facts}(U)$.

Informally, parallel-correctness states that the naive one-round evaluation algorithm that first distributes (reshuffles) the data over the computing nodes according to $\boldsymbol{P}$ and then evaluates Q in a subsequent parallel step at every computing node, always yields the correct result, for every possible instance. Notice that, since $\boldsymbol{P}$ is defined on the granularity of a fact, the reshuffling does not depend on the current distribution of the data and can be done in parallel as well.

While Definition 4.2 is in terms of general queries, in the rest of this section, we only consider (extensions of) conjunctive queries.

We first focus on a characterization of parallel-correctness. It is easy to see that a CQ Q is parallel-correct under distribution policy $\boldsymbol{P} = (U, \mathit{rfacts}_{\boldsymbol{P}})$ if, for each valuation for Q, the required facts meet at some node. That is, if the following condition holds:

For every valuation V for Q over U, there is a node $\kappa \in \mathcal{N}$ such that $V(\mathit{body}_Q) \subseteq \mathit{rfacts}_{\boldsymbol{P}}(\kappa)$. (PC_0)

Even though Condition (PC_0) is sufficient for parallel-correctness, it is not necessary as the following example shows.

Example 4.3. We consider the CQ Q,

$$H(x,z) \leftarrow R(x,y), R(y,z), R(x,x),$$

and the valuation $V = \{x \mapsto a, y \mapsto b, z \mapsto a\}$. Let further $\mathcal{N} = \{\kappa_1, \kappa_2\}$ and let $\boldsymbol{P}$ distribute every fact except $R(a,b)$ onto node κ_1 and every fact except $R(b,a)$ onto node κ_2. Since $R(a,b)$ and $R(b,a)$ do not meet under $\boldsymbol{P}$, valuation V witnesses the failure of Condition (PC_0) for $\boldsymbol{P}$ and Q.

However, Q is parallel-correct under $\boldsymbol{P}$. Indeed, every valuation that derives a fact $\boldsymbol{f}$ with the help of the facts $R(a,b)$ and $R(b,a)$, also requires the fact $R(a,a)$ (or $R(b,b)$). But then, $R(a,a)$ (or $R(b,b)$) alone is sufficient to derive $\boldsymbol{f}$ by mapping all variables to a (or b). Therefore, if $\boldsymbol{f} \in Q(I)$, for some instance I, then $\boldsymbol{f} \in [Q, \boldsymbol{P}](I)$ and thus Q is parallel-correct under $\boldsymbol{P}$. □

It turns out that for a semantical characterization of parallel-correctness, we need the notion of minimal valuations:

Definition 4.4. A valuation V for a CQ Q is *minimal* for Q if there does *not* exist a valuation V' for Q that derives the same head fact with a strict subset of body facts, that is, such that $V'(\mathit{body}_Q) \subsetneq V(\mathit{body}_Q)$ and $V'(\mathit{head}_Q) = V(\mathit{head}_Q)$.

Example 4.5. For a simple example of a minimal valuation and a non-minimal valuation, consider the CQ Q,

$$H(x,z) \leftarrow R(x,y), R(y,z), R(x,x).$$

[2]We mention that for Hypercube distributions, the view is reversed: facts are assigned to nodes. However, both views are essentially equivalent and we will freely adopt the view that fits best for the purpose at hand.

Both $V_1 = \{x \mapsto a, y \mapsto b, z \mapsto a\}$ and $V_2 = \{x \mapsto a, y \mapsto a, z \mapsto a\}$ are valuations for Q. Notice that both valuations agree on the head variables of Q, but they require different sets of facts. In particular, for V_1 to be satisfying on I, instance I must contain the facts $R(a,b), R(b,a)$, and $R(a,a)$, while V_2 only requires I to contain $R(a,a)$. This observation implies that V_1 is not minimal for Q. Further, since V_2 requires only one fact for Q, valuation V_2 must be minimal for Q. □

We are now ready to state the characterization of parallel-correctness for CQs.

Proposition 4.6. *[14] A CQ Q is parallel-correct under distribution policy $\boldsymbol{P} = (U, rfacts_{\boldsymbol{P}})$ if and only if the following holds:*

For every minimal valuation V for Q over U, there is a node $\kappa \in \mathcal{N}$ such that $V(body_Q) \subseteq rfacts_{\boldsymbol{P}}(\kappa)$. (PC_1)

The latter conditions are so fundamental when reasoning over parallel-correctness that they deserve their own terminology:

Definition 4.7. For a CQ Q and a distribution policy $\boldsymbol{P}$:

- $\boldsymbol{P}$ *saturates* Q if they fulfill Condition (PC_1); and,
- $\boldsymbol{P}$ *strongly saturates* Q if they fulfill Condition (PC_0).

We note that every Hypercube distribution for a conjunctive query Q strongly saturates Q (independent of the choices of the shares and the hash functions).

The quantifier structure in Condition (PC_1) hints at a Π_2^p upper bound for the complexity of testing parallel-correctness. Of course, the exact complexity can not be judged without having a bound on the number of nodes κ and the complexity of the test $V(body_Q) \subseteq rfacts_{\boldsymbol{P}}(\kappa)$. The largest classes of distribution policies for which an Π_2^p upper bound has been established, are gathered in the set $\mathfrak{P}_{\text{npoly}}$ that contains classes $\mathcal{P}$ of distribution policies, for which each policy comes with an algorithm $\mathcal{A}$ and a bound n on the representation size of nodes in the network, respectively, such that whether a node κ is responsible for a fact $\boldsymbol{f}$ is decided by $\mathcal{A}$ *non-deterministically* in time $\mathcal{O}(n^k)$, for some k that depends only on $\mathcal{P}$.

It turns out that the problem of testing parallel-correctness is also Π_2^p-hard, even for the simple class $\mathcal{P}_{\text{fin}}$ of distribution policies, for which all pairs $(\kappa, \boldsymbol{f})$ of a node and a fact are explicitly enumerated. Thus, in a sense, Condition (PC_1) can not be simplified.

To state the results more formally, we define the following two algorithmic problems.

PCI($\mathbf{CQ}, \mathcal{P}$)	
Input:	$Q \in \mathbf{CQ}$, $\boldsymbol{P} \in \mathcal{P}$, instance I
Question:	Is Q parallel-correct on I under $\boldsymbol{P}$?

PC($\mathbf{CQ}, \mathcal{P}$)	
Input:	$Q \in \mathbf{CQ}$, $\boldsymbol{P} \in \mathcal{P}$
Question:	Is Q parallel-correct under $\boldsymbol{P}$?

Here, **CQ** denotes the class of conjunctive queries.

Theorem 4.8. *[14] Problems PC($\boldsymbol{CQ}, \mathcal{P}$) and PCI($\boldsymbol{CQ}, \mathcal{P}$) are Π_2^p-complete, for every policy class $\mathcal{P} \in \{\mathcal{P}_{fin}\} \cup \mathfrak{P}_{npoly}$.*

We note that Proposition 4.6 continues to hold true in the presence of union and inequalities (under a suitable definition of minimal valuation for unions of CQs) leading to the same complexity bounds as stated in Theorem 4.8 [33].

When considering (unions) of conjunctive queries with negation the parallel-correctness problem becomes much more involved, since it might involve counterexample databases of exponential size. We emphasize that this exponential explosion can only occur if the arity of the relations in the database schema are not a-priori bounded by some constant. Below, $\mathbf{CQ}^{\neg}$ and $\mathbf{UCQ}^{\neg}$ denote the class of (unions) of conjunctive queries with negation.

Theorem 4.9. *[33] For every class $\mathcal{P} \in \mathfrak{P}_{npoly}$ of distribution policies,* PARALLEL-CORRECT($\boldsymbol{UCQ}^{\neg}, \mathcal{P}$) *and* PARALLEL-CORRECT($\boldsymbol{CQ}^{\neg}, \mathcal{P}$) *are coNEXPTIME-complete.*

The result and, in particular, the lower bound even holds if $\mathfrak{P}_{\text{npoly}}$ is replaced by the corresponding $\mathfrak{P}_{\text{poly}}$, where the decision algorithm for pairs $(\kappa, \boldsymbol{f})$ is deterministic and in polynomial time.

We note that, as queries in $\mathbf{CQ}^{\neg}$ are no longer monotone, parallel-correctness requires both parallel-soundness as well as parallel-completeness [33].

The proof of the lower bounds comes along an unexpected route and exhibits a reduction from query containment for $\mathbf{CQ}^{\neg}$ to parallel-correctness for $\mathbf{CQ}^{\neg}$. Specifically, query containment asks the question whether, given two queries Q and Q', it holds that $Q(I) \subseteq Q'(I)$ for all instances I. The latter is denoted by $Q \subseteq Q'$. It is shown in [33] that query containment for $\mathbf{CQ}^{\neg}$ is coNEXPTIME-complete, implying coNEXPTIME-hardness for parallel-correctness as well. The result regarding containment of $\mathbf{CQ}^{\neg}$ answers the observation in [44] that the Π_2^p-completeness result for query containment for $\mathbf{CQ}^{\neg}$ mentioned in [54] only holds for fixed database schemas (or a fixed arity bound, for that matter).

4.2 Parallel-Correctness Transfer

The one-round Shares and Hypercube algorithm require a reshuffling of the data before the evaluation of each new query. In the context of multiple query evaluation, where an optimizer tries to automatically partition the base data across multiple nodes to achieve overall optimal performance for a specific workload (see, e.g., [46, 51]), it makes sense to consider scenarios in which such reshuffling can be avoided. To this end, *parallel-correctness transfer* was introduced in [14] which states that a subsequent query Q' can always be evaluated over a distribution for which a query Q is parallel-correct.

Definition 4.10. For two queries Q and Q' over the same input schema, *parallel-correctness transfers from Q to Q'* if Q' is parallel-correct under every distribution policy for which Q is parallel-correct. In this case, we write $Q \xrightarrow{\text{pc}} Q'$.

Example 4.11. The next example is borrowed from [16]. We illustrate parallel-correctness transfer with the help of the following example queries:

$$Q_1 : H() \leftarrow S(x), R(x,x), T(x).$$
$$Q_2 : H() \leftarrow R(x,x), T(x).$$
$$Q_3 : H() \leftarrow S(x), R(x,y), T(y).$$
$$Q_4 : H() \leftarrow R(x,y), T(y).$$

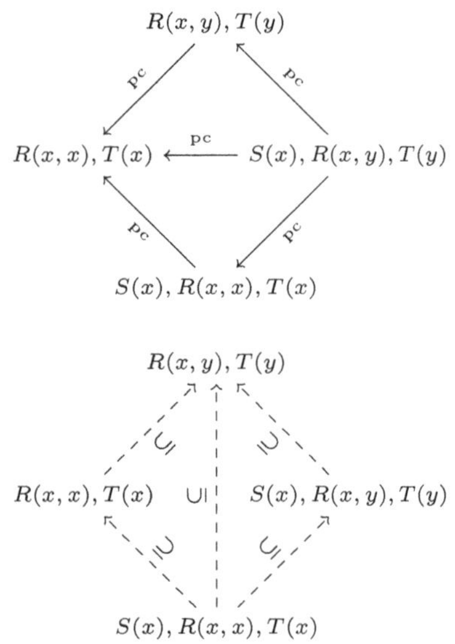

Figure 1: Relationship between the queries of Example 4.11 with respect to (a) parallel-correctness transfer and (b) query containment. (Figure taken from [16])

Figure 1 (a) shows how these queries relate with respect to parallel-correctness transfer. As an example, $Q_3 \xrightarrow{\text{pc}} Q_1$. As Figure 1 (b) illustrates, this relationships is entirely orthogonal to query containment. Indeed, there are examples where parallel-correctness transfer and query containment coincide (Q_3 vs. Q_4), where they hold in opposite directions (Q_4 vs. Q_2) and where one but not the other holds (Q_3 vs. Q_2 and Q_1 vs. Q_4, respectively). □

It turns out that, just like parallel-correctness, parallel-correctness transfer can be characterized in terms of minimal valuations. For this, we need the following notion:

Definition 4.12. For two CQs Q and Q', we say that Q *covers* Q' if the following holds:

> for every minimal valuation V' for Q', there is a minimal valuation V for Q, such that $V'(body_{Q'}) \subseteq V(body_Q)$.

Proposition 4.13. *[14] For two CQs Q and Q', parallel-correctness transfers from Q to Q' if and only if Q covers Q'.*[3]

Proposition 4.13, allows us to pinpoint the complexity of parallel-correctness transferability. For a formal statement we define the following algorithmic problem:

PC-TRANS (**CQ**)	
Input:	Queries Q and Q' from **CQ**
Question:	Does parallel-correctness transfer from Q to Q'?

When the defining condition of "covers" is spelled out by rewriting "minimal valuations" one gets a characterization with a Π_3-structure. Again, it can be shown that this is essentially optimal.

Theorem 4.14. *[14]* PC-TRANS(***CQ***) *is Π_3^p-complete.*

We note that the same complexity bounds continue to hold in the presence of inequalities and for unions of conjunctive queries [15].

It is shown in [14,15] that the complexity of deciding transferability can be lowered to NP in some cases when considering restricted classes of queries (as, for instance, the full queries) or when restricting the class of considered distribution policies (as, for instance, HyperCube distributions).

5. COORDINATION-FREE COMPUTATION

MPC is an inherent synchronized model that makes synchronization explicit by modeling computation as a sequence of rounds. In the remainder of this paper, we depart from synchronized systems and consider a setting where computing nodes are allowed to communicate freely. The particular setting we consider, is motivated by the work on declarative distributed computing, an approach where distributed computations are modeled and programmed using declarative formalisms based on extensions of Datalog (see, e.g., [1,2,13,34,35,41,42]).

The particular model we consider in the next section, operates under the assumption that messages can never be lost but can be arbitrarily delayed. Therefore, an *eventually consistent* semantics is adopted for queries entailing that the complete output is eventually produced after all messages have arrived and the system never outputs facts that later need to be retracted. An inherent source of inefficiency in such systems are the global barriers raised by the need for synchronization in computing the result of queries. Therefore, we consider systems that can communicate but are not allowed to coordinate, that is, they are restricted to so called coordination-free computation.

5.1 Relational Transducer Networks

In this section, we introduce relational transducer networks in a rather informal way. For a formal definition of this model we refer to [18,19].

On a logical level, programs (queries) are specified over a global schema and are computed by multiple computing nodes over which the input database is distributed. As every node in the network runs the same program Π, we refer to a specific relational transducer network by this name. Each node in the network is assigned a part of the database, referred to as the local database. This is modeled as a horizontal distribution H mapping each node κ to a database instance such that $\bigcup_{\kappa\in\mathcal{N}} H(\kappa)$ equals the global database. In addition, every node has access to some auxiliary relations for storing data and a designated output relation. The output relation is write-only. This means that once a fact is output it can never be retracted. All data available to the node is referred to as its relational state.

Nodes can communicate asynchronously with each other via messages. The only permitted operation is a broadcast to all. However, each node has access to a relation *All* containing the names of all the nodes in the network. In this way, direct messaging can be simulated (albeit in an inefficient way) by tagging tuples with the identity of the intended receiver. As mentioned before, messages can never be lost but can be arbitrarily delayed.

[3]The terminology *saturates*, *strongly saturates*, and *covers*, was not used in [14] but was introduced in [15] and also used in [16].

Computation is modeled as a transition system. At every point in time, one node is active and can perform a transition, that is, a computation. During this computation the node reads (and removes) an arbitrary message from its input buffer, updates its relational state (possibly writing to the output relation), and sends output messages to other nodes (updating the corresponding buffers). The input message is chosen nondeterministically to model arbitrary delay of messages. Every node runs the same program Π specifying how to perform a transition (computation) based on the message read from the input buffer and the current relational state. In this paper, we assume each node has arbitrary computational power. So, Π can be any computable (but generic) function. The paper [19] also considers more restricted settings where programs Π are expressed in various logics.

A run of the system is an infinite sequence of transitions and there is a fairness criteria ensuring that no computing nodes or messages are ignored infinitely often. The output of a particular run is then the union of the facts in the output relations at every node.

It remains to specify when Π computes a particular query Q: Π computes Q iff the output of every run is $Q(I)$ for every database I, for every network and for every horizontal distribution of I. In particular, the definition implies the following:

- every run computes Q: independence of order of messages and order of execution; the infinite nature of runs together with the fact that computations are generic ensures that there is a quiescence point after which no new output is produced, hence capturing eventual consistency;
- for every network: network independence;
- for every horizontal distribution: independence of how data is initially distributed.

The following example illustrates the just introduced model and prepares for the discussion of coordination-freeness handled next.

Example 5.1. (1) Consider the query $Q_\triangle$ computing all triangles:

$$H(x,y,z) \leftarrow E(x,y), E(y,z), E(z,x), x \neq y, y \neq z, z \neq x.$$

The following program $\Pi_\triangle$ run at node κ computes Q:

1. Output all triangles in $H(\kappa)$ (recall that $H(\kappa)$ is the data local to κ).
2. Broadcast $H(\kappa)$.
3. If a new edge is received, add it to $H(\kappa)$ and output any new triangles. Repeat step (3).

It should be clear that every run of $\Pi_\triangle$ computes Q on every network and for every horizontal distribution H. The reason this naive broadcast strategy work is because $Q_\triangle$ is monotone: adding more edges to the graph can never invalidate previously output triangles. While there definitely is communication between nodes, the communication is unidirectional and does not seem to require any coordination.

(2) Now, consider the following query selecting all open triangles:

$$H(x,y,z) \leftarrow E(x,y), E(y,z), \neg E(z,x).$$

This query is not monotone. A node κ can only output an open triangle (a,b,c) when it knows that the edge $E(c,a)$ is absent on every node in the network. This means that κ somehow needs to coordinate with every other node regarding the status of $E(c,a)$. An admittedly naive but correct program replicating the previous broadcasting strategy can be constructed by adding a coordination protocol. For instance, κ could acknowledge the receipt of an edge to the sender, who in turn could inform κ when it has received the acknowledgment for all data. Nodes then start to output open triangles when they have received all data from all nodes. Notice that this requires that every node knows all other nodes participating in the network. □

It remains to define coordination-freeness. Somehow Example 5.1(2) intuitively requires coordination while 5.1(1) does not. As it makes no sense to completely prohibit communication, the notion of coordination-freeness introduced in [19] tries to separates 'data-communication' from 'coordination-communication'. More specifically,

> a relational transducer network Π computing a query Q is *coordination-free* if for every database instance I there is at least one horizontal distribution of I such that Π computes Q without ever reading input messages from input buffers.[4]

So, the definition requires the existence of some 'ideal' initial horizontal distribution on which the query can be computed without any communication. To be more accurate, nodes can send messages to other nodes, but these are never read. The intuition is then as follows: because on the ideal distribution there is no coordination needed (as even communication is not needed there), and the transducer network has to correctly compute the query on all distributions (not just on the ideal one), communication is only used to transfer data on non-ideal distributions and is not used to coordinate. Furthermore, it is useful to note that the network is not aware that the data is ideally distributed (as it can not communicate).

The program $\Pi_\triangle$ presented in Example 5.1(1) is coordination-free. The required ideal distribution is the one that assigns the complete database to every node.[5]

5.2 Monotonicity and Coordination-freeness

Hellerstein [35] and Alvaro et al. [12] formulated the CALM-principle which suggests a link between logical monotonicity on the one hand and distributed consistency without the need for coordination on the other hand. Here, CALM stands for *Consistency And Logical Monotonicity.* A crucial property of monotone programs is that derived facts must never be retracted when new data arrives. As illustrated in Example 5.1 the latter implies a simple coordination-free execution strategy: every node sends all relevant data to every other node in the network and outputs new facts from the moment they can be derived. No coordination is needed and the output of all computing nodes is consistent. This observation motivated Hellerstein [35] to formulate the CALM-conjecture which, in its revised form, states

[4] The latter is modeled by so-called heartbeat transitions in [19].

[5] We remark that in general the ideal distribution can not always give the full input to all nodes, see [19].

a query has a coordination-free execution strategy if and only if the query is monotone.[6]

In this section, we address the correspondence between coordination-freeness and logical monotonicity. More specifically, we exhibit increasingly larger classes of coordination-free computations corresponding to increasingly weaker forms of monotonicity thereby providing a fine-grained answer to the CALM-conjecture.

5.2.1 CALM-theorem

We formally define monotonicity:

Definition 5.2. A query Q is *monotone* if $Q(I) \subseteq Q(I \cup J)$ for all database instances I and J.[7]

Let $\mathcal{M}$ denote the class of all monotone queries. We denote by $\mathcal{F}_0$ the class of queries that can be computed by coordination-free relational transducer networks. Furthermore, we denote by $\mathcal{A}_0$ the class of queries that can be computed by relational transducer networks that are not aware of all the other nodes in the network, that is, have no access to the relation *All* containing the names of all the nodes in the network. We note that $\mathcal{F}_0$ is an undecidable class while $\mathcal{A}_0$ is a syntactic class. In [19], $\mathcal{A}_0$ is referred to as the class of queries computed by *oblivious* transducer networks.

Example 5.1(1) illustrates that every monotone query can be evaluated in a coordination-free way. In fact, these are also the only queries having this property as indicated by the following theorem:

Theorem 5.3. *[19]* $\mathcal{F}_0 = \mathcal{A}_0 = \mathcal{M}$.

Proof. The inclusions $\mathcal{M} \subseteq \mathcal{A}_0$ and $\mathcal{M} \subseteq \mathcal{F}_0$ follow the strategy outlined in Example 5.1. The inclusion $\mathcal{A}_0 \subseteq \mathcal{F}_0$ holds by observing that the required ideal distribution is the one that places the whole database at every node. The inclusion $\mathcal{F}_0 \subseteq \mathcal{M}$ follows as the ideal distribution determines the behavior of Π on I independent of additions to other nodes. □

5.2.2 Extensions of the CALM-theorem

The previous theorem implies that computing open triangles can not be done in a coordination-free manner. We argue that when transducer networks have more knowledge on how the initial data is distributed, the open triangle query can in effect be evaluated in a coordination-free manner. For this, we assume that the initial horizontal distribution is defined in terms of a distribution policy $\boldsymbol{P}_H$ as defined in Section 4.1 and that every computing node can query $\boldsymbol{P}_H$. More specifically, when a and b are domain values occurring in the current relational state at κ, then κ can test whether κ is responsible for $E(a,b)$, that is, $\kappa \in \boldsymbol{P}_H(E(a,b))$. We stress that κ can not query $\boldsymbol{P}_H$ for values occurring outside of the local active domain at node κ. We refer to such transducer networks as *policy-aware.* We denote by $\mathcal{F}_1$ the class of queries that can be computed by coordination-free policy-aware relational transducer networks. We can likewise define the class $\mathcal{A}_1$ as the class of queries that can be computed by policy-aware relational transducer networks without access to the relation *All.*

[6]The original conjecture replaced monotone by Datalog [19].
[7]This definition is equivalent to the more standard definition of monotonicity but serves our purpose better: a query Q is *monotone* if $Q(I) \subseteq Q(J)$ for all database instances I and J with $I \subseteq J$.

Example 5.4. The open triangle query from Example 5.1 can now be computed in a coordination-free manner as follows:

1. Broadcast $H(\kappa)$.
2. If a new edge is received, add it to $H(\kappa)$. If there are edges in $E(a,b)$ and $E(b,c)$ in $H(\kappa)$, but edge $E(c,a) \notin H(\kappa)$ and $\kappa \in \boldsymbol{P}_H(E(c,a))$ then output (a,b,c). Repeat step (2).

□

We can now generalize Theorem 5.3 to a weaker notion of monotone queries. To this end, we say that a fact f is *domain distinct* from an instance I when $adom(f) \setminus adom(I) \neq \emptyset$. That is, f should contain an element not occurring in I. Furthermore, an instance J is domain distinct from I, when every fact in J is domain distinct from I.

Definition 5.5. A query Q is *domain-distinct-monotone* if $Q(I) \subseteq Q(I \cup J)$ for all database instances I and J for which J is domain distinct from I.

We denote the class of domain-distinct-monotone queries by $\mathcal{M}_{distinct}$.[8] Notice that $\mathcal{M} \subsetneq \mathcal{M}_{distinct}$ as the next example shows.

Example 5.6. The query $Q_\triangle$ of Example 5.1 selecting all open triangles in a graph is in $\mathcal{M}_{distinct}$. Indeed, towards a contradiction assume there are instances I and J with J domain distinct from I such that $Q(I) \not\subseteq Q(I \cup J)$. This means that there is a triple $(a,b,c) \in Q(I)$ for which $(a,b,c) \notin Q(I \cup J)$ implying that $\{E(a,b), E(b,c)\} \subseteq I$ and $E(c,a) \notin I$ but $E(c,a) \in J$. However, in that case J is not domain distinct from I which leads to the desired contradiction.

Consider the query $Q_{\neg\text{TC}}$ defining the complement of the transitive closure of E. We argue that $Q_{\neg\text{TC}} \notin \mathcal{M}_{distinct}$. Indeed, consider the empty instance I with $adom(I) = \{a,b\}$. Then, $(a,b) \in Q_{\neg\text{TC}}(I)$ but

$$(a,b) \notin Q_{\neg\text{TC}}(I \cup \{E(a,c), E(c,b)\})$$

and $\{E(a,c), E(c,b)\}$ is domain distinct from I for c different from a and b. □

The following lemma says that domain-distinct-monotone queries are in fact monotone w.r.t. induced subinstances. For $C \subseteq adom(I)$, let $I_{|C} = \{f \in I \mid adom(f) \subseteq C\}$. Then:

Lemma 5.7. *For $Q \in \mathcal{M}_{distinct}$, $Q(I_{|C}) \subseteq Q(I)$ for all I.*

We say that a set $C \subseteq \textbf{dom}$ is *distinct-complete* for κ, if for every fact f with $adom(f) \subseteq C$, κ received f from another node or $\kappa \in \boldsymbol{P}_H(f)$. In particular, κ knows for sure whether f belongs to the global instance I. Then the previous lemma implies that if a subset C is distinct-complete for κ, κ can safely output $Q(H(\kappa)_{|C})$. The latter leads to a simple coordination-free algorithm for every query $Q \in \mathcal{M}_{distinct}$:

1. Broadcast $H(\kappa)$.
2. If a new fact is received, add it to $H(\kappa)$. If $H(\kappa)$ contains a set C that is distinct-complete for κ, output $Q(H(\kappa)_{|C})$. Repeat step (2).

[8]Actually, $\mathcal{M}_{distinct}$ corresponds to the class of queries preserved under extensions (see, e.g., [4,38]).

It can easily be seen that this evaluation strategy is coordination-free: an ideal distribution is the one that assigns the whole database to every node. So, while there formally is no coordination or synchronization, unlike for monotone queries the just presented strategy does entail waiting: a compute node can only produce output for distinct-complete sets.

The following theorem provides the characterization:

Theorem 5.8. *[18]* $\mathcal{F}_1 = \mathcal{A}_1 = \mathcal{M}_{distinct}$.

We can weaken monotonicity even further beyond domain-distinct-monotonicity. We say that a fact f is *domain disjoint* from an instance I when $adom(f) \cap adom(I) = \emptyset$. That is, f consists solely of elements not occurring in I. Furthermore, an instance J is domain disjoint from I, when every fact in J is domain disjoint from I.

Definition 5.9. A query Q is *domain-disjoint-monotone* if $Q(I) \subseteq Q(I \cup J)$ for all database instances I and J for which J is domain disjoint from I.

We denote the class of domain-distinct-monotone queries by $\mathcal{M}_{disjoint}$.

Example 5.10. It can easily be seen that the query $Q_{\neg\text{TC}}$ from Example 5.6 is in $\mathcal{M}_{disjoint}$. Indeed, towards a contradiction assume there are instances I and J with J domain disjoint from I such that $Q(I) \not\subseteq Q(I \cup J)$. So, there has to be a pair $(a, b) \in Q(I)$ for which $(a, b) \notin Q(I \cup J)$. That is, there is no path from a to b in I while there is such a path in $I \cup J$. However, in that case J is not domain disjoint from I which leads to the desired contradiction.

Consider the query Q_{NT} returning the edge relation E when there is no three-node triangle present in the graph and the emptyset otherwise. Clearly, Q_{NT} is not in $\mathcal{M}_{disjoint}$. Indeed, set $I = \{E(a, a), E(b, b)\}$. Then $I = Q_{\text{NT}}(I)$ but $Q_{\text{NT}}(I \cup J) = \emptyset$ for every J domain disjoint from I containing a triangle. □

Hence, the previous example shows that

$$\mathcal{M} \subsetneq \mathcal{M}_{distinct} \subsetneq \mathcal{M}_{disjoint}.$$

The corresponding class of transducer networks is the one where the underlying distribution policies are domain-guided. More specifically, a domain assignment α for $\mathcal{N}$ is a total function from **dom** to the power set of $\mathcal{N}$. A domain assignment α now induces the domain-guided distribution policy $\boldsymbol{P}_\alpha$ where

$$P_\alpha(R(a_1, \ldots, a_k)) = \bigcup_{i=1}^{k} \alpha(a_i).$$

That is, every node in $\alpha(a)$ is responsible for every fact containing an occurrence of a. We refer to such transducer networks as *domain-guided*. We denote by $\mathcal{F}_2$ the class of queries that can be computed by coordination-free policy-aware relational transducer networks under domain-guided distribution policies. We can likewise define the class $\mathcal{A}_2$ as the class of queries that can be computed by policy-aware relational transducer networks under domain-guided distribution policies without access to the relation *All*.

There is an analog of Lemma 5.7. We say that J is a *component* of an instance I when $J \subseteq I$, $J \neq \emptyset$, $adom(J) \cap adom(I \setminus J) = \emptyset$ and J is minimal with this property. Then, the next lemma says that every domain-disjoint-monotone query is montone w.r.t. components.

Lemma 5.11. *For $Q \in \mathcal{M}_{disjoint}$, $Q(J) \subseteq Q(I)$ for all I and every component J of I.*

We say that a set $C \subseteq$ **dom** is *disjoint-complete* for κ if for every fact f with $adom(f) \cap C \neq \emptyset$, κ received f from another node or $\kappa \in \boldsymbol{P}_H(f)$. As every such C entails a union of components $H(\kappa)_{|C}$, κ can safely output $Q(H(\kappa)_{|C})$ for every domain-disjoint-monotone query Q. The coordination-free algorithm then operates at each node κ as follows (sketch):

1. Broadcast the active domain at κ, i.e., $adom(H(\kappa))$.
2. When a new domain element a is received, coordinate with at most one other node to transfer all tuples related to a. Notice that because the distribution is domain-guided, there is at least one computing node that contains all the facts related to a.
3. Evaluate Q on every disjoint-complete subset of I received at node κ.

We note that the previous algorithm is coordination-free: an ideal distribution is the one that assigns the whole database to every node. Still, it is quite obvious that the just presented algorithm does coordinate to some extend. Nevertheless, this coordination is not global but is pairwise and is determined by the concrete data distribution.

The following theorem provides the characterization:

Theorem 5.12. *[18]* $\mathcal{F}_2 = \mathcal{A}_2 = \mathcal{M}_{disjoint}$.

5.3 Datalog and Coordination-Freeness

As already remarked in Section 5.2, the original CALM-conjecture was formulated in terms of Datalog. It is therefore interesting to see how Datalog extensions correspond to classes of coordination-free queries. For a formal definition of Datalog we refer the interested reader to, for instance, [3].

Obviously, as all queries in Datalog are monotone, Theorem 5.3 implies that every Datalog query can be evaluated in a coordination-free manner. Afrati et al. [4] obtained that semi-positive Datalog, that is, Datalog extended with negation over base relations is in $\mathcal{M}_{distinct}$. Interestingly, Cabibbo [24] showed that Datalog with inequality and semi-positive Datalog extended with value invention capture the classes $\mathcal{M}$ and $\mathcal{M}_{distinct}$, respectively.

There also is a variant of Datalog that corresponds to $\mathcal{M}_{disjoint}$: semi-connected stratified Datalog. In particular, a Datalog program with negation is connected when the graph formed by the positive atoms is connected. Furthermore, a semi-connected stratified Datalog program is a stratified Datalog program where every stratum (except possibly the last one) is connected.

Example 5.13. The following program computing the complement of the transitive closure of E (query $Q_{\neg\text{TC}}$ of Example 5.10) is a semi-connected stratified Datalog program:

$$\begin{array}{lll} TC(x,y) & \leftarrow & E(x,y) \\ TC(x,y) & \leftarrow & TC(x,z), TC(z,y) \\ OUT(x,y) & \leftarrow & \text{ADom}(x), \text{ADom}(y), \neg TC(x,y) \end{array}$$

Here, ADom is a predicate defining the active domain of the instance.

Consider the following program defining query Q_{NT} of Example 5.10:

$$\begin{array}{lll} T(x,y,z) & \leftarrow & E(x,y), E(y,z), E(z,x), y \neq x, y \neq z, x \neq z \\ S(x) & \leftarrow & \text{ADom}(x), T(u,v,w) \\ OUT(x,y) & \leftarrow & E(x,y), \neg S(x) \end{array}$$

The above program is not semi-connected as the rule defining S is not connected. □

It is shown in [18] that when value invention is added to semi-connected stratified Datalog, the class $\mathcal{M}_{disjoint}$ is captured. Figure 2 (recycled from [18]) gives an overview of the presented results. Here, wILOG refers to Datalog extended with value invention while SP stands for semi-positive.

Finally, Ameloot et al. [17] obtained that connected stratified Datalog provides an effective syntax for Datalog programs that distribute over components. The authors also showed that under the well-founded semantics semi-connected Datalog programs with negation remain domain-disjoint-monotone and therefore in $\mathcal{F}_2$ providing a simple proof that win-move is coordination free for domain-guided transducer networks [59].

6. DISCUSSION

We considered the logical foundation of two different settings for parallel and distributed evaluation. Even within these particular settings there are quite a number of questions left unexplored and we touch upon some of these next.

Parallel-correctness and transfer.

For general conjunctive queries the complexity of parallel-correctness and transfer reside within different levels of the polynomial hierarchy. As these problems are static analysis problems, such high complexity does not rule out practical applicability. Still, it would be interesting to find tractable cases. Furthermore, even though containment and parallel-correctness transfer are incomparable, to take advantage of the large body of literature on query containment, it could be beneficial to investigate the relationship between these problems more deeply. The same holds true for the relationship with determinacy [45].

The notion of parallel-correctness is directly inspired by Hypercube where the result of the query is obtained by aggregating (through union) the evaluation of the original query over the distributed instance. Other possibilities are to consider more complex aggregator functions than union and to allow for a different query than the original one to be executed at computing nodes. Furthermore, it could be interesting to generalize the framework beyond one-round algorithms, that is, towards evaluation algorithms that comprise several rounds.

Coordination-free computation.

Figure 2 confirms that the notion of coordination-freeness as proposed by Ameloot et al [19] is a sensible one. In particular, as $\mathcal{A}_i = \mathcal{F}_i$ (for all $i = 0, 1, 2$) the notion seems to correspond to the intended semantics in that coordination-freeness avoids global synchronization barriers through the absence of knowledge about *all* the nodes in the network. That being said, the notion is not necessarily the best one as one could argue that, especially within $\mathcal{F}_1$ and $\mathcal{F}_2$, even though there is no global synchronization barrier, computing nodes are still prone to wait until complete subsets of the input data have been accumulated. Of course, this waiting is determined by the way the data is distributed and not by the evaluation algorithm.

The presented evaluation algorithms are very naive broadcast algorithms that essentially transfer all the data. It would be interesting to investigate efficient coordination-free algorithms. As an initial step, Ketsman and Neven [37] investigate more economical broadcasting strategies for full conjunctive queries without self-joins that only transmit a part of the local data necessary to evaluate the query at hand. In a sense, such approaches need to identify what part of the data is essential for answering a given query. An interesting related notion is that of scale independence, as introduced by Fan, Geerts and Libkin [31], where queries require only a relative small subset of the data whose size is determined by the structure of the query and the access methods rather than by the size of the data [25, 29, 30, 32].

Coordination-freeness is an all-or-nothing notion and might be too restrictive. It could be interesting to come up with ways to quantify coordination and relate it to Datalog programs. Interestingly, Alvaro et al. [11, 12] propose program analysis techniques to detect code fragments where coordination is perhaps overused. This way, some uses of coordination could be replaced with strategies like eventual consistency reducing the overall amount of coordination. Wang et al. [56] consider query plans incorporating failure-handling techniques for the evaluation of Datalog with bag-monotonic operators in synchronous as well as asynchronous settings.

Acknowledgments. I thank Tom Ameloot, Gaetano Geck, Bas Ketsman, Thomas Schwentick, Dan Suciu, and Tony Tan for helpful comments on a previous version of this paper.

7. REFERENCES

[1] S. Abiteboul, Z. Abrams, S. Haar, and T. Milo. Diagnosis of asynchronous discrete event systems: Datalog to the rescue! In *PODS*, pages 358–367, 2005.

[2] S. Abiteboul, M. Bienvenu, A. Galland, and E. Antoine. A rule-based language for Web data management. In *PODS*, pages 293–304, 2011.

[3] S. Abiteboul, R. Hull, and V. Vianu. *Foundations of Databases.* Addison-Wesley, 1995.

[4] F. Afrati, S. S. Cosmadakis, and M. Yannakakis. On Datalog vs polynomial time. *Journal of computer and system sciences*, 51:177–196, 1995.

[5] F. N. Afrati, V. R. Borkar, M. J. Carey, N. Polyzotis, and J. D. Ullman. Map-reduce extensions and recursive queries. In *EDBT*, pages 1–8, 2011.

[6] F. N. Afrati, M. Joglekar, C. Ré, S. Salihoglu, and J. D. Ullman. GYM: A multiround distributed join algorithm. *CoRR*, abs/1410.4156v4, 2015.

[7] F. N. Afrati, N. Stasinopoulos, J. D. Ullman, and A. Vasilakopoulos. Sharesskew: An algorithm to handle skew for joins in mapreduce. *CoRR abs/1512.03921*, cs.DB, 2015.

[8] F. N. Afrati and J. D. Ullman. Optimizing joins in a map-reduce environment. In *EDBT*, pages 99–110, 2010.

[9] F. N. Afrati and J. D. Ullman. Optimizing Multiway Joins in a Map-Reduce Environment. *IEEE Transactions on Knowledge and Data Engineering*, 23(9):1282–1298, 2011.

[10] F. N. Afrati and J. D. Ullman. Transitive closure and recursive datalog implemented on clusters. In *EDBT*, pages 132–143, 2012.

[11] P. Alvaro, N. Conway, J. M. Hellerstein, and D. Maier. Blazes: Coordination analysis for distributed

$$
\begin{array}{ccccccccc}
\text{Datalog}(\neq) & \subsetneq & \text{wILOG}(\neq) & = & \mathcal{M} & = & \mathcal{F}_0 & = & \mathcal{A}_0 \\
\cup\!\!\!\!\!\!\mid & & \cup\!\!\!\!\!\!\mid & & \cup\!\!\!\!\!\!\mid & & \cup\!\!\!\!\!\!\mid & & \cup\!\!\!\!\!\!\mid \\
\text{SP-Datalog} & \subsetneq & \text{SP-wILOG} & = & \mathcal{M}_{\text{distinct}} & = & \mathcal{F}_1 & = & \mathcal{A}_1 \\
\cup\!\!\!\!\!\!\mid & & \cup\!\!\!\!\!\!\mid & & \cup\!\!\!\!\!\!\mid & & \cup\!\!\!\!\!\!\mid & & \cup\!\!\!\!\!\!\mid \\
\text{semicon-datalog} & \subsetneq & \text{semicon-wILOG} & = & \mathcal{M}_{\text{disjoint}} & = & \mathcal{F}_2 & = & \mathcal{A}_2
\end{array}
$$

Figure 2: Correspondences between Datalog, monotone queries and classes of transducer networks.

programs. In *ICDE*, pages 52–63, 2014.

[12] P. Alvaro, N. Conway, J. M. Hellerstein, and W. R. Marczak. Consistency analysis in bloom: a CALM and collected approach. *CIDR*, pages 249–260, 2011.

[13] T. J. Ameloot. Declarative Networking: Recent Theoretical Work on Coordination, Correctness, and Declarative Semantics. *SIGMOD Record*, 43(2):5–16, 2014.

[14] T. J. Ameloot, G. Geck, B. Ketsman, F. Neven, and T. Schwentick. Parallel-correctness and transferability for conjunctive queries. In *PODS*, pages 47–58, 2015.

[15] T. J. Ameloot, G. Geck, B. Ketsman, F. Neven, and T. Schwentick. Parallel-correctness and transferability for conjunctive queries. Journal verion, 2015.

[16] T. J. Ameloot, G. Geck, B. Ketsman, F. Neven, and T. Schwentick. Data partitioning for single-round multi-join evaluation in massively parallel systems. *Sigmod Record*, 45(1), 2016.

[17] T. J. Ameloot, B. Ketsman, F. Neven, and D. Zinn. Datalog queries distributing over components. In *ICDT*, pages 308–323, 2015.

[18] T. J. Ameloot, B. Ketsman, F. Neven, and D. Zinn. Weaker forms of monotonicity for declarative networking: A more fine-grained answer to the CALM-conjecture. *ACM Transactions on Database Systems*, 40(4):A1–A45, 2015.

[19] T. J. Ameloot, F. Neven, and J. V. den Bussche. Relational transducers for declarative networking. *Journal of the ACM*, 60(2):15, 2013.

[20] P. Beame, P. Koutris, and D. Suciu. Communication steps for parallel query processing. In *PODS*, pages 273–284, 2013.

[21] P. Beame, P. Koutris, and D. Suciu. Skew in parallel query processing. In *PODS*, pages 212–223, 2014.

[22] P. Beame, P. Koutris, and D. Suciu. Communication cost in parallel query processing. *CoRR*, abs/1602.06236, 2016.

[23] S. Blanas, J. M. Patel, V. Ercegovac, J. Rao, E. J. Shekita, and Y. Tian. A comparison of join algorithms for log processing in mapreduce. In *SIGMOD*, pages 975–986, 2010.

[24] L. Cabibbo. The expressive power of stratified logic programs with value invention. *Information and Computation*, 147(1):22–56, 1998.

[25] Y. Cao, W. Fan, T. Wo, and W. Yu. Bounded Conjunctive Queries. *PVLDB*, 7(12):1231–1242, 2014.

[26] S. Chu, M. Balazinska, and D. Suciu. From theory to practice: Efficient join query evaluation in a parallel database system. In *SIGMOD*, pages 63–78, 2015.

[27] A. Das Sarma, F. N. Afrati, S. Salihoglu, and J. D. Ullman. Upper and lower bounds on the cost of a map-reduce computation. In *VLDB*, pages 277–288, 2013.

[28] J. Dean and S. Ghemawat. MapReduce: simplified data processing on large clusters. *Communications of the ACM*, 51(1):107–113, 2008.

[29] W. Fan and Y. Cao. An effective syntax for bounded relational queries. In *SIGMOD*, 2016.

[30] W. Fan, F. Geerts, Y. Cao, T. Deng, and P. Lu. Querying Big Data by Accessing Small Data. In *PODS*, pages 173–184, 2015.

[31] W. Fan, F. Geerts, and L. Libkin. On scale independence for querying big data. In *PODS*, pages 51–62. ACM Press, 2014.

[32] W. Fan, F. Geerts, and F. Neven. Making queries tractable on big data with preprocessing. *PVLDB*, 6(9):685–696, 2013.

[33] G. Geck, B. Ketsman, F. Neven, and T. Schwentick. Parallel-correctness and containment for conjunctive queries with union and negation. In *ICDT*, pages 9:1–9:17, 2016.

[34] S. Grumbach and F. Wang. Netlog, a rule-based language for distributed programming. In *PADL*, pages 88–103, 2010.

[35] J. M. Hellerstein. The declarative imperative: experiences and conjectures in distributed logic. *SIGMOD Record*, 39(1):5–19, 2010.

[36] M. Kaminski and N. Francez. Finite-memory automata. *Theor. Comput. Sci.*, 134(2):329–363, 1994.

[37] B. Ketsman and F. Neven. Optimal broadcasting strategies for conjunctive queries over distributed data. In *ICDT*, pages 291–307, 2015.

[38] P. G. Kolaitis and M. Y. Vardi. On the expressive power of Datalog: Tools and a case study. In *PODS*, pages 61–71, 1990.

[39] P. Koutris, P. Beame, and D. Suciu. Worst-Case Optimal Algorithms for Parallel Query Processing. In *ICDT*, pages 8:1–8:18, 2016.

[40] P. Koutris and D. Suciu. Parallel evaluation of conjunctive queries. In *PODS*, pages 223–234, 2011.

[41] B. T. Loo, T. Condie, M. N. Garofalakis, D. E. Gay, J. M. Hellerstein, P. Maniatis, R. Ramakrishnan, T. Roscoe, and I. Stoica. Declarative networking: language, execution and optimization. In *SIGMOD*, pages 97–108, 2006.

[42] J. Ma, F. Le, D. Wood, A. Russo, and J. Lobo. A

declarative approach to distributed computing: Specification, execution and analysis. *Theory and Practice of Logic Programming*, 13(4-5):815–830, 2013.

[43] S. Melnik, A. Gubarev, J. J. Long, G. Romer, S. Shivakumar, M. Tolton, and T. Vassilakis. Dremel: Interactive analysis of web-scale datasets. *PVLDB*, 3(1-2):330–339, 2010.

[44] M. Mugnier, G. Simonet, and M. Thomazo. On the complexity of entailment in existential conjunctive first-order logic with atomic negation. *Inf. Comput.*, 215:8–31, 2012.

[45] A. Nash, L. Segoufin, and V. Vianu. Views and queries: Determinacy and rewriting. *ACM Trans. Database Syst.*, 35(3), 2010.

[46] R. Nehme and N. Bruno. Automated partitioning design in parallel database systems. In *SIGMOD*, pages 1137–1148, 2011.

[47] F. Neven, N. Schweikardt, F. Servais, and T. Tan. Distributed streaming with finite memory. In *ICDT*, pages 324–341, 2015.

[48] F. Neven, T. Schwentick, and V. Vianu. Finite state machines for strings over infinite alphabets. *ACM Trans. Comput. Log.*, 5(3):403–435, 2004.

[49] C. Olston, B. Reed, U. Srivastava, R. Kumar, and A. Tomkins. Pig latin: A not-so-foreign language for data processing. In *SIGMOD*, pages 1099–1110, 2008.

[50] M. T. Özsu and P. Valduriez. *Principles of Distributed Database Systems, Third Edition.* Springer, 2011.

[51] J. Rao, C. Zhang, N. Megiddo, and G. Lohman. Automating physical database design in a parallel database. In *SIGMOD*, pages 558–569, 2002.

[52] T. Tan. Balancing the computation of distributed streaming with finite memory. Unpublished 2016.

[53] A. Thusoo, J. S. Sarma, N. Jain, Z. Shao, P. Chakka, S. Anthony, H. Liu, P. Wyckoff, and R. Murthy. Hive: A warehousing solution over a map-reduce framework. *PVLDB*, pages 1626–1629, 2009.

[54] J. D. Ullman. Information integration using logical views. *Theor. Comput. Sci.*, 239(2):189–210, 2000.

[55] J. D. Ullman. Designing good MapReduce algorithms. *ACM Crossroads*, 19(1):30–34, 2012.

[56] J. Wang, M. Balazinska, and D. Halperin. Asynchronous and fault-tolerant recursive Datalog evaluation in shared-nothing engines. *PVLDB*, 8(12):1542–1553, 2015.

[57] R. S. Xin, J. Rosen, M. Zaharia, M. J. Franklin, S. Shenker, and I. Stoica. Shark: SQL and rich analytics at scale. In *SIGMOD*, pages 13–24, 2013.

[58] M. Yannakakis. Algorithms for acyclic database schemes. In *VLDB*, pages 82–94, 1981.

[59] D. Zinn, T. J. Green, and B. Ludäscher. Win-move is coordination-free (sometimes). In *ICDT*, pages 99–113, 2012.

Counting Answers to Existential Positive Queries: A Complexity Classification

Hubie Chen
University of the Basque Country (UPV/EHU)
E-20018 San Sebastián, Spain
and IKERBASQUE, Basque Foundation for Science
E-48011 Bilbao, Spain

Stefan Mengel
CNRS, CRIL UMR 8188, France

ABSTRACT

Existential positive formulas form a fragment of first-order logic that includes and is semantically equivalent to unions of conjunctive queries, one of the most important and well-studied classes of queries in database theory. We consider the complexity of counting the number of answers to existential positive formulas on finite structures and give a trichotomy theorem on query classes, in the setting of bounded arity. This theorem generalizes and unifies several known results on the complexity of conjunctive queries and unions of conjunctive queries. We prove this trichotomy theorem by establishing a result which we call the *equivalence theorem*, which shows that for each class of existential positive formulas, there exists a class of conjunctive queries having the same complexity (in a sense made precise).

Keywords

counting complexity, query evaluation, existential positive queries

1. INTRODUCTION

1.1 Background

The computational problem of evaluating a formula (of some logic) on a finite relational structure is of central interest in database theory and logic. In the context of database theory, this problem is often referred to as *query evaluation*, as it models the posing of a query to a database, in a well-acknowledged way: the formula is the query, and the structure represents the database. We will refer to the results of such an evaluation as *answers*; logically, these are the satisfying assignments of the formula on the structure. The particular case of this problem where the formula is a sentence is often referred to as *model checking*, and even in just the case of first-order sentences, can capture a variety of well-known decision problems from all throughout computer science [11].

PODS'16, June 26-July 01, 2016, San Francisco, CA, USA

DOI: http://dx.doi.org/10.1145/2902251.2902279

In this article, we study the counting version of this problem, namely, given a formula and a structure, output the *number* of answers (see for example [18, 12, 10, 6] for previous studies). This problem of *counting query answers* generalizes model checking, which can be viewed as the particular case thereof where one is given a sentence and structure, and wants to decide if the number of answers is 1 or 0, corresponding to whether or not the empty assignment is satisfying. In addition to the counting problem's basic and fundamental interest, it can be pointed out that all practical query languages supported by database management systems have a counting operator. Indeed, it has been argued that database queries with counting are at the basis of decision support systems that handle large data volume [12].

As has been previously articulated, a typical situation in the database setting is the evaluation of a relatively short formula on a relatively large structure. Consequently, it has been argued that, in measuring the time complexity of query evaluation tasks, one could reasonably allow a slow (non-polynomial-time) preprocessing of the formula, so long as the desired evaluation can be performed in polynomial time following the preprocessing [17, 11]. Relaxing polynomial-time computation to allow arbitrary preprocessing of a *parameter* of a problem instance yields, in essence, the notion of *fixed-parameter tractability.* This notion of tractability is at the core of *parameterized complexity theory*, which provides a taxonomy for classifying problems where each instance has an associated parameter. We make use of this paradigm in this article; here, the formula is the parameter.

1.2 Contribution

Existential positive queries are the first-order formulas built from the two binary connectives ($\wedge$, $\vee$) and existential quantification. They include and are semantically equivalent to the so-called *unions of conjunctive queries*, also known as *select-project-join-union queries*; these have been argued to be the most common database queries [1]. Indeed, each union of conjunctive queries can be viewed as an existential positive query having a particular form, namely, a disjunction of primitive positive formulas; recall that a *primitive positive* query is an existential positive query that does not use disjunction.

We study the problem of counting query answers on existential positive queries. An established way to understand which types of queries are computationally well-behaved and exhibit desirable, tractable behavior is to consider this problem relative to a set of queries, and to attempt to understand on which sets this problem is tractable. Precisely, each set

Φ of existential positive queries yields a restricted version of the general problem, namely: count the number of answers of a given formula $\phi \in \Phi$ on a given finite structure $\mathbf{B}$. We hence have a family of problems, one problem for each such set Φ. Our study focuses on formula sets that have *bounded arity* (by which is meant that there is a constant that upper bounds the arity of all relation symbols used in formulas); let us assume this property of all formula sets in this discussion.[1]

In this article, we prove a trichotomy theorem (Theorem 3.2) on the parameterized complexity of the discussed family of problems, which describes the complexity of every such problem. In particular, our trichotomy theorem shows that—in a sense made precise—each such problem is fixed-parameter tractable, equivalent to the *clique* problem, or as hard as the *counting clique* problem (which generalizes the clique problem). Note that the hypothesis that the clique problem is not fixed-parameter tractable is an established one in parameterized complexity;[2] under this hypothesis, our trichotomy theorem yields a precise description of the problems (from those under consideration) that are fixed-parameter tractable. Our trichotomy theorem is in fact derived by invoking two theorems:

- A new theorem showing that, for each set of existential positive queries, there exists a set of primitive positive queries such that the two sets exhibit the same complexity behavior (see Theorem 3.1). This new theorem, which we call the *equivalence theorem*, can be conceived of as the primary technical contribution of this article.

- A previously presented trichotomy on primitive positive queries [6, 7] (discussed in Section 2.4.)

1.3 Related work

The statement of our new trichotomy theorem generalizes, unifies, and strengthens a number of existing parameterized complexity classification results in the literature, namely:

- The dichotomy for model checking primitive positive formulas [13], which built on a previous dichotomy [14]; see also [8].

- The dichotomy for model checking existential positive formulas [3].

- The dichotomy for counting answers to quantifier-free primitive positive formulas [9] (phrased as the problem of counting homomorphisms between relational structures).

- The trichotomy for counting answers to primitive positive formulas [6, 7], which trichotomy built on the previous work [10].

Let us emphasize that we only claim to generalize the parameterized complexity versions of the presented results. In some of the above works, such as the works [13] and [9], the problems that are classified as fixed-parameter tractable are also polynomial-time tractable. We can further remark that there are problems from the dichotomy theorem on model checking existential positive formulas [3] that are shown to be fixed-parameter tractable but also NP-complete.

The techniques used to prove our equivalence theorem are algebraic and combinatorial, and are quite different in nature from and contrast with those used to prove the previous classifications, which were more graph-theoretic and logical in flavor. Indeed, while the graph-theoretic measure of *treewidth* played a key role in the statement and proof of the previous trichotomy as well as of the previous dichotomies on primitive positive queries, it is not at all needed to prove our equivalence theorem. To establish the equivalence theorem, we make a key application of the inclusion-exclusion counting principle to translate an existential positive formula to a finite set of primitive positive formulas (see Section 5.3), which, in the setup considered by the article, is crucial to handling and understanding disjunction. We believe that the developed theory that supports said application should provide a valuable foundation for coping with disjunction in logics that are more expressive than the one considered here.

2. PRELIMINARIES

2.1 Basic definitions and notions

Note that $\cdot$ is sometimes used for multiplication of real numbers.

Polynomials. We remind the reader of some basic facts about polynomials which we will use throughout the paper. Here, a univariate polynomial p in a variable x is a function $p(x) = \sum_{i=0}^{d} a_i x^i$ where $d \geqslant 0$, each $a_i \in \mathbb{R}$ and $a_d \neq 0$, or the *zero polynomial* $p(x) = 0$. The a_i are called *coefficients* of p. The degree of a polynomial is defined as $-\infty$ in the case of the zero polynomial, and as d otherwise. Let $(x_0, y_0), \ldots, (x_n, y_n)$ be $n + 1$ pairs of real numbers. Then there is a uniquely determined polynomial of degree at most n such that $p(x_i) = y_i$ for each i; consequently, a polynomial p of degree n that has at least $n + 1$ zeroes (where a *zero* is a value x such that $p(x) = 0$) is the zero polynomial. If all x_i and y_i are rational numbers, then the coefficients a_i of this polynomial are rational numbers as well; moreover, the a_i can be computed in polynomial time.

Logic. We assume basic familiarity with the syntax and semantics of first-order logic. In this article, we focus on relational first-order logic where equality is not built-in to the logic. Hence, each *vocabulary/signature* under discussion consists only of relation symbols. We assume structures under discussion to be *finite* (that is, have finite universe); nonetheless, we sometimes describe structures as *finite* for emphasis. We assume that the relations of structures are represented as lists of tuples. We use the letters $\mathbf{A}$, $\mathbf{B}$, ... to denote structures, and the corresponding letters A, B, ... to denote their respective universes. When τ is a signature, we use $\mathbf{I}_\tau$ to denote the τ-structure with universe $\{a\}$ and where each relation symbol $R \in \tau$ has $R^{\mathbf{I}} = \{(a, \ldots, a)\}$. When $\mathbf{A}, \mathbf{B}$ are structures over the same signature τ, a *homomorphism* from $\mathbf{A}$ to $\mathbf{B}$ is a mapping $h : A \to B$ such that, for each $R \in \tau$ and each tuple $(a_1, \ldots, a_k) \in R^{\mathbf{A}}$, it holds that $(h(a_1), \ldots, h(a_k)) \in R^{\mathbf{B}}$.

We use the term *fo-formula* to refer to a first-order formula. An *ep-formula* (short for *existential positive formula*) is a fo-formula built from *atoms* (by which we refer to predicate applications of the form $R(v_1, \ldots, v_k)$, where R is a relation symbol and the v_i are variables), conjunction ($\wedge$),

[1]Note that in the case of unbounded arity, complexity may depend on the choice of representation of relations [5].

[2]It can be phrased in terms of complexity classes: FPT $\neq$ W[1].

disjunction ($\vee$), and existential quantification ($\exists$). A *pp-formula* (short for *primitive positive formula*) is defined as an ep-formula where disjunction does not occur. An fo-formula is *prenex* if it has the form $Q_1 v_1 \dots Q_n v_n \theta$ where θ is quantifier-free, that is, if all quantifiers occur in the front of the formula. The set of free variables of a formula ϕ is denoted by free(ϕ) and is defined as usual; a formula ϕ is a *sentence* if free(ϕ) $= \emptyset$.

We now present some definitions and conventions that are not totally standard. A primary concern in this article is in counting satisfying assignments of fo-formulas on a finite structure. The count is sensitive to the set of variables over which assignments are considered; and, we will sometimes (but not always) want to count relative to a set of variables that is strictly larger than the set of free variables. Hence, we will often associate with each fo-formula ϕ a set V of variables called the *liberal variables*, denoted by lib(ϕ), which is required to be a superset of free(ϕ), that is, we require lib(ϕ) $\supseteq$ free(ϕ). Note that lib(ϕ) may contain variables that do not occur at all in atoms of ϕ. To indicate that V is the set of liberal variables of ϕ, we often use the notation $\phi(V)$; we also use $\phi(v_1, \dots, v_n)$, where the v_i are a listing of the elements of V. Relative to a formula $\phi(V)$, when $\mathbf{B}$ is a structure, we will use $\phi(\mathbf{B})$ to denote the set of assignments $f : V \to B$ such that $\mathbf{B}, f \models \phi$. *We assume that, in each prenex formula with liberal variables associated with it, no variable is both liberal and quantified.* We call an fo-formula ϕ *free* if free(ϕ) $\neq \emptyset$, and *liberal* if lib(ϕ) is defined and lib(ϕ) $\neq \emptyset$.

Example 2.1. *Let us consider the formula $\phi(x, y, z) = R(x, y) \vee S(y, z)$. As indicated above, the notation $\phi(x, y, z)$ is used to indicate that* lib(ϕ) $= \{x, y, z\}$. *As* free(ϕ) $= \{x, y, z\}$, *we have* lib(ϕ) $=$ free(ϕ). *Define $\psi(x, y, z) = R(x, y)$ and $\psi'(x, y, z) = S(y, z)$. By the notation $\psi(x, y, z)$, we indicate that* lib(ψ) $= \{x, y, z\}$; *likewise, it holds that* lib(ψ') $= \{x, y, z\}$. *Notice that* free(ψ) $= \{x, y\}$, *so we have that* lib(ψ) *is a proper superset of* free(ψ); *in fact, the variable $z \in$* lib(ψ) *does not occur at all in an atom of ψ. Define also $\theta(x, y) = R(x, y)$; by the notation $\theta(x, y)$, we indicate that* lib(θ) $= \{x, y\}$.

Observe that, for any structure $\mathbf{B}$, we have $\phi(\mathbf{B}) = \psi(\mathbf{B}) \cup \psi'(\mathbf{B})$ (and hence $|\phi(\mathbf{B})| = |\psi(\mathbf{B}) \cup \psi'(\mathbf{B})|$). Observe, however, that for any structure $\mathbf{B}$ where $\theta(\mathbf{B})$ is non-empty, it does not hold that $\phi(\mathbf{B}) = \theta(\mathbf{B}) \cup \psi'(\mathbf{B})$, since $\phi(\mathbf{B})$ contains only assignments defined on lib(ϕ) $= \{x, y, z\}$, *whereas $\theta(\mathbf{B})$ contains only assignments defined on* lib(θ) $= \{x, y\}$. □

pp-formulas. It is well-known [2] that there is a correspondence between prenex pp-formulas and relational structures. In particular, each prenex pp-formula $\phi(S)$ (on signature τ) with lib(ϕ) $= S$ may be viewed as a pair $(\mathbf{A}, S)$ consisting of a structure $\mathbf{A}$ (on τ) and a set S; the universe A of $\mathbf{A}$ is the union of S with the variables appearing in ϕ, and the following condition defines the relations of $\mathbf{A}$: for each $R \in \tau$, a tuple $(a_1, \dots, a_k) \in A^k$ is in $R^{\mathbf{A}}$ if and only if $R(a_1, \dots, a_k)$ appears in ϕ. In the other direction, such a pair $(\mathbf{A}, S)$ can be viewed as a prenex pp-formula $\phi(S)$ where all variables in $A \backslash S$ are quantified and the atoms of ϕ are defined according to the above condition. A basic known fact [2] that we will use is that when $\phi(S)$ is a pp-formula corresponding to the pair $(\mathbf{A}, S)$, $\mathbf{B}$ is an arbitrary structure, and $f : S \to B$ is an arbitrary map, it holds that $\mathbf{B}, f \models \phi(S)$ if and only if there is an extension f' of f that is a homomorphism from $\mathbf{A}$ to $\mathbf{B}$. *We will freely interchange between the structure view and the usual notion of a prenex pp-formula.* For a pp-formula specified as a pair $(\mathbf{A}, S)$, we typically assume that $S \subseteq A$.

Example 2.2. *Consider the pp-formula $\phi(x, x', y, z) = \exists y' \exists u \exists v \exists w (E(x, x') \wedge E(y, y') \wedge F(u, v) \wedge G(u, w))$. The notation $\phi(x, x', y, z)$ indicates that* lib(ϕ) $= \{x, x', y, z\}$. *Note that* free(ϕ) $= \{x, x', y\}$. *To convert ϕ to a structure $\mathbf{A}$, we take the universe A of $\mathbf{A}$ to be the union of* lib(ϕ) *with all variables appearing in ϕ, so $A = \{x, x', y, z, y', u, v, w\}$. Then, we define the relations as just described above, so $E^{\mathbf{A}} = \{(x, x'), (y, y')\}$, $F^{\mathbf{A}} = \{(u, v)\}$, and $G^{\mathbf{A}} = \{(u, w)\}$. The resulting pair representation of ϕ is $(\mathbf{A}, \{x, x', y, z\})$.* □

Two structures are *homomorphically equivalent* if each has a homomorphism to the other. A structure is a *core* if it is not homomorphically equivalent to a proper substructure of itself. A structure $\mathbf{B}$ is a *core* of a structure $\mathbf{A}$ if $\mathbf{B}$ is a substructure of $\mathbf{A}$ that is a core and is homomorphically equivalent to $\mathbf{A}$. It is known that all cores of a structure are isomorphic and hence one sometimes speaks of *the* core of a structure.

For a prenex pp-formula $(\mathbf{A}, S)$ on signature τ, we define its *augmented structure*, denoted by $\mathsf{aug}(\mathbf{A}, S)$, to be the structure over the expanded vocabulary $\tau \cup \{R_a \mid a \in S\}$ (understood to be a disjoint union) where $R_a^{\mathsf{aug}(\mathbf{A}, S)} = \{a\}$; we define the *core* of the pp-formula $(\mathbf{A}, S)$ to be the core of $\mathsf{aug}(\mathbf{A}, S)$.

The following fundamental facts on pp-formulas will be used throughout.

Theorem 2.3 (follows from [2]). *Suppose that each of the pairs $(\mathbf{A}, V)$, $(\mathbf{B}, V)$ is a prenex pp-formula. The formula $(\mathbf{B}, V)$ logically entails the formula $(\mathbf{A}, V)$ if and only if there exists a homomorphism from the structure $\mathsf{aug}(\mathbf{A}, V)$ to the structure $\mathsf{aug}(\mathbf{B}, V)$. The formulas $(\mathbf{A}, V)$, $(\mathbf{B}, V)$ are logically equivalent if and only if they have isomorphic cores, or equivalently, when $\mathsf{aug}(\mathbf{A}, V)$ and $\mathsf{aug}(\mathbf{B}, V)$ are homomorphically equivalent.*

ep-formulas. In order to discuss ep-formulas, we will employ the following terminology. An ep-formula is *disjunctive* if it is the disjunction of prenex pp-formulas; when ϕ is a disjunctive ep-formula with lib(ϕ) defined, we typically assume that each of the pp-formulas ψ that appear as disjuncts of ϕ has lib(ψ) defined as lib(ϕ). (In this way, for an arbitrary finite structure $\mathbf{B}$, it holds that $|\phi(\mathbf{B})| = |\bigcup_{\psi} \psi(\mathbf{B})|$, where the union is over all such disjuncts ψ.) An ep-formula is *all-free* if it is disjunctive and each pp-formula appearing as a disjunct is free. An ep-formula $\phi(S)$ is *normalized* if it is disjunctive and for each sentence disjunct $(\mathbf{A}, S)$ and any other disjunct $(\mathbf{A}', S)$, there is no homomorphism from $\mathsf{aug}(\mathbf{A}, S)$ to $\mathsf{aug}(\mathbf{A}', S)$ (equivalently, there is no homomorphism from $\mathbf{A}$ to $\mathbf{A}'$). It is straightforward to verify that there is an algorithm that, given an ep-formula, outputs a logically equivalent normalized ep-formula.

Graphs. To every prenex pp-formula $(\mathbf{A}, S)$ we assign a graph whose vertex set is $A \cup S$ and where two vertices are connected by an edge if they appear together in a tuple of a relation of $\mathbf{A}$. A prenex pp-formula $(\mathbf{A}, S)$ is called *connected* if its graph is connected. A prenex pp-formula $(\mathbf{A}', S')$ is a *component* of a prenex pp-formula $(\mathbf{A}, S)$ over the same signature τ if there exists a set C that forms a connected component of the graph of $(\mathbf{A}, S)$, where:

- $S' = S \cap C$.
- For each relation $R \in \tau$, a tuple $(a_1, \ldots, a_k)$ is in $R^{\mathbf{A}'}$ if and only if $(a_1, \ldots, a_k) \in R^{\mathbf{A}} \cap C^k$.

Note that when this holds, the graph of $(\mathbf{A}', S')$ is the connected component of the graph of $(\mathbf{A}, S)$ on vertices C. We will use the fact that, if $\phi(V)$ is a prenex pp-formula and $\phi_1(V_1), \ldots, \phi_c(V_c)$ is a list of its components, then for any finite structure $\mathbf{B}$, it holds that $|\phi(\mathbf{B})| = \prod_{i=1}^{c} |\phi_i(\mathbf{B})|$.

EXAMPLE 2.4. *Let ϕ be the free prenex pp-formula from Example 2.2, and let $(\mathbf{A}, S)$ be the pair representation given there. The connected components of the graph of $(\mathbf{A}, S)$ are $\{x, x'\}$, $\{y, y'\}$, $\{z\}$, and $\{u, v, w\}$. There are thus four components of the formula $(\mathbf{A}, S)$; they are $(\mathbf{A}'_{\{x,x'\}}, \{x, x'\})$, $(\mathbf{A}'_{\{y,y'\}}, \{y\})$, $(\mathbf{A}'_{\{z\}}, \{z\})$, and $(\mathbf{A}'_{\{u,v,w\}}, \varnothing)$ (respectively), where each $\mathbf{A}'_C$ is the structure $\mathbf{A}'$ defined above, with respect to the set C.*

Written logically, these four components are $\psi_1(x, x') = E(x, x')$, $\psi_2(y) = \exists y' E(y, y')$, $\psi_3(z) = \top$, and $\psi_4(\varnothing) = \exists u \exists v \exists w (F(u, v) \wedge G(u, w))$, respectively. Here, $\top$ denotes the empty conjunction (considered to be true). □

2.2 Counting complexity

Throughout, we use Σ to denote an alphabet over which strings are formed. All problems to be considered are viewed as counting problems. So, a *problem* is a mapping $Q : \Sigma^* \to \mathbb{N}$. We view decision problems as problems where, for each $x \in \Sigma^*$, it holds that $Q(x)$ is equal to 0 or 1. A *parameterization* is a mapping $\kappa : \Sigma^* \to \Sigma^*$. A parameterized problem is a pair (Q, κ) consisting of a problem Q and a parameterization κ. Throughout, by π_i we denote the operator that projects a tuple onto its ith coordinate.

A partial function $T : \Sigma^* \to \mathbb{N}$ is *polynomial-multiplied* with respect to a parameterization κ if there exists a computable function $f : \Sigma^* \to \mathbb{N}$ and a polynomial $p : \mathbb{N} \to \mathbb{N}$ such that, for each $x \in \text{dom}(T)$, it holds that $T(x) \leqslant f(\kappa(x))p(|x|)$.

We now give a definition of FPT-computability for partial mappings.

DEFINITION 2.5. *Let $\kappa : \Sigma^* \to \Sigma^*$ be a parameterization. A partial mapping $r : \Sigma^* \to \Sigma^*$ is* FPT-computable *with respect to κ if there exist a polynomial-multiplied function $T : \Sigma^* \to \mathbb{N}$ (with respect to κ) with $\text{dom}(T) = \text{dom}(r)$ and an algorithm A such that, for each string $x \in \text{dom}(r)$, the algorithm A computes $r(x)$ within time $T(x)$; when this holds, we also say that r is* FPT-computable *with respect to κ* via *A.*

As is standard, we may and do freely interchange among elements of Σ^*, $\Sigma^* \times \Sigma^*$, and $\mathbb{N}$. We define FPT to be the class that contains a parameterized problem (Q, κ) if and only if Q is FPT-computable with respect to κ.

We now introduce a notion of reduction for counting problems, which is a form of Turing reduction. We use $\wp_{\text{fin}}(A)$ to denote the set containing all finite subsets of A.

DEFINITION 2.6. *A* counting FPT-reduction *from a parameterized problem (Q, κ) to another (Q', κ') consists of a computable function $h : \Sigma^* \to \wp_{\text{fin}}(\Sigma^*)$, and an algorithm A such that:*

- *on an input x, A may make oracle queries of the form $Q'(y)$ with $\kappa'(y) \in h(\kappa(x))$, and*
- *Q is FPT-computable with respect to κ via A.*

We use CLIQUE to denote the decision problem where (k, G) is a yes-instance when G is a graph that contains a clique of size $k \in \mathbb{N}$. By #CLIQUE we denote the problem of counting, given (k, G), the number of k-cliques in the graph G. The parameterized versions of these problems, denoted by p-CLIQUE and p-#CLIQUE, are defined via the parameterization $\pi_1(k, G) = k$.

2.3 Counting case complexity

We employ the framework of *case complexity* to develop some of our complexity results. We present the needed elements of this framework for counting problems. The definitions and results here are due to [6, 7], are based on the theory of [4], and are presented here for the sake of self-containment; see those articles for further discussion and motivation of the framework.

The case complexity framework was developed to prove results on restricted versions of parameterized problems where not all values of the parameter are permitted. This type of restricted problem arises naturally in query answering problems, where one often restricts the queries that are admissible, as is done here (for other examples, see [9, 13, 4]).

The case complexity framework provides a notion of *case problem* and a notion of reduction between case problem. A case problem was originally [4] defined as a language Q of pairs (that is, a subset of $\Sigma^* \times \Sigma^*$) where the first element of each pair is ultimately viewed as the parameter, along with a set $S \subseteq \Sigma^*$ restricting the permitted parameter values. In this article, as we are dealing with counting complexity, in lieu of considering languages, we will consider mappings $\Sigma^* \times \Sigma^* \to \mathbb{N}$. (Of course, a language of pairs can be naturally viewed as such a mapping by taking its characteristic function.)

One benefit of the framework is that the notion of reduction does not rely on any form of computability assumption on the sets S involved. Thus, in comparing case problems using this notion of reduction, one does not need to discuss the computability status of these sets S, even though in general, it is usual that authors ultimately assume some form of computability on these sets (typically computable enumerability or computability).

Let us turn to the formal presentation of the framework. A *case problem* consists of a problem $Q : \Sigma^* \times \Sigma^* \to \mathbb{N}$ and a subset $S \subseteq \Sigma^*$, and is denoted $Q[S]$. Note that, although a problem above is defined as a mapping from Σ^* to $\mathbb{N}$, here we work with a problem that is a mapping from $\Sigma^* \times \Sigma^*$ to $\mathbb{N}$; this is natural in the current paper, where an input to the studied problem consists of two parts, a formula and a structure. Note that a mapping $\Sigma^* \times \Sigma^* \to \mathbb{N}$ can be naturally viewed as a mapping $\Sigma^* \to \mathbb{N}$, as there are natural and well-known ways to encode the elements of $\Sigma^* \times \Sigma^*$ as elements of Σ^*. For each case problem $Q[S]$, we define param-$Q[S]$ as the parameterized problem (P, π_1) where $P(s, x)$ is defined as equal to $Q(s, x)$ if $s \in S$, and as 0 otherwise.

We have the following reduction notion for case problems.

DEFINITION 2.7. *A* counting slice reduction *from a case problem $Q[S]$ to a second case problem $Q'[S']$ consists of*

- *a computably enumerable language $U \subseteq \Sigma^* \times \wp_{\mathsf{fin}}(\Sigma^*)$, and*

- *a partial function $r : \Sigma^* \times \wp_{\mathsf{fin}}(\Sigma^*) \times \Sigma^* \to \Sigma^*$ that has domain $U \times \Sigma^*$ and is FPT-computable with respect to (π_1, π_2) via an algorithm A that, on input (s, T, y), may make queries of the form $Q'(t, z)$ where $t \in T$,*

such that the following conditions hold:

- *(coverage) for each $s \in S$, there exists $T \subseteq S'$ such that $(s, T) \in U$, and*

- *(correctness) for each $(s, T) \in U$, it holds (for each $y \in \Sigma^*$) that $Q(s, y) = r(s, T, y)$.*

Let us provide some intuition for this definition. Here, when discussing an instance (s, y) of a case problem, we refer to the first part s as the parameter. The role of U is to provide all pairs (s, T) such that instances (of the first problem) with parameter s can be reduced to instances (of the second problem) whose parameters lie in T. Correspondingly, the *coverage* condition posits that each $s \in S$ is covered by the second set S' in the sense that there exists a pair $(s, T) \in U$ with $T \subseteq S'$. The partial function r is the actual reduction; given a pair $(s, T) \in U$ along with a string y, it computes the value $Q(s, y)$—this is what the *correctness* condition asserts. As here in this article we are dealing with counting complexity, we permit a form of Turing reduction; so, the algorithm A of the partial function r, upon being given a triple (s, T, y), may make (possibly multiple) queries to the second problem, so long as the queries are about instances whose parameter falls into T.

We have the following key property of counting slice reducibility.

THEOREM 2.8. *[6] Counting slice reducibility is transitive.*

The following theorem shows that, from a counting slice reduction, one can obtain complexity results for the corresponding parameterized problems.

THEOREM 2.9. *[6] Let $Q[S]$ and $Q'[S']$ be case problems. Suppose that $Q[S]$ counting slice reduces to $Q'[S']$, and that both S and S' are computable. Then* param-$Q[S]$ *counting FPT-reduces to* param-$Q'[S']$.

2.4 Classification of pp-formulas

We present the complexity classification of pp-formulas previously presented in [6, 7]. The following definitions are adapted from that article. Let $(\mathbf{A}, S)$ be a prenex pp-formula, let $\mathbf{D}$ be the core thereof, and let $G = (D, E)$ be the graph of $\mathbf{D}$. An *$\exists$-component* of $(\mathbf{A}, S)$ is a graph of the form $G[V']$ where there exists $V \subseteq D$ that is the vertex set of a component of $G[D \backslash S]$ and V' is the union of V with all vertices in S having an edge to V. Define $\mathsf{contract}(\mathbf{A}, S)$ to be the graph on vertex set S obtained by starting from $G[S]$ and adding an edge between any two vertices that appear together in an $\exists$-component of $(\mathbf{A}, S)$.

Let Φ be a set of prenex pp-formulas. Let us say that Φ satisfies the *contraction condition* if the graphs in the set $\mathsf{contract}(\Phi) := \{\mathsf{contract}(\phi) \mid \phi \in \Phi\}$ are of bounded treewidth. Let us say that Φ satisfies the *tractability condition* if it satisfies the contraction condition and, in addition, the cores of Φ are of bounded treewidth; here, the treewidth of a prenex pp-formula is defined as that of its graph. We omit the definition of treewidth, as it is both well-known and not needed to understand the main technical proof of this article (which is in Section 5).

DEFINITION 2.10. *We define* count *to be the problem that maps a pair $(\phi(V), \mathbf{B})$ consisting of a fo-formula and a finite structure to the value $|\phi(\mathbf{B})|$.*

THEOREM 2.11. *[6] Let Φ be a set of prenex pp-formulas that satisfies the tractability condition. Then, the restriction of* param-count$[\Phi]$ *to $\Phi \times \Sigma^*$ is an FPT-computable partial function.*

THEOREM 2.12. *[6] Let Φ be a set of prenex pp-formulas of bounded arity that does not satisfy the tractability condition.*

1. *If Φ satisfies the contraction condition, then it holds that* count$[\Phi]$ *and* CLIQUE$[\mathbb{N}]$ *are interreducible, under counting slice reductions.*

2. *Otherwise, there exists a counting slice reduction from* #CLIQUE$[\mathbb{N}]$ *to* count$[\Phi]$.

We say that a set of formulas Φ has *bounded arity* if there exists a constant $k \geqslant 1$ that upper bounds the arity of each relation symbol appearing in a formula in Φ.

3. MAIN THEOREMS

The following theorem, which we call the *equivalence theorem* and which is proved in Section 5, is our primary technical result; it is used to derive our complexity trichotomy on ep-formulas from the known complexity trichotomy on pp-formulas (which was presented in Section 2.4).

THEOREM 3.1. *(Equivalence theorem) Let Φ be a set of ep-formulas. There exists a set Φ^+ of prenex pp-formulas with the following property: the two counting case problems* count$[\Phi]$ *and* count$[\Phi^+]$ *are interreducible under counting slice reductions. In particular, there exists an algorithm that computes, given an ep-formula ϕ, a finite set ϕ^+ of prenex pp-formulas such that for any set Φ of ep-formulas, the set Φ^+ defined as $\bigcup\{\phi^+ \mid \phi \in \Phi\}$ has the presented property.*

We now state our trichotomy theorem on the complexity of counting answers to ep-formulas, and show how to prove it using the equivalence theorem.

THEOREM 3.2. *(Trichotomy theorem) Let Φ be a computable set of ep-formulas of bounded arity, and let Φ^+ be the set of pp-formulas given by Theorem 3.1.*

1. *If Φ^+ satisfies the tractability condition, then it holds that* param-count$[\Phi]$ *is in FPT.*

2. *If Φ^+ does not satisfy the tractability condition but satisfies the contraction condition, then it holds that* param-count$[\Phi]$ *is interreducible with p-*CLIQUE *under counting FPT-reduction.*

3. *Otherwise, there is a counting FPT-reduction from the problem p-#*CLIQUE *to* param-count$[\Phi]$.

PROOF. For (1), we use the counting slice reduction (U, r) from $\mathsf{count}[\Phi]$ to $\mathsf{count}[\Phi^+]$ given by Theorem 3.1. In particular, given as input $(\phi, \mathbf{B})$, it is first checked if $\phi \in \Phi$; if not, 0 is output. Otherwise, the algorithm for r is invoked on $(\phi, \phi^+, \mathbf{B})$, where ϕ^+ is as defined in the statement of Theorem 3.1; queries to $\mathsf{count}(\psi, \mathbf{B})$ where $\psi \in \Phi^+$ are resolved according to the algorithm of Theorem 2.11.

For (2) and (3), we make use of the result (Theorem 3.1) that the problems $\mathsf{count}[\Phi]$ and $\mathsf{count}[\Phi^+]$ are interreducible under counting slice reductions. For (2), we have from Theorem 2.12 that $\mathsf{count}[\Phi^+]$ and CLIQUE[$\mathbb{N}$] are interreducible under counting slice reductions. Hence, we obtain that the problems CLIQUE[$\mathbb{N}$] and $\mathsf{count}[\Phi]$ are interreducible under counting slice reductions, and the result follows from Theorem 2.9. For (3), we have from Theorem 2.12 that there is a counting slice reduction from #CLIQUE[$\mathbb{N}$] to $\mathsf{count}[\Phi^+]$, and hence from #CLIQUE[$\mathbb{N}$] to $\mathsf{count}[\Phi]$; the result then follows from Theorem 2.9. □

Let us remark that when case (2) applies, a consequence of this theorem is that the problem $\mathsf{param\text{-}count}[\Phi]$ is not in FPT unless W[1] is in FPT, since p-CLIQUE is W[1]-complete; in a similar fashion, when case (3) applies, the problem $\mathsf{param\text{-}count}[\Phi]$ is not in FPT unless ♯W[1] is in FPT, since p-#CLIQUE is ♯W[1]-complete.

4. EXAMPLES

Before proving the equivalence theorem in full generality, we discuss some example ep-formulas to illustrate and preview some of the issues and difficulties with which the argument needs to cope.

EXAMPLE 4.1. *Consider the formula*

$$\phi(w, x, y, z) := E(x, y) \wedge (E(w, x) \vee (E(y, z) \wedge E(z, z))).$$

As a first simplification step, we bring disjunction to the outermost level in ϕ:

$$\phi(w, x, y, z) \equiv (E(x, y) \wedge E(w, x)) \vee (E(x, y) \wedge E(y, z) \wedge E(z, z)).$$

Now let us set $\phi_1(w, x, y, z) \equiv E(x, y) \wedge E(w, x)$ and also set $\phi_2(w, x, y, z) \equiv E(x, y) \wedge E(y, z) \wedge E(z, z)$. We can use inclusion-exclusion to count the number of satisfying assignments of ϕ on a structure $\mathbf{B}$ by

$$|\phi(\mathbf{B})| = |\phi_1(\mathbf{B})| + |\phi_2(\mathbf{B})| - |(\phi_1 \wedge \phi_2)(\mathbf{B})|.$$

One point to observe is that, in this last expression, the count $|\phi_1(\mathbf{B})|$ needs to be determined with respect to its set of liberal variabes $\mathrm{lib}(\phi_1) = \{w, x, y, z\}$, even though z does not appear in any atom of ϕ_1. If the count $|\phi_1(\mathbf{B})|$ is not computed in this way, the above expression for $|\phi(\mathbf{B})|$ fails to hold in general. The situation is analogous for the formula ϕ_2, where w does not appear in any atom. □

EXAMPLE 4.2. *In general, if we are given an ep-formula $\phi = \phi_1 \vee \ldots \vee \phi_n$ where the ϕ_i are pp-formulas, then to compute the count $|\phi(\mathbf{B})|$ of ϕ relative to $\mathbf{B}$, it suffices to know the count for each of the $2^n - 1$ pp-formulas obtained by taking a conjunction of a non-empty subset of the ϕ_i. In this example, we will see that, in fact, one does not always need to consider all of these conjunctions. To this end, set $V = \{w, x, y, z\}$ and set*

$$\phi(V) = \phi_1(V) \vee \phi_2(V) \vee \phi_3(V)$$

where $\phi_1(V) = E(x, y) \wedge E(y, z)$, $\phi_2(V) = E(z, w) \wedge E(w, x)$ and $\phi_3(V) = E(w, x) \wedge E(x, y)$. Applying inclusion-exclusion, we obtain

$$\begin{aligned} |\phi(\mathbf{B})| = &|\phi_1(\mathbf{B})| + |\phi_2(\mathbf{B})| + |\phi_3(\mathbf{B})| \\ &- |(\phi_1 \wedge \phi_2)(\mathbf{B})| - |(\phi_1 \wedge \phi_3)(\mathbf{B})| \\ &- |(\phi_2 \wedge \phi_3)(\mathbf{B})| + |(\phi_1 \wedge \phi_2 \wedge \phi_3)(\mathbf{B})|. \end{aligned}$$

Now observe that the formulas ϕ_1, ϕ_2 and ϕ_3 are actually equivalent to each other up to renaming variables; consequently, these formulas are equivalent in that, for any structure $\mathbf{B}$, they yield the same count: $|\phi_1(\mathbf{B})| = |\phi_2(\mathbf{B})| = |\phi_3(\mathbf{B})|$. In Section 5.1, we formalize and give a characterization of this notion of equivalence (on pp-formulas). The formulas $\phi_1 \wedge \phi_3$ and $\phi_2 \wedge \phi_3$ are also equivalent in this sense. We may thus obtain the following expression for $|\phi(\mathbf{B})|$.

$$\begin{aligned} |\phi(\mathbf{B})| = &3 \cdot |\phi_1(\mathbf{B})| - |(\phi_1 \wedge \phi_2)(\mathbf{B})| \\ &- 2 \cdot |(\phi_1 \wedge \phi_3)(\mathbf{B})| + |(\phi_1 \wedge \phi_2 \wedge \phi_3)(\mathbf{B})|. \end{aligned}$$

So far, we have only unified formulas that are equivalent up to renaming variables. In our parameterized complexity setting where ϕ is the parameter, this does not yield a significant decrease in the complexity of computing $|\phi(\mathbf{B})|$. However, we will now observe a simplification that is more substantial in this sense. Namely, one can verify that the formulas $\phi_1 \wedge \phi_2$ and $\phi_1 \wedge \phi_2 \wedge \phi_3$ are identical. So, if we identify their terms in this last expression for $|\phi(\mathbf{B})|$, we obtain a cancellation and arrive to the following expression:

$$|\phi(\mathbf{B})| = 3 \cdot |\phi_1(\mathbf{B})| - 2 \cdot |(\phi_1 \wedge \phi_3)(\mathbf{B})|.$$

The savings obtained by observing this cancellation are significant, in the following sense. The pp-formulas $\phi_1 \wedge \phi_2$ and $\phi_1 \wedge \phi_2 \wedge \phi_3$, which were cancelled, were the only formulas in the expression for $|\phi(\mathbf{B})|$ which did not have treewidth 1; they had treewidth 2. As it is known that the runtime of evaluation algorithms for quantifier-free pp-formulas scales with their treewidth [15], this reduction in treewidth yields a superior runtime for evaluating $|\phi(\mathbf{B})|$. □

As we have seen in the above examples, counting on an ep-formula can, via inclusion-exclusion, reduce to counting on a finite set of pp-formulas. (This is carried out in our argument; see Section 5.3). As just seen in Example 4.2, there can be some subtlety in choosing a desirable set of pp-formulas to reduce to. One question not addressed so far is how one can reduce from counting on a such obtained set of pp-formulas to counting on the original ep-formula. To this end, let us revisit our first example.

EXAMPLE 4.3. *Let us consider again the formulas of Example 4.1. Assume that we are given access to an oracle that lets us compute $|\phi(\mathbf{D})|$, for any structure $\mathbf{D}$ of our choice. We will see that, given a structure $\mathbf{B}$, we can compute $|\phi_1(\mathbf{B})|$, $|\phi_2(\mathbf{B})|$, and $|(\phi_1 \wedge \phi_2)(\mathbf{B})|$ efficiently using this oracle.*

To see this, consider the structure $\mathbf{C}$ with universe $C = \{1, 2, 3, 4\}$ and $E^{\mathbf{C}} = \{(1, 2), (2, 3), (3, 4), (4, 4)\}$. It is easy to check that the formulas ϕ_1, ϕ_2 and $\phi_1 \wedge \phi_2$ all have a different number of answers with respect to $\mathbf{C}$. Now note that for every pp-formula ψ and every pair of structures $\mathbf{D}_1$, $\mathbf{D}_2$ we have $|\psi(\mathbf{D}_1 \times \mathbf{D}_2)| = |\psi(\mathbf{D}_1)| \cdot |\psi(\mathbf{D}_2)|$. Querying the oracle for $|\phi(\cdot)|$ on $\mathbf{B} \times \mathbf{C}^i$ for the values $i = 0, 1, 2$, we *obtain the linear system*

$$A\begin{pmatrix}|\phi_1(\mathbf{B})|\\ |\phi_2(\mathbf{B})|\\ -|(\phi_1 \wedge \phi_2)(\mathbf{B})|\end{pmatrix} = \begin{pmatrix}(\phi(\mathbf{B})\\ \phi(\mathbf{B}\times\mathbf{C})\\ \phi(\mathbf{B}\times\mathbf{C}^2)\end{pmatrix}$$

with

$$A = \begin{pmatrix}1 & 1 & 1\\ |\phi_1(\mathbf{C})| & |\phi_2(\mathbf{C})| & |(\phi_1 \wedge \phi_2)(\mathbf{C})|\\ |\phi_1(\mathbf{C})|^2 & |\phi_2(\mathbf{C})|^2 & |(\phi_1 \wedge \phi_2)(\mathbf{C})|^2\end{pmatrix}.$$

Note that the entries of A can be computed efficiently, and the vector on the right-hand-side of the equation can be provided by our oracle. The matrix A is a Vandermonde matrix, as a consequence of the choice of $\mathbf{C}$. Thus, the system has a unique solution and can be solved to determine $|\phi_1(\mathbf{B})|$, $|\phi_2(\mathbf{B})|$, and $|(\phi_1 \wedge \phi_2)(\mathbf{B})|$, as desired. □

In Example 4.3 we have seen that, for the particular ep-formula ϕ discussed, counting on ϕ is in a certain sense interreducible with counting on the pp-formulas

$$\{\phi_1, \phi_2, \phi_1 \wedge \phi_2\}.$$

The statement of the equivalence theorem (Theorem 3.1) asserts that for *any* ep-formula ϕ, there exists a finite set ϕ^+ of pp-formulas such that one has this interreducibility.

5. PROOF OF EQUIVALENCE THEOREM

In this section, we give a decidable characterization of *counting equivalence* (Section 5.1); we then study a relaxation thereof which we call *semi-counting equivalence* (Section 5.2); we prove the equivalence theorem in the particular case of all-free ep-formulas (Section 5.3); and, we end by proving the equivalence theorem in its full generality (Section 5.4). Throughout this section, we generally assume pp-formulas to be prenex.

5.1 Counting equivalence

As we have seen in the examples of Section 4, it will be important to see when two different pp-formulas give same number of answers for every structure, because it will allow us to make simplifications in formulas we get by inclusion-exclusion. To this end, we make the following definition.

DEFINITION 5.1. *Define two fo-formulas $\phi(V), \phi'(V')$ to be* counting equivalent *if they are over the same vocabulary τ and for each finite τ-structure $\mathbf{B}$ it holds that $|\phi(\mathbf{B})| = |\phi'(\mathbf{B})|$.*

In this subsection, we characterize counting equivalence for pp-formulas. To approach the characterization, we start off with an example.

EXAMPLE 5.2. *It is apparent that logically equivalent formulas are counting equivalent, but the converse direction is not true. To see this, consider the pp-formulas $\phi_1(x, y) = E(x, y)$ and $\phi_2(w, z) = E(w, z)$. Obviously, ϕ_1 and ϕ_2 are counting equivalent (they just count the number of tuples in the relation E of a structure $\mathbf{B}$). But ϕ_1 and ϕ_2 are not logically equivalent; indeed, the assignments in $\phi_1(\mathbf{B})$ and $\phi_2(\mathbf{B})$ assign values to different variables.*

Note that one way of witnessing the counting equivalence of ϕ_1 and ϕ_2 is simply renaming the variable w to x and z to y to get equivalent formulas. Since this syntactic renaming obviously does not change the number of satisfying assignments, one can conclude that ϕ_1 and ϕ_2 are counting equivalent. □

Example 5.2 motivates the following definition.

DEFINITION 5.3. *We say that two pp-formulas*

$$(\mathbf{A}, S), (\mathbf{A}', S')$$

over the same signature are renaming equivalent *if there exist surjections $h : S \to S'$ and $h' : S' \to S$ that can be extended to homomorphisms $\bar{h} : \mathbf{A} \to \mathbf{A}'$ and $\bar{h}' : \mathbf{A}' \to \mathbf{A}$, respectively.*

Informally speaking, on pp-formulas, two formulas are renaming equivalent if they become logically equivalent after a renaming of variables, as occurred in Example 5.2. Hence, renaming equivalence is a relaxation of logical equivalence. Recall that logical equivalence of pp-formulas was characterized, in Theorem 2.3.

The main theorem of this subsection is that renaming equivalence does not only imply counting equivalence but is actually equivalent to it.

THEOREM 5.4. *Two pp-formulas*

$$\phi_1(S_1), \phi_2(S_2)$$

are counting equivalent if and only if they are renaming equivalent.

Note that Theorem 5.4 gives a syntactic/algebraic characterization of counting equivalence which makes counting equivalence decidable by a straightforward algorithm and in fact even puts it into NP.

Before we prove Theorem 5.4, we start off with an simple observation that will be helpful in the proof.

OBSERVATION 5.5. *Let ϕ and ϕ' be counting equivalent pp-formulas. Then $|\mathrm{lib}(\phi)| = |\mathrm{lib}(\phi')|$.*

PROOF. Let $\mathbf{C}$ be a structure that interprets every relation symbol in R of ϕ by $R^{\mathbf{C}} := \{0, 1\}^{\mathsf{arity}(R)}$. Then $|\phi(\mathbf{C})| = 2^{|\mathrm{lib}(\phi)|}$ and $|\phi'(\mathbf{C})| = 2^{|\mathrm{lib}(\phi')|}$ and the claim follows directly. □

PROOF. (Theorem 5.4) We begin with the backward direction; let $h_1 : S_1 \to S_2$ and $h_2 : S_2 \to S_1$ be the surjections from the definition of renaming equivalence. The existence of these surjections implies that $|S_1| = |S_2|$ and that each of h_1, h_2 is a bijection. Let $\mathbf{B}$ be an arbitrary structure. For each $f : S_2 \to B$ in $\phi_2(\mathbf{B})$, it is straightforward to verify that the composition $f(h_1)$ is in $\phi_1(\mathbf{B})$. Since the mapping that takes each such f to $f(h_1)$ is injective (due to h_1 being a bijection), we obtain that $|\phi_1(\mathbf{B})| \geqslant |\phi_2(\mathbf{B})|$. By symmetric reasoning, we can obtain that $|\phi_1(\mathbf{B})| \leqslant |\phi_2(\mathbf{B})|$, and we conclude that $|\phi_1(\mathbf{B})| = |\phi_2(\mathbf{B})|$.

For the other direction, let $\phi_1(S_1)$ and $\phi_2(S_2)$ be two pp-formulas over a common vocabulary τ that are not renaming equivalent; let $(\mathbf{A}_1, S_1)$ and $(\mathbf{A}_2, S_2)$ be the corresponding structures. By way of contradiction, assume that ϕ_1 and ϕ_2 are counting equivalent. If it holds that $|\mathrm{lib}(\phi_1)| \neq |\mathrm{lib}(\phi_2)|$, we are done by Observation 5.5. So we may assume, after potentially renaming some variables, that $\mathrm{lib}(\phi_1) = \mathrm{lib}(\phi_2) =: S$.

When $\mathbf{C}, \mathbf{D}$ are structures with $S \subseteq C \cap D$, let us define $\hom(\mathbf{C}, \mathbf{D}, S)$ to be the set of mappings from S to D

that can be extended to a homomorphism from $\mathbf{C}$ to $\mathbf{D}$; denote by $\text{surj}(\mathbf{C}, \mathbf{D}, S)$ the surjections $h : S \to S$ that lie in $\text{hom}(\mathbf{C}, \mathbf{D}, S)$.

As $(\mathbf{A}_1, S_1)$ and $(\mathbf{A}_2, S_2)$ are by hypothesis not renaming equivalent, we may assume, without loss of generality, that $\text{surj}(\mathbf{A}_1, \mathbf{A}_2, S) = \varnothing$. For $T \subseteq S$ let us use $\text{hom}_T(\mathbf{A}_1, \mathbf{A}_2, S)$ to denote the set of mappings $h \in \text{hom}(\mathbf{A}_1, \mathbf{A}_2, S)$ such that $h(S) \subseteq T$. By inclusion-exclusion we get

$$|\text{surj}(\phi_1, \phi_2, S)| = \sum_{T \subseteq S} (-1)^{|S|-|T|} |\text{hom}_T(\mathbf{A}_1, \mathbf{A}_2, S)|.$$

For $i \geqslant 0$ let $\text{hom}_{i,T}(\mathbf{A}_1, \mathbf{A}_2, S)$ be the set of mappings $h \in \text{hom}(\mathbf{A}_1, \mathbf{A}_2, S)$ such that h maps exactly i variables from S into T. Now for each $j = 1, \ldots, |S|$ we construct a new structure $\mathbf{D}_{j,T}$ over the domain $D_{j,T}$. To this end, let $a^{(1)}, \ldots, a^{(j)}$ be copies of $a \in T$ that are not in A_2. Then we set

$$D_{j,T} := \{a^{(k)} \mid a \in A_2, a \in T, k \in [j]\} \cup (A_2 \backslash T).$$

We define a mapping $B : A_2 \to \mathcal{P}(D_{j,T})$, where $\mathcal{P}(D_{j,T})$ is the power set of $D_{j,T}$, by

$$B(a) := \begin{cases} \{a^{(k)} \mid k \in [j]\}\}, & \text{if } a \in T \\ \{a\}, & \text{otherwise.} \end{cases}$$

For every relation symbol $R \in \tau$ we define

$$R^{\mathbf{D}_{T,j}} := \bigcup_{(d_1,\ldots,d_s) \in R^{\mathbf{A}_2}} B(d_1) \times \ldots \times B(d_s).$$

Then every $h \in \text{hom}_{i,T}(\mathbf{A}_1, \mathbf{A}_2, S)$ corresponds to j^i mappings in $\text{hom}(\mathbf{A}_1, \mathbf{D}_{j,T}, S)$. Thus for each j we get

$$\sum_{i=1}^{|S|} j^i |\text{hom}_{i,T}(\mathbf{A}_1, \mathbf{A}_2, S)| = |\text{hom}(\mathbf{A}_1, \mathbf{D}_{j,T}, S)|.$$

This is a linear system of equations and the corresponding matrix is a Vandermonde matrix; consequently, the value $\text{hom}_T(\mathbf{A}_1, \mathbf{A}_2, S) = \text{hom}_{|S|,T}(\mathbf{A}_1, \mathbf{A}_2, S)$ can efficiently be computed from $|\text{hom}(\mathbf{A}_1, \mathbf{D}, S)| = |\phi_1(\mathbf{D})|$ for some structures $\mathbf{D}$. We can similarly determine $|\text{hom}_T(\mathbf{A}_2, \mathbf{D}, S)|$ as a function of $|\phi_2(\mathbf{D})|$ for the same structures $\mathbf{D}$. Since $|\phi_1(\mathbf{D})| = |\phi_2(\mathbf{D})|$ for every structure $\mathbf{D}$ by assumption, it follows that for every subset $T \subseteq S$ we have

$$|\text{hom}_T(\mathbf{A}_1, \mathbf{A}_2, S)| = |\text{hom}_T(\mathbf{A}_2, \mathbf{A}_2, S)|.$$

But then we have

$$|\text{surj}(\mathbf{A}_1, \mathbf{A}_2, S)| = |\text{surj}(\mathbf{A}_2, \mathbf{A}_2, S)|.$$

Since $\text{surj}(\mathbf{A}_1, \mathbf{A}_2, S) = \varnothing$ and $\text{id} \in \text{surj}(\mathbf{A}_2, \mathbf{A}_2, S)$, this is a contradiction. Consequently, we obtain that ϕ_1 and ϕ_2 are not counting equivalent. □

5.2 Semi-counting equivalence

In this subsection, we study a relaxation of the notion of *counting equivalence*. This notion will be necessary when we emulate the approach of Example 4.3 in the proof of the Equivalence theorem: we will again construct a system of linear equations that we want to solve. In order to ensure solvability, we will make sure that the matrix of the system is again a Vandermonde matrix which in particular means that all its entries must be positive. Consequently, since the entries are of the form $|\phi(\mathbf{C})|^k$ for pp-formulas ϕ some carefully chosen structure $\mathbf{C}$ and integers k, it will be necessary to understand counting equivalence in the case where $\phi(\mathbf{C})$ is non-empty. The necessary notion is formalized by the following definition.

DEFINITION 5.6. *Call two prenex pp-formulas*

$$\phi_1(V_1), \phi_2(V_2)$$

on the same vocabulary semi-counting equivalent *if for each finite structure* $\mathbf{B}$ *such that* $|\phi_1(\mathbf{B})| > 0$ *and* $|\phi_2(\mathbf{B})| > 0$, *it holds that* $|\phi_1(\mathbf{B})| = |\phi_2(\mathbf{B})|$.

EXAMPLE 5.7. *The pp-formulas* $\phi_1(x, y) = E(x, y)$ *and* $\phi_2(x, y) = \exists z(E(x, y) \wedge F(z))$ *are not counting equivalent, because for every structure* $\mathbf{B}$ *for which* $F^{\mathbf{B}} = \varnothing$, *we have* $|\phi_2(\mathbf{B})| = 0$ *while* $|\phi_1(\mathbf{B})|$ *may be non-zero if* $E^{\mathbf{B}}$ *is non-empty. But if we have for a structure* $\mathbf{B}$ *such that* $|\phi_2(\mathbf{B})| > 0$, *then* $F^{\mathbf{B}} \neq \varnothing$ *and it is straightforward to verify that* $|\phi_1(\mathbf{B})| = |\phi_2(\mathbf{B})|$. *Consequently, we have that* ϕ_1 *and* ϕ_2 *are semi-counting equivalent.* □

For each free prenex pp-formula $\phi(V)$, define $\widehat{\phi}(V)$ to be the pp-formula obtained from ϕ by removing each atom that occurs in a non-liberal component of ϕ (a component of ϕ not having liberal variables).

EXAMPLE 5.8. *Consider the pp-formula* ϕ *discussed in Examples 2.2 and 2.4. This pp-formula has 4 components, namely, the pp-formulas* $\psi_1(x, x')$, $\psi_2(y)$, $\psi_3(z)$, *and* $\psi_4(\varnothing)$ *defined in Example 2.4. The formulas* ψ_1, ψ_2, *and* ψ_3 *are liberal, but the formula* ψ_4 *is not liberal. Recall that the formula* $\phi(x, x', y, z)$ *is equal to*

$$\exists y' \exists u \exists v \exists w (E(x, x') \wedge E(y, y') \wedge F(u, v) \wedge G(u, w))$$

and that we have $\psi_4(\varnothing) = \exists u \exists v \exists w (F(u, v) \wedge G(u, w))$. *We hence have that* $\widehat{\phi}(x, x', y, z)$ *is the formula*

$$\exists y' \exists u \exists v \exists w (E(x, x') \wedge E(y, y')).$$

□

The following characterization of semi-counting equivalence is the main theorem of this subsection.

THEOREM 5.9. *Let* $\phi_1(V_1), \phi_2(V_2)$ *be two free prenex pp-formulas. It holds that* $\phi_1(V_1)$ *and* $\phi_2(V_2)$ *are semi-counting equivalent if and only if* $\widehat{\phi_1}(V_1)$ *and* $\widehat{\phi_2}(V_2)$ *are counting equivalent.*

We will use the following proposition in the proof of Theorem 5.9.

PROPOSITION 5.10. *Let* $\phi(V)$ *be a free prenex pp-formula. Then for every structure* $\mathbf{B}$ *we have* $\phi(\mathbf{B}) = \varnothing$ *or* $\phi(\mathbf{B}) = \widehat{\phi}(\mathbf{B})$.

PROOF. Let $\mathbf{B}$ be a structure. Let ψ be the conjunction of the components deleted from ϕ to obtain $\widehat{\phi}$. If ψ is false on $\mathbf{B}$, then obviously $\phi(\mathbf{B}) = \varnothing$. Otherwise, ψ is true on $\mathbf{B}$, and for any assignment $f : V \to B$, it holds that $\mathbf{B}, f \models \phi$ if and only if $\mathbf{B}, f \models \widehat{\phi}$. □

PROOF. (Theorem 5.9) Assume first that $\widehat{\phi_1}$ and $\widehat{\phi_2}$ are counting equivalent. Let $\mathbf{B}$ be a structure. Then if $|\phi_1(\mathbf{B})| > 0$ and $|\phi_2(\mathbf{B})| > 0$, we have by Proposition 5.10 and counting equivalence of $\widehat{\phi_1}$ and $\widehat{\phi_2}$ that $|\phi_1(\mathbf{B})| = |\widehat{\phi_1}(\mathbf{B})| = |\widehat{\phi_2}(\mathbf{B})| = |\phi_2(\mathbf{B})|$, so ϕ_1 and ϕ_2 are semi-counting equivalent.

For the other direction let now ϕ_1 and ϕ_2 be semi-counting equivalent. By way of contradiction, we assume that $\widehat{\phi_1}$ and $\widehat{\phi_2}$ are not counting equivalent. Then by definition there is a structure $\mathbf{B}$ such that $|\widehat{\phi_1}(\mathbf{B})| \neq |\widehat{\phi_2}(\mathbf{B})|$. Note that each component of $\widehat{\phi_1}$ and $\widehat{\phi_2}$ has a liberal variable.

Let $\mathbf{I} = \mathbf{I}_\tau$, where τ is the vocabulary of ϕ_1 and ϕ_2. For each $k \in \mathbb{N}$ we denote by $\mathbf{B} + k\mathbf{I}$ the structure we get from $\mathbf{B}$ by disjoint union with k copies of $\mathbf{I}$. Note that for $k > 0$ we have $|\phi(\mathbf{B} + k\mathbf{I})| > 0$ for every pp-formula ϕ. Consequently, for every $k > 0$ we have $|\phi_1(\mathbf{B} + k\mathbf{I})| = |\widehat{\phi_1}(\mathbf{B} + k\mathbf{I})|$ and $|\phi_2(\mathbf{B} + k\mathbf{I})| = |\widehat{\phi_2}(\mathbf{B} + k\mathbf{I})|$ by Proposition 5.10. By the semi-counting equivalence of ϕ_1 and ϕ_2 we also have $|\phi_1(\mathbf{B}+k\mathbf{I})| = |\phi_2(\mathbf{B} + k\mathbf{I})|$ for all $k > 0$. It follows that $|\widehat{\phi_1}(\mathbf{B} + k\mathbf{I})| = |\widehat{\phi_2}(\mathbf{B} + k\mathbf{I})|$ for $k > 0$.

Let $\phi_{1,1}, \ldots, \phi_{1,n}$ denote the components of $\widehat{\phi_1}$, and let $\phi_{2,1}, \ldots, \phi_{2,m}$ denote the components of $\widehat{\phi_2}$. Because every component of $\widehat{\phi_1}$ has a liberal variable, we have

$$\begin{aligned}|\widehat{\phi_1}(\mathbf{B} + k\mathbf{I})| &= \sum_{J \subseteq [n]} k^{n-|J|} \prod_{j \in J} |\phi_{1,j}(\mathbf{B})| \\ &= \sum_{\ell=0}^{n} k^{n-\ell} \sum_{J \subseteq [n], |J|=\ell} \prod_{j \in J} |\phi_{1,j}(\mathbf{B})|.\end{aligned}$$

We can express $|\widehat{\phi_2}(\mathbf{B} + k\mathbf{I})|$ analogously. The expressions are polynomials in k and they are equal for every positive integer k by the observations above; thus the coefficients of the polynomials must coincide. The coefficients of k^0, namely the values $\prod_{j\in[n]} |\phi_{1,j}(\mathbf{B})|$ and $\prod_{j\in[m]} |\phi_{2,j}(\mathbf{B})|$, are thus equal. But then we get

$$|\widehat{\phi_1}(\mathbf{B})| = \prod_{j\in[n]} |\phi_{1,j}(\mathbf{B})| = \prod_{j\in[m]} |\phi_{2,j}(\mathbf{B})| = |\widehat{\phi_2}(\mathbf{B})|,$$

which is a contradiction to our assumption. □

Corollary 5.11. *Semi-counting equivalence is an equivalence relation (on pp-formulas).*

We now present a lemma that will be of utility; it is proved by induction.

Lemma 5.12. *Let $\phi_1(S_1), \ldots, \phi_n(S_n)$ be pp-formulas over the same vocabulary τ, which are liberal (that is, with each $|S_i| > 0$). Then there is a structure $\mathbf{C}$ (over τ) such that*

- *for all pp-formulas ϕ (over τ) it holds that $|\phi(\mathbf{C})| > 0$, and*
- *for all $i, j \in [n]$ such that ϕ_i and ϕ_j are not semi-counting equivalent, it holds that $|\phi_i(\mathbf{C})| \neq |\phi_j(\mathbf{C})|$.*

In order to establish this lemma, we first prove the following lemma.

Lemma 5.13. *Let $\phi_1(S_1)$ and $\phi_2(S_2)$ be two pp-formulas over a vocabulary τ that are not semi-counting equivalent. Then there is a structure $\mathbf{D}$ such that for every primitive positive formula ϕ over τ we have $|\phi(\mathbf{D})| > 0$ and $|\phi_1(\mathbf{D})| \neq |\phi_2(\mathbf{D})|$.*

Proof. Let $\mathbf{B}$ be any structure on which ϕ_1 and ϕ_2 have a non-zero but different number of solutions. Such a structure exists by definition of semi-counting equivalence. We claim that we can choose $\mathbf{D} = \mathbf{B} + k\mathbf{I}$ for some $k \in \mathbb{N}, k > 0$ where $\mathbf{B} + k\mathbf{I}$ is defined as in the proof of Theorem 5.9. By way of contradiction, assume that $|\phi_1(\mathbf{B} + k\mathbf{I})| = |\phi_2(\mathbf{B} + k\mathbf{I})|$ for all $k \in \mathbb{N}, k > 0$. Then with the same argument as in the proof of Theorem 5.9 we get the contradiction that $|\phi_1(\mathbf{B})| = |\phi_2(\mathbf{B})|$. □

Proof. (Lemma 5.12) We prove this by induction on n; the case $n = 2$ is implied by Lemma 5.13.

When $n > 2$, we first observe that it suffices to prove the result when the ϕ_i are pairwise not semi-counting equivalent, so we assume that this holds. Let $\mathbf{D}$ be the structure that we get by induction for $\phi_1, \ldots, \phi_{n-1}$. We may assume w.l.o.g. that

$$|\phi_1(\mathbf{D})| < |\phi_2(\mathbf{D})| < \ldots < |\phi_{n-1}(\mathbf{D})|.$$

If it holds that $|\phi_n(\mathbf{D})| \neq |\phi_i(\mathbf{D})|$ for every $i \in [n-1]$, then we are done. So we assume that there is an index $i \in [n-1]$ such that $|\phi_n(\mathbf{D})| = |\phi_i(\mathbf{D})|$.

Let $\mathbf{D}'$ be the structure we get by applying Lemma 5.13 to ϕ_n and ϕ_i.

Now choose k such that for every j with $1 < j \leqslant i$ we have

$$\frac{|\phi_{j-1}(\mathbf{D})|^k}{|\phi_j(\mathbf{D})|^k} < \frac{1}{|\mathrm{lib}(\phi_{j-1})|^{|D'|}}.$$

Then we have for every $\ell \geqslant k$ and $1 < j < i$

$$\begin{aligned}|\phi_{j-1}(\mathbf{D}^\ell \times \mathbf{D}')| &= |\phi_{j-1}(\mathbf{D}^\ell)| \cdot |\phi_{j-1}(\mathbf{D}')| \\ &\leqslant |\phi_{j-1}(\mathbf{D}^\ell)| \cdot |\mathrm{lib}(\phi_{j-1})|^{|D'|} \\ &< |\phi_j(\mathbf{D}^\ell)| \\ &\leqslant |\phi_j(\mathbf{D}^\ell)| \cdot |\phi_j(\mathbf{D}')| \\ &= |\phi_j(\mathbf{D}^\ell \times \mathbf{D}')|.\end{aligned}$$

Analogously, we get for every $\ell > k$ that

$$|\phi_{i-1}(\mathbf{D}^\ell \times \mathbf{D}')| < |\phi_n(\mathbf{D}^\ell \times \mathbf{D}')|.$$

Now choose k' such that for every j with $i \leqslant j < n$ we have

$$\frac{|\phi_{j+1}(\mathbf{D})|^{k'}}{|\phi_j(\mathbf{D})|^{k'}} > |\mathrm{lib}(\phi_j)|^{|D'|}.$$

Then we have for every $\ell > k'$ and every $i \leqslant j < n$

$$\begin{aligned}|\phi_j(\mathbf{D}^\ell \times \mathbf{D}')| &= |\phi_j(\mathbf{D}^\ell)| \cdot |\phi_j(\mathbf{D}')| \\ &\leqslant |\phi_j(\mathbf{D}^\ell)| \cdot |\mathrm{lib}(\phi_j)|^{|D'|} \\ &< |\phi_{j+1}(\mathbf{D}^\ell)| \\ &\leqslant |\phi_{j+1}(\mathbf{D}^\ell)| \cdot |\phi_j(\mathbf{D}')| \\ &= |\phi_{j+1}(\mathbf{D}^\ell \times \mathbf{D}')|.\end{aligned}$$

Similarly, we get for every $\ell > k$ that

$$|\phi_{i+1}(\mathbf{D}^\ell \times \mathbf{D}')| > |\phi_n(\mathbf{D}^\ell \times \mathbf{D}')|.$$

Now choosing $\ell = \max(k, k')$ and noting that

$$\begin{aligned}|\phi_i(\mathbf{D}^\ell \times \mathbf{D}')| &= |\phi_i(\mathbf{D}^\ell)| \cdot |\phi_i(\mathbf{D}')| \\ &\neq |\phi_n(\mathbf{D}^\ell)| \cdot |\phi_n(\mathbf{D}')| \\ &= |\phi_n(\mathbf{D}^\ell \times \mathbf{D}')|\end{aligned}$$

completes the proof with $\mathbf{C} = \mathbf{D}^\ell \times \mathbf{D}'$. □

The following is a consequence of this lemma.

LEMMA 5.14. *Let $\phi_1(S_1), \dots, \phi_n(S_n)$ be connected, liberal pp-formulas over the same vocabulary τ that are pairwise not counting equivalent. Then there exists a structure $\mathbf{C}$ (over τ) such that*

- *for all pp-formulas ϕ (over τ) it holds that $|\phi(\mathbf{C})| > 0$, and*
- *for all distinct $i, j \in [n]$, it holds that $|\phi_i(\mathbf{C})| \neq |\phi_j(\mathbf{C})|$.*

PROOF. By Lemma 5.12, it suffices to show that the pp-formulas ϕ_i are pairwise not semi-counting equivalent. Since each ϕ_i is connected and liberal, we have $\phi_i = \widehat{\phi_i}$. Thus, by the hypothesis that the ϕ_i are pairwise not counting equivalent in combination with Theorem 5.9, we obtain that the ϕ_i are pairwise not semi-counting equivalent. □

5.3 The all-free case

The aim of this subsection is the proof of Theorem 3.1 in the special case of all-free ep-formulas. Recall that an ep-formula is *all-free* if it is the disjunction of prenex pp-formulas, each of which is *free* in that it has a non-empty set of free variables. We will later in Section 5.4 use the result on all-free formulas to prove the general version of Theorem 3.1.

For every $\phi(V) \in \Phi$ we define a set ϕ^* of free pp-formulas; then, we define $\Phi^* = \bigcup_{\phi \in \Phi} \phi^*(V)$. Let $\phi(V) = \phi_1(V) \vee \dots \vee \phi_s(V)$ where the $\phi_i(V)$ are free pp-formulas. By inclusion-exclusion we have for every structure $\mathbf{B}$ that

$$\begin{aligned} |\phi(\mathbf{B})| &= \sum_{J \in [s]} (-1)^{|J|+1} |(\bigwedge_{j \in J} \phi_j)(\mathbf{B})| \\ &= \sum_{J \in [s]} (-1)^{|J|+1} |\phi_J(\mathbf{B})|, \end{aligned} \quad (1)$$

where the $\phi_J(V) = \bigwedge_{j \in J} \phi_j(V)$ are pp-formulas. Now iteratively do the following: If there are two summands $c|\phi_J(\mathbf{B})|$ and $c'|\phi_{J'}(\mathbf{B})|$ such that ϕ_J and $\phi_{J'}$ are counting equivalent, delete both summands and add $(c + c')|\phi_J|$ to the sum. When this operation can no longer be applied, delete all summands with coefficient zero. The pp-formulas that remain in the sum form the set ϕ^*.

EXAMPLE 5.15. *It shall be advantageous to again consider Example 4.2. There we started off with*

$$\phi(V) = \phi_1(V) \vee \phi_2(V) \vee \phi_3(V).$$

Inclusion-exclusion yields

$$\begin{aligned} |\phi(\mathbf{B})| =& |\phi_1(\mathbf{B})| + |\phi_2(\mathbf{B})| + |\phi_3(\mathbf{B})| \\ &- |(\phi_1 \wedge \phi_2)(\mathbf{B})| - |(\phi_1 \wedge \phi_3)(\mathbf{B})| \\ &- |(\phi_2 \wedge \phi_3)(\mathbf{B})| + |(\phi_1 \wedge \phi_2 \wedge \phi_3)(\mathbf{B})|. \end{aligned}$$

Now we simplify as described above and get

$$|\phi(\mathbf{B})| = 3 \cdot |\phi_1(\mathbf{B})| - 2 \cdot |(\phi_1 \wedge \phi_3)(\mathbf{B})|.$$

Consequently, for this example we have

$$\phi^* = \{\phi_1, \phi_1 \wedge \phi_3\}.$$

□

The algorithm discussed above directly yields the following proposition.

PROPOSITION 5.16. *There exists an algorithm that, when an all-free ep-formula ϕ is given as input, outputs a set $\phi^* := \{\phi_1^*, \dots, \phi_\ell^*\}$ of free pp-formulas, which are pairwise not counting equivalent, and coefficients $c_1, \dots, c_\ell \in \mathbb{Z}\backslash\{0\}$ such that for every structure $\mathbf{B}$, $|\phi(\mathbf{B})| = \sum_{i=1}^{\ell} c_i |\phi_i^*(\mathbf{B})|$.*

We will also require the following two facts for our proof.

PROPOSITION 5.17. *Let us presume that $\phi(S)$ and $\phi'(S')$ are two semi-counting equivalent free pp-formulas that are not counting equivalent and let $(\mathbf{A}, S)$ and $(\mathbf{A}', S')$ be the structures of ϕ and ϕ', respectively. Then $\mathbf{A}$ and $\mathbf{A}'$ are not homomorphically equivalent.*

PROOF. $\phi(S)$ and $\phi'(S')$ are semi-counting equivalent, so we have by Theorem 5.9 and Theorem 5.4 that $\widehat{\phi(S)}$ and $\widehat{\phi'(S')}$ are renaming equivalent. It follows that $\mathbf{A}$ and $\mathbf{A}'$ are homomorphically equivalent via homomorphisms $h : A \to A'$, $h' : A' \to A$ that act as bijections between S and S'.

If there exists a homomorphism g from $\mathbf{A}$ to $\mathbf{A}'$, then we can extend h (using the definition of g) to be defined on the components of ϕ deleted in the construction of $\widehat{\phi}$, to obtain a homomorphism from $\mathbf{A}$ to $\mathbf{A}'$ extending h. If there exists a homomorphism g' from $\mathbf{A}'$ to $\mathbf{A}$, we can extend h' in an analogous way. However, the existence of both such extensions would imply by definition that $\phi(S)$ and $\phi'(S')$ are counting equivalent. We may thus conclude that either there is no homomorphism $\mathbf{A} \to \mathbf{A}'$ or there is no homomorphism $\mathbf{A}' \to \mathbf{A}$. □

LEMMA 5.18. *There is an oracle FPT-algorithm that performs the following: given a set $\phi_1, \dots, \phi_s$ of semi-counting equivalent free pp-formulas that are pairwise not counting equivalent, a sequence $c_1, \dots, c_s \in \mathbb{Z}\backslash\{0\}$, and a structure $\mathbf{B}$, the algorithm computes $|\phi_i(\mathbf{B})|$ for every $i \in [s]$; it may make calls to an oracle that provides $\sum_{i=1}^{s} c_i \cdot |\phi_i(\mathbf{B}')|$ upon being given a structure $\mathbf{B}'$. Here, the ϕ_i with the c_i constitute the parameter.*

To establish this lemma, we first demonstrate the following proposition.

PROPOSITION 5.19. *Let $\phi_1, \dots, \phi_s$ be a sequence of semi-counting equivalent pp-formulas that are pairwise not counting equivalent. Then there is a structure $\mathbf{C}$ and $i \in [s]$ such that $\mathbf{C} \models \phi_i$ but $\mathbf{C} \not\models \phi_j$ for all $j \in [s]\backslash\{i\}$.*

PROOF. Let $\mathbf{A}_1, \dots, \mathbf{A}_n$ be the structures of the queries $\phi_1, \dots, \phi_n$. By Proposition 5.17 the structures $\mathbf{A}_i$ are pairwise not homomorphically equivalent. For $i, j \in [n]$, we write $\phi_i < \phi_j$ if there is a homomorphism from $\mathbf{A}_i$ to $\mathbf{A}_j$. It is easy to check that $<$ induces a partial order on the ϕ_i. Let ϕ_i be a minimal element of this partial order, then there is no homomorphism from any $\mathbf{A}_j$ to ϕ_i with $i \neq j$. Setting $\mathbf{C} = \mathbf{A}_i$ completes the proof. □

PROOF. (Lemma 5.18) We give and algorithm that recursively computes the $|\phi_i(\mathbf{B})|$ one after the other. So let the parameter and the input be given as in the statement of the lemma. By Proposition 5.19, there is an $i \in [n]$ and a structure $\mathbf{C}$ such that $\mathbf{C} \models \phi_i$ but $\mathbf{C} \not\models \phi_j$ for all $j \in [s]\backslash\{i\}$. W.l.o.g. assume $i = s$. Then $|\phi_i(\mathbf{B} \times \mathbf{C})| = 0$ for $i < s$. Consequently, we have that the oracle lets us compute $c_s \cdot |\phi_n(\mathbf{B} \times \mathbf{C})| = c_s \cdot |\phi_n(\mathbf{B})| \cdot |\phi_n(\mathbf{C})|$. Computing $|\phi_n(\mathbf{C})|$ by brute force then yields $|\phi_s(\mathbf{B})|$.

Now note that for every structure $\mathbf{B}'$ we can also compute $\sum_{i=1}^{s-1} c_i \cdot |\phi_i(\mathbf{B}')|$ by this approach with one subtraction. So we can apply the algorithm again for $\phi_1, \ldots, \phi_{s-1}$, answering oracle queries for the smaller sum $\sum_{i=1}^{s-1} c_i \cdot |\phi_i(\mathbf{B}')|$ with the help of the oracle for $\sum_{i=1}^{s} c_i \cdot |\phi_i(\mathbf{B}')|$. □

We can now prove Theorem 3.1 for all-free ep-formulas.

THEOREM 5.20. *Let Φ be a set of all-free ep-formulas. There exists a set Φ^* of free prenex pp-formulas such that the counting case problems* count[Φ] *and* count[Φ^*] *are equivalent under counting slice reductions.*

Before giving the technical details of the proof of Theorem 5.20, let us first descibe the ideas. The proof follows the approach presented in the examples of Section 4. In particular, the less straightforward reduction from count[Φ^*] to count[Φ] proceeds as we did in Example 4.3. Given ϕ and ϕ^*, we can evaluate $|\phi'(\mathbf{B})|$ for $\phi' \in \phi^*$ with an oracle for $|\phi(\mathbf{B} \times \mathbf{C}^\ell)|$ for a suitable structure $\mathbf{C}$ as in that example. The main difference is that, instead of having $\mathbf{C}$ explicitly as in Example 4.3, we here know from Lemma 5.12 that a structure $\mathbf{C}$ exists for which all formulas in ϕ^* have a different number of satisfying assignments. We can then compute $\mathbf{C}$ by brute force as it depends only on ϕ. This then allows to compute $\phi'(\mathbf{B})$ by solving a system of linear equations.

We now give the technical detail of the proof.

PROOF. Let us first specify the reduction from count[Φ] to count[Φ^*], which is quite straightforward. The relation U is the set of pairs (ϕ, ϕ^*) such that ϕ is an all-free ep-formula and ϕ^* is the output of the algorithm of Proposition 5.16 on input ϕ. Obviously, this satisfies the coverage condition. Then the oracle-FPT-algorithm to compute $\phi(\mathbf{B})$ given ϕ, ϕ^* and $\mathbf{B}$ first computes all of the $|\phi_i^*(\mathbf{B})|$ by oracle calls and then uses Proposition 5.16. This completes the reduction.

For the other direction, let $\phi' \in \Phi^*$. We set U to be the set of all pairs $(\phi', \{\phi\})$ such that ϕ is an all-free ep-formula and $\phi' \in \phi^*$. Given ϕ', ϕ and $\mathbf{B}$, we compute $|\phi'(\mathbf{B})| := r(\phi', \{\phi\}, \mathbf{B})$ as follows: Let $\phi_1^*, \ldots, \phi_s^*$ be the equivalence classes of ϕ^* with respect to semi-counting equivalence. Now choose a strucuture $\mathbf{C}$ as in Lemma 5.12. Then for $\psi, \psi' \in \phi^*$ we have $|\psi(\mathbf{C})| \neq |\psi'(\mathbf{C})|$ if ψ and ψ' are from different equivalence classes with respect to semi-counting equivalence, and otherwise $|\psi(\mathbf{C})| = |\psi'(\mathbf{C})| > 0$. Fix for each $j \in [s]$ a formula in ϕ_j^* and call it ψ_j. Moreover, denote by c_ψ the coefficiencent of ψ in Proposition 5.16. Using this notation and Proposition 5.16 we obtain, for every $\ell \in \mathbb{N}$, that

$$|\phi(\mathbf{B} \times \mathbf{C}^\ell)| = \sum_{j=1}^{s} |\psi_j(\mathbf{C})|^\ell \big(\sum_{\psi \in \phi_j^*} c_\psi |\psi(\mathbf{B})| \big).$$

Note that this is a linear equation where the coefficients have the form $|\psi_j(\mathbf{C})|^\ell$; these can be computed by brute force. Letting ℓ range from 0 to $s-1$ thus yields a system of linear equations whose coefficient matrix is a Vandermonde matrix. Consequently, with s oracle calls we can compute $\sum_{\psi \in \phi_j^*} c_\psi |\psi(\mathbf{B})|$ for each j. We use Lemma 5.18 to compute $\phi'(\mathbf{B})$. □

5.4 The general case

We now indicate how to prove Theorem 3.1 in its full generality.

We may assume that each ep-formula $\phi \in \Phi$ is normalized. For each ep-formula ϕ, define ϕ_{af} to be the all-free part of ϕ, that is, the disjunction of the ϕ-disjuncts that are free; define Φ_{af} to be $\{\phi_{\text{af}} \mid \phi \in \Phi\}$; and, define ϕ_{af}^- to be the set of formulas in ϕ_{af}^* that do not logically entail a sentence disjunct of ϕ. We define ϕ^+ to be the union of ϕ_{af}^- and the set containing each pp-sentence disjunct of ϕ; and, we define Φ^+ to be $\bigcup_{\phi \in \Phi} \phi^+$.

EXAMPLE 5.21. *Set $V = \{w, x, y, z\}$; we consider the formulas $\phi(V) = \phi_1(V) \vee \phi_2(V) \vee \phi_3(V)$ defined in Example 4.2. Define*

$$\theta_1(V) = \exists a \exists b \exists c \exists d E(a, b) \wedge E(b, c) \wedge E(c, d),$$

and define

$$\theta(V) = \phi_1(V) \vee \phi_2(V) \vee \phi_3(V) \vee \theta_1(V).$$

The all-free part of θ is $\theta_{\text{af}} = \phi_1(V) \vee \phi_2(V) \vee \phi_3(V)$, since each of these three disjuncts has a non-empty set of free variables, whereas θ_1 has an empty set of free variables. According to Example 5.15, we have

$$\theta_{\text{af}}^* = \{\phi_1, \phi_1 \wedge \phi_3\}.$$

Now, observe that $\phi_1 \wedge \phi_3$ logically entails the sentence disjunct θ_1 of θ; on the other hand, ϕ_1 does not logically entail θ_1. Hence, we have that $\theta_{\text{af}}^- = \{\phi_1\}$. We have θ^+ to be the union of θ_{af}^- and $\{\theta_1\}$, so

$$\theta^+ = \{\phi_1, \theta_1\}.$$

□

The idea of the proof of Theorem 3.1 is as follows. The counting slice reduction from count[Φ] to count[Φ^+] has U as the set of pairs (ϕ, ϕ^+) where ϕ is a normalized ep-formula; r on $(\phi(V), \phi^+, \mathbf{B})$ behaves as follows. First, it checks if there is a sentence disjunct θ of ϕ that is true on $\mathbf{B}$; if so, it outputs $|B|^{|V|}$; otherwise, it makes use of the counting slice reduction from count[Φ_{af}] to count[Φ_{af}^*]. The counting slice reduction from count[Φ^+] to count[Φ] has U as the set $\{(\psi, \{\phi\}) \mid \psi \in \phi^+\}$; r on $(\psi(V), \phi(V), \mathbf{B})$ is defined as follows. When $\psi \in \phi_{\text{af}}^-$, the counting slice reduction (U', r') from count[Φ_{af}^*] to count[Φ_{af}] is used to determine $|\psi(\mathbf{B})|$; this is performed by passing to r' a treated version of $\mathbf{B}$, on which no sentence disjunct of ϕ may hold. When ψ is a sentence disjunct of ϕ, an oracle query is made to obtain the count of ϕ on a treated version of $\mathbf{B}$; on this treated version, it is proved that all assignments satisfy ϕ if and only if $\mathbf{B} \models \psi$.

6. CONCLUSIONS

We have shown a trichotomy for the parameterized complexity of counting satisfying assignments to existential positive formulas of bounded arity. To this end, the main technical contribution was the equivalence theorem (Theorem 3.1) stating that for every set of existential positive formulas there is a set of primitive positive formulas that is computationally equivalent with respect to the counting problem studied. After showing this equivalence theorem, we could derive our trichotomy in a rather straightforward fashion by invoking a previous trichotomy for primitive positive formulas as a black-box.

In order to prove the equivalence theorem, we gave a syntactic characterization for when two pp-formulas are counting equivalent, that is, have the same number of satisfying assignments with respect to every finite structure. This result can be seen as an adaption, to the counting setting, of classical work of Chandra and Merlin [2] that characterizes logical equivalence of primitive positive formulas.

Let us note that the assumption of bounded arity is not needed in the proof of the equivalence theorem. It only appears in our trichotomy theorem because it is already present in the previous trichotomy on primitive positive formulas that we use. Consequently, if one could adapt the work of Marx [16] on model checking unbounded arity primitive positive formulas to counting to show a dichotomy or trichotomy for counting, this would directly give the corresponding result for existential positive formulas by applying our equivalence theorem.

Finally, let us remark that we are not aware of any fragment of first-order logic extending existential positive queries for which even model checking is understood, from the viewpoint of classifying the complexity of all sets of queries (for more information, see the discussion in the introduction of the article [4]). Hence, the research project of extending our complexity classification beyond existential positive queries would first require an advance in the study of model checking in first-order logic.

7. ACKNOWLEDGMENTS

The first author was supported by the Spanish Project MINECO COMMAS TIN2013-46181-C2-R, Basque Project GIU15/30, and Basque Grant UFI11/45.

The research presented in this paper was performed while the second author was a postdoc at Ecole Polytechnique, Université Paris-Saclay, France.

8. REFERENCES

[1] S. Abiteboul, R. Hull, and V. Vianu. *Foundations of Databases.* Addison-Wesley, 1995.

[2] A. K. Chandra and P. M. Merlin. Optimal implementation of conjunctive queries in relational data bases. In *Proceddings of STOC'77*, pages 77–90, 1977.

[3] H. Chen. On the complexity of existential positive queries. *ACM Trans. Comput. Log.*, 15(1), 2014.

[4] H. Chen. The tractability frontier of graph-like first-order query sets. In *Joint Meeting of the Twenty-Third EACSL Annual Conference on Computer Science Logic (CSL) and the Twenty-Ninth Annual ACM/IEEE Symposium on Logic in Computer Science (LICS), CSL-LICS '14, Vienna, Austria, July 14 - 18, 2014*, page 31, 2014.

[5] H. Chen and M. Grohe. Constraint satisfaction with succinctly specified relations. *Journal of Computer and System Sciences*, 76(8):847–860, 2010.

[6] H. Chen and S. Mengel. A trichotomy in the complexity of counting answers to conjunctive queries. *CoRR*, abs/1408.0890, 2014.

[7] H. Chen and S. Mengel. A trichotomy in the complexity of counting answers to conjunctive queries. In *18th International Conference on Database Theory, ICDT 2015, March 23-27, 2015, Brussels, Belgium*, pages 110–126, 2015.

[8] H. Chen and M. Müller. One hierarchy spawns another: graph deconstructions and the complexity classification of conjunctive queries. In *Joint Meeting of the Twenty-Third EACSL Annual Conference on Computer Science Logic (CSL) and the Twenty-Ninth Annual ACM/IEEE Symposium on Logic in Computer Science (LICS), CSL-LICS '14, Vienna, Austria, July 14 - 18, 2014*, pages 32:1–32:10, 2014.

[9] V. Dalmau and P. Jonsson. The complexity of counting homomorphisms seen from the other side. *Theor. Comput. Sci.*, 329(1-3):315–323, 2004.

[10] A. Durand and S. Mengel. Structural tractability of counting of solutions to conjunctive queries. In *Proceedings of the 16th International Conference on Database Theory (ICDT 2013)*, 2013.

[11] J. Flum and M. Grohe. *Parameterized Complexity Theory.* Springer, 2006.

[12] G. Greco and F. Scarcello. Counting solutions to conjunctive queries: structural and hybrid tractability. In *Proceedings of the 33rd ACM SIGMOD-SIGACT-SIGART Symposium on Principles of Database Systems*, pages 132–143, 2014.

[13] M. Grohe. The complexity of homomorphism and constraint satisfaction problems seen from the other side. *Journal of the ACM*, 54(1), 2007.

[14] M. Grohe, T. Schwentick, and L. Segoufin. When is the evaluation of conjunctive queries tractable? In *STOC 2001*, 2001.

[15] D. Marx. Can you beat treewidth? *Theory of Computing*, 6(1):85–112, 2010.

[16] D. Marx. Tractable hypergraph properties for constraint satisfaction and conjunctive queries. In *Proceedings of the 42nd ACM Symposium on Theory of Computing*, pages 735–744, 2010.

[17] C. Papadimitriou and M. Yannakakis. On the Complexity of Database Queries. *Journal of Computer and System Sciences*, 58(3):407–427, 1999.

[18] R. Pichler and S. Skritek. Tractable counting of the answers to conjunctive queries. In *Proceedings of the 5th Alberto Mendelzon International Workshop on Foundations of Data Management*, 2011.

Computing Join Queries with Functional Dependencies

Mahmoud Abo Khamis
LogicBlox Inc. and
SUNY Buffalo

Hung Q. Ngo
LogicBlox Inc. and
SUNY Buffalo

Dan Suciu
LogicBlox Inc. and
University of Washington

ABSTRACT

Recently, Gottlob, Lee, Valiant, and Valiant (GLVV) presented an output size bound for join queries with functional dependencies (FD), based on a linear program on polymatroids. GLVV bound strictly generalizes the bound of Atserias, Grohe and Marx (AGM) for queries with no FD, in which case there are known algorithms running within the AGM-bound and thus are worst-case optimal.

A main result of this paper is an algorithm for computing join queries with FDs, running within GLVV bound up to a poly-log factor. In particular, our algorithm is worst-case optimal for any query where the GLVV bound is tight. As an unexpected by-product, our algorithm manages to solve a harder problem, where (some) input relations may have prescribed maximum degree bounds, of which *both* functional dependencies and cardinality bounds are special cases.

We extend Gottlob et al. framework by replacing all variable subsets with the lattice of closed sets (under the given FDs). This gives us new insights into the structure of the worst-case bound and worst-case instances. While it is still open whether GLVV bound is tight in general, we show that it is tight on distributive lattices and some other simple lattices. Distributive lattices capture a strict superset of queries with no FD and with simple FDs. We also present two simpler algorithms which are also worst-case optimal on distributive lattices within a single-log factor, but they do not match GLVV bound on a general lattice. Our algorithms are designed based on a novel principle: we turn a proof of a polymatroid-based output size bound into an algorithm.

Keywords

Worst-case optimal; Join algorithm; Functional dependency; Entropy; Polymatroid

1. INTRODUCTION

Several results published in the last ten years or so have lead to tight worst-case output size bounds (*AGM-bound* [5, 13]) and the development of a new class of query processing algorithms running within the bound's time budget [18, 19, 23]. These new *worst-case optimal* algorithms are quite different from traditional query plans, in the sense that they no longer compute one pairwise join at a time, but instead process the query globally. The runtime is bounded by $O(N^{\rho^*})$, where N is the size of the database, while ρ^* is the value of the optimal fractional edge cover of the query. For example, they compute the query $Q(x, y, z)$:- $R(x, y), S(y, z), T(z, x)$ in time $O(N^{3/2})$, while any traditional query plan requires worst-case time $\Omega(N^2)$ [19].

While the vast majority of database engines today still rely on traditional query plans, new, complex data analytics engines increasingly switch to worst-case optimal algorithms: LogicBlox's engine [4] is built on a worst-case optimal algorithm called LeapFrog Triejoin [23] (LFTJ), the *Myria* data analytics platform supports a variant of LFTJ [8], and the increased role of SIMD instructions in modern processors also favors this new class of join algorithms [1].

When there are functional dependencies (FDs), however, the AGM-bound is no-longer tight. Gottlob, Lee, Valiant, and Valiant [12] initiated the study of the worst-case output size of a query in the presence of FDs and described an upper bound (reviewed in Sec.2), called the *GLVV-bound* henceforth. It remains open whether the GLVV-bound is tight; at present, it is the best known upper bound for the output size of a join query with FDs. A recent result by Gogacz and Toruńczyk [11] proved a weaker statement, namely that if we replace the polymatroidal constraints in the GLVV-bound with entropic constraints (of which there are infinitely many), then the bound is tight, albeit uncomputable.

Our paper proposes an approach to studying join queries in the presence of FDs by using lattice theory. The GLVV-bound is reformulated with a very simple linear program on the lattices' polymatroids, and output size bounds are obtained by studying formal inequalities satisfied by all these polymatroids. This approach allows us to derive both new lower and upper bounds on the worst-case output size. Furthermore, we present an algorithm which runs in time proportional to the GLVV-bound, within a polylogarithmic factor. We also describe two special cases where the polylogarithmic factor is reduced to a single log. Before discussing our results, we explain their significance.

1.1 Motivation

User-Defined Functions. UDF's, or interpreted predicates, significantly affect the runtime of a query. Consider:

$$Q(x, y, z, u) \text{ :- } R(x, y), S(y, z), T(z, u), u = f(x, z), x = g(y, u). \quad (1)$$

PODS'16, June 26-July 01, 2016, San Francisco, CA, USA
© 2016 ACM. ISBN 978-1-4503-4191-2/16/06...$15.00
DOI: http://dx.doi.org/10.1145/2902251.2902289

The predicates $u = f(x, z)$ and $x = g(y, u)$ represent two user-defined functions, f and g; for example $f(x, z)$ could be $x + z$, or the concatenation of two strings x and z. Any UDF can be modeled as a relation with a primary key, for example the function f can be viewed as a relation $F(x, z, u)$ of cardinality N^2 (with one entry for every x, z pair in their effective domains) satisfying the FD $xz \to u$; similarly g introduces the FD $yu \to x$. The addition of these two FD's significantly affects the output size and the query evaluation complexity: if we computed the intermediate query $R(x, y), S(y, z), T(z, u)$, and then applied the two predicates $u = f(x, z)$ and $x = g(y, u)$, then the runtime can be as high as N^2 because the size of the intermediate result is N^2 for $R = \{(i, 1) \mid i \in [N]\}$, $S = \{(1, 1)\}$, $T = \{(1, i) \mid i \in [N]\}$. However, as we will show, the GLVV-bound is $|Q| \leqslant N^{3/2}$. Our new algorithms run in $\tilde{O}(N^{3/2})$; and as we shall see this is worst-case optimal.

A related problem is querying relations with restricted access patterns [7]. In that setting, some of the relations in the database can only be read by providing the values of one or more attributes. As shown above, a user-defined function $f(x, z)$ can be modeled as an infinite relation $F(u, x, z) \equiv (u = f(x, z))$ with the restriction that F can be accessed only by providing inputs for the variables x and z. The work on querying under restricted access patterns has focused on the answerability question (whether a query can or cannot be answered). Our work extends that, by finding algorithms for answering the query within the GLVV-bound.

Known Frequencies. Systems often know an upper bound on the frequencies (or degrees) in the database. For example, consider the triangle query above, and assume that the binary graph defined by the relation $R(x, y)$ has a bounded degree: all outdegrees are $\deg(x) \leqslant d_1$ and all indegrees are $\deg(y) \leqslant d_2$. One can model this scenario by introducing an artificial color c_1 on outgoing edges, and a color c_2 for incoming edges of R:

$$Q(x, y, z, c_1, c_2) \text{ :- } R(x, c_1, c_2, y), S(y, z), T(z, x), C_1(c_1), C_2(c_2), xc_1 \to y, yc_2 \to x, xy \to c_1c_2 \quad (2)$$

where $|R| = |S| = |T| = N$ and $|C_1| = d_1, |C_2| = d_2$. Thus, each outgoing edge from x is colored with some distinct color c_1, and similarly each incoming edge to y is colored with some distinct color c_2. The new predicates C_1, C_2 limit the number of colors to d_1, d_2 respectively. We can show that the worst-case query output decreases from $N^{3/2}$ to $\min(N^{3/2}, Nd_1, Nd_2)$ [2]. Alternatively, one can use the linear program and algorithm in Sec 5.2 to capture queries with known maximum degree bounds. We note that, by adapting AYZ algorithm [3], degree information was used in [15] to obtain a sub-quadratic time algorithm for join on a special class of query graphs called *1-series-parallel graphs*. Their approach also uses a linear program similar to the one in Sec 5.2, *minus* the sub-modularity constraints.

1.2 Overview of the Results

Grohe and Marx [13] and later Atserias, Grohe and Marx [5] derived an elegant tight upper bound on the output size of a join query: $\prod_{j=1}^{m} |R_j|^{w_j}$, where $R_1, \ldots, R_m$ are the input relations to the query, and $(w_j)_{j=1}^{m}$ is any fractional edge cover of the query's hypergraph. This bound is known today as the AGM bound. They proved that the bound is tight by describing a simple database instance for any query, such that the query's output matches the bound. In that instance, every relation is a cross product of sets, one set per variable; we call it a *product instance.*

An obvious open question was whether a query Q can be evaluated on any database instance D in time that is no larger than the AGM bound of Q on databases with the same cardinalities as D; such an algorithm is called *worst-case optimal.* Ngo, Porat, Ré, and Rudra [18] described the first worst-case optimal algorithm; later Veldhuizen [23] proved that LFTJ, an algorithm already implemented at LogicBlox earlier, is also worst-case optimal. A survey and unification of these two algorithms can be found in [19].

Neither the AGM-bound nor the associated algorithms analytically exploit FDs in the database.[1] Such FDs can provably reduce the worst-case output of a query, but the upper bound and algorithms mentioned above cannot use this information, and instead treat the query by ignoring the FDs. Gottlob et al. [12] studied the upper bound of the query size in the presence of FDs, and established two classes of results. The first was a characterization of this bound in the case when the FD's are restricted to simple keys; as we will show, this case can be solved entirely using the AGM bound by simply replacing each relation with its closure. The second was a novel approach to reasoning about the worst-case output of a query, using information theory. They viewed the query output as a multivariate probability space, and introduced two constraints on the marginal entropies: a cardinality constraint for each input relation R, stating that the entropy of its variables cannot exceed the uniform entropy $H(\text{vars}(R)) \leqslant \log_2 |R|$, and one constraint for each FD $X \to Y$, stating $H(XY) = H(X)$. (Note that X and Y are sets of variables.) The largest answer to the query Q is then given by the largest possible value of $2^{H(\text{vars}(Q))}$, over all choices of entropic functions H that satisfy these constraints. Characterizing the space of all entropic functions H is a long-standing open problem in information theory [24]; to circumvent that, they relax the function H by allowing it to be any function that satisfies the *Shannon inequalities* [24]. Such a function is called a *polymatroid* in the literature, and we denote it with lower case h to distinguish it from entropic functions H. Thus, the problem in [12] can be stated equivalently as: find the maximum value $h(\text{vars}(Q))$ where h ranges over all polymatroids satisfying the given constraints.

In this paper, we continue the study of query evaluation under general FDs. We establish both bounds and algorithms. Our novelty is to model FDs as a lattice $\mathbf{L}$ of the closed sets of attributes, and to study polymatroids on lattices. The function h is now any non-negative and lattice-submodular function[2] that satisfies all cardinality constraints. FD constraints are enforced *automatically* by the lattice structure, and the upper bound on the query size is $2^{\max h(\text{vars}(Q))}$. When there are no FDs, the lattice is a Boolean algebra.

Our first question is whether the elegant AGM bound and worst-case product instance carry over to arbitrary FDs. We answer this question completely, by proving that both sides of the AGM bound hold iff the lattice has a special structure,

[1]Algorithmically, LFTJ handles FDs by binding variables at the earliest trie level at which they are functionally determined. For example, in $R(x, y), S(y, z), T(z, u), u = f(x, z), x = g(y, u)$ with a key order $[x, y, z, u]$, whenever z was bound the value of u would be immediately computed by $u = f(x, z)$.

[2]I.e. $h(X) + h(Y) \geqslant h(X \vee Y) + h(X \wedge Y)$

which we call a *normal lattice*. Both upper and lower bounds require minor extensions to be applicable to normal lattices. The standard AGM upper bound is given in terms of fractional edge covers of the query's hypergraph, but in a normal lattice one needs to consider a dual hypergraph, whose nodes are $\mathbf{L}$'s co-atoms. In a Boolean algebra, these two hypergraphs are isomorphic, but in a general lattice they can be significantly different. The notion of normal lattice seems novel, and strictly includes all distributive lattices, which in turn include all lattices corresponding to simple FDs (each FD is of the form $a \rightarrow b$, where a, b are attributes). The second minor change is that one needs to allow for a slight generalization of product instances, to what we call *quasi-product instances*. Importantly, both these properties fail on non-normal lattices; in particular, on non-normal lattices worst-case instances are not quasi-product instances.

Next, we examine algorithms whose runtime is bounded by the GLVV bound. We propose a novel methodology for designing such algorithms, starting from the observation that such an algorithm must provide a proof of the query's upper bound, equivalently, a proof of an inequality of the form $\sum_j w_j h(\text{vars}(R_j)) \geqslant h(\text{vars}(Q))$, where $R_1, R_2, \ldots$ are the input relations. In the case of a Boolean algebra, Shearer's lemma [9] is of this form; in a normal lattice this corresponds to a fractional edge cover of the co-atomic hypergraph; and, for a general lattice it is a general inequality. A key motivation behind NPRR [18] was to prove inequalities algorithmically. This paper completes the cycle by proceeding in the opposite direction: given a proof method for such inequalities, we design algorithms whose steps correspond to the proof steps. We design three such algorithms, corresponding to three methods for proving the above type of inequalities.

The first algorithm called the *chain algorithm* runs within the *chain bound*; the proof technique is adapted from Radhakrishnan's proof [20] of Shearer's lemma to general lattices. Both the chain bound and algorithm strictly generalize AGM-bound and worst-case optimal algorithms for join queries *without* FDs. The second algorithm, called the *sub-modular algorithm*, runs within the *sub-modularity bound*; the proof technique is that of Balister and Bollobás's [6]. The third algorithm, called the *conditional sub-modularity algorithm* (CSMA), runs within the general *GLVV-bound*, up to a polylogarithmic factor; the proof technique is our own, based on linear programming duality. As a bonus, CSMA can be used straightforwardly to handle input relations with known maximum degree bounds, which is a strict generalization of the problem of computing join queries with FDs. While GLVV bound is tighter than the other two in general lattices, we show that in distributive lattices all of them are tight, and thus our algorithms are worst-case optimal.

Outline. The paper is organized as follows. Background material is reviewed in Sec. 2, and basic definitions for our lattice-based approach are given in Sec. 3. We describe the main result on normal lattices in Sec. 4, then present two of our algorithms and bounds in Sec. 5. Due to space limitation, some details were left out of this extended abstract, including the sub-modularity bound and algorithm. Interested readers can find them in the full version [2].

2. NOTATIONS AND PRIOR RESULTS

For any positive integer n, $[n]$ denotes the set $\{1, \ldots, n\}$. All log in the paper are of base 2. We fix a relational schema $\mathbf{R} = \{R_1, \ldots, R_m\}$ whose attributes belong to a set of attributes $\mathbf{X} = \{x_1, \ldots, x_k\}$. We refer to $x_i \in \mathbf{X}$ interchangeably as an *attribute* or a *variable*; similarly we refer to R_j as a *relation*, or an *input*. We use lower case letters $x \in \mathbf{X}$ to denote single variables, and upper case letters $X \subseteq \mathbf{X}$ to denote sets of variables. The *domain* of variable x is denoted by $\mathsf{Dom}(x)$. For each relation R_j we denote $\text{vars}(R_j) \subseteq \mathbf{X}$ its set of attributes. Abusing notation, we blur the distinction between R_j and $\text{vars}(R_j)$, writing $R_j \subseteq \mathbf{X}$. We consider full conjunctive queries without self-joins:

$$Q(x_1, \ldots, x_k) \text{ :- } R_1(\text{vars}(R_1)), \ldots, R_m(\text{vars}(R_m)) \quad (3)$$

We will drop variables from the head, since it is understood that all variables need to be listed.

A database instance D consists of one relational instance R_j^D for each relation symbol; we denote $N_j = |R_j^D|$, $N = |D| = \sum_j N_j$, and use lower case for logs, $n_j = \log_2 N_j$. We denote Q^D the answer to Q on the database instance D. When D is implicit from context, we will simply write Q, R_j instead of Q^D, R_j^D. A *product database instance* is a database instance such that $R_j^D = \prod_{x_i \in R_j} \mathsf{Dom}(x_i)$ for $j \in [m]$; the query answer on a product database is the cross product of all domains, $Q^D = \prod_{i=1}^k \mathsf{Dom}(x_i)$.

The AGM Bound. A series of results over the last ten years [5, 13, 18, 19, 23] has established tight connections between the maximum output size of a query and the runtime of a query evaluation algorithm. The *query hypergraph* of a query Q is $H_Q = (\mathbf{X}, \mathbf{R})$; its nodes are the variables and its hyperedges are the input relations (where each $R_j \in \mathbf{R}$ is viewed as a set of variables). Consider the following two linear programs (LP's):

(Weighted) Edge Cover	(Weighted) Ver. Packing
$\text{minimize} \sum_{j=1}^{m} w_j n_j$	$\text{maximize} \sum_{i=1}^{k} v_i$
$\sum_{j: x_i \in R_j} w_j \geqslant 1, \forall i \in [k]$	$\sum_{i: x_i \in R_j} v_i \leqslant n_j, \forall j \in [m]$
$w_j \geqslant 0, \forall j \in [m]$	$v_i \geqslant 0, \forall i \in [k]$

We call a feasible solution to the first LP a *weighted fractional edge cover*, and to the second a *weighted fractional vertex packing*. The traditional (unweighted) notions correspond to $n_j = 1, \forall j$.

Theorem 2.1 (AGM bound). *[5, 13] (1) Let $(w_j)_{j=1}^m$ be a fractional edge cover. Then, for any input database D s.t. $|R_j^D| \leqslant N_j$ for all $j \in [m]$, the output size of Q is bounded by $2^{\sum_j w_j n_j}$. In other words, $|Q^D| \leqslant \prod_j N_j^{w_j}$. (2) Let $v_i, i \in [k]$ be a fractional vertex packing, and let D be the product database instance where $D_i = [2^{v_i}]$. Then, $|Q^D| = \prod_i 2^{v_i}$.*

(In the statement above, we ignore the issue of integrality of the v_i for the sake of clarity. There is a bit of loss when v_i are not integers, but this fact does not affect the asymptotics of the lowerbound [5].) Let $(w_j^*)_{j=1}^m$ be the optimal edge cover. The *AGM-bound* of the query Q is $\mathsf{AGM}(Q, (N_j)_{j=1}^m) \stackrel{\text{def}}{=} \prod_j N_j^{w_j^*}$, or simply $\mathsf{AGM}(Q)$ when the cardinalities $(N_j)_{j=1}^m$ are clear from the context. The query's output size is always $\leqslant \mathsf{AGM}(Q)$, and this bound is tight, because on the product database described above, the output size is $\mathsf{AGM}(Q)$. Several query evaluation algorithms have been described in the literature with runtime[3] $\tilde{O}(N + \mathsf{AGM}(Q))$: NPRR [18], LFTJ [23], Generic-join [19].

Functional Dependencies. A query with functional dependencies is a pair (Q, FD), where Q is a query and FD is a set of *functional dependencies* (fd), which are expressions of the form $U \to V$ where $U, V \subseteq \mathbf{X}$. An fd can be defined either by some input relation R_j, in which case we call it *guarded* (in particular $U, V \subseteq R_j$), or can be defined by a UDF (as we saw in Sec. 1.1), and then we call it *unguarded.* A *simple* fd is of the form $u \to v$ where both u, v are variables, and a *simple key* is a simple fd guarded in some R_j s.t. u is a key for R_j.

Gottlob et al. [12] studied output size bounds in the presence of FDs. Their bound is defined only in terms of the maximum cardinality, $\max_j N_j$, but in this paper we slightly generalize the discussion to all cardinalities $(N_j)_j$. The key technique introduced in [12] is to use information theory to upper bound the size of the query, as reviewed next.

Let Q^D be the query answer over some instance D. Define a probability distribution over $\prod_{i=1}^{k} \mathsf{Dom}(x_i)$ by randomly drawing one tuple from Q^D with probability $1/|Q^D|$ each. Then, the joint entropy of the k random variables $\mathbf{X}$ is $H(\mathbf{X}) = \log_2 |Q^D|$. Each subset of variables $X \subseteq \mathbf{X}$ defines a (marginal) distribution, with entropy $H(X)$. If $X = R_j$, then H must satisfy the following *cardinality constraint* $H(R_j) \leqslant \log_2 N_j = n_j$, because $\Pi_{R_j}(Q^D) \subseteq R_j^D$ and the marginal entropy is maximized when it is uniform. In addition, for any fd $U \to V$ the entropy must satisfy the *fd-constraint* $H(U) = H(UV)$.

We give here a very simple illustration of how the approach in [12] models the query output using entropy, by illustrating on the query Q :- $R(x,y), S(y,z), T(z,x)$ (without fd's) and output with five outcomes:

x	y	z	Q
a	3	r	$\frac{1}{5}$
a	2	q	$\frac{1}{5}$
b	2	q	$\frac{1}{5}$
d	3	r	$\frac{1}{5}$
a	3	q	$\frac{1}{5}$

x	y	R
a	3	$\frac{2}{5}$
a	2	$\frac{1}{5}$
b	2	$\frac{1}{5}$
d	3	$\frac{1}{5}$

y	z	S
3	r	$\frac{2}{5}$
2	q	$\frac{2}{5}$
3	q	$\frac{1}{5}$
4	q	0

x	z	T
a	r	$\frac{1}{5}$
a	q	$\frac{2}{5}$
b	q	$\frac{1}{5}$
d	r	$\frac{1}{5}$

Here $H(xyz) = \log 5$, $H(xy) \leqslant \log |R| = \log 4$, $H(yz) \leqslant \log |S| = \log 4$, and $H(xz) \leqslant \log |T| = \log 4$.

GLVV Bound. Gottlob et al. [12] observe that $\log |Q^D| \leqslant \max_H H(\mathbf{X})$, where H ranges over all *entropic* functions that satisfy the cardinality constraints and the fd-constraints, and this bound has recently been shown to be tight [11]. However, we do not know how to compute this upper bound. The entropic cone requires an infinite number of (independent) constraints to characterize, and the precise characterization is a long-standing open problem in information theory [24]. To circumvent this difficulty, in [12] the entropic function H is replaced with a *polymatroid* function h. A *polymatroid* over a set of variables $\mathbf{X}$ is a function $h : 2^{\mathbf{X}} \to \mathbb{R}^+$ that satisfies the following inequalities, called *the Shannon inequalities*:

$$h(X) + h(Y) \geqslant h(X \cap Y) + h(X \cup Y) \quad \text{Sub-modularity}$$

$$h(X \cup Y) \geqslant h(X) \quad \text{Monotonicity}$$

$$h(\emptyset) = 0 \quad \text{Zero}$$

[3] $\tilde{O}$ here hides log-factor in data complexity, and a polynomial factor in query size.

Every entropic function H is a polymatroid, and the converse fails when $\mathbf{X}$ has four or more variables [25]. Define $\mathsf{GLVV}(Q, \mathsf{FD}, (N_j)_j) \stackrel{\text{def}}{=} \max_h h(\mathbf{X})$, where h ranges over all polymatroids that satisfy all cardinality constraints $h(X_j) \leqslant n_j$, and all fd-constraints $h(UV) = h(U)$ for $U \to V \in \mathsf{FD}$. Formally, Gottlob et al. [12] proved:

Theorem 2.2 (GLVV-bound). *Let Q be a join query with functional dependencies FD and input relations R_j of size $|R_j| = N_j$. Then, $|Q| \leqslant \mathsf{GLVV}(Q, \mathsf{FD}, (N_j)_{j=1}^m)$.*

We abbreviate the bound by $\mathsf{GLVV}(Q)$ when FD and $(N_j)_{j=1}^m$ are clear from the context. Note the important fact that $\mathsf{GLVV}(Q)$ can be computed by solving a linear program (with $2^k - 1$ variables). As we shall show, the bound is tight on normal lattices and some non-normal lattices we examined in this paper; but in general it is open whether the bound is always tight.

Closure. Fix a set FD. The *closure* of a set $X \subseteq \mathbf{X}$ is the smallest set X^+ such that $X \subseteq X^+$, and that $U \to V \in \mathsf{FD}$ and $U \subseteq X^+$ imply $V \subseteq X^+$; X is *closed* if $X^+ = X$; the intersection of closed sets is closed. Denote by Q^+ the query obtained by replacing each relation $R_j(\text{vars}(R_j))$ with $R_j(\text{vars}(R_j)^+)$, then forgetting all functional dependencies; then a simple upper bound is $\max_D |Q^D| \leqslant \mathsf{AGM}(Q^+)$. This bound is tight when all fd's are simple keys, because any product database over the schema of Q^+ can be converted into a database over the schema for Q that satisfies all simple keys. Thus, for simple keys, $\mathsf{AGM}(Q^+)$ is a tight upper bound on $|Q^D|$. Theorem 4.4 in [12] proves essentially the same result. However, for fd's other than simple keys this technique fails, as illustrated by $Q(x,y,z) = R(x), S(y), T(x,y,z)$ where xy is a key in T (i.e. $xy \to z$): when $|R| = |S| = N$, $|T| = N^{100}$ we have $Q^+ = Q$ and $\mathsf{AGM}(Q^+) = N^{100}$, yet one can easily verify that $|Q^D| \leqslant N^2$.

The Expansion Procedure. All our algorithms use the following simple pre-processing subroutine, called an expansion. Fix a relation $R(X)$ and a database instance D. R may be an input relation, or some intermediate relation generated during query evaluation. An *expansion* of R^D is some relation $(R^+)^D$ over attributes X^+ such that $\Pi_{X^+}(Q^D) \subseteq (R^+)^D$ and $\Pi_X((R^+)^D) \subseteq R^D$. If $X^+ = X$, then the expansion could be R^D itself, or any partial semi-join reduction that removes dangling tuples from R^D (which do not join with tuples in other relations). If $X \neq X^+$, then the expansion fills in the extra attributes, by repeatedly applying functional dependencies $X \to y$: if the fd is guarded in R_j, then it joins R with $\Pi_{Xy}(R_j)$; otherwise, if the fd corresponds to a UDF $y = f(X)$ then it simply computes f for each tuple in R. The expansion of R can be done in time $\tilde{O}(N)$ using trivial techniques.

3. A LATTICE-BASED APPROACH

3.1 Lattice representation of queries with FDs

Fix a query with functional dependencies (Q, FD), over variables $\mathbf{X}$. It is well known [10, 14, 16] that the set of closed sets forms a lattice:

Definition 3.1 (Lattice representation). The lattice associated to FD is $\mathbf{L}_{\mathsf{FD}} = (\mathbf{L}, \preceq)$, where $\mathbf{L}$ consists of all closed sets and the partial order $\preceq$ is $\subseteq$. The *lattice representation* of a query (Q, FD) is the pair $(\mathbf{L}_{\mathsf{FD}}, \mathbf{R}^+)$, where

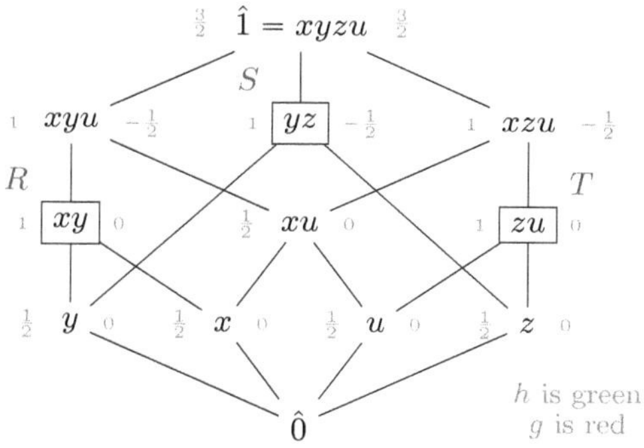

Figure 1: Q :- $R(x, y), S(y, z), T(z, u), xz \to u, yu \to x$

$\mathbf{R}^+ = \{R_1^+, \dots, R_m^+\} \subseteq \mathbf{L}$ is the set of closures of the attributes of the input relations. We will use $\mathbf{L}$ to directly denote the lattice, with FD understood from context. With the expansion procedure in place, w.l.o.g. we assume that all the input R_j are closed sets; thus, the lattice representation of the query can be denoted simply by $(\mathbf{L}, \mathbf{R})$, where $\mathbf{R} = \{R_1, \dots, R_m\} \subseteq \mathbf{L}$, and $\bigvee \mathbf{R} = \bigvee_{R_j \in \mathbf{R}} R_j = \hat{1}$. (If $\bigvee \mathbf{R} \prec \hat{1}$, then some output variables are unbound!)

Note that the size of the lattice may be exponential in that of the query, but this does not affect our complexity results, because they are given in terms of data complexity only. If Q has no functional dependencies, then $\mathbf{L}$ is the Boolean algebra $2^{\mathbf{X}}$. We will use Fig. 1 as a running example, which illustrates the lattice for query (1). Lattice elements corresponding to input relations are framed.

We briefly review some notions of lattice theory needed later and refer the reader to [22] for an extensive treatment. Let $\wedge, \vee, \hat{0}, \hat{1}$ denote the greatest lower bound (*meet*), least upper bound (*join*), minimum and maximum elements of the lattice. The following hold in $\mathbf{L}_{\mathsf{FD}}$: $X \wedge Y = X \cap Y$, $X \vee Y = (X \cup Y)^+$, $\hat{0} = \varnothing$, and $\hat{1} = \mathbf{X}$. We write $X \not\lesseqgtr Y$ to mean X and Y are incomparable. An element U is said to *cover* an element V of $\mathbf{L}$ if $U \succ V$ and $U \succeq W \succeq V$ implies $W = U$ or $W = V$. A *chain* is a sequence of elements, one below the next in partial order. A *maximal chain* is a sequence of elements from $\hat{0}$ to $\hat{1}$ where one is covered by the next. An *atom* is an element X that covers $\hat{0}$; a *co-atom* is an element covered by $\hat{1}$. X is called a *join-irreducible* if $Y \vee Z = X$ implies $Y = X$ or $Z = X$. X is called a *meet-irreducible* if $Y \wedge Z = X$ implies $Y = X$ or $Z = X$. For any $X \in \mathbf{L}$, let $\Lambda_X \stackrel{\text{def}}{=} \{Z \mid Z \preceq X, Z \text{ is a join-irreducible}\}$. The mapping $X \mapsto \Lambda_X$ defines a 1-1 mapping from $\mathbf{L}$ to the order ideals of the poset of join-irreducibles, with inverse $\Lambda_X \mapsto \bigvee \Lambda_X = X$.

Lattice representations and queries with FDs are in 1-to-1 correspondence, up to the addition/removal of variables functionally equivalent to some other set of variables. To see this in one direction, consider any pair $(\mathbf{L}, \mathbf{R})$ where $\mathbf{R} = \{R_1, \dots, R_m\} \subseteq \mathbf{L}$ and $\bigvee \mathbf{R} = \hat{1}$. Let $\mathbf{X}$ be the join-irreducibles of $\mathbf{L}$, and define a query (Q, FD) as follows. For $j \in [m]$, let R_j be a relation with attributes Λ_{R_j}. Define $\mathsf{FD} \stackrel{\text{def}}{=} \{X \to \Lambda_{\bigvee X} \mid X \subseteq \mathbf{X}\}$, then the closed sets are $\{\Lambda_U \mid U \in \mathbf{L}\}$; thus, the lattice representation of this query is isomorphic to $(\mathbf{L}, \mathbf{R})$. In the other direction, consider a query with functional dependencies, (Q, FD). Call a variable x redundant if $Y \leftrightarrow x$ for some set Y that does not contain x. W.l.o.g. we can remove all redundant variables from Q (and decrease accordingly the arity of the relations containing x), because the values of a redundant variable can be recovered through expansion (Sec. 2). We claim $x \mapsto x^+$ is a 1-to-1 mapping between the variables of Q and the join-irreducibles of $\mathbf{L}_{\mathsf{FD}}$. We first check that x^+ is join-irreducible: if $x^+ = Y \vee Z = (Y \cup Z)^+$ with $x \notin Y, x \notin Z$ then $x \leftrightarrow Y \cup Z$, contradicting the fact that x is not redundant. For injectivity, if $x \neq y$, then $x^+ = y^+$ implies $x \leftrightarrow y^+ - \{x\}$, again contradicting non-redundancy. Finally, surjectivity follows from the fact that $Y = \bigvee_{x \in Y} x^+$ for any closed set $Y \in \mathbf{L}$: if Y is join-irreducible then $Y = x^+$ for some $x \in Y$, proving surjectivity.

Thus, in the rest of the paper we shall freely switch between queries and lattices, using the following correspondence:

variable $x \in \mathbf{X}$	join-irreducible $X \in \mathbf{L}$
input $R_j(X_j)$	input $R_j \in \mathbf{L}$ with variables Λ_{R_j}
set of variables $X \subseteq \mathbf{X}$	set of join-irreducibles X
its closure X^+	$X^+ \stackrel{\text{def}}{=} \Lambda_Z$, where $Z = \bigvee X$
FD= $\varnothing$	Boolean Algebra

We prove the following in [2]:

Proposition 3.2. *If all functional dependencies are simple, then $\mathbf{L}$ is a distributive lattice.*

3.2 Database Instances for a Lattice

Let $\mathbf{X}$ denote the set of join-irreducibles of a lattice $\mathbf{L}$, and let $\mathsf{FD} = \{X \to \Lambda_{\bigvee X} \mid X \subseteq \mathbf{X}\}$ be all fd's implicitly defined by $\mathbf{L}$. A *database instance D for $\mathbf{L}$* is a relation with attributes $\mathbf{X}$ that satisfies FD. We denote $h_D : \mathbf{L} \to \mathbb{R}^+$ the restriction of its entropy function (as Sec. 2) to closed sets. If $(\mathbf{L}, \mathbf{R})$ is the lattice representation of a query (Q, FD), then any database instance for $\mathbf{L}$ defines a standard database instance for Q by $R_j^D \stackrel{\text{def}}{=} \Pi_{R_j}(D)$. For example, the query

$$Q \text{ :- } R(x), S(y), T(z), xy \to z, xz \to y, yz \to x$$

has corresponding lattice $\mathbf{L}$ isomorphic to M_3 in Fig. 6. The relation $D = \{(i, j, k) \in [N]^3 \mid i + j + k \mod N = 0\}$ is a database instance for M_3, which yields the standard instance: $R^D = S^D = T^D = [N]$. Notice that in this example, all fd's are unguarded and hence lost in the standard instance. Starting from Sec. 5.1 we will assume that during the query evaluation we have access to the UDF's that defined the unguarded fd's.

Definition 3.3 (Materializability). A function $h : \mathbf{L} \to \mathbb{R}^+$ is called *materializable* w.r.t. an input query $(\mathbf{L}, \mathbf{R})$ if there exists an instance D such that $\log |R_j^D| \leqslant h(R_j)$ forall $j \in [m]$ and $\log |Q^D| \geqslant h(\hat{1})$.

3.3 The Lattice Linear Program

Given a query $(\mathbf{L}, \mathbf{R})$ and log cardinalities $(n_j)_{j=1}^m$, define the following linear program

$$\begin{aligned} &\text{maximize } h(\hat{1}) \qquad (4)\\ \forall X \not\lesseqgtr Y &: h(X \wedge Y) + h(X \vee Y) \leqslant h(X) + h(Y) \\ \forall j \in [m] &: h(R_j) \leqslant n_j \end{aligned}$$

over *non-negative* variables $(h(X))_{X \in \mathbf{L}}$. This is called the *Lattice Linear Program*, or LLP; its optimal objective will be shown to be exactly GLVV-bound.

A feasible solution h to LLP is called a (non-negative) **L**-*sub-modular* function. If h is also **L**-*monotone*, i.e. $X \preceq Y \Rightarrow h(X) \leqslant h(Y)$, and $h(\hat{0}) = 0$, then h is called an **L**-*polymatroid*. When **L** is clear from context we drop the **L**-prefix from **L**-monotone, **L**-submodular, and **L**-polymatroid, respectively. LLP did not require h to be a polymatroid because, at optimality, h^* can always be taken to be a polymatroid thanks to *Lovász's monotonization*: if h is non-negative **L**-submodular, then the function $\bar{h}(\hat{0}) \stackrel{\text{def}}{=} 0$ and $\bar{h}(X) \stackrel{\text{def}}{=} \min_{Y:X \preceq Y} h(Y)$, $X \neq \hat{0}$, is an **L**-polymatroid (see e.g. [21], pp. 774) and satisfies: $\bar{h}(\hat{1}) = h(\hat{1})$ and $\forall X$, $\bar{h}(X) \leqslant h(X)$. The full version [2] has the (very short) proof of the following lattice-based formulation of GLVV-bound:

Proposition 3.4. *Let h^* be an optimal solution to the LLP of a query $(Q, \mathsf{FD}) = (\mathbf{L}, \mathbf{R})$. Then, $2^{h^*(\hat{1})} = \mathsf{GLVV}(Q)$.*

When $\mathsf{FD} = \varnothing$, **L** is a Boolean algebra in which case we show in [2] that $\mathsf{AGM}(Q) = 2^{h^*(\hat{1})}$.

3.4 Embeddings

The main goal in this paper is to design algorithms that compute a query (Q, FD) (i.e. $(\mathbf{L}, \mathbf{R})$) in time $\tilde{O}(2^{h^*(\hat{1})})$. Whenever GLVV-bound is tight such an algorithm is worst-case optimal, hence our second goal is to study cases when the bound is tight. This happens if and only if the LLP has some optimal solution h^* that is materializable w.r.t. $(\mathbf{L}, \mathbf{R})$. A secondary goal in this paper is to find sufficient conditions for h to be materializable. Embeddings allow us to "transfer" materializability of polymatroids from one lattice to another.

Definition 3.5. An *embedding* between two lattices **L** and $\mathbf{L}'$ is a function $f : \mathbf{L} \to \mathbf{L}'$ such that $f(\bigvee X) = \bigvee f(X)$ forall $X \subseteq \mathbf{L}$, and $f(\hat{1}_{\mathbf{L}}) = \hat{1}_{\mathbf{L}'}$. An embedding between two queries $f : (\mathbf{L}, \mathbf{R}) \to (\mathbf{L}', \mathbf{R}')$ is an embedding from **L** to $\mathbf{L}'$ that is a bijection from **R** to $\mathbf{R}'$.

If f is an embedding from **L** to $\mathbf{L}'$ and h' is a non-negative, sub-modular function on $\mathbf{L}'$, then one can check that $h \stackrel{\text{def}}{=} h' \circ f$ is also sub-modular. If f is an embedding between queries, then their relation symbols are in 1-1 correspondence: $R_1, \ldots, R_m$ and $R'_1, \ldots, R'_m$ respectively. Fix two queries $(Q, \mathsf{FD}), (Q', \mathsf{FD}')$ with variables $\mathbf{X}, \mathbf{X}'$ respectively. Call a function $\mathcal{L} : 2^{\mathbf{X}} \to 2^{\mathbf{X}'}$ a *variable renaming* if $\mathcal{L}(X) = \mathcal{L}(X^+)$, $\mathcal{L}(X) = (\bigcup_{x \in X} \mathcal{L}(x))^+$ ($\mathcal{L}$ is uniquely defined by its values on single variables), and $\mathcal{L}(\mathbf{X}) = \mathbf{X}'$ (all variables in Q' are used). One can check that every embedding f defines the variable renaming $\mathcal{L}(X) \stackrel{\text{def}}{=} f(X^+)$ for all $X \subseteq \mathbf{X}$, and vice versa.

Fix an embedding $f : \mathbf{L} \to \mathbf{L}'$, and an instance D' for $\mathbf{L}'$. Define the database instance $D \stackrel{\text{def}}{=} f^{-1}(D')$ as $D \stackrel{\text{def}}{=} \{t \circ \mathcal{L} \mid t \in D'\}$. In other words, every tuple $t' \in D'$ has attributes $\mathbf{X}'$, hence it can be viewed as a function $t' : \mathbf{X}' \to$ Dom: for each such t' we include in D a tuple $t' \circ \mathcal{L} : \mathbf{X} \to$ Dom, obtained from t' by renaming its attributes. One can check that $|D| = |D'|$ (because all variables in $\mathbf{X}'$ are used), and the same holds for all projections $|\Pi_X(D)| = |\Pi_{\mathcal{L}(X)}(D')|$ for all $X \subseteq \mathbf{X}$. This proves:

Proposition 3.6. *If $f : \mathbf{L} \to \mathbf{L}'$ is a lattice embedding, then for any instance D' for $\mathbf{L}'$, $h_D = h_{D'} \circ f$, where $D \stackrel{\text{def}}{=} f^{-1}(D')$. If $f : (\mathbf{L}, \mathbf{R}) \to (\mathbf{L}', \mathbf{R}')$ is a query embedding, and $h' : \mathbf{L}' \to \mathbb{R}^+$ is materializable, then $h \stackrel{\text{def}}{=} h' \circ f$ is also materializable.*

Definition 3.7. A *quasi-product database instance* for **L** is an instance of the form $f^{-1}(D')$ where f embeds **L** into a Boolean algebra A, and D' is a product instance for A.

In absence of fd's, the worst-case output size reaches the AGM-bound on some product instance. In Theorem 4.5 we characterize queries whose worst-case output size is the GLVV-bound, achieved on a quasi-product database instance.

3.5 Inequalities

In information theory, an *information inequality* is defined by a vector of real numbers $(w_X)_{X \subseteq \mathbf{X}}$ such that the inequality $\sum_{X \subseteq \mathbf{X}} w_X H(X) \geqslant 0$ holds for any entropic function H. Fix a query $(\mathbf{L}, \mathbf{R})$. An *output-inequality* is given by a vector of non-negative real numbers $(w_j)_{j \in [m]}$ such that the inequality

$$\sum_{j=1}^{m} w_j h(R_j) \geqslant h(\hat{1}) \tag{5}$$

holds for all polymatroids h on the lattice **L**. For example, in a Boolean algebra output inequalities correspond to Shearer's lemma: $\sum_j w_j h(R_j) \geqslant h(\mathbf{X})$ iff $(w_j)_{j=1}^m$ is a fractional edge cover of the hypergraph with nodes $\{x \mid x \in \mathbf{X}\}$ and hyperedges $\{R_j \mid j \in [m]\}$. *Any* output inequality gives us immediately an upper bound on the output size of a query, because (5) implies $h(\hat{1}) \leqslant \sum_j w_j n_j$ for any feasible solution h of the LLP with log-cardinalities $(n_j)_{j=1}^m$.

An output size upper bound is best if it is minimized, which is precisely the objective of the *dual-LLP*, which is defined over *non-negative* variables $(w_j)_{j=1}^m$ and $(s_{X,Y})_{X \not\lesseqgtr Y}$, corresponding to the input R_j and incomparable pairs of lattice elements (thus $s_{X,Y}$ is the same variable as $s_{Y,X}$). The definition of the dual-LLP and the proof of the following lemma can be found in the full version [2].

Lemma 3.8. *Let M denote the matrix of sub-modular inequalities (first inequality of the LLP (4)). Given a non-negative vector $(w_j)_{j \in [m]}$, define the vector $(c_X)_{X \in \mathbf{L}}$ by setting $c_{\hat{1}} \stackrel{\text{def}}{=} 1$, $c_{R_j} \stackrel{\text{def}}{=} -w_j$ and $c_X \stackrel{\text{def}}{=} 0$ otherwise. Then, the following statements are equivalent*

(i) (5) *holds for all polymatroids h*

(ii) (5) *holds for all non-negative sub-modular functions h*

(iii) there exists $s \geqslant 0$ such that $c^T \leqslant s^T M$. Equivalently, w is part of a feasible solution (s, w) of the dual-LLP.

Furthermore, if (s^*, w^*) and h^* are dual- and primal-optimal solutions, then $h^*(\hat{1}) = \sum_{j=1}^m w_j^* n_j$.

4. NORMAL LATTICES

This section shows that an **L**-polymatroid h can be materialized as a quasi-product database instance iff it satisfies all output inequalities given by fractional edge covers of a certain hypergraph; in that case we call h *normal*. Normal polymatroids are the largest class of polymatroids that preserve the elegant properties of the AGM bound: upper bound given in terms of a fractional edge cover, and lower bound given by a (quasi-) product database. We then extend normality to lattices, which we call normal if the lattice's optimal polymatroid h^* is normal. We show that every feasible solution to LLP on a normal lattice is materializable, and thus the GLVV-bound is tight on a normal lattice.

4.1 Normal polymatroids

Recall the Möbius inversion formula [22] in a lattice $\mathbf{L}$:

$$h(X) = \sum_{Y:X \preceq Y} g(Y) \quad \text{iff} \quad g(X) = \sum_{Y:X \preceq Y} \mu(X,Y)h(Y) \tag{6}$$

where $\mu(X,Y)$ is the Möbius function on $\mathbf{L}$ [22]. In information theory, when h is an entropy and $\mathbf{L}$ a Boolean algebra, the quantity $-g(X)$ is exactly the (multivariate) *conditional mutual information* $I(\hat{1}-X \mid X)$, which we abbreviate CMI. There is a simple sufficient condition on g which implies that h, defined by Eq.(6) is a polymatroid. (See Appendix A or the full version [2] for missing proofs.)

Lemma 4.1. *Let g be any function s.t. $g(Z) \leqslant 0$ for $Z \prec \hat{1}$, and $g(\hat{1}) = -\sum_{Z \prec \hat{1}} g(Z)$. Then the function h defined by Eq.(6) is a polymatroid. Furthermore, if $\mathbf{L}$ is distributive, then h is a modular polymatroid, i.e. $h(X) + h(Y) = h(X \vee Y) + h(X \wedge Y)$ for all $X, Y \in \mathbf{L}$.*

Any function h satisfying the property stated in Lemma 4.1 is called a *normal submodular function*. If, furthermore, $g(Z) = 0$ for all $Z \prec \hat{1}$ other than the co-atoms, then we say that h is *strictly normal*. The function h in our running example Fig. 1 is strictly normal because it is defined by the CMI g shown in the figure. The function h on the left of Fig. 6 is not normal, because its CMI satisfies $g(\hat{0}) > 0$.

Normal polymatroids are precisely non-negative linear combinations of "step functions". For every $Z \in \mathbf{L}$, *the step function h_Z at Z* is defined by $h_Z(X) = 1$ if $X \npreceq Z$, and 0 otherwise. Every step function is normal, because its Möbius inverse is $g_Z(\hat{1}) = 1$, $g_Z(Z) = -1$, and $g_Z(X) = 0$ otherwise. Any non-negative linear combination of step functions is normal. Conversely, if h is a normal polymatroid, then denoting $a_Z = -g(Z)$ for all $Z \neq \hat{1}$ we have $a_Z \geqslant 0$ (since h is normal) and $g = \sum_Z a_Z g_Z$, implying $h = \sum_Z a_Z h_Z$.

There are a couple of interesting properties of normal polymatroids, both of which allow us to prove lower bounds for $h^*(\hat{1})$. The first property is a generalization of the fact that the AGM-bound is tight.

Lemma 4.2. *Let h be an integral, non-negative, submodular function h on a lattice $\mathbf{L}$. Then h is normal iff it is the entropy function of a quasi-product instance (Definition 3.7).*

The second property is a generalization of AGM-bound. To state the second property, we need:

Definition 4.3. Let $(\mathbf{L}, \mathbf{R})$ be a query given in lattice representation. The co-atomic hypergraph $H_{\text{co}} = (V_{\text{co}}, E_{\text{co}})$ is defined as follows. The nodes V_{co} are the co-atoms of $\mathbf{L}$, and $E_{\text{co}} = \{e_1, \ldots, e_m\}$ with $e_j = \{Z \mid Z \in V_{\text{co}}, R_j \npreceq Z, R_j \in \mathbf{R}\}$. In other words, each relation R_j defines a hyperedge e_j consisting of those nodes that do *not* contain the variables of R_j. A simple illustration of a co-atomic hypergraph is in Fig.2.

Lemma 4.4. *Inequality (5) holds for all normal polymatroids h iff it holds for all strictly normal polymatroids iff $(w_j)_{j=1}^m$ is a fractional edge cover of H_{co}.*

The co-atomic hypergraph is the natural concept to capture Shearer's lemma in a general lattice. In fact, every vector $(w_j)_{j=1}^m$ for which the output inequality (5) holds is a fractional edge cover of the co-atomic hypergraph. One may wonder whether the output inequalities could also be described by the *atomic hypergraph*, defined in a similar way, however the latter does not seem to lead to any interesting properties, except for a Boolean algebra $2^{\mathbf{X}}$ where the atomic and co-atomic hypergraphs are isomorphic via $x \mapsto \mathbf{X} - \{x\}$.

4.2 Normal Lattices

A normal lattice is a lattice where, at optimality, the polymatroid is normal. This is captured by the following, which is the main result of this section. (See the full version [2] for a proof.)

Theorem 4.5. *Let $(\mathbf{L}, \mathbf{R})$ be a query in lattice representation. The following are equivalent:*

1. *For every non-negative, submodular function h there exists a normal polymatroid h' s.t. $h'(\hat{1}) = h(\hat{1})$ and $h'(R_j) \leqslant h(R_j)$ for all $R_j \in \mathbf{R}$.*
2. *The previous property holds for h' strictly normal.*
3. *Output inequality (5) holds for all non-negative, submodular functions h iff $\{w_j\}_{j=1}^m$ is a fractional edge cover of the co-atomic hypergraph.*
4. *Every non-negative submodular function h on $\mathbf{L}$ has a materialization that is a quasi-product database instance.*

We call $\mathbf{L}$ a *normal lattice w.r.t.* $\mathbf{R}$ if it satisfies any of these conditions, and a *normal lattice* if it is normal w.r.t. all $\mathbf{R}$. Normal lattices appear to be a new concept. It is decidable whether $\mathbf{L}$ is normal w.r.t. $\mathbf{R}$ using a brute-force procedure. In a normal lattice the GLVV-bound is tight (by item 4); we show [2] that every distributive lattice is normal, and thus the GLVV-bound is tight on those lattices.

Example 4.6. The lattice $\mathbf{L}$ in Fig.1 is normal w.r.t. inputs xy, yz, zu, which follows by exhaustively proving all inequalities defined by the fractional edge covers of the co-atomic hypergraph, shown in Fig. 2. For example, the edge cover $(1/2, 1/2, 1/2)$ corresponds to the inequality $h(xy) + h(yz) + h(zu) \geqslant 2h(\hat{1})$, which can be proven by $h(xy) + h(yz) \geqslant h(\hat{1}) + h(y)$ and $h(y) + h(zu) \geqslant h(\hat{1}) + h(0)$. In fact, $\mathbf{L}$ is normal w.r.t. any inputs. Notice that $\mathbf{L}$ is not distributive.

In the full version [2] we prove a necessary condition for normality, which we conjecture to be sufficient. Gottlob et al. [12] define a *coloring* of a query Q with variables $\mathbf{X}$ to be a function $\mathcal{L} : \mathbf{X} \to 2^{\mathbf{X}'}$ such that $\mathcal{L}(\mathbf{X}) \neq \varnothing$, and for any FD $X \to Y$, $\mathcal{L}(Y) \subseteq \mathcal{L}(X)$, where, for each set X, $\mathcal{L}(X) \stackrel{\text{def}}{=} \bigcup_{x \in X} \mathcal{L}(X)$. Then the *color number of $\mathcal{L}$* is defined as $C(\mathcal{L}) = |\mathcal{L}(\mathbf{X})| / \max_j |\mathcal{L}(R_j)|$ and the *color number of Q* is $\max_{\mathcal{L}} C(\mathcal{L})$. They prove two results: if the functional dependencies are restricted to simple keys then $|Q^D| \leqslant \left(\max_j |R_j^D|\right)^{C(Q)}$, and moreover this bound is essentially tight, even for general functional dependencies.

Colorings correspond one-to-one to integral, normal polymatroids, via $h(x) = |\bigcup_{x \in X} \mathcal{L}(x)|$. To see this, in one direction let $\mathcal{L} : \mathbf{X} \to 2^{\mathbf{X}'}$ be a coloring and define $h(X) \stackrel{\text{def}}{=} |\bigcup_{x \in X} \mathcal{L}(x)|$. The function $f(X) \stackrel{\text{def}}{=} \bigcup_{x \in X} \mathcal{L}(x)$ is an embedding $f : \mathbf{L} \to 2^{\mathbf{X}'}$ into a Boolean algebra (we assume w.l.o.g. that $f(\mathbf{X}) = \mathbf{X}'$, otherwise we redefine $\mathbf{X}'$), and we have $h = h' \circ f$ where $h'(Y) \stackrel{\text{def}}{=} |Y|$: since h' is a strictly normal polymatroid Lemma A.1 says that h is also normal.

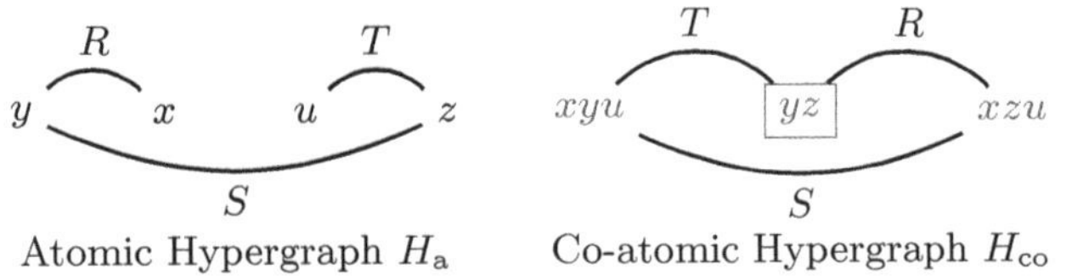

Figure 2: Atomic and Co-atomic hypergraphs for Fig.1

In the other direction, if h is an integral, normal polymatroid, then its canonical embedding (Definition A.2) defines a coloring $\mathcal{L}$ s.t. $h(X) \stackrel{\text{def}}{=} |\bigcup_{x \in X} \mathcal{L}(x)|$. Thus, colorings are essentially normal polymatroids. This implies the two results in [12] as follows. If FD consists only of simple keys, then the lattice **L** is distributive (Prop. 3.2), hence it is normal. Consequently, at optimality h^* can be assumed to be a normal polymatroid (Theorem 4.5 item 1), equivalently a coloring. The second result, tightness, follows from our Lemma 4.2, since any normal polymatroid (coloring) is the entropy of a quasi-product database instance.

5. PROOF SEQUENCE TO ALGORITHM

We aim to design an algorithm that, given an input query Q and database instance D, computes Q^D in time $\tilde{O}(2^{h^*(\hat{1})})$, where h^* is the optimal solution to the LLP (4). From Lemma 3.8, if (s^*, w^*) is dual-optimal then $h^*(\hat{1}) = \sum_{j=1}^m w_j^* n_j$ and the output inequality (5) holds with $w_j = w_j^*$, for *all* polymatroids. Our main algorithmic theme is to turn this process "inside-out": find a "proof" of inequality (5) consisting of a sequence of steps transforming the left-hand-side into the right-hand-side, then interpret these steps as algorithmic steps whose runtime does not exceed what the symbolic step allows.

We show that three different proof techniques for (5) lead to three different bounds and algorithms. The first two are known techniques for proving Shearer's lemma (i.e. the Boolean algebra case) that we adapt to lattices. The bounds are tight and the corresponding algorithms are worst-case optimal for some classes of lattices (such as distributive lattices, which include the Boolean algebra and the lattices of queries with simple fd's, subsuming results from [12,18,23]). However, for a generic lattice the bounds these techniques can prove are not $h(\hat{1}) \leqslant \sum_j w_j^* h(R_j)$, and thus the corresponding algorithms' runtimes in general can be worse than $\tilde{O}(2^{h^*(\hat{1})})$. An advantage of these two algorithms is that there is only one log-factor hidden in the $\tilde{O}$. Due to space limitations, the second bound and its corresponding algorithm are only described in the full version [2].

The last proof technique is our own, designed specifically to achieve the optimal LLP bound in an arbitrary lattice; this leads to an algorithm called CSMA running in the stated time of $\tilde{O}(2^{h^*(\hat{1})})$, where $\tilde{O}$ hides a polylogarithmic factor. This algorithm needs to regularize the data, somewhat similar in spirit to the uniformization step in [17] (see [2]).

5.1 Chain Bound and Chain Algorithm (CA)

Our first proof sequence adapts Jaikumar Radhakrishnan's proof of Shearer's lemma [20] to lattices, which is based on an arbitrary but fixed order of the random variables. We observe that a variable ordering corresponds to a maximal chain in the Boolean algebra. This idea allows us to generalize Radhakrishnan's proof to general lattices. Fix a chain $\mathbf{C} : \hat{0} = C_0 \prec C_1 \prec \cdots \prec C_k = \hat{1}$ in **L**. For $X \in \mathbf{L}$, we say that X *covers* i if $X \wedge C_i \neq X \wedge C_{i-1}$. Intuitively, X covers i if it contains some variable in C_i that does not appear in C_{i-1}. Fix a query represented by $(\mathbf{L}, \mathbf{R})$, where $\mathbf{R} = (R_1, \ldots, R_m)$.

Definition 5.1. The *chain hypergraph* associated with a chain $\mathbf{C}$ is $H_{\mathbf{C}} = ([k], \{e_j \mid j \in [m]\})$, where the hyperedge e_j contains all nodes i such that R_j covers i.

In a Boolean algebra all maximal chains have the same hypergraph, which is the same as the query hypergraph, and the co-atomic hypergraph. But in a general lattice all these hypergraphs may be different, and some output inequalities (5) can be derived only from non-maximal chains. For that reason, we relax the maximality requirement on the chain, as follows. We say that the chain $\mathbf{C}$ is *good* for R_j if:

$$\text{for all } i \in [k]: \quad i \in e_j \Rightarrow C_{i-1} \vee (R_j \wedge C_i) = C_i. \qquad (7)$$

The key property of "goodness" is that submodularity applies in the following way (see [2]):

Proposition 5.2. *If $\mathbf{C}$ is a maximal chain, then it is good for any R_j. Furthermore, if $\mathbf{C}$ is good for R_j, then, $\forall i \in e_j$,*

$$h(R_j \wedge C_i) - h(R_j \wedge C_{i-1}) \geqslant h(C_i) - h(C_{i-1}), \qquad (8)$$

*for every **L**-submodular function h.*

We say a chain $\mathbf{C}$ is *good* for $\mathbf{R}$ if it is good for all $R_j \in \mathbf{R}$. Radhakrishnan's proof is adapted to a lattice as follows.

Theorem 5.3 (The Chain Bound)**.** *Let $\mathbf{C}$ be any chain that is good for $\mathbf{R}$. If $(w_j)_{j=1}^m$ is any fractional edge cover of the chain hypergraph $H_{\mathbf{C}}$, then inequality (5) holds for any polymatroid h.*

Proof. By writing $h(R_j)$ as a telescoping sum, we obtain

$$\begin{aligned}
\sum_{j=1}^m w_j h(R_j) &= \sum_{j=1}^m w_j \cdot \left(\sum_{i \in e_j} (h(R_j \wedge C_i) - h(R_j \wedge C_{i-1})) \right) \\
\text{(from Eq.(8))} \quad &\geqslant \sum_{j=1}^m w_j \cdot \left(\sum_{i \in e_j} (h(C_i) - h(C_{i-1})) \right) \\
&= \sum_{i=1}^k \left(\sum_{j: i \in e_j} w_j \right) \cdot (h(C_i) - h(C_{i-1})) \\
&\geqslant \sum_{i=1}^k (h(C_i) - h(C_{i-1})) \\
&= h(\hat{1}),
\end{aligned}$$

where the last inequality holds because $(w_j)_{j=1}^m$ is a fractional edge cover of $H_{\mathbf{C}}$ and h is monotone. $\square$

Remark 5.4. Note that, if $\mathbf{C}$ is only good for a subset $\mathbf{R}'$ of $\mathbf{R}$, then we can apply the bound to $\mathbf{R}'$ with its corresponding chain hypergraph.

Example 5.5. Consider our running example from Figure 1; assume $|R| = |S| = |T| = N$. Consider the chain $\hat{0} \prec y \prec yz \prec xyzu = \hat{1}$, whose hypergraph has three vertices and hyperedges $e_R = \{y, xyzu\}$, $e_S = \{y, yz\}$, $e_T = \{yz, xyzu\}$. Thus, the chain bound on this chain is $N^{3/2}$, which is tight. (Consider the input $R = S = T = [\sqrt{N}] \times [\sqrt{N}]$, where the fd $xz \to u$ is defined by the UDF $f(x, z) = x$ and $yu \to x$ by $g(y, u) = u$.)

If there were no FD's, then the chain bound is exactly Shearer's lemma [9] (or, equivalently, AGM bound).

Corollary 5.6 (AGM bound and Shearer's lemma). *Consider a join query on n variables with no fd's. The chain bound on the chain $\mathbf{C}$: $C_0 = \emptyset \prec C_1 = [1] \prec C_2 = [2] \prec \cdots \prec C_n = [n]$ is exactly Shearer's lemma.*

Algorithm 1 The Chain Algorithm.

Input: A query $(\mathbf{L}, \mathbf{R})$, over $\mathbf{R} = \{R_1, \ldots, R_m\}$
Input: A good chain $\mathbf{C} : \hat{0} = C_0 \prec C_1 \prec \cdots \prec C_k = \hat{1}$
Input: Chain hypergraph $H_{\mathbf{C}} = ([k], \{e_1, \ldots, e_m\})$

```
1: Expand Q to Q+
2: Q0 = {()}
3: For i = 1 to k do
4:     Qi = ∅
5:     For each t ∈ Q(i-1) do
6:         T = ⋂_{j:i∈ej} (t ⋈ Π_{Rj∧Ci}(Rj))+        ▷ Takes time
       Õ( min_{j:i∈ej} |t ⋈ Π_{Rj∧Ci}(Rj)| ). See text.
7:         Qi = Qi ∪ T
8: Return Qk
```

The Chain Algorithm. In the proof above of the chain bound, the main idea is to take mixtures of conditional entropies (i.e. differences of two entropies), climbing up the chain. This strategy corresponds combinatorially to conditional search. From this proof, we derive Algorithm 1 that computes a query Q in time bounded by *any* fractional edge cover of the chain hypergraph. The algorithm assumes a fixed, good chain $\mathbf{C}$, where every node i is covered[4]. It pre-processes input relations by indexing them in an attribute order consistent with the chain. Then, it starts by expanding the query, as explained at the end of Sec. 2. Thus far it takes $\tilde{O}(N)$-time. Next, the algorithm computes inductively

$$Q_i \stackrel{\text{def}}{=} \left(\Join_{j:R_j \wedge C_i \neq \hat{0}} \Pi_{R_j \wedge C_i}(R_j)\right)^+,$$

for $i = 0, 1, \ldots, k$, where Q_i is an intermediate relation with attributes C_i. Initially Q_0 consists of just the empty tuple. Evidently, when $i = k$, Q_k is the output Q.

To compute Q_i, let R_j be some relation such that $i \in e_j$, in other words R_j has some new variable that occurs in C_i but not in C_{i-1}. Note that there exists at least one such R_j, because i is covered. Define

$$T_{ij} = Q_{i-1} \Join \Pi_{C_i \wedge R_j}(R_j),$$

whose attributes are $X_{ij} \stackrel{\text{def}}{=} C_{i-1} \cup (C_i \wedge R_j)$; and, by Eq.(7), its closure is $X_{ij}^+ = C_{i-1} \vee (C_i \wedge R_j) = C_i$. Consider T_{ij}'s expansion T_{ij}^+ (see Sec. 2): it has the same size as T_{ij} and has attributes $X_{ij}^+ = C_i$. Therefore,

$$Q_i = \bigcap_{j:i \in e_j} T_{ij}^+ = \bigcap_{j:i \in e_j} \left(Q_{i-1} \Join \Pi_{C_i \wedge R_j}(R_j)\right)^+.$$

[4]If i is not covered, in other words if $H_{\mathbf{C}}$ has an isolated vertex, then $\rho^*(H_{\mathbf{C}}) = \infty$, and the algorithm will not work.

However, we do not want to compute all the T_{ij}^+ and then compute the intersection to obtain Q_i, because this naïve strategy will push the runtime over the budget. In order to stay within the time budget, the algorithm computes this intersection differently: it iterates over all tuples $t \in Q_{i-1}$, and for each tuple computes the intersection T in line 6 in time $\tilde{O}(\min_{j:i \in e_j}(|t \Join \Pi_{R_j \wedge C_i}(R_j)|)$. This can be accomplished by first computing $j_* = \operatorname{argmin}_{j:i \in e_j}(|t \Join \Pi_{R_j \wedge C_i}(R_j)|)$ and tentatively setting $T = (t \Join \Pi_{R_{j_*} \wedge C_i}(R_{j_*}))^+$. Then, the algorithm removes from T any tuple t' that is not in the intersection defined in line 6. A tuple $t' \in T$ is not removed from T only if the following holds: for **every** $j \neq j_*$ s.t. R_j covers i, we have $\Pi_{C_i \wedge R_j}(t') \in \Pi_{C_i \wedge R_j}(R_j)$ **and** $(t \Join \Pi_{C_i \wedge R_j}(t'))^+ = t'$. Note the crucial fact that the relation R_{j_*} that is used to iterate over may depend on the tuple $t \in Q_{i-1}$. Due to the pre-processing step where every input relation is indexed with an attribute order consistent with the chain, j_* can easily be computed in logarithmic time in data complexity. The following is proved in Appendix B.

Theorem 5.7. *Assume the chain $\mathbf{C}$ is good for $\mathbf{R}$, and every node i is covered (i.e. no isolated vertices). Then, for any fractional edge cover of the chain hypergraph, $(w_j)_{j=1}^m$, the time taken by the Chain Algorithm to compute Q is $\tilde{O}(N + \prod_{j=1}^m N_j^{w_j})$, where $\tilde{O}$ hides a logarithmic factor needed for index lookup or binary search, and a small polynomial factor in query complexity.*

We present some examples.

Example 5.8. Continue with Example 5.5. The variable order corresponding to the chain $\hat{0} \prec y \prec yz \prec \hat{1}$ is $y, z, (xu)$, where x, u can be arranged in any order. The Chain Algorithm computes three intermediate relations:

$$\begin{aligned}
Q_1(y) &= \Pi_y(R(xy)) \cap \Pi_y(S(yz)) \\
Q_2(yz) &= Q_1(y) \Join S(yz) \\
Q_3(yzxu) &= (Q_2(yz) \Join R(xy))^+ \cap (Q_2(yz) \Join T(zu))^+
\end{aligned}$$

The first two steps are straightforward. In the third, the join $Q_2(yz) \Join R(xy)$ results in a relation with attributes xyz, which needs to be expanded with u (e.g. by computing the user-defined function $u = f(x, z)$), and similarly for the second join. However, the algorithm does not compute the joins first then intersect, instead it iterates over tuples $t \in Q_2(yz)$ and computes an intersection on a per-tuple basis using the less expensive option. In particular, for each $t = (y, z) \in Q_2$, it compares $|t \Join R(x, y)|$ and $|t \Join T(z, u)|$ (which can be done in logarithmic time given that R was indexed with attribute order (y, x) and T with order (z, u)). Suppose $|t \Join R(x, y)| \leqslant |t \Join T(z, u)|$, then for each $(y, z, x) \in t \Join R(x, y)$ the algorithm uses the $xz \to u$ FD to obtain the tuple (y, z, x, u). The next task is to verify that this tuple is indeed in the intersection as defined in line 6. This is done with *two* verifications: we make sure that $(z, u) \in T$, **and** that $yu \to x$ is indeed satisfied.[5]

On this chain the algorithm runs in optimal time $O(N^{3/2})$. We note that all previously proposed known worst-case optimal join algorithms for queries without FD's [18,19,23] require $\Omega(N^2)$ to compute the previous query on this instance: $R = S = T = \{(1, i) \mid i \in [N/2]\} \cup \{(i, 1) \mid i \in [N/2]\}$. For example, LFTJ with variable order y, z, x, u computes queries

[5]This is a subtle step in the algorithm that is easy to miss at the first read.

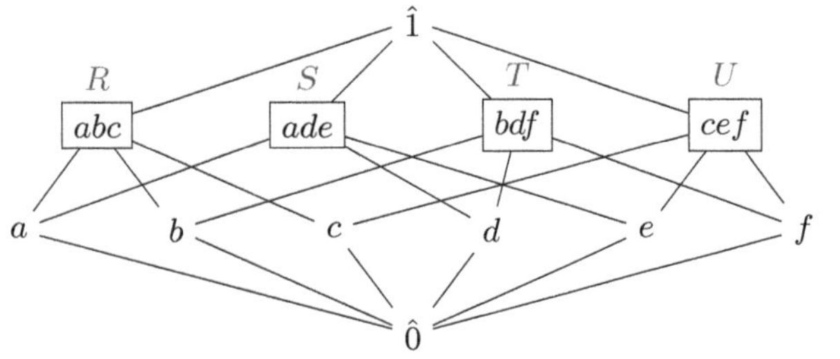

Figure 3: A query where the chain bound is not optimal

$Q_1(y), Q_2(yz), Q_3(xyz), Q_4(xyzu)$, where $|Q_3| = N^2$. Note, however, that not every maximal chain gives an optimal bound: for example the chain $\hat{0} \prec x \prec xu \prec xyu \prec xyzu = \hat{1}$ has hyperedges: $e_R = \{x, xyu\}$, $e_S = \{xyu, xyzu\}$, $e_T = \{xu, xyzu\}$ (isomorphic to the atomic hypergraph in Fig.2), and the optimal fractional edge covering number $\rho^* = 2$, hence the chain bound is $|Q^D| \leqslant N^2$, which is sub-optimal.

Example 5.9 (Chain bound is not always tight)**.** For some queries, even with normal lattices, no chains give a tight upper bound. This is illustrated by Q in Fig. 3. Consider the chain $\hat{0} \prec a \prec abc \prec \hat{1}$. Denoting $\{1, 2, 3\}$ the vertices of the chain hypergraph, its edges are $e_R = \{1, 2\}$, $e_S = \{1, 3\}$, $e_T = e_U = \{2, 3\}$. The optimal fractional edge cover is $(w_R, w_S, w_T, w_U) = (1/2, 1/2, 1/2, 0)$, $\rho^* = 3/2$, therefore the chain bound is $|Q^D| \leqslant N^{3/2}$ and the Chain Algorithm will run in this time. All other maximal chains give the same bound (non-maximal chains are not good). However, we show in [2] that $|Q^D| \leqslant N^{4/3}$, which means that no chain bound is tight.

Discussion. We show in [2] that the chain bound implies Shearer's lemma and AGM bound from the Boolean algebra; more generally it is tight on all distributive lattices. The lattice corresponding to simple FDs is distributive, thus the chain algorithm is worst-case optimal for simple FDs. We also presented examples and proved results on how to choose a good chain so that the chain hypergraph does not have an isolated vertex.

For brevity, we have described the Chain Algorithm using breadth-first search (or bottom-up). It can also be adapted to a depth-first implementation (or top-down), as used for example in LogicBlox' LFTJ [23], which does not materialize intermediate relations.

5.2 The CSMA Algorithm

There are lattices for which the chain bound and the SM-bound (for sub-modularity) [2] are not optimal.

Example 5.10. Consider the lattice in Fig. 4. It satisfies the inequality $h(M) + h(O) + h(P) \geqslant 2h(\hat{1}) + h(\hat{0})$, but the chain bound cannot derive it, and neither can the SM-proof [2]. It *can* be proved by summing up

$$h(M) + h(Z) \geqslant h(V) + h(G) \quad (9)$$
$$h(O) + h(Z) \geqslant h(W) + h(I) \quad (10)$$
$$h(P) + h(Z) \geqslant h(Y) + h(J) \quad (11)$$
$$h(V) + h(W) \geqslant h(\hat{1}) + h(R) \quad (12)$$
$$h(Y) + h(R) \geqslant h(\hat{1}) + h(Z) \quad (13)$$

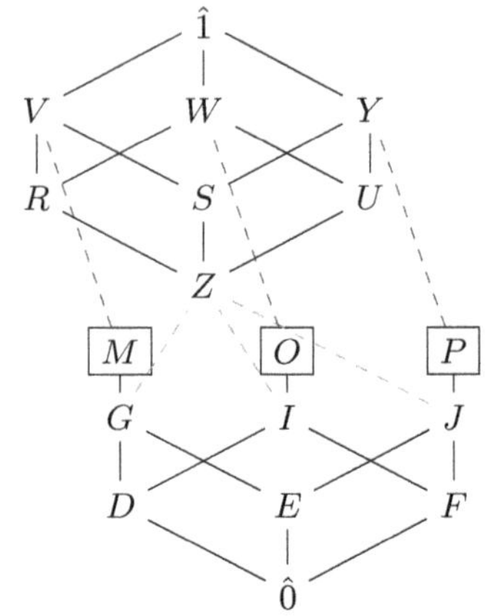

Figure 4: A lattice with a difficult-to-prove output inequality

$$h(G) + h(I) \geqslant h(Z) + h(D) \quad (14)$$
$$h(J) + h(D) \geqslant h(Z) + h(\hat{0}) \quad (15)$$

Our first goal in this section is to develop a set of rules that can prove any valid output inequality, including the one shown above in Example 5.10. In what follows, when $X \preceq Y$ we write $h(Y|X)$ as a short hand for $h(Y) - h(X)$. We assume h is a polymatroid. Our suggested proof strategy involves the following *three* basic rules:

- CD-rule: for $X \prec Y$, $h(Y) \to h(Y|X) + h(X)$.
- CC-rule: for $X \prec Y$, $h(Y|X) + h(X) \to h(Y)$.
- SM-rule: for $A \nleq B$, $h(A) + h(B|A \wedge B) \to h(A \vee B)$.

(CD stands for *conditional decomposition*, CC *conditional composition*, and SM *sub-modularity*.) Together, they are called the *CSM rules* (for *conditional submodularity*). The vision behind CSMA is to show that

- **(A)** every output inequality (5) can be proved by applying a series of CD, CC, and SM-rules: start with the left-hand side of an output inequality of the form (5), and repeatedly apply a CD/CC/SM-rule replacing the terms on the left-hand side of that rule with the terms on its right-hand side. In the end, we hope to end up with $h(\hat{1})$. The series of rules is then called a *CSM proof sequence* for the output inequality.
- **(B)** each rule can be interpreted combinatorially to become an algorithmic step, and together they constitute a join algorithm (called CSMA) that runs in time $\tilde{O}(2^{h^*(\hat{1})})$.

Interestingly, we fell short of objective (A) yet were able to achieve a *stronger* result than objective (B)! In particular, with respect to (A) we conjecture that the three rules above form a complete proof system. We only managed to prove a weaker version of the conjecture (Theorem 5.16) which is sufficient for CSMA to work, at the price of a poly-log factor. On the other hand, with respect to (B) we will work with output inequalities that are more general than (5), and with constraints that are more general than the fd-constraints.

Appendix C contains running examples illustrating the bound and algorithm of this section.

Conditional LLP *(*CLLP*)*. A key technical tool that helps realize the vision is a conditional version of LLP, called the *conditional* LLP (CLLP). A nice by-product of CLLP is that we will be able to compute join queries with given degree bounds, which is even more general than join queries with functional dependencies!

Definition 5.11 (Degree). Let $X, Y \in \mathbf{L}$ be two lattice elements, and $T(X)$, $T(Y)$ be two tables with attributes X, Y, respectively. Let $Z = X \wedge Y$ be the set of common variables in $T(X), T(Y)$. The $T(Y)$*-degree* of some value $v \in \prod_{z \in Z} \mathsf{Dom}(z)$ is the number of tuples in $T(Y)$ with $Z = v$:

$$\mathsf{degree}_{T(Y)}(v) \stackrel{\text{def}}{=} |\sigma_{Z=v}(T(Y))|. \tag{16}$$

Definition 5.12 (CLLP). Let $\mathcal{P}$ be some set of pairs $(X, Y) \in \mathbf{L}^2$ such that $X \prec Y$. Assume for every pair $(X, Y) \in \mathcal{P}$, there is a given non-negative number $n_{Y|X}$ called a *log-degree bound.* The CLLP is defined as:

$$\begin{array}{lll} \max & h(\hat{1}) & \\ \text{s.t.} & h(Y) - h(X) \leqslant n_{Y|X} & \forall (X,Y) \in \mathcal{P} \\ & h(A \vee B) + h(A \wedge B) \leqslant h(A) + h(B) & \forall A \lessgtr B \in \mathbf{L} \\ & h(X) - h(Y) \leqslant 0 & \forall X \prec Y \in \mathbf{L}. \end{array}$$

(By default, $h(\hat{0}) = 0$, and $h(X) \geqslant 0$.) In other words, CLLP requires h to be a polymatroid, subject to the additional constraints $h(Y) - h(X) \leqslant n_{Y|X}, \forall (X, Y) \in \mathcal{P}$, which are called log*-degree constraints.*

Both cardinality constraints and fd constraints are special cases of the log-degree constraints. Intuitively, cardinality constraints are degree bounds of the empty tuple (i.e. $h(Y) - h(\hat{0}) \leqslant n_{Y|\hat{0}} = n_Y$). An fd-constraint $X \to Y$ imposes the Y-degree bound of 1 for every X-tuple (i.e. $n_{Y|X} = 0$). The following is obvious:

Proposition 5.13. LLP *is exactly the same as* CLLP *for the special case when* $\mathcal{P} = \{(\hat{0}, R_j) \mid R_j \in \mathbf{R}\}$.

Furthermore, we can easily use the log-degree constraints to encode input relations with known maximum degree bounds.

We will also need the dual-CLLP.

Definition 5.14 (Dual-CLLP). Let $c_{Y|X}, s_{A,B}$ and $m_{X,Y}$ denote the (non-negative) dual variables corresponding to the log-degree, sub-modularity, and monotonicity constraints, respectively. For each $Z \in \mathbf{L} - \{\hat{0}\}$, define

$$\begin{aligned} \mathsf{netflow}(Z) \stackrel{\text{def}}{=} & \sum_{\substack{X:X \prec Z \\ (X,Z) \in \mathcal{P}}} c_{Z|X} - \sum_{\substack{Y:Z \prec Y \\ (Z,Y) \in \mathcal{P}}} c_{Y|Z} + \sum_{\substack{A \lessgtr B \\ A \wedge B = Z}} s_{A,B} \\ & + \sum_{\substack{A \lessgtr B \\ A \vee B = Z}} s_{A,B} - \sum_{A:A \lessgtr Z} s_{A,Z} - \sum_{X:X \prec Z} m_{X,Z} + \sum_{Y:Z \prec Y} m_{Z,Y}. \end{aligned}$$

Then, the dual-CLLP is

$$\begin{array}{lll} \min & \sum_{(X,Y) \in \mathcal{P}} n_{Y|X} c_{Y|X} & \\ \text{s.t.} & \mathsf{netflow}(\hat{1}) \geqslant 1 & \\ & \mathsf{netflow}(Z) \geqslant 0 & \forall Z \in \mathbf{L} - \{\hat{1}, \hat{0}\}. \end{array} \tag{17}$$

CSM proof sequence. The analog of output inequality (5) in the conditional world is

$$\sum_{(X,Y) \in \mathcal{P}} c_{Y|X} h(Y|X) \geqslant h(\hat{1}) \tag{18}$$

Identical to Lemma 3.8, we can show that (18) holds for all polymatroids if there are vectors s and m such that (c, s, m) is feasible to the dual-CLLP.

To answer question **(A)**, we prove a "reachability" lemma that helps us construct a CSM proof sequence. Let (c, s, m) be any feasible solution to the dual-CLLP (17). Let $K \subseteq \mathbf{L}$ be a set of lattice elements that contains $\hat{0}$. The *conditional closure* of K (with respect to (c, s, m)) is computed from K by repeatedly applying the following two steps: (1) CD-step ("Conditional Decomposition"): if $Y \in K$ and $X \prec Y$ then add X to K, (2) CC-step ("Conditional Composition"): if $X \in K$ and $c_{Y|X} > 0$ then add Y to K.

Lemma 5.15. *For any dual-feasible solution* (c, s, m)*, let* $K \subseteq \mathbf{L}$ *be a set that contains* $\hat{0}$*, and* $\bar{K}$ *be its conditional closure. If* $\hat{1} \notin \bar{K}$*, then there are two lattice elements* $A, B \in \bar{K}$ *such that* $A \vee B \notin \bar{K}$ *and* $s_{A,B} > 0$.

Proof. If $\hat{1} \notin \bar{K}$, then $S \stackrel{\text{def}}{=} \sum_{Z \notin \bar{K}} \mathsf{netflow}(Z) \geqslant 1$. If there is no such pair (A, B), then every dual variable $c_{Y|X}, m_{X,Y}, s_{A,B}$ contributes a non-positive amount to the sum S, which is a contradiction. □

The above lemma allows us to construct a "weak" CSM proof sequence for inequality (18), which is our answer to question **(A)** above. See Appendix C for a proof.

Theorem 5.16. *Let* (c, s, m) *be an arbitrary feasible solution to the dual-*CLLP*, where* $c_{Y|X} = q_{Y|X}/d$ *and* $s_{A,B} = q'_{A,B}/d$ *are rational numbers. Let* $\mathcal{B}$ *be a multiset of variables* $h(Y|X)$*,* $(X, Y) \in \mathcal{P}$*, where each variable* $h(Y|X)$ *occurs* $4^{|\mathbf{L}|} \cdot q_{Y|X}$ *times. Then, there is a sequence of CD-, CC-, and SM-rules* [6] *that transforms* $\mathcal{B}$ *into another multiset* $\bar{\mathcal{B}}$ *which contains the variable* $h(\hat{1})$*. Moreover, in this sequence all occurrences of identical rules are consecutive (hence, they can be combined into a single "rule with a multiplicity").*

Interpreted integrally, we think of the CSM proof sequence described in Theorem 5.16 as having $D \stackrel{\text{def}}{=} 4^{|\mathbf{L}|} d$ copies of $h(\hat{1})$ that it tries to reach, but at $\bar{\mathcal{B}}$ it reaches at least one copy and we stop. We call such a sequence *partial* in order to distinguish it from a *(full)* CSM proof sequence that reaches all D copies of $h(\hat{1})$.

The CSM algorithm (CSMA). CSMA is our answer to question **(B)**. The algorithm takes as input a join query with functional dependencies *and* maximum degree bounds (if any) from input relations. This input is represented by the set $\mathcal{P}^{(0)}$, corresponding log-degree bounds, and the linear program $\mathsf{CLLP}^{(0)}$. For example, if we use CSMA for the original join query with functional dependencies (with no other max-degree bounds), then we would be starting with $\mathcal{P}^{(0)} = \{(\hat{0}, R_j) \mid R_j \in \mathbf{R}\}$; in this case $\mathsf{CLLP}^{(0)}$ is equivalent to LLP.

Let $h^{(0)}$ and $(c^{(0)}, s^{(0)}, m^{(0)})$ be a pair of primal and dual optimal solutions to $\mathsf{CLLP}^{(0)}$, and OPT be its optimal objective value. CSMA takes the (partial) CSM-proof sequence for $\mathsf{CLLP}^{(0)}$ as symbolic *instructions.* For each instruction, CSMA does some computation, spawning a number of subproblems, creating new intermediate tables for the sub-problems if needed. The final output is contained in the union of outputs of the sub-problems.

[6]We can only apply SM-rules on pairs $A \lessgtr B$ if $s_{A,B} > 0$.

For each sub-problem, CSMA constructs a new set of pairs $\mathcal{P}'$, and a new linear program CLLP' with dual-feasible solution (c', s', m'). Note that to construct CLLP', there has to be a corresponding log-degree bound $n'_{Y|X}$ for each pair $(X, Y) \in \mathcal{P}'$. The following two invariants are maintained:

(Inv1) For any $(X, Y) \in \mathcal{P}'$, there is a table $T(Y)$ (a relation in the sub-problem) that "guards" the constraint $h(Y|X) \leqslant n'_{Y|X}$ of CLLP' in the sense that

$$\max_{v \in \Pi_X(T)} \log_2 \mathsf{degree}_T(v) \leqslant n'_{Y|X}.$$

(Note that if $X = \hat{0}$ then the above says $\log_2 |T| \leqslant n'_{Y|\hat{0}} = n'_Y$, which is a cardinality constraint.)

(Inv2) (c', s', m') is feasible to dual-CLLP' with objective value satisfying

$$\mathsf{OBJ}' \stackrel{\text{def}}{=} \sum_{(X,Y) \in \mathcal{P}} n'_{Y|X} c'_{Y|X} \leqslant \mathsf{OPT}.$$

It can be verified that the two invariants are satisfied at $\mathsf{CLLP}^{(0)}$. Next we describe how CSMA deals with each instruction from the CSM sequence.

(1) CD-rule $h(Y) \to h(Y|X) + h(X)$ with multiplicity t.

Recall that $h(Y)$ is just a short hand for $h(Y|\hat{0})$. By (Inv1) there is a table $T(Y)$ with $\log_2 |T| \leqslant n_Y$. Lemma C.1 shows that T can be partitioned into at most $\ell = 2 \log N$ sub-tables $T^{(1)}, \ldots, T^{(\ell)}$ such that $n^{(j)}_{Y|X} + n^{(j)}_X \leqslant n_Y$, for all $j \in [\ell]$, where

$$n^{(j)}_{Y|X} \stackrel{\text{def}}{=} \max_{v \in \Pi_X(T^{(j)})} \log_2 \mathsf{degree}_{T^{(j)}}(v),$$

$$n^{(j)}_X \stackrel{\text{def}}{=} \log_2 |\Pi_X(T^{(j)})|.$$

For each of these sub-tables $T^{(j)}$ of T, we create a sub-problem with T replaced by $T^{(j)}$. For the jth sub-problem, we add $(\hat{0}, X)$ and (X, Y) to $\mathcal{P}$ with corresponding log-degree constraints $h(X) \leqslant n^{(j)}_X$ and $h(Y|X) \leqslant n^{(j)}_{Y|X}$, respectively. We compute the projection of $T^{(j)}$ onto X so we have guards for the two new constraints. And we set $c'_{Y|X} = c_{Y|X} + t/D$, $c'_X = c_X + t/D$, $c'_Y = c_Y - t/D \geqslant 0$. If $c'_Y = 0$, then we remove $(\hat{0}, Y)$ from $\mathcal{P}$. By examining $\mathsf{netflow}(Z)$ at each node, we can verify that (c', s, m) is a feasible solution to the new CLLP' with a *reduction* in objective value of $(n_Y - n^{(j)}_{Y|X} - n^{(j)}_X)t/D$.

(2) CC-rule $h(Y|X) + h(X) \to h(Y)$ with multiplicity t.

Let R be the guard for $h(Y|X) \leqslant n_{Y|X}$ and S for $h(X) \leqslant n_X$. Let θ be a threshold to be determined. If $n_{Y|X} + n_X \leqslant \mathsf{OPT} + \theta$, then we can compute the table $T(Y) \stackrel{\text{def}}{=} S(X) \bowtie R(Y)$ by going over all tuples in S and expanding them using matching tuples in R. The runtime is $\tilde{O}(2^{n_X + n_{Y|X}}) = \tilde{O}(2^{\mathsf{OPT}+\theta})$. The dual solution is modified by setting

$$c'_{Y|X} = c_{Y|X} - t/D, \qquad c'_X = c_X - t/D,$$
$$c'_Y = c_Y + t/D, \qquad n'_Y = n_{Y|X} + n_X.$$

If $n_{Y|X} + n_X > \mathsf{OPT} + \theta$, we will start afresh from an optimal solution to the *current* CLLP. Lemma C.2 shows that the current CLLP has an optimal objective value at most $\mathsf{OPT} - \theta/(D-1)$.

(3) SM-rule $h(A) + h(B|A \wedge B) \to h(A \vee B)$ with multiplicity t.

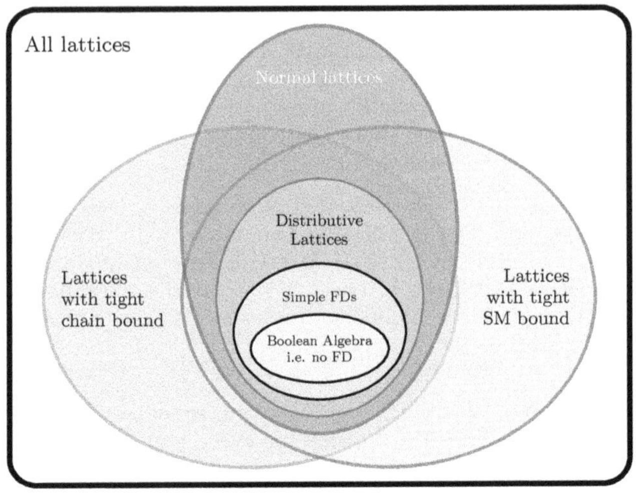

Figure 5: A summary of the lattices discussed in this paper

This is similar to case (2), and becomes identical to case (2) when $A = A \wedge B = X$ and $B = Y$. Let R be the guard for $h(A) \leqslant n_A$ and S for $h(B|A \wedge B) \leqslant n_{B|A \wedge B}$. If $n_A + n_{B|A \wedge B} \leqslant \mathsf{OPT} + \theta$, then we can compute $T(A \vee B) = R \bowtie S$ in time $\tilde{O}(2^{\mathsf{OPT}+\epsilon})$. If $n_A + n_{B|A \wedge B} > \mathsf{OPT} + \theta$, then we start afresh from a new optimal solution to the current CLLP. The minor difference to case (2) is that we have to modify the variable $s'_{A,B} = s_{A,B} - t/D$. By selecting the correct threshold θ, we prove (in Appendix C) that

Theorem 5.17. *CSMA runs in time $\tilde{O}(N + (\log N)^e 2^{OPT})$, where OPT is the optimal objective value for $\mathsf{CLLP}^{(0)}$, N is the input size, and e is a data-independent constant.*

6. CONCLUSIONS

We studied ways to prove worst-case output size bounds, and algorithms meeting the bounds for join queries with functional dependencies. A main aim was to design an algorithm running within time bounded by the entropy-based linear program proposed by Gottlob et al. [12]. For this purpose we developed new, lattice theoretic techniques, of independent interest. We described several classes of lattices, and several ways to prove upper or lower bounds on the worst-case query output, summarized in Fig. 5. On the algorithmic side, we devised the novel idea of turning a proof of an inequality into an algorithm. Three proof techniques lead to three different algorithms with increasing complexity. Our main algorithm does meet GLVV bound, up to a poly-log factor. The algorithm manages to solve a stronger problem, where input relations have prescribed maximum degree bounds, of which functional dependencies and cardinality bounds are special cases.

Acknowledgments

We thank Micheal Benedikt for thorough comments that significantly improved our presentation.

This work is partly supported by NSF grant 1535565, and by DARPA under agreement #FA8750-15-2-0009. The U.S. Government is authorized to reproduce and distribute reprints for Governmental purposes notwithstanding any copyright thereon.

7. REFERENCES

[1] C. R. Aberger, A. Nötzli, K. Olukotun, and C. Ré. Emptyheaded: Boolean algebra based graph processing. *CoRR*, abs/1503.02368, 2015.

[2] M. Abo Khamis, H. Q. Ngo, and D. Suciu. Computing join queries with functional dependencies. *CoRR*, abs/1604.00111, 2016.

[3] N. Alon, R. Yuster, and U. Zwick. Finding and counting given length cycles. *Algorithmica*, 17(3):209–223, 1997.

[4] M. Aref, B. ten Cate, T. J. Green, B. Kimelfeld, D. Olteanu, E. Pasalic, T. L. Veldhuizen, and G. Washburn. Design and implementation of the logicblox system. In T. K. Sellis, S. B. Davidson, and Z. G. Ives, editors, *Proceedings of the 2015 ACM SIGMOD International Conference on Management of Data, Melbourne, Victoria, Australia, May 31 - June 4, 2015*, pages 1371–1382. ACM, 2015.

[5] A. Atserias, M. Grohe, and D. Marx. Size bounds and query plans for relational joins. In *49th Annual IEEE Symposium on Foundations of Computer Science, FOCS 2008, October 25-28, 2008, Philadelphia, PA, USA*, pages 739–748, 2008.

[6] P. Balister and B. Bollobás. Projections, entropy and sumsets. *Combinatorica*, 32(2):125–141, 2012.

[7] M. Benedikt, J. Leblay, and E. Tsamoura. Querying with access patterns and integrity constraints. *PVLDB*, 8(6):690–701, 2015.

[8] S. Chu, M. Balazinska, and D. Suciu. From theory to practice: Efficient join query evaluation in a parallel database system. In *Proceedings of the 2015 ACM SIGMOD International Conference on Management of Data, Melbourne, Victoria, Australia, May 31 - June 4, 2015*, pages 63–78, 2015.

[9] F. R. K. Chung, R. L. Graham, P. Frankl, and J. B. Shearer. Some intersection theorems for ordered sets and graphs. *J. Combin. Theory Ser. A*, 43(1):23–37, 1986.

[10] J. Demetrovics, L. Libkin, and I. B. Muchnik. Functional dependencies in relational databases: A lattice point of view. *Discrete Applied Mathematics*, 40(2):155–185, 1992.

[11] T. Gogacz and S. Toruńczyk. Entropy bounds for conjunctive queries with functional dependencies. *CoRR*, abs/1512.01808, 2015.

[12] G. Gottlob, S. T. Lee, G. Valiant, and P. Valiant. Size and treewidth bounds for conjunctive queries. *J. ACM*, 59(3):16, 2012.

[13] M. Grohe and D. Marx. Constraint solving via fractional edge covers. In *SODA*, pages 289–298. ACM Press, 2006.

[14] P. Harremoës. Functional dependences and Bayesian networks. In *Proceedings WITMSE 2011*, Helsinki, 2011.

[15] M. Joglekar and C. Ré. It's all a matter of degree: Using degree information to optimize multiway joins. *CoRR*, abs/1508.01239, 2015.

[16] M. Levene. A lattice view of functional dependencies in incomplete relations. *Acta Cybern.*, 12(2):181–207, 1995.

[17] D. Marx. Tractable hypergraph properties for constraint satisfaction and conjunctive queries. *J. ACM*, 60(6):Art. 42, 51, 2013.

[18] H. Q. Ngo, E. Porat, C. Ré, and A. Rudra. Worst-case optimal join algorithms: [extended abstract]. In *PODS*, pages 37–48, 2012.

[19] H. Q. Ngo, C. Ré, and A. Rudra. Skew strikes back: new developments in the theory of join algorithms. *SIGMOD Record*, 42(4):5–16, 2013.

[20] J. Radhakrishnan. 6. entropy and counting. *Computational Mathematics, Modelling and Algorithms*, page 146, 2003.

[21] A. Schrijver. *Combinatorial optimization. Polyhedra and efficiency. Vol. B*, volume 24 of *Algorithms and Combinatorics*. Springer-Verlag, Berlin, 2003. Matroids, trees, stable sets, Chapters 39–69.

[22] R. P. Stanley. *Enumerative combinatorics. Volume 1*, volume 49 of *Cambridge Studies in Advanced Mathematics*. Cambridge University Press, Cambridge, second edition, 2012.

[23] T. L. Veldhuizen. Triejoin: A simple, worst-case optimal join algorithm. In N. Schweikardt, V. Christophides, and V. Leroy, editors, *Proc. 17th International Conference on Database Theory (ICDT), Athens, Greece, March 24-28, 2014.*, pages 96–106. OpenProceedings.org, 2014.

[24] R. W. Yeung. *Information Theory and Network Coding*. Springer Publishing Company, Incorporated, 1 edition, 2008.

[25] Z. Zhang and R. W. Yeung. On characterization of entropy function via information inequalities. *IEEE Transactions on Information Theory*, 44(4):1440–1452, 1998.

APPENDIX

A. ADDITIONAL MATERIAL FOR SEC 4

Lemma A.1. *Let $f : \mathbf{L} \to \mathbf{L}'$ be an embedding between two lattices, and let h' be a normal polymatroid on $\mathbf{L}'$. Then $h \stackrel{\text{def}}{=} h' \circ f$ is a normal polymatroid on $\mathbf{L}$.*

Proof. Recall that an embedding is the left adjoint of a Galois connection. Let $r : \mathbf{L}' \to \mathbf{L}$ be its right adjoint[7], in other words $f(X) \preceq Y$ iff $X \preceq r(Y)$. Let g' be the CMI for h'. The function $g(X) \stackrel{\text{def}}{=} \sum_{Y:r(Y)=X} g'(Y)$ is the CMI of h, because, for all $X \in \mathbf{L}$:

$$\begin{aligned}\sum_{Z:X\preceq Z} g(Z) &= \sum_{Z:X\preceq Z}\ \sum_{Z':r(Z')=Z} g'(Z') \\ &= \sum_{Z':X\preceq r(Z')} g'(Z') = \sum_{Z':f(X)\preceq Z'} g'(Z') \\ &= h'(f(X)) = h(X)\end{aligned}$$

In any Galois connection, $r(\hat{1}) = \hat{1}$ (since $f(\hat{1}) \preceq \hat{1}$ iff $\hat{1} \preceq r(\hat{1})$). By normality of h' we have $Y \neq \hat{1}$ implies $g'(Y) \leqslant 0$. Therefore, $X \neq \hat{1}$ implies $g(X) = \sum_{Y:r(Y)=X} g'(Y) \leqslant 0$, proving that h is normal. □

We need the following to prove Lemma 4.2:

[7] The standard notation is g, but we use g for the CMI.

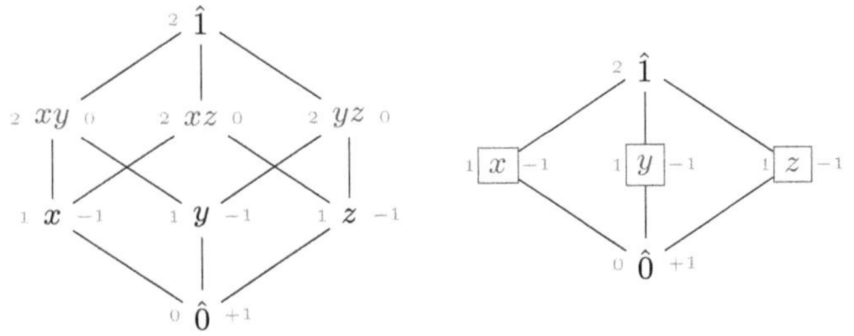

Figure 6: A non-normal function h (left) and the non-normal lattice M_3 (right)

Definition A.2. Let $A = 2^{\mathbf{X}}$ be a Boolean algebra. The canonical instance is the product database $D = [2]^{\mathbf{X}}$; note that $|\Pi_X(D)| = 2^{|X|}$, and thus $h_D(X) = |X|$, for all $X \subseteq \mathbf{X}$.

Let $\mathbf{L}$ be a lattice and h an integer-valued, normal polymatroid, and g its CMI. For all $X \in \mathbf{L}$, $X \neq \hat{1}$, let $C(X)$ be a set of $-g(X)$ arbitrary elements, such that the sets $(C(X))_{X \neq \hat{1}}$ are disjoint. Define $C(\hat{1}) = \emptyset$, and $\mathbf{C} \stackrel{\text{def}}{=} \bigcup_X C(X)$. The *canonical Boolean Algebra* is $A = (2^{\mathbf{C}}, \supseteq)$, and the *canonical embedding* of $\mathbf{L}$ is $f : \mathbf{L} \to A$, $f(X) \stackrel{\text{def}}{=} \bigcup_{Z: X \preceq Z} C(Z)$.

A is an "upside-down" Boolean algebra, where $Y \preceq Y'$ iff $Y \supseteq Y'$, and $\vee$ is set intersection; one can check that f commutes with $\vee$. We can now prove our result. (As in the AGM bound, there is a bit of loss when h are not integral, but this does not affect asymptotics)

Proof of Lemma 4.2. In one direction, let D be a quasi-product instance and h_D be its entropy function. By definition, $D = f^{-1}(D')$, where $f : \mathbf{L} \to A$ is an embedding into a Boolean algebra and D' is a product instance for A. Since $h_{D'}$ is normal (even strictly normal), h_D is also normal by Lemma A.1. In the opposite direction, assume h is normal. Let $f : \mathbf{L} \to A$ be the canonical embedding, and D' be the canonical instance for A. Then $D \stackrel{\text{def}}{=} f^{-1}(D')$ is the quasi-product instance, and one can check that $h = h_D = h_{D'} \circ f$. □

Proof of Lemma 4.4. Since each (stricly) normal polymatroid is a non-negative linear combination of (co-atomic) step functions, it suffices to assume that h is a step function. First consider a co-atomic step functions h_Z, i.e. Z is a co-atom: the left-hand side of Eq. (5) is $\sum_{j: Z \in e_j} w_j$, and the right-hand side is 1, meaning that the inequality holds iff $(w_j)_{j=1}^m$ covers node $Z \in V_{\text{co}}$. It remains to show that if (5) holds for all co-atomic step functions, then it holds for all step functions h_X: let Z be any co-atom s.t. $Z \succeq X$, then $h_Z \leq h_X$ and $h_Z(\hat{1}) = h_X(\hat{1}) = 1$ implying that (5) holds for h_X. □

Example A.3. The lattice on the left of Fig.6 is a Boolean algebra, hence it is normal: note that h in the figure is not normal[8], but we can simply increase $h(\hat{1})$ to 3 and now it is normal. The lattice M_3 on the right of Fig.6 is not normal. Its co-atomic hypergraph has edges $e_x = \{y, z\}$, $e_y = \{x, z\}$, $e_z = \{x, y\}$ and the inequality corresponding to the fractional edge cover $(1/2, 1/2, 1/2)$, $h(x) + h(y) + h(z) \geq 2h(\hat{1})$, fails for the submodular function shown in the figure. In particular, this polymatroid h is not materializable as a quasi-product database instance, but can be materialized as $\{(i, j, k) \mid i, j, k \in \{0, 1\}, i + j + k = 0 \mod 2\}$.

[8]The function XOR on three variables, $R(x, y, z) = \{(a, b, c) \mid a, b, c \in \{0, 1\}, a \text{ xor } b \text{ xor } c = 0\}$, is the canonical example of a distribution whose entropy has a negative mutual information.

B. ADDITIONAL MATERIAL FOR SEC 5.1

Proof of Theorem 5.7. We define some notation. For any tuple t and each relation R_j such that $R_j \wedge C_i \neq \hat{0}$, denote $n_{ijt} = |t \bowtie \Pi_{R_j \wedge C_i}(R_j)|$. Note that if $t = ()$ is the empty tuple, then $n_{ijt} = n_{ij()} = |\Pi_{R_j \wedge C_i}(R_j)|$.

Fix an iteration i. Denote by Time_i the time taken by iteration i (to compute Q_i). We will show that, for any $i \in [k]$,

$$\text{Time}_i = \tilde{O}\left(\prod_{j: R_j \wedge C_i \neq \hat{0}} n_{ij()}^{w_j} \right). \tag{19}$$

Since $n_{ij()} \leq |R_j|$, the sum over all Time_i will be at most $\tilde{O}(\prod_{j=1}^m |R_j|^{w_j})$, as desired. To bound Time_i, note that the number of steps taken to compute Q_i is

$$\sum_{t \in Q_{i-1}} \min_{j: i \in e_j} n_{ijt} \leq \sum_{t \in Q_{i-1}} \prod_{j: i \in e_j} n_{ijt}^{w_j} = \sum_{t \in Q_{i-1}} \prod_{j: R_j \wedge C_i \neq \hat{0}} n_{ijt}^{w_j}.$$

The equality follows from the fact that, if $t \in Q_{i-1}$ and $R_j \wedge C_i \neq \hat{0}$ but $i \notin e_j$, then $n_{ijt} = 1$. Hence, to show (19), it is sufficient to show the following:

$$\sum_{t \in Q_{i-1}} \prod_{j: R_j \wedge C_i \neq \hat{0}} n_{ijt}^{w_j} \leq \prod_{j: R_j \wedge C_i \neq \hat{0}} |n_{ij()}|^{w_j}. \tag{20}$$

For $0 \leq \ell \leq i - 1$, define

$$T_\ell \stackrel{\text{def}}{=} \Pi_{C_\ell}(Q_{i-1}), \qquad g(\ell) \stackrel{\text{def}}{=} \sum_{t \in T_\ell} \prod_{j: R_j \wedge C_i \neq \hat{0}} n_{ijt}^{w_j}.$$

By convention, T_0 has a single empty tuple $t = ()$. Then, (20) is equivalent to $g(i-1) \leq g(0)$. Thus, to show (20) it is sufficient to show that $g(\ell)$ is non-increasing in ℓ:

$$\begin{aligned}
g(\ell) &= \sum_{t \in T_\ell} \prod_{j: R_j \wedge C_i \neq \hat{0}} n_{ijt}^{w_j} \\
&= \sum_{u \in T_{\ell-1}} \sum_{\substack{v: \\ (u,v) \in T_\ell}} \prod_{j: R_j \wedge C_i \neq \hat{0}} n_{ij(u,v)}^{w_j} \\
&= \sum_{u \in T_{\ell-1}} \prod_{\substack{j: R_j \wedge C_i \neq \hat{0} \\ i-1 \notin e_j}} n_{iju}^{w_j} \sum_{\substack{v: \\ (u,v) \in T_\ell}} \prod_{\substack{j: R_j \wedge C_i \neq \hat{0} \\ i-1 \in e_j}} n_{ij(u,v)}^{w_j} \\
&\leq \sum_{u \in T_{\ell-1}} \prod_{\substack{j: R_j \wedge C_i \neq \hat{0} \\ i-1 \notin e_j}} n_{iju}^{w_j} \prod_{\substack{j: R_j \wedge C_i \neq \hat{0} \\ i-1 \in e_j}} \left(\sum_{\substack{v: \\ (u,v) \in T_\ell}} n_{ij(u,v)} \right)^{w_j} \\
&\leq \sum_{u \in T_{\ell-1}} \prod_{\substack{j: R_j \wedge C_i \neq \hat{0} \\ i-1 \notin e_j}} n_{iju}^{w_j} \prod_{\substack{j: R_j \wedge C_i \neq \hat{0} \\ i-1 \in e_j}} n_{iju}^{w_j} \\
&= \sum_{u \in T_{\ell-1}} \prod_{j: R_j \wedge C_i \neq \hat{0}} n_{iju}^{w_j} = g(\ell - 1).
\end{aligned}$$

The first inequality is generalized Hölder inequality, which applies because $(w_j)_{j=1}^m$ fractionally cover vertex $i-1$ of the chain hypergraph $H_{\mathbf{C}}$. The second inequality holds because, for every $u \in T_{\ell-1}$, $u \bowtie \Pi_{R_j \wedge C_i}(R_j) \supseteq T_\ell$. □

C. ADDITIONAL MATERIAL FOR SEC. 5.2

Example (5.10 **Continued**: CLLP)**.** Consider the lattice in Figure 4. Suppose the input relations are $T(M), T(O), T(P)$ (along with FDs imposing the lattice structure),[9] and we are not given any other bounds on degrees/cardinalities, then the CLLP has $\mathcal{P} = \{(\hat{0}, M), (\hat{0}, O), (\hat{0}, P)\}$ where $n_M = n_{M|\hat{0}} = \log_2 |T(M)|$, $n_O = n_{O|\hat{0}} = \log_2 |T(O)|$, and $n_P = n_{P|\hat{0}} = \log_2 |T(P)|$. In this case CLLP is just LLP. If in addition we also knew, for example, an upper bound d on the degree of G in table $T(M)$, then we can extend the CLLP by adding (G, M) to $\mathcal{P}$ where $n_{M|G} = \log_2 d$.

As mentioned earlier, this lattice satisfies the inequality $2h(\hat{1}) \leqslant h(M) + h(O) + h(P)$, which does not admit an SM-proof. In the CLLP, this inequality corresponds to the constraint $h(\hat{1}) \leqslant \frac{n_M+n_O+n_P}{2}$, which results from the following dual solution.

$$\begin{aligned} c_M = c_O = c_P &= 1/2, \\ s_{M,Z} = s_{O,Z} = s_{P,Z} &= 1/2, \\ s_{V,W} = s_{R,Y} = s_{G,I} = s_{D,J} &= 1/2, \end{aligned} \tag{21}$$

(where all dual variables not specified above are zeros). In this dual solution, $\mathsf{netflow}(\hat{1}) = 1$ and all other lattice nodes have a netflow value of 0. Hence, this solution is feasible.

Proof of Theorem 5.16. We prove the theorem with an algorithm. We start from the set $K = \{\hat{0}\}$, and keep adding elements to it using conditional closure (CC- and CD-) steps until K is conditionally closed; then we add a new element $A \vee B$ with an SM-step using the pair (A, B) found by Lemma 5.15. This process is repeated until $\hat{1} \in K$. With regard to $\mathcal{B}$, initially we will pretend that for each variable $h(Y|X) \in \mathcal{B}$ we have only $q_{Y|X}$ copies of it instead of $4^{|\mathbf{L}|}q_{Y|X}$ copies. While adding elements to K, we will also add variables to $\mathcal{B}$ so eventually $\mathcal{B}$ contains $\leqslant 4^{|\mathbf{L}|}q_{Y|X}$ of each variable.

We maintain the following invariants throughout the execution of the algorithm:

(1) For every $X \in K$, there is at least one copy of $h(X)$ in $\mathcal{B}$. To maintain this invariant, whenever we add a new element X to K while $\mathcal{B}$ does not contain any copy of $h(X)$, we apply some CSM rules on $\mathcal{B}$ to produce $h(X)$.

(2) For every copy of $h(Y|X)$ currently in $\mathcal{B}$, there will always remain at least one copy of $h(Y|X)$ after each step of the algorithm (i.e. in all subsequent multisets $\mathcal{B}$). To maintain this invariant, before applying any rule (where we will be losing one copy of each term on the left-hand side of that rule in order to gain one copy of each term on the right-hand side), we duplicate the multiplicities of all terms in the current $\mathcal{B}$, all previous multisets $\mathcal{B}$, and all rules that have been applied previously. (In effect, we re-run the entire history of rule application once.)

The above invariants are initially satisfied. Now we take the conditional closure of K. Whenever X is added to K due to some $Y \in K$ that satisfies $X \prec Y$ (signaling a CD-step), we first check whether $\mathcal{B}$ contains a copy of $h(X)$. If it does, then no further action is needed. If not, we duplicate multiplicities in the current and all previous $\mathcal{B}$ and all previous rules, and then we apply a CD-rule $h(Y) \to h(X) + h(Y|X)$.

[9] We abuse notation here, when the same notation symbol is used for different input relations. This is to avoid notation cluttering later in the description of the algorithm.

Whenever Y is added to K due to $c_{Y|X} > 0$ for some $X \in K$, we first check whether $h(Y)$ is in $\mathcal{B}$ already. If not, we duplicate all multiplicities as before, and then apply a CC-rule $h(X) + h(Y|X) \to h(Y)$.

Now, suppose K is already conditionally closed, we add $A \vee B$ using an SM-step guaranteed by Lemma 5.15. We check whether $h(A \vee B)$ is in $\mathcal{B}$. If it is not, we check whether $h(B|A \wedge B)$ is in $\mathcal{B}$. If it is not, we duplicate all multiplicities and apply a CD-rule $h(B) \to h(A \wedge B) + h(B|A \wedge B)$. Now, duplicate all multiplicities again, and apply an SM-rule $h(A) + h(B|A \wedge B) \to h(A \vee B)$.

For each element that is added to K, we have to duplicate its multiplicity at most twice, and there are at most $|\mathbf{L}|$ such elements.

Finally, we show that the same rule cannot be applied multiple times. In the above, before we applied any CC-rule that produced $h(Y)$, we checked whether $h(Y)$ was already in $\mathcal{B}$. Only if it was not, we applied the rule adding $h(Y)$ to $\mathcal{B}$, and letting the second invariant preserve it in $\mathcal{B}$. The same holds for SM-rules. In the above arguments, we applied CD-rules of the form $h(Y) \to h(X) + h(Y|X)$ in two different places: In the first, we checked that $h(X)$ was not in $\mathcal{B}$ before we added both $h(X)$ and $h(Y|X)$ to $\mathcal{B}$. In the second, we checked that $h(B|A \wedge B)$ was not in $\mathcal{B}$ before we added both $h(B|A \wedge B)$ and $h(A \wedge B)$ to $\mathcal{B}$. □

Example (5.10 **Continued**: CSM proof sequence)**.** Now, we simulate the proof of Theorem 5.16 on the dual solution in (21) (which corresponds to the inequality $h(\hat{1}) \leqslant \frac{h(M)+h(O)+h(P)}{2}$). We will start off with four copies of the right-hand side (i.e. $2h(M) + 2h(O) + 2h(P)$), and generate a CSM proof sequence that will produce one copy of $h(\hat{1})$ (out of 4 copies).

$$\begin{aligned}
2h(M) &\to 2h(M|G) + 2h(G) && (\,M \in \bar{K} \Rightarrow G \in \bar{K}) && (22)\\
2h(O) &\to 2h(O|I) + 2h(I) && (O \in \bar{K} \Rightarrow I \in \bar{K}) && (23)\\
2h(I) &\to 2h(I|D) + 2h(D) && (\text{extract } h(I|D)) && (24)\\
2h(G) + 2h(I|D) &\to 2h(Z) && (\text{SM-rule, } s_{G,I} > 0) && (25)\\
h(Z) + h(M|G) &\to h(V) && (\text{SM-rule, } s_{M,Z} > 0) && (26)\\
h(Z) + h(O|I) &\to h(W) && (\text{SM-rule, } s_{O,Z} > 0) && (27)\\
h(W) &\to h(W|R) + h(R) && (\text{extract } h(W|R)) && (28)\\
h(V) + h(W|R) &\to h(\hat{1}) && (\text{SM-rule, } s_{V,W} > 0) && (29)
\end{aligned}$$

Note that rules (22)...(25) above had multiplicities of 2, because we needed to produce two copies of $h(Z)$: one for (26) and another for (27).

Example (5.10 **Continued**: CSMA)**.** Consider a join query Q whose functional dependencies correspond to the lattice in Figure 4 and whose input relations are $T(M), T(O), T(P)$, all of size N. In the CLLP, we have $\mathcal{P} = \{(\hat{0}, M), (\hat{0}, O), (\hat{0}, P)\}$ where $n_M = n_O = n_P = (n \overset{\text{def}}{=} \log_2 N)$. The optimal objective value is $\mathsf{OPT} = \frac{3n}{2}$ (which implies that $|Q| \leqslant N^{\frac{3}{2}}$), and the feasible dual solution given by (21) is optimal. Consider the CSM sequence (22)...(29) that was constructed earlier for (21). We will explain how to run CSMA on this sequence in order to answer Q in time within a polylogarithmic factor of $2^{\mathsf{OPT}} = N^{\frac{3}{2}}$.

The first rule (22) in the sequence is a CD-rule: $h(M) \to h(M|G) + h(G)$. The corresponding algorithmic step would be to project $T(M)$ on G while making sure that the projection size times the maximum degree of the projection in

$T(M)$ does not exceed $|T(M)|$ (i.e. while making sure that the sum of $n'_G \stackrel{\text{def}}{=} \log_2 |\Pi_G(T(M))|$ and

$$n'_{M|G} \stackrel{\text{def}}{=} \max_{v \in \Pi_G(T(M))} \log_2 \mathsf{degree}_{T(M)}(v)$$

does not exceed n_M). If all tuples v in the projection $\Pi_G(T(M))$ have the same degree $\mathsf{degree}_{T(M)}(v)$ (i.e., if $T(M)$ is "uniform" with respect to G), then the required condition is met. Otherwise, let's assume for simplicity that all degrees $\mathsf{degree}_{T(M)}(v)$ are powers of 2 (and $|T(M)|$ is also a power of 2). If this is the case, then based on $\mathsf{degree}_{T(M)}(v)$ we can partition $T(M)$ into a logarithmic number (namely $n_M + 1$) of parts $T^{(0)}(M), T^{(1)}(M), \ldots$ such that the required condition is met in each one of them. (In particular, let $T^{(i)}(M)$ satisfy $n^{(i)}_{M|G} \leqslant i$ and $n^{(i)}_G \leqslant n_M - i$.) Now, the execution of CSMA will split into a logarithmic number of branches, each of which will continue on a different part of $T(M)$. For some arbitrarily-fixed i, let's track the execution of the i-th branch (i.e. the one on $T^{(i)}(M)$).

The second rule (23) is another CD-rule: $h(O) \to h(O|I) + h(I)$. Similar to above, it will result in the partitioning of $T(O)$ into $O(\log N)$ parts $T^{(0)}(O), T^{(1)}(O), \ldots$ (such that $T^{(j)}(O)$ satisfies $n^{(j)}_{O|I} \leqslant j$ and $n^{(j)}_I \leqslant n_O - j$.) The current i-th branch on $T^{(i)}(M)$ will now branch further into $O(\log N)$ branches corresponding to $T^{(0)}(O), T^{(1)}(O), \ldots$ Let's keep track of the j-th branch (on $T^{(j)}(O)$) for some arbitrary j.

The third rule (24) is yet another CD-rule: $h(I) \to h(I|D) + h(D)$. It will result in the partitioning of $T(I) \stackrel{\text{def}}{=} \Pi_I(T^{(j)}(O))$ (where $\Pi_I(T^{(j)}(O))$ resulted from the previous CD-step) into $O(\log N)$ parts: $T^{(0)}(I), T^{(1)}(I), \ldots$ (such that $T^{(k)}(I)$ satisfies $n^{(k)}_{I|D} \leqslant k$ and $n^{(k)}_D \leqslant n_I - k$.) Let's track the k-th branch (on $T^{(k)}(I)$).

The fourth rule (25) is an SM-rule: $h(G) + h(I|D) \to h(Z)$. The corresponding algorithmic step is to join the table $T(G)$ (or more precisely $\Pi_G(T^{(i)}(M))$ from Step 1) with the table $T(I)$ (or more precisely $T^{(k)}(I)$ from Step 3) in order to get a relation $T(Z)$. The time required to compute this join is bounded by the size of $T(G)$ times the maximum degree of D in $T(I)$. Depending on the current execution branch (i, j, k), this time might or might not exceed our budget of $2^{\mathsf{OPT}} = N^{3/2}$. For example, in the branch where both i and j are maximal, we will have $|T(G)| \leqslant 1$ and $|T(I)| \leqslant 1$, hence the join takes $O(1)$ time. On the other hand, in the branch where $i = j = 0$ and k is maximal, each one of $|T(G)|$, $|T(I)|$, and the maximum degree of D in $T(I)$ could be as large as N, hence the join could take time $O(N^2)$. Luckily, Lemma C.2 below implies that "when one door closes, another one opens": In those particular branches where the join cannot be computed within our time budget, there are extra constraints that if considered in the CLLP they would reduce the optimal objective value OPT. For example, in the branch where $i = j = 0$ and k is maximal, the value of D is already fixed. This is because the degree of D in table $T(I)$ is maximal, hence it is equal to $|T(I)|$.

The remaining rules (26)...(29) are similar to above.

Analysis of CSMA

Lemma C.1. *Let $X \prec Y$ be in the lattice $\mathbf{L}$. Let $T(Y)$ be a table with $\log_2 |T| \leqslant n_Y$. Then, T can be partitioned into at most $\ell = 2n_Y$ sub-tables $T^{(1)}, \ldots, T^{(\ell)}$ such that $n^{(j)}_{Y|X} + n^{(j)}_X \leqslant n_Y$, for all $j \in [\ell]$, where*

$$n^{(j)}_{Y|X} \stackrel{\text{def}}{=} \max_{v \in \Pi_X(T^{(j)})} \log_2 \mathsf{degree}_{T^{(j)}}(v)$$

$$n^{(j)}_X \stackrel{\text{def}}{=} \log_2 |\Pi_X(T^{(j)})|.$$

Proof. To obtain the copies $T^{(j)}$, observe that the number of elements $v \in \Pi_X(T)$ with log-degree in the interval $[j, j+1)$ is at most $|T|/2^j \leqslant 2^{n_Y - j}$. Hence, if we partition T based on which of the buckets $[j, j+1)$ the log-degree falls into, we would almost have the required inequality: $n^{(j)}_{Y|X} + n^{(j)}_X \leqslant (j+1) + (n_Y - j) = n_Y + 1$. To resolve the situation, we partition each $T^{(j)}$ into two equal-sized tables. Overall, we need $\ell = 2n_Y$. □

Lemma C.2. *Given a CLLP whose optimal objective value is OPT, and a feasible dual solution (c, s, m) whose objective value is $\mathsf{OBJ} = \sum_{(\bar{X},\bar{Y}) \in \mathcal{P}} c_{\bar{Y}|\bar{X}} n_{\bar{Y}|\bar{X}}$, let $c_Y > 0$ for some $(\hat{0}, Y) \in \mathcal{P}$.*

- *If $n_Y > \mathsf{OBJ}$, then $\mathsf{OPT} < \mathsf{OBJ}$.*
- *Given $\theta \geqslant 0$, $0 < \epsilon < 1$, $\epsilon \leqslant c_Y$, if $n_Y > \mathsf{OBJ} + \theta$, then $\mathsf{OPT} < \mathsf{OBJ} - \frac{\epsilon\theta}{1-\epsilon}$.*

Proof. Let (c', s, m') be a dual solution obtained by setting $c'_Y = c_Y - \epsilon$, $m'_{Y,\hat{1}} = m_{Y,\hat{1}} + \epsilon$ and keeping other c' and m' values identical to their c and m counterparts. (c', s, m') is not necessarily feasible. However, it satisfies $\mathsf{netflow}(\hat{1}) \geqslant 1 - \epsilon$ and $\mathsf{netflow}(Z) \geqslant 0$ for all $Z \in \mathbf{L} - \{\hat{1}, \hat{0}\}$. Let (c'', s'', m'') be a dual solution obtained by multiplying (c', s, m') by $\frac{1}{1-\epsilon}$. Now (c'', s'', m'') is indeed feasible. Let OBJ'' be its objective value. Because it is dual feasible, $\mathsf{OBJ}'' \geqslant \mathsf{OPT}$.

$$\begin{aligned}
\mathsf{OBJ}'' &= \sum_{(\bar{X},\bar{Y}) \in \mathcal{P}} c''_{\bar{Y}|\bar{X}} n_{\bar{Y}|\bar{X}} = \sum_{(\bar{X},\bar{Y}) \in \mathcal{P}} \frac{c'_{\bar{Y}|\bar{X}}}{1-\epsilon} n_{\bar{Y}|\bar{X}} \\
&= \frac{1}{1-\epsilon} \sum_{(\bar{X},\bar{Y}) \in \mathcal{P}} c_{\bar{Y}|\bar{X}} n_{\bar{Y}|\bar{X}} - \frac{\epsilon}{1-\epsilon} n_Y \\
&< \frac{1}{1-\epsilon} \mathsf{OBJ} - \frac{\epsilon}{1-\epsilon} (\mathsf{OBJ} + \theta) \\
&= \mathsf{OBJ} - \frac{\epsilon\theta}{1-\epsilon}.
\end{aligned}$$

□

Proof of Theorem 5.17. The number of CD-rules is at most $|\mathbf{L}|^2$ (these are rules with multiplicities, so no rule is repeated). The worst case is obtained when the algorithm branches as far as possible only to reduce the objective by $\epsilon = \frac{\theta}{D-1}$ at the very end and all leaf nodes of the execution tree have to be started afresh with the new optimal value. Let $x = 2^{\mathsf{OPT}}$ and $T(x)$ denote the runtime of the algorithm on the $\mathsf{CLLP}^{(0)}$ with objective value OPT. Then, the recurrence for the runtime is

$$\begin{aligned}
T(x) &= (\ell)^{|\mathbf{L}|^2} T\left(2^{\mathsf{OPT} - \frac{\theta}{D-1}}\right) + \ell^{|\mathbf{L}|^2} 2^\theta x \\
&= (\ell)^{|\mathbf{L}|^2} T\left(\frac{x}{2^{\theta/(D-1)}}\right) + \ell^{|\mathbf{L}|^2} 2^\theta x
\end{aligned}$$

To get the exponential decay effect we set θ so that $2^{\theta/(D-1)} = 2\ell^{|\mathbf{L}|^2}$, which means $\theta = (D-1)(|\mathbf{L}|^2 \log_2 \ell + 1)$. □

Semantic Acyclicity Under Constraints

Pablo Barceló
Center for Semantic Web Research & DCC
University of Chile
pbarcelo@dcc.uchile.cl

Georg Gottlob
Department of Computer Science
University of Oxford
georg.gottlob@cs.ox.ac.uk

Andreas Pieris
Institute of Information Systems
TU Wien
pieris@dbai.tuwien.ac.at

ABSTRACT

A conjunctive query (CQ) is semantically acyclic if it is equivalent to an acyclic one. Semantic acyclicity has been studied in the constraint-free case, and deciding whether a query enjoys this property is NP-complete. However, in case the database is subject to constraints such as tuple-generating dependencies (tgds) that can express, e.g., inclusion dependencies, or equality-generating dependencies (egds) that capture, e.g., functional dependencies, a CQ may turn out to be semantically acyclic under the constraints while not semantically acyclic in general. This opens avenues to new query optimization techniques. In this paper we initiate and develop the theory of semantic acyclicity under constraints. More precisely, we study the following natural problem: Given a CQ and a set of constraints, is the query semantically acyclic under the constraints, or, in other words, is the query equivalent to an acyclic one over all those databases that satisfy the set of constraints?

We show that, contrary to what one might expect, decidability of CQ containment is a necessary but not sufficient condition for the decidability of semantic acyclicity. In particular, we show that semantic acyclicity is undecidable in the presence of full tgds (i.e., Datalog rules). In view of this fact, we focus on the main classes of tgds for which CQ containment is decidable, and do not capture the class of full tgds, namely guarded, non-recursive and sticky tgds. For these classes we show that semantic acyclicity is decidable, and its complexity coincides with the complexity of CQ containment. In the case of egds, we show that if we focus on keys over unary and binary predicates, then semantic acyclicity is decidable (NP-complete). We finally consider the problem of evaluating a semantically acyclic query over a database that satisfies a set of constraints. For guarded tgds and functional dependencies the evaluation problem is tractable.

1. INTRODUCTION

Query optimization is a fundamental database task that amounts to transforming a query into one that is arguably more efficient to evaluate. The database theory community has developed several principled methods for optimization of conjunctive queries (CQs), many of which are based on *static-analysis* tasks such as containment [1]. In a nutshell, such methods compute a *minimal* equivalent version of a CQ, where minimality refers to number of atoms. As argued by Abiteboul, Hull, and Vianu [1], this provides a theoretical notion of "true optimality" for the reformulation of a CQ, as opposed to practical considerations based on heuristics. For each CQ q the minimal equivalent CQ is its *core* q' [21]. Although the static analysis tasks that support CQ minimization are NP-complete [12], this is not a major problem for real-life applications, as the input (the CQ) is small.

PODS'16, June 26-July 01, 2016, San Francisco, CA, USA

DOI: http://dx.doi.org/10.1145/2902251.2902302

It is known, on the other hand, that semantic information about the data, in the form of integrity constraints, alleviates query optimization by reducing the space of possible reformulations. In the previous analysis, however, constraints play no role, as CQ equivalence is defined over *all* databases. Adding constraints yields a refined notion of CQ equivalence, which holds over those databases that satisfy a given set of constraints only. But finding a minimal equivalent CQ in this context is notoriously more difficult than before. This is because basic static analysis tasks such as containment become undecidable when considered in full generality. This motivated a long research program for finding larger "islands of decidability" of such containment problem, based on syntactical restrictions on constraints [2, 8, 10, 11, 22, 23].

An important shortcoming of the previous approach, however, is that there is no theoretical guarantee that the minimized version of a CQ is in fact easier to evaluate (recall that, in general, CQ evaluation is NP-complete [12]). We know, on the other hand, quite a bit about classes of CQs that can be evaluated efficiently. It is thus a natural problem to ask whether constraints can be used to reformulate a CQ as one in such tractable classes, and if so, what is the cost of computing such reformulation. Following Abiteboul et al., this would provide us with a theoretical guarantee of "true efficiency" for those reformulations. We focus on one of the oldest and most studied tractability conditions for CQs; namely, *acyclicity*. It is known that acyclic CQs can be evaluated in linear time [27].

More formally, let us write $q \equiv_\Sigma q'$ whenever CQs q and q' are equivalent over all databases that satisfy Σ. In this work we study the following problem:

PROBLEM :	SEMANTIC ACYCLICITY
INPUT :	A CQ q and a finite set Σ of constraints.
QUESTION :	Is there an acyclic CQ q' s.t. $q \equiv_\Sigma q'$?

We study this problem for the two most important classes of database constraints; namely:

1. *Tuple-generating dependencies* (tgds), i.e., expressions of the form $\forall\bar{x}\forall\bar{y}(\phi(\bar{x},\bar{y}) \rightarrow \exists\bar{z}\psi(\bar{x},\bar{z}))$, where ϕ and ψ are conjuntions of atoms. Tgds subsume the important class of referential integrity constraints (or inclusion dependencies).

2. *Equality-generating dependencies* (egds), i.e., expressions of the form $\forall \bar{x}(\phi(\bar{x}) \rightarrow y = z)$, where ϕ is a conjunction of atoms and y, z are variables in $\bar{x}$. Egds subsume keys and functional dependencies (FDs).

A useful aspect of tgds and egds is that containment under them can be studied in terms of the *chase procedure* [25].

Coming back to semantic acyclicity, the main problem we study is, of course, decidability. Since basic reasoning with tgds and egds is, in general, undecidable, we cannot expect semantic acyclicity to be decidable for arbitrary such constraints. Thus, we concentrate on the following question:

Decidability: For which classes of tgds and egds is the problem of semantic acyclicity decidable? In such cases, what is the computational cost of the problem?

Since semantic acyclicity is defined in terms of CQ equivalence under constraints, and the latter has received a lot of attention, it is relevant also to study the following question:

Relationship to CQ equivalence: What is the relationship between CQ equivalence and semantic acyclicity under constraints? Is the latter decidable for each class of tgds and egds for which the former is decidable?

Notice that if this was the case, one could transfer the mature theory of CQ equivalence under tgds and egds to tackle the problem of semantic acyclicity.

Finally, we want to understand to what extent semantic acyclicity helps CQ evaluation. Although an acyclic reformulation of a CQ can be evaluated efficiently, computing such reformulation might be expensive. Thus, it is relevant to study the following question:

Evaluation: What is the computational cost of evaluating semantically acyclic CQs under constraints?

Semantic acyclicity in the absence of constraints. The semantic acyclicity problem in the absence of dependencies (i.e., checking whether a CQ q is equivalent to an acyclic one over the set of all databases) is by now well-understood. Regarding decidability, it is easy to prove that a CQ q is semantically acyclic iff its core q' is acyclic. (Recall that such q' is the minimal equivalent CQ to q). It follows that checking semantic acyclicity in the absence of constraints is NP-complete (see, e.g., [6]). Regarding evaluation, semantically acyclic CQs can be evaluated efficiently [13, 14, 19].

The relevance of constraints. In the absence of constraints a CQ q is equivalent to an acyclic one iff its core q' is acyclic. Thus, the only reason why q is not acyclic in the first hand is because it has not been minimized. This tells us that in this context semantic acyclicity is not really different from usual minimization. The presence of constraints, on the other hand, yields a more interesting notion of semantic acyclicity. This is because constraints can be applied on CQs to produce acyclic reformulations of them.

Example 1. This simple example helps understanding the role of tgds when reformulating CQs as acyclic ones. Consider a database that stores information about customers, records, and musical styles. The relation `Interest` contains pairs (c, s) such that customer c has declared interest in style s. The relation `Class` contains pairs (r, s) such that record r is of style s. Finally, the relation `Owns` contains a pair (c, r) when customer c owns record r.

Consider now a CQ $q(x, y)$ defined as follows:

$$\exists z\big(\texttt{Interest}(x, z) \wedge \texttt{Class}(y, z) \wedge \texttt{Owns}(x, y)\big).$$

This query asks for pairs (c, r) such that customer c owns record r and has expressed interest in at least one of the styles with which r is associated. This CQ is a core but it is not acyclic. Thus, from our previous observations it is not equivalent to an acyclic CQ (in the absence of constraints).

Assume now that we are told that this database contains compulsive music collectors only. In particular, each customer owns every record that is classified with a style in which he/she has expressed interest. This means that the database satisfies the tgd:

$$\tau = \texttt{Interest}(x, z), \texttt{Class}(y, z) \rightarrow \texttt{Owns}(x, y).$$

With this information at hand, we can easily reformulate $q(x, y)$ as the following acyclic CQ $q'(x, y)$:

$$\exists z\big(\texttt{Interest}(x, z) \wedge \texttt{Class}(y, z)\big).$$

Notice that q and q' are in fact equivalent over every database that satisfies τ. ∎

Contributions. We observe that semantic acyclicity under constraints is not only more powerful, but also theoretically more challenging than in the absence of them. We start by studying decidability. In the process we also clarify the relationship between CQ equivalence and semantic acyclicity.

Results for tgds: Having a decidable CQ containment problem is a necessary condition for semantic acyclicity to be decidable under tgds.[1] Surprisingly enough, it is not a sufficient condition. This means that, contrary to what one might expect, there are natural classes of tgds for which CQ containment but not semantic acyclicity is decidable. In particular, this is the case for the well-known class of *full* tgds (i.e., tgds without existentially quantified variables in the head). In conclusion, we cannot directly export techniques from CQ containment to deal with semantic acyclicity.

In view of the previous results, we concentrate on classes of tgds that (a) have a decidable CQ containment problem, and (b) do not contain the class of full tgds. These restrictions are satisfied by several expressive languages considered in the literature. Such languages can be classified into three main families depending on the techniques used for studying their containment problem: (i) *guarded* tgds [8], which contain inclusion and linear dependencies, (ii) *non-recursive* [16], and (iii) *sticky* sets of tgds [10]. Instead of studying such languages one by one, we identify two semantic criteria that yield decidability for the semantic acyclicity problem, and then show that each one of the languages satisfies one such criteria.

- The first criterion is *acyclicity-preserving chase*. This is satisfied by those tgds for which the application of the chase over an acyclic instance preserves acyclicity. Guarded tgds enjoy this property. We establish that semantic acyclicity under guarded tgds is decidable and has the same complexity than its associated CQ containment problem: 2EXPTIME-complete, and NP-complete for a fixed schema.

- The second criterion is *rewritability by unions of CQs (UCQs)*. Intuitively, a class $\mathbb{C}$ of sets of tgds has this property if the CQ containment problem under a set in $\mathbb{C}$ can always be reduced to a UCQ containment problem without constraints. Non-recursive and sticky sets of tgds enjoy this property. In the first case the complexity matches that of its associated CQ containment problem: NEXPTIME-complete, and NP-complete if the schema is fixed. In the second case, we get a NEXPTIME upper bound and an EXPTIME lower bound. For a fixed schema the problem is NP-complete.

[1]Modulo some mild technical assumptions elaborated in the paper.

The NP bounds (under a fixed schema) can be seen as positive results: By spending exponential time in the size of the (small) query, we can not only minimize it using known techniques but also find an acyclic reformulation if one exists.

Results for egds: After showing that the techniques developed for tgds cannot be applied for showing the decidability of semantic acyclicity under egds, we focus on the class of keys over unary and binary predicates and we establish a positive result, namely semantic acyclicity is NP-complete. We prove this by showing that in such context keys have acyclicity-preserving chase. Interestingly, this positive result can be extended to unary functional dependencies (over unconstrained signatures); this result has been established independently by Figueira [17]. We leave open whether the problem of semantic acyclicity under arbitrary egds, or even keys over arbitrary schemas, is decidable.

Evaluation: For tgds for which semantic acyclicity is decidable (guarded, non-recursive, sticky), we can use the following algorithm to evaluate a semantically acyclic CQ q over a database D that satisfies the constraints Σ:

1. Convert q into an equivalent acyclic CQ q' under Σ.
2. Evaluate q' on D.
3. Return $q(D) = q'(D)$.

The running time is $O(|D| \cdot f(|q|, |\Sigma|))$, where f is a double-exponential function (since q' can be computed in double-exponential time for each one of the classes mentioned above and acyclic CQs can be evaluated in linear time). This constitutes a *fixed-parameter tractable algorithm* for evaluating q on D. No such algorithm is believed to exist for CQ evaluation [26]; thus, semantically acyclic CQs under these constraints behave better than the general case in terms of evaluation.

But in the absence of constraints one can do better: Evaluating semantically acyclic CQs in such context is in polynomial time. It is natural to ask if this also holds in the presence of constraints. This is the case for guarded tgds and (arbitrary) FDs. For the other classes of constraints the problem remains to be investigated.

Further results: The results mentioned above continue to hold for a more "liberal" notion based on UCQs, i.e., checking whether a UCQ is equivalent to an acyclic union of CQs under the decidable classes of constraints identified above. Moreover, in case that a CQ q is not equivalent to an acyclic CQ q' under a set of constraints Σ, our proof techniques yield an *approximation of q under Σ* [4], that is, an acyclic CQ q' that is maximally contained in q under Σ. Computing and evaluating such approximation yields "quick" answers to q when exact evaluation is infeasible.

Finite vs. infinite databases. The results mentioned above interpret the notion of CQ equivalence (and, thus, semantic acyclicity) over the set of both *finite* and *infinite* databases. The reason is the wide application of the chase we make in our proofs, which characterizes CQ equivalence under arbitrary databases only. This does not present a serious problem though, as all the particular classes of tgds for which we prove decidability in the paper (i.e., guarded, non-recursive, sticky) are *finitely controllable* [3, 18]. This means that CQ equivalence under arbitrary databases and under finite databases coincide. In conclusion, the results we obtain for such classes can be directly exported to the finite case.

Organization. Preliminaries are in Section 2. In Section 3 we consider semantic acyclicity under tgds. Acyclicity-preserving chase is studied in Section 4, and UCQ-rewritability in Section 5. Semantic acyclicity under egds is investigated in Section 6. Evaluation of semantically acyclic CQs is in Section 7. Finally, we present further advancements in Section 8 and conclusions in Section 9.

2. PRELIMINARIES

Databases and conjunctive queries. Let $\mathbf{C}$, $\mathbf{N}$ and $\mathbf{V}$ be disjoint countably infinite sets of *constants*, *(labeled) nulls* and (regular) *variables* (used in queries and dependencies), respectively, and σ a relational schema. An *atom* over σ is an expression of the form $R(\bar{v})$, where R is a relation symbol in σ of arity $n > 0$ and $\bar{v}$ is an n-tuple over $\mathbf{C} \cup \mathbf{N} \cup \mathbf{V}$. An *instance* over σ is a (possibly infinite) set of atoms over σ that contain constants and nulls, while a *database* over σ is simply a finite instance over σ.

One of the central notions in our work is acyclicity. An instance I is acyclic if it admits a *join tree*; i.e., if there exists a tree T and a mapping λ that associates with each node t of T an atom $\lambda(t)$ of I, such that the following holds:

1. For each atom $R(\bar{v})$ in I there is a node t in T such that $\lambda(t) = R(\bar{v})$; and
2. For each null x occurring in I it is the case that the set $\{t \mid x \in \lambda(t)\}$ is connected in T.

A *conjunctive query* (CQ) over σ is a formula of the form:

$$q(\bar{x}) \ := \ \exists \bar{y} \big(R_1(\bar{v}_1) \wedge \cdots \wedge R_m(\bar{v}_m) \big), \qquad (1)$$

where each $R_i(\bar{v}_i)$ $(1 \leq i \leq m)$ is an atom without nulls over σ, each variable mentioned in the $\bar{v}_i$'s appears either in $\bar{x}$ or $\bar{y}$, and $\bar{x}$ are the free variables of q. If $\bar{x}$ is empty, then q is a *Boolean CQ*. As usual, the evaluation of CQs is defined in terms of *homomorphisms*. Let I be an instance and $q(\bar{x})$ a CQ of the form (1). A homomorphism from q to I is a mapping h, which is the identity on $\mathbf{C}$, from the variables and constants in q to the set of constants and nulls $\mathbf{C} \cup \mathbf{N}$ such that $R_i(h(\bar{v}_i)) \in I$,[2] for each $1 \leq i \leq m$. The *evaluation of $q(\bar{x})$ over I*, denoted $q(I)$, is the set of all tuples $h(\bar{x})$ over $\mathbf{C} \cup \mathbf{N}$ such that h is a homomorphism from q to I.

It is well-known that *CQ evaluation*, i.e., the problem of determining if a particular tuple $\bar{t}$ belongs to the evaluation $q(D)$ of a CQ q over a database D, is NP-complete [12]. On the other hand, CQ evaluation becomes tractable by restricting the syntactic shape of CQs. One of the oldest and most common such restrictions is *acyclicity*. Formally, a CQ q is acyclic if the instance consisting of the atoms of q (after replacing each variable in q with a fresh null) is acyclic. It is known from the seminal work of Yannakakis [27], that the problem of evaluating an acyclic CQ q over a database D can be solved in linear time $O(|q| \cdot |D|)$.

Tgds and the chase procedure. A *tuple-generating dependency* (tgd) over σ is an expression of the form:

$$\forall \bar{x} \forall \bar{y} \big(\phi(\bar{x}, \bar{y}) \rightarrow \exists \bar{z} \psi(\bar{x}, \bar{z}) \big), \qquad (2)$$

where both ϕ and ψ are conjunctions of atoms without nulls over σ. For simplicity, we write this tgd as $\phi(\bar{x}, \bar{y}) \rightarrow \exists \bar{z} \psi(\bar{x}, \bar{z})$, and use comma instead of $\wedge$ for conjoining atoms. Further, we assume that each variable in $\bar{x}$ is mentioned in some atom of ψ. We call ϕ and ψ the *body* and *head* of the tgd, respectively. The tgd in (2) is logically equivalent to the expression $\forall \bar{x}(q_\phi(\bar{x}) \rightarrow q_\psi(\bar{x}))$, where $q_\phi(\bar{x})$ and $q_\psi(\bar{x})$ are the CQs $\exists \bar{y} \phi(\bar{x}, \bar{y})$ and $\exists \bar{z} \psi(\bar{x}, \bar{z})$, respectively. Thus, an instance I over σ satisfies this tgd if and only if $q_\phi(I) \subseteq q_\psi(I)$. We say that an instance I satisfies a set Σ of tgds, denoted $I \models \Sigma$, if I satisfies every tgd in Σ.

[2] As usual, we write $h(v_1, \ldots, v_n)$ for $(h(v_1), \ldots, h(v_n))$.

The *chase* is a useful tool when reasoning with tgds [8, 16, 22, 25]. We start by defining a single chase step. Let I be an instance over schema σ and $\tau = \phi(\bar{x}, \bar{y}) \rightarrow \exists \bar{z} \psi(\bar{x}, \bar{z})$ a tgd over σ. We say that τ is *applicable* w.r.t. I if there exists a tuple $(\bar{a}, \bar{b})$ of elements in I such that $\phi(\bar{a}, \bar{b})$ holds in I. In this case, *the result of applying τ over I with $(\bar{a}, \bar{b})$* is the instance J that extends I with every atom in $\psi(\bar{a}, \bar{z}')$, where $\bar{z}'$ is the tuple obtained by simultaneously replacing each variable $z \in \bar{z}$ with a fresh distinct null not occurring in I. For such a single chase step we write $I \xrightarrow{\tau, (\bar{a}, \bar{b})} J$.

Let us assume now that I is an instance and Σ a finite set of tgds. A *chase sequence for I under Σ* is a sequence:

$$I_0 \xrightarrow{\tau_0, \bar{c}_0} I_1 \xrightarrow{\tau_1, \bar{c}_1} I_2 \ldots$$

of chase steps such that: (1) $I_0 = I$; (2) For each $i \geq 0$, τ_i is a tgd in Σ; and (3) $\bigcup_{i \geq 0} I_i \models \Sigma$. We call $\bigcup_{i \geq 0} I_i$ the *result* of this chase sequence, which always exists. Although the result of a chase sequence is not necessarily unique (up to isomorphism), each such result is equally useful for our purposes since it can be homomorphically embedded into every other result. Thus, from now on, we denote by $chase(I, \Sigma)$ the result of an arbitrary chase sequence for I under Σ. Further, for a CQ $q = \exists \bar{y}(R_1(\bar{v}_1) \wedge \cdots \wedge R_m(\bar{v}_m))$, we denote by $chase(q, \Sigma)$ the result of a chase sequence for the database $\{R_1(\bar{v}_1'), \ldots, R_m(\bar{v}_m')\}$ under Σ obtained after replacing each variable x in q with a fresh constant $c(x)$.

Egds and the chase procedure. An *equality-generating dependency* (egd) over σ is an expression of the form:

$$\forall \bar{x}(\phi(\bar{x}) \rightarrow x_i = x_j),$$

where ϕ is a conjunction of atoms without nulls over σ, and $x_i, x_j \in \bar{x}$. For clarity, we write this egd as $\phi(\bar{x}) \rightarrow x_i = x_j$, and use comma for conjoining atoms. We call ϕ the *body* of the egd. An instance I over σ satisfies this egd if, for every homomorphism h such that $h(\phi(\bar{x})) \subseteq I$, it is the case that $h(x_i) = h(x_j)$. An instance I satisfies a set Σ of egds, denoted $I \models \Sigma$, if I satisfies every egd in Σ.

Recall that egds subsume functional dependencies, which in turn subsume keys. A *functional dependency* (FD) over σ is an expression of the form $R : A \rightarrow B$, where R is a relation symbol in σ of arity $n > 0$, and A, B are subsets of $\{1, \ldots, n\}$, asserting that the values of the attributes of B are determined by the values of the attributes of A. For example, $R : \{1\} \rightarrow \{3\}$, where R is a ternary relation, is actually the egd $R(x, y, z), R(x, y', z') \rightarrow z = z'$. A FD $R : A \rightarrow B$ as above is called *key* if $A \cup B = \{1, \ldots, n\}$.

As for tgds, the chase is a useful tool when reasoning with egds. Let us first define a single chase step. Consider an instance I over schema σ and an egd $\epsilon = \phi(\bar{x}) \rightarrow x_i = x_j$ over σ. We say that ϵ is *applicable* w.r.t. I if there exists a homomorphism h such that $h(\phi(\bar{x})) \subseteq I$ and $h(x_i) \neq h(x_j)$. In this case, *the result of applying ϵ over I with h* is as follows: If both $h(x_i), h(x_j)$ are constants, then the result is "failure"; otherwise, it is the instance J obtained from I by identifying $h(x_i)$ and $h(x_j)$ as follows: If one is a constant, then every occurrence of the null is replaced by the constant, and if both are nulls, the one is replaced everywhere by the other. As for tgds, we can define the notion of the chase sequence for an instance I under a set Σ of egds. Notice that such a sequence, assuming that is not failing, always is finite. Moreover, it is unique (up to null renaming), and thus we refer to *the* chase for I under Σ, denoted $chase(I, \Sigma)$. Further, for a CQ $q = \exists \bar{y}(R_1(\bar{v}_1) \wedge \cdots \wedge R_m(\bar{v}_m))$, we denote by $chase(q, \Sigma)$ the result of a chase sequence for the database $\{R_1(\bar{v}_1'), \ldots, R_m(\bar{v}_m')\}$ under Σ obtained after replacing each variable x in q with a fresh constant $c(x)$; however, it is important to clarify that these are special constants, which are treated as nulls during the chase.

Containment and equivalence. Let q and q' be CQs and Σ a finite set of tgds or egds. Then, q is *contained* in q' under Σ, denoted $q \subseteq_\Sigma q'$, if $q(I) \subseteq q'(I)$ for every instance I such that $I \models \Sigma$. Further, q is *equivalent* to q' under Σ, denoted $q \equiv_\Sigma q'$, whenever $q \subseteq_\Sigma q'$ and $q' \subseteq_\Sigma q$ (or, equivalently, if $q(I) = q'(I)$ for every instance I such that $I \models \Sigma$). The following well-known characterization of CQ containment in terms of the chase will be widely used in our proofs:

LEMMA 1. *Let $q(\bar{x})$ and $q'(\bar{x}')$ be CQs and Σ be a finite set of tgds or egds. Then $q \subseteq_\Sigma q'$ if and only if $c(\bar{x})$ belongs to the evaluation of q' over $chase(q, \Sigma)$.*

A problem that is quite important for our work is *CQ containment under constraints* (tgds or egds), defined as follows: Given CQs q, q' and a finite set Σ of tgds or egds, is it the case that $q \subseteq_\Sigma q'$? Whenever Σ is bound to belong to a particular class $\mathbb{C}$ of sets of tgds, we denote this problem as $\mathsf{Cont}(\mathbb{C})$. It is clear that the above lemma provides a decision procedure for the containment problem under egds. However, this is not the case for tgds.

Decidable containment of CQs under tgds. It is not surprising that Lemma 1 does not provide a decision procedure for solving CQ containment under tgds since this problem is known to be undecidable [7]. This has led to a flurry of activity for identifying syntactic restrictions on sets of tgds that lead to decidable CQ containment (even in the case when the chase does not terminate).[3] Such restrictions are often classified into three main paradigms:

Guardedness: A tgd is *guarded* if its body contains an atom, called *guard*, that contains all the body-variables. Although the chase under guarded tgds does not necessarily terminate, query containment is decidable. This follows from the fact that the result of the chase has *bounded treewidth*. Let $\mathbb{G}$ be the class of sets of guarded tgds.

PROPOSITION 2. [8] $\mathsf{Cont}(\mathbb{G})$ *is* 2EXPTIME*-complete. It becomes* EXPTIME*-complete if the arity of the schema is fixed, and* NP*-complete if the schema is fixed.*

A key subclass of guarded tgds is the class of *linear* tgds, that is, tgds whose body consists of a single atom [9], which in turn subsume the well-known class of *inclusion dependencies* (linear tgds without repeated variables neither in the body nor in the head) [15]. Let $\mathbb{L}$ and $\mathbb{ID}$ be the classes of sets of linear tgds and inclusions dependencies, respectively. $\mathsf{Cont}(\mathbb{C})$, for $\mathbb{C} \in \{\mathbb{L}, \mathbb{ID}\}$, is PSPACE-complete, and NP-complete if the arity of the schema is fixed [22].

Non-recursiveness: A set Σ of tgds is *non-recursive* if its predicate graph contains no directed cycles. (Non-recursive sets of tgds are also known as *acyclic* [16, 24], but we reserve this term for CQs). Non-recursiveness ensures the termination of the chase, and thus decidability of CQ containment. Let $\mathbb{NR}$ be the class of non-recursive sets of tgds. Then:

PROPOSITION 3. [24] $\mathsf{Cont}(\mathbb{NR})$ *is complete for* NEXPTIME*, even if the arity of the schema is fixed. It becomes* NP*-complete if the schema is fixed.*

Stickiness: This condition ensures neither termination nor bounded treewidth of the chase. Instead, the decidability of query containment is obtained by exploiting *query rewriting* techniques. The

[3] In fact, these restrictions are designed to obtain decidable *query answering under tgds*. However, this problem is equivalent to query containment under tgds (Lemma 1).

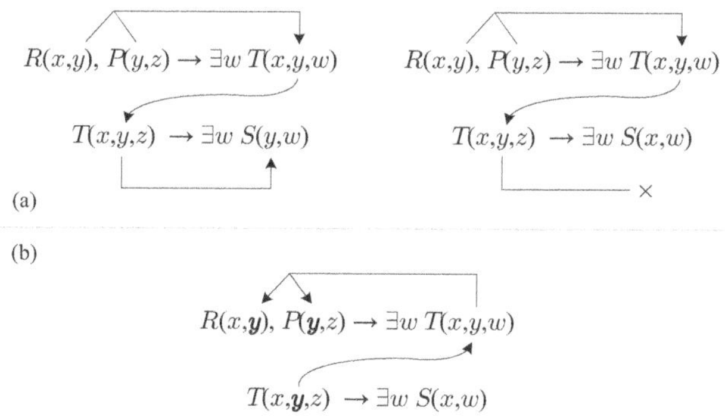

Figure 1: Stickiness and marking.

goal of stickiness is to capture joins among variables that are not expressible via guarded tgds, but without forcing the chase to terminate. The key property underlying this condition can be described as follows: During the chase, terms that are associated (via a homomorphism) with variables that appear more than once in the body of a tgd (i.e., join variables) are always propagated (or "stick") to the inferred atoms. This is illustrated in Figure 1(a); the first set of tgds is sticky, while the second is not. The formal definition is based on an inductive marking procedure that marks the variables that may violate the semantic property of the chase described above [10]. Roughly, during the base step of this procedure, a variable that appears in the body of a tgd τ but not in every head-atom of τ is marked. Then, the marking is inductively propagated from head to body as shown in Figure 1(b). Finally, a finite set of tgds Σ is *sticky* if no tgd in Σ contains two occurrences of a marked variable. Then:

PROPOSITION 4. [10] $\mathsf{Cont}(\mathbb{S})$ *is* EXPTIME-*complete. It becomes* NP-*complete if the arity of the schema is fixed.*

Weak versions: Each one of the previous classes has an associated weak version, called *weakly-guarded* [8], *weakly-acyclic* [16], and *weakly-sticky* [10], respectively, that guarantees the decidability of query containment. The underlying idea of all these classes is the same: Relax the conditions in the definition of the class, so that only those positions that receive null values during the chase procedure are taken into consideration. A key property of all these classes is that they extend the class of *full tgds*, i.e., those without existentially quantified variables. This is not the case for the "unrelaxed" versions presented above.

3. SEMANTIC ACYCLICITY WITH TGDS

One of the main tasks of our work is to study the problem of checking whether a CQ q is equivalent to an acyclic CQ over those instances that satisfy a set Σ of tgds. When this is the case we say that q is *semantically acyclic under* Σ. The semantic acyclicity problem is defined below; $\mathbb{C}$ is a class of sets of tgds (e.g., guarded, non-recursive, sticky, etc.):

PROBLEM :	$\mathsf{SemAc}(\mathbb{C})$
INPUT :	A CQ q and a finite set Σ of tgds in $\mathbb{C}$.
QUESTION :	Is there an acyclic CQ q' s.t. $q \equiv_\Sigma q'$?

3.1 Infinite Instances vs. Finite Databases

It is important to clarify that $\mathsf{SemAc}(\mathbb{C})$ asks for the existence of an acyclic CQ q' that is equivalent to q under Σ focussing on arbitrary (finite or infinite) instances. However, in practice we are concerned only with finite databases. Therefore, one may claim that the natural problem to investigate is $\mathsf{FinSemAc}(\mathbb{C})$, which accepts as input a CQ q and a finite set $\Sigma \in \mathbb{C}$ of tgds, and asks whether an acyclic CQ q' exists such that $q(D) = q'(D)$ for every finite database $D \models \Sigma$.

Interestingly, for all the classes of sets of tgds discussed in the previous section, SemAc and FinSemAc coincide due to the fact that they ensure the so-called *finite controllability* of CQ containment. This means that query containment under arbitrary instances and query containment under finite databases are equivalent problems. For non-recursive and weakly-acyclic sets of tgds this immediately follows from the fact that the chase terminates. For guarded-based classes of sets of tgds this has been shown in [3], while for sticky-based classes of sets of tgds it has been shown in [18]. Therefore, assuming that $\mathbb{C}$ is one of the above syntactic classes of sets of tgds, by giving a solution to $\mathsf{SemAc}(\mathbb{C})$ we immediately obtain a solution for $\mathsf{FinSemAc}(\mathbb{C})$.

The reason why we prefer to focus on $\mathsf{SemAc}(\mathbb{C})$, instead of $\mathsf{FinSemAc}(\mathbb{C})$, is given by Lemma 1: Query containment under arbitrary instances can be characterized in terms of the chase. This is not true for CQ containment under finite databases simply because the chase is, in general, infinite.

3.2 Semantic Acyclicity vs. Containment

There is a close relationship between semantic acyclicity and a restricted version of CQ containment under sets of tgds, as we explain next. But first we need to recall the notion of connectedness for queries and tgds. A CQ is *connected* if its *Gaifman graph* is connected – recall that the nodes of the Gaifman graph of a CQ q are the variables of q, and there is an edge between variables x and y iff they appear together in some atom of q. Analogously, a tgd τ is *body-connected* if its body is connected. Then:

PROPOSITION 5. *Let Σ be a finite set of body-connected tgds and q, q' two Boolean and connected CQs without common variables, such that q is acyclic and q' is not semantically acyclic under Σ. Then $q \subseteq_\Sigma q'$ iff $q \wedge q'$ is semantically acyclic under Σ.*

As an immediate corollary of Proposition 5, we obtain an initial boundary for the decidability of SemAc: We can only obtain a positive result for those classes of sets of tgds for which the restricted containment problem presented above is decidable. More formally, let us define $\mathsf{RestCont}(\mathbb{C})$ to be the problem of checking $q \subseteq_\Sigma q'$, given a set Σ of body-connected tgds in $\mathbb{C}$ and two Boolean and connected CQs q and q', without common variables, such that q is acyclic and q' is not semantically acyclic under Σ. Then:

COROLLARY 6. $\mathsf{SemAc}(\mathbb{C})$ *is undecidable for every class $\mathbb{C}$ of tgds such that* $\mathsf{RestCont}(\mathbb{C})$ *is undecidable.*

As we shall discuss later, RestCont is not easier than general CQ containment under tgds, which means that the only classes of tgds for which we know the former problem to be decidable are those for which we know CQ containment to be decidable (e.g., those introduced in Section 2).

At this point, one might be tempted to think that some version of the converse of Proposition 5 also holds; that is, the semantic acyclicity problem for $\mathbb{C}$ is reducible to the containment problem for $\mathbb{C}$. This would imply the decidability of SemAc for any class of sets of tgds for which the CQ containment problem is decidable. Our next result shows that the picture is more complicated than this as SemAc is undecidable even over the class $\mathbb{F}$ of sets of full tgds, which ensures the decidability of CQ containment:

THEOREM 7. *The problem* $\mathsf{SemAc}(\mathbb{F})$ *is undecidable.*

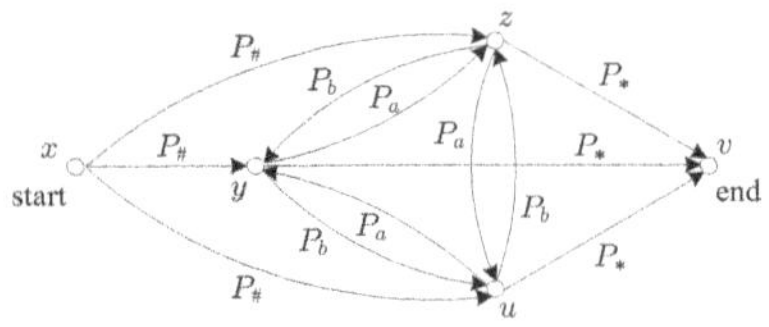

Figure 2: The query q from the proof of Theorem 7.

PROOF. We provide a sketch since the complete construction is long. We reduce from the *Post correspondence problem* (PCP) over the alphabet $\{a, b\}$. The input to this problem are two equally long lists $w_1, \dots, w_n$ and $w'_1, \dots, w'_n$ of words over $\{a, b\}$, and we ask whether there is a *solution*, i.e., a nonempty sequence $i_1 \dots i_m$ of indices in $\{1, \dots, n\}$ such that $w_{i_1} \dots w_{i_m} = w'_{i_1} \dots w'_{i_m}$.

Let $w_1, \dots, w_n$ and $w'_1, \dots, w'_n$ be an instance of PCP. In the full proof we construct a Boolean CQ q and a set Σ of full tgds over the signature $\{P_a, P_b, P_\#, P_*, \text{sync}, \text{start}, \text{end}\}$, where P_a, P_b, $P_\#$, P_* and sync are binary predicates, and start and end are unary predicates, such that the PCP instance given by $w_1, \dots, w_n$ and $w'_1, \dots, w'_n$ has a solution iff there exists an acyclic CQ q' such that $q \equiv_\Sigma q'$. In this sketch though, we concentrate on the case when the underlying graph of q' is a directed path; i.e, we prove that the PCP instance has a solution iff there is a CQ q' whose underlying graph is a directed path such that $q \equiv_\Sigma q'$. This does not imply the undecidability of the general case, but the proof of the latter is a generalization of the one we sketch below.

The restriction of the query q to the symbols that are not sync is graphically depicted in Figure 2. There, x, y, z, u, v denote the names of the respective variables. The interpretation of sync in q consists of all pairs in $\{y, u, z\}$.

Our set Σ of full tgds defines the *synchronization* predicate sync over those acyclic CQs q' whose underlying graph is a path. Assume that q' encodes a word $w \in \{a, b\}^+$. We denote by $w[i]$, for $1 \leq i \leq |w|$, the prefix of w of length i. In such case, the predicate sync contains those pairs (i, j) such that for some sequence $i_1 \dots i_m$ of indices in $\{1, \dots, n\}$ we have that $w_{i_1} \dots w_{i_m} = w[i]$ and $w'_{i_1} \dots w'_{i_m} = w[j]$. Thus, if w is a solution for the PCP instance, then $(|w|, |w|)$ belongs to the interpretation of sync.

Formally, Σ consists of the following rules:

1. An initialization rule:

$$\text{start}(x), P_\#(x, y) \rightarrow \text{sync}(y, y).$$

That is, the first element after the special symbol # (which denotes the beginning of a word over $\{a, b\}$) is synchronized with itself.

2. For each $1 \leq i \leq n$, a synchronization rule:

$$\text{sync}(x, y), P_{w_i}(x, z), P_{w'_i}(y, u) \rightarrow \text{sync}(z, u).$$

Here, $P_w(x, y)$, for $w = a_1 \dots a_t \in \{a, b\}^+$, denotes $P_{a_1}(x, x_1), \dots, P_{a_t}(x_{t-1}, y)$, where the x_i's are fresh variables. Roughly, if (x, y) is synchronized and the element z (resp., u) is reachable from x (resp., y) by word w_i (resp., w'_i), then (z, u) is also synchronized.

3. For each $1 \leq i \leq n$, a finalization rule:

$$\text{start}(x), P_a(y, z), P_a(z, u), P_*(u, v), \text{end}(v),$$
$$\text{sync}(y_1, y_2), P_{w_i}(y_1, y), P_{w'_i}(y_2, y) \rightarrow \psi,$$

where ψ is the conjunction of atoms:

$$P_\#(x, y), P_\#(x, z), P_\#(x, u), P_*(y, v), P_*(z, v),$$
$$P_b(z, y), P_b(u, z), P_a(u, y), P_b(y, u),$$
$$\text{sync}(y, y), \text{sync}(z, z), \text{sync}(y, z), \text{sync}(z, y),$$
$$\text{sync}(y, u), \text{sync}(u, y), \text{sync}(z, u), \text{sync}(u, z).$$

This tgd enforces $chase(q', \Sigma)$ to contain a "copy" of q whenever q' encodes a solution for the PCP instance.

We first show that if the PCP instance has a solution given by the nonempty sequence $i_1 \dots i_m$, with $1 \leq i_1, \dots, i_m \leq n$, then there exists an acylic CQ q' whose underlying graph is a directed path such that $q \equiv_\Sigma q'$. Let us assume that $w_{i_1} \dots w_{i_m} = a_1 \dots a_t$, where each $a_i \in \{a, b\}$. It is not hard to prove that $q \equiv_\Sigma q'$, where q' is as follows:

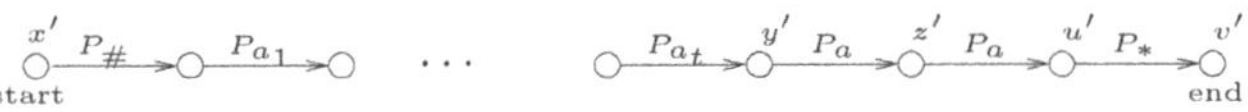

Here, again, x', y', z', u', v' denote the names of the respective variables of q'. All nodes in the above path are different. The main reason why $q \equiv_\Sigma q'$ holds is because the fact w is a solution implies that there are elements y_1 and y_2 such that $\text{sync}(y_1, y_2)$, $P_{w_1}(y_1, y)$ and $P_{w'_i}(y_2, y)$ hold in $chase(q', \Sigma)$. Thus, the finalization rule is fired. This creates a copy of q in $chase(q', \Sigma)$, which allows q to be homomorphically mapped to $chase(q', \Sigma)$.

Now we prove that if there exists an acyclic CQ q' such that $q \equiv_\Sigma q'$ and the underlying graph of q' is a directed path, then the PCP instance has a solution. Since $q \equiv_\Sigma q'$, Lemma 1 tells us that $chase(q, \Sigma) \equiv chase(q', \Sigma)$ are homomorphically equivalent. But then $chase(q', \Sigma)$ must contain at least one variable labeled start and one variable labeled end. The first variable cannot have incoming edges (otherwise, $chase(q', \Sigma)$ would not homomorphically map to $chase(q, \Sigma)$), while the second one cannot have outcoming edges (for the same reason). Thus, it is the first variable x' of q' that is labeled start and the last one v' that is labeled end. Further, all edges reaching v' in q' must be labeled P_* (otherwise q' does not homomorphically map to q). Thus, this is the label of the last edge of q' that goes from variable u' to v'. Analogously, the edge that leaves x' in q' is labeled $P_\#$. Further, any other edge in q' is labeled P_a, P_b, or sync.

Notice now that v' must have an incoming edge labeled P_* in $chase(q', \Sigma)$ from some node u'' that has an outgoing edge with label P_a (since q homomorphically maps to $chase(q', \Sigma)$). By definition of Σ, this could only have happened if the finalization rule is fired. In particular, u' is preceded by node z', which in turn is preceded by y', and there are elements y'_1 and y'_2 such that $\text{sync}(y'_1, y'_2)$, $P_{w_1}(y'_1, y')$ and $P_{w'_i}(y'_2, y')$ hold in $chase(q', \Sigma)$. In fact, the unique path from y'_1 (resp., y'_2) to y' in q' is labeled w_i (resp., w'_i). This means that the atom $\text{sync}(y'_1, y'_2)$ was not one of the edges of q', but must have been produced during the chase by firing the initialization or the synchronization rules, and so on. This process must finish in the second element x^* of q'. (Recall that $\text{sync}(x^*, x^*)$ belongs to $chase(q', \Sigma)$ due to the first rule of Σ). We conclude that our PCP instance has a solution. □

Theorem 7 rules out any class that captures the class of full tgds, e.g., weakly-guarded, weakly-acyclic and weakly-sticky sets of tgds. The question that comes up is whether the non-weak versions of the above classes, namely guarded, non-recursive and sticky sets of tgds, ensure the decidability of SemAc, and what is the complexity of the problem. This is the subject of the next two sections.

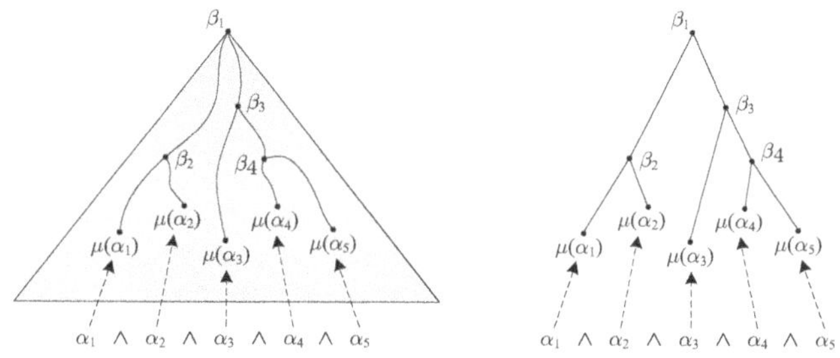

Figure 3: The compact acyclic query.

4. ACYCLICITY-PRESERVING CHASE

We propose a semantic criterion, the so-called *acyclicity-preserving chase*, that ensures the decidability of SemAc($\mathbb{C}$) whenever the problem Cont($\mathbb{C}$) is decidable. This criterion guarantees that, starting from an acyclic instance, it is not possible to destroy its acyclicity during the construction of the chase. We then proceed to show that the class of guarded sets of tgds has acyclicity-preserving chase, which immediately implies the decidability of SemAc($\mathbb{G}$), and we pinpoint the exact complexity of the latter problem. Notice that non-recursiveness and stickiness do not enjoy this property, even in the restrictive setting where only unary and binary predicates can be used; more details are given in the next section. The formal definition of our semantic criterion follows:

Definition 1. (**Acyclicity-preserving Chase**) We say that a class $\mathbb{C}$ of sets of tgds has *acyclicity-preserving chase* if, for every acyclic CQ q, set $\Sigma \in \mathbb{C}$, and chase sequence for q under Σ, the result of such a chase sequence is acyclic. ■

We can then prove the following small query property:

PROPOSITION 8. *Let Σ be a finite set of tgds that belongs to a class that has acyclicity-preserving chase, and q a CQ. If q is semantically acyclic under Σ, then there exists an acyclic CQ q', where $|q'| \leq 2 \cdot |q|$, such that $q \equiv_\Sigma q'$.*

The proof of the above result relies on the following technical lemma, established in [8] (using slightly different terminology), that will also be used later in our investigation:

LEMMA 9. *Let $q(\bar{x})$ be a CQ, I an acyclic instance, and $\bar{c}$ a tuple of distinct constants occurring in I such that $q(\bar{c})$ holds in I. There exists an acyclic CQ $q'(\bar{x})$, where $q' \subseteq q$ and $|q'| \leq 2 \cdot |q|$, such that $q'(\bar{c})$ holds in I.*

For the sake of completeness, we would like to recall the idea of the construction underlying Lemma 9, which is illustrated in Figure 3. Assuming that $\alpha_1, \ldots, \alpha_5$ are the atoms of q, there exists a homomorphism μ that maps $\alpha_1 \wedge \ldots \wedge \alpha_5$ to the join tree T of the acyclic instance I (the shaded tree in Figure 3). Consider now the subtree T_q of T consisting of all the nodes in the image of the query and their ancestors. From T_q we extract the smaller tree F also depicted in Figure 3; $F = (V, E)$ is obtained as follows:

1. V consists of all the root and leaf nodes of T_q, and all the inner nodes of T_q with at least two children; and
2. For every $v, u \in V$, $(v, u) \in E$ iff u is a descendant of v in T_q, and the only nodes of V that occur on the unique shortest path from v to u in T_q are v and u.

It is easy to verify that F is a join tree, and has at most $2 \cdot |q|$ nodes. The acyclic conjunctive query q' is defined as the conjunction of all atoms occurring in F.

Notice that a result similar to Lemma 9 is implicit in [4], where the problem of approximating conjunctive queries is investigated. However, from the results of [4], we can only conclude the existence of an exponentially sized acyclic CQ in the arity of the underlying schema, while Lemma 9 establishes the existence of an acyclic query of linear size. This is decisive for our later complexity analysis. Having the above lemma in place, it is not difficult to establish Proposition 8.

PROOF OF PROPOSITION 8. Since, by hypothesis, q is semantically acyclic under Σ, there exists an acyclic CQ $q''(\bar{x})$ such that $q \equiv_\Sigma q''$. By Lemma 1, $c(\bar{x})$ belongs to the evaluation of q over $chase(q'', \Sigma)$. Recall that Σ belongs to a class that has acyclicity-preserving chase, which implies that $chase(q'', \Sigma)$ is acyclic. Hence, by Lemma 9, there exists an acyclic CQ q', where $q' \subseteq q$ and $|q'| \leq 2 \cdot |q|$, such that $c(\bar{x})$ belongs to the evaluation of q' over $chase(q'', \Sigma)$. By Lemma 1, $q'' \subseteq_\Sigma q'$, and therefore $q \subseteq_\Sigma q'$. We conclude that $q \equiv_\Sigma q'$, and the claim follows. □

It is clear that Proposition 8 provides a decision procedure for SemAc($\mathbb{C}$) whenever $\mathbb{C}$ has acyclicity-preserving chase and Cont($\mathbb{C}$) is decidable. Given a CQ q, and a finite set $\Sigma \in \mathbb{C}$:

1. Guess an acyclic CQ q' of size at most $2 \cdot |q|$; and
2. Verify that $q \subseteq_\Sigma q'$ and $q' \subseteq_\Sigma q$.

The next result follows:

THEOREM 10. *Consider a class $\mathbb{C}$ of sets of tgds that has acyclicity-preserving chase. If the problem* Cont($\mathbb{C}$) *is decidable, then* SemAc($\mathbb{C}$) *is also decidable.*

4.1 Guardedness

We proceed to show that SemAc($\mathbb{G}$) is decidable and has the same complexity as CQ containment under guarded tgds:

THEOREM 11. SemAc($\mathbb{G}$) *is complete for* 2EXPTIME. *It becomes* EXPTIME-*complete if the arity of the schema is fixed, and* NP-*complete if the schema is fixed.*

The rest of this section is devoted to establish Theorem 11.

Decidability and Upper Bounds

We first show that:

PROPOSITION 12. $\mathbb{G}$ *has acyclicity-preserving chase.*

The above result, combined with Theorem 10, implies the decidability of SemAc($\mathbb{G}$). However, this does not say anything about the complexity of the problem. With the aim of pinpointing the exact complexity of SemAc($\mathbb{G}$), we proceed to analyze the complexity of the decision procedure underlying Theorem 10. Recall that, given a CQ q, and a finite set $\Sigma \in \mathbb{G}$, we guess an acyclic CQ q' such that $|q'| \leq 2 \cdot |q|$, and verify that $q \equiv_\Sigma q'$. It is clear that this algorithm runs in non-deterministic polynomial time with a call to a $\mathcal{C}$ oracle, where $\mathcal{C}$ is a complexity class powerful enough for solving Cont($\mathbb{G}$). Thus, Proposition 2 implies that SemAc($\mathbb{G}$) is in 2EXPTIME, in EXPTIME if the arity of the schema is fixed, and in NP if the schema is fixed. One may ask why for a fixed schema the obtained upper bound is NP and not Σ_2^P. Observe that the oracle is called only once in order to solve Cont($\mathbb{G}$), and since Cont($\mathbb{G}$) is already in NP when the schema is fixed, it is not really needed in this case.

Lower Bounds

Let us now show that the above upper bounds are optimal. By Proposition 5, $\mathsf{RestCont}(\mathbb{G})$ can be reduced in constant time to $\mathsf{SemAc}(\mathbb{G})$. Thus, to obtain the desired lower bounds, it suffices to reduce in polynomial time $\mathsf{Cont}(\mathbb{G})$ to $\mathsf{RestCont}(\mathbb{G})$. Interestingly, the lower bounds given in Section 2 for $\mathsf{Cont}(\mathbb{G})$ hold even if we focus on Boolean CQs and the left-hand side query is acyclic. In fact, this is true, not only for guarded, but also for non-recursive and sticky sets of tgds. Let $\mathsf{AcBoolCont}(\mathbb{C})$ be the following problem: Given an acyclic Boolean CQ q, a Boolean CQ q', and a finite set $\Sigma \in \mathbb{C}$ of tgds, is it the case $q \subseteq_\Sigma q'$?

From the above discussion, to establish the desired lower bounds for guarded sets of tgds (and also for the other classes of tgds considered in this work), it suffices to reduce in polynomial time $\mathsf{AcBoolCont}$ to $\mathsf{RestCont}$. To this end, we introduce the so-called connecting operator, which provides a generic reduction from $\mathsf{AcBoolCont}$ to $\mathsf{RestCont}$.

Connecting operator. Consider an acyclic Boolean CQ q, a Boolean CQ q', and a finite set Σ of tgds. We assume that both q, q' are of the form $\exists \bar{y}(R_1(\bar{v}_1) \wedge \cdots \wedge R_m(\bar{v}_m))$. The application of the *connecting operator* on (q, q', Σ) returns the triple $(\mathsf{c}(q), \mathsf{c}(q'), \mathsf{c}(\Sigma))$, where

- $\mathsf{c}(q)$ is the query

$$\exists \bar{y} \exists w \big(R_1^\star(\bar{v}_1, w) \wedge \cdots \wedge R_m^\star(\bar{v}_m, w) \wedge aux(w, w)\big),$$

where w is a new variable not in q, each $R_i^\star$ is a new predicate, and also aux is a new binary predicate;

- $\mathsf{c}(q')$ is the query

$$\exists \bar{y} \exists w \exists u \exists v \big(R_1^\star(\bar{v}_1, w) \wedge \cdots \wedge R_m^\star(\bar{v}_m, w) \wedge aux(w, u) \wedge aux(u, v) \wedge aux(v, w)\big),$$

where w, u, v are new variables not in q; and

- Finally, $\mathsf{c}(\Sigma) = \{\mathsf{c}(\tau) \mid \tau \in \Sigma\}$, where for a tgd $\tau = \phi(\bar{x}, \bar{y}) \rightarrow \exists \bar{z} \psi(\bar{x}, \bar{z})$, $\mathsf{c}(\tau)$ is the tgd

$$\phi^\star(\bar{x}, \bar{y}, w) \rightarrow \exists \bar{z} \psi^\star(\bar{x}, \bar{z}, w),$$

with $\phi^\star(\bar{x}, \bar{y}, w), \psi^\star(\bar{x}, \bar{z}, w)$ be the conjunctions obtained from $\phi(\bar{x}, \bar{y}), \psi(\bar{x}, \bar{z})$, respectively, by replacing each atom $R(x_1, \ldots, x_n)$ with $R^\star(x_1, \ldots, x_n, w)$, where w is a new variable not occurring in τ.

This concludes the definition of the connecting operator. A class $\mathbb{C}$ of sets of tgds is *closed under connecting* if, for every set $\Sigma \in \mathbb{C}$, $\mathsf{c}(\Sigma) \in \mathbb{C}$. It is easy to verify that $\mathsf{c}(q)$ remains acyclic and is connected, $\mathsf{c}(q')$ is connected and not semantically acyclic under $\mathsf{c}(\Sigma)$, and $\mathsf{c}(\Sigma)$ is a set of body-connected tgds. It can be also shown that $q \subseteq_\Sigma q'$ iff $\mathsf{c}(q) \subseteq_{\mathsf{c}(\Sigma)} \mathsf{c}(q')$.

From the above discussion, it is clear that the connecting operator provides a generic polynomial time reduction from $\mathsf{AcBoolCont}(\mathbb{C})$ to $\mathsf{RestCont}(\mathbb{C})$, for every class $\mathbb{C}$ of sets of tgds that is closed under connecting. Then:

PROPOSITION 13. *Let $\mathbb{C}$ be a class of sets of tgds that is closed under connecting such that* $\mathsf{AcBoolCont}(\mathbb{C})$ *is hard for a complexity class C that is closed under polynomial time reductions. Then,* $\mathsf{SemAc}(\mathbb{C})$ *is also C-hard.*

Back to guardedness. It is easy to verify that the class of guarded sets of tgds is closed under connecting. Thus, the lower bounds for $\mathsf{SemAc}(\mathbb{G})$ stated in Theorem 11 follow from Propositions 2 and 13. Note that, although Proposition 2 refers to $\mathsf{Cont}(\mathbb{G})$, the lower bounds hold for $\mathsf{AcBoolCont}(\mathbb{G})$; this is implicit in [8].

As said in Section 2, a key subclass of guarded sets of tgds is the class of linear tgds, i.e., tgds whose body consists of a single atom, which in turn subsume the well-known class of inclusion dependencies. By exploiting the non-deterministic procedure employed for $\mathsf{SemAc}(\mathbb{G})$, and the fact that both linear tgds and inclusion dependencies are closed under connecting, we can show that:

THEOREM 14. $\mathsf{SemAc}(\mathbb{C})$, *for* $\mathbb{C} \in \{\mathbb{L}, \mathbb{ID}\}$, *is complete for* PSPACE. *It becomes* NP*-complete if the arity of the schema is fixed.*

5. UCQ REWRITABILITY

Even though the acyclicity-preserving chase criterion was very useful for solving $\mathsf{SemAc}(\mathbb{G})$, it is of little use for non-recursive and sticky sets of tgds. As we show in the next example, neither $\mathbb{NR}$ nor $\mathbb{S}$ have acyclicity-preserving chase:

Example 2. Consider the acyclic CQ and the tgd

$$q = \exists \bar{x}(P(x_1) \wedge \ldots \wedge P(x_n)) \qquad \tau = P(x), P(y) \rightarrow R(x, y),$$

where $\{\tau\}$ is both non-recursive and sticky, but not guarded. In $chase(q, \{\tau\})$ the predicate R holds all the possible pairs that can be formed using the terms $x_1, \ldots, x_n$. Thus, in the Gaifman graph of $chase(q, \{\tau\})$ we have an n-clique, which means that is highly cyclic. Notice that our example illustrates that also other favorable properties of the CQ are destroyed after chasing with non-recursive and sticky sets of tgds, namely bounded (hyper)tree width.[4] ■

In view of the fact that the methods devised in Section 4 cannot be used for non-recursive and sticky sets of tgds, new techniques must be developed. Interestingly, $\mathbb{NR}$ and $\mathbb{S}$ share an important property, which turned out to be very useful for semantic acyclicity: *UCQ rewritability*. Recall that a *union of conjunctive queries (UCQ)* is an expression of the form $Q(\bar{x}) = \bigvee_{1 \leq i \leq n} q_i(\bar{x})$, where each q_i is a CQ over the same schema σ. The evaluation of Q over an instance I, denoted $Q(I)$, is defined as $\bigcup_{1 \leq i \leq n} q_i(I)$. The formal definition of UCQ rewritability follows:

Definition 2. (**UCQ Rewritability**) A class $\mathbb{C}$ of sets of tgds is *UCQ rewritable* if, for every CQ q, and $\Sigma \in \mathbb{C}$, we can construct a UCQ Q such that: For every CQ $q'(\bar{x})$, $q' \subseteq_\Sigma q$ iff $c(\bar{x}) \in Q(D_{q'})$, with $D_{q'}$ be the database obtained from q' after replacing each variable x with $c(x)$. ■

In other words, UCQ rewritability suggests that query containment can be reduced to the problem of UCQ evaluation. It is important to say that this reduction depends only on the right-hand side CQ and the set of tgds, but not on the left-hand side query. This is crucial for establishing the desirable small query property whenever we focus on sets of tgds that belong to a UCQ rewritable class. At this point, let us clarify that the class of guarded sets of tgds is not UCQ rewritable, which justifies our choice of a different semantic property, that is, acyclicity-preserving chase, for its study.

Let us now show the desirable small query property. For each UCQ rewritable class $\mathbb{C}$ of sets of tgds, there exists a computable function $f_{\mathbb{C}}(\cdot, \cdot)$ from the set of pairs consisting of a CQ and a set of tgds in $\mathbb{C}$ to positive integers such that the following holds: For every CQ q, set $\Sigma \in \mathbb{C}$, and UCQ rewriting Q of q and Σ, the *height* of Q, that is, the maximal size of its disjuncts, is at most $f_{\mathbb{C}}(q, \Sigma)$. The existence of the function $f_{\mathbb{C}}$ follows by the definition of UCQ rewritability. Then, we show the following:

[4]Notice that guarded sets of tgds over predicates of bounded arity preserve the bounded hyper(tree) width of the query.

PROPOSITION 15. *Let $\mathbb{C}$ be a UCQ rewritable class, $\Sigma \in \mathbb{C}$ a finite set of tgds, and q a CQ. If q is semantically acyclic under Σ, then there exists an acyclic CQ q', where $|q'| \leq 2 \cdot f_{\mathbb{C}}(q, \Sigma)$, such that $q \equiv_{\Sigma} q'$.*

PROOF. Since q is semantically acyclic under Σ, there exists an acyclic CQ $q''(\bar{x})$ such that $q \equiv_{\Sigma} q''$. As $\mathbb{C}$ is UCQ rewritable, there exists a UCQ Q such that $c(\bar{x}) \in Q(D_{q''})$, which implies that there exists a CQ q_r (one of the disjuncts of Q) such that $c(\bar{x}) \in q_r(D_{q''})$. Clearly, $|q_r| \leq f_{\mathbb{C}}(q, \Sigma)$. But $D_{q''}$ is acyclic, and thus Lemma 9 implies the existence of an acyclic CQ q', where $q' \subseteq q_r$ and $|q'| \leq 2 \cdot f_{\mathbb{C}}(q, \Sigma)$, such that $c(\bar{x}) \in q'(D_{q''})$. The latter implies that $q'' \subseteq q'$. By hypothesis, $q \subseteq_{\Sigma} q''$, and hence $q \subseteq_{\Sigma} q'$. For the other direction, we first show that $q_r \subseteq_{\Sigma} q$ (otherwise, Q is not a UCQ rewriting). Since $q' \subseteq q_r$, we get that $q' \subseteq_{\Sigma} q$. We conclude that $q \equiv_{\Sigma} q'$, and the claim follows. □

It is clear that Proposition 15 provides a decision procedure for $\mathsf{SemAc}(\mathbb{C})$ whenever $\mathbb{C}$ is UCQ rewritable, and $\mathsf{Cont}(\mathbb{C})$ is decidable. Given a CQ q, and a finite set $\Sigma \in \mathbb{C}$:

1. Guess an acyclic CQ q' of size at most $2 \cdot f_{\mathbb{C}}(q, \Sigma)$; and
2. Verify that $q \subseteq_{\Sigma} q'$ and $q' \subseteq_{\Sigma} q$.

The next result follows:

THEOREM 16. *Consider a class $\mathbb{C}$ of sets of tgds that is UCQ rewritable. If the problem $\mathsf{Cont}(\mathbb{C})$ is decidable, then $\mathsf{SemAc}(\mathbb{C})$ is also decidable.*

5.1 Non-Recursiveness

As already said, the key property of $\mathbb{NR}$ that we are going to exploit for solving $\mathsf{SemAc}(\mathbb{NR})$ is UCQ rewritability. For a CQ q and a set Σ of tgds, let $p_{q,\Sigma}$ and $a_{q,\Sigma}$ be the number of predicates in q and Σ, and the maximum arity over all those predicates, respectively. The next result is implicit in [20]:[5]

PROPOSITION 17. *$\mathbb{NR}$ is UCQ rewritable. Furthermore, $f_{\mathbb{NR}}(q, \Sigma) = p_{q,\Sigma} \cdot (a_{q,\Sigma} \cdot |q| + 1)^{a_{q,\Sigma}}$.*

The above result, combined with Theorem 16, implies the decidability of $\mathsf{SemAc}(\mathbb{NR})$. For the exact complexity of the problem, we simply need to analyze the complexity of the non-deterministic algorithm underlying Theorem 16. Observe that when the arity of the schema is fixed the function $f_{\mathbb{NR}}$ is polynomial, and therefore Proposition 17 guarantees the existence of a polynomially sized acyclic CQ. In this case, by exploiting Proposition 3, it is easy to show that $\mathsf{SemAc}(\mathbb{NR})$ is in NEXPTIME, and in NP if the schema is fixed. However, things are a bit cryptic when the arity of the schema is not fixed. In this case, $f_{\mathbb{NR}}$ is exponential, and thus we have to guess an acyclic CQ of exponential size. But now the fact that $\mathsf{Cont}(\mathbb{NR})$ is in NEXPTIME (by Proposition 3) alone is not enough to conclude that $\mathsf{SemAc}(\mathbb{NR})$ is also in NEXPTIME. We need to understand better the complexity of the query containment algorithm for $\mathbb{NR}$.

Recall that given two CQs $q(\bar{x}), q'(\bar{x})$, and a finite set $\Sigma \in \mathbb{NR}$, by Lemma 1, $q \subseteq_{\Sigma} q'$ iff $c(\bar{x}) \in q'(chase(q, \Sigma))$. By exploiting non-recursiveness, it can be shown that if $c(\bar{x}) \in q'(chase(q, \Sigma))$, then there exists a chase sequence

$$q = I_0 \xrightarrow{\tau_0, \bar{c}_0} I_1 \xrightarrow{\tau_1, \bar{c}_1} I_2 \dots I_{n-1} \xrightarrow{\tau_{n-1}, \bar{c}_{n-1}} I_n$$

of q and Σ, where $n = |q'| \cdot (b_{\Sigma})^{\mathcal{O}(p_{q',\Sigma})}$, with b_{Σ} be the maximum number of atoms in the body of a tgd of Σ, such that $c(\bar{x}) \in q'(I_n)$. The query containment algorithm for $\mathbb{NR}$ simply guesses such a chase sequence of q and Σ, and checks whether $c(\bar{x}) \in q'(I_n)$. Since n is exponential, this algorithm runs in non-deterministic exponential time. Now, recall that for $\mathsf{SemAc}(\mathbb{NR})$ we need to perform two containment checks where either the left-hand side or the right-hand side query is of exponential size. But in both cases the containment algorithm for $\mathbb{NR}$ runs in non-deterministic exponential time, and hence $\mathsf{SemAc}(\mathbb{NR})$ is in NEXPTIME. The lower bounds are inherited from $\mathsf{AcBoolCont}(\mathbb{NR})$ since $\mathbb{NR}$ is closed under connecting (see Proposition 13). Then:

THEOREM 18. *$\mathsf{SemAc}(\mathbb{NR})$ is complete for NEXPTIME, even if the arity of the schema is fixed. It becomes NP-complete if the schema is fixed.*

5.2 Stickiness

We now focus on sticky sets of tgds. As for $\mathbb{NR}$, the key property of $\mathbb{S}$ that we are going to use is UCQ rewritability. The next result has been explicitly shown in [20]:

PROPOSITION 19. *$\mathbb{S}$ is UCQ rewritable. Furthermore, $f_{\mathbb{S}}(q, \Sigma) = p_{q,\Sigma} \cdot (a_{q,\Sigma} \cdot |q| + 1)^{a_{q,\Sigma}}$.*

The above result, combined with Theorem 16, implies the decidability of $\mathsf{SemAc}(\mathbb{S})$. Moreover, Proposition 19 allows us to establish an optimal upper bound when the arity of the schema is fixed since in this case the function $f_{\mathbb{S}}$ is polynomial. In fact, we show that $\mathsf{SemAc}(\mathbb{S})$ is NP-complete when the arity of the schema is fixed. The NP-hardness is inherited from $\mathsf{AcBoolCont}(\mathbb{S})$ since $\mathbb{S}$ is closed under connecting (see Proposition 13). Now, when the arity of the schema is not fixed the picture is still foggy. In this case, the function $f_{\mathbb{S}}$ is exponential, and thus by following the usual guess and check approach we get that $\mathsf{SemAc}(\mathbb{S})$ is in NEXPTIME, while Proposition 13 implies an EXPTIME lower bound. To sum up, our generic machinery based on UCQ rewritability shows that:

THEOREM 20. *$\mathsf{SemAc}(\mathbb{S})$ is in NEXPTIME and hard for EXPTIME. It becomes NP-complete if the arity is fixed.*

An interesting question that comes up is whether for sticky sets of tgds a stronger small query property than Proposition 15 can be established, which guarantees the existence of a polynomially sized equivalent acyclic CQ. It is clear that such a result would allow us to establish an EXPTIME upper bound for $\mathsf{SemAc}(\mathbb{S})$. At this point, one might be tempted to think that this can be achieved by showing that the function $f_{\mathbb{S}}$ is actually polynomial even if the arity of the schema is not fixed. The next example shows that this is not the case. We can construct a sticky set Σ of tgds and a CQ q such that, for every UCQ rewriting Q for q and Σ, the height of Q is exponential in the arity.

Example 3. Let Σ be the sticky set of tgds given below; we write $\bar{x}_i^j$ for the tuple of variables $x_i, x_{i+1}, \dots, x_j$:

$$\{P_i(\bar{x}_1^{i-1}, Z, \bar{x}_{i+1}^n, Z, O), P_i(\bar{x}_1^{i-1}, O, \bar{x}_{i+1}^n, Z, O) \rightarrow P_{i-1}(\bar{x}_1^{i-1}, Z, \bar{x}_{i+1}^n, Z, O)\}_{i \in \{1,\dots,n\}}.$$

Consider also the Boolean CQ

$$P_0(0, \dots, 0, 0, 1).$$

It can be shown that, for every UCQ rewriting Q for q and Σ, the disjunct of Q that mentions only the predicate P_n contains exactly 2^n atoms. Therefore, there is no UCQ rewriting for q and Σ of polynomial height, which in turn implies that $f_{\mathbb{S}}$ cannot be polynomial in the arity of the schema. ■

[5] The work [20] does not consider $\mathbb{NR}$. However, the rewriting algorithm in that paper works also for non-recursive sets of tgds.

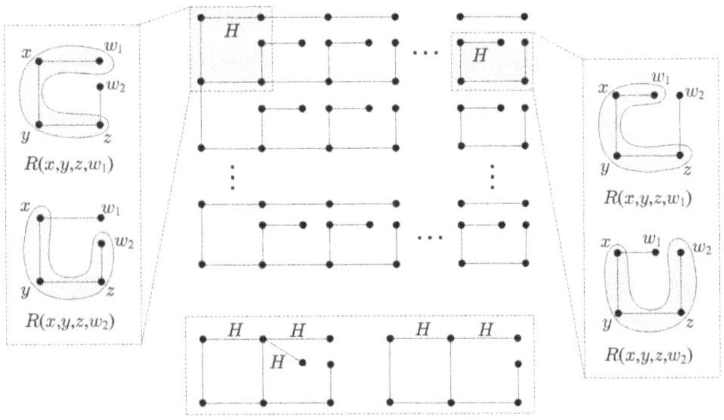

Figure 4: From a "tree" to a grid via key dependencies.

The above discussion reveals the need to identify a more refined property of stickiness than UCQ rewritability, which will allow us to close the complexity of SemAc($\mathbb{S}$) when the arity is not fixed. This is left as an interesting open problem.

6. SEMANTIC ACYCLICITY WITH EGDS

Up to now, we have considered classes of constraints that are based on tgds. However, semantic acyclicity can be naturally defined for classes of egds. Hence, one may wonder whether the techniques developed in the previous sections can be applied for egd-based classes of constraints. Unfortunately, the situation changes dramatically even for the simplest subclass of egds, i.e., keys.

6.1 Peculiarity of Keys

We show that the techniques developed in the previous sections for tgds cannot be applied for showing the decidability of semantic acyclicity under keys, and thus under egds. Although the notions of acyclicity-preserving chase (Definition 1) and UCQ rewritability (Definition 2) can be naturally defined for egds, are of little use even if we focus on keys.

Acyclicity-preserving chase. It is easy to show via a simple example that keys over binary and ternary predicates do not enjoy the acyclicity-preserving chase property:

Example 4. Let q be the acyclic query

$$R(x,y) \wedge S(x,y,z) \wedge S(x,z,w) \wedge S(x,w,v) \wedge R(x,v).$$

After applying on q the key $R(x,y), R(x,z) \rightarrow y = z$, which simply states that the first attribute of the binary predicate R is the key, we obtain the query

$$R(x,y) \wedge S(x,y,z) \wedge S(x,z,w) \wedge S(x,w,y),$$

which is clearly cyclic. ■

With the aim of emphasizing the peculiarity of keys, we give a more involved example, which shows that a tree-like query can be transformed via two keys into a highly cyclic query that contains a grid. Interestingly, this shows that also other desirable properties, in particular bounded (hyper)tree width, are destroyed when we chase a query using keys.

Example 5. Consider the CQ q depicted in Figure 4 (ignoring for the moment the dashed boxes). Although seemingly q contains an $n \times n$ grid, it can be verified that the grid-like structure in the figure is actually a tree. In addition, q contains atoms of the form $R(x,y,z,w)$ as explained in the figure. More precisely, for each of the open squares occurring in the first column (e.g., the upper-left shaded square), we have the two atoms $R(x,y,z,w_1)$ and $R(x,y,z,w_2)$ represented by the two hyperedges on the left. Moreover, for each of the internal open squares and the open squares occurring in the last column (e.g., the upper-right shaded square), we have the two atoms $R(x,y,z,w_1)$ and $R(x,y,z,w_2)$ represented by the two hyperedges on the right. Observe that q is an acyclic query. Consider now the set Σ of keys:

$$\epsilon_1 = R(x,y,z,w), R(x,y,z,w') \rightarrow w = w'$$
$$\epsilon_2 = H(x,y), H(x,z) \rightarrow y = z.$$

Notice that $H(\cdot,\cdot)$ stores the horizontal edges. It is not difficult to see that $chase(q,\Sigma)$ contains an $n \times n$ grid. Roughly, as described at the bottom of Figure 4, by first applying ϵ_1 we close the open squares of the first column, while the open squares of the second column have now the same shape as the ones of the first column, but with a dangling H-edge. Then, by applying ϵ_2, the two H-edges collapse into a single edge, and we obtain open squares that have exactly the same shape as those of the first column. After finitely many chase steps, all the squares are closed, and thus $chase(q,\Sigma)$ indeed contains an $n \times n$ grid. Therefore, although the query q is acyclic, $chase(q,\Sigma)$ is far from being acyclic. Observe also that the (hyper)tree width of $chase(q,\Sigma)$ depends on n, while q has (hyper)tree width 3. ■

UCQ rewritability. It is not hard to show that keys are not UCQ rewritable. This is not surprising due to the transitive nature of equality. Intuitively, the UCQ rewritability of keys implies that a first-order (FO) query can encode the fact that the equality relation is transitive. However, it is well-known that this is not possible due to the inability of FO queries to express recursion.

6.2 Keys over Constrained Signatures

Despite the peculiar nature of keys as discussed above, we can establish a positive result regarding semantic acyclicity under keys, providing that only unary and binary predicates can be used. This is done by exploiting the following generic result, which is actually the version of Theorem 10 for egd-based classes:

THEOREM 21. *Consider a class $\mathbb{C}$ of sets of egds. If $\mathbb{C}$ has acyclicity-preserving chase, then* SemAc($\mathbb{C}$) *is* NP*-complete, even if we allow only unary and binary predicates.*

The proof of the above result is along the lines of the proof for Theorem 10, and exploits the fact that the containment problem under egds is feasible in non-deterministic polynomial time (this can be shown by using Lemma 1). The lower bound follows from [14], which shows that the problem of checking whether a Boolean CQ over a single binary relation is equivalent to an acyclic one is NP-hard. We now show the following positive result for the class of keys over unary and binary predicates, denoted $\mathbb{K}_2$:

PROPOSITION 22. *$\mathbb{K}_2$ has acyclicity-preserving chase.*

Notice that the above result is not in a conflict with Examples 4 and 5, since both examples use predicates of arity greater than two. It is now straightforward to see that:

THEOREM 23. SemAc($\mathbb{K}_2$) *is* NP*-complete.*

Interestingly, Theorem 23 can be extended to *unary functional dependencies* (over unconstrained signatures), that is, FDs of the form $R : A \rightarrow B$, where R is a relational symbol of arity $n > 0$

and the cardinality of A is one. This result has been established independently by Figueira [17]. Let us recall that egds ensure the finite controllability of CQ containment. Consequently, Theorem 23 holds even for FinSemAc, which takes as input a CQ q and a set Σ of egds, and asks for the existence of an acyclic CQ q' such that q and q' are equivalent over all finite databases that satisfy Σ.

7. EVALUATION OF SEMANTICALLY ACYCLIC QUERIES

As it has been noted in different scenarios in the absence of constraints, semantic acyclicity has a positive impact on query evaluation [4, 5, 6]. We observe here that such good behavior extends to the notion of semantic acyclicity for CQs under the decidable classes of constraints we identified in the previous sections. In particular, evaluation of semantically acyclic CQs under constraints in such classes is a *fixed-parameter tractable* (fpt) problem, assuming the parameter to be $|q| + |\Sigma|$. (Here, $|q|$ and $|\Sigma|$ represent the size of reasonable encodings of q and Σ, respectively). Recall that this means that the problem can be solved in time $O(|D|^c \cdot f(|q|+|\Sigma|))$, for $c \geq 1$ and f a computable function.

Let $\mathbb{C}$ be a class of sets of tgds. We define SemAcEval($\mathbb{C}$) to be the following problem: The input consists of a set of constraints Σ in $\mathbb{C}$, a semantically acyclic CQ q under Σ, a database D such that $D \models \Sigma$, and a tuple $\bar{t}$ of elements in D. We ask whether $\bar{t} \in q(D)$.

PROPOSITION 24. SemAcEval($\mathbb{C}$) *can be solved in time*

$$O\left(|D| \cdot 2^{2^{O(|q|+|\Sigma|)}}\right),$$

where $\mathbb{C} \in \{\mathbb{G}, \mathbb{NR}, \mathbb{S}\}$.

PROOF. Our results state that for $\mathbb{C} \in \{\mathbb{G}, \mathbb{NR}, \mathbb{S}\}$, checking if a CQ q is semantically acyclic under $\mathbb{C}$ can be done in double-exponential time. More importantly, in case that q is in fact semantically acyclic under $\mathbb{C}$ our proof techniques yield an equivalent acyclic CQ q' of at most exponential size in $|q|+|\Sigma|$. We then compute and evaluate such a query q' on D, and return $q(D) = q'(D)$. Clearly, this can be done in time

$$O\left(2^{2^{O(|q|+|\Sigma|)}}\right) + O\left(|D| \cdot 2^{O(|q|+|\Sigma|)}\right).$$

The running time of this algorithm is dominated by

$$O\left(|D| \cdot 2^{2^{O(|q|+|\Sigma|)}}\right)$$

and the claim follows. □

This is an improvement over general CQ evaluation for which no fpt algorithm is believed to exist [26]. It is worth remarking, nonetheless, that SemAcEval($\mathbb{C}$) corresponds to a *promise version* of the evaluation problem, where the property that defines the class is EXPTIME-hard for all the $\mathbb{C}$'s studied in Proposition 24.

The above algorithm computes an equivalent acyclic CQ q' for a semantically acyclic CQ q under a set of constraints in $\mathbb{C}$. This might take double-exponential time. Surprisingly, computing such q' is not always needed at the moment of evaluating semantically acyclic CQs under constraints. In particular, this holds for the sets of guarded tgds. In fact, in such case evaluating a semantically acylic CQ q under Σ over a database D that satisfies Σ amounts to checking a polynomial time property over q and D. It follows, in addition, that the evaluation problem for semantically acyclic CQs under guarded tgds is tractable:

THEOREM 25. SemAcEval($\mathbb{G}$) *is in polynomial time.*

The idea behind the proof of the above theorem is as follows. When q is a semantically acyclic CQ in the absence of constraints, evaluating q on D amounts to checking the existence of a winning strategy for the duplicator in a particular version of the pebble game, known as the *existential 1-cover game*, on q and D [13]. We denote this by $q \equiv_{\exists 1c} D$. The existence of such winning strategy can be checked in polynomial time [13]. Now, when q is semantically acyclic under an arbitrary set Σ of tgds or egds, we show that evaluating q on D amounts to checking whether $chase(q, \Sigma) \equiv_{\exists 1c} D$. When Σ is a set of guarded tgds, we prove in addition that $chase(q, \Sigma) \equiv_{\exists 1c} D$ iff $q \equiv_{\exists 1c} D$. Thus, SemAcEval($\mathbb{G}$) is tractable since checking $q \equiv_{\exists 1c} D$ is tractable.

The fact that the evaluation of q on D boils down to checking whether $chase(q, \Sigma) \equiv_{\exists 1c} D$, when q is semantically acyclic under Σ, also yields tractability for SemAcEval($\mathbb{C}$), where $\mathbb{C}$ is any class of sets of egds for which the chase can be computed in polynomial time. This includes the central class of FDs. Notice, however, that we do not know whether SemAc under FDs is decidable.

8. FURTHER ADVANCEMENTS

In this section we informally discuss the fact that our previous results on semantic acyclicity under tgds and CQs can be extended to UCQs. Moreover, we show that our techniques establish the existence of maximally contained acyclic queries.

8.1 Unions of Conjunctive Queries

It is reasonable to consider a more *liberal* version of semantic acyclicity under tgds based on UCQs. In such case we are given a UCQ Q and a finite set Σ of tgds, and the question is whether there is a union Q' of acyclic CQs that is equivalent to Q under Σ. It can be shown that all the complexity results on semantic acyclicity under tgds presented above continue to hold even when the input query is a UCQ. This is done by extending the small query properties established for CQs (Propositions 8 and 15) to UCQs.

Consider a finite set Σ of tgds (that falls in one of the tgd-based classes considered above), and a UCQ Q. If Q is semantically acyclic under Σ, then one of the following holds: (i) for each disjunct q of Q, there exists an acyclic CQ q' of bounded size (the exact size of q' depends on the class of Σ) such that $q \equiv_\Sigma q'$, or (ii) q is redundant in Q, i.e., there exists a disjunct q' of Q such that $q \subseteq_\Sigma q'$. Having this property in place, we can then design a non-deterministic algorithm for semantic acyclicity, which provides the desired upper bounds. Roughly, for each disjunct q of Q, this algorithm guesses whether there exists an acyclic CQ q' of bounded size such that $q \equiv_\Sigma q'$, or q is redundant in Q. The desired lower bounds are inherited from semantic acyclicity in the case of CQs.

8.2 Query Approximations

Let $\mathbb{C}$ be any of the decidable classes of finite sets of tgds we study in this paper (i.e., $\mathbb{G}$, $\mathbb{NR}$, or $\mathbb{S}$). Then, for any CQ q without constants[6] and set Σ of constraints in $\mathbb{C}$, our techniques yield a *maximally contained* acyclic CQ q' under Σ. This means that $q' \subseteq_\Sigma q$ and there is no acyclic CQ q'' such that $q'' \subseteq_\Sigma q$ and $q' \subsetneq_\Sigma q''$. Following the recent database literature, such q' corresponds to an *acyclic CQ approximation of q under Σ* [4, 5, 6]. Notice that when q is semantically acyclic under Σ, this acyclic approximation q' is in fact equivalent to q under Σ. Computing and evaluating an acyclic CQ approximation for q might help finding "quick" (i.e., fixed-parameter tractable) answers to it when exact evaluation is infeasible.

[6]Approximations for CQs with constants are not well-understood, even in the absence of constraints [4].

The way in which we obtain approximations is by slightly reformulating the small query properties established in the paper (Propositions 8 and 15). Instead of dealing with semantically acyclic CQs only, we are now given an arbitrary CQ q. In all cases the reformulation expresses the following: For every acyclic CQ q' such that $q' \subseteq_\Sigma q$, there is an acyclic CQ q'' of the appropriate size $f(q, \Sigma)$ such that $q' \subseteq_\Sigma q'' \subseteq_\Sigma q$. It is easy to prove that for each CQ q there exists at least one acyclic CQ q' such that $q' \subseteq_\Sigma q$; take a single variable x and add a tuple $R(x, \dots, x)$ for each symbol R. It follows then that an acyclic CQ approximation of q under Σ can always be found among the set $\mathcal{A}(q)$ of acyclic CQs q' of size at most $f(q, \Sigma)$ such that $q' \subseteq_\Sigma q$. In fact, the acyclic CQ approximations of q under Σ are the maximal elements of $\mathcal{A}(q)$ under $\subseteq_\Sigma$.

9. CONCLUSIONS

We have concentrated on the problem of semantic acyclicity for CQs in the presence of database constraints; in fact, tgds or egds. Surprisingly, we have shown that there are cases such as the class of full tgds, where containment is decidable, while semantic acyclicity is undecidable. We have then focussed on the main classes of tgds for which CQ containment is decidable, and do not subsume full tgds, i.e., guarded, non-recusrive and sticky tgds. For these classes we have shown that semantic acyclicity is decidable, and obtained several complexity results. We have also shown that semantic acyclicity is NP-complete if we focus on keys over unary and binary predicates. Finally, we have considered the problem of evaluating a semantically acyclic CQ over a database that satisfies certain constraints, and shown that for guarded tgds and FDs is tractable. Here are some interesting open problems that we are planning to investigate: (i) The complexity of semantic acyclicity under sticky sets of tgds is still unknown; (ii) We do not know whether semantic acyclicity under keys over unconstrained signatures is decidable; and (iii) We do not know the complexity of evaluating semantically acyclic queries under $\mathbb{NR}$, $\mathbb{S}$ and egds.

Acknowledgements: Barceló would like to thank D. Figueira, M. Romero, S. Rudolph, and N. Schweikardt for insightful discussions about the nature of semantic acyclicity under constraints. We also thank the anonymous referees for their helpful feedback. Barceló is funded by the Millenium Nucleus Center for Semantic Web Research under grant NC120004. Gottlob is supported by the EPSRC Programme Grant EP/M025268/ "VADA: Value Added Data Systems – Principles and Architecture". Pieris is supported by the Austrian Science Fund (FWF), projects P25207-N23 and Y698, and Vienna Science and Technology Fund (WWTF), project ICT12-015.

10. REFERENCES

[1] S. Abiteboul, R. Hull, and V. Vianu. *Foundations of Databases*. Addison-Wesley, 1995.

[2] J.-F. Baget, M.-L. Mugnier, S. Rudolph, and M. Thomazo. Walking the complexity lines for generalized guarded existential rules. In *IJCAI*, pages 712–717, 2011.

[3] V. Bárány, G. Gottlob, and M. Otto. Querying the guarded fragment. *Logical Methods in Computer Science*, 10(2), 2014.

[4] P. Barceló, L. Libkin, and M. Romero. Efficient approximations of conjunctive queries. *SIAM J. Comput.*, 43(3):1085–1130, 2014.

[5] P. Barceló, R. Pichler, and S. Skritek. Efficient evaluation and approximation of well-designed pattern trees. In *PODS*, pages 131–144, 2015.

[6] P. Barceló, M. Romero, and M. Y. Vardi. Semantic acyclicity on graph databases. In *PODS*, pages 237–248, 2013.

[7] C. Beeri and M. Y. Vardi. The implication problem for data dependencies. In *ICALP*, pages 73–85, 1981.

[8] A. Calì, G. Gottlob, and M. Kifer. Taming the infinite chase: Query answering under expressive relational constraints. *J. Artif. Intell. Res.*, 48:115–174, 2013.

[9] A. Calì, G. Gottlob, and T. Lukasiewicz. A general Datalog-based framework for tractable query answering over ontologies. *J. Web Sem.*, 14:57–83, 2012.

[10] A. Calì, G. Gottlob, and A. Pieris. Towards more expressive ontology languages: The query answering problem. *Artif. Intell.*, 193:87–128, 2012.

[11] D. Calvanese, G. De Giacomo, and M. Lenzerini. Conjunctive query containment and answering under description logic constraints. *ACM Trans. Comput. Log.*, 9(3), 2008.

[12] A. K. Chandra and P. M. Merlin. Optimal implementation of conjunctive queries in relational data bases. In *STOC*, pages 77–90, 1977.

[13] H. Chen and V. Dalmau. Beyond hypertree width: Decomposition methods without decompositions. In *CP*, pages 167–181, 2005.

[14] V. Dalmau, P. G. Kolaitis, and M. Y. Vardi. Constraint satisfaction, bounded treewidth, and finite-variable logics. In *CP*, pages 310–326, 2002.

[15] R. Fagin. A normal form for relational databases that is based on domians and keys. *ACM Trans. Database Syst.*, 6(3):387–415, 1981.

[16] R. Fagin, P. G. Kolaitis, R. J. Miller, and L. Popa. Data exchange: Semantics and query answering. *Theor. Comput. Sci.*, 336(1):89–124, 2005.

[17] D. Figueira. Semantically acyclic conjunctive queries under functional dependencies. In *LICS*, 2016. To appear.

[18] T. Gogacz and J. Marcinkowski. Converging to the chase - A tool for finite controllability. In *LICS*, pages 540–549, 2013.

[19] G. Gottlob, G. Greco, and B. Marnette. Hyperconsistency width for constraint satisfaction: Algorithms and complexity results. In *Graph Theory, Computational Intelligence and Thought*, pages 87–99, 2009.

[20] G. Gottlob, G. Orsi, and A. Pieris. Query rewriting and optimization for ontological databases. *ACM Trans. Database Syst.*, 2014.

[21] P. Hell and J. Nešetřil. *Graphs and Homomorphisms*. Oxford University Press, 2004.

[22] D. S. Johnson and A. C. Klug. Testing containment of conjunctive queries under functional and inclusion dependencies. *J. Comput. Syst. Sci.*, 28(1):167–189, 1984.

[23] M. Krötzsch and S. Rudolph. Extending decidable existential rules by joining acyclicity and guardedness. In *IJCAI*, pages 963–968, 2011.

[24] T. Lukasiewicz, M. V. Martinez, A. Pieris, and G. I. Simari. From classical to consistent query answering under existential rules. In *AAAI*, pages 1546–1552, 2015.

[25] D. Maier, A. O. Mendelzon, and Y. Sagiv. Testing implications of data dependencies. *ACM Trans. Database Syst.*, 4(4):455–469, 1979.

[26] C. H. Papadimitriou and M. Yannakakis. On the complexity of database queries. *J. Comput. Syst. Sci.*, 58(3):407–427, 1999.

[27] M. Yannakakis. Algorithms for acyclic database schemes. In *VLDB*, pages 82–94, 1981.

Tractable Lineages on Treelike Instances: Limits and Extensions

Antoine Amarilli
LTCI, CNRS, Télécom ParisTech, Université Paris-Saclay, France
antoine.amarilli@telecom-paristech.fr

Pierre Bourhis
CRIStAL, UMR 9189, CNRS, Université Lille 1, France
pierre.bourhis@univ-lille1.fr

Pierre Senellart
LTCI, CNRS, Télécom ParisTech, Université Paris-Saclay, France & IPAL, CNRS, NUS, Singapore
pierre.senellart@telecom-paristech.fr

ABSTRACT

Query evaluation on probabilistic databases is generally intractable (#P-hard). Existing dichotomy results [19, 18, 23] have identified which queries are tractable (or *safe*), and connected them to tractable lineages [36]. In our previous work [2], using different tools, we showed that query evaluation is linear-time on probabilistic databases for arbitrary monadic second-order queries, if we bound the *treewidth* of the instance.

In this paper, we study limitations and extensions of this result. First, for probabilistic query evaluation, we show that MSO tractability cannot extend beyond bounded treewidth: there are even FO queries that are hard on *any* efficiently constructible unbounded-treewidth class of graphs. This dichotomy relies on recent polynomial bounds on the extraction of planar graphs as minors [10], and implies lower bounds in non-probabilistic settings, for query evaluation and match counting in subinstance-closed families. Second, we show how to explain our tractability result in terms of lineage: the lineage of MSO queries on bounded-treewidth instances can be represented as bounded-treewidth circuits, polynomial-size OBDDs, and linear-size d-DNNFs. By contrast, we can strengthen the previous dichotomy to lineages, and show that there are even UCQs with disequalities that have superpolynomial OBDDs on *all* unbounded-treewidth graph classes; we give a characterization of such queries. Last, we show how bounded-treewidth tractability explains the tractability of the *inversion-free* safe queries: we can rewrite their input instances to have bounded-treewidth.

1. INTRODUCTION

Many applications must deal with data which may be erroneous. This makes it necessary to extend relational database instances, to allow for uncertain facts. One of the simplest such formalisms [49] is that of *tuple-independent databases* (TID): each tuple in the database is annotated with an independent probability of being present. The semantics of a TID instance is to see it as a concise representation of a probability distribution on standard non-probabilistic instances.

PODS'16, June 26-July 01, 2016, San Francisco, CA, USA

ISBN 978-1-4503-4191-2/16/06...$15.00

DOI: http://dx.doi.org/10.1145/2902251.2902301

An important challenge when dealing with probabilistic data is that data management tasks become intractable. The main one is *query evaluation*: given an input database query q, for instance a conjunctive query, and given a relational instance I, determine the answers to q on I. When q is Boolean, we just ask whether I satisfies q. The corresponding problem in the TID setting asks for the *probability* that $I \models q$, that is, the total probability weight of the possible subsets of the TID instance I that satisfy q. The query q is usually assumed to be fixed, and we look at the complexity of this problem as a function of the input instance (or TID) I, that is, the *data complexity*. Sadly, while this task is highly tractable and parallelizable (in the complexity class AC^0) in the non-probabilistic context, exact computation is generally intractable (#P-hard) on TID instances, even for the simple conjunctive query $\exists xy\ R(x) \land S(x,y) \land T(y)$. See [17].

Faced with this intractability, two natural directions are possible. The first is to restrict the language of *queries* to focus on queries that are tractable on *all* instances, called *safe*. This has proven a very fruitful direction [19], culminating in the dichotomy result of Dalvi and Suciu [18]: the data complexity of a given union of conjunctive queries (UCQ) is either in PTIME or #P-hard. More recently, the safe non-repeated CQs *with negation* were characterized in [23].

The second approach is to restrict the *instances*, to focus on instance families that are tractable for *all* queries in highly expressive languages. In a recent work [2], going through the setting of semiring provenance [29], and using a celebrated result by Courcelle [13], we have started to explore this direction. We showed that, for queries in MSO (*monadic second-order*, a highly expressive language capturing UCQs), data complexity is linear-time on *treelike* instances, i.e., instances of *treewidth* bounded by a constant. Of course, this result says nothing of non-treelike instances, but covers use cases previously studied in their own right, such as probabilistic XML [11] (without data values).

This new direction raises several important questions:

- First, is this the best that one can hope for? For probability evaluation, could the tractability on bounded-treewidth instances be generalized, e.g., to bounded *clique-width* instances [14], as for MSO in the non-probabilistic case? More ambitiously, could we separate tractable and intractable instances with a dichotomy theorem?
- Second, can our bounded-treewidth tractability result be explained in terms of *lineage*? The *lineage* of a query intuitively represents how it can be satisfied on the instance,

and can be used to compute its probability: for many fragments of safe queries [36], tractability can be shown via a tractable representation of their lineage. In [2], we build a bounded-treewidth circuit representation of Boolean provenance. How does this compare to the usual lineage classes of OBDDs and d-DNNFs in knowledge compilation?

- Third, can we link the query-based tractability approach to our instance-based one? Can we explain the tractability of some safe queries by reducing them to query evaluation on treelike instances?

This paper answers all of these questions.

Contributions. Our *first main result* (in Section 4) is that bounded treewidth characterizes the tractable families of graphs for MSO queries in the probabilistic context. More precisely, we construct a query q_{h} for which probability evaluation is intractable on *any* unbounded-treewidth family of graphs satisfying mild constructibility requirements; query evaluation is precisely $\mathrm{FP}^{\#\mathrm{P}}$-complete under randomized polynomial-time (RP) reductions. Thus, tractability on bounded-treewidth instances is really the best we can get, on arity-2 signatures. Surprisingly, we show that q_{h} can be taken to be a (non-monotone) FO query; this is in stark contrast with non-probabilistic query evaluation [38, 26] where FO queries are fixed-parameter tractable under much milder conditions than bounded treewidth [37]. This provides the lower bound of a dichotomy, the upper bound being our result in [2].

In Section 5, we explain how this dichotomy result can be adapted to non-probabilistic MSO query evaluation and match counting on subgraph-closed graph families. While the necessity of bounded-treewidth for non-probabilistic query evaluation was studied before [38, 26], our use of a recent polynomial bound on grid minors [10] allows us to obtain stronger results in this context, which we review. Our work thus answers the conjecture of [30] (Conjecture 8.3) for MSO, which [38] answered for MSO_2, under similar complexity-theoretic assumptions.

In Section 6, we move from probability evaluation to the computation of tractable *lineages*. Our tractability result in [2] computes a bounded-treewidth lineage of linear size for MSO queries on bounded-treewidth instances. We revisit this upper bound and show that we can compute an OBDD lineage of polynomial size (by results in [35]) and a d-DNNF lineage of linear size (a new result). We show that on bounded-*pathwidth* instances (a notion more restrictive than that of bounded-treewidth), we obtain a bounded-pathwidth lineage, and hence a constant-width OBDD (by [35]). Further, all these representations can be efficiently constructed.

We then reexamine the choice of representing provenance as a *circuit* rather than a formula, because this is unusual in the semiring provenance context of [2]. We show in Section 7 that some of the previous tractability results for lineage representations *cannot* extend to formula representations, via conciseness bounds on Boolean circuits and formulae. This sheds some light on the conciseness gap between circuit and formula representations of lineage.

We then move in Section 8 to our *second main result*, which applies to tractable *OBDD lineages* rather than tractable query evaluation. It shows a dichotomy on arity-2 signatures, for the weaker query language of *UCQs with disequalities*: while bounded-treewidth instances admit efficient OBDDs for such queries, any constructible unbounded-treewidth instance family must have superpolynomial OBDDs for some query (depending only on the signature).

Last, in Section 9, we connect our approach to query-based tractability conditions [19, 18]. We show that, for safe UCQs that admit a concise OBDD representation (that is, precisely inversion-free UCQs from [36]), one can rewrite any instance to a bounded-treewidth instance (actually, to a bounded-pathwidth one), such that the query lineage, and hence the query probability, remain the same. Thus, in this sense, safe queries are tractable because their input instances may as well be bounded-pathwidth.

Related work. Bounded-treewidth has been shown to be a sufficient condition for tractability of query evaluation (this is by Courcelle's theorem [13], generalized to arbitrary relational structures in [24]), counting of query matches [4], and probabilistic query evaluation [2].

For MSO query evaluation on non-probabilistic instances, bounded-treewidth is known not to be necessary, e.g., query evaluation is tractable assuming bounded *clique-width* [14]. FO query evaluation is tractable assuming milder conditions [37]. Two separate lines of work investigated the necessity of bounding the treewidth of instances to ensure the tractability of other data management tasks.

First, in [43, 44], Marx shows that treewidth-based algorithms for binary constraint-satisfaction problems (CSP) are, assuming the exponential-time hypothesis, *almost optimal*: they can only be improved by a logarithmic factor. These works do not rely on the graph minor theorem [48] as we do, as they preceded the results of [10] that provide polynomial bounds on the size of grid minors: see the discussion in the Introduction of [44]. Instead, they characterize high treewidth via embeddings of low *depth*. The results of [43, 44] were further applied to inference in undirected [9] and directed [39] *graphical models*. All these works are specific to the setting and problem that they study, namely CSP and inference.

Second, another line of work [42, 38, 26] has shown necessity of bounded treewidth when a class of graphs is closed under some operations: extracting topological minors in [42], extracting subgraphs in [38], and extracting subgraphs and vertex relabeling in [26]. This requires that there are sufficiently many instances of high treewidth, through notions of *strong unboundedness* [38] and *dense unboundedness* [26]. We strengthen the results of [26] in Section 5.2 of this paper, using our techniques. None of these works consider probabilistic evaluation or match counting, which we do here.

Other related work is discussed throughout the paper, where relevant; in particular works related to lineages in Sections 6 to 8 and to safe queries in Section 9.

The next section (Section 2) presents preliminaries, and Section 3 gives our formal problem statement. We then move to our new results in Section 4 onwards.

For space reasons, we omit the full proofs for Sections 4, 5, and 8: they can be found in Chapter 6 of [1]. Full proofs of the other sections can be found in the appendix.

2. PRELIMINARIES

Instances. A *relational signature* σ is a set of relations $R, S, T, \ldots$, each having an *arity* denoted $\mathrm{arity}(R) \in \mathbb{N}_{>0}$. The signature σ is *arity-k* if k is the maximum arity of a relation in σ.

A *relational instance* (or simply σ-instance or instance) I is a finite set of ground *facts* on the signature σ, and a *class* or *family* of instances $\mathcal{I}$ is just a (possibly infinite) set of instances. A *subinstance* of I is a subset of its facts. We follow the *active domain semantics*, where the *domain* $\text{dom}(I)$ of I is the finite set of elements that occur in facts. Hence, for $I' \subseteq I$, $\text{dom}(I')$ is the (possibly strict) subset of $\text{dom}(I)$ formed of the elements that occur in facts of I'. The *size* of I, denoted $|I|$, is its number of facts.

A *homomorphism* from a σ-instance I to a σ-instance I' is a function $h : \text{dom}(I) \to \text{dom}(I')$ such that, for all $R(a_1, \ldots, a_k) \in I$, we have $R(h(a_1), \ldots, h(a_k)) \in I'$. A homomorphism is an *isomorphism* if it is bijective and its inverse is also a homomorphism.

Graphs. Throughout the paper, a *graph* will always be undirected, simple, and unlabeled, unless otherwise specified. Formally, we see a graph G as an instance of the *graph signature* with a single predicate E of arity 2 such that: (i) $\forall x\, E(x, x) \notin G$; and (ii) $\forall xy\, E(x, y) \in G \Rightarrow E(y, x) \in G$. As we follow the active domain semantics, this implies that we disallow *isolated vertices* in graphs. The facts of G are called *edges*. The set of *vertices* (or *nodes*) of a graph G, denoted $V(G)$, is its domain. Two vertices x and y of a graph G are *adjacent* if $E(x, y) \in G$, x and y are then called the *endpoints* of the edge, and the edge is *incident* to them; two edges are *incident* if they share a vertex.

The *degree* of a vertex x is the number of its adjacent vertices. For $k \in \mathbb{N}$, a graph is *k-regular* if all vertices have degree k. More generally, it is *K-regular*, where K is a finite set of integers, if every vertex has degree k for some $k \in K$. Finally, a graph is *degree-k* if k is the maximum of the degree of all its vertices, i.e., if it is $\{1, \ldots, k\}$-regular. A graph is *planar* if it can be drawn on the plane without edge crossings, in the standard sense [22].

A *path* of length $n \in \mathbb{N}_{>0}$ in a graph G is a set of edges $\{E(x_0, x_1), E(x_1, x_2), \ldots, E(x_{n-1}, x_n)\}$ that are all in G; the path is *simple* if all x_i's are distinct. A *cycle* is a path of length $n \geqslant 3$ where all vertices are distinct except that $x_0 = x_n$; a graph is *cyclic* if it has a cycle. A graph is *connected* if there is a path from every vertex to every other vertex. A *subdivision* of a graph G is a graph obtained by replacing each edge by an arbitrary non-empty simple path (every node on this path being fresh except the endpoints of the original edge).

Treewidth and pathwidth. A *tree* T is an acyclic connected graph (remember that graphs are undirected). A *tree decomposition* of a graph G is a tree with a labeling function λ from its nodes (called *bags*) to sets of vertices of G, ensuring: (i) for every edge $E(u, v) \in G$, there is a bag $n \in V(T)$ such that $\lambda(n)$ contains both u and v; (ii) for every node u of G, the subtree of T formed of all bags whose λ-image contains u must be connected. The *width* of T is $\max_{n \in V(T)} |\lambda(n)| - 1$. The *treewidth* of a graph G, denoted $\mathsf{tw}(G)$, is the minimum width of any tree decomposition of G.

The *treewidth* of a relational instance I, denoted $\mathsf{tw}(I)$, is defined as usual as the treewidth of its *Gaifman graph*, namely, the graph on the *domain* $\text{dom}(I)$ of I that connects any two elements that co-occur in a fact. When the signature is arity-2, we can see an instance I as a labeled graph, and the treewidth of I is then exactly the treewidth of this graph.

A *path decomposition* is a tree decomposition where T is also a path. The *pathwidth* of a graph G is the minimum width of any path decomposition of the graph. The *pathwidth* of a relational instance is the pathwidth of its Gaifman graph.

Queries. A *query* on the signature σ is a formula in second-order logic over predicates of σ, with its standard semantics. All queries that we consider have no constants; unless otherwise specified, they are *Boolean*, i.e., they have no free variable. We write $I \models q$ whenever an instance I satisfies the query q. We will be especially interested in the language FO of first-order logical sentences (where second-order quantifications are disallowed) and the language MSO of monadic second-order logical sentences (where the only second-order quantifications are over unary predicates).

We will also consider the language CQ of *conjunctive queries*, i.e., existentially quantified conjunctions of atoms over the signature; the language $\text{CQ}^{\neq}$ of conjunctive queries where additional atoms of the form $x \neq y$ (called *disequality* atoms) are allowed, where x and y are variables appearing in some regular atom; the language UCQ of *union of conjunctive queries*, namely, disjunctions of CQs; the language $\text{UCQ}^{\neq}$ of disjunctions of $\text{CQ}^{\neq}$ queries. The size $|q|$ of a $\text{UCQ}^{\neq}$ query q is its total number of atoms, i.e., the sum of the number of atoms in each $\text{CQ}^{\neq}$.

A *homomorphism* from a CQ q to an instance I is a mapping h from the variables of q to $\text{dom}(I)$ such that for each atom $R(x_1, \ldots, x_k)$ of q we have $R(h(x_1), \ldots, h(x_k)) \in I$. For $\text{CQ}^{\neq}$ queries, we require that $h(x) \neq h(y)$ whenever q contains the disequality atom $x \neq y$. A *homomorphism* from a $\text{UCQ}^{\neq}$ q to I is a homomorphism from some disjunct of q to I: it witnesses that $I \models q$. A *match* of a $\text{UCQ}^{\neq}$ q on an instance I is a subset of I which is the image of a homomorphism from q to I; a *minimal match* is a match that is minimal for inclusion.

A query is *monotone* if $I \models q$ and $I \subseteq I'$ imply $I' \models q$ for any two instances I, I'. A query is *closed under homomorphisms* if we have $I' \models q$ whenever $I \models q$ and I has a homomorphism to I', for any I and I'. UCQ is an example of query class that is both monotone and closed under homomorphisms, while $\text{UCQ}^{\neq}$ is monotone but not closed under homomorphisms.

3. PROBLEM STATEMENT

We study the problem of *probability evaluation*:

DEFINITION 3.1. *Given an instance I, a* probability valuation *is a function π that maps each fact of I to a value*[1] *in $[0, 1]$. A probability valuation defines a* probability distribution *on subinstances of I, which we also write π by a slight abuse of notation. The distribution π is intuitively obtained by seeing each fact F as kept with probability $\pi(F)$ and removed with probability $1 - \pi(F)$, all such choices being independent. Formally, the probability of $I' \subseteq I$ in this distribution is:*

$$\pi(I') := \prod_{F \in I'} \pi(F) \prod_{F \in I \setminus I'} (1 - \pi(F))$$

The probability evaluation problem *for a query q on a class $\mathcal{I}$ of relational instances asks, given an instance $I \in \mathcal{I}$ and a probability valuation π on I, what is the probability that q holds according to the probability distribution, i.e., it is the problem of computing $\pi(q, I) := \sum_{I' \subseteq I \text{ such that } I' \models q} \pi(I')$.*

[1] All non-integer numbers are rational numbers represented as the pair of their numerator and denominator.

In other words, probability evaluation asks for the probability of q over a TID instance defined by I and π. Note that we only consider classes $\mathcal{I}$ of instances with no associated probabilities, and the probability valuation π is given as an additional input — it is not indicated in $\mathcal{I}$. The complexity of the probability evaluation problem will always be studied in *data complexity*: the query q and class $\mathcal{I}$ is fixed, and the input is the instance $I \in \mathcal{I}$ and the probability valuation.

We also explore the problem of computing *tractable lineages* (or *provenance*), defined and studied in Section 6 onwards.

We rely on results of [2] that show the tractability in data complexity of provenance computation and probability evaluation on treelike (i.e., bounded-treewidth) instances. This holds for *guarded second-order* queries, but as such queries collapse to MSO under bounded treewidth [28], we always use MSO queries here. First, [2] shows that we can construct Boolean circuits that represent the provenance of MSO queries on treelike instances; we can also construct monotone circuits for monotone queries. The results also apply to other semirings, but this will not be our focus here. Second, [2] shows that probability evaluation is then tractable, namely, *ra-linear*: in linear time up to the (polynomial) cost of arithmetic operations.

Our goal is thus to investigate to what extent we can generalize the following tractability result from [2]:

THEOREM 3.2 [2]. *For any signature σ, for any (monotone) MSO query q, for any $k \in \mathbb{N}$, there is an algorithm which, given an input instance I of treewidth $\leqslant k$:*

- *Computes a (monotone) Boolean provenance circuit of q on I, in linear time in I;*
- *Given a probability valuation of I, computes the probability of q on I, in ra-linear time.*

We first focus on the second point (probability evaluation) in Section 4, followed by a digression about non-probabilistic evaluation in Section 5. We then study the first point (lineages) in Sections 6–8. We close with a connection to safe queries in Section 9.

4. PROBABILITY EVALUATION

This section studies whether we can extend the above tractability result by lifting the bounded-treewidth requirement. We answer in the negative by a *dichotomy result* on arity-two signatures: there are queries for which probabilistic evaluation is tractable on bounded-treewidth families but is intractable on *any* efficiently constructible unbounded-treewidth family. A first technical issue is to formalize what we mean by *efficiently* constructible. We use the following notion:

DEFINITION 4.1. *We call $\mathcal{I}$* treewidth-constructible *if for all $k \in \mathbb{N}$, if $\mathcal{I}$ contains instances of treewidth $\geqslant k$, we can construct one in polynomial time given k written in unary*[2].

In particular, this implies that $\mathcal{I}$ must contain a subfamily of unbounded-treewidth instances that are small, i.e., have size polynomial in their treewidth. We discuss the impact of this choice of definition, and alternate definitions of *efficiently* constructible instances, in Section 5.

A second technical issue is that we need to restrict to signatures of arity 2. We will then show our dichotomy for *any* such signature. This suffices to show that our Theorem 3.2 cannot be generalized: its generalization should apply to any signature, in particular arity-2 ones. Yet, we do not know whether the dichotomy applies to signatures of arity > 2.

Our *main result* on probability evaluation is as follows. In this result, $\mathrm{FP}^{\#\mathrm{P}}$ is the class of function problems which can be solved in PTIME with a deterministic Turing machine having access to a #P-oracle, i.e., an oracle for counting problems that can be expressed as the number of accepting paths for a nondeterministic PTIME Turing machine.

THEOREM 4.2. *Let σ be an arbitrary arity-2 signature. Let $\mathcal{I}$ be a treewidth-constructible class of σ-instances. Then the following dichotomy holds:*

- *If there is $k \in \mathbb{N}$ such that $\mathsf{tw}(I) \leqslant k$ for every $I \in \mathcal{I}$, then for every MSO query q, the probability evaluation problem for q on instances of $\mathcal{I}$ is solvable in ra-linear time.*
- *Otherwise, there is an FO query q_{h} (depending on σ but not on $\mathcal{I}$) such that the probability evaluation problem for q_{h} on $\mathcal{I}$ is $\mathrm{FP}^{\#\mathrm{P}}$-complete under randomized polynomial time (RP) reductions.*

The first part of this result is precisely the second point of Theorem 3.2. We thus sketch the proof of the hardness result of the second part. Pay close attention to the statement: while some FO queries (in particular, unsafe CQs [18]) may have $\mathrm{FP}^{\#\mathrm{P}}$-hard probability evaluation when *all* input instances are allowed, our goal here is to build a query that is hard even when input instances are restricted to *arbitrary families* satisfying our conditions, a much harder claim.

We reduce from the problem of counting graph *matchings*, namely, the number of edge subsets of a graph that have no pair of incident edges. This problem is known to be #P-hard on 3-regular planar graphs [52]. We define a FO query q_{h} that tests for matchings on such graphs (encoded in a certain way), and we rely on the connection between probability evaluation and model counting so that the probability of q_{h} on (an encoding of) a graph G reflects its number of matchings.

The main idea is that 3-regular planar graphs can be *extracted* from our family $\mathcal{I}$, using the following notion:

DEFINITION 4.3. *An* embedding *of a graph H in a graph G is an injective mapping f from the vertices of H to the vertices of G and a mapping g that maps the edges (u, v) of H to paths in G from $f(u)$ to $f(v)$, with all paths being vertex-disjoint. A graph H is a* topological minor *of a graph G if there is an embedding of H in G.*

We then use the following lemma, that rephrases the recent polynomial bound [10] on Robertson and Seymour's grid minor theorem [48] to the realm of topological minors; in so doing, we use the folklore observation that a degree-3 minor of a graph is always a topological minor:

LEMMA 4.4. *There is $c \in \mathbb{N}$ such that for any degree-3 planar graph H, for any graph G of treewidth $\geqslant |V(H)|^c$, H is a topological minor of G and an embedding of H in G can be computed in randomized polynomial time in $|G|$.*

Hence, intuitively, given an input 3-regular planar graph G (the input to the hard problem), we can extract it in randomized polynomial-time (RP) as a topological minor of (the

[2]The requirement that k be given in unary rather than in binary means that *more* instance families are treewidth-constructible, so treewidth-constructibility in this sense is a weaker assumption than if the input k could be written in binary.

Gaifman graph of) an instance I of our family $\mathcal{I}$ that we obtain using treewidth-constructibility. Once it is extracted, we show that, by choosing the right probability valuation for I, the probability of q_h on I allows us to reconstruct the answer to the original hard problem, namely, the number of matchings of G. The minor extraction step is what complicates the design of q_h, as q_h must then test for matchings in a way which is *invariant under subdivisions*: this is especially tricky in FO as we can only make local tests.

Choice of hard query. Not only is our query q_h independent from the class of instances $\mathcal{I}$, but it is also an FO query, so, in the *non-probabilistic* setting, its data complexity on any instance is in AC^0. In fact, our choice of q_h has also *linear-time* data complexity: one can determine in linear time in an input instance I whether $I \models q_h$. This contrasts sharply with the $FP^{\#P}$-completeness (under RP reductions) of *probability evaluation* for q_h on *any* unbounded-treewidth instance class (if it is treewidth-constructible).

The query q_h, however, is not monotone. We can alternatively show Theorem 4.2 for a MSO query which is *monotone*, but not in FO: more specifically, we use a query in $C2RPQ^{\neq}$, the class of *conjunctive two-way regular path queries* [7, 8] where we additionally allow disequalities between variables.

We will show an analogue of Theorem 4.2 in the setting of *tractable lineages* in Section 8, which applies to $UCQ^{\neq}$, an even weaker language. We do not know whether Theorem 4.2 itself can be shown with such queries, or with a *monotone* FO query. However, we know that Theorem 4.2 could not be shown with a query closed under homomorphism; this is implied by Proposition 8.9.

Providing valuations with the instances. When we fix the instance family $\mathcal{I}$, the probability valuation is not prescribed as part of the family, but can be freely chosen. If the instances of $\mathcal{I}$ were provided with their probability valuations, or if probability valuations were forced to be 1/2, then it is unlikely that an equivalent to Theorem 4.2 would hold.

Indeed, fix *any* query q such that, given any instance I, it is in #P to count how many subinstances of I satisfy q; e.g., let q be a CQ. Consider a family $\mathcal{I}$ of instances *with valuations* such that there is only one instance in $\mathcal{I}$ per encoding length: e.g., take the class of R-grids with probability 1/2 on each edge, for some binary relation R. Consider the problem, given the *length* of the encoding of an instance I (written in unary), of computing how many subinstances of I satisfy q. This problem is in the class $\#P_1$ [50]. Hence, the probability computation problem for q on $\mathcal{I}$ is in $FP^{\#P_1}$: rewrite the encoding of the input instance I to a word of the same length in a unary alphabet, use the $\#P_1$-oracle to compute the number of subinstances, and normalize the result by dividing by the number of possible worlds of I.

It thus seems unlikely that probabilistic evaluation of q on $\mathcal{I}$ with its valuations is #P-hard, so that our dichotomy result probably does not adapt if input instance families are provided with their valuations.

5. NON-PROBABILISTIC EVALUATION

Theorem 4.2 in Section 4 uses the recent technology of [10] that shows polynomial bounds for the grid minor theorem of [48]. These improved bounds also yield new results in the non-probabilistic setting. We accordingly study in this section the problem of *non-probabilistic* query evaluation, again defined in terms of data complexity:

DEFINITION 5.1. *The* evaluation problem *(or* model-checking problem*), for a fixed query q on an instance family $\mathcal{I}$, is as follows: given an instance $I \in \mathcal{I}$, decide whether $I \models q$.*

Observe that the probability evaluation problem in Section 4 allowed the valuation to set edges to have probability 0. We could thus restrict to any subinstance of an instance in the class $\mathcal{I}$. In other words, the freedom to choose valuations in probability evaluation gave us at least the possibility of choosing subinstances for non-probabilistic query evaluation. This is why we will study in this section the non-probabilistic query evaluation problem on instance classes $\mathcal{I}$ which are *closed under taking subinstances* (or *subinstance-closed*), namely, for any $I \in \mathcal{I}$ and $I' \subseteq I$, we have $I' \in \mathcal{I}$.

As before, we will prove dichotomy results for this problem on unbounded-treewidth instance families, though we will use an MSO query rather than an FO query. We give two phrasings of our results. The first one, in Section 5.1, still requires treewidth-constructibility, and shows hardness for every level of the polynomial hierarchy, again under RP reductions. The second phrasing, in Section 5.2, is inspired by the results of [26], which it generalizes: it relies on complexity assumptions (namely, the non-uniform exponential time hypothesis) but works with a weaker notion of constructibility, namely, it requires treewidth to be strongly unbounded poly-logarithmically.

Last, we study in Section 5.3 the problem of *match counting* in the non-probabilistic setting, for which no analogous results seemed to exist.

As in Section 4, we restrict to signatures of arity 2.

5.1 Hardness Formulation

Our first dichotomy result for non-probabilistic MSO query evaluation is as follows; it is phrased using the notion of treewidth-constructibility. In this result, Σ_i^P denotes the complexity class at the i-th existential level of the polynomial hierarchy.

THEOREM 5.2. *Let σ be an arbitrary arity-2 signature. Let $\mathcal{I}$ be a class of σ-instances which is treewidth-constructible and subinstance-closed. The following dichotomy holds:*

- *If there exists $k \in \mathbb{N}$ such that $\mathsf{tw}(I) \leqslant k$ for every $I \in \mathcal{I}$, then for every MSO query q, the evaluation problem for q on $\mathcal{I}$ is solvable in linear time.*
- *Otherwise, for each $i \in \mathbb{N}$, there is an MSO query q_h^i (depending only on σ, not on $\mathcal{I}$) such that the evaluation problem for q_h^i on $\mathcal{I}$ is Σ_i^P-hard under RP reductions.*

The upper bound is by Courcelle's results [13, 24], so our contribution is the hardness part, which we now sketch.

The main thing to change relative to the proof of Theorem 4.2 is the hard problems from which we reduce. We use hard problems on planar $\{1,3\}$-regular graphs, which we obtain from the *alternating coloring problem* as [26, 25], restricted to such graphs using techniques shown there, plus an additional construction to remove vertex labellings. Here is our formal claim about the existence of such hard problems:

LEMMA 5.3. *For any $i \in \mathbb{N}$, there exists an MSO formula ψ_i on the signature of graphs such that the evaluation of ψ_i on planar $\{1,3\}$-regular graphs is Σ_i^P-hard. Moreover, for any such graph G, we have $G \models \psi_i$ iff $G' \models \psi_i$ for any subdivision G' of G.*

The rest of the proof of Theorem 5.2 proceeds similarly as that of Theorem 4.2.

Table 1: **Summary of results for non-probabilistic query evaluation: if a graph class has unbounded treewidth in *some* sense, is closed under *some* operations, and has (in data complexity) tractable model checking in *some* sense for *some* logic, then *some* complexity assumption is violated**

Logic	Unboundedness	Closure	Tractability	Consequence	Source	
MSO	unbounded	subgraph	PTIME	no violation: holds for some classes	[42]	Prop. 32
MSO_2	unbounded	subgraph	PTIME	no violation: holds for some classes	[38]	(remark)
∃MSO	unbounded	topolog. minors	PTIME	P = NP	[42]	Thm. 11
MSO_2	strongly unb. polylog.	subgraph	PTIME	$PH \subseteq DTIME(2^{o(n)})$	[38]	Thm. 1.2
MSO	densely unb. polylog.	subgr., vert. lab.	quasi-poly	$PH \subseteq DTIME(2^{o(n)})/\text{SUBEXP}$	[26]	Thm. 5.5
MSO	unb., treewidth-constr.	subgraph	PTIME	$PH \subseteq RP$	**here**	**Thm. 5.2**
MSO	densely unb. polylog.	subgraph	quasi-poly	$PH \subseteq DTIME(2^{o(n)})/\text{SUBEXP}$	**here**	**Thm. 5.5**

Hypotheses. Theorem 5.2 relies crucially on the class $\mathcal{I}$ being *subinstance-closed.* Otherwise, considering the class $\mathcal{I}$ of cliques of a single binary relation E, this class is clearly unbounded-treewidth and treewidth-constructible, yet it has bounded clique-width so MSO query evaluation has linear data complexity on this class [15].

Further, the hypothesis of *treewidth-constructibility* is also crucial. Without this assumption, Proposition 32 of [42] shows the existence of graph families of unbounded treewidth which are subinstance-closed yet for which MSO query evaluation is in PTIME.

5.2 Alternate Formulation

We now give an alternative phrasing of Theorem 5.2 which connects it to the existing results of [38, 26]. Table 1 tersely summarizes their results in comparison to our own results and other related results. As [38, 26] are phrased in terms of graphs, and not arbitrary arity-2 relational instances, we do so as well in this subsection. Before stating our result, we summarize these earlier works to explain how our work relates to them.

[38, 26] show the intractability of MSO on any subgraph-closed unbounded-treewidth families of graphs, under finer notions than our *treewidth-constructibility.* Kreutzer and Tazari [38] proposed the notion of families of graphs with treewidth *strongly unbounded poly-logarithmically* and showed that MSO_2 (MSO with quantifications over both vertex- and edge-sets) over any such graph families is not fixed-parameter tractable in a strong sense (it is not in XP), unless the exponential-time hypothesis (ETH) fails. Ganian et al. [26] proved a related result, introducing the weaker notion of *densely unbounded poly-logarithmically* but requiring graph families to be closed under *vertex relabeling*; in such a setting, Theorem 4.1 of [26] shows that MSO (with vertex labels) cannot be fixed-parameter quasi-polynomial unless the *non-uniform* exponential-time hypothesis fails.

These two results of [38] and [26] are incomparable: [38] requires a stronger unboundedness notion (strongly unbounded vs densely unbounded) and a stronger query language (MSO_2 vs MSO), but it does not require vertex relabeling, and makes a weaker complexity theory assumption (ETH vs non-uniform ETH). See the Introduction of [26] for a detailed comparison.

Our Theorem 5.2 uses MSO and no vertex labeling, but it requires *treewidth-constructibility*, which is stronger than densely/strongly poly-logarithmic unboundedness: strongly unboundedness only requires constructibility in $o(2^n)$ and densely unboundedness does not require constructibility at all. The advantage of treewidth-constructibility is that we were able to show *hardness* of our problem (under RP reductions), without making *any* complexity assumptions. However, if we make the same complexity-theoretic hypotheses as [26], we now show that we can phrase our results in a similar way to theirs, and thus strengthen them.

We accordingly recall the notion of densely poly-logarithmic unboundedness, i.e., Definition 3.3 of [26]:

Definition 5.4. *A graph class $\mathcal{G}$ has treewidth* densely unbounded poly-logarithmically *if for all $c > 1$, for all $m \in \mathbb{N}$, there exists a graph $G \in \mathcal{G}$ such that $\mathsf{tw}(G) \geqslant m$ and $|V(G)| < O(2^{m^{1/c}})$.*

We now state our intractability result on densely unbounded poly-logarithmically graph classes. It is identical to Theorem 5.5 of [26] but applies to arbitrary MSO formulae, without a need for vertex relabeling: in the result, PH denotes the polynomial hierarchy. This result answers Conjecture 8.3 of [30] (as we pointed out in the Introduction).

Theorem 5.5. *Unless* $PH \subseteq DTIME(2^{o(n)})/\text{SUBEXP}$, *there is no graph class $\mathcal{G}$ satisfying all three properties:*

a) $\mathcal{G}$ is closed under taking subgraphs;

b) the treewidth of $\mathcal{G}$ is densely unbounded poly-logarithmically;

c) the evaluation problem for any MSO query q on $\mathcal{G}$ is quasi-polynomial, i.e., in time $O(n^{\log^d n \times f(|q|)})$ for $n = |V(G)|$, an arbitrary constant $d \geqslant 1$, and some computable function f.

The proof technique is essentially the same as in [26] up to using the newer results of [10]. It is immediate that an analogous result holds for probability query evaluation, as standard query evaluation obviously reduces to it (take the probability valuation giving probability 1 to each fact).

5.3 Match Counting

We conclude this section by moving to the problem of *match counting*, i.e., counting how many assignments satisfy a *non-Boolean MSO formula.* Match counting should not be confused with *model counting* (counting how many subinstances satisfy a Boolean formula) which is closely related[3] to probability evaluation.

To our knowledge, no dichotomy-like result on match counting for MSO queries was known. This section shows such a

[3]The number of models of a query q in an instance I of size n is 2^n multiplied by the probability of q under the probability valuation of I that gives probability $1/2$ to each fact of I.

Table 2: Bounds for lineage representations (including intractable ones)
Upper bounds (Section 6): computation bounds imply size bounds

Instance	Queries	Representation	Note	Time	Source	
bounded-pw	MSO	OBDD	$O(1)$ width	$O(n)$	**here**	**Thm. 6.7**
bounded-pw	(monotone) MSO	(monotone) circuit	bounded-pw	$O(n)$	**here**	**Prop. 6.8**
bounded-tw	MSO	OBDD		$O(\text{Poly}(n))$	**here**	**Thm. 6.5**
bounded-tw	(monotone) MSO	(monotone) circuit	bounded-tw	$O(n)$	[2]	Thm. 4.2
bounded-tw	MSO	d-DNNF		$O(n)$	**here**	**Thm. 6.11**
any	inversion-free UCQ	OBDD	$O(1)$ width	$O(\text{Poly}(n))$	[36]	Prop. 5
any	positive relational algebra	monotone formula		$O(\text{Poly}(n))$	[34]	Thm. 7.1
any	Datalog	monotone circuit		$O(\text{Poly}(n))$	[21]	Thm. 2

Lower bounds (Section 7)

Instance	Queries	Representation	Size	Source	
tree	$\text{CQ}^{\neq}$	formula	$\Omega(n \log \log n)$	**here**	**Prop. 7.1**
tree	$\text{CQ}^{\neq}$	monotone formula	$\Omega(n \log n)$	**here**	**Prop. 7.2**
tree	MSO	formula	$\Omega(n^2)$	**here**	**Prop. 7.3**
any	Datalog	monotone formula	$n^{\Omega(\log n)}$	[21]	Thm. 1

result; as in Section 5.1, we assume treewidth-constructibility, closure under subinstances, and arity-2 signatures.

We define the match counting problem as follows:

DEFINITION 5.6. *The* counting problem *for an MSO formula $q(\mathbf{X})$ (with free second-order variables) on an instance family $\mathcal{I}$ is the problem, given an instance $I \in \mathcal{I}$, of counting how many vectors $\mathbf{A}$ of domain subsets are such that I satisfies $q(\mathbf{A})$.*

The restriction to free second-order variables is without loss of generality, as free first-order variables can be rewritten to free second-order ones, asserting in the formula that they must be interpreted as singletons.

We show the following dichotomy result:

THEOREM 5.7. *Let σ be an arbitrary arity-2 signature. Let $\mathcal{I}$ be a subinstance-closed and treewidth-constructible class of σ-instances. The following dichotomy holds:*

- *If there exists $k \in \mathbb{N}$ such that $\mathsf{tw}(I) \leqslant k$ for every $I \in \mathcal{I}$, then for every MSO query $q(\mathbf{X})$ with free second-order variables, the counting problem for q on $\mathcal{I}$ is solvable in ra-linear time.*
- *Otherwise, there is an MSO query $q'_{\text{h}}(X)$ (depending only on σ, not on $\mathcal{I}$) with one free second order variable such that the counting problem for q'_{h} on $\mathcal{I}$ is $FP^{\#P}$-complete under RP reductions.*

The first claim is shown in [4]. The proof of the second claim proceeds as for Theorem 4.2. We reduce from the problem of counting Hamiltonian cycles in planar 3-regular graphs G, which is #P-hard [41], and which we express in MSO on the incidence graph of G.

Unlike in Theorem 4.2, the query q'_{h} does not have tractable model checking (as opposed to probability evaluation). We do not know whether we can show a similar result with such a tractable query.

6. LINEAGE UPPER BOUNDS

From *probability evaluation* in Section 4 (and its non-probabilistic variants in Section 5), we now turn to our second problem: the study of *tractable lineage representations.*

Indeed, a common way to achieve tractable probability evaluation is to represent the *lineage* of queries on input instances in a *tractable* formalism [36]. This section shows how the tractability of MSO probability evaluation on bounded-treewidth instances can be explained via lineages: Table 2 (upper part) summarizes the upper bounds that we prove.

Intuitively, the *lineage* of a query on an instance describes how the query depends on the facts of the instance. Formally:

DEFINITION 6.1. *The* lineage *of a query q on an instance I is a Boolean function φ whose variables are the facts of I, such that, for any $I' \subseteq I$, $I' \models q$ iff the corresponding valuation makes φ true. If q is monotone, then φ is a monotone Boolean function, in which case it can equivalently be called the* PosBool[X]*-provenance [29] of q on I.*

Lineages are related to probability evaluation, because evaluating the probability of query q under a probability valuation π of instance I amounts to evaluating the probability of the lineage φ, under the corresponding probability valuation on variables. Thus, if we can represent φ in a formalism that enjoys tractable probability computation, then we can tractably evaluate the probability $\pi(q, I)$ of q on I.

In this section, we show that MSO queries on bounded-treewidth instances admit tractable lineage representations in many common formalisms: they have linear-size bounded-treewidth Boolean circuits (as shown in [2]), but also have polynomial-size OBDDs [6, 47] (with a stronger claim for *bounded-pathwidth*), as well as linear-size d-DNNFs [20]. Further, as we show, all these lineage representations can be efficiently computed. Note that in all these results, as in [2], tractability only refers to *data complexity*, with large constant factors in the query and instance width: we leave to future work the study of query and instance classes for which lineage computation enjoys a lower *combined complexity.*

After our results on tractable lineage computations in this section, we will investigate in the next section whether we can represent the lineage as *Boolean formulae* (such as read-once formulae [36]), and we will show superlinear lower bounds for them. Section 8 will then study in which sense bounded-treewidth is *necessary* to obtain tractable lineages.

This section applies to signatures of arbitrary arity.

Bounded-treewidth circuits. We first recall our results from [2] and introduce a first representation of lineages: *Boolean circuits*, called *provenance circuits* in [2] and *expression DAGs* in [35]:

DEFINITION 6.2. *A* lineage circuit *for query q and instance I is a Boolean circuit with input gates and with NOT, OR, and AND internal gates, whose inputs are the facts of the database, and which computes the lineage of q on I. A* monotone *lineage circuit has no NOT gate. The* treewidth *and* pathwidth *of a lineage circuit are that of the circuit's graph.*

As recalled in Theorem 3.2, [2] showed that we can compute (monotone) lineage circuits for (monotone) MSO queries on bounded-treewidth instances in linear time. Further, these circuits themselves have *bounded-treewidth*, which is why probability evaluation is tractable on them, using message passing algorithms [40]. Hence:

THEOREM 6.3 ([2], Theorems 4.4 and 5.3). *For any fixed MSO query q and constant $k \in \mathbb{N}$, given an input instance I of treewidth $\leqslant k$, we can compute in linear time a bounded-treewidth lineage circuit C of q on I.*

If q is monotone then we can take C to be monotone.

We study how to adapt this to other tractable lineage representations.

OBDDs. We start by defining *OBDDs*, a common tractable representation of Boolean functions [6, 47]:

DEFINITION 6.4. *An* ordered binary decision diagram *(or* OBDD*) is a rooted directed acyclic graph (DAG) whose leaves are labeled* 0 *or* 1, *and whose non-leaf nodes are labeled with a variable and have two outgoing edges labeled* 0 *and* 1. *We require that there exists a total order Π on the variables such that, for every path from the root to a leaf, no variable occurs in two different internal nodes on the path, and the order in which the variables occur is compatible with Π.*

An OBDD defines a Boolean function on its variables: each valuation is mapped to the value of the leaf reached from the root by following the path given by the valuation.

The size *of an OBDD is its number of nodes, and its* width *is the maximum number of nodes at every* level, *where a level is the set of nodes reachable by enumerating all possible values of variables in a prefix of Π.*

Probability evaluation for OBDDs is tractable [47]. Our result is that we can compute polynomial-size OBDDs for MSO queries on bounded-treewidth instances in PTIME:

THEOREM 6.5. *For any fixed MSO query q and constant $k \in \mathbb{N}$, there is $c \in \mathbb{N}$ such that, given an input instance I of treewidth $\leqslant k$, one can compute in time $O(|I|^c)$ an OBDD (of size $O(|I|^c)$) for the lineage of q on I.*

We show this using Corollary 2.14 of [35]: any bounded-treewidth Boolean circuit can be represented by an equivalent OBDD of polynomial width. We complete this result and show that the OBDD can also be computed in polynomial time, which clearly implies Theorem 6.5 (using Theorem 6.3):

LEMMA 6.6. *For any $k \in \mathbb{N}$, there is $c \in \mathbb{N}$ such that, given a Boolean circuit C of treewidth k, we can compute an equivalent OBDD in time $O(|C|^c)$.*

Proof sketch. The variable order is that of [35] and can be constructed in PTIME. We then show that we can build the polynomial-size OBDD level by level, by testing the equivalence of partial valuations in PTIME. We do it using message passing, thanks to the tree decomposition of C. As in [35], c is doubly exponential in k. □

Bounded-pathwidth. We have explained the tractability of MSO probability evaluation on bounded-treewidth instances, showing that we could compute bounded-treewidth lineage circuits for them. We strengthen these results in the case of *bounded-pathwidth* instances, showing that we can compute *constant-width* OBDDs:

THEOREM 6.7. *For any fixed MSO query q and constant $k \in \mathbb{N}$, given an input instance I of pathwidth $\leqslant k$, one can compute in polynomial time an OBDD of constant width for the lineage of q on I.*

To prove the result, we first observe (adapting [2]) that we can compute *bounded-pathwidth* lineage circuits in linear time on bounded-pathwidth instances:

PROPOSITION 6.8. *For any fixed $k \in \mathbb{N}$ and (monotone) MSO query q, for any σ-instance I of* pathwidth *$\leqslant k$, we can construct a (monotone) lineage circuit C of q on I in time $O(|I|)$. The* pathwidth *of C only depends on k and q (not on I).*

By Corollary 2.13 of [35], this implies the existence of a constant-width OBDD representation, which we again show to be computable, proving Theorem 6.7.

LEMMA 6.9. *For any $k \in \mathbb{N}$, for any Boolean circuit C of pathwidth $\leqslant k$, we can compute in polynomial time in C an OBDD equivalent to C whose width depends only on k.*

d-DNNFs. We now turn to the more expressive tractable lineage formalism of *d-DNNFs*, introduced in [20]; we follow the definitions of [36]:

DEFINITION 6.10. *A* deterministic, decomposable negation normal form *(*d-DNNF*) is a Boolean circuit C that satisfies the following conditions:*

1. *Negation is only applied to input gates: the input of any NOT gate must always be an input gate.*
2. *The inputs of AND-gates depend on disjoint sets of input gates. Formally, for any AND-gate g, for any two gates $g_1 \neq g_2$ which are inputs of g, there is no input gate g' which is reachable (as a possibly indirect input) from both g_1 and g_2.*
3. *The inputs of OR-gates are mutually exclusive. Formally, for any OR-gate g, for any two gates $g_1 \neq g_2$ which are inputs of g, there is no valuation of the inputs of C under which g_1 and g_2 both evaluate to true.*

It is tractable to evaluate the probability of a d-DNNF [20], and d-DNNFs capture the tractability of probability evaluation for many safe queries (see [36]). We show that it also explains the ra-linearity of MSO probability evaluation on bounded-treewidth instances, as we can construct *linear* d-DNNFs for them:

THEOREM 6.11. *For any fixed MSO query q and constant $k \in \mathbb{N}$, given an input instance I of treewidth $\leqslant k$, one can compute in time $O(|I|)$ a d-DNNF representation of the lineage of q on I.*

Proof sketch. Our construction in [2] applies a tree automaton for the query to an annotated tree encoding of the instance. This yields a bounded-treewidth circuit representation of the lineage, in linear time in the instance (but with a constant factor that is nonelementary in the query). We show that, if the automaton is deterministic, the circuit that we obtain is already a d-DNNF. The result follows, as one can always make a tree automaton deterministic [12], at the cost of an increased constant factor in the data complexity. □

7. FORMULA LOWER BOUNDS

We have shown that MSO queries on bounded-treewidth instances have tractable lineages, and even linear-sized ones (bounded-treewidth circuits and d-DNNFs). All lineage representations that we have studied, however, are based on DAGs (circuits or OBDDs). In this section, we study whether we could obtain linear lineage representations as *Boolean formulae*, e.g., as *read-once formulae* [36].

This question is natural because existing work on probabilistic data seldom represents query lineages as Boolean circuits: they tend to use Boolean formulae, or other representations such as OBDDs, FBDDs and d-DNNFs [36]. Further, most prior works on provenance focus on formula representations of provenance (with the notable exception of [21], see below).

Intuitively, an important difference between formula and circuit representations is that circuits can share common subformulae whereas formulae cannot. We show in this section that this difference matters: formula-based representations of the lineage of MSO queries on bounded-treewidth instances *cannot* be linear in general, because of superlinear lower bounds. More specifically, we show that formula-based representations are *superlinear* even for some $\mathrm{CQ}^{\neq}$ queries, and that they are *quadratic* for some MSO queries.

A similar result was already known for lineage representations ([21], Theorem 1), which showed that circuit representations of provenance can be more concise than formulae; but this result applies to *arbitrary* instances, not bounded-treewidth ones. Hence, this section also sheds additional light on the compactness gain offered by the recent *circuit* representations of provenance in [21].

Our results in this section rely on classical lower bounds on the size of formulae expressing certain Boolean functions [51]. They apply to signatures of arbitrary arity. We summarize them in the lower part of Table 2.

$\mathrm{CQ}^{\neq}$ queries. We first show a mild conciseness gap for the comparatively simple language of $\mathrm{CQ}^{\neq}$. Formally, we exhibit a $\mathrm{CQ}^{\neq}$ query whose lineage cannot be represented by a linear-size formula, even on treelike instance families. By contrast, from the previous section, we know that its lineage has linear-size circuit representations.

PROPOSITION 7.1. *There is a $\mathrm{CQ}^{\neq}$ query q, and a family $\mathcal{I}$ of relational instances with treewidth 0, such that, for any $I \in \mathcal{I}$, for any Boolean formula ψ capturing the lineage of q on I, we have $|\psi| = \Omega(|I| \log\log |I|)$.*

Proof sketch. We show we can express the threshold function over n variables, for which [51] gives a lower bound on the formula size. □

As $\mathrm{CQ}^{\neq}$ queries are monotone, we can also ask for *monotone* lineage representations. From the previous section, we still have linear representations of the lineage as a *monotone* circuit. By contrast, if we restrict to *monotone* Boolean formulae, we obtain an improved lower bound:

PROPOSITION 7.2. *There is a $\mathrm{CQ}^{\neq}$ query q, and a family $\mathcal{I}$ of relational instances with treewidth 0, such that, for any $I \in \mathcal{I}$, for any* monotone *Boolean formula ψ capturing the lineage of q on I, we have $|\psi| = \Omega(|I| \log |I|)$.*

MSO queries. For the more expressive language of MSO queries, we show a wider gap: there is a query for which formula-based lineage representations must be *quadratic*, whereas we know that there are linear circuit representations of the lineage:

PROPOSITION 7.3. *There is an MSO query q, and a family $\mathcal{I}$ of relational instances with treewidth 1, such that, for any $I \in \mathcal{I}$, for any Boolean formula ψ capturing the lineage of q on I, we have $|\psi| = \Omega(|I|^2)$.*

Proof sketch. The proof is more subtle and constructs an MSO formula expressing the parity of the number of facts of a unary predicate, using a second auxiliary relation. The lower bound for parity comes again from [51]. □

We leave open the question of whether this bound can be further improved, but we note that even an $\Omega(|I|^3)$ lower bound would require new developments in the study of Boolean formulae. Indeed, the best currently known lower bound on formula size, for *any* explicit function of n variables with linear circuits, is in $\Omega(n^{3-o(1)})$ [33].

8. OBDD SIZE BOUNDS

We have shown in the previous sections that MSO queries on bounded-treewidth instances have tractable lineage representations as circuits and OBDDs. This section focuses on OBDDs and shows our *second main dichotomy result*: bounded-treewidth is necessary for MSO query lineages to have polynomial OBDDs.

We first state this result in Section 8.1. Its upper bound is Theorem 6.5, and its lower bound applies to a specific $\mathrm{UCQ}^{\neq}$ q_{p} (which only depends on the signature). We show that q_{p} has no polynomial-width OBDDs on *any* arity-2 instance family with treewidth densely unbounded polylogarithmically. This second dichotomy result thus shows that bounded-treewidth is necessary for some $\mathrm{UCQ}^{\neq}$ queries to have tractable OBDDs; it applies to a more restricted class than the FO query of our first main dichotomy result (Theorem 4.2), but applies to a different task (the computation of OBDD lineages, rather than probability evaluation).

We then study in Section 8.2 the language of *connected* $\mathrm{UCQ}^{\neq}$. For this language, we show that queries can be classified in a *meta-dichotomy* result: we characterize the *intricate* queries, such as q_{p}, which have no polynomial OBDDs on any unbounded treewidth family in the sense above; and we show that non-intricate queries actually have *constant-width* OBDDs on some well-chosen unbounded-treewidth instance family. Hence, if a connected $\mathrm{UCQ}^{\neq}$ has polynomial OBDDs on some unbounded-treewidth instance family, then it must have constant-width OBDDs on some other such family.

Finally, we investigate in Section 8.3 whether our second dichotomy result holds for more restricted fragments than $\mathrm{UCQ}^{\neq}$. First, we show that connected $\mathrm{CQ}^{\neq}$ queries are never intricate, so we cannot show our dichotomy result with such queries. Second, we show the same for connected UCQ; in fact, we show that no query *closed under homomorphisms* could be used. We last show that our meta-dichotomy fails for disconnected queries.

As in Sections 4 and 5, we limit ourselves to arity-2 signatures in this section.

8.1 A Dichotomy on OBDD Size

This section shows that our Theorem 6.5 on the existence of tractable lineage representations as OBDDs is unlikely to extend to milder conditions than bounded-treewidth. Indeed, there are even $\mathrm{UCQ}^{\neq}$ queries that have no polynomial-width OBDDs on any unbounded-treewidth input instance with treewidth densely unbounded poly-logarithmically, again on arity-two signatures. Here is our *second main dichotomy result* which shows this:

THEOREM 8.1. *There exists a constant $d \in \mathbb{N}$ such that the following holds. Let σ be an arbitrary arity-2 signature and $\mathcal{I}$ be a class of σ-instances. Assume there is a function $f(k) = O(2^{k^{1/d}})$ such that, for all $k \in \mathbb{N}$, if $\mathcal{I}$ contains instances of treewidth $\geqslant k$, one of them has size $\leqslant f(k)$. We have the following dichotomy:*

- *If there is $k \in \mathbb{N}$ such that $\mathsf{tw}(I) \leqslant k$ for every $I \in \mathcal{I}$, then for every MSO query q, an OBDD of q on I can be computed in time polynomial in $|I|$.*
- *Otherwise, there is a $\mathrm{UCQ}^{\neq}$ query q_{p} (depending on σ but not on $\mathcal{I}$) such that the width of any OBDD of q_{p} on $I \in \mathcal{I}$ cannot be bounded by any polynomial in $|I|$.*

This does *not* require treewidth-constructibility, and imposes instead a slight weakening[4] of densely unbounded poly-logarithmic treewidth. It does not require $\mathcal{I}$ to be subinstance-closed either, unlike in Section 5.

The first part of the theorem is by Theorem 6.5, so we sketch the proof of the second part. Our choice of $\mathrm{UCQ}^{\neq}$ q_{p} intuitively tests the existence of a path of length 2 in the Gaifman graph of the instance, i.e., a violation of the fact that the possible world is a matching of the original instance. Again, while we know that probability evaluation for q_{p} is $\mathrm{FP}^{\#\mathrm{P}}$-hard if we allow *arbitrary* input instances (as counting matchings reduces to it), our task is to show that q_{p} has no polynomial-width OBDDs when restricting to *any* instance family that satisfies the conditions, a much harder task.

To show this, we draw a link between treewidth and OBDD width for q_{p} on *individual* instances, with the following result (which is specific to q_{p}):

LEMMA 8.2. *Let σ be an arity-2 signature. There exist constants $d', k_0 \in \mathbb{N}$ such that for any instance I on σ of treewidth $\geqslant k_0$, the width of an OBDD for q_{p} on I is $\geqslant 2^{(\mathsf{tw}(I))^{1/d'}}$.*

Proof sketch. The proof is technical and uses Lemma 4.4 to extract high-treewidth topological minors of a specific shape: *skewed grids*. We then show that any variable order that enumerates the edges of the skewed grid must have a prefix that *shatters* the grid, i.e., sufficiently many independent grid nodes have both an enumerated incident edge and a non-enumerated one. This forces any OBDD for q_{p} to remember the exact configurations of the enumerated edges at the level for this shattering prefix of its variable order. Thus, the OBDD has superpolynomial width. We formalize this via the structure of the prime implicants of the lineage. □

8.2 A Meta-Dichotomy for $\mathrm{UCQ}^{\neq}$

For which queries does Theorem 8.1 adapt? It does not extend to all *unsafe* [18] queries, as a query may be unsafe and still be tractable on some unbounded-treewidth instance family: for instance, the standard unsafe query $R(x) \wedge S(x,y) \wedge T(y)$ from [17] has trivial OBDDs on the family of S-grids without unary relations.

We answer this question, again on arity-2 signatures, by introducing a notion of *intricate* queries. We show that it precisely characterizes the *connected* $\mathrm{UCQ}^{\neq}$ queries for which the dichotomy of Theorem 8.1 applies. Let us first recall the definition of *connected* $\mathrm{UCQ}^{\neq}$ queries:

DEFINITION 8.3. *A $\mathrm{CQ}^{\neq}$ is* connected *if, building the graph G on its atoms that connects those that share a variable (ignoring $\neq$-atoms), G is connected (in particular it has no isolated vertices, unless it consists of a single isolated vertex). A $\mathrm{UCQ}^{\neq}$ is* connected *if all its $\mathrm{CQ}^{\neq}$ disjuncts are* connected.

We now give our definition of *intricate* queries. We characterize them by looking at *line instances*:

DEFINITION 8.4. *A* line instance *is an instance I of the following form: a domain $a_1, \ldots, a_n$, and, for $1 \leqslant i < n$, one single binary fact between a_i and a_{i+1}: either $R(a_i, a_{i+1})$ for some $R \in \sigma$ or $R(a_{i+1}, a_i)$ for some binary $R \in \sigma$. (Recall that, as σ is* arity-two, *its maximal arity is two, so it must include at least one binary relation.)*

The intuition is that a query is intricate if, on any sufficiently long line instance, it must have a minimal match that contains the two middle facts (i.e., the ones that are incident to the middle element). Here is the formal definition of *intricate* queries:

DEFINITION 8.5. *A $\mathrm{UCQ}^{\neq}$ q is* n-intricate *for $n \in \mathbb{N}$ if, for every line instance I with $|I| = 2n + 2$, letting F and F' be the two facts of I incident to the middle element a_{n+2}, there is a* minimal *match of q on I that includes both F and F'.*
We call q intricate *if it is $|q|$-intricate.*

Observe that queries q with $|q| < 2$ clearly cannot be intricate. Further, if a query has no matches that include only binary facts, then it cannot be intricate; in other words, any disjunct that contains an atom for a unary relation can be ignored when determining whether a query is intricate. By contrast, our query q_{p} of Theorem 8.1 was designed to be intricate, in fact q_{p} is 0-intricate. Also note that an n-intricate query is always m-intricate for any $m > n$: consider the restriction of any line instance of size $2m + 2$ to a line instance of size $2n + 2$, and find a match in the restriction.

We note that we can decide whether $\mathrm{UCQ}^{\neq}$ queries are intricate or not, by enumerating line instances. We do not know the precise complexity of this task:

LEMMA 8.6. *Given a connected $\mathrm{UCQ}^{\neq}$ q, we can decide in PSPACE whether q is intricate.*

We can now state our *meta-dichotomy*: a dichotomy such as Theorem 8.1 holds for a connected $\mathrm{UCQ}^{\neq}$ q if and only if it is intricate. Further, *non-intricate* queries must actually have *constant-width* OBDD on some counterexample unbounded-treewidth family:

THEOREM 8.7. *For any connected $\mathrm{UCQ}^{\neq}$ q on an arity-2 signature:*

- *If q is not intricate, there is a treewidth-constructible and unbounded-treewidth family $\mathcal{I}$ of instances such that q has* constant-width *OBDDs on $\mathcal{I}$; the OBDDs can be computed in PTIME from the input instance.*
- *If q is intricate, then Theorem 8.1 applies to q: in particular, for any unbounded-treewidth family $\mathcal{I}$ of instances satisfying the hypotheses, q does not have polynomial-width OBDDs on $\mathcal{I}$.*

Proof sketch. We construct $\mathcal{I}$ for non-intricate $\mathrm{UCQ}^{\neq}$ q as a family of grids from a line instance which is a counterexample to intricacy. As we can disconnect facts that do not co-

[4]The condition is weaker because we require the subexponentiality to work for some fixed d, not an arbitrary c.

occur in a match, we can disconnect the grids to bounded-pathwidth instances in a lineage-preserving fashion.

Conversely, we adapt the hardness proof of Theorem 8.1 to any intricate UCQ$^{\neq}$ query q, extracting independent matches from any sufficiently subdivided skewed grid minor thanks to intricacy. □

8.3 Other Query Classes

We finish by investigating the status of other query classes relative to our meta-dichotomy, to see whether Theorem 8.1 could be shown for queries in an even less expressive class than UCQ$^{\neq}$, such as CQ$^{\neq}$ or UCQ.

Connected CQ$^{\neq}$ *queries.* We classify the connected CQ$^{\neq}$ queries relative to Theorem 8.7, by showing that a connected CQ$^{\neq}$ can never be intricate. This explains why, for instance, the query $R(x) \wedge S(x, y) \wedge T(y)$ is not intricate, as is witnessed by the family of S-grids.

PROPOSITION 8.8. *A connected* CQ$^{\neq}$ *is never intricate.*

Proof sketch. The signature σ must contain at most one binary relation R, as otherwise we can find for any CQ$^{\neq}$ q a family of grids where the query never holds, so that q would have trivial constant-width OBDDs. Now, if q contains a join pattern of the form $R(x, y) \wedge R(y, z)$, then q has no matches on line instances with R-facts of alternating directions. If q does not contain such a pattern, we consider line instances with a path of R-facts in the same direction, and show that q has no match that involves the two middle facts. □

By Theorem 8.7, this implies that any CQ$^{\neq}$ query q has an unbounded-treewidth, treewidth-constructible family of instances $\mathcal{I}$ such that q has constant-width OBDDs on $\mathcal{I}$ (that can be computed in PTIME); and it also implies that we could not have proven Theorem 8.1 with a connected CQ$^{\neq}$ query.

Homomorphism-closed. Second, we investigate the status in our meta-dichotomy of queries without inequalities, i.e., connected UCQs. We can in fact show a result for all queries that are *closed under homomorphisms*, no matter whether they are connected or not. Further, we can even choose a *single* class of instances which is easy for *all* query closed under homomorphisms. (Remember that our queries are always constant-free.)

PROPOSITION 8.9. *For any arity-2 signature, there is a treewidth-constructible instance family $\mathcal{I}$ with unbounded treewidth and $w \in \mathbb{N}$ such that any query q closed under homomorphisms has OBDDs of width w on $\mathcal{I}$ that can be computed in PTIME in the input instance.*

Proof sketch. Queries q closed under homomorphisms become essentially trivial on the class $\mathcal{I}$ of complete bipartite directed graphs: all minimal matches of q on $\mathcal{I}$ (if any) have a single fact, hence q has a constant-width OBDD. □

Hence, a connected UCQ is never intricate, so we could not have shown Theorem 8.1 with a UCQ query rather than a UCQ$^{\neq}$ query.

Again, this result should not be confused with those of [35, 36]. Of course, not all homomorphism-closed queries, or even UCQs, have constant-width OBDDs on arbitrary instances. We are merely claiming the *existence* of high-treewidth instance classes for which we have constant-width OBDDs whatever the query.

Beyond connected queries. We consider last whether our dichotomy in Theorem 8.1 could extend to *disconnected* CQ$^{\neq}$, which are not covered by Proposition 8.8 or by the meta-dichotomy of Theorem 8.7.

If the signature has more than one binary relation, this is hopeless: the easy argument used in the proof of Proposition 8.8 in this case can also apply to disconnected CQ$^{\neq}$.

However, quite surprisingly, on signatures with a *single* binary relation (and arbitrarily many unary ones) we can show a weakening of Theorem 8.1 for a disconnected CQ$^{\neq}$. The first part adapts (it holds for all MSO), so only the lower bound is interesting, which we can rephrase as before to a lower bound on OBDD width on individual input instances:

PROPOSITION 8.10. *Let σ be an arity-2 signature with only one binary relation. There exists a disconnected* CQ$^{\neq}$ *query q_{d}, a constant $d' > 1$ and integer $n_0 \in \mathbb{N}$ such that: for any instance I on σ of size $\geqslant n_0$, letting k be the treewidth of I, the width of any OBDD for q_{d} is $\Omega(k^{1/d'})$.*

Proof sketch. The query q_{d} tests whether there are at least two facts with disjoint domains. We adapt Lemma 8.2 and use a skewed grid minor of the instance, but show this time that the OBDD must remember linearly many configurations at some level. □

This implies that q_{d} does not satisfy the first part of the meta-dichotomy of Theorem 8.7. Surprisingly, however, we can show that the query q_{d} has OBDDs of width $O(k)$ on some unbounded-treewidth and treewidth-constructible instance class. Hence, q_{d} does not satisfy the second part of the meta-dichotomy either, so q_{d} witnesses that there are *disconnected* CQ$^{\neq}$ which do not follow our meta-dichotomy at all! We leave to future work a more precise study of disconnected queries.

9. CONNECTION TO SAFE QUERIES

We conclude this paper by connecting our results to *query-based* tractability conditions. More specifically, we focus on UCQs that have polynomial OBDD representations of their lineage: by the results of [36], those are the *inversion-free UCQs.* We will show that the tractability of such queries can be explained by our *data-based* tractability conditions: more precisely, for any inversion-free UCQ, there is a lineage-preserving rewriting of input instances to instances that have constant *tree-depth* [46], and hence (by Lemma 11 of [5]) have constant pathwidth and treewidth. The definition of *tree-depth* is as follows:

DEFINITION 9.1. An elimination forest *for an (undirected) graph G is a forest F on the vertices of G such that, for any edge $\{x, y\}$ of G, one of x and y is a descendant of the other in F. The* tree-depth *of G is the minimal height of an elimination forest of G. The* tree-depth *of an instance I is that of its Gaifman graph.*

This section applies to signatures of arbitrary arity.

Unfoldings. Our results are based on instance rewritings of a general kind, possibly of independent interest. We let I denote an arbitrary instance in this paragraph, and let q denote a query closed under homomorphisms.

DEFINITION 9.2. *An* unfolding *of instance I is an instance I' with a homomorphism h to I which is* bijective on facts*: for any fact $F(\mathbf{a})$ of I, there is exactly one fact $F(\mathbf{a}')$ in I such that $h(a'_i) = a_i$ for all i.*

The bijection defined by the homomorphism allows us to see the lineage of q on an unfolding I' of I as a Boolean function on the same variables as the lineage of q on I.

We use unfoldings as a tool to show lineage-preserving instance rewritings. Indeed, we can see from the homomorphism h from I' to I that any match of q in I' is preserved in I through h. In other words, the following is immediate:

LEMMA 9.3. *If I' is an unfolding of I and φ and φ' are the lineages of q on I and I', then for any valuation ν of the facts of I, if $\nu(\varphi') = 1$ then $\nu(\varphi) = 1$.*

The converse generally fails, but a sufficient condition is:

DEFINITION 9.4. *An unfolding I' of I* respects *q if, for any match $M \subseteq I$ of q on I, letting M' be its preimage in I', we have $M' \models q$.*

Intuitively, the unfolding does not "break" the matches of q. This ensures that the lineage is preserved exactly:

LEMMA 9.5. *If I' is an unfolding of I that respects q, then q has the same lineage on I and I'.*

Inversion-free UCQs. We use unfoldings to study Boolean constant-free *inversion-free* UCQ queries. We do not restate their formal definition here, and refer the reader to Section 2 of [36]. The following is known:

THEOREM 9.6 (Proposition 5 of [36]). *For any inversion-free UCQ q, for any input instance I, the lineage of q on I has an OBDD of constant width (i.e., the width only depends on q).*

When studying inversion-free UCQs, it is convenient to assume that the *ranking* transformation was applied to the query and instance [16, 18]. A UCQ is *ranked* if, defining a binary relation on its variables by setting $x < y$ when x occurs before y in some atom, then $<$ has no cycle. In particular, in a ranked query, no variable occurs twice in an atom. An instance is *ranked* if there is a total order $<$ on its domain such that for any fact $R(\mathbf{a})$ and $1 \leqslant i < j \leqslant \text{arity}(R)$, we have $a_i < a_j$. In particular, no element occurs twice in a fact. Up to changing the signature, we can always rewrite a UCQ q to a ranked UCQ q', and rewrite separately any instance I to a ranked instance I', so that the lineage of q on I is the same as that of q' on I'; see [16, 18] for details.

We will thus assume that the ranking transformation has been applied to the query, and to the instance. Note that this can be performed in linear time in the instance, and does not change its treewidth, pathwidth, or tree-depth, as the Gaifman graph is unchanged by this operation.

Once this ranking transformation has been performed, we can show the following:

THEOREM 9.7. *For any ranked inversion-free UCQ q, for any ranked instance I, there is an unfolding I' of I that respects q and has tree-depth $\leqslant \text{arity}(\sigma)$.*

Hence, in particular, q has the same lineage on I' and on I, as shown by Lemma 9.5. As pathwidth is less than tree-depth [5], by Theorem 6.7, this implies the result of Theorem 9.6, and (via Proposition 6.8) generalizes it slightly: it shows that the lineage can even be represented by a bounded-pathwidth circuit.

Proof sketch. We use an inversion-free expression [36] for q to define an order on relation attributes which is compatible across relations. We unfold each relation by distinguishing each element depending on the tuple of elements on the preceding positions; this is inspired by Proposition 5 of [36]. The result preserves the inversion-free expression and has a natural elimination tree defined by the prefix ordering on the distinguished elements. □

Theorem 9.7 thus suggests that the tractability of probability evaluation for inversion-free UCQs can be understood in terms of bounded-tree-depth and bounded-pathwidth tractability: what inversion-free UCQs "see" in an instance is a bounded tree-depth structure.

10. CONCLUSION

The main result of this work justifies that bounded treewidth is the right condition on instances to make probability evaluation tractable, with a dichotomy between *ra-linear* evaluation for *MSO* queries assuming bounded treewidth, and *$FP^{\#P}$-hardness* under RP reductions for *FO queries* otherwise. Our second main result extends this to $\text{UCQ}^{\neq}$ for tractable OBDD representations, specifically, to the *intricate* queries that we characterize: they have no polynomial OBDDs on *any* sufficiently dense unbounded-treewidth instance class.

We do not know whether our results extend beyond arity-2, e.g., using techniques from the CSP context [45]. Another question is whether the first dichotomy result extends to more restricted query classes, or even to the $\text{UCQ}^{\neq}$ q_{p} of Theorem 8.1: indeed, probability evaluation of q_{p} is #P-hard but we were unable to show this *under arbitrary subdivisions*. Another extension would be to use PTIME rather than RP reductions, which would follow from a derandomization of [10]. In terms of lineage, we do not know either whether our OBDD results extend to other lineage classes, e.g., FBDDs or d-DNNFs.

Our main hope, though, concerns the *unfolding* technique of Section 9. We showed that, for inversion-free UCQs, unfolding *always* reduces an instance to a bounded-treewidth one while preserving lineage. Could there be a *query-dependent*, lineage-preserving unfolding of instances, lowering the treewidth by undoing joins that the query does not "see"? Such a technique could yield a tractability condition on the instance *and* query, covering and extending *both* bounded-treewidth and safe queries. It could also be practically useful to approximate query probabilities, maybe in conjunction with the query-based *dissociation* technique [27].

Acknowledgements. We thank Mikaël Monet for careful proofreading, and Chandra Chekuri and Dan Suciu for technical clarifications on [10] and [36], respectively. We also thank the anonymous reviewers of PODS 2016 for their valuable comments, in particular for strengthening Theorem 9.7 to tree-depth. This work was partly funded by the Télécom ParisTech Research Chair on Big Data and Market Insights.

11. REFERENCES

[1] A. Amarilli. *Leveraging the Structure of Uncertain Data.* PhD thesis, Télécom ParisTech, 2016.

[2] A. Amarilli, P. Bourhis, and P. Senellart. Provenance circuits for trees and treelike instances. In *ICALP*, 2015.

[3] A. Amarilli, P. Bourhis, and P. Senellart. Provenance circuits for trees and treelike instances (extended version). http://arxiv.org/abs/1511.08723, 2015.

[4] S. Arnborg, J. Lagergren, and D. Seese. Easy problems for tree-decomposable graphs. *J. Algorithms*, 12(2), 1991.

[5] H. L. Bodlaender, J. R. Gilbert, H. Hafsteinsson, and T. Kloks. Approximating treewidth, pathwidth, frontsize, and shortest elimination tree. *J. Algorithms*, 18(2), 1995.

[6] R. E. Bryant. Symbolic boolean manipulation with ordered binary-decision diagrams. *ACM Comput. Surv.*, 24(3), 1992.

[7] D. Calvanese, G. De Giacomo, M. Lenzerini, and M. Y. Vardi. Containment of conjunctive regular path queries with inverse. In *KR*, 2000.

[8] D. Calvanese, G. De Giacomo, and M. Y. Vardi. Decidable containment of recursive queries. *Theor. Comput. Sci.*, 336(1), 2005.

[9] V. Chandrasekaran, N. Srebro, and P. Harsha. Complexity of inference in graphical models. In *UAI*, 2008.

[10] C. Chekuri and J. Chuzhoy. Polynomial bounds for the grid-minor theorem. In *STOC*, 2014.

[11] S. Cohen, B. Kimelfeld, and Y. Sagiv. Running tree automata on probabilistic XML. In *PODS*, 2009.

[12] H. Comon, M. Dauchet, R. Gilleron, C. Löding, F. Jacquemard, D. Lugiez, S. Tison, and M. Tommasi. Tree automata: Techniques and applications. Available on: http://www.grappa.univ-lille3.fr/tata, 2007.

[13] B. Courcelle. The monadic second-order logic of graphs. I. Recognizable sets of finite graphs. *Inf. Comput.*, 85(1), 1990.

[14] B. Courcelle, J. Engelfriet, and G. Rozenberg. Handle-rewriting hypergraph grammars. *JCSS*, 46(2), 1993.

[15] B. Courcelle, J. A. Makowsky, and U. Rotics. Linear time solvable optimization problems on graphs of bounded clique-width. *Theor. Comput. Sci.*, 33(2), 2000.

[16] N. Dalvi, K. Schnaitter, and D. Suciu. Computing query probability with incidence algebras. In *KR*, 2010.

[17] N. Dalvi and D. Suciu. Efficient query evaluation on probabilistic databases. *VLDBJ*, 16(4), 2007.

[18] N. Dalvi and D. Suciu. The dichotomy of probabilistic inference for unions of conjunctive queries. *JACM*, 59(6), 2012.

[19] N. N. Dalvi and D. Suciu. The dichotomy of conjunctive queries on probabilistic structures. In *PODS*, 2007.

[20] A. Darwiche. On the tractable counting of theory models and its application to truth maintenance and belief revision. *J. Applied Non-Classical Logics*, 11(1-2), 2001.

[21] D. Deutch, T. Milo, S. Roy, and V. Tannen. Circuits for Datalog provenance. In *ICDT*, 2014.

[22] R. Diestel. *Graph Theory.* Springer, 2005.

[23] R. Fink and D. Olteanu. A dichotomy for non-repeating queries with negation in probabilistic databases. In *PODS*, 2014.

[24] J. Flum, M. Frick, and M. Grohe. Query evaluation via tree-decompositions. *J. ACM*, 49(6), 2002.

[25] R. Ganian, P. Hlinený, J. Kneis, D. Meister, J. Obdrzálek, P. Rossmanith, and S. Sikdar. Are there any good digraph width measures? In *IPEC*, 2010.

[26] R. Ganian, P. Hliněný, A. Langer, J. Obdržálek, P. Rossmanith, and S. Sikdar. Lower bounds on the complexity of MSO1 model-checking. *JCSS*, 1(80), 2014.

[27] W. Gatterbauer and D. Suciu. Approximate lifted inference with probabilistic databases. *PVLDB*, 8(5), 2015.

[28] E. Grädel, C. Hirsch, and M. Otto. Back and forth between guarded and modal logics. *TOCL*, 3(3), 2002.

[29] T. J. Green, G. Karvounarakis, and V. Tannen. Provenance semirings. In *PODS*, 2007.

[30] M. Grohe. Logic, graphs, and algorithms. *Logic and Automata: History and Perspectives*, 2, 2007.

[31] G. Hansel. Nombre minimal de contacts de fermeture nécessaires pour réaliser une fonction booléenne symétrique de n variables. *C. R. Acad. Sc. Paris*, 258, 1964.

[32] C. Huang and A. Darwiche. Inference in belief networks: A procedural guide. *Int. J. Approximate Reasoning*, 1996.

[33] J. Håstad. The shrinkage exponent of de Morgan formulas is 2. *SIAM J. Comput.*, 27(1), 1998.

[34] T. Imieliński and W. Lipski, Jr. Incomplete information in relational databases. *J. ACM*, 31(4), 1984.

[35] A. K. Jha and D. Suciu. On the tractability of query compilation and bounded treewidth. In *ICDT*, 2012.

[36] A. K. Jha and D. Suciu. Knowledge compilation meets database theory: Compiling queries to decision diagrams. *Theory Comput. Syst.*, 52(3), 2013.

[37] S. Kreutzer. Algorithmic meta-theorems. In *Parameterized and Exact Computation.* Springer, 2008.

[38] S. Kreutzer and S. Tazari. Lower bounds for the complexity of monadic second-order logic. In *LICS*, 2010.

[39] J. Kwisthout, H. L. Bodlaender, and L. C. van der Gaag. The necessity of bounded treewidth for efficient inference in bayesian networks. In *ECAI*, 2010.

[40] S. L. Lauritzen and D. J. Spiegelhalter. Local computations with probabilities on graphical structures and their application to expert systems. *J. Royal Statistical Society. Series B*, 1988.

[41] M. Liskiewicz, M. Ogihara, and S. Toda. The complexity of counting self-avoiding walks in subgraphs of two-dimensional grids and hypercubes. *Theor. Comput. Sci.*, 1-3(304), 2003.

[42] J. A. Makowsky and J. Marino. Tree-width and the monadic quantifier hierarchy. *Theor. Comput. Sci.*, 303(1), 2003.

[43] D. Marx. Can you beat treewidth? In *FOCS*, 2007.

[44] D. Marx. Can you beat treewidth? *Theory of Computing*, 6(1), 2010.

[45] D. Marx. Tractable hypergraph properties for constraint satisfaction and conjunctive queries. *JACM*, 60(6), 2013.

[46] J. Nešetřil and P. O. Mendez. *Sparsity: Graphs, Structures, and Algorithms*, chapter Bounded Height Trees and Tree-Depth. 2012.

[47] D. Olteanu and J. Huang. Using OBDDs for efficient query evaluation on probabilistic databases. In *SUM*, 2008.

[48] N. Robertson and P. D. Seymour. Graph minors. V. Excluding a planar graph. *J. Comb. Theory, Ser. B*, 41(1), 1986.

[49] D. Suciu, D. Olteanu, C. Ré, and C. Koch. *Probabilistic Databases*. Morgan & Claypool, 2011.

[50] L. G. Valiant. The complexity of enumeration and reliability problems. *SIAM J. Comput.*, 8(3), 1979.

[51] I. Wegener. *The complexity of Boolean functions*. Wiley, 1987.

[52] M. Xia, P. Zhang, and W. Zhao. Computational complexity of counting problems on 3-regular planar graphs. *Theor. Comput. Sci.*, 384(1), 2007.

A. PROOFS FOR SECTION 6

LEMMA 6.6. *For any $k \in \mathbb{N}$, there is $c \in \mathbb{N}$ such that, given a Boolean circuit C of treewidth k, we can compute an equivalent OBDD in time $O(|C|^c)$.*

Proof. We rely on Corollary 2.14 of [35]: there is a doubly exponential function f such that, for any $k \in \mathbb{N}$, there is $c' := f(k) \in \mathbb{N}$ such that, for any tree decomposition T of width $\leqslant k$ of C, the OBDD O obtained for a certain variable order Π^R has width c'.

The order Π^R on variables is defined following an in-order traversal of T where children are ordered by the number of variables in this subtree; clearly this quantity can be computed over the entire tree in PTIME, so the order Π^R can be computed in PTIME. We show that we can construct the OBDD O in PTIME as well, in a level-wise manner inspired by [36].

Write $\Pi^R = X_1, \ldots, X_n$, and construct O level-by-level in the following way. Assuming that we have constructed O up to level $l-1$, create two children for each node at level $l-1$ (depending on the value of variable X_l), and then merge all such children n and n' that are *equivalent.* To define this, call *equivalent* two partial valuations ν and ν' of variables $X_1, \ldots, X_l$ if the Boolean function represented by C on the other variables $X_{l+1}, \ldots, X_n$ under ν is the same as under ν'. Now, call n and n' *equivalent* if, for any partial valuation ν leading to n (represented by a path from the root of O to n) and any partial valuation ν' leading to n', these two partial valuations of $X_1, \ldots, X_l$ are equivalent. As we will always ensure in the construction, any paths leading to the parent node of n are equivalent partial valuations of $X_1, \ldots, X_{l-1}$, so n and n' are equivalent iff, picking any two valuations ν for n and ν' for n' by following a path from the root to n and to n' respectively, ν and ν' are equivalent.

Hence, it suffices to show that there is a function g such that we can test in time $O(|C|^{g(k)})$ whether two partial valuations are equivalent. Indeed, we can then build O in the indicated time, because the maximal number of node pairs to test at any level of the OBDD is $\leqslant (2 \cdot |C|^{f(k)})^2$: we had at most $|C|^{f(k)}$ at the previous level, and each of them creates two children, before we merge the equivalent children. Hence, if we can test equivalence in the indicated time, then clearly we can construct O in time $O(|C|^c)$ for $c := 1 + 1 + 2 \cdot f(k) + g(k)$ (the first term accounts for the linear number of levels, and the second term accounts for the linear time required to find a partial valuation for a node).

We thus show that the equivalence of partial valuations can be tested in time $O(|C|^{g(k)})$ for some function g. Considering two partial valuations ν and ν' of the same set of variables $\mathcal{X}$, let C_ν and $C_{\nu'}$ be the two circuits obtained from C by substituting the input gates for $\mathcal{X}$ with constant gates according to ν and ν' respectively. Note that C_ν and $C_{\nu'}$ have the same set of input gates $\mathcal{X}'$, formed precisely of the variables not in $\mathcal{X}$. We rename the internal gates of $C_{\nu'}$ so that the only gates shared between C_ν and $C_{\nu'}$ are the input gates $\mathcal{X}'$. Now, C' be the circuit obtained by taking the union of C_ν and $C_{\nu'}$ (on the same set of variables), and adding an output gate and a constant number of gates such that the output gate is true iff the output gates of C_ν and $C_{\nu'}$ carry different values (this can be done with 5 additional gates in total). It is easy to see that there is a valuation of $\mathcal{X}'$ that makes the circuit C' evaluate to true iff the partial valuations ν and ν' are *not* equivalent. Now, observe that we can immediately construct from T a tree decomposition T'' of width $\leqslant 2k+5$ of C'. Indeed, it is obvious that T is a tree decomposition of C_ν, and we can rename gates to obtain from T a tree decomposition T' of $C_{\nu'}$, such that T and T' both have the same width k and the same skeleton. Now, construct T'' that has same skeleton as T and T' where each bag is the union of the corresponding bags of T and T', adding the 5 intermediate gates to each bag. The result T'' clearly has width $\leqslant 2k+5$ and it is immediate that it is a tree decomposition of C'.

We can then use message-passing techniques [40, 32] to determine in time exponential in $2k+5$ and polynomial in C' whether the bounded-treewidth circuit C' has a satisfying assignment, from which we deduce whether ν and ν' are equivalent. For details, see, e.g., Theorem D.2 of [2]. □

PROPOSITION 6.8. *For any fixed $k \in \mathbb{N}$ and (monotone) MSO query q, for any σ-instance I of* pathwidth *$\leqslant k$, we can construct a (monotone) lineage circuit C of q on I in time $O(|I|)$. The* pathwidth *of C only depends on k and q (not on I).*

Proof. Given a path decomposition of an instance I, which is a tree decomposition with a linear tree, the resulting tree encoding E of I (see [2, 3]) is clearly also a linear tree. From the proof of Theorem 4.4 of [3], we observe that the lineage circuit that we construct has a tree decomposition which can be made to be a path decomposition in this case, because it follows the structure of E. Hence, the circuit C has bounded pathwidth. □

LEMMA 6.9. *For any $k \in \mathbb{N}$, for any Boolean circuit C of pathwidth $\leqslant k$, we can compute in polynomial time in C an OBDD equivalent to C whose width depends only on k.*

Proof. As in the proof of Lemma 6.6, we can compute in PTIME the order Π^R on variables, and we can compute the OBDD under this order in the same way. This uses the fact that a path decomposition of circuit C is in particular a tree decomposition of C. □

THEOREM 6.11. *For any fixed MSO query q and constant $k \in \mathbb{N}$, given an input instance I of treewidth $\leqslant k$, one can compute in time $O(|I|)$ a d-DNNF representation of the lineage of q on I.*

Proof. We define a *bottom-up deterministic tree automaton* on alphabet Γ (or Γ-bDTA) in the standard manner. We start by adapting the proof of Proposition 3.1 of [3] to show the following result instead: a provenance d-DNNF of a *deterministic* $\overline{\Gamma}$-bDTA A on a $\overline{\Gamma}$-tree E can be constructed in time $O(|A| \cdot |E|)$. We construct the circuit exactly as in the proof of Proposition 3.1 of [3] and show that it is a d-DNNF.

First, observe that the only NOT gates that we use are the $g_n^{\neg \mathrm{i}}$, which are NOT gates of the g_n^{i}, which are input gates; so we only apply negation to leaf nodes.

Second, we show that the sets of leaves reachable from the children of any AND gate are pairwise disjoint. The AND gates that we create and that have multiple inputs are:

- The $g_n^{q_L,q_R}$, which are the AND of $g_{\mathrm{L}(n)}^{q_L}$ and $g_{\mathrm{R}(n)}^{q_L}$; now, $g_{\mathrm{L}(n)}^{q_L}$ only depends on the input gates $g_{n'}^{\mathrm{i}}$ for nodes n' of the subtree of E rooted at $\mathrm{L}(n)$, and likewise $g_{\mathrm{R}(n)}^{q_L}$ only depends on input gates in the right subtree;
- The $g_n^{q_L,q_R,\mathrm{i}}$, which are the AND of $g_n^{q_L,q_R}$ and g_n^{i}; now, the $g_n^{q_L,q_R}$ do not depend on g_n^{i}, only on input gates $g_{n'}^{\mathrm{i}}$ for n' a strict descendant of n in E;
- The $g_n^{q_L,q_R,\neg\mathrm{i}}$, which are the AND of $g_n^{q_L,q_R}$ and $g_n^{\neg\mathrm{i}}$; now, the $g_n^{q_L,q_R}$ do not depend on the sole input gate under $g_n^{\neg\mathrm{i}}$, i.e., g_n^{i}, but only on input gates $g_{n'}^{i}$ for n' a strict descendant of n in E.

Third, we show that the children of any OR gate are mutually exclusive. The OR gates that we create and that have multiple inputs are the following:

- The g_n^q when n is a leaf node of E, for which the claim is immediate, as the only two possible children are g_n^{i} and $g_n^{\neg\mathrm{i}}$ which are clearly mutually exclusive.
- The g_n^q when n is an internal node of E, which are the OR of gates of the form $g_n^{q_L,q_R,\mathrm{i}}$ or $g_n^{q_L,q_R,\neg\mathrm{i}}$ over several pairs q_L, q_R.
  To observe that these gates are mutually exclusive, remember that, for a valuation ν of the tree E, the gate $g_{n'}^q$ is true iff there is a run ρ of A on the subtree of $\nu(E)$ rooted at n' such that $\rho(n') = q$. However, as A is deterministic, for each n', there is at most one state q for which this is possible. Hence, for any valuation ν' of the circuit C, for our node n, there is at most one q'_L such that $g_{\mathrm{L}(n)}^{q'_L}$ is true under valuation ν', and only at most one q'_R such that $g_{\mathrm{R}(n)}^{q'_R}$ is true under ν'. Hence, by definition of the $g_n^{q_L,q_R}$, there is at most one of them which can be true under valuation ν', namely, $g_n^{q'_L,q'_R}$, which also means that only the gate $g_n^{q'_L,q'_R,\mathrm{i}}$ and the gate $g_n^{q'_L,q'_R,\neg\mathrm{i}}$ can be true under ν'. But these two gates are clearly mutually exclusive (only one can evaluate to true, depending on the value of $\nu(n)$), which proves the claim.
- The output gate g_0 which is the OR of gates of the form g_r^q for r the root node of E. Again, as A is deterministic, for any valuation ν' of C, letting ν be the corresponding valuation of the $\overline{\Gamma}$-tree E, there is only one state q' such that A has a run ρ on E with $\rho(r) = q'$, so at most one state q' such that $g_r^{q'}$ is true under ν.

Hence, the circuit constructed in the proof of Proposition 3.1 of [2] is a d-DNNF representation of the lineage of the automaton on the tree which has linear size.

We now adapt the proof of Theorem 4.2 of [3]. The theorem proceeds by constructing a bNTA for the query q [13] on the alphabet Γ_σ^k and modifying it to obtain a bNTA A' on $\overline{\Gamma_\sigma^k}$. We now additionally convert A' to a bDTA A'' on the same alphabet, which we can do using standard techniques [12]. All of this is performed independently of the instance.

Now, we conclude using the rest of the proof of Theorem 4.2 of [2]. The resulting circuit C' is the result of (bijectively) renaming the input gates, and replacing some input gates by constant gates, on the circuit C produced by Proposition 3.1 of [2]. However, by our previous observation, C is actually a d-DNNF circuit, so C' also is (up to evaluating negations of constant gates as constant gates). Hence, we have produced the desired d-DNNF, which by the statement of Theorem 4.2 of [2] is of linear size and is computed in linear time. □

B. PROOFS FOR SECTION 7

PROPOSITION 7.1. *There is a* $\mathrm{CQ}^{\neq}$ *query* q*, and a family* $\mathcal{I}$ *of relational instances with treewidth* 0*, such that, for any* $I \in \mathcal{I}$*, for any Boolean formula* ψ *capturing the lineage of* q *on* I*, we have* $|\psi| = \Omega(|I| \log\log |I|)$.

Proof. Consider the signature with a single unary predicate R, and consider the $\mathrm{CQ}^{\neq}$ $q : \exists xy\, R(x) \wedge R(y) \wedge x \neq y$. Consider the family of instances $\mathcal{I}$ defined as $\{R(a_1), \ldots, R(a_n)\}$ for all $n \in \mathbb{N}$. Clearly, for any $I \in \mathcal{I}$, the lineage of q on I is the threshold function checking whether at least two of its inputs are true.

By Chapter 8, Theorem 5.2 of [51], any formula using $\wedge$, $\vee$, $\neg$ expressing the threshold function over n variables has size $\Omega(n \log\log n)$, the desired bound. □

PROPOSITION 7.2. *There is a* $\mathrm{CQ}^{\neq}$ *query* q*, and a family* $\mathcal{I}$ *of relational instances with treewidth* 0*, such that, for any* $I \in \mathcal{I}$*, for any* monotone *Boolean formula* ψ *capturing the lineage of* q *on* I*, we have* $|\psi| = \Omega(|I| \log |I|)$.

Proof. We use the same proof as for Proposition 7.1 but relying on [31] (also Chapter 8, Theorem 1.2 of [51]), which shows that, for ψ built over the monotone basis $\wedge$ and $\vee$, we have $|\psi| = \Omega(n \log n)$. □

PROPOSITION 7.3. *There is an MSO query* q*, and a family* $\mathcal{I}$ *of relational instances with treewidth* 1*, such that, for any* $I \in \mathcal{I}$*, for any Boolean formula* ψ *capturing the lineage of* q *on* I*, we have* $|\psi| = \Omega(|I|^2)$.

Proof. Consider the signature σ with a unary predicate L and binary predicate E. We define the family $\mathcal{I} = (I_n)$ with I_n having domain $\{a_1, \ldots, a_n\}$ and facts $L(a_i)$ for each $1 \leqslant i \leqslant n$ and $E(a_i, a_{i+1})$ for each $1 \leqslant i < n$. Clearly, all instances in $\mathcal{I}$ have treewidth 1. We consider the MSO formula q that intuitively uses the E-facts to test whether the number of L-facts is odd. Formally, we define q as follows, inspired by the definition of an automaton:

$$q := \forall X_0 X_1\ \mathrm{Part}(X_0, X_1) \wedge \mathrm{Tr}(X_0, X_1) \wedge \mathrm{Init}(X_0, X_1)$$
$$\Rightarrow \forall x\ (\neg\exists y\ E(y, x) \Rightarrow x \in X_1)$$

where $\mathrm{Part}(X_0, X_1)$ asserts that X_0 and X_1 partition the domain (where $\oplus$ denotes exclusive OR):

$$\mathrm{Part}(X_0, X_1) := \forall x\ (x \in X_0) \oplus (x \in X_1)$$

$\mathrm{Tr}(X_0, X_1)$ is the conjunction of the following transition rules, for each $b \neq b'$ in $\{0, 1\}$:

$$\forall xy\ E(x, y) \wedge y \in X_b \wedge L(x) \Rightarrow x \in X_{b'}$$
$$\forall xy\ E(x, y) \wedge y \in X_b \wedge \neg L(x) \Rightarrow x \in X_b$$

and $\mathrm{Init}(X_0, X_1)$ asserts the initial states:

$$\forall x\ (\neg\exists y\ E(x, y)) \wedge \neg L(x) \Rightarrow x \in X_0$$
$$\forall x\ (\neg\exists y\ E(x, y)) \wedge L(x) \Rightarrow x \in X_1$$

Intuitively, on any possible world of I_n where all E-facts are present, q is true whenever the number of L-facts is odd. Indeed, it is clear that there is a unique choice of X_0 and X_1 in such worlds, defined by putting a_n in X_1 or X_0 depending on whether $L(a_n)$ holds, and, for $1 \leqslant i < n$, letting b such that $a_{i+1} \in X_b$ and b' be 1 or 0 depending on whether $L(a_i)$ holds or not, putting a_i in $X_{b \oplus b'}$. Hence, in worlds containing all E-facts, there is a unique choice of X_0 and X_1 where we have $a_i \in X_1$ iff the number of facts $L(a_j)$ with $i \leqslant j \leqslant n$ is odd. Hence, q is satisfied iff, in this unique assignment, a_1 (the only node with no incoming E-edge) is in X_1, that is, if the overall number of L-facts is odd.

Hence, pick $I \in \mathcal{I}$ and let ψ be a formula representation of the lineage of q on I. Replacing the input gates for the E-facts by constant 1-gates, we obtain a formula of the same size that computes the parity function of the inputs corresponding to the L-gates, the number of which is $\lceil |I| / 2 \rceil$.

Now, by Theorem 8.2, Chapter 8 of [51], any formula using $\wedge$, $\vee$, $\neg$ expressing the parity function over n variables has a number of variable occurrences that is at least n^2. Hence, we deduce that $|\psi| = \Omega(|I|^2)$, as claimed. □

C. PROOFS FOR SECTION 9

LEMMA 9.5. *If I' is an unfolding of I that respects q, then q has the same lineage on I and I'.*

Proof. By Lemma 9.3, it suffices to show that for any match M of q in I, the preimage M' of M by the bijection on facts is also a match of q; but this is precisely what is guaranteed by the fact that I respects q. □

THEOREM 9.7. *For any ranked inversion-free UCQ q, for any ranked instance I, there is an unfolding I' of I that respects q and has tree-depth $\leqslant$ arity(σ).*

The roadmap of the proof is as follows. We use an *inversion-free expression* [36] for q to define an order on relation attributes which is compatible across relations. We then unfold each relation by distinguishing each element depending on the tuple of elements on the preceding positions; this is inspired by Proposition 5 of [36]. The result preserves the inversion-free expression and has a path decomposition that enumerates the facts lexicographically. To follow the roadmap, we first define inversion-free expressions as in [36]:

DEFINITION C.1. *A* hierarchical expression *[36] is a logical sentence built out of atoms, conjunction, disjunction, and existential quantification, where each variable is a* root variable, *i.e., occurs in all atoms in the scope of its existential quantifier.*

An inversion-free expression *is a hierarchical expression such that, for each relation symbol R, we can define a total order $<_R$ on its positions $\{R^1, \ldots, R^{\text{arity}(R)}\}$, such that, in every R-atom $R(\mathbf{x})$, if $R^i <_R R^j$ then the quantifier $\exists x_j$ in the query is in the scope of the quantifier $\exists x_i$.*

By Proposition 2 of [36], a ranked UCQ is inversion-free iff it can be written as an inversion-free expression, so it suffices to show Theorem 9.7 for inversion-free expressions.

We first define our unfolding I' of an input instance I. For each fact $R(\mathbf{a})$ of I, we create the fact $R(\mathbf{b})$ defined as follows. Writing $R^{i_1} <_R \cdots <_R R^{i_n}$ the positions of R according to the total order $<_R$, we define b_{i_1} as the tuple (a_{i_1}), and define b_{i_j} as the tuple formed by concatenating $b_{i_{j-1}}$ and (a_{i_j}). We call f_R the operation thus defined, with $\mathbf{b} = f_R(\mathbf{a})$. Clearly the operation h mapping each tuple to its last element is a homomorphism from I' to I, and it is bijective on facts because it is the inverse of the operation that we described. Hence, I' is an unfolding of I. Note that this construction is similar to the one used in the proof of Proposition 5 in [36].

We must show that I' has bounded tree-depth. To do this, consider the elimination forest F defined on dom(I') by setting $\mathbf{b}$ to be the parent of $\mathbf{c}$ iff $\mathbf{b}$ is a longest strict prefix of $\mathbf{c}$. The forest F has one root per singleton element in dom(I'): these elements correspond the (possibly strict) subset of dom(I) of the elements occurring at the first position R^{i_1} for the order $<_R$ for some relation R. It is clear that F is indeed an elimination forest for the Gaifman graph of I', as by construction any fact $R(\mathbf{b})$ of I' is such that, letting $n :=$ arity(R) and R^{i_n} be the last position of R in the order $<_R$, the elements of $\mathbf{b}$ are exactly the non-empty prefixes of b_{i_n}, so, for any pair b_i, b_j of elements of $\mathbf{b}$, one is a prefix of the other, so one is an ancestor of the other in F. We conclude by noticing that the elimination forest F has height arity(σ), so the tree-depth of I' is at most arity(σ).

The only thing left to show is that I' respects q. For this, let us consider the inversion-free expression Q of q. For any subexpression φ of Q with free variables $\mathbf{x}$, let us define the *ordered free variables* of φ, denoted ofv(φ), as follows. If φ contains no atoms (i.e., it is the constant formula "true" or "false"), then $\mathbf{x}$ is empty and so is ofv(φ). Otherwise, as Q is inversion-free, it is in particular hierarchical, so all free variables of φ must occur in all atoms of φ: this is by definition, for any free variable x_i of φ, of the subexpression of Q that includes φ whose outermost operator is $\exists x_i$. Hence, consider any atom $A = R(\mathbf{x})$, and, remembering that no variable occurs twice in A (as Q is ranked), define ofv(φ) as the total order on $\mathbf{x}$ given by $x_i < x_j$ iff $R^i <_R R^j$.

It is clear that ofv(φ) is well-defined, i.e., that does not depend on our choice of atom in φ: this is because Q is an inversion-free expression, so the order of variables in atoms must reflect the order in which the variables are quantified.

We now show the claim that I' respects Q:

LEMMA C.2. *If I has a match M of Q, then, defining M' by mapping each fact $R(\mathbf{a})$ of M to the fact $R(f_R(\mathbf{a}))$ of I', M' is a match of Q in I'.*

Proof. Let f be defined on tuples of dom(I) by $f(\mathbf{a}) := (a_1, (a_1, a_2), \ldots, \mathbf{a})$. For any subformula φ with n free variables and any n-tuple $\mathbf{a}$ of dom(I), we write $I \models \varphi[\text{ofv}(\varphi){:=}\mathbf{a}]$ to mean the Boolean formula with constants obtained by substituting each variable in ofv(φ) by the corresponding element in $\mathbf{a}$ following the order of $\mathbf{a}$ and ofv(φ).

We proceed by induction on the subformulae of Q, showing that if a subformula φ and tuple $\mathbf{a} \in$ dom(M) is such that $M \models \varphi[\text{ofv}(\varphi){:=}\mathbf{a}]$, then $M' \models \varphi[\text{ofv}(\varphi){:=}f(\mathbf{a})]$.

- For atoms, this is by definition of ofv and of M'.
- For $\varphi \wedge \psi$, we observe that we have ofv(φ) = ofv($\varphi \wedge \psi$) = ofv(ψ): write $\mathbf{x}$ to refer to these ordered free variables. If $M \models (\varphi \wedge \psi)[\mathbf{x}{:=}\mathbf{a}]$, then $M \models \varphi[\mathbf{x}{:=}\mathbf{a}]$ and $M \models \psi[\mathbf{x}{:=}\mathbf{a}]$, as by induction $M' \models \varphi[\mathbf{x}{:=}f(\mathbf{a})]$ and $M' \models \psi[\mathbf{x}{:=}f(\mathbf{a})]$, we deduce $M' \models (\varphi \wedge \psi)[\mathbf{x}{:=}f(\mathbf{a})]$. For $\varphi \vee \psi$, the reasoning is the same.
- For $\varphi : \exists y\ \psi$, writing $\mathbf{x}{:=}$ofv(φ), by definition of ofv, y is the last variable of $\mathbf{x}'{:=}$ofv(ψ). As $M \models \varphi[\mathbf{x}{:=}\mathbf{a}]$, by definition there is $c \in$ dom(M) such that, letting $\mathbf{a}'$ be the concatenation of $\mathbf{a}$ and c, $M \models \psi[\mathbf{x}'{:=}\mathbf{a}']$. By induction hypothesis we have $M' \models \psi[\mathbf{x}'{:=}f(\mathbf{a}')]$, and as removing the last element of $f(\mathbf{a}')$ yields $f(\mathbf{a})$, we deduce that $M' \models (\exists y\ \psi)[\mathbf{x}{:=}f(\mathbf{a})]$.

The outcome of this induction is that $M \models Q$ implies $M' \models Q$, the desired claim. □

Towards Tight Bounds for the Streaming Set Cover Problem

Sariel Har-Peled* Piotr Indyk† Sepideh Mahabadi‡ Ali Vakilian§

ABSTRACT

We consider the classic Set Cover problem in the data stream model. For n elements and m sets ($m \geq n$) we give a $O(1/\delta)$-pass algorithm with a strongly sub-linear $\widetilde{O}(mn^{\delta})$ space and logarithmic approximation factor[1]. This yields a significant improvement over the earlier algorithm of Demaine et al. [11] that uses exponentially larger number of passes. We complement this result by showing that the tradeoff between the number of passes and space exhibited by our algorithm is tight, at least when the approximation factor is equal to 1. Specifically, we show that any algorithm that computes set cover exactly using $(\frac{1}{2\delta} - 1)$ passes must use $\widetilde{\Omega}(mn^{\delta})$ space in the regime of $m = O(n)$. Furthermore, we consider the problem in the geometric setting where the elements are points in $\mathbb{R}^2$ and sets are either discs, axis-parallel rectangles, or fat triangles in the plane, and show that our algorithm (with a slight modification) uses the optimal $\widetilde{O}(n)$ space to find a logarithmic approximation in $O(1/\delta)$ passes.

Finally, we show that any randomized one-pass algorithm that distinguishes between covers of size 2 and 3 must use a linear (i.e., $\Omega(mn)$) amount of space. This is the first result showing that a randomized, approximate algorithm cannot achieve a space bound that is sublinear in the input size.

This indicates that using multiple passes might be necessary in order to achieve sub-linear space bounds for this problem while guaranteeing small approximation factors.

*Department of Computer Science; University of Illinois; 201 N. Goodwin Avenue; Urbana, IL, 61801, USA; http://sarielhp.org/; sariel@illinois.edu.

†CSAIL; EECS; MIT; 32 Vassar Street; Cambridge, MA, 02139, USA; indyk@mit.edu.

‡CSAIL; EECS; MIT; 32 Vassar Street; Cambridge, MA, 02139, USA; mahabadi@mit.edu.

§CSAIL; EECS; MIT; 32 Vassar Street; Cambridge, MA, 02139, USA; vakilian@mit.edu.

[1]The notations $\widetilde{O}(f(n,m))$ and $\widetilde{\Omega}(f(n,m))$ are respectively short form for $O(f(n,m)\,\mathrm{polylog}(n,m))$ and $\Omega(f(n,m)/\,\mathrm{polylog}(n,m))$.

PODS'16, June 26-July 01, 2016, San Francisco, CA, USA

© 2016 ACM. ISBN 978-1-4503-4191-2/16/06...$15.00

DOI: http://dx.doi.org/10.1145/2902251.2902287

1. INTRODUCTION

The Set Cover problem is a classic combinatorial optimization task. Given a ground set of n elements $\mathsf{U} = \{e_1, \cdots, e_n\}$, and a family of m sets $\mathcal{F} = \{\mathsf{r}_1, \ldots, \mathsf{r}_m\}$ where $m \geq n$, the goal is to select a subset $\mathcal{I} \subseteq \mathcal{F}$ such that $\mathcal{I}$ *covers* U, i.e., $\mathsf{U} \subseteq \bigcup_{S \in \mathcal{I}} S$, and the number of the sets in $\mathcal{I}$ is as small as possible. Set Cover is a well-studied problem with applications in many areas, including operations research [18], information retrieval and data mining [31], web host analysis [7], and many others.

Although the problem of finding an optimal solution is NP-complete, a natural greedy algorithm which iteratively picks the "best" remaining set is widely used. The algorithm often finds solutions that are very close to optimal. Unfortunately, due to its sequential nature, this algorithm does not scale very well to massive data sets (e.g., see Cormode et al. [10] for an experimental evaluation). This difficulty has motivated a considerable research effort whose goal was to design algorithms that are capable of handling large data efficiently on modern architectures. Of particular interest are *data stream* algorithms, which compute the solution using only a small number of sequential passes over the data using a limited memory. In the *streaming* Set Cover problem [31], the set of elements U is stored in the memory in advance; the sets $\mathsf{r}_1, \cdots, \mathsf{r}_m$ are stored consecutively in a read-only repository and an algorithm can access the sets only by performing sequential scans of the repository. However, the amount of read-write memory available to the algorithm is limited, and is smaller than the input size (which could be as large as mn). The objective is to design an efficient approximation algorithm for the Set Cover problem that performs few passes over the data, and uses as little memory as possible.

The last few years have witnessed a rapid development of new streaming algorithms for the Set Cover problem, in both theory and applied communities, see [31, 10, 25, 13, 11, 6]. Figure 1.1 presents the approximation and space bounds achieved by those algorithms, as well as the lower bounds[2].

Related work. The semi-streaming Set Cover problem was first studied by Saha and Getoor [31]. Their result for Max k-Cover problem implies a $O(\log n)$-pass $O(\log n)$-approximation algorithm for the Set Cover problem that uses $\widetilde{O}(n^2)$ space. Adopting the standard greedy algorithm of Set Cover with a thresholding technique leads to $O(\log n)$-pass $O(\log n)$-

[2]Note that the simple greedy algorithm can be implemented by either storing the whole input (in one pass), or by iteratively updating the set of yet-uncovered elements (in at most n passes).

Result	Approx	Passes	Space	R
Greedy	$\ln n$	1	$O(mn)$	
algorithm	$\ln n$	n	$O(n)$	
[31]	$O(\log n)$	$O(\log n)$	$O(n^2 \ln n)$	
[13]	$O(\sqrt{n})$	1	$\widetilde{\Theta}(n)$	R
[6]	$O(n^\delta/\delta)$	$1/\delta - 1$	$\widetilde{\Theta}(n)$	R
[28]	$\frac{1}{2}\log n$	$O(\log n)$	$\widetilde{\Omega}(m)$	R
[11]	$O(4^{1/\delta}\rho)$	$O(4^{1/\delta})$	$\widetilde{O}(mn^\delta)$	R
[11]	$O(1)$	$O(\log n)$	$\widetilde{\Omega}(mn)$	
Theorem 2.8	$O(\rho/\delta)$	$2/\delta$	$\widetilde{O}(mn^\delta)$	R
Theorem 3.8	3/2	1	$\Omega(mn)$	R
Theorem 5.4	1	$1/2\delta - 1$	$\widetilde{\Omega}(mn^\delta)$	R
Geometric Set Cover (Theorem 4.6)	$O(\rho_g)$	$O(1)$	$\widetilde{O}(n)$	R
s-Sparse Set Cover (Theorem 6.6)	1	$1/2\delta - 1$	$\widetilde{\Omega}(ms)$	R

Figure 1.1: Summary of past work and our results. The last column indicates if the scheme is randomized, ρ denotes the approximation factor of an off-line algorithm solving Set Cover, which is $\ln n$ for the greedy, and 1 for exponential algorithm. Similarly, ρ_g denotes the approximation factor of an off-line algorithm solving geometric Set Cover. Finally, in the s-Sparse Set Cover problem, $s \leq n^\delta$ denotes an upper bound on the sizes of the input sets. Our lower bounds for Set Cover and s-Sparse Set Cover hold for $m = O(n)$. Moreover, [13] and [6] proved that their algorithms are tight. Here, and in the rest of the paper, all log are in base two.

approximation using $\widetilde{O}(n)$ space. In $\widetilde{O}(n)$ space regime, Emek and Rosen studied designing one-pass streaming algorithms for the Set Cover problem [13] and gave a *deterministic* greedy based $O(\sqrt{n})$-approximation for the problem. Moreover they proved that their algorithm is tight, even for randomized algorithms. The lower/upper bound results of [13] applied also to a generalization of the Set Cover problem, the ε-Partial Set Cover($\mathsf{U}, \mathcal{F}$) problem in which the goal is to cover $(1-\varepsilon)$ fraction of elements U and the size of the solution is compared to the size of an optimal cover of Set Cover($\mathsf{U}, \mathcal{F}$). Very recently, Chakrabarti and Wirth extended the result of [13] and gave a trade-off streaming algorithm for the Set Cover problem in *multiple passes* [6]. They gave a *deterministic* algorithm with p passes over the data stream that returns a $(p+1)n^{1/(p+1)}$-approximate solution of the Set Cover problem in $\widetilde{O}(n)$ space. Moreover they proved that achieving $0.99n^{1/(p+1)}/(p+1)^2$ in p passes using $\widetilde{O}(n)$ space is not possible even for randomized protocols which shows that their algorithm is tight up to a factor of $(p+1)^3$. Their result also works for the ε-Partial Set Cover problem.

In a different regime which was first studied by Demaine et al., the goal is to design a "low" approximation algorithms (depending on the computational model, it could be $O(\log n)$ or $O(1)$) in the smallest possible space [11]. They proved that any constant pass *deterministic* $(\log n/2)$-approximation algorithm for the Set Cover problem requires $\widetilde{\Omega}(mn)$ space. It shows that unlike the results in $\widetilde{O}(n)$-space regime, to obtain a sublinear "low" approximation streaming algorithm for the Set Cover problem in a constant number of passes, using *randomness* is necessary. Moreover, [11] presented a $O(4^{1/\delta})$-approximation algorithm that makes $O(4^{1/\delta})$ passes and uses $\widetilde{O}(mn^\delta)$ memory space.

The Set Cover problem is not polynomially solvable even in the restricted instances with points in $\mathbb{R}^2$ as elements, and geometric objects (either all disks or axis parallel rectangles or fat triangles) in plane as sets [15, 17, 22]. As a result, there has been a large body of work on designing approximation algorithms for the geometric Set Cover problems. See for example [27, 1, 3, 9] and references therein.

1.1 Our results

Despite the progress outlined above, however, some basic questions still remained open. In particular:

(A) Is it possible to design a *single* pass streaming algorithm with a "low" approximation factor[3] that uses sublinear (i.e., $o(mn)$) space?

(B) If such single pass algorithms are not possible, what are the achievable trade-offs between the number of passes and space usage?

(C) Are there special instances of the problem for which more efficient algorithms can be designed?

In this paper, we make a significant progress on each of these questions. Our upper and lower bounds are depicted in Figure 1.1.

On the algorithmic side, we give a $O(1/\delta)$-pass algorithm with a strongly sub-linear $\widetilde{O}(mn^\delta)$ space and logarithmic approximation factor. This yields a significant improvement over the earlier algorithm of Demaine et al. [11] which used exponentially larger number of passes. The trade-off offered by our algorithm matches the lower bound of Nisan [28] that holds at the endpoint of the trade-off curve, i.e., for $\delta = \Theta(1/\log n)$, up to poly-logarithmic factors in space[4]. Furthermore, our algorithm is very simple and succinct, and therefore easy to implement and deploy.

Our algorithm exhibits a natural tradeoff between the number of passes and space, which resembles tradeoffs achieved for other problems [19, 20, 21]. It is thus natural to conjecture that this tradeoff might be tight, at least for "low enough" approximation factors. We present the first step in this direction by showing a lower bound for the case when the approximation factor is equal to 1, i.e., the goal is to compute the optimal set cover. In particular, by an information theoretic lower bound, we show that any *streaming* algorithm that computes set cover using $(\frac{1}{2\delta} - 1)$ passes must use $\widetilde{\Omega}(mn^\delta)$ space (even assuming exponential computational power) in the regime of $m = O(n)$. Furthermore, we show that a stronger lower bound holds if all the input sets are sparse, that is if their cardinality is at most s. We prove a lower bound of $\widetilde{\Omega}(ms)$ for $s = O(n^\delta)$ and $m = O(n)$.

We also consider the problem in the geometric setting in which the elements are points in $\mathbb{R}^2$ and sets are either discs, axis-parallel rectangles, or fat triangles in the plane. We show that a slightly modified version of our algorithm achieves the *optimal* $\widetilde{O}(n)$ space to find an $O(\rho)$-approximation in $O(1)$ passes.

Finally, we show that any randomized one-pass algorithm that distinguishes between covers of size 2 and 3 must use a linear (i.e., $\Omega(mn)$) amount of space. This is the first result

[3]Note that the lower bound in [11] excluded this possibility only for deterministic algorithms, while the upper bound in [13, 6] suffered from a polynomial approximation factor.

[4]Note that to achieve a logarithmic approximation ratio we can use an off-line algorithm with the approximation ratio $\rho = 1$, i.e., one that runs in exponential time (see Theorem 2.8).

showing that a randomized, approximate algorithm cannot achieve a sub-linear space bound.

Very recently Assadi et al. [4] generalized this lower bound to any approximation ratio $\alpha = O(\sqrt{n})$. More precisely they showed that approximating Set Cover within any factor $\alpha = O(\sqrt{n})$ in a single pass requires $\Omega(\frac{mn}{\alpha})$ space.

Our techniques: Basic idea. Our algorithm is based on the idea that whenever a large enough set is encountered, we can immediately add it to the cover. Specifically, we guess (up to factor two) the size of the optimal cover k. Thus, a set is "large" if it covers at least $1/k$ fraction of the remaining elements. A small set, on the other hand, can cover only a "few" elements, and we can store (approximately) what elements it covers by storing (in memory) an appropriate random sample. At the end of the pass, we have (in memory) the projections of "small" sets onto the random sample, and we compute the optimal set cover for this projected instance using an offline solver. By carefully choosing the size of the random sample, this guarantees that only a small fraction of the set system remains uncovered. The algorithm then makes an additional pass to find the residual set system (i.e., the yet uncovered elements), making two passes in each iteration, and continuing to the next iteration.

Thus, one can think about the algorithm as being based on a simple iterative "dimensionality reduction" approach. Specifically, in two passes over the data, the algorithm selects a "small" number of sets that cover all but $n^{-\delta}$ fraction of the uncovered elements, while using only $\widetilde{O}(mn^{\delta})$ space. By performing the reduction step $1/\delta$ times we obtain a complete cover. The dimensionality reduction step is implemented by computing a small cover for a *random subset* of the elements, which also covers the vast majority of the elements in the ground set. This ensures that the remaining sets, when restricted to the random subset of the elements, occupy only $\widetilde{O}(mn^{\delta})$ space. As a result the procedure avoids a complex set of recursive calls as presented in Demaine et al. [11], which leads to a simpler and more efficient algorithm.

Geometric results. Further using techniques and results from computational geometry we show how to modify our algorithm so that it achieves *almost* optimal bounds for the Set Cover problem on geometric instances. In particular, we show that it gives a $O(1)$-pass $O(\rho)$-approximation algorithm using $\widetilde{O}(n)$ space when the elements are points in $\mathbb{R}^2$ and the sets are either discs, axis parallel rectangles, or fat triangles in the plane. In particular, we use the following surprising property of the set systems that arise out of points and disks: the the number of sets is nearly linear as long as one considers only sets that contain "a few" points.

More surprisingly, this property extends, with a twist, to certain geometric range spaces that might have quadratic number of shallow ranges. Indeed, it is easy to show an example of n points in the plane, where there are $\Omega(n^2)$ distinct rectangles, each one containing exactly two points, see Figure 1.2. However, one can "split" such ranges into a small number of canonical sets, such that the number of shallow sets in the canonical set system is near linear. This enables us to store the small canonical sets encountered during the scan explicitly in memory, and still use only near linear space.

We note that the idea of splitting ranges into small canonical ranges is an old idea in orthogonal range searching. It was used by Aronov et al. [3] for computing small ε-nets for these range spaces. The idea in the form we use, was further formalized by Ene et al. [14].

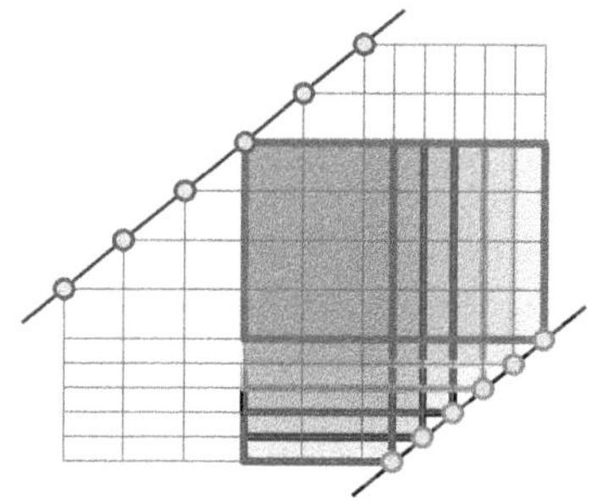

Figure 1.2: Consider two parallel lines in the plane with positive slope. Place $n/2$ points on each line such that all the points on the top line lie above and to the left of all the points on the bottom line. Consider all the rectangles whose upper left corner lie on the top line and their lower right corner lie on the bottom line. Clearly, we have $n^2/4$ distinct rectangles (i.e., sets), each containing two points.

Lower bounds. The lower bounds for multi-pass algorithms for the Set Cover problem are obtained via a careful reduction from Intersection Set Chasing. The latter problem is a communication complexity problem where n players need to solve a certain "set-disjointness-like" problem in p rounds. A recent paper [21] showed that this problem requires $\frac{n^{1+\Omega(1/p)}}{p^{O(1)}}$ bits of communication complexity for p rounds. This yields our desired trade-off of $\widetilde{\Omega}(mn^{\delta})$ space in $1/2\delta$ passes for exact protocols for Set Cover in the communication model and hence in the streaming model for $m = O(n)$. Furthermore, we show a stronger lower bound on memory space of sparse instances of Set Cover in which all input sets have cardinality at most s. By a reduction from a variant of Equal Pointer Chasing which maps the problem to a *sparse* instance of Set Cover, we show that in order to have an exact streaming algorithm for s-Sparse Set Cover with $o(ms)$ space, $\Omega(\log n)$ passes is necessary. More precisely, any $(\frac{1}{2\delta} - 1)$-pass *exact* randomized algorithm for s-Sparse Set Cover requires $\widetilde{\Omega}(ms)$ memory space, if $s \leq n^{\delta}$ and $m = O(n)$.

Our single pass lower bound proceeds by showing a lower bound for a one-way communication complexity problem in which one party (Alice) has a collection of sets, and the other party (Bob) needs to determine whether the complement of his set is covered by one of the Alice's sets. We show that if Alice's sets are chosen at random, then Bob can decode Alice's input by employing a small collection of "query" sets. This implies that the amount of communication needed to solve the problem is linear in the description size of Alice's sets, which is $\Omega(mn)$.

2. STREAMING ALGORITHM

2.1 Algorithm

In this section, we design an efficient streaming algorithm for the Set Cover problem that matches the lower bound results we already know about the problem. In the Set Cover problem, for a given set system $(\mathsf{U}, \mathcal{F})$, the goal is to find a subset $\mathcal{I} \subseteq \mathcal{F}$, such that $\mathcal{I}$ covers U and its cardinality

```
iterSetCover((U, F), δ):
// n = |U|
for k ∈ {2^i | 0 ≤ i ≤ log n} do in parallel:
  sol ← ∅
  Repeat for 1/δ times
    S be a sample of U of size cρkn^δ log m log n
    L ← S,   F_S ← ∅
    for r ∈ F do      // By doing one pass
      if |L ∩ r| ≥ |S|/k then    // Size Test
        sol ← sol ∪ {r},  L ← L \ r
      else
        F_S ← F_S ∪ {r ∩ L} //Store r ∩ L in mem
    D ← algOfflineSC(L, F_S, k),  sol ← sol ⋃ D
    U ← U \ ⋃_{r∈sol} r
return best sol computed in all parallel executions.
```

Figure 1.3: A tight streaming algorithm for the (unweighted) Set Cover problem. Here, algOfflineSC is an offline solver for Set Cover that provides ρ-approximation, and c is some appropriate constant.

is minimum. In the following, we sketch the iterSetCover algorithm (see also Figure 1.3).

In the iterSetCover algorithm, we have access to the algOfflineSC subroutine that solves the given Set Cover instance offline (using linear space) and returns a ρ-approximate solution where ρ could be anywhere between 1 and $\Theta(\log n)$ depending on the computational model one assumes. Under exponential computational power, we can achieve the optimal cover of the given instance of the Set Cover ($\rho = 1$); however, under $\mathbf{P} \neq \mathbf{NP}$ assumption, ρ cannot be better than $c \cdot \ln n$ where c is a constant [16, 29, 2, 26, 12] given polynomial computational power.

Let $n = |\mathsf{U}|$ be the initial number of elements in the given ground set. The iterSetCover algorithm, needs to guess (up to a factor of two) the size of the optimal cover of $(\mathsf{U}, \mathcal{F})$. To this end, the algorithm tries, in parallel, all values k in $\{2^i \mid 0 \leq i \leq \log n\}$. This step will only increase the memory space requirement by a factor of $\log n$.

Consider the run of the iterSetCover algorithm, in which the guess k is correct (i.e., $|\mathrm{OPT}| \leq k < 2|\mathrm{OPT}|$, where OPT is an optimal solution). The idea is to go through $O(1/\delta)$ iterations such that each iteration only makes two passes and at the end of each iteration the number of uncovered elements reduces by a factor of n^δ. Moreover, the algorithm is allowed to use $\widetilde{O}(mn^\delta)$ space.

In each iteration, the algorithm starts with the current ground set of uncovered elements U, and copies it to a *leftover* set L. Let S be a large enough uniform sample of elements U. In a single pass, using S, we estimate the size of all large sets in $\mathcal{F}$ and add $\mathsf{r} \in \mathcal{F}$ to the solution `sol` immediately (thus avoiding the need to store it in memory). Formally, if r covers at least $\Omega(|\mathsf{U}|/k)$ yet-uncovered elements of L then it is a heavy set, and the algorithm immediately adds it to the output cover. Otherwise, if a set is small, i.e., its covers less than $|\mathsf{U}|/k$ uncovered elements of L, the algorithm stores the set r in memory. Fortunately, it is enough to store its projection over the sampled elements explicitly (i.e., $\mathsf{r} \cap \mathsf{L}$) – this requires remembering only the $O(|\mathsf{S}|/k)$ indices of the elements of $\mathsf{r} \cap \mathsf{L}$.

In order to show that a solution of the Set Cover problem over the sampled elements is a good cover of the initial Set Cover instance, we apply the *relative (p, ε)-approximation* sampling result of [23] (see Definition 2.4) and it is enough for S to be of size $\widetilde{O}(\rho k n^\delta)$. Using relative (p, ε)-approximation sampling, we show that after two passes the number of uncovered elements is reduced by a factor of n^δ. Note that the relative (p, ε)-approximation sampling improves over the *Element Sampling* technique used in [11] with respect to the number of passes.

Since in each iteration we pick $O(\rho k)$ sets and the number of uncovered elements decreases by a factor of n^δ, after $1/\delta$ iterations the algorithm picks $O(\rho k/\delta)$ sets and covers all elements. Moreover, the memory space of the whole algorithm is $\widetilde{O}(\rho m n^\delta)$ (see Lemma 2.2).

2.2 Analysis

In the rest of this section we prove that the iterSetCover algorithm with high probability returns a $O(\rho/\delta)$-approximate solution of Set Cover$(\mathsf{U}, \mathcal{F})$ in $2/\delta$ passes using $\widetilde{O}(mn^\delta)$ memory space.

Lemma 2.1. *The number of passes the* iterSetCover *algorithm makes is $2/\delta$.*

PROOF. In each of the $1/\delta$ iterations of the iterSetCover algorithm, the algorithm makes two passes. In the first pass, based on the set of sampled elements S, it decides whether to pick a set or keep its projection over S (i.e., $\mathsf{r} \cap \mathsf{L}$) in the memory. Then the algorithm calls algOfflineSC which does not require any passes over $\mathcal{F}$. The second pass is for computing the set of uncovered elements at the end of the iteration. We need this pass because we only know the projection of the sets we picked in the current iteration over S and not over the original set of uncovered elements. Thus, in total we make $2/\delta$ passes. Also note that for different guesses for the value of k, we run the algorithm in parallel and hence the total number of passes remains $2/\delta$.

Lemma 2.2. *The memory space used by the* iterSetCover *algorithm is $\widetilde{O}(mn^\delta)$.*

PROOF. In each iteration of the algorithm, it picks during the first pass at most m sets (more precisely at most k sets) which requires $O(m \log m)$ memory. Moreover, in the first pass we keep the projection of the sets whose projection over the uncovered sampled elements has size at most $|\mathsf{S}|/k$. Since there are at most m such sets, the total required space for storing the projections is bounded by $O(\rho m n^\delta \log m \log n)$.

Since in the second pass the algorithm only updates the set of uncovered elements, the amount of space required in the second pass is $O(n)$. Thus, the total required space to perform each iteration of the iterSetCover algorithm is $\widetilde{O}(mn^\delta)$. Moreover, note that the algorithm does not need to keep the memory space used by the earlier iterations; thus, the total space consumed by the algorithm is $\widetilde{O}(mn^\delta)$.

Next we show the sets we picked before calling algOfflineSC has large size on U.

Lemma 2.3. *With probability at least $1 - m^{-c}$ all sets that pass the "Size Test" in the* iterSetCover *algorithm have size at least $|\mathsf{U}|/ck$.*

PROOF. Let r be a set of size less than $|\mathsf{U}|/ck$. In expectation, $|\mathsf{r} \cap \mathsf{S}|$ is less than $(|\mathsf{U}|/ck) \cdot (|\mathsf{S}|/|\mathsf{U}|) = \rho n^\delta \log m \log n$. By Chernoff bound for large enough c,

$$\mathbf{Pr}(|\mathsf{r} \cap \mathsf{S}| \geq c\rho n^\delta \log m \log n) \leq m^{-(c+1)}.$$

Applying the union bound, with probability at least $1-m^{-c}$, all sets passing "Size Test" have size at least $\frac{|\mathsf{U}|}{ck}$.

In what follows we define the *relative* (p,ε)*-approximation* sample of a set system and mention the result of Har-Peled and Sharir [23] on the minimum required number of sampled elements to get a relative (p,ε)-approximation of the given set system.

Definition 2.4. Let $(\mathsf{V},\mathcal{H})$ be a set system, i.e., V is a set of elements and $\mathcal{H} \subseteq 2^{\mathsf{V}}$ is a family of subsets of the ground set V. For given parameters $0<\varepsilon,p<1$, a subset $Z \subseteq \mathsf{V}$ is a *relative* (p,ε)*-approximation* for $(\mathsf{V},\mathcal{H})$, if for each $\mathsf{r} \in \mathcal{H}$, we have that if $|\mathsf{r}| \geq p|\mathsf{V}|$ then

$$(1-\varepsilon)\frac{|\mathsf{r}|}{|\mathsf{V}|} \leq \frac{|\mathsf{r} \cap Z|}{|Z|} \leq (1+\varepsilon)\frac{|\mathsf{r}|}{|\mathsf{V}|}.$$

If the range is light (i.e., $|\mathsf{r}| < p|\mathsf{V}|$) then it is required that

$$\frac{|\mathsf{r}|}{|\mathsf{V}|} - \varepsilon p \leq \frac{|\mathsf{r} \cap Z|}{|Z|} \leq \frac{|\mathsf{r}|}{|\mathsf{V}|} + \varepsilon p.$$

Namely, Z is $(1 \pm \varepsilon)$-multiplicative good estimator for the size of ranges that are at least p-fraction of the ground set.

The following lemma is a simplified variant of a result in Har-Peled and Sharir [23] – indeed, a set system with M sets, can have VC dimension at most $\log M$. This simplified form also follows by a somewhat careful but straightforward application of Chernoff's inequality.

Lemma 2.5. *Let* $(\mathsf{U},\mathcal{F})$ *be a finite set system, and* p,ε,q *be parameters. Then, a random sample of* U *such that* $|\mathsf{U}| = \frac{c'}{\varepsilon^2 p}\left(\log|\mathcal{F}|\log\frac{1}{p} + \log\frac{1}{q}\right)$, *for an absolute constant* c' *is a relative* (p,ε)*-approximation, for all ranges in* $\mathcal{F}$, *with probability at least* $(1-q)$.

Lemma 2.6. *Assuming* $|\mathrm{OPT}| \leq k \leq 2|\mathrm{OPT}|$, *after any iteration, with probability at least* $1-m^{1-c/4}$ *the number of uncovered elements decreases by a factor of* n^{δ}, *and this iteration adds* $O(\rho|\mathrm{OPT}|)$ *sets to the output cover.*

Proof. Let $\mathsf{V} \subseteq \mathsf{U}$ be the set of uncovered elements at the beginning of the iteration and note that the total number of sets that is picked during the iteration is at most $(1+\rho)k$ (see Lemma 2.3). Consider all possible such covers, that is $\mathcal{G} = \{\mathcal{F}' \subseteq \mathcal{F} \mid |\mathcal{F}'| \leq (1+\rho)k\}$, and observe that $|\mathcal{G}| \leq m^{(1+\rho)k}$. Let $\mathcal{H}$ be the collection that contains all possible sets of uncovered elements at the end of the iteration, defined as $\mathcal{H} = \left\{\mathsf{V} \setminus \bigcup_{\mathsf{r}\in\mathcal{C}} \mathsf{r} \mid \mathcal{C} \in \mathcal{G}\right\}$. Moreover, set $p = 2/n^{\delta}$, $\varepsilon = 1/2$ and $q = m^{-c}$ and note that $|\mathcal{H}| \leq |\mathcal{G}| \leq m^{(1+\rho)k}$. Since $\frac{c'}{\varepsilon^2 p}(\log|\mathcal{H}|\log\frac{1}{p} + \log\frac{1}{q}) \leq c\rho k n^{\delta}\log m \log n = |\mathsf{S}|$ for large enough c, by Lemma 2.5, S is a relative (p,ε)-approximation of $(\mathsf{V},\mathcal{H})$ with $(1-q)$ probability. Let $\mathcal{D} \subseteq \mathcal{F}$ be the collection of sets picked during the iteration which covers all elements in S. Since S is a relative (p,ε)-approximation sample of $(\mathsf{V},\mathcal{H})$ with probability at least $1-m^{-c}$, the number of uncovered elements of V (or U) by $\mathcal{D}$ is at most $\varepsilon p|\mathsf{V}| = |\mathsf{U}|/n^{\delta}$.

Hence, in each iteration we pick $O(\rho k)$ sets and at the end of iteration the number of uncovered elements reduces by n^{δ}.

Lemma 2.7. *The* iterSetCover *algorithm computes a set cover of* $(\mathsf{U},\mathcal{F})$, *whose size is within a* $O(\rho/\delta)$ *factor of the size of an optimal cover with probability at least* $1-m^{1-c/4}$.

Proof. Consider the run of iterSetCover for which the value of k is between $|\mathrm{OPT}|$ and $2|\mathrm{OPT}|$. In each of the $(1/\delta)$ iterations made by the algorithm, by Lemma 2.6, the number of uncovered elements decreases by a factor of n^{δ} where n is the number of initial elements to be covered by the sets. Moreover, the number of sets picked in each iteration is $O(\rho k)$. Thus after $(1/\delta)$ iterations, all elements would be covered and the total number of sets in the solution is $O(\rho|\mathrm{OPT}|/\delta)$. Moreover by Lemma 2.6, the success probability of all the iterations, is at least $1-\frac{1}{\delta m^{c/4}} \geq 1-(1/m)^{c/4-1}$.

Theorem 2.8. *The* iterSetCover$(\mathsf{U},\mathcal{F},\delta)$ *algorithm makes* $2/\delta$ *passes, uses* $\widetilde{O}(mn^{\delta})$ *memory space, and finds a* $O(\rho/\delta)$*-approximate solution of the* Set Cover *problem with high probability.*

Furthermore, given enough number of passes the iterSetCover *algorithm matches the known lower bound on the memory space of the streaming* Set Cover *problem up to a* polylog(m) *factor where* m *is the number of sets in the input.*

Proof. The first part of the proof implied by Lemma 2.1, Lemma 2.2, and Lemma 2.7.

As for the lower bound, note that by a result of Nisan [28], any randomized $(\frac{\log n}{2})$-approximation protocol for Set Cover$(\mathsf{U},\mathcal{F})$ in the one-way communication model requires $\Omega(m)$ bits of communication, no matter how many number of rounds it makes. This implies that any randomized $O(\log n)$-pass, $(\frac{\log n}{2})$-approximation algorithm for Set Cover$(\mathsf{U},\mathcal{F})$ requires $\widetilde{\Omega}(m)$ space, even under the exponential computational power assumption.

By the above, the iterSetCover algorithm makes $O(1/\delta)$ passes and uses $\widetilde{O}(mn^{\delta})$ space to return a $O(\frac{1}{\delta})$-approximate solution under the exponential computational power assumption ($\rho=1$). Thus by letting $\delta = c/\log n$, we will have a $(\frac{\log n}{2})$-approximation streaming algorithm using $\widetilde{O}(m)$ space which is optimal up to a factor of polylog(m).

Theorem 2.8 provides a strong indication that our tradeoff algorithm is optimal.

3. LOWER BOUND FOR SINGLE PASS ALGORITHMS

In this section, we study the Set Cover problem in the two-party communication model and give a tight lower bound on the communication complexity of the randomized protocols solving the problem in a single round. In the two-party Set Cover, we are given a set of elements U and there are two players Alice and Bob where each of them has a collection of subsets of U, $\mathcal{F}_A$ and $\mathcal{F}_B$. The goal for them is to find a minimum size cover $\mathcal{C} \subseteq \mathcal{F}_A \cup \mathcal{F}_B$ covering U while communicating the fewest number of bits from Alice to Bob (In this model Alice communicates to Bob and then Bob should report a solution).

Our main lower bound result for the single pass protocols for Set Cover is the following theorem which implies that the naive approach in which one party sends all of its sets to the the other one is optimal.

Theorem 3.1. *Any single round randomized protocol that approximates* Set Cover$(\mathsf{U},\mathcal{F})$ *within a factor better than* $3/2$ *and error probability* $O(m^{-c})$ *requires* $\Omega(mn)$ *bits of communication where* $n=|\mathsf{U}|$ *and* $m=|\mathcal{F}|$ *and* c *is a sufficiently large constant.*

We consider the case in which the parties want to decide whether there exists a cover of size 2 for U in $\mathcal{F}_A \cup \mathcal{F}_B$ or not. If any of the parties has a cover of size at most 2 for U, then it becomes trivial. Thus the question is whether there exist $r_a \in \mathcal{F}_A$ and $r_b \in \mathcal{F}_B$ such that $U \subseteq r_a \cup r_b$.

A key observation is that to decide whether there exist $r_a \in \mathcal{F}_A$ and $r_b \in \mathcal{F}_B$ such that $U \subseteq r_a \cup r_a$, one can instead check whether there exists $r_a \in \mathcal{F}_A$ and $r_b \in \mathcal{F}_B$ such that $\overline{r_a} \cap \overline{r_b} = \emptyset$. In other words we need to solve OR of a series of two-party Set Disjointness problems. In two-party Set Disjointness problem, Alice and Bob are given subsets of U, r_a and r_b and the goal is to decide whether $r_a \cap r_b$ is empty or not with the fewest possible bits of communication. Set Disjointness is a well-studied problem in the communication complexity and it has been shown that any randomized protocol for Set Disjointness with $O(1)$ error probability requires $\Omega(n)$ bits of communication where $n = |U|$ [5, 24, 30].

We can think of the following extensions of the Set Disjointness problem.

Many vs One: In this variant, Alice has m subsets of U, $\mathcal{F}_A$ and Bob is given a single set r_b. The goal is to determine whether there exists a set $r_a \in \mathcal{F}_A$ such that $r_a \cap r_b = \emptyset$.

Many vs Many: In this variant, each of Alice and Bob are given a collection of subsets of U and the goal for them is to determine whether there exist $r_a \in \mathcal{F}_A$ and $r_b \in \mathcal{F}_B$ such that $r_a \cap r_b = \emptyset$.

Note that deciding whether two-party Set Cover has a cover of size 2 is equivalent to solving the (Many vs Many)-Set Disjointness problem. Moreover, any lower bound for (Many vs One)-Set Disjointness clearly implies the same lower bound for the (Many vs Many)-Set Disjointness problem. In the following theorem we show that any single-round randomized protocol that solves (Many vs One)-Set Disjointness(m, n) with $O(m^{-c})$ error probability requires $\Omega(mn)$ bits of communication.

Theorem 3.2. *Any randomized protocol for* (Many vs One)-Set Disjointness(m, n) *with error probability* $O(m^{-c})$ *requires* $\Omega(mn)$ *bits of communication if* $n \geq c_1 \log m$ *where* c *and* c_1 *are large enough constants.*

The idea is to show that if there exists a single-round randomized protocol for the problem with $o(mn)$ bits of communication and error probability $O(m^{-c})$, then with constant probability one can distinguish $\Omega(2^{mn})$ distinct inputs using $o(mn)$ bits which is a contradiction.

Suppose that Alice has a collection of m uniformly and independently random subsets of U (in each of her subsets the probability that $e \in U$ is in the subset is 1/2). Lets assume that there exists a *single round* protocol **I** for (Many vs One)-Set Disjointness(n, m) with error probability $O(m^{-c})$ using $o(mn)$ bits of communication. Let algExistsDisj be Bob's algorithm in protocol **I**. Then we show that one can recover mn random bits with constant probability using algExistsDisj subroutine and the message s sent by the first party in protocol **I**. The algRecoverBit which is shown in Figure 3.1, is the algorithm to recover random bits using protocol **I** and algExistsDisj.

To this end, Bob gets the message s communicated by protocol **I** from Alice and considers all subsets of size $c_1 \log m$ and $c_1 \log m + 1$ of U. Note that s is communicated only once and thus the same s is used for all queries that Bob makes. Then at each step Bob picks a random subset r_b of size

```
algRecoverBit(U, s):
F_a ← ∅
for i = 1 to m^c log m do
    Let r_b be a random subset of U of size c_1 log m
    if algExistsDisj(s, r_b) = true
        r ← ∅
        for e ∈ U \ r_b
            if algExistsDisj(r_b ∪ e, s) = false
                r ← r ∪ e
        if ∃r' ∈ F_a s.t. r ⊂ r'    // Pruning step
            F_a ← F_a \ {r'},    F_a ← F_a ∪ {r}
        else if ∄r' ∈ F_a s.t. r' ⊂ r
            F_a ← F_a ∪ {r}
return F_a
```

Figure 3.1: algRecoverBit uses a protocol for (Many vs One)-Set Disjointness(m, n) to recover Alice's sets, $\mathcal{F}_A$ in Bob's side.

$c_1 \log m$ of U and solve the (Many vs One)-Set Disjointness problem with input $(\mathcal{F}_A, r_b)$ by running algExistsDisj(s, r_b). Next we show that if r_b is disjoint from a set in $\mathcal{F}_A$, then with high probability there is *exactly* one set in $\mathcal{F}_A$ which is disjoint from r_b (see Lemma 3.3). Thus once Bob finds out that his query, r_b, is disjoint from a set in $\mathcal{F}_A$, he can query all sets $r_b^+ \in \{r_b \cup e | e \in U \setminus r_b\}$ and recover the set (or union of sets) in $\mathcal{F}_A$ that is disjoint from r_b. By a simple *pruning step* we can detect the ones that are union of more than one set in $\mathcal{F}_A$ and only keep the sets in $\mathcal{F}_A$.

In Lemma 3.6, we show that the number of queries that Bob is required to make to recover $\mathcal{F}_A$ is $O(m^c)$ where c is a constant.

Lemma 3.3. *Let* r_b *be a random subset of* U *of size* $c \log m$ *and let* $\mathcal{F}_A$ *be a collection of* m *random subsets of* U. *The probability that there exists exactly one set in* $\mathcal{F}_A$ *that is disjoint from* r_b *is at least* $\frac{1}{m^{c+1}}$.

PROOF. The probability that r_b is disjoint from exactly one set in $\mathcal{F}_A$ is

$$\begin{aligned}&\Pr(r_b \text{ is disjoint from at least } \textbf{one} \text{ set in } \mathcal{F}_A)\\ &- \Pr(r_b \text{ is disjoint from at least } \textbf{two} \text{ sets in } \mathcal{F}_A)\\ &\geq (\frac{1}{2})^{c\log m} - \binom{m}{2}(\frac{1}{2})^{2c\log m} \geq \frac{1}{m^{c+1}}.\end{aligned}$$

First we prove the first term in the above inequality. For an arbitrary set $r \in \mathcal{F}_A$, since any element is contained in r with probability $\frac{1}{2}$, the probability that r is disjoint from r_b is $(1/2)^{c\log m}$.

$$\Pr(r_b \text{ is disjoint from at least } \textbf{one} \text{ set in } \mathcal{F}_A) \geq 2^{-c\log m}.$$

Moreover since there exist $\binom{m}{2}$ pairs of sets in $\mathcal{F}_A$, and for each $r_1, r_2 \in \mathcal{F}_A$, the probability that r_1 and r_2 are disjoint from r_b is m^{-2c},

$$\Pr(r_b \text{ disjoint from at least 2 sets in } \mathcal{F}_A) \leq m^{-(2c-2)}.$$

A family of sets $\mathcal{M}$ is called *intersecting* iff for any sets $A, B \in \mathcal{M}$ either both $A \setminus B$ and $B \setminus A$ are non-empty or both $A \setminus B$ and $B \setminus A$ are empty; in other words, there exists no $A, B \in \mathcal{M}$ such that $A \subseteq B$. Let $\mathcal{F}_A$ be a collection of subsets of U. We show that with high probability after testing $O(m^c)$ queries for sufficiently large constant c, the algRecoverBit algorithm recovers $\mathcal{F}_A$ completely if $\mathcal{F}_A$ is intersecting. First we show that with high probability the collection $\mathcal{F}_A$ is intersecting.

Observation 3.4. *Let $\mathcal{F}_A$ be a collection of m uniformly random subsets of U where $|\mathsf{U}| \geq c\log m$. With probability at least $1 - m^{-c/4+2}$, $\mathcal{F}_A$ is an intersecting family.*

PROOF. The probability that $\mathsf{r}_1 \subseteq \mathsf{r}_2$ is $(\frac{3}{4})^n$ and there are at most $m(m-1)$ pairs of sets in $\mathcal{F}_A$. Thus with probability at least $1 - m^2(\frac{3}{4})^n \geq 1 - 1/m^{\frac{c}{4}-2}$, $\mathcal{F}_A$ is intersecting.

Observation 3.5. *The number of distinct inputs of Alice (collections of random subsets of U), that is distinguishable by algRecoverBit is $\Omega(2^{mn})$.*

PROOF. There are 2^{mn} collections of m random subsets of U. By Observation 3.4, $\Omega(2^{mn})$ of them are intersecting. Since we can only recover the sets in the input collection and not their order, the distinct number of input collection that are distinguished by algRecoverBit is $\Omega(\frac{2^{mn}}{m!})$ which is $\Omega(2^{mn})$ for $n \geq c\log m$.

By Observation 3.4 and only considering the case such that $\mathcal{F}_A$ is intersecting, we have the following lemma.

Lemma 3.6. *Let $\mathcal{F}_A$ be a collection of m uniformly random subsets of U and suppose that $|\mathsf{U}| \geq c\log m$. After testing at most m^c queries, with probability at least $(1-\frac{1}{m})p^{m^c}$, $\mathcal{F}_A$ is fully recovered, where p is the success rate of protocol **I** for the* (Many vs One)-Set Disjointness *problem.*

PROOF. By Lemma 3.3, for each $\mathsf{r}_b \subset \mathsf{U}$ of size $c_1 \log m$ the probability that r_b is disjoint from exactly one set in a random collection of sets $\mathcal{F}_A$ is at least $1/m^{c_1+1}$. Given r_b is disjoint from exactly one set in $\mathcal{F}_A$, due to symmetry of the problem, the chance that r_b is disjoint from a specific set $\mathsf{r} \in \mathcal{F}_A$ is at least $\frac{1}{m^{c_1+2}}$. After $\alpha m^{c_1+2}\log m$ queries where α is a large enough constant, for any $\mathsf{r} \in \mathcal{F}_A$, the probability that there is not a query r_b that is only disjoint from r is at most $(1-\frac{1}{m^{c_1+2}})^{\alpha m^{c_1+2}\log m} \leq e^{-\alpha \log m} = \frac{1}{m^\alpha}$.

Thus after trying $\alpha m^{c_1+2}\log m$ queries, with probability at least $(1-\frac{1}{2m^{\alpha-1}}) \geq (1-\frac{1}{m})$, for each $\mathsf{r} \in \mathcal{F}_A$ we have at least one query that is only disjoint from r (and not any other sets in $\mathcal{F}_A \setminus \mathsf{r}$).

Once we have a query subset r_b which is only disjoint from a single set $\mathsf{r} \in \mathcal{F}_A$, we can ask $n - c\log m$ queries of size $c_1\log m + 1$ and recover r. Note that if r_b is disjoint from more than one sets in $\mathcal{F}_A$ simultaneously, the process (asking $n - c\log m$ queries of size $c_1\log m + 1$) will end up in recovering the union of those sets. Since $\mathcal{F}_A$ is an intersecting family with high probability (Observation 3.4), by *pruning step* in the algRecoverBit algorithm we are guaranteed that at the end of the algorithm, what we returned is exactly $\mathcal{F}_A$. Moreover the total number of queries the algorithm makes is at most

$$n \times (\alpha m^{c_1+2}\log m) \leq \alpha m^{c_1+3}\log m \leq m^c$$

for $c \geq c_1 + 4$.

Thus after testing m^c queries, $\mathcal{F}_A$ will be recovered with probability at least $(1-\frac{1}{m})p^{m^c}$ where p is the success probability of the protocol **I** for (Many vs One)-Set Disjointness(m,n).

Corollary 3.7. *Let **I** be a protocol for* (Many vs One)-Set Disjointness(m,n) *with error probability $O(m^{-c})$ and s bits of communication such that $n \geq c\log m$ for large enough c. Then algRecoverBit recovers $\mathcal{F}_A$ with constant success probability using s bits of communication.*

By Observation 3.5, since algRecoverBit distinguishes $\Omega(2^{mn})$ distinct inputs with constant probability of success (by Corollary 3.7), the size of message sent by Alice, should be $\Omega(mn)$. This proves Theorem 3.2.

Proof of Theorem 3.1: As we showed earlier, the communication complexity of (Many vs One)-Set Disjointness is a lower bound for the communication complexity of Set Cover. Theorem 3.2 showed that any protocol for (Many vs One)-Set Disjointness$(n, |\mathcal{F}_A)|$ with error probability less than $O(m^{-c})$ requires $\Omega(mn)$ bits of communication. Thus any single-round randomized protocol for Set Cover with error probability $O(m^{-c})$ requires $\Omega(mn)$ bits of communication. ∎

Since any p-pass streaming α-approximation algorithm for problem P that uses $O(s)$ memory space, is a p-round two-party α-approximation protocol for problem P using $O(sp)$ bits of communication [20], and by Theorem 3.1, we have the following lower bound for Set Cover problem in the streaming model.

Theorem 3.8. *Any single-pass randomized streaming algorithm for* Set Cover$(\mathsf{U},\mathcal{F})$ *that computes a $(3/2)$-approximate solution with probability $\Omega(1-m^{-c})$ requires $\Omega(mn)$ memory space (assuming $n \geq c_1\log m$).*

4. GEOMETRIC SET COVER

In this section, we consider the streaming Set Cover problem in the geometric settings. We present an algorithm for the case where the elements are a set of n points in the plane $\mathbb{R}^2$ and the m sets are either all disks, all axis-parallel rectangles, or all α-fat triangles (which for simplicity we call shapes) given in a data stream. As before, the goal is to find the minimum size cover of points from the given sets. We call this problem the Points-Shapes Set Cover problem.

Note that, the description of each shape requires $O(1)$ space and thus the Points-Shapes Set Cover problem is trivial to be solved in $O(m+n)$ space. In this setting the goal is to design an algorithm whose space is sub-linear in $O(m+n)$. Here we show that almost the same algorithm as iterSetCover (with slight modifications) uses $\widetilde{O}(n)$ space to find an $O(\rho)$-approximate solution of the Points-Shapes Set Cover problem in *constant* passes.

4.1 Preliminaries

A triangle $\triangle$ is called α*-fat* (or simply fat) if the ratio between its longest edge and its height on this edge is bounded by a constant $\alpha > 1$ (there are several equivalent definitions of α-fat triangles).

Definition 4.1. Let $(\mathsf{U},\mathcal{F})$ be a set system such that U is a set of points and $\mathcal{F}$ is a collection of shapes, in the plane $\mathbb{R}^2$. The *canonical representation* of $(\mathsf{U},\mathcal{F})$ is a collection $\mathcal{F}'$ of regions such that the following conditions hold. First, each $\mathsf{r}' \in \mathcal{F}'$ has $O(1)$ description. Second, for each $\mathsf{r}' \in \mathcal{F}'$, there exists $\mathsf{r} \in \mathcal{F}$ such that $\mathsf{r}' \cap \mathsf{U} \subseteq \mathsf{r} \cap \mathsf{U}$. Finally, for each $\mathsf{r} \in \mathcal{F}$, there exists c_1 sets $\mathsf{r}'_1, \cdots, \mathsf{r}'_{c_1} \in \mathcal{F}'$ such that $\mathsf{r} \cap \mathsf{U} = (\mathsf{r}'_1 \cup \cdots \cup \mathsf{r}'_{c_1}) \cap \mathsf{U}$ for some constant c_1.

The following two results are from [14] which are the formalization of the ideas in [3].

Lemma 4.2. (Lemma 4.18 in [14]) *Given a set of points* U *in the plane* $\mathbb{R}^2$ *and a parameter* w*, one can compute a set* $\mathcal{F}'_{total}$ *of* $O(|\mathsf{U}|w^2 \log |\mathsf{U}|)$ *axis-parallel rectangles with the following property. For an arbitrary axis-parallel rectangle* r *that contains at most* w *points of* U*, there exist two axis-parallel rectangles* $\mathsf{r}'_1, \mathsf{r}'_2 \in \mathcal{F}'_{total}$ *whose union has the same intersection with* U *as* r*, i.e.,* $\mathsf{r} \cap \mathsf{U} = (\mathsf{r}'_1 \cup \mathsf{r}'_2) \cap \mathsf{U}$.

Lemma 4.3. (Theorem 5.6 in [14]) *Given a set of points* U *in* $\mathbb{R}^2$*, a parameter* w *and a constant* α*, one can compute a set* $\mathcal{F}'_{total}$ *of* $O(|\mathsf{U}|w^3 \log^2 |\mathsf{U}|)$ *regions each having* $O(1)$ *description with the following property. For an arbitrary* α*-fat triangle* r *that contains at most* w *points of* U*, there exist nine regions from* $\mathcal{F}'_{total}$ *whose union has the same intersection with* U *as* r.

Using the above lemmas we get the following lemma.

Lemma 4.4. *Let* U *be a set of points in* $\mathbb{R}^2$ *and let* $\mathcal{F}$ *be a set of shapes (discs, axis-parallel rectangles or fat triangles), such that each set in* $\mathcal{F}$ *contains at most* w *points of* U*. Then, in a single pass over the stream of sets* $\mathcal{F}$*, one can compute the canonical representation* $\mathcal{F}'$ *of* $(\mathsf{U}, \mathcal{F})$*. Moreover, the size of the canonical representation is at most* $O(|\mathsf{U}|w^3 \log^2 |\mathsf{U}|)$ *and the space requirement of the algorithm is* $\widetilde{O}(|\mathcal{F}'|) = \widetilde{O}(|\mathsf{U}|w^3)$.

PROOF. For the case of axis-parallel rectangles and fat triangles, first we use Lemma 4.2 and Lemma 4.3 to get the set $\mathcal{F}'_{total}$ offline which require $\widetilde{O}(\mathcal{F}'_{total}) = \widetilde{O}(|\mathsf{U}|w^3 \log^2 |\mathsf{U}|)$ memory space. Then by making one pass over the stream of sets $\mathcal{F}$, we can find the canonical representation $\mathcal{F}'$ by picking all the sets $S' \in \mathcal{F}'_{total}$ such that $S' \cap \mathsf{U} \subseteq S \cap \mathsf{U}$ for some $S \in \mathcal{F}$. For discs however, we just make one pass over the sets $\mathcal{F}$ and keep a maximal subset $\mathcal{F}' \subseteq \mathcal{F}$ such that for each pair of sets $S'_1, S'_2 \in \mathcal{F}'$ their projection on U are different, i.e., $S'_1 \cap \mathsf{U} \neq S'_2 \cap \mathsf{U}$. By a standard technique of Clarkson and Shor [8], it can be proved that the size of the canonical representation, i.e., $|S'|$, is bounded by $O(|\mathsf{U}|w^2)$. Note that this is just counting the number of discs that contain at most w points, namely the at most w-level discs.

4.2 Algorithm

The outline of the Points-Shapes-Set-Cover algorithm (shown in Figure 4.1) is very similar to the iterSetCover algorithm presented earlier in Section 2.

In the first pass, the algorithm picks all the sets that cover a large number of yet-uncovered elements. Next, we sample S. Since we have removed all the ranges that have large size, in the first pass, the size of the remaining ranges *restricted to* the sample S is small. Therefore by Lemma 4.4, the canonical representation of $(\mathsf{S}, \mathcal{F}_\mathsf{S})$ has small size and we can afford to store it in the memory. We use Lemma 4.4 to compute the canonical representation $\mathcal{F}_\mathsf{S}$ in one pass. The algorithm then uses the sets in $\mathcal{F}_\mathsf{S}$ to find a cover $\mathtt{sol}_\mathsf{S}$ for the points of S. Next, in one additional pass, the algorithm replaces each set in $\mathtt{sol}_\mathsf{S}$ by one of its supersets in $\mathcal{F}$.

Finally, note that in the algorithm of Section 2, we are assuming that the size of the optimal solution is $O(k)$. Thus it is enough to stop the iterations once the number of uncovered elements is less than k. Then we can pick an arbitrary set for each of the uncovered elements. This would add only k more sets to the solution. Using this idea, we can reduce the size of the sampled elements down to $c\rho k(\frac{n}{k})^\delta \log m \log n$ which would help us in getting near-linear space in the geometric setting. Note that the final pass of the algorithm can be embedded into the previous passes but for the sake of clarity we write it separately.

```
algGeomSC(U, F, δ):
for k ∈ {2^i | 0 ≤ i ≤ log n} do in parallel:
  Let L ← U and sol ← ∅
  Repeat 1/δ times:
    for r ∈ F do    // Pass
      if |r ∩ L| ≥ |U|/k then
        sol ← sol ∪ {r}, L ← L \ r
    S ← sample of L of size cρk(n/k)^δ log m log n
    F_S ←compCanonicalRep(S, F, |S|/k) // Pass
    sol_S ← algOfflineSC(S, F_S)
    for r ∈ F do    // Pass
      if ∃r' ∈ sol_S s.t. r' ∩ S ⊆ r ∩ S then
        sol ← sol ∪ {r}, sol_S ← sol_S \ {r'}
        L ← L \ r
  for r ∈ F do    // Final Pass
    if r ∩ L ≠ ∅ then
      sol ← sol ∪ {r}, L ← L \ r
return smallest sol computed in parallel
```

Figure 4.1: A streaming algorithm for Points-Shapes Set Cover problem.

4.3 Analysis

By a similar approach to what we used in Section 2 to analyze the pass count and approximation guarantee of iterSetCover algorithm, we can show that the number of passes of the algGeomSC algorithm is $3/\delta+1$ (which can be reduced to $3/\delta$ with minor changes), and the algorithm returns an $O(\rho/\delta)$-approximate solution. Next, we analyze the space usage and the correctness of the algorithm. Note that our analysis in this section only works for $\delta \leq 1/4$.

Lemma 4.5. *The algorithm uses* $\widetilde{O}(n)$ *space.*

PROOF. Consider an iteration of the algorithm. The memory space used in the first pass of each iteration is $\widetilde{O}(n)$. The size of S is $c\rho k(n/k)^\delta \log m \log n$ and after the first pass the size of each set is at most $|\mathsf{U}|/k$. Thus using Chernoff bound for each set $\mathsf{r} \in \mathcal{F} \setminus \mathtt{sol}$,

$$\mathbf{Pr}\left[|\mathsf{r} \cap \mathsf{S}| > (1+2)\frac{|\mathsf{U}|}{k} \times \frac{|\mathsf{S}|}{|\mathsf{U}|}\right] \leq \exp\left(-\frac{4|\mathsf{S}|}{3k}\right) \leq (\frac{1}{m})^{c+1}.$$

Thus, with probability at least $1-m^{-c}$ (by the union bound), all the sets that are not picked in the first pass, cover at most $3|\mathsf{S}|/k = c\rho(n/k)^\delta \log m \log n$ elements of S. Therefore, we can use Lemma 4.4 to show that the number of sets in the canonical representation of $(\mathsf{S}, \mathcal{F}_\mathsf{S})$ is at most

$$O(|\mathsf{S}|\left(\frac{3|\mathsf{S}|}{k}\right)^3 \log^2 |\mathsf{S}|) = O(\rho^4 n \log^4 m \log^6 n),$$

as long as $\delta \leq 1/4$. To store each set in a canonical representation of $(\mathsf{S}, \mathcal{F})$ only constant space is required. Moreover, by Lemma 4.4, the space requirement of the second pass is $\widetilde{O}(|\mathcal{F}_\mathsf{S}|) = \widetilde{O}(n)$. Therefore, the total required space is $\widetilde{O}(n)$ and the lemma follows.

Theorem 4.6. *Given a set system defined over a set* U *of* n *points in the plane, and a set of* m *ranges* $\mathcal{F}$ *(which are either all disks, axis-parallel rectangles, or fat triangles). Let* ρ *be the quality of approximation to the offline set-cover solver we have, and let* $0 < \delta < 1/4$ *be an arbitrary parameter.*

Setting $\delta = 1/4$*, the algorithm* algGeomSC*, depicted in Figure 4.1, with high probability, returns an* $O(\rho)$*-approximate solution of the optimal set cover solution for the instance* $(\mathsf{U}, \mathcal{F})$*. This algorithm uses* $\widetilde{O}(n)$ *space, and performs constant passes over the data.*

Proof. As before consider the run of the algorithm in which $|\mathrm{OPT}| \leq k < 2|\mathrm{OPT}|$. Let V be the set of uncovered elements L at the beginning of the iteration and note that the total number of sets that is picked during the iteration is at most $(1 + c_1\rho)k$ where c_1 is the constant defined in Definition 4.1. Let $\mathcal{G}$ denote all possible such covers, that is $\mathcal{G} = \{\mathcal{F}' \subseteq \mathcal{F} \mid |\mathcal{F}'| \leq (1 + c_1\rho)k\}$. Let $\mathcal{H}$ be the collection that contains all possible set of uncovered elements at the end of the iteration, defined as $\mathcal{H} = \{\mathsf{V} \setminus \bigcup_{\mathsf{r} \in \mathcal{C}} \mathsf{r} \mid \mathcal{C} \in \mathcal{G}\}$. Set $p = (k/n)^{\delta}$, $\varepsilon = 1/2$ and $q = m^{-c}$. Since for large enough c, $\frac{c'}{\varepsilon^2 p}(\log |\mathcal{H}| \log \frac{1}{p} + \log \frac{1}{q}) \leq c\rho k (n/k)^{\delta} \log m \log n = |\mathsf{S}|$ with probability at least $1 - m^{-c}$, by Lemma 2.5, the set of sampled elements S is a relative (p, ε)-approximation sample of $(\mathsf{V}, \mathcal{H})$.

Let $\mathcal{C} \subseteq \mathcal{F}$ be the collection of sets picked in the third pass of the algorithm that covers all elements in S. By Lemma 4.4, $|\mathcal{C}| \leq c_1\rho k$ for some constant c_1. Since with high probability S is a relative (p, ε)-approximation sample of $(\mathsf{V}, \mathcal{H})$, the number of uncovered elements of V (or L) after adding $\mathcal{C}$ to `sol` is at most $\varepsilon p|\mathsf{V}| \leq |\mathsf{U}|(k/n)^{\delta}$. Thus with probability at least $(1 - m^{-c})$, in each iteration and by adding $O(\rho k)$ sets, the number of uncovered elements reduces by a factor of $(n/k)^{\delta}$.

Therefore, after 4 iterations (for $\delta = 1/4$) the algorithm picks $O(\rho k)$ sets and with high probability the number of uncovered elements is at most $n(k/n)^{\delta/\delta} = k$. Thus, in the final pass the algorithm only adds k sets to the solution `sol`, and hence the approximation factor of the algorithm is $O(\rho)$.

Remark 4.7. The result of Theorem 4.6 is similar to the result of Agarwal and Pan [1] – except that their algorithm performs $O(\log n)$ iterations over the data, while the algorithm of Theorem 4.6 performs only a constant number of iterations. In particular, one can use the algorithm of Agarwal and Pan [1] as the offline solver.

5. LOWER BOUND FOR MULTIPASS ALGORITHMS

In this section we give lower bound on the memory space of multipass streaming algorithms for the Set Cover problem. Our main result is $\Omega(mn^{\delta})$ space for streaming algorithms that return an optimal solution of the Set Cover problem in $O(1/\delta)$ passes for $m = O(n)$. Our approach is to reduce the communication Intersection Set Chasing(n, p) problem introduced by Guruswami and Onak [21] to the communication Set Cover problem.

Consider a communication problem P with n players $P_1, \cdots, P_n$. The problem P is a (n, r)-communication problem if players communicate in r rounds and in each round they speak in order $P_1, \cdots, P_n$. At the end of the rth round P_n should return the solution. Moreover we assume private randomness and public messages. In what follows we define the communication Set Chasing and Intersection Set Chasing problems.

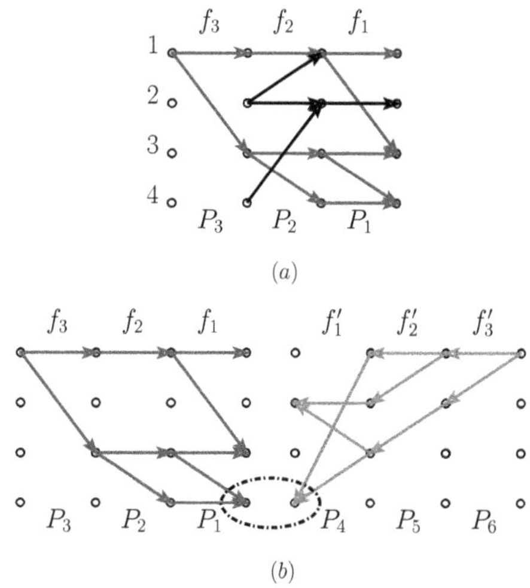

Figure 5.1: (a) shows an example of the communication Set Chasing(4, 3) and (b) is an instance of the communication Intersection Set Chasing(4, 3).

Definition 5.1 (Communication Set Chasing). The communication Set Chasing(n, p) problem is a $(p, p-1)$ communication problem in which the player i has a function $f_i : [n] \to 2^{[n]}$ and the goal is to compute $\vec{f_1}(\vec{f_2}(\cdots \vec{f_p}(\{1\}) \cdots))$ where $\vec{f_i}(S) = \bigcup_{s \in S} f_i(s)$. Figure 5.1(a) shows an instance of the communication Set Chasing $(4, 3)$.

Definition 5.2 (Communication Intersection Set Chasing). The communication Intersection Set Chasing(n, p) is a $(2p, p-1)$ communication problem in which the first p players have an instance of the Set Chasing(n, p) problem and the other p players have another instance of the Set Chasing(n, p) problem. The output of the Intersection Set Chasing(n, p) is 1 if the solutions of the two instances of the Set Chasing(n, p) intersect and 0 otherwise. Figure 5.1(b) shows an instance of the Intersection Set Chasing $(4, 3)$. The function f_i of each player P_i is specified by a set of directed edges form a copy of vertices labeled $\{1, \cdots, n\}$ to another copy of vertices labeled $\{1, \cdots, n\}$.

The communication Set Chasing problem is a generalization of the well-known communication Pointer Chasing problem in which player i has a function $f_i : [n] \to [n]$ and the goal is to compute $f_1(f_2(\cdots f_p(1) \cdots))$.

[21] showed that any randomized protocol that solves Intersection Set Chasing(n, p) with error probability less than $1/10$, requires $\Omega(\frac{n^{1+1/(2p)}}{p^{16} \log^{3/2} n})$ bits of communication where n is sufficiently large and $p \leq \frac{\log n}{\log \log n}$. In Theorem 5.4, we reduce the communication Intersection Set Chasing problem to the communication Set Cover problem and then give the first superlinear memory lower bound for the streaming Set Cover problem.

Definition 5.3 (Communication Set Cover$(\mathsf{U}, \mathcal{F}, p)$). The communication Set Cover(n, p) is a $(p, p-1)$ communication problem in which a collection of elements U is given to all players and each player i has a collection of subsets of U, $\mathcal{F}_i$. The goal is to solve Set Cover$(\mathsf{U}, \mathcal{F}_1 \cup \cdots \cup \mathcal{F}_p)$ using the minimum number of communication bits.

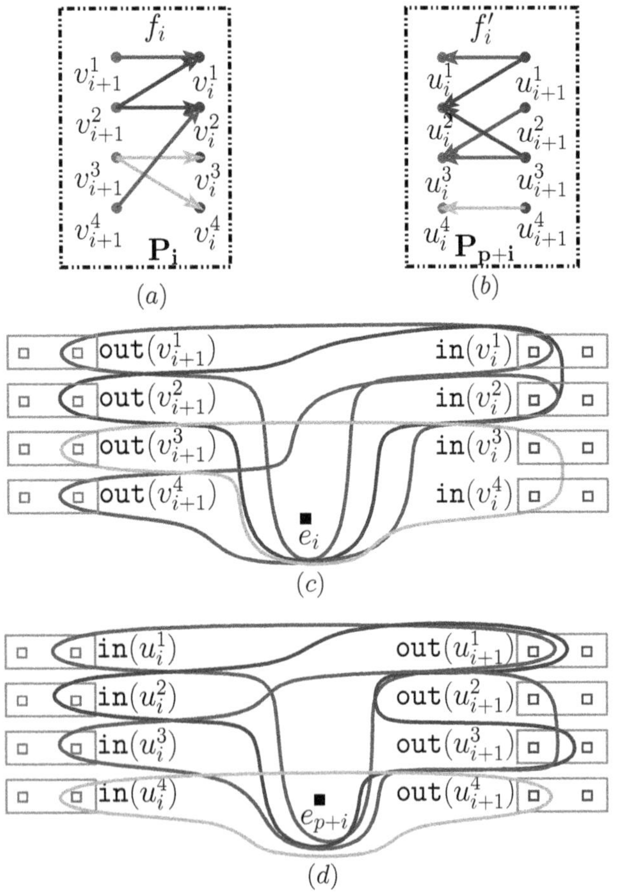

Figure 5.2: The gadgets used in the reduction of the communication Intersection Set Chasing problem to the communication Set Cover problem. (a) and (c) shows the construction of the gadget for players 1 to p and (c) and (d) shows the construction of the gadget for players $p+1$ to $2p$.

Theorem 5.4. *Any $(1/2\delta - 1)$ passes streaming algorithm that solves the* Set Cover(U, $\mathcal{F}$) *optimally with constant probability of error requires $\widetilde{\Omega}(mn^{\delta})$ memory space where $\delta \geq \frac{\log\log n}{\log n}$ and $m = O(n)$.*

Consider an instance ISC of the communication Intersection Set Chasing(n, p). We construct an instance of the communication Set Cover(U, $\mathcal{F}$, $2p$) problem such that solving Set Cover(U, $\mathcal{F}$) optimally determines whether the output of ISC is 1 or not.

The instance ISC consists of $2p$ players. Each player $1, \cdots, p$ has a function $f_i : [n] \to 2^{[n]}$ and each player $p+1, \cdots, 2p$ has a function $f'_i : [n] \to 2^{[n]}$ (see Figure 5.1). In ISC, each function f_i is shown by a set of vertices $v_i^1, \cdots, v_i^n$ and $v_{i+1}^1, \cdots, v_{i+1}^n$ such that there is a directed edge from v_{i+1}^j to v_i^ℓ iff $\ell \in f_i(j)$. Similarly, each function f'_i is denoted by a set of vertices $u_i^1, \cdots, u_i^n$ and $u_{i+1}^1, \cdots, u_{i+1}^n$ such that there is a directed edge from u_{i+1}^j to u_i^ℓ iff $\ell \in f'_i(j)$ (see Figure 5.2(a) and Figure 5.2(b)).

In the corresponding communication Set Cover instance of ISC, we add two elements $\texttt{in}(v_i^j)$ and $\texttt{out}(v_i^j)$ per each vertex v_i^j where $i \leq p+1, j \leq n$. We also add two elements $\texttt{in}(u_i^j)$ and $\texttt{out}(u_i^j)$ per each vertex u_i^j where $i \leq p+1, j \leq n$. In addition to these elements, for each player i, we add an element e_i (see Figure 5.2(c) and Figure 5.2(d)).

Next, we define a collection of sets in the corresponding Set Cover instance of ISC. For each player P_i, where $1 \leq i \leq p$, we add a single set S_i^j containing $\texttt{out}(v_{i+1}^j)$ and $\texttt{in}(v_i^\ell)$ for all out-going edges (v_{i+1}^j, v_i^ℓ). Moreover, all S_i^j sets contain the element e_i. Next, for each vertex v_i^j we add a set R_i^j that contains the two corresponding elements of v_i^j, $\texttt{in}(v_i^j)$ and $\texttt{out}(v_i^j)$. In Figure 5.2(c), the red rectangles denote R-type sets and the curves denote S-type sets for the first half of the players.

Similarly to the sets corresponding to players 1 to p, for each player P_{p+i} where $1 \leq i \leq p$, we add a set S_{p+i}^j containing $\texttt{in}(u_i^j)$ and $\texttt{out}(u_{i+1}^\ell)$ for all in-coming edges (u_{i+1}^ℓ, u_i^j) of u_i^j (denoting $f_i'^{-1}(j)$). The set S_{p+i}^j contains the element e_{p+i} too. Next, for each vertex u_i^j we add a set T_{p+i}^j that contains the two corresponding elements of u_i^j, $\texttt{in}(u_i^j)$ and $\texttt{out}(u_i^j)$. In Figure 5.2(d), the red rectangles denote T-type sets and the curves denote S-type sets for the second half of the players.

At the end, we merge v_1^is and u_1^is as shown in Figure 5.3. After merging the corresponding sets of v_1^js $(R_1^1, \cdots, R_1^n)$ and the corresponding sets of u_1^js $(T_1^1, \cdots, T_1^n)$, we call the merged sets $T_1^1, \cdots, T_1^n$.

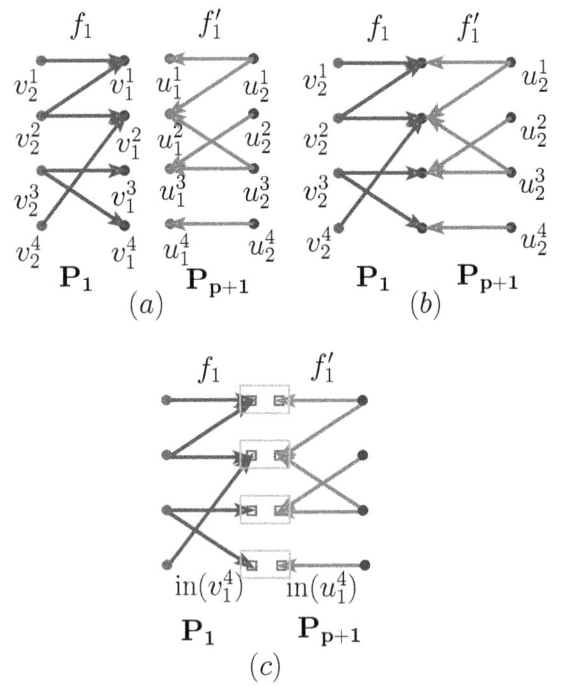

Figure 5.3: In (b) two Set Chasing instances merge in their first set of vertices and (c) shows the corresponding gadgets of these merged vertices in the communication Set Cover.

The main claim is that if the solution of ISC is 1 then the size of an optimal solution of its corresponding Set Cover instance SC is $(2p+1)n+1$; otherwise, it is $(2p+1)n+2$.

Lemma 5.5. *The size of any feasible solution of* SC *is at least $(2p+1)n+1$.*

Proof. For each player i $(1 \leq i \leq p)$, since $\texttt{out}(v_{i+1}^j)$s are only covered by R_{i+1}^j and S_i^j, at least n sets are required to cover $\texttt{out}(v_{i+1}^1), \cdots, \texttt{out}(v_{i+1}^n)$. Moreover for player P_p,

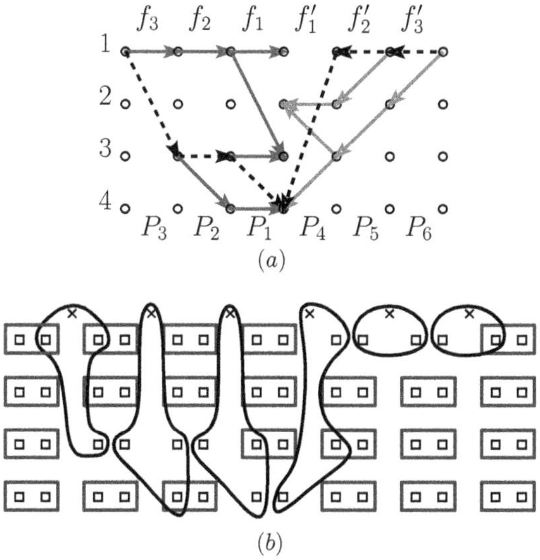

Figure 5.4: In (a), path Q is shown with black dashed arcs and (b) shows the corresponding cover of path Q.

since $\mathtt{in}(v^j_{p+1})$s are only covered by R^j_{p+1} and e_p is only covered by S^1_p, all $n+1$ sets $R^1_{p+1}, \cdots, R^n_{p+1}, S^1_p$ must be selected in any feasible solution of SC.

Similarly for each player $p+i$ $(1 \le i \le p)$, since $\mathrm{in}(u^j_i)$s are only covered by T^j_i and S^j_{p+i}, at least n sets are required to cover $\mathtt{in}(u^1_i), \cdots, \mathtt{in}(u^n_i)$. Moreover, considering $u^1_{p+1}, \cdots, u^n_{p+1}$, since $\mathtt{in}(u^j_{p+1})$ is only covered by T^j_{p+1}, all n sets $T^1_{p+1}, \cdots, T^n_{p+1}$ must be selected in any feasible solution of SC.

All together, at least $(2p+1)n+1$ sets should be selected in any feasible solution of SC.

Lemma 5.6. *Suppose that the solution of* ISC *is* 1. *Then the size of an optimal solution of its corresponding* Set Cover *instance is exactly* $(2p+1)n+1$.

PROOF. By Lemma 5.5, the size of an optimal solution of S is at least $(2p+1)n+1$. Here we prove that $(2p+1)n+1$ sets suffice when the solution of ISC is 1. Let $Q = v^1_{p+1}, v^{j_p}_p, \ldots, v^{j_2}_2, v^{j_1}_1, u^{\ell_1}_1, u^{\ell_2}_2, \ldots, u^{\ell_p}_p, u^1_{p+1}$ be a path in ISC such that $j_1 = \ell_1$ (since the solution of ISC is 1 such a path exists). The corresponding solution to Q can be constructed as follows (See Figure 5.4):

- Pick S^1_p and all R^j_{p+1}s $(n+1$ sets).
- For each $v^{j_i}_i$ in Q where $1 < i \le p$, pick the set $S^{j_i}_{i-1}$ in the solution. Moreover, for each such i pick all sets R^j_i where $j \ne j_i$ $(n(p-1)$ sets).
- For $v^{j_1}_1$ (or $u^{\ell_1}_1$), pick the set $S^{j_1}_{p+1}$. Moreover, pick all sets T^j_1 where $j \ne j_1$ (n sets).
- For each $u^{\ell_i}_i$ in Q where $1 < i \le p$, pick the set $S^{\ell_i}_{p+i}$ in the solution. Moreover, for each such i pick all sets T^ℓ_i where $\ell \ne \ell_i$ $(n(p-1)$ sets).
- Pick all T^j_{p+1}s (n sets).

It is straightforward to see that the solution constructed above is a feasible solution.

Lemma 5.7. *Suppose that the size of an optimal solution of the corresponding* Set Cover *instance of* ISC, SC, *is* $(2p+1)n+1$. *Then the solution of* ISC *is* 1.

PROOF. As we proved earlier in Lemma 5.5, any feasible solution of SC picks $R^1_{p+1}, \cdots, R^n_{p+1}, S^1_p$ and $T^1_{p+1}, \cdots, T^n_{p+1}$. Moreover, we proved that for each $1 \le i < p$, at least n sets should be selected from $R^1_{i+1}, \cdots, R^n_{i+1}, S^1_i, \cdots, S^n_i$. Similarly, for each $1 \le i \le p$, at least n sets should be selected from $T^1_i, \cdots, T^n_i, S^1_{p+i}, \cdots, S^n_{p+1}$. Thus if a feasible solution of SC, OPT, is of size $(2p+1)n+1$, it has exactly n sets from each specified group.

Next we consider the first half of the players and second half of the players separately. Consider i such that $1 \le i < p$. Let $S^{j_1}_i, \cdots, S^{j_k}_i$ be the sets picked in the optimal solution (because of e_i there should be at least one set of form S^j_i in OPT). Since each $\mathtt{out}(v^j_{i+1})$ is only covered by S^j_i and R^j_{i+1}, for all $j \notin \{j_1, \ldots, j_k\}$, R^j_{i+1} should be selected in OPT. Moreover, for all $j \in \{j_1, \cdots, j_k\}$, R^j_{i+1} should not be contained in OPT (otherwise the size of OPT would be larger than $(2p+1)n+1$). Consider $j \in \{j_1, \ldots, j_k\}$. Since R^j_{i+1} is not in OPT, there should be a set S^ℓ_{i+1} selected in OPT such that $\mathtt{in}(v^j_{i+1})$ is contained in S^ℓ_{i+1}. Thus by considering S_is in a decreasing order and using induction, if S^j_i is in OPT then v^j_{i+1} is reachable form v^1_{p+1}.

Next consider a set S^j_{p+i} that is selected in OPT $(1 \le i \le p)$. By similar argument, T^j_i is not in OPT and there exists a set S^ℓ_{p+i-1} (or S^ℓ_1 if $i = 1$) in OPT such that $\mathtt{out}(u^j_i)$ is contained in S^ℓ_{p+i-1}. Let $u^{\ell_1}_{i+1}, \cdots, u^{\ell_k}_{i+1}$ be the set of vertices whose corresponding $\mathtt{out}$ elements are in S^j_{p+i}. Then by induction, there exists an index r such that v^r_1 is reachable from v^1_{p+1} and u^r_1 is also reachable from all $u^{\ell_1}_{i+1}, \cdots, u^{\ell_k}_{i+1}$. Moreover, the way we constructed the instance SC guarantees that all sets $S^1_{2p}, \cdots, S^n_{2p}$ contains $\mathtt{out}(u^1_{p+1})$. Hence if the size of an optimal solution of SC is $(2p+1)n+1$ then the solution of ISC is 1.

Corollary 5.8. Intersection Set Chasing(n,p) *returns* 1 *iff the size of optimal solution of its corresponding* Set Cover *instance (as described here) is* $(2p+1)n+1$.

Observation 5.9. *Any streaming algorithm for* Set Cover, $\mathcal{I}$, *that in* ℓ *passes solves the problem optimally with a probability of error* $\mathtt{err}$ *and consumes* s *memory space, solves the corresponding communication* Set Cover *problem in* ℓ *rounds using* $O(s\ell^2)$ *bits of communication with probability error* $\mathtt{err}$.

PROOF. Starting from player P_1, each player runs $\mathcal{I}$ over its input sets and once P_i is done with its input, she sends the working memory of $\mathcal{I}$ publicly to other players. Then next player starts the same routine using the state of the working memory received from the previous player. Since $\mathcal{I}$ solves the Set Cover instance optimally after ℓ passes using $O(s)$ space with probability error $\mathtt{err}$, applying $\mathcal{I}$ as a black box we can solve P in ℓ rounds using $O(s\ell^2)$ bits of communication with probability error $\mathtt{err}$.

Proof of Theorem 5.4: By Observation 5.9, any ℓ-round $O(s)$-space algorithm that solves streaming Set Cover$(\mathsf{U}, \mathcal{F})$ optimally can be used to solve communication Set Cover$(\mathsf{U}, \mathcal{F}, p)$ problem in ℓ rounds using $O(s\ell^2)$ bits of communication. Moreover, by Corollary 5.8, we can decide the solution of the communication Intersection Set Chasing(n,p) by solving its corresponding communication Set Cover problem. Note that while working with the corresponding Set Cover instance of Intersection Set Chasing(n,p), all players know the collection of elements U and each player can construct its collection of sets $\mathcal{F}_i$ using f_i (or f_i').

However, by a result of [21], we know that any protocol that solves the communication Intersection Set Chasing(n,p) problem with probability of error less than $1/10$, requires $\Omega(\frac{n^{1+1/(2p)}}{p^{16}\log^{3/2}n})$ bits of communication. Since in the corresponding Set Cover instance of the communication Intersection Set Chasing(n,p), $|\mathsf{U}| = (2p+1)\times 2n + 2p = O(np)$ and $|\mathcal{F}| \leq (2p+1)n + 2pn = O(np)$, any $(p-1)$-pass streaming algorithm that solves the Set Cover problem optimally with a probability of error at most $1/10$, requires $\Omega(\frac{n^{1+1/(2p)}}{p^{18}\log^{3/2}n})$ bits of communication. Then using Observation 5.9, since $\delta \geq \frac{\log\log n}{\log n}$, any $(\frac{1}{2\delta}-1)$-pass streaming algorithmof Set Cover that finds an optimal solution with error probability less than $1/10$, requires $\widetilde{\Omega}(|\mathcal{F}|\cdot|\mathsf{U}|^{\delta})$ space. ■

6. LOWER BOUNDFOR SPARSE SET COVER IN MULTIPLE PASSES

In this part we give a stronger lower bound for the instances of the streaming Set Cover problem with sparse input sets. An instance of the Set Cover problem is s-Sparse Set Cover, if for each set $\mathsf{r} \in \mathcal{F}$ we have $|\mathsf{r}| \leq s$. We can us the same reduction approach described earlier in Section 5 to show that any $(1/2\delta - 1)$-pass streaming algorithm for s-Sparse Set Cover requires $\Omega(|\mathcal{F}|s)$ memory space if $s < |\mathsf{U}|^{\delta}$ and $|\mathcal{F}| = O(|\mathsf{U}|)$. To prove this, we need to explain more details of the approach of [21] on the lower bound of the communication Intersection Set Chasing problem. They first obtained a lower bound for Equal Pointer Chasing(n,p) problem in which two instances of the communication Pointer Chasing(n,p) are given and the goal is to decide whether these two instances point to a same value or not; $f_p(\cdots f_1(1)\cdots) = f_p'(\cdots f_1'(1)\cdots)$.

Definition 6.1 (r-non-injective functions). A function $f:[n]\to[n]$ is called *r-non-injective* if there exists $A\subseteq[n]$ of size at least r and $b\in[n]$ such that for all $a\in A$, $f(a)=b$.

Definition 6.2 (Pointer Chasing Problem). Pointer Chasing(n,p) is a $(p,p-1)$ communication problem in which the player i has a function $f_i:[n]\to[n]$ and the goal is to compute $f_1(f_2(\cdots f_p(1)\cdots))$.

Definition 6.3 (Equal Limited Pointer Chasing Problem). The communication Equal Pointer Chasing(n,p) is a $(2p,p-1)$ communication problem in which the first p players have an instance of the Pointer Chasing(n,p) problem and the other p players have another instance of the Pointer Chasing(n,p) problem. The output of the Equal Pointer Chasing(n,p) is 1 if the solutions of the two instances of Pointer Chasing(n,p) have the same value and 0 otherwise. Furthermore in Equal Limited Pointer Chasing(n,p,r), if there exists r-non-injective function f_i, then the output is 1. Otherwise, the output is the same as the value in Equal Pointer Chasing(n,p).

For a boolean communication problem P, OR_t(P) is defined to be OR of t instances of P and the output of OR_t(P) is `true` iff the output of any of the t instances is `true`. Using a direct sum argument, [21] showed that the communication complexity of OR_t(Equal Limited Pointer Chasing(n,p,r)) is t times the communication complexity of Equal Limited Pointer Chasing(n,p,r).

Lemma 6.4 ([21]). *Let n, p, t and r be positive integers such that $n\geq 5p$, $t\leq\frac{n}{4}$ and $r=O(\log n)$. Then the amount of bits of communication to solve* OR_t(Equal Limited Pointer Chasing(n,p,r)) *with error probability less than $1/3$ is $\Omega(\frac{tn}{p^{16}\log n}) - O(pt^2)$.*

Lemma 6.5 ([21]). *Let n, p, t and r be positive integers such that $t^{2p}r^{p-1} < n/10$. Then if there is a protocol that solves* Intersection Set Chasing(n,p) *with probability of error less than $1/10$ using C bits of communication, there is a protocol that solves* OR_t(Equal Limited Pointer Chasing(n,p,r)) *with probability of error at most $2/10$ using $C+2p$ bits of communication.*

Consider an instance of OR_t(Equal Limited Pointer Chasing (n,p,r)) in which $t\leq n^{\delta}, r=\log(n), p=\frac{1}{2\delta}-1$ where $\frac{1}{\delta}=o(\log n)$. By Lemma 6.4, the required amount of bits of communication to solve the instance with constant success probability is $\widetilde{\Omega}(tn)$. Then,applying Lemma 6.5, to solve the corresponding Intersection Set Chasing, $\widetilde{\Omega}(tn)$ bits of communication is required.

In the reduction from OR_t(Equal Limited Pointer Chasing (n,p,r)) to Intersection Set Chasing(n,p) (proof of Lemma 6.5), the r-non-injective property is preserved. In other words, in the corresponding Intersection Set Chasing instance each player's functions $f_i:[n]\to 2^{[n]}$ is union of t r-non-injective functions $f_i(a) := f_{i,1}(a)\cup\cdots\cup f_{i,t}(a)$[5]. Given that none of the $f_{i,j}$ functions is r-non-injective, the corresponding Set Cover instance will have sets of size at most rt (S-type sets are of size at most t for $1\leq i\leq p$ and of size at most rt for $p+1\leq i\leq 2p$). Since $r=O(\log n)$, the corresponding Set Cover instance is $\widetilde{O}(t)$-sparse. As we showed earlier in the reduction from Intersection Set Chasing to Set Cover, the number of elements (and sets) in the corresponding Set Cover instance is $O(np)$. Thus we have the following result for s-Sparse Set Cover problem.

Theorem 6.6. *For $s\leq|\mathsf{U}|^{\delta}$, any streaming algorithm that solves s-*Sparse Set Cover$(\mathsf{U},\mathcal{F})$ *optimally with probability of error less than $1/10$ in $(\frac{1}{2\delta}-1)$ passes requires $\widetilde{\Omega}(|\mathcal{F}|s)$ memory space for $|\mathcal{F}|=O(|\mathsf{U}|)$.*

Acknowledgment. Work on this paper by SHP was partially supported by NSF AF awards CCF-1421231, and CCF-1217462. Other authors were supported by NSF, Simons Foundation and MADALGO — Center for Massive Data Algorithmics — a Center of the Danish National Research Foundation.

[5]The Intersection Set Chasing instance is obtained by overlaying the t instances of Equal Pointer Chasing(n,p,r). To be more precise, the function of player i in instance j is $\pi_{i,j}\circ f_{i,j}\circ\pi_{i+1,j}^{-1}$ (π are randomly chosen permutation functions) and then stack the functions on top of each other.

7. REFERENCES

[1] P. K. Agarwal and J. Pan. Near-linear algorithms for geometric hitting sets and set covers. In *Proc. 30th Annu. Sympos. Comput. Geom.* (SoCG), pages 271–279, 2014.

[2] N. Alon, D. Moshkovitz, and S. Safra. Algorithmic construction of sets for k-restrictions. *ACM Trans. Algo.*, 2(2):153–177, 2006.

[3] B. Aronov, E. Ezra, and M. Sharir. Small-size ε-nets for axis-parallel rectangles and boxes. *SIAM J. Comput.*, 39(7):3248–3282, 2010.

[4] S. Assadi, S. Khanna, and Y. Li. Tight bounds for single-pass streaming complexity of the set cover problem. In *Proc. 48th Annu. ACM Sympos. Theory Comput.* (STOC), 2016.

[5] Z. Bar-Yossef, T. S. Jayram, R. Kumar, and D. Sivakumar. An information statistics approach to data stream and communication complexity. *J. Comput. Sys. Sci.*, 68(4):702–732, 2004.

[6] A. Chakrabarti and A. Wirth. Incidence geometries and the pass complexity of semi-streaming set cover. In *Proc. 27th ACM-SIAM Sympos. Discrete Algs.* (SODA), pages 1365–1373, 2016.

[7] F. Chierichetti, R. Kumar, and A. Tomkins. Max-cover in map-reduce. In *Proc. 19th Int. Conf. World Wide Web* (WWW), pages 231–240, 2010.

[8] K. L. Clarkson and P. W. Shor. Applications of random sampling in computational geometry, II. *Discrete Comput. Geom.*, 4:387–421, 1989.

[9] K. L. Clarkson and K. Varadarajan. Improved approximation algorithms for geometric set cover. *Discrete Comput. Geom.*, 37(1):43–58, 2007.

[10] G. Cormode, H. J. Karloff, and A. Wirth. Set cover algorithms for very large datasets. In *Proc. 19th ACM Conf. Info. Know. Manag.* (CIKM), pages 479–488, 2010.

[11] E. D. Demaine, P. Indyk, S. Mahabadi, and A. Vakilian. On streaming and communication complexity of the set cover problem. In *Proc. 28th Int. Symp. Dist. Comp.* (DISC), volume 8784 of *Lect. Notes in Comp. Sci.*, pages 484–498, 2014.

[12] I. Dinur and D. Steurer. Analytical approach to parallel repetition. pages 624–633. ACM, 2014.

[13] Y. Emek and A. Rosén. Semi-streaming set cover. In *Proc. 41st Int. Colloq. Automata Lang. Prog.* (ICALP), volume 8572 of *Lect. Notes in Comp. Sci.*, pages 453–464, 2014.

[14] A. Ene, S. Har-Peled, and B. Raichel. Geometric packing under non-uniform constraints. In *Proc. 28th Annu. Sympos. Comput. Geom.* (SoCG), pages 11–20, 2012.

[15] T. Feder and D. H. Greene. Optimal algorithms for approximate clustering. In *Proc. 20th Annu. ACM Sympos. Theory Comput.* (STOC), pages 434–444, 1988.

[16] U. Feige. A threshold of ln n for approximating set cover. *Journal of the ACM (JACM)*, 45(4):634–652, 1998.

[17] R. J. Fowler, M. S. Paterson, and S. L. Tanimoto. Optimal packing and covering in the plane are NP-complete. *Inform. Process. Lett.*, 12(3):133–137, 1981.

[18] T. Grossman and A. Wool. Computational experience with approximation algorithms for the set covering problem. *Euro. J. Oper. Res.*, 101(1):81–92, 1997.

[19] S. Guha and A. McGregor. Lower bounds for quantile estimation in random-order and multi-pass streaming. In *Proc. 34th Int. Colloq. Automata Lang. Prog.* (ICALP), volume 4596 of *Lect. Notes in Comp. Sci.*, pages 704–715, 2007.

[20] S. Guha and A. McGregor. Tight lower bounds for multi-pass stream computation via pass elimination. In *Proc. 35th Int. Colloq. Automata Lang. Prog.* (ICALP), volume 5125 of *Lect. Notes in Comp. Sci.*, pages 760–772, 2008.

[21] V. Guruswami and K. Onak. Superlinear lower bounds for multipass graph processing. In *Proc. 28th Conf. Comput. Complexity* (CCC), pages 287–298, 2013.

[22] S. Har-Peled and K. Quanrud. Approximation algorithms for polynomial-expansion and low-density graphs. In *Proc. 23nd Annu. European Sympos. Algorithms* (ESA), volume 9294 of *Lect. Notes in Comp. Sci.*, pages 717–728, 2015.

[23] S. Har-Peled and M. Sharir. Relative (p, ε)-approximations in geometry. *Discrete Comput. Geom.*, 45(3):462–496, 2011.

[24] B. Kalyanasundaram and G. Schintger. The probabilistic communication complexity of set intersection. *SIAM J. Discrete Math.*, 5(4):545–557, 1992.

[25] R. Kumar, B. Moseley, S. Vassilvitskii, and A. Vattani. Fast greedy algorithms in MapReduce and streaming. In *Proc. 25th ACM Sympos. Parallel Alg. Arch.* (SPAA), pages 1–10, 2013.

[26] D. Moshkovitz. The projection games conjecture and the NP-hardness of $\ln n$-approximating set-cover. In *Approximation, Randomization, and Combinatorial Optimization. Algorithms and Techniques*, pages 276–287. Springer, 2012.

[27] N. H. Mustafa, R. Raman, and S. Ray. Settling the apx-hardness status for geometric set cover. In *Proc. 55th Annu. IEEE Sympos. Found. Comput. Sci.* (FOCS), pages 541–550, 2014.

[28] N. Nisan. The communication complexity of approximate set packing and covering. In *Proc. 29th Int. Colloq. Automata Lang. Prog.* (ICALP), pages 868–875, 2002.

[29] R. Raz and S. Safra. A sub-constant error-probability low-degree test, and a sub-constant error-probability PCP characterization of NP. In *Proc. 29th Annu. ACM Sympos. Theory Comput.* (STOC), pages 475–484, 1997.

[30] A. A. Razborov. On the distributional complexity of disjointness. *Theo. Comp. Sci.*, 106(2):385–390, 1992.

[31] B. Saha and L. Getoor. On maximum coverage in the streaming model & application to multi-topic blog-watch. In *Proc. SIAM Int. Conf. Data Mining* (SDM), pages 697–708, 2009.

An Optimal Algorithm for ℓ_1-Heavy Hitters in Insertion Streams and Related Problems

Arnab Bhattacharyya
Indian Institute of Science, Bangalore
arnabb@csa.iisc.ernet.in

Palash Dey
Indian Institute of Science, Bangalore
palash@csa.iisc.ernet.in

David P. Woodruff
IBM Research, Almaden
dpwoodru@us.ibm.com

ABSTRACT

We give the first optimal bounds for returning the ℓ_1-heavy hitters in a data stream of insertions, together with their approximate frequencies, closing a long line of work on this problem. For a stream of m items in $\{1, 2, \ldots, n\}$ and parameters $0 < \varepsilon < \varphi \leqslant 1$, let f_i denote the frequency of item i, i.e., the number of times item i occurs in the stream. With arbitrarily large constant probability, our algorithm returns all items i for which $f_i \geqslant \varphi m$, returns no items j for which $f_j \leqslant (\varphi - \varepsilon)m$, and returns approximations $\tilde{f}_i$ with $|\tilde{f}_i - f_i| \leqslant \varepsilon m$ for each item i that it returns. Our algorithm uses $O(\varepsilon^{-1} \log \varphi^{-1} + \varphi^{-1} \log n + \log \log m)$ bits of space, processes each stream update in $O(1)$ worst-case time, and can report its output in time linear in the output size. We also prove a lower bound, which implies that our algorithm is optimal up to a constant factor in its space complexity. A modification of our algorithm can be used to estimate the maximum frequency up to an additive εm error in the above amount of space, resolving Question 3 in the IITK 2006 Workshop on Algorithms for Data Streams for the case of ℓ_1-heavy hitters. We also introduce several variants of the heavy hitters and maximum frequency problems, inspired by rank aggregation and voting schemes, and show how our techniques can be applied in such settings. Unlike the traditional heavy hitters problem, some of these variants look at comparisons between items rather than numerical values to determine the frequency of an item.

Keywords

Heavy hitters, frequent items, data streams, algorithms

1. INTRODUCTION

The data stream model has emerged as a standard model for processing massive data sets. Because of the sheer size of the data, traditional algorithms are no longer feasible, e.g., it may be hard or impossible to store the entire input, and algorithms need to run in linear or even sublinear time. Such algorithms typically need to be both randomized and approximate. Moreover, the data may not physically reside on any device, e.g., if it is internet traffic, and so if the data is not stored by the algorithm, it may be impossible to recover it. Hence, many algorithms must work given only a single pass over the data. Applications of data streams include data warehousing [6, 28, 31, 34], network measurements [3, 20, 23, 27], sensor networks [8, 65], and compressed sensing [12, 30]. We refer the reader to recent surveys on the data stream model [18, 59, 60].

One of the oldest and most fundamental problems in the area of data streams is the problem of finding the ℓ_1-heavy hitters (or simply, "heavy hitters"), also known as the top-k, most popular items, frequent items, elephants, or iceberg queries. Such algorithms can be used as subroutines in network flow identification at IP routers [27], association rules and frequent itemsets [2, 32, 35, 64, 68], iceberg queries and iceberg datacubes [6, 28, 31]. The survey [19] presents an overview of the state-of-the-art for this problem, from both theoretical and practical standpoints.

We now formally define the heavy hitters problem that we focus on in this paper:

Definition 1. **((ε, φ)-Heavy Hitters Problem)** *In the (ε, φ)-Heavy Hitters Problem, we are given parameters $0 < \varepsilon < \varphi \leqslant 1$ and a stream $a_1, \ldots, a_m$ of items $a_j \in \{1, 2, \ldots, n\}$. Let f_i denote the number of occurrences of item i, i.e., its frequency. The algorithm should make one pass over the stream and at the end of the stream output a set $S \subseteq \{1, 2, \ldots, n\}$ for which if $f_i \geqslant \varphi m$, then $i \in S$, while if $f_i \leqslant (\varphi - \varepsilon)m$, then $i \notin S$. Further, for each item $i \in S$, the algorithm should output an estimate $\tilde{f}_i$ of the frequency f_i which satisfies $|f_i - \tilde{f}_i| \leqslant \varepsilon m$.*

Note that other natural definitions of heavy hitters are possible and sometimes used. For example, *ℓ_2-heavy hitters* are those items i for which $f_i^2 \geqslant \varphi^2 \sum_{j=1}^n f_j^2$, and more generally, *$\ell_p$-heavy hitters* are those items i for which $f_i^p \geqslant \varphi^p \sum_{j=1}^n f_j^p$. It is in this sense that Definition 1 corresponds to ℓ_1-heavy hitters.

We are interested in algorithms which use as little space in bits as possible to solve the **(ε, φ)-Heavy Hitters Problem.** Further, we are also interested in minimizing the *update time* and *reporting time* of such algorithms. Here, the update time is defined to be the time the algorithm needs to update its data structure when processing a stream insertion. The reporting time is the time the algorithm needs to report the answer after having processed the stream. We allow the algorithm to be randomized and to succeed with probability at least $1 - \delta$ for $0 < \delta < 1$. We do not make

PODS'16, June 26-July 01, 2016, San Francisco, CA, USA

DOI: http://dx.doi.org/10.1145/2902251.2902284

any assumption on the ordering of the stream $a_1, \ldots, a_m$. This is desirable as often in applications one cannot assume a best-case or even a random order. We are also interested in the case when the length m of the stream is not known in advance, and give algorithms in this more general setting.

The first algorithm for the (ε, φ)-**Heavy Hitters Problem** was given by Misra and Gries [54], who achieved $O(\varepsilon^{-1}(\log n + \log m))$ bits of space for any $\varphi > \varepsilon$. This algorithm was rediscovered by Demaine et al. [23], and again by Karp et al. [38]. Other than these algorithms, which are deterministic, there are also a number of randomized algorithms, such as the CountSketch [16], Count-Min sketch [21], sticky sampling [48], lossy counting [48], space-saving [52], sample and hold [27], multi-stage bloom filters [15], and sketch-guided sampling [41]. Berinde et al. [5] show that using $O(k\varepsilon^{-1}\log(mn))$ bits of space, one can achieve the stronger guarantee of reporting, for each item $i \in S$, $\tilde{f}_i$ with $|\tilde{f}_i - f_i| \leqslant \varepsilon/k F_1^{res(k)}$, where $F_1^{res(k)} < m$ denotes the sum of frequencies of items in $\{1, 2, \ldots, n\}$ excluding the frequencies of the k most frequent items.

We emphasize that prior to our work the best known algorithms for the (ε, φ)-**Heavy Hitters Problem** used $O(\varepsilon^{-1}(\log n + \log m))$ bits of space. Two previous lower bounds were known. The first is a lower bound of $\log(\binom{n}{1/\varphi}) = \Omega(\varphi^{-1}\log(\varphi n))$ bits, which comes from the fact that the output set S can contain φ^{-1} items and it takes this many bits to encode them. The second lower bound is $\Omega(\varepsilon^{-1})$ which follows from a folklore reduction from the randomized communication complexity of the Index problem. In this problem, there are two players, Alice and Bob. Alice has a bit string x of length $(2\varepsilon)^{-1}$, while Bob has an index i. Alice creates a stream of length $(2\varepsilon)^{-1}$ consisting of one copy of each j for which $x_j = 1$ and copies of a dummy item to fill the rest of the stream. She runs the heavy hitters streaming algorithm on her stream and sends the state of the algorithm to Bob. Bob appends $(2\varepsilon)^{-1}$ copies of the item i to the stream and continues the execution. For $\varphi = 1/2$, it holds that $i \in S$. Moreover, f_i differs by an additive εm factor depending on whether $x_i = 1$ or $x_i = 0$. Therefore by the randomized communication complexity of the Index problem [40], the $(\varepsilon, 1/2)$-heavy hitters problem requires $\Omega(\varepsilon^{-1})$ bits of space. Although this proof was for $\varphi = 1/2$, no better lower bound is known for any $\varphi > \varepsilon$.

So, while the upper bound for the (ε, φ)-**Heavy Hitters Problem** is $O(\varepsilon^{-1}(\log n + \log m))$ bits, the best known lower bound is only $\Omega(\varphi^{-1}\log n + \varepsilon^{-1})$ bits. We note that we assume $\log(\varphi n) = \Omega(\log n)$, that is, that $\varphi \geqslant 1/n^{1-\Omega(1)}$. For constant φ, and $\log n \approx \varepsilon^{-1}$, this represents a nearly quadratic gap in upper and lower bounds. Given the limited resources of devices which typically run heavy hitters algorithms, such as internet routers, this quadratic gap can be critical in applications.

A problem related to the (ε, φ)-**Heavy Hitters Problem** is estimating the *maximum frequency* in a data stream, also known as the ℓ_∞-norm. In the IITK 2006 Workshop on Algorithms for Data Streams, Open Question 3 asks for an algorithm to estimate the maximum frequency of any item up to an additive εm error using as little space as possible. The best known space bound is still $O(\varepsilon^{-1}\log n)$ bits, as stated in the original formulation of the question (note that the "m" in the question there corresponds to the "n" here). Note that, if one can find an item whose frequency is the largest, up to an additive εm error, then one can solve this problem. The latter problem is independently interesting and corresponds to finding approximate plurality election winners in voting streams [24]. We refer to this problem as the ε-**Maximum** problem.

Finally, we note that there are many other variants of the (ε, φ)-**Heavy Hitters Problem** that one can consider. One simple variant of the above is to output an item of frequency within εm of the *minimum frequency* of any item in the universe. Note that an item of frequency 0 is considered an item of minimum frequency in our definition (see Section 2). We refer to this as the ε-**Minimum** problem. This only makes sense for small universes, as otherwise outputting a random item typically works. This is useful when one wants to count the "number of dislikes", or in anomaly detection; see more motivation below. In other settings, one may not have numerical scores associated with the items, but rather, each stream update consists of a "ranking" or "total ordering" of all stream items. This may be the case in ranking aggregation on the web (see, e.g., [47, 51]) or in voting streams (see, e.g., [13, 17, 24, 73]). One may consider a variety of aggregation measures, such as the Borda score of an item i, which asks for the sum, over rankings, of the number of items $j \neq i$ for which i is ranked ahead of j in the ranking. Alternatively, one may consider the Maximin score of an item i, which asks for the minimum, over items $j \neq i$, of the number of rankings for which i is ranked ahead of j. For these aggregation measures, one may be interested in finding an item whose score is an approximate maximum. This is the analogue of the ε-**Maximum** problem above. Or, one may be interested in listing all items whose score is above a threshold, which is the analogue of the (ε, φ)-**Heavy Hitters Problem**.

We give more motivation of these variants of heavy hitters in this section below, and precise definitions in Section 2.

1.1 Our Contributions

Our results are summarized in Table 1. We note that independently of this work and nearly parallelly, there have been improvements to the space complexity of the ℓ_2-heavy hitters problem in insertion streams [10, 11] and to the time complexity of the ℓ_p-heavy hitters problem in turnstile[1] streams [43] for all $p \in (0, 2]$. These works use very different techniques. See also [72] for a survey of some recent new algorithms for heavy hitters.

Our first contribution is an optimal algorithm and lower bound for the (ε, φ)-**Heavy Hitters Problem**. Namely, we show that there is a randomized algorithm with constant probability of success which solves this problem using

$$O(\varepsilon^{-1}\log\varphi^{-1} + \varphi^{-1}\log n + \log\log m)$$

bits of space, and we prove a lower bound matching up to constant factors. In the unit-cost RAM model with $O(\log n)$ bit words, our algorithm has $O(1)$ update time and reporting time linear in the output size, under the standard assumptions that the length of the stream and universe size are at least $\text{poly}(\varepsilon^{-1}\log(1/\varphi))$. Furthermore, we can achieve nearly the optimal space complexity even when the length

[1]In a turnstile stream, updates modify an underlying n-dimensional vector x initialized at the zero vector; each update is of the form $x \leftarrow x + e_i$ or $x \leftarrow x - e_i$ where e_i is the i'th standard unit vector. In an insertion stream, only updates of the form $x \leftarrow x + e_i$ are allowed.

Problem	Space complexity	
	Upper bound	Lower bound
(ε,φ)-Heavy Hitters	$O\left(\varepsilon^{-1}\log\varphi^{-1}+\varphi^{-1}\log n+\log\log m\right)$ [Theorem 2 and 7]	$\Omega\left(\varepsilon^{-1}\log\varphi^{-1}+\varphi^{-1}\log n+\log\log m\right)$ [Theorem 9 and 14]
ε-Maximum and ℓ_∞-approximation	$O\left(\varepsilon^{-1}\log\varepsilon^{-1}+\log n+\log\log m\right)$ [Theorem 1 and 7]	$\Omega\left(\varepsilon^{-1}\log\varepsilon^{-1}+\log n+\log\log m\right)$ [Theorem 9 and 14]
ε-Minimum	$O\left(\varepsilon^{-1}\log\log\varepsilon^{-1}+\log\log m\right)$ [Theorem 4 and 8]	$\Omega\left(\varepsilon^{-1}+\log\log m\right)$ [Theorem 11 and 14]
ε-Borda	$O\left(n(\log\varepsilon^{-1}+\log n)+\log\log m\right)$ [Theorem 5 and 8]	$\Omega\left(n(\log\varepsilon^{-1}+\log n)+\log\log m\right)$ [Theorem 12 and 14]
ε-Maximin	$O\left(n\varepsilon^{-2}\log^2 n+\log\log m\right)$ [Theorem 6 and 8]	$\Omega\left(n(\varepsilon^{-2}+\log n)+\log\log m\right)$ [Theorem 13]

Table 1: The bounds hold for constant success probability algorithms and for n sufficiently large in terms of ε. For the (ε,φ)-Heavy Hitters problem and the ε-Maximum problem, we also achieve $O(1)$ update time and reporting time which is linear in the size of the output. The upper bound for ε-Borda (resp. ε-Maximin) is for returning every item's Borda score (resp. Maximin score) up to an additive εmn (resp. additive εm), while the lower bound for ε-Borda (resp. ε-Maximin) is for returning only the approximate Borda score (resp. Maximin score) of an approximate maximum.

m of the stream is *not known in advance*. Although the results of [5] achieve stronger error bounds in terms of the tail, which are useful for skewed streams, here we focus on the original formulation of the problem.

Next, we turn to the problem of estimating the maximum frequency in a data stream up to an additive εm. We give an algorithm using

$$O(\varepsilon^{-1}\log\varepsilon^{-1}+\log n+\log\log m)$$

bits of space, improving the previous best algorithms which required space at least $\Omega(\varepsilon^{-1}\log n)$ bits, and show that our bound is tight. As an example setting of parameters, if $\varepsilon^{-1}=\Theta(\log n)$ and $\log\log m=O(\log n)$, our space complexity is $O(\log n\log\log n)$ bits, improving the previous $\Omega(\log^2 n)$ bits of space algorithm. We also prove a lower bound showing our algorithm is optimal up to constant factors. This resolves Open Question 3 from the IITK 2006 Workshop on Algorithms for Data Streams in the case of insertion streams, for the case of "ℓ_1-heavy hitters". Our algorithm also returns the the item with the approximate maximum frequency, solving the ε-**Maximum** problem.

We then focus on a number of variants of these problems. We first give nearly tight bounds for finding an item whose frequency is within εm of the minimum possible frequency. While this can be solved using our new algorithm for the $(\varepsilon,\varepsilon)$-**Heavy Hitters Problem**, this would incur $\Omega(\varepsilon^{-1}\log\varepsilon^{-1}+\log\log m)$ bits of space, whereas we give an algorithm using only $O(\varepsilon^{-1}\log\log(\varepsilon^{-1})+\log\log m)$ bits of space. We also show a nearly matching $\Omega(\varepsilon^{-1}+\log\log m)$ bits of space lower bound. We note that for this problem, a dependence on n is not necessary since if the number of possible items is sufficiently large, then outputting the identity of a random item among the first say, $10\varepsilon^{-1}$ items, is a correct solution with large constant probability.

Finally, we study variants of heavy hitter problems that are ranking-based. In this setting, each stream update consists of a total ordering of the n universe items. For the ε-**Borda** problem, we give an algorithm using $O(n(\log\varepsilon^{-1}+\log\log n)+\log\log m)$ bits of space to report the Borda score of every item up to an additive εmn. We also show this is nearly optimal by proving an $\Omega(n\log\varepsilon^{-1}+\log\log m)$ bit lower bound for the problem, even in the case when one is only interested in outputting an item maximum Borda score up to an additive εmn. For the ε-**Maximin** problem, we give an algorithm using $O(n\varepsilon^{-2}\log^2 n+\log\log m)$ bits of space to report the maximin score of every item up to an additive εm, and prove an $\Omega(n\varepsilon^{-2}+\log\log m)$ bits of space lower bound even in the case when one is only interested in outputting the maximum maximin score up to an additive εm. This shows that finding heavy hitters with respect to the maximin score is significantly more expensive than with respect to the Borda score.

1.2 Motivations for Variants of Heavy Hitters

While the (ε,φ)-**Heavy Hitters** and ε-**Maximum** problem are very well-studied in the data stream literature, the other variants introduced are not. We provide additional motivation for them here.

For the ε-**Minimum** problem, in our formulation, an item with frequency zero, i.e., one that does not occur in the stream, is a valid solution to the problem. In certain scenarios, this might not make sense, e.g., if a stream containing only a small fraction of IP addresses. However, in other scenarios we argue this is a natural problem. For instance, consider an online portal where users register complaints about products. Here, minimum frequency items correspond to the "best" items. That is, such frequencies arise in the context of voting or more generally making a choice: in cases for which one does not have a strong preference for an item, but definitely does not like certain items, this problem applies, since the frequencies correspond to "number of dislikes".

The ε-**Minimum** problem may also be useful for anomaly detection. Suppose one has a known set of sensors broadcasting information and one observes the "From:" field in the broadcasted packets. Sensors which send a small number of packets may be down or defective, and an algorithm for the ε-**Minimum** problem could find such sensors.

Finding items with maximum and minimum frequencies in a stream correspond to finding winners under plurality and veto voting rules respectively in the context of voting[2] [9].

[2]In fact, the first work [56] to formally pose the heavy hitters problem couched it in the context of voting.

The streaming aspect of voting could be crucial in applications like online polling [39], recommender systems [1, 33, 63] where the voters are providing their votes in a streaming fashion and at every point in time, we would like to know the popular items. While in some elections, such as for political positions, the scale of the election may not be large enough to require a streaming algorithm, one key aspect of these latter voting-based problems is that they are rank-based which is useful when numerical scores are not available. Orderings naturally arise in several applications - for instance, if a website has multiple parts, the order in which a user visits the parts given by its clickstream defines a voting, and for data mining and recommendation purposes the website owner may be interested in aggregating the orderings across users. Motivated by this connection, we define similar problems for two other important voting rules, namely Borda and maximin. The Borda scoring method finds its applications in a wide range of areas of artificial intelligence, for example, machine learning [14, 36, 62, 70], image processing [46, 55], information retrieval [4, 45, 61], etc. The Maximin score is often used when the spread between the best and worst outcome is very large (see, e.g., p. 373 of [58]). The maximin scoring method also has been used frequently in machine learning [37, 71], human computation [49, 50], etc.

2. PRELIMINARIES

We denote the disjoint union of sets by $\sqcup$. We denote the set of all permutations of a set $\mathcal{U}$ by $\mathcal{L}(\mathcal{U})$. For a positive integer ℓ, we denote $\{1, \dots, \ell\}$ by $[\ell]$. In most places, we ignore floors and ceilings for the sake of notational simplicity.

2.1 Model of Input Data

The input data is an insertion-only stream of elements from some universe $\mathcal{U}$. In the context of voting, the input data is an insertion-only stream over the universe of all possible rankings (permutations).

2.2 Communication Complexity

We will use lower bounds on *communication complexity* of certain functions to prove space complexity lower bounds for our problems. The communication complexity of a function measures the number of bits that need to be exchanged between two players to compute a function whose input is split among those two players [74]. In a more restrictive *one-way communication model*, Alice, the first player, sends only one message to Bob, the second player, and Bob outputs the result. A protocol is a method that the players follow to compute certain functions of their input. Also the protocols can be randomized; in that case, the protocol needs to output correctly with probability at least $1 - \delta$, for $\delta \in (0, 1)$ (the probability is taken over the random coin tosses of the protocol). The randomized one-way communication complexity of a function f with error probability δ is denoted by $\mathcal{R}_\delta^{\text{1-way}}(f)$. [42] is a standard reference for communication complexity.

2.3 Model of Computation

Our model of computation is the unit-cost RAM model on words of size $O(\log n)$, capable of generating uniformly random words and of performing arithmetic operations in $\{+, -, \log_2\}$ in one unit of time. We note that this model of computation has been used before [25]. We store an integer C using a variable length array of [7] which allows us to read and update C in $O(1)$ time and $O(\log C)$ bits of space.

2.4 Universal Family of Hash Functions

Definition 2. *(Universal family of hash functions) A family of functions $\mathcal{H} = \{h | h : A \to B\}$ is called a* universal family of hash functions *if for all $a \neq b \in A$, $\Pr\{h(a) = h(b)\} = 1/|B|$, where h is picked uniformly at random from $\mathcal{H}$.*

We know that there exists a universal family of hash functions $\mathcal{H}$ from $[k]$ to $[\ell]$ for every positive integer ℓ and every prime k [44]. Moreover, $|\mathcal{H}|$, the size of $\mathcal{H}$, is $O(k^2)$.

2.5 Problem Definitions

We now formally define the problems we study here. Suppose we have $0 < \varepsilon < \varphi < 1$.

Definition 3. (ε, φ)-LIST HEAVY HITTERS
Given an insertion-only stream of length m over a universe $\mathcal{U}$ of size n, find all items in $\mathcal{U}$ with frequency more than φm, along with their frequencies up to an additive error of εm, and report no items with frequency less than $(\varphi - \varepsilon)m$.

Definition 4. ε-MAXIMUM
Given an insertion-only stream of length m over a universe $\mathcal{U}$ of size n, find the maximum frequency up to an additive error of εm.

Next we define the *minimum* problem for $0 < \varepsilon < 1$.

Definition 5. ε-MINIMUM
Given an insertion-only stream of length m over a universe $\mathcal{U}$ of size n, find the minimum frequency up to an additive error of εm.

Next we define related heavy hitters problems in the context of rank aggregation. The input is a stream of rankings (permutations) over an item set $\mathcal{U}$ for the problems below. The *Borda score* of an item i is the sum, over all rankings, of the number of items $j \neq i$ for which i is ranked ahead of j in the ranking.

Definition 6. (ε, φ)-LIST BORDA
Given an insertion-only stream over a universe $\mathcal{L}(\mathcal{U})$ where $|\mathcal{U}| = n$, find all items with Borda score more than φmn, along with their Borda score up to an additive error of εmn, and report no items with Borda score less than $(\varphi - \varepsilon)mn$.

Definition 7. ε-BORDA
Given an insertion-only stream over a universe $\mathcal{L}(\mathcal{U})$ where $|\mathcal{U}| = n$, find the maximum Borda score up to an additive error of εmn.

The *maximin score* of an item i is the minimum, over all items $j \neq i$, of the number of rankings for which i is ranked ahead of j.

Definition 8. (ε, φ)-LIST MAXIMIN
Given an insertion-only stream over a universe $\mathcal{L}(\mathcal{U})$ where $|\mathcal{U}| = n$, find all items with maximin score more than φm along with their maximin score up to an additive error of εm, and report no items with maximin score less than $(\varphi - \varepsilon)m$.

Definition 9. ε-MAXIMIN
Given an insertion-only stream over a universe $\mathcal{L}(\mathcal{U})$ where $|\mathcal{U}| = n$, find the maximum maximin score up to an additive error of εm.

Notice that the maximum possible Borda score of an item is $m(n-1) = \Theta(mn)$ and the maximum possible maximin score of an item is m. This justifies the approximation factors in Definition 6 to 9. We note that finding an item with maximum Borda score within additive εmn or maximum maximin score within additive εm corresponds to finding an approximate winner of an election (more precisely, what is known as an ε-winner) [24].

3. ALGORITHMS

In this section, we present our upper bound results. All omitted proofs are in Appendix B. Before describing specific algorithms, we record some claims for later use. Lemma 1 follows by checking whether we get all heads in $\log m$ tosses of a fair coin.

Lemma 1. *Suppose m is a power of two[3]. Then there is an algorithm $\mathcal{A}$ for choosing an item with probability $1/m$ that has space complexity of $O(\log\log m)$ bits and time complexity of $O(1)$ in the unit-cost RAM model.*

Our second claim is a standard result for universal families of hash functions.

Lemma 2. *For $S \subseteq A$, $\delta \in (0,1)$, and universal family of hash functions $\mathcal{H} = \{h | h : A \to [\lceil |S|^2/\delta \rceil]\}$:*

$$\Pr_{h \in_{unif} \mathcal{H}} [\exists i \neq j \in S, h(i) = h(j)] \leqslant \delta$$

Our third claim is folklore and also follows from the celebrated DKW inequality [26]. We provide a simple proof here that works for constant δ.

We assume δ is a constant throughout this paper. This constant can be made arbitrarily small by independent repetition (in general, the complexity grows by a multiplicative factor of $\log(1/\delta)$), finding the heavy items that occur in a large constant fraction of the repetitions, and using the median of their estimated frequencies.

Lemma 3. *Let f_i and $\hat{f}_i$ be the frequencies of an item i in a stream $\mathcal{S}$ and in a random sample $\mathcal{T}$ of size r from $\mathcal{S}$, respectively. Then for $r \geqslant 2\varepsilon^{-2}\log(2\delta^{-1})$, with probability $1-\delta$, for every universe item i simultaneously,*

$$\left| \frac{\hat{f}_i}{r} - \frac{f_i}{m} \right| \leqslant \varepsilon.$$

PROOF FOR CONSTANT δ. This follows by Chebyshev's inequality and a union bound. Indeed, consider a given $i \in [n]$ with frequency f_i and suppose we sample each of its occurrences pairwise-independently with probability r/m, for a parameter r. Then the expected number $\mathbf{E}[\hat{f}_i]$ of sampled occurrences is $f_i \cdot r/m$ and the variance $\mathbf{Var}[\hat{f}_i]$ is $f_i \cdot r/m(1-r/m) \leqslant f_i r/m$. Applying Chebyshev's inequality,

$$\Pr\left[\left|\hat{f}_i - \mathbf{E}[\hat{f}_i]\right| \geqslant \frac{r\varepsilon}{2}\right] \leqslant \frac{\mathbf{Var}[\hat{f}_i]}{(r\varepsilon/2)^2} \leqslant \frac{4 f_i r}{m r^2 \varepsilon^2}.$$

Setting $r = \frac{C}{\varepsilon^2}$ for a constant $C > 0$ makes this probability at most $\frac{4f_i}{Cm}$. By the union bound, if we sample each element in the stream independently with probability $\frac{r}{m}$, then the probability there exists an i for which $|\hat{f}_i - \mathbf{E}[\hat{f}_i]| \geqslant \frac{r\varepsilon}{2}$ is at most $\sum_{i=1}^{n} \frac{4f_i}{Cm} \leqslant \frac{4}{C}$, which for $C \geqslant 400$ is at most $\frac{1}{100}$, as desired. □

For now, assume that the length of the stream is known in advance; we show in Section 3.5 how to remove this assumption.

3.1 List Heavy Hitters

For the (ε, φ)-LIST HEAVY HITTERS problem, we present two algorithms. The first is slightly suboptimal, but simple conceptually and already constitutes a very large improvement in the space complexity over known algorithms. We expect that this algorithm could be useful in practice as well. The second algorithm is more complicated, building on ideas from the first algorithm, and achieves the optimal space complexity upto constant factors.

We note that both algorithms proceed by sampling $O(\varepsilon^{-2}\ln(1/\delta))$ stream items and updating a data structure as the stream progresses. In both cases, the time to update the data structure is bounded by $O(1/\varepsilon)$, and so, under the standard assumption that the length of the stream is at least $\text{poly}(\ln(1/\delta)\varepsilon)$, the time to perform this update can be spread out across the next $O(1/\varepsilon)$ stream updates, since with large probability there will be no items sampled among these next $O(1/\varepsilon)$ stream updates. Therefore, we achieve worst-case[4] update time of $O(1)$.

3.1.1 A simpler, near-optimal algorithm

Theorem 1. *Assume the stream length is known beforehand, and $\delta > 0$ is any constant. Then there is a randomized one-pass algorithm $\mathcal{A}$ for the (ε, φ)-LIST HEAVY HITTERS problem which succeeds with probability at least $1-\delta$ using $O\left(\varepsilon^{-1}\log 1/\varepsilon + (1/\varphi)\log n + \log\log m\right)$ bits of space. Moreover, $\mathcal{A}$ has an update time of $O(1)$ and reporting time linear in its output size.*

Overview. The overall idea is as follows. We sample $\ell = O(\varepsilon^{-2})$ many items from the stream uniformly at random as well as hash the id's (the word "id" is short for identifier) of the sampled elements into a space of size $O(\varepsilon^{-4})$. Now, both the stream length as well as the universe size are $\text{poly}(\varepsilon^{-1})$. From Lemma 3, it suffices to solve the heavy hitters problem on the sampled stream. From Lemma 2, because the hash function is chosen from a universal family, the sampled elements have distinct hashed id's. We can then feed these elements into a standard Misra-Gries data structure with ε^{-1} counters, incurring space $O(\varepsilon^{-1}\log\varepsilon^{-1})$. Because we want to return the unhashed element id's for the heavy hitters, we also use $\log n$ space for recording the φ^{-1} top items according to the Misra-Gries data structure and output these when asked to report.

[3]In all our algorithms, whenever we pick an item with probability $p > 0$, we can assume, without loss of generality, that $1/p$ is a power of two. If not, then we replace p with p' where $1/p'$ is the largest power of two less than $1/p$. This does not affect correctness and performance of our algorithms.

[4]We emphasize that this is stronger than an amortized guarantee, as on every insertion, the cost will be $O(1)$.

Algorithm 1 for (ε, φ)-List heavy hitters

Input: A stream $\mathcal{S}$ of length m over $\mathcal{U} = [n]$; let $f(x)$ be the frequency of $x \in \mathcal{U}$ in $\mathcal{S}$

Output: A set $X \subseteq \mathcal{U}$ and a function $\hat{f} : X \to \mathbb{N}$ such that if $f(x) \geqslant \varphi m$, then $x \in X$ and $f(x) - \varepsilon m \leqslant \hat{f}(x) \leqslant f(x) + \varepsilon m$ and if $f(y) \leqslant (\varphi - \varepsilon)m$, then $y \notin X$ for every $x, y \in \mathcal{U}$

```
1: Initialize:
   2: ℓ ← 6 log(6/δ)/ε²
   3: Hash function h uniformly at random from a
      universal family H ⊆ {h : [n] → ⌈4ℓ²/δ⌉}.
   4: An empty table T1 of (key, value) pairs of length
      ε⁻¹. Each key entry of T1 can store an integer in
      [0, ⌈4ℓ²/δ⌉] and each value entry can store an
      integer in [0, 11ℓ]. ▷ The table T1 will be in sorted
      order by value throughout.
   5: An empty table T2 of length 1/φ. Each entry of T2
      can store an integer in [0, n].  ▷ The entries of T2
      will correspond to ids of the keys in T1 of the
      highest 1/φ values
6:
7: procedure Insert(x)
8:     With probability p = 6ℓ/m, continue. Otherwise, return .
9:     Perform Misra-Gries update using h(x) maintaining
       T1 sorted by values.
10:    if The value of h(x) is among the highest 1/φ valued
       items in T1 then
11:        if x_i is not in T2 then
12:            if T2 currently contains 1/φ many items then
13:                For y in T2 such that h(y) is not among
       the highest 1/φ valued items in T1, replace y with x.
14:            else
15:                We put x in T2.
16:        Ensure that elements in T2 are ordered according
       to corresponding values in T1.
17:
18: procedure Report( )
19:    return items in T2 along with their corresponding
       values in T1
```

Proof of Theorem 1. The pseudocode of our (ε, φ)-List heavy hitters algorithm is in Algorithm 1. By Lemma 3, if we select a subset $\mathcal{S}$ of size at least $\ell = 6\varepsilon^{-2}\log(6\delta^{-1})$ uniformly at random from the stream, then $\Pr[\forall i \in \mathcal{U}, |(\hat{f}_i/|\mathcal{S}|) - (f_i/n)| \leqslant \varepsilon] \geqslant 1 - \delta/3$, where f_i and $\hat{f}_i$ are the frequencies of item i in the input stream and $\mathcal{S}$ respectively. First we show that with the choice of p in line 10 in Algorithm 1, the number of items sampled is at least ℓ and at most 11ℓ with probability at least $(1 - \delta/3)$. Let X_i be the indicator random variable of the event that the item x_i is sampled for $i \in [m]$. Then the total number of items sampled $X = \sum_{i=1}^{m} X_i$. We have $\mathbb{E}[X] = 6\ell$ since $p = 6\ell/m$. Now we have the following.

$$\Pr[X \leqslant \ell \text{ or } X \geqslant 11\ell] \leqslant \Pr[|X - \mathbb{E}[X]| \geqslant 5\ell] \leqslant \delta/3$$

The inequality follows from the Chernoff bound and the value of ℓ. From here onwards we assume that the number of items sampled is in $[\ell, 11\ell]$.

We use (a modified version of) the Misra-Gries algorithm [54] to estimate the frequencies of items in $\mathcal{S}$. The length of the table in the Misra-Gries algorithm is ε^{-1}. We pick a hash function h uniformly at random from a universal family $\mathcal{H} = \{h | h : [n] \to \lceil 4\ell^2/\delta \rceil\}$ of hash functions of size $|\mathcal{H}| = O(n^2)$. Note that picking a hash function h uniformly at random from $\mathcal{H}$ can be done using $O(\log n + \log(1/\varepsilon) + \log(1/\delta))$ bits of space, which is $O(\log n)$ bits for constant δ and assuming that $\varepsilon \geqslant 1/n$ (as otherwise, there is an $\Omega(n)$ lower bound for the problem). Lemma 2 shows that there are no collisions in $\mathcal{S}$ under this hash function h with probability at least $1 - \delta/3$. From here onwards we assume that there is no collision among the ids of the sampled items under the hash function h.

We modify the Misra-Gries algorithm as follows. Instead of storing the id of any item x in the Misra-Gries table (table $\mathcal{T}_1$ in line 5 in Algorithm 1) we only store the hash $h(x)$ of the id x. We also store the ids (not the hash of the id) of the items with highest $1/\varphi$ values in $\mathcal{T}_1$ in another table $\mathcal{T}_2$. Moreover, we always maintain the table $\mathcal{T}_2$ consistent with the table $\mathcal{T}_1$ in the sense that the ith highest valued key in $\mathcal{T}_1$ is the hash of the ith id in $\mathcal{T}_2$.

Upon picking an item x with probability p, we create an entry corresponding to $h(x)$ in $\mathcal{T}_1$ and make its value one if there is space available in $\mathcal{T}_1$; decrement the value of every item in $\mathcal{T}_1$ by one if the table is already full; increment the entry in the table corresponding to $h(x)$ if $h(x)$ is already present in the table. When we decrement the value of every item in $\mathcal{T}_1$, the table $\mathcal{T}_2$ remains consistent and we do not need to do anything else. Otherwise there are three cases to consider. Case 1: $h(x)$ is not among the $1/\varphi$ highest valued items in $\mathcal{T}_1$. In this case, we do not need to do anything else. Case 2: $h(x)$ was not among the $1/\varphi$ highest valued items in $\mathcal{T}_1$ but now it is among the $1/\varphi$ highest valued items in $\mathcal{T}_1$. In this case the last item y in $\mathcal{T}_2$ is no longer among the $1/\varphi$ highest valued items in $\mathcal{T}_1$. We replace y with x in $\mathcal{T}_2$. Case 3: $h(x)$ was among the $1/\varphi$ highest valued items in $\mathcal{T}_1$. When the stream finishes, we output the ids of all the items in table $\mathcal{T}_2$ along with the values corresponding to them in table $\mathcal{T}_1$. Correctness follows from the correctness of the Misra-Gries algorithm and the fact that there is no collision among the ids of the sampled items. □

3.1.2 An optimal algorithm

Theorem 2. *Assume the stream length is known beforehand. Then there is a randomized one-pass algorithm $\mathcal{A}$ for the (ε, φ)-List heavy hitters problem which succeeds with constant probability using $O\left(\varepsilon^{-1}\log\varphi^{-1} + \varphi^{-1}\log n + \log\log m\right)$ bits of space. Moreover, $\mathcal{A}$ has an update time of $O(1)$ and reporting time linear in its output size.*

Overview. As in the simpler algorithm, we sample $\ell = O(\varepsilon^{-2})$ many stream elements and solve the $(\varepsilon/2, \varphi)$-List heavy hitters problem on this sampled stream. Also, the Misra-Gries algorithm for $(\varphi/2, \varphi)$-List heavy hitters returns a candidate set of $O(\varphi^{-1})$ items containing all items of frequency at least $\varphi\ell$. It remains to count the frequencies of these $O(\varphi^{-1})$ items with upto $\varepsilon\ell/2 = O(\varepsilon^{-1})$ *additive* error, so that we can remove those whose frequency is less than $(\varphi - \varepsilon/2)\ell$.

Fix some item $i \in [n]$, and let f_i be i's count in the sampled stream. A natural approach to count f_i approximately is to increment a counter probabilistically, instead of deterministically, at every occurrence of i. Suppose that we increment a counter with probability $0 \leqslant p_i \leqslant 1$ whenever item i

Algorithm 2 for (ε, φ)-List heavy hitters

Input: A stream $\mathcal{S}$ of length m over universe $\mathcal{U} = [n]$; let $f(x)$ be the frequency of $x \in \mathcal{U}$ in $\mathcal{S}$

Output: A set $X \subseteq \mathcal{U}$ and a function $\hat{f} : X \to \mathbb{N}$ such that if $f(x) \geqslant \varphi m$, then $x \in X$ and $f(x) - \varepsilon m \leqslant \hat{f}(x) \leqslant f(x) + \varepsilon m$ and if $f(y) \leqslant (\varphi - \varepsilon)m$, then $y \notin X$ for every $x, y \in \mathcal{U}$

Initialize:
- $\ell \leftarrow 10^5 \varepsilon^{-2}$
- $s \leftarrow 0$
- Hash functions $h_1, \ldots, h_{200 \log(12\varphi^{-1})}$ uniformly at random from a universal family $\mathcal{H} \subseteq \{h : [n] \to [100/\varepsilon]\}$.
- An empty table $\mathcal{T}_1$ of (key, value) pairs of length $2\varphi^{-1}$. Each key entry of $\mathcal{T}_1$ can store an element of $[n]$ and each value entry can store an integer in $[0, 10\ell]$.
- An empty table $\mathcal{T}_2$ with $100\varepsilon^{-1}$ rows and $200 \log(12\varphi^{-1})$ columns. Each entry of $\mathcal{T}_2$ can store an integer in $[0, 100\varepsilon\ell]$.
- An empty 3-dimensional table $\mathcal{T}_3$ of size at most $100\varepsilon^{-1} \times 200 \log(12\varphi^{-1}) \times 4 \log(\varepsilon^{-1})$. Each entry of $\mathcal{T}_3$ can store an integer in $[0, 10\ell]$. ▷ These are upper bounds; not all the allowed cells will actually be used.

procedure Insert(x)
- With probability ℓ/m, increment s and continue. Else, **return**
- Perform Misra-Gries update on $\mathcal{T}_1$ with x.
- **for** $j \leftarrow 1$ to $200 \log(12\varphi^{-1})$ **do**
  - $i \leftarrow h_j(x)$
  - With probability ε, increment $\mathcal{T}_2[i, j]$
  - $t \leftarrow \lfloor \log(10^{-6} \mathcal{T}_2[i, j]^2) \rfloor$ and $p \leftarrow \min(\varepsilon \cdot 2^t, 1)$
  - **if** $t \geqslant 0$ **then**
    - With probability p, increment $\mathcal{T}_3[i, j, t]$

procedure Report( )
- $X \leftarrow \emptyset$
- **for** each key x with nonzero value in $\mathcal{T}_1$ **do**
  - **for** $j \leftarrow 1$ to $200 \log(12\varphi^{-1})$ **do**
    - $\hat{f}_j(x) \leftarrow \sum_{t=0}^{4 \log(\varepsilon^{-1})} \mathcal{T}_3[h(x), j, t] / \min(\varepsilon 2^t, 1)$
  - $\hat{f}(x) \leftarrow \text{median}(\hat{f}_1, \ldots, \hat{f}_{10 \log \varphi^{-1}})$
  - **if** $\hat{f}(x) \geqslant (\varphi - \varepsilon/2)s$ **then**
    - $X \leftarrow X \cup \{x\}$
- **return** $X, \hat{f}$

arrives in the stream. Let the value of the counter be $\hat{c}_i$, and let $\hat{f}_i = \hat{c}_i / p_i$. We see that $\mathbb{E}\left[\hat{f}_i\right] = f_i$ and $\mathsf{Var}[\hat{f}_i] \leqslant f_i / p_i$. It follows that if $p_i = \Theta(\varepsilon^2 f_i)$, then $\mathsf{Var}[\hat{f}_i] = O(\varepsilon^{-2})$, and hence, $\hat{f}_i$ is an unbiased estimator of f_i with additive error $O(\varepsilon^{-1})$ with constant probability. We call such a counter an *accelerated counter* as the probability of incrementing accelerates with increasing counts. For each i, we can maintain $O(\log \varphi^{-1})$ accelerated counters independently and take their median to drive the probability of deviating by more than $O(\varepsilon^{-1})$ down to $O(\varphi)$. So, with constant probability, the frequency for the $O(\varphi^{-1})$ items in the Misra-Gries data structure is estimated within $O(\varepsilon^{-1})$ error, as desired.

However, there are two immediate issues with this approach. The first problem is that we may need to keep counts for $\Omega(\ell) = \Omega(\varepsilon^{-2})$ distinct items, which is too costly for our purposes. To get around this, we use a hash function from a universal family to hash the universe to a space of size $u = \Theta(\varepsilon^{-1})$, and we work throughout with the hashed id's. We can then show that the space complexity for each iteration is $O(\varepsilon^{-1})$. Also, the accelerated counters now estimate frequencies of hashed id's instead of actual items, but because of universality, the expected frequency of any hashed id is $\ell / u = O(\varepsilon^{-1})$, our desired error bound.

The second issue is that we need a constant factor approximation of f_i, so that we can set p_i to $\Theta(\varepsilon^2 f_i)$. But because the algorithm needs to be one-pass, we cannot first compute p_i in one pass and then run the accelerated counter in another. So, we divide the stream into *epochs* in which f_i stays within a factor of 2, and use a different p_i for each epoch. In particular, set $p_i^t = \varepsilon \cdot 2^t$ for $0 \leqslant t \leqslant \log(p_i/\varepsilon)$. We want to keep a running estimate of i's count to within a factor of 2 to know if the current epoch should be incremented. For this, we subsample each element of the (already sampled) stream with probability ε independently and maintain exact counts for the observed hashed id's. It is easy to see that this requires only $O(\varepsilon^{-1})$ bits in expectation. Consider any $i \in [u]$ and the prefix of the stream upto $b \leqslant \ell$, and let $f_i(b)$ be i's frequency in the prefix, let $\bar{c}_i(b)$ be i's frequency among the samples in the prefix, and $\bar{f}_i(b) = \frac{\bar{c}_i(b)}{\varepsilon}$. We see that $\mathbb{E}\left[\bar{f}_i(b)\right] = f_i(b)$, Moreover, we show that for any $b \in [\ell]$, $\bar{f}_i(b)$ is a 4-factor approximation of $f_i(b)$ with constant probability. By repeating $O(\log \varphi^{-1})$ times independently and taking the median, the error probability can be driven down to $O(\varphi)$.

Now, for every hashed id $i \in [u]$, we need not one accelerated counter but $O(\log(\varepsilon f_i))$ many, one corresponding to each epoch t. When an element with hash id i arrives at position b, we decide, based on $\bar{f}_i(b)$, the epoch t it belongs to and then increment the t'th accelerated counter with probability p_i^t. The storage cost over all i is still $O(1/\varepsilon)$. Also, we iterate the whole set of accelerated counters $O(\log \varphi^{-1})$ times, making the total storage cost $O(\varepsilon^{-1} \log \varphi^{-1})$.

Let $\hat{c}_{i,t}$ be the count in the accelerated counter for hash id i and epoch t. Then, let $\hat{f}_i = \sum_t \hat{c}_{i,t} / p_i^t$. Clearly, $\mathbb{E}\left[\hat{f}_i\right] = f_i$. The variance is $O(\varepsilon^{-2})$ in each epoch, and so, $\mathsf{Var}[\hat{f}_i] = O(\varepsilon^{-2} \log \varepsilon^{-1})$, not $O(\varepsilon^{-2})$ which we wanted. This issue is fixed by a change in how the sampling probabilities are defined, effectively making the sum a geometric series. We now go on to the formal proof.

Pseudocode appears in Algorithm 2 and the full proof in the appendix. Note that the numerical constants are chosen for convenience of analysis and have not been optimized. Also, for the sake of simplicity, the pseudocode does not have the optimal reporting time, but it can be modified to achieve this; see the proof for details.

3.2 Maximum

By tweaking Algorithm 1 slightly, we get the following result for the ε-Maximum problem.

Theorem 3. *Assume the length of the stream is known beforehand. Then there is a randomized one-pass algorithm $\mathcal{A}$ for the ε-Maximum problem which succeeds with probability at least $1 - \delta$ using $O(\min\{1/\varepsilon, n\}(\log 1/\varepsilon + \log\log 1/\delta) + \log n + \log\log m)$ bits* *of space. Moreover, the algorithm $\mathcal{A}$ has an update time of* $O(1)$.

PROOF. Instead of maintaining the table $\mathcal{T}_2$ in Algorithm 1, we just store the actual id of the item with maximum frequency in the sampled items. □

3.3 Minimum

Theorem 4. *Assume the length of the stream is known beforehand. Then there is a randomized one-pass algorithm $\mathcal{A}$ for the ε-MINIMUM problem which succeeds with probability at least $1-\delta$ using $O\left(({}^1/_\varepsilon) \log\log({}^1/_{\varepsilon\delta}) + \log\log m\right)$ bits of space. Moreover, the algorithm $\mathcal{A}$ has an update time of* $O(1)$.

Overview. Pseudocode is provided in Algorithm 3. The idea behind our ε-Minimum problem is as follows. It is most easily explained by looking at the REPORT(x) procedure starting in line 13. In lines 14-15 we ask, is the universe size $|U|$ significantly larger than $1/\varepsilon$? Note that if it is, then outputting a random item from $|U|$ is likely to be a solution. Otherwise $|U|$ is $O(1/\varepsilon)$.

The next point is that if the number of distinct elements in the stream were smaller than $1/(\varepsilon \log(1/\varepsilon))$, then we could just store all the items together with their frequencies with $O(1/\varepsilon)$ bits of space. Indeed, we can first sample $O(1/\varepsilon^2)$ stream elements so that all relative frequencies are preserved up to additive ε, thereby ensuring each frequency can be stored with $O(\log(1/\varepsilon))$ bits. Also, since the universe size is $O(1/\varepsilon)$, the item identifiers can also be stored with $O(\log(1/\varepsilon))$ bits. So if this part of the algorithm starts taking up too much space, we stop, and we know the number of distinct elements is at least $1/(\varepsilon \log(1/\varepsilon))$, which means that the minimum frequency is at most $O(m\varepsilon \log(1/\varepsilon))$. This is what is being implemented in steps 9-10 and 18-19 in the algorithm.

We can also ensure the minimum frequency is at least $\Omega(m\varepsilon/\log(1/\varepsilon))$. Indeed, by randomly sampling $O((\log(1/\varepsilon)/\varepsilon)$ stream elements, and maintaining a bit vector for whether or not each item in the universe occurs - which we can with $O(1/\varepsilon)$ bits of space since $|U| = O(1/\varepsilon)$ - any item with frequency at least $\Omega(\varepsilon m/\log(1/\varepsilon))$ will be sampled and so if there is an entry in the bit vector which is empty, then we can just output that as our solution. This is what is being implemented in steps 8 and 16-17 of the algorithm.

Finally, we now know that the minimum frequency is at least $\Omega(m\varepsilon/\log(1/\varepsilon))$ and at most $O(m\varepsilon \log(1/\varepsilon))$. At this point if we randomly sample $O((\log^6 1/\varepsilon)/\varepsilon)$ stream elements, then by Chernoff bounds all item frequencies are preserved up to a relative error factor of $(1 \pm 1/\log^2(1/\varepsilon))$, and in particular the relative minimum frequency is guaranteed to be preserved up to an additive ε. At this point we just maintain the exact counts in the sampled stream but truncate them once they exceed $\mathrm{poly}(\log(1/\varepsilon)))$ bits, since we know such counts do not correspond to the minimum. Thus we only need $O(\log\log(1/\varepsilon))$ bits to represent their counts. This is implemented in step 11 and step 20 of the algorithm.

3.4 Borda and Maximin

We defer describing the algorithms for Borda and Maximin to the appendix.

Algorithm 3 for ε-MINIMUM

Input: A stream $\mathcal{S} = (x_i)_{i\in[m]} \in \mathcal{U}^m$ of length m over $\mathcal{U}$; let $f(x)$ be the frequency of $x \in \mathcal{U}$ in $\mathcal{S}$

Output: An item $x \in \mathcal{U}$ such that $f(x) \leqslant f(y) + \varepsilon m$ for every $y \in \mathcal{U}$

1: **Initialize:**
2: $\ell_1 \leftarrow {}^{\log(6/\varepsilon\delta)}/_{\varepsilon}$, $\ell_2 \leftarrow {}^{\log(6/\delta)}/_{\varepsilon^2}$, $\ell_3 \leftarrow {}^{\log^6(6/\delta\varepsilon)}/_{\varepsilon}$
3: $p_1 \leftarrow {}^{6\ell_1}/_m$, $p_2 \leftarrow {}^{6\ell_2}/_m$, $p_3 \leftarrow {}^{6\ell_3}/_m$
4: $\mathcal{S}_1, \mathcal{S}_2, \mathcal{S}_3 \leftarrow \emptyset$
5: $\mathcal{B}_1 \leftarrow$ the bit vector for $\mathcal{S}_1$
6:
7: **procedure** INSERT(x)
8: Put x in $\mathcal{S}_1$ with probability p_1 by updating the bit vector $\mathcal{B}_1$
9: **if** the number of distinct items in the stream so far is at most ${}^1/_{(\varepsilon \log(1/\varepsilon))}$ **then**
10: Pick x with probability p_2 and put the id of x in $\mathcal{S}_2$ and initialize the corresponding counter to 1 if $x \notin \mathcal{S}_2$ and increment the counter corresponding to x by 1.
11: Pick x with probability p_3, put the id of x in $\mathcal{S}_3$ and initialize the corresponding counter to 1 if $x_i \notin \mathcal{S}_3$ and increment the counter corresponding to x_i by 1. Truncate counters of $\mathcal{S}_3$ at $2\log^7({}^2/_{\varepsilon\delta})$.
12:
13: **procedure** REPORT( )
14: **if** $|\mathcal{U}| \geqslant {}^1/_{((1-\delta)\varepsilon)}$ **then**
15: **return** an item x from the first ${}^1/_{((1-\delta)\varepsilon)}$ items in $\mathcal{U}$ (ordered arbitrarily) uniformly at random
16: **if** $\mathcal{S}_1 \neq \mathcal{U}$ **then**
17: **return** any item from $\mathcal{U} \setminus \mathcal{S}_1$
18: **if** the number of distinct items in the stream is at most ${}^1/_{(\varepsilon \log(1/\varepsilon))}$ **then**
19: **return** an item in $\mathcal{S}_2$ with minimum counter value in $\mathcal{S}_2$
20: **return** the item with minimum frequency in $\mathcal{S}_3$

Theorem 5. *Assume the length of the stream is known beforehand. Then there is a randomized one-pass algorithm $\mathcal{A}$ for (ε, φ)-LIST BORDA problem which succeeds with probability at least $1-\delta$ using $O\left(n\left(\log n + \log\frac{1}{\varepsilon} + \log\log\frac{1}{\delta}\right) + \log\log m\right)$ bits of space.*

Theorem 6. *Assume the length of the stream is known beforehand. Then there is a randomized one-pass algorithm $\mathcal{A}$ for (ε, φ)-LIST MAXIMIN problem which succeeds with probability at least $1-\delta$ using $O\left(n\varepsilon^{-2}\log^2 n + n\varepsilon^{-2}\log n \log\delta^{-1} + \log\log m\right)$ bits of space.*

3.5 Unknown stream length

Now we consider the case when the length of the stream is not known beforehand. We present below an algorithm for (ε, φ)-LIST HEAVY HITTERS and ε-MAXIMUM problems in this setting.

Theorem 7. *There is a randomized one-pass algorithm for (ε, φ)-LIST HEAVY HITTERS and ε-MAXIMUM problems with space complexity $O\left(\varepsilon^{-1}\log\varepsilon^{-1} + \varphi^{-1}\log n + \log\log m\right)$ bits and update time $O(1)$ even when the length of the stream is not known beforehand.*

PROOF. We describe below a randomized one-pass algorithm for the $(8\varepsilon, \varphi)$-LIST HEAVY HITTERS problem. We may assume that the length of the stream is at least $1/\varepsilon^2$; otherwise, we use the algorithm in Theorem 1 and get the result. Now we guess the length of the stream to be $1/\varepsilon^2$, but run an instance $\mathcal{I}_1$ of Algorithm 1 with $\ell = \log(6/\delta)/\varepsilon^3$ at line 2. By the choice of the size of the sample (which is $\Theta(\log(1/\delta)/\varepsilon^3)$), $\mathcal{I}_1$ outputs correctly with probability at least $(1-\delta)$, if the length of the stream is in $[1/\varepsilon^2, 1/\varepsilon^3]$. If the length of the stream exceeds $1/\varepsilon^2$, we run another instance $\mathcal{I}_2$ of Algorithm 1 with $\ell = \log(6/\delta)/\varepsilon^3$ at line 2. Again by the choice of the size of the sample, $\mathcal{I}_2$ outputs correctly with probability at least $(1-\delta)$, if the length of the stream is in $[1/\varepsilon^3, 1/\varepsilon^4]$. If the stream length exceeds $1/\varepsilon^3$, we discard $\mathcal{I}_1$, free the space it uses, and run an instance $\mathcal{I}_3$ of Algorithm 1 with $\ell = \log(6/\delta)/\varepsilon^3$ at line 2 and so on. At any point of time, we have at most two instances of Algorithm 1 running. When the stream ends, we return the output of the older of the instances we are currently running. We use the approximate counting method of Morris [57] to approximately count the length of the stream. We know that the Morris counter outputs correctly with probability $(1-2^{-k/2})$ using $O(\log\log m + k)$ bits of space at any point in time [29]. Also, since the Morris counter increases only when an item is read, it outputs correctly up to a factor of four at every position if it outputs correctly at positions $1, 2, 4, \ldots, 2^{\lfloor \log_2 m \rfloor}$; call this event E. Then we have $\Pr(E) \geqslant 1-\delta$ by choosing $k = 2\log_2(\log_2 m/\delta)$ and applying a union bound over the positions $1, 2, 4, \ldots, 2^{\lfloor \log_2 m \rfloor}$. The correctness of the algorithm follows from the correctness of Algorithm 1 and the fact that we are discarding at most εm many items in the stream (by discarding a run of an instance of Algorithm 1). The space complexity and the $O(1)$ update time of the algorithm follow from Theorem 1, the choice of k above, and the fact that we have at most two instances of Algorithm 1 currently running at any point of time.

The algorithm for the ε-MAXIMUM problem is same as the algorithm above except we use the algorithm in Theorem 3 instead of Algorithm 1. □

Note that this proof technique does not seem to apply to our optimal Algorithm 2. Similarly to Theorem 7, we get the following result for the other problems.

Theorem 8. *There are randomized one-pass algorithms for ε-MINIMUM, (ε, φ)-BORDA, and (ε, φ)-MAXIMIN problems with space complexity $O\left((1/\varepsilon)\log\log(1/\varepsilon\delta) + \log\log m\right)$, $O\left(n\left(\log\log n + \log\frac{1}{\varepsilon} + \log\log\frac{1}{\delta}\right) + \log\log m\right)$, and $O\left(n\log^2 n\log(1/\delta)/\varepsilon^2 + \log\log m\right)$ bits respectively even when the length of the stream is not known beforehand. Moreover, the update time for ε-MINIMUM is $O(1)$.*

4. HARDNESS

In this section, we prove space complexity lower bounds for the ε-HEAVY HITTERS, ε-MINIMUM, ε-BORDA, and ε-MAXIMIN problems. We present reductions from certain communication problems for proving space complexity lower bounds. Let us first introduce those communication problems with necessary results.

4.1 Communication Complexity

Definition 10. *(INDEXING$_{m,t}$)*
Let t and m be positive integers. Alice is given a string $x = (x_1, \cdots, x_t) \in [m]^t$. Bob is given an index $i \in [t]$. Bob has to output x_i.

The following is a well known result [42].

Lemma 4. *$\mathcal{R}_\delta^{1\text{-}way}(\text{INDEXING}_{m,t}) = \Omega(t\log m)$ for constant $\delta \in (0,1)$.*

[67] defines a communication problem called PERM, which we generalize to ε-PERM as follows.

Definition 11. *(ε-PERM)*
Alice is given a permutation σ over $[n]$ which is partitioned into $1/\varepsilon$ many contiguous blocks. Bob is given an index $i \in [n]$ and has to output the block in σ where i belongs.

Our lower bound for ε-PERM matches the lower bound for PERM in Lemma 1 in [67] when $\varepsilon = 1/n$.

Lemma 5. *$\mathcal{R}_\delta^{1\text{-}way}(\varepsilon - \text{PERM}) = \Omega(n\log(1/\varepsilon))$, for any constant $\delta < 1/10$.*

Finally, we consider the GREATER-THAN problem.

Definition 12. *(GREATER-THAN$_n$)*
Alice is given an integer $x \in [n]$ and Bob is given an integer $y \in [n], y \neq x$. Bob has to output 1 if $x > y$ and 0 otherwise.

The following result is due to [53, 66]. We provide a simple proof of it in the appendix for completeness[5].

Lemma 6. *$\mathcal{R}_\delta^{1\text{-}way}(\text{GREATER-THAN}_n) = \Omega(\log n)$, for every $\delta < 1/4$.*

4.2 Reductions

We observe that a trivial $\Omega((1/\varphi)\log n)$ bits lower bound for (ε, φ)-LIST HEAVY HITTERS, (ε, φ)-LIST BORDA, (ε, φ)-LIST MAXIMIN follows from the fact that any algorithm may need to output $1/\varphi$ many items from the universe. Also, there is a trivial $\Omega(n\log n)$ lower bound for (ε, φ)-LIST BORDA and (ε, φ)-LIST MAXIMIN because each stream item is a permutation on $[n]$, hence requiring $\Omega(n\log n)$ bits to read.

We show now a space complexity lower bound of $\Omega(\frac{1}{\varepsilon}\log\frac{1}{\varphi})$ bits for the ε-HEAVY HITTERS problem.

Theorem 9. *Suppose the size of universe n is at least $1/4\varepsilon(\varphi-\varepsilon)$. Any randomized one pass (ε, φ)-HEAVY HITTERS algorithm with success probability at least $(1-\delta)$ must use $\Omega((1/\varepsilon)\log 1/\varphi)$ bits of space, for constant $\delta \in (0,1)$.*

PROOF. Consider the INDEXING$_{1/2(\varphi-\varepsilon), 1/2\varepsilon}$ problem where Alice is given a string $x = (x_1, x_2, \cdots, x_{1/\varepsilon}) \in [1/2(\varphi-\varepsilon)]^{1/2\varepsilon}$ and Bob is given an index $i \in [1/2\varepsilon]$. We assume $\varphi > 2\varepsilon$. The stream we generate is over $[1/2(\varphi-\varepsilon)] \times [1/2\varepsilon] \subseteq \mathcal{U}$ (this is possible since $|\mathcal{U}| \geqslant 1/(4\varepsilon(\varphi-\varepsilon))$). Alice generates a stream of length $1/2\varepsilon$ by inserting one copy of (x_j, j) for each $j \in [1/2\varepsilon]$. Alice now sends the memory content of the algorithm to Bob. Bob resumes the run of the algorithm by generating another stream of length $1/2\varepsilon$ by inserting $\varphi/\varepsilon - 1$ copies of (j, i) for each $j \in [1/\varphi-\varepsilon]$. The length of the stream is ε^{-1}, the frequency of the item (x_i, i) is φ/ε, while the frequency of every other item is $\varphi/\varepsilon - 1$ or 1. Hence from the output of the (ε, φ)-HEAVY HITTERS algorithm, Bob knows i with probability at least $(1-\delta)$. Now the result follows from Lemma 4, since $\frac{1}{\varepsilon}\log\frac{1}{\varphi-\varepsilon} > \frac{1}{\varepsilon}\log\frac{1}{\varphi}$. □

[5] A similar proof appears in [40] but theirs gives a slightly weaker bound.

We now use the same idea as in the proof of Theorem 9 to prove an $\Omega(\frac{1}{\varepsilon}\log\frac{1}{\varepsilon})$ space complexity lower bound for the ε-Maximum problem.

Theorem 10. *Suppose the size of universe n is at least $\frac{1}{\varepsilon^2}$. Any randomized one pass ε-MAXIMUM algorithm with success probability at least $(1-\delta)$ must use $\Omega(\frac{1}{\varepsilon}\log\frac{1}{\varepsilon})$ bits of space, for constant $\delta \in (0,1)$.*

PROOF. Consider the $\text{INDEXING}_{1/\varepsilon,1/\varepsilon}$ problem where Alice is given a string $x = (x_1, x_2, \cdots, x_{1/\varepsilon}) \in [1/\varepsilon]^{1/\varepsilon}$ and Bob is given an index $i \in [1/\varepsilon]$. The stream we generate is over $[1/\varepsilon] \times [1/\varepsilon] \subseteq \mathcal{U}$ (this is possible since $|\mathcal{U}| \geqslant \frac{1}{\varepsilon^2}$). Alice generates a stream of length $m/2$ in such a way that the frequency of every item in $\{(x_j, j) : j \in [1/\varepsilon]\}$ is at least $\lfloor \varepsilon m/2 \rfloor$ and the frequency of any other item is 0. Alice now sends the memory content of the algorithm to Bob. Bob resumes the run of the algorithm by generating another stream of length $m/2$ in such a way that the frequency of every item in $\{(j,i) : j \in [1/\varepsilon]\}$ is at least $\lfloor \varepsilon m/2 \rfloor$ and the frequency of any other item is 0. The frequency of the item (x_i, i) is at least $\lfloor \varepsilon m \rfloor$ where as the frequency of every other item is at most $\lfloor \varepsilon m/2 \rfloor$. Hence the $\varepsilon/5$-MAXIMUM algorithm must output (x_i, i) with probability at least $(1-\delta)$. Now the result follows from Lemma 4. □

For ε-MINIMUM, we prove a space complexity lower bound of $\Omega(1/\varepsilon)$ bits.

Theorem 11. *Suppose the universe size n is at least $1/\varepsilon$. Then any randomized one pass ε-MINIMUM algorithm must use $\Omega(1/\varepsilon)$ bits of space.*

PROOF. We reduce from $\text{INDEXING}_{2,5/\varepsilon}$ to ε-MINIMUM thereby proving the result. Let the inputs to Alice and Bob in $\text{INDEXING}_{2,5/\varepsilon}$ be $(x_1, \ldots, x_{5/\varepsilon}) \in \{0,1\}^{5/\varepsilon}$ and an index $i \in [5/\varepsilon]$ respectively. Alice and Bob generate a stream $\mathcal{S}$ over the universe $[(5/\varepsilon)+1]$. Alice puts two copies of item j in $\mathcal{S}$ for every $j \in \mathcal{U}$ with $x_j = 1$ and runs the ε-MINIMUM algorithm. Alice now sends the memory content of the algorithm to Bob. Bob resumes the run of the algorithm by putting two copies of every item in $\mathcal{U} \setminus \{i, (5/\varepsilon)+1\}$ in the stream $\mathcal{S}$. Bob also puts one copy of $(5/\varepsilon)+1$ in $\mathcal{S}$. Suppose the size of the support of $(x_1, \ldots, x_{5/\varepsilon})$ be ℓ. Since $1/(2\ell+(2/\varepsilon)-1) > \varepsilon/5$, we have the following. If $x_i = 0$, then the ε-MINIMUM algorithm must output i with probability at least $(1-\delta)$. If $x_i = 1$, then the ε-MINIMUM algorithm must output $(5/\varepsilon)+1$ with probability at least $(1-\delta)$. Now the result follows from Lemma 4. □

We show next a $\Omega(n\log(1/\varepsilon))$ bits space complexity lower bound for ε-BORDA.

Theorem 12. *Any one pass algorithm for ε-BORDA must use $\Omega(n\log(1/\varepsilon))$ bits of space.*

PROOF. We reduce ε-PERM to ε-BORDA. Suppose Alice has a permutation σ over $[n]$ and Bob has an index $i \in [n]$. The item set of our reduced election is $\mathcal{U} = [n] \sqcup \mathcal{D}$, where $\mathcal{D} = \{d_1, d_2, \ldots, d_{2n}\}$. Alice generates a vote $\mathfrak{v}$ over the item set $\mathcal{U}$ from σ as follows. The vote $\mathfrak{v}$ is $\mathcal{B}_1 \succ \mathcal{B}_2 \succ \cdots \succ \mathcal{B}_{1/\varepsilon}$ where $\mathcal{B}_j$ for $j = 1, \ldots, 1/\varepsilon$ is defined as follows.

$$\begin{aligned}\mathcal{B}_j = d_{(j-1)2\varepsilon n+1} &\succ d_{(j-1)2\varepsilon n+2} \succ \cdots \succ d_{(2j-1)\varepsilon n}\\ &\succ \sigma_{j\varepsilon n+1} \succ \cdots \succ \sigma_{(j+1)\varepsilon n} \succ d_{(2j-1)\varepsilon+1} \succ \cdots \succ d_{2j\varepsilon n}\end{aligned}$$

Alice runs the ε-BORDA algorithm with the vote $\mathfrak{v}$ and sends the memory content to Bob. Let $\mathcal{D}_{-i} = \mathcal{D} \setminus \{i\}$, $\overrightarrow{\mathcal{D}_{-i}}$ be an arbitrary but fixed ordering of the items in $\mathcal{D}_{-i}$, and $\overleftarrow{\mathcal{D}_{-i}}$ be the reverse ordering of $\overrightarrow{\mathcal{D}_{-i}}$. Bob resumes the algorithm by generating two votes each of the form $i \succ \overrightarrow{\mathcal{D}_{-i}}$ and $i \succ \overleftarrow{\mathcal{D}_{-i}}$. Let us call the resulting election $\mathcal{E}$. The number of votes m in $\mathcal{E}$ is 5. The Borda score of the item i is at least $12n$. The Borda score of every item $x \in \mathcal{U}$ is at most $9n$. Hence for $\varepsilon < 1/15$, the ε-BORDA algorithm must output the item i. Moreover, it follows from the construction of $\mathfrak{v}$ that an εmn additive approximation of the Borda score of the item i reveals the block where i belongs in the ε-PERM instance. □

We next give a nearly-tight lower bound for the ε-MAXIMIN problem.

Theorem 13. *Any one-pass algorithm for ε-MAXIMIN requires $\Omega(n/\varepsilon^2)$ memory bits of storage.*

PROOF. We reduce from INDEXING. Let $\gamma = 1/\varepsilon^2$. Suppose Alice has a string y of length $(n-\gamma)\cdot\gamma$, partitioned into $n-\gamma$ blocks of length γ each. Bob has an index $\ell = i + (j-\gamma-1)\cdot\gamma$ where $i \in [\gamma], j \in \{\gamma+1, \ldots, n\}$. The INDEXING problem is to return y_ℓ for which there is a $\Omega(|y|) = \Omega(n/\varepsilon^2)$ lower bound (Lemma 4).

The initial part of the reduction follows the construction in the proof of Theorem 6 in [69], which we encapsulate in the following lemma.

Lemma 7 (Theorem 6 in [69]). *Given y, Alice can construct a matrix $P \in \{0,1\}^{n\times\gamma}$ using public randomness, such that if P^i and P^j are the i'th and j'th rows of P respectively, then with probability at least $2/3$, $\Delta(P^i, P^j) \geqslant \frac{\gamma}{2} + \sqrt{\gamma}$ if $y_\ell = 1$ and $\Delta(a,b) \leqslant \frac{\gamma}{2} - \sqrt{\gamma}$ if $y_\ell = 0$.*

Let Alice construct P according to Lemma 7 and then adjoin the bitwise complement of the matrix P below P to form the matrix $P' \in \{0,1\}^{2n\times\gamma}$; note that each column of P' has exactly n 1's and n 0's. Now, we interpret each row of P as a candidate and each column of P as a vote in the following way: for each $v \in [\gamma]$, vote v has the candidates in $\{c : P'_{c,v} = 1\}$ in ascending order in the top n positions and the rest of the candidates in ascending order in the bottom n positions. Alice inserts these γ votes into the stream and sends the state of the ε-MAXIMIN algorithm to Bob as well as the Hamming weight of each row in P'. Bob inserts γ more votes, in each of which candidate i comes first, candidate j comes second, and the rest of the $2n-2$ candidates are in arbitrary order.

Note that because of Bob's votes, the maximin score of j is the number of votes among the ones casted by Alice in which j defeats i. Since $i < j$, in those columns v where $P_{i,v} = P_{j,v}$, candidate i beats candidate j. Thus, the set of votes in which j defeats i is $\{v \mid P_{i,v} = 0, P_{j,v} = 1\}$. The size of this set is $\frac{1}{2}\left(\Delta(P^i, P^j) + |P^j| - |P^i|\right)$. Therefore, if Bob can estimate the maximin score of j upto $\sqrt{\gamma}/4$ additive error, he can find $\Delta(P^i, P^j)$ upto $\sqrt{\gamma}/2$ additive error as Bob knows $|P^i|$ and $|P^j|$. This is enough, by Lemma 7, to solve the INDEXING problem with probability at least $2/3$. □

Finally, we show a space complexity lower bound that depends on the length of the stream m.

Theorem 14. *Any one pass algorithm for ε-HEAVY HITTERS, ε-MINIMUM, ε-BORDA, and ε-MAXIMIN must use $\Omega(\log \log m)$ memory bits, even if the stream is over a universe of size 2, for every $\varepsilon < \frac{1}{4}$.*

PROOF. It is enough to prove the result only for ε-HEAVY HITTERS since the other three problems reduce to ε-HEAVY HITTERS for a universe of size 2. Suppose we have a randomized one pass ε-HEAVY HITTERS algorithm which uses $s(m)$ bits of space. Using this algorithm, we will show a communication protocol for the GREATER-THAN$_m$ problem whose communication complexity is $s(2^m)$ thereby proving the statement. The universal set is $\mathcal{U} = \{0,1\}$. Alice generates a stream of 2^x many copies of the item 1. Alice now sends the memory content of the algorithm. Bob resumes the run of the algorithm by generating a stream of 2^y many copies of the item 0. If $x > y$, then the item 1 is the only ε-winner; whereas if $x < y$, then the item 0 is the only ε-winner. □

References

[1] G. Adomavicius and A. Tuzhilin. Toward the next generation of recommender systems: A survey of the state-of-the-art and possible extensions. *IEEE Trans. Knowl. Data Eng.*, 17(6):734–749, 2005.

[2] R. Agrawal and R. Srikant. Fast algorithms for mining association rules in large databases. In *Proc. 20th International Conference on Very Large Data Bases*, pages 487–499, 1994.

[3] A. Arasu, S. Babu, and J. Widom. CQL: A language for continuous queries over streams and relations. In *Proc. 9th International Workshop on Database Programming Languages DBPL*, pages 1–19, 2003.

[4] J. A. Aslam and M. Montague. Models for metasearch. In *Proc. 24th Annual international ACM SIGIR conference on Research and Development in Information Retrieval*, pages 276–284. ACM, 2001.

[5] R. Berinde, P. Indyk, G. Cormode, and M. J. Strauss. Space-optimal heavy hitters with strong error bounds. *ACM Trans. Database Syst*, 35(4):26, 2010.

[6] K. S. Beyer and R. Ramakrishnan. Bottom-up computation of sparse and iceberg cubes. In *Proc. ACM SIGMOD International Conference on Management of Data*, pages 359–370, 1999.

[7] D. K. Blandford and G. E. Blelloch. Compact dictionaries for variable-length keys and data with applications. *ACM Trans. Algor.*, 4(2):17, 2008.

[8] P. Bonnet, J. Gehrke, and P. Seshadri. Towards sensor database systems. In *Proc. 2nd International Conference on Mobile Data Management, MDM*, pages 3–14, 2001.

[9] F. Brandt, V. Conitzer, U. Endriss, J. Lang, and A. Procaccia. Handbook of computational social choice, 2015.

[10] V. Braverman, S. R. Chestnut, N. Ivkin, J. Nelson, Z. Wang, and D. P. Woodruff. BPTree: an ℓ_2 heavy hitters algorithm using constant memory. 2016. arXiv:1603.00759.

[11] V. Braverman, S. R. Chestnut, N. Ivkin, and D. P. Woodruff. Beating countsketch for heavy hitters in insertion streams. Technical report, 2016. arXiv:1511.00661. To appear in STOC '16.

[12] E. J. Candes, J. Romberg, and T. Tao. Stable signal recovery from incomplete and inaccurate measurements. *Commun. Pur. Appl. Math.*, 59:1207–1223, 2006.

[13] I. Caragiannis and A. D. Procaccia. Voting almost maximizes social welfare despite limited communication. *Artif. Intell.*, 175(9–10):1655 – 1671, 2011.

[14] B. Carterette and D. Petkova. Learning a ranking from pairwise preferences. In *Proc. 29th Annual International ACM SIGIR Conference on Research and Development in Information Retrieval*, pages 629–630. ACM, 2006.

[15] Y. Chabchoub, C. Fricker, and H. Mohamed. Analysis of a bloom filter algorithm via the supermarket model. In *Proc. 21st International Teletraffic Congress, ITC*, pages 1–8, 2009.

[16] M. Charikar, K. Chen, and M. Farach-Colton. Finding frequent items in data streams. *Theor. Comput. Sci.*, 312(1):3–15, 2004.

[17] V. Conitzer and T. Sandholm. Communication complexity of common voting rules. In *Proc. 6th ACM Conference on Electronic Commerce*, pages 78–87. ACM, 2005.

[18] G. Cormode. Sketch techniques for massive data. In G. Cormode, M. Garofalakis, P. J. Haas, and C. Jermaine, editors, *Synopses for Massive Data: Samples, Histograms, Wavelets, Sketches*, volume 4 of *Foundations and Trends in Databases*, pages 1–294. Now Publishers Inc., Hanover, MA, USA, Jan. 2012.

[19] G. Cormode and M. Hadjieleftheriou. Finding frequent items in data streams. *Proceedings of the VLDB Endowment*, 1(2):1530–1541, 2008.

[20] G. Cormode, F. Korn, S. Muthukrishnan, and D. Srivastava. Finding hierarchical heavy hitters in streaming data. *ACM Trans. Knowl. Discov. Data*, 1(4), 2008.

[21] G. Cormode and S. Muthukrishnan. An improved data stream summary: the count-min sketch and its applications. *J. Algorithms*, 55(1):58–75, 2005.

[22] T. M. Cover and J. A. Thomas. *Elements of information theory*. John Wiley & Sons, 2012.

[23] E. D. Demaine, A. López-Ortiz, and J. I. Munro. Frequency estimation of internet packet streams with limited space. In *Proc. 10th Annual European Symposium on Algorithms*, pages 348–360. Springer, 2002.

[24] P. Dey and A. Bhattacharyya. Sample complexity for winner prediction in elections. In *Proc. 14th International Conference on Autonomous Systems and Multiagent Systems (AAMAS-15)*, 2015.

[25] M. Dietzfelbinger, T. Hagerup, J. Katajainen, and M. Penttonen. A reliable randomized algorithm for the closest-pair problem. *J. Algorithms*, 25(1):19–51, 1997.

[26] A. Dvoretzky, J. Kiefer, and J. Wolfowitz. Asymptotic minimax character of the sample distribution function and of the classical multinomial estimator. *Ann. Math. Stat.*, 27(3):642 – 669, 1956.

[27] C. Estan and G. Varghese. New directions in traffic measurement and accounting: Focusing on the elephants, ignoring the mice. *Theor. Comput. Syst.*, 21(3):270–313, 2003.

[28] M. Fang, N. Shivakumar, H. Garcia-Molina, R. Motwani, and J. D. Ullman. Computing iceberg queries efficiently. In *Proc. 24rd International Conference on*

Very Large Data Bases, pages 299–310, 1998.
[29] P. Flajolet. Approximate counting: a detailed analysis. *BIT Numerical Mathematics*, 25(1):113–134, 1985.
[30] A. C. Gilbert, M. J. Strauss, J. A. Tropp, and R. Vershynin. One sketch for all: fast algorithms for compressed sensing. In *Proc. 39th Annual ACM Symposium on Theory of Computing, San Diego, California, USA, June 11-13, 2007*, pages 237–246, 2007.
[31] J. Han, J. Pei, G. Dong, and K. Wang. Efficient computation of iceberg cubes with complex measures. In *Proc. 2001 ACM SIGMOD International Conference on Management of Data,*, pages 1–12, 2001.
[32] J. Han, J. Pei, and Y. Yin. Mining frequent patterns without candidate generation. In *Proc. 2000 ACM SIGMOD International Conference on Management of Data*, pages 1–12, 2000.
[33] J. L. Herlocker, J. A. Konstan, L. G. Terveen, and J. T. Riedl. Evaluating collaborative filtering recommender systems. *ACM Trans. Inf. Syst.*, 22(1):5–53, 2004.
[34] J. Hershberger, N. Shrivastava, S. Suri, and C. D. Tóth. Space complexity of hierarchical heavy hitters in multi-dimensional data streams. In *Proc. Twenty-fourth ACM SIGACT-SIGMOD-SIGART Symposium on Principles of Database Systems*, pages 338–347, 2005.
[35] C. Hidber. Online association rule mining. In *SIGMOD 1999, Proc. ACM SIGMOD International Conference on Management of Data*, pages 145–156, 1999.
[36] T. K. Ho, J. J. Hull, and S. N. Srihari. Decision combination in multiple classifier systems. *IEEE Trans. Pattern Anal. Mach. Intell.*, 16(1):66–75, 1994.
[37] A. Jiang, L. S. Marcolino, A. D. Procaccia, T. Sandholm, N. Shah, and M. Tambe. Diverse randomized agents vote to win. In *Proc. Annual Conference on Neural Information Processing Systems*, pages 2573–2581, 2014.
[38] R. M. Karp, S. Shenker, and C. H. Papadimitriou. A simple algorithm for finding frequent elements in streams and bags. *ACM Trans. Database Syst.*, 28(1):51–55, 2003.
[39] P. Kellner, J. Twyman, and A. Wells. Polling voting intentions. In *Political Communication in Britain*, pages 94–108. Springer, 2011.
[40] I. Kremer, N. Nisan, and D. Ron. On randomized one-round communication complexity. *Comput. Complex.*, 8(1):21–49, 1999.
[41] A. Kumar and J. J. Xu. Sketch guided sampling - using on-line estimates of flow size for adaptive data collection. In *Proc. 25th IEEE International Conference on Computer Communications, Joint Conference of the IEEE Computer and Communications Societies*, 2006.
[42] E. Kushilevitz and N. Nisan. *Communication Complexity*. Cambridge University Press, New York, NY, USA, 1997.
[43] K. G. Larsen, J. Nelson, H. L. Nguyen, and M. Thorup. Heavy hitters via cluster-preserving clustering. arXiv:1604.01357, Apr. 2016.
[44] C. E. Leiserson, R. L. Rivest, C. Stein, and T. H. Cormen. Introduction to algorithms. *The MIT press*, 5:2–2, 2001.
[45] H. Li. Learning to rank for information retrieval and natural language processing. In *Synthesis Lectures on Human Language Technologies*, volume 7, pages 1–121. Morgan & Claypool Publishers, 2014.
[46] A. Lumini and L. Nanni. Detector of image orientation based on borda count. *Pattern Recogn. Lett.*, 27(3):180–186, 2006.
[47] N. Mamoulis, M. L. Yiu, K. H. Cheng, and D. W. Cheung. Efficient top-k aggregation of ranked inputs. *ACM Trans. Database Syst*, 32(3):19, 2007.
[48] G. S. Manku and R. Motwani. Approximate frequency counts over data streams. In *Proc. 28th International Conference on Very Large Data Bases*, pages 346–357. VLDB Endowment, 2002.
[49] A. Mao, A. D. Procaccia, and Y. Chen. Social Choice for Human Computation. In *Proc. Fourth Workshop on Human Computation (HCOMP-12)*, 2012.
[50] A. Mao, A. D. Procaccia, and Y. Chen. Better Human Computation Through Principled Voting. In *Proc. 27th Conference on Artificial Intelligence (AAAI'13)*, 2013.
[51] A. Marian, N. Bruno, and L. Gravano. Evaluating top-k queries over web-accessible databases. *ACM Trans. Database Syst.*, 29(2):319–362, 2004.
[52] A. Metwally, D. Agrawal, and A. El Abbadi. Efficient computation of frequent and top-k elements in data streams. In *Proc. 10th International Conference on Database Theory*, ICDT'05, pages 398–412, Berlin, Heidelberg, 2005. Springer-Verlag.
[53] P. B. Miltersen, N. Nisan, S. Safra, and A. Wigderson. On data structures and asymmetric communication complexity. *J. Comput. Syst. Sci.*, 57(1):37–49, 1998.
[54] J. Misra and D. Gries. Finding repeated elements. *Sci. Comput. Program.*, 2(2):143–152, 1982.
[55] M. M. Monwar and M. L. Gavrilova. Multimodal biometric system using rank-level fusion approach. *IEEE Trans. Syst. Man. Cybern. B, Cybern.*, 39(4):867–878, 2009.
[56] J. S. Moore. J. Algorithm, June 1981. p. 208–209.
[57] R. Morris. Counting large numbers of events in small registers. *Commun. ACM*, 21(10):840–842, 1978.
[58] D. Mullen and B. Roth. *Decision making: Its logic and practice.* Savage, MD: Rowman and Littlefield Publishers, Inc., 1991.
[59] S. Muthukrishnan. *Data streams: Algorithms and applications.* Now Publishers Inc, 2005.
[60] J. Nelson. Sketching and streaming algorithms for processing massive data. *XRDS: Crossroads, The ACM Magazine for Students*, 19(1):14–19, 2012.
[61] R. Nuray and F. Can. Automatic ranking of information retrieval systems using data fusion. *Inf. Process Manag.*, 42(3):595–614, 2006.
[62] A. Prasad, H. Pareek, and P. Ravikumar. Distributional rank aggregation, and an axiomatic analysis. In *Proc. 32nd International Conference on Machine Learning (ICML-15)*, pages 2104–2112, 2015.
[63] P. Resnick and H. R. Varian. Recommender systems. *Commun. ACM*, 40(3):56–58, 1997.
[64] A. Savasere, E. Omiecinski, and S. B. Navathe. An efficient algorithm for mining association rules in large databases. In *Proc. 21th International Conference on Very Large Data Bases*, pages 432–444, 1995.
[65] N. Shrivastava, C. Buragohain, D. Agrawal, and

S. Suri. Medians and beyond: new aggregation techniques for sensor networks. In *Proc. 2nd International Conference on Embedded Networked Sensor Systems*, pages 239–249, 2004.
[66] D. Smirnov. Shannon's information methods for lower bounds for probabilistic communication complexity. Master's thesis, Moscow University, 1988.
[67] X. Sun and D. P. Woodruff. Tight bounds for graph problems in insertion streams. In *Proc. 18th. International Workshop on Approximation Algorithms for Combinatorial Optimization Problems (APPROX 2015)*, pages 435–448, 2015.
[68] H. Toivonen. Sampling large databases for association rules. In *Proc. 22th International Conference on Very Large Data Bases*, pages 134–145, 1996.
[69] D. Van Gucht, R. Williams, D. P. Woodruff, and Q. Zhang. The communication complexity of distributed set-joins with applications to matrix multiplication. In *Proc. 34th ACM Symposium on Principles of Database Systems*, pages 199–212. ACM, 2015.
[70] M. N. Volkovs and R. S. Zemel. New learning methods for supervised and unsupervised preference aggregation. *J. Mach. Learn. Res.*, 15(1):1135–1176, 2014.
[71] G. Wang and F. H. Lochovsky. Feature selection with conditional mutual information maximin in text categorization. In *Proc. 13th ACM International Conference on Information and Knowledge Management*, pages 342–349. ACM, 2004.
[72] D. P. Woodruff. New Algorithms for Heavy Hitters in Data Streams. 2016. arXiv 1603.01733. Appeared in ICDT '16.
[73] L. Xia. Computing the margin of victory for various voting rules. In *Proc. 13th ACM Conference on Electronic Commerce*, pages 982–999. ACM, 2012.
[74] A. C.-C. Yao. Some complexity questions related to distributive computing (preliminary report). In *Proc. 11th annual ACM Symposium on Theory of computing*, pages 209–213. ACM, 1979.

APPENDIX

Appendix A

Information Theory Facts

For a discrete random variable X with possible values $\{x_1, x_2, \ldots, x_n\}$, the Shannon entropy of X is defined as $H(X) = -\sum_{i=1}^{n} \Pr(X = x_i) \log_2 \Pr(X = x_i)$. Let $H_b(p) = -p \log_2 p - (1-p)\log_2(1-p)$ denote the binary entropy function when $p \in (0, 1)$. For two random variables X and Y with possible values $\{x_1, x_2, \ldots, x_n\}$ and $\{y_1, y_2, \ldots, y_m\}$, respectively, the conditional entropy of X given Y is defined as $H(X \mid Y) = \sum_{i,j} \Pr(X = x_i, Y = y_j) \log_2 \frac{\Pr(Y=y_j)}{\Pr(X=x_i, Y=y_j)}$. Let $I(X;Y) = H(X) - H(X \mid Y) = H(Y) - H(Y \mid X)$ denote the mutual information between two random variables X, Y. Let $I(X;Y \mid Z)$ denote the mutual information between two random variables X, Y conditioned on Z, i.e., $I(X;Y \mid Z) = H(X \mid Z) - H(X \mid Y, Z)$. The following summarizes several basic properties of entropy and mutual information.

Proposition 1. *Let X, Y, Z, W be random variables.*

1. *If X takes value in $\{1, 2, \ldots, m\}$, then $H(X) \in [0, \log m]$.*
2. *$H(X) \geqslant H(X \mid Y)$ and $I(X;Y) = H(X) - H(X \mid Y) \geqslant 0$.*
3. *If X and Z are independent, then we have $I(X;Y \mid Z) \geqslant I(X;Y)$. Similarly, if X, Z are independent given W, then $I(X;Y \mid Z, W) \geqslant I(X;Y \mid W)$.*
4. *(Chain rule of mutual information) $I(X,Y;Z) = I(X;Z) + I(Y;Z \mid X)$. More generally, for any random variables $X_1, X_2, \ldots, X_n, Y$, $I(X_1, \ldots, X_n; Y) = \sum_{i=1}^{n} I(X_i; Y \mid X_1, \ldots, X_{i-1})$. Thus, $I(X, Y; Z \mid W) \geqslant I(X; Z \mid W)$.*
5. *(Fano's inequality) Let X be a random variable chosen from domain $\mathcal{X}$ according to distribution μ_X, and Y be a random variable chosen from domain $\mathcal{Y}$ according to distribution μ_Y. For any reconstruction function $g : \mathcal{Y} \to \mathcal{X}$ with error δ_g,*
$$H_b(\delta_g) + \delta_g \log(|\mathcal{X}| - 1) \geqslant H(X \mid Y).$$

We refer readers to [22] for a nice introduction to information theory.

Appendix B

We now present the missing proofs.

Lemma 1. *Suppose m is a power of two*[6]*. Then there is an algorithm $\mathcal{A}$ for choosing an item with probability $1/m$ that has space complexity of $O(\log \log m)$ bits and time complexity of $O(1)$ in the unit-cost RAM model.*

PROOF. We generate a $\log_2 m$ bits integer C uniformly at random and choose the item, say x, only if $C = 0$. □

We remark that the algorithm in Lemma 1 has optimal space complexity as shown in Proposition 2 below which may be of independent interest.

Proposition 2. *[★] Any algorithm that chooses an item from a set of size n with probability p for $0 < p \leqslant \frac{1}{n}$, in unit cost RAM model must use $\Omega(\log \log m)$ bits of memory.*

PROOF. The algorithm generates t bits uniformly at random (the number of bits it generates uniformly at random may also depend on the outcome of the previous random bits) and finally picks an item from the say x. Consider a run $\mathcal{R}$ of the algorithm where it chooses the item x with *smallest number of random bits getting generated*; say it generates t random bits in this run $\mathcal{R}$. This means that in any other run of the algorithm where the item x is chosen, the algorithm must generate at least t many random bits. Let the random bits generated in $\mathcal{R}$ be $r_1, \cdots, r_t$. Let s_i be the memory content of the algorithm immediately after it generates i^{th} random bit, for $i \in [t]$, in the run $\mathcal{R}$. First notice that if $t < \log_2 n$, then the probability with which the item x is chosen is more than $\frac{1}{n}$, which would be a contradiction. Hence, $t \geqslant \log_2 n$. Now we claim that all the s_i's must be different. Indeed otherwise, let us assume $s_i = s_j$ for some $i < j$. Then the algorithm chooses the item

[6]In all our algorithms, whenever we pick an item with probability $p > 0$, we can assume, without loss of generality, that $1/p$ is a power of two. If not, then we replace p with p' where $1/p'$ is the largest power of two less than $1/p$. This does not affect correctness and performance of our algorithms.

x after generating $t-(j-i)$ many random bits (which is strictly less than t) when the random bits being generated are $r_1, \cdots, r_i, r_{j+1}, \cdots, r_t$. This contradicts the assumption that the run $\mathcal{R}$ we started with chooses the item x with smallest number of random bits generated. $\square$

Lemma 2. *For $S \subseteq A$, $\delta \in (0,1)$, and universal family of hash functions $\mathcal{H} = \{h | h : A \to [\lceil |S|^2/\delta \rceil]\}$:*

$$\Pr_{h \in_{unif} \mathcal{H}}[\exists i \neq j \in S, h(i) = h(j)] \leqslant \delta$$

PROOF. For every $i \neq j \in S$, since $\mathcal{H}$ is a universal family of hash functions, we have

$$\Pr_{h \text{ picked uniformly at random from } \mathcal{H}}\{h(i) = h(j)\} \leqslant 1/\lceil |S|^2/\delta \rceil$$

Now we apply a union bound to get

$$\Pr_{h \text{ picked uniformly at random from } \mathcal{H}}\{\exists i \neq j \in S, h(i) = h(j)\}$$
$$\leqslant |S|^2/\lceil |S|^2/\delta \rceil$$
$$\leqslant \delta$$

$\square$

PROOF OF THEOREM 2. Pseudocode appears in Algorithm 2. Note that the numerical constants are chosen for convenience of analysis and have not been optimized. Also, for the sake of simplicity, the pseudocode does not have the optimal reporting time, but it can be modified to achieve this; see the end of this proof for details.

By standard Chernoff bounds, with probability at least 99/100, the length of the sampled stream $\ell/10 \leqslant s \leqslant 10\ell$. For $x \in [n]$, let $f_{\text{samp}}(x)$ be the frequency of x in the sampled stream. By Lemma 3, with probability at least 9/10, for all $x \in [n]$:

$$\left|\frac{f_{\text{samp}}(x)}{s} - \frac{f(x)}{m}\right| \leqslant \frac{\varepsilon}{4}$$

Now, fix $j \in [10 \log \varphi^{-1}]$ and $x \in [n]$. Let $i = h_j(x)$ and $f_i = \sum_{y: h_j(y) = h_j(x)} f_{\text{samp}}(y)$. Then, for a random $h_j \in \mathcal{H}$, the expected value of $\frac{f_i}{s} - \frac{f_{\text{samp}}(x)}{s}$ is $\frac{\varepsilon}{100}$, since $\mathcal{H}$ is a universal mapping to a space of size $100\varepsilon^{-1}$. Hence, using Markov's inequality and the above:

$$\Pr\left[\left|\frac{f(x)}{m} - \frac{f_i}{s}\right| \geqslant \frac{\varepsilon}{2}\right]$$
$$\leqslant \Pr\left[\left|\frac{f(x)}{m} - \frac{f_{\text{samp}}}{s}\right| \geqslant \frac{\varepsilon}{4}\right] + \Pr\left[\left|\frac{f_{\text{samp}}(x)}{m} - \frac{f_i}{s}\right| \geqslant \frac{\varepsilon}{4}\right]$$
$$< \frac{1}{10} + \frac{1}{25} < \frac{3}{20} \tag{1}$$

In Lemma 8 below, we show that for each $j \in [200 \log(12\varphi^{-1})]$, with error probability at most 3/10, $\hat{f}_j(x)$ (in line 23) estimates f_i with additive error at most $5000\varepsilon^{-1}$, hence estimating $\frac{f_i}{s}$ with additive error at most $\frac{\varepsilon}{2}$. Taking the median over $200 \log(12\varphi^{-1})$ repetitions (line 24) makes the error probability go down to $\frac{\varphi}{6}$ using standard Chernoff bounds. Hence, by the union bound, with probability at least 2/3, for each of the $2/\varphi$ keys x with nonzero values in $\mathcal{T}_1$, we have an estimate of $\frac{f(x)}{m}$ within additive error ε, thus showing correctness.

Lemma 8. *Fix $x \in [n]$ and $j \in [200 \log 12\varphi^{-1}]$, and let $i = h_j(x)$. Then, $\Pr[|\hat{f}_j(x) - f_i| > 5000\varepsilon^{-1}] \leqslant 3/10$, where $\hat{f}_j$ is the quantity computed in line 23.*

PROOF. Index the sampled stream elements $1, 2, \ldots, s$, and for $b \in [s]$, let $f_i(b)$ be the frequency of items with hash id i restricted to the first b elements of the sampled stream. Let $\bar{f}_i(b)$ denote the value of $\mathcal{T}_2[i,j] \cdot \varepsilon^{-1}$ after the procedure INSERT has been called for the first b items of the sampled stream.

Claim 1. *With probability at least 9/10, for all $b \in [s]$ such that $f_i(b) \geqslant 100\varepsilon^{-1}$, $\bar{f}_i(b)$ is within a factor of 4 of $f_i(b)$.*

PROOF. Fix $b \in [s]$. Note that $\mathbb{E}\left[\bar{f}_i(b)\right] = f_i(b)$ as $\mathcal{T}_2$ is incremented with rate ε. $\mathsf{Var}[\bar{f}_i(b)] \leqslant f_i/\varepsilon$, and so by Chebyshev's inequality:

$$\Pr[|\bar{f}_i(b) - f_i(b)| > f_i(b)/2] < \frac{4}{f_i(b)\varepsilon}$$

We now break the stream into chunks, apply this inequality to each chunk and then take a union bound to conclude. Namely, for any integer $t \geqslant 0$, define b_t to be the first b such that $100\varepsilon^{-1}2^t \leqslant f_i(b) < 100\varepsilon^{-1}2^{t+1}$ if such a b exists. Then:

$$\Pr[\exists t \geqslant 0 : |\bar{f}_i(b_t) - f_i(b_t)| > f_i(b_t)/2] < \sum_t \frac{4}{100 \cdot 2^{t-1}}$$
$$< \frac{1}{10}$$

So, with probability at least 9/10, every $\bar{f}_i(b_t)$ and $f_i(b_t)$ are within a factor of 2 of each other. Since for every $b \geqslant b_0$, $f_i(b)$ is within a factor of 2 from some $f_i(b_t)$, the claim follows. $\square$

Assume the event in Claim 1 henceforth. Now, we are ready to analyze $\mathcal{T}_3$ and in particular, $\hat{f}_j(x)$. First of all, observe that if $t < 0$ in line 15, at some position b in the stream, then $\mathcal{T}_2[i,j]$ at that time must be at most 1000, and so by standard Markov and Chernoff bounds, with probability at least 0.85,

$$f_i(b) \begin{cases} < 4000\varepsilon^{-1}, & \text{if } t < 0 \\ > 100\varepsilon^{-1}, & \text{if } t \geqslant 0 \end{cases} \tag{2}$$

Assume this event. Then, $f_i - 4000\varepsilon^{-1} \leqslant \mathbb{E}\left[\hat{f}_j(x)\right] \leqslant f_i$.

Claim 2.

$$\mathsf{Var}(\hat{f}_j(x)) \leqslant 20000\varepsilon^{-2}$$

PROOF. If the stream element at position b causes an increment in $\mathcal{T}_3$ with probability $\varepsilon 2^t$ (in line 17), then $1000 \cdot 2^{t/2} \leqslant \mathcal{T}_2[i,j] \leqslant 1000 \cdot 2^{(t+1)/2}$, and so, $\bar{f}_i(b) \leqslant 1000\varepsilon^{-1}2^{(t+1)/2}$. This must be the case for the highest $b = \bar{b}_t$ at which the count for i in $\mathcal{T}_3$ increments at the t'th slot. The number of such occurrences of i is at most $f_i(\bar{b}_t) \leqslant 4\bar{f}_i(\bar{b}_t) \leqslant 4000\varepsilon^{-1}2^{(t+1)/2}$ by Claim 1 (which can be applied since $f_i(b) > 100\varepsilon^{-1}$ by Equation 2). So:

$$\mathsf{Var}[\hat{f}_j(x)] \leqslant \sum_{t \geqslant 0} \frac{f_i(\bar{b}_t)}{\varepsilon 2^t} \leqslant \sum_{t \geqslant 0} \frac{4000}{\varepsilon^2} 2^{-t/3} \leqslant 20000\varepsilon^{-2}$$

Elements inserted with probability 1 obviously do not contribute to the variance. $\square$

So, conditioning on the events mentioned, the probability that $\hat{f}_j(x)$ deviates from f_i by more than $5000\varepsilon^{-1}$ is at most 1/50. Removing all the conditioning yields what we wanted:

$$\Pr[|\hat{f}_j(x) - f_i| > 5000\varepsilon^{-1}] \leqslant \frac{1}{50} + \frac{3}{20} + \frac{1}{10} \leqslant 0.3$$

We next bound the space complexity.

Claim 3. *With probability at least 2/3, Algorithm 2 uses* $O(\varepsilon^{-1}\log\varphi^{-1} + \varphi^{-1}\log n + \log\log m)$ *bits of storage, if* $n = \omega(\varepsilon^{-1})$.

PROOF. The expected length of the sampled stream is $\ell = O(\varepsilon^{-2})$. So, the number of bits stored in $\mathcal{T}_1$ is $O(\varphi^{-1}\log n)$. For $\mathcal{T}_2$, note that in lines 13-15, for any given j, $\mathcal{T}_2$ is storing a total of $\varepsilon\ell = O(\varepsilon^{-1})$ elements in expectation. So, for $k \geqslant 0$, there can be at most $O((\varepsilon 2^k)^{-1})$ hashed id's with counts between 2^k and 2^{k+1}. Summing over all k's and accounting for the empty cells gives $O(\varepsilon^{-1})$ bits of storage, and so the total space requirement of $\mathcal{T}_2$ is $O(\varepsilon^{-1}\log\varphi^{-1})$.
.

The probability that a hashed id i gets counted in table $\mathcal{T}_3$ is at most $10^{-6}\varepsilon^3\bar{f}_i^2(s)$ from line 15 and our definition of $\bar{f}_i$ above. Moreover, from Claim 1, we have that this is at most $16\cdot 10^{-6}\varepsilon^3 f_i^2(s)$ if $f_i > 100\varepsilon^{-1}$. Therefore, if $f_i = 2^k \cdot 100\varepsilon^{-1}$ with $k \geqslant 0$, then the expected value of a cell in $\mathcal{T}_3$ with first coordinate i is at most $1600 \cdot 2^{2k}\varepsilon = 2^{O(k)}$. Taking into account that there are at most $O((\varepsilon 2^k)^{-1})$ many such id's i and that the number of epochs t associated with such an i is at most $\log(16 \cdot 10^{-6}\varepsilon^2 f_i^2) = O(\log(\varepsilon f_i)) = O(k)$ (from line 15), we get that the total space required for $\mathcal{T}_3$ is:

$$\sum_{j=1}^{O(\log\varphi^{-1})}\left(O(\varepsilon^{-1}) + \sum_{k=0}^{\infty} O((\varepsilon 2^k)^{-1}) \cdot O(k) \cdot O(k)\right) = O(\varepsilon^{-1}\log\varphi^{-1})$$

where the first $O(\varepsilon^{-1})$ term inside the summation is for the i's with $f_i < 100\varepsilon^{-1}$. Since we have an expected space bound, we obtain a worst-case space bound with error probability 1/3 by a Markov bound.

The space required for sampling is an additional $O(\log\log m)$, using Lemma 1. □

We note that the space bound can be made worst case by aborting the algorithm if it tries to use more space.

The only remaining aspect of Theorem 2 is the time complexity. As observed in Section 3.1, the update time can be made $O(1)$ per insertion under the standard assumption of the stream being sufficiently long. The reporting time can also be made linear in the output by changing the bookkeeping a bit. Instead of computing $\hat{f}_j$ and $\hat{f}$ at reporting time, we can maintain them after every insertion. Although this apparently makes INSERT costlier, this is not true in fact because we can spread the cost over future stream insertions. The space complexity grows by a constant factor.

Theorem 4. *Assume the length of the stream is known beforehand. Then there is a randomized one-pass algorithm* $\mathcal{A}$ *for the* ε-MINIMUM *problem which succeeds with probability at least* $1-\delta$ *using* $O\left((1/\varepsilon)\log\log(1/\varepsilon\delta) + \log\log m\right)$ *bits of space. Moreover, the algorithm* $\mathcal{A}$ *has an update time of* $O(1)$.

PROOF OF THEOREM 4. The pseudocode of our ε-MINIMUM algorithm is in Algorithm 3. If the size of the universe $|\mathcal{U}|$ is at least $1/((1-\delta)\varepsilon)$, then we return an item x chosen from $\mathcal{U}$ uniformly at random. Note that there can be at most $1/\varepsilon$ many items with frequency at least εm. Hence every item x among other remaining $\delta/((1-\delta)\varepsilon)$ many items has frequency less than εm and thus is a correct output of the instance. Thus the probability that we answer correctly is at least $(1-\delta)$. From here on, let us assume $|\mathcal{U}| < 1/((1-\delta)\varepsilon)$.

Now, by the value of p_j, it follows from the proof of Theorem 1 that we can assume $\ell_j < |\mathcal{S}_j| < 11\ell_j$ for $j = 1, 2, 3$ which happens with probability at least $(1 - (\delta/3))$. We first show that every item in $\mathcal{U}$ with frequency at least εm is sampled in $\mathcal{S}_1$ with probability at least $(1 - (\delta/6))$. For that, let X_i^j be the indicator random variable for the event that the jth sample in $\mathcal{S}_1$ is item i where $i \in \mathcal{U}$ is an item with frequency at least εm. Let $\mathcal{H} \subset \mathcal{U}$ be the set of items with frequencies at least εm. Then we have the following.

$$\Pr[X_i^j = 0] = 1 - \varepsilon$$
$$\Rightarrow \quad \Pr[X_i^j = 0 \ \forall j \in \mathcal{S}_1] \leqslant (1-\varepsilon)^{\ell_1} \leqslant \exp\{-\varepsilon\ell_1\} = \varepsilon\delta/6$$

Now applying a union bound we get the following.

$$\Pr[\exists i \in \mathcal{H}, X_i^j = 0 \ \forall j \in \mathcal{S}_1] \leqslant (1/\varepsilon)\varepsilon\delta/6 \leqslant \delta/6$$

Hence with probability at least $(1 - (\delta/3) - (\delta/6)) \geqslant (1-\delta)$, the output at line 17 is correct. Now we show below that if the frequency of any item $x \in \mathcal{U}$ is at most $\varepsilon \ln(6/\delta)/\ln(6/\varepsilon\delta)$, then $x \in \mathcal{S}_1$ with probability at least $(1 - (\delta/6))$.

$$\Pr[x \notin \mathcal{S}_1] = (1 - \varepsilon\ln(6/\delta)/\ln(6/\varepsilon\delta))^{\ln(6/\varepsilon\delta)/\varepsilon} \leqslant \delta/6$$

Hence from here onwards we assume that the frequency of every item in $\mathcal{U}$ is at least $\varepsilon m \ln(6/\delta)/\ln(6/\varepsilon\delta)$.

If the number of distinct elements is at most $1/(\varepsilon\ln(1/\varepsilon))$, then line 19 outputs the minimum frequency item up to an additive factor of εm due to Chernoff bound (see [24]). Note that we need only $O(\ln(1/((1-\delta)\varepsilon)))$ bits of space for storing ids. Hence $\mathcal{S}_2$ can be stored in space $O((1/\varepsilon\ln(1/\varepsilon))\ln(1/((1-\delta)\varepsilon)\ln\ln(1/\delta)) = O(1/\varepsilon \ln\ln(1/\delta))$.

Now we can assume that the number of distinct elements is at least $1/(\varepsilon\ln(1/\varepsilon))$. Hence if $f(t)$ is the frequency of the item t with minimum frequency, then we have $m\varepsilon/\ln(1/\varepsilon) \leqslant f(t) \leqslant m\varepsilon\ln(1/\varepsilon)$.

Let f_i be the frequency of item $i \in \mathcal{U}$, e_i be the counter value of i in $\mathcal{S}_3$, and $\hat{f}_i = e_i m/\ell_3$. Now again by applying Chernoff bound we have the following for any fixed $i \in \mathcal{U}$.

$$\begin{aligned}\Pr[|f_i - \hat{f}_i| > f_i/\ln^2(1/\varepsilon)] &\leqslant 2\exp\{-\ell_3 f_i/(m\ln^4(1/\varepsilon))\} \\ &\leqslant 2\exp\{-f_i\ln^2(6/\varepsilon\delta)/(\varepsilon m)\} \\ &\leqslant \varepsilon\delta/6.\end{aligned}$$

Now applying a union bound we get the following using the fact that $|\mathcal{U}| \leqslant 1/\varepsilon(1-\delta)$.

$$\Pr[\forall i \in \mathcal{U}, |f_i - \hat{f}_i| \leqslant f_i/\ln^2(1/\varepsilon)] > 1 - \delta/6$$

Again by applying Chernoff bound and union bound we get the following.

$$\Pr[\forall i \in \mathcal{U} \text{ with } f_i > 2m\varepsilon\ln(1/\varepsilon), |f_i - \hat{f}_i| \leqslant f_i/2] > 1 - \delta/6$$

Hence the items with frequency more than $2m\varepsilon\ln(1/\varepsilon)$ are approximated up to a multiplicative factor of $1/2$ from below in $\mathcal{S}_3$. The counters of these items may be truncated. The other items with frequency at most $2m\varepsilon\ln(1/\varepsilon)$ are be approximated up to $(1 \pm 1/\ln^2(1/\varepsilon))$ relative error and thus up to an additive error of $\varepsilon m/3$. The counters of these items would not get truncated. Hence the item with minimum counter value in $\mathcal{S}_3$ is the item with minimum frequency up to an additive εm.

We need $O(\ln(1/\varepsilon\delta))$ bits of space for the bit vector $\mathcal{B}_1$ for the set $\mathcal{S}_1$. We need $O(\ln^2(1/\varepsilon\delta))$ bits of space for the set $\mathcal{S}_2$ and $O((1/\varepsilon)\ln\ln(1/\varepsilon\delta))$ bits of space for the set $\mathcal{S}_3$ (by the choice of truncation threshold). We need an additional $O(\ln\ln m)$ bits of space for sampling using Lemma 1. Moreover, using the data structure of Section 3.3 of [23] Algorithm 3 can be performed in $O(1)$ time. Alternatively, we may also use the strategy described in Section 3.1 of spreading update operations over several insertions to make the cost per insertion be $O(1)$. $\square$

Theorem 3. *Assume the length of the stream is known beforehand. Then there is a randomized one-pass algorithm $\mathcal{A}$ for the ε-*MAXIMUM *problem which succeeds with probability at least $1-\delta$ using $O(\min\{1/\varepsilon, n\}(\log 1/\varepsilon + \log\log 1/\delta) + \log n + \log\log m)$ bits of space. Moreover, the algorithm $\mathcal{A}$ has an update time of $O(1)$.*

PROOF. Instead of maintaining the table $\mathcal{T}_2$ in Algorithm 1, we just store the actual ID of the item with maximum frequency in the sampled items. $\square$

Theorem 5. *Assume the length of the stream is known beforehand. Then there is a randomized one-pass algorithm $\mathcal{A}$ for (ε,φ)-*LIST BORDA *problem which succeeds with probability at least $1-\delta$ using $O\left(n\left(\log n + \log\frac{1}{\varepsilon} + \log\log\frac{1}{\delta}\right) + \log\log m\right)$ bits of space.*

PROOF. Let $\ell = 6\varepsilon^{-2}\log(6n\delta^{-1})$ and $p = 6\ell/m$. On each insertion of a vote v, select v with probability p and store for every $i \in [n]$, the number of candidates that candidate i beats in the vote v. Keep these exact counts in a counter of length n.

Then it follows from the proof of Theorem 1 that $\ell \leqslant |\mathcal{S}| \leqslant 11\ell$ with probability at least $(1-\delta/3)$. Moreover, from a straightforward application of the Chernoff bound (see [24]), it follows that if $\hat{s}(i)$ denotes the Borda score of candidate i restricted to the sampled votes, then:

$$\Pr\left[\forall i \in [n], \left|\frac{m}{|\mathcal{S}|}\hat{s}(i) - s(i)\right| < \varepsilon mn\right] > 1-\delta$$

The space complexity for exactly storing the counts is $O(n\log(n\ell)) = O(n(\log n + \log\varepsilon^{-1} + \log\log\delta^{-1}))$ and the space for sampling the votes is $O(\log\log m)$ by Lemma 1. $\square$

Theorem 6. *Assume the length of the stream is known beforehand. Then there is a randomized one-pass algorithm $\mathcal{A}$ for (ε,φ)-*LIST MAXIMIN *problem which succeeds with probability at least $1-\delta$ using $O\left(n\varepsilon^{-2}\log^2 n + n\varepsilon^{-2}\log n\log\delta^{-1} + \log\log m\right)$ bits of space.*

PROOF. Let $\ell = (8/\varepsilon^2)\ln(6n/\delta)$ and $p = 6\ell/m$. We put the current vote in a set $\mathcal{S}$ with probability p. Then it follows from the proof of Theorem 1 that $\ell \leqslant |\mathcal{S}| \leqslant 11\ell$ with probability at least $(1-\delta/3)$. Suppose $|\mathcal{S}| = \ell_1$; let $\mathcal{S} = \{v_i : i \in [\ell_1]\}$ be the set of votes sampled. Let $D_{\mathcal{S}}(x,y)$ be the weight of the edge in the weighted majority graph constructed from the votes in $\mathcal{S}$ for items $x, y \in \mathcal{U}$. Then by the choice of ℓ it follows that $|D_{\mathcal{S}}(x,y)m/\ell_1 - D_{\mathcal{E}}(x,y)| \leqslant \varepsilon m/2$ for every item $x, y \in \mathcal{U}$ [24]. Note that each vote can be stored in $O(n\ln n)$ bits of space. Hence simply finding $D_{\mathcal{S}}(x,y)$ for every $x, y \in \mathcal{U}$ by storing $\mathcal{S}$ and returning all the items with maximin score at least $\varphi\ell_1$ in $\mathcal{S}$ requires $O\left(n\ln^2 n\ln(1/\delta)/\varepsilon^2 + \ln\ln m\right)$ bits of memory.

Rather than simply storing all the items, we can do as follows. From $\mathcal{S}$, we generate another stream $\bar{\mathcal{S}}$ of elements belonging to the universe $\mathcal{U}\times\mathcal{U}$. Let a vote $v \in \mathcal{S}$ be $c_1 \succ c_2 \succ \cdots \succ c_n$. From v we put (c_j, c_k) in $\bar{\mathcal{S}}$ for every $j < k$. We count the frequency of every item in $\mathcal{S}$ by simply keeping one counter for every items in the universe $\mathcal{U}\times\mathcal{U}$ and output all the items with maximin score at least $\varphi\ell_1$ in $\mathcal{S}$. This requires $O\left(n^2\left(\ln\ln n + \ln(1/\varepsilon + \ln\ln(1/\delta))\right) + \ln\ln m\right)$ bits of space. The correctness of the algorithm follows from the argument above. $\square$

Lemma 5. *$\mathcal{R}_\delta^{1\text{-}way}(\varepsilon - \text{PERM}) = \Omega(n\log(1/\varepsilon))$, for any constant $\delta < 1/10$.*

PROOF. Let us assume σ, the permutation Alice has, is uniformly distributed over the set of all permutations. Let τ_j denotes the block the item j is in for $j \in [n]$, $\tau = (\tau_1, \ldots, \tau_n)$, and $\tau_{<j} = (\tau_1, \ldots, \tau_{j-1})$. Let $M(\tau)$ be Alice's message to Bob, which is a random variable depending on the randomness of σ and the private coin tosses of Alice. Then we have $\mathcal{R}^{1-way}(\varepsilon - \text{PERM}) \geqslant H(M(\tau)) \geqslant I(M(\tau);\tau)$. Hence it is enough to lower bound $I(M(\tau);\tau)$. Then we have the following by chain rule.

$$\begin{aligned}
I(M(\tau);\tau) &= \sum_{j=1}^{n} I(M(\tau);\tau_j|\tau_{<j}) \\
&= \sum_{j=1}^{n} H(\tau_j|\tau_{<j}) - H(\tau_j|M(\tau),\tau_{<j}) \\
&\geqslant \sum_{j=1}^{n} H(\tau_j|\tau_{<j}) - \sum_{j=1}^{n} H(\tau_j|M(\tau)) \\
&= H(\tau) - \sum_{j=1}^{n} H(\tau_j|M(\tau))
\end{aligned}$$

The number of ways to partition n items into $1/\varepsilon$ blocks is $n!/((\varepsilon n)!)^{(1/\varepsilon)}$ which is $\Omega((n/e)^n/(\varepsilon n/e)^n)$. Hence we have $H(\tau) = n\log(1/\varepsilon)$. Now we consider $H(\tau_j|M(\tau))$. By the correctness of the algorithm, Fano's inequality, we have $H(\tau_j|M(\tau)) \leqslant H(\delta) + (1/10)\log_2((1/\varepsilon) - 1) \leqslant (1/2)\log(1/\varepsilon)$. Hence we have the following.

$$I(M(\tau);\tau) \geqslant (n/2)\log(1/\varepsilon)$$

$\square$

Lemma 6. *$\mathcal{R}_\delta^{1\text{-}way}(\text{GREATER-THAN}_n) = \Omega(\log n)$, for every $\delta < 1/4$.*

PROOF. We reduce the AUGMENTED-INDEXING$_{2,\lceil\log n\rceil+1}$ problem to the GREATER-THAN$_n$ problem thereby proving the result. Alice runs the GREATER-THAN$_n$ protocol with its input number whose representation in binary is $a = (x_1 x_2 \cdots x_{\lceil\log n\rceil} 1)_2$. Bob participates in the GREATER-THAN$_n$ protocol with its input number whose representation in binary is $b = (x_1 x_2 \cdots x_{i-1} 1 \underbrace{0\cdots0}_{(\lceil\log n\rceil - i + 1)\ 0's})_2$. Now $x_i = 1$ if and only if $a > b$. $\square$

Better Algorithms for Counting Triangles in Data Streams*

Andrew McGregor
University of Massachusetts
mcgregor@cs.umass.edu

Sofya Vorotnikova
University of Massachusetts
svorotni@cs.umass.edu

Hoa T. Vu
University of Massachusetts
hvu@cs.umass.edu

ABSTRACT

We present space-efficient data stream algorithms for approximating the number of triangles in a graph up to a factor $1+\epsilon$. While it can be shown that determining whether a graph is triangle-free is not possible in sub-linear space, a large body of work has focused on minimizing the space required in terms of the number of triangles T (or a lower bound on this quantity) and other parameters including the number of nodes n and the number of edges m. Two models are important in the literature: the *arbitrary order* model in which the stream consists of the edges of the graph in arbitrary order and the *adjacency list order* model in which all edges incident to the same node appear consecutively. We improve over the state of the art results in both models. For the adjacency list order model, we show that $\tilde{O}(\epsilon^{-2}m/\sqrt{T})$ space is sufficient in one pass and $\tilde{O}(\epsilon^{-2}m^{3/2}/T)$ space is sufficient in two passes where the $\tilde{O}(\cdot)$ notation suppresses log factors. For the arbitrary order model, we show that $\tilde{O}(\epsilon^{-2}m/\sqrt{T})$ space suffices given two passes and that $\tilde{O}(\epsilon^{-2}m^{3/2}/T)$ space suffices given three passes and oracle access to the degrees. Finally, we show how to efficiently implement the "wedge sampling" approach to triangle estimation in the arbitrary order model. To do this, we develop the first algorithm for ℓ_p sampling such that multiple independent samples can be generated with $O(\text{polylog}\, n)$ update time; this primitive is widely applicable and this result may be of independent interest.

Categories and Subject Descriptors

F.2 [**Analysis of Algorithms & Problem Complexity**]

Keywords

data streams; triangles; clustering coefficients

1. INTRODUCTION

Estimating the number of triangles in a graph is a canonical problem in the data stream model of computation. The problem was first considered by Bar-Yossef et al. [6] nearly fifteen years ago and a significant body of work has since been devoted to designing more efficient and ingenious algorithms for the problem in both the single-pass [1, 2, 6, 9, 10, 22, 24, 29, 31, 37, 38, 41] and multi-pass models [8, 16, 28]. For a survey of existing graph stream algorithms, including triangle counting, see [32].

There appears to be two main reasons for the high level of interest in the problem. First, the number of triangles in a network and related quantities such as the *transitivity* or *global clustering coefficient* (the fraction of length two paths that are included in a triangle) play an important role in the analysis of real-world networks. Popular examples include motif detection in protein interaction networks [34], uncovering hidden thematic structure in the web graph [17], analysis of social networks [44], and the evaluation of large graph models [30]. Following Kutzkov et al. [9, 29], we direct the interested reader to Tsourakakis et al. [42] for an excellent overview of these and other applications. Second, the problem has a rich theory. The best exact algorithm in the RAM model runs in $O(m^{2\omega/(\omega+1)})$ time [2] where $\omega \leq 2.3728$ is the matrix multiplication exponent and m is the number of edges. This year, Eden et al. [18] designed the first sub-linear time algorithm. Finally, there are connections to a range of important problems in the field of fine-grained complexity [23]. Since many of the real world graphs of interest are massive, it is natural that the problem has also been studied in the appropriate computation models, e.g., the MapReduce model [40] and other parallel models [5, 7], external memory models [4], and the data stream model (see above for the long stream of references).

Two data stream models have been considered in the literature on triangle counting: the *arbitrary order* model in which the stream consists of the edges of the graph in arbitrary order and the *adjacency list order* model in which all edges incident to the same node appear consecutively.[1] Of the algorithms designed in both models, some are suitable when there are many triangles whereas others dominate if there are only a few triangles. We next discuss the state-of-the-art results and these trade-offs in the context of our new results.

1.1 Our Results and Related Work

In discussing our results and the related work we use n to denote the number of nodes in the input graph, m to be the number of edges, and T is the number of triangles in the graph.

Approximate Triangle Counting. We present four main algorithms that $(1+\epsilon)$-estimate the number of triangles: two algorithms for each data stream model (arbitrary order and adjacency list order)

*Work supported by NSF Awards CCF-0953754, IIS-1251110, CCF-1320719, and a Google Research Award.

PODS'16, June 26-July 01, 2016, San Francisco, CA, USA
© 2016 ACM. ISBN 978-1-4503-4191-2/16/06...$15.00
DOI: http://dx.doi.org/10.1145/2902251.2902283

[1]The adjacency list order model is closely related to the vertex arrival model that has been considered in the context of finding matchings in the data stream model [20, 26] and row-order arrival model consider in the context of linear algebra problems [12, 19].

where one is suitable for processing graphs with many triangles (in particular, when $T \geq m$) and the other is suitable for processing graphs with fewer triangles (i.e., $T \leq m$).[2] Specifically:

1. *Adjacency List Model:* We present a single-pass algorithm using $\tilde{O}(\epsilon^{-2}m/\sqrt{T})$ space and a two-pass algorithm using $\tilde{O}(\epsilon^{-2}m^{3/2}/T)$ space. We show that the space can be further reduced if we only need to distinguish triangle-free graphs from those with at least T triangles.

2. *Arbitrary Order Model:* We present a two-pass algorithm using $\tilde{O}(\epsilon^{-2}m/\sqrt{T})$ space and a three-pass algorithm using $\tilde{O}(\epsilon^{-2}m^{3/2}/T)$ space. However, the second algorithm assumes that we have oracle access to the degrees of the nodes.

It can be argued that using only $\approx m/\sqrt{T}$ space has become a natural goal in the context of estimating the number of triangles. In particular, Cormode and Jowhari [16] showed that any constant pass algorithm in the arbitrary order model required this amount of space when $m = \Theta(n\sqrt{T})$ and there is an existing two-pass algorithm that returns a 3-approximation using this amount of space. Furthermore, Jha et al. [22] showed that this space was sufficient for additively approximating T. Unfortunately, Braverman et al. [8] showed it was insufficient for achieving multiplicative approximation via a *single-pass* algorithm in the arbitrary order model. The significance of our results is showing that $\approx m/\sqrt{T}$ space is sufficient for $1+\epsilon$ approximation if we are given a single pass over a stream in adjacency list order or two passes over a stream in arbitrary order.

However, it is possible to improve upon $\approx m/\sqrt{T}$ space when T is large and our other two algorithms do just this. At a high level, the main difference between the two types of algorithms we present is as follows. The $m/\sqrt{T}$ dependence arises when we focus on distinguishing between edges that are involved in many triangles and those that are not, whereas the $m^{3/2}/T$ dependence arises when we distinguish between high and low degree nodes. The idea of distinguishing heavy and light edges or nodes is an important idea in the non-streaming work by Alon et al. [2], Eden et al. [18], Chiba and Nishizeki [11], among others. The main challenge in our work arises from the constraints of the data stream model. This necessitates new algorithms and new notions of heavy and light that may also depend on the ordering of the stream.

Wedge Sampling. An important technique developed in the context of triangle counting is that of *wedge sampling* [27, 39]. A wedge is a length-two path in a graph and the goal is to sample wedges uniformly from the graph. We use W to denote the number of wedges in a graph[3] and note that the global clustering coefficient equals $3T/W$. In the final section of this paper, we show the following:

3. *Fast Wedge Sampling via ℓ_p Sampling:* We show how to sample s independent wedges in the data stream model with $\tilde{O}(1)$ update time. We do this by first proving a new result for ℓ_p sampling, an important data stream primitive. See Section 4.2 for more details. Our second algorithm for the arbitrary order model is based on wedge sampling.

[2]For context, it can be shown that $T = O(m^{3/2})$ and there are graphs where $T = \Omega(m^{3/2})$ [2].

[3]For context, it can be shown that W is at least $m^2/(2n)$ (for $m \geq n$) and can be $\Omega(mn)$.

1.1.1 *Comparison to Previous Algorithms*

Adjacency List Model. Prior to our work, the state-of-the-art algorithms in the adjacency list model were a three-pass algorithm using $\tilde{O}(\sqrt{m} + \epsilon^{-2}m^{3/2}/T)$ space that was presented by Kolountzakis et al. [28] and a one-pass algorithm using $\tilde{O}(\epsilon^{-2}W/T)$ space that was presented by Buriol et al. [10]. Note that $\tilde{O}(\epsilon^{-2}W/T)$ is $\tilde{O}(\epsilon^{-2}mn/T)$ in the worst case and therefore the former algorithm may use significantly less space when $m \ll n^2$ but this improvement is limited by the additive $\sqrt{m}$ term. Our one-pass algorithm improves upon the Buriol et al. result for $T \leq n^2$ and improves upon the Kolountzakis et al. result for all values of T. This second observation follows because if $T \geq m$ then $m/\sqrt{T} \leq \sqrt{m}$ and if $T \leq m$ then $m/\sqrt{T} \leq m^{3/2}/T$. Our two-pass algorithm also dominates the algorithm of Kolountzakis et al. for all T since it uses only two passes rather than three passes and there is no additive $\sqrt{m}$ term in the space use.

Arbitrary Order Model. Prior to our work, the state-of-the-art results include another one-pass algorithm by Buriol et al. [10] that used $\tilde{O}(\epsilon^{-2}mn/T)$ space. Pavan et al. [38] showed that the dependence on n could be replaced by the maximum degree and Pagh and Tsourakakis [37] showed that this could be replaced by a dependence on the maximum number of triangles using a single edge. The other most relevant result is a one pass algorithm by Jha et al. [22] that returns an additive $\pm\epsilon W$ estimate (equivalently, an additive ϵ approximation of the transitivity coefficient) using $\tilde{O}(\epsilon^{-2}m/\sqrt{T})$ space. In establishing our first result for the arbitrary order model, we first revisit the Jha et al. algorithm to show that it can also be used to estimate the number of triangles multiplicatively using space that is almost identical to that required by Pagh and Tsourakakis' algorithm.

The most relevant previous work in the arbitrary order model is an $(1+\epsilon)$-approximation using $\tilde{O}(\epsilon^{-2}m/T^{1/3})$ space by Braverman et al. [8] and a $(3+\epsilon)$-approximation with $\tilde{O}(\epsilon^{-4.5}m/\sqrt{T})$ space by Cormode and Jowhari [16]. Note that Cormode and Jowhari initially claimed that their algorithm returned a $1+\epsilon$ but this claim is incorrect [13].[4] Subsequent to the submission of our paper, Cormode and Jowhari have independently designed a new algorithm [14]. This alternative algorithm, significantly different from their earlier algorithm and more complicated than our algorithm, uses $\tilde{O}(\epsilon^{-2.5}m/\sqrt{T})$ space.

1.2 Notation and Preliminaries

It will be convenient to assume the node set of the graph is $[n] = \{1, 2, \ldots, n\}$. Let $\Gamma(v)$ denote the neighbors of a node v and so $\deg(v) = |\Gamma(v)|$. We write (undirected) edges as sets of two nodes $\{u, v\}$ and write ordered pairs of nodes as uv. For example, $\{u, v\} = \{v, u\}$ but $uv \neq vu$. We use Δ to denote the set of triangles in the input graph and so $T = |\Delta|$. For a random variable X, we denote the expectation and variance as $\mathrm{E}[X]$ and $\mathrm{V}[X]$ respectively. $\mathbf{Bin}(n, p)$ denotes the binomial distribution with parameters n and p.

To simplify the presentation of our algorithms we adopt two main conventions that we explain here. Following Braverman et al. [8], we restrict our attention to bounding the expected space use of our randomized algorithm rather than bounding the space with high probability. Note that if the algorithm satisfies its accuracy guarantee with probability 99/100, for example, then it is straight-

[4]The error can be found in the proof of Theorem 3 [16]. Specifically, it is claimed that $Y \leq X$ and hence a lower bound on Y is a lower bound on X. However, all that can be shown is $Y \leq 3X$ and a factor of three is lost in the analysis.

forward to show that the algorithm satisfies its accuracy guarantee *and* doesn't exceed its expected space use by more than a factor 100 with probability at least $49/50$. Hence, by running a logarithmic number of copies of the algorithm in parallel, terminating any that exceed their space bound, and taking the median of the remaining estimates ensures an accurate answer with only a logarithmic space increase with $1-1/\operatorname{poly}(n)$ probability. Secondly, we parameterize our algorithms in terms of the actual number of triangles T in the graph and various quantities in the algorithm will depend on T. Obviously, we do not know T in advance (otherwise we wouldn't be trying to estimate it) but this convention is widely adopted in the literature. A natural way to formalize this is to phrase the problem as distinguishing between graphs with at most t triangles from those with at least $(1+\epsilon)t$ triangles where t is an input parameter. In practice, the quantities in the algorithm would be initialized based on a lower or upper bound (as appropriate) for the unknown quantities.

2. ADJACENCY LIST ALGORITHMS

In this model, we may assume that the stream consists of a sequence of ordered pairs xy. For each edge $\{x,y\}$, both xy and yx will be present in the stream. The promise on the ordering is that all tuples with the same first node appear consecutively in the stream. Aside from that constraint, the stream is ordered arbitrarily. For example, for the graph consisting of a cycle on three nodes $V=\{v_1,v_2,v_3\}$, a possible ordering of the stream could be

$$\langle v_3v_1, v_3v_2, v_1v_2, v_1v_3, v_2v_3, v_2v_1\rangle\ .$$

In this example, we say that the adjacency list for v_3 came first, then the adjacency list for v_1, and finally the adjacency list for v_2.

2.1 One Pass and $\tilde{O}(\epsilon^{-2}m/\sqrt{T})$ Space

Algorithm and Intuition. Define a total ordering on nodes $<_s$ based on stream ordering where $x <_s y$ if the adjacency list of x is specified before the adjacency list of y in the stream. Define

$$R_{xy}=\begin{cases}|\{z:\{x,y,z\}\in\Delta \text{ and } x<_s z<_s y\}| & \text{if } x<_s y\\ 0 & \text{if } y<_s x\end{cases}$$

and note that $\sum_{x,y} R_{xy}=T$.

The basic outline of the algorithm comprises of two interlocking parts. In the first part, we will sample each edge xy with probability p when it arrives and, until yx arrives, we count all nodes z such that $\{x,y,z\}$ forms a triangle. If we do not observe yx after xy was sampled (i.e., yx came before xy in the stream ordering) this counter will never be used. Otherwise, the counter equals R_{xy} when yx arrives. Hence, by summing these counters we get an estimator that equals $\sum_{xy} R_{xy} I[xy \text{ sampled}]$. In expectation it equals pT and has low variance if all R_{xy} are small.

The second part ensures that we estimate every R_{xy} if $R_{xy}\geq\sqrt{T}$ regardless of whether xy was sampled. This will allow us to restrict our attention to small R_{xy} in the first part of the algorithm (and hence get a good variance bound). The critical observation that allows us to estimate every large R_{xy} is as follows: when reading the neighbors of x, even if we did not sample xy, we will have probably sampled some of the edges in the set

$$\{xz:\{x,y,z\}\in\Delta \text{ and } x<_s z<_s y\}$$

if the number of edges in this set, i.e., R_{xy}, is large. Subsequently, each of these sampled edges form a triangle with the incident edges of y and the number of these triangles can be used to a) recognize R_{xy} is large and b) to estimate R_{xy}.

See Figure 1 for the detailed description of the algorithm with the appropriate bookkeeping.

Analysis. For the analysis, let $\mathcal{H}$ consist of all edges xy such that xy is defined as heavy by the algorithm. The final value of A can be written as $A=A_l+A_h$ where

$$A_l=\sum_{xy\notin\mathcal{H}} c_1(xy) \qquad \text{and} \qquad A_h=\sum_{xy\in\mathcal{H}} c_2(xy)$$

The next two lemmas establish that, with good probability, $A_l/p\approx\sum_{xy\notin\mathcal{H}}R_{xy}$ and $A_h/p\approx\sum_{xy\in\mathcal{H}}R_{xy}$.

LEMMA 1. *With probability at least* $99/100$,

$$A_h/p=\sum_{xy\in\mathcal{H}}R_{xy}\pm\epsilon T/2$$

and $R_{xy}\leq 2\sqrt{T}$ *for all* $xy\notin\mathcal{H}$.

PROOF. First note that $c_2(xy)\sim \mathbf{Bin}(R_{xy},p)$. If $R_{xy}\geq\sqrt{T}/2$, then by an application of the Chernoff bound,

$$\Pr\left[c_2(xy)=(1\pm\epsilon/2)pR_{xy}\right]\geq 1-2e^{-\epsilon^2 pR_{xy}/12}\geq 1-1/n^{10}\ .$$

Alternatively, if $R_{xy}\leq\sqrt{T}/2$ then $c_2(xy)<p\sqrt{T}$ with probability at least $1-1/n^{10}$. Taking the union bound over all xy establishes the lemma since

$$\sum_{xy:c_2(xy)\geq p\sqrt{T}} c_2(xy)=(1\pm\epsilon/2)p\sum_{xy\in\mathcal{H}}R_{xy}\ .$$

□

LEMMA 2. *With probability at least* $99/100$,

$$A_l/p=\sum_{xy\notin\mathcal{H}}R_{xy}\pm\epsilon T/2\ .$$

PROOF. First note that $c_1(xy)=R_{xy}$ with probability p and 0 otherwise. Furthermore, the $c_1(\cdot)$ values are independent because they each depend on whether a different tuple was sampled. Hence

$$\mathrm{E}\left[A_l\right]=p\sum_{xy\notin\mathcal{H}}R_{xy} \quad\text{and}\quad \mathrm{V}\left[A_l\right]\leq p\sum_{xy\notin\mathcal{H}}R_{xy}^2\leq 4pT^{3/2}\ .$$

since $R_{xy}\leq 2\sqrt{T}$ for $xy\notin\mathcal{H}$. By an application of the Chebyshev bound,

$$\Pr\left[|A_l-\mathrm{E}\left[A_l\right]|\geq\epsilon pT/2\right]\leq\frac{4pT^{3/2}}{(\epsilon pT/2)^2}=\frac{16}{p\epsilon^2T^{1/2}}\leq\frac{1}{100}\ .$$

□

We then use the above two lemmas to prove our first main result.

THEOREM 3. *There exists a* $\tilde{O}(\epsilon^{-2}m/\sqrt{T})$*-space algorithm using one pass in the adjacency list model that returns a* $(1+\epsilon)$*-approximation of* T *with probability* $49/50$.

PROOF. The accuracy guarantee follows from Lemmas 1 and 2. The expected space use is $\tilde{O}(pm)=\tilde{O}(\epsilon^{-2}m/\sqrt{T})$ since each edge is sampled with probability p and $\tilde{O}(1)$ bits of auxilary data is collected for each sampled node. □

2.2 Two Passes and $\tilde{O}(\epsilon^{-2}m^{3/2}/T)$ Space

Algorithm and Intuition. Define a total ordering on nodes $<_d$ based on degrees where $x<_d y$ if

$$\deg(x)<\deg(y) \ \text{ or } \ (\deg(x)=\deg(y) \text{ and } \mathrm{id}(x)<\mathrm{id}(x))\ ,$$

Algorithm TRIANGLES1

1. Initialize $A \leftarrow 0, S_1 \leftarrow \emptyset, S_2 \leftarrow \emptyset$ and $p \leftarrow \alpha \cdot \log n \cdot \epsilon^{-2}/T^{1/2}$ for some large constant α.
2. On seeing edges adjacent to v in the adjacency stream:
   (a) Update auxiliary information about sampled edges:
      i. For all $ab \in S_1$: If $a, b \in \Gamma(v)$ then $c(ab) \leftarrow c(ab) + 1$
      ii. For all $av \in S_2$: Let $\text{order}(av) = 1$
   (b) Sample additional edges and update estimator. For each incident edge vu:
      i. With probability p, $S_1 \leftarrow \{vu\} \cup S_1$ and set $c(vu) = 0$
      ii. With probability p, $S_2 \leftarrow \{vu\} \cup S_2$ and set $\text{order}(vu) = 0$
      iii. Define

$$c_1(uv) := \begin{cases} c(uv) & \text{if } uv \in S_1 \\ 0 & \text{otherwise} \end{cases}$$

$$c_2(uv) := |\{z : uz \in S_2, \text{order}(uz) = 1, z \in \Gamma(v)\}|$$

      and say uv is *heavy* if $c_2(uv) \geq p\sqrt{T}$. Update the estimator as follows:

$$A \leftarrow A + \begin{cases} c_1(uv) & \text{if } uv \text{ is not heavy} \\ c_2(uv) & \text{if } uv \text{ heavy} \end{cases}$$

3. Return A/p

Figure 1: The TRIANGLES1 Algorithm. The algorithm maintains two sets of edges S_1 and S_2 where each is generated by sampling each element of the stream with probability p. For each $xy \in S_1$, we maintain a counter $c(xy)$ that counts the number of triangles $\{x, y, z\}$ where $x <_s z <_s y$. For each $xy \in S_2$, we maintain a boolean order(xy) that is initially 0 but is set to 1 when yx is observed; at this point we have deduced $x <_s y$. The elements in S_2 will be used to determine whether each R_{xy} is large and, if so, to estimate it. The elements of S_1 will be used to estimate the contribution of all R_{xy} that are not large.

i.e., $<_d$ is ordering the nodes by degree with ties broken by the id of the node (recall, we assume the nodes are labelled in $1, 2, \ldots, n$). For each edge $e = \{x, y\}$, define

$$R_{\{x,y\}} = |\{z : \{x, y, z\} \in \Delta, x <_d z, y <_d z\}|$$

and note that $\sum_{e \in E} R_e = T$.

The basic idea for the algorithm in this section is as follows: In the first pass, we generate a sample of edges S along with the degree of each endpoint of the sample edges. In the second pass, for each $e \in S$ we compute R_e and return $\sum_{e \in S} R_e$. This will equal pT in expectation and we will be able to bound the variance by first showing that $R_e \leq \sqrt{2m}$ for all $e \in E$. See Figure 2 for the detailed description of the algorithm with the appropriate bookkeeping.

Analysis. We first prove a bound on $\max R_e$ that will be required to bound the variance of our estimator.

LEMMA 4. $\max R_e \leq \sqrt{2m}$.

PROOF. Let $e = \{x, y\}$ and suppose $R_e = R_{\{x,y\}} > \sqrt{2m}$. Then $\deg(x) \geq \sqrt{2m}$. Furthermore, there exist at least $\sqrt{2m}$ nodes $z_1, z_2, \ldots$ such that $\{x, y, z_i\}$ is a triangle and $\deg(z_i) \geq \deg(x) > \sqrt{2m}$. But then

$$\deg(z_1) + \deg(z_2) + \ldots > \sqrt{2m} \cdot \sqrt{2m} = 2m$$

which is a contradiction since the sum of degrees of every node in the graph is $2m$. □

THEOREM 5. *There exists an $\tilde{O}(\epsilon^{-2}m^{3/2}/T)$-space algorithm using two passes in the adjacency list model that returns a $(1+\epsilon)$-approximation of T with probability $99/100$.*

PROOF. Consider the above algorithm and note that each edge e is contained in S with probability p and $A = \sum_{e \in S} R_e$. Hence, by appealing to Lemma 4,

$$\mathrm{E}[A] = Tp \qquad \text{and} \qquad \mathrm{V}[A] < \sum_{e \in E} R_e^2 p \leq \sqrt{2m}Tp$$

Then, by the Chebyshev bound,

$$\begin{aligned} \Pr[|A/p - T| \geq \epsilon T] &\leq (\sqrt{2m}T/p)/(\epsilon^2 T^2) \\ &= p^{-1}\epsilon^{-2}\sqrt{2m}/T \leq 1/100. \end{aligned}$$

Hence the algorithm has the desired accuracy. The expected space use is $\tilde{O}(pm) = \tilde{O}(\epsilon^{-2}m^{3/2}/T)$. □

Improved Algorithm for Testing Triangle-Freeness. We conclude this section by showing that if we are only trying to distinguish triangle-free graphs from those with at least T triangles, less space is sufficient.

THEOREM 6. *There exists an $\tilde{O}(m/T^{2/3})$-space algorithm using two passes in the adjacency list model that distinguishes triangle-free graphs from those with at least T triangles with probability $99/100$.*

The basic observation is that a graph with T triangles has at least $T^{2/3}$ edges involved in these triangles. This follows because any graph with m edges can have at most $O(m^{3/2})$ triangles (see, e.g., [2]). Hence, if each edge is sampled with probability $p = \alpha/T^{2/3}$ for some large constant $\alpha > 0$ at least one edge $\{u, v\}$ in some triangle $\{u, v, z\}$ will the sampled. We do this sampling in the first pass. Then, in the second pass of the algorithm when the

Algorithm TRIANGLES2

1. *First pass:* Let $S = S' = \emptyset$ and $p = 200\epsilon^{-2}\sqrt{m}/T$. On seeing edges adjacent to v in the stream:
   (a) For each $a \in \Gamma(v)$, with probability p let $S' \leftarrow S' \cup \{va\}$ and store $\deg(v)$.
   (b) For each $bv \in S'$, let $S \leftarrow S \cup \{\{b, v\}\}$ and store $\deg(v)$.
2. *Second pass:* Let $A = 0$. On seeing edges adjacent to v in the stream:
   (a) For each edge $\{a, b\} \in S$ such that $a <_d v$, $b <_d v$, and $a, b \in \Gamma(v)$, $A \leftarrow A + 1$.
3. *Output:* Return A/p.

Figure 2: The TRIANGLES2 Algorithm. After the first pass, S contains each edge in the graph sampled with probability p along with the degrees of the endpoints. In the second pass, we count the number of triangles $\{a, b, v\}$ where $\{a, b\} \in S$, $a <_d v$, and $b <_d v$.

neighbors of z are observed we will identify a triangle by tracking which of the sampled edges have two endpoints in $\Gamma(z)$.

3. ARBITRARY ORDER ALGORITHMS

Recall that in the arbitrary order model, the m edges of the graph may arrive in any order. It will be useful to start by briefly revisiting an algorithm by Jha, Seshadri and Pinar [22] in this model. They designed a beautifully simple algorithm for estimating the transitivity coefficient of a graph up to small additive error. We show that the algorithm can be used to estimate the number of triangles and that, if one makes a small change to their algorithm (essentially sampling edges independently rather than sampling a fixed number of edges), this facilitates a simple analysis of the algorithm that is similar to that used by Pagh and Tsourakakis [37]. While we think that simplifying the analysis and generalizing the result is valuable in its own right, our main purpose in revisiting this algorithm is that we will need to build upon it in the next section.

The single-pass algorithm is as follows:

1. *Single Pass:* $S \leftarrow \emptyset$, $A \leftarrow 0$. On the arrival of the edge $\{u, v\}$:
   (a) $S \leftarrow S \cup \{\{u, v\}\}$ with probability p (to be determined).
   (b) $A \leftarrow A + |\{w : \{w, u\} \text{ and } \{w, v\} \in S\}|$
2. *Output:* Return A/p^2.

The following lemma bounds the probability that the output of the algorithm is far from T.

LEMMA 7. *Let $\tau = \sum_{e \in E} \binom{x_e}{2}$ and x_e is the number of triangles that include edge e. Then,*

$$\Pr\left[|A/p^2 - T| \geq B\right] \leq (T + \tau p)/(B^2 p^2) .$$

PROOF. Let $T_1, T_2, \ldots$ be the triangles in the graph and for each T_i let W_i be the length two path consisting of the first two edges in T_i that arrive in the stream. Let $A_i = 1$ if both edges in W_i are sampled and $A_i = 0$ otherwise. At the end of the stream $A = \sum A_i$. To analyze A, first note that $\mathrm{E}[A_i] = p^2$ and $\mathrm{V}[A_i] \leq p^2$. Furthermore, $\mathrm{Cov}[A_i, A_j] \leq \mathrm{E}[A_i A_j] = p^3$ if W_i and W_j share an edge (they can share at most one edge) and $\mathrm{Cov}[A_i, A_j] = 0$ otherwise. It follows that $\mathrm{E}[A] = Tp^2$ and

$$\begin{aligned} \mathrm{V}[A] &= \sum_{i \in T} \mathrm{V}[A_i] + \sum_{i \neq j} \mathrm{Cov}[A_i, A_j] \\ &\leq Tp^2 + \sum_{e \in E} \sum_{W_i \cap W_j = \{e\}} p^3 \\ &\leq Tp^2 + p^3 \sum_{e \in E} \binom{x_e}{2} = Tp^2 + \tau p^3 . \end{aligned}$$

The lemma follows from the Chebyshev's inequality. □

The parameter τ can be bounded as $O(Tx^*)$ where x^* is the maximum number of triangles that share the same edge. Hence, it follows that the variance of the estimate decreases with x^*. The following corollary follows by setting p appropriately. The first result is an algorithm with the same space bound as Pagh and Tsourakakis' algorithm [37] and the second result reproves the result of Jha et al. [22].

COROLLARY 8. *Setting p appropriately, the above single pass algorithm returns:*

- *$(1 \pm \epsilon)T$ with probability $99/100$ using $\tilde{O}(m(\epsilon^{-1}/\sqrt{T} + \epsilon^{-2}x^*/T))$ space.*
- *$T \pm \epsilon W$ with probability $99/100$ using $\tilde{O}(m\epsilon^{-2}/\sqrt{W})$ space.*

PROOF. First note that $\tau \leq \sum_{e \in E} x_e^2/2 \leq 1.5 \cdot x^* \cdot T$ and because $\binom{x_e}{2}$ is at most the square of the degree of an endpoint of e,

$$\begin{aligned} \tau = \sum_{e \in E} \binom{x_e}{2} &\leq \sum_{u:\deg(u)>1} (\deg(u))^3 \\ &\leq \left(\sum_{u:\deg(u)>1} (\deg(u))^2 \right)^{3/2} = O(W^{3/2}) . \end{aligned}$$

The expected space use of the algorithm is $\tilde{O}(pm)$. Hence, setting

$$p = \alpha \cdot \max(\epsilon^{-1}/\sqrt{T}, \epsilon^{-2}\tau/T^2)$$

in the algorithm for some sufficiently large constant α and appealing to Lemma 7 with $B = \epsilon T$ gives the first result. Similarly, setting $p = \alpha \cdot \epsilon^{-2}/\sqrt{W}$ in the algorithm and $B = \epsilon W$ gives the second result. □

3.1 Two Passes and $\tilde{O}(\epsilon^{-2}m/\sqrt{T})$ Space

From the analysis of the above one-pass algorithm, it is evident that the space required is very sensitive to the existence of edges that are involved in many triangles. In this section, we address this by considering two types of edges, *light* edges that are only involved in a small number of triangles and *heavy* that are involved in a large number of triangles. Using two passes, we estimate the number of triangles where every edge is light separately from the number of triangles with at least one heavy edge.

An oracle. Edges are characterized as heavy or light by an oracle defined by the following random process:

1. Sample each node z of the graph with probability
$$p = \beta\epsilon^{-2}\log n/\sqrt{T}$$
for some large constant $\beta > 0$. Let Z be the set of sampled nodes.

2. For any edge $e = \{u, v\}$, let $\tilde{x}_e = |\{z \in Z : u, v \in \Gamma(z)\}|$ and define
$$\text{oracle}(e) = \begin{cases} \mathtt{L} & \text{if } \tilde{x}_e < p\sqrt{T} \\ \mathtt{H} & \text{if } \tilde{x}_e \geq p\sqrt{T} \end{cases}.$$

Note that once Z is chosen, the value of oracle(e) is fixed for all e, including edges used to define the oracle. The following lemma establishes that x_e is relatively small if oracle$(e) = \mathtt{L}$ and relatively large if oracle$(e) = \mathtt{H}$.

LEMMA 9. *With high probability for all* $e = \{u, v\}$, oracle$(e) = \mathtt{L}$ *implies* $x_e \leq 2\sqrt{T}$ *and* oracle$(e) = \mathtt{H}$ *implies* $x_e \geq \sqrt{T}/2$.

PROOF. First, observe that for each e, $\tilde{x}(e) \sim \mathbf{Bin}(x_e, p)$. By an application of the Chernoff bound, if $x_e \geq 2\sqrt{T}$ then
$$\Pr\left[\tilde{x}(e) < p\sqrt{T}\right] \leq \exp(-2p\sqrt{T}/3) = n^{-10}.$$
Hence, by the union bound, with high probability oracle$(e) = \mathtt{H}$ if $x_e \geq 2\sqrt{T}$ for all edges e. The second case follows similarly. □

See Figure 3 for the two-pass algorithm. In the first pass, the algorithm instantiates the above oracle and samples some additional edges S_1. In the second pass, for each new edge that is light we increment a counter by a third of the number of triangles it forms with light edges from S_1. In expectation this counter will be p^2 times the total number of triangles involving three light edges. For each new edge that is heavy, we will use the oracle to estimate the number of triangles with i heavy edges that involve this edge for $i \in \{1, 2, 3\}$. If we incremented a counter by the sum of these estimates, we would count a triangle with i heavy edges i times. But by scaling appropriately we can ensure this counter is an estimate of the total number of triangles with at least one heavy edge.

THEOREM 10. *There exists a* $\tilde{O}(\epsilon^{-2}m/\sqrt{T})$*-space algorithm using two passes in the arbitrary order model that returns a* $(1+\epsilon)$*-approximation of* T *with probability at least* $49/50$.

PROOF. Let $T^{\mathtt{L}}$ be the number of triangles among the set of edges $E^{\mathtt{L}} = \{e \in E : \text{oracle}(e) = \mathtt{L}\}$. Let $W_1, W_2, \ldots$, be the length two paths in $E^{\mathtt{L}}$ that are involved in triangles in $E^{\mathtt{L}}$. Notice, there are three length two paths involved in every triangle. Let $A_i = 1$ if both edges in W_i are in S_1^L and $A_i = 0$ otherwise. Then, following the analysis in Lemma 7 and appealing to Lemma 9, we can show that $A^{\mathtt{L}}/p^2 = \sum_i A_i/(3p^2)$ equals $T^{\mathtt{L}} \pm \epsilon T/2$ with probability at least $99/100$.

Let $T^{\mathtt{H}}$ be the number of triangles in the input graph that have at least one heavy edge. For each heavy e, define x_e^i to be the number of triangles that include edge e and have exactly i heavy edges. Then
$$T^{\mathtt{H}} = \sum_{e:\text{oracle}(e)=\mathtt{H}} (x_e^1 + x_e^2/2 + x_e^3/3)$$
because every heavy triangle with i heavy edges occurs in i different summands. Since each $\tilde{x}_e^i \sim \mathbf{Bin}(x_e^i, p)$ we can apply the Chernoff bound to prove that
$$\tilde{x}_e^1 + \tilde{x}_e^2/2 + \tilde{x}_e^3/3 = (1 \pm \epsilon)p(x_e^1 + x_e^2/2 + x_e^3/3)$$
with probability at least
$$1 - 2\exp(-\epsilon^2 p(\sqrt{T}/6)/3) = 1 - 1/\operatorname{poly}(n).$$
We then apply the union bound.

To bound the space used by the algorithm observe that
$$\mathrm{E}\left[|S_1| + |S_2|\right] = pm + \sum_v p\deg(v) = 3pm$$
so the expected space used by the algorithm is $\tilde{O}(\epsilon^{-2}m/\sqrt{T})$ as claimed. □

4. WEDGE SAMPLING VIA ℓ_P SAMPLING

In this section, we consider the "wedge sampling approach" proposed by Schank and Wagner [39] and Kolda et al. [27]. This approach is most relevant to estimating the number of triangles when the global clustering coefficient of the graph is large. The previous work did not consider the data stream model, but we show that it is relatively straightforward to design a streaming algorithm based on their ideas. Our main results in this section are a) designing an $\tilde{O}(\epsilon^{-2}m^{3/2}/T)$-space algorithm based on the wedge sampling approach given certain assumptions and b) improving the update time of the algorithm to $\tilde{O}(1)$. To achieve the fast update time our main contribution is a new result on ℓ_p sampling, an important primitive in data stream algorithms. Throughout this section we assume that $m \geq 2n$. This guarantees there are a $\Omega(n)$ wedges in the graph.

4.1 Wedge Sampling Algorithms

The basic wedge sampling idea is to sample length-two paths *uniformly* and compute the fraction of these that are contained in a triangle. If there are W length-two paths or "wedges", then this fraction is $3T/W$ because each triangle contains three length-two paths. Thus, by an application of the Chernoff bound, if we sample $O(\epsilon^{-2}W/T)$ wedges then we can estimate T/W up to a factor $1 \pm \epsilon$ with good probability. Hence, the challenge becomes how to uniformly sample from the set of wedges in the graph and check whether there is an edge that "completes" this wedge to a triangle.

To sample and test a single wedge in the arbitrary order model we use the following two-pass algorithm:

- *First pass:* Use an ℓ_2-sampling algorithm [25] to sample a node v with probability proportional to $(1 \pm \epsilon)\deg(v)^2$. In Section 4.2, we discuss ℓ_2 sampling and show that this can be done with fast update time even if we need to sample many wedges simultaneously.

- *Second pass:* Independently sample two edges e_1 and e_2 incident to v uniformly at random using reservoir sampling [43] or ℓ_0-sampling algorithm [25]. If $e_1 = e_2$, output FAIL. Else, check if one of the edges arriving after e_1 and e_2 completes a triangle with e_1 and e_2.

The following lemma shows that the above algorithm outputs fail with probability at most $1/4$ and if not, finds a triangle with probability $\approx T/W$.

Algorithm TRIANGLES3

1. *Initialization:* Let Z be a random subset of nodes where each node is in Z with probability $p = \beta\epsilon^{-2}\log n/\sqrt{T}$.
2. *First pass:*
   (a) Sample a random subset of edges S_1 where each edge is in S_1 with probability p.
   (b) Collect all edges S_2 that are incident to any node in Z.
3. *Second pass:* Let $A_{\mathtt{L}} = A_{\mathtt{H}} = 0$. For each edge $e = \{u, v\}$ in the stream,
   (a) For $i \in \{1, 2\}$, define $S_i^{\mathtt{L}} = \{e \in S_i : \text{oracle}(e) = \mathtt{L}\}$ and $S_i^{\mathtt{H}} = \{e \in S_i : \text{oracle}(e) = \mathtt{H}\}$ where Z and S_2 define oracle as above.
   (b) If oracle$(e) = \mathtt{L}$ then $A_{\mathtt{L}} \leftarrow A_{\mathtt{L}} + |\{w : \{u, w\}, \{v, w\} \in S_1^{\mathtt{L}}\}|/3$
   (c) If oracle$(e) = \mathtt{H}$ then $A_{\mathtt{H}} \leftarrow A_{\mathtt{H}} + \tilde{x}_e^1 + \tilde{x}_e^2/2 + \tilde{x}_e^3/3$ where

$$\begin{aligned}
\tilde{x}_e^1 &= |\{w \in Z : \{u, w\}, \{v, w\} \in S_2^{\mathtt{L}}\}| \\
\tilde{x}_e^2 &= |\{w \in Z : \{u, w\} \in S_2^{\mathtt{L}}, \{v, w\} \in S_2^{\mathtt{H}}\}| \\
&\quad + |\{w \in Z : \{u, w\} \in S_2^{\mathtt{H}}, \{v, w\} \in S_2^{\mathtt{L}}\}| \\
\tilde{x}_e^3 &= |\{w \in Z : \{u, w\}, \{v, w\} \in S_2^{\mathtt{H}}\}|
\end{aligned}$$

   We will use $\tilde{x}_e^i/(ip)$ to estimate the number of triangles involving e that contain i heavy edges.
4. *Output:* Return $A_{\mathtt{L}}/p^2 + A_{\mathtt{H}}/p$

Figure 3: The TRIANGLES3 **Algorithm. In the first pass, we sample a set of edges S_2 that will be used to instantiate our oracle and a set of edges S_1. In the second pass, counter A_L will be used to estimate the number of triangles where all edges are light and counter A_H will be used to estimate the number of triangles that include at least one heavy edge.**

LEMMA 11. *Let F be the event that the above algorithms fails. Then if $m \geq 2n$, $\Pr[F] \leq 1/2$ and the probability of finding a triangle is $(1 \pm \epsilon)T/W$ conditioned on $\neg F$.*

PROOF. We assume the ℓ_2 sampling is performed perfectly since the $(1 \pm \epsilon)$ error will only introduce a factor $(1 \pm \epsilon)$ to all the probabilities. First observe that

$$\begin{aligned}
\Pr[F] &= \sum_{v \in V} \frac{\deg(u)^2}{\sum_{u \in V} \deg(u)^2} \cdot \frac{1}{\deg(v)} \\
&= \frac{\sum_{v \in V} \deg(v)}{\sum_{u \in V} \deg(u)^2} \\
&\leq \frac{2m}{4m^2/n} = \frac{n}{2m} \leq 1/4 \,.
\end{aligned}$$

Let R_v be the event that we sample node v and that $e_1 \neq e_2$.

$$\begin{aligned}
&\Pr[R_v | \neg F] \\
&= \frac{\Pr[R_v \wedge \neg F]}{\Pr[\neg F]} \\
&= \frac{\deg(v)^2}{\sum_u \deg(u)^2} \left(\frac{2}{\deg(v)^2}\right) \left(\frac{1}{1 - \sum_v \deg(v) / \sum_u \deg(u)^2}\right) \\
&= \frac{2}{\sum_u \deg(u)(\deg(u) - 1)} = 1/W \,.
\end{aligned}$$

Therefore e_1 and e_2 form a wedge chosen uniformly at random. Hence the probability that we find a triangle with edges e_1, e_2, e_3 where e_3 arrives in the stream after e_1 and e_2 are sampled in the second pass equals $\frac{3T}{W} \cdot \frac{1}{3} = T/W$ as required. Note that the fact that e_3 comes last is not true if we condition on the node v that was chosen as the "center" of the wedge; but since we chose a wedge uniformly at random, there was probability of $1/3$ that e_1 and e_2 were the first two edges of the triangle. ☐

Appealing to the previous lemma and the above discussion we can multiplicatively estimate T/W in two passes. Using the fact we can also multiplicatively approximate W in parallel (see details below), we can also multiplicatively approximate T.

THEOREM 12. *There is a two pass, $\tilde{O}(\epsilon^{-2}W/T)$-space algorithm in the arbitrary order model that returns a $(1+\epsilon)$-approximation to T with probability at least $99/100$.*

Three pass algorithm using $\tilde{O}(\epsilon^{-2}m^{3/2}/T)$ space and a degree oracle. Note that the above algorithm could be implemented in a single pass if the degrees of the nodes in the graph were known a priori. If we can assume oracle access to the degrees of the nodes in the graph (this may be reasonable in various systems), we can further improve the space use given additional passes. Given a degree oracle we can evaluate the $<_d$ ordering (as defined in Section 2.2) between the two endpoints of an edge when this edge arrives. This will allow us to focus on a smaller set of wedges when following the wedge sampling procedure above. Specifically, let W' be the number of length two-paths x-y-z where $y <_d x$ and $y <_d z$. We call such wedges "$<_d$-consistent". Note that $W' \leq W$ and it can be significantly less; W may be $\Omega(mn)$ whereas $W' = O(m^{3/2})$.

LEMMA 13. $W' < 2m^{3/2}$.

PROOF. Associate every wedge with its internal node y. The number of $z \in \Gamma(y)$ such that $y <_d z$ is at most $\sqrt{2m}$ using the same argument as used in Lemma 4. Hence, every edge participates in at most $(\sqrt{2m} - 1)$ wedges in W'. Therefore $W' < 2m^{3/2}$. ☐

Our three pass algorithm for sampling $<_d$-consistent wedges and checking if they participate in triangles is described in Figure 4. To output the estimate of the number of triangles, rather than T/W', we note that W' can be estimated via second frequency moment estimation [9] as explained shortly.

The analysis of this algorithm is analogous to that of the previous algorithm. Note that it is not clear whether it is possible to collapse

Algorithm TRIANGLES4

1. *Initialization:* $A = 0$, $B = 0$, $r = \alpha \log n \cdot \epsilon^{-2} m^{3/2}/T$ for a large constant α.
2. Repeat r times in parallel:
   (a) *First pass:* Use an ℓ_2-sampling algorithm to sample a node v with probability proportional to $(1 \pm \epsilon)|\{u \in \Gamma(v) : v <_d u\}|$.
   (b) *Second pass:* Given the node v chosen in the first pass, sample edges e_1 and e_2 from $\{\{u, v\} : u \in \Gamma(v), v <_d u\}$ via ℓ_0 sampling.
   (c) *Third pass:* If $e_1 \neq e_2$:
      i. $B \leftarrow B + 1$.
      ii. If for some edge e in the stream $\{e, e_1, e_2\}$ form a triangle, $A \leftarrow A + 1$.
3. *Output:* AW'/B

Figure 4: The TRIANGLES4 **Algorithm. The algorithm attempts to sample r wedges that are $<_d$-consistent in parallel. B stores the number of wedges found and A stores the number of these that participate in triangles.**

the second and third pass in a single pass, since the stream may be ordered such that edges on high degree nodes arrive before edges on low degree nodes.

THEOREM 14. *Given access to a degree oracle, there is a three pass, $\tilde{O}(\epsilon^{-2}m^{3/2}/T)$-space algorithm in the arbitrary order model that returns a $(1+\epsilon)$-approximation to T with probability at least* $99/100$.

Estimating W and W'. We start by rewriting W as follows:

$$W = 1/2 \cdot \sum_{v \in V} \deg(v)(\deg(v) - 1) = 1/2 \cdot \sum_{v \in V} \deg(v)^2 - m.$$

Assuming that $m \geq 2n$, then

$$1/2 \cdot \sum_{v \in V} \deg(v)^2 \geq 1/2 \cdot 4m^2/n \geq 4m.$$

Since m can be computed exactly, it follows that it is sufficient to $(1 + 3\epsilon/4)$-approximate $\sum_{v \in V} \deg(v)^2$ if we wish to approximate $(1+\epsilon)$-approximate W. This can be done using existing algorithms for estimating the second frequency moment estimation [9].

The case of W' can be argued similarly. Let

$$\deg'(v) = |\{u \in \Gamma(v) : u >_d v\}| \,.$$

Then,

$$W' = 1/2 \cdot \sum_{v \in V} \deg'(v)(\deg'(v) - 1) = 1/2 \cdot \sum_{v \in V} \deg'(v)^2 - m/2.$$

We also have

$$1/2 \cdot \sum_{v \in V} \deg'(v)^2 \geq 1/2 \cdot m^2/n \geq m\,.$$

Thus, $(1+\epsilon/2)$-approximating $\sum_{v \in V} \deg'(v)^2$ (which we can do given a degree oracle) is sufficient to $(1+\epsilon)$-approximate W'.

4.2 Running Time and Fast ℓ_p-Sampling

The above two algorithms require running many parallel copies of the corresponding wedge sampler. It may initially appear that running s copies would necessitate $\Omega(s)$ update time and thus make the algorithms prohibitively slow. Fortunately, this can be avoided and we can ensure $O(\text{polylog}\, n)$ update time. Specifically, it is easy to ensure that the third pass can be performed with $O(\log n)$ update time; we store the wedges in a hash table and when a new edge $\{x, y\}$ is read, we increment a counter by the number of wedges with endpoints x and y that are present. The more challenging problem is ensuring the s copies of an ℓ_0 and ℓ_2 sampler can be performed in parallel with update time that is independent of s. We do this in the next section.

4.2.1 Fast ℓ_p Sampling

We now introduce a fast ℓ_p-sampling technique which completes the argument that $O(\text{polylog}\, n)$ update time in the above wedge sampling algorithms is possible. Since ℓ_p-sampling is an important primitive for numerous streaming applications such as cascaded norms, duplicate detection, and higher moment estimation [36], our technique is also expected to be of independent interest. The case of fast ℓ_0-sampling is significantly simpler and a result was previously known [33].

Preliminaries and Intuition. Most streaming problems can be modeled by the evolution of an underlying n-dimensional integer vector x. In the *turnstile model*, the stream consists of $\text{poly}(n)$ updates in the form $x_i \leftarrow x_i + \delta$. In the context of the above algorithms, x_i would correspond to the degree of node i or the number of neighbors of i that have higher degree or a boolean to indicate that node i is neighbor of node v. An ℓ_p-sampler (see, [3, 15, 25, 36]) takes one pass over the stream and with high probability returns $(j, \tilde{x}_j)$ where $\tilde{x}_j = (1 \pm \epsilon)x_j$ and

$$\Pr[j = i] = (1 \pm \epsilon)x_i^p / F_p(x)$$

where $F_p(x) = \sum_i x_i^p$ and $F_0 = |\{i : x_i \neq 0\}|$.

The space and update time of existing ℓ_p-sampling algorithms are $O(\text{poly}(\epsilon^{-1}, \log n))$ and $O(\text{polylog}\, n)$ respectively per sample. If we want to draw s independent ℓ_p-samples, the naive implementation that maintains s different ℓ_p-samplers in parallel would need $\Omega(s)$ update time. We will prove the following theorem.

THEOREM 15. *For $p \in [0, 2]$, there exists a one-pass algorithm that, with high probability, outputs s independent ℓ_p-samples using $O(s \cdot \text{poly}(\epsilon^{-1}, \log n))$ space and $O(\text{polylog}\, n)$ update time.*

We achieve polylog n update time regardless of s and our result is most significant when $s = o(n)$ and $s = \omega(\text{polylog}\, n)$. The main idea behind our algorithm is as follows. We hash the coordinates of x into w groups and for each of these groups we maintain a small number of local ℓ_p-samplers restricting to the corresponding coordinates. To draw an ℓ_p-sample, we randomly pick a group with probability proportional to its mass contribution to $F_p(x)$ and pick an ℓ_p-sample from that group using a local ℓ_p-sampler. The main challenge is ensuring that each group's contribution is small so that we only need to maintain a small number of samplers in each group, hence, the fast update time. At a very high level, we achieve this by separating the heavy coordinates into one group using Heavy-Hitters algorithm.

Detailed Description. We restrict our attention to the case $p \in (0, 2]$. We make use of the following Heavy-Hitters result (see [25], Lemma 1 and Section 4.4) .

LEMMA 16. *For $p \in (0, 2]$, there exists a one-pass, $O(\epsilon^{-p}\phi^{-1} \cdot \text{polylog}\, n)$-space and $O(\log n)$-update time algorithm that with high probability returns $A \subseteq [n]$ and $B = \{\tilde{x}_i : \tilde{x}_i = (1 \pm \epsilon)x_i \text{ and } i \in A\}$ such that if $x_i^p \geq \phi F_p(x)$ then $i \in A$ and if $x_i^p < (\phi/8)F_p(x)$ then $i \notin A$.*

We next introduce some definitions. We consider a set of pairwise independent functions $\{h_i\}_{i\in[d]} : [n] \to [w]$ where $d = c \log n$ and $w = cs$ for some sufficiently large constant c. We let

$$A_{i,j} = \{k \in [n] : h_i(k) = j\} .$$

We use $a^{(i,j)}$ to denote the characteristic vector of the set $A_{i,j}$. Finally, we define the set of heavy coordinates as

$$H = \{j \in [n] : x_j^p \geq F_p(x)/s\}$$

and let H' be any superset of H. We consider the algorithm in Figure 5.

By running the Heavy-Hitters algorithm with $\phi = 1/s$, at the end of the stream, we have a set $H' \supseteq H$ as required. Moreover, for each $k \in H'$, the algorithm also returns $\tilde{x}_k^p = (1 \pm O(\epsilon))x_k^p$. One can use frequency moment approximation algorithm such as [21] that supports $O(\text{polylog}\, n)$ update time to maintain r and $\alpha^{(i,j)}$.

The update time during the stream is $O(\text{polylog}\, n)$. To see this, a stream update to coordinate k involves the following steps. First, the algorithm needs to compute $h_i(k)$ for each $i \in [d] = [c \log n]$. Then, it updates $O(\log n)$ data structures that are used to maintain $\{\alpha^{(i,j)}\}_{h_i(k)=j}$, r, and the ℓ_p-samplers on the vectors $\{a^{(i,j)}\}_{h_i(k)=j}$. Finally, the algorithm updates the Heavy-Hitters subroutine. Each of these updates can be done in $O(\text{polylog}\, n)$ time.

Based on the algorithm, we say group $A_{i,j}$ is *good* if $(i, j) \in G$. Let $I_{k\in H'}$ be the indicator variable for the event $k \in H'$. We define

$$g(k) = |\{(i, j) \in G : k \in A_{i,j}\}| + I_{k\in H'} .$$

Intuitively, we use $g(k)$ in the rejection probability to avoid bias toward the coordinates that appear in many groups. It is important to note that the rejection probability is valid. Since each coordinate is in at most d good groups, for sufficiently small ϵ,

$$\alpha \leq (1 + \epsilon) \sum_{(i,j)\in G} F_p(a^{(ij)}) \leq (1 + \epsilon)d \cdot F_p(x) \leq 2d \cdot r .$$

Furthermore, it is obvious that

$$\beta \leq (1 + \epsilon) \sum_{k\in H'} x_k^p \leq (1 + \epsilon)F_p(x) \leq 2d \cdot r .$$

LEMMA 17. *For all $k \notin H'$, k belongs to at least one good group with high probability.*

PROOF. Observe that if $k \notin H'$, then $x_k^p \leq F_p(x)/s$. Fix i and suppose $h_i(k) = j$. By pairwise independence,

$$\begin{aligned} \mathrm{E}\left[F_p(a^{(i,j)})\right] &\leq x_k^p + \sum_{z\neq k} x_z^p/w \\ &\leq x_k^p + F_p(x)/(c \cdot s) \leq 2F_p(x)/s. \end{aligned}$$

Applying Markov bound, $\Pr\left[F_p(a^{(i,j)}) > 8F_p(x)/s\right] \leq 1/4$. Hence,

$$\begin{aligned} \Pr\left[A_{i,j} \text{ is good}\right] &\geq \Pr\left[(1 + \epsilon)F_p(a^{(i,j)}) < 10(1 - \epsilon)F_p(x)/s\right] \\ &\geq \Pr\left[F_p(a^{(i,j)}) < 8F_p(x)/s\right] \geq 3/4. \end{aligned}$$

for sufficiently large c and small ϵ. Thus, the probability that there is no good group for k is at most $(1/4)^d = (1/4)^{c \log n} \leq n^{-c}$. The lemma follows by taking the union bound over all $k \in [n]$. ☐

Let $S_p(x_k)$ be the event of outputting $(k, \tilde{x}_k)$ as a sample and let $S_p(\text{success}) = \cup_{k\in[n]} S_p(x_k)$. The probability of successfully retrieving a sample is

$$\begin{aligned} \Pr\left[S_p(\text{success})\right] &= \sum_{k\in H'} \Pr\left[S_p(x_k) \mid \text{HEAD}\right] \Pr\left[\text{HEAD}\right] + \\ &\quad \sum_{\substack{(i,j)\in G \\ k\in A_{i,j}}} \Pr\left[S_p(x_k) \mid \text{TAIL}\right] \Pr\left[\text{TAIL}\right] \\ &= \sum_{k\in H'} \frac{1}{2} \cdot \frac{(1 \pm \epsilon)x_k^p}{\beta} \cdot \frac{\beta}{2dr \cdot g(k)} \\ &\quad + \sum_{\substack{(i,j)\in G \\ k\in A_{i,j}}} \frac{1}{2} \cdot \frac{\alpha^{(i,j)}}{\alpha} \cdot \frac{\alpha}{2dr} \cdot \frac{(1 \pm \epsilon)x_k^p}{F_p(a^{(i,j)})} \cdot \frac{1}{g(k)} \\ &= \sum_{k\in[n]} \frac{(1 \pm O(\epsilon))x_k^p}{4cF_p(x) \log n} = \Theta\left(\frac{1}{\log n}\right). \end{aligned}$$

The third step follows from the fact that $r = (1 \pm \epsilon)F_p(x)$ and $\alpha^{(i,j)} = (1 \pm \epsilon)F_p(a^{(i,j)})$. It is straight forward to verify that

$$\Pr\left[S_p(x_k) \mid S(\text{success})\right] = (1 \pm O(\epsilon))x_k^p/F_p(x)$$

as required.

Finally, we show that it suffices to maintain $O(\log n)$ ℓ_p-samplers on each vector $a^{(i,j)}$.

LEMMA 18. *With high probability, repeating $O(s \log n)$ times procedure S_p, we obtain s independent ℓ_p-samples. Furthermore, we need $O(\log n)$ different ℓ_p-samples from each good group.*

PROOF. As shown above, $\Pr\left[S_p(\text{success})\right] = \Omega(1/\log n)$. The first claim follows from Chernoff bound. On the other hand, $\alpha^{(i,j)} \leq 10r/s$ for all $(i, j) \in G$. Therefore, the probability that we require an ℓ_p-sample from a good group $A_{i,j}$ is

$$\alpha^{(i,j)}/(4dr) = O(1/(s \log n)) .$$

Therefore, for appropriate choice of constants, the probability that a good group needs more than $O(\log n)$ ℓ_p-samples is less than $1/\text{poly}(n)$. Finally, appealing to the union bound over all $O(s \log n)$ good groups concludes the second claim. ☐

5. CONCLUSIONS

We gave four main algorithms for estimating the number of triangles in the arbitrary order and adjacency list data stream models.

Algorithm FAST ℓ_p SAMPLING

1. During the stream,
   (a) Maintain $r = (1 \pm \epsilon)F_p(x)$ and $\alpha^{(i,j)} = (1 \pm \epsilon)F_p(a^{(i,j)})$ for each vector $a^{(i,j)}$.
   (b) Maintain $O(\log n)$ ℓ_p-samplers on each vector $a^{(i,j)}$.
   (c) Run the Heavy-Hitters algorithm with $\phi = 1/s$ on the vector x.
2. In post-processing:
   (a) $H' \leftarrow$ the indices returned by the Heavy-Hitters algorithm and compute $\beta := \sum_{k \in H'} \tilde{x}_k^p$.
   (b) Compute the set $G := \{(i,j) : \alpha^{(i,j)} < 10r/s\}$ and compute $\alpha := \sum_{(i,j) \in G} \alpha^{(i,j)}$.
   (c) Repeat the following procedure S_p until s samples are retrieved:
      i. Toss a fair coin.
      ii. If HEAD:
         A. Randomly pick $k \in H'$ where $k = k'$ with probability $\tilde{x}_{k'}^p/\beta$.
         B. Reject with probability $1 - \beta/(2d \cdot r \cdot g(k))$. Otherwise, output $(k, \tilde{x}_k)$ as a sample.
      iii. If TAIL:
         A. Randomly pick $(i,j) \in G$ where $(i,j) = (i',j')$ with probability $\alpha^{(i'j')}/\alpha$.
         B. Reject the current procedure with probability $1 - \alpha/(2 \cdot d \cdot r)$.
         C. Otherwise, use the next ℓ_p-sampler on $a^{(i,j)}$ to get $(k, \tilde{x}_k)$.
         D. Reject with probability $1 - 1/g(k)$. Otherwise, output $(k, \tilde{x}_k)$ as a sample.

Figure 5: The FAST ℓ_p-SAMPLING ALGORITHM

These algorithms use less space than the existing state-of-the-art algorithms for either all parameter settings (the number of nodes, edges, triangles etc.) or a large range of parameters depending on whether one or two passes over stream are permitted.

6. REFERENCES

[1] K. J. Ahn, S. Guha, and A. McGregor. Graph sketches: sparsification, spanners, and subgraphs. In *31st ACM SIGMOD-SIGACT-SIGART Symposium on Principles of Database Systems*, pages 5–14, 2012.

[2] N. Alon, R. Yuster, and U. Zwick. Finding and counting given length cycles. *Algorithmica*, 17(3):209–223, 1997.

[3] A. Andoni, R. Krauthgamer, and K. Onak. Streaming algorithms via precision sampling. In *Foundations of Computer Science (FOCS), 2011 IEEE 52nd Annual Symposium on*, pages 363–372. IEEE, 2011.

[4] L. Arge, M. T. Goodrich, and N. Sitchinava. Parallel external memory graph algorithms. In *24th IEEE International Symposium on Parallel and Distributed Processing, IPDPS 2010, Atlanta, Georgia, USA, 19-23 April 2010 - Conference Proceedings*, pages 1–11, 2010.

[5] S. Arifuzzaman, M. Khan, and M. V. Marathe. PATRIC: a parallel algorithm for counting triangles in massive networks. In *22nd ACM International Conference on Information and Knowledge Management, CIKM'13, San Francisco, CA, USA, October 27 - November 1, 2013*, pages 529–538, 2013.

[6] Z. Bar-Yossef, R. Kumar, and D. Sivakumar. Reductions in streaming algorithms, with an application to counting triangles in graphs. In *Proceedings of the Thirteenth Annual ACM-SIAM Symposium on Discrete Algorithms, January 6-8, 2002, San Francisco, CA, USA.*, pages 623–632, 2002.

[7] J. W. Berry, B. Hendrickson, S. Kahan, and P. Konecny. Software and algorithms for graph queries on multithreaded architectures. In *21th International Parallel and Distributed Processing Symposium (IPDPS 2007), Proceedings, 26-30 March 2007, Long Beach, California, USA*, pages 1–14, 2007.

[8] V. Braverman, R. Ostrovsky, and D. Vilenchik. How hard is counting triangles in the streaming model? In *Automata, Languages, and Programming - 40th International Colloquium, ICALP 2013, Riga, Latvia, July 8-12, 2013, Proceedings, Part I*, pages 244–254, 2013.

[9] L. Bulteau, V. Froese, K. Kutzkov, and R. Pagh. Triangle counting in dynamic graph streams. *CoRR*, abs/1404.4696, 2014.

[10] L. S. Buriol, G. Frahling, S. Leonardi, A. Marchetti-Spaccamela, and C. Sohler. Counting triangles in data streams. In *Proceedings of the Twenty-Fifth ACM SIGACT-SIGMOD-SIGART Symposium on Principles of Database Systems, June 26-28, 2006, Chicago, Illinois, USA*, pages 253–262, 2006.

[11] N. Chiba and T. Nishizeki. Arboricity and subgraph listing algorithms. *SIAM J. Comput.*, 14(1):210–223, 1985.

[12] K. L. Clarkson and D. P. Woodruff. Numerical linear algebra in the streaming model. In *Proceedings of the 41st Annual ACM Symposium on Theory of Computing, STOC 2009, Bethesda, MD, USA, May 31 - June 2, 2009*, pages 205–214, 2009.

[13] G. Cormode. Personal communication 8/23/15. 2015.

[14] G. Cormode. Personal communication 1/23/16. 2016.

[15] G. Cormode and D. Firmani. A unifying framework for ℓ_0-sampling algorithms. *Distributed and Parallel Databases*, 32(3):315–335, 2014.

[16] G. Cormode and H. Jowhari. A second look at counting triangles in graph streams. *Theor. Comput. Sci.*, 552:44–51, 2014.

[17] J.-P. Eckmann and E. Moses. Curvature of co-links uncovers hidden thematic layers in the world wide web. *Proceedings of the National Academy of Sciences*, 99(9):5825–5829, 2002.

[18] T. Eden, A. Levi, D. Ron, and C. Seshadhri. Approximately counting triangles in sublinear time. In *FOCS*, 2015.

[19] M. Ghashami, E. Liberty, J. M. Phillips, and D. P. Woodruff. Frequent directions : Simple and deterministic matrix sketching. *CoRR*, abs/1501.01711, 2015.

[20] A. Goel, M. Kapralov, and S. Khanna. On the communication and streaming complexity of maximum bipartite matching. In *Proceedings of the Twenty-Third Annual ACM-SIAM Symposium on Discrete Algorithms, SODA 2012, Kyoto, Japan, January 17-19, 2012*, pages 468–485, 2012.

[21] P. Indyk and D. Woodruff. Optimal approximations of the frequency moments of data streams. In *thirty-seventh annual ACM symposium on Theory of computing*, pages 202–208. ACM New York, NY, USA, 2005.

[22] M. Jha, C. Seshadhri, and A. Pinar. A space-efficient streaming algorithm for estimating transitivity and triangle counts using the birthday paradox. *TKDD*, 9(3):15:1–15:21, 2015.

[23] A. G. Jørgensen and S. Pettie. Threesomes, degenerates, and love triangles. In *55th IEEE Annual Symposium on Foundations of Computer Science, FOCS 2014, Philadelphia, PA, USA, October 18-21, 2014*, pages 621–630, 2014.

[24] H. Jowhari and M. Ghodsi. New streaming algorithms for counting triangles in graphs. In *Computing and Combinatorics, 11th Annual International Conference, COCOON 2005, Kunming, China, August 16-29, 2005, Proceedings*, pages 710–716, 2005.

[25] H. Jowhari, M. Saglam, and G. Tardos. Tight bounds for lp samplers, finding duplicates in streams, and related problems. In *PODS*, pages 49–58, 2011.

[26] M. Kapralov. Better bounds for matchings in the streaming model. In *Proceedings of the Twenty-Fourth Annual ACM-SIAM Symposium on Discrete Algorithms, SODA 2013, New Orleans, Louisiana, USA, January 6-8, 2013*, pages 1679–1697, 2013.

[27] T. G. Kolda, A. Pinar, and C. Seshadhri. Triadic measures on graphs: The power of wedge sampling. In *Proceedings of the 13th SIAM International Conference on Data Mining, May 2-4, 2013. Austin, Texas, USA.*, pages 10–18, 2013.

[28] M. N. Kolountzakis, G. L. Miller, R. Peng, and C. E. Tsourakakis. Efficient triangle counting in large graphs via degree-based vertex partitioning. *Internet Mathematics*, 8(1-2):161–185, 2012.

[29] K. Kutzkov and R. Pagh. Triangle counting in dynamic graph streams. In *Algorithm Theory - SWAT 2014 - 14th Scandinavian Symposium and Workshops, Copenhagen, Denmark, July 2-4, 2014. Proceedings*, pages 306–318, 2014.

[30] J. Leskovec, L. Backstrom, R. Kumar, and A. Tomkins. Microscopic evolution of social networks. In *Proceedings of the 14th ACM SIGKDD International Conference on Knowledge Discovery and Data Mining, Las Vegas, Nevada, USA, August 24-27, 2008*, pages 462–470, 2008.

[31] M. Manjunath, K. Mehlhorn, K. Panagiotou, and H. Sun. Approximate counting of cycles in streams. In *Algorithms - ESA 2011 - 19th Annual European Symposium, Saarbrücken, Germany, September 5-9, 2011. Proceedings*, pages 677–688, 2011.

[32] A. McGregor. Graph stream algorithms: a survey. *SIGMOD Record*, 43(1):9–20, 2014.

[33] A. McGregor, D. Tench, S. Vorotnikova, and H. T. Vu. Densest subgraph in dynamic graph streams. In *Mathematical Foundations of Computer Science 2015*, pages 472–482. Springer Berlin Heidelberg, 2015.

[34] R. Milo, S. Shen-Orr, S. Itzkovitz, N. Kashtan, D. Chklovskii, and U. Alon. Network motifs: simple building blocks of complex networks. In *Science*, pages 824–827, 2002.

[35] M. Mitzenmacher and E. Upfal. *Probability and Computing: Randomized Algorithms and Probabilistic Analysis.* Cambridge University Press, New York, NY, USA, 2005.

[36] M. Monemizadeh and D. P. Woodruff. 1-pass relative-error ℓ_p-sampling with applications. In *SODA*, pages 1143–1160, 2010.

[37] R. Pagh and C. E. Tsourakakis. Colorful triangle counting and a mapreduce implementation. *Inf. Process. Lett.*, 112(7):277–281, 2012.

[38] A. Pavan, K. Tangwongsan, S. Tirthapura, and K. Wu. Counting and sampling triangles from a graph stream. *PVLDB*, 6(14):1870–1881, 2013.

[39] T. Schank and D. Wagner. Approximating clustering coefficient and transitivity. *J. Graph Algorithms Appl.*, 9(2):265–275, 2005.

[40] S. Suri and S. Vassilvitskii. Counting triangles and the curse of the last reducer. In *Proceedings of the 20th International Conference on World Wide Web, WWW 2011, Hyderabad, India, March 28 - April 1, 2011*, pages 607–614, 2011.

[41] K. Tangwongsan, A. Pavan, and S. Tirthapura. Parallel triangle counting in massive streaming graphs. In *22nd ACM International Conference on Information and Knowledge Management, CIKM'13, San Francisco, CA, USA, October 27 - November 1, 2013*, pages 781–786, 2013.

[42] C. E. Tsourakakis, M. N. Kolountzakis, and G. L. Miller. Triangle sparsifiers. *J. Graph Algorithms Appl.*, 15(6):703–726, 2011.

[43] J. S. Vitter. Random sampling with a reservoir. *ACM Trans. Math. Softw.*, 11(1):37–57, 1985.

[44] B. F. Welles, A. V. Devender, and N. S. Contractor. Is a friend a friend?: investigating the structure of friendship networks in virtual worlds. In *Proceedings of the 28th International Conference on Human Factors in Computing Systems, CHI 2010, Extended Abstracts Volume, Atlanta, Georgia, USA, April 10-15, 2010*, pages 4027–4032, 2010.

Locating a Small Cluster Privately

Kobbi Nissim[*]
Ben-Gurion University *and*
Harvard University
kobbi@cs.bgu.ac.il

Uri Stemmer[†]
Ben-Gurion University
stemmer@cs.bgu.ac.il

Salil Vadhan[‡]
Harvard University
salil@seas.harvard.edu

ABSTRACT

We present a new algorithm for locating a small cluster of points with differential privacy [Dwork, McSherry, Nissim, and Smith, 2006]. Our algorithm has implications to private data exploration, clustering, and removal of outliers. Furthermore, we use it to significantly relax the requirements of the sample and aggregate technique [Nissim, Raskhodnikova, and Smith, 2007], which allows compiling of "off the shelf" (non-private) analyses into analyses that preserve differential privacy.

Keywords

Differential privacy, clustering, sample and aggregate

1. INTRODUCTION

Clustering – the task of grouping data points by their similarity – is one of the most commonly used techniques for exploring data, for identifying structure in uncategorized data, and for performing a variety of machine learning and optimization tasks. We present a new differentially private algorithm for a clustering-related task: Given a collection S of n points in the d-dimensional Euclidean space $\mathbb{R}^d$ and a parameter t reflecting a target number of points, our goal is to find a smallest ball containing at least t of the input points, while preserving differential privacy.

*Dept. of Computer Science, Ben-Gurion University *and* CRCS, Harvard University. Supported by NSF grant CNS-1237235, a grant from the Sloan Foundation, a Simons Investigator grant to Salil Vadhan, and ISF grant 276/12.

†Dept. of Computer Science, Ben-Gurion University. Supported by the Ministry of Science and Technology (Israel), and by the Frankel Center for Computer Science.

‡Center for Research on Computation & Society, John A. Paulson School of Engineering & Applied Sciences, Harvard University. `http://seas.harvard.edu/~salil`. Supported by NSF grant CNS-1237235, a grant from the Sloan Foundation, and a Simons Investigator grant. Work done in part when visiting the Shing-Tung Yau Center and the Department of Applied Mathematics at National Chiao-Tung University in Hsinchu, Taiwan.

PODS'16, June 26-July 01, 2016, San Francisco, CA, USA

DOI: http://dx.doi.org/10.1145/2902251.2902296

1.1 Problem and motivation

We recall the definition of differential privacy. We think of a dataset as consisting of n rows from a data universe U, where each row corresponds to one individual. Differential privacy requires that no individual's data has a significant effect on the distribution of what we output.

DEFINITION 1.1. *A randomized algorithm $M : U^n \to Y$ is (ϵ, δ)* differentially private *if for every two datasets $S, S' \in U^n$ that differ on one row, and every set $T \subseteq Y$, we have*

$$\Pr[M(S) \in T] \leq e^{\epsilon} \cdot \Pr[M(S') \in T] + \delta.$$

The common setting of parameters is to take ϵ to be a small constant and δ to be negligible in n, e.g., $\delta = 1/n^{\log n}$. For the introduction, we will assume that that $\delta < 1/(nd)$.

In this work we study the following problem under differential privacy:

DEFINITION 1.2. *A* 1-cluster problem *$\mathscr{C} = (X^d, n, t)$ consists of a d-dimensional domain X^d (where $X \subseteq \mathbb{R}$ is finite and totally ordered), and parameters $n \geq t$. We say that an algorithm $\mathcal{M}$ solves (X^d, n, t) with parameters (Δ, w) if for every input database $S \in (X^d)^n$, algorithm $\mathcal{M}(S)$ outputs a center c and a radius r s.t. the following holds with high probability probability:*

1. *The ball of radius r around c contains at least $t - \Delta$ input points (from S).*
2. *Let r_{opt} be the radius of the smallest ball in X^d containing at least t input points. Then $r \leq w \cdot r_{opt}$.*

The 1-cluster problem is very natural on its own, and furthermore, an algorithm for solving the 1-cluster problem can be used as a building block in other applications:

Data exploration. The 1-cluster problem has direct implications to performing data exploration privately, and, specifically to clustering. For example, one can think of an application involving map searches where one is interested in privately locating areas of certain "types" or "classes" of a given population to gain some insight of their concentration over different geographical areas.

Outlier detection. Consider using a solution to the 1-cluster problem to locate a small ball containing, say, 90% of the input points. This can be used as a basic private identification of outliers: The outcome of the algorithm can be viewed as defining a predicate h that evaluates to one inside the found ball and to zero otherwise. h can hence be useful for screening the inputs to a private analysis of the set of outlier points in the data. Outliers can skew and mislead the training of classification and regression algorithms, and hence, excluding them from further (privacy preserving) analysis can increase accuracy.

Furthermore, outlier detection can help in reducing the noise level required for the differentially private analysis itself, which in many cases would result in a dramatic improvement in accuracy. To see how this would happen, recall that the the most basic construction of differentially private algorithms is via the framework of *global sensitivity* [8] (see also Section 2 below). Noise is added to the outcome of a computation, and the noise magnitude is scaled to the *sensitivity* of the computation, i.e., the worst-case difference that a change of a single entry of the database may incur. Restricting the input space to a ball of (hopefully) a small diameter typically results in a smaller global sensitivity, and hence also significantly less noise.

Sample and aggregate. Maybe most importantly, an algorithm for the 1-cluster problem can be used in the Sample and Aggregate technique [16]. This generic technique allows using "off the shelf", *non-privacy preserving*, analyses and transform their outcome so as to preserve differential privacy.

Consider a (non-private) analysis f mapping databases to (a finite subset of) $\mathbb{R}^d$, and assume that f can be well approximated by evaluating f on a random subsample taken from the database. In the sample and aggregate framework, instead of applying the analysis f on the entire dataset, it is applied on several (say k) random sub-samples of the input dataset, obtaining k outputs $S = \{x_1, x_2, \dots, x_k\}$ in $\mathbb{R}^d$. The outputs are then *aggregated* to give a privacy-preserving result z that is "close" to some of the points in S. If f has the property that results that are in the vicinity of "good" results are also "good", then z will also be a "good" result. Furthermore, it suffices that (only) the aggregation procedure would be differentially private to guarantee that the entire construction satisfies differential privacy.

Using their aggregation function (discussed below), Nissim et al. constructed differentially private algorithms for k-means clustering and for learning mixtures of Gaussians [16]. Smith used the paradigm in dimension $d = 1$ to construct private statistical estimators [18]. One of the most appealing features of the paradigm is it that allows transforming programs that were not built with privacy in mind into differentially private analyses. For example, GUPT [15] is an implementation of differential privacy that uses differentially private averaging for aggregation. The development of better aggregators enables making the sample and aggregate paradigm more effective.

1.2 Existing techniques

As we will show (by reduction to a lower bound of Bun et al. [4]), solving the 1-cluster problem on infinite domains is impossible under differential privacy (for reasonable choices of parameters), so any private solution must assume a finite universe $X^d \subseteq \mathbb{R}^d$. We will consider the case that X^d is a discrete grid, identified with the real d dimensional unit cube quantized with grid step $1/(|X|-1)$.

We now list a few existing techniques that can be used to solve the 1-cluster problem (X^d, n, t):

Private aggregation. Nissim, Raskhodnikova, and Smith [16] introduced an efficient algorithm capable of identifying a ball of radius $O(r_{opt} \cdot \sqrt{d}/\epsilon)$ containing at least t points, provided that $t \geq 0.51n \geq O(\frac{d^2}{\epsilon^2}\log^2|X|)$.[1] There are three downsides here: (1) The error in the radius of the found ball grows with $\sqrt{d}$, which might be unacceptable in high dimensions. (2) The database size n needs to be as big as $d^2\log^2|X|$. (3) The algorithm can only identify a majority size cluster. If, e.g., the input points are split between several small balls such that none of them contains a majority of the points, then the algorithm results in an uninformative center z chosen almost at random.

Exponential mechanism. One of the first ideas for solving the 1-cluster problem is to use the exponential mechanism of McSherry Talwar [14] to choose among all balls: Given a radius r s.t. there exists a ball of radius r in X^d containing t points, the exponential mechanism is capable of identifying a ball of radius r containing $t - O(\log(|X|^d)/\epsilon)$ points. Privately finding the radius r could be done using a binary search, which would increase the loss in the size of the cluster by a factor of $O(\log(\sqrt{d}|X|))$. Overall, this strategy results in a ball of radius r_{opt} containing $t - \tilde{O}(d) \cdot \log^2(|X|)/\epsilon$ input points. Thus, the exponential mechanism can identify clusters even when they do not contain a majority of the points. However, we are seeking for an algorithm with running time $\mathrm{poly}(n, d, \log|X|)$, while the exponential mechanism runs in time $\mathrm{poly}(n, |X^d|)$.

Query release for threshold functions. For the special case where $d = 1$, the 1-cluster problem can be solved using algorithms for "query release for threshold functions": On input a database $S \in X^n$, a query release mechanism for threshold functions privately computes a database $S' \in X$ such that for every interval $I \subseteq X$ it holds that the number of points in S' differs from the number of points in S that lie in I by at most Δ. Searching for a smallest interval in S' containing $\gtrsim t$ points results in an interval of length $2r_{opt}$ (that is, of radius r_{opt}) containing at least $t - O(\Delta)$ input points. Known algorithms for query release for threshold functions [3, 4] achieve $\Delta = \max\left\{2^{(1+o(1))\log^*|X|} \cdot \log(\frac{1}{\delta}), \mathrm{polylog}(n)\right\}/\epsilon$. Note that the dependency on $|X|$ has improved substantially from the polylog$|X|$ of the above methods. Bun et al.[4] also showed that Δ must be at least $\Omega(\log^*|X|)$ and hence this problem is impossible to solve for infinite X (we show a similar lower bound for the 1-cluster problem).

1.3 Our contributions

We present an algorithm for the 1-cluster problem that achieves (almost) the best of all the above. Namely, it (a)

[1]The results of [16] do not assume a finite discrete grid universe. Instead, they allow both a multiplicative and an additive error in the radius of the found ball. The additive error in the radius is eliminated whenever $n \geq O(\frac{d^2}{\epsilon^2}\log^2|X|)$. More specifically, let z_0 denote the center of the smallest ball containing $t > 0.51n$ input points. The algorithm of [16] computes a center z s.t. that the error vector $(z_0 - z)$ has magnitude $O(\frac{r_{opt}}{\epsilon}) + \frac{1}{\epsilon} \cdot e^{-\Omega(\epsilon\sqrt{n}/d)}$ in each coordinate.

	Needed cluster size – t Additive loss in cluster size – Δ	Approximation factor in radius – w	Running time
Private aggregation [16]	$t \geq \max\left\{0.51n, O(\frac{d^2}{\epsilon^2}\log^2\lvert X\rvert)\right\}$ $\Delta = 0$	$w = O(\sqrt{d}/\epsilon)$	$\text{poly}(n, d, \log\lvert X\rvert)$
Exponential mechanism [14]	$t \geq \Delta = \tilde{O}(d) \cdot \log^2(\lvert X\rvert)/\epsilon$	$w = 1$	$\text{poly}(n, \lvert X^d\rvert)$
Query release for threshold functions ($d = 1$ only) [3, 4]	$t \geq \Delta = \max\left\{2^{(1+o(1))\log^*\lvert X\rvert} \cdot \log(\frac{1}{\delta}), \text{polylog}(n)\right\}/\epsilon$	$w = 1$	$\text{poly}(n, \log\lvert X\rvert)$
This work	$t \geq \frac{\sqrt{d}}{\epsilon}\log^{1.5}\left(\frac{1}{\delta}\right) \cdot 2^{O(\log^*(\lvert X\rvert d))}$ $\Delta = \frac{1}{\epsilon}\log\left(\frac{1}{\delta}\right) \cdot 2^{O(\log^*(\lvert X\rvert d))}$	$w = O(\sqrt{\log n})$	$\text{poly}(n, d, \log\lvert X\rvert)$

Table 1: Comparing different solutions from past work and our result.

handles a minority size cluster, of size only sublinear in d (better than all the above) and sublogarithmic in $|X|$ (as with query release), and loses even less than that in the size of the cluster; and (b) avoids paying $d^{\Omega(1)}$ factors in the error of the radius (instead paying $O(\sqrt{\log n})$). See Table 1 for a comparison with past work.

THEOREM 3.2 (INFORMAL). *There exists an efficient (ϵ, δ)-differentially private algorithm that, given a set S of n points in a discretized d-dimensional cube X^d, and a parameter t, outputs a ball of radius $O\left(\sqrt{\log n} \cdot r_{opt}\right)$ of size at least*

$$t - \frac{1}{\epsilon}\log\left(\frac{1}{\delta}\right) \cdot 2^{O(\log^*(|X|d))},$$

provided that

$$t \geq \frac{\sqrt{d}}{\epsilon}\log^{1.5}\left(\frac{1}{\delta}\right) \cdot 2^{O(\log^*(|X|d))}.$$

We note that the algorithm of [16] works in general metric output spaces, whereas ours is restricted to $\mathbb{R}^d$. We leave open the question of extending our construction to more general settings.

2. PRELIMINARIES

Notations. Throughout the paper, we use X to denote a finite totally ordered data universe, and use X^d for the corresponding d-dimensional domain. We will identify X^d with the real d-dimensional unit cube, quantized with grid step $1/(|X|-1)$. Datasets are (ordered) collections of elements from some data universe U (e.g., $U = X$ or $U = X^d$). Two datasets $S, S' \in U^n$ are called *neighboring* if they differ on at most one entry, i.e., $S' = (S_{-i}, x'_i)$ for some $1 \leq i \leq |S|$ and $x'_i \in U$.

We will construct algorithms that use several differentially private mechanisms as subroutines, and analyze the overall privacy using the following composition theorem:

THEOREM 2.1 ([6, 7]). *A mechanism that permits k adaptive interactions with (ϵ, δ)-differentially private mechanisms (and does not access the database otherwise) is $(k\epsilon, k\delta)$- differentially private.*

2.1 The framework of global sensitivity [8]

DEFINITION 2.2 (L_p-SENSITIVITY). *A function f mapping databases to $\mathbb{R}^d$ has L_p-*sensitivity *k if $\|f(S) - f(S')\|_p \leq k$ for all neighboring S, S'.*

The most basic constructions of differentially private algorithms are obtained by adding noise calibrated to the global sensitivity of the computation. We will use the Laplace mechanism of [8] to obtain noisy estimations to counting queries (e.g., how many points in S have 0 on their first coordinate? Such a query has sensitivity 1 since changing one database element can change the count by at most 1).

THEOREM 2.3 (LAPLACE MECHANISM [8]). *A random variable is distributed as $\text{Lap}(\lambda)$ if its probability density function is $f(y) = \frac{1}{2\lambda}\exp(-\frac{|y|}{\lambda})$. Let $\epsilon > 0$, and let $f : U^* \to \mathbb{R}^d$ be a function of L_1-sensitivity k. The mechanism $\mathcal{A}$ that on input $D \in U^*$ adds independently generated noise with distribution $\text{Lap}(\frac{k}{\epsilon})$ to each of the d output terms of $f(D)$ preserves $(\epsilon, 0)$-differential privacy.*

We will also use the Gaussian mechanism to obtain (noisy) averages of vectors in $\mathbb{R}^d$. See Appendix A for details.

THEOREM 2.4 (GAUSSIAN MECHANISM [6]). *Let $\epsilon, \delta \in (0, 1)$, and let $f : U^* \to \mathbb{R}^d$ be a function of L_2-sensitivity k. Denote $\sigma \geq \frac{k}{\epsilon}\sqrt{2\ln(1.25/\delta)}$. The mechanism $\mathcal{A}$ that on input $D \in U^*$ adds independently generated noise with distribution $\mathcal{N}(0, \sigma^2)$ to each of the d output terms of $f(D)$ preserves (ϵ, δ)-differential privacy.*

2.2 Stability based techniques [7, 19, 3]

Given a database $S \in U^*$, consider the task of choosing a "good" solution out of a possible set of solutions F, and assume that this "goodness" is quantified using a *quality function* $q : U^* \times F \to \mathbb{N}$ assigning "scores" to solutions from F (w.r.t. the given database S). One of the most useful constructions in differential privacy – the exponential mechanism [14] – shows that such scenarios are compatible with differential privacy, and that an approximately optimal solution $f \in F$ can be privately identified provided that q has low-sensitivity and that $|S| \gtrsim \log|F|$.

By limiting our attention to cases where the number of possible solutions with "high" scores is limited, it is possible to relax the requirement that $|S| \gtrsim \log|F|$, using what has come to be known as *stability based techniques*. In this work we use stability based techniques for the following task: Given a dataset $S \in U^n$ and a partition P of U, find a set $p \in P$ containing (approximately) maximum number of elements of S. This task can be privately solved using algorithms for query release for point functions.

THEOREM 2.5 ([3, 20]). *Fix ϵ, δ. Let U be a data universe, let P be a partition of U, and let $S \in U^n$ be an input database. There exists a $\mathrm{poly}(n, \log|U|)$-time (ϵ, δ)-differentially private algorithm s.t. the following holds. Let T denote the maximum number of input elements (from S) that are contained in a set in P. If $T \geq \frac{2}{\epsilon}\log(\frac{4n}{\beta\delta})$, then with probability at least $(1-\beta)$ the algorithm returns a set $q \in P$ containing at least $T - \frac{4}{\epsilon}\log(\frac{2n}{\beta})$ elements from S.*

3. OUR ALGORITHMS

In this paper we explore the following problem under differential privacy:

DEFINITION 3.1 (THE PROBLEM OF A MINIMAL BALL ENCLOSING t POINTS). *Given a set of n points in the Euclidean space $\mathbb{R}^d$ and an integer $t \leq n$, the goal is to find a ball of minimal radius r_{opt} enclosing at least t input points.*

To enhance readability, we are using this section as an informal presentation of our results, giving most of the ideas behind our construction. We will also briefly discuss some intuitive ideas which fail to solve the task at hand, but are useful for the presentation. Any informalities made hereafter will be removed in the sections that follow.

We start by recalling known facts (without concern for privacy) about the problem of a minimal ball enclosing t points:

1. It is NP-hard to solve exactly [17].
2. Agarwal et al. [1] presented an approximation scheme (PTAS) which computes a ball of radius $(1+\alpha)r_{opt}$ containing t points in time $O(n^{1/\alpha}d)$.
3. There is a trivial algorithm for computing a ball of radius $2r_{opt}$ containing t points: Consider only balls centered around input points, and return the smallest ball containing t points.

   Indeed, let B denote a ball of radius r_{opt} enclosing at least t input points, and observe that a ball of radius $2r_{opt}$ around any point in B contains all of B. Hence, there exists a ball of radius $2r_{opt}$ around an input point containing at least t points.

We present a (roughly) $\sqrt{\log n}$-approximation algorithm satisfying differential privacy:

THEOREM 3.2. *Let $n, t, \beta, \epsilon, \delta$ be s.t.*

$$t \geq O\left(\frac{\sqrt{d}}{\epsilon}\log\left(\frac{1}{\beta}\right)\log\left(\frac{nd}{\beta\delta}\right)\sqrt{\log\left(\frac{1}{\beta\delta}\right)} \cdot 9^{\log^*(2|X|\sqrt{d})}\right).$$

There exists a $\mathrm{poly}(n, d, 1/\beta, \log|X|)$-time (ϵ,δ)-differentially private algorithm that solves the 1-cluster problem (X^d, n, t) with parameters (Δ, w) and error probability β, where $w = O\left(\sqrt{\log n}\right)$ and

$$\Delta = O\left(\frac{1}{\epsilon}\log\left(\frac{n}{\delta}\right)\log\left(\frac{1}{\beta}\right) \cdot 9^{\log^*(2|X|\sqrt{d})}\right).$$

In words, there exists an efficient (ϵ,δ)-differentially private algorithm that (ignoring logarithmic factors) is capable of identifying a ball of radius $\tilde{O}(r_{opt})$ containing $t - \tilde{O}(\frac{1}{\epsilon})$ points, provided that $t \geq \tilde{O}(\sqrt{d}/\epsilon)$.

REMARK 3.3. *For simplicity, in the above theorem we identified X^d with the real d-dimensional unit cube, quantized with grid step $1/(|X|-1)$. Our results trivially extend to domains with minimal grid step ℓ and axis length $L = \max X - \min X$ by replacing $|X|$ with L/ℓ.*

REMARK 3.4. *Observe that the parameters t, Δ in Theorem 3.2 have some dependency on the domain size $|X|$. Although this dependency is very weak, it implies that our construction cannot be applied to instances with infinite domains. In Appendix B we show that this is a barrier one cannot cross with differential privacy, and that solving the 1-cluster problem on infinite domains is impossible under differential privacy (for reasonable choice of parameters).*

OBSERVATION 3.5. *Let $k \lesssim \frac{(\epsilon n)^{2/3}}{d^{1/3}}$. Our construction could be used as a heuristic for solving a k-clustering-type problem: Letting $t = n/k$, we can iterate our algorithm k times and find a collection of (at most) k balls that cover all the data points except at most $\approx \frac{\sqrt{dk}}{\epsilon}$ data points (ignoring logarithmic factors in $n, d, k, \frac{1}{\delta}$ and sublogarithmic factors in $|X|$).*

Towards proving Theorem 3.2 we design two algorithms. The first, `GoodRadius`, is given as input a collection S of n points and a parameter t, and returns a radius r such that there exists a ball of radius r containing $\gtrsim t$ of the points in S and, furthermore, r is within a constant factor of the smallest such ball.

The second algorithm, `GoodCenter`, is given as input the set S of input points, a parameter t, and a radius r computed by `GoodRadius`. The algorithm outputs a center z of a ball of radius $\tilde{O}(r)$ containing $\gtrsim t$ of the points in S. So, a simplified overview of our construction is:

Input: A set S of n points in X^d, and an integer $t \leq n$.

Step 1: Identify a radius $r = O(r_{opt})$ s.t. there is a ball of radius r containing $\gtrsim t$ input points.

Step 2: Given r, locate a ball of radius $O\left(\sqrt{\log n} \cdot r\right)$ containing $\gtrsim t$ input points.

3.1 Finding the cluster radius: algorithm GoodRadius

Let $S = (x_1, \ldots, x_n)$ be a database containing n points in X^d. Given S and $t \leq n$, our current task is to approximate the minimal radius r_{opt} for which there is a ball of that radius containing at least t points from S.

We start with the following notations: For a radius $r \geq 0$ and a point $p \in \mathbb{R}^d$, let $\mathcal{B}_r(p)$ denote the number of input points contained in a ball of radius r around p. That is, $\mathcal{B}_r(p) = |\{i : \|x_i - p\|_2 \leq r\}|$.

Recall that we are looking for (a radius of) a ball containing $\gtrsim t$ points from S, and that a ball containing t points is just as good as a ball of the same radius containing $100t$ points. Hence, we modify our notation of $\mathcal{B}_r(p)$ to cap counts at t:

$$\bar{\mathcal{B}}_r(p) = \min\left\{\, \mathcal{B}_r(p)\ ,\ t \,\right\}.$$

Using that notation, our goal is to approximate $r_{opt} = \min\{r \geq 0 : \exists p \in \mathbb{R}^d \text{ s.t. } \bar{\mathcal{B}}_r(p) \geq t\}$. Recall that a direct computation of r_{opt} is NP-hard, and let us turn to the simple 2-approximation algorithm that considers only balls centered at input points. To that end, for every $r \geq 0$ define $L(r)$ as the maximum number of input points contained in a ball of radius r around some input point (capped at t). That is,

$$L(r) = \max_{x_i \in S}\{\bar{\mathcal{B}}_r(x_i)\}.$$

As we next explain, using that notation, it suffices to compute a radius r s.t.

$$(i)\ L(r) \gtrsim t \qquad \text{and} \qquad (ii)\ L(r/2) < t.$$

We now argue that such an r satisfies the requirements of `GoodRadius`. By (i) there exists a ball of radius r containing $\gtrsim t$ input points, so we just need to argue that $r \leq O(r_{opt})$. Assume towards contradiction that $r_{opt} < r/4$, and hence there exists a subset $D \subseteq S$ of t input points which are contained in a ball of radius $r/4$. Observe that a ball radius $r/2$ around any point in D contains all of D, and therefore $L(r/2) \geq t$, contradicting (ii).

So we only need to compute a radius r satisfying properties (i) and (ii) above. However, the function L has high sensitivity, and hence it is not clear how to privately estimate $L(r)$ for a given radius r. To see why L has high sensitivity, consider a set S consisting of the unit vector $\vec{e_1}$ along with $t/2$ copies of the zero vector and $t/2$ copies of the vector $2 \cdot \vec{e_1}$. So, a ball of radius 1 around $\vec{e_1}$ contains all of the points, and $L(1) = t$. However, if we were to switch the vector $\vec{e_1}$ to $2 \cdot \vec{e_1}$, then the ball around $\vec{e_1}$ is no longer valid (since we only consider balls centered around input points), and every existing ball of radius 1 contains at most $t/2$ point. So the sensitivity of the function L is $\Omega(t)$.

In order to reduce the sensitivity of L we now redefine it using averaging (a related idea was also used in [16]). For $r \geq 0$ redefine L as

$$L(r) = \frac{1}{t} \max_{\text{distinct } i_1,\ldots,i_t \in [n]} \{\bar{\mathcal{B}}_r(x_{i_1}) + \ldots + \bar{\mathcal{B}}_r(x_{i_t})\}.$$

That is, to compute $L(r)$ we construct a ball of radius r around every input point, count the number of points contained in every such ball (counts are capped at t), and compute the average of the t biggest counts.

To see that the redefined function $L(r)$ has low sensitivity, consider a set of n input points and a ball of radius r around every input point. Adding a new input point can increase by at most 1 the number of points contained within every existing ball. In addition, we now have a new ball centered around the new input point, and as we cap counts at t, we count at most t points in this ball. Overall, adding the new input point can increase $L(r)$ by at most $t \cdot \frac{1}{t} + \frac{t}{t} = 2$. The function $L(r)$ has therefore sensitivity $O(1)$.

Utility wise, we are still searching for an r s.t.

$$(i)\ L(r) \gtrsim t \qquad \text{and} \qquad (ii)\ L(r/2) < t.$$

Again, such an r is useful since, by (i), there exists a ball of radius r containing $\gtrsim t$ input points, and by (ii) we have that $r \leq 4r_{opt}$: Otherwise (if $r_{opt} < r/4$) there exists a subset $D \subseteq S$ of t points which are contained in a ball of radius $r/4$. A ball of radius $r/2$ around *every* point in D contains all of D and therefore there are t balls of radius $r/2$ containing t points. Hence, $L(r/2) \geq t$, contradicting (ii).

So, the function L has low sensitivity, and we are searching for an r s.t. $L(r) \gtrsim t$ and $L(r/2) < t$. This can easily be done privately using binary search with noisy estimates of L for the comparisons, but as there are (roughly) $\log(\sqrt{d}|X|)$ comparisons such a binary search would only yield a radius r s.t. $L(r) \gtrsim t - \log(\sqrt{d}|X|)$.[2] In Section 4.1 we will use a tool from [3] (recursion on binary search) to improve the guarantee to $L(r) \gtrsim t - 9^{\log^*(\sqrt{d}|X|)}$.

LEMMA 3.6 (ALGORITHM `GoodRadius`). *Let $S \in (X^d)^n$ be a database containing n points from X^d and let $t, \beta, \epsilon, \delta$ be parameters. There exists a $\text{poly}(n, d, \log|X|)$-time (ϵ, δ)-differentially private algorithm that on input S outputs a radius $r \in \mathbb{R}$ s.t. with probability at least $(1 - \beta)$:*

1. *There is a ball in X^d of radius r containing at least $t - O\left(\frac{1}{\epsilon}\log(\frac{1}{\beta\delta}) \cdot 9^{\log^*(|X|\cdot d)}\right)$ points from S.*
2. *Let r_{opt} denote the radius of the smallest ball in X^d containing at least t points from S. Then $r \leq 4 \cdot r_{opt}$.*

3.2 Locating a cluster: algorithm GoodCenter

Let r be the outcome of Algorithm `GoodRadius` (so $r = O(r_{opt})$ and there exists a ball of radius r containing $\gtrsim t$ input points). Given the radius r, our next task is to locate, with differential privacy, a small ball in $\mathbb{R}^d$ containing $\gtrsim t$ input points. We begin by examining two intuitive (but unsuccessful) suggestions for achieving this goal.

First Attempt.

One of the first ideas for using the given radius r in order to locate a small ball is the following: Divide each axis into intervals of length $\approx r$, identify (for every axis) a "heavy" interval containing lots of input points, and return the resulting axis-aligned box. Such a "heavy" interval could be privately identified (on every axis) using known, stability-based techniques [7, 19, 3].

The main problem with our first attempt is that the resulting box might be empty. This is illustrated in Figure 1, where a "heavy" interval is identified on each axis s.t. their intersection is empty.

Second Attempt.

The failure point of our first strategy was the attempt to locate the cluster in an axis by axis manner. Trying to avoid that pitfall, consider the following idea for identifying a "heavy" *box* in $\mathbb{R}^d$: Let us denote by $P \subseteq S$ the guaranteed set of $\gtrsim t$ input points which are contained in a ball of radius r in $\mathbb{R}^d$. Observe that the set P is of diameter $2r$, and divide each axis into *randomly shifted* intervals of length $\approx 4dr$. For every axis we have that the projection of P onto that axis is contained within one interval w.p. $\gtrsim 1 - 1/(2d)$, and using the union bound, this is the case for all axes simultaneously w.p. $\gtrsim 1/2$. That is, without looking at the data, we have partitioned $\mathbb{R}^d$ into disjoint boxes of side length $\approx 4dr$ s.t. at least one of them contains $\gtrsim t$ input points, and such a "heavy" box can be privately identified

[2] Alternatively, an r s.t. $L(r) \gtrsim t$ and $L(r/2) < t$ could be privately computed using the sparse vector technique, which also yields a radius r s.t. $L(r) \gtrsim t - \log(\sqrt{d}|X|)$.

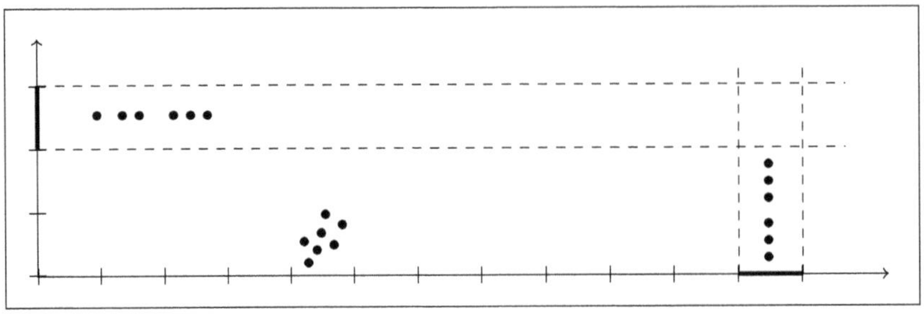

Figure 1: An illustration of "heavy" intervals s.t. their intersection is empty.

using known, stability-based techniques. While the resulting box is indeed "heavy", it is of side-length $\approx dr$ (i.e. of diameter $\approx d^{1.5}r$), which is not what we are looking for.

Towards a Solution.

Assume (for now) that we have privately identified a (concisely described) subset X' of X such that $S' = S \cap X'$ has $\gtrsim t$ points and is contained in a ball of radius r. Our current goal is, therefore, to identify a small ball enclosing all of S'. One option (which still does not preserve privacy, but has potential) it the following: Compute the average c of the points in S' and return a ball of radius r around c. This option has merit since computing the average of input points can be made private by adding random noise with magnitude proportional to the diameter of our subset S' divided by its size $|S'| \gtrsim t$ (the intuition is that random noise of that magnitude masks any possible change limited to one input element, see Theorem 2.4). In our case, we would like to use r (the diameter of S') as such a bound, and hence obtain a ball of radius (roughly) $2r$. However, all of our discussion above only holds with high probability, say with probability $1-\beta$. In particular, the diameter of S' is only bounded with probability $1-\beta$. In order for the privacy analysis to go through, we need this bound to hold with probability at least $1-\delta$, i.e., set $\beta = \delta$. Since δ is typically a negligible function of n, and since our running time depends on $1/\beta$, this is unacceptable.

As we next explain, our first (failed) attempt comes in handy for bounding the necessary noise magnitude. For the intuition, recall that our first attempt failed because we were misled by points outside the small cluster. By limiting our attention only to points in S' (which are clustered), this is no longer an issue.

Assume that the set S' contains $\gtrsim t$ points and that its diameter is r, and consider the following procedure: Partition every axis of $\mathbb{R}^d$ into intervals of length r. On every axis, at least one such interval contains (the projection of) $\gtrsim t/2$ points, and we can find such a "heavy" interval I using known, stability-based techniques. Afterwards, we can extend its length by r to the left and to the right to obtain an interval $\hat{I}$ of length $3r$ containing all of S'. See Figure 2 for an illustration. So, on every axis we identified an interval of length $3r$ containing *all* of the points in S'. Hence, the intersection of all those intervals is a box B of diameter $\approx \sqrt{d}r$ containing all of S'.

The thing that works in our favor here is that the above procedure *always* returns a box B of diameter $\approx \sqrt{d}r$, even if our assumptions on the set S' are invalid (in which case the box B might be empty, but its diameter is the same). Now consider the set $\tilde{S}$ where we truncate all points in S' to lie in B. Observe that (w.h.p.) we have that $S' \subseteq B$ and $\tilde{S} = S'$, and that, in any case, the diameter of $\tilde{S}$ is at most $\approx \sqrt{d}r$. We can therefore privately release the noisy average of the points in $\tilde{S}$, with noise magnitude proportional to $\lesssim \sqrt{d}r/|S'|$. Assuming that $|S'| \gtrsim t \geq \sqrt{d}$, the incurred noise is of magnitude $\lesssim r$, which results in a ball of radius $O(r)$ containing all of S'.

To summarize, it suffices to privately "ignore" all input points but $\gtrsim t$ points falling in some ball of radius $\approx r$.

Final Step.

Our final task is to identify a subset $S' \subseteq S$ of $\approx t$ input elements that are contained in a ball of radius roughly r. Using the Johnson-Lindenstrauss transform we project our input points onto $\mathbb{R}^k$, where $k \approx \log(n)$ (w.h.p. point distances are preserved up to a constant factor). We denote the projection of a point $x \in \mathbb{R}^d$ as $f(x) \in \mathbb{R}^k$. By the properties of the JL-transform, it suffices to identify a part of the input $S' \subseteq S$ s.t. its projection $f(S') := \{f(x) : x \in S'\}$ is contained within a ball of radius $\approx r$ in $\mathbb{R}^k$.

As we next explain, our second (unsuccessful) attempt could be used to identify such a subset $S' \subseteq S$. The intuition is that our second attempt incurred an unacceptable error factor of $\text{poly}(d)$ in the cluster radius when locating the ball in $\mathbb{R}^d$, and this error factor is mitigated by locating the ball in the lower-dimensional space $\mathbb{R}^k$ (where $k = O(\log n)$).

As above, let $P \subseteq S$ be the guaranteed set of $\gtrsim t$ input points contained within a ball of radius r in $\mathbb{R}^d$. Note that (w.h.p.) the set $f(P) := \{f(x) : x \in P\}$ is contained within a ball of radius $\lesssim r$ in $\mathbb{R}^k$, and assume that this is the case. Partition every axis i of $\mathbb{R}^k$ into randomly shifted intervals $\mathcal{I}_i = \{I^i_j\}_{j\in\mathbb{Z}}$ of length $\approx 4r$. On every axis i, with probability $\gtrsim 1/2$ the projection of $f(P)$ on the ith axis is completely contained within one interval in $\mathcal{I}_i$. Using the union bound, with probability $\gtrsim 0.5^k = 1/\text{poly}(n)$, this is the case for all of the k axes simultaneously, and $f(P)$ is completely contained within an axis aligned box whose projection onto every axis i of $\mathbb{R}^k$ is in $\mathcal{I}_i$. In other words, we have partitioned $\mathbb{R}^k$ into disjoint k-dimensional axis aligned boxes of side-length $\approx 4r$ s.t. with noticeable probability (we will later use repetitions to amplify this probability, and use the sparse vector technique to privately choose one of the repetitions) at least one of them contains $\gtrsim t$ (projected) input points. Such a "heavy" rectangle B could be privately identified using stability based techniques (its diameter is $\approx r\sqrt{k} \approx r\sqrt{\log n}$). Finally, we define the set $S' = \{x \in S : f(x) \in B\}$ as the set of points that are mapped (by

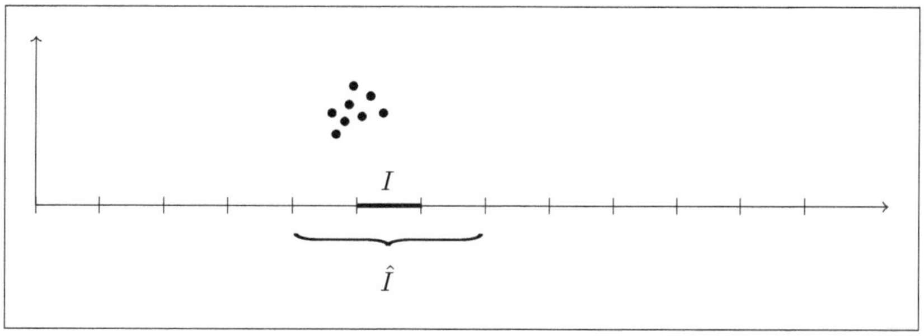

Figure 2: An illustration of an interval I of containing some of the points of S', and the corresponding interval $\hat{I}$ of length $3|I|$ containing all of S' (since S' is of diameter $r = |I|$).

the JL transform) into the rectangle B. We now have that S' contains $\gtrsim t$ input elements, since the box B is "heavy" in $\mathbb{R}^k$, and the diameter S' is $\lesssim r\sqrt{\log n}$, since that is the diameter of $B = f(S')$. The complete construction appears in Algorithm `GoodCenter` (algorithm 2).

LEMMA 3.7 (ALGORITHM GOODCENTER). *Let $S \in (\mathbb{R}^d)^n$ be a database containing n points in $\mathbb{R}^d$, and let $r, t, \beta, \epsilon, \delta$ be parameters s.t. $t \geq O\left(\frac{\sqrt{d}}{\epsilon}\log(\frac{1}{\beta})\log(\frac{nd}{\beta\epsilon\delta})\sqrt{\log(\frac{1}{\beta\delta})}\right)$. There exists a $\mathrm{poly}(n, d, 1/\beta)$-time (ϵ, δ)-differentially private algorithm that on input S, r, t outputs a point $z \in \mathbb{R}^d$ s.t. the following holds. If there exists a ball of radius r in $\mathbb{R}^d$ containing at least t points from S, then with probability at least $1 - \beta$, the ball of radius $O\left(r\sqrt{\log n}\right)$ around z contains at least $t - O\left(\frac{1}{\epsilon}\log(\frac{1}{\beta})\log(\frac{n}{\beta\epsilon\delta})\right)$ of the points in S.*

4. DETAILS OF ANALYSIS

4.1 Algorithm GoodRadius

As we explained in Section 3.1, it is possible to compute an approximation for the optimal radius using a binary search on a carefully chosen low sensitivity function. We use the following tool from [3] in order to reduce the sample cost of that binary search.

Quasi-concave promise problems [3].

A function $Q(\cdot)$ over a totally ordered domain is *quasi-concave* if $Q(\ell) \geq \min\{Q(i), Q(j)\}$ for every $i \leq \ell \leq j$.

DEFINITION 4.1 ([3]). *A* Quasi-Concave Promise Problem *consists of an ordered set F of possible solutions, a database $S \in U^n$, a sensitivity-1 quality function $Q : U^n \times F \to \mathbb{R}$, an approximation parameter α, and another parameter p (called a* quality promise*).*

If $Q(S, \cdot)$ is quasi-concave and if there exists a solution $f \in F$ for which $Q(S, f) \geq p$ then a good output for the problem is a solution $g \in F$ satisfying $Q(S, g) \geq (1 - \alpha)p$. The outcome is not restricted otherwise.

We will use Algorithm `RecConcave` from [3] to solve quasi-concave promise problems while preserving differential privacy:

THEOREM 4.2 (ALGORITHM RECCONCAVE [3]). *Let U be a domain, let F be a totally ordered (finite) set of solutions, and let $Q : U^n \times F \to \mathbb{R}$ be a sensitivity-1 quality function. Let $\alpha, \beta, \epsilon, \delta$ be parameters. There exists an (ϵ, δ)-differentially private algorithm s.t. the following holds. On input a database S and a quality promise p for which $Q(S, \cdot)$ is quasi-concave and*

$$\max_{f \in F}\{Q(S, f)\} \geq p \geq 8^{\log^* |F|} \cdot \frac{36\log^* |F|}{\alpha\epsilon}\log\left(\frac{12\log^* |F|}{\beta\delta}\right),$$

the algorithm outputs a solution $f \in F$ s.t. $Q(S, f) \geq (1 - \alpha)p$ with probability at least $(1 - \beta)$.

REMARK 4.3. *The computational efficiency of algorithm `RecConcave` depends on the quality function Q. It can be made efficient in cases where for every database $S \in U^n$, the totally ordered set of solutions F can be partitions into $k = \mathrm{poly}(n)$ intervals of sequential solutions $F_1, F_2, \ldots, F_k$ s.t. for every i and for every $f, f' \in F_i$ we have $Q(S, f) = Q(S, f')$. In such cases, the algorithm runs in time $\mathrm{poly}(n, \log|F|)$, assuming that the partition of F, and that evaluating Q, can be done in time $\mathrm{poly}(n, \log|F|)$.*

We now proceed with the privacy analysis of algorithm `GoodRadius`.

LEMMA 4.4. *Algorithm `GoodRadius` preserves (ϵ, δ)- differential privacy.*

PROOF. Algorithm `GoodRadius` interacts with its input database in step 2 using the Laplace mechanism and in step 4 using algorithm `RecConcave`. In order to show that those two interactions preserve privacy, we will now argue that $L(r, \cdot)$ is of sensitivity 2 (for every fixed r). To see why this is intuitively correct, consider a set of n input points and a ball of radius r around every input point. Adding a new input point can increase by at most 1 the number of points contained within every such ball. In addition, we now have a new ball centered around the new input point, and as we cap counts at t, we count at most t points in this ball. Overall, adding the new input point can increase $L(r, \cdot)$ by at most $t \cdot \frac{1}{t} + \frac{t}{t} = 2$.

More formally, let S, S' be two neighboring databases and assume that $S' = S \setminus \{y\} \cup \{y'\}$ and that $S = S' \setminus \{y'\} \cup \{y\}$. We have that

---

Algorithm 1 `GoodRadius`

Input: Database $S \in (X^d)^n$, desired ball volume t, failure probability bound β, and privacy parameters ϵ, δ.

Algorithm used: Algorithm `RecConcave` for privately solving quasi-concave problems. We denote the minimal quality promise needed for algorithm `RecConcave` (for our choice of parameters) as $\Gamma = 8^{\log^*(2|X|\sqrt{d})} \cdot \frac{144\log^*(2|X|\sqrt{d})}{\epsilon}\log\left(\frac{24\log^*(2|X|\sqrt{d})}{\beta\delta}\right)$.

Notation: For $x \in X^d$ and $0 \le r \in \mathbb{R}$ let $\mathcal{B}_r(x,S)$ denote the number of input points contained in a ball of radius r around x. For $r < 0$, let $\mathcal{B}_r(x,S) = 0$. Let $\bar{\mathcal{B}}_r(x,S) = \min\{\mathcal{B}_r(x,S), t\}$.

1. For $r \in \mathbb{R}$ define $L(r,S) = \frac{1}{t} \max\limits_{\text{distinct } i_1,\ldots,i_t \in [n]} \left(\bar{\mathcal{B}}_r(x_{i_1},S) + \ldots + \bar{\mathcal{B}}_r(x_{i_t},S)\right)$.
   % That is, for every input point $x \in S$ we count the number of input points contained in a ball of radius r around x, capped at t. We define $L(r,S)$ as the average of the t largest counts.
   % Note that $L(\cdot,S)$ is a non-decreasing function.
2. Let $\tilde{L}(0,S) = L(0,S) + \text{Lap}(4/\epsilon)$. If $\tilde{L}(0,S) > t - 2\Gamma - \frac{4}{\epsilon}\ln(2/\beta)$, then halt and return $z = 0$.
   % Step 2 handles the case where there exists a cluster of radius zero containing $\gtrsim t$ of the input points.
3. Define the quality function $Q(r,S) = \frac{1}{2}\min\{t - L(r/2,S),\ L(r,S) - t + 4\Gamma\}$.
4. Apply algorithm `RecConcave` with privacy parameters $(\frac{\epsilon}{2},\delta)$, utility parameters $(\alpha{=}\frac{1}{2}, \frac{\beta}{2})$, quality function Q, and quality promise Γ to choose and return $z \in \left\{0, \frac{1}{2|X|}, \frac{2}{2|X|}, \frac{3}{2|X|}, \ldots, \left\lceil\sqrt{d}\right\rceil\right\}$.
   % For simplicity, we identify X^d with the real d-dimensional unit cube, quantized with grid step $1/(|X|-1)$. Our results trivially extend to domains with grids steps ℓ by choosing the output out of $\left\{0, \frac{\ell}{2}, \frac{2\ell}{2}, \frac{3\ell}{2}, \ldots, \left\lceil|X|\ell\sqrt{d}\right\rceil\right\}$.

$$\begin{aligned}
L(r,S) &= \max_{\substack{\text{distinct}\\ x_1,\ldots,x_t \in S}} \frac{1}{t}\sum_{i=1}^{t} \bar{\mathcal{B}}_r(x_i,S) \\
&\le \max_{\substack{\text{distinct}\\ x_1,\ldots,x_{t-1} \in S\setminus\{y\}}} \frac{1}{t}\left(t + \sum_{i=1}^{t-1} \bar{\mathcal{B}}_r(x_i,S)\right) \\
&= \max_{\substack{\text{distinct}\\ x_1,\ldots,x_{t-1} \in S'\setminus\{y'\}}} \frac{1}{t}\left(t + \sum_{i=1}^{t-1} \bar{\mathcal{B}}_r(x_i,S)\right) \\
&\le \max_{\substack{\text{distinct}\\ x_1,\ldots,x_{t-1} \in S'\setminus\{y'\}}} \frac{1}{t}\left(t + \sum_{i=1}^{t-1} [\bar{\mathcal{B}}_r(x_i,S') + 1]\right) \\
&\le \max_{\substack{\text{distinct}\\ x_1,\ldots,x_{t-1} \in S'}} \frac{1}{t}\left(t + \sum_{i=1}^{t-1} [\bar{\mathcal{B}}_r(x_i,S') + 1]\right) \\
&\le L(r,S') + 2.
\end{aligned}$$

Similarly, $L(S,r) \ge L(S',r) - 2$, and $L(r,\cdot)$ is of sensitivity 2. Hence, the use of the laplace mechanism on step 2 preserves $(\frac{\epsilon}{2},0)$-differential privacy. Moreover, $\frac{1}{2}L(r,\cdot)$ is of sensitivity 1, and, therefore, $Q(r,\cdot)$ is of sensitivity 1 (defined as the minimum of two sensitivity 1 expressions). The application of algorithm `RecConcave` preserves $(\frac{\epsilon}{2},\delta)$-differential privacy. Overall, algorithm `GoodRadius` is (ϵ,δ)-differentially private by Composition Theorem 2.1. □

We now turn to proving the correctness of algorithm `GoodRadius`.

LEMMA 4.5. *Let* `GoodRadius` *be executed on a database S containing n points in X^d and on parameters $t, \beta, \epsilon, \delta$, and let Γ be as defined in algorithm* `GoodRadius`. *With probability at least $(1-\beta)$, the output z satisfies: (1) There exists a ball in X^d of radius z containing at least $(t - 4\Gamma - \frac{4}{\epsilon}\ln(1/\beta))$ input points from S. (2) Let r_{opt} denote the radius of the smallest ball in X^d containing at least t input points from S. Then $z \le 4r_{opt}$.*

PROOF. Note that if $L(0,S) \ge t - 2\Gamma$, then `GoodRadius` fails to output $z = 0$ in step 2 with probability at most $\beta/2$. We continue the proof assuming that $L(0,S) < t - 2\Gamma$.

We now argue that algorithm `RecConcave` returns (w.h.p.) a value z s.t. $Q(z,S)$ is significant. We need to show that $Q(\cdot,S)$ is quasi-concave, and that there exists an r s.t. $Q(r,S) \ge \Gamma$. To see that $Q(\cdot,S)$ is quasi-concave, note that $L(\cdot,S)$ is non-decreasing (as a function of r), and that, hence, for every $r_1 < r_2 < r_3$

$$\begin{aligned}
Q(r_2,S) &= \min\left\{\frac{t - L(r_2/2,S)}{2}, \frac{L(r_2,S) - t + 4\Gamma}{2}\right\} \\
&\ge \min\left\{\frac{t - L(r_3/2,S)}{2}, \frac{L(r_1,S) - t + 4\Gamma}{2}\right\} \\
&\ge \min\left\{Q(r_3,S), Q(r_1,S)\right\}.
\end{aligned}$$

To see that there exists an r s.t. $Q(r,S) \ge \Gamma$, recall that $L(0,S) = L\left(\frac{1}{2|X|}, S\right) < t - 2\Gamma$, and note that $L(\sqrt{d},S) = n \ge t$. Now consider the smallest

$$r \in \left\{0, \frac{1}{2|X|}, \frac{2}{2|X|}, \frac{3}{2|X|}, \ldots, \left\lceil\sqrt{d}\right\rceil\right\}$$

s.t. $L(r,S) \ge t - 2\Gamma$. For that r it holds that $Q(r,S) = \frac{1}{2}\min\{t - L(r/2,S),\ L(r,S) - t + 4\Gamma\} \ge \frac{1}{2}\min\{2\Gamma,\ 2\Gamma\} = \Gamma$.

By the properties of algorithm `RecConcave`, with probability at least $(1-\beta/2)$ the output z is s.t. $Q(z,S) \ge \frac{\Gamma}{2}$. Hence, by the definition of Q we have that

$$\text{(a) } L(z,S) \ge t - 4\Gamma \quad \text{and} \quad \text{(b) } L(z/2,S) \le t - \frac{\Gamma}{2}.$$

Recall that $L(z, S)$ averages $\bar{B}_z(x, S)$ over t points $x \in S$. Hence, by (a), there exists a ball of radius z in X^d that contains at least $t - 4\Gamma$ input points from S.

Let $P \subseteq S$ be a set of t input points, and assume towards contradiction that there is a ball of radius $z/4$ in X^d that contains all of the points in P. Now note that a ball of radius $z/2$ around every point in P contains all of the points in P. Hence, $L(z/2, S) \geq t$. This contradicts (b). We conclude that Algorithm GoodRadius returns a good radius with probability at least $1 - \beta$. □

4.2 Additional preliminaries

Before formally presenting algorithm GoodCenter, we introduce several additional tools.

4.2.1 Composition theorems

Recall that the privacy guaranties in composition theorem 2.1 deteriorates linearly with the number of interactions. By bounding the *expected* privacy loss in each interaction (as opposed to worst-case), Dwork et al. [10] showed the following stronger composition theorem, where privacy deteriorates (roughly) as $\sqrt{k}\epsilon + k\epsilon^2$ (rather than $k\epsilon$).

THEOREM 4.6 ([10]). *Let $\epsilon, \delta, \delta' > 0$. A mechanism that permits k adaptive interactions with (ϵ, δ)-differentially private mechanisms (and does not access the database otherwise) is $(\epsilon', k\delta + \delta')$-differentially private, for $\epsilon' = 2k\epsilon^2 + \epsilon\sqrt{2k\ln(1/\delta')}$.*

4.2.2 The sparse vector technique [9]

Consider a large number of low sensitivity functions $f_1, f_2, \ldots, f_k$, which are given (one by one) to a data curator (holding a database S). Given a dataset S, Algorithm AboveThreshold by Dwork et al. [9] identifies the queries f_i whose value $f_i(S)$ is greater than some threshold t:

THEOREM 4.7 (ALGORITHM ABOVETHRESHOLD). *There exists an $(\epsilon, 0)$-differentially private algorithm $\mathcal{A}$ such that for k rounds, after receiving a sensitivity-1 query $f_i : U^* \to \mathbb{R}$, algorithm $\mathcal{A}$ either outputs $\top$ and halts, or outputs $\perp$ and waits for the next round. If $\mathcal{A}$ was executed with a database $S \in U^*$ and a threshold parameter t, then the following holds with probability $(1-\beta)$: (i) If a query f_i was answered by $\top$ then $f_i(S) \geq t - \frac{8}{\epsilon}\log(2k/\beta)$; (ii) If a query f_i was answered by $\perp$ then $f_i(S) \leq t + \frac{8}{\epsilon}\log(2k/\beta)$.*

4.2.3 Geometric tools

We will use the Johnson Lindenstrauss transform to embed a set of points $S \in \mathbb{R}^d$ in $\mathbb{R}^k, k \ll d$ while preserving point distances.

LEMMA 4.8 (JL TRANSFORM [11]). *Let $S \subseteq \mathbb{R}^d$ be a set of n points, and let $\eta \in (0, 1/2)$. Let A be a $k \times d$ matrix whose entries are iid samples from $\mathcal{N}(0, 1)$, and define $f : \mathbb{R}^d \to \mathbb{R}^k$ as $f(x) = \frac{1}{\sqrt{k}}Ax$. Then,*

$$\Pr_A\left[\begin{array}{c} \forall x, y \in S \text{ it holds that} \\ (1-\eta)\|x-y\|_2^2 \\ \leq \|f(x) - f(y)\|_2^2 \\ \leq (1+\eta)\|x-y\|_2^2 \end{array}\right] \geq 1 - 2n^2\exp\left(-\frac{\eta^2 k}{8}\right).$$

4.3 Algorithm GoodCenter

Given the outcome of Algorithm GoodRadius, we now show that algorithm GoodCenter privately locates a small ball containing $\gtrsim t$ points. We start with its privacy analysis.

LEMMA 4.9. *Algorithm GoodCenter preserves (ϵ, δ)- differential privacy.*

PROOF. Algorithm GoodCenter interacts with its input database on steps 2, 5, 7, 8c, 10. Steps 2, 5 initialize and use Algorithm AboveThreshold, which is $(\frac{\epsilon}{4}, 0)$-differentially private. Step 7 invokes the algorithm from Theorem 2.5 (to choose a "heavy" box B), which is $(\frac{\epsilon}{4}, \frac{\delta}{4})$-private. Step 8c makes d applications of the algorithm from Theorem 2.5. By theorem 4.6 (composition), this preserves $(\frac{\epsilon}{4}, \frac{\delta}{4})$-differential privacy. Step 10 invokes the Gaussian mechanism, which is $(\frac{\epsilon}{4}, \frac{\delta}{4})$-private. Overall, GoodCenter is (ϵ, δ)-differentially private by composition. □

We now proceed with the utility analysis of algorithm GoodCenter.

LEMMA 4.10. *Let GoodCenter be executed on a database S containing n points in $\mathbb{R}^d$ with $r, t, \beta, \epsilon, \delta$ s.t.*

$$t \geq O\left(\frac{\sqrt{d}}{\epsilon}\log\left(\frac{nd}{\beta\delta}\right)\sqrt{\log(\frac{1}{\delta})}\right).$$

If there exists a ball of radius r in $\mathbb{R}^d$ containing at least t points from S, then with probability at least $1 - \beta$, the output z in Step 10 is s.t. at least $t - O\left(\frac{1}{\epsilon}\log(\frac{n}{\beta})\right)$ of the input points are contained in a ball of radius $O\left(r\sqrt{\log(\frac{n}{\beta})}\right)$ around z.

REMARK 4.11. *The dependency in $1/\beta$ can easily be removed from the radius of the resulting ball by applying GoodCenter with a constant β and amplifying the success probability using repetitions.*

PROOF. First note that by Theorem 4.8 (the JL transform), with probability at least $1 - \beta$, for every $x, y \in S$ it holds that $\|x-y\|$ and $\|f(x)-f(y)\|$ are similar up to a multiplicative factor of $(1 \pm \frac{1}{2})$. We continue the proof assuming that this is the case. Hence, there exists a ball of radius $3r$ in $\mathbb{R}^k$ containing at least t points from $\{f(x) : x \in S\}$. Denote this set of (at least t) projected points as W.

Clearly, the projection of the set W onto any axis of $\mathbb{R}^k$ lies in an interval of length $3r$. Recall that on Step 3a we partition every axis into randomly shifted intervals $\{A_j^i\}$ of length $300r$. Hence, for every axis i with probability 0.99 it holds that the projection of W onto the ith axis is contained within one of the $\{A_j^i\}$'s. The probability that this holds simultaneously for all of the k axes is $0.99^k \geq \frac{\beta}{2n}$. Note that in such a case there exists a rectangle in $\{B_{\vec{j}}\}$ containing all of the points in W, and hence, the corresponding query q (defined on step 5) satisfies $q(S) \geq t$. So, every (randomly constructed) query q satisfies $q(S) \geq t$ with probability $\beta/(2n)$.

Although the iteration of steps 3–6 might be repeated less than $2n\log(1/\beta)/\beta$ times, imagine that all of the (potential) $2n\log(1/\beta)/\beta$ queries were prepared ahead of time (and some may have never issued to AboveThreshold). With probability at least $(1-\beta)$ at least one such query q satisfies $q(S) \geq t$. We continue with the proof assuming that this is

Algorithm 2 `GoodCenter`

Input: Database $S \in \mathbb{R}^d$ containing n points, radius r, desired number of points t, failure probability β, and privacy parameters ϵ, δ.

1. Let $k = 46\log(2n/\beta)$ and let $f : \mathbb{R}^d \to \mathbb{R}^k$ be a mapping as in Theorem 4.8 (the JL transform).
2. Instantiate algorithm `AboveThreshold` (Theorem 4.7) with database S, privacy parameter $\epsilon/4$, and threshold $t - \frac{100}{\epsilon}\log(2n/\beta)$.
3. For every axis $1 \le i \le k$ of $\mathbb{R}^k$:
   (a) Choose a random $a_i \in [0, 300r]$. For $j \in \mathbb{Z}$, let A^i_j be the interval $[a_i + j \cdot 300r,\ a_i + (j+1) \cdot 300r)$.
   % $\{A^i_j\}_{j\in\mathbb{Z}}$ is a partition of the ith axis into (randomly shifted) intervals of length $300r$.
4. For every $\vec{j} = (j_1, \ldots, j_k) \in \mathbb{Z}^k$ let $B_{\vec{j}} \subseteq \mathbb{R}^k$ be the box whose projection on every axis i is $A^i_{j_i}$.
5. Issue query $q(S) = \max_{\vec{j}} |f(S) \cap B_{\vec{j}}|$ to `AboveThreshold`. Denote the received answer as a.
   % That is, $q(S)$ is the maximal number of (projected) input points that are contained within one box.
6. If this step was reached more than $2n\log(1/\beta)/\beta$ times, then halt and fail. Otherwise, if $a = \perp$ then goto Step 3.
   % That is, for at most $2n\log(1/\beta)/\beta$ rounds, we define a partition of $\mathbb{R}^k$ into disjoint rectangles $\{B_{\vec{j}}\}$, and query algorithm `AboveThreshold` to identify an iteration in which there is a rectangle in $\{B_{\vec{j}}\}$ containing $\gtrsim t$ points.
7. Use Theorem 2.5 with privacy parameters $(\frac{\epsilon}{4}, \frac{\delta}{4})$ to chose a box $B \in \{B_{\vec{j}}\}$ approximately maximizing $|f(S) \cap B|$. Denote $D = \{x \in S : f(x) \in B\}$.
   % That is, D is the set of input points from S that are mapped into B by the mapping f.
8. For every axis $1 \le i \le d$ of $\mathbb{R}^d$:
   (a) Partition axis i into intervals $\mathcal{I}_i = \{[j \cdot 450r\sqrt{k}\,,\ (j+1) \cdot 450r\sqrt{k})\ :\ j \in \mathbb{Z}\}$.
   (b) Define the quality $q(I)$ of every $I \in \mathcal{I}_i$ as the number of points $x \in D$ s.t. their i^{th} coordinate is in I.
   (c) Use Theorem2.5 with privacy parameters $\left(\frac{\epsilon}{10\sqrt{d\ln(8/\delta)}}, \frac{\delta}{8d}\right)$ to choose an interval $I_i \in \mathcal{I}_i$ with large $q(\cdot)$, and let $\hat{I}_i$ denote that chosen interval after extending it by $450r\sqrt{k}$ on each side (that is $\hat{I}_i$ is of length $1350r\sqrt{k}$).
9. Let c be the center of the box in $\mathbb{R}^d$ whose projection on every axis i is $\hat{I}_i$, and let C be the ball of radius $1350r\sqrt{kd}$ around c. Define $D' = D \cap C$.
   % Observe that we defined $D' = D \cap C$, even though we expect that $D \subseteq C$. While there is a small (but non negligible) probability β that the diameter of D is larger than $900r\sqrt{kd}$, we can now guarantee that the set D' is of bounded diameter. This will be useful in the privacy analysis.
10. Use the Gaussian mechanism with privacy parameters $(\frac{\epsilon}{4}, \frac{\delta}{4})$ to compute and return the noisy average of the points in D' (see Appendix A for details).

---

the case. Thus, by the properties of algorithm **AboveThreshold**, with probability at least $(1-\beta)$, the loop on Step 6 ended with **AboveThreshold** returning $\top$. Moreover, in that iteration we have that $q(S) \ge t - \frac{200}{\epsilon}\log(2n/\beta)$. Thus, by the definition of q, after Step 6 there exists a rectangle $\{B_{\vec{j}}\}$ containing at least $t - \frac{200}{\epsilon}\log(2n/\beta)$ projected input elements.

By Theorem 2.5, with probability at least $(1-\beta)$, the box B chosen on step 7 contains at least $t - \frac{216}{\epsilon}\log(\frac{2n}{\beta})$ projected input elements. We continue the proof assuming that this is the case, and denote the set of input points from S that are mapped into B as D.

Note that B is a box of diameter $300r\sqrt{k}$. Hence, by our assumption on the projection f, for any $x, y \in D$ it holds that $\|x - y\| \le 450r\sqrt{k}$. Therefore, when partitioning every axis i of $\mathbb{R}^d$ into intervals $\mathcal{I}_i$ of length $450r\sqrt{k}$ (on step 8a), at least one interval $I \in \mathcal{I}_i$ contains at least half of the points in D. Assuming that $|D| \ge \frac{280\sqrt{d}}{\epsilon}\log(\frac{6nd}{\beta\delta})\sqrt{\log(\frac{8}{\delta})}$, for every axis i Theorem 2.5 ensures that with probability at least $(1-\beta/d)$ the chosen interval $I_i \in \mathcal{I}_i$ (on step 8c) contains at least one input elements from D. Recall that the projection of D onto any axis lies in an interval of length $450r\sqrt{k}$. Hence, letting $\hat{I}_i$ be I_i after extending it by $450r\sqrt{k}$ on each side, we ensure that $\hat{I}_i$ contains *all* of the points in D. So, the box in $\mathbb{R}^d$ whose projection onto every axis i is $\hat{I}_i$ contains all of the points in D. Recall that (on step 9) we defined C to be the bounding sphere of that box, and hence, C contains all of D, and $D' = D \cap C = D$.

Let y denote the average of the point in $D' = D$, and observe that a ball of radius $450r\sqrt{k}$ around y contains all of the points in D. The output on step 10 is computed using the Gaussian mechanism as the noisy average of the points in $D' = D$, with noise magnitude proportional to the diameter of C (which is $1350r\sqrt{kd}$). By the properties of the Gaussian mechanism (see appendix A), with probability at least $(1-\beta)$ the output z satisfies $z = y + \eta$, where η is a random noise vector whose every coordinate is distributed as $\mathcal{N}(0, \sigma^2)$ for $\sigma \le \frac{43200r}{\epsilon|D'|}\sqrt{2kd\ln(\frac{8}{\delta})}$. Observe that $\|\eta\|_2^2$ is the sum of the squares of d independent normal random variables (this is the chi-squared distribution). Using tail bounds for the chi-squared distribution (see, e.g., [13], Lemma 1 page 1325), assuming that $|D| \ge \frac{86400}{\epsilon}\sqrt{d\ln(\frac{8}{\delta})\ln(\frac{1}{\beta})}$, with probability at least $(1-\beta)$ we have that $\|\eta\|_2 \leq r\sqrt{k}$, and hence $\|z - y\|_2 \leq r\sqrt{k}$. Using the triangle inequality, we get that a ball of radius $451r\sqrt{k}$ around the output z contains all of the points in D, where $|D| \geq t - \frac{216}{\epsilon}\log(\frac{2n}{\beta})$.

Overall, assuming that $t \geq \frac{866616\sqrt{d}}{\epsilon}\log(\frac{6nd}{\beta\delta})\sqrt{\log(\frac{8}{\delta})}$, with probability at least $(1-7\beta)$, the output on z is s.t. at least $t - \frac{216}{\epsilon}\log(\frac{2n}{\beta})$ of the input points are contained inside a ball of radius $451r\sqrt{k}$ around z. □

Theorem 3.2 now follows by combining lemmas 4.5, 4.4, 4.9, and 4.10.

5. SAMPLE AND AGGREGATE

Consider $f : U^* \to X^d$ mapping databases to X^d. Fix a database $S \in U^*$, and assume that evaluating f on a random sub-sample S' (containing iid samples from S) results in a good approximation to $f(S)$. Our goal is to design a private analogue to f.

DEFINITION 5.1. *Fix a function $f : U^* \to X^d$ and a database $S \in U^*$. A point $c \in X^d$ is an (m, r, α)-stable point of f on S if for a database S' containing m iid samples from S we have $\Pr[\|f(S') - c\|_2 \leq r] \geq \alpha$. If such a point c exists, we say that f is (m, r, α)-stable on S. We will call r the radius of the stable point c.*

In the sample and aggregate framework [16], the goal is to privately identify an (m, r, α)-stable point of a function f on the given input database S. Intuitively, if r is small and α is large, then such a point would be a good (private) substitute for (the non-private value) $f(S)$. Note that a stable point with small r and with large α might not exist.

THEOREM 5.2 ([16] RESTATED, INFORMAL). *Fix a desired stability parameters m, and let $n \geq 4d^2m$. There exists an efficient differentially private algorithm that given a database $S \in U^n$ and a function $f : U^* \to X^d$, identifies an $\left(m, O(\sqrt{d} \cdot r_{opt}) + \sqrt{d} \cdot e^{-\Omega(\sqrt{\frac{n}{m}}\frac{1}{d})}, 0.51\right)$-stable point of f on S, where r_{opt} is the smallest r s.t. f is $(m, r, 0.51)$-stable on S.*

Note the following caveats in Theorem 5.2: (1) The function f might only be $(m, r, 0.51)$-stable on S for very large values of r, in which case the similarity to (the non-private) $f(S)$ is lost. (2) The error in the radius of the stable point grows with $\sqrt{d}$, which might be unacceptable in high dimensions.[3] Using Theorem 3.2 it is possible to avoid those two caveats.

THEOREM 5.3. *Fix privacy parameters ϵ, δ, failure parameter β, and desired stability parameters m, α. Let*

$$\frac{n}{m} \geq O\left(\frac{\sqrt{d}\cdot\log\left(\frac{1}{\beta}\right)}{\alpha\cdot\min\{\alpha,\epsilon\}}\log\left(\frac{nd}{\alpha\beta\epsilon\delta}\right)\sqrt{\log\left(\frac{1}{\alpha\beta\epsilon\delta}\right)}\cdot 9^{\log^*(2|X|\sqrt{d})}\right).$$

There exists an efficient (ϵ, δ)-differentially private algorithm that given a database $S \in U^n$ and a function $f : U^* \to X^d$, with probability at least $(1-\beta)$, identifies an $(m, O(r_{opt} \cdot \sqrt{\log n}), \frac{\alpha}{8})$-stable point of f on S, where r_{opt} is the smallest r s.t. f is (m, r, α)-stable on S.

[3] Let c be an $(m, r, 0.51)$-stable point of f on S. In [16], the returned point c' is s.t. that the error vector $(c - c')$ has magnitude $O(r_{opt}) + e^{-\Omega(\sqrt{\frac{n}{m}}\frac{1}{d})}$ in each coordinate.

Theorem 5.3 is proved using algorithm **SA**. Similarly to [16], the idea is to apply f onto k random subsamples of the input database S (obtaining outputs $Y = \{y_1, y_2, \ldots, y_k\}$ in X^d), and then to privately identify a point $z \in X^d$ which is close to points in Y. We will use the following lemma to argue that the random subsampling step maintains privacy:

LEMMA 5.4 ([12, 4]). *Fix $\epsilon \leq 1$ and let $\mathcal{A}$ be an (ϵ, δ)-differentially private algorithm operating on databases of size m. For $n \geq 2m$, construct an algorithm $\tilde{\mathcal{A}}$ that on input a database D of size n subsamples (with replacement) m rows from D and runs $\mathcal{A}$ on the result. Then $\tilde{\mathcal{A}}$ is $(\tilde{\epsilon}, \tilde{\delta})$-differentially private for $\tilde{\epsilon} = 6\epsilon m/n$ and $\tilde{\delta} = \exp(6\epsilon m/n)\frac{4m}{n} \cdot \delta$.*

LEMMA 5.5. *Algorithm **SA** is (ϵ, δ)-differentially private.*

PROOF. Let $\mathcal{A}$ denote an algorithm identical to **SA**, except without the iid sampling on step 1 (the input to $\mathcal{A}$ is the database D), and observe that $\mathcal{A}$ preserve (ϵ, δ)-differential privacy. To see this, let D, D' be two neighboring databases, and consider the execution of $\mathcal{A}$ on D and D'. Next, note that there is at most one index i s.t. D_i differs from D'_i. Hence, Y and Y' are neighboring databases, and privacy is preserved by the properties of algorithm $\mathcal{M}$.

Algorithm **SA** (including the iid sampling) is (ϵ, δ)- differentially private by Lemma 5.4 (iid sampling). □

In the utility analysis of algorithm **SA** we first show that a ball around the returned point $z \in X^d$ contains $\gtrsim \alpha$ fraction of points in $Y = \{y_1 = f(D_1), y_2 = f(D_2), \ldots, y_k = f(D_k)\}$. Afterwards, we will argue that this ball also contains $\gtrsim \alpha$ mass of the underlying distribution (i.e., the distribution defined by applying f on a random subsample of S). The straightforward approach for such an argument would be to use VC bounds stating that for any ball (in particular, the ball around z) it holds that the fraction of points from Y in it is close to the weight of the ball w.r.t. the underlying distribution. However, for this argument to go through we would need $|Y|$ to be as big as the VC dimension of the class of d-dimensional balls, which is $d+1$. This seems wasteful since our private algorithm for locating the ball only requires the generation of a small cluster of size $\approx \sqrt{d}$. Instead, will make use of the inherent generalization properties of differential privacy, first proven by Dwork et al. [5]. Specifically, we will use the following theorem of Bassily et al. [2] stating that any predicate computed with differential privacy automatically provides generalization:

THEOREM 5.6 ([2]). *Let $\epsilon \in (0, 1/3)$, $\delta \in (0, \epsilon/4)$, and $n \geq \frac{1}{\epsilon^2}\log(\frac{4\epsilon}{\delta})$. Let $\mathcal{A} : U^n \to 2^U$ be an (ϵ, δ)-differentially private algorithm that operates on a database of size n and outputs a predicate $h : U \to \{0, 1\}$. Let $\mathcal{D}$ be a distribution over U, let S be a database containing n i.i.d. elements from $\mathcal{D}$, and let $h \leftarrow \mathcal{A}(S)$. Then,*

$$\Pr_{S,\mathcal{A}}\left[|h(S) - h(\mathcal{D})| > 18\epsilon\right] \leq \frac{\delta}{\epsilon},$$

where $h(S)$ is the empirical average of h on S, and $h(\mathcal{D})$ is the expectation of h over $\mathcal{D}$.

LEMMA 5.7. *Let **SA** be executed on a function f and on a database S of size n such that f is (m, r, α)-stable on S. Assume **SA** has access to an $(\epsilon \leq \frac{\alpha}{72}, \delta \leq \frac{\beta\epsilon}{3})$-private algorithm $\mathcal{M}$ for solving the 1-cluster problem (X^d, k, t) for*

Algorithm 3 SA

Input: Database S containing n elements from U, function $f : U^* \to X^d$, privacy parameters ϵ, δ, failure parameter β, and desired stability parameters m, α. We denote $k \triangleq \frac{n}{9m}$.

Algorithm used: An $(\epsilon \leq \frac{\alpha}{72}, \delta \leq \frac{\beta\epsilon}{3})$-private algorithm $\mathcal{M}$ for solving the 1-cluster problem (X^d, k, t) for every $t \geq t_{\min}$, with parameters $(\Delta \leq t/2, w)$ and error probability $\frac{\beta}{3}$.

1. Let D be the outcome of $n/9$ iid samples from S. Partition D into k databases $D_1, D_2, ..., D_k$ of size m each.
2. Let $Y = \{y_1 = f(D_1), y_2 = f(D_2), \ldots, y_k = f(D_k)\}$.
3. Apply $\mathcal{M}$ on the database Y with parameter $t = \frac{\alpha k}{2}$ to get a point z. Output z.

every $t \geq t_{\min}$ with parameters $(\Delta \leq t/2, w)$ and error probability $\frac{\beta}{3}$. With probability at least $(1-\beta)$, the output z is an $(m, wr, \frac{\alpha}{8})$-stable point of f on S, provided that

$$n \geq m \cdot O\left(\frac{t_{\min}}{\alpha} + \frac{1}{\alpha^2}\log\left(\frac{12}{\beta}\right)\right).$$

PROOF. Let algorithm SA be executed on a function f and on a database S such that f is (m, r, α)-stable on S. Let $c \in X^d$ be a stable point of f on S, and let $\mathcal{B}_r(c, Y)$ denote the number of points in Y within distance r from c.

By the definition of the stable point c, for every y_i (defined on step 2) we have that $\Pr[\|y_i - c\|_2 \leq r] \geq \alpha$. Hence, by the Chernoff bound, $\Pr[\mathcal{B}_r(c, Y) < \frac{\alpha k}{2}] \leq \exp(-\frac{\alpha k}{8}) \leq \beta/3$.

Assume that $\mathcal{B}_r(c, Y) \geq \frac{\alpha k}{2}$, i.e., there are at least $\frac{\alpha k}{2} = t$ points in Y within distance r from c. Hence, by the properties of algorithm $\mathcal{M}$, with probability at least $(1-\beta/3)$ the output z is s.t. $\mathcal{B}_{wr}(z, Y) \geq \frac{t}{2} = \frac{\alpha k}{4}$.

We now argue that the ball of radius wr around z not only contains a lot of points from Y, but is also "heavy" w.r.t. the underlying distribution (i.e., the distribution defined by applying f on a random subsample of S). To that end, consider the predicate $h : X^d \to \{0,1\}$ defined as $h(x) = 1$ iff $\|x - z\|_2 \leq wr$. That is, h evaluates to 1 exactly on points inside the ball of radius wr around z. So $h(Y) \geq \frac{\alpha}{4}$. By Theorem 5.6, assuming that $k \geq \frac{5184}{\alpha^2}\log(\frac{12}{\beta})$, with probability at least $1 - \delta/\epsilon \geq 1 - \beta/3$ we have that for a random subsample S' containing m i.i.d. samples from S, it holds that $\Pr[h(f(S')) = 1] = \Pr[\|f(S') - z\|_2 \leq wr] \geq \frac{\alpha}{4} - 18\epsilon \geq \frac{\alpha}{8}$.

All in all, provided that $n = 9mk \geq \frac{18m}{\alpha}t_{\min} + \frac{46646m}{\alpha^2}\log(\frac{12}{\beta})$, with probability at least $(1-\beta)$, the output z is an $(m, wr, \frac{\alpha}{8})$-stable point of f on S. ☐

Theorem 5.3 now follows from combining lemmas 5.5, and 5.7 with Theorem 3.2.

6. REFERENCES

[1] P. K. Agarwal, S. Har-Peled, and K. R. Varadarajan. Geometric approximation via coresets. In *COMBINATORIAL AND COMPUTATIONAL GEOMETRY, MSRI*, pages 1–30. University Press, 2005.

[2] R. Bassily, K. Nissim, A. D. Smith, T. Steinke, U. Stemmer, and J. Ullman. Algorithmic stability for adaptive data analysis. *STOC (to appear)*, 2016.

[3] A. Beimel, K. Nissim, and U. Stemmer. Private learning and sanitization: Pure vs. approximate differential privacy. In *APPROX-RANDOM*, volume 8096 of *Lecture Notes in Computer Science*, pages 363–378. Springer, 2013.

[4] M. Bun, K. Nissim, U. Stemmer, and S. P. Vadhan. Differentially private release and learning of threshold functions. In *FOCS*, pages 634–649, 2015.

[5] C. Dwork, V. Feldman, M. Hardt, T. Pitassi, O. Reingold, and A. L. Roth. Preserving statistical validity in adaptive data analysis. In *STOC*, pages 117–126. ACM, 2015.

[6] C. Dwork, K. Kenthapadi, F. McSherry, I. Mironov, and M. Naor. Our data, ourselves: Privacy via distributed noise generation. In S. Vaudenay, editor, *EUROCRYPT*, volume 4004 of *Lecture Notes in Computer Science*, pages 486–503. Springer, 2006.

[7] C. Dwork and J. Lei. Differential privacy and robust statistics. In M. Mitzenmacher, editor, *STOC*, pages 371–380. ACM, 2009.

[8] C. Dwork, F. McSherry, K. Nissim, and A. Smith. Calibrating noise to sensitivity in private data analysis. In *TCC*, volume 3876 of *Lecture Notes in Computer Science*, pages 265–284. Springer, 2006.

[9] C. Dwork, M. Naor, O. Reingold, G. N. Rothblum, and S. P. Vadhan. On the complexity of differentially private data release: efficient algorithms and hardness results. In M. Mitzenmacher, editor, *STOC*, pages 381–390. ACM, 2009.

[10] C. Dwork, G. N. Rothblum, and S. P. Vadhan. Boosting and differential privacy. In *FOCS*, pages 51–60. IEEE Computer Society, 2010.

[11] W. B. Johnson and J. Lindenstrauss. Extensions of Lipschitz maps into a Hilbert space. 1984.

[12] S. P. Kasiviswanathan, H. K. Lee, K. Nissim, S. Raskhodnikova, and A. Smith. What can we learn privately? *SIAM J. Comput.*, 40(3):793–826, 2011.

[13] B. Laurent and P. Massart. Adaptive estimation of a quadratic functional by model selection. *Ann. Statist.*, 28(5):1302–1338, 10 2000.

[14] F. McSherry and K. Talwar. Mechanism design via differential privacy. In *FOCS*, pages 94–103. IEEE Computer Society, 2007.

[15] P. Mohan, A. Thakurta, E. Shi, D. Song, and D. E. Culler. GUPT: privacy preserving data analysis made easy. In *Proceedings of the ACM SIGMOD International Conference on Management of Data, SIGMOD 2012, Scottsdale, AZ, USA, May 20-24, 2012*, pages 349–360, 2012.

[16] K. Nissim, S. Raskhodnikova, and A. Smith. Smooth sensitivity and sampling in private data analysis. In *STOC*, pages 75–84. ACM, 2007.
[17] V. Shenmaier. The problem of a minimal ball enclosing k points. *Journal of Applied and Industrial Mathematics*, 7(3):444–448, 2013.
[18] A. Smith. Privacy-preserving statistical estimation with optimal convergence rates. In *Proceedings of the 43rd ACM Symposium on Theory of Computing, STOC 2011, San Jose, CA, USA, 6-8 June 2011*, pages 813–822, 2011.
[19] A. Thakurta and A. Smith. Differentially private feature selection via stability arguments, and the robustness of the lasso. In S. Shalev-Shwartz and I. Steinwart, editors, *COLT*, volume 30 of *JMLR Proceedings*, pages 819–850. JMLR.org, 2013.
[20] S. Vadhan. *The Complexity of Differential Privacy.* 2016.

APPENDIX

A. NOISY AVERAGE OF VECTORS IN $\mathbb{R}^d$

THEOREM 2.4 (THE GAUSSIAN MECHANISM [6]). *Let $\epsilon, \delta \in (0,1)$, and let $f : X^* \to \mathbb{R}^d$ be a function of L_2-sensitivity k. Denote $\sigma \geq \frac{k}{\epsilon}\sqrt{2\ln(1.25/\delta)}$. The mechanism $\mathcal{A}$ that on input $D \in X^*$ adds independently generated noise with distribution $\mathcal{N}(0,\sigma^2)$ to each of the d output terms of $f(D)$ preserves (ϵ,δ)-differential privacy.*

We will use the Gaussian mechanism to obtain (noisy) averages of vectors in $\mathbb{R}^d$: Let $g : \mathbb{R}^d \to \{0,1\}$ be a predicate over vectors in $\mathbb{R}^d$, and denote

$$\Delta_g = \max_{\substack{v \in \mathbb{R}^d \text{ s.t.} \\ g(v)=1}} \|v\|_2.$$

Given a multiset of vectors V, we are interested in approximating $\frac{\sum_{v\in V:g(v)=1} v}{|\{v\in V:g(v)=1\}|}$. Since both the numerator and the denominator have bounded L_2-sensitivity, we could estimate each of them separately using the Gaussian mechanism. Alternatively, we could directly analyze the L_2-sensitivity of $g(V) \triangleq \frac{\sum_{v\in V:g(v)=1} v}{|\{v\in V:g(v)=1\}|}$ and apply the Gaussian mechanism directly to $g(V)$. This has the advantage of having only an additive Gaussian error, rather than a noisy numerator/denominator. It is easier to analyze.

We now bound the L_2 sensitivity of $g(V)$. Let V be a multiset of vectors in $\mathbb{R}^d$ and let $V' = V \cup \{u\}$ for some vector u. If $g(u) = 0$ then $g(V) = g(V')$ and $\|g(V) - g(V')\|_2 = 0$. We assume therefore that $g(u) = 1$.

Let $m = |\{v \in V : g(v) = 1\}|$. We need to analyze the L_2 norm of the error vector $\eta = \frac{1}{m}\left(\sum_{v\in V:g(v)=1} v\right) - \frac{1}{m+1}\left(u + \sum_{v\in V:g(v)=1} v\right)$. To that end, observe that the ith coordinate of η is

$$\begin{aligned}\eta_i &= \frac{1}{m}\left(\sum_{v\in V:g(v)=1} v_i\right) - \frac{1}{m+1}\left(u_i + \sum_{v\in V:g(v)=1} v_i\right)\\ &= \frac{\left(\sum_{v\in V:g(v)=1} v_i\right) - m u_i}{m(m+1)}\\ &= \frac{g(V)_i - u_i}{m+1}.\end{aligned}$$

Hence,

$$\begin{aligned}\|\eta\|_2 &= \sqrt{(\eta_1)^2 + \cdots (\eta_d)^2}\\ &= \frac{1}{m+1}\sqrt{\langle u,u\rangle - 2\langle u, g(V)\rangle + \langle g(V), g(V)\rangle}\\ &\leq \frac{2\Delta_g}{m+1},\end{aligned}$$

where the last inequality is since

$$\begin{aligned}&|\langle u, g(V)\rangle|\\ &= |u_1 \cdot g(V)_1 + \cdots + u_d \cdot g(V)_d|\\ &= \left|\frac{u_1}{m}\left(\sum_{v\in V:g(v)=1} v_1\right) + \cdots + \frac{u_d}{m}\left(\sum_{v\in V:g(v)=1} v_d\right)\right|\\ &\leq \frac{1}{m}\sum_{v\in V:g(v)=1} |\langle u, v\rangle|\\ &\leq \frac{1}{m}\sum_{v\in V:g(v)=1} \|u\|_2 \cdot \|v\|_2 \leq (\Delta_g)^2,\end{aligned}$$

and similarly

$$\begin{aligned}|\langle g(V), g(V)\rangle| &= \left|\left\langle \frac{1}{m}\sum_{v\in V:g(v)=1} v, g(V)\right\rangle\right|\\ &= \frac{1}{m}\left|\sum_{v\in V:g(v)=1} \langle v, g(V)\rangle\right| \leq (\Delta_g)^2.\end{aligned}$$

So, for any V and $V' = V \cup \{u\}$ we have that $\|g(V) - g(V')\|_2 \leq \frac{2\Delta_g}{m+1}$, where $m = |\{v \in V : g(v) = 1\}|$. Therefore, for any two neighboring sets $V_1 = V \cup \{u\}$ and $V_2 = V \cup \{v\}$ we have that $\|g(V_1) - g(V_2)\|_2 \leq \frac{4\Delta_g}{m+1}$ by the triangle inequality.

We will use algorithm `NoisyAVG` (algorithm 4) for privately obtaining (noisy) averages of vectors in $\mathbb{R}^d$.

OBSERVATION A.1. *Let V and g be s.t. $m = |\{v \in V : g(v) = 1\}| \geq \frac{16}{\epsilon}\ln(\frac{2}{\beta\delta})$. With probability at least $(1-\beta)$ algorithm `NoisyAVG`(V) returns $g(V) + \eta$ where η is a vector whose every coordinate is sampled i.i.d. from $\mathcal{N}(0,\sigma^2)$ for some $\sigma \leq \frac{16\Delta_g}{\epsilon m}\sqrt{2\ln(8/\delta)}$*

OBSERVATION A.2. *The requirement that*

$$\max_{v:g(v)=1} \|v\|_2 \leq \Delta_g$$

could easily be replaced by

$$\max_{u,v:g(u)=g(v)=1} \|u - v\|_2 \leq \Delta_g.$$

That is, the predicate g may define a subset of $\mathbb{R}^d$ of diameter $\leq \Delta_g$, not necessarily around the origin.

Algorithm 4 NoisyAVG

Input: Multiset V of vectors in $\mathbb{R}^d$, predicate g, parameters ϵ, δ.

1. Set $\hat{m} = |\{v \in V : g(v) = 1\}| + \text{Lap}(2/\epsilon) - \frac{2}{\epsilon}\ln(2/\delta)$. If $\hat{m} \leq 0$ then output $\perp$ and halt.
2. Denote $\sigma = \frac{8\Delta_g}{\epsilon\hat{m}}\sqrt{2\ln(8/\delta)}$, and let $\eta \in \mathbb{R}^d$ be a random noise vector with each coordinate sampled independently from $\mathcal{N}(0, \sigma^2)$. Return $g(V) + \eta$.

PROOF. Let $c \in \mathbb{R}^d$ be s.t. $\|c - v\|_2 \leq \Delta$ for every $v \in \mathbb{R}^d$ s.t. $g(v) = 1$. Given a vector set V, we could apply algorithm NoisyAVG on the set $\tilde{V} = \{v - c : v \in V\}$ with the predicate $\tilde{g} : \mathbb{R}^d \to \{0, 1\}$ s.t. $\tilde{g}(v) = g(v + c)$, and add the vector c to the result. □

THEOREM A.3. *Algorithm NoisyAVG is (ϵ, δ)- differentially private.*

PROOF. For a given parameter σ, let us denote by $\eta(\sigma)$ a random vector whose every coordinate is sampled iid from $\mathcal{N}(0, \sigma^2)$. Now fix two neighboring sets V, V' and a predicate g. Denote $m = |\{v \in V : g(v) = 1\}|$, and recall that $\|g(V) - g(V')\|_2 \leq \frac{4\Delta_g}{m}$. The standard analysis of the Gaussian mechanism shows that for any $F \subseteq \mathbb{R}^d$ and for any $\sigma \geq \frac{8\Delta_g}{\epsilon m}\sqrt{2\ln(8/\delta)}$ it holds that

$$\Pr_{\eta(\sigma)}[g(V) + \eta(\sigma) \in F] \leq e^{\epsilon/2} \cdot \Pr_{\eta(\sigma)}[g(V') + \eta(\sigma) \in F] + \frac{\delta}{6}.$$

We will use $\hat{m}(V)$ to denote $\hat{m}$ as it is on step 1 of the execution of NoisyAVG on V. Note that $\Pr[\hat{m}(V) > m] = \Pr[\text{Lap}(\frac{2}{\epsilon}) > \frac{2}{\epsilon}\ln(2/\delta)] \leq \frac{\delta}{2}$. Hence, for any set of outputs F s.t. $\perp \notin F$ we have that

$$\begin{aligned}
&\Pr[\texttt{NoisyAVG}(V) \in F] \\
&= \int_0^\infty \Pr[\hat{m}(V) = \tilde{m}] \\
&\qquad \cdot \Pr[\texttt{NoisyAVG}(V) \in F | \hat{m}(V) = \tilde{m}] d\tilde{m} \\
&\leq \frac{\delta}{2} + \int_0^m \Pr[\hat{m}(V) = \tilde{m}] \\
&\qquad \cdot \Pr[\texttt{NoisyAVG}(V) \in F | \hat{m}(V) = \tilde{m}] d\tilde{m} \\
&= \frac{\delta}{2} + \int_0^m \Pr[\hat{m}(V) = \tilde{m}] \\
&\qquad \cdot \Pr\left[g(V) + \eta\left(\frac{8\sqrt{2}}{\epsilon\tilde{m}}\sqrt{\ln(\frac{8}{\delta})}\right) \in F\right] d\tilde{m} \\
&\leq \frac{\delta}{2} + \int_0^m e^{\epsilon/2} \cdot \Pr[\hat{m}(V') = \tilde{m}] \cdot \\
&\left(e^{\epsilon/2} \Pr\left[g(V') + \eta\left(\frac{8\sqrt{2}}{\epsilon\tilde{m}}\sqrt{\ln(\frac{8}{\delta})}\right) \in F\right] + \frac{\delta}{6}\right) d\tilde{m} \\
&\leq \frac{\delta}{2} + \int_0^\infty e^{\epsilon/2} \cdot \Pr[\hat{m}(V') = \tilde{m}] \\
&\qquad \cdot \left(e^{\epsilon/2} \Pr\left[\texttt{NoisyAVG}(V') \in F | \hat{m}(V') = \tilde{m}\right] + \frac{\delta}{6}\right) d\tilde{m} \\
&\leq \delta + e^\epsilon \cdot \Pr[\texttt{NoisyAVG}(V') \in F].
\end{aligned}$$

For a set of outputs F s.t. $\perp \in F$ we have

$$\begin{aligned}
&\Pr[\texttt{NoisyAVG}(V) \in F] \\
&\quad = \Pr[\texttt{NoisyAVG}(V) = \perp] \\
&\qquad + \Pr[\texttt{NoisyAVG}(V) \in F \setminus \{\perp\}] \\
&\quad \leq e^\epsilon \Pr[\texttt{NoisyAVG}(V') = \perp] \\
&\qquad + e^\epsilon \Pr[\texttt{NoisyAVG}(V') \in F \setminus \{\perp\}] + \delta \\
&\quad = e^\epsilon \Pr[\texttt{NoisyAVG}(V') \in F] + \delta.
\end{aligned}$$

□

B. ON THE IMPOSSIBILITY OF SOLVING THE 1-CLUSTER PROBLEM ON INFINITE DOMAINS

In this section we will show that solving the 1-cluster problem on infinite domains (with a reasonable parameters) is impossible under differential privacy. Our lower bound is obtained through a reduction from the simple *interior point problem* defined below.

DEFINITION B.1. *An algorithm $A : X^n \to X$ solves the* interior point problem *on X with error probability β if for every $D \in X^n$,*

$$\Pr[\min D \leq A(D) \leq \max D] \geq 1 - \beta,$$

where the probability is taken over the coins of A. The sample complexity of the algorithm A is the database size n.

We call a solution x with $\min D \leq x \leq \max D$ an *interior point* of D. Note that x need not be a member of the database D. As was shown in [4], privately solving the interior point problem on a domain X requires sample complexity that grows with $|X|$. In particular, privately solving this problem over an *infinite* domain is impossible.

THEOREM B.2 ([4]). *Fix any constant $0 < \epsilon < 1/4$. Let $\delta(n) \leq 1/(50n^2)$. Then for every positive integer n, solving the interior point problem on X with probability at least $3/4$ and with $(\epsilon, \delta(n))$-differential privacy requires sample complexity $n \geq \Omega(\log^* |X|)$.*

As we will now see, solving the 1-Cluster problem over a domain X (or over X^d for any $d \geq 1$) implies solving the interior point problem on X.

THEOREM B.3. *Let $\beta, \epsilon, \delta, n, t, \Delta, w$ be such that $\Delta < t \leq n$. If there exists an (ϵ, δ)-private algorithm that solves the 1-cluster problem (X, n, t) with parameters (Δ, w) and error probability β, then there exist a $(2\epsilon, 2\delta)$-private algorithm that solves the interior point problem on X with error probability 2β using sample complexity*

$$m = n + 8^{\log^*(4w)} \cdot \frac{144\log^*(4w)}{\epsilon}\log\left(\frac{12\log^*(4w)}{\beta\delta}\right).$$

Algorithm 5 `IntPoint`

Input: Database $S \in X^m$ containing m points from X.

Algorithm used: Algorithm $\mathcal{A}$ for privately solving the 1-cluster problem (X, n, t) with parameters (Δ, w) and error probability β.

1. Sort the entries of S and let D be a multiset containing the middle n entries of S.
2. Apply $\mathcal{A}$ on D to obtain a center $c \in X$ and a radius $r \in \mathbb{R}$. Let $I \subseteq X$ denote the interval of length $2r$ centered at c. If $r = 0$ (i.e., I contains only the point c), then halt and return c.
   % If $\mathcal{A}$ succeeded, then the interval I contains at least 1 input points from D.
3. Partition I into intervals of length r/w, and let $\mathcal{J}$ be the set of all edge points of the resulting intervals.
   % As I contains points from D, at least one of the above intervals contains points from D. We will show that this interval cannot contain all of D, and hence, one of its two edge points is an interior point of D (and of S).
4. Define $q : X^* \times X \to \mathbb{N}$ as $q((x_1, \dots, x_n), a) = \min\{\ |\{i : x_i \leq a\}|\ ,\ |\{i : x_i \geq a\}|\ \}$. Apply algorithm `RecConcave` on the database S with privacy parameters (ϵ, δ), utility parameters $(\alpha = \frac{1}{2}, \beta)$, quality function q, and quality promise $\frac{m-n}{2}$ to choose and return $j \in \mathcal{J}$.
   % If a point $j^* \in \mathcal{J}$ is an interior point of D, then it is also an interior point of S with quality $q(S, j^*) \geq \frac{m-n}{2}$ (since D contains the middle n elements of S). Hence, w.h.p., algorithm `RecConcave` identifies an interior point of S.

Roughly speaking, Theorem B.3 states that any solution for the 1-cluster problem (with a reasonable parameter w) implies a solution for the interior point problem. Let us introduce the following notation for iterated exponentials:

$$\text{tower}(0) = 1 \quad \text{and} \quad \text{tower}(j) = 2^{\text{tower}(j-1)}.$$

COROLLARY B.4. *Fix any constants $0 < \epsilon, \beta < 1/8$, and let $\delta(n) \leq 1/(200n^2)$. Also let Δ, t, w be s.t. $\Delta < t \leq n$ and $w \leq \frac{1}{4}\,\text{tower}(\log(n^{1/5}/40))$. For every (ϵ, δ)-differentially private algorithm that solves the 1-cluster problem (X, n, t) with parameters (Δ, w) and error probability β, it holds that $n \geq \Omega(\log^* |X|)$.*

Hence, in any solution to the 1-cluster problem where w is smaller than an exponential tower in n, the sample size n must grow with $|X|$. In particular, privately solving such 1-cluster problems over infinite domains is impossible.

PROOF OF COROLLARY B.4. Denote $\delta(n) = 1/(200n^2)$, and let $\mathcal{A}$ be a $(\epsilon = \frac{1}{10}, \delta(n))$-differentially private algorithm that solves the 1-cluster problem (X, n, t) with parameters (Δ, w) and error probability $\beta = \frac{1}{10}$, where $\Delta < t \leq n$ and $w \leq \frac{1}{4}\,\text{tower}(\log(n^{1/5}/40))$. By Theorem B.3, there exist a $(2\epsilon = \frac{1}{5}, 2\delta(n))$-differentially private algorithm that solves the interior point problem on X with error probability $2\beta = \frac{1}{5}$ using sample complexity

$$m = n + 8^{\log^*(4w)} \cdot 1440 \log^*(4w) \log\Big(24000n^2 \log^*(4w)\Big).$$

Using the assumption that $w \leq \frac{1}{4}\,\text{tower}(\log(n^{1/5}/40))$, we get that $m \leq 2n$, and therefore $2\delta(n) = \frac{1}{100n^2} \leq \frac{1}{50m^2}$. Theorem B.2 now states that $m \geq \Omega(\log^* |X|)$, and hence, $n \geq \Omega(\log^* |X|)$. □

PROOF OF THEOREM B.3. The proof is via the construction of algorithm `IntPoint`. For the privacy analysis, observe that on step 1 the algorithm constructs a database D containing the n middle elements from the input database S. Fix two neighboring databases S_1, S_2 of size m, and consider the databases D_1, D_2 containing the middle n elements of S_1, S_2 respectively. As S_1, S_2 differ in at most one element, so does D_1, D_2 (our algorithms ignore the order of their input database). Hence, applying a private computation onto D preserves privacy. Algorithm `IntPoint` interacts with D using algorithm $\mathcal{A}$ (on step 1), and interacts with S using algorithm `RecConcave` (on step 4). Hence, by composition (see Theorem 2.1), Algorithm `IntPoint` is $(2\epsilon, 2\delta)$- differentially private.

As for the utility analysis, let $S \in X^m$ be an instance to the interior point problem, and consider the execution of algorithm `IntPoint` on S. Let D be the multiset defined on step 1 of the execution, and let c, r, I be the center, the radius, and the interval obtained on step 2. By the properties of algorithm $\mathcal{A}$, with probability $1 - \beta$, the interval I (of length $2r$ centered at c) contains at least $t - \Delta \geq 1$ input points from D, and moreover, $2r \leq 2w \cdot r_{opt}$ where $2r_{opt}$ is the length of the smallest interval containing t points from D. That is, *every* interval containing t points from D is of length at least $2r/w$. We continue with the analysis assuming that this is the case.

If $r = 0$, then the interval I contains only the point c, and c is therefore an interior point of D (and of S). We hence proceed with the analysis assuming that $r > 0$.

On step 3 we partition the interval I (of length $2r$) into intervals of length r/w. Let us denote them as $\mathcal{I} = \{I_i\}$. Since I contains at least 1 point from D, there exists an interval $I_\ell \in \mathcal{I}$ that contains a point from D. In addition, I_ℓ is of length r/w, and can hence contain at most $t-1$ points from D. So, there exists an interval $I_\ell \in \mathcal{I}$ containing some of the points in D, but not all of them. One of its edge points must be, therefore, an interior point of D. Thus, the set $\mathcal{J}$ of all end points of the intervals in $\mathcal{I}$ (defined on step 3) contains an interior point of D.

Recall that the input database S contains at least $\frac{m-n}{2}$ elements which are bigger than the elements in D and $\frac{m-n}{2}$ elements which are smaller. Hence, there exists a point $j^* \in \mathcal{J}$ s.t. $q(S, j^*) \geq \frac{m-n}{2}$, and the quality promise given to algorithm `RecConcave` is valid. Observe that $|\mathcal{J}| \leq 4w$ (this is the size of the solution set given to algorithm `RecConcave`). Hence, assuming that

$$m \geq n + 8^{\log^*(4w)} \cdot \frac{144 \log^*(4w)}{\epsilon} \log\left(\frac{12 \log^*(4w)}{\beta\delta}\right),$$

with probability at least $1 - \beta$, the output $j \in \mathcal{J}$ is s.t. $q(S, j) \geq \frac{m-n}{4}$, and j is an interior point of S as required. □

Parallel Algorithms for Constructing Range and Nearest-Neighbor Searching Data Structures*

Pankaj K. Agarwal Kyle Fox Kamesh Munagala
Abhinandan Nath
Duke University
{pankaj,kylefox,kamesh,abhinath}@cs.duke.edu

ABSTRACT

With the massive amounts of data available today, it is common to store and process data using multiple machines. Parallel programming platforms such as MapReduce and its variants are popular frameworks for handling such large data. We present the first provably efficient algorithms to compute, store, and query data structures for range queries and approximate nearest neighbor queries in a popular parallel computing abstraction that captures the salient features of MapReduce and other massively parallel communication (MPC) models. In particular, we describe algorithms for *kd*-trees, range trees, and BBD-trees that only require $O(1)$ rounds of communication for both preprocessing and querying while staying competitive in terms of running time and workload to their classical counterparts. Our algorithms are randomized, but they can be made deterministic at some increase in their running time and workload while keeping the number of rounds of communication to be constant.

1. INTRODUCTION

Rapid advances in sensing technologies as well as Internet applications such as social networks have led to unprecedented increase in the size and quantity of data sets. The term "big data" has become ubiquitous to describe data that cannot be stored or processed on a single machine. The MapReduce platform [18], its open source implementation Hadoop [43], and related platforms (such as Pregel [37], Spark [44], and Google Cloud Dataflow [7]) have emerged as dominant computing platforms for big-data processing. At a high level, these systems focus on computation local to the data stored on individual machines and have become popular due to their ability to abstract away the distributed nature of data storage and processing. The data itself is stored on disk in a distributed file system, for example, the Hadoop Distributed File System (HDFS) of the Hadoop platform [41]. A distributed file system can be treated as a cluster of machines, each with its own disk space where the data is stored. A high level programming language such as Pig [1] is used to write a program that is pushed to the machines where the data is stored and processed.

Motivated by social networks, target advertisements, and other applications, there has been a flurry of research activity on computing graph theoretic and machine learning primitives in MapReduce and other big data platforms. Moreover, advances in mapping and sensing technologies have led to the emergence of large geometric data sets as well. Even non-geometric data is often mapped to a set of points in a geometric space. One of the important problems in databases, GIS, and computational geometry is to answer various queries on such data. One could conceivably scan the entire data to answer each query, but since several queries are answered on the same data, it is desirable to preprocess data into a data structure so that a query can be answered quickly. A popular approach to cope with big data in the context of query processing is to work with a small summary of data such as random samples, coresets, sketches, *etc.* These methods are successful for answering aggregation queries, but they do not work well when queries involve analyzing local structure of data such as nearest-neighbor queries or range-reporting queries (especially for small ranges). In such instances, one has to work with the entire data. This difficulty raises the problem of constructing data structures on big data platforms. In this paper, we study data structures for range-reporting and nearest-neighbor queries – two very popular queries on geometric data – on big data platforms. In particular, we develop efficient algorithms for constructing some of the classical data structures such as *kd*-trees, BBD-trees, and range trees.

Our model. The technology for big data computation is in a constant state of flux. For instance, in MapReduce [18], the output data from a phase of computation is shuffled and stored on disk in the distributed file system. Spark [44] builds on MapReduce and attempts to keep data in memory to speed up machine learning applications that require multiple passes over the same data. Many of these platforms also incorporate streaming and real-time primitives.

To avoid dependence on specifics of a particular platform, we present our algorithms in a simple but popular abstract model called the (basic) *massively parallel communication* (MPC) model, originally proposed by Beame *et al.* [14] (see also Andoni *et al.* [9]).

*Work on this paper is supported by NSF under grants CCF-1161359, IIS-1408846, CCF-1408784, IIS-1447554, CCF-1546392, and CCF-1513816, by an ARO grant W911NF-15-1-0408, and by Grant 2012/229 from the U.S.-Israel Binational Science Foundation

PODS'16, June 26-July 01, 2016, San Francisco, CA, USA
© 2016 ACM. ISBN 978-1-4503-4191-2/16/06...$15.00
DOI: http://dx.doi.org/10.1145/2902251.2902303

Let n be the size of an input instance, and let I be a set of m machines. For simplicity, we assume I to be $\{0, \ldots, m-1\}$. Set $s = n/m$, and for simplicity, assume s is an integer.[1] Each machine has $O(s)$ memory (or space). As is standard, we assume $s \geq n^\alpha$ for some positive constant $\alpha < 1$. Computation proceeds in rounds. In each round, each machine reads its input, does some computation, and emits some output, where each output item is marked with the ID of the machine for which it is input in the next round. The size of the input to and output from any machine is bounded by $O(s)$ in each round. Communication across machines occurs only between rounds.

We explicitly allow data to persist on machines between rounds of computation and after all computation has been performed, as long as the total amount of data stored on each machine never exceeds $O(s)$. By considering data storage as we do, we are able to build and store data structures for massive geometric data. The explicit persistence of data between rounds and our hard requirements on the space of each machine are the main differences between our model and the MPC model as described by Beame *et al.* [14]. Andoni *et al.* [9] also limit the space on each machine, but they do not explicitly consider persistent storage. In fact, some work in similar models (*e.g.* Goodrich *et al.* [29]) require machines to communicate their own data to themselves in order for data to persist between rounds of computation.

Queries to our data structures behave as any other MPC computation. They simply take advantage of the distributed data structures already stored in the machines to reduce query time. When preprocessing a set of points P to build our data structures, we assume the points of P are distributed arbitrarily throughout the machines. Individual queries are sent to an arbitrary machine.

The efficiency of an algorithm is measured using three metrics: the number of rounds of computation R, the running time T, and the total work W. The first is obvious; we describe the latter two below. For machine $\beta \in I$, let $t_{\beta r}$ denote the computation time spent by this machine in round r. The *running time* is defined as

$$T = \sum_{r=1}^{R} \max_{\beta \in I} t_{\beta r}.$$

Note that this definition does not count the time it takes to communicate between the machines, which is accounted for separately by the quantity R.

The *total work* is defined as

$$W = \sum_{r=1}^{R} \sum_{\beta \in I} t_{\beta r}.$$

In order to make guarantees about our total work, we assume a machine performs zero work in a single round of computation if it does not receive any input or communication at the beginning of that round. This assumption can be interpreted as each machine "sleeping" through a round of computation unless it is given a reason to wake up, and this makes it possible for W to be significantly smaller than $m \cdot T$.

While most prior work on the MPC model focuses on minimizing the number of computation rounds R of an algorithm, e.g., [14, 23, 31], we must consider all three metrics in order to say anything interesting about geometric data structures. Consider processing a set of points $P \subseteq \mathbb{R}^2$ so that one may report the points lying within an axis-aligned query rectangle. If number of rounds were our only concern, we would build a trivial data structure in one round of computation by doing nothing. A query for rectangle $\square_q$ would then be performed in one round of computation as well by having each machine individually check which of its points lie inside $\square_q$. However, queries will take $O(s)$ time and require $O(n)$ work. We could slightly improve our data structure by building *kd*-trees for each machine's set of points using one round, $O(s \log s)$ time, and $O(n \log n)$ total work (see Section 3). The runtime of a query would improve to $O(\sqrt{s})$ in the worst case, but queries would still require $\Omega(m)$ work in the best case and $O(\sqrt{s}m) = O(n/\sqrt{s})$ work in the worst case. Unless s is nearly as large as n, these worst-case workloads are significantly higher than what is possible using classical sequential data structures. Therefore, we will focus on minimizing all three performance metrics.

Our results. Let P be a set of n points in $\mathbb{R}^d$, where d is a constant. We present efficient algorithms for building and querying *kd*-trees, range trees, and BBD-trees on P. The first two are used for range queries and the last one is used for approximate nearest-neighbor (NN) queries. They are formally defined in later sections; see [12, 17] for details. A *kd*-tree uses linear space and $O(n^{1-1/d} + k)$ query time to answer an orthogonal range query (*i.e.*, reporting all k points of P lying in a query axis-parallel rectangle). It can be computed in $O(n \log n)$ time. In contrast, a range tree uses $O(n \log^{d-1} n)$ space and $O(\log^{d-1} n + k)$ query time; range trees with slightly smaller space are also known [5]. A BBD-tree can answer an ε-approximate NN query in $O(c_{d,\varepsilon} \log n)$ time using $O(n)$ space where $c_{d,\varepsilon}$ is a constant dependent on d and ε.

For all of the data structures we consider, we will show a bound of $R = \text{poly}(\log_s n) = O(1)$ on the number of rounds of computation required both to build the data structure and to perform queries. Our running times T for building our data structures and performing queries will be comparable to the best sequential algorithms when performed on point sets of size s and our total work W will be comparable with the best sequential algorithms for point sets of size n. More precisely, we obtain the following results; see Table 1 for a summary.

- A *kd*-tree on P can be built in $O(1)$ rounds, $O(s \log s)$ time, and $O(n \log n)$ work with probability at least $1 - \frac{1}{n^{\Omega(1)}}$.[2] Queries can be answered using $O(1)$ rounds and $O(n^{1-1/d} + k)$ work where k is the output size; the running time is $O(s^{1-1/d} + k')$ where k' is the maximum number of points reported by a machine.
- A BBD-tree on P can be built in $O(1)$ rounds, $O(s \log s)$ time, and $O(n \log n)$ work with probability at least $1 - \frac{1}{n^{\Omega(1)}}$. Queries can be answered in $O(1)$ rounds, $O\left(\frac{1}{\varepsilon^d} \log\left(\frac{1}{\varepsilon}\right) \log n\right)$ time, and $\frac{1}{\varepsilon^{O(d)}} \log n$ work.
- A range tree on P can be built in $O(1)$ rounds, $O(s \log^d s)$

[1]For simplicity, we will ignore floor and ceiling operators throughout this paper and assume appropriate choice of parameters so that the ratios are integers when needed.

[2]The *kd*-tree we build is a slight variant of the standard *kd*-tree in that unlike the latter, our tree is not exactly balanced in partitioning the points. Nevertheless, we show that the space, query, and preprocessing requirements are asymptotically identical.

time, and $O(n \log^d n)$ work.[3] Queries can be answered in $O(\log^d n + k)$ time and work in $O(1)$ rounds of computation, where k is the number of points reported.

The algorithm for *kd*-trees can be extended to many variants of *kd*-trees such as hB-trees [36], hB^π-trees [24], and box trees [4]. It can also be extended to construct a partition tree [15] that is used for answering simplex range searching queries, *i.e.*, reporting all points that lie inside a query simplex.

The algorithms for building *kd*-trees and BBD-trees use randomization. However, they can be derandomized while keeping the number of computation rounds constant by increasing the running time – we obtain a tradeoff between the number of rounds and the running time.

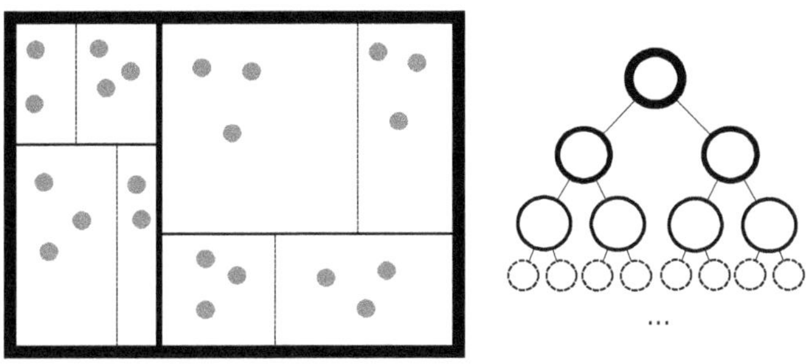

Figure 1. A *kd*-tree partitions space into a hierarchy of boxes. Each box is represented by a node in a tree, and nesting boxes are represented by ancestor-descendant relationships within the tree.

We remark that there is extensive work on I/O-efficient data structures in databases. For example, the *kdB*-tree is an I/O-efficient version of a *kd*-tree [10]. Similarly I/O-efficient range trees have been proposed [10]. Our algorithms can be modified easily to construct I/O-efficient versions of the data structures.

Our techniques. Our algorithms for constructing data structures depend upon the concept of ε-approximations defined formally in Section 2.1. Intuitively, an ε-approximation is a small subset of points $S \subset P$ such that any low complexity region $\mathcal{R}$ of $\mathbb{R}^d$ contains about the same fraction of points of S as that of P. One property common to most of the data structures we build is that they induce a hierarchical decomposition of $\mathbb{R}^d$ represented by a balanced tree. See Figure 1. In a constant number of rounds of computation, we sample an ε-approximation S of P. We choose S to be small enough to fit on a single machine, so we use a sequential algorithm to build the first few layers of the tree data structure using only points in S. The regions of $\mathbb{R}^d$ associated with the leaves of the partial tree partition S into approximately equal sized subsets. Because S is an ε-approximation of P, these same regions partition P into almost equal sized subsets as well. We recursively build the lower levels of the data structure on each piece of the partition.

Our algorithms are simple, and our analysis shows that a simple sampling based technique gives essentially the best possible running time in the MPC model, without using additional features that some modern data processing techniques may enable.

Sampling and the similar concept of filtering have been used before for the design of efficient algorithms for models based on MapReduce [22, 23, 32, 33]. However, these algorithms complete their work on a single machine after acquiring a small set of samples. In contrast, the partial trees our algorithms compute using their sample sets are not an entire solution; the algorithms must continue processing the remaining points in the input set using the partial trees to aid in the remaining computation.

Related work. A common concern when designing data structures for massive amounts of (geometric) data is the cost of reading and writing from disk, called an I/O operation. Aggarwal and Vitter [6] described the two-level I/O-memory model in an attempt to understand those costs. Extensive work has been done on developing range-searching data structures in this model. See the survey by Arge [10]. Agarwal *et al.* [3] describe I/O-optimal algorithms for constructing *kd*-trees and BBD-trees; however their techniques are not easily parallelizable.

An alternative to the two-level I/O model described above is the cache-oblivious model introduced by Frigo *et al.* [25]. In essence, algorithms for the traditional RAM model are evaluated in terms of performance using the two-level I/O model with *unknown* internal memory size and unknown block size. The analysis assumes transfers between internal and external memory are done using an optimal caching strategy. Again, there is extensive study of range-searching data structures in this model; see Arge *et al.* [11] for a survey.

While the I/O models above are designed with the storage of massive data in mind, they are still inherently *sequential*. In contrast, the Parallel Random Access Machine (PRAM) model ignores I/O complexities and instead models parallel processors sharing a common memory pool. Many efficient PRAM algorithms have been described; see Goodrich [28] for a survey.

The Bulk Synchronous Parallel (BSP) model [42] of Valiant models parallel processing, communication, and synchronization. A specialization of this model to multiprocessors is termed coarse grained parallelism (CGP) [19]. This model is similar to MPC; there are $p \leq n^\epsilon$ processors (where n is the input size and $\epsilon \leq 0.5$), each of which is allowed $O(n/p)$ communication between rounds, and arbitrary sequential computation. The goal is to simultaneously optimize the number of rounds, as well as the sequential computation done per processor. Dehne *et al.* [19] present optimal algorithms for several geometric problems. Simple deterministic partitioning of the point sets, however, suffice for the problems they consider. Furthermore, they do not focus on the more challenging problem of constructing data structures.

In order to theoretically model modern distributed programming frameworks, many authors have focused on variations of the MapReduce model [9, 14, 26, 29, 31, 33]. There is extensive work in database systems on developing algorithms under MapReduce and its variants, e.g., algorithms for large graph processing, join operations, query processing etc. See e.g. [30, 34, 40].

From a theoretical perspective, Goodrich *et al.* [29] describe a connection between MapReduce and the BSP model mentioned above, which leads to efficient implementation of some geometric algorithms. Andoni *et al.* [9] develop geometric approximation algorithms under MapReduce; see

[3]In order to have sufficient space just to store the range tree, we slightly amend our model so the memory and per-round input and output size of each machine is $O(s \log^{d-1} n)$.

Performance metric		kd-tree	BBD-tree	Range tree
Pre-processing	Rounds	$O(1)$	$O(1)$	$O(1)$
	Time	$O(s \log s)$	$O(s \log s)$	$O(s \log^d s)$
	Work	$O(n \log n)$	$O(n \log n)$	$O(n \log^d n)$
Query	Rounds	$O(1)$	$O(1)$	$O(1)$
	Time	$O(s^{1-1/d} + k')$	$O(\log n)$	$O(\log n + k)$
	Work	$O(n^{1-1/d} + k)$	$O(\log n)$	$O(\log^d n + k)$

Table 1. Our results.

also [19]. However the partitioning scheme used in [9] is based on randomly shifted quadtrees, hence largely independent of the input point set. On the other hand, we use a small sample of the input points in a clever way to partition the points. There is some work on similarity search in high dimensions in the distributed setting [13]. However, their focus is on reducing the amount of communication per round and is based on distributed locality-sensitive hashing, whereas our approach is quite different and is tailored for low dimensions. The most closely related works to this paper is MapReduce implementations for analyzing and querying spatial and geometric data, see [2, 8, 20–22] and references there in. For example, SpatialHadoop [22] is a full-fledged MapReduce framework that adapts traditional spatial index structures like R-tree and R+-tree to form a two-level spatial index. It is also equipped with other operations, including range query, k-nearest neighbors, and spatial join. However, we are not aware of any work on constructing range-searching and other geometric query data structures with *provable bounds* on performance, which is the main focus of this paper.

The rest of the paper is organized as follows. We describe some primitive operations useful for building geometric data structures in Section 2. We discuss *kd*-trees and an extension of our techniques to partition trees [15] in Section 3. We discuss BBD-trees and range trees in Sections 4 and 5, respectively. Finally, we conclude in Section 6 by mentioning some directions for future research.

2. MPC PRIMITIVES

Before describing our MPC primitives, we introduce the notion of an ε-approximation, which will be constructed by one of the primitives and which will be used by many of our algorithms.

2.1 Range spaces and ε-approximations

A *range space* Σ is a pair $(X, \mathcal{R})$, where X is a ground set and $\mathcal{R}$ is a family of subsets (*ranges*) of X. For example, X is a set of points in $\mathbb{R}^2$ and

$$\mathcal{R} = \{X \cap \square \mid \square \text{ is a rectangle in } \mathbb{R}^2\}.$$

A subset $X' \subseteq X$ is *shattered* by Σ if $\{X' \cap R \mid R \in \mathcal{R}\} = 2^{X'}$. The *VC dimension* of Σ is the size of the largest subset of X shattered by Σ. If there are arbitrarily large shattered subsets, the VC dimension of Σ is set to ∞.

Given range spaces $\Sigma_1 = (X, \mathcal{R}_1)$ and $\Sigma_2 = (X, \mathcal{R}_2)$ with VC dimensions δ_1 and δ_2 respectively, the union of Σ_1 and Σ_2 is defined as

$$(X, \mathcal{R}) = (X, \{R_1 \cup R_2 \mid R_1 \in \mathcal{R}_1, R_2 \in \mathcal{R}_2\}),$$

and has VC dimension $O(\delta_1 + \delta_2)$. The complement of Σ is defined as $(X, \overline{\mathcal{R}}) = (X, \{X \setminus R \mid R \in \mathcal{R}\})$ and has the same VC dimension as Σ. See Chazelle [16] for details.

Given a range space $\Sigma = (X, \mathcal{R})$ and $0 \le \varepsilon \le 1$, a subset $X' \subseteq X$ is called an *ε-approximation* of Σ if for any range $R \in \mathcal{R}$, we have

$$\left| \frac{|X' \cap R|}{|X'|} - \frac{|R|}{|X|} \right| \le \varepsilon.$$

The following bound on an ε-approximation was proved by Li *et al.* [35].

THEOREM 2.1 ([35]). *There is a positive constant c such that if $\Sigma = (X, \mathcal{R})$ is a range space with VC dimension δ, then a random subset of X of size $\frac{c}{\varepsilon^2}\left(\delta + \log \frac{1}{\psi}\right)$ is an ε-approximation of X with probability at least $1 - \psi$.*

For range spaces with constant VC dimension, a random subset of size $O\left(\frac{1}{\varepsilon^2} \log n\right)$ is an ε-approximation with probability at least $1 - 1/n^{\Omega(1)}$, where n is the size of the ground set.[4] The ranges that we consider in this paper are induced by axis-aligned boxes, simplices, and rectilinear regions defined by constant number of rectangles. Since these regions can be formed by taking a Boolean combination of a constant number of halfspaces, the range spaces induced by these regions have constant VC dimension.

2.2 Geometric primitives and techniques

We define a few primitive operations that we use to build our distributed data structures :

`PrefixSum`$(P, I, \text{rank}, \text{value})$**:** Given a set of points P stored on a contiguous subset of machines $I = \{i_0, i_0{+}1, \dots\}$, a rank function rank : $P \to \mathbb{Z}^+$, and a value function value : $P \to \mathbb{R}$, compute the prefix sum of values for each point $p \in P$ where rank(p) is the rank of point p in some sorted order.

`Broadcast`$(\mathcal{S}, I, \beta)$**:** Given a set of words $\mathcal{S}$, a contiguous set of machines $I = \{i_0, i_0 + 1, \dots\}$, and a machine β storing $\mathcal{S}$, copy $\mathcal{S}$ to all machines in I. We require $\mathcal{S}$ has size $O(s^{1/2})$.

`Partition`(P, I, Π, β)**:** Given a spatial subdivision Π of $\mathbb{R}^d$ into simple regions (e.g., rectangles, simplices), reorganize the points of P so that all points lying in a cell π of Π lie on a distinct contiguous subset of machines

[4]Better bounds for the size of ε-approximations exist for range spaces with finite VC dimension [16], but the bounds given here suffice for our purposes.

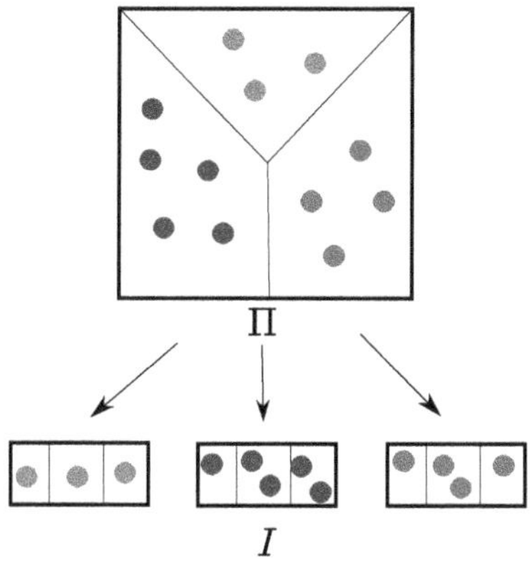

Figure 2. `Parition`(Π, I, β) reorganizes the points stored on I as dictated by the partition Π.

$I_\pi \subseteq I$. See Figure 2. We assume I itself is also a contiguous subset of machines $\{i_0, i_0+1, \dots\}$. We require that $|\Pi| = O(s^{1/2})$, $|\Pi| \leq |I|$, and each cell π of Π contains $O(|P|/|\Pi|)$ points.

`Sample`(P, I, r, β)**:** Given a set of points P stored on a contiguous subset of machines $I = \{i_0, i_0+1, \dots\}$, compute a $(1/r)$-approximation $S \subseteq P$ of size $O(r^2 \log n)$ and send it to machine β. We require $|S| = O(s^{1/2})$.[5]

Before describing how to implement these primitives efficiently, we describe a procedure that will be used by these primitives.

To facilitate transfer of information between a given contiguous subset of machines $I = \{i_0, i_0+1, \dots\}$, we construct a tree T, a *complete* $s^{1/2}$*-ary tree* with $|I|$ leaves. Each node v of T is associated with a single machine $\beta(v) \in I$ such that each machine is used at most once per level of T. We let r_T denote the root of T and set $\beta(r_T)$ appropriately depending on the primitive. Let λ_T denote the depth of T. We have $\lambda_T = O(\log_{s^{1/2}} |I|) = O(1)$. Goodrich *et al.* [29] use a similar tree to compute prefix sums. A number of simple operations can be completed in a constant number of rounds of computation guided by T, by passing information between machines belonging to parent and child nodes. For example, it is straightforward to compute the max and sum of several numbers stored across the machines. While sending information from parent to children, the parent node's machine sends $O(s^{1/2})$ data to each child node's machine. If information is sent from children to parent, each child's machine sends $O(s^{1/2})$-size data to the parent's machine. Since each node has $s^{1/2}$ children, the input and output size for each machine is bounded by $O(s)$ in one round.
We now describe an implementation of above primitives.

`PrefixSum`$(P, I, \text{rank}, \text{value})$**:** It can be implemented in $O(1)$ rounds with linear time and work using an algorithm of Goodrich *et al.* [29]. Without giving details here, we state the bounds :

LEMMA 2.2. `PrefixSum`$(P, I, \text{rank}, \text{value})$ *can be implemented by a deterministic algorithm in $O(1)$ rounds, $O(s)$ time, and $O(n)$ total work.*

[5]Strictly speaking, the algorithm for computing a $(1/r)$-approximation depends on the underlying range space. In our applications, the range space associated with P will be clear from the context and will have constant VC dimension.

`Broadcast`$(\mathcal{S}, I, \beta)$**:** We use the tree T over the machines in I. Our broadcast procedure takes exactly $\lambda_T + 1 = O(1)$ rounds of computation. In round i, each machine $\beta(v)$ for a node v at level $i-1$ receives a copy of $\mathcal{S}$. If it has not done so already, $\beta(v)$ stores a copy of $\mathcal{S}$. When the round of computation ends, $\beta(v)$ sends a copy of $\mathcal{S}$ to each machine $\beta(v')$ where v' is a child of v in T.

LEMMA 2.3. `Broadcast`$(\mathcal{S}, I, \beta)$ *can be implemented by a deterministic algorithm using $O(1)$ rounds of computation, $O(s)$ time, and $O(n)$ total work.*

`Partition`(P, I, Π, β)**:** Order the cells of Π in an arbitrary way, and let $\{\pi_0, \pi_1, \dots\}$ be the cells of Π. We let $I_{\pi_k} = \{i_0 + k(|I|/|\Pi|), \dots, i_0 + (k+1)(|I|/|\Pi|) - 1\}$. We begin by running `Broadcast`(Π, I, β) to store Π on all the machines. In order to distribute the points of each partition cell π evenly across I_π, we use the `PrefixSum` primitive to count for each machine-cell pair (i, k) the points that are either in cells $\{\pi_0, \dots, \pi_{k-1}\}$ or in cell π_k and stored on machines $\{i_0, \dots, i-1\}$. Using these counts, we can then quickly finish the partitioning procedure.

Each machine $i \in I$ creates a set of $|\Pi|$ *counting points* C_i to be given to the `PrefixSum` primitive. The point $q_{i,k} \in C_i$ is associated with the cell π_k. Let $\text{rank}(q_{i,k}) = k|I| + i - i_0 + 1$, and let $\text{value}(q_{i,k})$ be equal to the number of points on machine i in cell π_k. Let $C = \bigcup_{i \in I} C_i$. We run `PrefixSum`$(C, I, \text{rank}, \text{value})$. The prefix sum of counting point $q_{i,k}$ is the number of points in cell π_k stored on machines $\{i_0, \dots, i-1\}$ plus the number of points in cells $\{\pi_0, \dots, \pi_{k-1}\}$. Now, let $\{p_0, p_1, \dots\} \subseteq P$ be a set of points in arbitrary order belonging to some machine i and partition cell π_k. Let $q_{|I|+1,k} = q_{|I|,k} + \text{value}(|I|, k)$. Each value $q_{i+1,k}$ can be sent to machine i in one round of communication. Machine i then sends point p_j to machine $i_0 + k(|I|/|\Pi|) + \lfloor (q_{i+1,k} - q_{i,k} + j)/(|P|/|\Pi|) \rfloor$.

LEMMA 2.4. `Partition`(P, Π, I, β) *can be implemented by a deterministic algorithm using $O(1)$ rounds of computation, $O(s \log s)$ time, and $O(n \log n)$ total work.*

`Sample`(P, I, r, β)**:** We first describe a simple Las Vegas algorithm for computing the sample $S \subseteq P$. Each machine i selects a subset of its points S_i by selecting points independently, each with probability $p = c(r^2/|P|) \ln n$ for some constant c that depends on the VC dimension of the underlying range space. We then use the tree T to compute the total *number* of selected points in $\lambda_T + 1 = O(1)$ rounds of computation by summing the values $|S_i|$ across each machine. If this number is more than $2cr^2 \ln n$ or less than $(c/2)r^2 \ln n$, an incorrect number of points have been selected and the procedure restarts. Otherwise, all the selected points from each machine are sent to β to form the set S. A standard Chernoff bound [39] guarantees the probability of restarting even once is at most $\exp(-(c/8)r^2 \ln n) \leq 1/n^2$ for large enough c. Each sample of size $|S|$ is chosen with equal probability, so S is an $(1/r)$-approximation with probability at least $1 - 1/n^2$ as well by Theorem 2.1.

We can also choose S deterministically as follows. We use the tree T and let $\beta(r_T) = \beta$. Our sampling procedure still takes $\lambda_T + 1 = O(1)$ rounds of computation. In round i, each machine $\beta(v)$ for a node v at depth $\lambda_T - i + 1$ receives a set S_v of $O(s)$ points from its children that may be used in the $(1/r)$-approximation. If v is a leaf of T, then $\beta(v)$ simply uses the members of P initially found at $\beta(v)$. Machine $\beta(v)$

computes a (c/r)-approximation $S'_v \subseteq S_v$, for some sufficiently small constant c, of size $O(r^2 \log n) = O(s^{1/2})$ using the deterministic algorithm of Matoušek [38] in $O(s(r^2 \log r)^\delta)$ time. If $v = r_T$, then S'_v is the final $(1/r)$-approximation desired by the algorithm. When the round of computation ends, $\beta(v)$ sends set S'_v to $\beta(p(v))$, the machine corresponding to the parent of v.

LEMMA 2.5. *The above procedure computes a $(1/r)$-approximation of P.*

PROOF. Let P_v be the subset of points contained in the subtree of T rooted at v, and let λ_v be the depth of v. Fix a node v, and assume inductively that $S'_{v'}$ is a $(\gamma^{\lambda_{v'}-\lambda_T} c/r)$-approximation of $P_{v'}$ for each descendant v' of v for some constant γ. The children of v can be divided into three groups: the children where every descendant leaf has depth λ_T, children where every descendant leaf has depth $\lambda_T - 1$, and the solitary child with descendant leaves of both depths. Let V_1, V_2, and V_3 be these respective groups of child nodes. For any pair of children v_1, v_2 in a single group, there exist constants c' and c'' such that $c'|P_{v_2}| \le |P_{v_1}| \le c''|P_{v_2}|$ and $c'|S'_{v_2}| \le |S'_{v_1}| \le c''|S'_{v_2}|$. Let v' be an arbitrary node of V_i, and let $x_i = |S'_{v'}|$ and $y_i = |P_{v'}|$. Let R be an arbitrary range in our range space. We have

$$\left|\frac{|S_v \cap R|}{|S_v|} - \frac{|P_v \cap R|}{|P_v|}\right|$$
$$\le \sum_{i=1}^{3} \left|\frac{|(\bigcup_{v' \in V_i} S'_{v'}) \cap R|}{|\bigcup_{v' \in V_i} S'_{v'}|} - \frac{|(\bigcup_{v' \in V_i} P_{v'}) \cap R|}{|\bigcup_{v' \in V_i} P_{v'}|}\right|$$
$$\le \sum_{i=1}^{3} \left|\frac{|(\bigcup_{v' \in V_i} S'_{v'}) \cap R|}{c'|V_i|x_i} - \frac{|(\bigcup_{v' \in V_i} P_{v'}) \cap R|}{c''|V_i|y_i}\right|$$
$$\le \sum_{i=1}^{3} \frac{1}{|V_i|} \sum_{v' \in V_i} c''' \left(\left|\frac{|S'_{v'} \cap R|}{|S'_{v'}|} - \frac{|P_{v'} \cap R|}{|P_{v'}|}\right|\right)$$
$$\le \gamma^{\lambda_v - \lambda_T} c/2r$$

where c''' is a constant.

Therefore, S_v is a $(\gamma^{\lambda_v - \lambda_T} c/2r)$-approximation of P_v. Set S'_v is a $(\gamma^{\lambda_v - \lambda_T} c/r)$-approximation [38, Observation 4.3]. T has depth $O(1)$, so S'_{r_T} is a $(1/r)$-approximation of $P_{r_T} = P$ when c is sufficiently small.[6] □

LEMMA 2.6. *(i) $\texttt{Sample}(P, I, r, \beta)$ can be implemented by a Las Vegas algorithm using $O(1)$ rounds of computation, $O(s)$ time, and $O(|P|)$ total work, with probability at least $1 - 1/n^{\Omega(1)}$.*
(ii) The procedure can be implemented by a deterministic algorithm using $O(1)$ rounds of computation, $O(s(r^2 \log r)^\delta)$ time, and $O(|P|(r^2 \log r)^\delta)$ total work.

3. KD-TREE

Given a set of n points $P \in \mathbb{R}^d$, a *kd*-tree on P can answer an orthogonal range-reporting query in $O(n^{1-1/d} + k)$ time using $O(n)$ space, where k is the number of points lying inside the query rectangle. Each node v of the tree is associated with a d-dimensional rectangle $\square_v$, called the cell of v, with the root cell being large enough to contain the entire set P. Let $P_v = P \cap \square_v$. If $|P_v| \le 1$, v is a leaf and P_v is stored at v. If $|P_v| > 1$, then $\square_v$ is split into two cells $\square_w$ and $\square_z$ by an axis-parallel hyperplane h_v such that the interior of each cell contains at most $|P_v|/2$ points of P_v. If the depth of v is i, then h_v is parallel to the $((i \bmod d)+1)$-th axis. The cell $\square_w$ (resp. $\square_z$) is associated with the child w (resp. z) of v. Since the partitions are balanced, the tree has height $O(\log n)$. The size of the tree is $O(n)$. It is well known that the tree can be constructed in $O(n \log n)$ time by first sorting P along each axis and then constructing it level by level in a top-down manner, spending $O(n)$ time at each level. See [17] for details.

Queries are performed recursively in a top-down manner starting with the root node. Given a query rectangle ρ and a node v of the tree, there are three cases : (a) $\square_v \subseteq \rho$, then all points of P_v are reported , (b) $\square_v \cap \rho = \varnothing$, there is nothing to be done, (c) $\square_v \cap \partial\rho \ne \varnothing$, we recurse on the children of v.

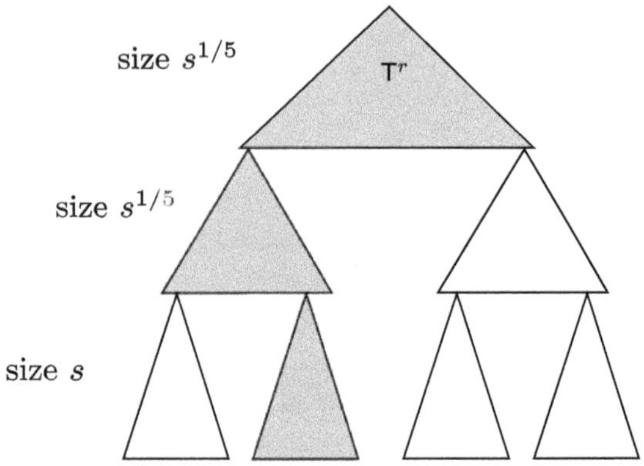

Figure 3. T^r is stored on a single machine. The leaves of T^r partition P into smaller subsets, each represented by their own recursively constructed *kd*-trees. Shaded subtrees may be stored on a single machine; however the space used on a single machine is still $O(s)$.

3.1 An MPC algorithm

We now describe an algorithm for constructing the *kd*-tree, denoted by $\mathsf{T} := \mathsf{T}(P)$, of linear size that has $O(s^{1-1/d} + k)$ query time. Our algorithm uses only $O(1)$ rounds of computation to build the tree. T is constructed and stored recursively in a distributed fashion across all machines. If $|P| = O(s)$, T is stored on a single machine and constructed using the sequential algorithm mentioned above. Otherwise we choose a parameter r, and the top subtree T^r of T containing $\log_2 r$ levels and $\Theta(r)$ leaves is built and stored on one machine, say β. The leaves of T^r partition P into subsets, each subset P_i associated with leaf l_i residing on its own consecutive set of machines I_i (the sets of machines being pairwise disjoint). For each such set P_i, $\mathsf{T}(P_i)$ is built and stored recursively using the machines in I_i. A machine may store multiple subtrees, one from each level of the recursion. However, the space used on a single machine is still $O(s)$. See Figure 3.

The key to our $O(1)$ round algorithm is the use of an ε-approximation to build the top subtree T^r. While the size of all $P_i's$, the subsets associated with the leaves of T^r, will

[6]Our procedure and its proof require a fairly small constant c. One can increase the constant by guaranteeing each set $P_{v'}$ has equal size and each set $S_{v'}$ has equal size by choosing T carefully and adding $O(n)$ additional points. While possible, doing so would be very tedious in our model.

not be *exactly* the same, as for the standard *kd*-tree, the usage of ε-approximation will ensure that $|P_i| \le 2|P|/r$, which in turn will guarantee that the height of T is at most $\log_2 n + O(1)$.

We now describe the recursive procedure `Build-kd-tree`$(S, \Box, I)$, which for a rectangle $\Box$, builds the tree $T(S)$ on $S = P \cap \Box$ using a contiguous subset I of $\frac{|S|}{n} m$ machines, say $\{\beta, \beta+1, \ldots, \beta + \frac{|S|}{n} m - 1\}$. If $|I| = 1$, i.e., $|S| = O(s)$, then $\mathsf{T}(S)$ is constructed on machine β using the sequential algorithm. So assume $|I| > 1$.

Set $r = s^{1/5}$. Let $\Sigma = (S, \mathcal{R})$ be the range space where the ranges are induced by rectangles, i.e., $\mathcal{R} = \{S \cap \Box \mid \Box \text{ is a rectangle}\}$. We compute a $(1/r)$-approximation R of Σ of size $cr^2 \ln n$, for some constant $c > 0$, by calling the (randomized) procedure `Sample`(S, r, β). We compute on machine β the top subtree T^r of the standard *kd*-tree on R so that $|\mathsf{R}_v| \le cr \ln n$ for every leaf v of T^r. The height of T^r is $\log_2 r$. Let `Partial-kd-tree`(R, r) denote this procedure. We assume this procedure returns the tree T^r as well as the partition Π' of $\Box$ induced by the rectangles associated with the leaves of T^r. By calling `Partition`(S, I, Π', β), we partition S so that for each rectangle $\Box_v$ of Π', $S_v = S \cap \Box_v$ lies in a contiguous subset I_v of machines of I; $|I_v| = \frac{|S_v|}{n} \cdot m$. If $|S_v| > \frac{2|S|}{r}$ for some leaf v of T^r, we discard R and T^r, and repeat the above step. Otherwise, we recursively compute $(S_v, \Box_v, I_v)$ for all leaves v of T^r. Algorithm 1 describes the pseudocode.

Algorithm 1 `Build-kd-tree`$(S, \Box, I)$

```
1: If |I| = 1, compute T(S) sequentially.
2: r = s^{1/5}.
3: R ← Sample(S, r, β).
4: T^r, Π' ← Partial-kd-tree(R, r).
5: Partition(S, I, Π', β).
6: for all □_v ∈ Π' in parallel do
7:     Build-kd-tree(S_v, □_v, I_v)
8: end for
```

LEMMA 3.1. *T^r has $\Theta(r)$ leaves. If R is a $(1/r)$-approximation of Σ then $|S_v| \le \frac{2|S|}{r}$ for all leaves of T^r.*

PROOF. Since the depth of T^r is $\log_2 r$, it has $\Theta(r)$ leaves. For any leaf $v \in \mathsf{T}^r$, let $\mathsf{R}_v = \mathsf{R} \cap \Box_v$. If R is a $(1/r)$-approximation of Σ, then

$$\left| \frac{|S_v|}{|S|} - \frac{|\mathsf{R}_v|}{|\mathsf{R}|} \right| \le \frac{1}{r}.$$

Therefore,

$$|S_v| \le |S| \left(\frac{1}{r} + \frac{|\mathsf{R}_v|}{|\mathsf{R}|} \right) \le |S| \left(\frac{1}{r} + \frac{cr \ln n}{cr^2 \ln n} \right) = \frac{2|S|}{r}.$$

□

Since R is a $(1/r)$-approximation with probability at least $1 - 1/n^{\Omega(1)}$, the algorithm succeeds in one attempt with probability at least $1 - 1/n^{\Omega(1)}$. The depth of recursion is $O(\log_r n)$. Since $r = s^{1/5}$ and we assume $s = n^\alpha$ for some constant $\alpha > 0$, the depth of recursion is $O(1)$. By Lemmas 2.4 and 2.6 (i), the running time of the algorithm is $O(s \log s)$ and the total work performed is $O(n \log n)$ with probabillity at least $1 - 1/n^{\Omega(1)}$.

LEMMA 3.2. *The height of the tree constructed by the algorithm is at most $\log_2 n + O(1)$.*

PROOF. The base case, i.e. $|I| = 1$, constructs a subtree of height $\log_2 s$. `Partial-kd-tree` constructs a subtree of height at most $\log_2 r$. Since the depth of the recursion is at most $\log_{r/2}\left(\frac{n}{s}\right)$, the total height of the tree is at most

$$\begin{aligned}
&\log_2 s + \log_{r/2}\left(\frac{n}{s}\right) \cdot \log_2 r \\
\le\ & \log_2 s + \log_{r/2}\left(\frac{n}{s}\right)\left(1 + \log_2\left(\frac{r}{2}\right)\right) \\
\le\ & \log_2 s + \log_2\left(\frac{n}{s}\right) + \left(\frac{\log_2(n/s)}{\log_2 r - 1}\right) \\
\le\ & \log_2 n + \frac{(1-\alpha)\log_2 n}{(\alpha/5)\log_2 n - 1} \\
=\ & \log_2 n + O(1).
\end{aligned}$$

□

Alternatively, the deterministic version of `Sample`(S, r, β) can be used to construct a $(1/r)$-approximation R. Since the deterministic procedure is more expensive, we choose $r = s^\beta$ where $\beta \le 1/5$ is a sufficiently small constant. The depth of recursion remains $O(\log_r n) = O(1/\beta)$. By Lemma 2.6 (ii), the running time of the algorithm is $s^{1+O(\beta)}$ and the total work peformed by the algorithm is $n^{1+O(\beta)}$.

3.2 Query procedure

Given a query rectangle ρ and the set of machines I containing T, in the first round we perform the query locally on the machine β containing the top subtree T^r. This gives us a set of leaves of T^r whose squares intersect with ρ. For each such leaf v, the query is performed recursively in parallel on the subtree rooted at v contained in the machines I_v.

The number of levels of recursion is the same as that of the construction algorithm, i.e., $O(1)$. This is also the number of rounds of computation required. The following lemma bounds the query procedure's work.

LEMMA 3.3. *The total work performed by the query procedure is $O(n^{1-1/d} + k)$ where k is the number of points in the query rectangle.*

PROOF. For simplicity, we prove the lemma for $d = 2$; the proof is similar for higher values of d. Let ρ be a query rectangle. The total work performed by the query procedure is $O(k)$ plus the number of nodes v in$\mathsf{T}$ such that $\partial\rho$ intersects $\Box_v$. Fix an edge e of ρ. Since the splitting line alternates between being horizontal and vertical, e intersects the cells associated with at most two grandchildren of a node v; see [17]. Let $\varphi(h)$ denote the number of nodes in a subtree of height h that intersect e. We obtain the following recurrence:

$$\varphi(h) \le 2\varphi(h-2) + 3.$$

The solution to the above recurrence is $\varphi(h) = O(2^{h/2})$. By Lemma 3.2, the height of T is at most $\log_2 n + O(1)$. We obtain that e intersects the cells associated with $O(\sqrt{n})$ nodes of T. Hence, $\partial\rho$ intersects $O(\sqrt{n})$ cells of T. This completes the proof of the lemma. □

The time required by the query procedure can be similarly bounded by $O(s^{1-1/d}+k')$, where k' is the maximum number of points reported by a single machine. We thus have the following.

THEOREM 3.4. *Let P be a set of n points in $\mathbb{R}^d$. A kd-tree on P can be constructed in the MPC model so that an orthogonal range-reporting query can be answered using $O(1)$ rounds of computation and $O(n^{1-1/d}+k)$ work, where k is the output size; the running time is $O(s^{1-1/d}+k')$ where k' is the maximum number of points reported by a machine. The tree can be built in $O(1)$ rounds, $O(n\log n)$ work, and $O(s\log s)$ time with probability $1-1/n^{\Omega(1)}$. Alternatively, for a parameter $\beta \le 1/5$, it can be constructed deterministically in $O(1/\beta)$ rounds, $s^{1+O(\beta)}$ time, and $n^{1+O(\beta)}$ work.*

3.3 Partition trees

Given a set of n points P in $\mathbb{R}^d$, Chan [15] described a partition tree that can answer simplex range-reporting queries (*i.e.*, reporting points lying in a simplex) in $O(n^{1-1/d}+k)$ time using $O(n)$ space. The expected time to construct the partition tree is $O(n\log n)$. Like *kd*-trees, partition trees represent a hierarcical decomposition of space into cells; however each cell is a simplex. The number of points within a cell decreases by a constant factor at every level, so the tree has height $O(\log n)$. Any arbitrary hyperplane intersects at most $O(n^{1-1/d})$ cells in the tree, hence a simplicial range-reporting query can be answered in $O(n^{1-1/d}+k)$ time, where k is the number of points reported.

Our algorithm for constructing a *kd*-tree can be extended to build a partition tree in the MPC model in $O(1)$ rounds of computation. Omitting all the details, we conclude the following:

THEOREM 3.5. *Let P be a set of n points in $\mathbb{R}^d$. A partition tree on P can be constructed in the MPC model so that a simplicial range-reporting query can be answered using $O(1)$ rounds of computation and $O(n^{1-1/d}+k)$ work, where k is the output size; the running time is $O(s^{1-1/d}+k')$ where k' is the maximum number of points reported by a machine. The tree can be built in $O(1)$ rounds in expected time $O(s\log s)$ and $O(n\log n)$ expected work. Alternatively, for a parameter $\beta \le 1/5$, it can be constructed deterministically in $O(1/\beta)$ rounds, $s^{1+O(\beta)}$ time, and $n^{1+O(\beta)}$ work.*

4. NN SEARCHING AND BBD-TREE

Given a set of points P and a query point q in $\mathbb{R}^d$, a $(1+\varepsilon)$-nearest neighbor (ε-NN) of q is a point in P whose distance from q is within a factor of $(1+\varepsilon)$ of the distance between q and its closest point in P. The goal is to process P into a data structure so that for a query point q, an ε-NN of q in P can be reported quickly. Arya et al. [12] proposed the *balanced-box decomposition* (BBD) tree for answering ε-NN queries. This section describes building a BBD tree in the MPC model.

Given n points $P \in \mathbb{R}^d$, the BBD-tree of P, denoted by $\mathsf{B}(P) := \mathsf{B}$, is a binary tree of height $O(\log n)$. A node $v \in \mathsf{B}$ stores a cell $\square_v$ and a representative point $p_{\square_v} \in P$ lying inside $\square_v$. The cell $\square_v$ is either a d-dimensional rectangle or the region between two nested rectangles. All rectangles have *aspect ratio* (the ratio between the longest and the shortest side) bounded by 3. The root cell is large enough to contain the entire set P. The cell $\square_v$ (with possibly a hole inside) is split into two cells $\square_w$ and $\square_z$ in one of two ways:

(a) by an axis-parallel hyperplane not intersecting the hole (if any), or

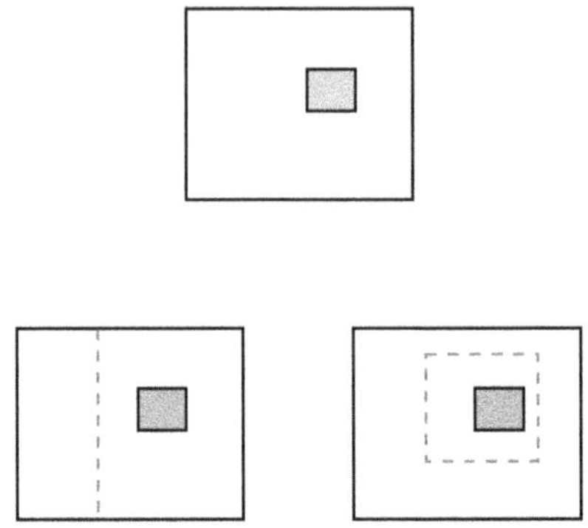

Figure 4. Two ways to divide a cell (with one hole) into two cells in a BBD tree.

(b) by an axis-parallel rectangle containing the hole (if any).

See Figure 4. The cell $\square_w$ (resp. $\square_z$) is associated with the child w (resp. z) of v. Like a *kd*-tree, a BBD-tree induces a hierarchical partition of $\mathbb{R}^d$. The *size* of a cell is the length of its longest side. Arya et al. show that cells at each node can be split in a way so that the number of points inside the cells reduces by at least a factor of 2/3 every 4 levels of B, and the size of cells decreases by at least a factor of 2/3 every $4d$ levels of the tree. Each leaf cell contains at most one input point. The crucial observation is that the range space induced by the cells in a BBD-tree has constant VC-dimension (see Section 2.1), and we can adapt the *kd*-tree construction algorithm for building the BBD-tree. The only difference is that instead of building a *kd*-tree locally in the procedure `Partial-kd-tree`, we build a local BBD-tree. The tree is also stored in a manner similar to the *kd*-tree, i.e., $\mathsf{B}(P)$ is stored in a distributed fashion across all machines.

Query procedure. We first describe a sequential query procedure that is slightly different from the one in [12], and then show how to implement it in the MPC model.

Given a query point q, the query procedure proceeds top-down, level by level. At each step, it maintains an estimate r_{curr} of distance from q to its nearest neighbor, and it stores the set of active nodes in a queue Q. Algorithm 2 summarizes the query procedure.

Algorithm 2 `NN-Query`(q)

```
r_curr ← ||q p_root||, p_curr ← p_root.
Q ← {root}.
while Q ≠ ∅ do
    v ← Dequeue(Q).
    if ||q p_v|| < r_curr then
        r_curr ← ||q p_v||, p_curr ← p_v.
    end if
    if dist(q, □_v) < r_curr/(1+ε) and v not a leaf then
        Enqueue(w, Q) for all child w of v.
    end if
end while
Return p_curr.
```

LEMMA 4.1. *The above query procedure returns an ε-NN of q.*

PROOF. Let p^* be the actual nearest neighbor of q. We show that at the end of the procedure $r_{curr} \le (1+\varepsilon)||qp^*||$.

Note that the value of r_{curr} is non-increasing throughout the procedure. Let v be the last node examined by the procedure such that $p^* \in \Box_v$. If v is a leaf, then $r_{curr} = ||qp^*||$. Otherwise, v was discarded, in which case $\text{dist}(q, \Box_v) \ge \frac{r_{curr}}{1+\varepsilon}$. However, $||qp^*|| \ge \text{dist}(q, \Box_v)$ and hence $r_{curr} \le (1+\varepsilon)||qp^*||$. □

We use the following fact, proved as Lemma 4 in [12], to bound the number of cells examined at each level.

FACT 4.2. *Given a BBD-tree for a set of data points in* $\mathbb{R}^d$, *the number of cells of size at least* $\Delta > 0$ *that intersect a ball of radius* r *is at most* $\lceil 1 + 6r/\Delta \rceil^d$.

The next lemma is then a simple variant of Lemma 5 in [12].

LEMMA 4.3. *The query procedure visits at most* $\lceil 1 + 6d/\varepsilon \rceil^d$ *cells at any level.*

The MPC implementation of the query procedure is obtained by modifying Algorithm 2 as follows. Let q be a query point, and let I be the set of machines that store B. The first round runs Algorithm 2 on the machine β containing the top subtree B^r, having $O(\log r)$ levels. When the procedure finishes traversing B^r, by Lemma 4.3, Q has $O(\frac{1}{\varepsilon^d})$ leaves of B^r. For each such leaf v, we pass the values p_{curr} and r_{curr} to the machines I_v containing the subtree B_v rooted at v, and Algorithm 2 is then run recursively in parallel on all B_v for $v \in Q$. At the end, we return the point that is nearest to q among all the points returned by these subtrees.

The query procedure performs $O(1)$ rounds of computation. The number of recursive subproblems increases by a factor of $O\left(\frac{1}{\varepsilon^d}\right)$ at every level of recursion. The subproblems at each level of recursion run in parallel and take time $O\left(\frac{1}{\varepsilon^d} \log\left(\frac{1}{\varepsilon}\right) \log n\right)$. Since the number of recursive subproblems is $\frac{1}{\varepsilon^{O(d)}}$, the total work done is $\frac{1}{\varepsilon^{O(d)}} \log n$. We thus have the following.

THEOREM 4.4. *Given a set* P *of* n *points in* $\mathbb{R}^d$, *a BBD-tree on* P *can be built in the MPC model that can answer* $(1+\varepsilon)$*-nearest neighbor queries in* $O(1)$ *computation rounds,* $O\left(\frac{1}{\varepsilon^d} \log\left(\frac{1}{\varepsilon}\right) \log n\right)$ *time and* $\frac{1}{\varepsilon^{O(d)}} \log n$ *work, for some constant* $c \ge 2$. *The tree can be built in* $O(1)$ *rounds of computation,* $O(n \log n)$ *work, and* $O(s \log s)$ *time with probabillity* $1 - 1/n^{\Omega(1)}$. *Alternatively, for a parameter* $\beta \le 1/5$, *it can be constructed deterministically in* $O(1/\beta)$ *rounds,* $s^{1+O(\beta)}$ *time, and* $n^{1+O(\beta)}$ *work.*

5. RANGE TREE

Given a set P of n points in $\mathbb{R}^d$, a d-dimensional range tree on P, denoted by $\mathsf{T} := \mathsf{T}(P)$, can answer orthogonal range queries in $O(\log^{d-1} n + k)$ time using $O(n \log^{d-1} n)$ space, where k is the number of points reported [17]. T is defined recursively. For $d = 1$, T is a sorted array or a balanced binary search tree. For $d > 1$, T consists of a primary tree $\mathsf{T}_0 := \mathsf{T}_0(P)$, and each node of T_0 stores a $(d-1)$-dimensional range tree as a secondary structure. T_0 is a balanced binary search tree on the x_1-coordinates of P. Each node $v \in \mathsf{T}_0$ stores an interval δ_v. Let P_v be the points whose x_1-coordinates lie in δ_v (the root has the set P and the interval spanning all of P). The interval δ_v is split into δ_w and δ_z so that $|P_w|, |P_z| \le \lceil |P_v|/2 \rceil$, where w and z are the children of v. Let $P_v^\perp$ denote the projection of P_v onto the hyperplane $x_1 = 0$. Node v also has a secondary data structure $\mathsf{T}(P_v^\perp)$, a $(d-1)$-dimensional range tree on $P_v^\perp$. A simple recursive argument shows that the size of T is $O(n \log^{d-1} n)$, and that it can be constructed in $O(n \log^{d-1} n)$ time after sorting P along each of its coordinates.

Let $\rho = [a_1, b_1] \times \ldots \times [a_d, b_d]$ be a query rectangle, and let $\rho^\perp = [a_2, b_2] \times \ldots \times [a_d, b_d]$. Let w_a (resp. w_b) be the leaf of the primary tree such that $a_1 \in \delta_{w_a}$ (resp. $b_1 \in \delta_{w_b}$), and let v^* be the lowest common ancestor of w_a and w_b. Let V_ρ be the set of nodes v such that either v is the right child of its parent and the left sibling of v lies on the path from v^* to w_a or v is the left child of its parent and its right sibling lies on the path from v^* to w_b. It is known [17] that $P \cap \rho = \bigcup_{v \in V_\rho} (P_v \cap \rho)$ and a point $p \in P_v \cap \rho$, for $v \in V_\rho$, if and only if $p^\perp \in P_v^\perp \cap \rho^\perp$. Hence, we recursively query $P_v^\perp$ with $\rho^\perp$ for all $v \in V_\rho$.

5.1 An MPC algorithm

Since the total space required by T is $O(n \log^{d-1} n)$, we slightly amend our model so that the memory and I/O size for each machine per round is $O(s \log^{d-1} n)$. We still have m machines with $s = n/m$ and $s \ge n^\alpha$ for some positive constant $\alpha < 1$. For each $\ell \in \{1, \ldots, d\}$, let $s_\ell = s \log^{\ell-1} n$. We assume that the input points are initially distributed so that each machine contains $O(s_1) = O(s)$ points. This assumption can be guaranteed by redistributing the points using an algorithm similar to the `Partition` procedure described in Section 2.2. Our construction procedure recursively builds primary trees for each coordinate x_ℓ using $O(s_\ell)$ memory and I/O size per machine.

T is stored in a distributed fashion. Suppose we are building an ℓth level structure of the range tree (initially, $\ell = 1$). The primary tree T_0 for this level is built and stored in a manner similar to the *kd*-tree, using a procedure we call `Build-primary-tree`(P, I, ℓ), which is nearly the same as the one used to build the *kd*-tree. The only difference is that the range space is induced by intervals over the real line, whose VC-dimension is a constant. Briefly, if $|P| = O(s_\ell)$, then T_0 is stored on a single machine and constructed using the sequential algorithm. Otherwise, we choose a parameter r, and the top subtree T_0^r of T_0 containing $\log_2 r$ levels and $\Theta(r)$ leaves is built and stored on a machine β. The leaves of T_0^r again partition P, and the subtrees of T_0 rooted at these leaves are built and stored recursively using disjoint sets of machines. We can also build T_0 deterministically in the same amount of time, work, and rounds by using a simpler deterministic `Sample` procedure since our ranges are just intervals over the real line. We omit details for the deterministic procedure.

Each node v of T_0 has a pointer to a secondary structure. Each bottom-most subtree of T_0 of size $O(s_\ell)$ stored on a single machine has all the secondary structures of its nodes stored on the same machine. These secondary structures are built using the sequential algorithm in $O(s_\ell \log^{d-\ell} n)$ time and space each. The secondary structures for the remaining nodes are stored on disjoint subsets of I. See Figure 5.

To build the secondary structures, each point p is copied $\Theta(\log |P|)$ times, sending the copies to the disjoint sets of machines that will store $\mathsf{T}(P_v^\perp)$ for all P_v containing p. We name our copying procedure Copy-points(P, I, T_0). Each machine of $I = \{i_0, i_0 + 1, \ldots\}$ contains several points lying in the leaves of T_0. To facilitate our copying procedure, we inform each machine about the nodes of T_0 that lie above its points. Let β be the machine storing T_0^r. We run the procedure Broadcast(T_0^r, I, β) and then recursively repeat the broadcast procedure with the child subtrees of T_0^r and their disjoint sets of machines. In $O(1)$ rounds, each machine will receive the ancestor subtrees for its points.

Let $\lambda = \Theta(\log |P|)$ be the depth of T_0. Intuitively, the set I is divided into λ equal-sized sets of size $|I|/\lambda$, one for each level of T_0. Sets P_v are then distributed among disjoint subsets of machines from those machines set aside for level λ. Now, consider a node v of T_0. Let λ_v be the depth of node v in T_0, $\{v_0, v_1, \ldots\}$ be the nodes of T_0 lying at depth λ_v, and $v_j = v$. Let $I_v = \{i_v, i_v + 1, \ldots, \}$ be the set of machines storing the points P_v. Let $p \in P_v$, and let i be the machine storing p. Finally, let c be a sufficiently small constant. Machine i sends a copy of p to machine $i_0 + \lambda_v \cdot cm/\lambda + cmj/(2^{\lambda_v}\lambda) + \lfloor c(i - i_v)/\lambda \rfloor - 1$. Let I'_v be the set of machines that receive the points of P_v, the set that is used to construct the secondary structure for v. Each point is copied $\Theta(\log |P|)$ times, so the total communication out of i while copying points is $O(s_\ell \log |P|)$.

Our construction algorithm concludes by recursively building the secondary structures (at the $(\ell + 1)$st level) for each node v on the set of machines I'_v. We describe our construction procedure in Algorithm 3. The procedure Build-range-tree takes ℓ as one of its parameters to account for the storage required when building each level of the data structure.

Algorithm 3 Build-range-tree(P, I, ℓ)

```
1: If |I| = 1, build T(P) sequentially.
2: T0(P) ← Build-primary-tree(P, I, ℓ).
3: Copy-points(P, I, T0).
4: for all v ∈ T0 do
5:     Build-range-tree(P, I'_v, k + 1)
6: end for
```

LEMMA 5.1. *Algorithm* Build-range-tree($P, I, 1$) *takes* $O(1)$ *rounds of computation,* $O(n \log^d n)$ *work, and* $O(s \log^d n)$ *time.*

PROOF. Consider running Build-range-tree(P, I, ℓ) for an arbitrary $\ell \in \{1, \ldots, d\}$. Step 1 can be done locally in $O(s_\ell \log^{d-\ell} n)$ time. Step 2 can be done in $O(1)$ rounds using $O(s_\ell \log n)$ time and $O(m \cdot s_\ell \log n)$ work. Copying points can also be done in one round using $O(s_\ell \log n)$ time and $O(m \cdot s_\ell \log n)$ work. There are $O(1)$ levels in the data structure, and each is built in $O(1)$ rounds, so the entire construction procedure takes $O(1)$ rounds of computation. The running time $T(\ell)$ for building ℓth and lower levels of a d-dimensional range tree with $O(s_\ell)$ points initially stored on each machine can be expressed using the recurrence $T(\ell) = O(s_\ell \log n) + T(\ell+1)$ with a base case of $T(d) = O(s_d \log n) = O(s \log^d n)$. This recurrence solves to $T(\ell) = O(s \log^d n)$. Similarly, the total work is $O(n \log^d n)$. □

5.2 Query procedure

Given a query ρ, we run it through the primary structure T_0 to get the $O(\log n)$ nodes whose secondary structures have to be probed further (as described in the beginning of Section 5). This takes $O(\log n)$ time and work and $O(1)$ rounds. Each secondary structure is then probed recursively.

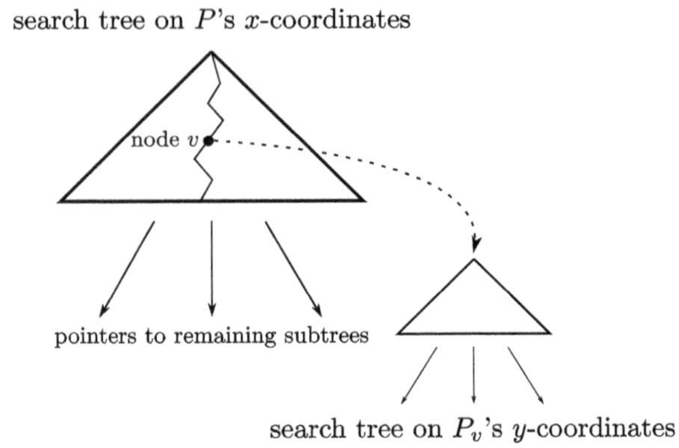

Figure 5. A distributed range tree in 2 dimensions. A balanced binary search tree over the x-coordinates is stored in a recursive manner. Each node points to a distributed binary search tree over the y-coordinates.

In total, we take $O(\log n)$ time and $O(\log^{d-1})$ work over $O(1)$ rounds finding secondary structures to probe that are stored in the distributed manner described above. The actual time and work bottleneck is the $O(\log^d n + k)$ time and work required to query the bottom-most subtrees stored entirely within individual machines.

We thus have the following theorem.

THEOREM 5.2. *Given a set P of n points in $\mathbb{R}^d$, a range tree $\mathsf{T}(P)$ on P of size $O(n \log^{d-1} n)$ can be constructed that can answer an orthogonal range-reporting query in $O(\log^d n + k)$ time and work in the MPC model in $O(1)$ rounds of computation, where k is the number of points reported. The tree can be built in $O(1)$ rounds, $O(n \log^d n)$ work, and $O(s \log^d s)$ time.*

6. CONCLUSIONS

We presented efficient algorithms to build and query *kd*-trees, range trees, and BBD-trees in the MPC model. Our algorithms were based on recursively partitioning a set of points in $\mathbb{R}^d$ by first sampling a small set of points and then computing the partition based on the sample. We believe our framework may be useful in designing efficient data structures in other domains or in the direct analysis of data.

We leave several questions open for future research. The one most closely related to our current work is whether our algorithms for *kd*-trees and BBD-trees can be made deterministic while remaining work-optimal. Our algorithms use $\mathrm{poly}(\log_s n) = O(1)$ rounds; it will be interesting to see if this can be improved to $O(\log_s n)$. A lower bound result from [27] says that $\Omega(\log_s n)$ rounds are needed to construct the data structures. Further afield, we ask what other data structures can be constructed efficiently in massively parallel models like MPC; can we efficiently build geometric data structures with more direct GIS applications such as those supporting fast point location queries? Can we efficiently parallelize geometric and topological data analysis methods such as persistent homology? Finally, can our techniques be used outside the geometric domain? In particular, it would be interesting to see if similar hierarchical data structures can be used to efficiently answer graph connectivity and related queries after some preprocessing.

7. REFERENCES

[1] http://pig.apache.org/.

[2] F. N. Afrati, A. D. Sarma, S. Salihoglu, and J. D. Ullman. Upper and lower bounds on the cost of a MapReduce computation. *Proc. VLDB Endow.*, 6(4):277–288, 2013.

[3] P. K. Agarwal, L. Arge, O. Procopiuc, and J. S. Vitter. A framework for index bulk loading and dynamization. In *Proc. 28th Int. Colloq. Automata, Lang. and Program.*, pages 115–127, 2001.

[4] P. K. Agarwal, M. de Berg, J. Gudmundsson, M. Hammar, and H. J. Haverkort. Box-trees and R-trees with near-optimal query time. *Disc. Comput. Geom.*, 28(3):291–312, 2002.

[5] P. K. Agarwal and J. Erickson. Geometric range searching and its relatives. In B. Chazelle, J. Goodman, and R. Pollack, editors, *Advances in Discrete and Computational Geometry*, pages 1–56. American Mathematical Society, 1998.

[6] A. Aggarwal and J. S. Vitter. The input/output complexity of sorting and related problems. *Comm. ACM*, 31(9):1116–1127, 1988.

[7] T. Akidau, R. Bradshaw, C. Chambers, S. Chernyak, R. J. Fernandez-Moctezuma, R. Lax, S. McVeety, D. Mills, F. Perry, E. Schmidt, and S. Whittle. The Dataflow model: A practical approach to balancing correctness, latency, and cost in massive-scale, unbounded, out-of-order data processing. *Proc. VLDB Endow.*, 8(12):1792–1803, 2015.

[8] L. Alarabi, A. Eldawy, R. Alghamdi, and M. F. Mokbel. TAREEG: a MapReduce-based system for extracting spatial data from OpenStreetMap. In *Proc. 22nd ACM SIGSPATIAL Int. Conf. Advances Geo. Inf. Systems*, pages 83–92, 2014.

[9] A. Andoni, A. Nikolov, K. Onak, and G. Yaroslavtsev. Parallel algorithms for geometric graph problems. In *Proc. 46th ACM Annu. Symp. Theory Comput.*, pages 574–583, 2014.

[10] L. Arge. External memory data structures. In J. Abello, P. M. Pardalos, and M. G. Resende, editors, *Handbook of Massive Data Sets*, pages 313–357. Springer, 2002.

[11] L. Arge, G. S. Brodal, and R. Fagerberg. Cache-oblivious data structures. In D. Mehta and S. Sahni, editors, *Handbook of Data Structures and Applications*. CRC Press, 2005.

[12] S. Arya, D. M. Mount, N. S. Netanyahu, R. Silverman, and A. Y. Wu. An optimal algorithm for approximate nearest neighbor searching in fixed dimensions. *J. ACM*, 45(6):891–923, 1998.

[13] B. Bahmani, A. Goel, and R. Shinde. Efficient distributed locality sensitive hashing. In *Proc. 21st ACM Int. Conf. Info. Know. Manage.*, pages 2174–2178, 2012.

[14] P. Beame, P. Koutris, and D. Suciu. Communication steps for parallel query processing. In *Proc. 32nd Symp. Princ. Database Systems*, pages 273–284, 2013.

[15] T. M. Chan. Optimal partition trees. *Disc. Comput. Geom.*, 47(4):661–690, 2012.

[16] B. Chazelle. *The Discrepancy Method - Randomness and Complexity*. Cambridge University Press, 2001.

[17] M. de Berg, M. van Kreveld, M. Overmars, and O. Cheong. *Computational geometry*. Springer, 3rd edition, 2000.

[18] J. Dean and S. Ghemawat. MapReduce: simplified data processing on large clusters. *Comm. ACM*, 51(1):107–113, 2008.

[19] F. Dehne, A. Fabri, and A. Rau-Chaplin. Scalable parallel geometric algorithms for coarse grained multicomputers. In *Proc. 9th Annu. Symp. Comput. Geom.*, pages 298–307, 1993.

[20] A. Eldawy, L. Alarabi, and M. F. Mokbel. Spatial partitioning techniques in SpatialHadoop. *Proc. VLDB Endow.*, 8(12):1602–1613, 2015.

[21] A. Eldawy, Y. Li, M. F. Mokbel, and R. Janardan. CG_Hadoop: computational geometry in MapReduce. In *Proc. 21st ACM SIGSPATIAL Int. Conf. Advances Geo. Inf. Systems*, pages 284–293, 2013.

[22] A. Eldawy and M. F. Mokbel. SpatialHadoop: A MapReduce framework for spatial data. In *Proc. 31st IEEE Int. Conf. Data Eng.*, pages 1352–1363, 2015.

[23] A. Ene, S. Im, and B. Moseley. Fast clustering using MapReduce. In *Proc. 17th ACM SIGKDD Int. Conf. Know. Discovery and Data Mining*, pages 681–689, 2011.

[24] G. Evangelidis, D. B. Lomet, and B. Salzberg. The hB-Pi-tree: A multi-attribute index supporting concurrency, recovery and node consolidation. *VLDB J.*, 6(1):1–25, 1997.

[25] M. Frigo, C. E. Leiserson, H. Prokop, and S. Ramachandran. Cache-oblivious algorithms. In *Proc. 40th IEEE Annu. Symp. Found. Comp. Sci.*, pages 285–298, 1999.

[26] A. Goel and K. Munagala. Complexity measures for MapReduce, and comparison to parallel computing. *CoRR*, abs/1211.6526, 2012.

[27] M. T. Goodrich. Communication-efficient parallel sorting. *SIAM J. Comput.*, 29(2):416–432, 1999.

[28] M. T. Goodrich. Parallel algorithms in geometry. In *Handbook of Discrete and Computational Geometry, Second Edition.*, pages 953–967. 2004.

[29] M. T. Goodrich, N. Sitchinava, and Q. Zhang. Sorting, searching, and simulation in the MapReduce framework. In *Proc. 22nd Int. Symp. Alg. Comput.*, pages 374–383, 2011.

[30] E. Jahani, M. J. Cafarella, and C. Ré. Automatic optimization for MapReduce programs. *Proc. VLDB Endow.*, 4(6):385–396, 2011.

[31] H. Karloff, S. Suri, and S. Vassilvitskii. A model of computation for MapReduce. In *Proc. 21st ACM-SIAM Annu. Symp. Disc. Alg.*, pages 938–948, 2010.

[32] R. Kumar, B. Moseley, S. Vassilvitskii, and A. Vattani. Fast greedy algorithms in MapReduce and streaming. *ACM Trans. Parallel Comput.*, 2(3):14:1–14:22, 2015.

[33] S. Lattanzi, B. Moseley, S. Suri, and S. Vassilvitskii. Filtering: A method for solving graph problems in MapReduce. In *Proc. 23rd ACM Annu. Symp. Parall. Alg. Arch.*, pages 85–94, 2011.

[34] K.-H. Lee, Y.-J. Lee, H. Choi, Y. D. Chung, and

B. Moon. Parallel data processing with MapReduce: A survey. *SIGMOD Rec.*, 40(4):11–20, 2012.

[35] Y. Li, P. M. Long, and A. Srinivasan. Improved bounds on the sample complexity of learning. *J. Comp. Syst. Sci.*, 62(3):516–527, 2001.

[36] D. B. Lomet and B. Salzberg. The hb-tree: A multiattribute indexing method with good guaranteed performance. *ACM Trans. Database Syst.*, 15(4):625–658, 1990.

[37] G. Malewicz, M. H. Austern, A. J. C. Bik, J. C. Dehnert, I. Horn, N. Leiser, and G. Czajkowski. Pregel: a system for large-scale graph processing. In *Proc. 2010 ACM SIGMOD Int. Conf. Manage. Data*, pages 135–146, 2010.

[38] J. Matoušek. Approximations and optimal geometric divide-and-conquer. *J. Comp. Syst. Sci.*, 50(2):203–208, 1995.

[39] M. Mitzenmacher and E. Upfal. *Probability and Computing - Randomized Algorithms and Probabilistic Analysis.* Cambridge University Press, 2005.

[40] L. Qin, J. X. Yu, L. Chang, H. Cheng, C. Zhang, and X. Lin. Scalable big graph processing in MapReduce. In *Proc. 2014 ACM SIGMOD Int. Conf. Manage. Data*, pages 827–838, 2014.

[41] K. Shvachko, H. Kuang, S. Radia, and R. Chansler. The hadoop distributed file system. In *Proc. 26th IEEE Symp. Mass Storage Syst. Tech.*, pages 1–10, 2010.

[42] L. G. Valiant. A bridging model for parallel computation. *Comm. ACM*, 33(8):103–111, 1990.

[43] T. White. *Hadoop: The Definitive Guide.* O'Reilly Media, Inc., 2012.

[44] M. Zaharia, M. Chowdhury, M. J. Franklin, S. Shenker, and I. Stoica. Spark: Cluster computing with working sets. In *Proc. 2nd USENIX Conf. Hot Topics Cloud Comput.*, pages 10–10, 2010.

Space Lower Bounds for Itemset Frequency Sketches

Edo Liberty
Yahoo Research
New York

Michael Mitzenmacher*
Harvard University
School of Engineering and Applied Sciences

Justin Thaler†
Yahoo Research
New York

Jonathan Ullman
Northeastern University
College of Computer and Information Sciences

ABSTRACT

Given a database, computing the fraction of rows that contain a query itemset or determining whether this fraction is above some threshold are fundamental operations in data mining. A uniform sample of rows is a good sketch of the database in the sense that all sufficiently frequent itemsets and their approximate frequencies are recoverable from the sample, and the sketch size is independent of the number of rows in the original database. For many seemingly similar problems there are better sketching algorithms than uniform sampling. In this paper we show that for itemset frequency sketching this is not the case. That is, we prove that there exist classes of databases for which uniform sampling is a space optimal sketch for approximate itemset frequency analysis, up to constant or iterated-logarithmic factors.

CCS Concepts

•**Theory of computation → Sketching and sampling;** Lower bounds and information complexity;

Keywords

sketching, itemset mining, marginal queries, conjunction queries, lower bounds

1. INTRODUCTION

Identifying frequent itemsets is one of the most basic and well-studied problems in data mining. Formally, we are given a binary database $\mathcal{D} \in (\{0,1\}^d)^n$ consisting of n rows and d columns, or attributes.[1] An *itemset* $T \subseteq [d]$ is a subset of the attributes, and the *frequency* f_T of T is the fraction of rows of $\mathcal{D}$ that have a 1 in all columns in T.

Computing itemset frequencies is a central primitive that can be used to solve the following problems (and countless others): given a large corpus of text files, compute the number of documents containing a specific search query; given user records, compute the fraction of users who belong to a specific demographic; given event logs, compute sets of events that are observed together; given shopping cart data, identify bundles of items that are frequently bought together.

In many settings, an approximation of f_T, as opposed to an exact result, suffices. Alternatively, in some settings it suffices to recover a single bit indicating whether or not $f_T \geq \epsilon$ for some user defined threshold ϵ; such frequent itemsets may require additional study or processing. It is easy to show that uniformly sampling poly(d/ϵ) rows from $\mathcal{D}$ and computing the approximate frequencies on the sample $\mathcal{S}(\mathcal{D})$ provides good approximations to f_T up to additive error ϵ. Our main contribution is to provide lower bounds establishing that uniform sampling is an essentially optimal *sketch*, in terms of the space/accuracy tradeoff, for many parameter regimes. Here, a sketch $\mathcal{S}(\mathcal{D})$ of a database is a bit string that enables recovery of accurate approximations to itemset frequencies.

Note that, unlike a row sample, in general a sketch is not limited to containing a subset of the database rows. Our lower bounds hold for any summary data structure and recovery algorithm that constitute a valid sketch.

1.1 Motivation

1.1.1 *The Case Against Computing Frequent Itemsets Exactly*

If the task is only to identify frequent itemsets ($f_T \geq \epsilon$ for some ϵ), it is natural to ask whether we can compute all ϵ-frequent itemsets and store only those. Assuming that only a small fraction of itemsets are ϵ-frequent, this will result in significant space saving relative to naïve solutions. The extensive literature on exact mining of frequent itemsets dates back to work of Agrawal et al. [AIS93], whose motivation stemmed from the field of market basket analysis. As the

*Michael Mitzenmacher was supported by grants NSF CNS-1228598, NSF CCF-1320231, and NSF CCF-1535795.

†Parts of this work were performed while Justin Thaler was a Research Fellow at the Simons Institute for the Theory of Computing. Supported by a Research Fellowship from the Simons Institute for the Theory of Computing.

PODS'16, June 26-July 01, 2016, San Francisco, CA, USA

ISBN 978-1-4503-4191-2/16/06...$15.00

DOI: http://dx.doi.org/10.1145/2902251.2902278

[1]Throughout, we use the terms *attributes* and *items* interchangeably. While attributes may be non-binary in many applications, any attribute with m possible values can be decomposed into $2\lceil \log m \rceil$ binary attributes, using two binary attributes to mark whether the value is 0 or 1 in the ith bit. We therefore focus on the binary case.

search space for frequent itemsets is exponentially large (i.e., size 2^d), substantial effort was devoted to developing algorithms that rapidly prune the search space and minimize the number of scans through the database. While the algorithms developed in this literature offer substantial concrete speedups over naive approaches to frequent itemset mining, they may still take time $2^{\Omega(d)}$, simply because there may be these many frequent itemsets. For example, if there is a frequent itemset of cardinality $d/10$, each of its $2^{d/10}$ subsets is also frequent. Motivated by this simple observation, there is now an extensive literature on condensed or non-redundant representations of exact frequent itemsets. Reporting only *maximal* and *closed* frequent itemsets often works well in practice, but it still requires exponential size in the worst case (see the survey [CG07]).

Irrespective of space complexity, the above methods face computational challenges. Yang [Yan04] determined that counting all frequent itemsets is #P-complete, and a bottleneck for enumeration is that the number of frequent itemsets can be exponentially large. Hamilton et al. [HCW06] provide further hardness results based on parametrized complexity. Here we observe that finding even a single frequent itemset of approximately maximal size is NP-hard. (The authors of [LLSW05] noticed this connection as well but did not mention approximation-hardness.)

Consider the bipartite graph containing n nodes (rows) on one side and d nodes (attributes) on the other. An edge exists between the two sides if and only if the row contains the attribute with value 1. Assume there exists a frequent itemset of cardinality ϵn and frequency ϵ. This itemset induces a balanced complete bipartite subgraph with ϵn nodes on each side. Likewise, any balanced complete bipartite subgraph with ϵn nodes per side implies the existence of an itemset of cardinality ϵn and frequency ϵ. Finding the maximal balanced complete bipartite subgraph is NP-hard, and approximating it requires superpolynomial time assuming that SAT cannot be solved in subexponential time [FK04]. Hence, finding an itemset of approximately maximal frequency requires superpolynomial time under the same assumption.

1.1.2 The Case for Itemset Sketches

Determining the smallest possible itemset sketches (as defined in § 1.3) is of interest in several data analysis settings.

Interactive Knowledge Discovery. Knowledge discovery in databases is often an interactive process: an analyst poses a sequence of queries to the dataset, with later queries depending on the answers to earlier ones [MT96]. For large databases, it may be inefficient or even infeasible to reread the entire dataset every time a query is posed. Instead, a user can keep around an itemset sketch only; this sketch will be much smaller than the original database, while still providing fast and accurate answers to itemset frequency queries.

Efficient Data Release. Itemset oracles capture a central problem in *data release*. Here, a data curator (such as a government agency like the US Census Bureau) wants to make a dataset publicly available. Due to their utility and ease of interpretation, the data format of choice in these settings is typically *marginal contingency tables* (marginal tables for short). For any itemset $T \subseteq [d]$ with $|T| = k$, the marginal table corresponding to T has 2^k entries, one for each possible setting of the attributes in T; each entry counts how many rows in the database are consistent with the corresponding setting of the k attributes. Notice that marginal tables are essentially just a list of itemset frequencies for $\mathcal{D}$.[2]

However, marginal tables can be extremely large (as any k-attribute marginal table has 2^k entries and there $\binom{d}{k}$ such tables), and each released table may be downloaded by an enormous number of users. Rather than releasing marginal tables in their entirety, the data curator can instead choose to release an itemset summary. This summary can be much smaller than even a single k-attribute marginal table, while still permitting any user to obtain fast and accurate estimates for the frequency of any k-attribute marginal query.

Mitigating Runtime Bottlenecks. While the use of itemset sketches cannot circumvent the hardness results discussed in Section 1.1.1, in many settings the empirical runtime bottleneck is the number of scans through the database, rather than the total runtime of the algorithm. The use of itemset sketches eliminates the need for the user to repeatedly scan or even keep a copy of the original database. The user can instead run a computationally intensive algorithm on the sketch to solve (natural approximation variants) of the hard decision or search problems. Indeed, there has been considerable work in the data mining community devoted to bounding the magnitude of errors that build up as a result of using approximate itemset frequency information when performing more complicated data mining tasks, such as rule identification [MT96].

1.2 Other Prior Work

The idea of producing condensed representations of approximate frequent itemsets is not new. Most relevant to our work, an influential paper by Mannila and Toivonen defined the notion of an *ϵ-adequate representation* of any class of queries [MT96]. Our For-All-Itemset-Frequency-Estimator sketching task essentially asks for an ϵ-adequate representation for the class of all itemset frequency queries. Mannila and Toivonen analyzed the magnitude of errors that build up when using ϵ-adequate representations to perform more complicated data mining tasks, such as rule identification. Subsequent work by Boulicaut et al. [BBR03] presented algorithms yielding ϵ-adequate representations for the class of all itemset queries, while Pei et al. [PDZH04] gave algorithms for approximating the frequency of all *frequent* itemsets to error ϵ. Unlike the trivial algorithms that we describe in Section 2, the algorithms presented in [MT96, BBR03, PDZH04] take exponential time in the worst case, and do not come with worst-case guarantees on the size of the output.

Streaming algorithms for both exact and approximate variants of frequent itemset mining have also been extensively studied, in a line of work dating back to Manku and Motwani [MM02] — see the survey [CKN08]. None of these works have been able to show that these algorithms use less space than uniform random sampling of database rows, and our results justify why. In particular, to our knowledge there has been almost no work establishing lower bounds on the space complexity of streaming algorithms for identifying approximate frequent itemsets that are better than the lower bounds that hold for the much simpler *approximate frequent items* problem (a.k.a. the heavy hitters problem). The one exception that we are aware of is work by Campagna and Pagh [CP10], who proved a simple lower bound on the space complexity of streaming algorithms that solve a variant of the

[2]More precisely, itemset frequency queries are equivalent to *monotone conjunction* queries on a database, while marginal tables are equivalent to general (non-monotone) conjunction queries.

For-All-Itemset-Frequency-Indicator sketches [CP10, Theorem 1]. Note that the lower bounds that we establish in this work apply even to summaries computed by non-streaming algorithms.

Related Work by Price [Pri14]. An earlier version of this manuscript by the first three authors [LMT14] gave lower bounds on the size of sketches for frequent itemset mining that are quantitatively weaker than the bounds presented here [LMT14]. In work subsequent to [LMT14], and contemporaneous with the work presented here, Price [Pri14] discovered a short proof of an optimal lower bound for the For-All-Itemset-Frequency-Indicator sketching problem (defined in Section 1.3 below) for itemsets T of size $|T| = O(1)$. We compare our results to Price's in more detail in Section 3.1.

1.3 Notation and Problem Statements

Throughout, $\mathcal{D} \in (\{0,1\}^d)^n$ will denote a binary database consisting of n rows and d columns, or attributes. We denote the set $\{1, \ldots, d\}$ by $[d]$. An *itemset* $T \subseteq [d]$ is a subset of the attributes; abusing notation, we also use T to refer to the *indicator vector* in $\{0,1\}^d$ whose ith entry is 1 if and only if $i \in T$. We refer to any itemset T with $|T| = k$ as a *k-itemset.* The ith row of $\mathcal{D}$ will be denoted by $\mathcal{D}(i)$, and the jth entry of the ith row will be denoted by $\mathcal{D}(i,j)$. We say that a row *contains* an itemset T if the row has a 1 in all columns in T. The *frequency* $f_T(\mathcal{D})$ of T is the fraction of rows of $\mathcal{D}$ that contain T. Alternatively, $f_T(\mathcal{D}) = \frac{1}{n}\sum_{i=1}^{n} \mathbb{I}_{\{T \subseteq \mathcal{D}(i)\}}$. We use the simplified notation f_T instead of $f_T(\mathcal{D})$ when the meaning is clear. Note that we may view a row $\mathcal{D}(i)$ of $\mathcal{D}$ as a one-row database in its own right; hence, $f_T(\mathcal{D}(i))$ equals 1 if $\mathcal{D}(i)$ contains T, and equals 0 otherwise.

We consider *four* different sketching problems that each capture a natural notion of approximate itemset frequency analysis. All four sketching problems permit randomized sketching algorithms, and require that the sketching algorithm succeeds with high probability. Success can be interpreted in two different ways: (1) with high probability, for all k-itemsets the answer is correct; or (2) for each k-itemset, with high probability the answer is correct (but it may be very unlikely that one can recover accurate estimates for all k-itemsets from the sketch simultaneously). These two different notions of success are often termed, respectively, "for all" and "for each" in the compressed sensing literature [AKW14]. Our first two problem definitions (Definitions 1 and 2) correspond to the "for all" notion, while our latter two problem problem definitions (Definitions 3 and 4) correspond to the weaker "for each" notion.

Definition 1. *A For-All-Itemset-Frequency-Indicator sketch is a tuple $(\mathcal{S}, \mathcal{Q})$. The first term $\mathcal{S}$ is a randomized sketching algorithm. It takes as input a database $\mathcal{D} \in (\{0,1\}^d)^n$, a precision ϵ, an itemset size k, and a failure probability δ. It outputs a* summary $\mathcal{S}(\mathcal{D}, k, \epsilon, \delta) \in \{0,1\}^s$ *where s is the size of the sketch in bits. The second term is a deterministic query procedure $\mathcal{Q} : \{0,1\}^s \times \{0,1\}^d \to \{0,1\}$. It takes as input a summary $\mathcal{S}$ and a k-itemset T and outputs a single bit indicating whether T is frequent in $\mathcal{D}$ or not. More precisely, for a triple of input parameters (k, ϵ, δ), the following two conditions must hold with probability $1-\delta$ over the randomness of the sketching algorithm $\mathcal{S}$, for every database $\mathcal{D}$:*

$$\forall\ k\text{-itemsets } T \text{ s.t. } f_T > \epsilon,\quad \mathcal{Q}(\mathcal{S}(\mathcal{D}, k, \epsilon, \delta), T) = 1, \quad (1)$$

and

$$\forall\ k\text{-itemsets } T \text{ s.t. } f_T < \epsilon/2,\quad \mathcal{Q}(\mathcal{S}(\mathcal{D}, k, \epsilon, \delta), T) = 0. \quad (2)$$

Note that if $\epsilon/2 \le f_T \le \epsilon$ then either bit value can be returned.

Definition 2. *A For-All-Itemset-Frequency-Estimator sketch is a tuple $(\mathcal{S}, \mathcal{Q})$. Here $\mathcal{S}$ is defined as above but $\mathcal{Q} : \{0,1\}^s \times \{0,1\}^d \to [0,1]$ outputs an approximate frequency. To be precise, the pair $(\mathcal{S}, \mathcal{Q})$ is a valid For-All-Itemset-Frequency-Estimator sketch for a triple of input parameters (k, ϵ, δ) if for every database $\mathcal{D}$:*

$$\Pr[\forall\ k\text{-itemsets } T,\ |\mathcal{Q}(\mathcal{S}(\mathcal{D}, k, \epsilon, \delta), T) - f_T| \le \epsilon] \ge 1-\delta. \quad (3)$$

Definition 3. *A For-Each-Itemset-Frequency-Indicator sketch is identical to a For-All-Itemset-Frequency-Indicator sketch, except that Equations (1) and (2) are replaced with the requirement that for every database $\mathcal{D}$ and any (single) k-itemset T:*

- *If $f_T > \epsilon$, then $\mathcal{Q}(\mathcal{S}(\mathcal{D}, k, \epsilon, \delta), T) = 1$ with probability at least $1-\delta$.*
- *If $f_T < \epsilon/2$, then $\mathcal{Q}(\mathcal{S}(\mathcal{D}, k, \epsilon, \delta), T) = 0$ with probability at least $1-\delta$.*

Definition 4. *A For-Each-Itemset-Frequency-Estimator sketch is identical to a For-All-Itemset-Frequency-Estimator sketch, except that Equation (3) is replaced with the requirement that for every database $\mathcal{D}$ and any (single) k-itemset T:* $\Pr[|\mathcal{Q}(\mathcal{S}(\mathcal{D}, k, \epsilon, \delta), T) - f_T| \le \epsilon] \ge 1-\delta$.

Definition 5. *The space complexity of a sketch, denoted by $|\mathcal{S}(n, d, k, \epsilon, \delta)|$, is the maximum sketch size generated by $\mathcal{S}$ for any database with n rows and d columns. That is,* $|\mathcal{S}(n, d, k, \epsilon, \delta)| = \max_{\mathcal{D} \in (\{0,1\}^d)^n} |\mathcal{S}(\mathcal{D}, k, \epsilon, \delta)|$.

For brevity, we typically omit the parameters $(n, d, k, \epsilon, \delta)$ when the meaning is clear, and simply write $|\mathcal{S}|$ to denote the space complexity of a sketch.

1.4 Techniques

At a high level our lower bounds are proven via the standard approach of encoding arguments. That is, to prove that $\Omega(s)$ bit sketches are necessary to solve one of the problems above, we construct a distribution over s-bit databases $\mathcal{D} \in (\{0,1\}^d)^{s/d}$ such that 1) the entropy of the distribution is $\Omega(s)$ and 2) any itemset frequency sketch can be used to reconstruct the database. Thus, the sketch must have size $\Omega(s)$ bits in the worst case.

For the simplest case of $k = 1$ and $\epsilon = 1/3$, it is easy to show that $\Omega(d)$ bits are necessary to solve every version of the itemset sketching problem, since any non-trivial estimation of the 1-itemset frequencies is sufficient to exactly encode a database consisting of a single row. In order to prove larger space lower bounds for larger values of k and smaller values of ϵ, we must show that if we are given either k-itemset queries for $k = \omega(1)$, or sketches with accuracy $\epsilon = o(1)$, then we can encode databases consisting of more than one row.

To do so, we combine some new arguments with information-theoretic techniques that were previously developed to solve problems in *differential privacy* [DMNS06]. The problem of constructing differentially private sketches for frequent itemset queries has been studied intensely in recent years (see e.g. [BCD+07, KRSU10, De12, GHRU13, TUV12, CTUW14, BUV14]; in these works frequent itemset queries are called monotone conjunction queries and sometimes contingency tables). It turns out that the techniques in these works provide exactly the information-theoretic tools that we need to devise our encoding arguments. Although the connection between the two problems appears coincidental, we believe that information-theoretic tools from the privacy literature may find future applications outside of privacy.[3]

We now sketch roughly how our encoding arguments work. Suppose we have already proven a lower bound of $\Omega(s)$ bits for any sufficiently accurate k-itemset sketch via an encoding argument. For this informal discussion, the precise definition of accuracy will not be important. We then have a high-entropy distribution $\mathcal{D}$ on databases $D \in (\{0,1\}^d)^{s/d}$ such that a sufficiently accurate sketch for k-itemset frequency queries on D must encode D. For example, as we discussed above, we can trivially start with a lower bound of d bits for any non-trivial approximation to the 1-itemset queries, although sometimes we will need to start with stronger lower bounds. We then obtain a lower bound of $\Omega(t \cdot s)$ for any sufficiently accurate sketch for k'-itemset frequency queries using the following amplification technique, inspired by the technique in [BUV14] for amplifying lower bounds in differential privacy. Roughly, the technique allows us to construct a new distribution $\mathcal{D}'$ on databases $D' \in (\{0,1\}^{2d})^{ts/d}$ such that any sufficiently accurate sketch for k'-itemset frequency queries can be used to reconstruct an accurate k-itemset sketch on each of t different draws from the distribution $\mathcal{D}$ over $(\{0,1\}^d)^{s/d}$. Since we have started by assuming that such a sketch for k-itemset frequency queries requires $\Omega(s)$ bits, we conclude that any sufficiently accurate sketch of for k'-itemset frequency queries requires $\Omega(t \cdot s)$ bits of space. The above outline is overly simplified, and the resulting reconstruction will only be approximate. Thus, we need to make sure that the approximation is good enough for our arguments to go through, especially in some of our bounds that require applying the above amplification arguments twice, where the approximation becomes even weaker.

2. NAÏVE UPPER BOUNDS

In the following we describe three trivial sketching algorithms.

DEFINITION 6 (RELEASE–DB). *This algorithm simply releases the database verbatim. In other words, the function $\mathcal{S}$ is the identity and $\mathcal{Q}$ is a standard database query.*

The space complexity of RELEASE–DB is clearly $|\mathcal{S}| = O(nd)$ and it produces exact estimates for both For-All-Itemset-Frequency-Estimator and For-All-Itemset-Frequency-Indicator sketches and their For-Each analogs.

DEFINITION 7 (RELEASE–ANSWERS). *This algorithm precomputes and stores the results to all possible queries.*

Since there are $\binom{d}{k}$ possible k-itemset queries, the space complexity of RELEASE–ANSWERS is $|\mathcal{S}| = O(\binom{d}{k})$ for For-All-Itemset-Frequency-Indicator sketches and their For-Each analogs, and $|\mathcal{S}| = O\left(\binom{d}{k}\log(1/\epsilon)\right)$ for For-All-Itemset-Frequency-Estimator sketches and their For-Each analogs. The extra $\log(1/\epsilon)$ factor is needed to represent frequencies as floating point numbers up to precision ϵ.

DEFINITION 8 (SUBSAMPLE). *This algorithm samples rows uniformly at random with replacement from the database. The samples constitute the sketch $\mathcal{S}(\mathcal{D}, k, \epsilon, \delta)$. The recovery algorithm $\mathcal{Q}(\mathcal{S}(\mathcal{D}), T)$ returns the frequency of T in the sampled rows via a standard database query.*

LEMMA 9 (SUBSAMPLING). SUBSAMPLE *outputs*

- *a valid For-All-Itemset-Frequency-Indicator sketch of space complexity $|\mathcal{S}| = O\left(\epsilon^{-1} d \log\left(\binom{d}{k}/\delta\right)\right)$,*
- *a valid For-All-Itemset-Frequency-Estimator sketch of space complexity $|\mathcal{S}| = O\left(\epsilon^{-2} d \log\left(\binom{d}{k}/\delta\right)\right)$,*
- *a valid For-Each-Itemset-Frequency-Indicator sketch of space complexity $|\mathcal{S}| = O\left(\epsilon^{-1} d \log(1/\delta)\right)$, and*
- *a valid For-Each-Itemset-Frequency-Estimator sketch of space complexity $|\mathcal{S}| = O\left(\epsilon^{-2} d \log(1/\delta)\right)$.*

PROOF. Each row sample requires d bits to represent. Thus to prove each of the above statements it suffices to bound the number of row samples required to ensure the accuracy goal. We can do so using standard probabilistic inequalities: Chernoff bounds for sums of independent random variables and union bounds. We will need the following standard forms of the Chernoff bound.

LEMMA 10. *Suppose $X_1, \ldots, X_s$ are independent random $\{0,1\}$-valued random variables with expectation p, and let $\overline{X} = \frac{1}{s}\sum_{i=1}^{s} X_i$. Then for any $\epsilon < 2e - 1$, $\mathbb{P}[\overline{X} \notin [(1-\epsilon)p, (1+\epsilon)p] \leq 2\exp(-sp\epsilon^2/4)$.*

LEMMA 11. *Suppose $X_1, \ldots, X_s$ are independent random $\{0,1\}$-valued random variables with expectation p, and let $\overline{X} = \frac{1}{s}\sum_{i=1}^{s} X_i$. Then for any $\epsilon < 1$, $\mathbb{P}[\overline{X} \notin [p - \epsilon, p + \epsilon] \leq 2\exp(-2s\epsilon^2)$.*

For-Each-Itemset-Frequency-Indicator sketches: Fix a dataset $\mathcal{D}$ and an itemset T and let $p = f_T(\mathcal{D})$. Consider drawing s independent uniform random samples of rows $\mathcal{D}'(1), \ldots, \mathcal{D}'(s)$ with replacement from $\mathcal{D}$. Let $\mathcal{D}'$ be the database consisting of the s row samples. For $i = 1, \ldots, s$, define the random variable $X_i = 1$ if $T \subseteq D'(i)$ and 0 otherwise. Let $\overline{X} = f_T(\mathcal{D}') = \frac{1}{s}\sum_{i=1}^{s} X_i$. Since the samples $\mathcal{D}'(i)$ are independent, the random variables X_i are independent. Moreover, for every i, $\mathbb{E}[X_i] = p$, and by linearity of expectation $\mathbb{E}[\overline{X}] = p$. Then by Lemma 10, we have that

$$\mathbb{P}[f_T(\mathcal{D}') \notin [p/2, 2p]] \leq 2\exp(-sp/16).$$

[3]Indeed, our use of techniques from the privacy literature may not be purely coincidental, as there is a formal (though quantitatively loose) connection between the problems of developing private and non-private sketches for itemset frequency queries. Suppose that there is a way to take any dataset $D \in (\{0,1\}^d)^n$ and create a sketch $\mathcal{S}$ of s bits that encodes the answer to every itemset query $f_T(D)$ to within additive error $\pm\epsilon$. Then we can obtain a differentially private sketch that encodes the answers to every query $f_T(D)$ to within additive error $\epsilon + O(s/n)$ as follows. Output a sketch S with probability proportional to $\exp(-n \cdot \max_T |f_T(D) - \mathcal{Q}(S,T)|)$. Our claims that the output S will be differentially private and that with high probability the chosen sketch will have additive error $\epsilon + O(s/n)$ can both be proven by an elementary analysis, or by using the fact that this algorithm is a special case of the exponential mechanism [MT07] and thus standard results can be applied. Now, suppose that we had a lower bound saying that any differentially private algorithm must incur error t/n (lower bounds in differential privacy are often of the form t/n for some t independent of n). Then we would immediately obtain a lower bound saying that any ϵ-accurate sketch for itemsets requires $s = \Omega(t - \epsilon n)$ bits. Thus, accuracy lower bounds in differential privacy *immediately* imply space lower bounds for the associated sketching problem. However, this generic connection rarely leads to bounds that are quantitatively tight.

The right hand side will be at most δ if $s \geq 16\ln(2/\delta)/p$ for a sufficiently large constant C. From this bound, we can deduce that, for For-Each-Itemset-Frequency-Indicator sketches, it suffices to take $s = O(\epsilon^{-1}\log(1/\delta))$ row samples to ensure that the accuracy requirement of Definition 3 is satisfied.

For-Each-Itemset-Frequency-Estimator skeches: The setup is the same, except that we apply Lemma 11 instead of Lemma 10 to obtain:

$$\mathbb{P}[f_T(\mathcal{D}') \notin [p-\epsilon, p+\epsilon]] \leq 2\exp(-2s\epsilon^2).$$

The right hand side will be at most δ if $s \geq \epsilon^{-2}\ln(2/\delta)$. Thus, for For-Each-Itemset-Frequency-Estimator sketches it suffices to take $s = O(\epsilon^{-2}\log(1/\delta))$ row samples to ensure that the accuracy requirement of Definition 4 is satisfied.

For-All-Itemset-Frequency-Indicator sketches: By the analysis above, we know that for any $\delta' > 0$ and any itemset T, $f_T(\mathcal{D}')$ is accurate with probability at least $1-\delta'$ if $s = O(\epsilon^{-1}\log(1/\delta'))$. Thus, by a union bound

$$\mathbb{P}[\exists\, T \subseteq [d], |T| = k,\ f_T(\mathcal{D}') \text{ is not accurate}] \leq \binom{d}{k}\mathbb{P}[f_T(\mathcal{D}') \text{ is not accurate}] \leq \binom{d}{k}\delta'.$$

Now, by setting $\delta' = \delta/\binom{d}{k}$, we can see that it suffices to take $s = O(\epsilon^{-1}\log(\binom{d}{k}/\delta))$ samples to ensure accuracy.

For-All-Itemset-Frequency-Estimator sketches: Here we apply the same union bound argument to our analysis of For-Each-Itemset-Frequency-Estimator sketches. We can easily see that it suffices to take $s = O(\epsilon^{-2}\log(\binom{d}{k}/\delta))$. $\square$

For any setting of the parameters $(n, d, k, \epsilon, \delta)$, the minimal space usage among the above three trivial algorithms constitutes our naïve upper bound for all four sketching problems that we consider, formalized in Theorem 12 below.

THEOREM 12. *(a) For any (k, ϵ, δ), there is a randomized algorithm that, given any database $\mathcal{D} \in (\{0,1\}^d)^n$, outputs a For-All-Itemset-Frequency-Indicator sketch of size* $O\left(\min\left\{nd, \binom{d}{k}, \epsilon^{-1}d\log\left(\binom{d}{k}/\delta\right)\right\}\right)$.

(b) For any (k, ϵ, δ), there is a randomized algorithm that, given any database $\mathcal{D} \in (\{0,1\}^d)^n$, outputs a For-All-Itemset-Frequency-Estimator sketch of size $O\left(\min\left\{nd, \binom{d}{k}\log(1/\epsilon), \epsilon^{-2}d\log\left(\binom{d}{k}/\delta\right)\right\}\right)$.

(c) For any (k, ϵ, δ), there is a randomized algorithm that, given any database $\mathcal{D} \in (\{0,1\}^d)^n$, outputs a For-Each-Itemset-Frequency-Indicator sketch of size $O\left(\min\left\{nd, \binom{d}{k}, \epsilon^{-1}d\log(1/\delta)\right\}\right)$.

(d) For any (k, ϵ, δ), there is a randomized algorithm that, given any database $\mathcal{D} \in (\{0,1\}^d)^n$, outputs a For-Each-Itemset-Frequency-Estimator sketch of size $O\left(\min\left\{nd, \binom{d}{k}\log(1/\epsilon), \epsilon^{-2}d\log(1/\delta)\right\}\right)$.

3. LOWER BOUNDS

In this section, we turn to proving lower bounds on the size of For-All-Itemset-Frequency-Indicator and For-All-Itemset-Frequency-Estimator sketches. Notice that the algorithms RELEASE–ANSWERS and SUBSAMPLE produce sketches whose size is independent of n; hence, it is impossible to prove lower bounds that grow with n. Consequently, we state our lower bounds in terms of the parameters $(d, k, 1/\epsilon)$, with all of our lower bounds holding as long as n is sufficiently large relative to these three parameters. This parameter regime — with n a sufficiently large polynomial in d, k, and $1/\epsilon$ — is consistent with typical usage scenarios, where the number of rows in a database far exceeds the number of attributes. In our formal theorem statements, we make explicit precisely how large a polynomial n must be in terms of d, k, and $1/\epsilon$ for the lower bound to hold.

Each of our lower bounds also requires d, k, and $1/\epsilon$ to satisfy certain mild technical relationships with each other — for example, Theorems 13 and 14 require that $1/\epsilon < \binom{d/2}{k-1}$. In all cases, the assumed technical relationship between the parameters is necessary or close to necessary for the claimed lower bound to hold. For instance, the $\Omega(d/\epsilon)$ lower bound of Theorems 13 and 14 is false for $1/\epsilon \gg \binom{d/2}{k-1}$, as the algorithm RELEASE–ANSWERS would output a sketch of size $o(d/\epsilon)$ in this parameter regime.

3.1 Overview of the Lower Bounds

We now formally state all of the lower bounds that we prove, and place our results in context. Throughout this section, we assume that the failure probability δ of the sketching algorithm is a constant less than one.

Resolving the complexity of For-Each-Itemset-Frequency-Indicator sketches. The main result stated in this section is a relatively simple $\Omega(d/\epsilon)$ lower bound for the For-Each-Itemset-Frequency-Indicator sketching problem (Theorem 14 below), which is essentially optimal despite its simplicity. For expository purposes, it will be convenient to first state an analogous lower bound for the (harder) For-All-Itemset-Frequency-Indicator sketching problem. In Section 3.2, we prove the For-All lower bound first, and then explain how to modify the proof to handle the For-Each case.

THEOREM 13. *Let $k \geq 2$. Suppose that $1/\epsilon \leq \binom{d/2}{k-1}$, and the failure probability $\delta < 1$ is constant. Then for $n \geq 1/\epsilon$, the space complexity of any valid For-All-Itemset-Frequency-Indicator sketch is $|\mathcal{S}(n, k, d, \epsilon, \delta)| = \Omega(d/\epsilon)$.*

THEOREM 14. *Let $k \geq 2$. Suppose that $1/\epsilon \leq \binom{d/2}{k-1}$, and $\delta < 1/3$. Then for $n \geq 1/\epsilon$, the space complexity of any valid For-Each-Itemset-Frequency-Indicator sketch is $|\mathcal{S}(n, k, d, \epsilon, \delta)| = \Omega(d/\epsilon)$.*

Theorem 14 is tight whenever it applies (i.e., when $1/\epsilon < \binom{d/2}{k-1}$), as it matches the $O(d/\epsilon)$ upper bound obtained by the algorithm SUBSAMPLE for the For-Each-Itemset-Frequency-Indicator sketching problem (see Theorem 12). And the algorithm RELEASE–ANSWERS achieves a summary size of $\binom{d}{k}$ for the For-Each-Itemset-Frequency-Indicator sketching problem, which is asymptotically optimal when $1/\epsilon \geq \binom{d/2}{k-1}$ and $k = O(1)$. Therefore, Theorems 12 and 14 together precisely resolve the complexity of For-Each-Itemset-Frequency-Indicator sketches for all values of d and ϵ, when $k = O(1)$.

Resolving the complexity of For-All-Itemset-Frequency-Indicator sketches. Theorem 13 is tight for For-All-Itemset-Frequency-Indicator sketches when $1/\epsilon$ is small relative to the other input parameters n or d. In particular, when $n = 1/\epsilon$, RELEASE–DB provides a trivial matching sketch that is $O(nd) = O(d/\epsilon)$ bits in size. In addition, when $k = O(1)$ and $1/\epsilon \geq \binom{d/2}{k-1}$, RELEASE–ANSWERS provides a matching sketch that is $O(\binom{d}{k}) = O(d/\epsilon)$ bits in size.

The tightness of Theorem 13 in these parameter regimes is arguably surprising, as it shows that the For-All-Itemset-Frequency-Indicator sketching problem is *equivalent* in complexity to its For-Each analog in these regimes.

However, when $1/\epsilon \ll \binom{d/2}{k-1}$, Theorem 13 is not tight for For-All-Itemset-Frequency-Indicator sketches, because it has suboptimal dependence on d and k. Our main result for the For-All-Itemset-Frequency-Indicator sketching problem establishes a tight lower bound, matching the $O(\epsilon^{-1} d \log \binom{d}{k})$ upper bound for the problem obtained by the algorithm SUBSAMPLE.

THEOREM 15. *Let $k \geq 3$, and suppose that $1/\epsilon = O\left(\binom{d/3}{\lfloor (k-1)/2 \rfloor}\right)$ and the failure probability $\delta < 1$ is a constant. Then for any $n \geq kd\log(d/k)/\epsilon$, the space complexity of any valid For-All-Itemset-Frequency-Indicator sketch is $|\mathcal{S}(n,k,d,\epsilon,\delta)| = \Omega(kd\log(d/k)/\epsilon)$.*

Comparison to Price's work. Price independently proved an $\Omega(d\log(d)/\epsilon)$ lower bound on the size of For-All-Itemset-Frequency-Indicator sketches for $k \geq 2$ and $1/\epsilon \leq d^{.99}$ [Pri14]. This matches the lower bound of Theorem 15 for any $k = O(1)$, but not for $k = \omega(1)$. One advantage of Price's result is that it holds for $k = 2$ and any value of ϵ satisfying $1/\epsilon \leq d^{.99}$; in contrast, Theorem 15 holds for $k \geq 3$. We remark that our proof of Theorem 15 actually establishes the $\Omega(d\log(d))$ lower bound even for $k = 2$, but our extension of the proof to sub-constant values of ϵ requires $k \geq 3$.

Essentially resolving the complexity of For-All-Itemset-Frequency-Estimator sketches. Theorem 16 below establishes a lower bound for the For-All-Itemset-Frequency-Estimator sketching problem with a quadratically stronger dependence on $1/\epsilon$, relative to the linear dependence that is necessary and sufficient for the For-All-Itemset-Frequency-Indicator problem. Our lower bound matches the space usage of SUBSAMPLE (cf. Lemma 9) up to a factor of $\log_{(q)}(1/\epsilon)$ for any desired constant $q > 0$, where $\log_{(q)}$ denotes the logarithm function iterated q times (e.g. $\log_{(3)}(x) = \log\log\log(x)$).[4]

THEOREM 16. *Fix any integer constants $c \geq 2$, $q \geq 1$, and let $\delta < 1$ be a constant. Let $k \geq c+1$, let d, ϵ satisfy $1/\epsilon^2 \leq d^{c-1}/\log_{(q)}(1/\epsilon^2)$, and let $\delta < 1$ be a constant. Let $\mathcal{S}$ be a For-All-Itemset-Frequency-Estimator sketching algorithm capable of answering all k-itemset frequency queries to error $\pm\epsilon$ on databases $\mathcal{D} \in \left(\{0,1\}^d\right)^n$ for any $n > d\log(d/k)\log_{(q)}(1/\epsilon^2)/\epsilon^2$. Then*

$$|\mathcal{S}(n,d,k,\epsilon,\delta)| = \Omega\left(\frac{kd\log(d/k)}{\epsilon^2\log_{(q)}(1/\epsilon)}\right).$$

For illustration, consider fixing the constants $c = q = 10$. Then theorem says that for every $k \geq 11$, if $1/\epsilon = O(d^{4.5}/\log_{(10)}(d))$, and the database size n is sufficiently large, then there is a space lower bound of

$$|\mathcal{S}| = \Omega\left(kd\log(d/k)/\left(\epsilon^2\log_{(10)}(1/\epsilon)\right)\right).$$

Finally, we use a simple reduction to show that the above theorem also implies a lower bound for the For-Each case, which is optimal up to a factor of $\log_{(q)}(1/\epsilon)$.[5]

THEOREM 17. *Fix any integer constants $c \geq 2$, $q \geq 1$. Let $k \geq \max\{3, c+1\}$, let d, ϵ satisfy $1/\epsilon^2 \leq d^{c-1}/\log_{(q)}(1/\epsilon^2)$, and let $\delta < 1/2$ be a constant. Let $\mathcal{S}$ be an For-Each-Itemset-Frequency-Estimator sketching algorithm capable of answering any (single) k-itemset frequency queries to error $\pm\epsilon$ on databases $\mathcal{D} \in \left(\{0,1\}^d\right)^n$ for any $n > d\log(d/v)\log_{(q)}(1/\epsilon^2)/\epsilon^2$. Then $|\mathcal{S}(n,d,k,\epsilon,\delta)| = \Omega\left(\frac{d}{\epsilon^2\log_{(q)}(1/\epsilon)}\right)$.*

3.2 Lower Bound Proofs for Itemset-Frequency-Indicator Sketches

3.2.1 *First Lower Bound Proofs: Theorems 13 and 14*

We begin by proving our two simplest bounds (Theorems 13 and 14). Recall that the former applies to For-All-Itemset-Frequency-Indicator sketches, and the latter applies even to their For-Each analogs. The proofs consider databases in which even a single appearance of an itemset already makes it frequent. We show that, unsurprisingly, essentially no compression is possible in this setting. (For simplicity, we assume that $1/\epsilon$ is an integer throughout.)

PROOF OF THEOREM 13. Our proof uses an encoding argument. Consider the following family of databases. There will be $1/\epsilon$ possible settings for each row; as $n \geq 1/\epsilon$, some rows may be duplicated. For expository purposes, we begin by describing the setting with $n = 1/\epsilon$, in which case there are no duplicated rows. The first $d/2$ columns in each row contain a unique set of exactly $k-1$ attributes. The last $d/2$ attributes in each row are unconstrained. The only minor technicality is that to ensure that each row can receive a unique set of $k-1$ items from the first $d/2$ attributes, we require $1/\epsilon \leq \binom{d/2}{k-1}$.

Given a valid For-All-Itemset-Frequency-Indicator or For-All-Itemset-Frequency-Estimator sketch for this database, one can recover all of the values $\mathcal{D}(i,j)$ where $j \geq d/2$ as follows. For any $j \geq d/2$, let $T_{i,j}$ be a set of k attributes, where the first $k-1$ attributes in $T_{i,j}$ correspond to the $k-1$ attributes in the first $d/2$ columns in the ith row, and the final attribute in $T_{i,j}$ is j. Notice that $T_{i,j} \in \mathcal{D}$ if and only if $\mathcal{D}(i,j) = 1$. Moreover, since $n = 1/\epsilon$ we have that $f_T \geq \epsilon$ if and only if $\mathcal{D}(i,j) = 1$. Given a valid For-All-Itemset-Frequency-Indicator or For-All-Itemset-Frequency-Estimator sketch for this database, one can iterate over all

[4] An anonymous reviewer has pointed out that subsequent work of Van Gucht et al. [GWWZ15, Theorem 6] can be combined with our amplification techniques to remove the $\log_{(q)}(1/\epsilon)$ factor in the bound of Theorem 16, when $\epsilon > 1/\sqrt{d}$; the resulting bound matches the size of the sketch produced by SUBSAMPLE up to a constant factor. (Note that Theorem 16 holds even for values of ϵ smaller than $1/\sqrt{d}$, whenever $k > 3$.) In more detail, the proof of [GWWZ15, Theorem 6] implies an $\Omega(d/\epsilon^2)$ lower bound on the size of any For-All-Itemset-Frequency-Estimator sketch answering 99% of all 2-itemset queries, when $\epsilon > 1/\sqrt{d}$. By combining this result with our amplification techniques, it is possible to prove an $\Omega\left(\frac{kd\log(d/k)}{\epsilon^2}\right)$ lower bound on the size of any For-All-Itemset-Frequency-Estimator sketch answering all k-itemset queries for $k \geq 3$, whenever $\epsilon > 1/\sqrt{d}$.

[5] Footnote 4 implies that one can remove the $\log_{(q)}(1/\epsilon)$ factor in the bound of Theorem 17 when $\epsilon > 1/\sqrt{d}$. The resulting bound matches the size of the sketch produced by SUBSAMPLE in this parameter regime up to a constant factor.

itemsets $T_{i,j}$ to recover all the values $\mathcal{D}(i,j)$ where $j \geq d/2$. Since these are an unconstrained set of $d/(2\epsilon)$ bits, the space complexity of storing them (with $1-\Omega(1)$ failure probability) is $\Omega(d/\epsilon)$ by standard information theory.

For n a multiple of $1/\epsilon$, we construct a database with $1/\epsilon$ rows as above, and duplicate each row $n\epsilon$ times; in this case we have $f_T \geq \epsilon$ if and only if $\mathcal{D}(i,j) = n\epsilon$. More generally, when $n \geq 1/\epsilon$, duplicating each row at least $\lfloor n\epsilon \rfloor$ times, we have $f_T \geq \epsilon$ if and only if $\mathcal{D}(i,j) \geq \lfloor n\epsilon \rfloor$. □

We remark that the condition $1/\epsilon \leq \binom{d/2}{k-1}$ can be relaxed to $1/\epsilon \leq \binom{\alpha d}{k-1}$ for any constant $\alpha < 1$, by a simple modification of the proof. We now extend the argument used to prove Theorem 13 to the For-Each case.

Proof of Theorem 14. Recall that in the setting of one-way randomized communication complexity, there are two parties, Alice and Bob. Alice has an input $x \in \mathcal{X}$, Bob has an input $y \in \mathcal{Y}$, and Alice and Bob both have access to a public random string r. Their goal is to compute $f(x,y)$ for some agreed upon function $f\colon \mathcal{X} \times \mathcal{Y} \to \{0,1\}$. Alice sends a single message $m(x,r)$ to Bob. Based on this message, Bob outputs a bit, which is required to equal $f(x,y)$ with probability at least $2/3$.

We consider the well-known INDEX function. In this setting, Alice's input x is an N-dimensional binary vector, Bob's input y is an index in $[N]$, and $f(x,y) = x_y$, the y'th bit of x. It is well-known that one-way randomized communication protocols for INDEX require communication $\Omega(N)$ [Abl96]. We show how to use any For-Each-Itemset-Frequency-Indicator sketching algorithm $\mathcal{S}$ to obtain a one-way communication protocol for INDEX on vectors of length $N = (d/2) \cdot 1/\epsilon$, with communication proportional to $|\mathcal{S}(n,d,\epsilon,k,\delta)|$.

Specifically, let (n,d,k,ϵ,δ) be as in the statement of the theorem. Consider any Boolean vector $x \in \{0,1\}^N$, where $N = (d/2) \cdot 1/\epsilon$. We associate each index $y \in [N]$ with a unique k-itemset $T_y \subseteq [d]$ of the following form: the first $k-1$ attributes in T_y are each in $[d/2]$, and the final attribute in T_y is in $\{d/2+1,\ldots,d\}$. The proof of Theorem 13 established the following fact: given any vector $x \in \{0,1\}^N$, there exists a database $\mathcal{D}_x$ with d columns and n rows satisfying the following two properties for all $y \in [N]$:

$$x_y = 1 \Longrightarrow f_{T_y}(\mathcal{D}_x) \geq \epsilon, \text{ and } x_y = 0 \Longrightarrow f_{T_y}(\mathcal{D}_x) = 0 < \epsilon/2. \tag{4}$$

Hence, we obtain a one-way randomized protocol for the INDEX function as follows: Alice sends to Bob $\mathcal{S}(\mathcal{D}_x,k,\epsilon,\delta)$ at a total communication of $|\mathcal{S}(n,d,\epsilon,k,\delta)|$ bits, and Bob outputs $\mathcal{Q}(\mathcal{S}(\mathcal{D}_x,k,\epsilon,\delta),T_y)$. It follows immediately from Equation (4) and Definition 3 that Bob's output equals x_y with probability $1-\delta$. We conclude that $|\mathcal{S}(n,d,\epsilon,k,\delta)| = \Omega(N) = \Omega(d/\epsilon)$, completing the proof. □

3.2.2 A Tight Lower Bound for For-All-Itemset-Frequency-Indicator Sketches: Proof of Theorem 15

Our proof of Theorem 15 is inspired by an approach from [BUV14] for "bootstrapping" two weak privacy lower bounds into a stronger lower bound.

Proof of Theorem 15. We begin by proving an $\Omega(kd\log(d/k))$ lower bound for $\epsilon = 1/50$ and every $k \geq 2$ (the specific choice $\epsilon = 1/50$ is for convenience; the lower bound holds for any suitably small constant). We then use the ideas underlying the proof of Theorem 14 to extend the lower bound to sub-constant values of ϵ, for any $k \geq 3$.

The case of $\epsilon = 1/50$. We begin by recalling a basic combinatorial fact about k-itemset frequency queries on databases with d attributes.

Fact 18. *For any $k' \geq 1$, let $v = k' \cdot \log(d/k')$. There exist strings $x_1,\ldots,x_v \in \{0,1\}^d$ such that for every string $s \in \{0,1\}^v$, there is a k'-itemset T_s such that $f_{T_s}(x_i) = s_i$ for all $i \in [v]$.*

Proof of Fact 18. It is well-known that the set of k'-itemset frequency queries (equivalently, k'-way monotone conjunction queries), when evaluated on d-bit vectors (i.e., on d-attribute database rows), has VC dimension at least $k' \cdot \log(d/k')$. The desired strings $x_1,\ldots,x_v$ are simply the shattered set whose existence is guaranteed by having VC dimension v. It is also not difficult to directly construct the shattered set; we provide such a direct construction in Appendix A for completeness. □

Let $k' = k-1$, let $v = (k-1)\log(d/(k-1))$, and let $x_1,\ldots,x_v \in \{0,1\}^d$ be the strings promised by Fact 18. Let $y_1,\ldots,y_v \in \{0,1\}^d$ be an arbitrary set of v strings of length d. We will show how to construct a database $\mathcal{D}$ with v rows and $2d$ columns such that, with probability at least $1-\delta$, at least 96% of the dv bits in $(y_1,\ldots,y_v)$ can be reconstructed from any For-All-Itemset-Frequency-Indicator sketch $\mathcal{S}(\mathcal{D},k,1/50,\delta)$. This will imply an $\Omega(dv)$ space lower bound. Specifically, define row i of $\mathcal{D}$ to be

$$\mathcal{D}(i) := (x_i, y_i). \tag{5}$$

That is, the first d bits in $\mathcal{D}(i)$ are equal to x_i and the last d bits are equal to y_i.

The key observation behind the reconstruction of the y_i's is that, given *exact* answers to all k-way itemset frequency queries, one can compute the inner product between the last d columns of $\mathcal{D}$ and any desired vector. Moreover, it is easy to see that, given sufficiently many inner products, any column of $\mathcal{D}$ can be exactly reconstructed. However, For-All-Itemset-Frequency-Indicator sketches do not provide exact answers to itemset frequency queries; they merely indicate whether the frequency of an itemset is larger than ϵ or smaller than $\epsilon/2$. Nonetheless, we show that in order to reconstruct 96% of the bits in any given column of $\mathcal{D}$, it is enough to know, for sufficiently many vectors, whether the inner product of the column with the vector is larger than $\epsilon = 1/50$ or smaller than $\epsilon/2 = 1/100$.

In more detail, fix a column $j \in \{d+1,\ldots,2d\}$. Let $t := (y_{1,j},\ldots,y_{v,j}) \in \{0,1\}^v$ be the bits in this column of $\mathcal{D}$. Fix a string s in $\{0,1\}^v$, and for any $j \in [d]$, let $T_{s,j} = T_s \cup \{j\}$, where T_s is defined as in Fact 18. We claim that the correct answer to the itemset frequency query $f_{T_{s,j}}(\mathcal{D})$ is $\langle s,t\rangle/v$. To see this, notice that by the definition of $\mathcal{D}$ (Equation (5)), $T_{s,j}$ is contained in any row i of $\mathcal{D}$ such that $s_i = y_{ij} = 1$, and $T_{s,j}$ is not contained in any other rows. Hence, $f_{T_{s,j}}(\mathcal{D}) = \frac{1}{v}|\{i : s_i = 1, y_{ij} = 1\}| = \langle s,t\rangle/v$.

It follows that any For-All-Itemset-Frequency-Indicator sketch $\mathcal{S}$ of $\mathcal{D}$ that provides answers with error parameter $\epsilon = 1/50$ for all k-itemsets, provides a bit b_s for every $s \in \{0,1\}^v$ such that the following holds: $b_s = 1$ if $\langle s,t\rangle/v > \epsilon$, and $b_s = 0$ if $\langle s,t\rangle/v < \epsilon/2$. The following lemma implies that we can use the b_s values to reconstruct a vector t' that is close to t in Hamming distance.

Lemma 19. *Suppose for every $s \in \{0,1\}^v$, we are given a bit b_s satisfying $b_s = 1$ if $\langle s,t\rangle/v > \epsilon$, and $b_s = 0$ if $\langle s,t\rangle/v < \epsilon/2$. Let $t' \in \{0,1\}^v$ be any vector that is consistent with all of the b_s values, in the sense that $\langle s,t'\rangle/v > \epsilon$ for all s such* *that $b_s = 1$, and $\langle s, t' \rangle / v < \epsilon/2$ for all s such that $b_s = 0$. Then the Hamming distance between t and t' is at most $v/25$.*

PROOF OF LEMMA 19. Consider any vector $t' \in \{0,1\}^v$ such that t and t' differ in more than $v/25$ fraction of bits. Then there must a set of coordinates $S \subseteq [v]$ of size at least $v/50$ such that at least one of the two conditions is satisfied: (a) $t'_j = 1$ and $t_j = 0$ for all $j \in S$, or (b) $t'_j = 0$ and $t_j = 1$ for all $j \in S$.

Assume without loss of generality that Condition (a) is satisfied (the proof in the case that Condition (b) is satisfied is analogous). Consider the vector $s \in \{0,1\}^v$ that is the indicator vector of S. Then $\langle s, t \rangle = 0$, so $b_s = 0$. However, $\langle s, t' \rangle \geq v/50$. This implies that t' is not consistent with the value b_s returned by the For-All-Itemset-Frequency-Indicator sketch, proving the lemma. □

Lemma 19 implies that, for any $k \geq 2$, given the For-All-Itemset-Frequency-Indicator sketch $\mathcal{S}(\mathcal{D}, k, 1/50, \delta)$, we can recover at least 96% of the bits of $(y_1, \ldots, y_v)$ with probability at least $1-\delta$. Suppose we let $(y_1, \ldots, y_v)$ be the error-corrected encoding of a vector $(y'_1, \ldots, y'_z) \in \{0,1\}^z$, using a code with constant rate that is uniquely decodable from 4% errors (e.g. using a Justesen code [Jus72]). Then $z = \Omega(v)$, and it follows from the above that $(y'_1, \ldots, y'_z)$ can be *exactly* reconstructed from $\mathcal{S}(\mathcal{D}, k, 1/50, \delta)$ with probability at least $1-\delta$. Hence, $\mathcal{S}(\mathcal{D})$ allows for exact reconstruction of $z = \Omega(dv)$ arbitrary bits with probability $1-\delta$. Basic information theory then implies that $|\mathcal{S}| = \Omega(dv) = \Omega\left(kd \log(d/k)\right)$.

The case of $\epsilon = o(1)$. For any $k \geq 3$, suppose that we are given a For-All-Itemset-Frequency-Indicator sketching algorithm $\mathcal{S}$ that is capable of answering For-All-Itemset-Frequency-Indicator queries with error parameter ϵ for all k-itemsets. For simplicity, we assume k is odd. At a high level, we show that, given $m = \frac{1}{50\epsilon}$ independent databases $\mathcal{D}_i$, each with v rows and $2d$ columns, we can construct a single "larger" database $\mathcal{D}$ with mv rows and $3d$ columns such that the following holds: for *every* $\mathcal{D}_i$, $\mathcal{S}(\mathcal{D}, k, \epsilon, \delta)$ can be used to answer all For-All-Itemset-Frequency-Indicator queries on $\mathcal{D}_i$ with error parameter $\epsilon' = 1/50$ for all $(k+1)/2$-itemsets. Since we have assumed $k \geq 3$, it holds that $(k+1)/2 \geq 2$; hence, we can apply our earlier analysis to conclude that any such summary for $\mathcal{D}_i$ contains $\Omega\left(kd \log(d/k)\right)$ bits of information, in the sense that it can encode an arbitrary bit vector of this length. It follows that $\mathcal{S}(\mathcal{D}, k, \epsilon, \delta)$ contains $\Omega\left(kd \log(d/k)/\epsilon\right)$ bits of information, proving the theorem. Details follow.

Let $T_1, \ldots, T_m \subseteq [d]$ be distinct $((k-1)/2)$-itemsets (note that as in the proof of Theorem 13, we can indeed choose m such T_i's as long as $1/\epsilon < \binom{d}{(k-1)/2}$). Now consider any m independent databases $\mathcal{D}_1, \ldots, \mathcal{D}_m$, each with v rows and $2d$ columns. We construct a new $(mv) \times 3d$ database $\mathcal{D}$ by appending the d-bit indicator vector of T_i to each row of $\mathcal{D}_i$, and letting $\mathcal{D}$ be the concatenation of all of the resulting databases.

For each T_i, let $T' \subseteq [3d]$ be defined via $T'_i = \{j + 2d : j \in T_i\}$. That is, T'_i is simply T "shifted" to operate on the final d of the $3d$ attributes over which the "larger" database $\mathcal{D}$ is defined. Let $T^* \subseteq [2d]$ be any $(k+1)/2$-itemset, and for each $i \in [m]$, let $T^*_i \subseteq [3d]$ be the k-itemset defined via: $T^*_i = T^* \cup T'_i$. Observe that $f_{T^*}(\mathcal{D}_i) = m \cdot f_{T^*_i}(\mathcal{D}')$. Hence, $f_{T^*_i}(\mathcal{D}) > \epsilon$ if and only if $f_{T^*}(\mathcal{D}_i) > 1/50$, and $f_{T^*_i}(\mathcal{D}) < \epsilon/2$ if and only if $f_{T^*}(\mathcal{D}_i) < 1/100$. That is, one can use $\mathcal{S}(\mathcal{D}, k, \epsilon, \delta)$ to answer all For-All-Itemset-Frequency-Indicator queries on $\mathcal{D}_i$ with error parameter $1/50$ for all k-itemsets (this holds simultaneously for all i with probability $1-\delta$).

By the argument for the case $\epsilon = 1/50$, this implies that $\mathcal{S}(\mathcal{D}, k, \epsilon, \delta)$ can be used to losslessly encode an arbitrary vector of length $\Omega(d \cdot v \cdot m) = \Omega((kd \log(d/k)/\epsilon)$, and thus $|\mathcal{S}(\mathcal{D}, k, \epsilon, \delta)| = \Omega\left((kd \log(d/k)/\epsilon)\right)$. This completes the proof of Theorem 15.

4. LOWER BOUNDS PROOFS FOR ITEMSET-FREQUENCY-ESTIMATOR SKETCHES

4.1 The For-All Case: Proof of Theorem 16

4.1.1 *Informal Overview of the Proof*

For constant $k' \geq 2$, an $\tilde{\Omega}(d/\epsilon^2)$ lower bound on the size of For-All-Itemset-Frequency-Estimator sketches follows fairly directly from existing work in the literature on differential privacy (cf. Kasiviswanathan et al. [KRSU10]; we refer to this work as KRSU). The idea of KRSU's result is the following. Itemset frequency queries are a linear class of queries, in the sense that we can represent any database as a vector z (in which each entry of z corresponds to a possible record in $\{0,1\}^d$ and its value is the number of such records in the database), and the vector of answers to all k'-itemset frequency queries on z can be written as Az for some matrix A. Given a vector y of approximate answers to these queries, on can try to reconstruct z via the approximation $\hat{z} = A^{-1}y$, where A^{-1} denotes the Moore-Penrose pseudo-inverse of A (this is essentially reconstruction via L_2-distance minimization). If the matrix A has a "nice" spectrum, then it is possible to bound the distance between $\hat{z}$ and z. If this distance is small enough, then any description of y contains many bits of information, since it essentially encodes an entire database z.

However, KRSU do not actually look at the matrix A corresponding to k'-itemset frequency queries. Instead, they look at a matrix $M^{(k')}$ they define as follows. Consider a database $\mathcal{D}$ with n rows and k' columns, where the first $k'-1$ columns of $\mathcal{D}$ are generated at random. For any fixed setting of the first $k'-1$ columns, the vector of answers to k'-itemset frequency queries on $\mathcal{D}$ are a function only of column k' of $\mathcal{D}$. Denoting column k' of $\mathcal{D}$ by x, these answers can be written in the form $M^{(k')}x$, for a particular matrix $M^{(k')}$ derived from the first $k'-1$ columns of $\mathcal{D}$.

KRSU show that $M^{(k')}$ behaves a lot like a matrix with truly random entries from $\{0,1\}$, and hence has a "nice" spectrum (with high probability over the random choice of the first $k'-1$ columns of $\mathcal{D}$). This ensures that $\hat{x} = A^{-1}y$ is a "good" approximation to the last column x of $\mathcal{D}$ as long as all answers in y have error $\epsilon \lesssim \sqrt{n}$. Put another way, if the error in the answers is ϵ, then it is possible to reconstruct column k' of $\mathcal{D}$ as long as the number of rows is at most (roughly) $1/\epsilon^2$.

This shows that one can use a summary providing ϵ-approximate answers to all k'-itemset frequency queries on a database with k' columns and $1/\epsilon^2$ rows to reconstruct $\tilde{\Omega}(1/\epsilon^2)$ arbitrary bits. It is possible to extend this argument to databases with $d+k'-1$ columns and $\tilde{\Omega}(1/\epsilon^2)$ rows, yielding a $\tilde{\Omega}(d/\epsilon^2)$ lower bound on the size of For-All-Itemset-Frequency-Estimator sketches for such databases.

Our main contribution for the For-All-Itemset-Frequency-Estimator problem is to combine such an $\tilde{\Omega}(d/\epsilon^2)$ lower bound for sketches for k'-way marginals with a technique for "amplifying" the lower bound to $\tilde{\Omega}(k \cdot \log(d/k) \cdot d/\epsilon^2)$ for $(k+k')$-way marginal queries (we used essentially the same amplification technique, which was inspired by work of Bun et al. [BUV14] in the context of differential privacy, in Section 3.2.2). This technique says that, given $v = k \cdot \log(d/k)$ databases $\mathcal{D}'_1, ..., \mathcal{D}'_v$, each with $d + k' - 1$ columns and $1/\epsilon^2$ rows, we can construct a bigger database $\mathcal{D}$ such that one can use ϵ-approximate answers to all $(k + k')$-way marginal queries on $\mathcal{D}$ to obtain ϵ-approximate answers to the k'-way marginals on every database $\mathcal{D}'_i$.

This amplification technique actually requires the $\tilde{\Omega}(d/\epsilon^2)$ lower bound for k'-way marginals to hold even if the answer vector y only has error ϵ "on average", rather than having error at most ϵ for every single answer. Hence, we cannot directly use the KRSU lower bound in our argument. In fact, to reconstruct a database from answers that have error at most ϵ only "on average", one cannot use L_2 distance minimization as in KRSU's lower bound argument, since L_2-minimization is highly sensitive to a few answers having large error. Fortunately, De [De12] shows how to use L_1-minimization to establish an $\tilde{\Omega}(1/\epsilon^2)$ lower bound even in the setting in which answers are only required to have error at most ϵ "on average". We use his techniques to obtain a lower bound suitable for our argument.

4.1.2 Proof Details

In the context of differential privacy, De [De12], building on [KRSU10, Rud12], described an algorithm for reconstructing a database $\mathcal{D}$, given sufficiently accurate answers to all k-itemset frequency queries on $\mathcal{D}$. In our terminology, De's result establishes that any For-All-Itemset-Frequency-Estimator-sketch can be used to losslessly encode $\Omega(\frac{d}{\epsilon^2 \log_{(q)}(1/\epsilon)})$ bits of information. Here $\log_{(q)}(\cdot)$ denotes the logarithm function iterated q times. Formally, we use the following slight refinement of De's result.

LEMMA 20 (VARIANT OF THEOREM 5.12 OF [DE12]). *For any constant integers $k \geq 2$ and $q \geq 1$, there exists a constant $\gamma = \gamma(k, q) > 0$ and a distribution μ over k-itemset queries such that the following holds.*

Let d and ϵ be parameters satisfying $1/\epsilon^2 \leq d^{k-1}/\log_{(q)}(1/\epsilon^2)$. Suppose $\mathcal{S}$ is any summary algorithm that can answer a $1 - \gamma$ fraction of all k-itemset frequency queries under μ on databases with d columns to error $\pm\epsilon$. Then there exists a $b = b(d, \epsilon) = \Omega(d/\epsilon^2 \log_{(q)}(1/\epsilon))$, an $n = n(d, \epsilon) = O(\log_{(q)}(d)/\epsilon^2)$, a database-generation algorithm $\mathcal{A}$ that takes as input a Boolean vector $y \in \{0, 1\}^b$ and outputs a database $\mathcal{A}(y) \in \left(\{0, 1\}^d\right)^n$, and a decoding algorithm $\mathcal{A}'$ such that $\mathcal{A}'$ outputs y with high probability given $\mathcal{S}(\mathcal{A}(y))$.

We prove Lemma 20 in Appendix B.

Lemma 20 alone is enough to yield a lower bound of $\Omega\left(d/\epsilon^2 \log_{(q)}(1/\epsilon)\right)$ on the size of For-All-Itemset-Frequency-Estimator sketches capable of answering all k-itemset frequency queries to error $\pm\epsilon$, for any $k \geq 2$. The technical contribution of this section is to "bootstrap" this result to obtain a lower bound of $\Omega\left(kd \log(d/k)/\epsilon^2 \log_{(q)}(1/\epsilon)\right)$ bits, which improves over the bound that follows from a direct application of Lemma 20 even for $k = 3$. This lower bound is essentially optimal, matching the $O(kd \log(d/k)/\epsilon^2)$ upper bound achieved by algorithm SUBSAMPLE up to a $\log_{(q)}(1/\epsilon)$ factor (for an arbitrarily large constant q).

PROOF OF THEOREM 16. Let $v = (k - c) \log(d/(k - c))$ and $x_1, \ldots, x_v \in \{0, 1\}^d$ be the strings promised by Fact 18 applied with $k' = k - c$. Recall that for every vector $s \in \{0, 1\}^v$, there is a $(k-c)$-itemset T_s such that $f_{T_s}(x_i) = s_i$ for all $i \in [v]$. Recall that $c \geq 2$ is a parameter of the theorem.

Let $\gamma = \gamma(c, q)$ be the constant in Lemma 20. Fix $\epsilon' = 100\epsilon/\gamma$. Suppose that we are given v strings $y_1, \ldots, y_v \in \{0, 1\}^b$, where $b = b(d, \epsilon')$ is as in Lemma 20 for $k = c$. Let $\mathcal{A}(y_i) = \mathcal{D}_i \in \left(\{0, 1\}^d\right)^n$, where $\mathcal{A}$ is the database generation algorithm promised by Lemma 20. We show how to construct a single "large" database $\mathcal{D}$ with $2d$ columns and nv rows such that 96% of the bits of $y_1, \ldots, y_v$ can be recovered from $\mathcal{S}(\mathcal{D}, k, \epsilon, \delta)$. Note that Lemma 20 applies, since $c \geq 2$. Also note that γ is indeed a constant since we required that c and q are constants; therefore $\epsilon' = O(\epsilon)$.

Definition of $\mathcal{D}$. Recall that $\mathcal{D}_i(j)$ denotes the jth row of $\mathcal{D}_i$. Define $\mathcal{D}'_i$ to be the database with $2d$ columns and n rows defined via $\mathcal{D}'_i(j) = (x_i, \mathcal{D}_i(j))$. That is, $\mathcal{D}'_i$ is obtained from $\mathcal{D}_i$ by appending the string x_i to the front of every row. We define $\mathcal{D}$ to be the concatenation of all of the $\mathcal{D}'_i$ databases. We index the vn rows of $\mathcal{D}$ as $(i, j) : i \in [v], j \in [n]$.

Reconstructing $y_1, \ldots, y_v$ from $\mathcal{S}(\mathcal{D})$. For any c-itemset query $T \subseteq [d]$, let z_T denote the vector $z_T = (f_T(\mathcal{D}_1), \ldots, f_T(\mathcal{D}_v))$. Let $s \in \{0, 1\}^v$ be any vector. Define $T' = T'(T, s) \subseteq [2d]$ to be the k-itemset whose indicator vector is the concatenation of the indicator vectors of T_s and T; that is, $T' := T_s \cup \{j + d : j \in T\}$.

We claim that $\frac{1}{v}\langle s, z_T\rangle = f_{T'(s,T)}(\mathcal{D})$. To see this, note that T' is contained in row (i, j) of $\mathcal{D}$ if and only if $s_i = 1$ and T is contained in row j of $\mathcal{D}_i$. Hence,

$$\begin{aligned}
\frac{1}{v}\langle s, z_T\rangle &= \frac{1}{v} \cdot \sum_{i \in [v] : s_i = 1} f_T(\mathcal{D}_i) \\
&= \frac{1}{v} \sum_{i \in [v]} \frac{1}{n} |\{j \in [n] : T \text{ is contained in } D_i(j)\}| \\
&= \frac{1}{nv} \sum_{(i,j) \in [v] \times [n]} |\{T' \text{ is contained in row } (i, j) \text{ of } \mathcal{D}\}| \\
&= f_{T'(T,s)}(\mathcal{D}).
\end{aligned}$$

Hence, from any For-All-Itemset-Frequency-Estimator sketch $\mathcal{S}(\mathcal{D}, k, \epsilon, \delta)$, one can compute for every c-itemset T, an estimate $\hat{f}_{T'(T,s)}$ satisfying $|\hat{f}_{T'(T,s)} - \frac{1}{v}\langle s, z_T\rangle| \leq \epsilon$. The following lemma describes why these estimates are useful in reconstructing $y_1, \ldots, y_v$.

LEMMA 21. *Fix a c-itemset $T \subset [d]$. Given values $\hat{f}_{T'(s,T)}$ satisfying $|\hat{f}_{T'(s,T)} - \frac{1}{v}\langle s, z_T\rangle| \leq \epsilon$ for all $s \in \{0, 1\}^v$, it is possible to identify a vector $\hat{z}_T \in [0, 1]^v$ satisfying $\frac{1}{v}\|\hat{z}_T - z_T\|_1 \leq 4\epsilon$.*

PROOF. Consider the algorithm that outputs any vector $\hat{z}_T \in [0, 1]^v$ satisfying the following property:

$$\text{For all } s \in \{0, 1\}^v, \left|\frac{1}{v}\langle \hat{z}_T, s\rangle - \hat{f}_{T'(s,T)}\right| \leq \epsilon. \quad (6)$$

Note that at least one such vector always exists, because setting $\hat{z}_T = z_T$ satisfies Equation (6). Thus, the algorithm always produces some output.

We claim that any $\hat{z}_T$ output by the algorithm satisfies $\frac{1}{v}\|\hat{z}_T - z_T\|_1 \leq 4\epsilon$. Indeed, suppose otherwise. Define $s^{(1)} \in \{0, 1\}^v$ via $s^{(1)}_i = 1$ if and only if $\hat{z}_{T,i} \geq z_{T,i}$ and $s^{(2)} \in \{0, 1\}^v$ via $s^{(2)}_i = 1$ if and only if $z_{T,i} > \hat{z}_{T,i}$. Then either $\frac{1}{v}\left(\langle \hat{z}_T, s^{(1)}\rangle - \langle z_T, s^{(1)}\rangle\right) > 2\epsilon$, or $\frac{1}{v}\left(\langle \hat{z}_T, s^{(2)}\rangle - \langle z_T, s^{(2)}\rangle\right) > 2\epsilon$. Assume without loss of generality that the former case holds. Then

$$\left|\frac{1}{v}\langle \hat{z}_T, s^{(1)}\rangle - \hat{f}_{T'(s^{(1)},T)}\right| \geq$$

$$\frac{1}{v}\left(\langle \hat{z}_T, s^{(1)}\rangle - \langle z_T, s^{(1)}\rangle\right) - \left|\frac{1}{v}\langle z_T, s\rangle - \hat{f}_{T'(s,T)}\right| >$$

$$2\epsilon - \epsilon = \epsilon,$$

where the inequality holds by the triangle inequality. But this contradicts the assumption that $\hat{z}_T$ satisfies (6). □

For each c-itemset T, let $\hat{z}_T$ be as in Lemma 21. We think of $\hat{z}_{T,i}$ as an estimate of $z_{T,i} = f_T(\mathcal{D}_i)$. Lemma 21 guarantees that *for any distribution* μ *over c-itemsets* T, this estimate has error at most 4ϵ on average, when the averaging is done over a random c-itemset T chosen according to μ, and databases $\mathcal{D}_i$. In symbols:

$$\mathbf{E}_{T\leftarrow\mu}\mathbf{E}_{i\in v}|\hat{z}_{T,i} - z_{T,i}| = \sum_T \mu(T)\left(\mathbf{E}_{i\in v}|\hat{z}_{T,i} - z_{T,i}|\right)$$
$$\leq \sum_T \mu(T)\cdot 4\epsilon \leq 4\epsilon.$$

Here, $\mathbf{E}_{T\leftarrow\mu}$ denotes the expectation operation when T is chosen according to the distribution μ, and the penultimate inequality holds by Lemma 21.

By Markov's inequality we conclude that for at least 96% of the databases $\mathcal{D}_i$, the estimates $\hat{z}_{T,i}$ have error at most 100ϵ on average, where the averaging is over the choice of T according to distribution μ. That is, for at least 96% of databases $\mathcal{D}_i$, it holds that

$$\mathbf{E}_{T\leftarrow\mu}\mathbf{E}_{i\in v}|\hat{z}_{T,i} - z_{T,i}| \leq 100\epsilon. \quad (7)$$

For any $\mathcal{D}_i$ satisfying Equation (7) and any $\gamma > 0$, another application of Markov's inequality implies that the $|\hat{z}_{T,i} - f_T(\mathcal{D}_i)| \leq 100\epsilon/\gamma = \epsilon'$ for a $1-\gamma$ fraction of all c-itemsets T under distribution μ. By Lemma 20, this implies that y_i can be exactly recovered from the $\hat{z}_{T,i}$ values, using algorithm $\mathcal{A}'$.

Since 96% of the y_i vectors can be *exactly* recovered, it follows that at least 96% of the bv total bits in the vectors of $y_1, \ldots, y_v$ can be recovered. Suppose we let the bv bits in the collection of vectors $(y_1, \ldots, y_v)$ be the error-corrected encoding of a single vector $(y'_1, \ldots, y'_z) \in \{0,1\}^z$, using a code with constant rate that is uniquely decodable from 4% errors (e.g. using a Justesen code [Jus72]). Then $z = \Omega(bv)$, and it follows from the above that $(y'_1, \ldots, y'_z)$ can be *exactly* reconstructed from $\mathcal{S}(\mathcal{D}, k, \epsilon, \delta)$ with probability $1-\delta$. Basic information theory then implies that

$$|\mathcal{S}(\mathcal{D}, k, \epsilon, \delta)| = \Omega(bv)$$

$$= \Omega\left(\frac{kd\log(d/k)}{(\epsilon')^2\log_{(q)}(1/(\epsilon'))}\right) = \Omega\left(\frac{kd\log(d/k)}{\epsilon^2\log_{(q)}(1/\epsilon)}\right),$$

where we have used the fact that $\epsilon' = O(\epsilon)$. This completes the proof of the theorem.

4.2 The For-Each Case: Proof of Theorem 17

Recall that Theorem 17 establishes a lower bound against For-Each-Itemset-Frequency-Estimator sketches that is tight up to a $\log_{(q)}(d)$ factor. We prove Theorem 17 via a simple argument that shows how to transform any For-Each-Itemset-Frequency-Estimator sketch into a For-All-Itemset-Frequency-Estimator sketch with a modest increase in space. This allows us to transform Theorem 16 into the claimed lower bound against For-Each-Itemset-Frequency-Estimator sketches.

PROOF OF THEOREM 17. Suppose that we are given an For-Each-Itemset-Frequency-Estimator sketching algorithm $\mathcal{S}$ using space $|\mathcal{S}|$. We show how to transform $\mathcal{S}$ into a For-All-Itemset-Frequency-Estimator sketching algorithm $\mathcal{S}'$ using space $O\left(|\mathcal{S}|\cdot\log\binom{d}{k}\right) = O\left(|\mathcal{S}(k,\epsilon,\delta)|\cdot k\cdot\log(d/k)\right)$. It then follows from Theorem 16 that $|\mathcal{S}| = \Omega\left(\frac{d}{\epsilon^2\log_{(q)}(1/\epsilon)}\right)$.

The For-All-Itemset-Frequency-Estimator sketching algorithm $\mathcal{S}'$ simply outputs $10\cdot\log\left(\binom{d}{k}/\delta\right)$ independent copies of $\mathcal{S}(\mathcal{D})$ (i.e., using fresh randomness for each of the $10\cdot\log\left(\binom{d}{k}/\delta\right)$ runs of $\mathcal{S}$). Given any k-itemset T, the query procedure $\mathcal{Q}'$ associated with $\mathcal{S}'$ simply runs the query procedure $\mathcal{Q}$ associated with $\mathcal{S}$ on each of the copies of $\mathcal{S}(\mathcal{D})$, and outputs the median of the results. Since each copy of $\mathcal{S}$ outputs an estimated frequency that has error at most ϵ with probability $1-\delta > 1/2$, standard Chernoff Bounds imply that for any fixed k-itemset T, the median estimate will have error at most ϵ with probability at least $1-\delta/\binom{d}{k}$. A union bound implies that the median estimate will have error at most ϵ for all $\binom{d}{k}$ itemsets with probability at least $1-\delta$. Thus, $\mathcal{S}'$ is a For-All-Itemset-Frequency-Estimator sketching algorithm with failure probability at most δ. □

5. CONCLUSION

We introduced four closely related notions that capture the problem of approximating itemset frequencies in databases. For all four problems, we studied the minimal size of sketches that permit a user to recover sufficiently accurate information about itemset frequencies. After identifying three naive algorithms that apply to all four problems, we turned to proving sketch size lower bounds. Our results establish that random sampling achieves optimal or essentially optimal sketch size for all four problems. This stands in contrast to several seemingly similar problems, such as identifying approximate frequent items in data streams, and various matrix approximation problems, for which uniform sampling is not an optimal sketching algorithm.

We proved our lower bounds by adapting and extending techniques developed in the literature on differentially privacy data analysis. It is an interesting open question whether there are other problems in non-private data analysis that can be resolved using techniques from the literature on differential privacy.

In addition, our lower bound arguments specify a "hard" distribution over databases, for which it is impossible to improve upon the space usage of the uniform sampling sketching algorithm for answering approximate itemset frequency queries. But real-world databases are likely to be substantially more structured than the databases appearing in our hard distribution, and real-world query loads are likely to be highly non-uniform. In these settings, *importance sampling* is a natural candidate for improving upon the space usage of the uniform sampling sketching algorithm. It would be interesting to identify rigorous yet realistic conditions on databases and query loads that allow for such an improvement. Subsequent work by Lang et al. [LLS16] takes some initial steps in this direction.

Acknowledgements. The authors are grateful to Amit Chakrabarti, Graham Cormode, Nikhil Srivastava, and Suresh Venkatasubramanian for several helpful conversations during the early stages of this work.

6. REFERENCES

[Abl96] Farid M. Ablayev. Lower bounds for one-way probabilistic communication complexity and their application to space complexity. *Theor. Comput. Sci.*, 157(2):139–159, 1996.

[AIS93] Rakesh Agrawal, Tomasz Imieliński, and Arun Swami. Mining association rules between sets of items in large databases. *SIGMOD Rec.*, 22(2):207–216, 1993.

[AKW14] Alexandr Andoni, Robert Krauthgamer, and David P. Woodruff. The sketching complexity of graph cuts. *CoRR*, abs/1403.7058, 2014.

[BBR03] Jean-François Boulicaut, Artur Bykowski, and Christophe Rigotti. Free-sets: A condensed representation of boolean data for the approximation of frequency queries. *Data Min. Knowl. Discov.*, 7(1):5–22, 2003.

[BCD+07] Boaz Barak, Kamalika Chaudhuri, Cynthia Dwork, Satyen Kale, Frank McSherry, and Kunal Talwar. Privacy, accuracy, and consistency too: a holistic solution to contingency table release. In Leonid Libkin, editor, *PODS*, pages 273–282. ACM, 2007.

[BUV14] Mark Bun, Jonathan Ullman, and Salil Vadhan. Fingerprinting codes and the price of approximate differential privacy. In *Proceedings of the 46th Annual ACM Symposium on Theory of Computing*, STOC '14, pages 1–10, New York, NY, USA, 2014. ACM.

[CG07] Toon Calders and Bart Goethals. Non-derivable itemset mining. *Data Min. Knowl. Discov.*, 14(1):171–206, February 2007.

[CKN08] James Cheng, Yiping Ke, and Wilfred Ng. A survey on algorithms for mining frequent itemsets over data streams. *Knowl. Inf. Syst.*, 16(1):1–27, 2008.

[CP10] Andrea Campagna and Rasmus Pagh. On finding similar items in a stream of transactions. In Wei Fan, Wynne Hsu, Geoffrey I. Webb, Bing Liu, Chengqi Zhang, Dimitrios Gunopulos, and Xindong Wu, editors, *ICDMW 2010, The 10th IEEE International Conference on Data Mining Workshops, Sydney, Australia, 13 December 2010*, pages 121–128. IEEE Computer Society, 2010.

[CTUW14] Karthekeyan Chandrasekaran, Justin Thaler, Jonathan Ullman, and Andrew Wan. Faster private release of marginals on small databases. In Moni Naor, editor, *ITCS*, pages 387–402. ACM, 2014.

[De12] Anindya De. Lower bounds in differential privacy. In Ronald Cramer, editor, *TCC*, volume 7194 of *Lecture Notes in Computer Science*, pages 321–338. Springer, 2012.

[DMNS06] Cynthia Dwork, Frank McSherry, Kobbi Nissim, and Adam Smith. Calibrating noise to sensitivity in private data analysis. In *Theory of Cryptography, Third Theory of Cryptography Conference, TCC 2006, New York, NY, USA, March 4-7, 2006, Proceedings*, pages 265–284, 2006.

[FK04] Uriel Feige and Shimon Kogan. Hardness of approximation of the Balanced Complete Bipartite Subgraph problem. Technical Report MCS04-04, Weizmann Institute of Science, 2004.

[GHRU13] Anupam Gupta, Moritz Hardt, Aaron Roth, and Jonathan Ullman. Privately releasing conjunctions and the statistical query barrier. *SIAM J. Comput.*, 42(4):1494–1520, 2013.

[GWWZ15] Dirk Van Gucht, Ryan Williams, David P. Woodruff, and Qin Zhang. The communication complexity of distributed set-joins with applications to matrix multiplication. In Tova Milo and Diego Calvanese, editors, *Proceedings of the 34th ACM Symposium on Principles of Database Systems, PODS 2015, Melbourne, Victoria, Australia, May 31 - June 4, 2015*, pages 199–212. ACM, 2015.

[HCW06] Matthew Hamilton, Rhonda Chaytor, and Todd Wareham. The parameterized complexity of enumerating frequent itemsets. In *Proceedings of the Second International Conference on Parameterized and Exact Computation*, IWPEC'06, pages 227–238, Berlin, Heidelberg, 2006. Springer-Verlag.

[Jus72] J. Justesen. A class of constructive asymptotically good algebraic codes. *IEEE Transactions on Information Theory*, 18(5):652–656, 1972.

[KRSU10] Shiva Prasad Kasiviswanathan, Mark Rudelson, Adam Smith, and Jonathan Ullman. The price of privately releasing contingency tables and the spectra of random matrices with correlated rows. In *STOC*, pages 775–784, 2010.

[LLS16] Kevin Lang, Edo Liberty, and Konstantin Shmakov. Stratified sampling meets machine learning, 2016. Manuscript. Available at `www.cs.yale.edu/homes/el327/papers/lls15.pdf`.

[LLSW05] Jinyan Li, Haiquan Li, Donny Soh, and Limsoon Wong. A correspondence between maximal complete bipartite subgraphs and closed patterns. In *PKDD*, PKDD'05, pages 146–156, Berlin, Heidelberg, 2005. Springer-Verlag.

[LMT14] Edo Liberty, Michael Mitzenmacher, and Justin Thaler. Space lower bounds for itemset frequency sketches. *CoRR*, abs/1407.3740, 2014.

[MM02] Gurmeet Singh Manku and Rajeev Motwani. Approximate frequency counts over data streams. In *Proceedings of the 28th International Conference on Very Large Data Bases*, VLDB '02, pages 346–357. VLDB Endowment, 2002.

[MT96] Heikki Mannila and Hannu Toivonen. Multiple uses of frequent sets and condensed representations. In *KDD*, 1996.

[MT07] Frank McSherry and Kunal Talwar. Mechanism design via differential privacy. In *Proceedings of the 48th Annual IEEE Symposium on Foundations of Computer Science*, FOCS '07, pages 94–103, Washington, DC, USA, 2007. IEEE Computer Society.

[PDZH04] Jian Pei, Guozhu Dong, Wei Zou, and Jiawei Han. Mining condensed frequent-pattern bases. *Knowl. Inf. Syst.*, 6(5):570–594, 2004.

[Pri14] Eric Price. Optimal lower bound for itemset frequency indicator sketches. *CoRR*, abs/1410.2640, 2014.

[Rud12] Mark Rudelson. Row products of random

matrices. *Advances in Mathematics*, 231(6):3199 – 3231, 2012.

[TUV12] Justin Thaler, Jonathan Ullman, and Salil P. Vadhan. Faster algorithms for privately releasing marginals. In Artur Czumaj, Kurt Mehlhorn, Andrew M. Pitts, and Roger Wattenhofer, editors, *ICALP (1)*, volume 7391 of *Lecture Notes in Computer Science*, pages 810–821. Springer, 2012.

[Yan04] Guizhen Yang. The complexity of mining maximal frequent itemsets and maximal frequent patterns. In *KDD*, KDD '04, pages 344–353, New York, NY, USA, 2004. ACM.

APPENDIX

A. PROOF OF FACT 18

We provide a direct construction of the vectors whose existence is guaranteed by Fact 18, restated here for convenience.

Fact 18. *For any $k' \geq 1$, let $v = k' \cdot \log(d/k')$. There exist strings $x_1, \ldots, x_v \in \{0,1\}^d$ such that for every string $s \in \{0,1\}^v$, there is a k'-itemset T_s such that $f_{T_s}(x_i) = s_i$ for all $i \in [v]$.*

Proof of Fact 18. For expository purposes, we first describe a set of vectors $w_1, \ldots, w_{k'} \in \{0,1\}^{k'}$ that are "shattered" by k'-itemset frequency queries, i.e., for every string $s \in \{0,1\}^{k'}$, there is a k'-itemset T_s such that $f_{T_s}(y_i) = s_i$ for all $i \in [k']$. We then describe a set of vectors $y_1, \ldots, y_{\log d} \in \{0,1\}^d$ that are shattered even by 1-itemset frequency queries. Finally, we explain how to "glue together" the w_i's and y_i's to obtain the full set $x_1, \ldots, x_v \in \{0,1\}^d$ whose existence is claimed in the statement of Fact 18.

Description of the w_i's. For each $i \in [k']$, define $w_i \in \{0,1\}^{k'}$ via:

$$\begin{cases} w_{i,j} = 1 : & 1 \leq j \leq k', j \neq i \\ w_{i,j} = 0 & j = i \end{cases}$$

To restate the above in matrix notation, we define the $k' \times k'$ matrix $W^{(k')}$ whose rows are the w_i's via:

$$W^{(k')} := \begin{pmatrix} w_1 \\ w_2 \\ \vdots \\ w_{k'-1} \\ w_{k'} \end{pmatrix} = \begin{pmatrix} 0 & 1 & 1 & \ldots & 1 & 1 \\ 1 & 0 & 1 & \ldots & 1 & 1 \\ \vdots & \vdots & \vdots & \ldots & \vdots & \vdots \\ 1 & 1 & 1 & \ldots & 0 & 1 \\ 1 & 1 & 1 & \ldots & 1 & 0 \end{pmatrix}$$

For any string $s \in \{0,1\}^{k'}$, let $T_s := \{i : s_i = 0\}$. It is straightforward to check that $f_{T_s}(w_i) = s_i$ as desired.

Description of the y_i's. For each $i \in [\log d]$, we define each $y_i \in \{0,1\}^d$ to ensure that the matrix whose rows are the y_i's contains every possible $\log(d)$-bit string as a column. In matrix notation, we define the $\log(d) \times d$ matrix $Y^{(d)}$ via:

$$Y^{(d)} := \begin{pmatrix} y_1 \\ y_2 \\ \vdots \\ y_{\log(d)-1} \\ y_{\log d} \end{pmatrix} = \begin{pmatrix} 0 & 0 & 0 & \ldots & 1 & 1 \\ 0 & 0 & 0 & \ldots & 1 & 1 \\ \vdots & \vdots & \vdots & \ldots & \vdots & \vdots \\ 0 & 0 & 1 & \ldots & 1 & 1 \\ 0 & 1 & 0 & \ldots & 0 & 1 \end{pmatrix}$$

For any string $s \in \{0,1\}^{\log d}$, we interpret s as the binary representation of an integer $\text{int}(s) \in \{0, \ldots, d-1\}$, and define $T_s := \{\text{int}(s)\}$. It is straightforward to check that $f_{T_s}(y_i) = s_i$ as desired.

Description of the x_i's. Recall that $v = k' \cdot \log(d/k')$. Consider the $v \times d$ matrix X whose rows are the x_i's. We view this matrix as a collection of sub-matrices, where each sub-matrix has dimension $k' \times (d/k')$. More specifically, let $\mathbf{J}$ denote the $k' \times (d/k')$ matrix of all-ones. We define X to be the matrix obtained from $W^{(d/k')}$ by replacing each entry of $W^{(d/k')}$ that is equal to 1 with the matrix $\mathbf{J}$, and replacing each entry of $W^{(d/k')}$ that is equal to 0 with the matrix $Y^{(d/k')}$. In more detail, define:

$$X := \begin{pmatrix} x_1 \\ x_2 \\ \vdots \\ x_{k'-1} \\ x_{k'} \end{pmatrix} = \begin{pmatrix} Y^{(d/k')} & \mathbf{J} & \mathbf{J} & \ldots & \mathbf{J} & \mathbf{J} \\ \mathbf{J} & Y^{(d/k')} & \mathbf{J} & \ldots & \mathbf{J} & \mathbf{J} \\ \vdots & \vdots & \vdots & \ldots & \vdots & \vdots \\ \mathbf{J} & \mathbf{J} & \mathbf{J} & \ldots & Y^{(d/k')} & \mathbf{J} \\ \mathbf{J} & \mathbf{J} & \mathbf{J} & \ldots & \mathbf{J} & Y^{(d/k')} \end{pmatrix}$$

Given any vector $s \in \{0,1\}^v$, we interpret s as specifying k' integers $\ell_1, \ldots, \ell_{k'} \in \{0, \ldots, d/k'\}$ in the natural way. We view $[d]$ as the cross-product $[k'] \cdot [d/k']$, and associate each $j \in [d]$ with a pair $(r_1, r_2) \in [k'] \times [d/k']$ in the natural way. We then define $T_s := \{(i, \ell_i) : i \in [k']\}$. It is then straightforward to observe that $f_{T_s}(x_i) = s_i$. □

B. PROOF OF LEMMA 20

We restate Lemma 20 for convenience, before providing its proof.

Lemma 20. (Refinement of Theorem 5.12 of [De12]) *For any constant integers $k \geq 2$ and $q \geq 1$, there exists a constant $\gamma = \gamma(k,q) > 0$ and a distribution μ over k-itemset queries such that the following holds.*

Let d and ϵ be parameters satisfying $1/\epsilon^2 \leq d^{k-1}/\log_{(q)}(1/\epsilon^2)$. Suppose $\mathcal{S}$ is any summary algorithm that can answer a $1-\gamma$ fraction of all k-itemset frequency queries under μ on databases with d columns to error $\pm\epsilon$. Then there exists a $b = b(d,\epsilon) = \Omega(d/\epsilon^2 \log_{(q)}(1/\epsilon))$, an $n = n(d,\epsilon) = O(\log_{(q)}(d)/\epsilon^2)$, a database-generation algorithm $\mathcal{A}$ that takes as input a Boolean vector $y \in \{0,1\}^h$ and outputs a database $\mathcal{A}(y) \in (\{0,1\}^d)^n$, and a decoding algorithm $\mathcal{A}'$ such that $\mathcal{A}'$ outputs y with high probability given $\mathcal{S}(\mathcal{A}(y))$.

As Lemma 20 is a refinement of Theorem 5.12 of De's work [De12], the presentation of our proof borrows heavily from De's.

Proof. We begin by defining the Hadamard product of matrices.

Definition 22 (Hadamard product of matrices). *Let $A_1, \ldots, A_s \in \mathbb{R}^{\ell_i \times n}$. Then, the Hadamard product of $A_1, \ldots, A_s$ is denoted by $A = A_1 \circ A_2 \circ \cdots \circ A_s \in \mathbb{R}^{L \times n}$, where $L = \ell_1 \cdot \cdots \cdot \ell_s$ and is defined as follows: Every row of A is identified with a unique element of $[\ell_1] \times \cdots \times [\ell_s]$. For*

$i = (i_1, \ldots i_s)$, *define*

$$A[i,h] = \prod_{j=1}^{s} A_j[i_j, h]$$

where $A[i,h]$ *represents the element in row* i *and column* h *of* A.

We will also require the definition of Euclidean sections, which play an important role in the analysis of LP decoding algorithms.

DEFINITION 23 (EUCLIDEAN SECTIONS). $V \subseteq \mathbb{R}^z$ *is said to be a* (δ, d', z) *Euclidean Section if* V *is a linear subspace of dimension* d' *and for every* $x \in V$, *the following holds:*

$$\sqrt{z}\|x\|_2 \geq \|x\|_1 \geq \delta\sqrt{z}\|x\|_2.$$

A linear operator $A\colon \mathbb{R}^{d'} \to \mathbb{R}^z$ *is said to be* δ*-Euclidean if the range of* A *is a Euclidean* (δ, d', z) *section.*

The following lemma follows directly from the proof of [De12, Lemma 5.9].

LEMMA 24 (REFORMULATION OF LEMMA 5.9 OF [DE12]). *Let* $d_0^{k-1} > n$. *Suppose there exist Boolean matrices* $A_1, \ldots, A_{\ell-1} \in \mathbb{R}^{d_0 \times n}$ *such that* $A = A_1 \circ A_2 \circ \cdots \circ A_{k-1}$, *all the singular values of* A *are at least* σ, *and the range of* A *is a* (δ, n, d_0^{k-1})*-Euclidean section.*

Let $\mathcal{D}_0$ *denote the database with* n *rows and* $(k-1) \cdot d_0$ *columns obtained from the* A_i*'s as follows: the* j*th row of* $\mathcal{D}_0$ *is the concatenation of the* j*th row of each of the matrices* $A_1^T, A_2^T, \ldots, A_{k-1}^T$. *Let* $\mathcal{A}_1$ *denote the database generation algorithm that takes as input a Boolean vector* $y \in \{0,1\}^n$, *and outputs the database* $\mathcal{D}_1(y)$ *with* n *rows and* $d_1 := (k-1) \cdot d_0 + 1$ *columns obtained from* $\mathcal{D}_0$ *by appending an additional column equal to* y.

Then, there exists a constant $\gamma_1 = \gamma_1(\delta) > 0$, *a distribution* μ_1 *over* k*-itemsets* $T \subseteq [d_1]$, *and a reconstruction algorithm* $\mathcal{R}$ *satisfying the following. Fix any* $\zeta_1 \in o(\sqrt{n}\sigma/\sqrt{d_1^{k-1}})$. *Suppose* $\mathcal{R}$ *is given* $\mathcal{D}_0$ *and approximate itemset frequencies* $\hat{f}_T$ *for all* k*-itemsets* $T \subseteq [d_1]$. *Let* S_1 *denote the set of all* k*-itemsets* T *satisfying* $n \cdot |\hat{f}_T - f_T(\mathcal{D}_2(y))| \leq \zeta_1$, *and suppose that* $\sum_{T \in S_1} \mu(T) \geq 1 - \gamma_1$. *Then* $\mathcal{R}$ *outputs a vector* $\hat{y}$ *of Hamming distance* $o(n)$ *from* y.

We use Lemma 24 to establish the following stronger statement.

LEMMA 25. *Let* $A_1, \ldots, A_{k-1}$, δ, $\mathcal{D}_0$, μ_1, d_0, d_1, n, γ_1, *and* ζ_1 *be as in Lemma 24. There is a* $b = b(d_0, n) \in \Omega(d_0 \cdot n)$ *and database generation algorithm* $\mathcal{A}_2$ *that takes as input a Boolean vector* $y' \in \{0,1\}^b$, *and outputs a database* $\mathcal{D}_2$ *with* n *rows and* $d_2 := (k-1) \cdot d_0 + d_0 = k \cdot d_0$ *columns such that the following holds.*

There exists a constant $\gamma_2 = \gamma_2(\delta) > 0$, *a distribution* μ_2 *over* k*-itemsets* $T \subseteq [d_2]$, *and a reconstruction algorithm* $\mathcal{R}_2$ *satisfying the following. Suppose* $\mathcal{R}_2$ *is given* $\mathcal{D}_0$ *and approximate itemset frequencies* $\hat{f}_T$ *for all* k*-itemsets* $T \subseteq [d_2]$. *Let* S_2 *denote the set of all* k*-itemsets* T *satisfying* $n \cdot |\hat{f}_T - f_T(\mathcal{D}_2(y'))| \leq \zeta_1$, *and suppose that* $\sum_{T \in S_2} \mu_2(T) \geq 1 - \gamma_2$. *Then* $\mathcal{R}_2$ *outputs* y'.

PROOF. Let $\mathcal{A}_2$ be the database generation algorithm that takes as input a Boolean vector $y' \in \{0,1\}^b$, and first replaces y' with an error-corrected encoding $\text{Enc}(y') \in \{0,1\}^{d_0 \cdot n}$ of y', using an error-correcting code of constant rate that is uniquely decodable from 2% errors. $\mathcal{A}_2$ then outputs the database $\mathcal{D}_2(y')$ with n rows and d_2 columns obtained from $\mathcal{D}_0$ by appending d_0 additional columns, with the first additional column equal to the first n bits of $\text{Enc}(y')$, the second additional column equal to the second n bits of $\text{Enc}(y')$, and so on. We refer to the d_0 attributes corresponding to these additional columns as *special attributes*. Similarly, we call an itemset $T \subseteq [d_2]$ *special* if T contains exactly one special attribute.

For each $i \in [d_0]$, let $y^{(i)} \in \{0,1\}^n$ denote the vector $(\text{Enc}(y')_{(i-1)\cdot n+1}, \ldots, \text{Enc}(y')_{i \cdot n})$; that is, $y^{(i)}$ is the ith "block" of n bits from $\text{Enc}(y')$. Let $\mathcal{D}_1(y^{(i)})$ be as in the statement of Lemma 24. Note that $\mathcal{D}_1(y^{(i)})$ is a sub-database of $\mathcal{D}_2(y')$, in the sense that $\mathcal{D}_1(y^{(i)})$ equals $\mathcal{D}_2(y')$ with several columns removed. Hence, for any k-itemset $T_1 \subseteq [d_1]$, there is a unique itemset $g_i(T_1) \subseteq [d_2]$ such that $f_{T_1}(\mathcal{D}_1(y^{(i)})) = f_{g_i(T_1)}(\mathcal{D}_2(y'))$. Notice that $g_i(T_1)$ is a special itemset, for any i and T_1. Moreover, the g_i's are all invertible: for any special itemset $T_2 \subseteq [d_2]$, there is a unique itemset $h(T_2) \subseteq [d_1]$ and a unique i satisfying $g_i(h(T_2)) = T_2$.

Let $\gamma_2 = \gamma/100$. We define the distribution μ_2 over k-itemsets $T \subseteq [d_2]$ as follows.

$$\mu_2(T) = \begin{cases} 0 & \text{if } T \text{ is not special.} \\ (1/d_0) \cdot \mu_1(h(T)) & \text{if } T \text{ is special.} \end{cases}$$

As per the hypothesis of the lemma, suppose $\mathcal{R}_2$ is given $\mathcal{D}_0$ and approximate itemset frequencies $\hat{f}_T$ for all k-itemsets $T \subseteq [d_2]$. Let S_2 denote the set of all k-itemsets T satisfying $n \cdot |\hat{f}_T - f_T(\mathcal{D}_2(y'))| \leq \zeta_1$, and suppose that $\sum_{T \in S_2} \mu_2(T) \geq 1 - \gamma_2$.

The recovery algorithm $\mathcal{R}_2$ will reconstruct y' by first constructing a vector $y'' \in \{0,1\}^{d_0 \cdot n}$ such that the fractional Hamming distance between y'' and $\text{Enc}(y')$ is at most .02, and then running the decoding algorithm for the error-correcting code on y''. $\mathcal{R}_2$ constructs the vector y'' as follows. For each $i \in [d_0]$, $\mathcal{R}_2$ constructs the i'th block of n bits of y'' by simulating $\mathcal{R}_1$ on $\mathcal{D}_1(y^{(i)})$ in the natural way: whenever $\mathcal{R}_1$ requests a value $\hat{f}_{T_1}$, $\mathcal{R}_2$ returns the value $f_{g_i(T_1)}$. $\mathcal{R}_2$ then sets $(y''_{(i-1)\cdot n+1}, \ldots, y''_{i \cdot n})$ to the vector $\hat{y}$ output by $\mathcal{R}_1$.

Showing y'' is close to $\text{Enc}(y')$ in Hamming distance. For each special attribute i, let $S_{1,i}$ denote the set of itemsets $T \subseteq [d_2]$ in $\text{Range}(g_i)$ satisfying $n \cdot |\hat{f}_T - f_T(\mathcal{D}_2(y'))| \leq \zeta_1$. Since a $1 - \gamma_2$ fraction of the estimates $\hat{f}_T$ under μ_2 satisfy $n \cdot |\hat{f}_T - f_T(\mathcal{D}_2(y'))| \leq \zeta_1$, Markov's inequality implies that 99% of the i's satisfy $\sum_{T \in S_{1,i}} \mu_2(T)/d_0 \geq 1 - 100\gamma_2 = 1 - \gamma_1$. Lemma 24 implies that for each such i, the ith block output by $\mathcal{R}_2$, namely $(y''_{(i-1)\cdot n+1}, \ldots, y''_{i \cdot n})$, will have Hamming distance $o(n)$ from the ith block of $\text{Enc}(y')$. Hence, y'' has fractional Hamming distance at most $.01 + o(1) \leq .02$ from $\text{Enc}(y')$. □

Rudelson [Rud12] proved the existence of matrices $A_1, \ldots, A_{k-1}$ satisfying the conditions of Lemmas 24 and 25.

LEMMA 26 (RUDELSON [RUD12]). *Let* q, k *be constants. Also, let* $\nu \sim \mathbb{R}^{d' \times n}$ *be a distribution over matrices such that every entry of the matrix is an independent and unbiased* $\{0,1\}$ *random variable. Let* $A_1, \ldots, A_{k-1}$ *be i.i.d. copies of random matrices drawn from the distribution* ν *and* A *be the Hadamard product of* $A_1, \ldots, A_{k-1}$. *Then, provided that* $d^{k-1} = o(n \log_{(q)}(n))$, *with probability* $1 - o(1)$, *the smallest singular value of* A, *denoted by* $\sigma_n(A)$, *satisfies* $\sigma_n(A) =$

$\Omega\left(\sqrt{d^{k-1}}\right)$. *Also, the range of A is a $(\gamma(q,\ell),n,d^{k-1})$ Euclidean section for some $\gamma(q,\ell)>0$.*

Combining Lemmas 26 and Lemma 25, we obtain the following lemma.

LEMMA 27. *For any positive constants q,k, and any pair $d_0,n>0$ satisfying $n\log_{(q)}(n)<d_0^{k-1}$, there is a $b=b(d_0,n)\in\Omega(d_0\cdot n)$ and database generation algorithm $\mathcal{A}_2$ that takes as input a Boolean vector $y\in\{0,1\}^b$, and outputs a database $\mathcal{D}_2$ with n rows and $d_2:=(k-1)\cdot d_0+d_0=k\cdot d_0$ columns such that the following holds.*

There exists a constant $\gamma_2=\gamma_2(k,q)>0$, a distribution μ_2 over k-itemsets $T\subseteq[d_2]$, and a reconstruction algorithm $\mathcal{R}_2$ satisfying the following. Let $\zeta_1=\sqrt{n}/\log_{(q+1)}(n)$. Suppose $\mathcal{R}_2$ is given $\mathcal{D}_0$ and approximate itemset frequencies $\hat{f}_T$ for all k-itemsets $T\subseteq[d_2]$. Let S_2 denote the set of all k-itemsets T satisfying $n\cdot|\hat{f}_T-f_T(\mathcal{D}_2(y'))|\leq\zeta_1$, and suppose that $\sum_{T\in S_2}\mu_2(T)\geq 1-\gamma_2$. Then $\mathcal{R}_2$ outputs y'.

Remark: Note that Lemma 27 actually holds for any $\zeta_1=o(\sqrt{n})$; we choose a particular ζ_1 that makes the lemma particularly convenient to apply in our context.

For any $\epsilon>0$, suppose we set $n=1/(\epsilon^2\cdot\log_{(q)}(n))$ in the statement of Lemma 27. This causes ζ_1/n to equal $1/(\sqrt{n}\cdot\log_{(q+1)}(n))=\epsilon\sqrt{\log_{(q)}(n)}/\log_{(q+1)}(n)>\epsilon$. Hence, we conclude that an For-All-Itemset-Frequency-Estimator sketch that can answer all k-itemset frequency queries with error bounded by ϵ provides sufficiently accurate itemset frequency estimates $\hat{f}_T$ to apply Lemma 27 with $n=1/(\epsilon^2\cdot\log_{(q)}(n))$, and Lemma 20 follows.

Are Few Bins Enough: Testing Histogram Distributions

Clément L. Canonne
Columbia University
New York, USA
ccanonne@cs.columbia.edu

ABSTRACT

A probability distribution over an ordered universe $[n] = \{1, \ldots, n\}$ is said to be a k-histogram if it can be represented as a piecewise-constant function over at most k contiguous intervals. We study the following question: given samples from an arbitrary distribution D over $[n]$, one must decide whether D is a k-histogram, or is far in ℓ_1 distance from any such succinct representation. We obtain a sample and time-efficient algorithm for this problem, complemented by a nearly-matching information-theoretic lower bound on the number of samples required for this task. Our results significantly improve on the previous state-of-the-art, due to Indyk, Levi, and Rubinfeld [18] and Canonne, Diakonikolas, Gouleakis, and Rubinfeld [7].

1. INTRODUCTION

1.1 Motivation and background

Large datasets have become the norm over recent decades, a trend that if anything has been hastening lately – and most likely will for the foreseeable future. This rapid increase in the amount of information to store, analyze, and process comes with many challenges; and in particular calls for succinct ways of *representing* the data, as well as (very) fast algorithms to operate on it.

One of the oldest and most widely used representations is that of *histograms*, where the range of possible values the data can take is divided into groups, or "bins" [24]. The number of records from the dataset falling in each bin is then recorded, and serves as summary of the records themselves. Whenever the dataset can be well-approximated by histograms with few bins, this provides a space-efficient and flexible way of storing, querying, and analyzing the data and its distribution; specifically, whenever the number of bins k is much smaller than the size n of the universe. For these reasons, the study of histograms and algorithms that operate on them has received significant interest in databases [22, 25, 14, 11, 20, 31, 32] and many other fields, such as statistics [28, 13, 5], streaming [15, 29, 16], and learning theory [18, 8, 9, 17, 2] (see also [19] for a survey).

In this work we will be concerned with the framework of *property testing of distributions*, as first introduced in the seminal work of Batu et al. [4] (see also [26, 27, 6] for surveys on property and distribution testing). In this setting, access to the data is provided *via* random samples drawn independently from the dataset (that is, from the probability distribution that underlies it).[1] The algorithm must then decide, after looking at as a few samples as possible, whether this probability distribution satisfies some fixed property of interest – e.g., if the records are uniformly distributed. This setting is particularly relevant when confronted to massive datasets, whose sheer size makes the perspective of reading the whole input impractical, or even impossible. In this case, a standard approach to meet the memory and computational constraints is by random sampling of the data, which enables one to instead only perform computations on a small representative portion of the dataset. In view of this, we consider here the following testing question: *given some input parameters k and ε, can the distribution of the data be represented as a histogram on at most k bins, or is it significantly different (at distance at least ε) from any such "k-histogram" representation?*

An efficient primitive answering this question could then be used to represent or sketch the dataset as compactly as possible, when invoked as a subroutine to perform model selection. In more detail, given a bound ε on the desired approximation error, one can iteratively run such an algorithm (e.g., by doubling search) to look for the "smallest corresponding k," that is the smallest number of bins needed to accurately capture the statistical properties of the dataset (within error ε). Once this parameter identified, calling an agnostic learning algorithm as that of e.g. [3] with this k will yield a succinct approximation of the dataset, achieving an optimal tradeoff between accuracy and conciseness. (The efficiency of the testing procedure, notably the number of samples required, is in this case crucial. Indeed, this approach is only advantageous as long as the subroutine only takes $o(n)$ samples – if not, then the overhead it brings completely eclipses the savings made in the learning stage, as one can always approximate the whole dataset and compute the closest histogram "offline" from $O(n)$ data points.)

1.2 Our results

We obtain an efficient algorithm, complemented by a nearly matching lower bound, that together settle the question of

[1] See Section 2 for the formal definition of the model.

PODS'16, June 26-July 01, 2016, San Francisco, CA, USA

ISBN 978-1-4503-4191-2/16/06...$15.00
DOI: http://dx.doi.org/10.1145/2902251.2902274

testing whether an unknown probability distribution can be represented as a k-histogram, for any k in the range of interest (with regard to the size of the universe $\Omega = \{1, \ldots, n\}$). Specifically, we prove the following theorems:

THEOREM 1.1 (UPPER BOUND). *For any $1 \leq k \leq n$, there exists an efficient testing algorithm for the class of k-histograms with sample complexity $O\Big(\frac{\sqrt{n}}{\varepsilon^2}\log k + \frac{k}{\varepsilon^3}\log^2 k\Big)$.*

THEOREM 1.2 (LOWER BOUND). *For any $1 \leq k \leq \frac{n}{120}$, any (non-necessarily efficient) testing algorithm for the class of k-histograms must have sample complexity $\Omega\Big(\frac{\sqrt{n}}{\varepsilon^2} + \frac{1}{\varepsilon}\frac{k}{\log k}\Big)$.*

Indeed, this essentially resolves the sample complexity of testing k-histograms, up to polylogarithmic factors in k and the dependence on ε of the second term. Moreover, we note that the proof of Theorem 1.2 implies the same lower bound on the sample complexity of testing *k-modal distributions*, that is the class of distributions whose probability mass function is allowed to go "up and down" or "down and up" at most k times.

Comparison with previous work.

Our results significantly improve upon the previous algorithmic results of Indyk, Levi, and Rubinfeld [18], which required $O\Big(\frac{\sqrt{kn}}{\varepsilon^5}\log n\Big)$ samples; as well as on later work by Canonne, Diakonikolas, Gouleakis, and Rubinfeld [7], where this upper bound is brought down to $O\Big(\frac{\sqrt{kn}}{\varepsilon^3}\log n\Big)$. Moreover, these results crucially left open the question of the interplay between the domain size n and the parameter k of the class to be tested.

At a high level, our results (almost) answer this question, by "decoupling" these two parameters. In particular, ignoring ε in the statement of Theorem 1.1 one can see the first term as capturing the (sublinear) dependence on the domain size, while the other second only depends on the complexity of the class to be tested.

Turning to the negative results, prior to our work the best lower bounds for this question were due to Paninski [23], who establishes an $\Omega(\sqrt{n}/\varepsilon^2)$ sample lower bound for testing *uniformity* (that is, the case $k = 1$), and to Indyk, Levi, and Rubinfeld [18] where a lower bound of $\Omega(\sqrt{kn})$ samples is proven for $k \leq 1/\varepsilon$. Theorem 1.2 unifies and extends both results, obtaining a nearly-tight lower bound featuring the same decoupling between n and k as in our upper bound.

Importantly, the question we consider is the setting where one does *not* know beforehand the decomposition of the domain in k intervals on which the unknown distribution D "should be piecewise-constant," but instead must decide if such a decomposition exists. The (easier) problem of testing, given as input an explicit partition Π of the domain in k intervals, if D is indeed a histogram with regard to this *specific* Π has been recently considered in [12], where the authors obtain tight upper and lower bounds on the question.

1.3 Techniques

Upper bound.

To obtain our algorithmic result, we follow an approach similar to that of Acharya, Daskalakis, and Kamath [1], who show how to apply the "testing by learning" paradigm to the setting of distribution testing. At a high-level, the idea is to first learn an approximation of the unknown distribution *as if it satisfied the property of interest* (which can usually be achieved with relatively few samples); before verifying that the output of this learning stage is both (a) close to having the property and (b) close to the unknown distribution. While standard in property testing of *functions*, this method was believed to inherently fail in the case of probability distributions, due to the hardness of efficiently estimating the distance between distributions from samples [30] – as required for (b). Namely, the result of [30] implies that this last step would by itself cost a prohibitive number of samples, almost linear in the domain size n. The main idea of [1] is to circumvent this impossibility result by first choosing to learn the unknown distribution not with regard to the total variation, but instead in χ^2 distance; and showing that the corresponding variant of distance estimation (deciding whether two distributions are close in χ^2 distance, versus far in total variation) *can* be achieved with only $\sqrt{n}$ samples.[2]

In order to establish Theorem 1.1, we adapt the above approach, with several crucial modifications. Namely, applying the ideas of [1] out-of-the-box would require an efficient algorithm to learn the class of k-histograms in χ^2 distance, i.e. one with sample complexity poly$(k, 1/\varepsilon)$ (independent of n). To the best of our knowledge, such learning algorithm does not appear in the literature, and it is not clear whether one can even exist. Instead, we settle for a weaker guarantee: that of learning a good approximation of an unknown k-histogram except on a small (but unknown) portion of the domain, *where the accuracy can be arbitrarily poor.* To handle this, we then need to adapt the second stage (testing in χ^2 vs. total variation) to identify and discard this small portion of the domain. This is done by iteratively applying (a modification of) the testing algorithm of [1] several times, removing "bad chunks of the domain" one at a time. The challenge here is to do this in a careful and controlled manner, in order to keep the number of such iterations (and therefore samples) as small as possible. (Intuitively, this is where the $\log k$ factor in the first term of the sample complexity stems from – a union bound over k outcomes of the testing subroutine.)

Lower bound.

Turning now to the converse result, we split the proof of Theorem 1.2 in two parts, establishing separately each term of the lower bound. The first one, $\Omega(\sqrt{n}/\varepsilon^2)$, is essentially a direct modification of the lower bound of Paninski on testing uniformity (i.e., 1-histograms). The second term, however, proves to be much less straightforward: the main ingredient in our $\Omega(k/\log k)$ bound is a reduction from a seemingly unrelated question, that of *estimating the support size* [30]. A key aspect of this reduction is to lift the corresponding lower bound of Valiant and Valiant – which heavily relies on the support size to be a symmetric property,[3] to our

[2]The use and analysis of a χ^2-based statistic to obtain optimal testing algorithms already appears in [10], where the authors consider the (related) question of distinguishing whether two distributions are *equal* vs. far in total variation distance.

[3]That is, a property invariant to relabeling of the domain elements: D has a property if and only if, for every permutation σ of the domain, $D \circ \sigma$ has the property.

setting – a property that is clearly *not* symmetric, and thus at first glance intrinsically different. Perhaps surprisingly, we manage to connect these two questions in a black-box and conceptually simple way; moreover, we believe our reduction to be of independent interest, and applicable to other properties as well.

1.4 Organization

After introducing the required definitions and notations in Section 2, we establish our algorithmic result, Theorem 1.1, in Section 3. Finally, Section 4 contains the details of our lower bound, Theorem 1.2.

2. NOTATIONS AND PRELIMINARIES

All throughout this paper, we denote by $[n]$ the set $\{1,\dots,n\}$, and by log the logarithm in base 2. We write $\Delta([n])$ for the set of discrete probability distributions over domain $[n]$, i.e. the set of all real-valued functions $D\colon [n]\to[0,1]$ such that $\sum_{i=1}^n D(i)=1$. A *property* of distributions over $[n]$ is a subset $\mathcal{P}\subseteq\Delta([n])$, consisting of all distributions that have the property.

For any fixed $1\leq k\leq n$, we let $\mathcal{H}_k\subseteq\Delta([n])$ denote the class of *k-histograms*, i.e. the property of being piecewise-constant with at most k "pieces." Formally, $D\in\mathcal{H}_k$ if and only if there exists a partition $\mathcal{I}=(I_1,\dots,I_k)$ of $[n]$ into k intervals such that D is constant on each I_j.

In this work, we will measure the distance between two distributions D_1, D_2 on $[n]$ by their *total variation distance*

$$\mathrm{d_{TV}}(D_1,D_2)\stackrel{\text{def}}{=}\frac{1}{2}\|D_1-D_2\|_1=\max_{S\subseteq[n]}(D_1(S)-D_2(S))$$

which takes value in $[0,1]$. (Note that this metric, sometimes referred to as *statistical distance* and equivalent to the ℓ_1 distance, is one of the most stringent ones and the standard distance measure in distribution testing.) To prove some of our results, we will also require as a tool the definition of the (asymmetric) χ^2*-distance* between two distributions $D_1,D_2\in\Delta([n])$,

$$\mathrm{d}_{\chi^2}(D_1\mid\mid D_2)=\sum_{i=1}^n\frac{(D_1(i)-D_2(i))^2}{D_2(i)}=-1+\sum_{i=1}^n\frac{D_1(i)^2}{D_2(i)}.$$

Finally, recall that a *testing algorithm* for a fixed property $\mathcal{P}$ is a randomized algorithm TESTER which takes as input n, $\varepsilon\in(0,1]$, and is granted access to independent samples from an unknown distribution D:

(i) if $D\in\mathcal{P}$, the algorithm outputs accept with probability at least 2/3;

(ii) if $\mathrm{d_{TV}}(D,D')\geq\varepsilon$ for every $D'\in\mathcal{P}$, it outputs reject with probability at least 2/3.

That is, TESTER must accept if the unknown distribution has the property, and reject if it is ε*-far* from having it. The *sample complexity* of the algorithm is the number of samples it draws from the distribution in the worst case.

Poissonization.

We hereafter follow, for our upper bounds, the standard "Poissonization trick": specifically, we assume that instead of drawing a fixed number m of samples from a distribution D, the algorithms instead randomly select $m'\sim\mathrm{Poisson}(m)$, and then draw m' independent samples from D. While greatly simplifying the analysis by making the number of times different domain elements appear in the samples independent, this can be achieved at only a negligible cost in both the sample complexity and the probability of error, due to the tight concentration of the Poisson distribution around its mean.

On discrete domains.

Although the setting we consider is that of *discrete* domains, our techniques can be easily extended to continuous ones by suitably gridding the range of values. This approach may not in general be optimal, and will depend on the step chosen for the discretization; however, it is not clear how to even phrase distribution testing questions in a continuous setting without either additional assumptions on the unknown distribution or changing the metric.

3. UPPER BOUND: AN EFFICIENT TESTING ALGORITHM

In this section, we prove our upper bound, Theorem 1.1. More specifically, we establish the following, more detailed, result:

THEOREM 3.1. *For any $k\geq 1$, there exists a testing algorithm for $\mathcal{H}_k$ with sample complexity*

$$O\left(\frac{\sqrt{n}}{\varepsilon^2}\log k+\frac{k}{\varepsilon^3}\log k+\frac{k}{\varepsilon}\log^2\frac{k}{\varepsilon}\right).$$

Moreover, its running time is $\sqrt{n}\,\mathrm{poly}(\log k,1/\varepsilon)+\mathrm{poly}(k,1/\varepsilon)$.

We first state in the next subsection some results from the literature we shall rely upon, before delving into the proof of the theorem.

3.1 Tools from previous work

Our starting point will be a recent result of Acharya, Daskalakis, and Kamath, which shows how to efficiently perform a specific relaxation of *tolerant identity testing*,[4] with regard to a χ^2 guarantee:

THEOREM 3.2 ([1], REPHRASED). *There exists an algorithm* TESTER *that, on input n, $\varepsilon\in(0,1]$ as well as the explicit description of a distribution $D^*\in\Delta([n])$, takes $O(\sqrt{n}/\varepsilon^2)$ samples from an unknown distribution $D\in\Delta([n])$ and satisfies the following.*

(i) If $\mathrm{d}_{\chi^2}(D\mid\mid D^*)\leq\frac{\varepsilon^2}{500}$, then TESTER *outputs* accept *with probability at least 2/3;*

(ii) If $\mathrm{d_{TV}}(D,D^*)\geq\varepsilon$, then TESTER *outputs* reject *with probability at least 2/3.*

Moreover, TESTER *runs in time $O(\sqrt{n}/\varepsilon^2)$.*

For our purpose, instead of invoking this result as a blackbox we will rely on the following refinement (which already appears in the section of [1] dealing with unimodality):[5] given

[4]In tolerant identity testing, the goal is, provided the full description of a distribution D^* and samples from an unknown distribution D, to distinguish between $\mathrm{d_{TV}}(D,D^*)\leq\varepsilon$ and $\mathrm{d_{TV}}(D,D^*)\geq 2\varepsilon$. Valiant and Valiant [30] showed that even in the case of D^* being the uniform distribution, $\Omega\left(\frac{n}{\log n}\right)$ samples were required for this task.

[5]See Appendix D of the full version of [1].

an explicit partition of $[n]$ on K intervals $I_1, \dots, I_K$ and a fully specified distribution D^*, the algorithm from Theorem 3.2 takes (Poisson) $m = O(\sqrt{n}/\varepsilon^2)$ samples from D, and computes the K (independent) statistics $Z_1, \dots, Z_K$ defined as

$$Z_j = \sum_{i \in I_j \cap \mathcal{A}_\varepsilon} \frac{(N_i - mD^*(i))^2 - N_i}{mD^*(i)}$$

where $\mathcal{A}_\varepsilon = \left\{ i \in [n] : D^*(i) \geq \frac{\varepsilon}{50n} \right\}$ and N_i is the number of occurrences of $i \in [n]$ among the samples drawn from D. Observing that N_i is distributed according to Poisson$(mD(i))$, standard computations yield that $\mathbb{E}Z_j = m\sum_{i \in I_j \cap \mathcal{A}_\varepsilon} \frac{(D(i)-D^*(i))^2}{D^*(i)}$. Letting $Z = \sum_{j=1}^K Z_j$, we get the quantity analyzed by Acharya, Daskalakis, and Kamath, for which they show the following:

Proposition 3.3 ([1], Lemmata 1 and 2). *The statistic Z above has the following guarantees, provided that $m \geq 20000\sqrt{n}/\varepsilon^2$.*

- *If $\mathrm{d}_{\chi^2}(D \,\|\, D^*) \leq \frac{\varepsilon^2}{500}$, then $\mathbb{E}Z \leq \frac{m\varepsilon^2}{500}$, which implies $\operatorname{Var} Z \leq \frac{m^2\varepsilon^4}{500000}$.*
- *If $\mathrm{d}_{\mathrm{TV}}(D, D^*) \geq \varepsilon$, then $\mathbb{E}Z \geq \frac{m\varepsilon^2}{5}$, which implies $\operatorname{Var} Z \leq \frac{\mathbb{E}[Z]^2}{100}$.*

Moreover, for any $j \in [K]$ such that $\mathbb{E}Z_j \geq \frac{m\varepsilon^2}{5}$, we have $\operatorname{Var} Z_j \leq \frac{\mathbb{E}[Z_j]^2}{100}$ (as per the second item).

We will also leverage another characteristic of the tester of Theorem 3.2; specifically, that it also works for *subdistributions* (i.e., considering only a portion of the domain, on which the two distributions do not necessarily sum to one nor to the same value), considering the natural restrictions of χ^2 and total variation to intervals (the latter as half the ℓ_1 norm, as defined above).[6]

Finally, we will make use of the fact below, which can be shown by a standard application of Chernoff bounds.

Proposition 3.4 ([1], Claim 1 (Full version)). *There exists an algorithm* ApproxPart *that, given a parameter $b > 1$, takes $O(b \log b)$ samples from a distribution D and, with probability at least $9/10$, outputs a partition of $[n]$ in $K \leq 2b + 2$ intervals $I_1, \dots, I_K$ such that the following holds:*

(i) For each $i \in [n]$ such that $D(i) \geq 1/b$, there exists $\ell \in [K]$ such that $I_\ell = \{i\}$;

(ii) There are at most two intervals I such that $D(I) < 1/(2b)$;

(iii) Every other interval is such that $D(I) \in [1/(2b), 2/b]$.

Moreover, the algorithm runs in time $O(b \log b)$.

3.2 Proof of Theorem 3.1

As described in Section 1.3, our algorithm relies on two main components: the first is an (almost) learning procedure for k-histograms which outputs an approximation $\hat{D}$ of an unknown distribution D, with the guarantee that *if $D \in \mathcal{H}_k$*, then $\hat{D}$ is close to D in χ^2 distance *except possibly on a small but unknown portion S of the domain.* The second is a testing procedure, inspired by the work of [1], which takes this $\hat{D}$ as input and iteratively "sieves" the domain, in order to discard a set S' (the algorithm's "guess" for S); and eventually checks if $\hat{D}$ and D are indeed close in χ^2 distance on the sieved domain $[n] \setminus S'$.

Algorithm 1

Require: Parameters k and $\varepsilon \in (0, 1]$; sample access to a distribution D over $[n]$

Set $b \stackrel{\text{def}}{=} \frac{20k \log k}{\varepsilon}$, and $\varepsilon' \stackrel{\text{def}}{=} \frac{13\varepsilon}{30}$.

Learning

Run ApproxPart (from Proposition 3.4) with parameter b; let $\mathcal{I}$ be the partition of $[n]$ into K intervals it outputs.

Run Learner (from Lemma 3.5) with parameters K, $\frac{\varepsilon}{60}$, and $\mathcal{I}$; let $\hat{D} \in \mathcal{H}_K$ be its output.

Sieving

Identify $O(k \log k)$ intervals from $\mathcal{I}$ to discard (with regard to $D, \hat{D}$), as detailed in Section 3.2.1. Let $\mathcal{I}' \subseteq \mathcal{I}$ be the set of remaining intervals, and $G = \cup_{I \in \mathcal{I}'} I$.

Checking

Check there exists $D^* \in \mathcal{H}_k$ such that $\mathrm{d}^G_{\mathrm{TV}}(\hat{D}, D^*) \leq \frac{\varepsilon}{60}$; otherwise, **return** reject. ▷ Can be done in time poly$(k, 1/\varepsilon)$ by dynamic programming, as in [7] (Lemma 4.11)

Testing

Run Tester (from Theorem 3.2) on D with parameters n, ε', and $\hat{D}$, restricted to the subdomain G; if the tester rejects, **return** reject.

return accept

A learning lemma. Let $\mathcal{I}$ be a partition of $[n]$ into intervals. For a subset of intervals $\mathcal{J} \subseteq \mathcal{I}$ define $\widetilde{D}^{\mathcal{J}}$ as follows. For every $i \notin \cup_{J \in \mathcal{J}} J$, $\widetilde{D}^{\mathcal{J}}(i) = D(i)$ and otherwise $\widetilde{D}^{\mathcal{J}}(i) = D(I)/|I|$ where I is such that $I \in \mathcal{I}$ and $i \in I$. Given a histogram $D \in \mathcal{H}_k$, we say that $i \in [n]$ is a *breakpoint* of D if $D(i) \neq D(i+1)$. Similarly, an interval $I \in \mathcal{I}$ is a *breakpoint interval* of D (with respect to $\mathcal{I}$) if it contains a breakpoint of D. (Note that there can be at most $k-1$ such breakpoints and breakpoint intervals).

Lemma 3.5. *There exists an algorithm* Learner *that, on input n, a partition of $[n]$ into ℓ intervals $\mathcal{I} = \{I_1, \dots, I_\ell\}$ and $\varepsilon \in (0, 1]$, takes $O(\ell/\varepsilon^2)$ samples from an unknown distribution $D \in \Delta([n])$ and outputs (the succinct description of) a distribution $\hat{D} \in \mathcal{H}_\ell$ that satisfies the following. For every $k \leq \ell$, if $D \in \mathcal{H}_k$ and $\mathcal{J} = \{J_1, \dots, J_{r-1}\} \subseteq \mathcal{I}$ (with $r \leq k$) are the breakpoints intervals of D, then $\mathrm{d}_{\chi^2}\left(\widetilde{D}^{\mathcal{J}} \,\|\, \hat{D}\right) \leq \varepsilon^2$ with probability at least $9/10$. Moreover, the algorithm runs in time $O(\ell/\varepsilon^2)$.*

Proof. We follow the analysis of the Laplace estimator from [21], first defining a modified estimator (from m independent samples $s_1, \dots, s_m$ from a distribution D on $[n]$)

[6]Namely, for an interval I define $\mathrm{d}^I_{\chi^2}(D_1 \,\|\, D_2) = \sum_{i \in I} \frac{(D_1(i) - D_2(i))^2}{D_2(i)}$ and $\mathrm{d}^I_{\mathrm{TV}}(D_1, D_2) = \frac{1}{2}\sum_{i \in I} |D_1(i) - D_2(i)|$.

by

$$\hat{D}(j) \stackrel{\text{def}}{=} \frac{m_{I_i}+1}{m+\ell}\cdot\frac{1}{|I_i|}, \quad i\in[\ell], j\in I_i$$

where $m_{I_i} \stackrel{\text{def}}{=} \sum_{j\in I_i} m_j$ and $m_i \stackrel{\text{def}}{=} |\{\, j\in[m] : s_j = i \,\}|$.

Suppose D is a k-histogram. The expected value of $\mathrm{d}_{\chi^2}\left(\widetilde{D}^{\mathcal{J}} \mid\mid \hat{D}\right)$, over the draws of the m samples, can be written

$$\mathbb{E}\left[\mathrm{d}_{\chi^2}\left(\widetilde{D}^{\mathcal{J}} \mid\mid \hat{D}\right)\right] = -1 + \sum_{I\in\mathcal{I}} |I|\cdot\mathbb{E}\left[\frac{\left(\frac{D(I)}{|I|}\right)^2}{\frac{m_I+1}{m+\ell}\cdot\frac{1}{|I|}}\right]$$

$$= -1 + \sum_{I\in\mathcal{I}} \mathbb{E}\left[\frac{D(I)^2(m+\ell)}{m_I+1}\right]$$

Now, for a fixed $I\in\mathcal{I}$, we have

$$\mathbb{E}\left[\frac{1}{m_I+1}\right] = \sum_{s=0}^{m}\frac{1}{s+1}\binom{m}{s}D(I)^s(1-D(I))^{m-s} \leq \frac{1}{D(I)(m+1)}.$$

Plugging it back, this implies

$$\mathbb{E}\left[\mathrm{d}_{\chi^2}\left(\widetilde{D}^{\mathcal{J}} \mid\mid \hat{D}\right)\right] \leq -1 + \sum_{I\in\mathcal{I}}\frac{D(I)(m+\ell)}{m+1} \leq \frac{\ell}{m}$$

Letting $m \geq c\cdot\frac{\ell}{\varepsilon^2}$ (where $c>0$ is an absolute constant), this together with Markov's inequality yields the result. □

Outline and correctness.

The idea is to first run the algorithm ApproxPart of Proposition 3.4 on D with parameter b set to $(20k\log k)/\varepsilon$, getting $K = O((k\log k)/\varepsilon)$ intervals $I_1,\dots,I_K$ (meeting the stated guarantee with probability at least 9/10), after taking $O(K\log K)$ samples. We then run the χ^2 learner of Lemma 3.5 with parameter $\frac{\varepsilon}{60}$ (which requires $O\left(\frac{K}{\varepsilon^2}\right)$ samples from D) to output a histogram $\hat{D}$ on this partition.

- In the completeness case, $D\in\mathcal{H}_k$: meaning that there exists a fixed and fully determined, albeit unknown, subset $\mathcal{B}$ of at most k intervals among the K which contain the "breakpoints intervals" for the piecewise-constant D. (Note that the only possible intervals that can be "bad" must be non-singletons.) Conditioning on the learning algorithm to meet its guarantees on $G \stackrel{\text{def}}{=} \bigcup_{j\in[K]\setminus\mathcal{B}} I_j$ (which happens with probability at least 9/10), we obtain that $\mathrm{d}^G_{\chi^2}\left(D \mid\mid \hat{D}\right) \leq \frac{\varepsilon^2}{3600}$.
- In the soundness case, $\mathrm{d}_{\mathrm{TV}}(D,\mathcal{H}_k)\geq\varepsilon$. Since $D(I)\leq\frac{2}{b}$ for any non-singleton interval, this implies that no matter which set $\mathcal{B}$ of at most $k\log k$ intervals we discard, it amounts for no more than $\frac{\varepsilon}{10}$ total probability weight under D, and we can safely ignore it in the rest of the procedure. Indeed, for any such $\mathcal{B}$ and the corresponding remaining domain $G = \bigcup_{j\in[K]\setminus\mathcal{B}} I_j$, $\mathrm{d}^G_{\mathrm{TV}}(D,D')\geq\frac{9\varepsilon}{20}$ for any $D'\in\mathcal{H}_k$.

The goal is therefore to remove $k\log k$ (non-singleton) intervals, out of the K intervals, which together contribute the maximum amount to Z; that is, to remove $Z_{i_1},\dots,Z_{i_k}$ such that $\sum_{\ell=1}^k \mathbb{E}Z_{i_\ell}$ is maximized (call this stage (‡)). Indeed, assuming this has been done (which corresponds to identifying a good restricted domain G), the two items above together ensure correctness of Algorithm 1, conditioning on all subroutines meeting their specification (which by a union bound happens with probability at least 2/3). In more detail, assuming the sieving stage to have gone through, the algorithm will check that (a) $\hat{D}$ is $\frac{\varepsilon}{60}$-close in "total variation restricted to G" to some k-histogram D' (as it should if $D\in\mathcal{H}_k$); and then (b) run the tester of Theorem 3.2 on $D,\hat{D}$ (on G) with parameter $\varepsilon' \stackrel{\text{def}}{=} \frac{13\varepsilon}{30}$.

Completeness. if $D\in\mathcal{H}_k$ then the learning algorithm of Step 4 outputs $\hat{D}$ such that $\mathrm{d}^G_{\chi^2}\left(D \mid\mid \hat{D}\right) \leq \frac{\varepsilon^2}{3600}$, so that Tester will accept in Step 13; and as this also implies $\mathrm{d}^G_{\mathrm{TV}}\left(\hat{D},D\right)\leq\frac{\varepsilon}{60}$, Step 10 accepts as well.

Soundness. Conversely, suppose $\mathrm{d}_{\mathrm{TV}}(D,\mathcal{H}_k)\geq\varepsilon$ and the algorithm accepts in Step 10 there is a $D^*\in\mathcal{H}_k$ such that $\mathrm{d}^G_{\mathrm{TV}}\left(\hat{D},D^*\right)\leq\frac{\varepsilon}{60}$. But by the above discussion we must have $\mathrm{d}^G_{\mathrm{TV}}(D,D^*)\geq\frac{9\varepsilon}{20}$, and from the triangle inequality $\mathrm{d}^G_{\mathrm{TV}}\left(D,\hat{D}\right)\geq\mathrm{d}^G_{\mathrm{TV}}(D,D^*)-\mathrm{d}^G_{\mathrm{TV}}\left(\hat{D},D^*\right)\geq\frac{13\varepsilon}{30}$: the algorithm will output reject in Step 13.

The correctness having been established, the main question is therefore *how* to perform the "sieving stage" (‡), which we detail next.

3.2.1 *Sieving: removing up to $k\log k$ possible bad intervals.*

In what follows, we will compute the statistics Z_j from Proposition 3.3 several times, computed independently each time. Furthermore, by standard arguments (repeating the test, and taking the median value), we can assume the probability of success/correctness of this test to be $1-\delta$, at the price of an extra $\log\frac{1}{\delta}$ factor in the sample complexity. (In particular, we shall take δ to depend on k, in order to apply a union bound over many tests.)

For simplicity, we deal with the following scenario (where the constants have been changed): among the K indices, there is a fixed but unknown subset $\mathcal{B}=\{i_1,\dots,i_k\}$ of k indices such that

1. $\sum_{j\notin\mathcal{B}}\mathbb{E}Z_j\leq m\alpha^2$;
2. $\sum_{j\in\mathcal{B}}\mathbb{E}Z_j > 100m\alpha^2$

and we want to remove a subset $\mathcal{B}'$ of $2k$ indices such that $\sum_{j\notin\mathcal{B}'}\mathbb{E}Z_j\leq 100m\alpha^2$. (This will deal with the completeness case, and setting $\alpha=\frac{\varepsilon}{C}$ for some big enough constant C in the learning stage will give us what we want.)

Discarding the heavy ones: Let $\mathcal{B}^+\subseteq\mathcal{B}$ be the indices such that $\mathbb{E}Z_j\geq 100m\alpha^2$. By assumption, $\left|\mathcal{B}^+\right|\leq k$, and this is a fixed (albeit unknown) set of indices fully determined by D. In particular, if we compute the statistics as in Proposition 3.3 with failure probability $\delta=\frac{1}{10(k+1)}$, by a union bound we can condition on (i) each Z_j, $j\in\mathcal{B}^+$ behaving as expected: $Z_j > 10m\alpha^2$, and (ii) the fixed set $[K]\setminus\mathcal{B}$ also behaving as expected, so that $\sum_{j\notin\mathcal{B}}Z_j\leq 10m\alpha^2$. By removing all j's such that $Z_j > 10m\alpha^2$, and outputting reject if there are more than k, we thus have filtered all intervals from $\mathcal{B}^+$ (with success probability at least 9/10), and no other. Let ℓ' be the number of elements removed, and $k' = k - \ell$ the number of "possible remaining bad elements."

Iteratively removing the rest: we therefore can now assume we have at most k' indices to remove (call this set $\mathcal{B}^-$), such that for each $\mathbb{E}Z_j < 100m\alpha^2$. In particular, $\sum_{j\in\mathcal{B}^-} \mathbb{E}Z_j < 100mk\alpha^2$. We repeat the following at most $\log k$ times, until either the test accepts at some step, or we performed more than $O(\log k)$ such steps (in which cases we proceed to the last stage, the sieving part being over); or we removed more than k' indices in total (in the latter case, we output reject and stop)

- compute the statistics Z_j for all remaining indices, and check the value of their sum Z.
- if $Z < 10m\alpha^2$, accept.
- otherwise, sort the Z_j's by decreasing order, and remove the first ℓ indices, where $\ell \leq k'$ is the smallest integer such that $\sum_{j>\ell} Z_j \leq 2m\alpha^2$.

Define $\mathcal{B}^-_{\rm rem} \subseteq \mathcal{B}^-$ as the set of bad indices remaining at the current step. By a conditioning on the two subsets of indices $\mathcal{B}^-_{\rm rem}$ and $[K] \setminus \mathcal{B}$, we have that $\sum_{j\notin\mathcal{B}} Z_j \leq 2m\alpha^2$, and if $\sum_{j\in\mathcal{B}^-_{\rm rem}} \mathbb{E}Z_j > 100m\alpha^2$ then $\sum_{j\in\mathcal{B}^-_{\rm rem}} Z_j > \frac{1}{2}\sum_{j\in\mathcal{B}^-_{\rm rem}} \mathbb{E}Z_j$.

By assumption, we remove at least $\frac{1}{2}\sum_{j\in\mathcal{B}^-_{\rm rem}} \mathbb{E}Z_j - 2m\alpha^2 > \frac{1}{3}\sum_{j\in\mathcal{B}^-_{\rm rem}} \mathbb{E}Z_j$ of the "bad weight" as long as $\sum_{j\in\mathcal{B}^-_{\rm rem}} \mathbb{E}Z_j > 100m\alpha^2$ and we know that at the beginning $\sum_{j\in\mathcal{B}^-} \mathbb{E}Z_j < 100mk\alpha^2$. This implies that after $O(\log k)$ such steps, we have that the sum of $\mathbb{E}Z_j$ for the remaining Z_j's is at most $101m\alpha^2$ (from what remains in the "bad" intervals, and the contribution of the "good" ones). Moreover, in total we removed at most $O(\log k)\cdot k' = O(k\log k)$ intervals, and ran $O(\log k)$ "tests" with $\delta = \Theta\left(\frac{1}{\log k}\right)$ (which costs $O\left(\frac{\sqrt{n}}{\alpha^2}\log\log k\right)$ samples).

Overall, over these two stages we end up paying $O\left(\frac{\sqrt{n}}{\alpha^2}\log k\right) + O\left(\frac{\sqrt{n}}{\alpha^2}\log\log k\right) = O\left(\frac{\sqrt{n}}{\alpha^2}\log k\right)$ samples, and perform the "sieving" (‡). This concludes the proof of Theorem 3.1: the total sample complexity is

$$O\left(\frac{\sqrt{n}}{\varepsilon^2}\log k\right) + O\left(\frac{k}{\varepsilon^3}\log k\right) + O\left(\frac{k\log k}{\varepsilon}\log\frac{k\log k}{\varepsilon}\right)$$
$$= O\left(\frac{\sqrt{n}}{\varepsilon^2}\log k\right) + O\left(\frac{k}{\varepsilon^3}\log k\right) + O\left(\frac{k}{\varepsilon}\log^2\frac{k}{\varepsilon}\right)$$

as stated. The running time of the overall algorithm is easily seen to be as claimed, as each of the learning and testing subroutines runs in time linear in the number of samples. □

4. AN INFORMATION-THEORETIC LOWER BOUND

In this section, we prove Theorem 1.2, that is both an $\Omega(\sqrt{n}/\varepsilon^2)$ and an $\Omega(k/(\varepsilon\log k))$ lower bound on testing k-histograms (the latter for $k = \omega(1)$):

PROPOSITION 4.1. *There exists an absolute constant $\varepsilon_0 > 0$ such that the following holds. For any $1 \leq k < \frac{n}{3}$ and $\varepsilon \in (0, \varepsilon_0]$, any (non-necessarily efficient) testing algorithm for $\mathcal{H}_k$ must take $\Omega\left(\frac{\sqrt{n}}{\varepsilon^2}\right)$ samples.*

PROPOSITION 4.2. *There exists an absolute constant $\varepsilon_1 > 0$ such that the following holds. For any large enough $k \leq \frac{n}{120}$ and $\varepsilon \in (0, \varepsilon_1]$, any (non-necessarily efficient) testing algorithm for $\mathcal{H}_k$ must take $\Omega\left(\frac{1}{\varepsilon}\frac{k}{\log k}\right)$ samples.*

As mentioned earlier, the first lower bound builds on a proof of Paninski [23] on testing uniformity; while our argument for the second will rely on a result of Valiant and Valiant [30], namely a lower bound on estimating a *symmetric* property: support size. While $\mathcal{H}_k$ is clearly *not* a symmetric class (i.e., it is not invariant by permutation of the support), we show how one can still leverage this lower bound for our purpose.

4.1 Proof of Proposition 4.1

The result follows from adapting the proof of [23], intended for the case of uniformity testing, or equivalently $\mathcal{H}_1$. In this argument, Paninski defines a family of distributions $\mathcal{Q}$, parameterized as follows. A distribution $D \in \mathcal{Q}_\varepsilon$ is defined by $\frac{n}{2}$ bits $z_1, \dots, z_{n/2} \in \{0,1\}$, and

$$D(2i) = \frac{1+(-1)^{z_i}\cdot c\varepsilon}{n}, \qquad D(2i-1) = \frac{1-(-1)^{z_i}\cdot c\varepsilon}{n}$$

for $i \in [n/2]$, where $c > 0$ is a suitably chosen constant. The result then follows from observing that any distribution in $\mathcal{Q}_\varepsilon$ is ε-far from uniform, and yet that $\Omega(\sqrt{n}/\varepsilon^2)$ samples are necessary to distinguish a uniformly chosen $D \sim \mathcal{Q}_\varepsilon$ from the uniform distribution with probability at least 2/3.

To apply this argument to our case, it is sufficient to observe that for $k < \frac{n}{3}$ (and the right choice of the constant c), a random $D \sim \mathcal{Q}_\varepsilon$ will be ε-far from $\mathcal{H}_k$ as well. To see why, fix $D \in \mathcal{Q}_\varepsilon$, and let $D^* \in \mathcal{H}_k$ be a k-histogram minimizing $d_{\rm TV}(D, D^*)$. Define $S \subseteq [n/2]$ as the set of indices such that $D^*(2i-1) = D^*(2i)$; note that by the triangle inequality, for all $i \in S$ we have $|D(2i-1) - D^*(2i-1)| + |D(2i) - D^*(2i)| \geq |D(2i) - D(2i-1)| = \frac{2c\varepsilon}{n}$. Since one must have $|S| \geq \frac{n}{2} - k + 1 > \frac{n}{6}$ as $D^* \in \mathcal{H}_k$, this implies that

$$2d_{\rm TV}(D, D^*) = \sum_{i=1}^{\frac{n}{2}} \left(|D(2i-1) - D^*(2i-1)| + |D(2i) - D^*(2i)|\right)$$
$$\geq \sum_{i\in S} \left(|D(2i-1) - D^*(2i-1)| + |D(2i) - D^*(2i)|\right)$$
$$\geq \frac{n}{6}\cdot\frac{2c\varepsilon}{n} = \frac{c\varepsilon}{3}$$

so that taking $c \geq 6$ (and $\varepsilon_0 \leq 1/c$) yields the result. □

REMARK 4.3. *We observe that a simpler proof of this lower bound, albeit restricted to the range $k = o(\sqrt{n})$, can be obtained by applying the framework of [7]. Specifically, one can invoke [7] (Theorem 6.1), using as a blackbox the uniformity testing lower bound of Paninski along with the fact that k-histograms can be learned agnostically from $O(k/\varepsilon^2)$ samples ([3]).*

4.2 Proof of Proposition 4.2

Outline.

We start by considering a scalar *symmetric* property, support size. The corresponding problem SUPPSIZE_m is as follows: given sample access to an unknown distribution $D \in \Delta([m])$ with the promise that $D(i) \in \{0\} \cup [\frac{1}{m}, 1]$ for all $i \in [m]$,[7] one must distinguish between (i) $\text{supp}(D) \leq \frac{2m}{3} + 1$ and (ii) $\text{supp}(D) \geq \frac{7m}{8}$. This problem is known to require $c \cdot \frac{m}{\log m}$ samples, where $c > 0$ is an absolute constant, for m sufficiently large ([30] (Theorem 1)).

We then argue that any tester for the property of being a k-histogram can be used to solve this problem, with only a constant factor blowup in the sample complexity. Indeed, if TESTER is a *bona fide* $q(n, k, \varepsilon)$-sample tester for testing k-histograms (with probability of success 2/3), then it can be converted to a symmetric tester TESTER′ for the weak support size problem as follows: first, "enlarge" the domain $[m]$ of D by embedding it in $[n]$, for some $n > m$ (that is, setting $D(i) = 0$ for all $m + 1 \leq i \leq n$). Second, pick uniformly at random a permutation $\sigma \in \mathcal{S}_n$ of the "enlarged domain", where $\mathcal{S}_n$ denote the set of all permutations of $[n]$. Then, given samples of a distribution D it remains to feed TESTER with q samples from a distribution $D_\sigma = D \circ \sigma^{-1}$ ("re-building" the identity of the samples according to σ: for $i \in [n]$, $D_\sigma(i) = D(\sigma^{-1}(i))$). The key point is to argue that with high constant probability over the choice of σ:

- If D has support size at most $\frac{m}{3}$, then D_σ is a k-histogram for $k \stackrel{\text{def}}{=} 2 \cdot \frac{m}{3} + 1$ (with probability one);
- If D has support size in $[\frac{7m}{8}, m]$, then D_σ is far from any k-histogram, as with high constant probability its support is "sprinkled" over many *isolated* points – say at least $\frac{3m}{4}$. Whenever this happens, D_σ needs at least $\frac{6m}{4} - 1$ intervals to be a histogram, and incurs constant distance ε_1 (where $\varepsilon_1 = \left(\frac{3}{4}m - k + 1\right)\frac{1}{2m} = \frac{1}{24}$) from any k-histogram, from a similar argument as in Proposition 4.1 and the lower bound $1/m$ on any non-zero probability.

Independently repeating a constant number of times this procedure (that is, drawing a new permutation σ, and applying TESTER on D_σ using fresh samples from D) and taking the majority vote then allows the test to succeed with probability at least 5/9. But this in turn implies a lower bound on q, as otherwise it would contradict the lower bound on the number of samples required to tolerantly test the symmetric property SUPPSIZE_m.

The last piece we need in our reduction is the guarantee that, when permuting the domain at random, (a) a distribution with support size at most ℓ will be a $(2\ell + 1)$ histogram (this point is obvious); but also (b) with high probability over the permutation, a distribution with support size $\ell \ll n$ will keep its support "sprinkled" over the domain, and therefore need much more than $(2\ell + 1)$ pieces to be represented as a histogram. The following lemma makes this intuition precise, showing that for reasonable values of ℓ a random permutation will keep the points of the support isolated with constant probability:

[7]That is, $1/m$ is a lower bound on the probability weight of any element in the support.

LEMMA 4.4. *Let $\ell \leq \frac{n}{70}$. For any set $S \subseteq [n]$, define $s = \text{cover}(S)$ as the minimum number of disjoint intervals $I_1, \ldots, I_s \subseteq S$ necessary to cover S. (That is, $\text{cover}(S)$ is the number of disjoint "chunks" S induces in $[n]$). Then, fixing $S \subseteq [n]$ of size ℓ, we have*

$$\Pr_{\sigma \sim \mathcal{S}_n}\left[\text{cover}(\sigma(S)) \leq \frac{6\ell}{7}\right] \leq \frac{7\ell}{n} \leq \frac{1}{10}$$

where the probability is taken over a uniform choice of permutation $\sigma \in \mathcal{S}_n$.

PROOF. Let $X_1, \ldots, X_{n-1}$ be the $n - 1$ (identically distributed, but non-independent) indicator random variables defined as follows. X_i is 1 if $\sigma^{-1}(i) \leq \ell$, but $\sigma^{-1}(i+1) > \ell$ (that is, one of the ℓ "good" points ends up on i, but one of the $n - \ell$ "bad points" ends up on $i + 1$).

Let $X = \sum_{i=1}^{n-1} X_i$ be their sum: note that X is a lower bound on the number of clusters, up to an additive one (X counts the number of "right borders," and may only be off if the last cluster-interval ends at n). Moreover,

$$\mathbb{E}X_i = \frac{\ell}{n} \cdot \frac{n - \ell}{n - 1}$$

so that $\mathbb{E}X = \ell \cdot \frac{n-\ell}{n} = \ell\left(1 - \frac{\ell}{n}\right)$ by linearity. Define $Y = \ell - X \geq 0$ (with $\mathbb{E}Y = \frac{\ell^2}{n}$); by Markov's inequality

$$\Pr\left[X \leq \frac{6\ell}{7}\right] = \Pr\left[Y \geq \frac{\ell}{7}\right] \leq \frac{\mathbb{E}Y}{\ell/7} = \frac{\ell/n}{1/7} = \frac{7\ell}{n}.$$

□

Now, this in particular imply that for $m \leq \frac{n}{70}$, a distribution D with support size in $[\frac{7m}{8}, m]$ will, after a random permutation σ of the larger domain $[n]$, have at least $\frac{6}{7} \cdot \frac{7m}{8} = \frac{3m}{4}$ isolated "chunks." But that also implies that $D_\sigma \notin \mathcal{H}_{\frac{3m}{4}-2}$ (i.e., needs a partition of at least $\frac{3m}{4} - 1$ intervals to be a histogram).

Details.

We can now make precise the reduction outlined above: assume we have a tester TESTER for the property of being a histogram, which takes as input n, k, ε as well as $q(n, k, \varepsilon)$ independent samples from an unknown distribution D; and distinguishes with success probability at least 2/3 between (a) $D \in \mathcal{H}_k$ and (b) $\ell_1(D, \mathcal{H}_k) > \varepsilon_1$.

Given sufficiently large integer n, and k satisfying $k \leq \frac{n}{120}$, we define $m \stackrel{\text{def}}{=} \left\lceil \frac{3}{2}(k-1) \right\rceil \leq \frac{n}{70}$. Now, we can embed any instance D' of SUPPSIZE_m (i.e., a distribution $D' \in \Delta([m])$ meeting the promise of the problem) by seeing it as a distribution on $[n]$, and use TESTER to solve SUPPSIZE_m as follows:

1. Draw uniformly a random a permutation $\sigma \in \mathcal{S}_n$;
2. Run TESTER on $D'_\sigma \in \Delta([n])$ with parameters n, k, and $\varepsilon_1 \stackrel{\text{def}}{=} \frac{1}{24}$;
3. accept if and only if TESTER accepted.

By the foregoing discussion and Lemma 4.4, the above test succeeds in solving SUPPSIZE_m with probability at least $1 - \frac{1}{10} - \frac{1}{3} = \frac{17}{30}$; repeating constantly many times independently and taking a majority vote brings this success probability to 2/3. The overall sample complexity being $O(q(n, k))$, the lower bound of [30] (Theorem 1) implies that, for some absolute constant $c > 0$ and k large enough, $q(n, k, \varepsilon_1) \geq c \cdot \frac{k}{\log k}$, as claimed.

Finally, using a standard "trick" (embedding the hard instance by adding an extra element with weight $1 - \frac{\varepsilon}{\varepsilon_1}$), this yields an $\Omega\left(\frac{1}{\varepsilon}\frac{k}{\log k}\right)$ lower bound on testing $\mathcal{H}_k$, for any $\varepsilon \leq \varepsilon_1$. $\square$

5. ACKNOWLEDGMENTS

The author would like to thank Reut Levi for many insightful discussions and comments.

Research supported by NSF grants CCF-1115703 and CCF-1319788.

6. REFERENCES

[1] J. Acharya, C. Daskalakis, and G. Kamath. Optimal testing for properties of distributions. In C. Cortes, N. Lawrence, D. Lee, M. Sugiyama, R. Garnett, and R. Garnett, editors, *Advances in Neural Information Processing Systems 28*, pages 3577–3598. Curran Associates, Inc., 2015. Full version available on arXiv at abs/1507.05952. 1.3, 3.2, 3.1, 5, 3.3, 3.4, 3.2

[2] J. Acharya, I. Diakonikolas, C. Hegde, J. Z. Li, and L. Schmidt. Fast and near-optimal algorithms for approximating distributions by histograms. In T. Milo and D. Calvanese, editors, *Proceedings of the 34th ACM Symposium on Principles of Database Systems, PODS 2015, Melbourne, Victoria, Australia, May 31 - June 4, 2015*, pages 249–263. ACM, 2015. 1.1

[3] J. Acharya, I. Diakonikolas, J. Z. Li, and L. Schmidt. Sample-optimal density estimation in nearly-linear time. *CoRR*, abs/1506.00671, 2015. 1.1, 4.3

[4] T. Batu, L. Fortnow, R. Rubinfeld, W. D. Smith, and P. White. Testing that distributions are close. In *Proceedings of FOCS*, pages 189–197, 2000. 1.1

[5] L. Birgé. On the risk of histograms for estimating decreasing densities. *The Annals of Statistics*, 15(3):pp. 1013–1022, 1987. 1.1

[6] C. L. Canonne. A Survey on Distribution Testing: your data is Big. But is it Blue? *Electronic Colloquium on Computational Complexity (ECCC)*, 22:63, Apr. 2015. 1.1

[7] C. L. Canonne, I. Diakonikolas, T. Gouleakis, and R. Rubinfeld. Testing Shape Restrictions of Discrete Distributions. In N. Ollinger and H. Vollmer, editors, *33rd Symposium on Theoretical Aspects of Computer Science, STACS 2016, February 17-20, 2016, Orléans, France*, volume 47 of *LIPIcs*, pages 25:1–25:14. Schloss Dagstuhl - Leibniz-Zentrum fuer Informatik, 2016. Also available on arXiv at abs/1507.03558. (document), 1.2, 10, 4.3

[8] S. Chan, I. Diakonikolas, R. A. Servedio, and X. Sun. Learning mixtures of structured distributions over discrete domains. In *Proceedings of SODA*, pages 1380–1394, 2013. 1.1

[9] S. Chan, I. Diakonikolas, R. A. Servedio, and X. Sun. Near-optimal density estimation in near-linear time using variable-width histograms. In *Annual Conference on Neural Information Processing Systems (NIPS)*, pages 1844–1852, 2014. 1.1

[10] S. Chan, I. Diakonikolas, G. Valiant, and P. Valiant. Optimal algorithms for testing closeness of discrete distributions. In *Proceedings of SODA*, pages 1193–1203, 2014. 2

[11] S. Chaudhuri, R. Motwani, and V. R. Narasayya. Random sampling for histogram construction: How much is enough? In L. M. Haas and A. Tiwary, editors, *SIGMOD 1998, Proceedings ACM SIGMOD International Conference on Management of Data, June 2-4, 1998, Seattle, Washington, USA.*, pages 436–447. ACM Press, 1998. 1.1

[12] I. Diakonikolas and D. M. Kane. A New Approach for Testing Properties of Discrete Distributions. *ArXiv e-prints*, Jan. 2016. 1.2

[13] D. Freedman and P. Diaconis. On the histogram as a density estimator: L_2 theory. *Zeitschrift für Wahrscheinlichkeitstheorie und Verwandte Gebiete*, 57(4):453–476, 1981. 1.1

[14] P. B. Gibbons, Y. Matias, and V. Poosala. Fast incremental maintenance of approximate histograms. In M. Jarke, M. J. Carey, K. R. Dittrich, F. H. Lochovsky, P. Loucopoulos, and M. A. Jeusfeld, editors, *VLDB'97, Proceedings of 23rd International Conference on Very Large Data Bases, August 25-29, 1997, Athens, Greece*, pages 466–475. Morgan Kaufmann, 1997. 1.1

[15] A. C. Gilbert, S. Guha, P. Indyk, Y. Kotidis, S. Muthukrishnan, and M. Strauss. Fast, small-space algorithms for approximate histogram maintenance. In J. H. Reif, editor, *Proceedings on 34th Annual ACM Symposium on Theory of Computing, May 19-21, 2002, Montréal, Québec, Canada*, pages 389–398. ACM, 2002. 1.1

[16] S. Guha, N. Koudas, and K. Shim. Approximation and streaming algorithms for histogram construction problems. *ACM Trans. Database Syst.*, 31(1):396–438, 2006. 1.1

[17] S. Guha, K. Shim, and J. Woo. REHIST: relative error histogram construction algorithms. In M. A. Nascimento, M. T. Özsu, D. Kossmann, R. J. Miller, J. A. Blakeley, and K. B. Schiefer, editors, *(e)Proceedings of the Thirtieth International Conference on Very Large Data Bases, Toronto, Canada, August 31 - September 3 2004*, pages 300–311. Morgan Kaufmann, 2004. 1.1

[18] P. Indyk, R. Levi, and R. Rubinfeld. Approximating and Testing k-Histogram Distributions in Sub-linear Time. In *Proceedings of PODS*, pages 15–22, 2012. (document), 1.1, 1.2

[19] Y. E. Ioannidis. The history of histograms (abridged). In *VLDB*, pages 19–30, 2003. 1.1

[20] H. V. Jagadish, N. Koudas, S. Muthukrishnan, V. Poosala, K. C. Sevcik, and T. Suel. Optimal histograms with quality guarantees. In A. Gupta, O. Shmueli, and J. Widom, editors, *VLDB'98, Proceedings of 24rd International Conference on Very Large Data Bases, August 24-27, 1998, New York City, New York, USA*, pages 275–286. Morgan Kaufmann, 1998. 1.1

[21] S. Kamath, A. Orlitsky, D. Pichapati, and A. T. Suresh. On learning distributions from their samples. In P. Grünwald, E. Hazan, and S. Kale, editors, *Proceedings of The 28th Conference on Learning*

Theory, COLT 2015, Paris, France, July 3-6, 2015, volume 40 of *JMLR Proceedings*, pages 1066–1100. JMLR.org, 2015. 3.2

[22] R. Kooi. *The Optimization of Queries in Relational Databases.* PhD thesis, Case Western Reserve University, Sept. 1980. 1.1

[23] L. Paninski. A coincidence-based test for uniformity given very sparsely sampled discrete data. *IEEE Transactions on Information Theory*, 54(10):4750–4755, 2008. 1.2, 4, 4.1

[24] K. Pearson. Contributions to the Mathematical Theory of Evolution. II. Skew Variation in Homogeneous Material. *Philosophical Transactions of the Royal Society of London A: Mathematical, Physical and Engineering Sciences*, 186:343–414, 1895. 1.1

[25] V. Poosala, Y. E. Ioannidis, P. J. Haas, and E. J. Shekita. Improved histograms for selectivity estimation of range predicates. In H. V. Jagadish and I. S. Mumick, editors, *Proceedings of the 1996 ACM SIGMOD International Conference on Management of Data, Montreal, Quebec, Canada, June 4-6, 1996.*, pages 294–305. ACM Press, 1996. 1.1

[26] D. Ron. Property Testing: A Learning Theory Perspective. *Foundations and Trends in Machine Learning*, 1(3):307–402, 2008. 1.1

[27] D. Ron. Algorithmic and Analysis Techniques in Property Testing. *Foundations and Trends in Theoretical Computer Science*, 5:73–205, 2010. 1.1

[28] D. W. Scott. On optimal and data-based histograms. *Biometrika*, 66(3):605–610, 1979. 1.1

[29] N. Thaper, S. Guha, P. Indyk, and N. Koudas. Dynamic multidimensional histograms. In M. J. Franklin, B. Moon, and A. Ailamaki, editors, *Proceedings of the 2002 ACM SIGMOD International Conference on Management of Data, Madison, Wisconsin, June 3-6, 2002*, pages 428–439. ACM, 2002. 1.1

[30] G. Valiant and P. Valiant. A CLT and tight lower bounds for estimating entropy. *Electronic Colloquium on Computational Complexity (ECCC)*, 17:179, 2010. 1.3, 1.3, 4, 4, 4.2, 4.2

[31] W. Wang, H. Jiang, H. Lu, and J. X. Yu. Bloom histogram: Path selectivity estimation for XML data with updates. In *Proceedings of the Thirtieth International Conference on Very Large Data Bases - Volume 30*, VLDB '04, pages 240–251. VLDB Endowment, 2004. 1.1

[32] J. Xu, Z. Zhang, X. Xiao, Y. Yang, G. Yu, and M. Winslett. Differentially private histogram publication. *VLDB J.*, 22(6):797–822, 2013. 1.1

Range-Max Queries on Uncertain Data*

Pankaj K. Agarwal† Nirman Kumar‡ Stavros Sintos§ Subhash Suri¶

ABSTRACT

Let P be a set of n uncertain points in $\mathbb{R}^d$, where each point $p_i \in P$ is associated with a real value v_i and a probability $\alpha_i \in (0, 1]$ of existence, i.e., each p_i exists with an independent probability α_i. We present algorithms for building an index on P so that for a d-dimensional query rectangle ρ, the expected maximum value or the most-likely maximum value in ρ can be computed quickly. The specific contributions of our paper include the following: (i) The first index of sub-quadratic size to achieve a sub-linear query time in any dimension $d \geq 1$. It also provides a trade-off between query time and size of the index. (ii) A conditional lower bound for the most-likely range-max queries, based on the conjectured hardness of the set-intersection problem, which suggests that in the worst case the product (query time)^2 $\times$ (index size) is $\Omega(\frac{n^2}{\mathrm{polylog}(n)})$. (iii) A linear-size index for estimating the expected range-max value within approximation factor 1/2 in $O(\log^c n)$ time, for some constant $c > 0$; that is, if the expected maximum value is μ then the query procedure returns a value μ' with $\mu/2 \leq \mu' \leq \mu$. (iv) Extensions of our algorithm to more general uncertainty models and for computing the top-k values of the range-max.

*Work by Agarwal and Sintos is supported by NSF under grants CCF-11-61359, CCF-15-13816, CCF-15-46392, and IIS-14-08846, by ARO grant W911NF-15-1-0408, and by Grant 2012/229 from the U.S.-Israel Binational Science Foundation. Work by Suri and Kumar is supported by NSF under grants CCF-11-61495 and CCF-15-25817.

†Department of Computer Science, Duke University, Durham, NC 27708-0129, USA; pankaj@cs.duke.edu.

‡Department of Computer Science, University of California, Santa Barbara, CA 93106, USA; nirman@cs.ucsb.edu.

§Department of Computer Science, Duke University, Durham, NC 27708-0129, USA; ssintos@cs.duke.edu.

¶Department of Computer Science, University of California, Santa Barbara, CA 93106, USA; suri@cs.ucsb.edu.

PODS'16, June 26-July 01, 2016, San Francisco, CA, USA

© 2016 ACM. ISBN 978-1-4503-4191-2/16/06...$15.00

DOI: http://dx.doi.org/10.1145/2902251.2902281

1. INTRODUCTION

Query-driven data management is an important function in most database systems, and range query is a common tool for summarizing information on the objects lying in a query range. In recent years, motivated by applications in sensor networks, data cleaning, data integration, pervasive computing and scientific data analysis, there has been a growing interest in managing *uncertain data* [6, 14]. In these settings, uncertainty is typically captured using stochastic data models, and summarizing or querying data requires computing *statistics* about the probabilistic behavior of the underlying data.

In this paper we study the *range-max* query on uncertain data—return statistics on the maximum value of the data inside a query range. Formally, we consider database records of the form (p, v, α), where p is a *point* in $\mathbb{R}^d$ (attribute values of the record) with $d \geq 1$ a constant, along with a positive *scalar value* $v \in \mathbb{R}^+$ and a probability $\alpha \in (0, 1]$. We refer to this simple model as the *existence-uncertainty* model. The value v is the metric of interest in our range queries and the probability α reflects our confidence in this record. Given a collection of n such records, our goal is to construct an index to answer queries of the following form efficiently: report the *expected maximum value* (the EM problem) or the *most likely maximum value* (MLM problem) of the records whose attribute values (points) lie in a d-dimensional orthogonal query rectangle ρ. We use P to denote the set of points corresponding to the input records. Throughout the paper, we assume the real-RAM model of computation, which counts word-level operations instead of bits: specifically, each memory cell can store an arbitrary real number and any arithmetic or relational operation between two operands takes $O(1)$ time.

The max is a special case of the widely studied top-k summary of data (i.e. $k = 1$) but is also a popular aggregation operator in its own right. For example, the suprema of random processes (a collection of random variables arising from given distributions) are widely studied in random matrix theory, control of empirical processes in statistics and machine learning, random optimization problems, and Banach spaces probabilities. The reason for this keen interest can be understood from the following hypothetical but representative application. The points might represent a set of geographical locations (cities) $\{p_1, p_2, \ldots, p_n\}$, each associated with a probability α_i of being struck by a natural disaster (flood, earthquake, fire) during next year, and v_i a measure of the *cost* (damage) incurred at that location due to that disaster.[1] In this case, a range query asks for the expected value of the maximum damage suffered within the range. Similarly, an insurance company may associate probabilities of financial claims with various entities, and need to analyze the profile of its maximum loss portfolio. Indeed, in natural disasters such as earthquakes or flooding, the impact is highly *non-linear*—even hundreds of small quakes hardly cause serious financial or social harm, but a single large one can be catastrophic. Thus, it is far more important to be able to carry out analysis on the profile of the *maximum values*, and not on simpler aggregates such as sum or average.

Range-max queries on uncertain data are also relevant when dealing with spatially distributed noisy data sources (e.g. sensors) where unusually high measurements might be cause for concern, but only if they deviate from the norm. A probabilistic profile of the expected max in a range can serve as the benchmark for deciding when a sensor measurement is abnormal.

We point out that, given a query rectangle ρ, the expected value of *range-SUM*, namely, $\sum_{p_i \in \mathsf{P} \cap \rho} \alpha_i v_i$ is easy to compute: we simply assign each point p_i a *weight* of $\alpha_i v_i$ and compute the weighted range sum using traditional (non-uncertain) techniques. In contrast, computing the expected value of *range-max*, our EM problem, seems much harder and it is not clear how to use any existing range-aggregation index to answer this query. The difficulty arises in part because the EM problem is not *range decomposable*, i.e., if P_1, P_2 is a partition of P then for a query rectangle ρ, the EM value of $\mathsf{P} \cap \rho$ cannot be quickly computed from the EM values of $\mathsf{P}_1 \cap \rho$ and $\mathsf{P}_2 \cap \rho$. The interaction of probabilities rules out traditional tree-style range-searching indexes where the value at each node is inferred simply from values at its children. On the positive side, while the probability distribution of range-SUM can take exponentially many possible values, the probability distribution of range-max only has linear size. Therefore, computing statistics on the distribution of range-max (e.g. most likely max) might be easier than a similar statistics on range-SUM; the latter is known to be $\#P$-hard [19].

[1]More generally, each point can be associated with not just a single pair (value, probability) but an entire distribution. For the ease of exposition, we initially focus on the single value case, but remark on how to generalize our results to distributional settings later.

For both the EM and MLM queries in 1-dimension, an index structure with $O(n^2)$ size and $O(\log n)$ query time is straightforward: we can precompute answers for each of the $O(n^2)$ *combinatorially distinct* intervals defined by pairs of input points. The interesting question is whether these queries can be answered in sublinear time using subquadratic space. In this paper, we answer this question affirmatively.

Our results. Our main results are shown in Table 1, and can be summarized as follows:

(A) We design the first sub-quadratic size index that achieves a sub-linear query time in any dimension $d \geq 1$ for both EM and MLM problems. For any $t \in [0, 1]$, the index answers a query in $O(n^{1-t} + \log n)$ time, has size $O(n^{(2d-1)t+1})$, and takes $O(n^{(2d-1)t+1} \log n)$ time to build. The tunable parameter t gives the index a continuum of trade-offs between query time and its size. In particular, for $d = 1$ the index can achieve a query time of $O(\sqrt{n})$ with $O(n^{3/2})$ size and $O(n^{3/2} \log n)$ preprocessing. (Section 2)

(B) Our above result raises a natural question: is there a near-linear-size index that can answer an EM or MLM query in polylog(n) time. Although no such lower bound is known, we show that such an index is unlikely. In particular, we prove a conditional lower bound for the most-likely range-max queries, based on the conjectured hardness of the following set-intersection problem: Preprocess a family $S_1, \ldots, S_m$ of sets so that for a query pair $i, j \leq m$, one can quickly determine whether $S_i \cap S_j = \emptyset$. It is conjectured that the size of any data structure with query time $t_q = \Omega(\log n)$ is $\Omega((\frac{n}{t_q \,\mathrm{polylog}(n)})^2)$, where $n = \sum_i |S_i|$. We reduce the MLM problem for $d \geq 2$ to the set-intersection problem. (Section 3)

Since the EM and MLM problems seem hard in the worst-case, we consider approximation algorithms and algorithms under some assumptions on the input, as discussed below.

(C) Suppose the values of input points are chosen according to a random permutation model (RPM), i.e., first a set of values are chosen and then they are assigned in a random order to the input points (see Section 4). We present an index of size $O(n \log^{d+1} n)$ that can answer a MLM query in expected time $O(\log^{d+3} n)$. (Section 4)

(D) We design a linear-size index for estimating the expected maximum value (denoted by $\mu(\mathsf{P} \cap \rho)$), for a query rectangle ρ, within approximation factor $1/2$ in $O(\log^{d+1} n)$ time; that is, the query procedure returns a value μ' such that

$$\frac{1}{2}\mu(\mathsf{P} \cap \rho) \leq \mu' \leq \mu(\mathsf{P} \cap \rho).$$

(Section 5)

Finally we extend our algorithms in two directions:

(E) First, we extend our algorithms to the *location-uncertainty* model, in which the location of each point

Model	Algorithm	EM		MLM	
		Space	Query	Space	Query
Existence	Exact	$O\left(n^{(2d-1)t+1}\right)$	$O\left(n^{1-t}+\log n\right)$	$O\left(n^{(2d-1)t+1}\right)$	$O\left(n^{1-t}+\log n\right)$
				$\Omega\left(\left(\frac{n}{t_q\ \mathrm{polylog}(n)}\right)^2\right)$	t_q
	Approx.	$O\left(n\log^d n\right)$	$O\left(\log^{d+1} n\right)$		
	RPM			$O\left(n\log^{d+1} n\right)$	$O\left(\log^{d+3} n\right)$
Location	Exact	$O\left(n^{(2d-1)t+1}f^{2d}\right)$	$O\left(n^{1-t}+\log(nf)\right)$	$O\left(n^{(2d-1)t+1}f^{2d}\right)$	$O\left(n^{1-t}+\log(nf)\right)$
		$\Omega\left(\left(\frac{n}{t_q\ \mathrm{polylog}(n)}\right)^2\right)$	t_q	$\Omega\left(\left(\frac{n}{t_q\ \mathrm{polylog}(n)}\right)^2\right)$	t_q
	Approx.	$O\left(nf\log^d(nf)\right)$	$O\left(\log^{d+1}(nf)\right)$		
	RPM			$O\left(nf^{2d}\log^{2d+1}(nf)\right)$	$O\left(\log^{2d+3}(nf)\right)$

Table 1. Summary of results. Lower bounds are conditional to the set-intersection conjecture and hold for $d \geq 2$; RPM is the random permutation model; and t_q is the query time.

is described as a probability distribution over a set of f discrete locations. We propose generalizations of the subquadratic index in (A) to compute the EM or the MLM in sublinear time and generalizations of (D) to compute an $1/2$-approximation of the expected maximum value in polylog(n) time. We also provide a conditional lower bound for the EM problem in location distributions. Second, we provide an indexing scheme for returning k records with the highest probabilities of being the maximum. (Sections 2, 6)

Our paper makes significant progress in advancing the state of art for computing range-max statistics over uncertain data. Despite the fundamental role and practical applications of the max statistic, and top-k summaries more generally, prior to our work no sublinear query scheme with subquadratic storage was known for either the EM or the MLM problem. In achieving sublinear query time using subquadratic space, our proposed algorithms break a conceptual barrier, and introduce novel indexing techniques both for exact and approximate range-max queries. In the exact setting, the idea of first partitioning data by value (instead of range attributes), and then applying range searching within each group turns out to be a key insight for range-max queries. In the approximation setting, the use of Prophet inequality for range queries is novel. Finally, our hardness proof adapts a construction originally designed for deterministic range queries, and applies it to derive complexity lower bounds for uncertain data ranges.

Related work. There is extensive work on managing, querying, and analyzing uncertain data. See the book [6] and the survey paper [14] for an overview of known results on this topic.

In the context of query processing, early work focused on top-k queries over uncertain data. Numerous algorithms under different semantics of top-k queries have been proposed; see [11, 16, 17, 22, 27, 30] and references therein. In another line of work, Jayram *et al.* [18] describe algorithms for computing aggregation statistics on uncertain data in the streaming model. Cormode *et al.* [13] used the expected rank of the uncertain entries across all possible worlds to compute the ranking of the data. All these papers compute the desired statistics over the entire data, and do not consider query ranges. Extending these results to top-k (even for $k = 1$) or aggregation statistics inside a query range seems particularly challenging, partly because the problem is not range decomposable, as mentioned above.

A few algorithms have been proposed for answering range-reporting queries on uncertain data [28, 31]. Cheng *et al.* [12] considered the 1D range-reporting query when the location of each input point is given as a uniform distribution and the goal is to report all points that lie inside a query range with probability at least τ, for some fixed $\tau \in [0, 1]$. They proposed an index of $O(n\tau^{-1})$ size with $O(\tau^{-1}\log n + k)$, where k is is the output size. Note that both the size and the query time depend on τ. Tao *et al.* [28] considered the problem in higher dimensions, and gave indexes based on space partitioning heuristics. In the worst case, their procedure visits all points.

Agarwal *et al.* [4] described an index for 1D range reporting when the location of each point is given as a piecewise-constant pdf. For a fixed τ, they described an index of linear size that can report in $O(\log n + k)$ time all k points lying inside a query interval with probability at least τ. If τ is part of the query, then the query time is $O(\log^3 n + k)$ and the size of the index is $O(n\log^2 n)$. They also presented a near-linear-size index that can handle more general probability distributions for input points and answer queries in $O(\log n + k)$ time. Recently Li and Wang [21] extended the approach in [4] to return the t points, for a given t (instead of all points), that lie in the query interval with the highest probability. Singh *et al.* [26] presented some heuristic solutions for querying uncertain data that are categorical. All these results are customized for range-*reporting* queries, and they require linear time in the worst case for computing range-aggregate statistics.

As mentioned above, computing the expected value of range-SUM for a query rectangle ρ can be reduced to computing range-SUM on data without uncertainty. However no efficient index is known for computing the most-likely value of range-SUM, or approximating the distribution of range-SUM (unless we make some assumptions on the probabilities of existence). The only result in this direction is by Abdullah *et al.* [1] who proved the existence of small-size coresets for some range-SUM problems on uncertain data.

The only paper on range top-k we are aware of is [29], which studies the problem for $d = 1$. For a query interval I and a parameter $\tau \in [0, 1]$, the data structure returns points that lie in I and their rank of being at most k is at least τ. They present some pruning techniques to reduce the query time, but the worst-case query time is super linear.

Finally we note that there is also some work on nearest neighbor queries on uncertain data [3, 5, 8, 9] but they cannot be adapted to range-max queries.

2. EXACT ALGORITHMS

Let $\mathsf{P} = \{p_1, \ldots, p_n\} \subseteq \mathbb{R}^d$ be a set of n uncertain points where each p_i is associated with a value $v_i \in \mathbb{R}^+$ and an independent probability $\alpha_i \in (0, 1]$ of its existence; multiple points may have the same value. Throughout, we assume that dimension d is a fixed constant. We present indexing schemes for computing the expected or the most-likely maximum value among the points lying in a query orthogonal rectangle in $\mathbb{R}^d$. We begin with some definitions, and then describe our index structure.

Let $X = \{x_1, \ldots, x_m\}$, for $m \le n$, be the set of (distinct) values associated with the points in P. (Recall that the values of the points need not be all distinct.) Given a subset of points $\mathsf{R} \subseteq \mathsf{P}$, we define $\pi(\mathsf{R})$ as the probability that *none* of its points are present. That is,

$$\pi(\mathsf{R}) = \prod_{p_i \in \mathsf{R}} (1 - \alpha_i),$$

where we assume $\pi(\mathsf{R}) = 1$ if $\mathsf{R} = \emptyset$. For any value $x \in X$, let $\alpha(x, \mathsf{R})$ denote the probability that some point with associated value x exists:

$$\begin{aligned} \alpha(x, \mathsf{R}) &= 1 - \pi(\{p_i \in \mathsf{R} \mid v_i = x\}) \\ &= 1 - \prod_{p_i \in \mathsf{R}: v_i = x} (1 - \alpha_i), \end{aligned}$$

with the convention that $\alpha(x, \mathsf{R}) = 0$ if there is no point with value x in R; in particular, $\alpha(x, \mathsf{R}) = 0$ if $\mathsf{R} = \emptyset$. Define $\beta(x, \mathsf{R})$ as the probability that no point with value larger than x is present in R:

$$\beta(x, \mathsf{R}) = \pi(\{p_i \in \mathsf{R} \mid v_i > x\}).$$

It follows that the probability of x being the maximum value of a point in R, denoted $\gamma(x, \mathsf{R})$, can be written as

$$\gamma(x, \mathsf{R}) = \alpha(x, \mathsf{R})\beta(x, \mathsf{R}).$$

Note that $\gamma(x, \mathsf{R}) = 0$ if $\mathsf{R} = \emptyset$ or x is not associated with any point of R. If $\mu(\mathsf{R})$ denotes the expected maximum (EM) value in R, then we have

$$\mu(\mathsf{R}) = \sum_{x \in X} x\gamma(x, \mathsf{R}).$$

By our convention, $\mu(\mathsf{R}) = 0$ if $\mathsf{R} = \emptyset$. The most likely maximum (MLM) value, denoted by $\lambda(\mathsf{R})$, is

$$\lambda(\mathsf{R}) = \operatorname*{argmax}_{x \in X} \gamma(x, \mathsf{R}).$$

If $\mathsf{R} = \emptyset$, $\lambda(\mathsf{R})$ is undefined.

We describe our index structure in detail for computing EM for $d = 1$, and then sketch its extension to higher dimensions and to computing MLM.

Indexing scheme. We fix a parameter $t \in [0, 1]$, and partition the input P into $k \le 2\lceil n^{1-t} \rceil$ subsets $\mathsf{P}_1, \ldots, \mathsf{P}_k$ such that (i) all points in P_i have strictly higher values than those in P_{i+1}, and (ii) either $|\mathsf{P}_i| \le 2n^t$ or all points in P_i have the same value.

We call P_i *uniform* if all of its points have the same value, and non-uniform otherwise. If P_i is uniform, then we compute and store the value $\pi(\mathsf{P}_i \cap (-\infty, p_j])$, for all $p_j \in \mathsf{P}_i$. Otherwise (for non-uniform P_i) we compute and store $\pi(\mathsf{P}_i \cap [a, b])$ and $\mu(\mathsf{P}_i \cap [a, b])$, for all pairs $a, b \in \mathsf{P}_i$ with $a < b$.

We also sort each P_i (by position) and store the sorted lists $\mathsf{P}_1, \ldots \mathsf{P}_k$ so that for any $q \in \mathbb{R}$ its predecessor and successor in each P_i, denoted by $pred(q, \mathsf{P}_i)$ and $succ(q, \mathsf{P}_i)$ respectively, can be computed efficiently. We use the so-called fractional-cascading scheme [10] to expedite this process, which augments each sequence P_i by adding some points to P_i and stores the augmented list $\mathsf{P}_i^\star$. More precisely, starting with the bottom-most set $\mathsf{P}_k^\star = \mathsf{P}_k$, we construct the remaining augmented lists as follows. Suppose $\mathsf{P}_i^\star = \langle a_1, a_2, a_3, \ldots, a_{n_i} \rangle$, and let $\frac{1}{2}\mathsf{P}_i^\star = \langle a_2, a_4, a_6, \ldots \rangle$ be the subsequence of $\mathsf{P}_i^\star$ consisting of every other item. Then, we define $\mathsf{P}_{i-1}^\star = \mathsf{P}_{i-1} \cup \frac{1}{2}\mathsf{P}_i^\star$, and with each item $a \in \mathsf{P}_i^\star$, we store the indices of $pred(a, \mathsf{P}_i)$, $succ(a, \mathsf{P}_i)$ and of $succ(a, \mathsf{P}_{i+1}^\star)$ in $\mathsf{P}_{i+1}^\star$. The total size of all the augmented list is $\sum_{i=1}^k |\mathsf{P}_i^\star| \le 2n$. With these augmented lists, we can find $pred(q, \mathsf{P}_i)$ and $succ(q, \mathsf{P}_i)$ for any $q \in \mathbb{R}$ in all the set P_i, $i = 1, 2, \ldots, k$, in total time $O(\log n + k)$, improving the obvious bound of $O(k \log n)$. See [10] for details. This completes the description of the index.

The index needs $O(|\mathsf{P}_i|^2) = O(n^{2t})$ space when P_i is non-uniform, and $O(|\mathsf{P}_i|)$ space otherwise. Since $\sum_{i=1}^k |\mathsf{P}_i| = n$, the total space for the index is $O(n) + O(n^{1-t}n^{2t}) = O(n^{1+t})$. We now discuss how to answer a query using this index, and then discuss its construction details.

Query procedure. Given a query interval $I = [a, b]$, we wish to compute $\mu(\mathsf{P} \cap I)$ using the index. For $j = 1, \ldots, k$, let $a_j = succ(a, \mathsf{P}_j)$ and $b_j = pred(b, \mathsf{P}_j)$. Define $I_j = [a_j, b_j]$ as the projection of the query range onto the subset P_j, where we assume $I_j = \emptyset$ if $a_j > b_j$, see Figure 1 for an example. We use the shorthand notation $\mathsf{P}_{<j} = \bigcup_{l=0}^{j-1} \mathsf{P}_l$ to denote the union of all subsets with index smaller than j, with the convention that $\mathsf{P}_{<1} = \emptyset$. The following lemma explains our main idea for computing the expected max value $\mu(\mathsf{P} \cap I)$.

Lemma 2.1 *The partition $\mathsf{P}_1, \ldots, \mathsf{P}_k$ satisfies the following properties:*

(i) $\mu(I \cap \mathsf{P}) = \sum_{j=1}^{k} \pi(I \cap \mathsf{P}_{<j})\mu(I_j \cap \mathsf{P}_j)$.

(ii) For $j \geq 1$, $\pi(I \cap \mathsf{P}_{<j}) = \pi(I \cap \mathsf{P}_{<j-1})\pi(I_{j-1} \cap \mathsf{P}_{j-1})$.

PROOF. To prove (i), let $X_j \subseteq X$ be the set of distinct values among the points of P_j. Then the following holds:

$$\mu(I \cap \mathsf{P}) = \sum_{x \in X} x\alpha(x, I \cap \mathsf{P})\beta(x, I \cap \mathsf{P})$$
$$= \sum_{j=1}^{k} \sum_{x \in X_j} x\alpha(x, I \cap \mathsf{P})\beta(x, I \cap \mathsf{P})$$

The values in X_{j-1} are all larger than those in X_j and x belongs to at most one such X_j, therefore $\alpha(x, I \cap \mathsf{P}) = \alpha(x, I \cap \mathsf{P}_j)$, and

$$\beta(x, I \cap \mathsf{P}) = \pi(I \cap \mathsf{P}_{<j})\pi(I \cap \{p_i \in \mathsf{P}_j \mid v_i > x\})$$
$$= \pi(I \cap \mathsf{P}_{<j})\beta(x, \mathsf{P}_j \cap I).$$

We also have $\alpha(x, I \cap \mathsf{P}_j) = \alpha(x, I_j \cap \mathsf{P}_j)$ and $\beta(x, I \cap \mathsf{P}_j) = \beta(x, I_j \cap \mathsf{P}_j)$, which follows because $\mathsf{P}_j \cap (I \backslash I_j) = \emptyset$, by definition. Thus, we can conclude that

$$\mu(I \cap \mathsf{P}) = \sum_{j=1}^{k} \sum_{x \in X_j} x\pi(I \cap \mathsf{P}_{<j})\alpha(x, I_j \cap \mathsf{P}_j)\beta(x, I_j \cap \mathsf{P}_j)$$
$$= \sum_{j=1}^{k} \pi(I \cap \mathsf{P}_{<j})\mu(x, I_j \cap \mathsf{P}_j).$$

The proof of (ii) follows from the fact that $\mathsf{P}_{<j} = \mathsf{P}_{<j-1} \cup \mathsf{P}_{j-1}$ and $\mathsf{P}_{<j-1} \cap \mathsf{P}_{j-1} = \emptyset$. $\square$

If P_j is non-uniform, then the index stores the values of $\mu(I_j \cap \mathsf{P}_j)$ and $\pi(I_j \cap \mathsf{P}_j)$. For a uniform P_j, we observe that $\pi(I_j \cap \mathsf{P}_j) = \pi(\mathsf{P}_j \cap (-\infty, b_j])/\pi(\mathsf{P}_j \cap (-\infty, a_j))$ and $\mu(I_j \cap \mathsf{P}_j) = x(1 - \pi(I_j \cap \mathsf{P}_j))$. Since we store $\pi(\mathsf{P}_j \cap (-\infty, p])$ for all $p \in \mathsf{P}_j$, the values $\pi(I_j \cap \mathsf{P}_j)$ and $\mu(I_j \cap \mathsf{P}_j)$ can be computed in $O(1)$ time. The pseudo-code in Algorithm 1 below describes the query procedure and Figure 1 shows the intervals in each group given the query interval I.

Algorithm 1. EXACT_EM_QUERY

```
Input: I = [a, b]
Output: μ(I ∩ P)
for j = 1 to k do
    a_j = succ(a, P_j),    b_j = pred(b, P_j)
end for
EM = 0,   p = 1
for j = 1 to k do
    EM = EM + p · μ(I_j ∩ P_j)
    p = p · π(I_j ∩ P_j)
end for
return EM
```

We note that a_j and b_j can be found for all $j = 1, 2, \ldots, k$, in $O(\log n + k)$ time using fractional-cascading. We spend $O(1)$ time in each iteration of the second for loop, so the total query time is $O(\log n + k) = O(\log n + n^{1-t})$.

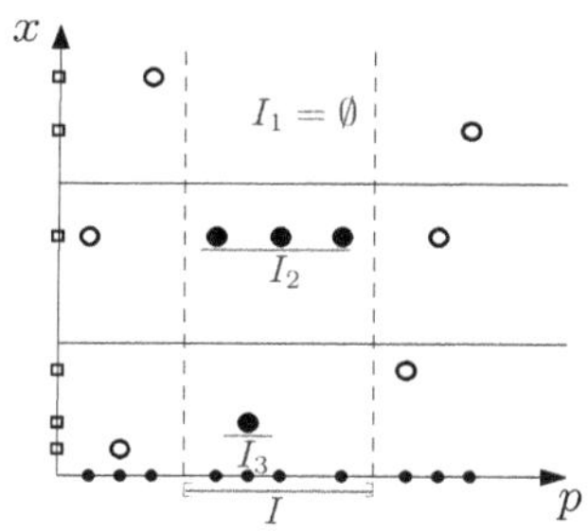

Figure 1. Points (x-axis), values (y-axis), and a partition of P into 3 sets; $\{(p_i, v_i) \mid 1 \leq i \leq n\}$ are drawn as $2D$ points.

Preprocessing. We now describe how to build the index structure. Given a subset $S \subseteq \mathsf{P}$, let $S[x] = \{p_i \in S \mid v_i = x\}$ be the set of points in S that have value x. We sort the set of distinct values X in descending order and construct the partition of P by scanning the elements of X in sorted order. Suppose the sets $\mathsf{P}_1, \ldots, \mathsf{P}_{j-1}$ have been constructed, we are building the set P_j, and $x_i \in X$ is the next value in the sorted sequence. If either $|\mathsf{P}_j| \geq n^t$ or $|\mathsf{P}[x_i]| \geq n^t$, we close P_j, and start the new subset P_{j+1} by adding $\mathsf{P}[x_i]$ to it. Otherwise we have both $|\mathsf{P}_j| < n^t$ and $|\mathsf{P}[x_i]| < n^t$, in which case we add $\mathsf{P}[x_i]$ to P_j, and continue to the next value of X. The total time for constructing $\mathsf{P}_1, \ldots, \mathsf{P}_k$ is clearly $O(n \log n)$. Finally, the number of sets k is at most $2\lceil n^{1-t} \rceil$ because if $|\mathsf{P}_i| < n^t$, then $|\mathsf{P}_{i+1}| \geq n^t$. The construction of the fractional-cascaded sequences to expedite searching in these sets is straightforward, and takes $O(n)$ time, as shown in [10].

The preprocessing cost of the uniform sets is only linear because computing $\pi(\mathsf{P}_j \cap (-\infty, a])$, for all $a \in \mathsf{P}_j$, takes $O(|\mathsf{P}_j|)$ time if P_j is uniform. The main part of the construction is the preprocessing of the non-uniform sets, which we describe in detail below.

Suppose $X_j = \langle x_1 < \ldots < x_s \rangle$ is the sequence of distinct values for the points of P_j. Let T be a complete binary tree whose leaves store x_j's in the sorted order and let $X_u \subseteq X_j$ be the subset of values stored at the leaves of the subtree rooted at a node $u \in T$. We will dynamically maintain a set $S \subseteq \mathsf{P}_j$ in T under insertion of points, and each node $u \in T$ will store $\pi_u = \pi(S_u)$ and $\mu_u = \mu(S_u)$, where $S_u = \{p_i \in S \mid v_i \in X_u\}$ is the set of points associated with values in X_u. More specifically, if u is a leaf, with $X_u = \{x\}$, then $\pi_u = \prod_{p_i \in S[x]}(1 - \alpha_i)$ and $\mu_u = x(1 - \pi(S_u))$. If u is an internal node whose left and right children are w and z, then we can see that (using the same argument as Lemma 2.1)

$$\pi_u = \pi_w \cdot \pi_z \quad \text{and} \quad \mu_u = \mu_z + \pi_z \mu_w. \qquad (1)$$

When inserting a point p_i into S, we only need to update the nodes along the root-to-leaf path between the root of T and the leaf z storing v_i. Starting at the leaf, whose values π_z and μ_z are easily updated in $O(1)$ time, we update the remaining nodes of the path in the bottom-up order, using the equation (1). The total time spent in updating T is $O(\log |\mathsf{P}_j|)$. With this structure in place, we can now describe how to finish the preprocessing of P_j.

Suppose the points of P_j are $p_1 < \ldots < p_r$, in left to right order. We need to compute $\pi(\cdot)$ and $\mu(\cdot)$ values for all of its $\binom{r}{2}$ intervals, in total time $O(r^2 \log r)$. We do this in batches where for a fixed $u \le r$, we compute in $O(r \log r)$ time $\pi(\mathsf{P}_j \cap [p_u, p_v])$ and $\mu(\mathsf{P} \cap [p_u, p_v])$, for all v with $u \le v \le r$, as follows. We initialize $S = \emptyset$, and $\pi_v = 1$, $\mu_v = 0$ for all $v \in T$. Then we add $p_u, p_{u+1}, \ldots$ one by one. After $p_u, \ldots, p_v$ have been inserted, the values π_{root}, μ_{root} at the root of T are precisely $\pi(\mathsf{P}_j \cap [p_u, p_v])$ and $\mu(\mathsf{P}_j \cap [p_u, p_v])$. Because each insertion takes $O(\log r)$ time, the total time spent is $O(r \log r)$. We repeat this procedure for all $u \le r$, which bounds the total preprocessing time for a non-uniform set P_j as $O(r^2 \log r) = O(n^{2t} \log n)$. We, therefore, have the following theorem.

Theorem 2.2 *Let P be a set of n uncertain points in $\mathbb{R}^1$. For any $t \in [0, 1]$, an index of size $O(n^{1+t})$ can be constructed in $O(n^{1+t} \log n)$ time so that $\mu(\mathsf{P} \cap I)$, for a query interval I, can be computed in $O(n^{1-t} + \log n)$ time.*

The 1-dimensional indexing algorithm can be extended to higher dimensions easily as follows. We begin by fixing a parameter t and partitioning the input into $k \le 2\lceil n^{1-t} \rceil$ subsets $\mathsf{P}_1, \ldots, \mathsf{P}_k$ by value, as in one dimension. The main change needed is in lines 1-3 of Algorithm 1, where instead of "canonical intervals" we need to preprocess for canonical d-dimensional rectangles. In particular, for each non-uniform set P_j, there are now $|\mathsf{P}_j|^{2d} = O(n^{2dt})$ "combinatorially distinct" rectangles which we refer to as *canonical* rectangles. For each canonical rectangle ρ, we compute $\mu(\mathsf{P}_j \cap \rho)$ and $\pi(\mathsf{P}_j \cap \rho)$. By adapting the 1D preprocessing algorithm, these values can be computed in a total of $O(n^{2dt} \log n)$ time. The preprocessing of the uniform sets is the same as in 1-dimension, namely, sorting of points in each dimension.

Summing over all j, the total space and preprocessing time are $O(n^{(2d-1)t+1})$ and $O(n^{(2d-1)t+1} \log n)$ respectively. Given a query rectangle ρ, we "project" it onto its canonical rectangles $\rho_1, \ldots, \rho_k$, i.e., for each j a rectangle ρ_j such that, $\rho \cap \mathsf{P}_j = \rho_j \cap \mathsf{P}_j$. This requires finding the predecessor and successor within P_j of its extent in each dimension, which can be done in $O(\log n)$ time using fractional cascading. Since there are $k = n^{1-t}$ sets P_j, the total time to find all the canonical rectangles is $O(\log n + n^{1-t})$ using fractional cascading. The remaining part of Algorithm 1, namely, lines 4-9 then compute $\mu(\mathsf{P} \cap \rho)$ as before. We thus obtain the following:

Theorem 2.3 *Let P be a set of n uncertain points in $\mathbb{R}^d$. For any $t \in [0, 1]$, an index of size $O(n^{(2d-1)t+1})$ can be constructed in $O(n^{(2d-1)t+1} \log n)$ time so that $\mu(\mathsf{P} \cap \rho)$, for a query rectangle ρ, can be computed in $O(n^{1-t} + \log n)$ time.*

The index just described can be adapted easily to compute the most likely maximum value $\lambda(\mathsf{P} \cap I)$ with the same performance bounds. For each non-uniform set P_j and for each pair $p_u, p_v \in \mathsf{P}_j$ with $p_u < p_v$, we compute the values $x_{uv} = \lambda(\mathsf{P}_j \cap [p_u, p_v])$, $\gamma(x_{uv}, \mathsf{P}_j \cap [p_u, p_v])$, and $\pi(\mathsf{P}_j \cap [p_u, p_v])$. The query algorithm is a simple adaptation of Algorithm 1, leading to the following result:

Theorem 2.4 *Let P be a set of n uncertain points in $\mathbb{R}^d$. For any $t \in [0, 1]$, an index of size $O(n^{(2d-1)t+1})$ can be constructed in $O(n^{(2d-1)t+1} \log n)$ time so that $\lambda(\mathsf{P} \cap \rho)$, for a query rectangle ρ, can be computed in $O(n^{1-t} + \log n)$ time.*

Extensions. (i) Our index can be generalized to return the k values with the highest probabilities of being the range-max for a query rectangle ρ, as follows. For each combinatorially distinct rectangle, we store the k most likely maximum values instead of the single most likely maximum leading to an index of size $O(kn^{(2d-1)t+1})$. Given a query rectangle ρ, we search among the k most-likely values stored at the relevant canonical rectangle in each subset P_i and find the k most likely values in $O(n^{1-t} + k \log n)$ time.

(ii) The algorithm can be extended to the case in which each point p_i is associated with a discrete distribution over its values of constant support f, i.e., $\{v_{i1}, \ldots, v_{if}\} \subset \mathbb{R}^+$ with probabilities $\{\alpha_{i1}, \ldots, \alpha_{if}\} \subset [0, 1]$, where the point assumes value v_{ij} with probability α_{ij}. An instance of the EM (MLM) problem with n points of value uncertainty can be mapped to an instance of EM (MLM) problem with nf independent points of existential uncertainty; we omit the details from this abstract.

3. HARDNESS OF MLM

The range-max query problem for uncertain data seems significantly harder than its deterministic counterpart. Indeed, the latter can be solved easily in $O(\log^{d-1} n)$ query time and $O(n \log^{d-1} n)$ space using orthogonal range trees with fractional cascading, for $d \ge 2$ [2]. This stands in sharp contrast to what we are able to achieve for the uncertain data model; to wit, if the space requirement of our data structure is nearly linear, our query time goes up to near linear as well. In this section, we offer evidence for the hardness of uncertain range-max problem through a reduction from the *set-intersection* problem, which suggests that indexes with near-linear space and poly-logarithmic query time are unlikely to exist even for $d = 2$. Our lower bound is in the real-RAM model, mentioned above.

The set-intersection problem is defined as follows. Given a family of sets $S_1, S_2, \ldots, S_m$, with real-valued items, preprocess them so that the intersection queries of the following form can be answered efficiently: given indices i, j, do the sets S_i and S_j have a non-empty intersection? It is widely believed that any index that can answer such queries in worst-case time $O(t)$ must use at least $\Omega((n/t)^2)$ space, ignoring polylog factors [15, 23, 24], where $n = \sum |S_i|$ is the total size of all the sets. We show in the following that any index for solving the MLM problem in $\mathbb{R}^d$ for $d \geq 2$ can also solve the set-intersection problem, and is therefore subject to the same query-space tradeoff.

Reduction. We transform an instance of the set-intersection problem of size n into an instance of the MLM problem with $2n$ points in $\mathbb{R}^2$. Specifically, let $S_1, \ldots, S_m$ be the input to the set-intersection problem, where $\sum_{i=1}^{m} |S_i| = n$. Let $n_0 = 0$ and $n_i = n_{i-1} + |S_i|$ for $i = 1, \ldots, m$. We use s_{ik} to denote the (value of) the kth item of S_i, for $1 \leq k \leq |S_i|$. We create a 2-dimensional instance of the MLM problem corresponding to these sets as follows. All the points in the MLM lie on two parallel lines, $L : y = x + n$ and $L' : y = x - n$. For each member of the set S_i, we create two points, one on each of these lines. Specifically, the points corresponding to the kth item $s_{ik} \in S_i$ are: $(-(k + n_{i-1}), -(k + n_{i-1}) + n))$ on L, and $((k + n_{i-1}), (k + n_{i-1}) - n))$ on L'. The existence probability of these two points is $\alpha = 1 - 2^{-\frac{1}{n+1}}$ and their value is s_{ik}. Let P_i and P'_i denote the set of points corresponding to S_i that lie on L and L', respectively. Finally, let $\mathsf{P} = \bigcup_i (\mathsf{P}_i \cup \mathsf{P}'_i)$ denote the set of all the $2n$ points that form the input to the MLM problem. Note that all points of P have the same existence probability α, and for any pair i, j, all points in $\mathsf{P}_i \cup \mathsf{P}'_j$ have distinct values if and only if $S_i \cap S_j = \emptyset$.

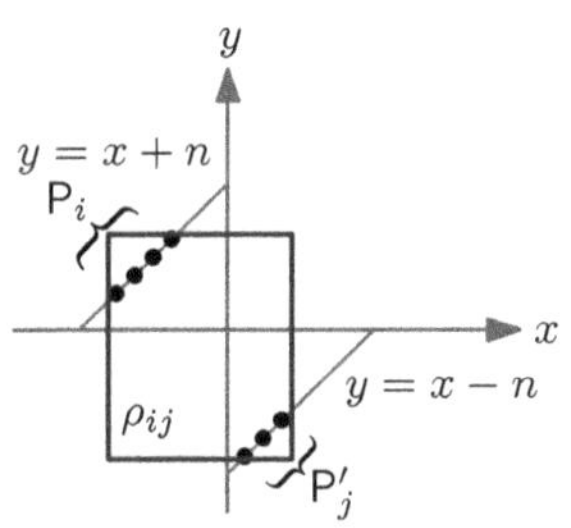

Figure 2. Illustration for the lower bound construction.

Clearly the construction takes $O(n)$ time, and one can easily verify that (1) all points on L lie in the northwest quadrant while those on L' lie in the southeast quadrant, and (2) the points corresponding to S_i are placed in consecutive order on both L and L', and they lie between the points corresponding to S_{i-1} and S_{i+1}.

The placement of the points in opposite quadrants ensures the following geometric property: given any two indices i, j, there is a rectangular range ρ_{ij} that includes only P_i and P'_j, namely, $\rho_{ij} \cap \mathsf{P} = \mathsf{P}_i \cup \mathsf{P}'_j$. See Figure 2.

Given a set-intersection query: "Does S_i intersect S_j?" we compute the MLM for the query range ρ_{ij}. If the answer is value v, then we check if v belongs to both S_i and S_j. If it does, then we return "Yes," meaning that the sets intersect; otherwise, we answer "No."

Thus, we answer a set-intersection query using one MLM range query and two set membership queries to decide if $v \in S_i \cap S_j$. The membership queries are easily performed in $O(\log n)$ time, using any standard balanced search tree, and so the set-intersection query time is dominated by the MLM query time, as long as the latter is $\Omega(\log n)$. The correctness of the reduction follows from the following lemma.

Lemma 3.1 *In the preceding reduction, $S_i \cap S_j \neq \emptyset$ if and only if $\lambda(\mathsf{P} \cap \rho_{ij})$ belongs to $S_i \cap S_j$.*

PROOF. If $\lambda(\mathsf{P} \cap \rho_{ij})$ belongs to $S_i \cap S_j$, then $S_i \cap S_j \neq \emptyset$, and the claim holds trivially. Conversely, assume $S_i \cap S_j \neq \emptyset$. Let $\mathsf{P}_{ij} = \mathsf{P} \cap \rho_{ij}$, $v = \lambda(\mathsf{P}_{ij})$, and r the number of points in P_{ij} with values larger than v. If v is associated with only one point of P_{ij}, then $\gamma(v, \mathsf{P}_{ij}) = \alpha(1 - \alpha)^r \leq \alpha$.

On the other hand if v is associated with two points of P_{ij} (note that each value of P_{ij} is associated with at most two points), then

$$\gamma(v, \mathsf{P}_{ij}) = (2\alpha - \alpha^2)(1 - \alpha)^r \geq (2\alpha - \alpha^2)(1 - \alpha)^n > \alpha$$

because $\alpha = 1 - 2^{-\frac{1}{n+1}}$. Since $S_i \cap S_j \neq \emptyset$, there are two points in P_{ij} with the same value, corresponding to an item of $S_i \cap S_j$. Therefore v belongs to $S_i \cap S_j$ in this case, as claimed. □

We have established the following result.

Theorem 3.2 *If there is an index to solve the MLM problem for n points in $\mathbb{R}^2$ with $S(n)$ space and $Q(n)$ query time, for $Q(n) \geq \Omega(\log n)$, then the set-intersection problem can be solved in $Q(2n)$ time with space $S(2n)$.*

The set intersection problem is conjectured to require $\Omega((n/t)^2)$ space, ignoring polylog factors, as long as the query time is $t = \Omega(\log n)$. Subject to this conjecture, Theorem 3.2 implies that any data structure that uses near-linear space cannot hope to achieve polylog query time. More formally, the theorem suggests that in the worst-case the product (query time)^2 × (index size) is $\Omega(n^2)$, ignoring polylog factors, for $d \geq 2$.

4. RANDOM PEMUTATION MODEL

We describe an index of $O(n \operatorname{polylog}(n))$ size that can answer an MLM query in $O(\operatorname{polylog}(n))$ expected time if the values of points are distinct and they are assigned using the so-called *random permutation model.* More precisely, we assume that the existence probabilities α_i's of points are arbitrary but their *values* v_i's are assigned randomly as follows: Let $x_1 \geq x_2 \geq \ldots \geq x_n$ be an arbitrary set of real values. We choose a random permutation σ of $[1 : n]$ and set $v_i = x_{\sigma(i)}$.

We map each point $p_i \in \mathsf{P}$ to a two-dimensional point $\hat{p}_i = (\alpha_i, v_i) \in \mathbb{R}^2$. Let $\hat{\mathsf{P}} = \{\hat{p}_i \mid p_i \in \mathsf{P}\}$. A point $a = (a_1, a_2)$ *dominates* another point $b = (b_1, b_2)$ if $a_1 > a_2$ and $b_1 \geq b_2$ or $a_1 \geq a_2$ and $b_1 > b_2$. The *skyline* of a point set $S \subseteq \mathbb{R}^2$ is the subset of points in S that are not dominated by another point of S. The following simple lemma is the basis of our index.[2]

Lemma 4.1 *Let $\mathsf{R} \subseteq \mathsf{P}$ such that the values of all points in R are distinct. If $v_k = \lambda(\mathsf{R})$, then $\hat{p}_k$ belongs to the skyline of $\hat{\mathsf{R}} = \{\hat{p}_i \mid p_i \in \mathsf{R}\}$.*

PROOF. If $\hat{p}_k$ is not on the skyline of $\hat{\mathsf{R}}$, then it is dominated by some other point $\hat{p}_j \in \hat{\mathsf{R}}\backslash\{\hat{p}_k\}$. Thus, we have $\alpha_j \geq \alpha_k$ and $v_j \geq v_k$. Since the values are distinct, the second inequality must be strict, namely, $v_j > v_k$. It is easy to check that

$$\beta(v_k, \mathsf{R}) \leq (1 - \alpha_j)\beta(v_j, \mathsf{R}).$$

Therefore, we have the following inequality:

$$\begin{aligned}\gamma(v_k, \mathsf{R}) &= \alpha(v_k, \mathsf{R})\beta(v_k, \mathsf{R}) \leq \alpha_k(1 - \alpha_j)\beta(v_j, \mathsf{R}) \\ &< \alpha_j\beta(v_j, \mathsf{R}) = \gamma(v_j, \mathsf{R})\end{aligned}$$

which contradicts the assumption that

$$\gamma(v_k, \mathsf{R}) = \operatorname*{argmax}_{x \in X} \gamma(x, \mathsf{R}).$$

This completes the proof. $\square$

For a rectangle ρ, let $\mathsf{P}_\rho = \mathsf{P} \cap \rho$, $\hat{\mathsf{P}}_\rho = \{\hat{p} \mid p \in \mathsf{P}_\rho\}$, and $S_\rho \subseteq \mathsf{P}_\rho$ the set of points p_i such that $\hat{p}_i$ belongs to the skyline of $\hat{\mathsf{P}}_\rho$. By Lemma 4.1,

$$\lambda(\mathsf{P}_\rho) = \arg\max_{p_i \in S_\rho} \gamma(v_i, \mathsf{P}_\rho).$$

If the values of P are assigned using a random permutation model, then we note that the same holds for an arbitrary subset $\mathsf{R} \subseteq \mathsf{P}$ as well. A classical result in stochastic geometry implies that the expected size of the skyline of $\hat{\mathsf{P}}_\rho$ is $O(\log n)$, see e.g. [20, 7]. Using these observations, we compute $\lambda(\mathsf{P}_\rho)$ in two stages: First, we compute S_ρ, and then compute $\gamma(v_i, \mathsf{P}_\rho)$ for every $p_i \in S_\rho$.

Rahul and Janardan [24] have presented an index for storing P and $\hat{\mathsf{P}}$ of size $O(n \log^{d+1} n)$, that can be constructed in time $O(n \log^{d+1} n)$ so that for any query rectangle ρ, S_ρ can be computed in time $O(|S_\rho| \log^{d+2} n)$). For $d = 1$, the size, the preprocessing time, and the query time are $O(n)$, $O(n \log^2 n)$ time, and $O(|S_\rho| + \log n)$, respectively.

To compute $\gamma(v_i, \mathsf{P}_\rho)$, for every $p_i \in S_\rho$, we map each point $p_i \in \mathsf{P}$ to $\bar{p}_i := (p_i, v_i) \in \mathbb{R}^{d+1}$ and set its weight $w(\bar{p}_i) = 1 - \alpha_i$. Set $\bar{\mathsf{P}} = \{\bar{p}_i \mid 1 \leq i \leq n\}$. We build, in $O(n \log^d n)$ time, a $(d+1)$-dimensional range tree of size $O(n \log^d n)$ so that for any $(d+1)$-dimensional rectangle $\bar{\rho}$, $w(\bar{\rho}) = \prod_{\bar{p} \in \bar{\mathsf{P}} \cap \bar{\rho}} w(\bar{p})$ can be computed in $O(\log^d n)$ time [2]. For $p_i \in S_\rho$, let $\bar{\rho}_i = \rho \times (v_i, \infty)$. Then $\gamma(v_i, \mathsf{P}_\rho) = \alpha_i w(\bar{\rho}_i)$ can be computed in $O(\log^d n)$ time using this index.

Putting everything together, we obtain the following result:

[2]The lemma does not assume the values to be assigned using a random permutation. It holds for arbitrarily assigned values, as long as they are distinct.

Theorem 4.2 *Let P be a set of n uncertain points in $\mathbb{R}^d$, such that the values of P are all distinct and chosen according to a random permutation model. An index of size $O(n \log^{d+1} n)$ on P can be built in $O(n \log^{d+1} n)$ time so that for a query rectangle ρ, $\lambda(\mathsf{P} \cap \rho)$ can be computed in expected time $O(\log^{d+3} n)$. For $d = 1$, the size and expected query time can be improved to $O(n)$ and $O(\log^2 n)$, respectively.*

5. APPROXIMATION ALGORITHMS

In this section we describe approximation algorithms for EM and MLM problems. We begin by discussing two simple algorithms. The first one can be used for both EM and MLM problems but the running time depends on the probabilities of the points. The second one works only for MLM and gives an additive approximation. In the end, we propose a constant-factor approximation algorithm for the EM problem, whose running time is independent of the input probabilities.

Suppose the existence probability of each point in P is at least α. Set $t = \lceil \frac{1}{\alpha} \ln \frac{n}{\varepsilon\alpha} \rceil$ for any $\varepsilon > 0$. A simple calculation shows that for any rectangle ρ and for any value $x \in X$ that is not among the t largest ones in $\mathsf{P}_\rho = \mathsf{P} \cap \rho$, $\gamma(x, \mathsf{P}_\rho) \leq \frac{\varepsilon\alpha}{n}$, i.e., it is negligible and such a point can be ignored. Using a standard index for reporting top t values inside ρ [2], we can construct an index of size $O(n \log^{d-1} n)$ in time $O(n \log^{d-1} n)$ that returns, in $O(\log^{d-1} n + t \log n)$ time, values $\eta_\rho \in \mathbb{R}^+$ and $x_\rho \in X$ such that $(1 - \varepsilon)\mu(\mathsf{P}_\rho) \leq \eta_\rho \leq \mu(\mathsf{P}_\rho)$ and $\gamma(x_\rho, \mathsf{P}_\rho) \geq (1 - \varepsilon)\max_{x \in X} \gamma(x, \mathsf{P}_\rho)$.

If there are input points with small existence probabilities, for example $\alpha = \frac{1}{\sqrt{n}}$, then the previous scheme is not efficient. In these cases a straightforward sampling-based Monte Carlo approach can estimate $\gamma(x, \mathsf{P}_\rho)$ with additive error ε, for any $x \in X$ and rectangle ρ, with high probability. We instantiate P, $s = O(\frac{1}{\varepsilon} \log n)$ times. Each time the point p_j is chosen with probability α_j. Let S_i be the i-th instance of P. For each $i \leq s$, we build a range-MAX index, like a range-tree, for the set S_i. Given a query rectangle ρ, we find the maximum value in $\rho \cap S_i$ for each i, and return the value that was the maximum in most of the indexes. This procedure returns a value x_ρ such that $\gamma(x_\rho, \mathsf{P}_\rho) \geq \max_{x \in X} \gamma(x, \mathsf{P}_\rho) - \varepsilon$ with high probability, in time $O(\frac{1}{\varepsilon} \log^d n)$, using $O(\frac{1}{\varepsilon} n \log^d n)$ space.

This simple sampling-based approach, however, does not work for estimating $\mu(\mathsf{P}_\rho)$, for a query rectangle, because a point in P_ρ with very small existence probability may have a very large value. We describe a novel $O(n\,\text{polylog}(n))$-size index that estimates $\mu(\mathsf{P}_\rho)$ within relative error $1/2$ in $O(\text{polylog}(n))$ time. The index is based on the following lemma.

Lemma 5.1 *Let $Y_1, \ldots, Y_m$ be Bernoulli random variables such that Y_i assumes value v_i with probability α_i and 0 otherwise. Then,*

$$\mathbf{E}\left[\max_j Y_j\right] \geq w \geq \frac{1}{2}\mathbf{E}\left[\max_j Y_j\right],$$

where w is a solution of the equation

$$w = \sum_j \mathbf{E}\left[\max\{Y_j - w, 0\}\right].$$

The second part of this inequality is the well-known Prophet inequality [25]. The first part of the inequality can be shown by induction on i; we omit the proof from this abstract.[3] We now discuss how to use this lemma to devise an index for the range-max queries.

For a point $p_j \in \mathsf{P}$, let Y_j be a random variable that has value v_j with probability α_j and 0 otherwise. For a subset $\mathsf{R} \subseteq \mathsf{P}$ and a real-valued parameter $t > 0$, we define

$$F_{\mathsf{R}}(t) = \sum_{p_j \in \mathsf{R}} \mathbf{E}\left[\max\{Y_j - t, 0\}\right]. \quad (2)$$

Let $X = \langle x_1, \ldots, x_m \rangle$ be the sequence of distinct values of points of P in decreasing order. The proof of the following lemma is straightforward.

Lemma 5.2 *For any subset $\mathsf{R} \subseteq \mathsf{P}$,*

(i) $F_{\mathsf{R}}(t)$ is a monotonically decreasing, piecewise-linear continuous function.

(ii) For any $1 \le i \le m$, $F_{\mathsf{R}}(t)$ is a linear function in the interval $[x_i, x_{i-1}]$ with the following form:

$$F_{\mathsf{R},i}(t) = \sum_{p_j \in \mathsf{R}: v_j \ge x_{i-1}} \alpha_j (v_j - t). \quad (3)$$

The following corollary is an easy consequence of Lemma 5.2 (i).

Corollary 5.3 *There is a unique value t, denoted by $\tau(\mathsf{R})$, for which $F_{\mathsf{R}}(t) = t$.*

Given a subset $\mathsf{R} \subseteq \mathsf{P}$, $\tau(\mathsf{R})$ can be computed in two stages. The first stage computes the value $i := i(\mathsf{R})$ such that $\tau(\mathsf{R}) \in [x_i, x_{i-1}]$ by performing a binary search on X. The second stage computes $\tau(\mathsf{R})$ by solving the linear equation $F_{\mathsf{R},i}(t) - t = 0$ (cf. 3).

Indexing scheme. Define $\bar{\mathsf{P}} = \{\bar{p}_i \mid 1 \le i \le n\}$, where $\bar{p}_i = (p_i, v_i) \in \mathbb{R}^{d+1}$, for $p_i \in \mathsf{P}$. We build an index on $\bar{\mathsf{P}}$ so that for any query $(d+1)$-dimensional rectangle $\bar{\rho}$, quantities $b_{\bar{\rho}} = \sum_{\bar{p}_i \in \bar{\rho} \cap \bar{\mathsf{P}}} \alpha_i v_i$ and $a_{\bar{\rho}} = \sum_{\bar{p}_i \in \bar{\rho} \cap \bar{\mathsf{P}}} \alpha_i$ can be computed quickly, using an instance of a $(d+1)$-dimensional range-SUM query. In particular, an index of size $O(n \log^d n)$ can be built in time $O(n \log^d n)$ so that $a_{\bar{\rho}}$, $b_{\bar{\rho}}$ can be computed in $O(\log^d n)$ time [2].

Query procedure. Let ρ be a query rectangle in $\mathbb{R}^d$, and we wish to estimate $\mu(\mathsf{P}_\rho)$. We perform a binary search on X to compute $i := i(\mathsf{P}_\rho)$ such that $\tau(\mathsf{P}_\rho) \in [x_i, x_{i-1}]$. Each step of the binary search chooses a value $x_r \in X$ and queries the index with the rectangle $\bar{\rho}_r = \rho \times [x_r, \infty)$, which returns

$$a_{\bar{\rho}_r} = \sum_{\bar{p}_i \in \bar{\rho}_r \cap \bar{\mathsf{P}}} \alpha_i, \quad b_{\bar{\rho}_r} = \sum_{p_i \in \bar{\rho}_r \cap \bar{\mathsf{P}}} \alpha_i v_i. \quad (4)$$

By Lemma 5.2

$$F_{\mathsf{P}_\rho}(x_r) = b_{\bar{\rho}_r} - a_{\bar{\rho}_r} x_r. \quad (5)$$

Therefore, by comparing $F_{\mathsf{P}_\rho}(x_r)$ with x_r, we can determine in $O(1)$ time whether $\tau(\mathsf{P}_\rho) = x_r$, $\tau(\mathsf{P}_\rho) > x_r$, or $\tau(\mathsf{P}_\rho) < x_r$. In the first case, we have the value of $\tau(\mathsf{P}_\rho)$ and return $F_{\mathsf{P}_\rho}(x_r)$ as an estimate of $\mu(\mathsf{P}_\rho)$. Otherwise, we proceed with the binary search.

After having computed the value $i(\mathsf{P}_\rho)$, we can compute $\tau(\mathsf{P}_\rho)$ in another $O(1)$ time. Putting everything together, we obtain the following:

Theorem 5.4 *Let P be a set of n uncertain points in $\mathbb{R}^d$. An index of size $O(n \log^d n)$ can be built on P in time $O(n \log^d n)$ that for a query rectangle ρ returns in $O(\log^{d+1} n)$ time a value η_ρ such that $\frac{1}{2}\mu(\mathsf{P} \cap \rho) \le \eta_\rho \le \mu(\mathsf{P} \cap \rho)$.*

6. LOCATION UNCERTAINTY MODEL

In the interest of exposition and to highlight the conceptual framework, we have described our range-max index structures for a simple model of data uncertainty. The methodology, however, extends naturally to more general uncertainty models. We already discussed one such extension—uncertainty in values—at the end of Section 2. In this section, we discuss *location uncertainty*, where the position of each point has a probability distribution.

In the location-uncertainty model, the location of a point P is represented as a probability distribution. We assume P is specified by a point set $\{p_1, \ldots, p_f\}$ with associated probabilities $\{\alpha_1, \ldots, \alpha_f\}$, i.e., $\alpha_j = \mathbf{Pr}[P \text{ is at location } p_j]$, $\sum_{j=1}^f \alpha_j \le 1$, and P does not appear with probability $1 - \sum_{j=1}^f \alpha_j$. We refer to f as the *support size* of P. Let $\mathsf{P} = \{P_1, \ldots, P_n\}$ be a set of n points in $\mathbb{R}^d$ in the location uncertainty model. Without loss of generality, we assume that the support size of each point is f, i.e., $P_i = \{p_{i1}, \ldots, p_{if}\}$ and $\alpha_{ij} = \mathbf{Pr}[P_i \text{ is at } p_{ij}]$.

Each P_i is associated with a scalar $v_i > 0$. Note that the model described in Section 1 is a special case of this model with $f = 1$. With a slight abuse of notation we will use P_i to define an uncertain point as well as the set of its possible locations. We wish to compute the expected or most-likely value of the maximum in a query rectangle ρ.

The algorithms described in Sections 2, 4, and 5 can be extended to the location uncertainty model. Since the location uncertainty model is more general, the lower bound described in Section 3 holds for this model but we also prove a similar lower bound for the EM problem in this model. Due to lack of space we only describe how to extend the exact and approximation algorithms, and we briefly sketch the lower-bound construction.

[3]We thank Kamesh Munagala for pointing out the usage of Prophet inequality.

Exact algorithm. For simplicity we assume the values of points in P are distinct; the case of multiple points having the same value can be handled by adapting the definitions and Algorithm 1 in Section 2. We show that the expected and the most-likely value of maximum inside a rectangle can be defined analogously to Section 2.

For a rectangle ρ, let $P_i(\rho)$ denote the restriction of P_i inside ρ. That is, $P_i(\rho)$ is an uncertain point with possible locations $P_i \cap \rho$ and for $p_{ij} \in P_i \cap \rho$, $\mathbf{Pr}[P_i(\rho) \text{ is at } p_{ij}] = \alpha_{ij}$. We define $\alpha_i(\rho)=\sum_{p_{ij}\in P_i\cap\rho}\alpha_{ij}$ to be the probability of P_i appearing inside ρ, and $\pi_i(\rho) = 1 - \alpha_i(\rho)$ to be the probability of P_i not appearing inside ρ. For a subset $\mathsf{Q} \subseteq \mathsf{P}$ and for a rectangle ρ let $\gamma_i(\mathsf{Q}, \rho)$ be the probability of v_i, with $P_i \in \mathsf{Q}$, being the maximum value among the points of Q in ρ, then [4]

$$\gamma_i(\mathsf{Q},\rho) = \alpha_i(\rho) \prod_{P_j\in\mathsf{Q}:v_j>v_i} \pi_j(\rho),$$

$$\mu(\mathsf{Q},\rho) = \sum_{i=1}^{n} v_i\gamma_i(\mathsf{Q},\rho),$$

$$\lambda(\mathsf{Q},\rho) = \arg\max_{1\le i\le n} \gamma_i(\mathsf{Q},\rho).$$

With these definitions γ_i, μ, and λ in place, the overall structure of the algorithm is the same as before. We partition P into $O(n^{1-t})$ subsets $\mathsf{P}_1, \dots, \mathsf{P}_k$, each of size at most $2n^t$, so that all points in P_i have higher values than those in P_{i+1}. For each P_i, there is a set $S_i = \bigcup_{P_j\in\mathsf{P}_i} P_j$ of $O(n^t f)$ possible locations. Therefore, there are $O((n^t f)^{2d})$ "combinatorially distinct" rectangles with respect to P_i, each defined by a subset of $2d$ locations in S_i, in the sense that $\gamma(\mathsf{P}_i,\rho)$, $\mu(\mathsf{P}_i,\rho)$, and $\lambda(\mathsf{P}_i,\rho)$, for any rectangle ρ, are the same as for one of these rectangles. We store $\mu(\mathsf{P}_i,\rho)$ and $\pi(\mathsf{P}_i,\rho) = \prod_{P_j\in\mathsf{P}_i}\pi_j(\rho)$ for every combinatorially distinct rectangle. The total size of the index is $O(n^{(2d-1)t+1}f^{2d})$, and it can be constructed in time $O(n^{(2d-1)t+1}f^{2d}\log n)$. Algorithm 1 can be adapted in a straightforward manner to compute $\mu(\mathsf{P},\rho)$ and $\lambda(\mathsf{P},\rho)$ in time $O(n^{1-t} + \log(nf))$. We thus obtain the following:

Theorem 6.1 *Let P be a set of n locationally uncertain points in $\mathbb{R}^d$, each of support size f. For any $t \in [0,1]$, an index of size $O(n^{(2d-1)t+1}f^{2d})$ can be constructed in $O(n^{(2d-1)t+1}f^{2d}\log n)$ time so that the expected or most-likely maximum value inside a query rectangle can be computed in $O(n^{1-t} + \log(nf))$ time.*

Approximation algorithm. We now show that the approximation algorithm described in Section 5 for the EM problem can be extended to the location uncertainty model.

For a rectangle ρ and for a point $P_i \in \mathsf{P}$, we define a random variable $Y_{i,\rho}$ whose value is v_i if P_i lies inside ρ and 0 otherwise. Then

$$\mathbf{Pr}[Y_{i,\rho} = v_i] = \alpha_i(\rho) = \sum_{p_{ij}\in P_i(\rho)} \alpha_{ij}.$$

and $\mu(\mathsf{P},\rho) = \mathbf{E}[\max Y_{j,\rho}]$. Lemma 5.1 still holds for the Bernoulli random variables $Y_{i,\rho}$. We also define the function

$$F_\rho(t) = \sum_{j=1}^{n} \mathbf{E}[\max\{Y_{j,\rho} - t, 0\}].$$

Let $v_1, \dots, v_n$ be the values of points in decreasing order, then analogously to Lemma 5.2, $F_\rho(t)$ has the following form in $[v_i, v_{i-1}]$:

$$F_{\rho,i}(t) = \sum_{v_j\ge v_{i-1}} \alpha_j(\rho)(v_j - t) := b_{\rho,i} - a_{\rho,i}t,$$

where

$$a_{\rho,i} = \sum_{v_j\ge v_{i-1}} \alpha_j(\rho), \quad b_{\rho,i} = \sum_{v_j\ge v_{i-1}} \alpha_j(\rho)v_j.$$

As in Section 5, we construct an index to compute $a_{\rho,i}$, $b_{\rho,i}$ quickly for a given rectangle ρ and an integer $i \in [2,n]$. More precisely, for $1 \le i \le n$ and $1 \le j \le f$, let $\bar{p}_{ij} = (p_{ij}, v_i) \in \mathbb{R}^{d+1}$. We assign a pair of weights $w_a(\bar{p}_{ij}) = \alpha_{ij}$ and $w_b(\bar{p}_{ij}) = \alpha_{ij}v_j$ for each $\bar{p}_{ij}$. Set $\bar{S} = \{\bar{p}_{ij} \mid 1 \le i \le n, 1 \le j \le f\}$. For a rectangle ρ in $\mathbb{R}^d$ and for an integer $i \in [2,n]$, let $\bar{\rho}_i = \rho \times [v_{i-1}, \infty)$. Then

$$a_{\rho,i} = \sum_{\bar{p}_{jk}\in\bar{S}\cap\bar{\rho}_i} w_a(\bar{p}_{jk}), \quad b_{\rho,i} = \sum_{\bar{p}_{jk}\in\bar{S}\cap\bar{\rho}_i} w_b(\bar{p}_{jk}).$$

By building an index on $\bar{S}$ for range-SUM queries, $a_{\rho,i}$, $b_{\rho,i}$ can be computed in $O(\log^d n)$ time. The size of the index is $O(nf\log^d(nf))$, and it can be constructed in the same time [2]. The query procedure is the same as in Section 5. We thus obtain the following:

Theorem 6.2 *Let P be a set of n locationally uncertain points in $\mathbb{R}^d$, each with support size f. An index of size $O(nf\log^d(nf))$ can be constructed in time $O(nf\log^d(nf))$ that for a query rectangle ρ returns in $O(\log^{d+1}(nf))$ time a value η_ρ, such that $\frac{1}{2}\mu(\mathsf{P},\rho) \le \eta_\rho \le \mu(\mathsf{P},\rho)$.*

Lower bound. We sketch the reduction of the set-intersection problem to the EM problem[5]. We may assume all the integers in the sets $S_1, \dots, S_m$ are divisible by 3. If not, we can work with the instance $S_i' = \{3x \mid x \in S_i\}$, without a change to the answer of any set-intersection query. We use almost the same construction as in the proof of Theorem 3.2, with four important differences.

[4]In the location uncertainty model, P is a family of sets of points, so the notation here is slightly different from earlier sections.

[5]In the lower bound, we use sets with *integer-valued* items, as opposed to real-valued items. However, the set-intersection problem over reals is easily reduced to an integer-valued instance, and so the former is just as hard [15, 23, 24].

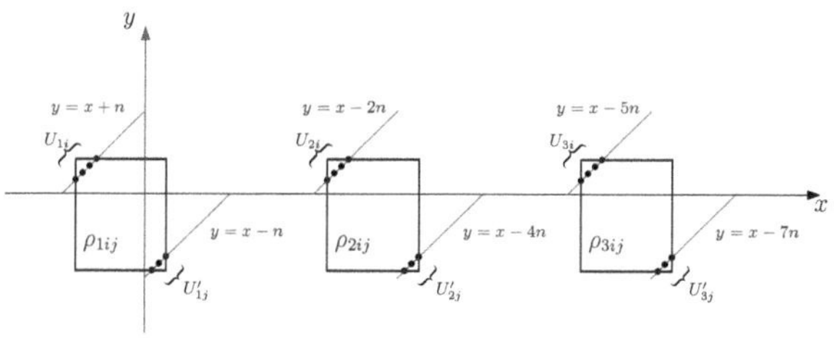

Figure 3. Illustration - lower bound for EM in location uncertainty model.

(i) The entire configuration is shifted parallel to itself by $3n$ and $6n$ to get three non-interfering configurations;

(ii) the associated values of the points above the x-axis come from the sets as before, but for the points below the x-axis they are increased by 1 for the second instance, by 2 for the third instance and are unchanged in the first instance;

(iii) points with the same value are all considered as belonging to one uncertain point in the location model, and,

(iv) all points are assigned probability α which can be chosen small enough so that each uncertain point is deficient, i.e., the sum of probabilities of locations is less than 1, see Figure 3 for illustration.

To answer a query, "Does S_i intersect S_j?" where $i \neq j$, we consider the rectangles $\rho_{1ij}, \rho_{2ij}, \rho_{3ij}$ as shown in Figure 3, and we query the EM value for each of them - denote these by Ψ_1, Ψ_2, Ψ_3. We can show that:

Lemma 6.3 $\Psi_2 = (\Psi_1 + \Psi_3)/2$ *if and only if the sets* S_i, S_j *do not intersect.*

Intuitively, we can see the above as follows. The EM value $\mu(\mathsf{P}, \rho_{ij})$ is the sum $\sum_{k=1}^{n} v_k \gamma_k(\mathsf{P}, \rho_{ij})$, and if the queried sets S_i, S_j are disjoint, all the values occurring inside all the rectangles are distinct and one can easily show that the sum for each of the Ψ_k is formed by two distinct components - one coming from contributions from values for points corresponding to S_i and the other by those from S_j, and thus $\Psi_2 - \Psi_1 = \Psi_3 - \Psi_2$, because of the equal shifts in values. On the other hand, if the sets intersect, some points inside the first rectangle belong to the same uncertain point - but this does not happen for the second and third rectangles because the numbers involved are distinct modulo 3. In this case, Ψ_2, Ψ_3 behave similar to the case when S_i, S_j are disjoint but Ψ_1 increases. Thus we have, $\Psi_2 - \Psi_1 < \Psi_3 - \Psi_2$. Finally, we can show the following result where n, m come from the construction, as there are $O(n)$ uncertain points now, with support size bounded by $O(m)$.

Theorem 6.4 *Suppose there exists an index with size $S(n, f)$ and query time $Q(n, f)$ for solving the* EM *problem for n points in $\mathbb{R}^2$ under the location uncertainty model, where each point has a distribution over at most f possible locations. Then an instance of the set-intersection problem, for sets $S_1, \ldots, S_m$, with $\sum_{i=1}^{m} |S_i| = n$, can be solved in $O(Q(n, m))$ query time using space $O(S(n, m))$.*

7. CONCLUSION

In this paper, we studied the range-max query problem for uncertain data, and designed efficient index structures for answering these queries both exactly and approximately under two models of data uncertainty (existential and locational). Our exact algorithms are the first to achieve sublinear query time using sub-quadratic space, while our approximation algorithms utilize novel tools such as the Prophet inequality. We also prove a hardness result for the MLM, which shows that range-max queries over uncertain data are provably more difficult than their deterministic counterparts. Our work suggests several avenues of future research, including the following:
(i) Our query-space bounds represent an important advance but are unlikely to be optimal, so improving them is an obvious goal. In particular, is sublinear query time possible for the EM and MLM problems using only a linear size index?

(ii) Our lower bound for the MLM problem is conditioned on the (widely) conjectured hardness of the set intersection problem. Is an *unconditional* lower bound possible? Can the lower bound be shown for dimension $d = 1$?

(iii) Our Prophet Inequality based approximation works only for the EM problem. Can a similar scheme be designed for the MLM problem?

(iv) Extend our results to other range queries, such as range-SUM. Can we efficiently approximate the *distribution* of the range-SUM statistic?

Acknowledgments. We thank Kamesh Munagala for pointing out the prophet inequality, and Ke Yi and Wuzhou Zhang for helpful discussions.

8. REFERENCES

[1] A. Abdullah, S. Daruki, and J. M. Phillips. Range counting coresets for uncertain data. In *Proc. 29th Annu. Sympos. Comput. Geom.*, pages 223–232, 2013.

[2] P. K. Agarwal. Range searching. In J. E. Goodman and J. O'Rourke, editors, *Handbook of Discrete and Computational Geometry, 2nd Edition.*, pages 809–837. CRC, 2004.

[3] P. K. Agarwal, B. Aronov, S. Har-Peled, J. M. Phillips, K. Yi, and W. Zhang. Nearest neighbor searching under uncertainty ii. In *Proc. 32nd Annu. sympos. Princ. Database Sys.*, pages 115–126, 2013.

[4] P. K. Agarwal, S.-W. Cheng, and K. Yi. Range searching on uncertain data. *ACM Trans. Algorithms*, 8(4):43, 2012.

[5] P. K. Agarwal, A. Efrat, S. Sankararaman, and W. Zhang. Nearest neighbor searching under uncertainty. In *Proc. 31st Annu. ACM sympos. Princ. Database Sys.*, pages 225–236, 2012.

[6] C. C. Aggarwal. *Managing and Mining Uncertain Data: 3, A.*, volume 35. Springer Science & Business Media, 2010.

[7] Z. Bai, L. Devroye, H. Hwang, and T. Tsai. Maxima in hypercubes. *Random Structures & Algorithms*, 27(3):290–309, 2005.

[8] T. Bernecker, T. Emrich, H.-P. Kriegel, N. Mamoulis, M. Renz, and A. Zuefle. A novel probabilistic pruning approach to speed up similarity queries in uncertain databases. In *Proc. 27th Annu. IEEE Int. Conf. Data Eng.*, pages 339–350, 2011.

[9] G. Beskales, M. A. Soliman, and I. F. Ilyas. Efficient search for the top-k probable nearest neighbors in uncertain databases. *Proc. 34th Very Large Data Bases*, 1(1):326–339, 2008.

[10] B. Chazelle and L. J. Guibas. Fractional cascading: I. A data structuring technique. *Algorithmica*, 1(1-4):133–162, 1986.

[11] J. Chen and L. Feng. Efficient pruning algorithm for top-k ranking on dataset with value uncertainty. In *Proc. 22nd ACM Conf. Inf. Knowl. Manag.*, pages 2231–2236, 2013.

[12] R. Cheng, Y. Xia, S. Prabhakar, R. Shah, and J. S. Vitter. Efficient indexing methods for probabilistic threshold queries over uncertain data. In *Proc. 30th Very Large Data Bases*, pages 876–887, 2004.

[13] G. Cormode, F. Li, and K. Yi. Semantics of ranking queries for probabilistic data and expected ranks. In *Proc. 25th Annu. IEEE Int. Conf. Data Eng.*, pages 305–316, 2009.

[14] N. Dalvi, C. Ré, and D. Suciu. Probabilistic databases: diamonds in the dirt. *Comm. ACM*, 52(7):86–94, 2009.

[15] P. Davoodi, M. Smid, and F. van Walderveen. Two-dimensional range diameter queries. In *Proc. 10th Latin American Theo. Inform. Sympos.*, pages 219–230, 2012.

[16] T. Ge, S. Zdonik, and S. Madden. Top-k queries on uncertain data: on score distribution and typical answers. In *Proc. SIGMOD*, pages 375–388, 2009.

[17] M. Hua, J. Pei, and X. Lin. Ranking queries on uncertain data. *The VLDB Journal*, 20(1):129–153, 2011.

[18] T. Jayram, S. Kale, and E. Vee. Efficient aggregation algorithms for probabilistic data. In *Proc. 18th Annu. ACM-SIAM Sympos. Discrete Alg.*, pages 346–355, 2007.

[19] J. Kleinberg, Y. Rabani, and É. Tardos. Allocating bandwidth for bursty connections. *SIAM Journal on Computing*, 30(1):191–217, 2000.

[20] A. I. Kuksa and N. Z. Šor. The method of estimating the number of conditionally optimal trajectories of discrete separable dynamic programming (in russian). *Kibernetika (Kiev)*, 6:37–44, 1972.

[21] J. Li and H. Wang. Range queries on uncertain data. In *Algorithms and Computation*, pages 326–337. 2014.

[22] X. Lian and L. Chen. Probabilistic top-k dominating queries in uncertain databases. *Information Sciences*, 226:23–46, 2013.

[23] M. Patrascu and L. Roditty. Distance oracles beyond the Thorup-Zwick bound. In *Proc. 51st Annu. IEEE Found. Comp. Sci.*, pages 815–823, 2010.

[24] S. Rahul and R. Janardan. Algorithms for range-skyline queries. In *20th ACM Int. Conf. Adv. Geogr. Inf. Sys.*, 2012.

[25] E. Samuel-Cahn. Comparison of threshold stop rules and maximum for independent nonnegative random variables. *Ann. Probab.*, 12(4):1213–1216, 11 1984.

[26] S. Singh, C. Mayfield, S. Prabhakar, R. Shah, and S. Hambrusch. Indexing uncertain categorical data. In *Proc. 23rd Annu. IEEE Int. Conf. Data Eng.*, pages 616–625, 2007.

[27] M. A. Soliman, I. F. Ilyas, and K. Chen-Chuan Chang. Top-k query processing in uncertain databases. In *Proc. 23rd Annu. IEEE Int. Conf. Data Eng.*, pages 896–905, 2007.

[28] Y. Tao, X. Xiao, and R. Cheng. Range search on multidimensional uncertain data. *ACM Trans. Database Sys.*, 32(3):15, 2007.

[29] G. Xiao, K. Li, K. Li, and X. Zhou. Efficient top-(k, l) range query processing for uncertain data based on multicore architectures. *Distributed & Parallel Databases*, pages 1–33, 2014.

[30] K. Yi, F. Li, G. Kollios, and D. Srivastava. Efficient processing of top-k queries in uncertain databases. In *Proc. 24th Annu. IEEE Int. Conf. Data Eng.*, pages 1406–1408, 2008.

[31] M. L. Yiu, N. Mamoulis, X. Dai, Y. Tao, and M. Vaitis. Efficient evaluation of probabilistic advanced spatial queries on existentially uncertain data. *IEEE Trans. Knowl. Data Eng.*, 21(1):108–122, 2009.

Fast Algorithms for Parsing Sequences of Parentheses with Few Errors

Arturs Backurs
MIT

Krzysztof Onak
IBM Research

ABSTRACT

We consider the problem of fixing sequences of unbalanced parentheses. A classic algorithm based on dynamic programming computes the optimum sequence of edits required to solve the problem in cubic time. We show the first algorithm that runs in linear time when the number of necessary edits is small. More precisely, our algorithm runs in $O(n) + d^{O(1)}$ time, where n is the length of the sequence to be fixed and d is the minimum number of edits.

The problem of fixing parentheses sequences is related to the task of repairing semi-structured documents such as XML and JSON.

Keywords

Dyck language; edit distance; parsing

1. INTRODUCTION

Balanced sequences of parentheses can be used to describe arbitrary rooted trees. Their popular application is to specify the order in which binary operations are performed in algebraic and arithmetic expressions. The language of well-balanced sequences on k different types of parentheses is also known as the Dyck(k) language and can easily be expressed as a context-free grammar.

The Dyck(k) language is inherently present in both numerous semi-structured document formats—such as XML and JSON—and essentially all programming languages that allow for recursively nesting blocks and loops. In XML and—most of the time—in HTML,[1] an opening tag **<xyz>** has to be accompanied by the corresponding closing tag **</xyz>**, where **xyz** is an arbitrary allowed identifier. Pairs of tags can be nested as in **<a><b></b></a>**. They can also appear alongside as in **<a></a><b></b>**, but they cannot be interleaved as in **<b><a></b></a>**.

A large fraction of HTML documents on the web are malformed or do not conform to HTML standards. Unfortunately, there is no mechanism allowing to notify the content creator about the issue and speedily receive a corrected document. Therefore, at the risk of losing their market share, major web browsers are forced to routinely display malformed HTML documents. While many tags such as section headers cannot be meaningfully nested, an arbitrary proper nesting of text formatting elements such as **<i>**, **<b>**, **<sub>**, **<sup>**, etc. is allowed within a paragraph.[2]

Given an incorrectly formatted text paragraph, what is the best way to interpret it in order to visualize it? One way to approach this problem is to find a way of fixing the formatting by making the minimum number of tag modifications such as substitutions, deletions, and insertions. This corresponds to expressing the formatting tags as a sequence of parentheses and finding the minimum number of edits converting the input sequence into a sequence in Dyck(k).

Unfortunately, the best known algorithm for this problem requires time that is cubic in the length of the input (it also uses quadratic space), which is prohibitively expensive even for relatively small documents. A linear time algorithm would be ideal from the practical perspective, but there is evidence that such algorithms may not exist [2]. However, this does not preclude the existence of more efficient algorithms if the edit distance is *small*. If the distance to Dyck(k) is large, then the document is likely to be too corrupt to permit a meaningful recovery.

In this paper we focus on the small distance regime, and show an algorithm that finds a minimum number of edits in time and space $O(n) + d^{O(1)}$, where n is the length of the sequence and d is the distance to Dyck(k).

Potential applications of our algorithm go beyond correcting HTML documents. Our techniques can be applied to correcting a wider class of semi-structured documents, the topic discussed in the papers by Korn et al. [7] and Saha [10]. The work by Korn at al. [7] gives an algorithm that returns few edits needed to repair a sequence of parentheses. It discusses the practical aspects of parentheses repairing in depth. Furthermore, compilers often do not stop processing the input immediately after encountering the first syntax error but attempt to correct it in order to list more errors at once. Frequently, syntax errors are a result of incorrectly nested blocks. The authors of this paper have suffered from

[1]Formally, HTML is not an XML-adherent language. Attempts at making it follow a more restrictive set of rules, such as XHTML, have not been very widely adopted. However, the differences are not important for the discussion here, which focuses on an XML-like part of HTML.

[2]See any HTML standard definition, e.g., [1], or tutorial for more information on the function of these tags.

PODS'16, June 26-July 01, 2016, San Francisco, CA, USA

DOI: http://dx.doi.org/10.1145/2902251.2902304

mismatched LaTeX `\begin{...}` and `\end{...}` tags multiple times while writing this work. A fast tag correcting algorithm could also be used in an integrated development environment to provide feedback to the user about structural problems in the document being created. The Dyck language arises naturally in many biological applications like RNA folding [14].

1.1 Our results

Table 1 summarizes previous results and our results on computing distance to Dyck(k). We give two algorithms. We start our presentation with an easier and faster algorithm for the case that only deletions are allowed. Its running time is $O(n+d^6)$, where n is the length of the sequence and d is the distance. If substitutions are allowed as well, we give a slower $O(n+d^{16})$-time algorithm. In either case, the running time does not depend on k as long as all parentheses are represented as positive integers bounded by $n^{O(1)}$. (Under this condition, an underlying suffix tree can be built in $O(n)$ time.)

A note on computing an optimal sequence of edits.

For simplicity, we focus our presentation on computing distance to the closest well-balanced sequence of parentheses. In a more practical setting, one would most likely be interested in obtaining an optimal sequence of edits as well. The sequence of edits provides a possible way of interpreting the corrupt input sequence as a well balanced sequence of parentheses. Our algorithms construct and retain a dynamic programming table that is sufficient for reconstructing the optimal sequence of edits in the same running time. We note that if the distance is larger than d, our algorithms detect this fact in the same running time.

A note on the presentation.

In the presentation of our algorithms, we assume that d is an upper bound on edit distance to Dyck(k). Our general result can be obtained by first setting $d = 1$ and then doubling d as long as the algorithm fails. This is enough to obtain an $O(n \log d) + d^{O(1)}$-algorithm, where d is the actual distance. The part of our algorithm that takes linear time is preprocessing, which is independent of the bound on d. Hence the $O(\log d)$ factor in the running time is not necessary.

1.2 Previous results and related work

We list related results in Table 1. A cubic-time algorithm for computing distance to Dyck(k) was given by Aho and Peterson [3], who studied the distance to general context-free grammars (see also [9]). Valiant [13] studied subcubic algorithms for the problem. Combining his techniques with state-of-the-art algorithms for distances in graphs, one obtains exact algorithms of running times $O(n^3/2^{\Omega(\sqrt{\log n})})$ and $O(d \cdot n^{\omega})$.

Saha [10] studied the problem of *approximating* the distance to Dyck(k) in near-linear time. She gave meta-algorithms that reduce the problem to a small number of executions of an approximate edit distance algorithm. In Table 1, we list three applications of her results. The most related to the topic of this paper is an algorithm that computes an $O(\log d)$-approximation in $O(n + d^2)$ time. Her meta-algorithms are based on cleverly guessing an alignment of strings with a neat analysis based on random walks. Since whenever a parsing algorithm gets stuck, the optimal edit decision that enables proceeding comes from a constant-size set of options, one can enumerate over all possible sets of at most d edit decisions in order to find an optimal edit sequence. This leads to an exact algorithm that runs in $2^{O(d)} \cdot n$ time. In another work, Saha [11] gave an algorithm for computing a $(1+\epsilon)$-approximation to distance to a fixed context-free grammar. The running time of the algorithm is $\tilde{O}(n^{\omega}/\epsilon^{O(1)})$.

Finally, Abboud et al. [2] showed that under plausible complexity assumptions, there is no exact algorithm that runs significantly faster than in time $O(n^{\omega})$. Hence, it is unlikely that there is an exact algorithm for distance to Dyck(k) that runs in near-linear time even for large d.

1.3 Our techniques

We first preprocess the input sequence to align pairs of parentheses that can already be matched. Eliminating them does not change the distance to Dyck(k). After this step, one can show that the input consists of $O(d)$ blocks, where each block is first a sequence of opening and then closing parentheses. We also define a height function that describes how deeply nested each parenthesis is. Parentheses at very different heights can only be matched with a large number of edits. This together with a bound on the number of blocks leads to a poly(d) bound on what other parentheses each parenthesis could be matched to (perhaps after a substitution).

Our algorithms enumerate over all possible matches of borders between blocks in the above decomposition. The number of all such matches can be shown to be polynomial in d. Assuming that we know how to efficiently compute the number of edits required to align potentially long but very simple sequences of opening—on one side—and closing—on the other side—parentheses, we build a dynamic programming instance on top of poly(d) different subsequences. The dynamic program gives eventually the solution to the edit distance problem.

The missing piece, a subroutine for quickly computing how well two "simple" subsequences of parentheses align, is an adaptation of techniques from the $O(n + d^2)$-time edit distance algorithm [8], which largely inspired our work. A "simple" subsequence consists of only opening or closing parentheses. In particular, out algorithms have have to align very distant subsequences of parentheses efficiently. This is what our adaptation of techniques of Landau et al. [8] can do in $O(d^2)$ time, independently of the length of subsequences involved, after an initial linear-time preprocessing.

1.4 Future work

We see our algorithm as a proof of concept that near-linear time algorithms can be constructed when the edit distance to Dyck(k) is polynomially small. We believe that further research will result in improved running time and, simultaneously, more practical algorithms. We predict, however, that constructing an $O(n+d^3)$-time algorithm will turn out to be a very challenging task. If it is not possible at all, it would be very interesting to prove a conditional lower bound that uses a popular complexity assumption that computing edit distance to Dyck(k) requires $\omega(n)$ time for $d = o(n^{1/3})$ (see [4, 2] for examples of related conditional lower bounds).

	Runtime	Approximation factor	Comments
Theorem 40	$O(n + d^{16})$	Exact	
Theorem 26	$O(n + d^6)$	Exact	No substitutions
[3, 9]	$O(n^3)$	Exact	
	$O\left(n^3/2^{\Omega(\sqrt{\log n})}\right)$	Exact	Follows from [15] and [13]
	$O(d \cdot n^\omega)$	Exact	Follows from [5, 12] and [13]
[10]	$O(n^{1+\epsilon})$	$(\log n)^{O(1/\epsilon)}$	
[10]	$O(n)$	$O(d)$	
[10]	$O(n + d^2)$	$O(\log d)$	
	$2^{O(d)} \cdot n$	Exact	Follows from [10]
[11]	$\tilde{O}\left(n^\omega/\epsilon^{O(1)}\right)$	$1 + \epsilon$	
[2]	$\Omega\left(n^{\omega - o(1)}\right)$	Exact	Conditional lower bound

Table 1: Summary of our and previous results on computing distance to Dyck(k). n is the length of the sequence of parentheses. d is the upper bound on the Parentheses language edit distance. $\omega < 2.373$ is the matrix multiplication constant [16, 6].

In the long run, it would be interesting to develop similar algorithms for a wider class of grammars relevant for programming languages.

2. PRELIMINARIES

We write $[n]$ to denote the set $\{1, 2, \ldots, n\}$ for any integer n. For integers n, m, we write $[n, m]$ to denote $\{n, \ldots, m\}$. For a sequence X, $|X|$ denotes its length (the number of symbols in it) and X_i denotes the i-th symbol of X for $i \in [|X|]$. For a sequence X of symbols, $\text{rev}(X)$ is X reversed. More precisely, for every $i \in [|X|]$, we set $(\text{rev}(X))_i := X_{|X|+1-i}$. Given two sequences X and Y, we write $X \circ Y$ to denote the product of their concatenation. From now on, whenever we use the variable k, it will *not* be the number of different types of parentheses k (as in Dyck(k)). Remember that our runtimes do not depend on k (as long as integers representing parentheses are reasonably bounded).

Parentheses.

The input sequences consist of parentheses of different types. For two matching parentheses, one of them is *opening* and the other is *closing*. They can match only if the opening occurs before the closing. Under the usual interpretation, "(" and ")" are a matching pair of parentheses, and so are "{" and "}." Among them, "(" and "{" are opening parentheses, and ")" and ")" are closing parentheses.

DEFINITION 1. *We say that two parentheses are of the same* type *if they are equal or can be matched.*

According to the above definition, "(" and ")" are of the same type, "(" and "(" are also of the same type, but "(" and "]" are *not* of the same type.

We define an operation that removes a sequence of parentheses the information about whether each parenthesis is opening or closing. It keeps, however, the information about the type of each of them.

DEFINITION 2. *We assign integers* 1, 2, ... *to all possible types of parentheses. Given a sequence X of parentheses, we define a sequence $U(X)$ of symbols as follows. For every $i \in [|X|]$, if the parenthesis X_i belongs to the j-th type (it can be a closing or an opening parenthesis), we replace it with a formal symbol a_j.*

For completeness, we state a recursive definition of balanced sequences.

DEFINITION 3. *A sequence X of parentheses is balanced if any of the following holds:*

- *X is an empty string,*
- *$X = Y \circ Z$, where Y and Z are non-empty balanced sequences,*
- *$X = Y_1 \circ Z \circ Y_2$, where Z is a balanced sequence and Y_1 are Y_2 are sequences of length 1 that contain matching opening and closing parentheses, respectively.*

As an example, "((){})" is balanced and "((()()" is not.

Distance.

We consider two distance measures. In one, only deletions are allowed. In the other, substitutions are allowed as well.

DEFINITION 4. *Let S be a sequence of possibly unbalanced parentheses. We write*

- *$\text{edit}_1(S)$ to denote the minimum number of parenthesis deletions necessary to turn S into a balanced sequence of parentheses,*
- *$\text{edit}_2(S)$ to denote the minimum number of parenthesis deletions and substitutions (of one parenthesis with another) necessary to turn S into a balanced sequence of parentheses.*

3. ALGORITHM FOR DISTANCE WITH NO SUBSTITUTIONS

We start by describing a simpler and faster algorithm for the case of only deletions allowed. When substitutions are allowed, we have to handle a few more cases, which inflate both the descriptive and computational complexity of the algorithm.

3.1 Fast distance computation for a simple case

In this subsection, we describe a subroutine that we repeatedly use for computing edit distance (with no substitutions) when the sequence consists of first opening and then closing parenthesis. More generally, we construct a data structure that allows for efficiently computing this kind of information, when the two parts of the sequence are arbitrary disjoint subsequences of the input. We heavily borrow techniques from Landau et al. [8], who designed them for their $O(n+d^2)$ edit distance algorithm.

We start with a definition.

DEFINITION 5. *Let X be a sequence of opening parentheses and Y be a sequence of closing parentheses. By* $\text{edit}_1(X,Y)$ *we denote the quantity* $\text{edit}_1(XY)$.

There is a simple algorithm based on dynamic programming for computing $\text{edit}_1(X,Y)$ in time $O(|X|\cdot|Y|)$. We describe the algorithm here in full because this allows us to introduce a notation that we will find helpful later.

DEFINITION 6. *For any sequences A and B, we define* $\text{edit}'_1(A,B)$ *as the minimum total number of symbol deletions in A and B necessary to make both sequences equal.*

The following fact is straightforward (see Definition 2 for U).

FACT 7. $\text{edit}_1(X,Y) = \text{edit}'_1(U(X), \text{rev}(U(Y)))$.

Therefore, to compute $\text{edit}_1(X,Y)$, it suffices to compute $\text{edit}'_1(U(X), \text{rev}(U(Y)))$. We now show that, given two sequences A, B of symbols, $\text{edit}'_1(A,B)$ can be computed in $O(|A|\cdot|B|)$ time.

The algorithm for $\text{edit}'_1(A,B)$ proceeds as follows. It builds dynamic programming table D with entries $D_{r,c}$ for $r=0,\ldots,|A|$ and $c=0,\ldots,|B|$. It sets $D_{0,c}=c$ for all c and $D_{r,0}=r$ for all r. Then the algorithm fills in the rest of the table D using the following rule:

$$D_{r,c} := \min(D_{r-1,c}+1, D_{r,c-1}+1, 2\cdot\delta_{A_r\neq B_c} + D_{r-1,c-1}), \tag{1}$$

where $\delta_E = 1$ if event E happens and $\delta_E = 0$ if event E does not happen. The last entry $D_{|A|,|B|}$ that we fill in equals $\text{edit}'_1(A,B)$.

DEFINITION 8. *For any integer i, let $T_i := \{(r,c) \mid r-c = i\}$ be the i-th diagonal of entries of D.*

The following two properties of D follow from (1).

PROPERTY 9. *For any r and c, $D_{r+1,c+1} \geq D_{r,c}$.*

Property 9 says that if we move along any diagonal T_i in D, the entries do not decrease.

PROPERTY 10. *Let d be an arbitrary integer. For any integer i with $|i| > d$, we have that $D_{r,c} > d$ for any $(r,c) \in T_i$.*

Property 10 says that all entries in a diagonal far from the main diagonal are large. This implies that if we know that the overall distance is at most d, we do not need to compute entries in diagonals T_i for $|i| > d$ in order to compute the total distance between the strings.

DEFINITION 11. *For integer $i = 0,\ldots,d$, we define*

$$\text{wave}(i) := \{(r,c) \mid D_{r,c} = i \text{ and } D_{r+1,c+1} > i\}.$$

THEOREM 12. *Let C be a sequence of symbols of length n. We can preprocess C in time $O(n)$ so that the following holds. Let $d \geq 0$ be an arbitrary integer, independent of the preprocessing step. Given two arbitrary substrings C_1 and C_2 of C, we can output* $\text{wave}(0),\ldots,\text{wave}(d)$ *(corresponding to* $\text{edit}'_1(C_1,C_2)$*) in time $O(d^2)$.*

PROOF. By Property 10, we have that $|\text{wave}(i)| \leq 2d+1$ for all $i = 0,\ldots,d$. This is because $\text{wave}(i)$ contains at most one (r,c) from each diagonal T_j. The total size of the waves is at most $O(d^2)$. The proof of the theorem appears in [8] (see subsection 2.3 in [8]). The theorem is proved for a slightly different matrix D. It is proved for the case when $\text{edit}'_1(C_1,C_2)$ is the minimum number of insertions, deletions, *and substitutions* necessary to transform C_1 into C_2. However, the proof can be straightforwardly generalized to our definition of edit'_1. More precisely, we change Lemma 2.8 from [8] by replacing expression $\max\{L^{h-1}(d+1)+1, L^{h-1}(d)+1, L^{h-1}(d-1)+1\}$ with $\max\{L^{h-1}(d+1)+1, L^{h-1}(d-1)+1\}$, that is, we remove the second argument from max. Also, notice that we added "+1" to the third argument. We believe that the current statement of Lemma 2.3 in [8] without "+1" is not correct.

The only application of the suffix tree both in [8] and in this theorem is for finding the length of the longest identical substring starting at two specified indices in constant time. Formally, given a sequence $S = S_1 \ldots S_n$, we want to answer queries of the following form: given i and j, what is the largest q such that for all $t \in \{0,\ldots,q-1\}$, $S(i+t) = S(j+t)$? The linear time precomputation involves building the suffix tree and constructing an LCA (=lowest common ancestor) data structure on the suffix tree. The answer to queries can be provided in constant time by finding the leaves corresponding to the suffixes starting at i and j and finding their LCA. The weighted depth of the LCA provides the length of the string.

The algorithm described in Section 2.3 of [8] computes consecutive waves $\text{wave}(0),\ldots,\text{wave}(d)$ using only answers to the above queries, where $S = AxYy$ and x and y are unique symbols (x and y can be removed if one trims the answers provided by the data structure). The algorithm doesn't need to know anything else about the input. Therefore, the same data structure works for arbitrary substrings C_1 and C_2 of any fixed string $S = C$ (as long as we trim the answers to within C_1 and C_2). The precomputation has to be done only once for the entire string S. This is how our algorithm works. For any pair of substrings, the computation time and number of queries to the data structure are bounded by $O(d^2)$. □

THEOREM 13. *Let C be a sequence of symbols of length n. We can preprocess C in time $O(n)$ so that the following holds. Let $d \geq 0$ be an arbitrary integer, independent of the preprocessing step. Given two arbitrary substrings C_1 and C_2 of C, we can output a data structure in time $O(d^2)$ that satisfies the following property. Let D be the dynamic programming table corresponding to* $\text{edit}'_1(C_1,C_2)$*. Given arbitrary (r,c), we can in $O(\log d)$ time output $D_{r,c}$, if $D_{r,c} \leq d$. If $D_{r,c} > d$, we output that $D_{r,c} > d$ in constant time by comparing (r,c) to* $\text{wave}(d)$.

PROOF. By Theorem 12, given two substring C_1, C_2, we can in $O(d^2)$ output $\text{wave}(0),\ldots,\text{wave}(d)$. This is our data structure. Suppose we are given arbitrary (r,c). If $D_{r,c} \leq d$, we can output $D_{r,c}$ in $O(\log d)$ by doing binary search among values wave(i). We can do binary search because wave(0) $\cap T_{r-c}, \ldots,$ wave(d) $\cap T_{r-c}$ are nondecreasing by Property 9. We store each wave(i) indexed by diagonals $-d, \ldots, -1, 0, 1, \ldots, d$. If $D_{r,c} > d$, we output that $D_{r,c} > d$ in constant time. □

We use the following theorem later in the paper.

THEOREM 14. *For any sequence S of parentheses, we can preprocess S in time $O(n)$, where $n = |S|$, so that the following holds. Given any two substrings S_1 and S_2 of S and a parameter d, we can, in $O(d^2)$ time, build a data structure, corresponding to S_1 and S_2, that provides the following two operations:*

- *For any prefix S_1' of S_1 and any suffix S_2' of S_2, such that $\text{edit}_1(S_1', S_2') \leq d$, we can output $\text{edit}_1(S_1', S_2')$ in $O(\log d)$ time.*
- *We can check whether $\text{edit}_1(S_1', S_2') \leq d$ in $O(1)$ time.*

PROOF. We set $C := U(S) \circ \text{rev}(U(S))$ and preprocess C as in Theorem 13. $U(S_1)$ is substring of $U(S)$. $\text{rev}(U(S_2))$ is substring of $\text{rev}(U(S))$. $U(S_1')$ is a prefix of $U(S_1)$. $\text{rev}(U(S_2'))$ is a prefix of $\text{rev}(U(S_2))$. By Fact 7 and Theorem 13, we get the required algorithm. □

3.2 Algorithm

Let S be a sequence of parentheses. We denote the length of S by $n = |S|$. We are given integer d such that $\text{edit}_1(S) \leq d$. In this section we show how to compute $\text{edit}_1(S)$ in time $O(n + d^6)$.

The following height function is very convenient in further analysis.

DEFINITION 15. *We define function $h : [n] \to \mathbb{Z}$ as follows: $h(1) := 0$ and, for $n \geq i \geq 2$,*

$$h(i) := \begin{cases} h(i-1) & \text{if } S_{i-1} \text{ and } S_i \\ & \text{are of different classes;} \\ h(i-1) - 1 & \text{if } S_{i-1} \text{ and } S_i \text{ are both opening;} \\ h(i-1) + 1 & \text{if } S_{i-1} \text{ and } S_i \text{ are both closing.} \end{cases}$$

We see that function h decreases if it has consecutive opening parentheses and increases if it has consecutive closing parentheses. Otherwise function does not change its value. See Figure 1 for an example and visualization. Consider the i-th symbol of S, we call $h(i)$ the height of the i-th symbol. h is the height function for sequence S.

We decompose sequence S as

$$S = D_1 U_1 D_2 U_2 \ldots D_{k-1} U_{k-1} D_k U_k \tag{2}$$

for some integer $k \geq 1$. Each D_i consists of opening parentheses only and each U_i consists of closing parentheses only. We require that all U_i, $i < k$ are non-empty sequences. We require that all D_i, $i > 1$ are non-empty sequences. Only D_1 and U_k may be empty. Note that the decomposition is unique.

DEFINITION 16. *For $i \in [k]$, we call sequence $D_i U_i$ the i-th* valley *of S.*

DEFINITION 17. *If D_1 is nonempty, we call the first symbol of D_1 the 0-th peak of S. We call the last symbol of U_1 and the first symbol of D_2 the 1-st peak of S. In general, for $i = 1, \ldots, k-1$, we call the last symbol of U_i and the first symbol of D_{i+1} the i-th peak of S. If U_k is nonempty, we call the last symbol of U_k the k-th peak of S.*

Consider any series of deletions of parentheses that produce a balanced final sequence S' of parentheses. If we visualize the height function of S', we observe the following property. Consider any two parentheses that are aligned (in particular, they are of the same type, the left one is an opening parenthesis and the right one is a closing parenthesis). These have the same height and, if we connect them with a horizontal line, there will be no intersection with the graph of the height function. See an example in Figure 2.

Consider the aligned parentheses in the original sequence S. It is possible to connect all pairs of the aligned parentheses without one line crossing another line or a line crossing the graph of the height function. See Figure 3 for an example. We call the set of aligned parentheses an alignment of S.

Now we describe a recursive algorithm that computes edit_1 distance. Its running time is large, but after a series of improvements, we obtain the desired running time of $O(n+d^6)$.

We first preprocess S as follows. As long as there are two *neighboring* symbols that can be aligned, remove them. Let S'' be the resulting sequence after the preprocessing. We state the next simple fact without a proof.

FACT 18. $\text{edit}_1(S) = \text{edit}_1(S'')$.

The intuition is that if we don't match the two symbols (one of them is matched to a symbol somewhere else), one of the two symbols will be deleted or substituted which contributes 1 to the distance. We can rematch the two symbols in a pair and we don't increase the total distance.

We can check that the preprocessing can be done in time $O(n)$. Therefore, because of this and Fact 18, we can assume that the input sequence is already preprocessed. Thus, we can assume that S satisfies the following property.

PROPERTY 19. *No two neighbouring symbols of S can be aligned.*

We use several times the following simple fact which we state without a proof.

FACT 20. *Consider subsequence $S_i S_{i+1} \ldots S_j$ of S for some integers $j \geq i$. If $|h(j) - h(i)| > d$, then*

$$\text{edit}_1(S_i S_{i+1} \ldots S_j) > d.$$

CLAIM 21. *$k \leq d$ (see (2) for the definition of k).*

PROOF. Suppose that D_1 and U_k are not empty. By Property 19, the last symbol of D_i and the first symbol of U_i cannot be aligned for every $i \in [k]$. It means that at least one of them has to be deleted. Therefore, $\text{edit}_1(S) \geq k$ and the claim follows from the promise that d upper bounds $\text{edit}_1(S)$. If D_1 is empty then the first symbol of U_1 must be deleted. If U_k is empty the the last symbol of D_k must be deleted. If one of these cases or both cases happen, we still have that $\text{edit}_1(S) \geq k$. Which implies that $k \leq d$. □

3.2.1 First improvement

In this section we prove the following theorem.

THEOREM 22. *Let S be a sequence of parentheses that satisfy Property 19. Assume that $\text{edit}_1(S) \leq d$. Then we can compute $\text{edit}_1(S)$ in time $O(n^2 d^6)$.*

Notice that this running time is already better by a polynomial factor than the trivial $O(n^3)$ running time when $d \leq o(n^{\frac{1}{6}})$.

The recursive algorithm is as follows. It considers three cases.

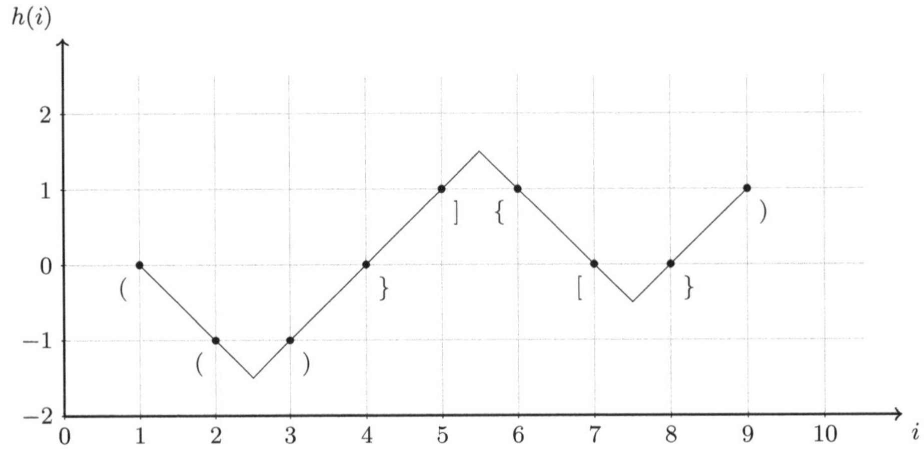

Figure 1: Height function $h : [9] \to \mathbb{Z}$ corresponding to sequence $S = (()\}]\{[\})$. See Definition 15.

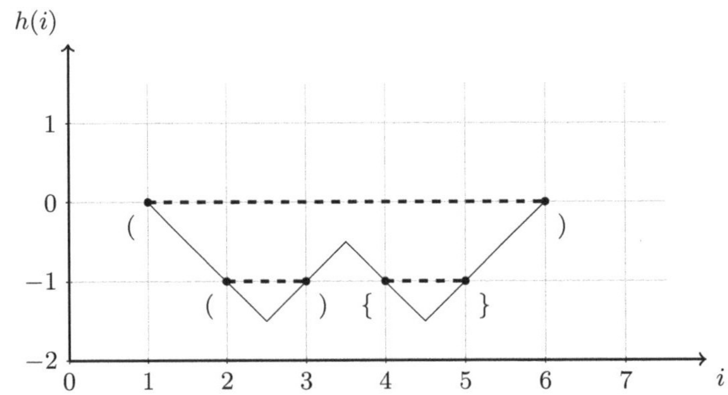

Figure 2: Height function $h : [6] \to \mathbb{Z}$ corresponding to a balanced sequence of parentheses $S = (()\{\})$. Dashed lines connect the aligned pairs of sequences. Notice that the horizontal dashed lines do not cross the graph of the function h.

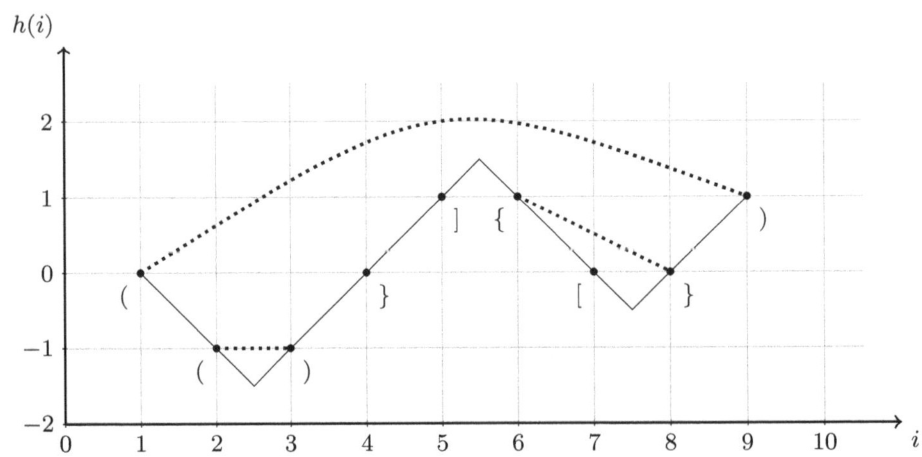

Figure 3: Height function $h : [9] \to \mathbb{Z}$ corresponding to an unbalanced sequence of parentheses $S = (()\}]\{[\})$. Notice that the balanced sequence of parentheses $S' = (()\{\})$ corresponding to Figure 2 is subsequence of S. For every aligned pair of parentheses in S', we connect the corresponding parentheses with dotted line in the graph corresponding to sequence S. Notice that the dotted lines do not cross the graph of the function h. The dotted lines can't be always drawn horizontally as opposed to the dashed lines in Figure 2.

Case 1.

$k = 1$. In this case we compute $\text{edit}_1(D_1, U_1)$ and output the result.

If Case 1 does not occur (that is, $k > 1$), we consider the next two cases. Case 2 results in quantity M_1, Case 3 results in quantity M_2. The algorithm outputs $\min(M_1, M_2)$.

Case 2.

There is an optimal alignment for S in which there is a parenthesis in D_1 that is aligned to a parenthesis in U_k. We call such aligned pair of parentheses *good.* Fix an optimal alignment that has a good pair. Choose good pair for which the parenthesis in D_1 is the rightmost one in D_1 among all good pairs. Suppose that this good pair aligns parenthesis S_i (in D_1) with parenthesis S_j (in U_k). We write $D_1 = D_1'D_1''$ such that D_1' ends with S_i. Similarly, we write $U_k = U_k''U_k'$ such that U_k' starts with S_j.

LEMMA 23. *There exists $r \in \{1, \ldots, k-1\}$ with the following property. There is no symbol in any of the sequences*

$$D_1'', D_2, D_3, D_4, \ldots, D_r$$

that is matched to a symbol from any of the sequences

$$U_{r+1}, \ldots, U_{k-3}, U_{k-2}, U_{k-1}, U_k''.$$

PROOF. Consider $r = k-1$. If this r does not satisfy the condition, there must be alignment of U_k'' with $D_{r'}$ for $r \geq r' \geq 2$ or with D_1''. We can exclude alignment between U_k'' and D_1'' because that contradicts the choice of S_i and S_j. Consider $r = r'-1$. If this r does not satisfy the condition, there must be alignment of U_k'' with $D_{r''}$ for $r \geq r'' \geq 2$. Consider $r = r''-1$. We continue this until $r = 1$ or we find r that satisfies the condition in the statement of the lemma. If we continue until $r = 1$, this value $r = 1$ satisfies the condition because otherwise there is an alignment between D_1'' and U_k'', which contradicts the choice of S_i and S_j. □

By the assumption, there is an optimal alignment for S in which there is a parenthesis in D_1 that is aligned to a parenthesis in U_k. This means that we can write $D_1 = D_1'D_1''$ and $U_k = U_k''U_k'$ as described above. Now, using Lemma 23, we can split the problem into three independent parts for some $r \in \{1, \ldots, k-1\}$.

$$\begin{aligned}\text{edit}_1(S) = {} & \text{edit}_1(D_1', U_k') \\ & + \text{edit}_1(D_1''U_1D_2U_2D_3U_3 \ldots D_rU_r) \\ & + \text{edit}_1(D_{r+1}U_{r+1} \ldots D_{k-1}U_{k-1}D_kU_k'').\end{aligned}$$

We observe that $\text{edit}_1(D_1', U_k')$ is edit_1 distance between two sequences and we don't do recursion on it. We do recursion on the remaining two parts.

Our recursive algorithm proceeds now as follows. For $t = 1, \ldots, k-1$, we define i_t such that the last symbol of U_t is S_{i_t}. We set $l := \max_t h(i_t)$. By Fact 20, it suffices to consider all parentheses S_i in D_1 such that $|h(i) - l| \leq 10d$. Similarly, it suffices to consider all parentheses S_j in U_k such that $|h(j) - l| \leq 10d$. We conclude that we have $\leq 20d+1$ choices for i, $\leq 20d+1$ choices for j and $\leq d$ choices for r.

Therefore, if we compute recursively

$$\begin{aligned}M_1 := \min_{\substack{D_1 = D_1'D_1'' \\ U_k = U_k''U_k' \\ r \in \{1,\ldots,k-1\}}} & \text{edit}_1(D_1', U_k') \\ & + \text{edit}_1(D_1''U_1D_2U_2 \ldots D_rU_r) \\ & + \text{edit}_1(D_{r+1}U_{r+1} \ldots D_{k-1}U_{k-1}D_kU_k''),\end{aligned} \tag{3}$$

we make at most $2 \cdot (20d+1) \cdot (20d+1) \cdot d \leq O(d^3)$ different recursive calls (one for each triple i, j, r).

Case 3.

We consider this case if one of the following two things happen.

- D_1 or U_k is empty.
- There is an optimal alignment where there are no symbols matched between D_1 and U_k (one from D_1 and one from U_k).

The analysis is similar to Case 2 but simpler. Fix any optimal alignment. We have similar lemma as in Case 2.

LEMMA 24. *There exists $r \in \{1, \ldots, k-1\}$ with the following property. There is no symbol in any of the sequences $D_1, D_2, D_3, D_4, \ldots, D_r$ that is matched to a symbol from any of the sequences*

$$U_{r+1}, \ldots, U_{k-3}, U_{k-2}, U_{k-1}, U_k.$$

PROOF. The proof is analogous to the proof of Lemma 23. □

Using Lemma 24, we can split the problem into two independent parts for some r. We have that

$$\begin{aligned}\text{edit}_1(S) = {} & \text{edit}_1(D_1U_1D_2U_2 \ldots D_rU_r) \\ & + \text{edit}_1(D_{r+1}U_{r+1} \ldots D_{k-1}U_{k-1}D_kU_k).\end{aligned}$$

We recurse on the two subproblems. There are at most d choices for r. Therefore, if we compute recursively

$$\begin{aligned}M_2 := \min_r \; & \text{edit}_1(D_1U_1D_2U_2 \ldots D_rU_r) \\ & + \text{edit}_1(D_{r+1}U_{r+1} \ldots D_{k-1}U_{k-1}D_kU_k),\end{aligned}$$

where we make at most $2d$ recursive calls.

We also notice that, similarly as in Case 2, by Fact 20, if the height difference between the first symbol of S and the last symbol of U_r is $\geq 10d$, we don't need to consider subcall $\text{edit}_1(D_1U_1D_2U_2 \ldots D_rU_r)$. Also, if the height difference between the last symbol of S and the first symbol of D_{r+1} is $\geq 10d$, we don't need to consider subcall $\text{edit}_1(D_{r+1}U_{r+1} \ldots D_{k-1}U_{k-1}D_kU_k)$. We will use this property below.

This finishes the description of the algorithm and Cases 1, 2 and 3.

The correctness of the algorithm follows from the discussions in the description of Cases 1, 2 and 3. We see that the runtime of the algorithm is exponential because we make many recursive calls. However, we can easily fix this by noticing that the number of *different* recursive calls is small. We see that for every subproblem, sequence S starts or ends with a symbol that is in a peak of the original sequence. There are at most $d+1$ peaks in the original problem. For every peak, there are two possibilities: a subproblem can start or end at this peak.

The subproblem ends at the peak.

The subproblem can start in any of at most d sequences $D_1, D_2, \ldots$ of the original problem. In any of D_i, the subproblem can start with any of at most $20d + 1$ symbols.

The subproblem starts at the peak.

The subproblem can end in any of at most d sequences $U_k, D_{k-1}, \ldots$ of the original problem. In any of U_i, the subproblem can start with any of at most $20d + 1$ symbols.

Over all, we see that there are at most $(d+1) \cdot 2 \cdot d \cdot (20d+1) \leq O(d^3)$ subproblems of the original problem to solve. Whenever we solve a subproblem, we store the answer to it so that, when the same subproblem is queried later, we don't need to recompute it. Every subproblem requires $O(d^3)$ subcalls (see the description of Cases 2 and 3). For a subcall we might need to compute $\text{edit}_1(D_1, U_1)$ (which takes $O(n^2)$ time), if we happen to be in Case 1 or we might possibly need to compute $\text{edit}_1(D'_1, U'_k)$ (which takes $O(n^2)$ time), if we happen to be in Case 2. We get that the final running time is $O(d^3) \cdot O(d^3) \cdot O(n^2) \leq O(n^2 d^6)$ as required.

3.2.2 Second improvement

In the next theorem we improve the runtime of the algorithm described in Theorem 22.

THEOREM 25. *Let S be a sequence of parentheses that satisfy Property 19. Assume that* $\text{edit}_1(S) \leq d$. *Then we can compute* $\text{edit}_1(S)$ *in time* $O(d^3(n^2 + d^3))$.

The algorithm described in Theorem 22 considers three cases. If a subproblem falls in Case 1, we can solve it in time $O(n^2)$. Since there are at most $O(d^3)$ subproblems, the total runtime corresponding to Case 1 is upper bounded by $O(d^3 n^2) \leq O(d^3(n^2 + d^3))$. If a subproblem falls in Case 3, then it requires time $O(d)$ (choosing r). Thus, the total runtime corresponding to Case 3 can be upper bounded by $O(d^4) \leq O(d^3(n^2 + d^3))$.

Now we modify the algorithm corresponding to Case 2. Consider a subproblem, where we are given sequence $S = D_1 U_1 \ldots D_k U_k$. We compute dynamic programming table for problem $\text{edit}_1(D_1, U_k)$, which takes time $O(n^2)$. This allows us to answer queries $\text{edit}_1(D'_1, U'_k)$ in time $O(1)$ (by single look-up in the dynamic programming table). Since there are at most $O(d^3)$ subproblems, the total time corresponding to Case 2 is $O(d^3)(O(n^2) + O(d^3))$.

We see that in all three Cases 1,2 and 3, the total runtime is upper bounded by $O(d^3(n^2 + d^3))$ as required.

Notice that the runtime bottleneck are cases 1 and 2. In the final improvement below we use the result of Landau et al. [8] to preprocess the input sequence and improve the corresponding runtimes.

3.2.3 Final improvement

In the next theorem we improve the runtime of the algorithm described in Theorem 25.

THEOREM 26. *Let S be a sequence of parentheses. Assume that* $\text{edit}_1(S) \leq d$. *Then we can compute* $\text{edit}_1(S)$ *in time* $O(n + d^6)$.

As per discussion above, we can assume that S satisfies Property 19.

We further improve the algorithm presented in Theorem 22.

As was discussed in the proof of Theorem 25, we have:

- The total runtime corresponding to Case 1 is upper bounded by $O(d^3 n^2)$, which we improve to $O(n + d^5) \leq O(n + d^6)$.
- The total runtime corresponding to Case 2 is upper bounded by $O(d^3)(O(n^2) + O(d^3))$, which we will improve to $O(n + d^6)$.
- The total runtime corresponding to Case 3 is upper bounded by $O(d^4) \leq O(n + d^6)$.

Improvement of the total runtime for Case 1.

In Case 1 we have to compute $\text{edit}_1(D_1, U_1)$, where D_1 and U_1 are substrings of the original sequence S. Notice that D_1 and U_1 do not necessarily come from the first valley of the original sequence S since the algorithm is recursive. We preprocess S according to Theorem 14. We build the data structure for substring D_1 and U_1 in time $O(d^2)$. From Theorem 14, we can now answer query $\text{edit}_1(D_1, U_k)$ in $O(\log d)$ time. We had to preprocess the original sequence S but this needs to be done only once. Since we make $O(d^3)$ queries (each taking time $O(d^2) + O(\log d)$), the total runtime bound for Case 1 is

$$O(n) + O(d^3) \cdot \left(O(d^2) + O(\log d)\right) \leq O(n + d^5)$$

as required.

Improvement of the total runtime for Case 2.

In Case 2 we have to compute $\text{edit}_1(D'_1, U'_k)$ many times (see (3)). D'_1 is prefix of D_1 and U'_k is suffix of U_k. D_1 and U_k are substrings of the original sequence S. Notice that D_1 and U_k do not necessarily come from the first and the last valley of the original sequence S respectively since the algorithm is recursive. It is not sufficient to preprocess sequences D_1 and U_k in linear time to be able to answer the corresponding queries in $O(1)$. The reason is that we would have to do such preprocessing $d^{O(1)}$ times and the final runtime would be $n \cdot d^{O(1)}$ instead of $O(n + d^{O(1)})$. To avoid this, we preprocess S according to Theorem 14. This allows us to build the data structure for substring D_1 and U_k in time $O(d^2)$ for arbitrary two D_1 and U_k (in the recursive calls). From Theorem 14, we can now answer every query $\text{edit}_1(D'_1, U'_k)$ in $O(\log d)$ time. We had to preprocess the original sequence S but this needs to be done only once. For every one of $O(d^3)$ subproblems:

- Build a data structure in time $O(d^2)$ for D_1 and U_k.
- Answer at most $(20d+1)^2$ queries of the form $\text{edit}_1(D'_1, U'_k)$, each in time $O(\log d)$.
- Explore $O(d^3)$ subcalls.

Thus, the total running time is bounded by

$$O(n) + O(d^3)(O(d^2) + (20d+1)^2 \cdot O(\log d) + O(d^3))$$

$$= O(n + d^6)$$

as required.

4. ALGORITHM FOR DISTANCE WITH SUBSTITUTIONS

In this section, we present an algorithm for computing edit distance to a well-balanced sequence of parentheses when both insertions and substitutions are allowed. This section partially mimics the previous one, but also adds another layer of complexity. For instance, when substitutions are allowed, two unrelated opening parentheses, say, "(" and "{," can be matched after "{" is transformed into ")." This operation costs one unit, which is better than just deleting both the parentheses, which comes at the higher cost of two. Unfortunately, this shows that now there is no more clear partition into two classes of symbols, opening and closing, with opening always being aligned with closing. Since closing parentheses can be transformed into opening parentheses and vice verse, the number of subproblems (and their handling) grows non-trivially.

4.1 Fast distance computation for a simple case

We start by modifying the subroutine designed in Section 3.1 to the case of substitutions allowed.

DEFINITION 27. *Let X be a sequence of opening parentheses and Y be a sequence of closing parentheses. By* $\mathrm{edit}_2(X, Y)$ *we denote the quantity* $\mathrm{edit}_2(XY)$.

DEFINITION 28. *Let A and B be two sequences of symbols. We define* $\mathrm{edit}'_2(A, B)$ *as the minimum number of operations necessary to transform A and B in to the same sequence, where the allowed operations are*

- *delete a symbol from A or B,*
- *substitute a symbol in A or B with another symbol,*
- *delete* two consecutive *symbols from A or B.*

The next fact is easy to verify by case analysis, which we omit. We just note that the last operation in the definition of edit'_2 stems from the following property. For edit_2 with substitutions, if we have two consecutive opening parentheses, we can modify the second (make it closing) to match the first one. Namely, consider the sequences $A =$"((" and $B = \epsilon$ (B is an empty sequence). Then $\mathrm{edit}_2(A, B) = 1$ since we replace the second symbol "(" in A by ")" and we get $AB =$"()" which is a balanced sequence.

FACT 29. $\mathrm{edit}_2(X, Y) = \mathrm{edit}'_2(U(X), \mathrm{rev}(U(Y)))$.

Therefore, to compute $\mathrm{edit}_2(X, Y)$, it suffices to compute $\mathrm{edit}'_2(U(X), \mathrm{rev}(U(Y)))$. We now show that, given two sequences A and B, $\mathrm{edit}'_2(A, B)$ can be computed in $O(n+d^2)$ time, where d upper bounds $\mathrm{edit}'_2(A, B)$ and n upper bounds $|A|$ and $|B|$. To achieve this goal, we modify the algorithm of [8]. [8] gives an algorithm with these guarantess except for a slightly different distance edit'_2. They give an algorithm where deletions of two consecutive symbols are not allowed. (That is, they give algorithm for the *standard* definition of edit distance.) We now describe the changes to the algorithm from [8] that we make.

We show the following variant of Lemma 2.3 from [8].

LEMMA 30. *Let A and B be two sequences of symbols. Let a and b be symbols. Then*

$$\mathrm{edit}'_2(Aa, Bb) - \mathrm{edit}'_2(A, B) \in \{0, 1\}.$$

Let x be a symbol. Then

$$\mathrm{edit}'_2(Ax, Bx) = \mathrm{edit}'_2(A, B).$$

PROOF. We show that $\mathrm{edit}'_2(Ax, Bx) = \mathrm{edit}'_2(A, B)$. Clearly, $\mathrm{edit}'_2(Ax, Bx) \le \mathrm{edit}'_2(A, B)$ since we can match symbols x (which contributes 0 to the cost) and we are left with $\mathrm{edit}'_2(A, B)$. Now we prove that $\mathrm{edit}'_2(Ax, Bx) \ge \mathrm{edit}'_2(A, B)$. If symbols x at the end of Ax and Bx get matched, we get equality. Suppose that a symbol x at the end of Ax or Bx gets deleted. W.l.o.g., symbol x at the end of Ax gets deleted. This costs 1. Now we have

$$\mathrm{edit}'_2(Ax, Bx) = 1 + \mathrm{edit}'_2(A, Bx) \ge \mathrm{edit}'_2(A, B),$$

where in the last inequality we used $\mathrm{edit}'_2(A, Bx) \ge \mathrm{edit}'_2(A, B) - 1$ which is easy to verify. It remains to consider the last case when the last symbol from A gets deleted together with x for unit cost (if the same happens to sequence Bx, the proof is analogous). We write $A = A'y$. We have to show that $\mathrm{edit}'_2(Ax, Bx) = \mathrm{edit}'_2(A'yx, Bx) = 1 + \mathrm{edit}'_2(A', Bx)$ is at least $\mathrm{edit}'_2(A, B)$. Consider the last symbol x in Bx. If it gets deleted, we have

$$\begin{aligned} 1 + \mathrm{edit}'_2(A', Bx) &= 2 + \mathrm{edit}'_2(A', B) \\ &\ge 1 + \mathrm{edit}'_2(A'y, B) = 1 + \mathrm{edit}'_2(A, B), \end{aligned}$$

which suffices for our goal. Suppose that the last symbol x from Bx gets deleted togeher with the last symbol of B. Write $B = B'z$. Then

$$\begin{aligned} 1 + \mathrm{edit}'_2(A', Bx) &= 2 + \mathrm{edit}'_2(A', B') \\ &\ge 1 + \mathrm{edit}'_2(A'y, B'z) = 1 + \mathrm{edit}'_2(A, B), \end{aligned}$$

which is sufficient for our goal. Consider the last operation that can happen to the last symbol x from Bx. It gets aligned to a symbol in A'. Suppose that this x gets to symbol w in A'. Every symbol to the right of w in Ax must be deleted. Let's write $A = A''wA'''$. We have

$$\begin{aligned} \mathrm{edit}'_2(Ax, Bx) &= \mathrm{edit}'_2(A'', B) + \mathit{delete}(A'''x) \\ &= \mathrm{edit}'_2(A'', B) + \mathit{delete}(wA''') \ge \mathrm{edit}'_2(A, B), \end{aligned}$$

which is what we need.

We show that $\mathrm{edit}'_2(Aa, Bb) - \mathrm{edit}'_2(A, B) \in \{0, 1\}$. Clearly, $\mathrm{edit}'_2(Aa, Bb) \le \mathrm{edit}'_2(A, B) + 1$ since we can substitute a with b. We need to show that $\mathrm{edit}'_2(Aa, Bb) \ge \mathrm{edit}'_2(A, B)$. In the proof that $\mathrm{edit}'_2(Ax, Bx) \ge \mathrm{edit}'_2(A, B)$, we never used the fact that Ax and Bx ends with the same symbol. Therefore, we also have $\mathrm{edit}'_2(Aa, Bb) \ge \mathrm{edit}'_2(A, B)$. □

We replace Lemma 2.8 from [8] with the following lemma.

LEMMA 31. *For all $h > 0$,*

$$L^h(d) = \mathit{Slide}_d \left(\max \begin{cases} L^{h-1}(d+2) + 1 & \text{if } d < h-2 \\ L^{h-1}(d+1) + 1 & \text{if } d < h-1 \\ L^{h-1}(d) + 1 & \text{if } -h < d < h \\ L^{h-1}(d-1) + 1 & \text{if } d > -h+1 \\ L^{h-1}(d-2) + 1 & \text{if } d > -h+2 \end{cases} \right).$$

The rest of the algorithm from [8] remains unchanged. We get an algorithm with the following guarantees:

THEOREM 32. *We are given two sequences A and B of length at most n. Let d be such that* $\mathrm{edit}'_2(A, B) \le d$. *Then we can output* $\mathrm{edit}'_2(A, B)$ *in* $O(n + d^2)$ *time.*

We will need the following further consequence of the algorithm from [8].

THEOREM 33. *We are given two sequences A and B of length at most n. We can preprocess A and B in $O(n)$ time so that the following holds. Let A' and B' be two substring of A and B, respectively. Let d be such that* $\text{edit}'_2(A', B') \leq d$. *Then we can in $O(n + d^2)$ time output* $\text{edit}'_2(A', B')$.

PROOF. See [8] for the proof. The algorithm in Theorem 32 *preprocesses* the sequences A and B in such a way that we can answer queries $\text{edit}'_2(A', B')$ in time $O(d^2)$.

The only difference between Theorem 32 and this theorem is that we don't know substrings A' and B' of A and B, respectively. However, as in Theorem 12, we only need to be able to answer in constant time queries about longest identical substrings. A data structure answering them can be precomputed in linear time, independently of what A' and B'. □

Now we can get the following theorem that we will use later.

THEOREM 34. *We are given sequence S of parentheses of length n. We can preprocess S in time $O(n)$ time so that the following holds. Given any two substrings S_1 and S_2 of S such that* $\text{edit}_2(S_1, S_2) \leq d$ *for some d, we can output* $\text{edit}_2(S_1, S_2)$ *in time $O(d^2)$.*

PROOF. We set $A = B = U(S) \circ \text{rev}(U(S))$ and preprocess A and B as in Theorem 33. Now $U(S_1)$ is substring of $U(S)$ and $\text{rev}(U(S_2))$ is substring of $\text{rev}(U(S))$. Since, by Fact 29,

$$\text{edit}_2(S_1, S_2) = \text{edit}'_2(U(S_1), \text{rev}(U(S_2))),$$

we get the required algorithm. □

4.2 Algorithm

Let S be a set of parentheses of length n. Define $A_{i,j} := \text{edit}_2(S_i S_{i+1} \dots S_{j-1} S_j)$. We want to compute $\text{edit}_2(S) = A_{1,|S|}$. Consider the following dynamic programming solution for this problem:

$$A_{i,j} = \min \begin{Bmatrix} A_{i+1,j-1} \text{ if } S_i \text{ and } S_j \text{ aligns,} \\ \min_{r=i,\dots,j-1} A_{i,r} + A_{r+1,j} \end{Bmatrix} \tag{4}$$

with base cases $A_{i,i} = 1$ and $A_{i+1,i} = 0$ for all i.

The runtime of this algorithm is $O(n^3)$ and our goal is to obtain an algorithm that runs in time $O(n + d^{16})$, where d upper bounds $\text{edit}_2(S)$. The runtime of the $O(n^3)$ time algorithm comes from the fact that we are examining $O(n^3)$ triples (i, j, r). Our idea is to improve this algorithm by examining only $O(n + d^{16})$ triples. The rest of this section is devoted to implementing this idea with the help of Theorem 34.

Recall Definitions 15, 16, and 17 as well as the decomposition (2) from Section 3. The following claim is an analogue of Claim 21 with a very similar proof.

CLAIM 35. *$k \leq 2d$.*

We need the following fact, which is a slight variation of Fact 20.

FACT 36. *Consider subsequence $S_i S_{i+1} \dots S_j$ of S for some integers $j \geq i$. If $|h(j) - h(i)| > 2d$, then*

$$\text{edit}_2(S_i S_{i+1} \dots S_j) > d.$$

The fact follows from the observations that a deletion or insertion change $|h(j) - h(i)|$ by at most 1 and that a substitution change $|h(j) - h(i)|$ by at most 2.

We also need the following definition.

DEFINITION 37. *We call the last symbol of D_1 (if D_1 is nonempty) and the first symbol of U_1 the 1-th base of S. For $i = 2, \dots, k-1$, we call the last symbol of D_i and the first symbol of U_i the i-th base of S. We call the last symbol of D_k and the first symbol of U_k (if U_k is nonempty) the k-th base of S.*

We define set H:

$$\begin{aligned} H := &\{h(i) \mid S_i \text{ belongs to the } j\text{-th peak} \\ &\quad \text{for some } j = 0, \dots, k\} \\ \cup &\{h(i) \mid S_i \text{ belongs to the } j\text{-th base} \\ &\quad \text{for some } j = 1, \dots, k\}. \end{aligned} \tag{5}$$

We define set L:

$$L := \{[v - 100d, v + 100d] \mid v \in H\}. \tag{6}$$

We can think of set L as the set of heights where alignments between parentheses between more than two slopes can happen. We will see that for sequences of symbols S_i with $h(i) \notin L$, we can deal fairly easy - by using Theorem 34.

As long as there exist $[a, b], [c, d] \in L$ with $[a, b] \neq [c, d]$ and $[a, b] \cap [c, d] \neq \emptyset$, we update

$$L \leftarrow (L \setminus \{[a, b], [c, d]\}) \cup \{[a, b] \cup [c, d]\}.$$

That is, we merge any two intersecting intervals into one. Let $L = \{[a_1, b_1], \dots, [a_l, b_l]\}$ be the resulting set L for $a_1 < b_1 < a_2 < b_2 < \dots < a_l < b_l$. We call $[a_t, b_t] \in L$ the t-th *layer* of S. Since the total number of peaks and bases is upper bounded by $2d + 1$, the number l of layers is upper bounded by $l \leq 2d + 1$. Also, we have

$$|[a_t, b_t]| = b_t - a_t + 1 \leq (200d + 1) \cdot l + 1 \leq O(d^2).$$

That is, the length of every layer is upper bounded by $O(d^2)$.

We define the following set of pairs of indices:

$$E := \{(i, j) \mid \exists t : \; h(i), h(j) \in [a_t, b_t]\}.$$

Since the number of valleys is $k \leq 2d$ (by Claim 35), we get

$$|E| \leq \left(\sum_{t=1}^{l} (k \cdot |[a_t, b_t]|) \right)^2 \leq O(d^8).$$

Now let's reconsider Algorithm (4). The idea is to preprocess S in $O(n)$ time so that we can consider only triples (i, j, r) that satisfy $(i, j), (i, r), (j, r) \in E$. There are at most $O(|E|^2)$ such triples. Additionally, per every tuple (i, j), we will have to spend time $O(d^4)$ (see the algorithm below). There are at most $O(|E|)$ such tuples. The total runtime, including the preprocessing is

$$O(n) + O(|E|^2) + O(|E|) \cdot O(d^4) \leq O(n + d^{16}),$$

which is what we wanted.

To implement the new algorithm, we need the following definitions.

DEFINITION 38. *Let $[a_t, b_t] \in L$ be the t-th layer. We call $[a_t, a_t + 10d]$ the* bottom *of the t-th layer. We call $[b_t - 10d, b_t]$ the* top *of the t-th layer.*

DEFINITION 39. *We call i and j to be* top neighbors *(*bottom neighbors, *respectively) in layer t if the following conditions hold:*

- $i < j$.
- *$h(i)$ and $h(j)$ are both in the top (bottom, respectively) of the t-th layer.*
- *S_i is a symbol in D_r for some r and S_j is a symbol in $U_{r'}$ for some r'. Consider smallest $j' > i$ such that $h(j')$ belongs to the top (bottom, resp.) of t-th layer and $S_{j'}$ belongs to $U_{r''}$ for some r''. Then we have property that $r' = r''$.*

Now we can describe our recursive algorithm that is based on Algorithm (4) and that runs in time $O(n + d^{16})$.

Before running the recursive algorithm, we first preprocess S in $O(n)$ time according to Theorem 34. Then we run the recursive algorithm:

1. We are given $(i, j) \in E$ with $i < j$. If we already computed $A_{i,j}$ before, we return the previously computed answer.
2. If i and j are *not* bottom neighbors in any layer t, then:
   (a) For $r = i, \ldots, j-1$, define M_r as follows. If $(i, r) \notin E$ or $(r+1, j) \notin E$, set $M_r = +\infty$. Otherwise, recursively compute $A_{i,r}$ and $A_{r+1,j}$ and set $M_r = A_{i,r} + A_{r+1,j}$.
   (b) Set $M := \min_{r=i,\ldots,j-1} M_r$.
   (c) If parentheses S_i and S_j align, recursively compute $A_{i+1,j-1}$ and set $M' := A_{i+1,j-1}$. Otherwise, set $M' := +\infty$.
   (d) return $\min(M, M')$.
3. Let layer t be such that i and j are bottom neighbors in this layer. By the definition of L, there must be i' and j' that satisfy:
   (a) i' and j' are top neighbors in layer $t-1$.
   (b) $i < i' < j' < j$.

   There are at most $(10d+1)^2 \leq O(d^2)$ such tuples (i', j') by Definition 39. Because of the preprocessing and Theorem 34, we can compute

   $$\mathrm{edit}_2(S_i \ldots S_{i'-1}, S_{j'+1} \ldots S_j)$$

   in time $O(d^2)$.

   For every i', j', we recursively compute $A_{i',j'}$ and set

   $$M_{i',j'} := \mathrm{edit}_2(S_i \ldots S_{i'-1}, S_{j'+1} \ldots S_j) + A_{i',j'}.$$
4. Return $\min_{i',j'} M_{i',j'}$.

Output.

$\mathrm{edit}_2(S)$ is equal to $A_{1,|S|}$. $(1, |S|) \in E$ holds by the definition of E and L and the fact that $h(1) - h(|S|) \leq 2d$ (remember assumption that $\mathrm{edit}_2(S) \leq d$ and see Claim 35).

The runtime analysis.

Preprocessing is done in time $O(n)$. The total time corresponding to Step 2 is $O(|E|^2)$. This holds due to at most $|E|$ choices for tuple (i, j) and, for every choice of tuple (i, j), there are at most $|E|$ choices for r. The total runtime corresponding to Step 3 is $O(|E|d^4)$. This is so because there are $O(|E|)$ choices for tuple (i, j). And for every choice of tuple we have at most $O(d^2)$ choices of tuple (i', j'). And for every choice of i, j, i', j', we must do computational task taking $O(d^2)$ time (computing an instance of edit_2 problem). Thus, the total runtime is:

$$O(n) + O(|E|^2) + O(|E|) \cdot O(d^2) \cdot O(d^2) \leq O(n + d^{16})$$

as required.

The correctness of the algorithm.

We prove correctness inductively. We show that we compute $A_{i,j}$ correctly, if the recursive calls that we make, all return correct answers. We consider two cases.

i and j are such that we do Step 2.

i and j are not bottom neighbors in any layer t. By definition of set E, Definition 38 and Fact 36, we have that it is sufficient to consider all $r = i, \ldots, j-1$ for which $(i, r), (r+1, j) \in E$. Correctness for this step follows from the correctness of Algorithm 4.

i and j are such that we do Step 3.

i and j are bottom neighbors in layer t. Consider an optimal alignment for $S_i \ldots S_j$ achieving cost $\mathrm{edit}_2(S_i \ldots S_j)$. There must be i' and j' with $i < i' < j' < j$ such that

$$\mathrm{edit}_2(S_i \ldots S_j) = \mathrm{edit}_2(S_i \ldots S_{i'-1}, S_{j'+1} \ldots S_j) + \mathrm{edit}_2(S_{i'} \ldots S_{j'}).$$

This is so because $h(i)$ and $h(j)$ belong to bottom of layer t. We can choose i' and j' so that i' and j' are top neighbors in layer $t-1$. This follows from Definitions 38 and 39.

This finishes the correctness proof.

We get the following theorem.

THEOREM 40. *Let S be a sequence of parentheses. In $O(n + d^{16})$ time we can compute* $\mathrm{edit}_2(S)$.

5. ACKNOWLEDGMENTS

We thank Piotr Sankowski for early discussions. We thank Piotr Indyk for many helpful comments on the early version of the write-up and suggesting the title. We also thank anonymous reviewers for many helpful comments on how to improve the presentation. Arturs Backurs was supported by NSF and the Simons Foundation.

6. REFERENCES

[1] WHATWG's HTML Living Standard. https://html.spec.whatwg.org/. Accessed: 2015-12-03.

[2] A. Abboud, A. Backurs, and V. Vassilevska Williams. If the current clique algorithms are optimal, so is Valiant's parser. *FOCS*, 2015.

[3] A. V. Aho and T. G. Peterson. A minimum distance error-correcting parser for context-free languages. *SIAM Journal on Computing*, 1(4):305–312, 1972.

[4] A. Backurs and P. Indyk. Edit distance cannot be computed in strongly subquadratic time (unless SETH is false). In *Proceedings of the Forty-Seventh Annual ACM on Symposium on Theory of Computing, STOC 2015, Portland, OR, USA, June 14-17, 2015*, pages 51–58, 2015.

[5] Z. Galil and O. Margalit. All pairs shortest distances for graphs with small integer length edges. *Information and Computation*, 134(2):103 – 139, 1997.

[6] F. L. Gall. Powers of tensors and fast matrix multiplication. In *International Symposium on Symbolic and Algebraic Computation, ISSAC '14, Kobe, Japan, July 23-25, 2014*, pages 296–303, 2014.

[7] F. Korn, B. Saha, D. Srivastava, and S. Ying. On repairing structural problems in semi-structured data. *Proceedings of the VLDB Endowment*, 6(9):601–612, 2013.

[8] G. M. Landau, E. W. Myers, and J. P. Schmidt. Incremental string comparison. *SIAM J. Comput.*, 27(2):557–582, Apr. 1998.

[9] G. Myers. Approximately matching context-free languages. *Information Processing Letters*, 54(2):85–92, 1995.

[10] B. Saha. The Dyck language edit distance problem in near-linear time. In *Foundations of Computer Science (FOCS), 2014 IEEE 55th Annual Symposium on*, pages 611–620. IEEE, 2014.

[11] B. Saha. Language edit distance and maximum likelihood parsing of stochastic grammars: Faster algorithms and connection to fundamental graph problems. In *Foundations of Computer Science (FOCS), 2015 IEEE 56th Annual Symposium on*, pages 118–135. IEEE, 2015.

[12] A. Shoshan and U. Zwick. All pairs shortest paths in undirected graphs with integer weights. In *In IEEE Symposium on Foundations of Computer Science*, pages 605–614, 1999.

[13] L. G. Valiant. General context-free recognition in less than cubic time. *Journal of computer and system sciences*, 10(2):308–315, 1975.

[14] B. Venkatachalam, D. Gusfield, and Y. Frid. Faster algorithms for rna-folding using the four-russians method. *Algorithms for Molecular Biology*, 9(1):1, 2014.

[15] R. Williams. Faster all-pairs shortest paths via circuit complexity. In *Proceedings of the 46th Annual ACM Symposium on Theory of Computing*, pages 664–673. ACM, 2014.

[16] V. V. Williams. Multiplying matrices faster than Coppersmith-Winograd. In *Proceedings of the 44th symposium on Theory of Computing*, pages 887–898. ACM, 2012.

Author Index

Abdulla, Parosh Aziz 195
Abo Khamis, Mahmoud 13, 327
Agarwal, Pankaj K. 429, 465
Ahle, Thomas D. 151
Aiswarya, C. 195
Amarilli, Antoine 355
Arenas, Marcelo 11, 225
Atig, Mohamed Faouzi 195
Backurs, Arturs 477
Barceló, Pablo 343
Bender, Michael A. 289
Berry, Jonathan W. 289
Bhattacharyya, Arnab 385
Bourhis, Pierre 355
Braverman, Vladimir 261
Buneman, Peter 11
Canonne, Clément L. 455
Cao, Yang 107
Chen, Hubie 315
Chestnut, Stephen R. 261
Cohen, Sara 165
Czerwiński, Wojciech 43
Deutsch, Alin 179
Dey, Palash 385
Fagin, Ronald 55
Fan, Wenfei 107
Felber, David 251
Fox, Kyle 429
Geerts, Floris 107
Gogacz, Tomasz 121
Gottlob, Georg 57, 343
Greco, Gianluigi 57
Guagliardo, Paolo 211
Har-Peled, Sariel 371
Hu, Xiao 135
Indyk, Piotr 371
Joglekar, Manas 91
Johnson, Rob 289
Koch, Christoph 75
Kroeger, Thomas M. 289
Kumar, Nirman 465
Leone, Nicola 57
Li, Yuliang 179
Liberty, Edo 441
Libkin, Leonid 211
Lu, Ping 107
Lupei, Daniel 75
Mahabadi, Sepideh 371
Marcinkowski, Jerzy 121
Martens, Wim 43
McCauley, Samuel 289
McGregor, Andrew 401
Mengel, Stefan 315
Mitzenmacher, Michael 441
Montali, Marco 195
Munagala, Kamesh 429
Murlak, Filip 237
Nath, Abhinandan 429
Neven, Frank 303
Ngo, Hung Q. 13, 327
Niewerth, Matthias 43
Nissim, Kobbi 413
Onak, Krzysztof 477
Ostrovsky, Rafail 251
Pagh, Rasmus 151
Paperman, Charles 237
Parys, Paweł 43
Phillips, Cynthia A. 289
Pieris, Andreas 343
Pilipczuk, Michał 237
Puttagunta, Rohan 91
Rahul, Saladi 277
Razenshteyn, Ilya 151
Ré, Christopher 91
Rezine, Othmane 195
Rudra, Atri 13
Scarcello, Francesco 57
Sealfon, Adam 29
Senellart, Pierre 355
Silvestri, Francesco 151
Simon, Bertrand 289
Singh, Shikha 289
Sintos, Stavros 465
Stemmer, Uri 413
Suciu, Dan 327
Suri, Subhash 465
Tannen, Val 75
Tao, Yufei 277
Thaler, Justin 441
Ugarte, Martín 225
Ullman, Jonathan 441
Vadhan, Salil 413
Vakilian, Ali 371
Van den Bussche, Jan 11
Vardi, Moshe Y. 1
Vianu, Victor 179
Vorotnikova, Sofya 401
Vu, Hoa T. 401
Woodruff, David P. 261, 385
Yang, Lin F. 261
Yi, Ke 135
Zage, David 289

www.ingramcontent.com/pod-product-compliance
Ingram Content Group UK Ltd.
Pitfield, Milton Keynes, MK11 3LW, UK
UKHW051241300926
15471UKWH00015B/1602

9 781450 346078